567

# Adventures in American Literature

REWEY BELLE INGLIS     FORMERLY UNIVERSITY HIGH SCHOOL
MINNEAPOLIS, MINNESOTA

MARY RIVES BOWMAN     ASSOCIATE PROFESSOR OF ENGLISH
EAST TEXAS STATE TEACHERS COLLEGE, COMMERCE, TEXAS

JOHN GEHLMANN     OAK PARK HIGH SCHOOL, OAK PARK, ILLINOIS

WILBUR SCHRAMM     DIRECTOR, SCHOOL OF JOURNALISM
UNIVERSITY OF IOWA, IOWA CITY, IOWA

FOURTH *1949* EDITION

*New York*     HARCOURT, BRACE AND COMPANY     *Chicago*

# PREFACE

MANY YEARS of experience have built up the basic materials of *Adventures in American Literature*. But the book must be true to its title; there are always adventures into the realms of the new. A fourth edition must combine the substantial old with the exploratory new. We believe that by careful screening we have retained those readings of former editions that most fully meet with the enthusiasm of teachers and students. Here in a nutshell are the new features we offer: fifty-eight new selections, eighteen new authors, a new form of organization, a completely new history of the literature and its background, an entirely new set of illustrations.

IMPROVEMENTS IN ORGANIZATION. In this fourth edition we believe that we have found a happy solution to the problem often debated by teachers: whether American literature should be presented by types or by chronology. This book is divided into two parts of approximately equal length, each suitable for one semester's work. Part I presents *only literature of the twentieth century* arranged by types much as in preceding editions. Part II gives a chronological treatment of American literature to the end of the nineteenth century. The book is now more flexible. Those who wish to teach the entire course on a chronological basis may begin with Part II and conclude with Part I, without the confusion arising from dipping into different parts of the book. We editors, however, have placed the type arrangement of modern material first because we believe this makes a more effective teaching sequence than the purely chronological order, for these reasons:

a. First impressions often color a pupil's entire reactions to a course. Colonial literature has little immediate appeal to the young person, because it seems remote, unexciting, and often full of language stumbling blocks. On the other hand, experience has shown the strong Short Story section to be the most enticing doorway to the course. Interest is at a high pitch, and the teen-age student often reads ahead voluntarily out of pure pleasure. Such an attitude at the beginning of the year is a boon to any teacher.

b. The literature of the youth's own century is more easily understood by him. He can read it rapidly without being perplexed by historical background or outmoded style. If he is well grounded in good writings of his own day, he is more likely to see significance in the earlier literature when he turns to it.

c. Teachers who begin with the older material are often tempted to spend too much time on it. The twentieth century is then crowded into a few hurried weeks at the end of the year, and the student receives the impression that the writings of our own century are not very important. This unfortunately tends to widen the gulf between " literature " as taught in the classroom and " interesting reading " as boys and girls pick it up for themselves. With the modern literature first the teacher can more easily lay the foundation for good reading habits by familiarizing the students with the best current writers and by affording some needed guidance through the maze of modern reading matter.

d. Arrangement by types is not just for the purpose of recognizing type differences. In addition, it is the best grouping to promote class discussion of the relative merits of selections. It is as futile to try to compare the values of a short story and a lyric poem as it would be to pronounce on the relative skills displayed in running a railroad and carving a cameo. Within the same classification, however, differences in the authors' purposes and styles may produce worthwhile discussion.

IMPROVEMENTS IN PART I. Obviously the greater number of new authors appear in Part I. In the Short Story section there are four significant new names. Stephen Vincent Benét, represented previously only by poetry, is now also represented in the fiction group by a story which has already become an American classic, " The Devil and Daniel Webster." Three younger story tellers now included are William Saroyan, James Street, and Wilbur Schramm. More effective stories from O. Henry and Pearl Buck bring the total of fresh stories up to six. With seven old favorites retained, there are now thirteen varied and fascinating stories from our own century.

The Prose section shows the greatest innovations in Part I. Ten new authors are scattered through the illuminating reorganization of this section under five heads. To The Informal Essay the well-known names of James Thurber and Thomas Wolfe are added. New selections by Christopher Morley and E. B. White bring fresh flavor to the group. Howard Vincent O'Brien's appealing " So Long, Son " has been added to the section entitled The Magazine and Newspaper Article. The Book Review section is entirely changed, with reviews of three recent books from three outstanding critical magazines. Moreover, the names of two of the new reviewers, William Rose Benét and Eudora Welty, are significant in the fields of poetry and fiction. In key with the times an entirely new subdivision — Reportage — has been included. Here William Shirer and Ernie Pyle report significant episodes in World War II, while Daniel Lang gives a vivid picture of " The Atomic City." Biography has been strengthened by selections from two recent best sellers: Catherine Drinker Bowen's *Yankee from Olympus,* and that inimitable account of the experiences of a Russian-American, *Anything Can Happen,* by George and Helen Papashvily.

In its entirety, then, we believe that we have a superb presentation of modern prose. With the transfer of the more difficult authors of an older day to Part II, the student will now find little or nothing that he wants to brand as " dry," and will therefore escape the let-down he sometimes felt after leaving the livelier fiction section.

The Poetry and Drama sections offer less reason for innovation. However, in Poetry the names of Robert Tristram Coffin and T. S. Eliot have been added, and nineteen new poems appear, most of them to strengthen the representation of major figures previously chosen. In Drama, Thornton Wilder's *Our Town* seems unsurpassed in appeal and appropriateness, while Eugene O'Neill's name retains its high rank. But two new selections have been added to represent radio drama, a form still in its infancy. One of these selections, adapted from a famous story by Paul Gallico, *The Snow Goose,* centers around the heroic evacuation of troops from

Dunkirk in World War II; the other, equally timely, is an effective sketch by Pearl Buck of some of the sacrifices made by the Chinese people in order to help bring the war to a successful conclusion.

IMPROVEMENTS IN PART II. Linked by an entirely new historical survey, the selections in Part II now form a clear and representative succession of great American literature from its beginning to the end of the nineteenth century. The historical comments are alive! They speak to the student directly, challenging him with great questions that America has always propounded, stirring him with high faiths that America has always affirmed. The student is led to see the how, why, and wherefore of momentous events, and to be heartened by the rollcall of our greatest leaders and thinkers. Nineteen new selections give added point and significance to the work of the standard authors. Among these are two stories by Poe and two by Hawthorne. The addition of major poems strengthens the total picture of three important poets. Whittier's *Snow-Bound* is given in a somewhat abridged form; Longfellow's *Song of Hiawatha* is represented by the episode of Hiawatha's courtship; and Lanier's " The Marshes of Glynn " is given entire, with marginal gloss to help interpret this somewhat difficult but highly rewarding poem. Probably the most pleasing additions from the students' point of view are two new Mark Twain selections, one from *Roughing It* and one from *Innocents Abroad.* Following the chapters from his *Autobiography* and from *Life on the Mississippi,* which have been retained from previous editions, they build up a fascinating picture of the early life of this distinguished American.

Teachers will be glad to see that the new organization of the book permits the assemblage of all work by one author in a single place. No longer need they pursue Emerson or Holmes from one section to another to present the man as a whole.

The book ends with a short interpretive chapter on the significance of twentieth-century literature, from which the student can turn back to Part I for a quick review of a panorama already familiar to him. Thus the circle of the year is completed.

IMPROVEMENTS IN EDITORIAL MATTER. All introductions to sections, authors, and selections have been revised and brought up to date. Footnotes now include pronunciation of all difficult proper names. The vocabulary studies running through the entire book have been enriched in content, with pronunciations also added. Many new suggestions among the study helps enable the teacher to parallel the teaching of composition with the study of literature. Reading lists have all been revised and some new ones added in Part II. The illustrations are closely correlated with the selections in order to give the student a visual acquaintance with both authors and subjects.

In presenting this fourth edition, we wish to thank the many teachers, librarians, and students (acknowledged in detail at the end of the book) who have helped with suggestions and with reactions to proposed new selections. We hope that those who study this volume will find continued satisfaction and stimulation in its pages.

THE EDITORS

*Adventures in American Literature* is part of a series for junior and senior high schools which includes *Adventures for Readers: Books I and II, Adventures in Reading, Adventures in Appreciation, Adventures in English Literature, Adventures in Modern Literature, Adventures in World Literature.*

# Contents

## Part One: MODERN AMERICAN LITERATURE

## *Part Two:* THE GROWTH OF AMERICAN LITERATURE

# THE GROWTH OF REALISM

# AMERICA IN THE MODERN WORLD

# PART ONE

# Modern American Literature

CITY RIVER SCENE, 1947. (Carew from Monkemeyer)

THE STORY of America is a thrilling revelation of man's determination to be free. Our first settlers sought in the new world the religious and political freedom which they could not find under the tyrannies of Europe. In 1776 our forefathers proclaimed that " all men . . . are endowed by their Creator with certain inalienable rights, that among these are life, *liberty,* and the pursuit of happiness." Later our Constitution provided a Bill of Rights, guaranteeing freedom of religion, freedom of speech, freedom of the press, and freedom of assembly. In the nineteenth century human slavery was abolished, and Abraham Lincoln voiced our determination that " government of the people, by the people, and for the people shall not perish from the earth." And today we are daring to seek, in addition to freedom of religion and freedom of speech, freedom from fear and freedom from want. Small wonder, then, that modern American literature draws its most outstanding characteristic from this rich heritage of freedom.

This spirit of independence manifests itself, first of all, in the selection of *subject matter.* Today the most important American books are the product of young Americans examining their environment more closely, more challengingly — and with more brutal frankness — than ever before. Gone are the old taboos and inhibitions; modern authors write about everything. Novelists and dramatists do not hesitate to record the ugly, sordid phases of American life. Biographers no longer whitewash their subjects in flattering " official " biographies, but try to interpret both the strength and the weakness in a man's life. In all types of literature authors feel free to use whatever material they can find to suit their purpose.

Not only in the subject matter but also in the *forms* of literature modern American writers feel no compulsion to respect convention and tradition. Modern poets no longer follow exclusively the regular metrical forms of the older poetry, but make wide use of the large, free, loosely patterned rhythms of " free verse." Indeed, much modern poetry varies from Bryant and Longfellow as much as George Gershwin and Duke Ellington vary from Mozart and Beethoven. Biographical material is treated so freely that the distinction between novel and biography has all but broken down, and a number of modern " novels " are in reality fictionalized biographies. In the drama, to the old forms have been added the movie script and the radio play, while on the stage itself we are offered all sorts of experiments and innovations: old plays in modern dress, revolving stages, Greek masks, plays with no scenery, even plays running from late afternoon to nearly midnight with intermission between acts for dinner!

Just as the modern poet, by turning to " free verse," has liberated himself from many restrictions of established poetic forms, so the modern short-story writer and novelist have refused any longer to be hampered by the standard requirements of novel and short-story technique. " If you feel the significance of life, the design builds itself," says John Steuart Curry about painting. The famous architect Frank Lloyd Wright says that the outside of the house should not be created in a pleasing design and then the inside accommodated to this pattern. Rather, Mr. Wright believes, the function for which the house is intended should dictate the plan for the interior; and the exterior must then be accepted as it turns out to be, even if it does look unconventional or even formless. In the same way, many authors of today have abandoned the old " contrived " story forms with regulation plot and stereotyped technique, and have given their stories freedom to grow into any pattern that the author's purpose may dictate.

In Part I of this book you will find modern American literature arranged in four sections: fiction, nonfiction prose, poetry, and drama. As you read the various selections in each section, keep alert to detect the new subjects and the new forms which indicate the amazing vitality of our twentieth-century American writing.

# Modern American Fiction

## THE SHORT STORY

### GUIDE TO SHORT STORIES

An American first defined the short story, Americans first developed it into a popular favorite, and Americans still read thousands of short stories every month. When you pick up a magazine, whether it is a slick-paper journal for the sophisticates or one of the unpretentious but swarming pulps, the chances are strong that short stories will be one of its important features. If you can learn to distinguish the good stories from the poorer ones, and if you can develop a preference for the better ones, you will increase the dividends on many an hour of your leisure reading for years to come.

### CENTRAL IMPRESSION

What makes a short story good? Fortunately for the amateur critic, the starting point for study of the short story is simply the main interest of the story. The one all-important requirement, first recognized by Edgar Allan Poe, is that the story must give one central impression. All the parts of the story — the familiar narrative elements of action, character, and setting — must be skillfully combined to give a single effect. The satisfying sense of completeness thus achieved is the great charm of the short story. We read for the story, but it is the central effect that makes the story impressive.

In any collection of short stories we find a great variety of central impressions. A writer may want to create a mood; or he may want to illustrate some idea about life and human nature; or, as in mystery and detective stories, so popular just now, he may make the chief interest the intellectual one of unraveling the plot. Hawthorne usually concentrated on presenting a serious truth about character or destiny. Poe sometimes sought to arouse his reader's emotions, often by the fascination of horror; and sometimes he wrote detective stories to puzzle the mind. Stories in which mood is the thing — such as humorous stories, adventure stories, and horror and ghost stories — may have no underlying idea about life, since they deal with unusual happenings, not typical ones. Often both thought and mood are strong in a story; but they must be harmonious, so that the central impression is strengthened and not divided. Unfortunately some modern magazine publishers demand that stories be padded in order to be continued among the advertisements from which the real income of the magazines is derived. Consequently many of our modern stories are spoiled by rambling digressions, " talkiness," and the resulting confusion of impressions. In our better magazines, where literary quality is not sacrificed to revenue from advertising, the stories are technically sound, each making one definite point, one single impression.

As soon as you have finished reading a story, while the details are still clear in your mind, examine the total impression it has made on you and try to reduce that impression to a clear statement, such as " This

JAMES STREET          BOOTH TARKINGTON          SINCLAIR LEWIS

revenge was horrible "; " The grass is always greener on the other side of the fence "; or " This practical joke backfired on the joker with comic effect." If the story has achieved artistic unity, the central impression will stand out clearly. And all the details of action, character, and setting will contribute to the single effect; there will be no padding, no " talky " digressions.

### ACTION

In his handling of action the author is greatly influenced by his main purpose. He chooses and arranges the happenings of the story so as to bring out most effectively the central impression he wishes to leave in the mind of the reader. If he wishes to present some truth about real life, he chooses incidents that are typical and presents them so that they are convincingly realistic. In particular, the ending of a realistic story must seem probable, the outcome logically expected from the earlier happenings and the sort of people involved in them. But if the author is amusing you with a humorous tale or entertaining you with exciting adventure, he can present odd and unexpected happenings without in the least damaging his central effect. It is only the realistic stories that are open to criticism if the incidents are improbable.

But, whether the story is realistic or romantic, the reader must be convinced (for the time being at least) that the happenings are real. This quality of seeming real we call " verisimilitude." While you are reading, it may be a matter of small importance whether the happenings are probable or not; if they seem real to you, they will hold you absorbed. Various methods serve to achieve verisimilitude. Sometimes not the plot itself but the skillful handling of the other interwoven parts, character and setting, builds up the feeling of reality. But always the author's best means is to write narrative so vividly that you feel the motives which impel the characters to action and you actually see and hear those happenings.

Every story must have action, but in most stories the action is more than just a series of incidents; it takes the form of a *plot*. The basis of the plot is a struggle or conflict, with the opposing forces so evenly balanced that there is real doubt about the outcome. The struggle need not be a physical one. The forces pitted against each other may be mental or spiritual. Many of our best stories are purely psychological; that is, important " events " in the story are changes of mind or attitude on the part of the characters. But the struggle, whether mental or physical, carries us on through the story; and when the struggle is over, the story must end and end quickly. The turning point in the plot, at which you first

JOHN STEINBECK        JESSE STUART        WILLIAM SAROYAN

foresee the ending, is called the *climax;* and the late climax is one of the marked characteristics of the short story.

Above everything else, a plot must have *suspense*. Suspense is a combination of two elements, uncertainty as to the outcome of the struggle and strong interest in that outcome. If you feel too sure of the way the story will end or if you do not much care how it will end, suspense is greatly weakened if not lost. So the writer must balance the opposing forces to keep the outcome uncertain, and he must stir your interest so that the outcome holds your attention.

In evaluating the author's handling of action ask yourself these questions: Do the incidents all contribute to the central impression? Is the ending logical? Do the happenings seem vivid and real while you are reading them? Is there a real plot? (If so, what are the two opposing forces?) Is the suspense well handled? When your answers to these questions are in general negative, the story is weak in the handling of action and plot. It may be, however, that the story has merit because of the author's treatment of the two other major elements of a story, characters and setting.

## CHARACTERS

In the portrayal of characters, as in the handling of action, a good writer is strongly influenced by the central impression he

wishes to make. If the author wishes the main idea of his story to center on a character, he will subordinate action and setting and make his story primarily a character sketch. If his purpose is merely to entertain, he may concentrate on humorous or exciting action and scarcely develop the characters at all. If the central impression is a general truth about life, the author will select representative people rather than marked individuals, just as he selects happenings which frequently occur; in this case, he will bring to our attention only those traits and qualities of his characters which are typical of the class each character represents.

Since the short story must remain short, descriptions of characters cannot be long. The sentence or two that can be spared to present a character must be keenly illuminating. A gifted writer can often sketch his characters by presenting them in action, so that the story goes forward while the reader is forming his impression, just as he does of people about him in real life, by observing what they say and do. Whatever method is used, the characters must seem real; you must feel, as you read, that they are living people.

Though the writer must limit severely the space he devotes to portraying his characters, the writers who command our most serious attention are those whose skillful presentation of characters and penetrating analysis of their motives and reactions increase our knowledge of human nature.

The author's treatment of characters, then, may be judged by its contribution to the central impression, its success in making the characters seem real, and the extent to which it increases your knowledge of human nature.

## SETTING

Setting is seldom a main interest of the short story. In only two types is it really stressed: in the local-color story, focused on the interesting peculiarities of one section of a country; and in period stories about earlier times, when the way people lived is a main interest in itself. In such stories even the action should be conditioned by the setting — concerned with happenings that are typical of the locality or of the period, not with events that could occur at any place or time.

But even when setting is not a main interest, it can be definitely important. In stories that concentrate on a mood, description of the setting is used to build up atmosphere. Both the details chosen and the words used have a share in giving description an emotional tone, so that, almost without realizing why, the reader slips into the mood the author wants to create. Another frequent use of descriptive detail is to build up an impression of reality by providing a full background for the happenings. Poe began " The Gold Bug " with a matter-of-fact account of the island, so that the reader would fall into the habit of believing him before he came to the fantastic search for the treasure.

To discover just how successful an author has been in his use of the setting, you must first decide whether the setting furnishes the central impression or whether it is used merely to put the reader into a desired mood or to build up an impression of reality.

## INDIVIDUALITY AND STYLE

Skill can make a good short-story writer, but it takes individuality as well to make a great one. The writer must have a distinctive touch of his own. He may have favorite localities or groups of people that he writes about. He may have personal convictions about life which he repeats in his different stories. But the quality which can be relied upon more than any other to distinguish one man's work from another's is style.

Style is simply a man's own way of using words and shaping them into statements. It is as personal as the tone of his speaking voice — and almost as hard to describe. But a few keys to the style of a writer will be disclosed by the answers to these questions: Does he write in a leisurely fashion as if he had all evening to chat with you, or does he clip off his remarks as if he were rushing off to a busy day's work? Are you aware of his personality as if he were telling the story directly to you, or is the personal element completely suppressed? Does he use words solemnly for their exact meaning, or does he enjoy using lively language? Does he give much conversation, and does it have sparkle and flavor? You can answer all these and many more questions without really knowing what makes a man's style individual. But if you notice his manner of writing closely enough to answer these with conviction, you will develop the feeling for style that is so hard to outline and so satisfying to possess.

In the following pages you will find representatives of most of the important types of the short story. But this group of stories is probably only a handful compared with the ones you read in magazines in the course of a year. You can acquire genuine discrimination along with your diversion if you take a few minutes to check over each story you read in terms of the central impression at which the author aims; how he achieves the impression through his use of action, characters, and setting; and whether the finished product is commonplace or distinguished by originality or individuality. It is not particularly important just why you like the stories you choose. It *is* important that you realize why you like them.

In this section you will find first two up-to-date stories, followed by earlier stories from twentieth century literature in chronological order according to the date of the author's birth.

## James Street 1903–

James Street is one of the most widely read of modern American writers of fiction. Of his five novels more than half a million copies have been distributed. And his numerous short stories, published in the popular magazines of large circulation, have delighted millions of readers. Writing frankly as an entertainer, Mr. Street denies any purpose in his stories except to spin a good yarn.

### THE BISCUIT EATER

This is James Street's best-known story. First published in the *Saturday Evening Post,* it has been reprinted in numerous books, made several appearances on the radio, and been turned into a moving picture voted among the ten best of the year.

This story of two Mississippi boys and their dog will make you understand why James Street is often bracketed with Mark Twain and Booth Tarkington as one of the best portrayers of the American boy in fiction. Lonnie and Text deserve a place in your hearts beside Tom Sawyer and Huck Finn and Penrod.

Lonnie poked out his lower lip and blew as hard as he could, trying to blow back the tousled brown hair that flopped over his forehead and got in his eyes. He couldn't use his hands to brush back his hair, for his hands were full of puppies. He held the puppies up, careful to protect their eyes from the sun, and examined them.

Then he cocked his head as his father often did and said solemnly, as though he were an expert on such matters, " Yes siree bobtail. Fine litter of puppies. Pure D scutters, sure as my name is Lonnie McNeil."

" Think so, Son? " Harve McNeil glanced up at his only son. He wanted to laugh at Lonnie's solemn expression, but he wouldn't. Never treat a child as a child,

treat him as an equal. That's what Harve McNeil believed. The boy was serious, so the father must be serious, too. " Mighty glad you think so. You're an A No. 1 bird-dog man and I have a heap of respect for your judgment."

Lonnie's heart swelled until it filled his chest and lapped over into his throat. He stuck out his chest and swaggered a bit. Then he put the puppies back into the big box where he and his father were working.

They were Bonnie Blue's pups, seven squirming, yelping little fellows that tumbled over themselves in greedy attempts to reach their mother, lying in a corner of the box and watching her litter proudly. They were nine days old and their eyes were open.

The boy sat on his feet next to his father in the crowded box and helped him doctor the puppies. Now that their eyes were open they must be prepared to face a blinding sun. Soon they must have shots to ward off diseases, but first their eyes and ears must be cleaned. A bird dog with defective sight and hearing is no 'count.

This was the first time Lonnie had ever been allowed to help his father with a new litter. Harve held a puppy in his big hand, wiped each eye with a clean piece of cotton, then bathed the pup's ears.

" Hand me another, Son," he said. " But handle him gently. Ol' Bonnie's got her eye on you, and if you hurt one of them she'll jump you like a jay jumps a June bug."

Lonnie picked up a puppy and cuddled it. " Hi, puppy dog. How you doing, ol' puppy dog? Know me now that you got your eyes open? " The pup flicked out his tongue and ran it across Lonnie's face. Then he caught Lonnie's ear and began sucking it. The boy laughed and handed the puppy to his father.

Harve looked the dog over carefully. " He's a beaut all right." He ran his finger over a small knot on the pup's head. " Ummhh. Little knot there. But it'll go away. Then he'll be perfect. Ought to be. Good blood line in this litter. Hey, Bonnie Blue, ol' girl. I'm bragging on your pups."

Bonnie Blue perked up her ears and

rubbed her nose against Harve. She was a champion. She was almost as good a dog as Silver Belle, the pride of the place. Bonnie had won more than her share of field trials, and once she had run in the Grand National up at Grand Junction, Tennessee, the world series for bird dogs. But the puppies had a doubtful strain in them, inherited from their father, a fair to middlin' bird dog until he killed one of Farmer Eben's sheep, and was shot, according to the code of the piney woods. Farmer Eben lived across the hollow from the McNeils.

Mr. Eben warned Harve that any puppies that had the sheep killer's blood in them were bound to be no 'count by the law of heritage. Bonnie's litter was on the way when the father was killed, and Harve believed he could cure the pups of any bad habits. The father had had a lot of courage, a strong heart, and a good nose. Maybe the pups would be all right.

Harve scratched the pup on the belly, then passed him back to a huge grinning Negro, the handyman around the place. The Negro was First-and-Second-Thessalonians. Everybody in the community called him Thes.

" Yas suh, Mistah Harve," Thes said as he put the pup into another box. " Me and you and Mistah Lon and ol' Bonnie Blue got us a good litter this go-round. And ol' Mistah Lon handles 'em just like he was born with a pup in each hand. Just like a natchel bird-dawg man."

It was too much for Lonnie. He was so happy he wanted to cry. Everybody bragging on him. His father beamed and resumed his work. It was good working there in the shade, with his son at his side and good dogs to work with. Harve McNeil was very proud of his boy and his dogs and his job. He trained dogs for Mr. Ames, the Philadelphia sportsman, and Ames's dogs, handled by McNeil, were known at every important field trial from Virginia to Texas. The Ames plantation, almost hidden in the piney woods of South Mississippi, was Lonnie's home. There were many bird dogs in the kennel, pointers and setters, and some were as valuable as race horses. Mr. Ames could have named his own price for Bonnie Blue and Silver Belle, but money couldn't buy them.

Cicadas sang in the water oaks as Harve worked. Hummingbirds darted around the red cannas and the mellow Cape jasmine. June bugs buzzed around the fig trees. Jay birds scolded in a pecan tree and mockingbirds warbled. In a field near by, a bobwhite whistled, and Bonnie Blue lifted her ears. Yes, Harve McNeil thought, it was good, working there with his boy in such a beautiful, peaceful land. So he began humming:

Went to the river and couldn't get across,
    Singing polly-wolly-doodle all day —

Lonnie took up the melody:

Paid five dollars for an old gray hoss,
    Singing polly-wolly-doodle all day.

Thes doubled up with laughter. " Listen to ol' Mistah Lon sing that gray-hoss song. Just like a natchel man. Know this 'un, Mistah Lon?"

The big Negro tilted his head, shuffled his feet, and chanted:

Peckerwood a-sittin' on a swingin' limb,
    Bluejay a-struttin' in the garden —

Lonnie joined in:

Ol' gray goose a-settin' in the lane,
    She'll hatch on the other side of Jordan.

Thes slapped his thigh. " Hot ziggity-dog. How 'bout this 'un: ' Thought I heard somebody say —' "

" Soda pop, soda pop, take it away." Lonnie sang so loudly that the pups quit yelping and looked up at him.

They doctored six pups, and as Harve finished the last one he told his son, " Run in the house and tell Mamma we'll be in for dinner in a minute."

Lonnie jumped up and started away. Then he stopped suddenly. " But we got another puppy, Papa. We only done six. There's seven in the litter."

Harve looked over at Thes and the big Negro turned his head. The father reached down and lifted the seventh pup. "We won't fix him, Son."

"How come?" asked Lonnie. He stared at the pup, a scrawny little fellow with spots that looked like freckles, a stringy tail, and watery brown eyes. He was the most forlorn looking pup Lonnie had ever seen.

"He's no 'count, Son," Harve said sadly. "He's the runt of the litter. Thes will get rid of him."

"You mean kill him?" Lonnie said.

"Now don't look at me that way," Harve said. "He'll go easy. You're a bird-dog man, Son. You know there's a bad 'un in 'most every litter. All these dogs got one strike on them 'cause their papa was a sheep killer. But this one has got two strikes on him."

All the blood drained from Lonnie's face and his heart went to the pit of his stomach. "I was a runt," he said. "And I got freckles. Why didn't you drown me?"

"Don't talk that away, Mistah Lon," Thes said. "It's hard 'nuff to kill him without you carryin' on so."

Harve McNeil looked at his boy a long time, then at the runt. Slowly he began cleaning the puppy's ears. "We'll keep him, Thes," he said. "If my boy wants to keep this dog, we'll keep him."

Lonnie's heart climbed from his stomach back to his chest and he choked up again. "Is he mine, Papa?"

"He's yours." Harve got up and put his hand on his boy's shoulder. "He's your dog, Son. But don't feel bad if he's no good. I'll help you train him, but he looks like a biscuit eater."

"He sho' do," said Thes.

"He don't neither," said Lon. It was his dog now and nobody could defame him. "He ain't no biscuit eater. Are you, puppy dog?"

He held the dog close to him and began running toward the branch, beyond which lived his friend, Text. Text was Thes's little brother and was just as black.

Harve and Thes watched the boy out of sight. "How come Mistah Lon want that li'l ol' pup, you reckon?" Thes scratched his head.

"Nobody, Thes," Harve said, "has ever understood the way of a boy with a dog. I reckon the boy wanted him because nobody else did."

"Reckon he's a biscuit eater?" Thes asked.

"It sticks out all over him," Harve said. "He ain't worth a shuck. But he's Lonnie's dog, and Heaven help the boy who calls him a biscuit eater."

A biscuit eater is an ornery dog. He won't hunt anything except his own biscuits. And he'll suck eggs and steal chickens and run coons and jump rabbits. To a bird-dog man, a biscuit eater is the lowest form of animal life. Strangers in Mississippi often are puzzled by the expression until natives, who usually eat biscuits instead of light bread, explain that a biscuit eater is a no 'count hound that isn't good for anything except to hunt his meat and biscuits.

Lonnie found Text down at the branch, fishing for shiners, long silver minnows that thrived near the bank. Text was the youngest of Aunt Charity's brood. A sanctified Baptist, Aunt Charity lived close to God and had given her children names that should be fitting in the eyes of the Lord. She had heard her preacher take text from this and text from that, so she reckoned Text was a superfine name.

The white boy held the puppy in his arms so Text couldn't see him and said, "Guess what I got."

"A gopher," Text suggested.

Lonnie sat on the ground and opened his arms. The puppy tumbled out, and Text's eyes popped open. "A puppy dawg. Be John dogged, Lon. And he's ours!"

"Mine," said Lonnie.

Text took the dog in his arms and ignored Lonnie's claim of complete possession. "We finally got us a dawg. Heah, pup."

The pup's tail drooped, but his big eyes watched Text. He was awkward, scrawny, and wobbly-legged. "Ain't he a beaut, Lon?" Text said. "Boy, we got us a dawg."

There was no denying Text a claim to the pup, so Lonnie said, "You tell 'um. We got us a dog."

The pup whimpered and licked Lonnie's hand. " Knows me already. Better get him back to his mamma."

Text went with him, but before they put the pup in the kennel, the little Negro turned him over, placed his hand over the pup's heart, and muttered:

Possum up a sweetgum stump, raccoon in the holler,
Wake, snake! June bug done stole yo' half-a-dollar.

Lonnie said, " What's that for? "

" Luck," said Text. " I put the ol' charm on him. I got better charms than that, but I'm savin' 'em."

The boys hung around Bonnie Blue's kennel all day, watching their dog. They called him Pup for lack of a better name, and in the weeks that followed they worked hard at his training. The dog developed fast. The freckles grew into big spots. His chest filled out and the muscles rippled in his legs. The boys saw only love and loyalty in his eyes, but Harve and Thes saw meanness there, and stubbornness. He was slow to learn, but the boys were patient.

A bird dog must know many things. How to carry an egg in his mouth without breaking it. How to get bird scents from the air and how to stand motionless for an hour if necessary, pointing birds, showing the master where the covey is. A bird dog knows instinctively that quail live in flocks, or coveys, usually a brood. They feed on the ground and fly in coveys until scattered. A bird dog must know all the habits of quail and never try to round them up, or crawl and putter around them. Only a biscuit eater who can't catch air scents rounds up birds in an effort to sight-point them. A quail's only protection is his color, and when a dog sight-points him the bird knows he's been seen and will take off. Good dogs must know how to keep their heads up and hold birds on the ground until the master is ready to flush the covey by frightening the quail. Then, when the birds take wing fast as feathered lightning, bird dogs must stand

still until the hunter shoots the birds and orders his dog to fetch the kill.

He must know how to cover every likely looking spot, passing up bare ground where quail can't hide. He should have a merry tail that whips back and forth. And he must cast [1] with wisdom and range wide.

He must know how to honor the other dog's point by backing him up and standing still while the other dog holds the birds. A good dog knows that if he moves while another dog is on a point he might flush the birds. Such behavior is instinct with good dogs and not really a sense of honor.

Harve tried to help the boys train the pup, but was not able to get close to his affections. There was no feeling between him and the pup, no understanding. The pup cowered at Lonnie's feet when Harve ordered him into the fields to hunt. And then one night Harve caught him in the henhouse, sucking eggs.

An egg-sucking dog simply is not tolerated. It hurt Harve to get rid of the dog, but there was nothing else to do. He walked with Lonnie out to the barn and they sat down. Harve told his son, " You're a bird-dog man, Son. A hunter. It's in your blood."

Lonnie sensed what was coming and asked, " What's my dog done now? "

" Sucked eggs. I caught him last night."

" No, Papa. Not that. He ain't no suck-egger."

" Yes, he is, Son, and remember his father was a sheep killer. The bad streak's coming out. He's a biscuit eater, and there's no cure for a biscuit eater. We've got to get rid of him. He'll teach my good dogs bad habits. He's got to go."

Lonnie didn't say anything. He compressed his lips, knowing that if he opened them he would cry. He walked out of the barn and down to the branch [2] where he could think over his problem. Text could keep the dog. That was the solution. They could keep him away from Harve's fine dogs. Lonnie ran to tell Text the plan, but while he was away Harve took the dog

[1] cast: to range about seeking game. [2] branch: a small creek.

across the ridge and gave him to a Negro. He didn't have the heart to kill him or let Thes kill him.

Harve shoved the dog toward the Negro and said, " He's yours, if you want him. He'll run rabbits. But I warn you, he's no good. He's a suck-egg biscuit eater."

The Negro accepted the dog because he knew he could swap him. That very night, however, the dog stole eggs from the Negro's henhouse, and the Negro tied a block and rope around his neck and beat him and called him a low-life biscuit eater. The dog immediately associated the block and rope and the beating with the term biscuit eater and he was sorely afraid and hurt. He was hurt because the man was displeased with him and he didn't know why. So when the Negro called him biscuit eater, he ran under the cabin and sulked.

When Lonnie learned what his father had done with the outcast, he went to Text, and together they went over the ridge to bargain for the dog. On the way, Text paused, crossed his fingers and muttered:

> Green corn, sweet corn,
> Mister, fetch a demijohn,
> Fat meat, fat meat,
> That's what the Injuns eat.

Lonnie said, " Puttin' on a good-luck spell? "

" Uh huh. That's one of my best charms. We going to need luck to make this swap."

The Negro man was wily. He sensed a good bargain and was trader enough to know that if he low-rated the dog, the boys would want him more than ever. The dog had a cotton rope around his neck, and the rope was fastened to a block, and when the dog walked, his head pulled sideways as he tugged the block. The dog walked to Lonnie and rubbed against his legs. The boy ignored him. He mustn't let the Negro man know how badly he wanted the dog. The man grabbed the rope and jerked the dog away.

" He's a biscuit eater! " The Negro nudged the dog with his foot. The animal looked sideways at his master and slunk away. " He ain't worth much."

" He's a suck-egg biscuit eater, ain't he? " Lonnie asked. The dog watched him, and when the boy said " biscuit eater," the dog ran under the cabin, pulling the block behind him. " He's scared," Lonnie said. " You been beating him. And ever' time you jump him, you call him ' biscuit eater.' That's how come he's scared. Whatcha take for him? "

The man said, " Whatcha gimme? "

" I'll give you my frog-sticker." Lonnie showed his knife. " And I got a pretty good automobile tire. Ain't but one patch on it. It'd make a prime superfine swing for your young 'uns."

The Negro asked Text, " What'll you chip in to boot? "

Text said, " You done cussed out the dawg so much I don't want no share of him. You done low-rated him too much. If he sucks eggs at my house, my Maw'll bust me in two halves. Whatcha want to boot? "

" Whatcha got? "

" Nothin'," said Text, " cep'n two big hands what can tote a heap of wood. Tote your shed full of light'r knots for boot."

" What else? "

Text thought for a minute, weighing the deal. " Lon wants that dawg. I know where there's a pas'l of May haws and a honeybee tree."

The Negro man said, " It's a deal, boys, if'n you pick me a lard bucket full of May haws and show me the bee tree."

Lonnie took the block from the dog and led him across the field. Then Text led him awhile. Out of sight of the Negro's shack, the boys stopped and examined their possession.

Text ran his hand over the dog, smoothing the fur. " He's a good dawg, ain't he, Lon? Look at them big ol' eyes, and them big ol' feet, and that big ol' short tail. Bet he can point birds from here to yonder. Betcha if he tries, he can point partridge on light bread." He looked down at the big, brooding dog. " We got to give him a name. We can't keep on calling him Pup. He's a big dawg and if'n you call a big dawg Pup it's like calling a growed-up man young 'un. What we going to name him, Lon? "

Lonnie said, " Dunno, Text. But listen, don't ever call him — " He looked at the dog, then at Text. " You know." He held his fingers in the shape of a biscuit and pantomimed as though he were eating. The dog didn't understand. Neither did Text. So Lonnie whispered, " You know, ' biscuit eater.' Don't ever call him that. That's what's the matter with him. He expects a beating when he hears it."

" It's a go," Text whispered. " Let's name him Moreover. It's in the Bible."

" Where 'bouts? "

" I heard the preacher say so. He said, ' Moreover, the dog,' and he was reading from the Bible."

Lonnie held the dog's chin with one hand and stroked his chest with the other. " If Moreover is good enough for the Bible, then it's good enough for us. He's Moreover then. He's a good dog, Text. And he's ours. You keep him and I'll furnish the rations. I can snitch 'em from Papa. Will Aunt Charity raise cain if you keep him? "

" Naw," said Text. " I 'member the time that big ol' brother of mine, ol' First-and-Second-Thessalonians, fetched a goat home, and Maw didn't low-rate him. She just said she had so many young 'uns she didn't mind a goat. I 'spects she feels the same way 'bout a dawg, if'n he's got a Bible name."

" I reckon so, too," said Lonnie and ran home and told his father about the deal.

Harve told his son, " It's all right for you and Text to keep the dog, but keep him away from over here. I don't want him running around my good dogs. You know why."

Lonnie said, " He's a good dog, Papa. He just ain't had no chance."

Harve looked at his son. The boy was growing, and the man was proud.

He noticed his son collecting table scraps the next morning, but didn't mention it. " I'm going to work Silver Belle today. Want to come along? "

Lonnie shook his head. Harve knew then how much the boy loved Moreover for, ordinarily, Lonnie would have surrendered any pleasure to accompany his father when he worked Silver Belle. She was the finest pointer in the Ames kennels and Harve had trained her since puppyhood. Already, she had won the Grand National twice. A third win would give his employer permanent possession of the Grand National trophy, and Harve wanted to win the prize for Mr. Ames more than he wanted anything in the world. He pampered Silver Belle. She was a magnificent pointer, trim and beautiful. There were no characteristics of a biscuit eater in Silver Belle. She was everything that Moreover was not, and when hunting she ranged so far and so fast that she had to wear a bell so the hunters could keep track of her. She had seen Moreover only once and that was from a distance. The aristocrat had sniffed and Moreover had turned his big head and stared at her, awe and admiration in his eyes. And then he had tucked his head and run away. He knew his place.

Lonnie set the greasy bag of table scraps on a hummock of wire grass and leaned over the branch, burying his face in the cool water.

A lone ant poked its head from around a clover leaf, surveyed the scene, and scurried boldly to the scraps. The adventurer scrambled about the sack and then turned away. Soon the ant reappeared with a string of fellow workers and they circled the bag, seeking an opening. But the boy didn't notice the ants. He lifted his head out of the water, took a deep breath, and plunged it in again.

A beetle lumbered from behind a clod and stumbled toward the scraps. One of the working ants spied it and signaled the others, and the little army retreated into the grass to get reinforcements. The beetle went to the scraps and was preparing for a feast when the ants attacked.

Lonnie paid no mind to the drama of life. He wiped his mouth with the back of his hand. Hundreds of black, frisky water bugs, aroused at his invasion of their playground, scooted to the middle of the stream, swerved as though playing follow-the-leader, and scooted back to the bank.

The boy laughed at their capers. Slowly,

he stooped over the water. His hand darted as a cottonmouth strikes, and he snatched one of the bugs and smelled it. There was a sharp, sugary odor on the bug.

" A sweet stinker, sure as I'm born," the boy muttered. If you caught a sweet stinker among water bugs, it meant good luck, maybe. Lonnie mumbled slowly:

Eerie, oarie, eekerie, Nan,
Fillison, follison, Nicholas, Buck,
Queavy, quavy, English navy,
Sticklum, stacklum, come good luck.

That should help the charm. Everybody knew that. Lonnie held the mellow bug behind him, closed his eyes, tilted his head, and whispered to the pine trees, the branch, the wire grass, and anything else in the silence that wanted to hear him and would never tell his wish: " I hope Moreover is always a good dog."

Then Lonnie put the bug back in the branch. It darted in circles for a second and skedaddled across the creek, making a bee-line for the other bugs. There were tiny ripples in its wake. The boy grinned. He was in for some good luck. If the sweet stinker had changed its course, it would have broken the charm.

He picked up his bag of scraps and brushed off the beetle and ants, crushing some of the ants. The beetle landed on its back, and a blue jay swooped down and snatched it. Lonnie watched the bird fly away. Then he studied the earth near the stream. No telling what a fellow would find if he looked around. Maybe he would find a doodlebug hole and catch one on a straw. That was good luck, too; better luck than finding a ladybug and telling her, " Ladybug, ladybug, fly away home; your house is on fire and your children are alone." He found no doodlebug hole, but there was a crawdad castle, a house of mud that a crawfish had built. There was no luck in a crawdad, but Lonnie marked the place. Crawdads are good fish bait. He crossed the branch on a log and moseyed to the edge of the woods where the cleared land began. The land was choked with grass and stumps.

Lonnie pursed his lower lip and whistled the call of the catbird, watching the cabin in the field where Text lived.

Lonnie saw Text run to the rickety front gallery of the cabin and listen. He whistled again. Text answered and ran around the house, and a minute later he was racing across the field with Moreover at his heels. The white boy opened his arms and the dog ran to him and tried to lick his face. The dog almost bowled the boy over. Lonnie jerked off his cap and his long, brown uncombed hair fell over his face. He put his face very close to the dog's right ear and muttered to him the things that boys always mutter to dogs. The dog's tail wagged and his big eyes looked quizzically at the boy. He rubbed against the boy's legs and Lonnie scratched him.

Text waited until Lonnie and the dog had greeted each other properly and then he said, " Hydee, Lon. Ol' Moreover is glad to see you. Me and him bof'."

Lonnie said, " Hi, Text. He looks slick as el-lem sap, don't he? Been working him? "

" A heap and whole lot," said Text. " Turned him loose in the wire grass yestiddy and he pointed two coveys 'fore I could say, ' Lawd 'a' mercy.' He's a prime superfine bird dawg, Lon. He ain't no no 'count biscuit eater."

Lonnie put his arm around his friend. " You mighty come a'right he ain't no biscuit eater."

The dog had wiped away all class and race barriers between Lonnie and Text, and they were friends in a way that grownups never understand. They didn't brag about their friendship or impose upon it, but each knew he could count upon the other.

They worked hard and patiently trying to train the dog, and sometimes the task seemed hopeless. Once he pointed a flock of chickens, a disgraceful performance. Again he ran a rabbit and once he left a point to dash across a field and bark at Mr. Eben, who was plowing a mule. Mr. Eben threw a clod at him.

The boys couldn't teach the dog to carry an egg in his mouth, for he always broke the egg and ate it. Once when he sucked an egg, Lon put his arms around the dog and cried, not in anger but in anguish.

Cotton hung loosely in the bolls and dog days passed. Indian summer came and the forest smelled woodsy and smoky. Sumac turned to yellow and gold, and the haze of autumn hugged the earth.

Moreover improved slowly, but the boys still were not satisfied. " Let's work him across the ridge today," Lon said. " Papa's got Silver Belle in the south forty and he won't want us and Moreover around."

Text said, " It's a go, Lon. I'll snitch ol' Thes's shotgun and meet you 'cross the ridge. But that there lan' over there is pow'-ful close to Mister Eben's place. I don't want no truck with that man."

" I ain't afraid of Mr. Eben," said Lonnie.

" Well, I am. And so are you! And so is your Paw! "

Lonnie's face flushed and he clenched his fists. It was the first time he had ever clenched his fists at Text, but nobody could talk about his papa. " Papa's not afraid of anything and I'll bust you in two halves if you say so." He jerked off his cap and hurled it to the ground.

Text rolled his eyes until the whites showed. He had never seen Lon angry before, but he wasn't afraid. " Then how come your Paw didn't whup Mister Eben when Mister Eben kicked his dawg about two years ago? "

Negroes heard everything and forgot nothing. Everybody in the country had wondered why Harve McNeil hadn't thrashed Eben when the farmer kicked one of McNeil's dogs without cause. The code of the county was, " Love me, love my dog." And one of the favorite sayings was, " It makes no difference if he is a hound, don't you kick my dog around."

But Harve had done nothing when Eben kicked his dog. Harve didn't believe in set-tling disputes with his fists. As a young man he had fought often for many reasons, but now that he was a father he tried to set a good example for his son. So he had taken

the Eben insult although it was hard to do.

Lonnie often had wondered why his father didn't beat up Mr. Eben. His mother tried to explain and had said, " Gentlemen don't go around fighting. Your father is a gentleman and he wants you to be one."

Lonnie was ashamed and embarrassed because some of the other boys had said Harve was afraid of Eben. And now Text said the same thing. " Papa didn't whip Mr. Eben 'cause Mother asked him not to, that's why," Lonnie said defiantly.

Text realized that his friend was hurt and he 'lowed that Mr. McNeil was the best bird-dog man in the county. The flattery might help to offset the charge of cowardice that the little Negro had made against his friend's father. Text couldn't stand to see Lonnie hurt. He jammed his hands in his overall pockets and grinned at Lonnie. " Lady folks sho' are buttinskies," Text said. " All time trying to keep men folks from whupping each other. Lady folks sho' are scutters. All 'cept your maw and my maw, huh, Lon? "

Lonnie said, " Mr. Eben is just a crotch-ety man. Mother said so. He don't mean no harm."

" That's what you say," Text said. " But he's a scutter from 'way back. Maw says when he kills beeves he drinks the blood, and I'se popeyed scared of him. His lan' say, ' Posted. Keep off. Law.' And I ain't messin' around over there."

They turned Moreover loose near a field of stubble and watched him range. Lonnie often had worked dogs with his father and had seen the best run at field trials. He trained Moreover by inspiring confidence in him. The first time Text shot over him, Moreover cowered, but now he no longer was gun shy, and he worked for the sheer joy of working. Lonnie never upbraided him. When Moreover showed a streak of good traits, the boys patted him; when he erred, they simply ignored him. The dog had a marvelous range and moved through the saw grass at an easy gait, never tiring.

He had a strange point. He cocked his long head in the air, then turned slowing

BIRD DOG. When Moreover froze to a point he held his head high, his tail stiff as a ramrod. (Ewing Galloway)

toward Lonnie as he froze to his point. But having caught Lonnie's eye, he always turned his head back and pointed his nose toward the birds, his head high, his tail as stiff as a ramrod. He was not spectacular, but constant. He ran at a sort of awkward lope, twisting his head as though he still were tugging a block. But he certainly covered ground.

"He sho' is a good dawg," Text said.

They were working him near Eben's farm and Moreover, catching wind of a huge covey, raced through the stubble and disappeared in the sage. When the boys found him he was frozen on a point far inside Farmer Eben's posted land. And watching Moreover from a pine thicket was Eben, a shotgun held loosely in the crook of his arm.

Text was terror-stricken and gaped at Eben as though the stubble-faced man were an ogre. Lonnie took one look at his dog, then at the man, and walked to the thicket. Text was in his shadow. "Please don't shoot him, Mr. Eben," Lonnie said.

The farmer said, "Huh?"

"Naw, suh, please don't shoot him." Text found his courage. "He couldn't read yo' posted sign."

Eben scowled. "I don't aim to shoot him. That is, less'n he gets 'round my sheep. I was watching his point. Right pretty, ain't it?"

Lonnie said. "Mighty pretty. He's a good dog, Mr. Eben. If ever you want a mess of birds, I'll give you the loan of him."

"Nothin' shaking," Eben said. "He's that biscuit eater your paw gave that Negro over the ridge."

Moreover still was on the point and when Lon heard the dreaded word he turned quickly to his dog. The dog's eyes blinked, but he didn't break his point. Text protested, " Don't go callin' him that, please, suh. He don't like it."

" He can't read my posted sign, but he can understand English, huh? " Eben laughed. He admired the dog's point again and then flushed the birds by rustling the grass. The quail got up and Eben shot one. Moreover didn't flinch. Eben ordered him to fetch, but the big, brooding dog turned his head toward Lonnie and just stood there. He wouldn't obey Mr. Eben and the farmer was furious. He picked up a stick and started toward the dog, but Lon and Text jumped beside Moreover.

The dog showed his fangs.

" I'll teach that biscuit eater to fetch dead birds," Eben snarled.

" If you touch my dog, I'll tell Papa," Lon said, slowly.

" I'm not afraid of your papa. And get that dog off'n my land or I'll sprinkle him with bird shot." He glared at Moreover, and the dog crouched to spring. " I believe that dog would jump me," Eben said.

" He will if'n you bother me or Lon," said Text. " He won't 'low nobody to bother us."

Lonnie patted his dog and whistled, and Moreover followed him and Text.

Lonnie was moody at supper and his mother reckoned he needed a tonic or something. He didn't eat but one helping of chicken pie, corn on the cob, string beans, light bread, molasses, butter, and sweet-potato pie. Usually he had two helpings and at least two glasses of buttermilk. His mother was worried about him, but his father knew that something was bothering the boy and kept his peace.

Finally, Lon took a deep breath and asked his father, " How come you didn't whip Mr. Eben that time he kicked your dog? "

Harve looked quickly at his wife and swallowed. " What made you think of that question? "

" Nothin'," said Lon. " I was just wonder-ing. If a man kicked my dog, I'd bust him open."

" Well, I tell you, Son. I've had my share of fighting. It never proves anything. Anything can fight. Dogs, cats, skunks, and such things. But a man is supposed to be different. He's supposed to have some sense. I don't mind a good fight if there's something to fight for. I'd fight for you and your mother and our country, but I won't fight for foolishness." He knew his wife was pleased with his words, but he wasn't pleased with himself. He wished there was some way he could meet Eben without everybody knowing about it. He was a peace-loving man, but not too peace-loving.

Harve knew his son wasn't satisfied with the explanation. He frowned and glanced at his wife. He hadn't punished Eben simply because he didn't think the crime of kicking a dog justified a beating. There had been a time when he thought differently. But he was older now, and respected. He wondered if Lonnie thought he was afraid of Eben, and the thought bothered him.

" I wish we had the papers on Moreover," Lonnie changed the subject. " I want to register him."

Harve said, " I got the papers, Son. You can have 'em. What you gonna do, run your dog against my Belle in the county-seat trials? " He was joshing the boy. Ordinarily, Harve wouldn't enter Silver Belle in such two-bit trials as the county meets. She was a national champion and no dogs in the little meet would be in her class. But Harve wanted to get her in perfect shape for the big meet, and the county trials would help.

Lonnie looked at his father. " That's what I aim to do," he said. " Run my dog against yours."

The father laughed loudly, and his laughter trailed off into a chuckle. Lonnie enjoyed hearing his father laugh that way. " It's a great idea, Son. So you have trained that biscuit eater for the trials! Where are you going to get your entry fee? "

" He ain't no biscuit eater! " Lonnie said defiantly.

His mother was startled at his impudence

to his father. But Harve shook his head at his wife and said, " 'Course he ain't, Son. I'm sorry. And just to show that me and Belle ain't scared of you and Moreover, I'll give you and Text the job of painting around the kennels. You can earn your entry fee. Is it a go? "

" Yes siree bob." Lonnie stuffed food in his mouth and hurried through his meal. " I'm going to high-tail it over and tell Text and Moreover."

Harve walked down the front path with his son. It was nice to walk down the path with his son. The father said simply and in man's talk, " Maybe I'm batty to stake you and your dog to your entry fee. You might whip me and Belle, and Mr. Ames might give you my job of training his dogs."

Lonnie didn't reply. But at the gate he paused and faced his father. " Papa, you ain't scared of Mr. Eben, are you? "

The trainer leaned against the gate and lit his pipe. " Son," he said, " I ain't scared of nothing but God. But don't tell your mother." He put his hand on his boy's shoulder. " You're getting to be a big boy, Lonnie. Before long you'll be a man. I'm mighty proud of you."

" I'm proud of you, too, Papa, even if you didn't whip Mr. Eben."

" You and Text have done a mighty fine job with your dog. It takes a good man to handle a dog like yours. He ain't had much chance in life. He really ain't much 'count. But you boys have shown patience and courage with him. So I'll tell you what I'll do. If you fellows make a good showing at the trials, I'll let you bring that dog back to the kennels."

" Is it a deal, Papa? If we do good, can I bring my li'l ol' dog back home? "

" It's a deal," said Harve, and they shook hands.

Lonnie ran down to the branch and whistled for Text and told him the good news.

" Gee m'netty," Text said. " But who's going to handle him, me or you? Can't but one of us work him."

" Count out," said Lonnie. " That'll make it fair and square."

Text began counting out, pointing his finger at Lon, then at himself as he recited slowly:

> William come Trimble-toe,
> He is a good fisherman.
> Catches hens, puts 'em in pens,
> Some lay eggs, some lay none.
> Wire, brier, Limberlock,
> Three geese in a flock,
> One flew east, one flew west,
> One flew over the cuckoo's nest.
> O–U–T spells out and out you go,
> You dirty old dish rag you.

Text was pointing at himself when he said the last word, so he was out. " You're it, Lon," he said. " You work him and I'll help."

Mr. Ames sat on the steps of the gun-club lodge and laughed when he saw his truck coming up the driveway. His cronies, who had come to the county seat for the trials — a sort of minor-league series — laughed, too. Harve was driving. Silver Belle was beside him. Lonnie and Text were on the truck bed with dogs all around them, and behind the truck, tied with cotton rope, loped Moreover. Mr. Ames shook hands with his trainer and met the boys.

" We got competition," Harve said, and nodded toward Moreover.

Ames studied the big dog. " By Joe, Harve! That used to be my dog. Is that the old bis — "

" Sh-h-h! " Harve commanded. " Don't say it. It hurts the dog's feelings. Or so the boys say."

Ames understood. He had a son at home. He walked around Moreover and looked at him. " Mighty fine dog, boys. . . . If he beats Belle, I might hire you, Lonnie, and fire your father." He winked at Harve, but the boys didn't see him.

They took Moreover to the kennels. They didn't have any money to buy rations, so Text ran to the kitchen of the lodge and soon had a job doing chores. Moreover's food was assured, for it was easy for Text to slip liver and bits of good beef for the dog.

Lonnie bedded his dog down carefully and combed him and tried to make him look spruce. But Moreover would not be spruce. There was a quizzical look in his eyes. The other dogs took attention as though they expected it, but Moreover rubbed his head along the ground and scratched his ears against the kennel box and mussed himself up as fast as Lonnie cleaned him. But he seemed to know that Lonnie expected something of him. All the other dogs were yelping and were nervous. But Moreover just flopped on his side and licked Lonnie's hands.

Inside the lodge, Ames asked Harve, " How's Belle? "

" Tiptop," said Harve. " She'll win hands down here, and I'm laying that she'll take the Grand National later. I'm gonna keep my boy with me, Mr. Ames. Text can stay with the help."

" What do those kids expect to do with that biscuit eater? " Ames laughed.

" You know how boys are. I'll bet this is the first time in history a colored boy and a white boy ever had a joint entry in a field trial. They get riled if anybody calls him a biscuit eater."

" Can't blame them, Harve," Ames said. " I get mad if anybody makes fun of my dogs. We are all alike, men and boys."

" You said it. Since the first, I reckon, boys have got mad if a fellow said anything against their mothers or dogs."

" Or fathers? " Ames suggested.

" Depends on the father," said Harve. " Wish Lonnie's dog could make a good showing. Do the boy a heap of good."

They were standing by the fireplace and Ames said, " I hope that big brute is not in a brace with Belle. She's a sensitive dog." Then he laughed. " Be funny, Harve, if that dog whipped us. I'd run you bowlegged."

All the men laughed, but when a waiter told the pantry maid the story, he neglected to say that the threat was a jest. The pantry maid told the barkeeper. The barkeeper told the cook, and by the time the story was circulated around the kitchen, the servants were whispering that rich Mr. Ames had threatened to fire poor Mr. Harve because his son had fetched a biscuit eater to the field trials.

The morning of the first heat, Text met Lonnie at the kennels, and together they fed Moreover. " Let's put some good ol' gunpowder in his vittles," Text said. " Make him hunt better."

" Aw, that's superstition," said Lonnie.

" I don't care what it is, it helps," said Text.

Lonnie didn't believe in tempting luck, so Moreover was fed a sprinkling of gunpowder.

Text said, " I got my lucky buckeye along. We bound to have luck, Lon."

Lonnie was getting too big for such foolishness, but then he remembered. " I caught a sweet stinker not so long ago," he whispered, " and he swum the right way."

" A good ol' sweet-stinking mellow bug? " asked Text eagerly. " Lon, good luck gonna bust us in two halves."

Harve took Silver Belle out in an early brace and the pointer completely outclassed her rival. Her trainer sent her back to her kennel and went into the fields with Ames to watch Moreover in his first race. He was braced with a rangy setter. Even the judges smiled at the two boys and their dog. Text, in keeping with the rules of the sport, gave no orders.

The spectators and judges were mounted, but the handlers were on foot. Lonnie put his dog down on the edge of a clover field and the judges instructed that the dogs be set to work. Moreover's competitor leaped away and began hunting, but Moreover just rolled over, then jumped up and loped around the boy, leaping on him and licking his face. The judges scowled. It was bad behavior for a bird dog. Lonnie and Text walked into the field, and Moreover followed. Lonnie leaned over his dog and whispered in his ear. The big dog jerked up his head, cocked it, and began casting. He ranged to the edge of the field and worked in. He loped past a patch of saw grass, slowed suddenly, wheeled and pointed, his head high, his right leg poised, and his tail stiff as a poker.

Lonnie kept his dog on the point until the judges nodded approval, and then the boy threw a stick among the birds and flushed them. Moreover didn't blink an eye when the birds whirred away and Lonnie shot over him. Then the boy called his dog to the far edge of a field and set him ranging again. He was on a point in a flash.

Ames looked at Harve. " That's a good dog, McNeil. He's trained beautifully. He'll give us a run for our money sure as shooting. If that dog beats Belle, it'll make us look bad."

Harve was beaming with pride. " It proves what I've always preached. A bird dog will work for a man, if the man understands him. I couldn't do anything with that dog, but he'll work his heart out for my boy and Text. But don't worry, Mr. Ames, he can't beat Belle."

To the utter amazement of everybody, except Lonnie and Text, Moreover swept through to the final series, or heat, and was pitted against Silver Belle for the championship. Harve regretted then that he had entered Belle. He wasn't worried about his dog winning. He had confidence in Silver Belle, but the mere fact that a grand champion was running against a biscuit eater was bad. And, too, Harve hated to best his own son in the contest. News that father and son were matched, with the famous Belle against a biscuit eater, brought sportsmen and sportswriters swarming to the county seat. Harve and Lonnie slept and ate together, but the man didn't discuss the contest with his son. He didn't want to make him nervous. He treated Lonnie as he would treat any other trainer.

Neither Harve nor Lonnie had much to say that morning at breakfast. Once the father, his mouth full of batter cakes, looked over at his son and winked. Lonnie winked back. But the boy didn't eat much. He was too excited. The excitement, however, didn't interfere with Text's eating. The other sportsmen kidded Harve and joshed him about the possibility of a biscuit eater beating Silver Belle.

The spectators and judges rode to the edge of a field of stubble, and Harve snapped a bell on his dog's collar. It was the first time he had used the bell during the trials and Lonnie knew what it meant. His father was going to give Silver Belle her head, let her show all that was in her, let her range far and wide. Lonnie's heart sank and Text rolled his eyes. Silver Belle stood there beautifully, but Moreover tucked his head and flopped his ears. The judges gave the signal and Harve said, " Go get 'em, girl."

The champion dashed into the stubble and soon was out of sight. Moreover didn't leap away as he should have, but rubbed against Lonnie's legs and watched Silver Belle for a minute, then began running along her trail. There was no order between Lonnie and his dog, only understanding. Moreover looked like a biscuit eater all right. He didn't race as most bird dogs do, but he sort of trotted away, taking his time. The judges smiled.

The men heard the tinkling of the bell on Silver Belle and knew that the champion was still casting. The dog had ranged far beyond a ridge and Harve did his best to keep her in sight. Suddenly, the bell was silent and Harve ran to his dog. Belle was on a point and was rigid. Her trim body was thrown forward a bit; her nose, perfectly tilted, was aimed toward a clump of sage. She didn't flex a muscle. She might have been made of marble.

" Point! " Harve shouted, and the judges came.

Moreover crept behind Silver Belle and stopped, honoring her point. Harve smiled at his son and Lonnie's heart beat faster. It was a beautiful point. The judges nodded approval, and Harve flushed the birds and shot over his dog, and Belle took it as a champion should.

When the echo of the shot died away, Belle walked to her master and he patted her. Lonnie took Moreover by the collar and the judges gave the signal that the dogs be released again. Belle raced into the stubble, but Moreover swung along at an easy gait. He cast a bit to the right, sniffed, and found the trail that Belle had just made. He never depended on ground scents but on body scents, and kept his nose high enough to catch any smells the wind blew his way.

He got the odor of birds and the muscles of his legs suddenly bunched. He leaped away, easing his nose higher in the air, and raced back up the trail Belle had made. Suddenly, he crouched. Slowly, noiselessly, he took two steps, then three, and froze to a point. His right leg came up slowly, deliberately. He cocked his head in that strange fashion, and the quizzical, comical look came into his eyes. Moreover was a still hunter and never waited for orders. Lonnie clicked the safety off his gun and watched his dog. Text was beside him. The judges and spectators were far away.

" Look at that li'l ol' dawg," said Text. " He's got himself a mess of birds."

Lonnie cupped his hands and shouted to the judges, " Point! "

" Pint! " Text whooped.

Moreover held his point as Lonnie shot over him. Belle honored his point, and as soon as the gun sounded and Moreover got a nod from Lonnie, the big dog dashed to the right and flashed to another point.

The judges whistled softly. " Most beautiful work I ever saw," whispered one. Ames's face took on a worried look. So did Harve's. The big dog had picked up a covey almost under Belle's nose.

Belle settled down to hunt. She seemed everywhere. She dashed to a point on the fringe of a cornfield and got a big covey. She raced over the ridge, her nose picking up scents in almost impossible places. Moreover sort of ambled along, never wasting energy, but every time Belle got a covey he honored her and then cast for a few minutes, pointed, and held. He waited for her to set the pace and it was a killing pace.

Belle held a covey for ten minutes near a rabbit's den. The smell of rabbit was strong in her nose, but she knew birds were there and she handled them.

It was then that Moreover pulled his downwind point. He was running with the wind and didn't get the odor of the covey until he had passed it. But when the hot odor of birds filled his nose, he leaped, reversed himself in mid-air and landed on a point, his front feet braced, his choke-bore nose held high.

It was the most beautiful performance of the morning. Belle tried to match it, but couldn't. She was hunting because she was bred to hunt. Moreover was hunting from habit and because Lonnie expected him to.

It was exasperating. Belle tried every trick of her training, but her skill was no match for his stamina. Her heart was pumping rapidly and she was tired when the crowd passed near the clubhouse and the judges suggested refreshments. Harve and Lon rubbed their dogs while they waited. Belle's tongue was hanging out, but Moreover just sat on his haunches and watched his master. Text ran into the lodge to help fetch food and drink to the crowd. He strutted into the kitchen and told the servants that Moreover was running Silver Belle ragged.

The servants shook their heads, and one told him that Mr. Ames would fire Harve if Moreover beat Belle. Text couldn't swallow his food. He ran out of the lodge and called Lonnie aside. Lonnie's throat hurt when he heard the story that Moreover's victory would cost his father the job of training Mr. Ames's dogs. He stared at Moreover and then at Text.

" That Mr. Ames sho' is a scutter," said Text. " A frazzlin' scutter. He's worse'n Mr. Eben. What we gonna do, Lon? "

Lonnie said sadly, " He's half your dog, Text. What you say? "

The little Negro put his hand on his friend's arm. " We can't let yo' paw get in no trouble on account of us. He got to have a job. He got to eat, ain't he? "

Lonnie nodded and bit his lip. He noticed that his father's face was drawn as the contest was renewed. Ames was nervous. The two men had worked for years to get Belle to perfection and win the Grand National for the third time. And here an outcast dog was hunting her heart out at a minor meet. Lonnie thought his father was worried about his job and that Ames was angry.

His mind was made up. He watched Moreover leap across a branch, then race toward a rail fence. He and Text were right behind him.

The big dog held his head high for a split second, then sprang. He balanced himself perfectly on the rail fence, turned his face to Lonnie, and seemed to smile. Then he tilted his nose and pointed a covey just beyond the fence.

Lonnie and Text just stood there for a minute, their mouths wide open. Pointing quail from a rail fence! Lonnie choked up with pride, but he didn't shout " point." He didn't want the judges to know, but the judges saw Moreover.

They stopped their horses and gaped. One judge said in a whisper, " That's the best dog I ever saw."

Harve said, " Pointing from a fence. I'm looking right at him but I can't believe it. No dog's that good. That beats Belle."

A judge told Lonnie to flush the birds and shoot over his dog. The boy didn't move, however. His tongue was frozen to the roof of his mouth. Then he cupped his hands and said, hoarsely, " Hep! " It was an order Moreover had never heard. Lonnie thought the strange order would startle his dog and cause him to break his point, but Moreover stood rigid.

Again Lon called, " Hep! " The dog didn't budge. The judges couldn't understand the action of the boy and Harve was puzzled.

Lonnie tried again, and Moreover turned his head and faced his master, amazement in his eyes.

Ames whispered, " He's breaking. That good-for-nothing streak is cropping out."

Moreover didn't break, however. He settled to the point, and in desperation Lonnie walked close to him and hissed, " Biscuit eater! Low-life, no 'count, egg-sucking biscuit eater."

Text cringed when he heard the words.

Moreover faced the boy again and blinked his eyes. Slowly his tail dropped. Then his head. Lonnie repeated it. " Biscuit eater." There were tears in his eyes and his voice quivered.

Moreover tucked his tail between his legs and leaped from the fence, flushing the birds. Then he turned his big, sad eyes toward Lonnie. He couldn't believe his ears and must see for himself that his master had thrown him down. Lonnie stood there by the fence, his fists clenched and tears rolling down his face. Moreover ran to the lodge and hid under it. He wanted to be alone, away from the sight and smell of men.

Lonnie and Text ran after him. They couldn't face the crowd. The judges didn't know what to make of it and the spectators muttered at the strange performance.

Ames looked at Harve for an explanation, and Harve said, " I don't get it. My son called his dog off. He quit. He threw his dog down."

The judges awarded the trophy to Mr. Ames, but the sportsman wouldn't touch it. " We didn't earn it. Those kids and their dog beat us. I won't have it. You take it, Harve."

Harve shook his head slowly. " It's not mine. I don't want the thing. I can't understand my son. I can't understand why he quit. That dog worked hard for those boys and they double-crossed him. I heard my boy call his dog a biscuit eater. He would fight anybody else who called him a biscuit eater. My boy broke his dog's heart. . . ."

It took Lonnie and Text a long time to coax Moreover from under the lodge. The dog crawled to Lonnie's feet and rolled over. Lonnie patted him, but Moreover didn't lick his face. " He's mad at us," Text said. " He don't like us no more."

" His feelings are hurt," Lonnie said, as Moreover lay down and thumped his tail. . . . " I'm sorry I said it, Moreover. I had to."

Text said, " We sorry, puppy dawg. We didn't mean it. But us had to say it, huh,

Lon? Aw, don't cry, Lon. Ol' Moreover knows you didn't mean it. Please don't cry. Don't let ol' Moreover see us bawlin'."

Harve didn't speak to the boys as they loaded the truck. Mr. Ames wanted to tell the boys good-by, but they walked away from him. Harve had his boy sit on the front seat by him. They said good-by to the crowd and rolled away.

Finally, Harve asked Lonnie, " How come you did that, Son? "

Lonnie didn't reply and the father didn't press the point. " Don't ever quit, Son, if you're winning or losing. It ain't fair to the dog."

" My dog is mad at me," Lonnie said.

" We'll give him a beef heart when we get home. His feelings are hurt because you threw him down. But he'll be all right. Dogs are not like folks. They'll forgive a fellow." He knew then that Lonnie had a reason for what he had done, and he knew that if his son wanted him to know the reason, he would tell him.

Back home, Lonnie cooked a beef heart and took the plate to the back gallery where the dog was tied. Moreover slunk into the shadows and Harve said, " Untie him, Son. You can let him run free over here. I made a deal with you and I'll stick to it. You can keep your dog right here. He needn't go back to Text's house."

The boy hugged his father gratefully and untied his dog. Moreover sniffed the food and toyed with it. He never had had such good food before. Lonnie and his father went back into the house.

After supper, Lonnie went to see about his dog. The meat hadn't been eaten and Moreover was gone.

" He's still mad at me," Lon said. " He don't like me no more. He's gone off and I'm going after him."

" I'll go with you," said Harve, and got a lantern.

Text hadn't seen the dog. He joined the search and the three hunted through the woods for an hour or so, Lonnie whistling for Moreover, and Text calling him, " Heah, heah, fellow. Heah."

Harve sat on a stump, put the lantern down, and called the boys to him. He had seen only a few dogs that would refuse to eat beef heart as Moreover had done.

" Text," he said sharply, " did Moreover ever suck eggs at your place? "

Text rolled his eyes and looked at Lonnie. " Yas, suh." He was afraid to lie to Harve. " But I didn't tell Lon. I didn't want to hurt his feelings. Moreover was a suck-egger, good and proper."

Harve said, " Go on, tell us about it."

" Maw put hot pepper in a raw egg, but it didn't break him. My ol' brother, ol' First-and-Second Thessalonians, reckoned he'd kill Moreover less'n he quit suck-egging. So I got to snitching two eggs ever' night and feeding them to him. He sho' did like eggs."

Lonnie said sharply. " You hadn't ought to have done that, Text."

Harve said, " Did you feed him eggs tonight? "

" Naw, suh," said Text. " I reckoned he had vittles at yo' house. We had done gathered all the eggs, and Maw had counted them by nightfall."

Harve got up. " I'm worried. Let's walk up the branch. . . . Text, you take the left side . . . Lonnie, you take the right side. I'll walk up the bank."

Lonnie found Moreover's body, still warm, only a few feet from the water. He stooped over his dog, put the lantern by his head, and opened his mouth. The dog had been poisoned. Lonnie straightened. He didn't cry. His emotions welled up within him, and having no outlet, hurt him.

He knelt beside his dog and stroked Moreover's head. Then he pulled the dog's body into his lap and whispered, " My li'l ol' dog, my li'l ol' dog. . . ."

He looked up at his father and said simply, " I'm sorry I called him a biscuit eater."

Harve was too choked up to speak, and Text sat down by Lonnie and stroked the dog, too. " He was trying to get to water. I sho' hate to think of him dying, wanting just one swallow of good ol' water."

" Who killed him, Papa? " Lonnie got to his feet and faced his father.

"That's what I'm aiming to find out."
The man picked up the lantern and walked away, the boys at his heels. They walked over the ridge to Eben's house, and Harve pounded on the front gallery until the farmer appeared.

"My boy's dog is dead," Harve said. "Reckoned you might know something about it."

Eben said, "If he was poisoned, I do. He's a suck-egg dog. I put poison in some eggs and left them in the field. Seems he mout' have committed suicide, McNeil."

"Seems you made it powerful easy for him to get those poisoned eggs," Harve said.

"Ain't no room round here for suck-egg dogs. His daddy was a sheep killer, too. It's good riddance. You ain't got no cause to jump me, Harve McNeil."

Harve said, "He's right, boys. A man's got a right to poison eggs on his own land, and if a dog sucks 'em and dies, the dog's to blame."

Eben said, "Reckon you young 'uns want to bury that dog. Buzzards will be thick to-morrow. You can have the loan of my shovel."

Lonnie looked at the man a long time. He bit his lip so he couldn't cry. "Me and Text will dig a hole with a stick," he said, and turned away.

"You boys go bury him," Harve said. "I'll be home in a few minutes."

Lonnie and Text walked silently into the woods. Text said, "He sho' was a good dawg, huh, Lon? You ain't mad at me 'cause I fed him eggs, are you, Lon?"

"No, Text. Ain't no use in being mad at you. Getting mad at you won't bring ol' Moreover back. Let's wait up here and watch Papa. He can't see us."

Back at Eben's gallery, Harve propped against a post and spoke slowly, "I would have paid you for all the eggs the dog took. My boy loved that dog, Eben."

"Looka heah!" Eben said. "I know my rights."

"I know mine," Harve said. "I always pay my debts, Eben. And I always collect

them. I ain't got no cause to get riled be-cause that dog stole poisoned eggs. But I ain't got no use for a man who will poison a dog. If a dog is mad, shoot him. It's low-life to plant poisoned eggs where a dog can find them. But you were within your rights. I ain't forgot another little thing, however. Two years ago you kicked one of my dogs . . ."

"He barked at me and scared my team on the road," Eben said.

"A dog has got a right on the road, and he's got a right to bark." Harve straightened slowly. A look of fear came into Eben's eyes and he backed away. Harve said softly, "You're a bully. I don't like bullies. I don't like folks who go around causing trouble, picking on their neighbors and keeping everything upset. I'm a peace-loving man, but even peace-loving folks get fed up some-times." He reached out and grabbed Eben by the collar.

"I'll law you!"[1] Eben shouted.

Harve didn't reply. He slapped the man with his open palm, and when Eben squared off to fight, Harve knocked him down.

In the shadows of the woods, Lonnie whispered to Text, "What did I tell you? Papa ain't scared of nothing, cep'n God."

They buried their dog near the branch. Text poured water in the grave. "I can't stand to think of him wanting water when there's a heap of water so close. Reckon if he could have got to the ol' branch he could have washed out that poison? Reckon, Lon?"

"Maybe so."

They were walking to Lonnie's house. "My ol' buckeye and your sweet-stinking mellow bug ain't helped us much, eh, Lon? Luck is plum' mad at us, ain't it, Lon?"

Lonnie waited at the gate until his father arrived. "Me and Text saw the fight," he said. "I won't tell Mother. Women are scut-ters, ain't they, Papa? Always trying to keep men folks from fighting."

Harve smiled and kept his right hand in his pocket. He didn't offer the boys another dog. He could have easily, but he was too

[1] **law you:** have the law on you.

wise. Lonnie and Text would have other dogs, but there would never be another dog like their first dog. And Harve knew it would be crude to suggest another dog might replace Moreover.

He peered into the darkness and saw a car parked behind the house, then hurried inside. Mr. Ames was warming himself by the fire and talking with Mrs. McNeil. She went to the kitchen to brew coffee, and left the men alone, after calling for Lonnie and Text to follow her.

Ames said, " I heard why your boy called his dog off. Call him and that little colored boy in here. I can't go back East with those boys thinking what they do of me."

Lonnie and Text stood by the fire, and Ames said, " That story you heard about me isn't true. I wouldn't have fired this man if your dog had won. We were joking about it and the servants got the story all wrong. I just wanted you boys to know that."

Harve said, " Yes. But even if Mr. Ames would have fired me, it wouldn't have made any difference. You did what you thought was right, but you were wrong. Don't ever quit a race once you start it."

Lonnie told Mr. Ames, " My dog is dead. I'm sorry I called him a biscuit eater. He wasn't. I just want you to know that."

Ames lit his pipe and passed his tobacco pouch to Harve. He saw Harve's bloody hand as the trainer accepted the tobacco.

" Ran into some briars," Harve said.

"Lots of them around here." Ames's eyes twinkled. " Just been thinking, Harve. We got some fine pups coming along. You need help down here. Better hire a couple of good men."

" Good men are sort of scarce," Harve said.

" The kind I want are mighty scarce," said Ames. " They've got to be men with a lot of courage who can lose without grumbling and win without crowing."

" Believe I know where I can get hold of a couple to fill the bill." Harve put his hand on Lon's shoulder and smiled at his son and at Text.

" Well, I'll trust your judgment," Ames said. He shook hands all around. " I've got to be going. Good night, men."

## Suggestions for Study

1. In your opinion does this story make a single central impression? If so, what is it? Can you name any details which do not seem to contribute to this central idea?

2. What effect, if any, did this story have upon your notions of racial relations?

3. Name any pet superstition which you may cherish.

4. With whom did you sympathize in the matter of fighting — Lonnie, or his father, or his mother?

5. Vocabulary: scutter, cicadas, hummock, pursed, quizzical, crotchety.

## Wilbur Schramm     1907–

Wilbur Schramm's main job is that of director of the School of Journalism at the University of Iowa. But he is a man of numerous activities: newspaper correspondent, educational consultant for the Army and Navy, magazine and textbook editor, and author. As a writer he has in recent years produced a unique series of short stories which are really tall tales based upon American legends and folklore. Among the best-known of these are " Windwagon Smith," " Dan Peters and Casey Jones," and " The Wonderful Life of Wilbur the Jeep."

### BOONE OVER THE PACIFIC

This is a typical Schramm story — perhaps not so funny as some, but typical in that into its warp and woof are woven heroic characters of American legend. Trapped in a tropical foxhole were three American soldiers, one from Kentucky, one from Minnesota, and one from Texas. And with them were Daniel Boone, and Paul Bunyan, and Davy Crockett of Texas. Yes, they were there — unless you are one of those poor, benighted souls who don't believe in ghosts. And if you are, what's that to men like Daniel and Paul and Davy?

The first day the Japs came. The second day the rains came. The third day — well, I'll tell you what happened, and let you decide who came the third day.

But answer this first: What if you were caught in a foxhole seven thousand miles from home, and every time you stuck your head an inch above ground level, you asked the Japs to part your hair with a bullet? And suppose that every ten minutes or so a big tree with leaves like elephant's ears would flip a leaf full of water on you. Your wound began to smell, and you could feel the fever and ache begin to creep in on you. You knew the Japs were all around you, and where your own troops were you didn't know. And then suppose someone said to you, " If you had one choice, if you could bring in one man to help you out of this," how would you answer that?

That is the question we tried to answer, those three days.

The first day, the Japs hit us with as neat a one-two punch as I ever saw. They set up a mortar on the far side of the river and began to drop shells all around us. We thought that was their main position and started out to get it. Then they swung the haymaker. They attacked on the flank and behind. We couldn't see them. All we could see were streaks of fire and the air full of bits of tree and leaves. For those of us who were left, there wasn't anything to do except get out if we could.

Some of the boys managed to drop back into the woods. Some jumped into the river and tried to swim downstream under water, with bullets kicking up waterspouts around them. Some of us had to stay where we were.

Tex and Swede and I crawled into a foxhole on the far edge of the woods. We might have got away clean if we hadn't been nicked. But from where we were, we saw probably more Japs than anyone else did. You don't see much of jungle fighting. That's the object. You can't shoot what you don't see. And we didn't see a single Jap until no more shots came from the Americans. Then the little fellows swarmed out of trees and holes and bushes, stationed guards, policed the riverbank and worked over the bodies. They didn't seem to be interested in uniforms or helmets, but cut off the regimental insignia and took the shoes. They gathered

GUADALCANAL FOXHOLE. Trapped three days in a foxhole, beleaguered by Japs and rain, these soldiers needed help from real heroes. (Acme)

guns and knives and ration tins and canteens, and went through all the pockets. If they weren't quite sure the man was dead, they fired a couple more shots into him.

That was hard for us to take. I saw Tex getting redder and redder, and finally he raised his Garand and began to take aim on one of the vultures. I pulled him down. There was no use tipping them off. We squatted in our hole and tried to look like tropical mud and waited for it. But the little green-suited fellows finished their job, made a quick, nervous inspection, and melted away into the undergrowth.

For a long time after that we squeezed our knives and stared out into the greenery until dusk turned it from green to gray and we could afford time to check up on ourselves.

I had a stiff arm and Tex a crease in his side. Swede had caught two bullets in one leg. When we moved it a little to see whether we could find a comfortable position, the pieces of bone ground like a nutmeg grater. Swede lay there with that yellow hair sticking out from under his helmet and his wide, honest face all white and stiff, and put one hand in his mouth to keep from yelling. We tied a bayonet on the leg like a splint to keep him from bending the knee.

Then we had a council of war in whis· pers. Swede couldn't be moved without a stretcher. But Tex or I could go for help.

" Go where? " whispered Tex.

" Texas," Swede suggested, with a grin.

The truth was, we didn't know where to go. Our patrol had been a long way forward. Another unit might be four hundred yards or four miles away. We didn't know which, and we didn't know what direction. We didn't dare signal, because the one thing we were pretty sure of was that Japs were all around us thicker than wood ticks.

Even so, Tex wanted to go out that night and try. But Swede said no.

" The boys have got to come up this way to cross the river," he whispered. " Let 'em find us. Give 'em two or three days, anyway."

" In three days General Douglas MacArthur will be sitting personally in your lap," I promised. But I wondered what kind of shape Swede would be in after three days.

We divided the K rations into three parts. We each took a sulfa tablet, and Tex and I put aside our extra ones for Swede. Then we took turns standing watch.

I had first watch. Tex wasn't sleepy and wanted to talk. That was when he asked the funny question. He said, " What if you could choose one man, any man, to help you out of this. Who would you choose? "

" General MacArthur," I whispered back. " General MacArthur and the Umptyumpth Division."

" One man," he said. " Who do you think you are that anybody would send a whole division after you? "

I thought a minute. " How about Daniel Boone? " I suggested.

Tex threw back his head in a soundless laugh. " Stout fellow," he said. " At least he could find his way around a woods."

" How would you like to have him trailing for you? " I said. " They say he could pick up a footprint and follow the trail back as far as the fellow's father and grandfather. They say he followed one Indian back three generations."

" Do tell," said Tex.

" And there's another great thing about him," I said. " He comes from Kentucky. Go to sleep."

I kept thinking about that question Tex asked me, while I watched. You watch with your ears in the jungle at night. You can't see the jungle, but you hear it. The movement of the leaves, the voices of insects, the crackling steps of small animals, the drip of water — you become accustomed to all these, and you listen for anything unusual. I lay on my back, braced at a fortyfive degree angle against the side of the foxhole, and tried to identify what I heard in terms of the night sounds I had been used to in Kentucky. There was something that sang like a cricket, but lower in pitch, and something that whirred softly, like a moth at the window. Ordinarily, jungle night sounds would have been rather pleasant. The nasty thing about keeping watch was the sensation of waiting for something to come out of the dark and get you. I found myself wondering what I would do if a son of heaven were suddenly to look down into the foxhole and say " So solly." I judged that I could use some help from Boone.

I woke in the morning with a headache. The rains had come. Rain back in Kentucky falls in separate drops and sounds like a thousand little tack hammers. Tropical rain falls in soft heavy blobs, and so thickly that you can't separate the drops. But the biggest difference from rain back in the States is that out here it keeps on coming. And coming. And coming.

All day the rain kept coming down. We thought we were lucky at first because the trees sheltered us. But old elephant ears, the big tree above us, had a better system for soaking us.

Its huge leaves would catch the rain. As each leaf filled, it would turn gracefully over and deposit half a bucketful of water on one of us below. Water began to ooze out of the ground, and the mud we sat in took on the consistency of jelly.

"Jehoshaphat, what a country!" said Tex.

That started us talking about the country we came from. We didn't dare talk aloud; we whispered. The thing that Tex remembered with most pleasure was the long stretch of treeless plain in Texas under the mountains.

He said he had never realized how much he disliked trees until he learned about them from old elephant ears above our foxhole. Trees were probably a Japanese invention, he said. Swede grinned and talked about Minnesota birches. I asked him whether Minnesota dug all those big football players out of the Iron Range, and he surprised us by saying that he had played end for Minnesota under Bernie Bierman. Swede had never talked much about himself. Tex, of course, wouldn't admit that there was any such thing as football outside Texas, and pretty soon he was diagramming the Texas double-pass play with the point of his bayonet in the mud.

"I know who I'd take," Tex said suddenly. "Who I'd take if I had one man to get me out of this mess."

"Who?" said Swede.

"Davy Crockett," Tex said. "David Q. Crockett, of Texas."

"He didn't come from Texas," I said. "He came from Tennessee, about a spit and a throw from where I was born in Kentucky."

"He came to Texas as soon as he had time," argued Tex. "He died at the Alamo."

"Was he the fellow who grinned coons out of trees?" asked Swede.

"The same," said Tex. "He didn't have to shoot 'em. All he had to do was grin at 'em. One time he grinned at what he thought was a coon, and peeled all the bark off a tree."

Swede leaned over to slap Tex playfully, and grimaced with pain.

"He used to pick cherries off a tree half a mile away, shoot their stems in two because it was easier than climbing," said Tex. "He called his rifle Old Betsy. She was almost human. All he had to do was point her toward the woods and she would pick out an animal or an Indian to hit."

"Those were the days," Swede whispered.

"How would it be to have Betsy picking out Japs for us?" I asked.

We talked about Boone and Crockett a lot. We would keep coming back to them. It seems funny now that I remember it, but I suppose that when a fellow gets in that kind of spot he always dreams about some easy way out.

We listened awhile for Japs, and then just sat still and remembered. I could guess what Tex was thinking of — the feel of a good cow pony under you, and the roundups in West Texas where there weren't any trees. And Swede would be remembering the coolness of the wind through the birches, the smell of Swedish cookies on the stove, and maybe the yelling of football crowds in the stadium at Minneapolis. As for me, I seemed to keep calling up things out of my boyhood — the way a steamboat whistles on the Ohio River, the smell of green tobacco just out of the field, the sheen of bluegrass, the clot-clot of a horse on a hard track. We all sat there in the mud and the dripping water, listening and waiting, but our memories were seven thousand miles away, and I wanted to be back in Kentucky so bad it hurt.

Then we started talking about girls, and traded our pictures around. Tex had a brown-eyed beauty who was just graduating from Texas College for Women, and a black-haired beauty who came from the Creole country and went to dances with him in Austin. I had Ellen, who was working for the ration board in Lexington and waiting for me, I hoped. Swede was married. We hadn't known that either. He had a fat youngster with hair like white sand. The kid had come after Swede joined up.

All this information we exchanged in whispers. After a few hours, whispering became the natural way of communication, and talking aloud would have seemed unnatural. Tex drawled even when he whispered. I wished that I could laugh aloud at him to relieve the strain.

We whispered on through the afternoon while the water oozed. Swede's voice got hoarser and hoarser, and his cheeks flushed. Toward the end of the afternoon he went to sleep, and Tex and I winked at each other and quit talking. I sat back against the jellylike side of the foxhole and thought how three Americans could get together in the mud of a South Pacific island, and in a few minutes make that spot a little America and begin arguing about football and Boone and Crockett.

That night was the dangerous one. The rain slackened. We knew that if it slackened enough, the Japs would be out. Tex and I took over all the watches and let Swede rest. Every few minutes he would moan softly in his sleep, and we would put a hand on him to soothe him and keep him quiet.

Watches dragged. The rain muffled other sounds, and we strained our ears to pick out a human noise. Once a six-inch spider walked over my hand, and another time a big night bird dived down on us and flapped his wings almost in my face. I found myself hanging on to my gun, with icy sweat running down my legs and across my stomach and standing in beads on my face. I tried to get a grip on myself before it was time to shake Tex and whisper, " Your ride, cowboy."

I fell into sleep like a stone into water, but was tireder than ever when Tex shook me and whispered, " Steer the boat awhile, will you? "

" Anything happen? " I asked.

" Nope. Rain about over," he answered. " Watch right smart."

" How's Swede? "

" Moaning a little more. Wake him up if he gets too noisy."

About half a lifetime later I shook Tex again. " Your turn, boy."

But it seemed like only five minutes later when Tex's hand was on my shoulder and his whisper in my ear, " You're at bat, stout fellow."

And so we listened through the night.

I was glad when light came, and I could relax ears and use eyes again and see longlegged, lean Tex sleeping like a baby, with a smile on his face, and big, rawboned Swede, face twisted, stirring uneasily, and once in a while thrashing out with a fist.

I woke Tex first, and we had a little conference. Things didn't look good. Swede was in bad shape. Through the torn trousers, his leg showed signs of discoloring. I felt feverish. Tex said he did too. We agreed, if Gen. Douglas MacArthur didn't come for us by night, one of us had to go look for the general. But the big question we avoided: whether by evening, when going would be safer, either of us would be in shape to go.

We were quieter that day. Swede was too sick to do much talking. We sat in our muddy jelly and listened, and felt the fever and the ache creep into our muscles. Once Tex had a chill. It hurt me to move even a finger, and Tex said he felt as though he had just had his first horseback ride, and on a bronco. Swede's leg was beginning to smell.

We didn't say a word about the big question, but by dusk we knew the answer. Neither of us was going to be able to go for help. If we got any help, it would have to come to us. And if it didn't come soon — well, it would have to come soon.

We didn't want to talk about the big question, so we went back again to the question that had teased us ever since Tex asked it.

" These are funny things for us to be talking about out here," said Swede. " Out where they never heard of Crockett or Boone."

" Let's introduce 'em to the South Pacific," I said.

" I reckon wherever Americans go, Boone and Crockett go with them," said Tex.

" Do you remember about Boone and the traveling church? " I asked. " It was when whole churches with their preachers used to travel west over the Wilderness Road, and Boone guided one of them. He came on the track of an Indian war party. There wasn't an Indian fighter in the church, but he told them all, even the women and the children, to go and get tin pans out of the wagons, and sticks to beat them with, and hide in the woods. When the war party came near, he gave a signal and all the church people began to beat on the pans and yell and sing hymns, and I guess the Indians are running yet."

"That's my team," said Tex. "Boone to guide us out of here, and Crockett to pick off the little buzzards when we flush 'em. Have you got any Swedes up in Minnesota to play on that team?" he asked Swede.

"How about Paul Bunyan?" Swede whispered.

"I remember something about a Blue Ox," said Tex. "Which was the Swede — Paul Bunyan or the ox?"

Swede stretched his fever-cracked lips into a grin. "If Old Paul was here," he said, "he wouldn't trifle with your Japs. He'd pick 'em up in one hand and throw 'em in the river."

"What's your favorite Paul Bunyan story?" I asked him.

Swede lay there with his leg stiff out in front of him, and told us in his feverish croak how Paul dug Niagara; how they could never keep telegraph poles around where Paul was working, because he always pulled them up and used them for toothpicks.

"I believe every word of it," said Tex.

"Did you ever know that Old Paul had a wife?" Swede asked.

"No," I lied.

"Old Paul never let anybody see her," Swede said. "He hid her in a cabin in the North. But every time he did a big job, like building the Black Hills or digging Niagara Falls, he would call her name just before he did it."

"What was her name?" Tex asked.

"Olga Christina," said Swede.

"It would be," said Tex.

It was nearly dark. Tex was trying to count on his fingers. "What day of the month is this?" he asked suddenly.

"Not so loud," I said, trying to listen into the shadows.

"We came in on March second," Tex said. "We got hit on the fourth, and yesterday was the fifth, and today," he said impressively, "is March sixth. This is Alamo Day. The day Davy Crockett died at the Alamo with twenty-five dead Mexicans around him."

"Pipe down," I said. "Don't tell Tojo."

"Gentlemen," said Tex, "let us drink to Davy Crockett who on this day in 1836 died for the freedom of Texas and the honor of its womanhood. May he always watch over Texans." He waved his canteen grandly.

"And to Boone," I added. "May he always take care of Kentucky."

"And to Old Paul," croaked Swede. "We could sure use him here."

We sat there with a great show of elegance and drank rain water out of our canteens. I shushed them down because I kept thinking I heard an alien sound near by in the darkened woods.

"They say Old Paul is living yet," said Swede. "Up in the North, waiting for the right time to come back."

"The Indians say Davy never died either," said Tex. "They say that whenever it lightnings and thunders he is shooting his gun, Old Betsy, up in the sky."

"Sh'h," I said.

Just then came the biggest flash and clap of thunder I've ever heard. It wouldn't have been unusual back in Kentucky, but down in the Pacific there isn't much thunder and lightning. The rain doesn't need a storm for an excuse. And so, without any warning at all, this brilliant flash split the sky, and almost at the same moment a thunderclap burst like an H.E.[1] shell.

"There's Crockett," said Tex, forgetting to whisper.

But in the same second he spoke we both saw a sight that froze our backbones to the

---

[1] **H.E.:** high explosive.

sides of the foxhole. About ten yards away, a Jap, crouched on his hands and knees, rifle slung over his back and grenade in his hand, was turning his head in little jerks this way and that, trying to locate the voice he heard.

Tex stood bolt upright in the foxhole and pointed his Garand in the direction we had seen the Jap. In the next flash of lightning he squeezed the trigger. The Jap was ready to throw the grenade, but he was too late.

*They'll come after us now,* I said to myself, and mentally calculated how long it would take a Jap patrol to find us. Probably there was a circle of Japs around us now. In a couple of minutes, a grenade —

I don't know why Tex did what he did then. I don't know why any of us did what we did. I guess maybe we all were delirious and didn't know it. We just couldn't wait any longer for whatever was coming out of the jungle to get us.

Tex began to blaze away with his rifle into the shadows. " Come on, Betsy! " he yelled, and fired away. I started to pull him down, and then something came over me, too, and I jumped up, grabbed my knife in my one good hand, and began to beat on my canteen. Out there in the quiet jungle, it sounded like an Indian war drum. Even as I did it, I wondered why I was doing it. Some voice in my feverish brain said that I was doing it because that was the way Dan Boone trapped an Indian war party on the Wilderness Road. A more rational part of me said that this wasn't the Wilderness Road and I wasn't Boone and we weren't fighting Indians. But I drummed like mad and yelled, and all the time my head was as light as a balloon and felt as though it might sail away.

I heard a croaking beside me, and saw that poor crippled Swede was trying to enter the game too. And then I understood what he was croaking. He was trying to yell, " Olga Christina," like Paul Bunyan.

I helped him out. I yelled, " Olga Christina! " over and over again. It made a pretty good cheer. And there we were, three crazy, sick fools, in the middle of a jet-black jungle, shooting at what we couldn't see, beating an imitation war drum, yelling and whooping and repeating magic names out of Paul Bunyan stories.

I remember thinking, *What does it matter? This is the way to go out — go out in a blaze, not a whimper.* The forest around us began to light up with rifle flashes, and we could hear men moving fast. There were shouts, and a splashing in the river, and then the sweetest sound we had ever heard in our lives — the deep-throated bellow of American heavy machine guns, the smooth rattle of Thompsons, and the firm crack of Garands. That's all. That's all I remember. I went out like a light, with those American sounds in my ears. I guess I got nicked by another bullet or else I fainted and got nicked later. The next I remember, Tex and Swede and I were side by side on three cots in a field hospital. Our bandages were clean, our blankets were clean, and everything around had the sweetish, clean smell of ether and antiseptic. I felt a little sick to my stomach, but awfully comfortable.

They told Tex and me there wasn't anything wrong with us that a week in the hospital and a good furlough wouldn't fix, and they told Swede he wouldn't lose his leg, although it might take a long time to heal, and they were going to ship him back to the States for a while. They said we were heroes, and would get the Purple Heart and maybe something more. They said a big shot was coming to see us.

The big shot was a colonel. No less. He said that our ambuscade was a brilliant maneuver. The Japs were going to try to hit his party on two sides, just as they had hit our party three days earlier. But when we began to shout and yell from our foxhole, the Japs thought they were outsmarted and outflanked in turn. Our first shots picked off two of their officers; the colonel didn't know how we could see to aim. He said we sounded like a whole company. The Japs must have thought so, too, because they gave up their flanking movement, and ran from us right into the path of the American heavy machine guns.

To make it still worse for the Japs, the colonel said, they had gathered all their mortars and some of their machine guns on the riverbank. And a good fifty feet of the bank collapsed and fell into the river, carrying all the guns and a full company of Nips.

I turned my head to look at Swede and to see whether he was thinking the same thing I was. He was. His eyes looked as big as dinner plates.

The colonel said we were heroes and were going to get the Purple Heart and the Silver Star. And Swede and Tex and I couldn't tell him that Bunyan and Boone and Crockett had anything to do with what happened that night, even if we believed it. Could we?

## Suggestions for Study

1. What is a haymaker? What are K rations? Why are Japanese soldiers called "sons of heaven"?

2. What is *your* favorite Paul Bunyan story?

3. Cite from your own experience an incident that illustrates the Kentucky boy's remark, " I suppose when a fellow gets in that kind of spot he always dreams about some easy way out."

4. What other legendary American heroes do you know? You might enjoy looking up the tall tales about Mike Fink, Pecos Bill, John Henry, Tony Beaver, and Johnny Appleseed.

## O. Henry      1862–1910

O. Henry (William Sydney Porter) had an exceedingly varied life. Born in North Carolina, he migrated to a Texas cattle ranch in search of health; edited a paper; worked in a bank; became entangled in a charge of embezzlement, which caused him to flee to Central America; returned to this country and paid the penalty of his lack of business sense; and eventually landed in New York where success but not fortune awaited him. Most of his stories are brief; and as many of them were written for a newspaper, it is small wonder that they smack of journalism. This type of writing was fostered around the beginning of the century by the rapidly increasing cheap magazines and the syndication of stories by daily newspapers. Designed for a large, nonliterary audience, its

conciseness and directness are often in marked contrast to the more elegant, leisurely prose of previous generations. In this type of writing O. Henry is a recognized master.

## THE COP AND THE ANTHEM

O. Henry's sense of plot was phenomenal. The surprise ending, the ability to throw the reader off the scent, the suggestive use of a clue which reveals the whole situation at a glance — these were tricks in his kit which he used over and over again, but always with a fresh and original touch. Besides, his warmth of human understanding and sympathy with the " underdog " give poignancy to many of his stories, even while the reader is convulsed by his amusing speech idioms and absurd situations. The following story has the traditional earmarks of an O. Henry story — wit, humor, irony, cleverness, individuality, and local color.

On his bench in Madison Square, Soapy moved uneasily. When wild geese honk high of nights, and when women without sealskin coats grow kind to their husbands, and when Soapy moves uneasily on his bench in the park, you may know that winter is near at hand.

A dead leaf fell in Soapy's lap. That was Jack Frost's card. Jack is kind to the regular denizens of Madison Square and gives fair warning of his annual call. At the corners of four streets he hands his pasteboards to the North Wind, footman of the mansion of All Outdoors, so that the inhabitants thereof may make ready.

Soapy's mind became cognizant of the fact that the time had come for him to resolve himself into a singular Committee of Ways and Means to provide against the coming rigor. And therefore he moved uneasily on his bench.

The hibernatorial ambitions of Soapy were not of the highest. In them there were no considerations of Mediterranean cruises, of soporific Southern skies, or drifting in the Vesuvian Bay. Three months on the Island [1] was what his soul craved. Three months of

---

[1] **the Island:** Blackwell's Island lying in the East River is the site of the city workhouse to which vagrants are sentenced.

assured board and bed and congenial company, safe from Boreas and bluecoats, seemed to Soapy the essence of things desirable.

For years the hospitable Blackwell's had been his winter quarters. Just as his more fortunate fellow New Yorkers had bought their tickets to Palm Beach and the Riviera each winter, so Soapy had made his humble arrangements for his annual hegira to the Island. And now the time was come. On the previous night three Sabbath newspapers, distributed beneath his coat, about his ankles, and over his lap, had failed to repulse the cold as he slept on his bench near the spurting fountain in the ancient square. So the Island loomed big and timely in Soapy's mind. He scorned the provisions made in the name of charity for the city's dependents. In Soapy's opinion the Law was more benign than Philanthropy. There was an endless round of institutions, municipal and eleemosynary, on which he might set out and receive lodging and food accordant with the simple life. But to one of Soapy's proud spirit the gifts of charity are encumbered. If not in coin you must pay in humiliation of spirit for every benefit received at the hands of philanthropy. As Caesar had his Brutus, every bed of charity must have its toll of a bath, every loaf of bread its compensation of a private and personal inquisition. Wherefore it is better to be a guest of the law which, though conducted by rules, does not meddle unduly with a gentleman's private affairs.

Soapy, having decided to go to the Island, at once set about accomplishing his desire. There were many easy ways of doing this. The pleasantest was to dine luxuriously at some expensive restaurant; and then, after declaring insolvency, be handed over quietly and without uproar to a policeman. An accommodating magistrate would do the rest.

Soapy left his bench and strolled out of the square and across the level sea of asphalt, where Broadway and Fifth Avenue flow together. Up Broadway he turned, and halted at a glittering café, where are gathered together nightly the choicest products of the grape, the silkworm, and the protoplasm.

Soapy had confidence in himself from the lowest button of his vest upward. He was shaven, and his coat was decent and his neat, black, ready-tied four-in-hand had been presented to him by a lady missionary on Thanksgiving Day. If he could reach a table in the restaurant unsuspected, success would be his. The portion of him that would show above the table would raise no doubt in the waiter's mind. A roasted mallard duck, thought Soapy, would be about the thing — with a bottle of Chablis, and then Camembert, a demi-tasse and a cigar. One dollar for the cigar would be enough. The total would not be so high as to call forth any supreme manifestation of revenge from the café management; and yet the meat would leave him filled and happy for the journey to his winter refuge.

But as Soapy set foot inside the restaurant door the head waiter's eye fell upon his frayed trousers and decadent shoes. Strong and ready hands turned him about and conveyed him in silence and haste to the sidewalk and averted the ignoble fate of the menaced mallard.

Soapy turned off Broadway. It seemed that his route to the coveted island was not to be an epicurean one. Some other way of entering limbo must be thought of.

At a corner of Sixth Avenue electric lights and cunningly displayed wares behind plate glass made a shop window conspicuous. Soapy took a cobblestone and dashed it through the glass. People came running around the corner, a policeman in the lead. Soapy stood still, with his hands in his pockets, and smiled at the sight of brass buttons.

" Where's the man that done that? " inquired the officer excitedly.

" Don't you figure out that I might have had something to do with it? " said Soapy, not without sarcasm, but friendly, as one greets good fortune.

The policeman's mind refused to accept Soapy even as a clue. Men who smash windows do not remain to parley with the law's minions. They take to their heels. The policeman saw a man halfway down the block running to catch a car. With drawn club he joined in the pursuit. Soapy, with disgust in his heart, loafed along, twice unsuccessful.

On the opposite side of the street was a restaurant of no great pretensions. It catered to large appetites and modest purses. Its crockery and atmosphere were thick; its soup and napery thin. Into this place Soapy took his accusive shoes and telltale trousers without challenge. At a table he sat and consumed beefsteak, flapjacks, doughnuts, and pie. And then to the waiter he betrayed the fact that the minutest coin and himself were strangers.

"Now, get busy and call a cop," said Soapy. "And don't keep a gentleman waiting."

"No cop for youse," said the waiter, with a voice like butter cakes and an eye like the cherry in a Manhattan cocktail. "Hey, Con!"

Neatly upon his left ear on the callous pavement two waiters pitched Soapy. He arose, joint by joint, as a carpenter's rule opens, and beat the dust from his clothes. Arrest seemed but a rosy dream. The Island seemed very far away. A policeman who stood before a drugstore two doors away laughed and walked down the street.

Five blocks Soapy traveled before his courage permitted him to woo capture again. This time the opportunity presented what he fatuously termed to himself a "cinch." A young woman of a modest and pleasing guise was standing before a show window gazing with sprightly interest at its display of shaving mugs and inkstands, and two yards from the window a large policeman of severe demeanor leaned against a water plug.

It was Soapy's design to assume the role of the despicable and execrated "masher." The refined and elegant appearance of his victim and the contiguity of the conscientious cop encouraged him to believe that he would soon feel the pleasant official clutch upon his arm that would insure his winter quarters on the right little, tight little isle.

Soapy straightened the lady missionary's ready-made tie, dragged his shrinking cuffs into the open, set his hat at a killing cant, and sidled toward the young woman. He made eyes at her, was taken with sudden coughs and "hems," smiled, smirked, and went brazenly through the impudent and contemptible litany of the "masher." With half an eye Soapy saw that the policeman was watching him fixedly. The young woman moved away a few steps, and again bestowed her absorbed attention upon the shaving mugs. Soapy followed, boldly stepping to her side, raised his hat and said:

"Ah there, Bedelia! Don't you want to come and play in my yard?"

The policeman was still looking. The persecuted young woman had but to beckon a finger and Soapy would be practically en route for his insular haven. Already he imagined he could feel the cozy warmth of the station house. The young woman faced him and, stretching out a hand, caught Soapy's coat sleeve.

"Sure, Mike," she said joyfully, "if you'll blow me to a pail of suds. I'd have spoke to you sooner, but the cop was watching."

With the young woman playing the clinging ivy to his oak, Soapy walked past the policeman overcome with gloom. He seemed doomed to liberty.

At the next corner he shook off his companion and ran. He halted in the district where by night are found the lightest streets, hearts, vows, and librettos. Women in furs and men in greatcoats moved gaily in the wintry air. A sudden fear seized Soapy that some dreadful enchantment had rendered him immune to arrest. The thought brought a little of panic upon it, and when he came upon another policeman lounging grandly in front of a transplendent theater he caught at the immediate straw of "disorderly conduct."

On the sidewalk Soapy began to yell drunken gibberish at the top of his harsh voice. He danced, howled, raved, and otherwise disturbed the welkin.

CITY STREET SCENE. Will Soapy succeed in getting arrested this time? (Frederic Lewis)

The policeman twirled his club, turned his back to Soapy and remarked to a citizen:

" 'Tis one of them Yale lads celebratin' the goose egg they give to the Hartford College. Noisy; but no harm. We've instructions to lave them be."

Disconsolate, Soapy ceased his unavailing racket. Would never a policeman lay hands on him? In his fancy the Island seemed an unattainable Arcadia. He buttoned his thin coat against the chilling wind.

In a cigar store he saw a well-dressed man lighting a cigar at a swinging light. His silk umbrella he had set by the door on entering. Soapy stepped inside, secured the umbrella, and sauntered off with it slowly. The man at the cigar light followed hastily.

" My umbrella," he said, sternly.

" Oh, is it? " sneered Soapy, adding insult to petit larceny. " Well, why don't you call a policeman? I took it. Your umbrella! Why don't you call a cop? There stands one on the corner."

The umbrella owner slowed his steps. Soapy did likewise, with a presentiment that luck would again run against him. The policeman looked at the two curiously.

" Of course," said the umbrella man — " that is — well, you know how these mistakes occur — I — if it's your umbrella I hope you'll excuse me — I picked it up this morning in a restaurant — if you recognize it as yours, why — I hope you'll — "

" Of course it's mine," said Soapy, viciously.

The ex-umbrella man retreated. The policeman hurried to assist a tall blonde in an opera cloak across the street in front of a streetcar that was approaching two blocks away.

Soapy walked eastward through a street damaged by improvements. He hurled the umbrella wrathfully into an excavation. He muttered against the men who wear helmets and carry clubs. Because he wanted to fall into their clutches, they seemed to regard him as a king who could do no wrong.

At length Soapy reached one of the avenues to the east where the glitter and turmoil was but faint. He set his face down this toward Madison Square, for the homing instinct survives even when the home is a park bench.

But on an unusually quiet corner Soapy came to a standstill. Here was an old church, quaint and rambling and gabled. Through one violet-stained window a soft light glowed, where, no doubt, the organist loitered over the keys, making sure of his mastery of the coming Sabbath anthem. For there drifted out to Soapy's ears sweet music that caught and held him transfixed against the convolutions of the iron fence.

The moon was above, lustrous and serene; vehicles and pedestrians were few; sparrows twittered sleepily in the eaves — for a little while the scene might have been a country churchyard. And the anthem that the organist played cemented Soapy to the iron fence, for he had known it well in the days when his life contained such things as mothers and roses and ambitions and friends and immaculate thoughts and collars.

The conjunction of Soapy's receptive state of mind and the influences about the old church wrought a sudden and wonderful change in his soul. He viewed with swift horror the pit into which he had tumbled, the degraded days, unworthy desires, dead hopes, wrecked faculties, and base motives that made up his existence.

And also in a moment his heart responded thrillingly to this novel mood. An instantaneous and strong impulse moved him to battle with his desperate fate. He would pull himself out of the mire; he would make a man of himself again; he would conquer the evil that had taken possession of him. There was time; he was comparatively young yet; he would resurrect his old eager ambitions and pursue them without faltering. Those solemn but sweet organ notes had set up a revolution in him. Tomorrow he would go into the roaring downtown district and find work. A fur importer had once offered him a place as driver. He would find him tomorrow and ask for the position. He would be somebody in the world. He would —

Soapy felt a hand laid on his arm. He looked quickly around into a broad face of a policeman.

" What are you doin' here? " asked the officer.

" Nothin'," said Soapy.

" Then come along," said the policeman.

" Three months on the Island," said the Magistrate in the Police Court the next morning.

## Suggestions for Study

1. What is meant by " the choicest products of the grape, the silkworm, and the protoplasm "? Mention other neat phrases in the story.

2. In your case how successful was the surprise ending? There are two tests of a good surprise ending: (a) you should not be able to see it coming; (b) you should be obliged to admit, on looking back over the story, that all the necessary clues were there. Point out the clues which O. Henry gave to prepare the reader for the ending.

3. What details show that O. Henry was familiar with the New York setting he used in this story?

4. What are the two opposing forces in the plot of this story? What is the single effect?

5. Vocabulary: denizens, cognizant, hibernatorial, soporific, hegira, benign, eleemosynary, insolvency, epicurean, limbo, fatuously, despicable, execrated, contiguity.

## For Your Vocabulary

WORD ANALYSIS. Many long words that look strange at first glance are actually made up of familiar words at the core, with prefixes and suffixes added. It is a profitable habit to look at long words closely. You can often recognize parts and discover for yourself what the meaning must be. Examine *disconsolate* (page 34) and you find the prefix *dis-*, indicating the lack or opposite of, and the adjective suffix *-ate* on the familiar word *console*. But notice how a shift of accent changes the sound — dĭs-kŏn'-sŏ-lĭt. *Unavailing* (page 34) and *unattainable* (page 34) are similarly formed by adding to simple verbs, but accent and pronunciation of the base-words are unchanged. The prefix *un-* never makes the accent of the base-word shift forward. *Presentiment* (prĕ-zĕn'tĭ-mĕnt) takes a little more figuring; *sentiment* here means " feeling," and *pre-*, " before." Thus a presentiment is a feeling before a happening that it is going to occur. Check on page 34 to see what Soapy's *presentiment* was. *Decadent* (page 32) and *despicable* (page 33) make slight changes in the spelling of the familiar base-words but are still recognizable. *Decadent* keeps the sound of *decay*, but *despicable* (dĕs'-pĭ-ká-b'l) changes the sound as well as the spelling of *despise*. Keep an eye out for other such built-up words. Some will be listed in the vocabulary notes for you to analyze.

## Booth Tarkington          1869–1946

For about a quarter of a century Booth Tarkington has been known for his humorous portrayals of youth, especially lovelorn youth in the late teen age.

Like Riley, who encouraged him to become an author, Tarkington was a Hoosier, and lived for many years in his birthplace, Indianapolis. After Princeton he tried for six years to write, and earned $22.50. Success came at last with *Monsieur Beaucaire* (1900), which is one of the best of the historical romances that flourished at the turn of the century. His next important success came when he turned to humorous stories of boyhood with *Penrod* (1914) and *Seventeen* (1916). All the world knows Penrod and Willy Baxter. They are in the characteristic Tarkington vein, which never seemed to give out. Even in his plays, like *Clarence* (1919), characters of the same type appear. Possibly his more serious novels of American life, like *The Turmoil* (1915), *The Magnificent Ambersons* (1918), or his masterpiece, *Alice Adams* (1921), will be longer remembered; but to thousands of American boys and girls " Tarkington " means characters like Penrod, Willy Baxter, or Mr. Indiana in the following story.

## HENRY THE GREAT

This story gives a vivid and humorous picture of a self-conscious youth whose personal problems — chiefly emotional — are to him more important than the fate of nations. Mr. Tarkington seems to find amusement, too, in two rather absurd phases of the great game of advertising: the amateur radio contest and the Miss America competition. In short, you are about to read a typical Tarkington story.

A brisk young couple noisily laughed their way across the lobby of the Arlington Hotel in Boston — a girl whose summer blouse displayed a gold satin ribbon lettered in black, Miss Vermont, and a tall youth similarly labeled Mr. California. " Make me sick! " an elderly guest complained to a clerk at the desk. " In all the nineteen years I've been living at the Arlington, I've never heard so much noise. Who are all these juveniles? Convention of defectives? "

" Defectives? " the clerk said, humorously affecting shock. " Nay! Our country's chosen intelligentsia! "

Here he acquired another listener. This was a blue-eyed, sandy-haired boy of appearance so youthful that perhaps his reason for wearing a derby hat was to make him look older. The weather was warm; all other hats in sight were of straw, and maybe, too, he hoped that this derby hat, a new one, lent knowingness to a face both bright and timid. Carrying a new leatherine

suitcase of which no bellboy had sought to relieve him, he had been standing not far from the desk for five or ten minutes, sometimes clearing his throat authoritatively to show that he wasn't worrying about anything. Hearing the word " intelligentsia," however, he moved nearer.

" There's to be ninety-six of 'em altogether," the clerk continued. " It's the Sidex Corporation's Intellect Prize Contest. Two Intellect Prize Winners, a male and a female, from every state in the Union."

" What? " The complaining guest looked again at Miss Vermont and Mr. California, now waiting for an elevator, and his staring eyes threatened to become bloodshot. " Intellect? Oh, my soul! "

" Intellect, sure! " The clerk tried to mollify him. " You don't object to beauty contests where bathing girls get elected Miss Florida or Miss New Jersey, do you? The Sidex people simply got up a broadcasting Intellect Contest, instead, open to everybody twenty-two years old or younger. The candidates sent in eight-minute essays and the best ones in each state were picked out to make speeches over the radio, and the listeners-in of that state sent in votes on which were the best. The young man and young lady that had the most votes in each state got the prize of a free trip to Boston, and the Sidex people put them up at the Arlington, of course, because they read our circulars! " The clerk laughed affably. " See? Shows Boston's still the right place for Intellect Prize Winners to come to."

" As if poor old Boston didn't have enough troubles of her — " The guest interrupted himself as the leatherine suitcase bumped the calf of his leg. " Don't crowd me, bud. I'm on my way, anyhow, if you want to register."

He departed, and the boy in the derby hat, nervous, swallowed nothing so plainly that the operation could be traced along the surface of his slender throat.

" Room? " the clerk asked. " Got a reservation? "

" Sir? I — I guess I ought to sign the book."

" I see."

The clerk handed him a dipped pen.

The boy in the derby hat hesitated, grew red, then applied the pen to the register and wrote carefully:

*Mr. Indiana, R.R., No. 2*
*Emmonsville, Indiana*

The clerk looked at the inscription, glanced at the inscriber, and seemed surprised. " Well, well! So you're one of the Intellect Prize Winners, too, are you? You must be the youngest of the whole bunch." He smiled amiably. " I expect you might as well put your name down, though."

" Sir? "

" Just write your own name there alongside of ' Mr. Indiana,' " the clerk explained. " Just in Boston we're more or less supposed to rather keep track of our guests' real names."

" Yes, sir." Even redder than he had been, the boy wrote as requested, " Henry Hopgood Dilmer."

" Excellent," the clerk said with gravity. " Quite all right, Mr. Indiana. Shoot you right up, Mr. Indiana."

" Up? Where — "

" To your room. Might like to brush your hat or wash your face or something. After that you're supposed to join up with the Sidex people on the mezzanine." The clerk rang a bell, and then, seeing that the boy had removed his derby hat and was looking at it, added, " I didn't mean it's dusty; it's just a custom. This bellboy'll carry your bag for you, Mr. Indiana. Four-fourteen."

Mr. Indiana, or, as he had theretofore been generally known to those who knew him, Henry Hopgood Dilmer, looked rather anxiously at the bellboy and also at the suitcase; then gave up the one to the other, and, as the bellboy carried the suitcase immediately to an elevator, decided after a moment's hesitation to follow him. The bellboy took the suitcase into the elevator, rose to the fourth floor, went down a corridor, opened a door marked 414, and entered a bedchamber; Mr. Indiana was still following. The room had two beds, and, at the foot of one, a closed traveling bag lay upon a portable stool.

" You're doubled up with Mr. Idaho," the bellboy said, placed Mr. Indiana's suitcase upon a stand at the foot of the other bed, went to the open window, adjusted the shade slightly, coughed several times, and then walked slowly toward the door. " That all? " he asked. " Anything else I can do for you? "

" No, I don't guess so."

The bellboy lingered one moment longer, then made a brief sound with his breath only and left the room. Henry Hopgood Dilmer, uncertain about the meaning of the sound the bellboy had made, looked again at his hat, then went to a dressing table over which hung a mirror, looked at himself, and forgot the bellboy. After a time he extended his hand toward his reflection.

" Listen, good ole Mr. Indiana," he said earnestly. " Well, here we are in Boston! Shake."

He moved his extended hand up and down several times, replaced the derby hat upon his head, returned to the corridor, found the elevator doors, and pressed a button — the wrong one. A door opened, he stepped within the car and ascended to the tenth floor; whereupon, as he remained in a corner, the attendant, a cold and elderly blonde, glanced at him.

" This is the top," she said.

" Ma'am? " he asked. " Is it? "

She made no response; the car went down, taking in several passengers on its way. At the office floor these stepped out, others stepped in, and the car ascended again. At the top floor the attendant again looked at Henry. " Listen," she said. " Say, listen. What floor you want? "

Another slight undulation of his neck became visible. " Well, I — I'm supposed to be looking for the — the mezzanine."

" Then whyn't you get off at it? "

" Ma'am? "

" Oh, me! " she said. " Oh, me! "

She was kinder, however, than she seemed, for, near the conclusion of the next descent, she stopped the elevator, opened the door, and spoke in a loud and distinct voice: " Mezzanine floor."

Henry Hopgood Dilmer, abruptly breathless, stepped out of the elevator and found himself in a corridor thronged and noisy with young Intellect Prize Winners. To Henry, however, they didn't appear to be young; in his eyes they possessed a daunting maturity, most of them being apparently as much as twenty-one or even twenty-two years old, and he was discomfited by their seeming to be already upon terms of lively familiarity with one another. Mr. California, in particular, was appalling to Henry. Tall Mr. California, hooked by the arm to laughing Miss Vermont, strolled up and down the corridor, confident, loud-voiced, and jovial in his blue serge coat, white trousers, and impressive white-and-black shoes. He seemed to know everybody, exchanged laughter and slang with almost all groups; and there were others like him — easy, free-spoken, and free-moving — swarthy Mr. New York, merry Mr. South Carolina, handsome Mr. Kentucky, and, largest and noisiest of all the girls, Miss Delaware.

Henry had the guilty feeling that all these people immediately wondered who he was and, since he alone was badgeless, looked upon him as an intruder. He stood with his back to the wall near the closed elevator shaft, removed his hat, and stared at it frowningly. He protracted his inspection longer than he thought plausible and began to blush, thinking, " They won't believe I'm looking for a speck on my hat this long. I got to do something else; I simply got to. They'll get the idea I'm embarrassed and think I don't know anything. I can't keep on doing this the whole day! " He turned the hat over, looked inside it, frowned more deeply. " Maybe they'll think I put my railroad ticket in it and can't find it," he thought. " No, they won't. I simply got to quit this! "

Opposite him, across the corridor, four girls sat rather bleakly together upon a sofa — a group neglected by Mr. California and other conspicuous male Prize Winners. Even among Intellectuals, it appeared, there could be wallflowers. One of these four was stout and spectacled; one was thin, tall, and severe; one was noticeably what is called plain of feature. The fourth was small, a delicate and almost childlike figure; and the extreme forward dip of her white straw hat so obscured her face in shadow that her interested observation of Henry Hopgood Dilmer went unnoticed. The golden badges of the four showed them to be Miss Massachusetts, Miss Minnesota, Miss Oklahoma, and Miss Virginia. The little one with the down-bent hat brim was Miss Virginia.

Miss Virginia whispered to her neighbors on the sofa, " That poor young little thing ovuh yonduh's scared out of his wits. Somebody's got to do something for him or he'll run home! " She rose, crossed the corridor, and spoke to Henry in a pretty voice. " I wonduh you lookin' for Mr. Heilbrenner? His desk's out on the mezzanine gall'ry. Like me to show you? "

" Well, I — " Henry said. " Who? I guess from your badge you must be Miss Virginia."

" Wonderful! " she returned. " But how's anybody goin' to tell who you are? "

Henry began to regain some self-confidence. " I come from out West." He coughed boldly. " I am Mr. Indiana."

She laughed. " Mr. California wouldn't say you from very out Wes'! I thought I ought to come help you some 'cause looks like maybe you and I got kind of a tie between us, as it were."

" Tie? What kind of a — "

" Looks like we two the very littles' young Prize Winnuhs in the whole United States, Mr. Indiana. I'm the younges' of all the girls. How old you? "

" Me? I'll be eighteen next year," Henry said.

" You will? You mean by the far end of next year, don't you? I won't. It's the ever-lastin' livin' truth I'll only be seventeen even then. I expect you and me about the same age and liable to get lost in Boston if we don't look out for ourselves! " Under the concealing hat brim there was a twinkle of kind brown eyes already become maternal. " Expect I'll have to be the one does the lookin' out too! Tell the truth now; don't brag, mistuh. You evuh been this far from home before? "

" Well — no, not altogether." All at once Henry became confidential. " I been on motor trips with my family to Wyandotte Cave and Indianapolis and Terre Haute lots of times, and my father and I went to the Century of Progress, but we stayed in kind of a boarding-house. I never been upstairs exactly in exactly this kind of a hotel before — I mean not exactly." He followed an impulse toward further conversation. " What was your topic in the contest? Mine was ' Fascism Unmasked.' " He laughed with a modest carelessness. " I don't s'pose you happened to be listening in and heard it maybe? "

" I'm awful sorry. We get so much static in our radio some nights we jus' miss everything, 'specially what's the very bes'. I don't know how I happened to win the contest in my state, myself; I jus' wrote a little no-'count piece and spoke it."

Henry looked judicial. " Well, it might have been on account of your voice."

" Think it might? That's awful sweet of you, Mr. Indiana."

" Oh, no," Henry said. " I never say anything except what I mean. I always believe in being sincere, don't you? I think it's the highest quality there is. Don't you? "

" 'Deed I do," she said. " Listen, Mr. Indiana; you haven't even got your badge yet. I'm goin' march you straight out to Mr. Heilbrenner on the mezzanine gall'ry, 'cause you got to show him your Sidex card from home and get your MR. INDIANA ribbon pinned onto you. We may be the younges', but anyways we goin' show people who us two little things are! "

Henry felt himself adopted, sweetly owned, and looked out for. The feathery touch of Miss Virginia's fingers upon his sleeve guided him through the crowd, led him out upon an open gallery beyond the

corridor and to a table where sat a stout middle-aged man and two young women, his assistants.

" This gentleman's Mr. Indiana, Mr. Heilbrenner," Miss Virginia said. . . . " Hand Mr. Heilbrenner your Sidex card from home, Mr. Indiana. . . . That's right. Now you goin' get your badge pinned onto you, pretty as a picture! " Then, when one of the assistants had properly decorated Henry's lapel, Miss Virginia inquired, " Now don't that strong little chest o' yours feel proud as Satan, Mr. Indiana? "

" Satan? " Henry asked, somewhat disturbed. " Well, I'd hardly say — "

" Come on," she interrupted cozily, and again he felt her light touch on his arm. " We goin' back to that sofa where Miss Massachusetts, Miss Minnesota, and Miss Oklahoma sittin' all alone. I wouldn't like 'em to think I'd run away from 'em, 'cause I'm scared they kind o' feel a little outside the big show, as it were. You be nice to them, Mr. Indiana, so now they goin' feel they got a man to escort 'em round, show 'em attentions. Come on! "

Henry returned with her to the sofa in the corridor and, upon Miss Virginia's warm presentation of him, was received affably by Miss Massachusetts, Miss Minnesota, and Miss Oklahoma. " Look a-here, ladies," big-hearted Miss Virginia said. " Look what we got! Anybody accuse us of bein' too much intellect now, we can prove our softuh natures, 'cause now we got a man — and goin' to hold onto him too! From now on we four goin' to claim Indiana jus' about almos' the very grandes' state in the Union! "

" It's got the center of population of the United States in it," Henry said seriously. " Thirty miles from Columbus, Indiana, statistics show that — "

He was interrupted by a loud clapping of hands for silence. Mr. Heilbrenner appeared in the corridor and sonorously made an announcement. " Now we're all going downstairs," he said. " Busses are waiting there, and we'll get in and be taken to the Public Library, the Art Museum, Faneuil

Hall, Bunker Hill Monument, and the State House, after which we return here for lunch. After lunch the busses will leave to show us other sights of Boston, Cambridge, Longfellow's Home, and Harvard University. Afterward we meet for dinner in the dining room, after which there will be dancing for those who care to indulge. Tomorrow morning at ten o'clock the busses will conduct us on a motor trip to Concord, Lexington, and other historic points of interest, and in the evening we will return here for the big Prize Winners' Banquet, when there will be a Surprise Announcement made that I'm sure will bring each and every one of you a thrill of the highest pleasure. You will all be immensely pleased with the surprise Sidex has for you at the banquet tomorrow night. Now please all follow me downstairs to the busses. Sidex thanks you! "

" You walk with Miss Massachusetts," Miss Virginia whispered to Henry, pushing him gently forward; and as he frankly looked blank, she added, " Don't worry; the rest of us three goin' stick closer to you than the buttons on your jacket! "

She was almost as good as her word, and in the bus he had the pleasure of finding himself beside her. In the bright summer daylight he had another pleasure too; rather gradually he discovered that under the obscuring hat was one of the very prettiest piquant faces he had ever seen. This was not bad news to Henry; he became almost as conscious of Miss Virginia as he was of himself and of his golden badge. Moreover, in chatting with him she sometimes used a half-smothered monosyllable that warmed his spine.

" Why, of course I love my grandma, hon," she said, on the way from Bunker Hill Monument to the State House. " What makes you say you hate yours so bad? "

Henry drew a deep breath. " Look, Miss Virginia, did — did — do — do — do you mean it when you call me ' hon ' that way? "

" Now! " she said, and laughed. " Don't get mad at my little ways! What makes you hate your grandma? "

" I don't mean I hate her exactly," Henry

explained. " I guess it's mostly because she lives at our house and's pretty faultfinding with me and always takes my sister's part. I guess I'm pretty critical, because I got a critical nature. I wish she was like you."

" Who? Your grandma? "

" Yes," Henry said. " I wish she was and I wish my sister was, too. There'd be a lot more peace in our house if both of 'em were like you."

" Tell me some more about your grandma and your sister."

" Well," Henry said, " there's something wrong with both of 'em."

Miss Virginia looked sympathetic. " You mean they got something they don't feel well? "

• " No," Henry said. " They never had a day's sickness in their lives. The trouble is they can't stand the slightest criticism. Well, I got to be sincere, haven't I? I think sincerity's the highest quality there is; don't you? " He paused. " Oh, yes; we did talk about that. What else do you think ought to be in a person's nature if you were really going to care for them? "

She looked solemn. " Well, maybe I think they ought to come from Indiana! "

" Do — do you? " he said in a husky whisper; then saw that under her hat she was laughing at him charmingly.

Henry felt bewitched; all at once he was even more conscious of Miss Virginia than he was of himself or his golden ribbon, and during the rest of that day his condition continually got more so. Even Longfellow's Home was only a hazy background for the bright little figure from the South; Henry's Intellect Prize Winning visit to Boston hadn't really taken him to New England. Mr. Indiana walked in a dream of sunnier fields and softer skies.

Miss Virginia, not dreamy at all, continued to share him honorably with Miss Massachusetts, Miss Minnesota, and Miss Oklahoma. Most of the Prize Winners, like Mr. California and Miss Vermont, had coupled up, so to speak, with a stag element left over — youths who held together defensively, a masculine clique apart. Miss Virginia made Henry as much of a substitute for these as she could. Whenever she saw a lonely girl standing neglected, Miss Virginia would tuck her arm in Henry's, join that girl, introduce Henry, and stay for a little chat. Miss Virginia and Henry became gratefully known to all the friendless.

That night at the dance, however, Miss Virginia became known to everybody else. Henry's first sight of her without a hat and wearing the daintiest white silk dancing dress he'd ever seen undid his vocal organs. He looked at her, gasped, " Oh, my! " and was unable to speak further. Then they danced together, and, when she murmured, " I jus' knew you'd turn out to be the bes' little dancer in the worl'! " he could only swallow and respond with a breathless " Um-hum " that fatuously sounded affirmative.

He didn't dance with her long. Miss Virginia, an unnoticeable little person all that day, was revealed in her evening gown and hatlessness transformed — nay, transfigured. She had that ever-fascinating contrast of rippled hair lighter than trim dark eyebrows, dark appealing eyes, and dark coquettish lashes; her subtle little figure seemed woven out of grace itself; and she danced, as forebears of hers would have said, with the foot of a fairy. Many eyes began to follow her; wolfish stags cut in on Henry, and so did young gentlemen somewhat committed in other directions — Miss Vermont began to be peevish with tall Mr. California. In a word, Miss Virginia was the belle of the ball.

" Listen! " Henry said to her emotionally, late in the evening, during a short whirl round the room. " Look! You don't act the way you did all day any more. I know some of 'em got tucks and I haven't, but there's one thing I got to know."

" Only one? What? "

" Do you — do you call all of 'em, ' hon,' too, the way you did me? "

The lovely eyes, profoundly reproachful, seemed about to fill with tears. " My own

bes' little man bringin' accusations agains' me already? "

" No, not accusations exactly, but — "

" That's right! " Her eyes shed sunshine again and the light hand upon his shoulder was lifted to give his cheek a little pat. " Listen, hon; you danced with Miss Massachusetts and Miss Minnesota and Miss Oklahoma and Miss South Dakota and Miss Wisconsin and everybody else I told you to? "

" Yes, I did," he said resentfully. " I was pretty near an hour getting away from that big ole Miss South Dakota too; and all that time you were — "

" Listen, hon," she said. " You haven't danced with Miss Indiana yet, and you certainly owe it to her the mos' of any. You go straight and dance with her, and I want you to promise me something. Promise? "

" You know I'd promise you anything."

" Goody," she said. " You promise me not to cut in to dance with me one more time tonight! "

" What? "

" You promised! You keep cuttin' in on every girl here that's too long with one partner."

" But I — " The heavy hand of Mr. Iowa fell upon his shoulder; he had to relinquish her.

" Remembuh, you promised! " her sweet voice called as she swung away with Mr. Iowa.

Henry danced with plain girls, with girls taller than himself, with girls who couldn't dance; and all the while a painful question perplexed him: Had she decided that he was too ignoble to be seen with, or was it really a compliment to him that she bestowed him, as it were, upon less-favored girls? Then, at the end of the evening, when the musicians were departing, he saw her at the other end of the big room — laughing, happy, brilliantly surrounded — and his question seemed to be answered.

" Ha-ha! " he said ironically to himself aloud, though in a low voice. " No use for you if you haven't got a tuck! Just wanted to get rid of me. A lot of use being Mr. Indiana if all this had to happen to me, isn't it? "

In his bedchamber, whither he went without giving her another glance, he was morose with his roommate, Mr. Idaho, who would fain have been talkative.

" Boy! " Mr. Idaho exclaimed. " Is that Miss Virginia some on her feet? Boy! Has she got eyes? Oh, man! Listen, Hoosier lad, if that big contest comes off, does Miss Virginia get the vote of Idaho? Boy! Didn't meet her, did you? "

" I did, too," Henry said heavily. " What contest? "

" Well, it's only a rumor; but it's supposed to've leaked out through one of Mr. Heilbrenner's lady secretaries' being a cousin of Miss Massachusetts. Miss Mass. spilled it to a couple of other girls she's got intimate with, and they promised to keep it secret; but it seems Miss Minnesota passed it out snub nosa [1] to somebody else, so it kind of leaked around here and there tonight. It may be baloney; but it's supposed to be the inside of the big secret surprise Mr. Heilbrenner's going to announce at the banquet tomorrow night."

Henry got into bed, gloomily laid his head upon the pillow. " I don't know what you're talking about."

" Well, keep it under your hat, baby; but this rumor is that the whole forty-eight states at the banquet's going to elect a Miss America. Hot diggety! Watch Miss Virginia in that race! Boy! Listen, Middle East; then, after the convention elects Miss America, the rumor is that — "

" Look," Henry said. " Put out the light if you got your night clo'es on, will you? I'd like to get a little sleep."

Rebuffed, breezy Mr. Idaho satirically paraphrased a lullaby fragment, instructed Henry to rest his little woolly Indiana head on his Mammy's breast; but at the same time, for his own sake, did put out the light and almost immediately afterward slept.

Mr. Indiana's state of mind was less for-

[1] snub nosa: a humorous and intentional corruption of *sub rosa*, which means secretly.

tunate. Far, far from kith and kin, lying restless in a vast Boston hotel, Henry was tormented by imaginings; tall glittering Mr. California in a tuck, darkly fashionable Mr. New York in a tuck, handsome Mr. Kentucky betucked, others in tucks — all old-looking, men-about-town figures that swept Miss Virginia gleaming with them in a hateful dance across the sky, while she made cruel music with her sweet and cozy laughter. So she might even become Miss America, might she? And once he'd thought — ha-ha! — that she had time for him!

In the morning, when the ninety-six Prize Winners again met in the corridor, Henry was chill though tremulous when she hurried to join him. " I bid you good morning," he said repellently.

" What? " she asked, astonished. " What in the livin' worl's the mattuh with you, Mr. Indiana? "

" Nothing," he said. " Nothing at all. I can't help seeing I've gotten disgusting to you, can I? "

" Gotten what? "

" Disgusting," Henry said. " Do you think simply because I don't wear a tuck at some ole dance, I can't tell when I've gotten disgusting to some girl? "

She put her small hands upon his shoulders and shook him. " Why, you sweet little thing! " she cried.

Henry, dazed, spoke swallowingly. " You — you don't mean it. You say it, but — but you don't mean it."

" You'll see! " she said, and gave him another ineffable pat upon his cheek. " Listen, hon, you be good as gol' today and keep pickin' up Miss Louisiana's parasol and gloves and handkerchief when she drops 'em, and carrying Miss Oregon's camera for her and Miss Minnesota's notebooks, same as I got you to yesterday. Talk nice to Miss Vermont whenever you get a chance, too, 'cause it looks like she begins to feel kind o' left out. You rastle roun' among 'em jus' like yesterday and don't worry about me, 'cause — "

" No? " Henry said, frosty again. " Excuse me; but you needn't be scared I desire to intrude my presence on you, since you think I'm so dis — "

" Aw, hon! " Miss Virginia was tender with him, irresistibly. " You so far from home, aren't you goin' to let me be your little mamma for you? "

" Yes," Henry gulped. " If you say so."

He was wax again; but ten minutes later, seated beside Miss Oregon on the way to Lexington and Concord, he once more felt the hollowness of representing the state of Indiana intellectually — Miss Virginia was not even in the same bus with him.

" All right," he said to himself. " I'll do what she told me, and then, if she ever comes near me again, I'll laugh. I'll look at her — then I'll laugh! "

But Miss Virginia, even more the belle of the ball today than last night, wasn't near him again until the ninety-six were seating themselves for lunch in the dining room of a hotel on the Gloucester rocks. Then, just as he sat down next to Miss Vermont, there was the touch of a hand upon his shoulder, and, looking up, but not laughing, he found her fondly approving face close to his own.

" You doin' fine, hon! " she whispered hurriedly, and, attended by Mr. California, Mr. Idaho, Mr. Maine, and Mr. Ohio, went on gaily to a distant table.

For the one magnetizing moment Henry was warm, breathless, convinced. Alas, that moment was but a drop of honey in a gallon of vinegar! The rest of the day was all sour; Henry had only glimpses of her, remote from him and resplendent — the center of every group to which she fluttered; but fluttering not again to him. What time [1] the busses returned to Boston and the Arlington Hotel in twilight, Henry felt that for him all was ended — he had but one desire, a bitter one.

He wished to confront her, to unpin from his lapel the golden ribbon with MR. IN-DIANA large-lettered upon it, to cast it at her feet and say, " There! Long as I live I'll never write another essay or deliver

[1] **What time:** by the time.

another oration or win another prize trip. That's all you've done to me! "

This was still his mood as he found the place reserved for him at the Sidex Intellect Prize Winners' Banquet that evening; and jubilating music issuing from a grilled balcony made him feel more dramatic, but not happier. Henry's seat, alphabetic, was at a small table with Miss Indiana, Miss Illinois and Mr. Illinois, while upon a long dais at the head of the room gleamed with cutlery the flower-decked white plateau where sat Mr. Heilbrenner and thirteen representatives of the thirteen original states. Mr. Heilbrenner had proved human. At his right hand, sparkling, heartbreakingly gay and beautiful, sat Miss Virginia. Through the music and all other sounds her laughter ran as distinctly as if uttered by little bells of silver.

Henry heard that cruel tinkling almost continually. The back of his chair was toward the dais, and he turned only four times during the serving of the meal to look at her. Not once did he find her looking at him.

" All right, Miss Unsincere! " he said, almost audibly. " You can go! "

When the coffee had been brought, Mr. Heilbrenner rose and rapped loudly upon the table with a gavel. " Sidex congratulates each and every one of you! " he proclaimed, while a microphone was being placed before him. " We are now come to the last and most important session of this great Sidex enterprise, and a few minutes hence our proceedings will begin to be broadcast over a wide hookup. Yesterday morning I promised you the announcement of a surprise at this banquet, and I know that each and every heart here is beating high with excitement as I rise to tell you what it is."

" Mine isn't." Henry, with his chair now facing the dais, was mutteringly sardonic. " What I care? Puh! "

" In these two days," Mr. Heilbrenner continued, " you, from all parts of the Union, have associated together, have learned one another's characters, have

HIGH SCHOOL CONVENTION. Who will be elected? That is the big question, especially if the convention is choosing a Miss or a Mr. America. (Acme)

formed estimates and opinions. Previously, listening in at home, many of you heard one another's prize speeches during the Sidex Hour. Sidex believes you will judge justly. Before each and every one of you, at your tables, you have doubtless noticed a small pencil and an envelope, each envelope containing two blank cards. Ladies and gentlemen, Sidex congratulates you again. Out of your number you, the representatives of the states of the Union, are now about to elect two representatives of the Union itself. Ladies and gentlemen, you are now going to elect Miss America and Mr. America! "

He paused, waiting for an almost shriekingly excited applause to subside. " Mr. America, too? " Henry muttered, sickened.

" It'll be that great big squirt from California." His nostrils widened in a sneer of pain. " All right, go ahead and marry him! You'll see someday how he turns out."

" Five minutes will now be given," Mr. Heilbrenner announced, " while you kindly write upon one card your selection for Miss America and upon the other your choice for Mr. America. Sidex officials will then pass among you, collecting the sealed envelopes containing your ballots for Miss America and Mr. America. After that, the broadcasting will begin with your all rising and singing ' America.' The result of the balloting will then be announced to you and broadcast simultaneously, after which the mayor of Boston has graciously consented to congratulate the two winners and they will be escorted to the microphone, where each will make a one-minute address to the nation." Mr. Heilbrenner placed a watch before him. " Ladies and gentlemen, you have five minutes in which to write your ballots and return them to the envelopes. Sidex thanks you."

A great buzzing filled the room. Henry, not contributing to it, removed the two cards from the envelope before him, took up the pencil, and, swallowing profoundly, slowly wrote " Miss Virginia " upon one of the cards and replaced it in the envelope. After that, he sat for some moments in studious doubt.

Certainly he didn't intend to vote for Mr. California or for any other of those show-offs. In fact, he couldn't conscientiously vote for any one of his male colleagues to be exalted as the Premier Intellectual of the whole United States. He hadn't observed greatness in any of them and didn't feel justified in contributing to an enormous reputation falsely achieved. Would the whole ballot be announced, he wondered, so that everybody who received even one vote would at least be mentioned? It'd be pretty ignominious for anybody not to get a single vote, especially with her sitting up there in triumph! Yes, and far, far away, out in Emmonsville, Indiana, the whole family listening in, and everybody else in Emmonsville, too, and —

Hurriedly, though using his left hand to shield the writing from the observation of his neighbors, Henry wrote his choice for Mr. America upon the second card, slid it quickly into the envelope, and sealed the envelope tightly.

The ballots were collected, taken to a table in a corner of the room, and the counting began. The mayor of Boston made his appearance upon the dais, was applauded. Excited voices filled the room with conglomerate sound until the gavel again struck the table. Mr. Heilbrenner stood with two sheets of paper in his hand. "The ballot is concluded and the broadcast has begun," he said solemnly. " We will all now please rise and sing ' America.' "

Henry rose with the rest and sang, though his voice was heard but faintly, even by himself. What heart had he to sing? Miss Virginia was going to be elected Miss America, going to be topmost, brightest figure in all the light of fame — high, high above even the reach of his bitterness. He knew her now — at last. Of course, Miss Massachusetts had told her the secret of the surprise, and for two days Miss Virginia had been lobbying — making herself popular — yes, and making him into a mere tool to increase that popularity! Henry laughed raspingly, caring little who heard him.

On the dais the chairman's solemnity deepened. " Mr. Mayor, representatives of the states, my friends of the radio audience," he said, " Sidex announces the result of the balloting. Sidex congratulates beautiful Miss Clara Pattle Brown, Virginia's charming Sidex Intellect Prize Winner. She, as Miss Virginia, has received a total of sixty-one votes out of the ninety-six, and I do therefore now and herewith proclaim Clara Pattle Brown to be Miss America! "

Thereupon, while ardent cheers arose, the orchestra first played " Dixie " and then " Carry Me Back to Old Virginny." Henry couldn't see triumphant Clara Pattle Brown; the mayor of Boston was congratulating her; everybody at the high table had risen and rushed about her. " Look at 'em! " Henry groaned. " Didn't I tell you? "

Mr. Heilbrenner's gavel pounded upon the table again, and again silence fell. " In announcing the election of Mr. America, Sidex wishes to mention a fact that should be gratifying to all the male representatives of the states and their friends," Mr. Heilbrenner said. " Every single male representative has received at least one vote. That should please us all. Of those who have received more than two votes, Idaho has received three; Michigan, four; Ohio, four; Kentucky, seven; but the fine old state of Indiana has received the highest number, sixteen, which carries with it the election. I therefore now and herewith proclaim that Henry Hopgood Dilmer, heretofore Mr. Indiana merely, has been and is duly elected Mr. America. I appoint Miss Massachusetts and Mr. Rhode Island to escort Mr. America to the platform to receive the congratulations of the mayor of Boston and to follow Miss America in delivering a one-minute radio address to the nation. Mr. America, Sidex congratulates you! Mr. America, we all congratulate you!"

Deafeningly the orchestra played "On the Banks of the Wabash," and seldom indeed has anybody ever been paler than was Mr. America while being escorted to the platform by Miss Massachusetts and Mr. Rhode Island. Henry's ears heard the voice of the mayor of Boston congratulating him; Henry's upper chest felt the touch of Mr. Heilbrenner affixing the white ribbon upon which MR. AMERICA was printed in letters of gold; Henry's right hand felt the grasp of other hands; his eyes were aware of blushing lovely Miss America, happy beside him; but his mind had no true consciousness of any of these things.

Mr. America! Was it true? It was. Suddenly a light of incredible brightness enveloped Henry; he was dazzled by himself. Mr. America!

Miss America's little speech into the microphone was but a buzzing in his ears. "It's your turn!" Mr. Heilbrenner whispered to Mr. America urgently. "Speak up! Put your face closer to the mike. Speak up, can't you?"

"I —" Henry addressed the instrument hoarsely. "I —" he said again, and choked.

Miss America whispered in his ear, "Don't be scared. You tell 'em, hon!"

Henry told them. "I — I wish to thank," he said — "I wish to thank every citizen of the United States for this honor that — that has come upon me. I wish to thank the citizens of Emmonsville and the citizens of the nation and the mayor of Boston and all others I grew up with in high school and — and elsewhere. I will try to deserve it and I will live such a life so that I will never feel worthy of — I mean unworthy — so I will be worthy of being Mr. America. Wherever

I glo — I mean go — I hope I will always be looked upon as Mr. America."

He was removed from the microphone, though in the kindest manner, just after taking breath and saying, "I hope I —" again. "Your time's up, honey," glowing Miss America told him. "You did fine! Are you happy — Henry?"

"Henry?" he repeated, in a tone of vague inquiry.

Not otherwise did he respond to her sweet question. The orchestra was playing "The Star-Spangled Banner," and the former Mr. Indiana officially joined the mayor of Boston in trying to sing it. Henry looked upward, over the heads of the mere state representatives below him; he looked upward and sang "The Star-Spangled Banner" mainly without words, but as loudly as he could. Henry sang, and, in that supreme moment, was really unaware of Miss America's very existence.

This, of course, doesn't mean that he entirely forgot her for any considerable time, though it can't be said that during the brief remainder of his visit to Boston he became quite himself again. Only the old Indiana home could restore Henry's faculties.

On the train I was on [he wrote to her from Emmonsville] it seemed as if traveling people are not much of listeners in and a man in the diner across from me thought my badge meant advertising some show or something until I told him. Well yesterday the *Emmonsville News* had it in in "Notes about Town," but I have quit wearing the badge because I do not like to be ostentatious and I could see it was causing ill feeling among my own circle of young people.

So I have learned in this life we must expect this and since returning home I have scarcely been able to say a single thing in my own family or perform any action that I would not hear comments from the two members, one oldest and the other one next to me in age I told you about. "Oh I would not think Mr. America would say that" they keep squawking and "Oh I would not think Mr. America would do thus and so" or else "Oh only to think of somebody that had been elected Mr. America behaving in this manner" and so forth &c &c &c. It seems in this life if we receive honors outside the family circle it is certain members of our own family that it brings out the worst side of.

Well, it seems Miss Indiana and Miss Missouri were on the train in another car so I did not see them except on the platform at Indianapolis when I got off to take the bus for Emmonsville but had a short chat. They both told me it was you suggested voting for me and might not thought of it if you had not spoken to them. So I feel I ought to thank you as I might not rec'd so much a majority if you had not.

You said you were going to college next year and I would like to plan attending the same one because if we both go to some good coeducational college together they would know what it means for it having us both in it and I have gotten a feeling that every man needs the good influence of a woman and I have gotten a feeling that both of us would be a success in life wherever you are. So please write soon and say you meant what you said at the good old South Station in Boston when you said what you said because I have gotten a feeling there was a higher Fate in this whole thing and it will be better for us to make the same plans from now on. So please write soon which college because I have made up my mind nothing on earth can stop me from going any place you do.

Now it is getting late and so Mr. America will have to stop writing to Miss America. But I will always sign myself

Yours only<br>*Henry*

## Suggestions for Study

1. When did you first become aware of Miss Virginia's plot? How did the author make you feel interested in the outcome?

2. Why did Miss Virginia electioneer for Mr. Indiana? Let the boys give their opinions of Clara to the class, and the girls give theirs of Henry. Do the characters seem real, or are they caricatures?

3. Is Henry's tendency to treat with exaggerated seriousness matters which to anyone else would seem inconsequential really characteristic of immature youth? Is the trait confined to youth? Is immaturity a matter of age?

4. Do you think, as some critics have said, that Tarkington's humorous portrayals of

youth are also warmly sympathetic? Is there any significance in the title?

5. What is your opinion of Miss America contests? of other radio contests? Do you think Sidex's contest did anything of value for the contestants? To what extent are Mr. and Miss America justified in being proud of their election?

6. Do you think Clara's manner of talking is an accurate representation of Virginian speech? Discuss other regional mannerisms you have heard.

7. What errors can you find in Henry's letter to Miss America?

8. Vocabulary: defectives, mollify, undulation, piquant, fatuously, morose, ineffable, sardonic, ignominious, conglomerate, ardent.

## For Your Vocabulary

BASE-WORD. Henry made a mistake when he wrote "ostentitious" for *ostentatious* (page 46), but he was at least trying to use a very good word. You will find it and some of its relatives used a number of times in this book. They are made from the base-word usually appearing as *ostent* or *ostens*, which means, literally, to hold out, as for someone to look at, therefore to show. *Ostentatious* (ŏs-tĕn-tā'-shŭs) means deliberately showy or pretentious. The noun for the quality, *ostentation,* is used of manners or behavior and of such things as dress and house-furnishings. A person may be fond of *ostentation,* or he may be offended by it. A related word is *ostensible* (ŏs-tĕn'sĭ-b'l), which describes that which is shown, often as opposed to that which is real. A person's *ostensible* motive may not be his real motive at all. Remember that when you come to Mark Twain's use of the word in telling of tricks he played on his mother.

## Jack London      1876–1916

" Jack London, California waif, water-front street gamin, barroom 'tough,' and hoodlum, leader of the oyster pirates, deck hand on a North Pacific sealer, millworker, hobo, college student for a time, gold seeker in Alaska during the first wild days of the Klondike rush, adventurer among the islands of the South Seas!" Surely here is a wealth of experience for a writer to draw upon for stories! London's stories are filled with an atmosphere which convinces his reader that authentic pictures of life are being painted. Written early in the present century, they embody both the localized realism and the journalistic style which first appeared between the years 1890 and 1900. Their virility and power make them epic in scope. They are " crisp and crackling and interesting, terse in style and vigorous of phrase," as he himself declared that stories should be.

## TO BUILD A FIRE

In this story notice how London piles detail upon detail to accomplish his effect. There are no digressions, and no time is wasted in getting from introduction to conclusion. " Cold " is the fourth word, and the story ends with the phrase " fire providers." In technique this is an almost perfect story. Give it a fair chance at your emotions by reading it through without an interruption.

Day had broken cold and gray, exceedingly cold and gray, when the man turned aside from the main Yukon trail and climbed the high earth bank, where a dim and little-traveled trail led eastward through the fat spruce timberland. It was a steep bank, and he paused for breath at the top, excusing the act to himself by looking at his watch. It was nine o'clock. There was no sun nor hint of sun, though there was not a cloud in the sky. It was a clear day, and yet there seemed an intangible pall over the face of things, a subtle gloom that made the day dark, and that was due to the absence of sun. This fact did not worry the man. He was used to the lack of sun. It had been days since he had seen the sun, and he knew that a few more days must pass before that cheerful orb, due south, would just peep above the sky line and dip immediately from view.

The man flung a look back along the way he had come. The Yukon lay a mile wide and hidden under three feet of ice. On top of this ice were as many feet of snow. It was all pure white, rolling in gentle undulations where the ice jams of the freeze-up had formed. North and south, as far as his eye could see, it was unbroken white, save for a dark hairline that curved and twisted from around the spruce-covered island to the south, and that curved and twisted away into the north, where it disappeared behind another spruce-covered island. This dark hairline was the trail — the main trail — that led south five hundred miles to the Chilkoot Pass, Dyea, and salt water; and that led north seventy miles to Dawson, and still on to the north a thousand miles to Nulato, and finally to St. Michael on Bering Sea, a thousand miles and half a thousand more.

But all this — the mysterious, far-reaching hairline trail, the absence of sun from the sky, the tremendous cold, and the strangeness and weirdness of it all — made no impression on the man. It was not because he was long used to it. He was a newcomer in the land, a cheechako, and this was his first winter. The trouble with him was that he was without imagination. He was quick and alert in the things of life, but only in the things, and not in the significances. Fifty degrees below zero meant eighty-odd degrees of frost. Such fact impressed him as being cold and uncomfortable, and that was all. It did not lead him to meditate upon his frailty as a creature of temperature, and upon man's frailty in general, able only to live within certain narrow limits of heat and cold, and from there on it did not lead him to the conjectural field of immortality and man's place in the universe. Fifty degrees below zero stood for a bite of frost that hurt and that must be guarded against by the use of mittens, ear flaps, warm moccasins, and thick socks. Fifty degrees below zero was to him just precisely fifty degrees below zero. That there should be anything more to it than that was a thought that never entered his head.

As he turned to go on, he spat speculatively. There was a sharp, explosive crackle that startled him. He spat again. And again, in the air, before it could fall to the snow, the spittle crackled. He knew that at fifty

" To Build a Fire," from *Lost Face*, by Jack London. Reprinted by permission of The Macmillan Company, publishers.

below spittle crackled on the snow, but this spittle had crackled in the air. Undoubtedly it was colder than fifty below — how much colder he did not know. But the temperature did not matter. He was bound for the old claim on the left fork of Henderson Creek, where the boys were already. They had come over across the divide from the Indian Creek country, while he had come the roundabout way to take a look at the possibilities of getting out logs in the spring from the islands in the Yukon. He would be into camp by six o'clock; a bit after dark, it was true, but the boys would be there, a fire would be going, and a hot supper would be ready. As for lunch, he pressed his hand against the protruding bundle under his jacket. It was also under his shirt, wrapped up in a handkerchief and lying against the naked skin. It was the only way to keep the biscuits from freezing. He smiled agreeably to himself as he thought of those biscuits, each cut open and sopped in bacon grease, and each inclosing a generous slice of fried bacon.

He plunged in among the big spruce trees. The trail was faint. A foot of snow had fallen since the last sled had passed over, and he was glad he was without a sled, traveling light. In fact, he carried nothing but the lunch wrapped in the handkerchief. He was surprised, however, at the cold. It certainly was cold, he concluded, as he rubbed his numb nose and cheekbones with his mittened hand. He was a warm-whiskered man, but the hair on his face did not protect the high cheekbones and the eager nose that thrust itself aggressively into the frosty air.

At the man's heels trotted a dog, a big native husky, the proper wolf dog, gray-coated and without any visible or temperamental difference from its brother, the wild wolf. The animal was depressed by the tremendous cold. It knew that it was no time for traveling. Its instinct told it a truer tale than was told to the man by the man's judgment. In reality, it was not merely colder than fifty below zero; it was colder than sixty below, than seventy below. It was seventy-five below zero. Since the freezing point is thirty-two above zero, it meant that one hundred and seven degrees of frost obtained. The dog did not know anything about thermometers. Possibly in its brain there was no sharp consciousness of a condition of very cold such as was in the man's brain. But the brute had its instinct. It experienced a vague but menacing apprehension that subdued it and made it slink along at the man's heels, and that made it question eagerly every unwonted movement of the man, as if expecting him to go into camp or to seek shelter somewhere and build a fire. The dog had learned fire, and it wanted fire, or else to burrow under the snow and cuddle its warmth away from the air.

The frozen moisture of its breathing had settled on its fur in a fine powder of frost, and especially were its jowls, muzzle, and eyelashes whitened by its crystaled breath. The man's red beard and mustache were likewise frosted, but more solidly, the deposit taking the form of ice and increasing with every warm, moist breath he exhaled. Also, the man was chewing tobacco, and the muzzle of ice held his lips so rigidly that he was unable to clear his chin when he expelled the juice. The result was that a crystal beard of the color and solidity of amber was increasing its length on his chin. If he fell down it would shatter itself, like glass, into brittle fragments. But he did not mind the appendage. It was the penalty all tobacco chewers paid in that country, and he had been out before in two cold snaps. They had not been so cold as this, he knew, but by the spirit thermometer at Sixty Mile he knew they had been registered at fifty below and at fifty-five.

He held on through the level stretch of woods for several miles, crossed a wide flat of niggerheads, and dropped down a bank to the frozen bed of a small stream. This was Henderson Creek, and he knew he was ten miles from the forks. He looked at his watch. It was ten o'clock. He was making four miles an hour, and he calculated that he would arrive at the forks at half-past twelve. He decided to celebrate that event by eating his lunch there.

The dog dropped in again at his heels, with a tail drooping discouragement, as the man swung along the creek bed. The furrow of the old sled trail was plainly visible, but a dozen inches of snow covered the marks of the last runners. In a month no man had come up or down that silent creek. The man held steadily on. He was not much given to thinking, and just then particularly he had nothing to think about save that he would eat lunch at the forks and that at six o'clock he would be in camp with the boys. There was nobody to talk to; and, had there been, speech would have been impossible because of the ice muzzle on his mouth. So he continued monotonously to chew tobacco and to increase the length of his amber beard.

Once in a while the thought reiterated itself that it was very cold and that he had never experienced such cold. As he walked along he rubbed his cheekbones and nose with the back of his mittened hand. He did this automatically, now and again changing hands. But rub as he would, the instant he stopped his cheekbones went numb, and the following instant the end of his nose went numb. He was sure to frost his cheeks; he knew that, and experienced a pang of regret that he had not devised a nose strap of the sort Bud wore in cold snaps. Such a strap passed across the cheeks, as well, and saved them. But it didn't matter much, after all. What were frosted cheeks? A bit painful, that was all; they were never serious.

Empty as the man's mind was of thought, he was keenly observant, and he noticed the changes in the creek, the curves and bends and timber jams, and always he sharply noted where he placed his feet. Once, coming around a bend, he shied abruptly, like a startled horse, curved away from the place where he had been walking, and retreated several paces back along the trail. The creek, he knew, was frozen clear to the bottom — no creek could contain water in that arctic winter — but he knew also that there were springs that bubbled out from the hillsides and ran along under the snow and on top of the ice of the creek. He knew that the coldest snaps never froze these springs, and he knew likewise their danger. They were traps. They hid pools of water under the snow that might be three inches deep, or three feet. Sometimes a skin of ice half an inch thick covered them, and in turn was covered by the snow. Sometimes there were alternate layers of water and ice skin, so that when one broke through he kept on breaking through for a while, sometimes wetting himself to the waist.

That was why he had shied in such panic. He had felt the give under his feet and heard the crackle of a snow-hidden ice skin. And to get his feet wet in such a temperature meant trouble and danger. At the very least it meant delay, for he would be forced to stop and build a fire, and under its protection to bare his feet while he dried his socks and moccasins. He stood and studied the creek bed and its banks, and decided that the flow of water came from the right. He reflected a while, rubbing his nose and cheeks, then skirted to the left, stepping gingerly and testing the footing for each step. Once clear of the danger, he took a fresh chew of tobacco and swung along at his four-mile gait.

In the course of the next two hours he came upon several similar traps. Usually the snow above the hidden pools had a sunken, candied appearance that advertised the danger. Once again, however, he had a close call; and once, suspecting danger, he compelled the dog to go on in front. The dog did not want to go. It hung back until the man shoved it forward, and then it went quickly across the white, unbroken surface. Suddenly it broke through, floundered to one side, and got away to firmer footing. It had wet its forefeet and legs, and almost immediately the water that clung to it turned to ice. It made quick efforts to lick the ice off its legs, then dropped down in the snow and began to bite out the ice that had formed between the toes. This was a matter of instinct. To permit the ice to remain would mean sore feet. It did not know this. It merely obeyed the mysterious prompting that arose from the deep crypts of its being. But the man knew, having achieved a judgment on the subject, and he removed the mitten from his right hand and helped tear out the ice particles. He did not expose his fingers more than a minute, and was astonished at the swift numbness that smote them. It certainly was cold. He pulled on the mitten hastily, and beat the hand savagely across his chest.

At twelve o'clock the day was at its brightest. Yet the sun was too far south on its winter journey to clear the horizon. The bulge of the earth intervened between it and Henderson Creek, where the man walked under a clear sky at noon and cast no shadow. At half-past twelve, to the minute, he arrived at the forks of the creek. He was pleased at the speed he had made. If he kept it up, he would certainly be with the boys by six. He unbuttoned his jacket and shirt and drew forth his lunch. The action consumed no more than a quarter of a minute, yet in that brief moment the numbness laid hold of the exposed fingers. He did not put the mitten on, but, instead, struck the fingers a dozen sharp smashes against his leg. Then he sat down on a snow-covered log to eat. The sting that followed upon the striking of his fingers against his leg ceased so quickly that he was startled. He had had no chance to take a bite of biscuit. He struck the fingers repeatedly and returned them to the mitten, baring the other hand for the purpose of eating. He tried to take a mouthful, but the ice muzzle prevented. He had forgotten to build a fire and thaw out. He chuckled at his foolishness, and as he chuckled he noted the numbness creeping into the exposed fingers. Also he noted that the stinging which had first come to his toes when he sat down was already passing away. He wondered whether the toes were warm or numb. He moved them inside the moccasins and decided that they were numb.

He pulled the mitten on hurriedly and stood up. He was a bit frightened. He stamped up and down until the stinging returned into the feet. It certainly was cold, was his thought. That man from Sulphur Creek had spoken the truth when telling how cold it sometimes got in the country. And he had laughed at him at the time! That showed one must not be too sure of things. There was no mistake about it, it *was* cold. He strode up and down, stamping his feet and threshing his arms, until reassured by the returning warmth. Then he got out matches and proceeded to make a fire. From the undergrowth, where high water of the previous spring had lodged a supply of seasoned twigs, he got his firewood. Working carefully from a small beginning, he soon had a roaring fire, over which he thawed the ice from his face and in the protection of which he ate his biscuits. For the moment the cold of space was outwitted. The dog took satisfaction in the fire, stretching out close enough for warmth and far enough away to escape being singed.

When the man had finished, he filled his pipe and took his comfortable time over a smoke. Then he pulled on his mittens, settled the ear flaps of his cap firmly about his ears, and took the creek trail up the left fork. The dog was disappointed and yearned back toward the fire. This man did not know cold. Possibly all the generations of his ancestry had been ignorant of cold, of real cold, of cold one hundred and seven degrees below freezing point. But the dog knew; all its ancestry knew, and it had inherited the knowledge. And it knew that it was not good to walk abroad in such fearful cold. It was the time to lie snug in a hole in the snow and wait for a curtain of cloud to be drawn across the face of outer space whence this cold came. On the other hand, there was no keen intimacy between the dog and the man. The one was the toil-slave of the other, and the only caresses it had ever received were the caresses of the whiplash and of harsh and menacing throat sounds that threatened the whiplash. So the dog made no effort to communicate its apprehension to the man. It was not concerned in the welfare of the man; it was for its own sake that it yearned back toward the fire. But the man whistled, and spoke to it with the sound of whiplashes, and the dog swung in at the man's heels and followed after.

The man took a chew of tobacco and proceeded to start a new amber beard. Also, his moist breath quickly powdered with white his mustache, eyebrows, and lashes. There did not seem to be so many springs on the left fork of the Henderson, and for half an hour the man saw no signs of any. And then it happened. At a place where there were no signs, where the soft, unbroken snow seemed to advertise solidity beneath, the man broke through. It was not deep. He wet himself halfway to the knees before he floundered out to the firm crust.

He was angry, and cursed his luck aloud. He had hoped to get into camp with the boys at six o'clock, and this would delay him an hour, for he would have to build a fire and dry out his footgear. This was imperative at that low temperature — he knew that much; and he turned aside to the bank, which he climbed. On top, tangled in the underbrush about the trunks of several small spruce trees, was a high-water deposit of dry firewood — sticks and twigs, principally, but also larger portions of seasoned branches and fine, dry, last year's grasses. He threw down several large pieces on top of the snow. This served for a foundation and prevented the young flame from drowning itself in the snow it otherwise would melt. The flame he got by touching a match to a small shred of birch bark that he took from his pocket. This burned even more readily than paper. Placing it on the foundation, he fed the young flame with wisps of dry grass and with the tiniest dry twigs.

He worked slowly and carefully, keenly aware of his danger. Gradually, as the flame grew stronger, he increased the size of the twigs with which he fed it. He squatted in the snow, pulling the twigs out from their entanglement in the brush and feeding directly to the flame. He knew there must be no failure. When it is seventy-five below

zero a man must not fail in his first attempt to build a fire — that is, if his feet are wet. If his feet are dry, and he fails, he can run along the trail for half a mile and restore his circulation. But the circulation of wet and freezing feet cannot be restored by running when it is seventy-five below. No matter how fast he runs, the wet feet will freeze the harder.

All this the man knew. The old-timer on Sulphur Creek had told him about it the previous fall, and now he was appreciating the advice. Already all sensation had gone out of his feet. To build the fire, he had been forced to remove his mittens, and the fingers had quickly gone numb. His pace of four miles an hour had kept his heart pumping blood to the surface of his body and to all the extremities. But the instant he stopped, the action of the pump eased down. The cold of space smote the unprotected tip of the planet, and he, being on that unprotected tip, received the full force of the blow. The blood of his body recoiled before it. The blood was alive, like the dog, and like the dog it wanted to hide away and cover itself up from the fearful cold. So long as he walked four miles an hour, he pumped that blood, willy-nilly, to the surface; but now it ebbed away and sank down into the recesses of his body. The extremities were the first to feel its absence. His wet feet froze the faster, and his exposed fingers numbed the faster, though they had not yet begun to freeze. Nose and cheeks were already freezing, while the skin of all his body chilled as it lost its blood.

But he was safe. Toes and nose and cheeks would be only touched by the frost, for the fire was beginning to burn with strength. He was feeding it with twigs the size of his finger. In another minute he would be able to feed it with branches the size of his wrist, and then he could remove his wet footgear, and, while it dried, he could keep his naked feet warm by the fire, rubbing them at first, of course, with snow. The fire was a success. He was safe. He remembered the advice of the old-timer on Sulphur Creek, and smiled. The old-timer had been very serious in laying down the law that no man must travel alone in the Klondike after fifty below. Well, here he was; he had had the accident; he was alone; and he had saved himself. Those old-timers were rather womanish, some of them, he thought. All a man had to do was to keep his head, and he was all right. Any man who was a man could travel alone. But it was surprising the rapidity with which his cheeks and nose were freezing. And he had not thought his fingers could go lifeless in so short a time. Lifeless they were, for he could scarcely make them move together to grip a twig, and they seemed remote from his body and from him. When he touched a twig he had to look and see whether or not he had hold of it. The wires were pretty well down between him and his finger ends.

All of which counted for little. There was the fire, snapping and crackling and promising life with every dancing flame. He started to untie his moccasins. They were coated with ice; the thick German socks were like sheaths of iron halfway to the knees; and the moccasin strings were like rods of steel all twisted and knotted as by some conflagration. For a moment he tugged with his numb fingers, then, realizing the folly of it, he drew his sheath knife.

But before he could cut the strings it happened. It was his own fault, or, rather, his mistake. He should not have built the fire under the spruce tree. He should have built it in the open. But it had been easier to pull the twigs from the bush and drop them directly on the fire. Now the tree under which he had done this carried a weight of snow on its boughs. No wind had blown for weeks, and each bough was fully freighted. Each time he had pulled a twig he had communicated a slight agitation to the tree — an imperceptible agitation, so far as he was concerned, but an agitation sufficient to bring about the disaster. High up in the tree one bough capsized its load of snow. This fell on the boughs beneath, capsizing them. This process continued, spreading out and involving the whole tree. It grew like

ALASKAN TRAPPER. In frozen Alaska, the building of a fire may mean the difference between life and death. (Ewing Galloway)

an avalanche, and it descended without warning upon the man and the fire, and the fire was blotted out! Where it had burned was a mantle of fresh and disordered snow.

The man was shocked. It was as though he had just heard his own sentence of death. For a moment he sat and stared at the spot where the fire had been. Then he grew very calm. Perhaps the old-timer on Sulphur Creek was right. If he had only had a trailmate he would have been in no danger now. The trailmate could have built the fire. Well, it was up to him to build the fire over again, and this second time there must be no failure. Even if he succeeded, he would most likely lose some toes. His feet must be badly frozen by now, and there would be some time before the second fire was ready.

Such were his thoughts, but he did not sit and think them. He was busy all the time they were passing through his mind. He made a new foundation for a fire, this time in the open, where no treacherous tree could blot it out. Next he gathered dry grasses and tiny twigs from the high-water flotsam. He could not bring his fingers together to pull them out, but he was able to gather them by the handful. In this way he got many rotten twigs and bits of green moss that were undesirable, but it was the best he could do. He worked methodically, even collecting an armful of the larger branches to be used later when the fire gathered strength. And all the while the dog sat and watched him, a certain yearning wistfulness in its eyes, for it looked upon him as the fire provider, and the fire was slow in coming.

When all was ready, the man reached in his pocket for a second piece of birch bark. He knew the bark was there, and, though he could not feel it with his fingers, he could hear its crisp rustling as he fumbled for it. Try as he would, he could not clutch hold of it. And all the time, in his consciousness, was the knowledge that each instant his feet were freezing. This thought tended to put him in a panic, but he fought against it and kept calm. He pulled on his mittens with his teeth, and threshed his arms back and forth, beating his hands with all his might against his sides. He did this sitting down, and he stood up to do it; and all the while the dog sat in the snow, its wolf brush of a tail curled around warmly over its forefeet, its sharp wolf ears pricked forward intently as it watched the man. And the man, as he beat and threshed with his arms and hands, felt a great surge of envy as he regarded the creature that was warm and secure in its natural covering.

After a time he was aware of the first faraway signals of sensation in his beaten fingers. The faint tingling grew stronger till it evolved into a stinging ache that was excruciating, but which the man hailed with satisfaction. He stripped the mitten from his right hand and fetched forth the birch bark. The exposed fingers were quickly going numb again. Next he brought out his bunch of sulphur matches. But the tremendous cold had already driven the life out of his fingers. In his effort to separate one match from the others, the whole bunch fell in the snow. He tried to pick it out of the snow, but failed. The dead fingers could neither touch nor clutch. He was very careful. He drove the thought of his freezing feet, and nose, and cheeks, out of his mind, devoting his whole soul to the matches. He watched, using the sense of vision in place of that of touch, and when he saw his fingers on each side the bunch, he closed them — that is, he willed to close them, for the wires were down, and the fingers did not obey. He pulled the mitten on the right hand, and beat it fiercely against his knee. Then, with both mittened hands, he scooped the bunch of matches, along with much snow, into his lap. Yet he was no better off.

After some manipulation he managed to get the bunch between the heels of his mittened hands. In this fashion he carried it to his mouth. The ice crackled and snapped when by a violent effort he opened his mouth. He drew the lower jaw in, curled the upper lip out of the way, and scraped the bunch with his upper teeth in order to separate a match. He succeeded in getting one, which he dropped on his lap. He was no better off. He could not pick it up. Then he devised a way. He picked it up in his teeth and scratched it on his leg. Twenty times he scratched before he succeeded in lighting it. As it flamed he held it with his teeth to the birch bark. But the burning brimstone went up his nostrils and into his lungs, causing him to cough spasmodically. The match fell into the snow and went out.

The old-timer on Sulphur Creek was right, he thought in the moment of controlled despair that ensued: after fifty below, a man should travel with a partner. He beat his hands, but failed in exciting any sensation. Suddenly he bared both hands, removing the mittens with his teeth. He caught the whole bunch between the heels of his hands. His arm muscles, not being frozen, enabled him to press the hand heels tightly against the matches. Then he scratched the bunch along his leg. It flared into flame, seventy sulphur matches at once! There was no wind to blow them out. He kept his head to one side to escape the strangling fumes, and held the blazing bunch to the birch bark. As he so held it, he became aware of sensation in his hand. His flesh was burning. He could smell it. Deep down below the surface he could feel it. The sensation developed into pain that grew acute. And still he endured it, holding the flame of the matches clumsily to the bark that would not light readily because his own burning hands were in the way, absorbing most of the flame.

At last, when he could endure no more, he jerked his hands apart. The blazing matches fell sizzling into the snow, but the birch bark was alight. He began laying dry grasses and the tiniest twigs on the flame. He could not pick and choose, for he had to lift the fuel between the heels of his hands. Small pieces of rotten wood and green moss clung to the twigs, and he bit them off as well as he could with his teeth. He cherished the flame carefully and awkwardly. It meant life, and it must not perish. The withdrawal of blood from the surface of his body now made him begin to shiver, and he grew more awkward. A large piece of green moss fell squarely on the little fire. He tried to poke it out with his fingers, but his shivering frame made him poke too far, and he disrupted the nucleus of the little fire, the burning grasses and tiny twigs separating and scattering. He tried to poke them together again, but, in spite of the tenseness of the effort, his shivering got away with him, and the twigs were hopelessly scattered. Each twig gushed a puff of smoke and went out. The fire provider had failed. As he looked apathetically about him, his eyes chanced on the dog, sitting across the ruins of the fire from him, in the snow, making restless, hunching movements, slightly lifting one forefoot and then the other, shifting its weight back and forth on them with wistful eagerness.

The sight of the dog put a wild idea into his head. He remembered the tale of the man, caught in a blizzard, who killed a steer and crawled inside the carcass, and so was saved. He would kill the dog and bury his hands in the warm body until the numbness went out of them. Then he could build another fire. He spoke to the dog, calling it to him; but in his voice was a strange note of fear that frightened the animal, who had never known the man to speak in such way before. Something was the matter, and its suspicious nature sensed danger — it knew not what danger, but somewhere, somehow, in its brain arose an apprehension of the man. It flattened its ears down at the sound of the man's voice, and its restless, hunching movements and the liftings and shiftings of its forefeet became more pronounced; but it would not come to the man. He got on his hands and knees and crawled toward the dog. This unusual posture again excited suspicion, and the animal sidled mincingly away.

The man sat up in the snow for a moment and struggled for calmness. Then he pulled on his mittens, by means of his teeth, and got upon his feet. He glanced down at first in order to assure himself that he was really standing up, for the absence of sensation in his feet left him unrelated to the earth. His erect position in itself started to drive the webs of suspicion from the dog's mind; and when he spoke peremptorily with the sound of whiplashes in his voice, the dog rendered its customary allegiance and came to him. As it came within reaching distance, the man lost his control. His arms flashed out to the dog, and he experienced genuine surprise when he discovered that his hands could not clutch, that there was neither bend nor feeling in the fingers. He had forgotten for the moment that they were frozen and that they were freezing more and more. All this happened quickly, and before the animal could get away, he encircled its body with his arms. He sat down in the snow, and in this fashion held the dog, while it snarled and whined and struggled.

But it was all he could do, hold its body encircled in his arms and sit there. He realized that he could not kill the dog. There was no way to do it. With his helpless hands he could neither draw nor hold his sheath knife nor throttle the animal. He released it, and it plunged wildly away, with tail between its legs, and still snarling. It halted forty feet away and surveyed him curiously, with ears sharply pricked forward. The man looked down at his hands in order to locate them, and found them hanging on the ends of his arms. It struck him as curious that one should have to use his eyes in order to find out where his hands were. He began threshing his arms back and forth, beating the mittened hands against his sides. He did this for five minutes, violently, and his heart pumped enough blood up to the surface to put a stop to his shivering. But no sensation was aroused in the hands. He had an impression that they hung like weights on the ends of his arms, but when he tried to run the impression down, he could not find it.

A certain fear of death, dull and oppressive, came to him. This fear quickly became poignant as he realized that it was no longer a mere matter of freezing his fingers and toes, or of losing his hands and feet, but that it was a matter of life and death, with the chances against him. This threw him into a panic, and he turned and ran up the creek bed along the old dim trail. The dog joined in behind and kept up with him. He ran blindly, without intention, in fear such as he had never known in his life. Slowly, as he plowed and floundered through the snow, he began to see things again — the banks of the creek, the old timber jams, the leafless aspens, and the sky. The running made him feel better. He did not shiver. Maybe, if he ran on, his feet would thaw out; and, anyway, if he ran far enough, he would reach the camp and the boys. Without doubt he would lose some fingers and toes and some of his face; but the boys would take care of him, and save the rest of him when he got there. And at the same time there was another thought in his mind that said he would never get to the camp and the boys; that it was too many miles away, that the freezing had too great a start on him, and that he would soon be stiff and dead. This thought he kept in the background and refused to consider. Some-

times it pushed itself forward and demanded to be heard, but he thrust it back and strove to think of other things.

It struck him as curious that he could run at all on feet so frozen that he could not feel them when they struck the earth and took the weight of his body. He seemed to himself to skim along above the surface, and to have no connection with the earth. Somewhere he had once seen a winged Mercury, and he wondered if Mercury felt as he felt when skimming over the earth.

His theory of running until he reached camp and the boys had one flaw in it: he lacked the endurance. Several times he stumbled, and finally he tottered, crumpled up, and fell. When he tried to rise, he failed. He must sit and rest, he decided, and next time he would merely walk and keep on going. As he sat and regained his breath, he noted that he was feeling quite warm and comfortable. He was not shivering, and it even seemed that a warm glow had come to his chest and trunk. And yet, when he touched his nose or cheeks, there was no sensation. Running would not thaw them out. Nor would it thaw out his hands and feet. Then the thought came to him that the frozen portions of his body must be extending. He tried to keep this thought down, to forget it, to think of something else; he was aware of the panicky feeling that it caused, and he was afraid of the panic. But the thought asserted itself, and persisted, until it produced a vision of his body totally frozen. This was too much, and he made another wild run along the trail. Once he slowed down to a walk, but the thought of the freezing extending itself made him run again.

And all the time the dog ran with him, at his heels. When he fell down a second time, it curled its tail over its forefeet and sat in front of him, facing him, curiously eager and intent. The warmth and security of the animal angered him, and he cursed it till it flattened down its ears appeasingly. This time the shivering came more quickly upon the man. He was losing in his battle with the frost. It was creeping into his body from all sides. The thought of it drove him on, but he ran no more than a hundred feet, when he staggered and pitched headlong. It was his last panic. When he had recovered his breath and control, he sat up and entertained in his mind the conception of meeting death with dignity. However, the conception did not come to him in such terms. His idea of it was that he had been making a fool of himself, running around like a chicken with its head cut off — such was the simile that occurred to him. Well, he was bound to freeze anyway, and he might as well take it decently. With this new-found peace of mind came the first glimmerings of drowsiness. A good idea, he thought, to sleep off to death. It was like taking an anesthetic. Freezing was not so bad as people thought. There were lots worse ways to die.

He pictured the boys finding his body next day. Suddenly he found himself with them, coming along the trail and looking for himself. And, still with them, he came around a turn in the trail and found himself lying in the snow. He did not belong with himself any more, for even then he was out of himself standing with the boys and looking at himself in the snow. It certainly was cold, was his thought. When he got back to the States, he could tell the folks what real cold was. He drifted on from this to a vision of the old-timer on Sulphur Creek. He could see him quite clearly, warm and comfortable, and smoking a pipe.

" You were right, old hoss; you were right," the man mumbled to the old-timer of Sulphur Creek.

Then the man drowsed off into what seemed to him the most comfortable and satisfying sleep he had ever known. The dog sat facing him and waiting. The brief day drew to a close in a long, slow twilight. There were no signs of a fire to be made, and, besides, never in the dog's experience had it known a man to sit like that in the snow and make no fire. As the twilight drew on, its eager yearning for the fire mastered it, and with a great lifting and shifting of forefeet, it whined softly, then flattened its ears down in anticipation of being chidden by the man. But the man remained silent. Later, the dog whined loudly. And still later it crept close to the man and caught the scent of death. This made the animal bristle and back away. A little longer it delayed, howling under the stars that leaped and danced and shone brightly in the cold sky. Then it turned and trotted up the trail in the direction of the camp it knew, where were the other food providers and fire providers.

## Suggestions for Study

1. In a plot, interest may depend on suspense — your uncertainty as to which side is going to win in the struggle — or, when you are sure of the outcome, curiosity as to just how victory will be achieved. Which kind of interest is there in " To Build a Fire "? Draw up a list of the places where the struggle seems to turn in the man's favor and where it seems to turn against him. Does this make you uncertain as to the outcome?

2. What are the opposing forces of this plot? When were you sure that one had been triumphant in the struggle? How near the end of a good story should the reader know the outcome of the struggle?

3. How would the quality of the story have been affected had the man been rescued?

4. What effect is obtained by not naming the man? Owen Wister did not name the hero in *The Virginian*. Do you know any other stories using this device?

5. Locate on a map the Yukon and other places mentioned on page 48.

6. Write an account of the struggle of a person against a succession of difficulties. Try to balance success and failure so as to keep the reader in suspense as to the outcome.

7. To become better acquainted with Jack London's work, read " All-Gold Canyon," one of his best short stories, or others in *Tales of the Fish Patrol, Children of the Frost,* and *Lost Face.* If you have read and enjoyed *The Call of the Wild,* try other long stories: *The Sea-Wolf* and *White Fang. Martin Eden* is his autobiographical novel.

8. London was influenced by the writings of Rudyard Kipling, an Englishman. If you have read some of Kipling's stories, point out similarities between the two writers.

## For Your Vocabulary

WORD POWER. Having a general idea of the meaning of a word is a help to understanding, but knowing its exact meaning gives you the full power of the word in reading — and the power to use it forcefully yourself. Two sensations of this ill-fated arctic traveler are described with words that are particularly expressive, *excruciating* (page 54) and *poignant* (page 56). An intensely sharp physical pain is said to be *excruciating* (ĕks-krōō′shĭ-āt-ĭng), or like being crucified. But *poignant* (poin′-yănt), which literally means piercing, is used of intense emotions more often than of physical feeling. Another difference is that although *poignant* is often used of painful feelings, like regret and fear, it can also be used of keenly pleasant feelings, such as *poignant* delight.

## Sinclair Lewis    1885–

To win the Nobel prize in literature is to be recognized as a writer of world importance. The first American author to be honored by the Nobel prize was Sinclair Lewis, who is probably the ablest exponent in America of the art of satire, and a ceaseless crusader against those features of our social and political life which he considers vicious.

Sinclair Lewis has always been a nonconformist. Instead of going to the state university like most of his schoolmates in Sauk Center, Minnesota, he decided to go to an eastern college. At Yale he cared nothing for fraternities or the usual outside activities and none too much for the curriculum; while there he earned the enduring nickname "Red," because of his hair and his radical ideas.

Mr. Lewis has chosen to write about the contemporary American scene, not maintaining a strict realism, but coloring the narrative in order to bring home his social messages.

While Mr. Lewis's characters are typical and his settings recognizable, the ideas which he is trying to develop are much more important to him than a clear, objective portrayal of life. This is equally true of any propagandist or of any satirist; in his characters he must exaggerate those qualities, good and bad, on which he wants us to focus attention and form judgments. And since Mr. Lewis's social and political views are not the conventional ones, his novels are always challenging; each new novel brings out angry protests, either from those who have been made the butt of his none-too-kindly satire or from those who disapprove of his doctrines.

## RING AROUND A ROSY

This story is a good-natured satire on those people who are never happy where they are. Each character has a reason for thinking his own country no longer tolerable. It is interesting to read in this story, which was written in 1931, that an Italian professor, annoyed by the loss of free speech and discussion in Italy, goes, of all places, to Germany — because there he can say anything he pleases!

T. Eliot Hopkins was a nice young man at forty-two, and he had done nicely all the nice things — Williams College, a New York brokerage office, his first million, his first Phyfe table, careful polo at Del Monte, the discovery that it was smart to enjoy the opera and the discovery that it was much smarter to ridicule it. In fact, by the time he had a penthouse on Park Avenue, Eliot understood the theory of relativity as applied to the world of fashion — that a man is distinguished not by what he likes but by what he is witty enough to loathe.

As for Eleanor, his wife, she came from Chicago, so naturally she had a cousin married to a French count and another cousin who would have married an Italian marquis if it had not been discovered that he was already married and not a marquis. Still, he really was Italian.

Their first year in the penthouse was ecstatic. Thirty stories up, atop 9999 Park Avenue, looking to east and north and south, it had a terrace exclamatory with scarlet wicker chairs, Pompeian marble benches, and a genuine rose garden attended by a real gardener — at three dollars an hour, from the florist's. On the terrace opened the duplex living room, fifty feet long, its Caen stone walls and twenty-foot windows soaring up to a raftered ceiling of English oak. But to a nosy and domestic mind, to one who had known Eleanor when she lived in a six-room bungalow in

Wilmette, these glories of city-dominating terrace and castle hall were less impressive than the little perfections of the apartment: the kitchen, which was a little like a chemist's laboratory and more like the cabin of an electric locomotive; the bathrooms of plate glass and purple tile, and the master's bathroom with an open fireplace. Through this domain Eleanor bustled for a year, slipping out to look across the East River to the farthest hills and gashouses of Long Island, dashing inside to turn on the automatic pipe organ, plumping down at her most *art moderne* desk of silver, aluminum, and black glass to write dinner invitations. And they entertained. Vastly. These gigantic rooms demanded people, and sometimes there were forty guests at the unique diamond-shaped dinner table, with five old family retainers sneaked in from the caterer's. With such a turnover of guests, there weren't always enough bank vice-presidents and English authors and baronets and other really worth-while people on the market, and Eleanor had to fall back on persons who were nothing but old friends, which was pretty hard on a girl. So she was not altogether contented, even before things happened.

They were important things. Eliot sold short before the stock-market depression. His first million was joined by two others, and he immediately took up reading, art criticism, and refined manners. He also bought new jodhpurs. I am not quite sure what jodhpurs are, but then T. Eliot hadn't known, either, six years before. They have to do with polo, though whether they are something you ride or wear or hit the ball with, I have not been informed. But I do know that Eliot's jodhpurs were singularly well spoken of at Meadowbrook, and whatever else they may have been, they were not cursed by being American. They were as soundly English as cold toast.

Now, selling short at a time when everyone else is dismally long is likely to have a large effect on nice people, and Eleanor agreed with Eliot that it was shocking — it was worse than shocking, it was a bore —

that they should have to go on slaving their lives away among commercial lowbrows, when in England, say, people of Their Class led lives composed entirely of beauty, graciousness, leisure, and servants who didn't jiggle the tea tray.

The penthouse seemed to her a little gaudy, a little difficult. With the stupidity of servants, it took her hours a day to prepare for even the simplest dinner party. It was like poor Eliot's having to dash out and be in his office in the dawn, at ten o'clock, and often give up his afternoons of golf because his clerks were so idiotically dumb that he couldn't trust them.

When they had taken the penthouse, a friend of Eleanor's had been so conservative as to buy a quiet little house in Turtle Bay and furnish it with English antiques. Mahogany. White fireplaces. Just a shack. But now Eleanor found the shack restful. The drawing room did not seem empty with but two of them for tea, and the little befrilled maid was not too humble, as she would have been in the vastnesses of the penthouse.

All the way home Eleanor looked wistfully out of the limousine. She wished that there weren't a law against her walking, this warm June evening. But she wanted to be walking, not on an avenue but in a real certificated English lane — rosy cottages, old women curtsying, nightingales rising from the hedges, or whatever nightingales do rise from; witty chatter at the gate with their neighbor, General Wimbledom, former C. in C.[1] in India; not one of these horrid New Yorkers who talk about bond issues.

When Eliot dragged home, hot, his eyes blurred with weariness, he groaned at Eleanor, " I'm glad we're not going out tonight! Let's dine on the terrace."

" But we are going out, my pet! I'm restless. I can't stand this private Grand Central. I feel like a redcap. Let's go to that nice little French speak-easy on Forty-ninth and try to make ourselves believe we've had sense enough to go to Europe."

[1] C. in C.: Commander in Chief.

" All right. I wish we had gone. If nothing begins to happen in the market — Maybe we'll be abroad before the summer's over."

The Chez Edouard has, like all distinguished French restaurants, a Swiss manager, Czech waiters, a Bavarian cook, a Greek coat checker, and scenes from Venice painted on the walls of a decayed drawing room, and, unlike most of them, it has German wine. Eleanor crooned over the thought of onion soup, chicken cutlet Pojarski, *crêpes Suzette,* and *Oppenheimer Kreuz Spätlese.*

" America — New York — isn't so bad after all, if you belong, if you know where to go," exulted Eleanor.

Then the waiter wouldn't wait.

Eleanor raised a gracious finger, Eleanor raised an irritated hand, Eliot sank so low as to snap his fingers, and the waiter merely leered at them and did not come. He was attending a noisy group of six businessmen, who were beginning a sound meal with six cocktails apiece — tip after each round.

" It's absolutely dreadful what America does even to good foreign servants! " Eleanor raged. " They become so impertinent and inefficient! It's something in the air of this awful country. They're so selfish and inconsiderate — and yet so nice as long as they stay abroad. I wish we were there — in Europe — where we could lead a civilized life." |

" Yes," said Eliot. " Little inns. Nice."

When they were finally served with chicken cutlets Pojarski, and Eleanor had come to believe that after all she would live through it, she encountered the most terrible affliction of all. One of the six noisy interlopers wambled across and addressed her: " Sister, I just noticed we're taking more of the waiter's time than we ought to. You had to bawl him out before he brought your chicken croquettes. Excuse us! If you and the gentleman would come over and join us in a little libation — Excuse the liberty, but we've got some pretty decent, old-fashioned, housebroken rye, and if we could have the pleasure — "

During this shocking affront Eleanor had gaped at Eliot in terror. He rescued her in a brave and high-toned manner; he said dryly to the intruder, " Very kind of you, but we have quite enough to drink here, thank you, and we must be going immediately."

" Imagine a dreadful thing like that happening in any other country! England, for instance! " Eleanor murmured afterward. " Simply no privacy anywhere in America. Dreadful! Let's get out of this dreadful restaurant."

Nor was she any the more pleased when the checking girl, whisking her white flannel topcoat across the counter, gurgled, " Here you are, dearie."

" And no respect for their betters! Just Bolsheviks! " pronounced Eleanor.

They had sent away the car. Eleanor — as a girl she had often walked six miles on a picnic — suggested to Eliot, " It would be awfully jolly and adventurous to walk home! "

They came on the new Titanic Talkie Theater — Cooled Air — Capacity 4,000. Eliot yawned, " Ever been in one of these super-movies palaces? I never have. Let's see what it's like."

" You know what it will be like. Dreadful. Vulgar. But let's see."

The lobby was a replica, but somewhat reduced, of Seville Cathedral. A bowing doorman, in gold lace, scarlet tunic, and a busby with a purple plume, admitted them through gilded bronze doors to an inner lobby, walled with silk tapestry, floored with the largest Oriental rug in the world, and dotted with solid silver statues of negligent ladies, parakeets in golden cages on pedestals of Chinese lacquer, a fountain whose stream was illuminated with revolving lights, lemon-colored and green and crimson, and vast red club chairs beside which, for ash receivers, were Florentine wine jars.

" Oh! This hurts! " wailed Eleanor.

A line of ushers, young men in the uniforms of West Point cadets, stood at attention. One of them galloped forward and, bending from the waist, held out a white-gloved hand for their tickets.

" I'm paralyzed! This is like an opium eater's dream of a mid-Victorian royal palace. Must we go in? " fretted Eleanor.

" No! Let's go home. Think how nice a cool Tom Collins would be on the terrace," said Eliot, and to the usher: " Thanks, I think we've seen enough."

The stateliness, the choiceness and aristocracy of their exit were a little crumpled by the military usher's blatting behind them, " Well, can you lay that! The Prince of Wales and Tex Guinan — that's who they are! " And at the door they heard from a comfortable woman enthroned in a tall Spanish chair, addressing her lady friend, " I always did like a good artistic talkie with Doug Fairbanks and some old antique castles, and like that. I can't stand this low-down sex stuff. Gotta have art or nothing."

Eleanor had lived in New York so long that she rarely saw it. She did tonight, with liveliness and hatred.

Broadway was turned into a county fair, with orange-juice stands, pineapple-juice stands, show windows with nuts arranged in circles and diamonds, radio shops blaring, shops jammed with clothing models draped in aching brown suits with green shirts, green ties, green-bordered handkerchiefs. The people on Broadway Eleanor lumped as " impossible " — hoarse newsboys, Hungarians and Sicilians and Polish Jews guffawing on corners, tight-mouthed men with gray derbies concealing their eyes, standing in snarling conferences, silk-stockinged girls laughing like grackles.

" Dreadful! " she observed.

They looked east to a skyscraper like a gigantic arm threatening the sky with the silver mace that was its tower.

" Our buildings are so big and pretentious! Nothing kindly, nothing civilized about them. So — oh, so new! " complained Eleanor.

" Um — yes," said Eliot.

At home, from their terrace, they looked across the East River, then south and west to the wriggling electricity of Broadway, where tawdry signs, high on hotels, turned crimson and gold and aching white with hysterical quickness. A searchlight wounded the starless dark. And the noises scratched her nerves. Once she had felt that together they made a symphony; now she distinguished and hated them. Tugboats brayed and howled on the river. Trains on the three elevated railways clanked like monstrous shaken chains, and streetcars bumped with infuriating dullness. A million motors snarled, four million motor tires together joined in a vast hissing, like torn silk, and through all the uproar smashed the gong of an ambulance.

" Let's get out of it! Let's have a house in England! " cried Eleanor. " Peace! Civilized society! Perfect servants! Old tradition! Let's go! "

In the offices of Messrs. Trottingham, Strusby and Beal, Estate Agents, London, Eliot and Eleanor, once they had convinced a severe lady reception clerk that, though they were Americans, they really did want to lease a house, were shown a portfolio of houses with such ivy-dripping Tudor walls, such rose gardens, such sunny slopes of lawn between oaks ancient as Robin Hood, that they wriggled like children in a candy shop. They had been well trained by reading fiction and the comic papers; they knew enough not to laugh when they read " 16 bd., 2 bthrms., usual offices, choice fernery, stbling., 12, garge., 1 car." So they were taken into favor, and young Mr. Claude Beal himself drove them down to Tiberius Hall, in Sussex.

" The Hall," he said, " belongs to Sir Horace and Lady Mingo. You will remember that Sir Horace was formerly solicitor general."

" Oh, yes," said Eliot.

" Quite," said Eleanor.

" Sir Horace wishes to rent only because his health is not good. He is no longer a young man. He requires a hotter climate. He is thinking of Italy. Naturally Lady Mingo and he hate to leave so charming a place, you will understand."

" I see," said Eliot.

" Hush," said Eleanor.

" But if they find really reliable tenants, they might — you see? But you understand that I'm not trying to do a bit of selling, as you Yankees say."

" I see. Yes," said Eliot.

They passed through the gateway of Tiberius Hall — the stone gateposts were worn by three centuries — and saw the gatekeeper's lodge. On the shoulder of the stone chimney were gargoyles that had looked on the passing Queen Elizabeth, and before the latticed windows, with crocus-yellow curtains, were boxes of red geraniums.

Laburnums edged the quarter mile of driveway and shut off most of the estate, but they saw a glade with deer feeding in a mistiness of tender sunlight. " Not," mused Eleanor, " like our dreadful, glaring, raw sunlight at home." They came suddenly on the Hall. It was of Tudor, pure, the stone mellow. The chimneys were fantastically twisted; the red-tiled roof was soft with mosses; the tall windows of the ground floor gave on a terrace of ancient flagging. But what grasped at her, caressed her, more than the house itself was the lawn at one side where, under the shadow of oaks, half a dozen people sat in basket chairs at tea, attended by a butler whose cheeks were venerable pouches of respectability, and by a maid fresh as a mint drop in her cap and apron.

" We're going to take it," Eleanor whispered.

" We certainly are! "

" Here, we'll really live! "

" Yes! Tea, with servants like that! Polo and golf with gentlemen, not with money-grubbers! Neighbors who've actually read a book! Nell, we've come home! "

" This country," said Sir Horace Mingo, " has gone utterly to the dogs."

" It has indeed," said Lady Mingo. " No competent servants since the war. Not one. The wages they demand, and their incredible stupidity — impossible to find a cook who can do a gooseberry trifle properly — and their impertinence! Did I tell you how pertly Bindger answered me when I spoke to her about staying out till ten? "

" You did, beloved. *In extenso,* if you will permit me to say so, I agree with you. My man — and to think of paying him twenty-two bob [1] a week; when I was a youngster the fellow would have been delighted to have ten — he cannot press trousers so that they won't resemble bags. ' Higgs,' I often say to him, ' I don't quite understand why it is that when you have given your loving attention to my trousers they always resemble bags '; and as to his awakening me when I tell him to, he never fails to be either five minutes late or, what is essentially more annoying, ten minutes early, and when your confounded Bindger brings my tea in the morning it is invariably cold, and if I speak to her about it she merely sniffs and tosses her head and — but — "

While Sir Horace is catching his breath it must be interjected that this conversation of the Mingos, before the James II fireplace at Tiberius Hall, had been patriotically enjoyed three months before Eliot and Eleanor Hopkins, on their penthouse terrace, had decided to flee from the land of electricity and clamor.

" But," rumbled Sir Horace, in that port-and-Stilton voice which had made him the pursuing fiend to the sinful when he had been solicitor general, " the fact that in the entire length and breadth of England to-day, and I dare say Scotland as well, it is utterly impossible, at any absurd wage, to find a servant who is not lazy, ignorant, dirty, thieving — and many of them dare to be impertinent, even to me! — this indisputable decay in English service is no more alarming than the fact that in our own class, good manners, sound learning, and simple decency appear to have vanished. Young men up at Oxford who waste their time on socialism and chemistry — chemistry! for a gentleman! — instead of acquiring a respectable knowledge of the classics! Young

[1] **bob:** slang for shilling, about twenty-five cents.

women who smoke, curse, go about exhibiting their backs — "

" Horace! "

" Well, they do! I'm scarcely to blame, am I? Have I ever gone about exhibiting my back? Have I caused whole restaurants to be shocked by the spectacle of my back? And that is not all. Everywhere! The pictures instead of Shakespeare! Motors making our lanes a horror and a slaughter! Shops that have electric lights and enormous windows and everything save honest wares and shop attendants with respectful manners! Shopkeepers setting themselves up to be better and certainly richer than the best county families! In fact, the whole blasted country becoming Americanized. . . . And cocktails! Cocktails! My word, if anybody had ever offered my old father a cocktail, I should think he would have knocked him down!

" England has always had a bad climate. But there was a day when the manners of the gentry and the charms of domestic life made up for it. But now I can see no reason why we should remain here. Why can't we go to Italy? That fellow Mussolini, he may not be English, but he has taught the masses discipline. You don't find impertinent servants and obscene gentlewomen there, I'll wager! "

" Yes. Why don't we go, Horace? "

" How can we? With this expensive place on our hands? If I were some petrol johnny, or a City bloke, or someone who had made his money selling spurious remedies, we might be able to afford it. But having been merely a servant of His Majesty all my life, merely devoting such legal knowledge and discernment as I might chance to have to the cause of justice and — "

" But we might rent the place, Horace. Oh! Think of a jolly little villa at San Remo or on Lake Maggiore, with the lovely sunshine and mountains and those too sweet Italian servants who retain some sense of the dignity and joy of service! "

" Rent it to whom — whom? Our class are all impoverished."

" But there's the Argentines and Ameri-

cans and Armenians. You know. All those curious A races where everyone is a millionaire. How they would appreciate a place with lawns! I'm told there isn't a single pretty lawn in America. How could there be? They would be so glad — "

" Though I couldn't imagine any American being trusted with our Lord Penzance sweetbriers! "

" But, Horace, a sweet little peasant villa at Baveno; just ten or twelve rooms."

" Well — After all, Victoria, why should people of some breeding, as I flatter myself we do possess, be shut up in this shocking country, when we might be in the sun of Italy — and Dr. Immens-Bourne says it would be so much better for my rheumatism. Shall we speak to an estate agent? If there are any honest and mannerly estate johnnys left in this atrocious country! "

On the terrace of crumbling pink and yellow tiles, sufficiently shaded by the little orange trees in pots, Sir Horace and Lady Mingo sat looking across Lake Maggiore to the bulk of Sasso del Ferro, along whose mountain trails perched stone villages. A small steamer swaggered up the lake; after its puffing there was no sound save goat bells and a clattering cart.

" Oh, the peace of it! Oh, the wise old peace of Italy! " sighed Lady Mingo, and the wrinkles in her vellumlike cheeks seemed smoother, her pale old eyes less weary.

" Yes! " said Sir Horace. He was not so pontifical as he had been at Tiberius Hall. " Peace. No jazz! No noisy English servants yelping music-hall songs and banging things about! "

From the kitchen, a floor below the terrace, a sound of the cook banging his copper pots, and a maid yelping a few bars of *Traviata*.

" Yes! The sweet Italian servants! So gay and yet so polite! Smiling! And the lovely sun all day! Why we ever stayed — Oh, Horace, I do hope I shan't be punished for saying such things. Of course England is the greatest country in the world, and when I think of people like my father and the dean, of course no other country could ever produce great gentlemen like them, but at the same time, I really don't care if we never leave Italy again! And those sweet ruins at Fiesole! And the trains always quite absolutely on time since Mussolini came! And — Oh, Horace, it's really quite too simply perfect! "

" Rather! Quite! You know, I'd thought I should worry about Tiberius Hall. But that's a very decent chap — that Hoffman Eliot — Hopkins — Eliot Hopkins — what is the chap's absurd name? — quite gentlemanly, for an American. I was astonished. None of these strange clothes Americans wear. I really quite took him for an English gentleman, until he opened his mouth. Astonishing! He hadn't a red sweater or a great, huge felt hat or a velvet dinner jacket, or any of these odd things that Americans ordinarily wear. And now we must dress, my dear. Professor Pulciano will be here at half after seven. So decent of him to rent us this — this paradise! "

He was youngish and rather rich; but Carlo Pulciano had not remained in the Italian army after the war, though his brother was commanding general of one of the departments, nor would he listen to his sister-in-law's insistence that he blossom in the *salons* of Rome.

He had previously scandalized them by teaching economics in the University of Pisa, by sitting over buckram-bound books full of tedious figures, and when the Black Shirts had marched on Rome and taken over the country, when it was not wise to speculate too much about economics, Pulciano had the more offended his people by buying this largish villa on the Pallanza peninsula at Lake Maggiore and retiring to his books and bees.

But in that still paradise he became restless and a little confused. All through the morning he would, in discussions nonetheless mad because they were entirely within his head, be completely pro-Fascist, admiring the Fascist discipline, the ideal of planned industry, the rousing of youngsters

from sun loafing into drilling. Then, all afternoon, he would be communistic or Social Democratic.

But whatever he was, here he was forever nothing. He had no one with whom to talk. It was not safe. And to Carlo Pulciano talking was life; talking late at night, feverishly, over cigarettes and Lacrima Cristi [1]; talking on dusty walks; talking through elegant dinners so ardently that he did not notice whether he was eating veal stew or zabaglione.[2] Forever talking!

He would not have minded turning Fascist complete, provided he might have lived in a place where everyone hated Fascismo, so that furiously, all night, he might have defended it. He admitted, with one of the few grins this earnest young man ever put on, that he didn't so much want any particular social system as the freedom to discuss, in any way, at any time, over any kind of liquor, all social systems.

He longed for Germany, where he had studied economics as a young man. Germany! There was the land where he could talk unendingly! There was the land where, though the *Polizei* [3] might harry you off the grass, you could say precisely what you thought or, greater luxury yet, say what you didn't think at all, just for the pleasure of it.

Pulciano cursed the fact that he had sunk most of his money in this villa and could not afford to go live in Germany. He had loved Italy; for it he had been wounded on the Piave. He had loved this villa and the peace of its blue lake waters. He had come to hate them both.

He hated the servants — so ready to promise everything and so unlikely to do anything; so smiling of eye and so angry in their hearts. He hated the climate. " It would be in Italy that we have the chilliest and wettest winters in Christendom, yet the mushheaded people insist it's always sunny and will not put in even fireplaces." He

---

[1] **Lacrima Cristi** (làk′rĭm-à krĭs′tĭ): an Italian wine with the strange name Tears of Christ. [2] **zabaglione** (tsä-bäl-yō′nà): an Italian confection made of egg yolks, sugar, and wine. [3] **Polizei** (pŏ-lĭ-tsī′): police. (German.)

hated the food. " I'd give all the confounded pastes and fruits in the world for a decent *Mass*[1] of dark beer and a pig's knuckle at Munich! " He hated funeral processions, policemen with cocks' plumes on their hats, plaster shrines, the silly wicker on wine bottles, wax matches that burned his fingers, and even — so far was he gone in treason against Italy — cigars with straws in them. But he did nothing about it. He was too busy hating to do much of anything.

He was delighted when the manager of the Grand Hotel d'Isola Bella came inquiring whether he might not care to lease his villa to a crazy English nobleman named Sir Mingo. Yes, for a year.

A week later, with many bundles and straw suitcases, Carlo Pulciano was on the train for Berlin and free talk, freethinking — long free thought over long cheap beers.

The doctrine of most American and British caricaturists, and all French ones, is that every German is fat, towheaded, and given to vast beers, while every German woman is still fatter, and clad invariably in a chip hat and the chintz covering for a wing chair.

Baron Helmuth von Mittenbach, Silesian Junker[2] and passionate mechanical engineer, had ruddy hair and blue eyes filled with light. He was slender, and looked rather more English than the Prince of Wales. The Baroness, Hilda, was slim as an icicle and as smooth, and she liked dancing in the night clubs off the Kurfürstendamm, in Berlin, till four of the morning. Neither of them liked beer, nor had ever drunk it since school days.

During the war, which ended when he was thirty, Helmuth had tried to join the flying circus of his friend Von Richthofen. He would have enjoyed swooping, possibly even being swooped upon. But he was too good a designer, and headquarters kept him improving the tank, and the one time when he sneaked off to try out his own tank at the front, they strafed him so that he stayed

back of the line after that, fuming in a room verminous with steel shavings.

He was, therefore, more excited after the war than during it. Now he could take a real part! Now engineers were to be not assistants and yes men, like quartermasters or photographers or royal princes, but the real lords, shaping a new Germany.

He believed that the struggle to rebuild German glory would be a crusade holy and united. Now that the republic had come, with so little bloodspilling, the political parties would join; the politicians would give up that ultimate selfishness of insisting on the superiority of their own ideals.

He was certain that the salvation of Germany was in industrial efficiency. They hadn't the man power and raw stuffs of America or Russia, nor the army of France, nor the ships and empire of Great Britain. They must make things more swiftly, better, and more economically than any other land. They must no longer grudgingly adopt machinery when they had to admit that a machine could do the work of a hundred men, but take machinery as a religion.

Helmuth took it so. It is definitely not true that Helmuth and the youngish men who worked with him in those driving days thought mostly, or even much at all, about the profits they and their bosses might make out of machinery and rationalization. It was not true that they saw machinery as the oppressor of ordinary men. Rather, they saw it as the extension of man's force and dignity.

Here you had an ordinary human, with an ordinary, clumsy fist. Put a lever or an electric switch into it, and it had the power of a thousand elephants. Man that walked wearily, swam like a puppy, and flew not at all, man that had been weakest and most despicable of all the major mammals, was with motor and submarine and plane, with dynamo and linotype, suddenly to be not mammal at all but like the angels. So dreamed Baron Mittenbach, while he grunted and hunched his shoulders over his drawing board, while in the best parade-ground manner he called a careless foreman

[1] **Mass** (mäs): literally, a measure; here a pot of beer. [2] **Junker** (yŏŏng′kĕr): a German aristocrat.

an accursed-swine-hound-thunder-weather-
once-again-for-the-sake-of-Heaven.

He had gone as chief engineer to the great
A. A. G. — the so-called Universal Automobile Trust. His hobbies were light, cheap
tractors for small farms, and light, cheap
cars. He planned sedans which would sell,
when exchange was normal again, for what,
in American, would be a hundred and fifty
dollars. By night, at home, he planned other
devices, some idiotic, some blandly practical — eighteen-thousand-ton liners to leave
out the swimming pools and marble pillars
streaked like oxtail soup and to cross the Atlantic in three days; floating aviation fields,
a string of fifteen of them across the ocean,
so that a fallen plane would never be more
than an hour from rescue; a parachute to
ease down an entire plane, should the motor
die or a wing drop off. Crazy as any other
poet, and as excited. But happier.

He had reason at first for his excitement
and his happiness. Though the Germans
gabbled of every known political scheme,
from union with Russia to union with England, they jumped into the deification of
modern industry as schoolboys into a summer lake. They worked ten hours a day,
twelve, fourteen, not wearily but with a
zest in believing that their sweat was ce-
menting a greater Germany. They ruthlessly stripped factories and at whatever
cost put in rows of chemical retorts a quarter mile long, conveyer belts, automatic oil
furnaces, high-speed steel.

Helmuth was fortunate in being able to
have a decent and restful house not too far
from his factory, for though he drove at a
speed which caused the police to look
pained, he could not, he told himself, take
all morning getting to work. There were too
many exciting things to do. The factory was
in the Spandau district of Berlin, and reasonably near, among the placid villas and
linden rows of Grünewald, Hilda and Helmuth took a brick-and-stucco house with a
mosaic eagle shining over the tile balcony.

The attic floor had been a private gaming
room. Snorting at these signs of idleness and
pride, Helmuth stripped out the card tables,

roulette wheel, billiard table, dumped
them in the basement, and set up a lathe, a
workbench, a drawing board, an electric
furnace.

Here all evening, while Hilda restlessly
studied Russian or yawned over crossword
puzzles, this grandson of a field marshal, in
a workman's jumper and atrocious felt slippers, experimented with aluminum alloys
or drew plans of a monorail which would do
the six hundred and sixty miles from Berlin
to Paris in six hours, with carriages like
drawing rooms, glass-walled, twenty feet
wide.

It was a good time — for a year. The destruction of the currency did not worry Helmuth; he was convinced that man should
be saved by gasoline alone. But after two
years, or three, he roused from his dream to
see that the German recovery was not altogether a pure, naïve crusade; that the politicians would not forget their petty little
differences. There were not two or three parties, as in Britain and America, but eight,
ten, a dozen; and these parties clamorously
advocated almost everything save total immersion. They advocated the return of the
Kaiser, or immediate communism; they advocated a cautious state socialism, or wider
power for the industrialists; they advocated
combining with Austria, or the independence of Bavaria.

Outside the political parties, there were
some thousands of noisy and highly admired prophets who had no interest in Helmuth's turret lathes and r.p.m.'s,[1] but who
shouted in little halls and little blurry magazines that the world was to be saved by
vegetarianism, or going naked, or abolishing armies, or integrating spoken plays with
the movie film, or growing carrots instead
of wheat, or colonizing Brazil, or attending
spiritualist seances, or mountain climbing,
or speaking Esperanto.

In his worship of clean, driving, unsenti-
mental steel, Helmuth despised equally all
cult mongers and all politicians, however
famous. They talked; they chewed over old
straw; they pushed themselves into per-

[1] **r.p.m.'s:** revolutions per minute.

sonal notoriety. He didn't, just now, care a hang whether he lived under a democracy or a monarchy or a soviet, so long as they would let him make more tractors.

The more eloquent the politicians were, in their bright oratory in the Reichstag or the jolly conferences at Lausanne and Geneva, the more he hated them. His gods were Duisberg and Citroen and Ford and Edison and the Wright brothers, and since most of the pantheon were Americans, he came to worship that country as his Olympus.

The German politicians talked — all the Germans talked, he snarled. They were so proud of having mental freedom. Yes, snorted Helmuth, and the Irish were so proud of having fairies! Freedom for what — for escape from discipline into loquacious idleness, or for the zest of hard work? He hated peculiarly — doubtless unjustly — the intellectuals whom he had known in the university, who gabbled that there was something inescapably evil about machines; that because the transition from handicrafts to machinery had certainly produced unemployment, this unemployment must always continue; who whimpered that we must all go back to the country and live perfectly simple old-fashioned lives — with, however, telephones and open plumbing and typewriters and automobiles and electric lights and quick mail and newspapers.

" Yah! My picture of those gentry," Helmuth grumbled to Hilda, " is that they sit in machine-made modernistic metal chairs, telephoning to one another that they want us to stop manufacturing telephones and just beautifully write them! Good-night. Tomorrow I must be up early and write a carburetor and sculp a grease gun."

Thus irritated, he looked daily more toward America. There, he believed, everybody was united in the one common purpose of solving economic injustices, not by turning every capitalist into a starved proletarian but by making all competent proletarians into capitalists. The more he read American magazines and yearned for American vitality and ingenuity, the more he

grumbled about Germany. And his Hilda, who was most of the time happily ignorant of everything he was saying, here joined him.

In America, she had heard, there was no need of servants, because everything was done, and perfectly, by machinery. And she was so sick, she confided, of German servants since the war. What had got into them? Regular communists! They no longer had respect for the better classes, and the government was supporting them in their demands. What with compulsory insurance and the law that you couldn't, without notice, kick out even the most impertinent maid, there was no running a house. She longed for electric dishwashers and washing machines, but their landlord was old-fashioned; he would not put them in.

America!

Just when Helmuth and Hilda were keenest about it, he met McPherson Jones, of the Engel & Jones High Speed Tractor Company of Long Island City, who was scouting about Europe looking for new efficiencies. Helmuth spoke a photographic English. Jones and he went to Essen, to the Ruhr, and argued about beer and about torque in aviation. Jones offered him a place high on the staff of Engel & Jones, with a breath-taking salary; and a month later Helmuth and Hilda were on the high seas — to the miserable Hilda it was evident why they were called high.

Helmuth had sublet his house to an Italian, a Professor Carlo Pulciano, who was going to study something or other at the university. Helmuth did not leave Berlin till a fortnight after he had turned the house over to Pulciano. He called to say good-by, and Pulciano proudly showed him the changes he had made. On the top floor Helmuth did a little youthful suffering. Pulciano had ripped out the lathe, the workbench, the drawing board, and fitted up the room in imitation of an old Bavarian inn, with heavy wooden tables, stone beer mugs, a barrel of beer, and painted mottoes announcing that men who gave earnest attention to anything save drinking, kissing, singing, and snoring were invariably jackasses.

" I tell you," cried Pulciano, " here I shall have again the good free talk of my German student days! I am in your Germany so happy! You Germans realize that the purpose of life is not just doing, but thinking, and setting thoughts in jeweled words — and again I get decent red cabbage! "

" *Ja?* " said Helmuth. It can sound extraordinarily like " Yeah? "

He groaned to himself, " Just the old, thick-necked, beer-steaming Germany we have been trying to kill! I want a race stark and lean and clear and cold-bathed and unafraid of the song of flywheels! "

With Hilda seasick, Helmuth found solace in the smoking room of the steamer. By the end of three days he knew a dozen Americans — a banker, the superintendent of a steel plant, two automobile-foreign-sales men, a doctor who had been studying gross pathology in Vienna.

He expected them to resent his coming to America in rivalry with their earnings; he expected them to smile at his English. But they welcomed him to the tournament. " Come on! If you can get anything away from us in America, it just makes the game better," they said; and: " Your English? Listen, baron. The only trouble with you is, you went to a school where they let the teams weaken themselves by looking at books between the halves. By the way, will you happen to be in Detroit, time of the Michigan-Notre Dame game? Wish you'd come stay with us and I'll drive you down. Like to have you meet the wife and show her up — she thinks she can parley Deutsch."

" They are," Helmuth glowed to Hilda, " the kindest and politest people I have ever known. But just the same, *ich sage Dir bestimmt,*[1] that Mr. Tolson is all wrong about the front-wheel drive. . . . I wonder about the market for speedboats in Norway? "

He had accepted invitations to Bar Har-

[1] ich sage Dir bestimmt (ĭk sä'gĕ dēr bĕ-shtĭmt'): I tell you definitely. (German.)

bor, Seattle, Moose Jaw, Gramercy Square, Franconia Notch, and Social Circle, Georgia, before he saw the skyscrapers from New York harbor.

" They are my friends! I have never had so many friends — not in my life! " he rejoiced, and with a feeling that the towers of New York were his own, he pointed them out to a slightly shaky Hilda beside him.

" They are very pretty. They are not all worn, like cathedral spires," he said. " I wonder what the wind pressure per square meter is with a sixty-kilometer wind? I wonder if electric welding costs more than riveting? I wonder whether the marble here comes from Italy or Vermont? Yes, it is exciting; I am very thrilled. . . . I wonder what is the tensile strength of the steel in these buildings? "

But his friend, Dr. Moore, the Omaha surgeon, could not answer any of these obvious questions, though he was a real American.

A week after their arrival, Baron and Baroness Mittenbach leased a penthouse atop the apartment house at 9999 Park Avenue. It belonged to some people named Hopkins, now living in the south of England.

They took possession on an autumn afternoon. Hilda raced through the great living room ecstatically. " I say to you, Helmuth, so beautiful a room have I never seen! Stone walls! And the rafters! Windows like a cathedral! And the organ, quite gold! It is no larger than the Great Hall in my father's *Schloss,* but so much more wonderful. Always I hated those tattered tapestries and the moldy stag horns! But this room is indeed something noble! "

Squealing, with Helmuth beside her and not much less childish, she explored the wonders of the kitchen and butler's pantry — electric dishwasher and coffee urn and toaster and vacuum cleaner and clock and egg cooker. She couldn't quite make out the electric waffle iron; she wasn't sure whether it was for cooking or pleating. But on the automatic refrigerator they both fell with shouts. This was a possession they had en-

NEW YORK SKYLINE. Sinclair Lewis demonstrates that there are two ways of looking at this view from a New York penthouse. "One man's meat is another man's poison." (Ewing Galloway)

vied their richer friends in Berlin. They cautiously pulled out an ice tray and gazed with fatuous admiration on the beautiful cubes of ice.

" Much better than diamonds," said Helmuth.

Refrigerator, gas stove, small electric range, luxurious enameled sink and kitchen cabinet were all finished in white and canary yellow; the kitchen was gayer than any boudoir.

" Already I am a — how is it called? — hunnerd-procent American," observed Helmuth in what he believed to be English. " The old system, it was to make beautiful the salon and the chapel, and make hateful the kitchen, the heart of the house. Yes, I am a modern! We do something, we engineers. We do not believe that the more a

room is used, the less *gemütlich* [1] it should be. Modern, yes, and very old. We go back to medieval days, when men were not ashamed to eat and love, and when kitchens were more important than reception rooms, and when — "

" Here," said Hilda, " I would be happy if we had no servants at all, and I did all the work. I shall cook the dinner — tomorrow. Tonight let us find that lovely spikizzy — is right? — of which the doctor has spoken on the steamer."

When, on the wine list of the Chez Edouard, they found an *Oppenheimer Kreuz Spätlese,* they asked each other why anyone should go to Europe. Their only trouble was that the waiter was a bit slow. But they understood, for he was much engaged with

[1] **gemütlich** (gĕ-müt′lĭк): pleasant. (German.)

a jolly group of six men at the next table.

One of the six noticed the plight of the Von Mittenbachs and, coming to their table, said, " Sorry we're grabbing off so much of the waiter's time. Afraid we're holding up your dinner. So, meanwhile — if you'll excuse the liberty — won't you folks come have a drink with us? "

" That would be very nice," said Helmuth.

He was, after all, a shy young man, and he was grateful for the way in which these strangers took him in. They were all, it seemed, in motor manufacturing. When they learned that he had just come from Germany to join them, instantly a card was out of every pocket, an address was scribbled, and each had insisted that when he went to South Bend, or Toledo, or Detroit, he must dine with them — " and I hope the missus will be along with you."

In a glow that burned out of him all the loneliness he had felt that afternoon in the cold shadow of the monstrous skyscrapers, Helmuth returned with Hilda to their table and dinner.

" So kind to a foreigner, a poor unknown engineer," said Helmuth. " No wonder no American ever wants to go abroad for more than a visit of a month! "

From the terrace before their penthouse they stared across the East River, then south and west to the wriggling electricity of Broadway. They were thirty stories up; they seemed to be looking on the whole world, but a world transformed into exultant light.

" It is as though we were in a castle on a huge sheer cliff, a castle on the Matterhorn himself, and yet in the midst of Berlin and London and Paris joined into one," said Helmuth. " This is perhaps — not true, Hilda? — the greatest spectacle of the world! Why speak they of the Acropolis, the Colosseum, the Rhineland, when they have this magic? "

Tugboats shouted cheerily on the East River; liners roared gallantly from the North River; the elevated trains, streaks of golden light, chanted on their three tracks; and the million motor horns spoke of the beautiful and exciting places to which the cars were going.

" And it's ours now! We've found our home! We shall know all this city, all those people in the lovely motors down there! I think we stay here the rest of our lives! " said Helmuth.

Hilda pondered, " Yes, except — except neither Germany nor America has any mystery. I want us someday to go to China, Japan. There it gives mystery. And I hear the servants are divine, and so cheap. Don't you think we might go live in China — soon? "

## Suggestions for Study

1. Do you understand the title? Each of these groups of people has practically the same point of view. What is it?

2. Notice how in the very first sentence Mr. Lewis makes fun of T. Eliot Hopkins, an apparently successful man. Point out the contrast between his career and that of Mr. Lewis himself. Pick out several other passages in which the author is satirizing characters in the story or attitudes they exhibit.

3. One of the trade-marks of Mr. Lewis's style is his habit of listing specific details for purposes of satire. Find examples of such listing and read them aloud. When you catch their tone of mockery, you have heard the authentic voice of Sinclair Lewis.

4. Do the characters seem like cartoons, or like photographs? Explain.

5. Which of your opinions — ones you have always taken for granted — does this story challenge?

6. Show that this story has no true plot. Compare the ending of this story with that of " The Cop and the Anthem."

7. Vocabulary: ecstatic, jodhpurs, spurious, pontifical, deification, immersion, pantheon, proletarian, rationalization, verminous.

## For Your Vocabulary

CONTEXT. After using the word *caricaturists* (kăr'ĭ-kȧ-tŭr-ĭsts) Lewis goes on to describe their work and give you an excellent idea of the meaning of the term (page 65). A *caricaturist* is an artist who in his drawings exaggerates traits or features to give a desired impression. In any campaign year you can find in newspaper cartoons *caricatures* of prominent candidates which will show you how the real appearance of men is exaggerated to make the impression which best suits the political interests of a newspaper. Sinclair Lewis himself is a *satirist* (săt′ĭ-rĭst), a writer who exaggerates for a special purpose just as the *caricaturist* does. Another type of artistic exaggeration mentioned in the story is a *gargoyle* (gär′goil), a sculptural work. Find a picture of a *gargoyle* in the encyclopedia and see if you can tell why gargoyles have been described as " caricatures on the whole animal kingdom."

WORD ANALYSIS. Analyze *indisputable* (ĭn-dĭs′pŭ-tà-b′l), *impoverished* (ĭm-pŏv′ẽr-ĭsht), and *infuriating* (ĭn-fū′rĭ-āt-ĭng). All are built on familiar English words. One difficulty with the prefix *in-* or *im-* is that it can mean either " in " or " not." Context will help you decide which meaning fits. The words are used on pages 62, 63, and 61, in that order.

## Wilbur Daniel Steele    1886–

Wilbur Daniel Steele belongs to the North and the South, the East and the West. He was born in North Carolina, graduated from the University of Denver, studied art in Boston and New York, and has resided in Nantucket, Massachusetts, in the midst of the Cape Cod life he portrays so well in many of his stories. Twenty-five years ago he had no recognized superior in the field of the American short story, and today he still rates high.

### FOOTFALLS

" This is not an easy story," says Mr. Steele in his first sentence. But when you have forgotten many of the short stories of this collection you will still remember Boaz Negro, the blind Portuguese cobbler, listening through nine years for the footfalls of " that *cachorra*." You will remember the " act of almost incredible violence " with which the story ends.

This is not an easy story; not a road for tender or for casual feet. Better the meadows. Let me warn you, it is as hard as that old man's soul and as sunless as his eyes. It has its inception in catastrophe, and its end in an act of almost incredible violence; between them it tells barely how one long blind can become also deaf and dumb.

He lived in one of those old Puritan sea towns where the strain has come down austere and moribund, so that his act would not be quite unbelievable. Except that the town is no longer Puritan and Yankee. It has been betrayed; it has become an outpost of the Portuguese islands.

This man, this blind cobbler himself, was a Portuguese from St. Michael, in the Western Islands, and his name was Boaz Negro.

He was happy. An unquenchable exuberance lived in him. When he arose in the morning he made vast, as it were uncontrollable, gestures with his stout arms. He came into his shop singing. His voice, strong and deep as the chest from which it emanated, rolled out through the doorway and along the street, and the fishermen, done with their morning work and lounging and smoking along the wharves, said, " Boaz is to work already." Then they came up to sit in the shop.

In that town a cobbler's shop is a club. One sees the interior always dimly thronged. They sit on the benches watching the artisan at his work for hours, and they talk about everything in the world. A cobbler is known by the company he keeps.

Boaz Negro kept young company. He would have nothing to do with the old. On his own head the gray hairs set thickly.

He had a grown son. But the benches in his shop were for the lusty and valiant young, men who could spend the night drinking, and then at three o'clock in the morning turn out in the rain and dark to pull at the weirs, sing songs, buffet one another among the slippery fish in the boat's bottom, and make loud jokes about the fundamental things, love and birth and death. Hearkening to their boasts and strong prophecies, his breast heaved and his heart beat faster. He was a large, full-blooded fellow, fashioned for exploits; the flame in his darkness burned higher even to hear of them.

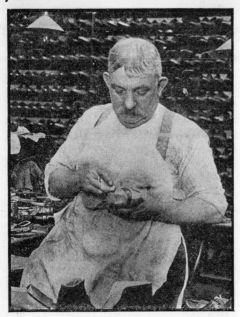

SHOEMAKER AT WORK. Year after year, Boaz tapped on his last and shaped his shoes until his arms were as strong as iron. (Keystone View)

It is scarcely conceivable how Boaz Negro could have come through this much of his life still possessed of that unquenchable and priceless exuberance; how he would sing in the dawn; how, simply listening to the recital of deeds in gale or brawl, he could easily forget himself a blind man, tied to a shop and a last; easily make of himself a lusty young fellow breasting the sunlit and adventurous tide of life.

He had had a wife, whom he had loved. Fate, which had scourged him with the initial scourge of blindness, had seen fit to take his Angelina away. He had had four sons. Three, one after another, had been removed, leaving only Manuel, the youngest. Recovering slowly, with agony, from each of these recurrent blows, his unquenchable exuberance had lived. And there was another thing quite as extraordinary. He had never done anything but work, and that sort of thing may kill the flame where an abrupt catastrophe fails. Work in the dark. Work, work, work! And accompanied by privation; an almost miserly scale of per-

sonal economy. Yes, indeed, he had " skinned his fingers," especially in the earlier years. When it tells most.

How he had worked! Not alone in the daytime, but also sometimes, when orders were heavy, far into the night. It was strange for one, passing along that deserted street at midnight, to hear issuing from the black shop of Boaz Negro the rhythmical tap-tap-tap of hammer on wooden peg.

Nor was that sound all: no man in town could get far past that shop in his nocturnal wandering unobserved. No more than a dozen footfalls, and from the darkness Boaz's voice rolled forth, fraternal, stentorian, " Good night, Antone! " " Good night to you, Caleb Snow! "

To Boaz Negro it was still broad day.

Now, because of this, he was what might be called a substantial man. He owned his place, his shop, opening on the sidewalk, and behind it the dwelling house with trellised galleries upstairs and down.

And there was always something for his son, a " piece for the pocket," a dollar, five, even a ten-dollar bill if he had " got to have it." Manuel was " a good boy." Boaz not only said this; he felt that he was assured of it in his understanding, to the infinite peace of his heart.

It was curious that he should be ignorant only of the one nearest to him. Not because he was physically blind. Be certain he knew more of other men and of other men's sons than they or their neighbors did. More, that is to say, of their hearts, their understandings, their idiosyncrasies, and their ultimate weight in the balance pan of eternity.

His simple explanation of Manuel was that Manuel " wasn't too stout." To others he said this, and to himself. Manuel was not indeed too robust. How should he be vigorous when he never did anything to make him so? He never worked. Why should he work, when existence was provided for, and when there was always that " piece for the pocket "? Even a ten-dollar bill on a Saturday night! No, Manuel " wasn't too stout."

In the shop they let it go at that. The

missteps and frailties of everyone else in the world were canvassed there with the most shameless publicity. But Boaz Negro was a blind man, and in a sense their host. Those reckless, strong young fellows respected and loved him. It was allowed to stand at that. Manuel was " a good boy." Which did not prevent them, by the way, from joining later in the general condemnation of that father's laxity — " the ruination of the boy! "

" He should have put him to work, that's what."

" He should have said to Manuel, ' Look here, if you want a dollar, go earn it first.' "

As a matter of fact, only one man ever gave Boaz the advice direct. That was Campbell Wood. And Wood never sat in that shop.

In every small town there is one young man who is spoken of as " rising." As often as not he is not a native, but " from away."

In this town Campbell Wood was that man. He had come from another part of the state to take a place in the bank. He lived in the upper story of Boaz Negro's house, the ground floor now doing for Boaz and the meager remnant of his family. The old woman who came in to tidy up for the cobbler looked after Wood's rooms as well.

Dealing with Wood, one had first of all the sense of his incorruptibility. A little ruthless perhaps, as if one could imagine him, in defense of his integrity, cutting off his friend, cutting off his own hand, cutting off the very stream flowing out from the wellsprings of human kindness. An exaggeration, perhaps.

He was by long odds the most eligible young man in town; good-looking in a spare, ruddy, sandy-haired Scottish fashion; important, incorruptible, " rising." But he took good care of his heart. Precisely that; like a sharp-eyed duenna to his own heart. One felt that here was the man, if ever was the man, who held his destiny in his own hand. Failing, of course, some quite gratuitous and unforeseeable catastrophe.

Not that he was not human, or even incapable of laughter or passion. He was, in a way, immensely accessible. He never clapped one on the shoulder; on the other hand, he never failed to speak. Not even to Boaz.

Returning from the bank in the afternoon, he had always a word for the cobbler. Passing out again to supper at his boarding place, he had another, about the weather, the prospects of rain. And if Boaz were at work in the dark when he returned from an evening at the Board of Trade, there was a " Good night, Mr. Negro! "

On Boaz's part, his attitude toward his lodger was curious and paradoxical. He did not pretend to anything less than reverence for the young man's position; precisely on account of that position he was conscious toward Wood of a vague distrust. This was because he was an uneducated fellow.

To the uneducated the idea of large finance is as uncomfortable as the idea of the law. It must be said for Boaz that, responsive to Wood's unfailing civility, he fought against this sensation of dim and somehow shameful distrust.

Nevertheless his whole parental soul was in arms that evening, when, returning from the bank and finding the shop empty of loungers, Wood paused a moment to propose the bit of advice already referred to.

" Haven't you ever thought of having Manuel learn the trade? "

A suspicion, a kind of premonition, lighted the fires of defense.

" Shoemaking," said Boaz, " is good enough for a blind man."

" Oh, I don't know. At least it's better than doing nothing at all."

Boaz's hammer was still. He sat silent, monumental. Outwardly. For once his unfailing response had failed him, " Manuel ain't too stout, you know." Perhaps it had become suddenly inadequate.

He hated Wood; he despised Wood; more than ever before, a hundredfold more, quite abruptly, he distrusted Wood.

How could a man say such things as Wood had said? And where Manuel himself might hear!

Where Manuel had heard! Boaz's other

emotions — hatred and contempt and distrust — were overshadowed. Sitting in darkness, no sound had come to his ears, no footfall, no infinitesimal creaking of a floor plank. Yet by some sixth uncanny sense of the blind he was aware that Manuel was standing in the dusk of the entry joining the shop to the house.

Boaz made a Herculean effort. The voice came out of his throat, harsh, bitter, and loud enough to have carried ten times the distance to his son's ears.

"Manuel is a good boy!"

"Yes — h'm — yes — I suppose so."

Wood shifted his weight. He seemed uncomfortable.

"Well. I'll be running along, I — ugh! Heavens!"

Something was happening. Boaz heard exclamations, breathings, the rustle of sleeve cloth in large, frantic, and futile graspings — all without understanding. Immediately there was an impact on the floor, and with it the unmistakable clink of metal. Boaz even heard that the metal was minted, and that the coins were gold. He understood. A coin sack, gripped not quite carefully enough for a moment under the other's overcoat, had shifted, slipped, escaped, and fallen.

And Manuel had heard!

It was a dreadful moment for Boaz, dreadful in its native sense, as full of dread. Why? It was a moment of horrid revelation, ruthless clarification. His son, his link with the departed Angelina, that "good boy" — Manuel, standing in the shadow of the entry, visible alone to the blind, had heard the clink of falling gold, and — *and Boaz wished that he had not!*

There, amazing, disconcerting, destroying, stood the sudden fact.

Sitting as impassive and monumental as ever, his strong, bleached hands at rest on his work, round drops of sweat came out on Boaz's forehead. He scarcely took the sense of what Wood was saying. Only fragments.

"Government money, understand — for the breakwater workings — huge — too

many people know here, everywhere — don't trust the safe — tin safe — 'Noah's Ark' — give you my word — Heavens, no!"

It boiled down to this — the money, more money than was good for that antiquated "Noah's Ark" at the bank — and whose contemplated sojourn there overnight was public to too many minds — in short, Wood was not only incorruptible, he was canny. To what one of those minds, now, would it occur that he should take away that money bodily, under casual cover of his coat, to his own lodgings behind the cobbler shop of Boaz Negro? For this one, this important night!

He was sorry the coin sack had slipped, because he did not like to have the responsibility of secret sharer cast upon anyone, even upon Boaz, even by accident. On the other hand, how tremendously fortunate that it had been Boaz and not another. So far as that went, Wood had no more anxiety now than before. One incorruptible knows another.

"I'd trust you, Mr. Negro" (that was one of the fragments which came and stuck in the cobbler's brain), "as far as I would myself. As long as it's only you. I'm just going up here and throw it under the bed. Oh, yes, certainly."

Boaz ate no supper. For the first time in his life food was dry in his gullet. Even under those other successive crushing blows of Fate the full and generous habit of his functionings had carried on unabated; he had always eaten what was set before him. Tonight, over his untouched plate, he watched Manuel with his sightless eyes, keeping track of his every mouthful, word, intonation, breath. What profit he expected to extract from this catlike surveillance it is impossible to say.

When they arose from the supper table Boaz made another Herculean effort: "Manuel, you're a good boy!"

The formula had a quality of appeal, of despair, and of command.

"Manuel, you should be short of money, maybe. Look, what's this? A tenner? Well, there's a piece for the pocket; go and enjoy yourself."

He would have been frightened had Manuel, upsetting tradition, declined the offering. With the morbid contrariness of the human imagination, the boy's avid grasping gave him no comfort.

He went out into the shop, where it was already dark, drew to him his last, his tools, mallets, cutters, pegs, leather. And having prepared to work, he remained idle. He found himself listening.

It has been observed that the large phenomena of sunlight and darkness were nothing to Boaz Negro. A busy night was broad day. Yet there was a difference; he knew it with the blind man's eyes, the ears.

Day was a vast confusion, or rather a wide fabric, of sounds; great and little sounds all woven together, voices, footfalls, wheels, far-off whistles and foghorns, flies buzzing in the sun. Night was another thing. Still there were voices and footfalls, but rarer, emerging from the large, pure body of silence as definite, surprising, and yet familiar entities.

Tonight there was an easterly wind, coming off the water and carrying the sound of waves. So far as other fugitive sounds were concerned it was the same as silence. The wind made little difference to the ears. It nullified, from one direction at least, the other two visual processes of the blind, the sense of touch and the sense of smell. It blew away from the shop, toward the living-house.

As has been said, Boaz found himself listening, scrutinizing with an extraordinary attention, this immense background of sound. He heard footfalls. The story of that night was written, for him, in footfalls.

He heard them moving about the house, the lower floor, prowling here, there, halting for long spaces, advancing, retreating softly on the planks. About this aimless, interminable perambulation there was something to twist the nerves, something led and at the same time driven like a succession of frail and indecisive charges.

Boaz lifted himself from his chair. All his impulse called him to make a stir, join battle, cast in the breach the reinforcement of his presence, authority, good will. He sank back again; his hands fell down. The curious impotence of the spectator held him.

He heard footfalls, too, on the upper floor, a little fainter, borne to the inner rather than the outer ear, along the solid causeway of partitions and floor, the legs of his chair, the bony framework of his body. Very faint indeed. Sinking back easily into the background of the wind. They, too, came and went, this room, that, to the passage, the stairhead, and away. About them, too, there was the same quality of being led and at the same time of being driven.

Time went by. In his darkness it seemed to Boaz that hours must have passed. He heard voices. Together with the footfalls, that abrupt, brief, and (in view of Wood's position) astounding interchange of sentences made up his history of the night. Wood must have opened the door at the head of the stair; by the sound of his voice he would be standing there, peering below perhaps; perhaps listening.

"What's wrong down there?" he called. "Why don't you go to bed?"

After a moment, came Manuel's voice, "Ain't sleepy."

"Neither am I. Look here, do you like to play cards?"

"What kind? Euchre! I like euchre all right. Or pitch."

"Well, what would you say to coming up and having a game of euchre then, Manuel? If you can't sleep?"

"That'd be all right."

The lower footfalls ascended to join the footfalls on the upper floor. There was the sound of a door closing.

Boaz sat still. In the gloom he might have been taken for a piece of furniture, of machinery, an extraordinary lay figure, perhaps, for the trying on of the boots he made. He seemed scarcely to breathe, only the sweat starting from his brow giving him an aspect of life.

He ought to have run, and leaped up that inner stair and pounded with his fists on that door. He seemed unable to move. At rare intervals feet passed on the sidewalk outside, just at his elbow, so to say, and yet somehow, tonight, immeasurably far away. Beyond the orbit of the moon. He heard Rugg, the policeman, noting the silence of the shop, muttering, " Boaz is to bed tonight," as he passed.

The wind increased. It poured against the shop with its deep, continuous sound of a river. Submerged in its body, Boaz caught the note of the town bell striking midnight.

Once more, after a long time, he heard footfalls. He heard them coming around the corner of the shop from the house, footfalls half swallowed by the wind, passing discreetly, without haste, retreating, merging step by step with the huge, incessant background of the wind.

Boaz's muscles tightened all over him. He had the impulse to start up, to fling open the door, shout into the night, " What are you doing? Stop there! Say! What are you doing and where are you going? "

And as before, the curious impotence of the spectator held him motionless. He had not stirred in his chair. And those footfalls, upon which hinged, as it were, that momentous decade of his life, were gone.

There was nothing to listen for now. Yet he continued to listen. Once or twice, half arousing himself, he drew toward him his unfinished work. And then relapsed into immobility.

As has been said, the wind, making little difference to the ears, made all the difference in the world with the sense of feeling and the sense of smell. From the one important direction of the house. That is how it could come about that Boaz Negro could sit, waiting and listening to nothing in the shop and remain ignorant of disaster until the alarm had gone away and come back again, pounding, shouting, clanging.

" *Fire!* " he heard them bawling in the street. " *Fire! Fire!* "

Only slowly did he understand that the fire was in his own house.

There is nothing stiller in the world than the skeleton of a house in the dawn after a fire. It is as if everything living, positive, violent, had been completely drained in the one flaming act of violence, leaving nothing but negation till the end of time. It is worse than a tomb. A monstrous stillness! Even the footfalls of the searchers cannot disturb it, for they are separate and superficial. In its presence they are almost frivolous.

Half an hour after dawn the searchers found the body, if what was left from that consuming ordeal might be called a body. The discovery came as a shock. It seemed incredible that the occupant of that house, no cripple or invalid but an able man in the prime of youth, should not have awakened and made good his escape. It was the upper floor which had caught; the stairs had stood to the last. It was beyond calculation. Even if he had been asleep!

And he had not been asleep. This second and infinitely more appalling discovery began to be known. Slowly. By a hint, a breath of rumor here; there an allusion, half taken back. The man, whose incinerated body still lay curled in its bed of cinders, had been dressed at the moment of disaster; even to the watch, the cuff buttons, the studs, the very scarf pin. Fully clothed to the last detail, precisely as those who had dealings at the bank might have seen Campbell Wood any weekday morning for the past eight months. A man does not sleep with his clothes on. The skull of the man had been broken, as if with a blunt instrument of iron. On the charred lacework of the floor lay the leg of an old andiron with which Boaz Negro and his Angelina had set up housekeeping in that new house.

It needed only Mr. Asa Whitelaw, coming up the street from that gaping "Noah's Ark " at the bank, to round out the scandalous circle of circumstance.

" Where is Manuel? "

Boaz Negro still sat in his shop, impassive, monumental, his thick, hairy arms resting on the arms of his chair. The tools and materials of his work remained scattered about him, as his irresolute gathering of the night before had left them. Into his eyes no change could come. He had lost his house, the visible monument of all those years of " skinning his fingers." It would seem that he had lost his son. And he had lost something incalculably precious — that hitherto unquenchable exuberance of the man.

" Where is Manuel? "

When he spoke his voice was unaccented and stale, like the voice of a man already dead.

" Yes, where is Manuel? "

He had answered them with their own question.

" When did you last see him? "

Neither he nor they seemed to take note of that profound irony.

" At supper."

" Tell us, Boaz; you knew about this money? "

The cobbler nodded his head.

" And did Manuel? "

He might have taken sanctuary in a legal doubt. How did he know what Manuel knew? Precisely! As before, he nodded his head.

" After supper, Boaz, you were in the shop? But you heard something? "

He went on to tell them what he had heard: the footfalls, below and above, the extraordinary conversation which had broken for a moment the silence of the inner hall. The account was bare, the phrases monosyllabic. He reported only what had been registered on the sensitive tympanums of his ears, to the last whisper of footfalls stealing past the dark wall of the shop. Of all the formless tangle of thoughts, suspicions, interpretations, and the special and personal knowledge given to the blind which moved in his brain, he said nothing.

He shut his lips there. He felt himself on the defensive. Just as he distrusted the higher ramifications of finance (his house had gone down uninsured), so before the rites and processes of that inscrutable creature, the Law, he felt himself menaced by

the invisible and the unknown, helpless, oppressed; in an abject sense, skeptical.

" Keep clear of the Law! " they had told him in his youth. The monster his imagination had summoned up then still stood beside him in his age.

Having exhausted his monosyllabic and superficial evidence, they could move him no farther. He became deaf and dumb. He sat before them, an image cast in some immensely heavy stuff, inanimate. His lack of visible emotion impressed them. Remembering his exuberance, it was only the stranger to see him unmoving and unmoved. Only once did they catch sight of something beyond. As they were preparing to leave he opened his mouth. What he said was like a swan song to the years of his exuberant happiness. Even now there was no color of expression in his words, which sounded mechanical.

" Now I have lost everything. My house. My last son. Even my honor. You would not think I would like to live. But I go to live. I go to work. That *cachorra*, one day he shall come back again, in the dark night, to have a look. I shall go to show you all. That *cachorra!* "

(And from that time on, it was noted, he never referred to the fugitive by any other name than *cachorra*, which is a kind of dog. " That *cachorra!* " As if he had forfeited the relationship not only of the family, but of the very genus, the very race! " That *cachorra!* ")

He pronounced this resolution without passion. When they assured him that the culprit would come back again indeed, much sooner than he expected, " with a rope around his neck," he shook his head slowly.

" No, you shall not catch that *cachorra* now. But one day — "

There was something about its very colorlessness which made it sound oracular. It was at least prophetic. They searched, laid their traps, proceeded with all their placards, descriptions, rewards, clues, trails. But on Manuel Negro they never laid their hands.

Months passed and became years. Boaz Negro did not rebuild his house. He might have done so, out of his earnings, for upon himself he spent scarcely anything, reverting to his old habit of almost miserly economy. Yet perhaps it would have been harder after all. For his earnings were less and less. In that town a cobbler who sits in an empty shop is apt to want for trade. Folk take their boots to mend where they take their bodies to rest and their minds to be edified.

No longer did the walls of Boaz's shop resound to the boastful recollections of young men. Boaz had changed. He had become not only different, but opposite. A metaphor will do best. The spirit of Boaz Negro had been a meadowed hillside giving upon the open sea, the sun, the warm, wild winds from beyond the blue horizon. And covered with flowers, always hungry and thirsty for the sun and the fabulous wind and bright showers of rain. It had become an intrenched camp, lying silent, sullen, verdureless, under a gray sky. He stood solitary against the world. His approaches were closed. He was blind, and he was also deaf and dumb.

Against that what can young fellows do who wish for nothing but to rest themselves and talk about their friends and enemies? They had come and they had tried. They had raised their voices even higher than before. Their boasts had grown louder, more presumptuous, more preposterous, until, before the cold separation of that unmoving and as if contemptuous presence in the cobbler's chair, they burst of their own air, like toy balloons. And they went and left Boaz alone.

There was another thing which served, if not to keep them away, at least not to entice them back. That was the aspect of the place. It was not cheerful. It invited no one. In its way that fire-bitten ruin grew to be almost as great a scandal as the act itself had been. It was plainly an eyesore. A valuable property, on the town's main thoroughfare — and an eyesore! The neighboring owners protested.

Their protestations might as well have gone against a stone wall. That man was deaf and dumb. He had become, in a way, a kind of vegetable, for the quality of a vegetable is that, while it is endowed with life, it remains fixed in one spot. For years Boaz was scarcely seen to move foot out of that shop that was left him, a small, square, blistered promontory on the shores of ruin.

He must indeed have carried out some rudimentary sort of domestic program under the debris at the rear (he certainly did not sleep or eat in the shop). One or two lower rooms were left fairly intact. The outward aspect of the place was formless; it grew to be no more than a mound in time; the charred timbers, one or two still standing, lean and naked against the sky, lost their blackness and faded to a silvery gray. It would have seemed strange, had they not grown accustomed to the thought, to imagine that blind man, like a mole, or some slow slug, turning himself mysteriously in the bowels of that gray mound — that time-silvered " eyesore."

When they saw him, however, he was in the shop. They opened the door to take in their work (when other cobblers turned them off), and they saw him seated in his chair in the half-darkness, his whole person, legs, torso, neck, head, as motionless as the vegetable of which we have spoken — only his hands and his bare arms endowed with visible life. The gloom had bleached the skin to the color of damp ivory, and against the background of his immobility they moved with a certain amazing monstrousness, interminably. No, they were never still. One wondered what they could be at. Surely he could not have had enough work now to keep those insatiable hands so monstrously in motion. Even far into the night. Tap-tap-tap! Blows continuous and powerful. On what? On nothing? On the bare iron last? And for what purpose? To what conceivable end?

Well, one could imagine those arms, growing paler, also growing thicker and more formidable with that unceasing labor; the muscles feeding themselves, omnivorously on their own waste, the cords toughening, the bone tissues revitalizing themselves without end. One could imagine the whole aspiration of that mute and motionless man pouring itself out into those pallid arms, and the arms taking it up with a kind of blind greed. Storing it up. Against a day!

"That *cachorra!* One day —"

What were the thoughts of this man? What moved within that motionless cranium covered with long hair? Who can say? Behind everything, of course, stood that bitterness against the world — the blind world — blinder than he would ever be. And against " that *cachorra*." But this was no longer a thought; it was the man.

Just as all muscular aspiration flowed into his arms, so all the energies of his senses turned to his ears. The man had become, you might say, two arms and two ears. Can you imagine a man listening, intently, through the waking hours of nine years?

Listening to footfalls. Marking with a special emphasis of concentration the beginning, rise, full passage, falling away, and dying of all footfalls. By day, by night, winter and summer and winter again. Unraveling the skein of footfalls passing up and down the street!

For three years he wondered when they would come. For the next three years he wondered if they would ever come. It was during the last three that a doubt began to trouble him. It gnawed at his huge moral strength. Like a hidden seepage of water, it undermined (in anticipation) his terrible resolution. It was a sign, perhaps of age, a slipping away of the reckless infallibility of youth.

Supposing, after all, that his ears should fail him. Supposing they were capable of being tricked, without his being able to know it. Supposing that that *cachorra* should come and go, and he, Boaz, living in some vast delusion, some unrealized distortion of memory, should let him pass unknown. Supposing precisely this thing had already happened!

Or the other way around. What if he

should hear the footfalls coming, even into the very shop itself? What if he should be as sure of them as of his own soul? What, then, if he should strike? And what then, if it were not that *cachorra* after all? How many tens and hundreds of millions of people were there in the world? Was it possible for them all to have footfalls distinct and different?

Then they would take him and hang him. And that *cachorra* might then come and go at his own will, undisturbed.

As he sat there sometimes the sweat rolled down his nose, cold as rain.

Supposing!

Sometimes, quite suddenly, in broad day, in the booming silence of the night, he would start. Not outwardly. But beneath the pale integument of his skin all his muscles tightened and his nerves sang. His breathing stopped. It seemed almost as if his heart stopped.

What was it? Were those the feet, there emerging faintly from the distance? Yes, there was something about them. Yes! Memory was in travail. Yes, yes, yes! No! How could he be sure? Ice ran down into his empty eyes. The footfalls were already passing. They were gone, swallowed up already by time and space. Had that been that *cachorra?*

Nothing in his life had been so hard to meet as this insidious drain of distrust in his own powers; this sense of a traitor within the walls. His iron-gray hair had turned white. It was always this now, from the beginning of the day to the end of the night: how was he to know? How was he to be inevitably, unshakably, sure?

Curiously, after all this purgatory of doubts, he did know them. For a moment at least, when he had heard them, he was sure. It was on an evening of the winter holidays, the Portuguese festival of *Menin' Jesus*. Christ was born again in a hundred mangers on a hundred tiny altars; there was cake and wine; songs went shouting by to the accompaniment of mandolins and tramping feet. The wind blew cold under a clear sky. In all the houses there were lights; even in Boaz Negro's shop a lamp was lit just now, for a man had been in for a pair of boots which Boaz had patched. The man had gone out again. Boaz was thinking of blowing out the light. It meant nothing to him.

He leaned forward, judging the position of the lamp chimney by the heat on his face, and puffed out his cheeks to blow. Then his cheeks collapsed suddenly, and he sat back again.

It was not odd that he had failed to hear the footfalls until they were actually within the door. A crowd of merrymakers was passing just then; their songs and tramping almost shook the shop.

Boaz sat back. Beneath his passive exterior his nerves thrummed; his muscles had grown as hard as wood. Yes! Yes! But no! He had heard nothing; no more than a single step, a single foot-pressure on the planks within the door. Dear God! He could not tell!

Going through the pain of an enormous effort, he opened his lips.

" What can I do for you? "

" Well, I — I don't know. To tell the truth — "

The voice was unfamiliar, but it might be assumed. Boaz held himself. His face remained blank, interrogating, slightly helpless.

" I am a little deaf," he said. " Come nearer."

The footfalls came halfway across the intervening floor, and there appeared to hesitate. The voice, too, had a note of uncertainty.

" I was just looking around. I have a pair of — well, you mend shoes? "

Boaz nodded his head. It was not in response to the words, for they meant nothing. What he had heard was the footfalls on the floor.

Now he was sure. As has been said, for a moment at least after he had heard them he was unshakably sure. The congestion of his muscles had passed. He was at peace.

The voice became audible once more. Before the massive preoccupation of the blind man it became still less certain of itself.

" Well, I haven't got the shoes with me. I was — just looking around."

It was amazing to Boaz, this miraculous sensation of peace.

" Wait! " Then, bending his head as if listening to the winter wind, " It's cold tonight. You've left the door open. But wait! " Leaning down, his hand fell on a rope's end hanging by the chair. The gesture was one continuous, undeviating movement of the hand. No hesitation. No groping. How many hundreds, how many thousands of times, had his hand schooled itself in that gesture!

A single strong pull. With a little *bang* the front door had swung to and latched itself. Not only the front door. The other door, leading to the rear, had closed, too, and latched itself with a little *bang*. And leaning forward from his chair, Boaz blew out the light.

There was not a sound in the shop. Outside, feet continued to go by, ringing on the frozen road; voices were lifted; the wind hustled about the corners of the wooden shell with a continuous, shrill note of whistling. All of this outside, as on another planet. Within the blackness of the shop the complete silence persisted.

Boaz listened. Sitting on the edge of his chair, half crouching, his head, with its long, unkempt, white hair, bent slightly to one side, he concentrated upon this chambered silence the full power of his senses. He hardly breathed. The other person in that room could not be breathing at all, it seemed.

No, there was not a breath, not the stirring of a sole on wood, not the infinitesimal rustle of any fabric. It was as if, in this utter stoppage of sound, even the blood had ceased to flow in the veins and arteries of that man, who was like a rat caught in a trap.

It was appalling even to Boaz; even to the cat. Listening became more than a labor. He began to have a fight against a growing impulse to shout out loud, to leap, sprawl forward without aim in that un-stirred darkness — do something. Sweat rolled down from behind his ears, into his shirt collar. He gripped the chair arms. To keep quiet he sank his teeth into his lower lip. He would not! He would not!

And of a sudden he heard before him, in the center of the room, an outburst of breath, an outrush from lungs in the extrem-ity of pain, thick, laborious, fearful. A coughing up of dammed air.

Pushing himself from the arms of the chair, Boaz leaped.

His fingers, passing swiftly through the air, closed on something. It was a sheaf of hair, bristly and thick. It was a man's beard.

On the road outside, up and down the street for a hundred yards, merrymaking people turned to look at one another. With an abrupt cessation of laughter, of speech. Inquiringly. Even with an unconscious dilation of the pupils of their eyes.

" What was that? "

There had been a scream. There could be no doubt of that. A single, long-drawn note. Immensely high-pitched. Not as if it were human.

" God's sake! What was that? Where'd it come from? "

Those nearest said it came from the cob-bler shop of Boaz Negro.

They went and tried the door. It was closed; even locked, as if for the night. There was no light behind the window shade. But Boaz would not have a light. They beat on the door. No answer.

But from where, then, had that pro-longed, as if animal, note come?

They ran about, penetrating into the side lanes, interrogating, prying. Coming back at last, inevitably, to the neighborhood of Boaz Negro's shop.

The body lay on the floor at Boaz's feet, where it had tumbled down slowly after a moment from the spasmodic embrace of his arms; those ivory-colored arms which had beaten so long upon the bare iron surface of the last. Blows continuous and powerful. It seemed incredible. They were

so weak now. They could not have lifted the hammer now.

But that beard! That bristly, thick, square beard of a stranger!

His hands remembered it. Standing with his shoulders fallen forward and his weak arms hanging down, Boaz began to shiver. The whole thing was incredible. What was on the floor there, upheld in the vast gulf of darkness, he could not see. Neither could he hear it; smell it. Nor (if he did not move his foot) could he feel it. What he did not hear, smell, or touch did not exist. It was not there. Incredible!

But that beard! All the accumulated doubtings of those years fell down upon him. After all, the thing he had been so fearful of in his weak imaginings had hap-pened. He had killed a stranger. He, Boaz Negro, had murdered an innocent man!

And all on account of that beard. His deep panic made him lightheaded. He be-gan to confuse cause and effect. If it were not for that beard, it would have been that *cachorra*.

On this basis he began to reason with a crazy directness. And to act. He went and pried open the door into the entry. From a shelf he took down his razor. A big, heavy-heeled strop. His hands began to hurry. And the mug, half full of soap. And water. It would have to be cold water. But after all, he thought (lightheadedly), at this time of night —

Outside, they were at the shop again. The crowd's habit is to forget a thing quickly, once it is out of sight and hearing. But there had been something about that solitary cry which continued to bother them, even in memory. Where had it been? Where had it come from? And those who had stood nearest the cobbler shop were heard again. They were certain now, dead certain. They could swear!

In the end they broke down the door.

If Boaz heard them he gave no sign. An absorption as complete as it was monstrous wrapped him. Kneeling in the glare of the lantern they had brought, as impervious as his own shadow sprawling behind him, he continued to shave the dead man on the floor.

No one touched him. Their minds and imaginations were arrested by the gigantic proportions of the act. The unfathomable presumption of the act. As throwing murder in their faces to the tune of a jig in a barbershop. It is a fact that none of them so much as thought of touching him. No less than all of them, together with all other men, shorn of their imaginations — that is to say, the expressionless and imperturbable creature of the Law — would be sufficient to touch that ghastly man.

On the other hand, they could not leave him alone. They could not go away. They watched. They saw the damp, lather-soaked beard of that victimized stranger falling away, stroke by stroke of the flashing, heavy razor. The dead denuded by the blind!

It was seen that Boaz was about to speak. It was something important he was about to utter; something, one would say, fatal. The words would not come all at once. They swelled his cheeks out. His razor was arrested. Lifting his face, he encircled the watchers with a gaze at once of imploration and of command. As if he could see them. As if he could read his answer in the expressions of their faces.

" Tell me one thing now. Is it that *cachorra?* "

For the first time those men in the room made sounds. They shuffled their feet. It was as if an uncontrollable impulse to ejaculation, laughter, derision, forbidden by the presence of death, had gone down into their boot soles.

" Manuel? " one of them said. " You mean *Manuel?* "

Boaz laid the razor down on the floor beside its work. He got up from his knees slowly, as if his joints hurt. He sat down in his chair, rested his hands on the arms, and once more encircled the company with his sightless gaze.

" Not Manuel. Manuel was a good boy. But tell me now, is it that *cachorra?* "

Here was something out of their calculations; something for them, mentally, to chew on. Mystification is a good thing sometimes. It gives to the brain a fillip, stirs memory, puts the gears of imagination in mesh. One man, an old, tobacco-chewing fellow, began to stare harder at the face on the floor. Something moved in his intellect.

" No, but look here now, by God — "

He had even stopped chewing. But he was forestalled by another.

" Say now, if it don't look like that fellow Wood, himself. The bank fellow — that was burned — remember? Himself."

" That *cachorra* was not burned. Not that Wood. You darned fool! "

Boaz spoke from his chair. They hardly knew his voice, emerging from its long silence: it was so didactic and arid.

" That *cachorra* was not burned. It was my boy that was burned. It was that *cachorra* called my boy upstairs. That *cachorra* killed my boy. That *cachorra* put his clothes on my boy, and he set my house on fire. I knew that all the time. Because when I heard those feet come out of my house and go away, I knew they were the feet of that *cachorra* from the bank. I did not know where he was going to. Something said to me — you better ask him where he is going to. But then I said, you are foolish. He had the money from the bank. I did not know. And then my house was on fire. No, it was not my boy that went away; it was that *cachorra* all the time. You darned fools! Did you think I was waiting for my own boy?

" Now I show you all," he said at the end. " And now I can get hanged."

No one ever touched Boaz Negro for that murder. For murder it was in the eye and letter of the Law. The Law in a small town is sometimes a curious creature; it is sometimes blind only in one eye.

Their minds and imaginations in that town were arrested by the romantic proportions of the act. Simply, no one took it up. I believe the man, Wood, was understood to have died of heart failure.

When they asked Boaz why he had not told what he knew as to the identity of that fugitive in the night, he seemed to find it hard to say exactly. How could a man of no education define for them his own but half-defined misgivings about the Law, his sense of oppression, constraint, and awe, of being on the defensive, even, in an abject way, his skepticism? About his wanting, come what might, to " keep clear of the Law "?

He did say this, " You would have laughed at me."

And this, " If I told folks it was Wood went away, then I say he would not dare come back again."

That was the last. Very shortly he began to refuse to talk about the thing at all. The act was completed. Like the creature of fable, it had consumed itself. Out of that old man's consciousness it had departed. Amazingly. Like a dream dreamed out.

Slowly at first, in a makeshift, piece-at-a-time, poor man's way, Boaz commenced to rebuild his house. That " eyesore " vanished.

And slowly at first, like the miracle of a green shoot pressing out from the dead earth, that priceless and unquenchable exuberance of the man was seen returning. Unquenchable, after all.

## Suggestions for Study

1. If the ending surprised you, you have nobody but yourself to blame; for Mr. Steele has played the game fairly. Consider how absolutely wrong, after all, would have been the ending you expected. Read the story again and see how emphatically you were told that Wood was a villain and that he was preparing a trap.

2. Have any other characters in these stories been as real to you as Boaz Negro? If so, what ones?

3. Write a radio script dramatizing this story.

4. Note how short, direct, and abrupt are most of the sentences and paragraphs in this story. What short-story writer in this book provides the greatest contrast to these features of Steele's journalistic style?

5. Vocabulary: moribund, weirs, stentorian, ruthless, duenna, canny, fillip, paradoxical, perambulation.

## For Your Vocabulary

CONTEXT. One of the most natural ways to add a word to your vocabulary is to read it in a sentence or group of sentences that makes its meaning fairly clear — that is, in enlightening *context*. Writers are not always so helpful to a growing reader, but Steele uses three good words in illuminating context: " the pale *integument* (ĭn-tĕg'ŭ-mĕnt) of his skin " (page 79); " not the *infinitesimal* (ĭn-fĭn-ĭ-tĕs'ĭ-măl) rustle of any fabric " (page 80); and " the dead *denuded* (dĕ-nūd'ĕd) by the blind " (page 82). Reread the passages in which they occur, and state the meaning of each word for yourself. Don't jump at the conclusion that *integument* means *color*. Word analysis throws additional light on the last two words.

WORD ANALYSIS. Pick out the separate parts that make up *unquenchable* (ŭn-kwĕnch'à-b'l), *incorruptibility* (ĭn-kŏ-rŭp'tĭ-bĭl-ĭ-tĭ), *clarification* (klăr-ĭ-fĭ-kā'shŭn), *immobility* (ĭm-ō-bĭl'-ĭ-tĭ), and *incalculably* (ĭn-kăl'kŭ-là-blĭ). What is the simplest form of the base-word for each? What prefixes used in these words have the same meaning, though slightly different in form? Do you recognize the kinship of *-able*, *-ibility*, and *-bly?* Remember that the suffix *-fy*, to make, adds another suffix, *-cation*, to form a noun meaning the process of making.

## Pearl S. Buck 1892–

In some happier future time, when the Chinese people have taken their rightful place in the culture of the world and the family of nations, Pearl Buck will be remembered for *The Good Earth*, " a book which made us feel of the Chinese peasant that all men are brothers." But Pearl Buck's fame has not had to wait upon time. Attaining the best-seller lists at once, *The Good Earth* remained there for twenty-one months, won the Pulitzer prize for 1932, was translated into about twenty languages, and as a movie went around the world. It was probably also the decisive reason for the 1938 award of the Nobel prize for literature to Pearl Buck, which surprised the author and deeply gratified her readers.

Pearl Buck's work is a fine example of the principle that an author should write about what he knows. Boasting a pre-Revolutionary American ancestry, she was born of American missionaries to China; grew up in China, where she talked Chinese before learning English; came back to go to college in Virginia; and returned to China, where she taught in universities in Nanking for ten years. She now lives in Pennsylvania with her husband, Richard Walsh, and several adopted children. Her writing career began in earnest in 1929. Her best novels are in the trilogy called *House of Earth: The Good Earth, Sons,* and *A House Divided.* The experiences of her own parents furnish the material for two biographies, *Fighting Angel* and *The Exile.* She has also written some fine short stories and radio plays and many serious articles on social and artistic problems. Her contribution to American knowledge of the Chinese includes a translation of a Chinese folk novel, *All Men Are Brothers* (1933). Her work is marked by complete sincerity and a style of Biblical flavor. In her fiction East at last meets West on a common ground of sympathy and understanding.

## THE ENEMY

In " The Enemy " Pearl Buck extends her study of Oriental peoples to include the Japanese. This thrilling story of World War II may give you some insight into the meaning of the statement that " science is international."

Dr. Sadao Hoki's house was built on a spot of the Japanese coast where as a little boy he had often played. The low square stone house was set upon rocks well above a narrow beach that was outlined with bent pines. As a boy Sadao had climbed the pines, supporting himself on his bare feet, as he had seen men do in the South Seas when they climbed for coconuts. His father had taken him often to the islands of those seas, and never had he failed to say to the little grave boy at his side, " Those islands yonder, they are the stepping-stones to the future for Japan."

" Where shall we step from them? " Sadao had asked seriously.

" Who knows? " his father had answered. " Who can limit our future? It depends on what we make it."

Sadao had taken this into his mind as he did everything his father said, his father who never joked or played with him but who spent infinite pains upon him who was his only son. Sadao knew that his education was his father's chief concern. For this reason he had been sent at twenty-two to America to learn all that could be learned of surgery and medicine. He had come back at thirty, and before his father died he had seen Sadao become famous not only as a surgeon but as a scientist. Because he was now perfecting a discovery which would render wounds entirely clean, he had not been sent abroad with the troops. Also, he knew, there was some slight danger that the old General might need an operation for a condition for which he was now being treated medically, and for this possibility Sadao was being kept in Japan.

Clouds were rising from the ocean now. The unexpected warmth of the past few days had at night drawn heavy fog from the cold waves. Sadao watched mists hide outlines of a little island near the shore and then come creeping up the beach below the house, wreathing around the pines. In a few minutes fog would be wrapped about the house too. Then he would go into the room where Hana, his wife, would be waiting for him with the two children.

But at this moment the door opened and she looked out, a dark-blue woolen *haori* [1] over her kimono. She came to him affectionately and put her arm through his as he stood, smiled, and said nothing. He had met Hana in America, but he had waited to fall in love with her until he was sure she was Japanese. His father would never have received her unless she had been pure in her race. He wondered often whom he would have married if he had not met Hana, and by what luck he had found her in the most casual way, by chance literally, at an American professor's house. The professor and his wife had been kind people anxious to do something for their few foreign students, and the students, though bored, had accepted this kindness. Sadao had often told Hana how nearly he had not gone to Professor Harley's house that night — the rooms were so small, the food so bad, the professor's wife so voluble. But he had gone

[1] haori (hä'ō-rĭ).

and there he had found Hana, a new student, and had felt he would love her if it were at all possible.

Now he felt her hand on his arm and was aware of the pleasure it gave him, even though they had been married years enough to have the two children. For they had not married heedlessly in America. They had finished their work at school and had come home to Japan, and when his father had seen her the marriage had been arranged in the old Japanese way, although Sadao and Hana had talked everything over beforehand. They were perfectly happy. She laid her cheek against his arm.

It was at this moment that both of them saw something black come out of the mists. It was a man. He was flung up out of the ocean — flung, it seemed, to his feet by a breaker. He staggered a few steps, his body outlined against the mist, his arms above his head. Then the curled mists hid him again.

" Who is that? " Hana cried. She dropped Sadao's arm and they both leaned over the railing of the veranda. Now they saw him again. The man was on his hands and knees crawling. Then they saw him fall on his face, and lie there.

" A fisherman perhaps," Sadao said, " washed from his boat." He ran quickly down the steps and behind him Hana came, her wide sleeves flying. A mile or two away on either side there were fishing villages, but here was only the bare and lonely coast, dangerous with rocks. The surf beyond the beach was spiked with rocks. Somehow the man had managed to come through them — he must be badly torn.

They saw when they came toward him that indeed it was so. The sand on one side of him had already a stain of red soaking through.

" He is wounded," Sadao exclaimed. He made haste to the man, who lay motionless, his face in the sand. An old cap stuck to his head soaked with sea water. He was in wet rags of garments. Sadao stooped, Hana at his side, and turned the man's head. They saw the face.

" A white man! " Hana whispered.

Yes, it was a white man. The wet cap fell away, and there was his wet yellow hair, long, as though for many weeks it had not been cut, and upon his young and tortured face was a rough yellow beard. He was unconscious and knew nothing that they did to him.

Now Sadao remembered the wound, and with his expert fingers he began to search for it. Blood flowed freshly at his touch. On the right side of his lower back Sadao saw that a gun wound had been reopened. The flesh was blackened with powder. Sometime, not many days ago, the man had been shot and had not been tended. It was bad chance that the rock had struck the wound.

" Oh, how he is bleeding! " Hana whispered again in a solemn voice. The mists screened them now completely, and at this time of day no one came by. The fishermen had gone home and even the chance beachcombers would have considered the day at an end.

" What shall we do with this man? " Sadao muttered. But his trained hands seemed of their own will to be doing what they could to stanch the fearful bleeding. He packed the wound with the sea moss that strewed the beach. The man moaned with pain in his stupor but he did not awaken.

" The best thing that we could do would be to put him back in the sea," Sadao said, answering himself.

Now that the bleeding was stopped for the moment, he stood up and dusted the sand from his hands.

" Yes, undoubtedly that would be best," Hana said steadily. But she continued to stare down at the motionless man.

" If we sheltered a white man in our house we should be arrested and if we turned him over as a prisoner, he would certainly die," Sadao said.

" The kindest thing would be to put him back into the sea," Hana said. But neither of them moved. They were staring with a curious repulsion upon the inert figure.

" What is he? " Hana whispered.

" There is something about him that

looks American," Sadao said. He took up the battered cap. Yes, there, almost gone, was the faint lettering. " A sailor," he said, " from an American warship." He spelled it out: " U. S. Navy." The man was a prisoner of war!

" He has escaped," Hana cried softly, " and that is why he is wounded."

" In the back," Sadao agreed.

They hesitated, looking at each other. Then Hana said with resolution:

" Come, are we able to put him back into the sea? "

" If I am able, are you? " Sadao asked.

" No," Hana said. " But if you can do it alone . . ."

Sadao hesitated again. " The strange thing is," he said, " that if the man were whole I could turn him over to the police without difficulty. I care nothing for him. He is my enemy. All Americans are my enemy. And he is only a common fellow. You see how foolish his face is. But since he is wounded . . ."

" You also cannot throw him back to the sea," Hana said. " Then there is only one thing to do. We must carry him into the house."

" But the servants? " Sadao inquired.

" We must simply tell them that we intend to give him to the police — as indeed we must, Sadao. We must think of the children and your position. It would endanger all of us if we did not give this man over as a prisoner of war."

" Certainly," Sadao agreed. " I would not think of doing anything else."

Thus agreed, together they lifted the man. He was very light, like a fowl that has been half starved for a long time until it is only feathers and skeleton. So, his arms hanging, they carried him up the steps and into the side door of the house. This door opened into a passage and down the passage they carried the man toward an empty bedroom. It had been the bedroom of Sadao's father and since his death it had not been used. They laid the man on the deeply matted floor. Everything here had been Japanese to please the old man, who would never in his own home sit on a chair or sleep in a foreign bed. Hana went to the wall cupboards and slid back a door and took out a soft quilt. She hesitated. The quilt was covered with flowered silk and the lining was pure white silk.

" He is so dirty," she murmured in distress.

" Yes, he had better be washed," Sadao agreed. " If you will fetch hot water I will wash him."

" I cannot bear for you to touch him," she said. " We shall have to tell the servants he is here. I will tell Yumi now. She can leave the children for a few minutes and she can wash him."

Sadao considered a moment. " Let it be so," he agreed. " You tell Yumi and I will tell the others."

But the utter pallor of the man's unconscious face moved him first to stoop and feel his pulse. It was faint but it was there. He put his hand against the man's cold breast. The heart too was yet alive.

" He will die unless he is operated on," Sadao said, considering. " The question is whether he will not die anyway."

Hana cried out in fear. " Don't try to save him! What if he should live? "

" What if he should die? " Sadao replied. He stood gazing down on the motionless man. This man must have extraordinary vitality or he would have been dead by now. But then he was very young — perhaps not yet twenty-five.

" You mean die from the operation? " Hana asked.

" Yes," Sadao said.

Hana considered this doubtfully, and when she did not answer Sadao turned away. " At any rate something must be done with him," he said, " and first he must be washed." He went quickly out of the room and Hana came behind him. She did not wish to be left alone with the white man. He was the first she had seen since she left America and now he seemed to have nothing to do with those whom she had known there. Here he was her enemy, a menace, living or dead.

She turned to the nursery and called, "Yumi!"

But the children heard her voice, and she had to go in for a moment and smile at them and play with the baby boy, now nearly three months old.

Over the baby's soft black hair she motioned with her mouth, "Yumi — come with me!"

"I will put the baby to bed," Yumi replied. "He is ready."

She went with Yumi into the bedroom next to the nursery and stood with the boy in her arms while Yumi spread the sleeping quilts on the floor and laid the baby between them.

Then Hana led the way quickly and softly to the kitchen. The two servants were frightened at what their master had just told them. The old gardener, who was also a house servant, pulled the few hairs on his upper lip.

"The master ought not to heal the wound of this white man," he said bluntly to Hana. "The white man ought to die. First he was shot. Then the sea caught him and wounded him with her rocks. If the master heals what the gun did and what the sea did, they will take revenge on us."

"I will tell him what you say," Hana replied courteously. But she herself was also frightened, although she was not superstitious as the old man was. Could it ever be well to help an enemy? Nevertheless she told Yumi to fetch the hot water and bring it to the room where the white man was.

She went ahead and slid back the partitions. Sadao was not yet there. Yumi, following, put down her wooden bucket. Then she went over to the white man. When she saw him her thick lips folded themselves into stubbornness. "I have never washed a white man," she said, "and I will not wash so dirty a one now."

Hana cried at her severely, "You will do what your master commands you!"

"My master ought not to command me to wash the enemy," Yumi said stubbornly.

There was so fierce a look of resistance upon Yumi's round dull face that Hana felt

unreasonably afraid. After all, if the servants should report something that was not as it happened?

"Very well," she said with dignity. "You understand we only want to bring him to his senses so that we can turn him over as a prisoner?"

"I will have nothing to do with it," Yumi said. "I am a poor person and it is not my business."

"Then please," Hana said gently, "return to your own work."

At once Yumi left the room. But this left Hana with the white man alone. She might have been too afraid to stay had not her anger at Yumi's stubbornness now sustained her.

"Stupid Yumi," she muttered fiercely. "Is this anything but a man? And a wounded helpless man!"

In the conviction of her own superiority she bent impulsively and untied the knotted rags that kept the white man covered. When she had his breast bare she dipped the small clean towel that Yumi had brought into the steaming hot water and washed his face carefully. The man's skin, though rough with exposure, was of a fine texture and must have been very blond when he was a child.

While she was thinking these thoughts, though not really liking the man better now that he was no longer a child, she kept on washing him until his upper body was quite clean. But she dared not turn him over. Where was Sadao? Now her anger was ebbing, and she was anxious again and she rose, wiping her hands on the wrung towel. Then, lest the man be chilled, she put the quilt over him.

"Sadao!" she called softly.

He had been about to come in when she called. His hand had been on the door and now he opened it. She saw that he had brought his surgeon's emergency bag and that he wore his surgeon's coat.

"You have decided to operate!" she cried.

"Yes," he said shortly. He turned his back to her and unfolded a sterilized towel upon the floor of the *tokonoma* [1] alcove, and put his instruments out upon it.

" Fetch towels," he said.

She went obediently, but how anxious now, to the linen shelves and took out the towels. There ought also to be old pieces of matting so that the blood would not ruin the fine floor covering. She went out to the back veranda where the gardener kept strips of matting with which to protect delicate shrubs on cold nights and took an armful of them.

But when she went back into the room, she saw this was useless. The blood had already soaked through the packing in the man's wound and had ruined the mat under him.

" Oh, the mat! " she cried.

" Yes, it is ruined," Sadao replied, as though he did not care. " Help me to turn him," he commanded her.

She obeyed him without a word, and he began to wash the man's back carefully.

" Yumi would not wash him," she said.

" Did you wash him then? " Sadao asked, not stopping for a moment his swift concise movements.

" Yes," she said.

He did not seem to hear her. But she was used to his absorption when he was at work. She wondered for a moment if it mattered to him what was the body upon which he worked so long as it was for the work he did so excellently.

" You will have to give the anesthetic if he needs it," he said.

" I? " she repeated blankly. " But never have I! "

" It is easy enough," he said impatiently.

He was taking out the packing now and the blood began to flow more quickly. He peered into the wound with the bright surgeon's light fastened on his forehead. " The bullet is still there," he said with cool interest. " Now I wonder how deep this rock wound is. If it is not too deep it may be that I can get the bullet. But the bleeding is not superficial. He has lost much blood."

[1] **tokonoma** (tŏ′kŏ-nō′mȧ): a recess for the display of art objects.

At this moment Hana choked. He looked up and saw her face the color of sulphur.

" Don't faint," he said sharply. He did not put down his exploring instrument. " If I stop now, the man will surely die." She clapped her hands to her mouth and leaped up and ran out of the room. Outside in the garden he heard her retching. But he went on with his work.

" It will be better for her to empty her stomach," he thought. He had forgotten that of course she had never seen an operation. But her distress and his inability to go to her at once made him impatient and irritable with this man who lay like dead under his knife.

" This man," he thought, " there is no reason under heaven why he should live."

Unconsciously this thought made him ruthless and he proceeded swiftly. In his dream the man moaned, but Sadao paid no heed except to mutter at him.

" Groan," he muttered, " groan if you like. I am not doing this for my own pleasure. In fact, I do not know why I am doing it."

The door opened and there was Hana again. She had not stopped even to smooth back her hair.

" Where is the anesthetic? " she asked in a clear voice.

Sadao motioned with his chin. " It is as well that you came back," he said. " This fellow is beginning to stir."

She had the bottle and some cotton in her hand.

" But how shall I do it? " she asked.

" Simply saturate the cotton and hold it near his nostrils," Sadao replied without delaying for one moment the intricate detail of his work. " When he breathes badly move it away a little."

She crouched close to the sleeping face of the young American. It was a piteously thin face, she thought, and the lips were twisted. The man was suffering whether he knew it or not. Watching him, she wondered if the stories they heard sometimes of the sufferings of prisoners were true. They came like flickers of rumor, told by word of mouth and always contradicted. In the newspapers the reports were always that wherever the Japanese armies went the people received them gladly, with cries of joy at their liberation. But sometimes she remembered such men as General Takima, who at home beat his wife cruelly, though no one mentioned it now that he had fought so victorious a battle in Manchuria. If a man like that could be so cruel to a woman in his power, would he not be cruel to one like this, for instance?

She hoped anxiously that this young man had not been tortured. It was at this moment that she observed deep red scars on his neck, just under the ear. " Those scars," she murmured, lifting her eyes to Sadao.

But he did not answer. At this moment he felt the tip of his instrument strike against something hard, dangerously near the kidney. All thought left him. He felt only the purest pleasure. He probed with his fingers, delicately, familiar with every atom of this human body. His old American professor of anatomy had seen to that knowledge. " Ignorance of the human body is the surgeon's cardinal sin, sirs! " he had thundered at his classes year after year. " To operate without as complete knowledge of the body as if you had made it — anything less than that is murder."

" It is not quite at the kidney, my friend," Sadao murmured. It was his habit to murmur to the patient when he forgot himself in an operation. " My friend," he always called his patients and so now he did, forgetting that this was his enemy.

Then quickly, with the cleanest and most precise of incisions, the bullet was out. The man quivered, but he was still unconscious. Nevertheless he muttered a few English words.

" Guts," he muttered, choking. " They got . . . my guts . . ."

" Sadao! " Hana cried sharply.

" Hush," Sadao said.

The man sank again into silence so profound that Sadao took up his wrist, hating the touch of it. Yes, there was still a pulse so faint, so feeble, but enough, if he wanted the man to live, to give hope.

" But certainly I do not want this man to live," he thought.

" No more anesthetic," he told Hana.

He turned as swiftly as though he had never paused and from his medicines he chose a small vial and from it filled a hypodermic and thrust it into the patient's left arm. Then, putting down the needle, he took the man's wrist again. The pulse under his fingers fluttered once or twice and then grew stronger.

" This man will live in spite of all," he said to Hana and sighed.

The young man woke, so weak, his blue eyes so terrified when he perceived where he was, that Hana felt compelled to apology. She served him herself, for none of the servants would enter the room.

When she came in the first time she saw him summon his small strength to be prepared for some fearful thing.

" Don't be afraid," she begged him softly.

" How come . . . you speak English . . ." he gasped.

" I was a long time in America," she replied.

She saw that he wanted to reply to that, but he could not, and so she knelt and fed him gently from the porcelain spoon. He ate unwillingly, but still he ate.

" Now you will soon be strong," she said, not liking him and yet moved to comfort him.

He did not answer.

When Sadao came in the third day after the operation, he found the young man sitting up, his face bloodless with the effort.

" Lie down," Sadao cried. " Do you want to die? "

He forced the man down gently and strongly and examined the wound. " You may kill yourself if you do this sort of thing," he scolded.

" What are you going to do with me? " the boy muttered. He looked just now barely seventeen. " Are you going to hand me over? "

For a moment Sadao did not answer. He finished his examination and then pulled the silk quilt over the man.

" I do not know myself what I shall do with you," he said. " I ought of course to give you to the police. You are a prisoner of war — no, do not tell me anything." He put up his hand as he saw the young man about to speak. " Do not even tell me your name unless I ask it."

They looked at each other for a moment, and then the young man closed his eyes and turned his face to the wall.

" Okay," he whispered, his mouth a bitter line.

Outside the door Hana was waiting for Sadao. He saw at once that she was in trouble.

" Sadao, Yumi tells me the servants feel they cannot stay if we hide this man here any more," she said. " She tells me that they are saying that you and I were so long in America that we have forgotten to think of our own country first. They think we like Americans."

" It is not true," Sadao said harshly, " Americans are our enemies. But I have been trained not to let a man die if I can help it."

" The servants cannot understand that," she said anxiously.

" No," he agreed.

Neither seemed able to say more, and somehow the household dragged on. The servants grew daily more watchful. Their courtesy was as careful as ever, but their eyes were cold upon the pair to whom they were hired.

" It is clear what our master ought to do," the old gardener said one morning. He had worked with flowers all his life, and had been a specialist too in moss. For Sadao's father he had made one of the finest moss gardens in Japan, sweeping the bright green carpet constantly so that not a leaf or a pine needle marred the velvet of its surface. " My old master's son knows very well what he ought to do," he now said, pinching a bud from a bush as he spoke. " When the man was so near death, why did he not let him bleed? "

" That young master is so proud of his skill to save life that he saves any life," the cook said contemptuously. She split a fowl's neck skillfully and held the fluttering bird and let its blood flow into the roots of a wistaria vine. Blood is the best of fertilizers, and the old gardener would not let her waste a drop of it.

" It is the children of whom we must think," Yumi said sadly. " What will be their fate if their father is condemned as a traitor? "

They did not try to hide what they said from the ears of Hana as she stood arranging the day's flowers in the veranda near by, and she knew they spoke on purpose that she might hear. That they were right she knew too in most of her being. But there was another part of her which she herself could not understand. It was not sentimental liking of the prisoner. She had come to think of him as a prisoner. She had not liked him even yesterday when he had said in his impulsive way, " Anyway, let me tell you that my name is Tom." She had only bowed her little distant bow. She saw hurt in his eyes but she did not wish to assuage it. Indeed, he was a great trouble in this house.

As for Sadao, every day he examined the wound carefully. The last stitches had been pulled out this morning, and the young man would in a fortnight be nearly as well as ever. Sadao went back to his office and carefully typed a letter to the chief of police reporting the whole matter. " On the twenty-first day of February an escaped prisoner was washed up on the shore in front of my house." So far he typed and then he opened a secret drawer of his desk and put the unfinished report into it.

On the seventh day after that two things happened. In the morning the servants left together, their belongings tied in large square cotton kerchiefs. When Hana got up in the morning nothing was done, the house not cleaned and the food not prepared, and she knew what it meant. She was dismayed and even terrified, but her pride as a mistress would not allow her to show it. Instead, she inclined her head gracefully when

JAPANESE HOME. In a typical middle-class house like this, Sadao and Hana concealed "the enemy." (Philip Gendreau)

they appeared before her in the kitchen, and she paid them off and thanked them for all that they had done for her. They were crying, but she did not cry. The cook and the gardener had served Sadao since he was a little boy in his father's house, and Yumi cried because of the children. She was so grieving that after she had gone she ran back to Hana.

"If the baby misses me too much to-night, send for me. I am going to my own house and you know where it is."

"Thank you," Hana said smiling. But she told herself she would not send for Yumi however the baby cried.

She made the breakfast and Sadao helped with the children. Neither of them spoke of the servants beyond the fact that they were gone. But after Hana had taken morning food to the prisoner she came back to Sadao.

"Why is it we cannot see clearly what we ought to do?" she asked him. "Even the servants see more clearly than we do. Why are we different from other Japanese?"

Sadao did not answer. But a little later he went into the room where the prisoner was and said brusquely, "Today you may get up on your feet. I want you to stay up only five minutes at a time. Tomorrow you may try it twice as long. It would be well that you get back your strength as quickly as possible."

He saw the flicker of terror on the young face that was still very pale.

"Okay," the boy murmured. Evidently he was determined to say more. "I feel I ought to thank you, doctor, for having saved my life."

"Don't thank me too early," Sadao said coldly. He saw the flicker of terror again in the boy's eyes — terror as unmistakable as an animal's. The scars on his neck were crimson for a moment. Those scars! What were they? Sadao did not ask.

In the afternoon the second thing happened. Hana, working hard on unaccustomed labor, saw a messenger come to the door in official uniform. Her hands went weak and she could not draw her breath. The servants must have told already. She ran to Sadao, gasping, unable to utter a word. But by then the messenger had simply followed her through the garden and there he stood. She pointed at him helplessly.

Sadao looked up from his book. He was in his office, the outer partition of which was thrown open to the garden for the southern sunshine.

"What is it?" he asked the messenger, and then he rose, seeing the man's uniform.

"You are to come to the palace," the man said, "the old General is in pain again."

"Oh," Hana breathed, "is that all?"

"All?" the messenger exclaimed. "Is it not enough?"

"Indeed it is," she replied. "I am very sorry."

When Sadao came to say good-by, she was in the kitchen, but doing nothing. The children were asleep and she sat merely resting for a moment, more exhausted from her fright than from work.

"I thought they had come to arrest you," she said.

He gazed down into her anxious eyes. "I must get rid of this man for your sake," he said in distress. "Somehow I must get rid of him."

"Of course," the General said weakly, "I understand fully. But that is because I once took a degree in Princeton. So few Japanese have."

"I care nothing for the man, Excellency," Sadao said, "but having operated on him with such success . . ."

"Yes, yes," the General said. "It only makes me feel you more indispensable to me. Evidently you can save anyone — you are so skilled. You say you think I can stand one more such attack as I have had today?"

"Not more than one," Sadao said.

"Then certainly I can allow nothing to happen to you," the General said with anxi-

ety. His long pale Japanese face became expressionless, which meant that he was in deep thought. "You cannot be arrested," the General said, closing his eyes. "Suppose you were condemned to death and the next day I had to have my operation?"

"There are other surgeons, Excellency," Sadao suggested.

"None I trust," the General replied. "The best ones have been trained by Germans and would consider the operation successful even if I died. I do not care for their point of view." He sighed. "It seems a pity that we cannot better combine the German ruthlessness with the American sentimentality. Then you could turn your prisoner over to execution and yet I could be sure you would not murder me while I was unconscious." The General laughed. He had an unusual sense of humor. "As a Japanese, could you not combine these two foreign elements?" he asked.

Sadao smiled. "I am not quite sure," he said, "but for your sake I would be willing to try, Excellency."

The General shook his head. "I had rather not be the test case," he said. He felt suddenly weak and overwhelmed with the cares of his life as an official in times such as these when repeated victory brought great responsibilities all over the south Pacific. "It is very unfortunate that this man should have washed up on your doorstep," he said irritably.

"I feel it so myself," Sadao said gently.

"It would be best if he could be quietly killed," the General said. "Not by you, but by someone who does not know him. I have my own private assassins. Suppose I send two of them to your house tonight — or better, any night. You need know nothing about it. It is now warm — what would be more natural than that you should leave the outer partition of the white man's room open to the garden while he sleeps?"

"Certainly it would be very natural," Sadao agreed. "In fact, it is so left open every night."

"Good," the General said, yawning. "They are very capable assassins — they make no noise and they know the trick of inward bleeding. If you like I can even have them remove the body."

Sadao considered. " That perhaps would be best, Excellency," he agreed, thinking of Hana.

He left the General's presence then and went home, thinking over the plan. In this way the whole thing would be taken out of his hands. He would tell Hana nothing, since she would be timid at the idea of assassins in the house, and yet certainly such persons were essential in an absolute state such as Japan was. How else could rulers deal with those who opposed them?

He refused to allow anything but reason to be the atmosphere of his mind as he went into the room where the American was in bed. But as he opened the door, to his surprise he found the young man out of bed, and preparing to go into the garden.

" What is this! " he exclaimed. " Who gave you permission to leave your room? "

" I'm not used to waiting for permission," Tom said gaily. " Gosh, I feel pretty good again! But will the muscles on this side always feel stiff? "

" Is it so? " Sadao inquired surprised. He forgot all else. " Now I thought I had provided against that," he murmured. He lifted the edge of the man's shirt and gazed at the healing scar. " Massage may do it," he said, " if exercise does not."

" It won't bother me much," the young man said. His young face was gaunt under the stubbly blond beard. " Say, doctor, I've got something I want to say to you. If I hadn't met a Jap like you — well, I wouldn't be alive today. I know that."

Sadao bowed but he could not speak.

" Sure, I know that," Tom went on warmly. His big thin hands gripping a chair were white at the knuckles. " I guess if all the Japs were like you there wouldn't have been a war."

" Perhaps," Sadao said with difficulty. " And now I think you had better go back to bed."

He helped the boy back into bed and then bowed. " Good night," he said.

Sadao slept badly that night. Time and time again he woke, thinking he heard the rustling of footsteps, the sound of a twig broken or a stone displaced in the garden — a noise such as men might make who carried a burden.

The next morning he made the excuse to go first into the guest room. If the American were gone, he then could simply tell Hana that so the General had directed. But when he opened the door he saw at once that it was not last night. There on the pillow was the shaggy blond head. He could hear the peaceful breathing of sleep and he closed the door again quietly.

" He is asleep," he told Hana. " He is almost well to sleep like that."

" What shall we do with him? " Hana whispered her old refrain.

Sadao shook his head. " I must decide in a day or two," he promised.

But certainly, he thought, the second night must be the night. There rose a wind that night, and he listened to the sounds of bending boughs and whistling partitions.

Hana woke too. " Ought we not to go and close the sick man's partition? " she asked.

" No," Sadao said. " He is able now to do it for himself."

But the next morning the American was still there.

Then the third night of course must be the night. The wind changed to quiet rain, and the garden was full of the sound of dripping eaves and running springs. Sadao slept a little better, but he woke at the sound of a crash and leaped to his feet.

" What was that? " Hana cried. The baby woke at her voice and began to wail. " I must go and see."

But he held her and would not let her move.

" Sadao," she cried, " what is the matter with you? "

" Don't go," he muttered, " don't go! "

His terror infected her and she stood breathless, waiting. There was only silence. Together they crept back into the bed, the baby between them.

Yet, when he opened the door of the guest room in the morning, there was the young man. He was very gay and had already washed and was now on his feet. He had asked for a razor yesterday and had shaved himself, and today there was a faint color in his cheeks.

" I am well," he said joyously.

Sadao drew his kimono round his weary body. He could not, he decided suddenly, go through another night. It was not that he cared for this young man's life. No, simply it was not worth the strain.

" You are well," Sadao agreed. He lowered his voice. " You are so well that I think if I put my boat on the shore tonight, with food and extra clothing in it, you might be able to row to that little island not far from the coast. It is so near the coast that it has not been worth fortifying. Nobody lives on it because in storm it is submerged. But this is not the season of storm. You could live there until you saw a Korean fishing boat pass by. They pass quite near the island because the water is many fathoms deep there."

The young man stared at him, slowly comprehending. " Do I have to? " he asked.

" I think so," Sadao said gently. " You understand — it is not hidden that you are here."

The young man nodded in perfect comprehension. " Okay," he said simply.

Sadao did not see him again until evening. As soon as it was dark he had dragged the stout boat down to the shore and in it put food and bottled water that he had bought secretly during the day, as well as two quilts he had bought at a pawnshop. The boat he tied to a post in the water, for the tide was high. There was no moon and he worked without a flashlight.

When he came to the house he entered as though he were just back from his work, and so Hana knew nothing. " Yumi was here today," she said as she served his supper. Though she was so modern, still she did not eat with him. " Yumi cried over the baby," she went on with a sigh. " She misses him so."

" The servants will come back as soon as the foreigner is gone," Sadao said.

He went into the guest room that night before he went to bed and himself checked carefully the American's temperature, the state of the wound, and his heart and pulse. The pulse was irregular, but that was perhaps because of excitement. The young man's pale lips were pressed together and his eyes burned. Only the scars on his neck were red.

" I realize you are saving my life again," he told Sadao.

" Not at all," Sadao said. " It is only inconvenient to have you here any longer."

He had hesitated a good deal about giving the man a flashlight. But he had decided to give it to him after all. It was a small one, his own, which he used at night when he was called.

" If your food runs out before you catch a boat," he said, " signal me two flashes at the same instant the sun drops over the horizon. Do not signal in darkness, for it will be seen. If you are all right but still there, signal me once. You will find fish easy to catch but you must eat them raw. A fire would be seen."

" Okay," the young man breathed.

He was dressed now in the Japanese clothes which Sadao had given him, and at the last moment Sadao wrapped a black cloth about his blond head.

" Now," Sadao said.

The young American without a word shook Sadao's hand warmly, and then walked quite well across the floor and down the step into the darkness of the garden. Once — twice — Sadao saw his light flash to find his way. But that would not be suspected. He waited until from the shore there was one more flash. Then he closed the partition. That night he slept.

" You say the man escaped? " the General asked faintly. He had been operated upon a week before, an emergency operation to which Sadao had been called in the night. For twelve hours Sadao had not been sure the General would live. The gall bladder was much involved. Then the old man had begun to breathe deeply again and to demand food. Sadao had not been able to ask about the assassins. So far as he knew they had never come. The servants had returned, and Yumi had cleaned the guest room thoroughly and had burned sulphur in it to get the white man's smell out of it. Nobody said anything. Only the gardener was cross because he had got behind with his chrysanthemums.

But after a week Sadao felt the General was well enough to be spoken to about the prisoner.

"Yes, Excellency, he escaped," Sadao now said. He coughed, signifying that he had not said all he might have said, but was unwilling to disturb the General farther. But the old man opened his eyes suddenly.

"That prisoner," he said with some energy, "did I not promise you I would kill him for you?"

"You did, Excellency," Sadao said.

"Well, well!" the old man said in a tone of amazement, "so I did! But you see, I was suffering a good deal. The truth is, I thought of nothing but myself. In short, I forgot my promise to you."

"I wondered, Your Excellency," Sadao murmured.

"It was certainly very careless of me," the General said, "But you understand it was not lack of patriotism or dereliction of duty." He looked anxiously at his doctor. "If the matter should come out, you would understand that, wouldn't you?"

"Certainly, Your Excellency," Sadao said. He suddenly comprehended that the General was in the palm of his hand and that as a consequence he himself was perfectly safe. "I can swear to your loyalty, Excellency," he said to the old General, "and to your zeal against the enemy."

"You are a good man," the General murmured and closed his eyes. "You will be rewarded."

But Sadao, searching the spot of black in the twilighted sea that night, had his reward. There was no prick of light in the dusk. No one was on the island. His prisoner was gone — safe, doubtless, for he had warned him to wait only for a Korean fishing boat.

He stood for a moment on the veranda, gazing out to the sea from whence the young man had come that other night. And into his mind, although without reason, there came other white faces he had known — the professor at whose house he had met Hana, a dull man, and his wife had been a silly talkative woman, in spite of her wish to be kind. He remembered his old teacher of anatomy, who had been so insistent on mercy with the knife, and then he remembered the face of his fat and slatternly landlady. He had had great difficulty in finding a place to live in America because he was a Japanese. The Americans were full of prejudice, and it had been bitter to live in it, knowing himself their superior. How he had despised the ignorant and dirty old woman who had at last consented to house him in her miserable home! He had once tried to be grateful to her because she had in his last year nursed him through influenza, but it was difficult, for she was no less repulsive to him in her kindness. But then, white people were repulsive, of course. It was a relief to be openly at war with them at last. Now he remembered the youthful, haggard face of his prisoner — white and repulsive.

"Strange," he thought, "I wonder why I could not kill him?"

## Suggestions for Study

1. In what ways was Sadao different from his father? How do you account for these differences?

2. In your opinion, why was Sadao unable to kill Tom or turn him over to the authorities?

3. Reverse the story in your mind: let an escaped Japanese prisoner of war be rescued by Americans. In what ways do you think the typical American would be different from Sadao, Hana, and the servants?

4. Did this story affect in any way your opinion of the Japanese? Explain.

5. American scientists who worked on the atom bomb steadfastly opposed government censorship of scientific work after World War II was ended. What light does "The Enemy"

throw upon their statement that "science knows no national boundaries"?

6. For your vocabulary: voluble, repulsion, inert, retching.

# Stephen Vincent Benét

## 1898–1943

Stephen Vincent Benét was born in Bethlehem, Pennsylvania. He graduated from Yale and took his master's degree there. He published two volumes before leaving college; and within ten years after graduation he had won both the *Nation's* poetry prize and the Pulitzer prize, the latter for *John Brown's Body*. In the late thirties he turned his attention also to short-story writing and wrote a large number of extraordinary stories. They are greatly varied in subject, in method, and in style, but perhaps those which will be longest remembered are his stories of fantasy, of the strange and unusual. In this field Benét was acknowledged master during his lifetime. Most of his short stories were collected in the volumes *Thirteen O'Clock* and *Tales before Midnight*.

## THE DEVIL AND DANIEL WEBSTER

Of all of Stephen Benét's short stories, this one is the most famous. It is generally regarded as a minor American classic, and has been turned into a successful movie ("All That Money Can Buy"), a one-act play, and even a grand opera. It is an excellent illustration of the delightful folklore and of the fantasy to be found in many of Benét's stories.

It's a story they all tell in the border country, where Massachusetts joins Vermont and New Hampshire.

Yes, Dan'l Webster's dead — or, at least, they buried him. But every time there's a thunderstorm around Marshfield, they say you can hear his rolling voice in the hollows of the sky. And they say that if you go to his grave and speak loud and clear, "Dan'l Webster — Dan'l Webster!" the ground'll begin to shiver and the trees begin to shake. And after a while you'll hear a deep voice saying, "Neighbor, how stands the Union?" Then you better answer the Union stands as she stood, rock-bottomed and copper-sheathed, one and indivisible, or he's liable to rear right out of the ground. At least, that's what I was told when I was a youngster.

You see, for a while, he was the biggest man in the country. He never got to be President, but he was the biggest man. There were thousands that trusted in him right next to God Almighty, and they told stories about him and all the things that belonged to him that were like the stories of patriarchs and such. They said when he stood up to speak stars and stripes came right out in the sky, and once he spoke against a river and made it sink into the ground. They said when he walked the woods with his fishing rod, Killall, the trout would jump out of the streams right into his pockets, for they knew it was no use putting up a fight against him; and, when he argued a case, he could turn on the harps of the blessed and the shaking of the earth underground. That was the kind of man he was, and his big farm up at Marshfield was suitable to him. The chickens he raised were all white meat down through the drumsticks, the cows were tended like children, and the big ram he called Goliath had horns with a curl like a morning-glory vine and could butt through an iron door. But Dan'l wasn't one of your gentlemen farmers; he knew all the ways of the land, and he'd be up by candlelight to see that the chores got done. A man with a mouth like a mastiff, a brow like a mountain, and eyes like burning anthracite — that was Dan'l Webster in his prime. And the biggest case he argued never got written down in the books, for he argued it against the devil, nip and tuck, and no holds barred. And this is the way I used to hear it told:

There was a man named Jabez Stone, lived at Cross Corners, New Hampshire. He wasn't a bad man to start with, but he was an unlucky man. If he planted corn, he got borers; if he planted potatoes, he got blight. He had good-enough land, but it didn't prosper him; he had a decent wife and children, but the more children he had, the less there was to feed them. If stones cropped up in his neighbor's field, boulders boiled up in his; if he had a horse with the spavins, he'd trade it for one with the staggers and give something extra. There's some folks bound to be like that, apparently. But one day Jabez Stone got sick of the whole business.

He'd been plowing that morning and he'd just broke the plowshare on a rock that he could have sworn hadn't been there yesterday. And, as he stood looking at the plowshare, the off horse began to cough — that ropy kind of cough that means sickness and horse doctors. There were two children down with the measles, his wife was ailing, and he had a whitlow on his thumb. It was about the last straw for Jabez Stone. " I vow," he said, and he looked around him kind of desperate — " I vow it's enough to make a man want to sell his soul to the devil! And I would, too, for two cents! "

Then he felt a kind of queerness come over him at having said what he'd said; though, naturally, being a New Hampshire-man, he wouldn't take it back. But, all the same, when it got to be evening and, as far as he could see, no notice had been taken, he felt relieved in his mind, for he was a religious man. But notice is always taken, sooner or later, just like the Good Book says. And, sure enough, the next day, about suppertime, a soft-spoken, dark-dressed stranger drove up in a handsome buggy and asked for Jabez Stone.

Well, Jabez told his family it was a lawyer, come to see him about a legacy. But he knew who it was. He didn't like the looks of the stranger, nor the way he smiled with his teeth. They were white teeth, and plentiful — some say they were filed to a point, but I wouldn't vouch for that. And he didn't like it when the dog took one look at the stranger and ran away howling, with his tail between his legs. But having passed his word, more or less, he stuck to it, and they went out behind the barn and made their bargain. Jabez Stone had to prick his finger to sign, and the stranger lent him a silver pen. The wound healed clean, but it left a little white scar.

After that, all of a sudden, things began to pick up and prosper for Jabez Stone. His cows got fat and his horses sleek, his crops were the envy of the neighborhood, and lightning might strike all over the valley, but it wouldn't strike his barn. Pretty soon, he was one of the prosperous people of the county; they asked him to stand for selectman, and he stood for it; there began to be talk of running him for state senate. All in all, you might say the Stone family was as happy and contented as cats in a dairy. And so they were, except for Jabez Stone.

He'd been contented enough, the first few years. It's a great thing when bad luck turns; it drives most other things out of your head. True, every now and then, especially in rainy weather, the little white scar on his finger would give him a twinge. And once a year, punctual as clockwork, the stranger with the handsome buggy would come driving by. But the sixth year, the stranger lighted, and, after that, his peace was over for Jabez Stone.

The stranger came up through the lower field, switching his boots with a cane — they were handsome black boots, but Jabez Stone never liked the look of them, particularly the toes. And, after he'd passed the time of day, he said, " Well, Mr. Stone, you're a hummer! It's a very pretty property you've got here, Mr. Stone."

" Well, some might favor it and others might not," said Jabez Stone, for he was a New Hampshireman.

" Oh, no need to decry your industry! " said the stranger, very easy, showing his teeth in a smile. " After all, we know what's been done, and it's been according to contract and specifications. So when — ahem — the mortgage falls due next year, you shouldn't have any regrets."

" Speaking of that mortgage, mister," said Jabez Stone, and he looked around for help to the earth and the sky, " I'm beginning to have one or two doubts about it."

"Doubts?" said the stranger, not quite so pleasantly.

"Why, yes," said Jabez Stone. "This being the U. S. A. and me always having been a religious man." He cleared his throat and got bolder. "Yes, sir," he said, "I'm beginning to have considerable doubts as to that mortgage holding in court."

"There's courts and courts," said the stranger, clicking his teeth. "Still, we might as well have a look at the original document." And he hauled out a big black pocketbook, full of papers. "Sherwin, Slater, Stevens, Stone," he muttered. "I, Jabez Stone, for a term of seven years — Oh, it's quite in order, I think."

But Jabez Stone wasn't listening, for he saw something else flutter out of the black pocketbook. It was something that looked like a moth, but it wasn't a moth. And as Jabez Stone stared at it, it seemed to speak to him in a small sort of piping voice, terrible small and thin, but terrible human.

"Neighbor Stone!" it squeaked. "Neighbor Stone! Help me! For God's sake, help me!"

But before Jabez Stone could stir hand or foot, the stranger whipped out a big bandanna handkerchief, caught the creature in it, just like a butterfly, and started tying up the ends of the bandanna.

"Sorry for the interruption," he said. "As I was saying — "

But Jabez Stone was shaking all over like a scared horse.

"That's Miser Stevens' voice!" he said, in a croak. "And you've got him in your handkerchief!"

The stranger looked a little embarrassed.

"Yes, I really should have transferred him to the collecting box," he said with a simper, "but there were some rather unusual specimens there and I didn't want them crowded. Well, well, these little contretemps [1] will occur."

"I don't know what you mean by contertan," said Jabez Stone, "but that was

Miser Stevens' voice! And he ain't dead! You can't tell me he is! He was just as spry and mean as a woodchuck, Tuesday!"

"In the midst of life — " said the stranger, kind of pious. "Listen!" Then a bell began to toll in the valley, and Jabez Stone listened, with the sweat running down his face. For he knew it was tolled for Miser Stevens and that he was dead.

"These long-standing accounts," said the stranger with a sigh; "one really hates to close them. But business is business."

He still had the bandanna in his hand, and Jabez Stone felt sick as he saw the cloth struggle and flutter.

"Are they all as small as that?" he asked hoarsely.

"Small?" said the stranger. "Oh, I see what you mean. Why, they vary." He measured Jabez Stone with his eyes, and his teeth showed. "Don't worry, Mr. Stone," he said. "You'll go with a very good grade. I wouldn't trust you outside the collecting box. Now, a man like Dan'l Webster, of course — well, we'd have to build a special box for him, and even at that, I imagine the wing spread would astonish you. He'd certainly be a prize. I wish we could see our way clear to him. But, in your case, as I was saying — "

"Put that handkerchief away!" said Jabez Stone, and he began to beg and to pray. But the best he could get at the end was a three years' extension, with conditions.

But till you make a bargain like that, you've got no idea of how fast four years can run. By the last months of those years, Jabez Stone's known all over the state and there's talk of running him for governor — and it's dust and ashes in his mouth. For every day, when he gets up, he thinks, "There's one more night gone," and every night when he lies down, he thinks of the black pocketbook and the soul of Miser Stevens, and it makes him sick at heart. Till, finally, he can't bear it any longer, and, in the last days of the last year, he hitches up his horse and drives off to seek Dan'l Webster. For Dan'l Webster was born in

---

[1] **contretemps** (kôn′trĕ-täɴ): an embarrassing situation. Note Stone's pronunciation of the word in the next line.

New Hampshire, only a few miles from Cross Corners, and it's well known that he has a particular soft spot for old neighbors.

It was early in the morning when he got to Marshfield, but Dan'l was up already, talking Latin to the farm hands and wrestling with the ram, Goliath, and trying out a new trotter and working up speeches to make against John C. Calhoun. But when he heard a New Hampshireman had come to see him, he dropped everything else he was doing, for that was Dan'l's way. He gave Jabez Stone a breakfast that five men couldn't eat, went into the living history of every man and woman in Cross Corners, and finally asked him how he could serve him.

Jabez Stone allowed that it was a kind of mortgage case.

"Well, I haven't pleaded a mortgage case in a long time, and I don't generally plead now, except before the Supreme Court," said Dan'l, " but if I can, I'll help you."

"Then I've got hope for the first time in ten years," said Jabez Stone, and told him the details.

Dan'l walked up and down as he listened, hands behind his back, now and then asking a question, now and then plunging his eyes at the floor, as if they'd bore through it like gimlets. When Jabez Stone had finished, Dan'l puffed out his cheeks and blew. Then he turned to Jabez Stone, and a smile broke over his face like the sunrise over Monadnock.

"You've certainly given yourself the devil's own row to hoe, Neighbor Stone," he said, " but I'll take your case."

"You'll take it?" said Jabez Stone, hardly daring to believe.

"Yes," said Dan'l Webster. "I've got about seventy-five other things to do and the Missouri Compromise [1] to straighten

[1] **Missouri Compromise:** An act passed by Congress in 1820 which provided for the admission of Missouri to the Union as a slave state but established a boundary at latitude 36°30', north of which slavery would not be permitted in any future state to be admitted.

out, but I'll take your case. For if two New Hampshiremen aren't a match for the devil, we might as well give the country back to the Indians."

Then he shook Jabez Stone by the hand and said, " Did you come down here in a hurry? "

"Well, I admit I made time," said Jabez Stone.

"You'll go back faster," said Dan'l Webster, and he told 'em to hitch up Constitution and Constellation to the carriage. They were matched grays with one white forefoot, and they stepped like greased lightning.

Well, I won't describe how excited and pleased the whole Stone family was to have the great Dan'l Webster for a guest, when they finally got there. Jabez Stone had lost his hat on the way, blown off when they overtook a wind, but he didn't take much account of that. But after supper he sent the family off to bed, for he had most particular business with Mr. Webster. Mrs. Stone wanted them to sit in the front parlor, but Dan'l Webster knew front parlors and said he preferred the kitchen. So it was there they sat, waiting for the stranger, with a jug on the table between them and a bright fire on the hearth — the stranger being scheduled to show up on the stroke of midnight, according to specification.

Well, most men wouldn't have asked for better company than Dan'l Webster and a jug. But with every tick of the clock Jabez Stone got sadder and sadder. His eyes roved round, and though he sampled the jug you could see he couldn't taste it. Finally, on the stroke of 11:30 he reached over and grabbed Dan'l Webster by the arm.

"Mr. Webster, Mr. Webster! " he said, and his voice was shaking with fear and a desperate courage. " For God's sake, Mr. Webster, harness your horses and get away from this place while you can! "

"You've brought me a long way, neighbor, to tell me you don't like my company," said Dan'l Webster, quite peaceable, pulling at the jug.

" Miserable wretch that I am! " groaned Jabez Stone. " I've brought you a devilish way, and now I see my folly. Let him take me if he wills. I don't hanker after it, I must say, but I can stand it. But you're the Union's stay and New Hampshire's pride! He mustn't get you, Mr. Webster! He mustn't get you! "

Dan'l Webster looked at the distracted man, all gray and shaking in the firelight, and laid a hand on his shoulder.

" I'm obliged to you, Neighbor Stone," he said gently. " It's kindly thought of. But there's a jug on the table and a case in hand. And I never left a jug or a case half finished in my life."

And just at that moment there was a sharp rap on the door.

" Ah," said Dan'l Webster, very coolly, " I thought your clock was a trifle slow, Neighbor Stone." He stepped to the door and opened it. " Come in! " he said.

The stranger came in — very dark and tall he looked in the firelight. He was carrying a box under his arm — a black, japanned box with little air holes in the lid. At the sight of the box, Jabez Stone gave a low cry and shrank into a corner of the room.

" Mr. Webster, I presume," said the stranger, very polite, but with his eyes glowing like a fox's deep in the woods.

" Attorney of record for Jabez Stone," said Dan'l Webster, but his eyes were glowing too. " Might I ask your name? "

" I've gone by a good many," said the stranger carelessly. " Perhaps Scratch will do for the evening. I'm often called that in these regions."

Then he sat down at the table and poured himself a drink from the jug. The liquor was cold in the jug, but it came steaming into the glass.

" And now," said the stranger, smiling and showing his teeth, " I shall call upon you, as a law-abiding citizen, to assist me in taking possession of my property."

Well, with that the argument began — and it went hot and heavy. At first, Jabez Stone had a flicker of hope, but when he saw Dan'l Webster being forced back at point after point, he just sat scrunched in his corner, with his eyes on that japanned box. For there wasn't any doubt as to the deed or the signature — that was the worst of it. Dan'l Webster twisted and turned and thumped his fist on the table, but he couldn't get away from that. He offered to compromise the case; the stranger wouldn't hear of it. He pointed out the property had increased in value, and state senators ought to be worth more; the stranger stuck to the letter of the law. He was a great lawyer, Dan'l Webster, but we know who's the King of Lawyers, as the Good Book tells us, and it seemed as if, for the first time, Dan'l Webster had met his match.

Finally, the stranger yawned a little. " Your spirited efforts on behalf of your client do you credit, Mr. Webster," he said, " but if you have no more arguments to adduce, I'm rather pressed for time — " and Jabez Stone shuddered.

Dan'l Webster's brow looked dark as a thundercloud. " Pressed or not, you shall not have this man! " he thundered. " Mr. Stone is an American citizen, and no American citizen may be forced into the service of a foreign prince. We fought England for that in '12 and we'll fight all hell for it again! "

" Foreign? " said the stranger. " And who calls me a foreigner? "

" Well, I never yet heard of the dev — of your claiming American citizenship," said Dan'l Webster with surprise.

" And who with better right? " said the stranger, with one of his terrible smiles. " When the first wrong was done to the first Indian, I was there. When the first slaver put out for the Congo, I stood on her deck. Am I not in your books and stories and beliefs, from the first settlements on? Am I not spoken of, still, in every church in New England? 'Tis true the North claims me for a Southerner, and the South for a Northerner, but I am neither. I am merely an honest American like yourself — and of the best descent — for, to tell the truth, Mr. Webster, though I don't like to boast of it, my name is older in this country than yours."

" Aha! " said Dan'l Webster, with the veins standing out in his forehead. " Then I stand on the Constitution! I demand a trial for my client! "

" The case is hardly one for an ordinary court," said the stranger, his eyes flickering. " And, indeed, the lateness of the hour — "

" Let it be any court you choose, so it is an American judge and an American jury! " said Dan'l Webster in his pride. " Let it be the quick [1] or the dead; I'll abide the issue! "

" You have said it," said the stranger, and pointed his finger at the door. And with that, and all of a sudden, there was a rushing of wind outside and a noise of footsteps. They came, clear and distinct, through the night. And yet, they were not like the footsteps of living men.

" In God's name, who comes by so late? " cried Jabez Stone, in an ague of fear.

" The jury Mr. Webster demands," said the stranger, sipping at his boiling glass. " You must pardon the rough appearance of one or two; they will have come a long way."

And with that the fire burned blue and the door blew open and twelve men entered, one by one.

If Jabez Stone had been sick with terror before, he was blind with terror now. For there was Walter Butler, the loyalist, who spread fire and horror through the Mohawk Valley in the times of the Revolution; and there was Simon Girty, the renegade, who saw white men burned at the stake and whooped with the Indians to see them burn. His eyes were green, like a catamount's, and the stains on his hunting shirt did not come from the blood of the deer. King Philip was there, wild and proud as he had been in life, with the great gash in his head that gave him his death wound, and cruel Governor Dale, who broke men on the wheel. There was Morton of Merry Mount, who so vexed the Plymouth Colony, with his

[1] the quick: the living.

flushed, loose, handsome face and his hate of the godly. There was Teach, the bloody pirate, with his black beard curling on his breast. The Reverend John Smeet, with his strangler's hands and his Geneva gown,[2] walked as daintily as he had to the gallows. The red print of the rope was still around his neck, but he carried a perfumed handkerchief in one hand. One and all, they came into the room with the fires of hell still upon them, and the stranger named their names and their deeds as they came, till the tale of twelve was told. Yet the stranger had told the truth — they had all played a part in America.

" Are you satisfied with the jury, Mr. Webster? " said the stranger mockingly, when they had taken their places.

The sweat stood upon Dan'l Webster's brow, but his voice was clear.

" Quite satisfied," he said. " Though I miss General Arnold from the company."

" Benedict Arnold is engaged upon other business," said the stranger, with a glower. " Ah, you asked for a justice, I believe."

He pointed his finger once more, and a tall man, soberly clad in Puritan garb, with the burning gaze of the fanatic, stalked into the room and took his judge's place.

" Justice Hathorne is a jurist of experience," said the stranger. " He presided at certain witch trials once held in Salem. There were others who repented of the business later, but not he."

" Repent of such notable wonders and undertakings? " said the stern old justice. " Nay, hang them — hang them all! " And he muttered to himself in a way that struck ice into the soul of Jabez Stone.

Then the trial began, and, as you might expect, it didn't look anyways good for the defense. And Jabez Stone didn't make much of a witness in his own behalf. He took one look at Simon Girty and screeched, and they had to put him back in his corner in a kind of swoon.

It didn't halt the trial, though; the trial went on, as trials do. Dan'l Webster had faced some hard juries and hanging judges

[2] Geneva gown: minister's robe.

THE DEVIL AND DAN-
IEL WEBSTER. Walter
Huston and Edward Ar-
nold in the movie version
of this story are pitted
against each other in the
courtroom scene before the
jury of lost souls. (RKO
Radio Pictures)

in his time, but this was the hardest he'd ever faced, and he knew it. They sat there with a kind of glitter in their eyes, and the stranger's smooth voice went on and on. Every time he'd raise an objection, it'd be " Objection sustained," but whenever Dan'l objected, it'd be " Objection denied." Well, you couldn't expect fair play from a fellow like this Mr. Scratch.

It got to Dan'l in the end, and he began to heat, like iron in the forge. When he got up to speak he was going to flay that stranger with every trick known to the law, and the judge and jury too. He didn't care if it was contempt of court or what would happen to him for it. He didn't care any more what happened to Jabez Stone. He just got madder and madder, thinking of what he'd say. And yet, curiously enough, the more he thought about it, the less he was able to arrange his speech in his mind.

Till, finally, it was time for him to get up on his feet, and he did so, all ready to bust out with lightnings and denunciations. But before he started he looked over the judge and jury for a moment, such being his custom. And he noticed the glitter in their eyes was twice as strong as before, and they all leaned forward. Like hounds just before they get the fox, they looked, and the blue mist of evil in the room thickened as he watched them. Then he saw what he'd been about to do, and he wiped his forehead, as a man might who's just escaped falling into a pit in the dark.

For it was him they'd come for, not only Jabez Stone. He read it in the glitter of their eyes and in the way the stranger hid his mouth with one hand. And if he fought them with their own weapons, he'd fall into their power; he knew that, though he couldn't have told you how. It was his own anger and horror that burned in their eyes; and he'd have to wipe that out or the case was lost. He stood there for a moment, his black eyes burning like anthracite. And then he began to speak.

He started off in a low voice, though you could hear every word. They say he could call on the harps of the blessed when he chose. And this was just as simple and easy as a man could talk. But he didn't start out by condemning or reviling. He was talking about the things that make a country a country, and a man a man.

And he began with the simple things that everybody's known and felt — the freshness of a fine morning when you're young, and the taste of food when you're hungry, and the new day that's every day when you're a child. He took them up and he turned them in his hands. They were good things for any man. But without freedom, they sickened. And when he talked of those enslaved, and the sorrows of slavery, his voice got like a big bell. He talked of the early days of America and the men who had made those days. It wasn't a spread-eagle speech, but he made you see it. He admitted all the wrong that had ever been done. But he showed how, out of the wrong and the right, the suffering and the starvations, something new had come. And everybody had played a part in it, even the traitors.

Then he turned to Jabez Stone and showed him as he was — an ordinary man who'd had hard luck and wanted to change it. And, because he'd wanted to change it, now he was going to be punished for all eternity. And yet there was good in Jabez Stone, and he showed that good. He was hard and mean, in some ways, but he was a man. There was sadness in being a man, but it was a proud thing too. And he showed what the pride of it was till you couldn't help feeling it. Yes, even in hell, if a man was a man, you'd know it. And he wasn't pleading for any one person any more, though his voice rang like an organ. He was telling the story and the failures and the endless journey of mankind. They got tricked and trapped and bamboozled, but it was a great journey. And no demon that was ever foaled could know the inwardness of it — it took a man to do that.

The fire began to die on the hearth and the wind before morning to blow. The light was getting gray in the room when Dan'l Webster finished. And his words came back at the end to New Hampshire ground, and the one spot of land that each man loves and clings to. He painted a picture of that, and to each one of that jury he spoke of things long forgotten. For his voice could search the heart, and that was his gift and his strength. And to one, his voice was like the forest and its secrecy, and to another like the sea and the storms of the sea; and one heard the cry of his lost nation in it, and another saw a little harmless scene he hadn't remembered for years. But each saw something. And when Dan'l Webster finished he didn't know whether or not he'd saved Jabez Stone. But he knew he'd done a miracle. For the glitter was gone from the eyes of judge and jury, and, for the moment, they were men again, and knew they were men.

"The defense rests," said Dan'l Webster, and stood there like a mountain. His ears were still ringing with his speech, and he didn't hear anything else till he heard Judge Hathorne say, "The jury will retire to consider its verdict."

Walter Butler rose in his place and his face had a dark, gay pride on it.

"The jury has considered its verdict," he said, and looked the stranger full in the eye. "We find for the defendant, Jabez Stone."

With that, the smile left the stranger's face, but Walter Butler did not flinch.

"Perhaps 'tis not strictly in accordance with the evidence," he said, "but even the damned may salute the eloquence of Mr. Webster."

With that, the long crow of a rooster split the gray morning sky, and judge and jury were gone from the room like a puff of smoke and as if they had never been there. The stranger turned to Dan'l Webster, smiling wryly. "Major Butler was always a bold man," he said. "I had not thought him quite so bold. Nevertheless, my congratulations, as between two gentlemen."

"I'll have that paper first, if you please," said Dan'l Webster, and he took it and tore it into four pieces. It was queerly warm to the touch. "And now," he said, "I'll have you!" and his hand came down like a bear

trap on the stranger's arm. For he knew that once you bested anybody like Mr. Scratch in fair fight, his power on you was gone. And he could see that Mr. Scratch knew it too.

The stranger twisted and wriggled, but he couldn't get out of that grip. "Come, come, Mr. Webster," he said, smiling palely. "This sort of thing is ridic — ouch! — is ridiculous. If you're worried about the costs of the case, naturally, I'd be glad to pay — "

"And so you shall!" said Dan'l Webster, shaking him till his teeth rattled. "For you'll sit right down at that table and draw up a document, promising never to bother Jabez Stone nor his heirs or assigns nor any other New Hampshireman till doomsday! For any hades we want to raise in this state, we can raise ourselves, without assistance from strangers."

"Ouch!" said the stranger. "Ouch! Well, they never did run very big to the barrel, but — ouch! — I agree!"

So he sat down and drew up the document. But Dan'l Webster kept his hand on his coat collar all the time.

"And, now, may I go?" said the stranger, quite humble, when Dan'l'd seen the document was in proper and legal form.

"Go?" said Dan'l, giving him another shake. "I'm still trying to figure out what I'll do with you. For you've settled the costs of the case, but you haven't settled with me. I think I'll take you back to Marshfield," he said, kind of reflective. "I've got a ram there named Goliath that can butt through an iron door. I'd kind of like to turn you loose in his field and see what he'd do."

Well, with that the stranger began to beg and to plead. And he begged and he pled so humble that finally Dan'l, who was naturally kindhearted, agreed to let him go. The stranger seemed terrible grateful for that and said, just to show they were friends, he'd tell Dan'l's fortune before leaving. So Dan'l agreed to that, though he didn't take much stock in fortunetellers ordinarily.

But, naturally, the stranger was a little different. Well, he pried and he peered at the lines in Dan'l's hands. And he told him one thing and another that was quite remarkable. But they were all in the past.

" Yes, all that's true, and it happened," said Dan'l Webster. " But what's to come in the future? "

The stranger grinned, kind of happily, and shook his head. " The future's not as you think it," he said. " It's dark. You have a great ambition, Mr. Webster."

" I have," said Dan'l firmly, for everybody knew he wanted to be President.

" It seems almost within your grasp," said the stranger, " but you will not attain it. Lesser men will be made President and you will be passed over."

" And, if I am, I'll still be Daniel Webster," said Dan'l. " Say on."

" You have two strong sons," said the stranger, shaking his head. " You look to found a line. But each will die in war and neither reach greatness."

" Live or die, they are still my sons," said Dan'l Webster. " Say on."

" You have made great speeches," said the stranger. " You will make more."

" Ah," said Dan'l Webster.

" But the last great speech you make will turn many of your own against you," said the stranger. " They will call you Ichabod; [1] they will call you by other names. Even in New England some will say you have turned your coat and sold your country, and their voices will be loud against you till you die."

" So it is an honest speech, it does not matter what men say," said Dan'l Webster. Then he looked at the stranger and their glances locked.

" One question," he said. " I have fought for the Union all my life. Will I see that fight won against those who would tear it apart? "

" Not while you live," said the stranger, grimly, " but it will be won. And after you are dead, there are thousands who will fight

for your cause, because of words that you spoke."

" Why, then, you long-barreled, slab-sided, lantern-jawed, fortunetelling noteshaver! " said Dan'l Webster, with a great roar of laughter, " be off with you to your own place before I put my mark on you! For, by the thirteen original colonies, I'd go to the Pit itself to save the Union! "

And with that he drew back his foot for a kick that would have stunned a horse. It was only the tip of his shoe that caught the stranger, but he went flying out of the door with his collecting box under his arm.

" And now," said Dan'l Webster, seeing Jabez Stone beginning to rouse from his swoon, " let's see what's left in the jug, for it's dry work talking all night. I hope there's pie for breakfast, Neighbor Stone."

But they say that whenever the devil comes near Marshfield, even now, he gives it a wide berth. And he hasn't been seen in the state of New Hampshire from that day to this. I'm not talking about Massachusetts or Vermont.

## Suggestions for Study

1. What is the single central impression of this story? Show that Benét makes characters, action, and setting all contribute to this central idea.

2. What contribution is made by the folk language in which the story is told?

3. What is the meaning of " till the tale of twelve was told " (page 101)? Only seven men are mentioned. Suggest suitable persons for the other five.

4. Point out places in the story that have poetic qualities.

5. Finish the quotation, " In the midst of life —." Name the source of the quotation. These five words are the title of a collection of excellent short stories by Ambrose Bierce. What kind of endings would you expect these stories to have?

6. Who was John C. Calhoun, and why is he mentioned in this story?

7. Vocabulary: patriarchs, anthracite, spavins, staggers, whitlow, legacy, selectman, decry, japanned, adduce, catamount.

---

[1] **Ichabod** (ĭk'å-bŏd): the title of Whittier's poem criticizing Webster's speech of March 7, 1850, in which he denounced the Abolitionists. Because of this speech many Northerners considered Webster a traitor. Ichabod is a Hebrew name meaning "where is the glory?" or, as it is usually translated, "the glory is departed."

## For Your Vocabulary

FIGURATIVE USE OF WORDS. A sure way to improve your command of language is to learn new words. An equally certain way to achieve effective speech is to use familiar words vividly, with imagination. By now, you have studied figures of speech and know the effectiveness of comparisons: " gone from the room like a puff of smoke," " as contented as cats in a dairy "; and of symbols: " no better company than Daniel Webster and a jug "; and of exaggeration: " when he spoke, stars and stripes came right out in the sky." You can probably name them: *simile* (sĭm′ĭ-lē), *metonymy* (mē-tŏn′ĭ-mĭ), *hyperbole* (hī-pûr′bŏ-lē). But it is even better to be able to use them effectively. Look at the way Benét puts life into his story with figures of speech. The story is full of them. Let's narrow it down to his picturing of eyes. Daniel Webster had eyes *like burning anthracite*. Simon Girty, the renegade, had eyes *green, like a catamount's*. The devil had eyes *glowing like a fox's deep in the woods*. Now those are all similes, expressed comparisons with *like* for a label. But Benét uses single verbs figuratively of the look in these men's eyes. He describes Webster as " *plunging* his eyes at the floor as if they'd bore through it like gimlets." The devil's eyes were *flickering*. Justice Hathorne had " the *burning* eyes of the fanatic." Not one of these words is used literally, yet each one gives you the impression more clearly than a detailed realistic description. Some figurative uses of words have become so general that we forget they are figurative. What is the literal and the figurative meaning of " a particular *soft spot* for old neighbors "; of " gives New Hampshire *a wide berth* "?

## John Steinbeck        1902–

To read John Steinbeck is to enlarge one's understanding and sympathies. His characters are for the most part California workers and farmers — Mexican cannery workers, transient fruit pickers, cattle ranchers, labor organizers. Steinbeck, California born and reared, knows these people intimately from having worked and lived among them, and in his stories he presents them with great vividness and realism. But Steinbeck is not content merely to display the character in action. He wants to show why the character acts and reacts as he does. To this greater task, Steinbeck brings a profound understanding of and sympathy with people, all kinds of people. Many of his characters are alien to the ordinary reader's experience; they are violent, or frustrated, or abnormal. But by masterly and compassionate presentation of their backgrounds and their motives, Steinbeck induces understanding in the reader — understanding, and oftentimes overwhelming pity.

John Steinbeck's first novels and stories were published in the early thirties. In 1937 he won a national audience with *Of Mice and Men*, and *The Grapes of Wrath* was the most talked-about novel of 1939, as well as winner of the Pulitzer prize. During the war he wrote *The Moon Is Down*, an anti-Nazi novel which was dramatized for both stage and screen and whose theme created much discussion.

## FLIGHT

Across the California country that Steinbeck knows best, from the Monterey coast line to the desert interior, Pepé,[1] the Mexican-Indian boy, a murderer, makes his flight. Steinbeck lays a careful foundation; he takes time to show us Pepé's background and to enlist our sympathies. But once the flight has begun, the story moves with terrible directness. We do not swerve our attention to ask about the pursuers. It is only Pepé who matters, his desperation and his anguish and his fate.

About fifteen miles below Monterey, on the wild coast, the Torres family had their farm, a few sloping acres above a cliff that dropped to the brown reefs and to the hissing white waters of the ocean. Behind the farm the stone mountains stood up against the sky. The farm buildings huddled like little clinging aphids on the mountain skirts, crouched low to the ground as though the wind might blow them into the sea. The little shack, the rattling, rotting barn were gray-bitten with sea salt, beaten by the damp wind until they had taken on the color of the granite hills. Two horses, a red cow and a red calf, half a dozen pigs and a flock of lean, multicolored chickens stocked the place. A little corn was raised on the sterile

[1] **Pepé** (pā-pā′).

slope, and it grew short and thick under the wind, and all the cobs formed on the landward sides of the stalks.

Mama Torres, a lean, dry woman with ancient eyes, had ruled the farm for ten years, ever since her husband tripped over a stone in the field one day and fell full length on a rattlesnake. When one is bitten on the chest there is not much that can be done.

Mama Torres had three children, two undersized black ones of twelve and fourteen, Emilio [1] and Rosy, whom Mama kept fishing on the rocks below the farm when the sea was kind and when the truant officer was in some distant part of Monterey County. And there was Pepé, the tall smiling son of nineteen, a gentle, affectionate boy, but very lazy. Pepé had a tall head, pointed at the top, and from its peak coarse black hair grew down like a thatch all around. Over his smiling little eyes Mama cut a straight bang so he could see. Pepé had sharp Indian cheekbones and an eagle nose, but his mouth was as sweet and shapely as a girl's mouth, and his chin was fragile and chiseled. He was loose and gangling, all legs and feet and wrists, and he was very lazy. Mama thought him fine and brave, but she never told him so. She said, " Some lazy cow must have got into thy father's family, else how could I have a son like thee." And she said, " When I carried thee, a sneaking lazy coyote came out of the brush and looked at me one day. That must have made thee so."

Pepé smiled sheepishly and stabbed at the ground with his knife to keep the blade sharp and free from rust. It was his inheritance, that knife, his father's knife. The long heavy blade folded back into the black handle. There was a button on the handle. When Pepé pressed the button, the blade leaped out ready for use. The knife was with Pepé always, for it had been his father's knife.

One sunny morning when the sea below the cliff was glinting and blue and the white surf creamed on the reef, when even the

stone mountains looked kindly, Mama Torres called out the door of the shack, " Pepé, I have a labor for thee."

There was no answer. Mama listened. From behind the barn she heard a burst of laughter. She lifted her full long skirt and walked in the direction of the noise.

Pepé was sitting on the ground with his back against a box. His white teeth glistened. On either side of him stood the two black ones, tense and expectant. Fifteen feet away a redwood post was set in the ground. Pepé's right hand lay limply in his lap, and in the palm the big black knife rested. The blade was closed back into the handle. Pepé looked smiling at the sky.

Suddenly Emilio cried, " Ya! "

Pepé's wrist flicked like the head of a snake. The blade seemed to fly open in midair, and with a thump the point dug into the redwood post, and the black handle quivered. The three burst into excited laughter. Rosy ran to the post and pulled out the knife and brought it back to Pepé. He closed the blade and settled the knife carefully in his listless palm again. He grinned self-consciously at the sky.

" Ya! "

The heavy knife lanced out and sunk into the post again. Mama moved forward like a ship and scattered the play.

" All day you do foolish things with the knife, like a toy baby," she stormed. " Get up on thy huge feet that eat up shoes. Get up! " She took him by one loose shoulder and hoisted at him. Pepé grinned sheepishly and came halfheartedly to his feet. " Look! " Mama cried. " Big lazy, you must catch the horse and put on him thy father's saddle. You must ride to Monterey. The medicine bottle is empty. There is no salt. Go thou now, Peanut! Catch the horse."

A revolution took place in the relaxed figure of Pepé. " To Monterey, me? Alone? *Sí*, Mama."

She scowled at him. " Do not think, big sheep, that you will buy candy. No, I will give you only enough for the medicine and the salt."

Pepé smiled. " Mama, you will put the hatband on the hat? "

She relented then. " Yes, Pepé. You may wear the hatband."

His voice grew insinuating, " And the green handkerchief, Mama? "

" Yes, if you go quickly and return with no trouble, the silk green handkerchief will go. If you make sure to take off the handkerchief when you eat so no spot may fall on it."

" Sí, Mama. I will be careful. I am a man."

" Thou? A man? Thou art a peanut."

He went into the rickety barn and brought out a rope, and he walked agilely enough up the hill to catch the horse.

When he was ready and mounted before the door, mounted on his father's saddle that was so old that the oaken frame showed through torn leather in many places, then Mama brought out the round black hat with the tooled leather band, and she reached up and knotted the green silk handkerchief about his neck. Pepé's blue denim coat was much darker than his jeans, for it had been washed much less often.

Mama handed up the big medicine bottle and the silver coins. " That for the medicine," she said, " and that for the salt. That for a candle to burn for the papa. That for dulces [1] for the little ones. Our friend Mrs. Rodriguez [2] will give you dinner and maybe a bed for the night. When you go to the church say only ten paternosters and only twenty-five Ave Marias. Oh! I know, big coyote. You would sit there flapping your mouth over Aves all day while you looked at the candles and the holy pictures. That is not good devotion to stare at the pretty things."

The black hat, covering the high pointed head and black thatched hair of Pepé, gave him dignity and age. He sat the rangy horse well. Mama thought how handsome he was, dark and lean and tall. " I would not send thee now alone, thou little one, except for the medicine," she said softly. " It is not

good to have no medicine, for who knows when the toothache will come, or the sadness of the stomach. These things are."

" Adiós, [3] Mama," Pepé cried. " I will come back soon. You may send me often alone. I am a man."

" Thou art a foolish chicken."

He straightened his shoulders, flipped the reins against the horse's shoulder and rode away. He turned once and saw that they still watched him, Emilio and Rosy and Mama. Pepé grinned with pride and gladness and lifted the tough buckskin horse to a trot.

When he had dropped out of sight over a little dip in the road, Mama turned to the black ones, but she spoke to herself. " He is nearly a man now," she said. " It will be a nice thing to have a man in the house again." Her eyes sharpened on the children. " Go to the rocks now. The tide is going out. There will be abalones to be found." She put the iron hooks into their hands and saw them down the steep trail to the reefs. She brought the smooth stone metate to the doorway and sat grinding her corn to flour and looking occasionally at the road over which Pepé had gone. The noonday came and then the afternoon, when the little ones beat the abalones on a rock to make them tender and Mama patted the tortillas to make them thin. They ate their dinner as the red sun was plunging down toward the ocean. They sat on the doorsteps and watched a big white moon come over the mountaintops.

Mama said, " He is now at the house of our friend Mrs. Rodriguez. She will give him nice things to eat and maybe a present."

Emilio said, " Someday I, too, will ride to Monterey for medicine. Did Pepé come to be a man today? "

Mama said wisely, " A boy gets to be a man when a man is needed. Remember this thing. I have known boys forty years old because there was no need for a man."

Soon afterward they retired, Mama in her big oak bed on one side of the room, Emilio

---

[1] dulces (dōōl'sās): sweets. (Spanish.) [2] Rodriguez (rŏd-rē'gĕs).

[3] adiós (ä-dē-ōs'): good-by.

and Rosy in their boxes full of straw and sheepskins on the other side of the room.

The moon went over the sky and the surf roared on the rocks. The roosters crowed the first call. The surf subsided to a whispering surge against the reef. The moon dropped toward the sea. The roosters crowed again.

The moon was near down to the water when Pepé rode on a winded horse to his home flat. His dog bounced out and circled the horse yelping with pleasure. Pepé slid off the saddle to the ground. The weathered little shack was silver in the moonlight and the square shadow of it was black to the north and east. Against the east the piling mountains were misty with light; their tops melted into the sky.

Pepé walked wearily up the three steps and into the house. It was dark inside. There was a rustle in the corner.

Mama cried out from her bed. " Who comes? Pepé, is it thou? "

" *Sí*, Mama."

" Did you get the medicine? "

" *Sí*, Mama."

" Well, go to sleep, then. I thought you would be sleeping at the house of Mrs. Rodriguez." Pepé stood silently in the dark room. " Why do you stand there, Pepé? Did you drink wine? "

" *Sí*, Mama."

" Well, go to bed then and sleep out the wine."

His voice was tired and patient, but very firm. " Light the candle, Mama. I must go away into the mountains."

" What is this, Pepé? You are crazy." Mama struck a sulphur match and held the little blue burr until the flame spread up the stick. She set light to the candle on the floor beside her bed. " Now, Pepé, what is this you say? " She looked anxiously into his face.

He was changed. The fragile quality seemed to have gone from his chin. His mouth was less full than it had been, the lines of the lips were straighter, but in his eyes the greatest change had taken place. There was no laughter in them any more, nor any bashfulness. They were sharp and bright and purposeful.

He told her in a tired monotone, told her everything just as it had happened. A few people came into the kitchen of Mrs. Rodriguez. There was wine to drink. Pepé drank wine. The little quarrel — the man started toward Pepé and then the knife — it went almost by itself. It flew, it darted before Pepé knew it. As he talked, Mama's face grew stern, and it seemed to grow more lean. Pepé finished. " I am a man now, Mama. The man said names to me I could not allow."

Mama nodded. " Yes, thou art a man, my poor little Pepé. Thou art a man. I have seen it coming on thee. I have watched you throwing the knife into the post, and I have been afraid." For a moment her face had softened, but now it grew stern again. " Come! We must get you ready. Go. Awaken Emilio and Rosy. Go quickly."

Pepé stepped over to the corner where his brother and sister slept among the sheepskins. He leaned down and shook them gently. " Come, Rosy! Come, Emilio! The Mama says you must arise."

The little black ones sat up and rubbed their eyes in the candlelight. Mama was out of bed now, her long black skirt over her nightgown. " Emilio," she cried. " Go up and catch the other horse for Pepé. Quickly, now! Quickly." Emilio put his legs in his overalls and stumbled sleepily out the door.

" You heard no one behind you on the road? " Mama demanded.

" No, Mama. I listened carefully. No one was on the road."

Mama darted like a bird about the room. From a nail on the wall she took a canvas water bag and threw it on the floor. She stripped a blanket from her bed and rolled it into a tight tube and tied the ends with string. From a box beside the stove she lifted a flour sack half full of black stringy jerky. " Your father's black coat, Pepé. Here, put it on."

Pepé stood in the middle of the floor watching her activity. She reached behind the door and brought out the rifle, a long

38–56, worn shiny the whole length of the barrel. Pepé took it from her and held it in the crook of his elbow. Mama brought a little leather bag and counted the cartridges into his hand. " Only ten left," she warned. " You must not waste them."

Emilio put his head in the door. " *'Qui 'st 'l caballo*,[1] Mama."

" Put on the saddle from the other horse. Tie on the blanket. Here, tie the jerky to the saddle horn."

Still Pepé stood silently watching his mother's frantic activity. His chin looked hard, and his sweet mouth was drawn and thin. His little eyes followed Mama about the room almost suspiciously.

Rosy asked softly, " Where goes Pepé? "

Mama's eyes were fierce. " Pepé goes on a journey. Pepé is a man now. He has a man's thing to do."

Pepé straightened his shoulders. His mouth changed until he looked very much like Mama.

At last the preparation was finished. The loaded horse stood outside the door. The water bag dripped a line of moisture down the bay shoulder.

The moonlight was being thinned by the dawn, and the big white moon was near down to the sea. The family stood by the shack. Mama confronted Pepé. " Look, my son! Do not stop until it is dark again. Do not sleep even though you are tired. Take care of the horse in order that he may not stop of weariness. Remember to be careful with the bullets — there are only ten. Do not fill thy stomach with jerky or it will make thee sick. Eat a little jerky and fill thy stomach with grass. When thou comest to the high mountains, if thou seest any of the dark watching men, go not near to them nor try to speak to them. And forget not thy prayers." She put her lean hands on Pepé's shoulders, stood on her toes and kissed him formally on both cheeks, and Pepé kissed her on both cheeks. Then he went to Emilio and Rosy and kissed both of their cheeks.

[1] *'Qui 'st 'l caballo* (kēst'l kä-bä'yō): Here is the horse. (Colloquial Spanish.)

Pepé turned back to Mama. He seemed to look for a little softness, a little weakness in her. His eyes were searching, but Mama's face remained fierce. " Go now," she said. " Do not wait to be caught like a chicken."

Pepé pulled himself into the saddle. " I am a man," he said.

It was the first dawn when he rode up the hill toward the little canyon which let a trail into the mountains. Moonlight and daylight fought with each other, and the two warring qualities made it difficult to see. Before Pepé had gone a hundred yards, the outlines of his figure were misty; and long before he entered the canyon, he had become a gray, indefinite shadow.

Mama stood stiffly in front of her doorstep, and on either side of her stood Emilio and Rosy. They cast furtive glances at Mama now and then.

When the gray shape of Pepé melted into the hillside and disappeared, Mama relaxed. She began the high, whining keen of the death wail. " Our beautiful — our brave," she cried. " Our protector, our son is gone." Emilio and Rosy moaned beside her. " Our beautiful — our brave, he is gone." It was the formal wail. It rose to a high piercing whine and subsided to a moan. Mama raised it three times and then she turned and went into the house and shut the door.

Emilio and Rosy stood wondering in the dawn. They heard Mama whimpering in the house. They went out to sit on the cliff above the ocean. They touched shoulders. " When did Pepé come to be a man? " Emilio asked.

" Last night," said Rosy. " Last night in Monterey." The ocean clouds turned red with the sun that was behind the mountains.

" We will have no breakfast," said Emilio. " Mama will not want to cook." Rosy did not answer him. " Where is Pepé gone? " he asked.

Rosy looked around at him. She drew her knowledge from the quiet air. " He has gone on a journey. He will never come back."

" Is he dead? Do you think he is dead? "

Rosy looked back at the ocean again. A

little steamer, drawing a line of smoke, sat on the edge of the horizon. " He is not dead," Rosy explained. " Not yet."

Pepé rested the big rifle across the saddle in front of him. He let the horse walk up the hill and he didn't look back. The stony slope took on a coat of short brush so that Pepé found the entrance to a trail and entered it.

When he came to the canyon opening, he swung once in his saddle and looked back, but the houses were swallowed in the misty light. Pepé jerked forward again. The high shoulder of the canyon closed in on him. His horse stretched out its neck and sighed and settled to the trail.

It was a well-worn path, dark soft leaf-mold earth strewn with broken pieces of sandstone. The trail rounded the shoulder of the canyon and dropped steeply into the bed of the stream. In the shallows the water ran smoothly, glinting in the first morning sun. Small round stones on the bottom were as brown as rust with sun moss. In the sand along the edges of the stream the tall, rich wild mint grew, while in the water itself the cress, old and tough, had gone to heavy seed.

The path went into the stream and emerged on the other side. The horse sloshed into the water and stopped. Pepé' dropped his bridle and let the beast drink of the running water.

Soon the canyon sides became steep and the first giant sentinel redwoods guarded the trail, great round red trunks bearing foliage as green and lacy as ferns. Once Pepé was among the trees, the sun was lost. A perfumed and purple light lay in the pale green of the underbrush. Gooseberry bushes and blackberries and tall ferns lined the stream, and overhead the branches of the redwoods met and cut off the sky.

Pepé drank from the water bag, and he reached into the flour sack and brought out a black string of jerky. His white teeth gnawed at the string until the tough meat parted. He chewed slowly and drank occasionally from the water bag. His little eyes

were slumberous and tired, but the muscles of his face were hard-set. The earth of the trail was black now. It gave up a hollow sound under the walking hoofbeats.

The stream fell more sharply. Little waterfalls splashed on the stones. Five-fingered ferns hung over the water and dripped spray from their finger tips. Pepé rode half over in his saddle, dangling one leg loosely. He picked a bay leaf from a tree beside the way and put it into his mouth for a moment to flavor the dry jerky. He held the gun loosely across the pommel.

Suddenly he squared in his saddle, swung the horse from the trail and kicked it hurriedly up behind a big redwood tree. He pulled up the reins tight against the bit to keep the horse from whinnying. His face was intent and his nostrils quivered a little.

A hollow pounding came down the trail, and a horseman rode by, a fat man with red cheeks and a white stubble beard. His horse put down its head and blubbered at the trail when it came to the place where Pepé had turned off. " Hold up! " said the man, and he pulled up his horse's head.

When the last sound of the hoofs died away, Pepé came back into the trail again. He did not relax in the saddle any more. He lifted the big rifle and swung the lever to throw a shell into the chamber, and then he let down the hammer to half cock.

The trail grew very steep. Now the redwood trees were smaller and their tops were dead, bitten dead where the wind reached them. The horse plodded on; the sun went slowly overhead and started down toward the afternoon.

Where the stream came out of a side canyon, the trail left it. Pepé dismounted and watered his horse and filled up his water bag. As soon as the trail had parted from the stream, the trees were gone and only the thick brittle sage and manzanita and chaparral edged the trail. And the soft black earth was gone, too, leaving only the light tan broken rock for the trail bed. Lizards scampered away into the brush as the horse rattled over the little stones.

Pepé turned in his saddle and looked

back. He was in the open now: he could be seen from a distance. As he ascended the trail the country grew more rough and terrible and dry. The way wound about the bases of great square rocks. Little gray rabbits skittered in the brush. A bird made a monotonous high creaking. Eastward the bare rock mountaintops were pale and powder-dry under the dropping sun. The horse plodded up and up the trail toward a little V in the ridge which was the pass.

Pepé looked suspiciously back every minute or so, and his eyes sought the tops of the ridges ahead. Once, on a white barren spur, he saw a black figure for a moment; but he looked quickly away, for it was one of the dark watchers. No one knew who the watchers were, nor where they lived, but it was better to ignore them and never to show interest in them. They did not bother one who stayed on the trail and minded his own business.

The air was parched and full of light dust blown by the breeze from the eroding mountains. Pepé drank sparingly from his bag and corked it tightly and hung it on the horn again. The trail moved up the dry shale hillside, avoiding rocks, dropping under clefts, climbing in and out of old water scars. When he arrived at the little pass he stopped and looked back for a long time. No dark watchers were to be seen now. The trail behind was empty. Only the high tops of the redwoods indicated where the stream flowed.

Pepé rode on through the pass. His little eyes were nearly closed with weariness, but his face was stern, relentless, and manly. The high mountain wind coasted sighing through the pass and whistled on the edges of the big blocks of broken granite. In the air, a red-tailed hawk sailed over close to the ridge and screamed angrily. Pepé went slowly through the broken jagged pass and looked down on the other side.

The trail dropped quickly, staggering among broken rock. At the bottom of the slope there was a dark crease, thick with brush, and on the other side of the crease a little flat, in which a grove of oak trees

grew. A scar of green grass cut across the flat. And behind the flat another mountain rose, desolate with dead rocks and starving little black bushes. Pepé drank from the bag again, for the air was ·so dry that it encrusted his nostrils and burned his lips. He put the horse down the trail. The hoofs slipped and struggled on the steep way, starting little stones that rolled off into the brush. The sun was gone behind the westward mountain now, but still it glowed brilliantly on the oaks and on the grassy flat. The rocks and the hillsides still sent up waves of the heat they had gathered from the day's sun.

Pepé looked up to the top of the next dry withered ridge. He saw a dark form against the sky, a man's figure standing on top of a rock, and he glanced away quickly not to appear curious. When a moment later he looked up again, the figure was gone.

Downward the trail was quickly covered. Sometimes the horse floundered for footing, sometimes set his feet and slid a little way. They came at last to the bottom where the dark chaparral was higher than Pepé's head. He held up his rifle on one side and his arm on the other to shield his face from the sharp brittle fingers of the brush.

Up and out of the crease he rode, and up a little cliff. The grassy flat was before him, and the round comfortable oaks. For a moment he studied the trail down which he had come, but there was no movement and no sound from it. Finally he rode out over the flat, to the green streak, and at the upper end of the damp he found a little spring welling out of the earth and dropping into a dug basin before it seeped out over the flat.

Pepé filled his bag first, and then he let the thirsty horse drink out of the pool. He led the horse to the clump of oaks, and in the middle of the grove, fairly protected from sight on all sides, he took off the saddle and the bridle and laid them on the ground. The horse stretched his jaws sideways and yawned. Pepé knotted the lead rope about the horse's neck and tied him to a sapling among the oaks, where he could graze in a fairly large circle.

When the horse was gnawing hungrily at the dry grass, Pepé went to the saddle and took a black string of jerky from the sack and strolled to an oak tree on the edge of the grove, from under which he could watch the trail. He sat down in the crisp dry oak leaves and automatically felt for his big black knife to cut the jerky, but he had no knife. He leaned back on his elbow and gnawed at the tough strong meat. His face was blank, but it was a man's face.

The bright evening light washed the eastern ridge, but the valley was darkening. Doves flew down from the hills to the spring, and the quail came running out of the brush and joined them, calling clearly to one another.

Out of the corner of his eye Pepé saw a shadow grow out of the bushy crease. He turned his head slowly. A big spotted wildcat was creeping toward the spring, belly to the ground, moving like thought.

Pepé cocked his rifle and edged the muzzle slowly around. Then he looked apprehensively up the trail and dropped the hammer again. From the ground beside him he picked an oak twig and threw it toward the spring. The quail flew up with a roar and the doves whistled away. The big cat stood up: for a long moment he looked at Pepé with cold yellow eyes, and then fearlessly walked back into the gulch.

The dusk gathered quickly in the deep valley. Pepé muttered his prayers, put his head down on his arm and went instantly to sleep.

The moon came up and filled the valley with cold blue light, and the wind swept rustling down from the peaks. The owls worked up and down the slopes looking for rabbits. Down in the brush of the gulch a coyote gabbled. The oak trees whispered softly in the night breeze.

Pepé started up, listening. His horse had whinnied. The moon was just slipping behind the western ridge, leaving the valley in darkness behind it. Pepé sat tensely gripping his rifle. From far up the trail he heard an answering whinny and the crash of shod hoofs on the broken rock. He jumped to his feet, ran to his horse and led it under the trees. He threw on the saddle and cinched it tight for the steep trail, caught the unwilling head and forced the bit into the mouth. He felt the saddle to make sure the water bag and the sack of jerky were there. Then he mounted and turned up the hill.

It was velvet-dark. The horse found the entrance to the trail where it left the flat, and started up, stumbling and slipping on the rocks. Pepé's hand rose up to his head. His hat was gone. He had left it under the oak tree.

The horse had struggled far up the trail when the first change of dawn came into the air, a steel grayness as light mixed thoroughly with dark. Gradually the sharp snaggled edge of the ridge stood out above them, rotten granite tortured and eaten by the winds of time. Pepé had dropped his reins on the horn, leaving direction to the horse. The brush grabbed at his legs in the dark until one knee of his jeans was ripped.

Gradually the light flowed down over the ridge. The starved brush and rocks stood out in the half-light, strange and lonely in high perspective. Then there came warmth into the light. Pepé drew up and looked back, but he could see nothing in the darker valley below. The sky turned blue over the coming sun. In the waste of the mountainside, the poor dry brush grew only three feet high. Here and there, big outcroppings of unrotted granite stood up like moldering houses. Pepé relaxed a little. He drank from his water bag and bit off a piece of jerky. A single eagle flew over, high in the light.

Without warning Pepé's horse screamed and fell on its side. He was almost down before the rifle crash echoed up from the valley. From a hole behind the struggling shoulder, a stream of bright crimson blood pumped and stopped and pumped and stopped. The hoofs threshed on the ground. Pepé lay half stunned beside the horse. He looked slowly down the hill. A piece of sage clipped off beside his head and another crash echoed up from side to side of the canyon. Pepé flung himself frantically behind a bush.

He crawled up the hill on his knees and one hand. His right hand held the rifle up off the ground and pushed it ahead of him. He moved with the instinctive care of an animal. Rapidly he wormed his way toward one of the big outcroppings of granite on the hill above him. Where the brush was high he doubled up and ran; but where the cover was slight he wriggled forward on his stomach, pushing the rifle ahead of him. In the last little distance there was no cover at all. Pepé poised and then he darted across the space and flashed around the corner of the rock.

He leaned panting against the stone. When his breath came easier he moved along behind the big rock until he came to a narrow split that offered a thin section of vision down the hill. Pepé lay on his stomach and pushed the rifle barrel through the slit and waited.

The sun reddened the western ridges now. Already the buzzards were settling down toward the place where the horse lay. A small brown bird scratched in the dead sage leaves directly in front of the rifle muzzle. The coasting eagle flew back toward the rising sun.

Pepé saw a little movement in the brush far below. His grip tightened on the gun. A little brown doe stepped daintily out on the trail and crossed it and disappeared into the brush again. For a long time Pepé waited. Far below he could see the little flat and the oak trees and the slash of green. Suddenly his eyes flashed back at the trail again. A quarter of a mile down there had been a quick movement in the chaparral. The rifle swung over. The front sight nestled in the V of the rear sight. Pepé studied for a moment and then raised the rear sight a notch. The little movement in the brush came again. The sight settled on it. Pepé squeezed the trigger. The explosion crashed down the mountain and up the other side, and came rattling back. The whole side of the slope grew still. No more movement.

And then a white streak cut into the granite of the slit and a bullet whined away and a crash sounded up from below. Pepé felt a sharp pain in his right hand. A sliver of granite was sticking out from between his first and second knuckles and the point protruded from his palm. Carefully he pulled out the sliver of stone. The wound bled evenly and gently. No vein nor artery was cut.

Pepé looked into a little dusty cave in the rock and gathered a handful of spider web, and he pressed the mass into the cut, plastering the soft web into the blood. The flow stopped almost at once.

The rifle was on the ground. Pepé picked it up, levered a new shell into the chamber. And then he slid into the brush on his stomach. Far to the right he crawled, and then up the hill, moving slowly and carefully, crawling to cover and resting and then crawling again.

In the mountains the sun is high in its arc before it penetrates the gorges. The hot face looked over the hill and brought instant heat with it. The white light beat on the rocks and reflected from them and rose up quivering from the earth again, and the rocks and bushes seemed to quiver behind the air.

Pepé crawled in the general direction of the ridge peak, zigzagging for cover. The deep cut between his knuckles began to throb. He crawled close to a rattlesnake before he saw it, and when it raised its dry head and made a soft beginning whir, he backed up and took another way. The quick gray lizards flashed in front of him, raising a tiny line of dust. He found another mass of spider web and pressed it against his throbbing hand.

Pepé was pushing the rifle with his left hand now. Little drops of sweat ran to the ends of his coarse black hair and rolled down his cheeks. His lips and tongue were growing thick and heavy. His lips writhed to draw saliva into his mouth. His little dark eyes were uneasy and suspicious. Once when a gray lizard paused in front of him on the parched ground and turned

VIEW OF THE HIGH SIERRAS. Against the harsh beauty of the bleak California mountains, young Pepé made his last fight. (Muench from Frederic Lewis)

its head sideways he crushed it flat with a stone.

When the sun slid past noon he had not gone a mile. He crawled exhaustedly a last hundred yards to a patch of high sharp manzanita, crawled desperately, and when the patch was reached he wriggled in among the tough gnarly trunks and dropped his head on his left arm. There was little shade in the meager brush, but there was cover and safety. Pepé went to sleep as he lay and the sun beat on his back. A few little birds hopped close to him and peered and hopped away. Pepé squirmed in his sleep and he raised and dropped his wounded hand again and again.

The sun went down behind the peaks and the cool evening came, and then the dark. A coyote yelled from the hillside. Pepé started awake and looked about with misty eyes. His hand was swollen and heavy; a little thread of pain ran up the inside of his arm and settled in a pocket in his armpit. He peered about and then stood up, for the mountains were black and the moon had not yet risen. Pepé stood up in the dark. The coat of his father pressed on his arm. His tongue was swollen until it nearly filled his mouth. He wriggled out of the coat and dropped it in the brush, and then he struggled up the hill, falling over rocks and tearing his way through the brush. The rifle knocked against stones as he went. Little dry avalanches of gravel and shattered stone went whispering down the hill behind him.

After a while the old moon came up and showed the jagged ridgetop ahead of him. By moonlight Pepé traveled more easily. He bent forward so that his throbbing arm hung away from his body. The journey uphill was made in dashes and rests, a frantic rush up a few yards and then a rest. The wind coasted down the slope rattling the dry stems of the bushes.

The moon was at meridian when Pepé came at last to the sharp backbone of the ridgetop. On the last hundred yards of the rise no soil had clung under the wearing winds. The way was on solid rock. He clambered to the top and looked down on the other side. There was a draw like the last below him, misty with moonlight, brushed with dry struggling sage and chaparral. On the other side the hill rose up sharply and at the top the jagged rotten teeth of the mountain showed against the sky. At the bottom of the cut the brush was thick and dark.

Pepé stumbled down the hill. His throat was almost closed with thirst. At first he tried to run, but immediately he fell and rolled. After that he went more carefully. The moon was just disappearing behind the mountains when he came to the bottom. He crawled into the heavy brush, feeling with his fingers for water. There was no water in the bed of the stream, only damp earth. Pepé laid his gun down and scooped up a handful of mud and put it in his mouth, and then he spluttered and scraped the earth from his tongue with his finger, for the mud drew at his mouth like a poultice. He dug a hole in the stream bed with his fingers, dug a little basin to catch water; but before it was very deep his head fell forward on the damp ground and he slept.

The dawn came and the heat of the day fell on the earth, and still Pepé slept. Late in the afternoon his head jerked up. He looked slowly around. His eyes were slits of weariness. Twenty feet away in the heavy brush a big tawny mountain lion stood looking at him. Its long thick tail waved gracefully; its ears were erect with interest, not laid back dangerously. The lion squatted down on its stomach and watched him.

Pepé looked at the hole he had dug in the earth. A half inch of muddy water had collected in the bottom. He tore the sleeve from his hurt arm, with his teeth ripped out a little square, soaked it in the water and put it in his mouth. Over and over he filled the cloth and sucked it.

Still the lion sat and watched him. The evening came down but there was no movement on the hills. No birds visited the dry bottom of the cut. Pepé looked occasionally at the lion. The eyes of the yellow beast drooped as though he were about to sleep.

He yawned and his long thin red tongue curled out. Suddenly his head jerked around and his nostrils quivered. His big tail lashed. He stood up and slunk like a tawny shadow into the thick brush.

A moment later Pepé heard the sound, the faint far crash of horses' hoofs on gravel. And he heard something else, a high whining yelp of a dog.

Pepé took his rifle in his left hand and he glided into the brush almost as quietly as the lion had. In the darkening evening he crouched up the hill toward the next ridge. Only when the dark came did he stand up. His energy was short. Once it was dark he fell over the rocks and slipped to his knees on the steep slope, but he moved on and on up the hill, climbing and scrabbling over the broken hillside.

When he was far up toward the top, he lay down and slept for a little while. The withered moon, shining on his face, awakened him. He stood up and moved up the hill. Fifty yards away he stopped and turned back, for he had forgotten his rifle. He walked heavily down and poked about in the brush, but he could not find his gun. At last he lay down to rest. The pocket of pain in his armpit had grown more sharp. His arm seemed to swell out and fall with every heartbeat. There was no position lying down where the heavy arm did not press against his armpit.

With the effort of a hurt beast, Pepé got up and moved again toward the top of the ridge. He held his swollen arm away from his body with his left hand. Up the steep hill he dragged himself, a few steps and a rest, and a few more steps. At last he was nearing the top. The moon showed the uneven sharp back of it against the sky.

Pepé's brain spun in a big spiral up and away from him. He slumped to the ground and lay still. The rock ridgetop was only a hundred feet above him.

The moon moved over the sky. Pepé half turned on his back. His tongue tried to make words, but only a thick hissing came from between his lips.

When the dawn came, Pepé pulled himself up. His eyes were sane again. He drew his great puffed arm in front of him and looked at the angry wound. The black line ran up from his wrist to his armpit. Automatically he reached in his pocket for the big black knife, but it was not there. His eyes searched the ground. He picked up a sharp blade of stone and scraped at the wound, sawed at the proud flesh and then squeezed the green juice out in big drops. Instantly he threw back his head and whined like a dog. His whole right side shuddered at the pain, but the pain cleared his head.

In the gray light he struggled up the last slope to the ridge and crawled over and lay down behind a line of rocks. Below him lay a deep canyon exactly like the last, waterless and desolate. There was no flat, no oak trees, not even heavy brush in the bottom of it. And on the other side a sharp ridge stood up, thinly brushed with starving sage, littered with broken granite. Strewn over the hill there were giant outcroppings, and on the top the granite teeth stood out against the sky.

The new day was light now. The flame of the sun came over the ridge and fell on Pepé where he lay on the ground. His coarse black hair was littered with twigs and bits of spider web. His eyes had retreated back into his head. Between his lips the tip of his black tongue showed.

He sat up and dragged his great arm into his lap and nursed it, rocking his body and moaning in his throat. He threw back his head and looked up into the pale sky. A big black bird circled nearly out of sight, and far to the left another was sailing near.

He lifted his head to listen, for a familiar sound had come to him from the valley he had climbed out of; it was the crying yelp of hounds, excited and feverish, on a trail.

Pepé bowed his head quickly. He tried to speak rapid words but only a thick hiss came from his lips. He drew a shaky cross on his breast with his left hand. It was a long struggle to get to his feet. He crawled slowly and mechanically to the top of a big rock on the ridge peak. Once there, he arose slowly, swaying to his feet, and stood erect. Far below he could see the dark brush where he had slept. He braced his feet and stood there, black against the morning sky.

There came a ripping sound at his feet. A piece of stone flew up and a bullet droned off into the next gorge. The hollow crash echoed up from below. Pepé looked down for a moment and then pulled himself straight again.

His body jarred back. His left hand fluttered helplessly toward his breast. The second crash sounded from below. Pepé swung forward and toppled from the rock. His body struck and rolled over and over, starting a little avalanche. And when at last he stopped against a bush, the avalanche slid slowly down and covered up his head.

## Suggestions for Study

1. Find Mama Torres's statement about a boy's becoming a man. Discuss the changes that came over Pepé as a result of the murder. Of what significance is the fact that Pepé chose the manner of his death?

2. Discuss whether it was right for the mother to help Pepé escape.

3. Compare this story and " To Build a Fire." How are they similar in plot structure and in use of detail? Compare the two leading characters. What contrast do you feel between London's attitude toward his character and John Steinbeck's attitude toward Pepé? Read again the first question on " To Build a Fire." Which kind of interest do you have in " Flight " — curiosity or suspense? Enumerate the details by which the author renders the outcome increasingly certain.

4. The play The Emperor Jones by Eugene O'Neill tells of another dramatic and terrible flight. Read it and compare the two stories.

5. Read The Yearling by Marjorie Kinnan Rawlings to find a more extended treatment of the ordeal of growing up.

6. Write an account of some journey against odds, such as one to escape from an approaching storm or to rush an injured person to a hospital. Use a setting with which you are familiar, and include details of the background which contribute to the vividness and suspense.

7. Vocabulary: aphids, metate, abalones, tortillas, jerky, pommel, chaparral, manzanita.

## Jesse Stuart            1907–

A product of the Kentucky back country, the first member of his family ever to get a college education, Jesse Stuart has the earnestness and courage to write about his own region and folk and to tell their stories in the simple, colloquial style that is native to them and to him. He wrote his first poems on pale poplar leaves. He literally fought his own way through school and college, as you may see if you read his autobiography, Beyond the Dark Hills, or his first novel, Trees of Heaven (1940).

Earnestness is perhaps the outstanding characteristic of this young man; he is too earnest to exploit his locale merely for its picturesqueness. He has expressed his love for the beauty of the dark hills of Kentucky in simple, earthy poems which have caused some critics to hail him as the American Burns. He loves the backward people of the hill country and, feeling himself one of them, seeks to present them in his stories with insight and without distortion. His earnestness shows not only in his writing. A teacher of English in county high schools in Kentucky and Ohio, he says, " I've had nine years of experience with high-school students. If I know anything on earth, it is I do know how to get literature over to them — even the toughest boys. Last year I taught remedial English in Portsmouth High School. I had 'most all the boys on the football team — they never lost a game in Ohio — big boys — two-hundred-pounders. They thought to get a teacher whose poetry had appeared in books and magazines, they'd get a ' sissy ' or ' softie ' — they changed their minds. I had those boys reading poetry and stories and loving to do it. I'd read them my stories before I sent them away — they turned out to be my best critics."

Of one of his best stories, " Eustacia," he says, " I wrote a short story about a high-school girl — revised it seven times and sent it thirty-one trips to magazines. The story eventually sold to Household Magazine and was selected this year by Edward J. O'Brien for his 1939 collection of The Best Short Stories. The story is a struggle for a girl to get an education among the hills of Kentucky — an honest, actual portrait. When I sold the story, I gave the girl the proceeds to enter college — she is in Berea College, Berea, Kentucky, today."

A writer so vigorous, honest, and individual is peculiarly American. Jesse Stuart is a young man still. Remember his name and watch his progress.

## SPLIT CHERRY TREE

In contrast to the carefully plotted and shrewdly integrated stories of most writers, " Split Cherry Tree " will seem to you somewhat formless and loose-jointed. Reading this story is like listening to a storyteller who is propped in the sun against the side of a mountain cabin and whittling away as he drawls; " Split Cherry Tree " is a yarn in the vernacular. Yet it is more than that, too, for in it is revealed Jesse Stuart's sincere interest in the problem of bringing education to the hill people.

" I don't mind staying after school," I says to Professor Herbert, " but I'd rather you'd whip me with a switch and let me go home early. Pa will whip me anyway for getting home two hours late."

" You are too big to whip," says Professor Herbert, " and I have to punish you for climbing up in that cherry tree. You boys knew better than that! The other five boys have paid their dollar each. You have been the only one who has not helped pay for the tree. Can't you borrow a dollar? "

" I can't," I says. " I'll have to take the punishment. I wish it would be quicker punishment. I wouldn't mind."

Professor Herbert stood and looked at me. He was a big man. He wore a gray suit of clothes. The suit matched his gray hair.

" You don't know my father," I says to Professor Herbert. " He might be called a little old-fashioned. He makes us mind him until we're twenty-one years old. He believes: ' If you spare the rod you spoil the child.' I'll never be able to make him understand about the cherry tree. I'm the first of my people to go to high school."

" You must take the punishment," says Professor Herbert. " You must stay two hours after school today and two hours after school tomorrow. I am allowing you twenty-five cents an hour. That is good

money for a high-school student. You can sweep the schoolhouse floor, wash the blackboards, and clean windows. I'll pay the dollar for you."

I couldn't ask Professor Herbert to loan me a dollar. He never offered to loan it to me. I had to stay and help the janitor and work out my fine at a quarter an hour.

I thought as I swept the floor, " What will Pa do to me? What lie can I tell him when I go home? Why did we ever climb that cherry tree and break it down for anyway? Why did we run crazy over the hills away from the crowd? Why did we do all of this? Six of us climbed up in a little cherry tree after one little lizard! Why did the tree split and fall with us? It should have been a stronger tree! Why did Eif Crabtree just happen to be below us plowing and catch us in his cherry tree? Why wasn't he a better man than to charge us six dollars for the tree? "

It was six o'clock when I left the schoolhouse. I had six miles to walk home. It would be after seven when I got home. I had all my work to do when I got home. It took Pa and me both to do the work. Seven cows to milk. Nineteen head of cattle to feed, four mules, twenty-five hogs, firewood and stovewood to cut, and water to draw from the well. He would be doing it when I got home. He would be mad and wondering what was keeping me!

I hurried home. I would run under the dark, leafless trees. I would walk fast uphill. I would run down the hill. The ground was freezing. I had to hurry. I had to run. I reached the long ridge that led to our cow pasture. I ran along this ridge. The wind dried the sweat on my face. I ran across the pasture to the house.

I threw down my books in the chipyard. I ran to the barn to spread fodder on the ground for the cattle. I didn't take time to change my clean school clothes for my old work clothes. I ran out to the barn. I saw Pa spreading fodder on the ground to the cattle. That was my job. I ran up to the fence. I says, " Leave that for me, Pa. I'll do it. I'm just a little late."

" I see you are," says Pa. He turned and looked at me. His eyes danced fire. " What in th' world has kept you so? Why ain't you been here to help me with this work? Make a gentleman out'n one boy in th' family and this is what you get! Send you to high school and you get too onery fer th' buzzards to smell! "

I never said anything. I didn't want to tell why I was late from school. Pa stopped scattering the bundles of fodder. He looked at me. He says, " Why are you gettin' in here this time o' night? You tell me or I'll take a hickory withe to you right here on th' spot! "

I says, " I had to stay after school." I couldn't lie to Pa. He'd go to school and find out why I had to stay. If I lied to him it would be too bad for me.

" Why did you haf to stay atter school? " says Pa.

I says, " Our biology class went on a field trip today. Six of us boys broke down a cherry tree. We had to give a dollar apiece to pay for the tree. I didn't have the dollar. Professor Herbert is making me work out my dollar. He gives me twenty-five cents an hour. I had to stay in this afternoon. I'll have to stay in tomorrow afternoon! "

" Are you telling me th' truth? " says Pa.

" I'm telling you the truth," I says. " Go and see for yourself."

" That's jist what I'll do in th' mornin'," says Pa. " Jist whose cherry tree did you break down? "

" Eif Crabtree's cherry tree! "

" What was you doin' clear out in Eif Crabtree's place? " says Pa. " He lives four miles from th' county high school. Don't they teach you no books at that high school? Do they jist let you get out and gad over th' hillsides? If that's all they do I'll keep you at home, Dave. I've got work here fer you to do! "

" Pa," I says, " spring is just getting here. We take a subject in school where we have to have bugs, snakes, flowers, lizards, frogs, and plants. It is biology. It was a pretty day today. We went out to find a few of these. Six of us boys saw a lizard at the same time sunning on a cherry tree. We all went up the tree to get it. We broke the tree down. It split at the forks. Eif Crabtree was plowing down below us. He ran up the hill and got our names. The other boys gave their dollar apiece. I didn't have mine. Professor Herbert put mine in for me. I have to work it out at school."

" Poor man's son, huh," says Pa. " I'll attend to that myself in th' mornin'. I'll take keer o' 'im. He ain't from this county nohow. I'll go down there in th' mornin' and see 'im. Lettin' you leave your books and galavant all over th' hills. What kind of a school is it nohow! Didn't do that, my son, when I's a little shaver in school. All fared alike too."

" Pa, please don't go down there," I says, " just let me have fifty cents and pay the rest of my fine! I don't want you to go down there! I don't want you to start anything with Professor Herbert! "

" Ashamed of your old Pap are you, Dave," says Pa, " atter th' way I've worked to raise you! Tryin' to send you to school so you can make a better livin' than I've made.

" I'll straighten this thing out myself! I'll take keer o' Professor Herbert myself! He ain't got no right to keep you in and let the other boys off jist because they've got th' money! I'm a poor man. A bullet will go in a professor same as it will any man. It will go in a rich man same as it will a poor man. Now you get into this work before I take one o' these withes and cut the shirt off'n your back! "

I thought once I'd run through the woods above the barn just as hard as I could go. I thought I'd leave high school and home forever! Pa could not catch me! I'd get away! I couldn't go back to school with him. He'd have a gun and maybe he'd shoot Professor Herbert. It was hard to tell what he would do. I could tell Pa that school had changed in the hills from the way it was when he was a boy, but he wouldn't understand. I could tell him we studied frogs, birds, snakes, lizards, flowers, insects. But Pa wouldn't understand. If I did run away from home it wouldn't matter to Pa. He would see Professor Herbert anyway. He would think that high school and Professor Herbert had run me away from home. There was no need to run away. I'd just have to stay, finish foddering the cattle, and go to school with Pa the next morning.

I would take a bundle of fodder, remove the hickory witheband from around it, and scatter it on rocks, clumps of green briers, and brush so the cattle wouldn't tramp it under their feet. I would lean it up against the oak trees and the rocks in the pasture just above our pigpen on the hill. The fodder was cold and frosty where it had set out in the stacks. I would carry bundles of the fodder from the stack until I had spread out a bundle for each steer. Pa went to the barn to feed the mules and throw corn in the pen to the hogs.

The moon shone bright in the cold March sky. I finished my work by moonlight. Professor Herbert really didn't know how much work I had to do at home. If he had known he would not have kept me after school. He would have loaned me a dollar to have paid my part on the cherry tree. He had never lived in the hills. He didn't know the way the hill boys had to work so that they could go to school. Now he was teaching in a county high school where all the boys who attended were from hill farms.

After I'd finished doing my work I went to the house and ate my supper. Pa and Mom had eaten. My supper was getting cold. I heard Pa and Mom talking in the front room. Pa was telling Mom about me staying in after school.

" I had to do all th' milkin' tonight, chop th' wood myself. It's too hard on me atter I've turned ground all day. I'm goin' to take a day off tomorrow and see if I can't remedy things a little. I'll go down to that high school tomorrow. I won't be a very good scholar fer Professor Herbert nohow. He won't keep me in atter school. I'll take a different kind of lesson down there and make 'im acquainted with it."

" Now, Luster," says Mom, " you jist stay away from there. Don't cause a lot o' trouble. You can be jailed fer a trick like that. You'll get th' Law atter you. You'll jist go down there and show off and plague your own boy Dave to death in front o' all th' scholars! "

" Plague or no plague," says Pa, " he don't take into consideration what all I haf to do here, does he? I'll show 'im it ain't right to keep one boy in and let the rest go scot free. My boy is good as th' rest, ain't he? A bullet will make a hole in a schoolteacher same as it will anybody else. He can't do me that way and get by with it. I'll plug 'im first. I aim to go down there bright and early in the mornin' and get all this straight! I aim to see about bug larnin' and this runnin' all over God's creation huntin' snakes, lizards, and frogs. Ransackin' th' country and goin' through cherry orchards and breakin' th' trees down atter lizards! Old Eif Crabtree ought to a-poured th' hot lead to 'em instead o' chargin' six dollars fer th' tree! He ought to a-got old Herbert th' first one! "

I ate my supper. I slipped upstairs and lit the lamp. I tried to forget the whole thing. I studied plane geometry. Then I studied my biology lesson. I could hardly study for thinking about Pa. " He'll go to school with me in the morning. He'll take a gun for Professor Herbert! What will Professor Herbert think of me! I'll tell him when Pa leaves that I couldn't help it. But Pa might shoot him. I hate to go with Pa. Maybe he'll cool off about it tonight and not go in the morning."

Pa got up at four o'clock. He built a fire in the stove. Then he built a fire in the fireplace. He got Mom up to get breakfast. Then he got me up to help feed and milk. By the time we had our work done at the barn, Mom had breakfast ready for us. We ate our breakfast. Daylight came and we could see the bare oak trees covered white with frost. The hills were white with frost. A cold wind was blowing. The sky was clear. The sun would soon come out and melt the frost. The afternoon would be warm with sunshine and the frozen ground with thaw. There would be mud on the hills again.

Muddy water would then run down the little ditches on the hills.

" Now, Dave," says Pa, " let's get ready fer school. I aim to go with you this mornin' and look into bug larnin', frog larnin', lizard and snake larnin', and breakin' down cherry trees! I don't like no sicha foolish way o' larnin' myself! "

Pa hadn't forgot. I'd have to take him to school with me. He would take me to school with him. We were going early. I was glad we were going early. If Pa pulled a gun on Professor Herbert there wouldn't be so many of my classmates there to see him.

I knew that Pa wouldn't be at home in the high school. He wore overalls, big boots, a blue shirt and a sheepskin coat and a slouched black hat gone to seed at the top. He put his gun in its holster. We started trudging toward the high school across the hill.

It was early when we got to the county high school. Professor Herbert had just got there. I just thought as we walked up the steps into the schoolhouse, " Maybe Pa will find out Professor Herbert is a good man. He just doesn't know him. Just like I felt toward the Lambert boys across the hill. I didn't like them until I'd seen them and talked to them. After I went to school with them and talked to them, I liked them and we were friends. It's a lot in knowing the other fellow."

" You're th' Professor here, ain't you? " says Pa.

" Yes," says Professor Herbert, " and you are Dave's father."

" Yes," says Pa, pulling out his gun and laying it on the seat in Professor Herbert's office. Professor Herbert's eyes got big behind his black-rimmed glasses when he saw Pa's gun. Color came into his pale cheeks.

" Jist a few things about this school I want to know," says Pa. " I'm tryin' to make a scholar out'n Dave. He's the only one out'n eleven youngins I've sent to high school. Here he comes in late and leaves me all th' work to do! He said you's all out bug huntin' yesterday and broke a cherry

tree down. He had to stay two hours atter school yesterday and work out money to pay on that cherry tree! Is that right? "

" Wwwwy," says Professor Herbert, " I guess it is."

He looked at Pa's gun.

" Well," says Pa, " this ain't no high school. It's a bug school, a lizard school, a snake school! It ain't no school nohow! "

" Why did you bring that gun? " says Professor Herbert to Pa.

" You see that little hole," says Pa as he picked up the long blue forty-four and put his finger on the end of the barrel, " a bullet can come out'n that hole that will kill a schoolteacher same as it will any other man. It will kill a rich man same as a poor man. It will kill a man. But atter I come in and saw you, I know'd I wouldn't need it. This maul o' mine could do you up in a few minutes."

Pa stood there, big, hard, brown-skinned, and mighty beside of Professor Herbert. I didn't know Pa was so much bigger and harder. I'd never seen Pa in a schoolhouse before. I'd seen Professor Herbert. He'd aways looked big before to me. He didn't look big standing beside of Pa.

" I was only doing my duty," says Professor Herbert, " Mr. Sexton, and following the course of study the state provided us with."

" Course o' study," says Pa, " what study, bug study? Varmint study? Takin' youngins to th' woods and their poor old Ma's and Pa's at home a-slavin' to keep 'em in school and give 'em a education! You know that's dangerous, too, puttin' a lot o' boys and girls out together like that! "

Students were coming into the schoolhouse now.

Professor Herbert says, " Close the door, Dave, so others won't hear."

I walked over and closed the door. I was shaking like a leaf in the wind. I thought Pa was going to hit Professor Herbert every minute. He was doing all the talking. His face was getting red. The red color was coming through the brown, weather-beaten skin on Pa's face.

KENTUCKY MOUNTAIN HOME. People from remote dwellings like this are often suspicious of schools and book learning — at first. (Ewing Galloway)

"I was right with these students," says Professor Herbert. "I know what they got into and what they didn't. I didn't send one of the other teachers with them on this field trip. I went myself. Yes, I took the boys and girls together. Why not?"

"It jist don't look good to me," says Pa, "a-takin' all this swarm of youngins out to pillage th' whole deestrict. Breakin' down cherry trees. Keepin' boys in atter school."

"What else could I have done with Dave, Mr. Sexton?" says Professor Herbert. "The boys didn't have any business all climbing that cherry tree after one lizard. One boy could have gone up in the tree and got it. The farmer charged us six dollars. It was a little steep, I think, but we had it to pay. Must I make five boys pay and let your boy off? He said he didn't have the dollar and couldn't get it. So I put it in for him. I'm letting him work it out. He's not working for me. He's working for the school!"

"I jist don't know what you could a-done

with 'im," says Pa, "only a-larruped 'im with a withe! That's what he needed!"

"He's too big to whip," says Professor Herbert, pointing at me. "He's a man in size."

"He's not too big fer me to whip," says Pa. "They ain't too big until they're over twenty-one! It jist didn't look fair to me! Work one and let th' rest out because they got th' money. I don't see what bugs has got to do with a high school! It don't look good to me nohow!"

Pa picked up his gun and put it back in its holster. The red color left Professor Herbert's face. He talked more to Pa. Pa softened a little. It looked funny to see Pa in the high-school building. It was the first time he'd ever been there.

"We were not only hunting snakes, toads, flowers, butterflies, lizards," says Professor Herbert, "but, Mr. Sexton, I was hunting dry timothy grass to put in an incubator and raise some protozoa."

" I don't know what that is," says Pa. " Th' incubator is th' new-fangled way o' cheatin' th' hens and raisin' chickens. I ain't so sure about th' breed o' chickens you mentioned."

" You've heard of germs, Mr. Sexton, haven't you? " says Professor Herbert.

" Jist call me Luster, if you don't mind," says Pa, very casual-like.

" All right, Luster, you've heard of germs, haven't you? "

" Yes," says Pa, " but I don't believe in germs. I'm sixty-five years old and I ain't seen one yet! "

" You can't see them with your naked eye," says Professor Herbert. " Just keep that gun in the holster and stay with me in the high school today. I have a few things I want to show you. That scum on your teeth has germs in it."

" What," says Pa, " you mean to tell me I've got germs on my teeth! "

" Yes," says Professor Herbert. " The same kind as we might be able to find in a living black snake if we dissect it! "

" I don't mean to dispute your word," says Pa, " but I don't believe it. I don't believe I have germs on my teeth! "

" Stay with me today and I'll show you. I want to take you through the school any-way! School has changed a lot in the hills since you went to school. I don't guess we had high schools in this county when you went to school! "

" No," says Pa, " jist readin', writin', and cipherin'. We didn't have all this bug larnin', frog larnin', and findin' germs on your teeth and in the middle o' black snakes! Th' world's changin'."

" It is," says Professor Herbert, " and we hope all for the better. Boys like your own there are going to help change it. He's your boy. He knows all of what I've told you. You stay with me today."

" I'll shore stay with you," says Pa. " I want to see th' germs off'n my teeth. I jist want to see a germ. I've never seen one in my life. ' Seein' is believin',' Pap allus told me."

Pa walks out of the office with Professor Herbert. I just hoped Professor Herbert didn't have Pa arrested for pulling his gun. Pa's gun has always been a friend to him when he goes to settle disputes.

The bell rang. School took up. I saw the students when they marched in the school-house look at Pa. They would grin and punch each other. Pa just stood and watched them pass in at the schoolhouse door. Two long lines marched in the house. The boys and girls were clean and well dressed. Pa stood over in the schoolyard under a leaf-less elm, in his sheepskin coat, his big boots laced in front with buckskin, and his heavy socks stuck above his boot tops. Pa's over-alls legs were baggy and wrinkled be-tween his coat and boot tops. His blue work shirt showed at the collar. His big black hat showed his gray-streaked black hair. His face was hard and weather-tanned to the color of a ripe fodder blade. His hands were big and gnarled like the roots of the elm tree he stood beside.

When I went to my first class I saw Pa and Professor Herbert going around over the schoolhouse. I was in my geometry class when Pa and Professor Herbert came in the room. We were explaining our propo-sitions on the blackboard. Professor Her-bert and Pa just quietly came in and sat down for a while. I heard Fred Wurts whis-per to Glenn Armstrong, " Who is that old man? Lord, he's a rough-looking scamp." Glenn whispered back, " I think he's Dave's Pap." The students in geometry looked at Pa. They must have wondered what he was doing in school. Before the class was over, Pa and Professor Herbert got up and went out. I saw them together down on the play-ground. Professor Herbert was explaining to Pa. I could see the prints of Pa's gun under his coat when he'd walk around.

At noon in the high-school cafeteria Pa and Professor Herbert sat together at the little table where Professor Herbert always ate by himself. They ate together. The stu-dents watched the way Pa ate. He ate with his knife instead of his fork. A lot of the stu-dents felt sorry for me after they found out he was my father. They didn't have to feel sorry for me. I wasn't ashamed of Pa after I found out he wasn't going to shoot Professor Herbert. I was glad they had made friends. I wasn't ashamed of Pa. I wouldn't be as long as he behaved. He would find out about the high school as I had found out about the Lambert boys across the hill.

In the afternoon when we went to biology Pa was in the class. He was sitting on one of the high stools beside the microscope. We went ahead with our work just as if Pa wasn't in the class. I saw Pa take his knife and scrape tartar from one of his teeth. Professor Herbert put it on the lens and adjusted the microscope for Pa. He adjusted it and worked awhile. Then he says: " Now Luster, look! Put your eye right down to the light. Squint the other eye! "

Pa put his head down and did as Professor Herbert said. " I see 'im," says Pa. " Who'd a ever thought that? Right on a body's teeth! Right in a body's mouth. You're right certain they ain't no fake to this, Professor Herbert? "

" No, Luster," says Professor Herbert. " It's there. That's the germ. Germs live in a world we cannot see with the naked eye. We must use the microscope. There are millions of them in our bodies. Some are harmful. Others are helpful."

Pa holds his face down and looks through the microscope. We stop and watch Pa. He sits upon the tall stool. His knees are against the table. His legs are long. His coat slips up behind when he bends over. The handle of his gun shows. Professor Herbert pulls his coat down quickly.

" Oh, yes," says Pa. He gets up and pulls his coat down. Pa's face gets a little red. He knows about his gun and he knows he doesn't have any use for it in high school.

" We have a big black snake over here we caught yesterday," says Professor Herbert. " We'll chloroform him and dissect him and show you he has germs in his body, too."

" Don't do it," says Pa. " I believe you. I jist don't want to see you kill the black snake. I never kill one. They are good

mousers and a lot o' help to us on the farm. I like black snakes. I jist hate to see people kill 'em. I don't allow 'em killed on my place."

The students look at Pa. They seem to like him better after he said that. Pa with a gun in his pocket but a tender heart beneath his ribs for snakes, but not for man! Pa won't whip a mule at home. He won't whip his cattle.

" Man can defend hisself," says Pa, " but cattle and mules can't. We have the drop on 'em. Ain't nothin' to a man that'll beat a good pullin' mule. He ain't got th' right kind o' a heart! "

Professor Herbert took Pa through the laboratory. He showed him the different kinds of work we were doing. He showed him our equipment. They stood and talked while we worked. Then they walked out together. They talked louder when they got out in the hall.

When our biology class was over I walked out of the room. It was our last class for the day. I would have to take my broom and sweep two hours to finish paying for the split cherry tree. I just wondered if Pa would want me to stay. He was standing in the hallway watching the students march out. He looked lost among us. He looked like a leaf turned brown on the tree among the treetop filled with growing leaves.

I got my broom and started to sweep. Professor Herbert walked up and says. " I'm going to let you do that some other time. You can go home with your father. He is waiting out there."

I laid my broom down, got my books, and went down the steps.

Pa says, " Ain't you got two hours o' sweepin' yet to do? "

I says, " Professor Herbert said I could do it some other time. He said for me to go home with you."

" No," says Pa. " You are goin' to do as he says. He's a good man. School has changed from my day and time. I'm a dead leaf, Dave. I'm behind. I don't belong here. If he'll let me I'll get a broom and we'll both sweep one hour. That pays your debt.

I'll hep you pay it. I'll ast 'im and see if he won't let me hep you."

" I'm going to cancel the debt," says Professor Herbert. " I just wanted you to understand, Luster."

" I understand," says Pa, " and since I understand, he must pay his debt fer th' tree and I'm goin' to hep 'im."

" Don't do that," says Professor Herbert. " It's all on me."

" We don't do things like that," says Pa, " we're just and honest people. We don't want somethin' fer nothin'. Professor Herbert, you're wrong now and I'm right. You'll haf to listen to me. I've larned a lot from you. My boy must go on. Th' world has left me. It changed while I've raised my family and plowed th' hills. I'm a just and honest man. I don't skip debts. I ain't larned 'em to do that. I ain't got much larnin' myself but I do know right from wrong atter I see through a thing."

Professor Herbert went home. Pa and I stayed and swept one hour. It looked funny to see Pa use a broom. He never used one at home. Mom used the broom. Pa used the plow. Pa did hard work. Pa says, " I can't sweep. Durned if I can. Look at th' streaks o' dirt I leave on th' floor! Seems like no work a-tall fer me. Brooms is too light 'r somethin'. I'll jist do th' best I can, Dave. I've been wrong about th' school."

I says, " Did you know Professor Herbert can get a warrant out for you for bringing your pistol to school and showing it in his office! They can railroad you for that! "

" That's all made right," says Pa. " I've made that right. Professor Herbert ain't goin' to take it to court. He likes me. I like 'im. We jist had to get together. He had the remedies. He showed me. You must go on to school. I am as strong a man as ever come out'n th' hills fer my years and th' hard work I've done. But I'm behind, Dave. I'm a little man. Your hands will be softer than mine. Your clothes will be better. You'll allus look cleaner than your old Pap. Jist remember, Dave, to pay your debts

and be honest. Jist be kind to animals and don't bother th' snakes. That's all I got agin th' school. Puttin' black snakes to sleep and cuttin' 'em open."

It was late when we got home. Stars were in the sky. The moon was up. The ground was frozen. Pa took his time going home. I couldn't run like I did the night before. It was ten o'clock before we got the work finished, our suppers eaten. Pa sat before the fire and told Mom he was going to take her and show her a germ sometime. Mom hadn't seen one either. Pa told her about the high school and the fine man Professor Herbert was. He told Mom about the strange school across the hill and how different it was from the school in their day and time.

## Suggestions for Study

1. To get the flavor of Jesse Stuart's style, read half a dozen paragraphs aloud. What do you notice about the diction and the sentences? Does his style seem natural or artificial?

2. Why was Pa so unjust to the school before he went to visit it? What is the remedy for most faulty, emotional reasoning? Discuss the shrewdness of the principal in his handling of Pa. How does the story support Pa's contention that he is " a just and honest man "?

3. Cite passages in this story which show that Jesse Stuart believes in education for the hill people.

4. Show that the setting furnishes the central impression of this story. What details make this story vivid and seemingly real? What convinces you that these details are true to Kentucky hill-country life?

5. Review the details of different regions of our country given in the stories in this book. Which of these regions were new to you? which were made most vivid? which would you most like to visit?

6. Find out about Berea College in Kentucky and tell the class. What other states besides Kentucky have similar problems of the education of " mountain whites "? What can you find out about illiteracy and educational progress in these regions?

7. Write a composition in which you try to present life in some region as vividly as does this story.

# William Saroyan    1908–

William Saroyan baffles description. He admits that he is a genius, and his brash self-assurance prejudices many against him. But even those who most resent his conceit find that they cannot dismiss him as unimportant. His stories and plays violate all the rules, but they live and breathe.

Saroyan is a Californian of Armenian descent. He left school after two years in junior high and moved from one job to another in rapid succession: telegraph messenger, office worker, farm laborer, newspaper reporter. In 1934 he achieved instant success with his story, "The Daring Young Man on the Flying Trapeze." In 1940 he won the Pulitzer prize for drama (which he refused to accept!) for *The Time of Your Life.* Perhaps his best-known book is *The Human Comedy.*

*Don Freeman*

## LOCOMOTIVE 38, THE OJIBWAY

If you have never read anything by Saroyan, you will find this story different from any story you have ever read before. The fact that Saroyan does not bother to use quotation marks takes the story at once out of the orthodox pattern; but Saroyan's style is different in many other ways, also. If you like this story of the millionaire Ojibway, you will find other equally entertaining stories in *My Name Is Aram,* which contains some of Saroyan's best writing.

One day a man came to town on a donkey and began loafing around in the public library where I used to spend most of my time in those days. He was a tall young Indian of the Ojibway tribe. He told me his name was Locomotive 38. Everybody in town believed he had escaped from an asylum.

Six days after he arrived in town his animal was struck by the Tulare Street trolley and seriously injured. The following day the animal passed away, most likely of internal injuries, on the corner of Mariposa and Fulton streets. The animal sank to the pavement, fell on the Indian's leg, groaned and died. When the Indian got his leg free he got up and limped into the drugstore on the corner and made a long-distance telephone call. He telephoned his brother in Oklahoma. The call cost him a lot of money, which he dropped into the slot as requested by the operator as if he were in the habit of making such calls every day.

I was in the drugstore at the time, eating a Royal Banana Special, with crushed walnuts.

When he came out of the telephone booth he saw me sitting at the soda fountain eating this fancy dish.

Hello, Willie, he said.

He knew my name wasn't Willie — he just liked to call me that.

He limped to the front of the store where the gum was, and bought three packages of Juicy Fruit. Then he limped back to me and said, What's that you're eating, Willie? It looks good.

This is what they call a Royal Banana Special, I said.

The Indian got up on the stool next to me.

Give me the same, he said to the soda fountain girl.

That's too bad about your animal, I said.

There's no place for an animal in this world, he said. What kind of an automobile should I buy?

Are you going to buy an automobile? I said.

I've been thinking about it for several minutes now, he said.

I didn't think you had any money, I said. I thought you were poor.

That's the impression people get, he said. Another impression they get is that I'm crazy.

I didn't get the impression that you were

crazy, I said, but I didn't get the impression that you were rich, either.

Well, I am, the Indian said.

I wish I was rich, I said.

What for? he said.

Well, I said, I've been wanting to go fishing at Mendota for three years in a row now. I need some equipment and some kind of an automobile to get out there in.

Can you drive an automobile? the Indian said.

I can drive anything, I said.

Have you ever driven an automobile? he said.

Not yet, I said. So far I haven't had any automobile to drive, and it's against my family religion to steal an automobile.

Do you mean to tell me you believe you could get into an automobile and start driving? he said.

That's right, I said.

Remember what I was telling you on the steps of the public library the other evening? he said.

You mean about the machine age? I said.

Yes, he said.

I remember, I said.

All right, he said. Indians are born with an instinct for riding, rowing, hunting, fishing, and swimming. Americans are born with an instinct for fooling around with machines.

I'm no American, I said.

I know, the Indian said. You're an Armenian. I remember. I asked you and you told me. You're an Armenian born in America. You're fourteen years old and already you know you'll be able to drive an automobile the minute you get into one. You're a typical American, although your complexion, like my own, is dark.

Driving a car is no trick, I said. There's nothing to it. It's easier than riding a donkey.

All right, the Indian said. Just as you say. If I go up the street and buy an automobile, will you drive for me?

Of course, I said.

How much in wages would you want? he said,

You mean you want to give me wages for driving an automobile? I said.

Of course, the Ojibway said.

Well, I said, that's very nice of you, but I don't want any money for driving an automobile.

Some of the journeys may be long ones, he said.

The longer the better, I said.

Are you restless? he said.

I was born in this little old town, I said.

Don't you like it? he said.

I like mountains and streams and mountain lakes, I said.

Have you ever been in the mountains? he said.

Not yet, I said, but I'm going to reach them some day.

I see, he said. What kind of an automobile do you think I ought to buy?

How about a Ford roadster? I said.

Is that the best automobile? he said.

Do you want the *best*? I said.

Shouldn't I have the best? he said.

I don't know, I said. The best costs a lot of money.

What is the best? he said.

Well, I said, some people think the Cadillac is the best. Others like the Packard. They're both pretty good. I wouldn't know which is best. The Packard is beautiful to see going down the highway, but so is the Cadillac. I've watched a lot of them fine cars going down the highway.

How much is a Packard? he said.

Around three thousand dollars, I said. Maybe a little more.

Can we get one right away? he said.

I got down off the stool. He sounded crazy, but I knew he wasn't.

Listen, Mr. Locomotive, I said, do you really want to buy a Packard right away?

You know my animal passed away a few minutes ago, he said.

I saw it happen, I said. They'll probably be arresting you any minute now for leaving the animal in the street.

They won't arrest me, he said.

They will if there's a law against leaving a dead donkey in the street, I said.

No, they won't, he said.

Why not? I said.

Well, he said, they won't after I show them a few papers I carry around with me all the time. The people of this country have a lot of respect for money, and I've got a lot of money.

I guess he is crazy after all, I thought.

Where'd you get all this money? I said.

I own some land in Oklahoma, he said. About fifty thousand acres.

Is it worth money? I said.

No, he said. All but about twenty acres of it is worthless. I've got some oil wells on them twenty acres. My brother and I.

How did you Ojibways ever get down to Oklahoma? I said. I always thought the Ojibways lived up north, up around the Great Lakes.

That's right, the Indian said. We used to live up around the Great Lakes but my grandfather was a pioneer. He moved west when everybody else did.

Oh, I said. Well, I guess they won't bother you about the dead donkey at that.

They won't bother me about anything, he said. It won't be because I've got money. It'll be because they think I'm crazy. Nobody in this town but you knows I've got money. Do you know where we can get one of them automobiles right away?

The Packard agency is up on Broadway, two blocks beyond the public library, I said.

All right, he said. If you're sure you won't mind driving for me, let's go get one of them. Something bright in color, he said. Red, if they've got red. Where would you like to drive to first?

Would you care to go fishing at Mendota? I said.

I'll take the ride, he said. I'll watch you fish. Where can we get some equipment for you?

Right around the corner at Homan's, I said.

We went around the corner to Homan's and the Indian bought twenty-seven dollars' worth of fishing equipment for me. Then we went up to the Packard agency on Broadway. They didn't have a red Packard,

but there was a beautiful green one. It was light green, the color of new grass. This was back there in 1922. The car was a beautiful sports touring model.

Do you think you could drive this great big car? the Indian said.

I *know* I can drive it, I said.

The police found us in the Packard agency and wanted to arrest the Indian for leaving the dead donkey in the street. He showed them the papers he had told me about and the police apologized and went away. They said they'd removed the animal and were sorry they'd troubled him about it.

I'll take this car, he said.

He turned to the manager of the Packard agency, Jim Lewis, who used to run for Mayor every time election time came around.

I'll take this car, he said.

I'll draw up the papers immediately, Jim said.

What papers? the Indian said. I'm going to pay for it now.

You mean you want to pay three thousand two hundred seventeen dollars and sixty-five cents *cash?* Jim said.

Yes, the Indian said. It's ready to drive, isn't it?

Of course, Jim said. I'll have the boys go over it with a cloth to take off any dust on it. I'll have them check the motor too, and fill the gasoline tank. It won't take more than ten minutes. If you'll step into the office I'll close the transaction immediately.

Jim and the Indian stepped into Jim's office.

About three minutes later Jim came over to me, a man shaken to the roots.

Aram, he said, who is this guy? I thought he was a nut. I had Johnny telephone the Pacific-Southwest and they said his bank account is being transferred from somewhere in Oklahoma. They said his account is something over a million dollars. I thought he was a nut. Do you know him?

He told me his name is Locomotive 38, I said. That's no name.

That's a translation of his Indian name,

Jim said. We've got his full name on the contract. Do you know him?

I've talked to him every day since he came to town on that donkey that died this morning, I said, but I never thought he had any money.

He says you're going to drive for him, Jim said. Are you sure you're the man to drive a great big car like this, son?

Wait a minute now, Mr. Lewis, I said. Don't try to push me out of this chance of a lifetime. I can drive this big Packard as well as anybody else in town.

I'm not trying to push you out of anything, Jim said. I just don't want you to drive out of here and run over six or seven innocent people and maybe smash the car. Get into the car and I'll give you a few pointers. Do you know anything about the gearshift?

I don't know anything about anything yet, I said, but I'll soon find out.

All right, Jim said. Just let me help you.

I got into the car and sat down behind the wheel. Jim got in beside me.

From now on, son, he said, I want you to regard me as a friend who will give you the shirt off his back. I want to thank you for bringing me this fine Indian gentleman.

He told me he wanted the best car on the market, I said. You know I've always been crazy about driving a Packard. Now how do I do it?

Well, Jim said, let's see.

He looked down at my feet.

Great Scott, son, he said, your feet don't reach the pedals.

Never mind that, I said. You just explain the gearshift.

Jim explained everything while the boys wiped the dust off the car and went over the motor and filled the gasoline tank. When the Indian came out and got into the car, in the back where I insisted he should sit, I had the motor going.

He says he knows how to drive, the Indian said to Jim Lewis. By instinct, he said. I believe him, too.

You needn't worry about Aram here, Jim said. He can drive all right. Clear the way

there, boys, he shouted. Let him have all the room necessary.

I turned the big car around slowly, shifted, and shot out of the agency at about fifty miles an hour, with Jim Lewis running after the car and shouting, Take it easy, son. Don't open up until you get out on the highway. The speed limit in town is twenty-five miles an hour.

The Indian wasn't at all excited, even though I was throwing him around a good deal.

I wasn't doing it on purpose, though. It was simply that I wasn't very familiar with the manner in which the automobile worked.

You're an excellent driver, Willie, he said. It's like I said. You're an American and you were born with an instinct for mechanical contraptions like this.

We'll be in Mendota in an hour, I said. You'll see some great fishing out there.

How far is Mendota? the Indian said.

About ninety miles, I said.

Ninety miles is too far to go in an hour, the Indian said. Take two hours. We're passing a lot of interesting scenery I'd like to look at a little more closely.

All right, I said, but I sure am anxious to get out there and fish.

Well, all right then, the Indian said. Go as fast as you like this time, but some time I'll expect you to drive a little more slowly, so I can see some of the scenery. I'm missing everything. I don't even get a chance to read the signs.

I'll travel slowly *now* if you want me to, I said.

No, he insisted. Let her go. Let her go as fast as she'll go.

Well, we got out to Mendota in an hour and seventeen minutes. I would have made better time except for the long stretch of dirt road.

I drove the car right up to the riverbank. The Indian asked if I knew how to get the top down, so he could sit in the open and watch me fish. I didn't know how to get the top down, but I got it down. It took me twenty minutes to do it.

I fished for about three hours, fell into

the river twice, and finally landed a small one.

You don't know the first thing about fishing, the Indian said.

What am I doing wrong? I said.

Everything, he said. Have you ever fished before?

No, I said.

I didn't think so, he said.

What am I doing wrong? I said.

Well, he said, nothing in particular, only you're fishing at about the same rate of speed that you drive an automobile.

Is that wrong? I said.

It's not exactly wrong, he said, except that it'll keep you from getting anything to speak of, and you'll go on falling into the river.

I'm not falling, I said. They're pulling me in. They've got an awful pull. This grass is mighty slippery, too. There ain't nothing around here to grab hold of.

I reeled in one more little one and then I asked if he'd like to go home. He said he would if I wanted to, too, so I put away the fishing equipment and the two fish and got in the car and started driving back to town.

I drove that big Packard for this Ojibway Indian, Locomotive 38, as long as he stayed in town, which was all summer. He stayed at the hotel all the time. I tried to get him to learn to drive, but he said it was out of the question. I drove that Packard all over the San Joaquín Valley that summer, with the Indian in the back, chewing eight or nine sticks of gum. He told me to drive anywhere I cared to go, so it was either to some place where I could fish, or some place where I could hunt. He claimed I didn't know anything about fishing or hunting, but he was glad to see me trying. As long as I knew him he never laughed, except once. That was the time I shot at a jack rabbit with a twelve-gauge shotgun that had a terrible kick, and killed a crow. He tried to tell me all the time that that was my average. To shoot at a jack rabbit and kill a crow. You're an American, he said. Look at the way you took to this big automobile.

One day in November that year his brother came to town from Oklahoma, and the next day when I went down to the hotel to get him, they told me he'd gone back to Oklahoma with his brother.

Where's the Packard? I said.

They took the Packard, the hotel clerk said.

Who drove? I said.

The Indian, the clerk said.

They're both Indians, I said. Which of the brothers drove the car?

The one who lived at this hotel, the clerk said.

Are you sure? I said.

Well, I only saw him get into the car out front and drive away, the clerk said. That's all.

Do you mean to tell me he knew how to shift gears? I said.

It *looked* as if he did, the clerk said. He looked like an expert driver to me.

Thanks, I said.

On the way home I figured he'd just wanted me to *believe* he couldn't drive, so *I* could drive all the time and feel good. He was just a young man who'd come to town on a donkey, bored to death or something, who'd taken advantage of the chance to be entertained by a small-town kid who was bored to death, too. That's the only way I could figure it out without accepting the general theory that he was crazy.

## Suggestions for Study

1. What peculiarities of style did you find in this story? In your opinion did they improve or harm it?

2. What did you think of the ending? Did Mr. Saroyan prepare you for it?

3. Was Locomotive 38, to you, a credible character? What details about him did you find hard to accept as possible?

## Maureen Daly    1922–

Unquestionably the United States has produced some of the world's finest short stories, and the roster of authors' names is a list to make Americans proud. But even the humblest of us are storytellers; and one of the sources

MAUREEN DALY. At sixteen, Miss Daly wrote the story which established her reputation as an author.

of student interest in the short story as a type is that students, too, write short stories, and sometimes very good ones. So, to complete this section, we are presenting a student's story — a story written by a high-school girl in Fond du Lac, Wisconsin. Maureen Daly was only sixteen when she wrote this story and submitted it to *Scholastic Magazine,* where it won the National High School Short Story Contest in 1938; but, though only sixteen, she had learned the most important principle of good writing: Cultivate awareness of your own surroundings and write about things you understand.

Miss Daly was recently graduated from Rosary College, River Forest, Illinois, and has continued to win literary laurels with a successful first novel, *Seventeenth Summer.*

### SIXTEEN

Now don't get me wrong. I mean, I want you to understand from the beginning that I'm not really so dumb. I know what a girl should do and what she shouldn't. I get around. I read. I listen to the radio. And I have two older sisters. So you see, I know what the score is. I know it's smart to wear tweedish skirts and shaggy sweaters with the sleeves pushed up and pearls and ankle socks and saddle shoes that look as if they've seen the world. And I know that your hair should be long, almost to your shoulders, and sleek as a wet seal, just a little fluffed on the ends, and you should wear a campus hat or a dink or else a peasant hankie if you've that sort of face. Properly, a peasant hankie should make you think of edelweiss, mist and sunny mountains, yodeling and Swiss cheese. You know, that kind of peasant. Now, me, I never wear a hankie. It makes my face seem wide and Slavic and I look like a picture always in one of those magazine articles that run — " And Stalin says the future of Russia lies in its women. In its women who have tilled its soil, raised its children — " Well, anyway. I'm not exactly too small-town either. I read Winchell's column. You get to know what New York boy is that way about some pineapple princess on the West Coast and what Paradise pretty is currently the prettiest, and why someone, eventually, will play Scarlett O'Hara. It gives you that cosmopolitan feeling. And I know that anyone who orders a strawberry sundae in a drugstore instead of a lemon coke would probably be dumb enough to wear colored ankle socks with high-heeled pumps or use Evening in Paris with a tweed suit. But I'm sort of drifting. This isn't what I wanted to tell you. I just wanted to give you the general idea of how I'm not so dumb. It's important that you understand that.

You see, it was funny how I met him. It was a winter night like any other winter night. And I didn't have my Latin done, either. But the way the moon tinseled the twigs and silver-plated the snowdrifts, I just couldn't stay inside. The skating rink isn't far from our house — you can make it in five minutes if the sidewalks aren't slippery — so I went skating. I remember it took me a long time to get ready that night because I had to darn my skating socks first. I don't know why they always wear out so fast — just in the toes, too. Maybe it's because I have metal protectors on the toes of my skates. That probably *is* why. And then I brushed my hair — hard, so hard it clung to my hand and stood up around my head in a hazy halo.

My skates were hanging by the back door all nice and shiny, for I'd just gotten them for Christmas and they smelled so queer — just like fresh smoked ham. My dog walked with me as far as the corner. She's a red chow, very polite and well mannered, and she kept pretending it was me she liked when all the time I knew it was the ham smell. She panted along beside me and her hot breath made a frosty little balloon balancing on the end of her nose. My skates thumped me good-naturedly on my back as I walked and the night was breathlessly quiet and the stars winked down like a million flirting eyes. It was all so lovely.

It was all so lovely I ran most of the way and it was lucky the sidewalks had ashes on them or I'd have slipped surely. The ashes crunched like crackerjack and I could feel their cindery shape through the thinness of my shoes. I always wear old shoes when I go skating.

I had to cut across someone's back garden to get to the rink and last summer's grass stuck through the thin ice, brown and discouraged. Not many people came through this way and the crusted snow broke through the little hollows between corn stubbles frozen hard in the ground. I was out of breath when I got to the shanty — out of breath with running and with the loveliness of the night. Shanties are always such friendly places. The floor all hacked to wet splinters from skate runners and the wooden wall frescoed with symbols of dead romance. There was a smell of singed wool as someone got too near the glowing isinglass grin of the iron stove. Girls burst through the door laughing, with snow on their hair, and tripped over shoes scattered on the floor. A pimply-faced boy grabbed the hat from the frizzled head of an eighth-grade blonde and stuffed it into an empty galosh to prove his love and then hastily bent to examine his skate strap with innocent unconcern.

It didn't take me long to get my own skates on and I stuck my shoes under the bench — far back where they wouldn't get knocked around and would be easy to find when I wanted to go home. I walked out on my toes and the shiny runners of my new skates dug deep into the sodden floor.

It was snowing a little outside — quick, eager little Luxlike flakes that melted as soon as they touched your hand. I don't know where the snow came from, for there were stars out. Or maybe the stars were in my eyes and I just kept seeing them every time I looked up into the darkness. I waited a moment. You know, to start to skate at a crowded rink is like jumping on a moving merry-go-round. The skaters go skimming round in a colored blur like gaudy painted horses and the shrill musical jabber re-echoes in the night from a hundred human calliopes. Once in, I went all right. At least after I found out exactly where that rough ice was. It was " round, round, jump the rut, round, round, round, jump the rut, round, round — "

And then he came. All of a sudden his arm was around my waist so warm and tight and he said very casually, " Mind if I skate with you? " and then he took my other hand. That's all there was to it. Just that and then we were skating. It wasn't that I'd never skated with a boy before. Don't be silly. I told you before I get around. But this was different. He was a smoothie! He was a big shot up at school and he went to all the big dances and he was the best dancer in town except Harold Wright, who didn't count because he'd been to college in New York for two years! Don't you see? This was different.

I can't remember what we talked about at first; I can't even remember if we talked at all. We just skated and skated and laughed every time we came to that rough spot and pretty soon we were laughing all the time at nothing at all. It was all so lovely.

Then we sat on the big snowbank at the edge of the rink and just watched. It was cold at first even with my skating pants on, sitting on that hard heap of snow, but pretty soon I got warm all over. He threw a handful of snow at me and it fell in a little white shower on my hair and he leaned over to brush it off. I held my breath. The night stood still.

The moon hung just over the warming shanty like a big quarter slice of muskmelon and the smoke from the pipe chimney floated up in a sooty fog. One by one the houses around the rink twinked out their lights and somebody's hound wailed a mournful apology to a star as he curled up for the night. It was all so lovely.

Then he sat up straight and said, " We'd better start home." Not " Shall I take you home? " or " Do you live far? " but " We'd better start home." See, that's how I know he wanted to take me home. Not because he *had* to but because he *wanted* to. He went to the shanty to get my shoes. " Black ones," I told him. " Same size as Garbo's." And he laughed again. He was still smiling when he came back and took off my skates and tied the wet skate strings in a soggy knot and put them over his shoulder. Then he held out his hand and I slid off the snow-bank and brushed off the seat of my pants and we were ready.

It was snowing harder now. Big, quiet flakes that clung to twiggy bushes and snuggled in little drifts against the tree trunks. The night was an etching in black and white. It was all so lovely I was sorry I lived only a few blocks away. He talked softly as we walked, as if every little word were a secret. " Did I like Wayne King, and did I plan to go to college next year, and had I a cousin who lived in Appleton and knew his brother? " A very respectable Emily Post sort of conversation, and then finally " how nice I looked with snow in my hair and had I ever seen the moon so — close? " For the moon was following us as we walked and ducking playfully behind a chimney every time I turned to look at it. And then we were home.

The porch light was on. My mother always puts the porch light on when I go away at night. And we stood there a moment by the front steps and the snow turned pinkish in the glow of the colored light and a few feathery flakes settled on his hair. Then he took my skates and put them over my shoulder and said, " Good night now. I'll call you." " I'll call you," he said.

I went inside then and in a moment he was gone. I watched him from my window as he went down the street. He was whistling softly and I waited until the sound faded away so I couldn't tell if it was he or my heart whistling out there in the night. And then he was gone, completely gone.

I shivered. Somehow the darkness seemed changed. The stars were little hard chips of light far up in the sky and the moon stared down with a sullen yellow glare. The air was tense with sudden cold and a gust of wind swirled his footprints into white oblivion. Everything was quiet.

But he'd said, " I'll call you." That's what he said — " I'll call you." I couldn't sleep all night.

And that was last Thursday. Tonight is Tuesday. Tonight is Tuesday and my homework's done, and I darned some stockings that didn't really need it, and I worked a crossword puzzle, and I listened to the radio, and now I'm just sitting. I'm just sitting because I can't think of anything else to do. I can't think of anything, anything but snowflakes and ice skates and yellow moons and Thursday night. The telephone is sitting on the corner table with its old black face turned to the wall so I can't see its leer. I don't even jump when it rings any more. My heart still prays, but my mind just laughs. Outside the night is still, so still I think I'll go crazy, and the white snow's all dirtied and smoked into grayness and the wind is blowing the arc light so it throws weird, waving shadows from the trees onto the lawn — like thin, starved arms begging for I don't know what. And so I'm just sitting here and I'm not feeling anything; I'm not even sad, because all of a sudden I know. All of a sudden I know. I can sit here now forever and laugh and laugh and laugh while the tears run salty in the corners of my mouth. For all of a sudden I know, I know what the stars knew all the time — he'll never, never call — never.

## Suggestions for Study

1. By her title Miss Daly says that here is a picture of life as it is lived by a girl of sixteen. What is the distinguishing quality of youth in her story? What other story in this book makes this same point?

2. How does the first paragraph inspire the reader's confidence?

3. Name the four different moods the girl experiences. Show that the description of scene is in key with each of these moods.

4. Pick out passages of effective description which show Maureen Daly's ability to observe and appreciate her environment.

5. Can you remember something that you wanted desperately to have happen although it might seem a trifle to your elders? Try writing of your experience as simply and frankly as this girl writes of hers. Or perhaps you would like to tell this same incident from the boy's point of view.

## For Your Vocabulary

FIGURATIVE USE OF WORDS. This story gains a large part of its charm from its vividness. And its vividness is the result of figures of speech and figurative use of single words. The similes are easy to spot, from the key words *like* and *as:*

hair sleek as a wet seal
stars winked like flirting eyes
ashes crunched like crackerjack
the moon like a big quarter slice of muskmelon.

Did you notice the single words used figuratively to just as good effect?

the moon *tinseled* the twigs and *silver-plated* the snowdrifts
the dog's hot breath made a frosty little *balloon balancing* on the tip of her nose
the shrill musical jabber (of the skaters) re-echoes from a hundred human *calliopes*
a hound wailed a mournful *apology* to a star
a very nice *Emily Post* sort of conversation
the moon was *ducking playfully* behind a chimney every time I turned to look at it.
the telephone's black *face* turned to the wall so I can't see its *leer*

Apply this method on the narrative suggested in question 5, or choose a place where you have a particularly good time, and write a short description which gives its feeling as well as its appearance. Don't say anything *was* thus and so. Use nouns and verbs figuratively for the impressions, and go easy on *like* phrases.

## Short Story Reading List

OTHER SHORT STORIES IN THIS BOOK

By reading the short stories in Part II of this book you can trace the history of the short story from Irving (whose " Rip Van Winkle," written in 1819, was the first American short story) to the moderns.

SHORT STORIES IN MAGAZINES

Current magazines contain many short stories, ranging from poor to excellent. Since most of us do not have time to read more than a small fraction of these stories, we welcome any guidance we can find to the better ones. To this end two annual anthologies are most helpful: *The Best Short Stories of 19—* (a series which began in 1915, formerly edited by Edward J. O'Brien, and since his death edited by Martha Foley) and the *O. Henry Memorial Award Prize Stories of 19—* (a series which began in 1919 and is now edited by Herschel Brickell).

A study of these anthologies indicates that many of the best American short stories are published in the following magazines:

*The Atlantic Monthly*
*Harper's Bazaar*
*Harper's Magazine*
*The New Yorker*
*The Saturday Evening Post*
*Story*

Mention should also be made of *Post Stories of 1937*, etc., a series running through 1941. The stories were selected from the *Saturday Evening Post* of each year.

The following collections assemble outstanding stories in convenient form. Many of the stories by individual authors mentioned below are to be found in these, and also in collections not limited to American stories.

Atlantic Monthly Press: *Modern Atlantic Stories*

Becker, M. L., ed.: *Golden Tales of Our America; Growing Up with America; Golden Tales of the Old South; Golden Tales of the Prairie States; Golden Tales of the Far West; Golden Tales of the Southwest*

Burrell, A. and Cerf, B., eds.: *The Bedside Book of Famous American Stories*

Fagin, N. B.: *America through the Short Story*

Flanagan, John T., ed.: *America Is West*

Heydrick, Benjamin, ed.: *Americans All*

Howells, W. D., ed.: *The Great American Short Stories; Great Modern American Stories*

Jessup, Alexander, ed.: *Representative American Short Stories; The Best American Humorous Stories; Representative Modern Short Stories*

Maule, H. E., ed.: *Great Tales of the American West*

O'Brien, E. J., ed.: *Modern American Short Stories; 50 Best American Short Stories, 1915–1939*

Pattee, F. L., ed.: *American Short Stories*

Williams, B. C., ed.: *Great American Short Stories; O. Henry Memorial Prize Winning Stories*

Wood, W. R., and Husband, J. D., eds.: *Short Stories As You Like Them* (a collection of short stories by American authors)

In case of trouble in finding a given story, you can always consult the *Index to Short Stories* compiled by Ina Ten Eyck Firkins. This gives the place of original publication and every other work in which a given story may be found. All libraries have this volume.

Following is a recommended list of American short stories. Italicized titles are those of volumes of short stories, and often also of the first story in the volume.

Aldrich, T. B.: *Marjorie Daw and Other Stories*

Allen, J. L.: *Flute and Violin;* " King Solomon of Kentucky "; " Two Gentlemen of Kentucky "

Andrews, M. R. S.: " The Counsel Assigned "; " The Three Things "; " The Perfect Tribute "; " American, Sir! "

Bacon, J. D.: " Edgar, the Choir Boy Uncelestial "

Benét, S. V.: *Tales before Midnight; Thirteen O'Clock; Twenty-five Short Stories*

Bercovici, Konrad: *Ghitza*

Bierce, Ambrose: *In the Midst of Life*

Biggers, E. D.: *Earl Derr Biggers Tells Ten Stories*

Brown, Alice: *Meadow Grass; Tiverton Tales; The Flying Teuton*

Buck, Pearl: " The Good River "; " A Rainy Day "; " Wang Lung "; " Father Andrea "; " The Old Mother "; " The Frill "; *Today and Forever*

Bunner, H. C.: *Short Sixes;* " A Sisterly Scheme "; " The Love Letters of Smith "; " The Tenor "; " The Nice People "; " Zenobia's Infidelity "

Butler, E. P.: *The Behind Legs of the 'Orse, and Other Stories; Ghosts What Ain't; Goat Feathers; Pups and Pies; Pigs Is Pigs!*

Cable, G. W.: *Old Creole Days*

Cather, Willa: *Obscure Destinies; Youth and the Bright Medusa*

Clemens, S. L. (Mark Twain): " The Jumping Frog "; " A Dog Story "

Cobb, I. S.: *The Escape of Mr. Trimm;* " The Belled Buzzard"; *Old Judge Priest*

Cohen, O. R.: *Polished Ebony; Come Seven; Black and Blue*

Connell, Richard: *The Sin of Monsieur Pettipon; Apes and Angels; Variety*

Connolly, J. B.: *Out of Gloucester; Deep Waters*

Craddock, C. E. (Mary N. Murfree): *In the Tennessee Mountains*

Davis, R. H.: *The Bar Sinister; Gallegher; From Gallegher to the Deserter*

Deland, Margaret: *Old Chester Tales; Dr. Lavendar's People*

Dreiser, Theodore: " The Lost Phoebe "

Edmonds, W. D.: *Rome Haul*

Fast, Howard M.: *Patrick Henry and the Frigate's Keel*

Ferber, Edna: *Cheerful — by Request; Roast Beef Medium; Mother Knows Best*

Fisher, D. C.: *Hillsboro People; Home Fires in France; Made-to-Order Stories; The Real Motive*

Fitch, G. H.: *At Good Old Siwash*

Freeman, M. E. W.: *A New England Nun; A Humble Romance; Best Stories of Mary E. Wilkins,* ed. by H. W. Lanier

Gale, Zona: *Friendship Village; Old-Fashioned Tales*

Garland, Hamlin: *Main-Traveled Roads; Other Main-Traveled Roads*

Hale, E. E.: " The Man without a Country "; " My Double and How He Undid Me "

Harris, J. C.: *Uncle Remus Stories;* " The Wonderful Tar Baby "; " How a Witch Was Caught "; " The Creature with No Claws "

Harte, Bret: *The Luck of Roaring Camp;* " An Ingénue of the Sierras "; " Tennessee's Partner "; " The Postmistress of Laurel Run "; " Left Out on Lone Star Mountain "; " M'liss "; " How Santa Claus Came to Simpson's Bar "

Hawthorne, Nathaniel: *Twice-Told Tales; Mosses from an Old Manse; The Snow Image*

Irving, Washington: *The Alhambra; Tales of a Traveler;* " Rip Van Winkle "; " The Specter Bridegroom "; " The Legend of Sleepy Hollow "; " The Stout Gentleman "

James, Henry: " The Real Thing "; *Daisy Miller* (novelette)

Jewett, S. O.: *A White Heron; A Native of Winby; Best Stories of Sarah Orne Jewett,* ed. by Willa Cather

Johnson, Owen: *The Tennessee Shad*

Kelly, Myra: *Little Citizens; Little Aliens*

La Farge, Oliver: *All the Young Men*

Lardner, Ring: *Round Up*

Lewis, Sinclair: " Let's Play King "; " The Willow Walk "; " Land "; " A Letter from the Queen "; " Young Man Axelbrod "

Lincoln, J. C.: *Back Numbers*

London, Jack: *Tales of the Fish Patrol; The Faith of Men; Children of the Frost; Lost Face; Moon-Face; The Son of the Wolf*

Marshall, Edison: " The Elephant Remembers "; " The Heart of Little Shikara "

Montague, M. P.: *England to America; Uncle Sam of Freedom Ridge; Closed Doors; Up Eel River*

O'Brien, Fitz-James: " The Diamond Lens "; " What Was It? "

Page, T. N.: *In Ole Virginia; Marse Chan*

Parker, Dorothy: *Here Lies; After Such Pleasures*

Poe, E. A.: " The Black Cat "; " A Descent into the Maelstrom "; " The Fall of the House of Usher "; " The Gold Bug "; " MS. Found in a Bottle "; " The Masque of the Red Death "; " Murders in the Rue Morgue "; " The Oblong Box "; " The Oval Portrait "; " A Cask of Amontillado "; " The Purloined Letter "

Porter, W. S. (O. Henry): *The Four Million; The Heart of the West; Roads of Destiny; Whirligigs; The Voice of the City; Sixes and Sevens; Cabbages and Kings; The Gentle Grafter*

Rinehart, M. R.: *Tish Marches On*

Schramm, Wilbur: " Wilbur the Jeep "; " Grandpa Hopewell and the Flying Tractor "

Shaw, Irwin: " Faith at Sea "

Smith, E. V.: " 'Lijah "; " Prelude "

Smith, F. H.: *Forty Minutes Late; A Gentleman Vagabond; The Other Fellow*

Steele, W. D.: " Land's End "; " White Horse Winter "; " Down on Their Knees "; " The Yellow Cat "; " Blue Murder "; " Autumn Bloom "; " Lightning "; " Sooth "; " Luck "; " Sailor! Sailor! "

Steinbeck, John: *The Red Pony; The Long Valley*

Stockton, F. R.: *The Lady or the Tiger and Other Stories*

Street, James: " The Golden Key "; " In Full Glory Reflected "; " The Old Gordon Place "; *Short Stories*

Stuart, Jesse: " Eustacia "; " Brothers "; " Three Hundred Acres of Elbow Room "

Stuart, R. McE.: *Sonny; A Golden Wedding*

Suckow, Ruth: *Country People; Iowa Interiors; Children and Older People*

Van Dyke, Henry: *The Blue Flower; The Ruling Passion; Half-Told Tales; The Unknown Quantity; The Other Wise Man*

Wharton, Edith: *Xingu and Other Stories; Certain People; Tales of Men and Ghosts*

White, S. E.: *Blazed Trail Stories; Arizona Nights; The Two-Gun Man*

White, W. A.: *The Court of Boyville; In Our Town; The Real Issue*

Williams, B. A.: *Thrifty Stock;* " Sheener "; " They Grind Exceeding Small "; " One Crowded Hour "

Wood, F. G.: " Shoes "; " Turkey Red "

Yezierska, Anzia: *Children of Loneliness; Hungry Hearts*

# THE NOVEL

## GUIDE TO THE NOVEL

While reading the short stories in this volume, you must not forget the other great branch of fiction — the novel. Since the length of novels forbids their adequate representation in a general collection, it is recommended that you read outside of class at least one, and as many more as you can, from the list of novels on pages 140–142. For your outside reading in the novel your teacher will probably wish you to make either an oral or a written report to him or to the class. For these reports he may have a particular scheme or outline, for which he will give you specific instructions. Or, perhaps, you will be given a free rein to make any sort of report that you desire. If you are left to your own devices, you may find the following brief suggestions helpful.

First of all, decide what you are trying to do with your report. If you liked the book, you may wish to " sell " it to the class — to get as many as possible of your classmates to read it. If this is your purpose, be sure not to spoil the story for them by revealing too much. Another type of report is intended to save others the trouble of reading the book; you tell them so much about the story that they feel familiar with it and need investigate it no further. Still a third purpose in reporting on a novel is to discuss its theme. In this case you use the book as a starting point and draw material not only from this story but from other books and from your personal experiences. Probably the most mature purpose for a book report is to give a critical evaluation of the book; that is, to attempt to tell what merit the book has and what gives it this merit. If you wish to try your hand at a critical report, perhaps you can use one of the two following procedures:

1. Open with a brief statement of the author's position in the history of our literature: when he lived, where he lived, what sort of reputation he has as a writer. Next, place the particular book you have read by telling whether it is one of the author's early or later books and whether it is considered one of his best. You might mention a few of his other books.

Then make the main part of your report an answer to these three questions: What was the author's purpose in writing the story? How well did he succeed in carrying out his purpose? How worthy was his purpose? Fortify each point that you make by citing incidents or quotations from the book.

Among the many purposes for writing novels are the following: to give the reader an escape from reality by means of a thrilling vicarious adventure; to entertain by humorous incidents or characters; to present a picture of life and thought at some given place at a given time; to present a psychological study of some specific character; to teach some great truth; to present propaganda for a cause; to satirize some situation or some group. If you make many reports of this nature, you may find some value in noting the purpose of the novels you most enjoy. When you can find true enjoyment in the novel of character or of theme, you have become much more mature than you were when your chief enjoyment was merely in a thrilling plot.

2. Since novels, like short stories, are made up of action, characters, and setting, you might, after identifying the author, report on one of these elements, or each of them in turn, using the questions suggested for the short story on pages 3–6. In this kind of report, as in the one suggested first, you should be careful to cite material from the book to justify your various estimates.

Novels are usually more complicated in plot structure than are short stories. If you find several subplots, you might point out their interrelations and state just how each subplot contributes to the author's purpose. Sometimes a subplot is included to present a situation in contrast to the main plot, or perhaps merely to give variety. In discussing the plot, give some attention to the outcome. Did it please you? If it did not, examine your reaction carefully to discover whether a happy ending is more important to you than the feeling that the book is true to life and character.

Even more than the short story, the novel takes you into the experience of other human beings; for instead of glimpsing only brief, significant periods in their lives, you often follow them through a lifetime of development and come to feel that you have known them intimately. In discussing the characters, note particularly how any character develops or changes as the story advances. Try to decide whether the change grows logically out of the given situation and characters.

# DEVELOPMENT
# OF THE AMERICAN NOVEL

Although English settlements in America date from 1607, when Captain John Smith founded Jamestown, Virginia, no novelist of genuine importance appeared in America before 1800. For two centuries the American colonists were too busy conquering the wilderness and founding a new nation to have much time for such luxuries as art, music, and literature. By 1800 America had become a nation; she felt pride in her past, confidence in her future, the thrill of national unity — emotions which are fertile soil for the growth of a national literature.

During the romantic early years of the nineteenth century James Fenimore Cooper and William Gilmore Simms became our first important novelists. Cooper's reputation rests primarily upon the five romantic adventure novels about the early American frontier which compose the famous Leatherstocking series. Simms popularized American themes and achieved noteworthy success with his novels of the Revolution.

Before the War between the States broke out in 1861, two other important American novelists had appeared: Nathaniel Hawthorne and Herman Melville. Hawthorne lifted the novel above the plane of mere entertainment and made of it an artistic vehicle for the teaching of profound truths concerning man's spiritual and moral nature. His novels are only four in number. Of these *The Scarlet Letter* and *The House of the Seven Gables* are the most famous; the former is considered by many the greatest American novel. Herman Melville's most important book, *Moby Dick*, the saga of the white whale, is not only a vivid picture of the whaling industry painted on a vast canvas but an allegorical presentation of man's struggle with nature and his own soul. Although it was shamefully neglected until the twentieth century, today critics acclaim it a masterpiece.

In contrast with the romantic tales of Cooper, Simms, Hawthorne, and Melville, the fiction of the last quarter of the nineteenth century turned realistic and has remained predominantly so ever since. The two leaders in this movement were William Dean Howells and Henry James.

An important contemporary of Howells and James is the greatest of American humorists, Mark Twain, whose sense of humor made the most of the awkward age of a growing nation. In *The Adventures of Huckleberry Finn*, the epic of the Mississippi River vagabond, the American humorous novel reaches its highest point.

In the last decade of the century several authors turned from William Dean Howells' dictum that " the smiling aspects of life are the most American " and insisted upon presenting pictures of the disagreeable, sordid, brutal phases of life. These writers are sometimes called " naturalists " because they, like the Frenchman Zola, the father of naturalism, broke down the restraints and taboos which formerly existed and began to write about the ugly and the vicious. Among these early American naturalists, Stephen Crane is probably the greatest.

At the turn of the century, perhaps in

reaction to too much realism, there was a great vogue for historical novels, among which Winston Churchill's *Richard Carvel* and *The Crisis* are noteworthy. Romantic as are these stories when compared with more recent historical novels, they are considerably more true to life than the adventurous romances of Cooper and Simms.

In recent years the most obvious development in American fiction is found in the critical attitude of authors toward various unpleasant phases of American life. Distinguished among these writers is Sinclair Lewis, who was awarded the Nobel prize for literature in 1930, Pearl S. Buck, who won the Nobel prize for 1938, Ernest Hemingway, and John Steinbeck.

If you wish to pursue a course of reading which will reveal to you the development of the American novel, you should find the following list helpful. Any high-school student who reads these novels understandingly may well feel that he has made considerable progress in obtaining a fine literary background in this field. This list, however, is an adult list for mature readers. These are not books for easy, free reading; they are some of the greatest writings in American literature.

Cooper, James Fenimore: *The Last of the Mohicans* (1826)
Hawthorne, Nathaniel: *The Scarlet Letter* (1850)
Melville, Herman: *Moby Dick* (1851)
James, Henry: *The American* (1877)
Howells, William Dean: *The Rise of Silas Lapham* (1885)
Clemens, Samuel L. (Mark Twain): *The Adventures of Huckleberry Finn* (1885)
Crane, Stephen: *The Red Badge of Courage* (1893)
Norris, Frank: *McTeague* (1899)
Dreiser, Theodore: *Sister Carrie* (1900)
Lewis, Sinclair: *Arrowsmith* (1924)
Wolfe, Thomas: *Look Homeward, Angel* (1929)
Buck, Pearl S.: *The Good Earth* (1931)
Steinbeck, John: *The Grapes of Wrath* (1939)
Hemingway, Ernest: *For Whom the Bell Tolls* (1940)

## Novels for Home Reading

### GOOD ENTERTAINMENT: THRILLS, LAUGHS, AND TEARS

Alcott, Louisa M.: *Little Women*
Allen, J. L.: *A Kentucky Cardinal*
Bangs, John Kendrick: *A Houseboat on the Styx*
Clemens, Samuel L. (Mark Twain): *The Adventures of Tom Sawyer*
Davis, R. H.: *Soldiers of Fortune*
James, Will: *Smoky*
Johnson, Owen: *The Varmint*
London, Jack: *The Call of the Wild; The Sea Wolf; White Fang*
Morley, Christopher: *Parnassus on Wheels*
O'Hara, Mary, pseud.: *My Friend Flicka; Thunderhead*
Stockton, F. R.: *The Casting Away of Mrs. Lecks and Mrs. Aleshine; Rudder Grange*
Tarkington, Booth: *Seventeen; The Plutocrat*
Tunis, John R.: *The Iron Duke*
Westcott, E. N.: *David Harum*
Wilson, H. L.: *Merton of the Movies; Ruggles of Red Gap*

### HISTORICAL NOVELS WITH FOREIGN SETTINGS

Buck, Pearl: *House of Earth* (trilogy including *The Good Earth, Sons,* and *A House Divided*
Clemens, Samuel L. (Mark Twain): *The Prince and the Pauper; A Connecticut Yankee in King Arthur's Court*
Crawford, F. M.: *In the Palace of the King*
Davis, W. S.: *A Friend of Caesar; The Victor of Salamis; The Beauty of the Purple*
Douglas, Lloyd C.: *The Robe*
Nordhoff, C. B., and Hall, J. N.: *Mutiny on the Bounty; Men against the Sea; Pitcairn's Island; The Hurricane; The High Barbaree*
Tarkington, Booth: *Monsieur Beaucaire* (novelette)
Wallace, Lew: *Ben Hur*

### THE STORY OF AMERICA
#### Colonial Days

Bacheller, Irving: *In the Days of Poor Richard*
Cather, Willa: *Shadows on the Rock* (Quebec)
Cooper, J. F.: *The Deerslayer; The Pioneers*

Johnston, Mary: *To Have and To Hold;*
   *Prisoners of Hope; 1492*
Roberts, Kenneth: *Northwest Passage*
Simms, William G.: *The Yemassee*

### The Revolution

Atherton, Gertrude: *The Conqueror*
Boyd, James: *Drums*
Cannon, Le Grand: *Look to the Mountain*
Churchill, Winston: *Richard Carvel*
Cooper, J. F.: *The Pilot; The Spy*
Edmonds, W. D.: *Drums along the Mohawk*
Fast, Howard: *Citizen Tom Paine*
Forbes, Esther: *Johnny Tremaine*
Ford, P. L.: *Janice Meredith*
Mitchell, S. W.: *Hugh Wynne, Free Quaker*
Roberts, Kenneth: *Arundel; Rabble in Arms*
Thompson, Maurice: *Alice of Old Vincennes*
Turnbull, Agnes: *Day Must Dawn*

### From the Revolution to the Civil War

Cable, G. W.: *Dr. Sevier*
Cather, Willa: *Death Comes for the Archbishop*
Churchill, Winston: *The Crossing*
Coatsworth, E. J.: *Here I Stay*
Eggleston, Edward: *The Hoosier Schoolmaster*
Hergesheimer, Joseph: *Java Head*
Hough, Emerson: *The Covered Wagon*
Jackson, H. H.: *Ramona*
Lovelace, M. H.: *Early Candlelight*
Melville, Herman: *Typee*
Roberts, E. M.: *The Great Meadow*
Stowe, Harriet Beecher: *Uncle Tom's Cabin*
Twain, Mark, and Warner, C. D.: *The Gilded
   Age*
White, S. E.: *Long Rifle; The Gray Dawn*

### The Civil War and Reconstruction

Bacheller, Irving: *A Man for the Ages*
Boyd, James: *Marching On*
Churchill, Winston: *The Crisis*
Fox, J.: *The Little Shepherd of Kingdom Come*
Johnston, Mary: *The Long Roll*
Kantor, McKinlay: *Long Remember*
Mitchell, Margaret: *Gone with the Wind*
Page, Thomas Nelson: *Red Rock*
Stone, Irving: *Immortal Wife*
Young, S.: *So Red the Rose*

### The Later Frontier and the Rise of Industry

Aldrich, B. S.: *A Lantern in Her Hand*
Cather, Willa: *My Ántonia; O Pioneers!*
Churchill, Winston: *Coniston*
Fairbank, J. A.: *Bright Land*
Ferber, Edna: *Cimarron; Show Boat*

Ford, P. L.: *The Honorable Peter Stirling*
Garland, Hamlin: *Trail-Makers of the Middle
   Border*
Lane, Rose Wilder: *Let the Hurricane Roar*
Norris, Frank: *The Octopus; The Pit*
Rölvaag, O. E.: *Giants in the Earth*
Walker, Mildred: *Winter Wheat*
White, S. E.: *The Blazed Trail*
White, W. A.: *A Certain Rich Man*
Wister, Owen: *The Virginian*

### Modern American Life (Twentieth Century)

Barnes, M. A.: *Years of Grace; Within This
   Present*
Boyd, Thomas: *Through the Wheat*
Brown, H. P. M.: *A Walk in the Sun*
Carroll, G. H.: *As the Earth Turns*
Cather, Willa: *One of Ours*
Ferber, Edna: *So Big*
Hobart, Alice Tisdale: *Oil for the Lamps of
   China*
Lawrence, Josephine: *If I Have Four Apples*
Lewis, Sinclair: *Main Street; Babbitt; It Can't
   Happen Here*
Rawlings, Marjorie Kinnan: *The Yearling*
Saroyan, William: *The Human Comedy*
Tarkington, Booth: *The Magnificent Amber-
   sons*

### NOVELS OF CHARACTER DEVELOPMENT

#### Youth and Romance

Chase, M. E.: *Mary Peters; Windswept*
Fisher, D. C.: *The Bent Twig; The Deepening
   Stream*
Poole, Ernest: *The Harbor*
Tarkington, Booth: *The Turmoil; Alice Adams*

#### More Mature Studies

Deland, Margaret: *The Iron Woman*
Gale, Zona: *Miss Lulu Bett*
Hawthorne, Nathaniel: *The House of the
   Seven Gables; The Marble Faun*
Hersey, John: *A Bell for Adano*
Howells, W. D.: *A Modern Instance*
James, Henry: *The Portrait of a Lady*
Lewis, Sinclair: *Dodsworth*
London, Jack: *Martin Eden*
Marquand, John P.: *The Late George Apley;
   H. M. Pulham, Esquire; So Little Time*
Suckow, Ruth: *The Folks*
Wharton, Edith: *Ethan Frome* (novelette);
   *The Age of Innocence*
Wilder, Thornton: *The Bridge of San Luis Rey*

THE WRITER of informal essays takes his subject matter from his own pastimes and interests. (Frederic Lewis)

# Modern American Prose

## THE INFORMAL ESSAY

I F WE were making a list of the things we really enjoy doing in this world, most of us would put near the top the simple, everyday act of sitting down and chatting with our best friends about things in general. Our minds are then comfortable and relaxed; our ideas flow without great effort. We may surprise ourselves occasionally by a sudden realization of how well we have been talking, or perhaps we may forget ourselves completely in listening to the engrossing conversation of a friend. The best informal essays are such pieces of glorified conversation. They take us into the confidence of the writer on an informal, everyday plane. They are the literary form which is nearest to human friendship.

Our daily lives are full of essays. Wherever people are thrown together for an hour's chat, be it train, hotel lobby, party, picnic, or what not, you will hear little essays in progress on " The Weather," " What I Like to Eat," " How to Reduce," " Where to Spend a Vacation," " The Kind of People I Like," " The Best Make of Car," and so on and on.

Besides being personal in tone, most good informal essays tend to be gay rather than serious. They are pervaded by an easy and sprightly humor. They have the light touch.

A third characteristic of the informal essay is a graceful, literary style. The essayist is a cultivated citizen of the world. He has read widely. He assumes that the reader is equally well read, equally sophisticated, equally appreciative of a neat turn of phrase.

So far we have been discussing the essay as a comparatively short unit of writing. But there are certain types of nonfiction books which are closely allied to the essay. It is easy enough to identify the collection of essays — a book of more or less unrelated short pieces, sometimes by one author, or again by various authors. Paul de Kruif's *Microbe Hunters,* a selection from which concludes this section, would be a good example of a book of unrelated essays by a single writer. But in another book an author may present a series of short essays, each a separate unit but so closely related in theme that when put together they build up a unified picture or experience in the mind of the reader. An outstanding example of this is Clarence Day's *Life with Father,* which leaves one with as vivid impressions of characters as a novel does; yet it is definitely a series of short separate essays.

The six essays which follow are by six outstanding modern writers. Among them are our most successful modern essayists. These men seem to have a way of taking us at once into the circle of their personal friends. Their essays are " good talk." If these essayists make you want to " talk back " on paper, so much the better. A good essayist is like an electric current sent through the brain. He makes us tingle with ideas.

THOMAS WOLFE          CLARENCE DAY              E. B. WHITE

## James Thurber                1894–

James Thurber, an artist as well as a writer, is perhaps as well known for his " inspired doodling " as for his stories and essays. Perhaps you have seen some of his indescribable drawings in his latest book of cartoons, *Men, Women and Dogs*. If so, you will never forget his determined, somewhat frightening women, his overstuffed men who are so valiantly and so unsuccessfully trying to achieve a thought, or his huge, resigned dogs with their floppy ears. Especially the dogs. He has made that sort of dog immortal.

Mr. Thurber's writings are as difficult to describe as his drawings. Although they have a deceptive air of casualness, they have often been rewritten as many as ten times. Along with his humor there is wisdom and penetrating comment on modern man. He is a true humorist, and a genuine humorist is much more than a man who is merely funny.

James Thurber was graduated from Ohio State University in 1919. He served an apprenticeship on various newspapers and was for a while managing editor of the *New Yorker*. He still contributes many of his drawings and articles to that magazine.

Among his better-known books are *My Life and Hard Times, Let Your Mind Alone, Fables for Our Time, My World — and Welcome to It*. With Elliott Nugent he wrote the Broadway success, *The Male Animal*. His most recent book, *The White Deer*, is a sly parody of the old-time fairy tale in the form of a fantasy for moderns.

## UNIVERSITY DAYS

Mr. Thurber's amusing account of some of his college experiences may remind you of similar happenings in high school. Perhaps the very first sentence will win from you a sympathetic response.

I passed all the other courses that I took at my university, but I could never pass botany. This was because all botany students had to spend several hours a week in a laboratory looking through a microscope at plant cells, and I could never see through a microscope. I never once saw a cell through a microscope. This used to enrage my instructor. He would wander around the laboratory pleased with the progress all the students were making in drawing the involved and, so I am told, interesting structure of flower cells, until he came to me. I would just be standing there. " I can't see anything," I would say. He would begin patiently enough, explaining how anybody can see through a microscope, but he would always end up in a fury, claiming that I could *too* see through a microscope but just pretended that I couldn't. " It takes away from the beauty of flowers anyway," I used to tell him. " We are not concerned with beauty in this course," he would say. " We are concerned solely with what I may call the *mechanics* of flars." " Well," I'd say, " I can't see anything." " Try it just once again," he'd say, and I would put my eye to the microscope and see nothing at all, except now and again a nebulous milky substance — a phenomenon of maladjustment. You were supposed to see a vivid, restless clock-work of sharply defined plant cells. " I see what looks like a lot of milk," I would tell him. This, he claimed, was the result of my not having adjusted the microscope properly, so he would readjust it for me, or rather, for himself. And I would look again and see milk.

I finally took a deferred pass, as they called it, and waited a year and tried again. (You had to pass one of the biological sciences or you couldn't graduate.) The professor had come back from vacation brown as a berry, bright-eyed, and eager to explain cell structure again to his classes. " Well," he said to me, cheerily, when we met in the first laboratory hour of the semester, " we're going to see cells this time, aren't we? " " Yes, sir," I said. Students to right of me and to left of me and in front of me were seeing cells; what's more, they were quietly drawing pictures of them in their notebooks. Of course, I didn't see anything.

" We'll try it," the professor said to me, grimly, " with every adjustment of the microscope known to man. As God is my witness, I'll arrange this glass so that you see cells through it or I'll give up teaching. In twenty-two years of botany, I — " He cut off abruptly for he was beginning to quiver all over, like Lionel Barrymore, and he genuinely wished to hold onto his temper; his scenes with me had taken a great deal out of him.

So we tried it with every adjustment of the microscope known to man. With only one of them did I see anything but blackness or the familiar lacteal opacity, and that time I saw, to my pleasure and amazement, a variegated constellation of flecks, specks, and dots. These I hastily drew. The instructor, noting my activity, came back from an adjoining desk, a smile on his lips and his eyebrows high in hope. He looked at my cell drawing. " What's that? " he demanded, with a hint of a squeal in his voice. " That's what I saw," I said. " You didn't, you didn't, you *did*n't! " he screamed, losing control of his temper instantly, and he bent over and squinted into the microscope. His head snapped up. " That's your eye! " he shouted. " You've fixed the lens so that it reflects! You've drawn your eye! "

Another course that I didn't like, but somehow managed to pass, was economics. I went to that class straight from the botany class, which didn't help me any in understanding either subject. I used to get them mixed up. But not as mixed up as another student in my economics class who came there direct from a physics laboratory. He was a tackle on the football team, named Bolenciecwcz. At that time Ohio State University had one of the best football teams in the country, and Bolenciecwcz was one of its outstanding stars. In order to be eligible to play it was necessary for him to keep up in his studies, a very difficult matter, for while he was not dumber than an ox he was not any smarter. Most of his professors were lenient and helped him along. None gave him more hints, in answering questions, or asked him simpler ones than the economics professor, a thin, timid man named Bassum. One day when we were on the subject of transportation and distribution, it came Bolenciecwcz's turn to answer a question. " Name one means of transportation," the professor said to him. No light came into the big tackle's eyes. " Just any means of transportation," said the professor. Bolenciecwcz sat staring at him. " That is," pursued the professor, " any medium, agency, or method of going from one place to another." Bolenciecwcz had the look of a man who is being led into a trap. " You may choose among steam, horse-drawn, or electrically propelled vehicles," said the instructor. " I might suggest the one which we

THURBER DRAWING. Bolenciecwcz was trying to think.

commonly take in making long journeys across land." There was a profound silence in which everybody stirred uneasily, including Bolenciecwcz and Mr. Bassum. Mr. Bassum abruptly broke this silence in an amazing manner. " Choo-choo-choo," he said, in a low voice, and turned instantly scarlet. He glanced appealingly around the room. All of us, of course, shared Mr. Bassum's desire that Bolenciecwcz should stay abreast of the class in economics, for the Illinois game, one of the hardest and most important of the season, was only a week off. " Toot, toot, too-tooooooot! " some student with a deep voice moaned, and we all looked encouragingly at Bolenciecwcz. Somebody else gave a fine imitation of a locomotive letting off steam. Mr. Bassum himself rounded off the little show. " Ding, dong, ding, dong," he said, hopefully. Bolenciecwcz was staring at the floor now, trying to think, his great brow furrowed, his huge hands rubbing together, his face red.

" How did you come to college this year, Mr. Bolenciecwcz? " asked the professor. "*Chu*ffa chuffa, *chu*ffa chuffa."

" M'father sent me," said the football player.

" What on? " asked Bassum.

" I git an 'lowance," said the tackle, in a low, husky voice, obviously embarrassed.

" No, no," said Bassum. " Name a means of transportation. What did you *ride* here on? "

" Train," said Bolenciecwcz.

" Quite right," said the professor. " Now, Mr. Nugent, will you tell us — "

If I went through anguish in botany and economics — for different reasons — gymnasium work was even worse. I don't even like to think about it. They wouldn't let you play games or join in the exercises with your glasses on and I couldn't see with mine off. I bumped into professors, horizontal bars, agricultural students, and swinging iron rings. Not being able to see, I could take it but I couldn't dish it out. Also, in order to pass gymnasium (and you had to pass it to graduate) you had to learn to swim if you didn't know how. I didn't like the swimming pool, I didn't like swimming, and I didn't like the swimming instructor, and after all these years I still don't. Another thing I didn't like about gymnasium work was that they made you strip the day you registered. It is impossible for me to be happy when I am stripped and being asked a lot of questions. Still, I did better than a lanky agricultural student who was cross-examined just before I was. They asked each student what college he was in — that is, whether Arts, Engineering, Commerce, or Agriculture. " What college are you in? " the instructor snapped at the youth in front of me. " Ohio State University," he said promptly.

It wasn't that agricultural student but it was another a whole lot like him who decided to take up journalism, possibly on the ground that when farming went to pot he could fall back on newspaper work. He didn't realize, of course, that that would be very much like falling back full-length on a kit of carpenter's tools. Haskins didn't seem cut out for journalism, being too embarrassed to talk to anybody and unable to use a typewriter, but the editor of the college paper assigned him to the cow barns, the sheep house, the horse pavilion, and the animal husbandry department generally. This was a genuinely big " beat," for it took up five times as much ground and got ten times as great a legislative appropriation as the College of Liberal Arts. The agricultural student knew animals, but nevertheless his stories were dull and colorlessly written. He took all afternoon on each of them, on account of having to hunt for each letter on the typewriter. Once in a while he had to ask somebody to help him hunt. " C " and " L," in particular, were hard letters for him to find. His editor finally got pretty much annoyed at the farmer-journalist because his pieces were so uninteresting. " See here, Haskins," he snapped at him one day, " why is it we never have anything hot from you on the horse pavilion? Here we have two hundred head of horses on this campus — more than any other university in the Western Conference except Purdue — and yet you never get any real low-down on them. Now shoot over to the horse barns and dig up something lively." Haskins shambled out and came back in about an hour; he said he had something. " Well, start it off snappily," said the editor. " Something people will read." Haskins set to work and in a couple of hours brought a sheet of typewritten paper to the desk; it was a two-hundred word story about some disease that had broken out among the horses. Its opening sentence was simple but arresting. It read: " Who has noticed the sores on the tops of the horses in the animal husbandry building? "

Ohio State was a land-grant university and therefore two years of military drill was compulsory. We drilled with old Springfield rifles and studied the tactics of the Civil War even though the World War [1] was going on at the time. At eleven o'clock each morning thousands of freshmen and sophomores used to deploy over the campus, moodily creeping up on the old chemistry building. It was good training for the kind of warfare that was waged at Shiloh but it had no connection with what was going on in Europe. Some people used to think there was Ger-

[1] **World War:** This was World War I, 1917-18.

man money behind it, but they didn't dare say so or they would have been thrown in jail as German spies. It was a period of muddy thought and marked, I believe, the decline of higher education in the Middle West.

As a soldier I was never any good at all. Most of the cadets were glumly indifferent soldiers, but I was no good at all. Once General Littlefield, who was commandant of the cadet corps, popped up in front of me during regimental drill and snapped, " You are the main trouble with this university! " I think he meant that my type was the main trouble with the university but he may have meant me individually. I was mediocre at drill, certainly — that is, until my senior year. By that time I had drilled longer than anybody else in the Western Conference, having failed at military at the end of each preceding year so that I had to do it all over again. I was the only senior still in uniform. The uniform which, when new, had made me look like an interurban railway conductor, now that it had become faded and too tight made me look like Bert Williams in his bellboy act. This had a definitely bad effect on my morale. Even so, I had become by sheer practice little short of wonderful at squad maneuvers.

One day General Littlefield picked our company out of the whole regiment and tried to get it mixed up by putting it through one movement after another as fast as we could execute them: squads right, squads left, squads on right into line, squads right about, squads left front into line, etc. In about three minutes one hundred and nine men were marching in one direction and I was marching away from them at an angle of forty degrees, all alone. " Company, halt! " shouted General Littlefield, " That man is the only man who has it right! " I was made a corporal for my achievement.

The next day General Littlefield summoned me to his office. He was swatting flies when I went in. I was silent and he was silent too, for a long time. I don't think he remembered me or why he had sent for me, but he didn't want to admit it. He swatted some more flies, keeping his eyes on them narrowly before he let go with the swatter. " Button up your coat! " he snapped. Looking back on it now I can see that he meant me although he was looking at a fly, but I just stood there. Another fly came to rest on a paper in front of the general and began rubbing its hind legs together. The general lifted the swatter cautiously. I moved restlessly and the fly flew away. " You startled him! " barked General Littlefield, looking at me severely. I said I was sorry. " That won't help the situation! " snapped the General, with cold military logic. I didn't see what I could do except offer to chase some more flies toward his desk, but I didn't say anything. He stared out the window at the faraway figures of coeds crossing the campus toward the library. Finally, he told me I could go. So I went. He either didn't know which cadet I was or else he forgot what he wanted to see me about. It may have been that he wished to apologize for having called me the main trouble with the university; or maybe he had decided to compliment me on my brilliant drilling of the day before and then at the last minute decided not to. I don't know. I don't think about it much any more.

## Suggestions for Study

1. What is the difference between a college and a university?

2. In your school are most of the athletes good students, or is there a distinct cleavage between the " athletic type " and the " student type "? Name some students who excel in both lines. To what extent would you support a teacher who refused to lie about the scholastic standing of an outstanding athlete?

3. What are the advantages of military training in college? in high school?

4. Point out passages which show that this is a light, informal treatment of the subject rather than a serious discussion.

5. Relate some experience of your own in dealing with a school subject which you found difficult. Don't be afraid to poke a little fun at yourself.

6. Vocabulary: nebulous, lacteal, opacity.

## Clarence Day                    1874-1935

Clarence Day's family, one of New York's prominent and prosperous ones, lived in a typical brownstone front on Madison Avenue in the seventies and eighties. The father, Clarence Day, Sr., son of the founder of the New York *Sun*, was a successful stockbroker. The mother had been a beautiful debutante before her marriage. The four little boys were brought up with all the advantages of that day. Servants kept the household routine running smoothly. From without, the family would seem to inspire awe or envy, perhaps, but certainly not laughter. Yet seen through the eyes of the eldest son, this family has become one of the chief American mirth producers.

Clarence Day's mature life was a struggle against disease, mention of which he never allowed to creep into his books or his conversation. After leaving Yale, he enlisted in the Navy to escape the seat on the stock exchange which his father insisted on buying for him. Here he developed arthritis, which crippled him to such an extent that he spent much of the rest of his life on crutches, in a wheel chair, or in bed. But this did not deter him from trying ranch life in Colorado, managing a glove business, making and losing money on the stock exchange, marrying a charming New England girl, and gaining a reputation as one of the wittiest conversationalists in New York. He could draw clever sketches as well as write — all the more remarkable when we learn that because of his disease he had to hold his pencil awkwardly between thumb and third finger and move his muscles from the shoulder.

## FATHER AND HIS HARD-ROCKING SHIP

Although he wrote several other witty books, Clarence Day's real place in American literature has been won by the three comparatively short books of sketches about his own family — *God and My Father, Life with Father*, and *Life with Mother*. Since the author's death, incidents and conversation from these books have been cleverly woven into a comedy called *Life with Father*, one of the greatest successes in the history of the theater. It is no wonder that this amazing family of redheads has won popular favor on the stage as well as between the covers of a book.

Father, strong-willed, authoritative, expecting to dominate his home as he does his business, finds unaccountable obstacles in mother's quiet determination, in boy nature, in social conventions, and in things in general which do not bow immediately to his will. His explosions rock the household, but the reader feels underneath the tempest the saving foundation of family affection and solidarity, and Clarence remarked once that he actually pitied those dull families that were always quiet and mannerly.

Father said that one great mystery about the monthly household expenses was what made them jump up and down so. " Anyone would suppose that there would be some regularity after a while which would let a man try to make plans, but I never know from one month to another what to expect."

Mother said she didn't, either. Things just seemed to go that way.

" But they have no business to go that way, Vinnie," Father declared. " And, what's more, I won't allow it."

Mother said she didn't see what she could do about it. All she knew was that when the bills mounted up it didn't mean that she had been extravagant.

" Well, it certainly means that you've spent a devil of a lot of money," said Father.

Mother looked at him obstinately. She couldn't exactly deny this, but she said that it wasn't fair.

Appearances were often hopelessly against Mother, but that never daunted her. She wasn't afraid of Father or anybody. She was a woman of great spirit who would have flown at and pecked any tyrant. It was only when she had a bad conscience that she had no heart to fight. Father had the best of her there because he never had a bad conscience. And he didn't know that he was a tyrant. He regarded himself as a long-suffering man who asked little of anybody, and who showed only the greatest moderation in his encounters with unreasonable beings like Mother. Mother's one advantage over him was that she was quicker. She was particularly elusive when Father was trying to hammer her into shape.

When the household expenses shot up very high, Father got frightened. He would then, as Mother put it, yell his head off. He always did some yelling anyhow, merely on general principles, but when his alarm was genuine he roared in real anguish.

Usually this brought the total down again, at least for a while. But there were times when no amount of noise seemed to do any good and when every month for one reason or another the total went on up and up. And then, just as Father had almost resigned himself to this awful outgo, and just as he had eased up on his yelling and had begun to feel grim, the expenses, to his utter amazement, would take a sharp drop.

Mother didn't keep track of these totals; she was too busy watching small details, and Father never knew whether to tell her the good news or not. He always did tell her, because he couldn't keep things to himself. But he always had cause to regret it.

When he told her, he did it in as disciplinary a manner as possible. He didn't congratulate her on the expenses having come down. He appeared at her door, waving the bills at her with a threatening scowl, and said, " I've told you again and again that you could keep the expenses down if you tried, and this shows I was right."

Mother was always startled at such attacks, but she didn't lose her presence of mind. She asked how much less the amount was and said it was all due to her good management, of course, and Father ought to give her the difference.

At this point Father suddenly found himself on the defensive, and the entire moral lecture that he had intended to deliver was wrecked. The more they talked, the clearer it seemed to Mother that he owed her that money. Only when he was lucky could he get out of her room without paying it.

He said that this was one of the things about her that was enough to drive a man mad.

The other thing was her lack of system,

which was always cropping up in new ways. He sometimes looked at Mother as though he had never seen her before. " Upon my soul," he said, " I almost believe you don't know what system is. You don't even want to know, either."

He had at last invented what seemed a perfect method of recording expenses. Whenever he gave any money to Mother, he asked her what it was for and made a note of it in his pocket notebook. His idea was that these items, added to those in the itemized bills, would show him exactly where every dollar had gone.

But they didn't.

He consulted his notebook. " I gave you six dollars in cash on the twenty-fifth of last month," he said, " to buy a new coffee-pot."

" Yes," Mother said, " because you broke your old one. You threw it right on the floor."

Father frowned. " I'm not talking about that," he answered. " I am simply endeavoring to find out from you, if I can — "

" But it's so silly to break a nice coffee-pot, Clare, and that was the last of those French ones, and there was nothing the matter with the coffee that morning; it was made just the same as it always is."

" It wasn't," said Father. " It was made in a barbaric manner."

" And I couldn't get another French one," Mother continued, " because that little shop the Auffmordts told us about has stopped selling them. They said the tariff wouldn't let them any more, and I told Monsieur Duval he ought to be ashamed of himself to stand there and say so. I said that if I had a shop I'd like to see the tariff keep me from selling things."

" But I gave you six dollars to buy a new pot," Father firmly repeated, " and now I find that you apparently got one at Lewis and Conger's and charged it. Here's their bill: ' One brown earthenware drip coffee-pot, five dollars.' "

" So I saved you a dollar," Mother triumphantly said, " and you can hand it right over to me."

" Bah! What nonsense you talk! " Father cried. " Is there no way to get this thing straightened out? What did you do with the six dollars? "

" Why, Clare! I can't tell you now, dear. Why didn't you ask at the time? "

" Oh, great Scott! " Father groaned.

" Wait a moment," said Mother. " I spent four dollars and a half for that new umbrella I told you I wanted, and you said I didn't need a new one; but I did, very much."

Father got out his pencil and wrote " New Umbrella for V." in his notebook.

" And that must have been the week," Mother went on, " that I paid Mrs. Tobin for two extra days' washing, so that was two dollars more out of it, which makes it six-fifty. There's another fifty cents that you owe me."

" I don't owe you anything," Father said. " You have managed to turn a coffee-pot for me into a new umbrella for you. No matter what I give you money for, you buy something else with it; and if this is to keep on, I might as well not keep account books at all."

" I'd like to see you run this house without having any money on hand for things," Mother said.

" I am not made of money," Father replied. " You seem to think I only have to put my hand in my pocket to get some."

Mother not only thought this, she knew it. His wallet always was full. That was the provoking part of it — she knew he had the money right there, but he tried to keep from giving it to her. She had to argue it out of him.

" Well, you can put your hand in your pocket and give me that dollar-fifty this minute," she said. " You owe me that, anyhow."

Father said that he didn't have a dollar-fifty to spare and tried to get back to his desk, but Mother wouldn't let him go till he paid her. She said she wouldn't put up with injustice.

Mother said it hampered her dreadfully never to have any cash. She was always

LIFE WITH FATHER. Here father is having difficulty in getting mother to understand household bookkeeping. The play version is one of the most successful Broadway productions of all time. (Photo, Vandamm, courtesy of Oscar Serlin, producer)

having to pay out small amounts for demands that she had forgot to provide for, and in such emergencies the only way to do was to juggle things around. One result, however, of all these more or less innocent shifts was that in this way she usually took care of all her follies herself. All the small ones, at any rate. They never got entered on Father's books, except when they were monstrous.

She came home one late afternoon in a terrible state. " Has it come yet? " she asked the waitress.

The waitress said nothing had come that she knew of.

Mother ran upstairs with a hunted expression and flung herself down on her bed. When we looked in, she was sobbing.

It turned out that she had gone to an auction, and she had become so excited that she had bought but not paid for a grandfather's clock.

Mother knew in her heart that she had no business going to auctions. She was too suggestible; and if an hypnotic auctioneer once got her eye, she was lost. Besides, an auction aroused all her worst instincts — her combativeness, her recklessness, and her avaricious love of a bargain. And the worst of it was that this time it wasn't a bargain at all. At least she didn't think it was now. The awful old thing was about eight feet tall, and it wasn't the one she had wanted. It wasn't half as nice as the clock that old Miss Van Derwent had bought. And inside the hood over the dial, she said, there was a little ship which at first she hadn't noticed, a horrid ship that rocked up and down every time the clock ticked. It made her ill just to look at it. And she didn't have the money, and the man said he'd have to send it this evening, and what would Father say?

She came down to dinner, and left halfway through. Couldn't stand it. But an hour or two later, when the doorbell rang, she bravely went to tell Father.

She could hardly believe it; but she found that luck was with her, for once. If the clock had come earlier, there might have been a major catastrophe; but Father was in a good mood, and he had had a good dinner. And though he never admitted it or spoke of it, he had a weakness for clocks. There were clocks all over the house, which he would allow no one to wind but himself. Every Sunday between breakfast and church he made the rounds, setting them at the right time by his infallible watch, regulating their speed, and telling us about every clock's little idiosyncrasies. When he happened to be coming downstairs on the hour, he cocked his ear, watch in hand, to listen to as many of them as he could, in the hope that they would all strike at once. He would reprove the impulsive pink clock in the spare room for striking too soon, and the big solemn clock in the dining room for being a minute too late.

So when Mother led him out in the hall to confess to him and show him what she had bought, and he saw it was a clock, he fell in love with it and made almost no fuss at all.

The letdown was too much for Mother. She tottered off to her room without another word and went straight to bed, leaving Father and the auctioneer's man setting up the new clock alongside the hatrack. Father was especially fascinated by the hard-rocking ship.

## Suggestions for Study

1. What characteristics of Father and Mother are most evident in this selection? How do you feel toward each of them? What evidence is there of the financial standing of the family?

2. Which parts of the essay appealed to you as especially funny? Could a similar situation be treated with tragic rather than comic ef-

fect? What essential differences are there between comic bickering and tragic quarreling?

3. Why is this classed as an essay rather than as a short story? Discuss differences between the two forms.

4. Read other parts of the Day books mentioned in the introduction, and report or read to the class especially choice bits.

5. The play *Life with Father*, made from the Day books by Howard Lindsay and Russel Crouse, is available in book form and offers some fine opportunities for class dramatization.

6. Write an essay on some situation in your own family that lends itself to comic treatment.

## For Your Vocabulary

FIGURATIVE USE OF WORDS. It would be nearly impossible to picture the lively atmosphere of this home without figures of speech. The troublesome household expenses would " jump up and down " and sometimes they " shot up very high." Mother was a woman " who would have flown at and pecked any tyrant." To what is Mother compared? (Don't pick a meek fowl like a chicken!) In addition to comparison, exaggeration is appropriately used to give the mood of the Day household. No ordinary auctioneer could force a purchase on Mother. The clock was sold to her by a *hypnotic* (hĭp-nŏt′ĭk) auctioneer. Do you think he could really *hypnotize* (hĭp′nŏ-tīz) people? Father would " yell his head off " when the expenses indulged in their acrobatics. Such exaggeration is called *hyperbole* (hī-pûr′bŏ-lê), and it is a favorite figure of speech with young people. Did you ever say " I nearly died laughing " or " I waited ages for the phone to ring "? What are some of the common hyperboles in the talk of your crowd?

## Thomas Wolfe                1900–1938

On the tombstone of Thomas Wolfe in Asheville, North Carolina, are these words from one of his novels: " Death bent to touch his chosen son with mercy, love, and pity, and put the seal of honor on him when he died." These words suggest the tragedy of Thomas Wolfe's life, cut short by death at the early age of thirty-eight.

Born into comparative poverty, Wolfe, who

was a giant in both body and intellect, overcame all obstacles and entered the University of North Carolina at the age of fifteen. Later he received his M.A. from Harvard and attempted unsuccessfully to become a playwright. He then turned to the novel, and achieved a spectacular success, though some critics violently contended that his books were amateurish and unskillful, and — in their use of autobiographical material — inexcusably offensive.

Writing was never a light task for Thomas Wolfe. He was obsessed with the need to say what was on his mind, and on his mind was much which demanded to be expressed. " As I prowled the streets of Brooklyn," he says, " the staggering impact of man's inhumanity to his fellow man left a scar upon my life, a conviction in my soul which I shall never lose."

## CIRCUS AT DAWN

It is a far cry from Thomas Wolfe's long novels to the informal essay. But one of his books, *From Death to Morning,* contains some shorter, lighter pieces which Wolfe himself said were as good writing as he had ever done. You will not wish to read *Look Homeward, Angel* or *Of Time and the River* till you are considerably older, but you ought to find in " Circus at Dawn " a pleasant introduction to a modern writer who created " some of the noblest prose that ever came out of America."

There were times in early autumn — in September — when the greater circuses would come to town — the Ringling Brothers, Robinson's, and Barnum and Bailey shows, and when I was a route-boy on the morning paper, on those mornings when the circus would be coming in I would rush madly through my route in the cool and thrilling darkness that comes just before break of day, and then I would go back home and get my brother out of bed.

Talking in low excited voices we would walk rapidly back toward town under the rustle of September leaves, in cool streets just grayed now with that still, that unearthly and magical first light of day which seems suddenly to rediscover the great earth out of darkness, so that the earth emerges with an awful, a glorious sculptural stillness, and one looks out with a feeling of joy and disbelief, as the first men on this earth must have done, for to see this happen is one of the things that men will remember out of life forever and think of as they die.

At the sculptural still square where at one corner, just emerging into light, my father's shabby little marble shop stood with a ghostly strangeness and familiarity, my brother and I would " catch " the first streetcar of the day bound for the " depot " where the circus was — or sometimes we would meet someone we knew, who would give us a lift in his automobile.

Then, having reached the dingy, grimy, and rickety depot section, we would get out, and walk rapidly across the tracks of the station yard, where we could see great flares and steamings from the engines, and hear the crash and bump of shifting freight cars, the swift sporadic thunders of a shifting engine, the tolling of bells, the sounds of great trains on the rails.

And to all these familiar sounds, filled with their exultant prophecies of flight, the voyage, morning, and the shining cities — to all the sharp and thrilling odors of the trains — the smell of cinders, acrid smoke, of musty, rusty freight cars, the clean pineboard of crated produce, and the smells of fresh stored food — oranges, coffee, tangerines and bacon, ham and flour and beef — there would be added now, with an unforgettable magic and familiarity, all the strange sounds and smells of the coming circus.

The gay yellow sumptuous-looking cars in which the star performers lived and slept, still dark and silent, heavily and powerfully still, would be drawn up in long strings upon the tracks. And all around them the sounds of the unloading circus would go on furiously in the darkness. The receding gulf of lilac and departing night would be filled with the savage roar of the lions, the murderously sudden snarling of great jungle cats, the trumpeting of the elephants, the stamp of the horses, and with the musty, pungent, unfamiliar odor of the jungle ani-

CIRCUS AT DAWN. What boy wouldn't get up at dawn to superintend raising the big top? (Frederic Lewis)

mals: the tawny camel smells, and the smells of panthers, zebras, tigers, elephants, and bears.

Then, along the tracks, beside the circus trains, there would be the sharp cries and oaths of the circus men, the magical swinging dance of lanterns in the darkness, the sudden heavy rumble of the loaded vans and wagons as they were pulled along the flats and gondolas, and down the runways to the ground. And everywhere, in the thrilling mystery of darkness and awakening light, there would be the tremendous conflict of a confused, hurried, and yet orderly movement.

The great iron-gray horses, four and six to a team, would be plodding along the road of thick white dust to a rattling of chains and traces and the harsh cries of their drivers. The men would drive the animals to the river which flowed by beyond the tracks, and water them; and as first light came one could see the elephants wallowing in the familiar river and the big horses going slowly and carefully down to drink.

Then, on the circus grounds, the tents were going up already with the magic speed of dreams. All over the place (which was near the tracks and the only space of flat land in the town that was big enough to hold a circus) there would be this fierce, savagely hurried, and yet orderly confusion. Great flares of gaseous circus light would blaze down on the seared and battered faces of the circus toughs as, with the rhythmic precision of a single animal — a human riveting machine — they swung their sledges at the stakes, driving a stake into the earth with the incredible instancy of accelerated figures in a motion picture. And everywhere, as light came, and the sun appeared, there would be a scene of magic, order, and of violence. The drivers would curse and talk their special language to their teams, there would be the loud, gasping, and uneven labor of a gasoline engine, the shouts and curses of the bosses, the wooden riveting of driven stakes, and the rattle of heavy chains.

Already in an immense cleared space of dusty beaten earth, the stakes were being driven for the main exhibition tent. And an elephant would lurch ponderously to the field, slowly lower his great swinging head at the command of a man who sat perched upon his skull, flourish his gray wrinkled snout a time or two, and then solemnly wrap it around a tent pole big as the mast of a racing schooner. Then the elephant would back slowly away, dragging the great pole with him as if it were a stick of matchwood. . . .

Meanwhile, the circus food-tent — a huge canvas top without concealing sides — had already been put up, and now we could see the performers seated at long trestled tables underneath the tent, as they ate breakfast. And the savor of the food they ate — mixed as it was with our strong excitement, with the powerful but wholesome smells of the animals, and with all the joy, sweetness, mystery, jubilant magic and glory of the morning and the coming of the circus — seemed to us to be of the most maddening and appetizing succulence of any food that we had ever known or eaten.

We could see the circus performers eating tremendous breakfasts, with all the savage relish of their power and strength: they ate big fried steaks, pork chops, rashers of bacon, a half dozen eggs, great slabs of fried ham and great stacks of wheat cakes which a cook kept flipping in the air with the skill of a juggler, and which a husky-looking waitress kept rushing to their tables on loaded trays held high and balanced marvelously on the fingers of a brawny hand. And above all the maddening odors of the wholesome and succulent food, there brooded forever the sultry and delicious fragrance — that somehow seemed to add a zest and sharpness to all the powerful and thrilling life of morning — of strong boiling coffee, which we could see sending off clouds of steam from an enormous polished urn, and which the circus performers gulped down, cup after cup.

And the circus men and women themselves — these star performers — were such fine-looking people, strong and handsome, yet speaking and moving with an almost stern dignity and decorum, that their lives seemed to us to be as splendid and wonderful as any lives on earth could be. There was never anything loose, rowdy, or tough in their comportment. . . .

Rather, these people in an astonishing way seemed to have created an established community which lived an ordered existence on wheels, and to observe with a stern fidelity unknown in towns and cities the decencies of family life. There would be a powerful young man, a handsome and magnificent young woman with blonde hair and the figure of an Amazon, and a powerfully-built, thickset man of middle age, who had a stern, lined, responsible-looking face and a bald head. They were probably the members of a trapeze team — the young man and woman would leap through space like projectiles, meeting the grip of the older man and hurtling back again upon their narrow perches, catching the swing of their trapeze in mid-air, and whirling thrice before they caught it, in a perilous and beautiful exhibition of human balance and precision.

But when they came into the breakfast tent, they would speak gravely yet courteously to other performers, and seat themselves in a family group at one of the long tables, eating their tremendous breakfast with an earnest concentration, seldom speaking to one another, and then gravely, seriously, and briefly.

And my brother and I would look at them with fascinated eyes; my brother would watch the man with the bald head for a while and then turn toward me, whispering:

" D-d-do you see that f-f-fellow there with the bald head? W-w-well, he's the heavy man," he whispered knowingly. " He's the one that c-c-c-catches them! That f-f-fellow's got to know his business! You know what happens if he m-m-misses, don't you? " said my brother.

" What? " I would say in a fascinated tone.

My brother snapped his fingers in the air. " Over! " he said. " D-d-done for! W-w-why, they'd be d-d-d-dead before they knew what happened. Sure! " he said, nodding vigorously. " It's a f-f-f-fact! If he ever m-m-m-misses it's all over! That boy has g-g-g-got to know his s-s-s-stuff! " my brother said. " W-w-w-why," he went on in a low tone of solemn conviction, " it w-w-w-wouldn't surprise me at all if they p-p-p-pay him s-s-seventy-five or a hundred dollars a week! It's a fact! " my brother cried vigorously.

And we would turn our fascinated stares again upon these splendid and romantic creatures, whose lives were so different from our own, and whom we seemed to know with such familiar and affectionate intimacy. And at length, reluctantly, with full light come and the sun up, we would leave the circus grounds and start for home.

And somehow the memory of all we had seen and heard that glorious morning, and the memory of the food-tent with its wonderful smells, would waken in us the pangs of such a ravenous hunger that we could not wait until we got home to eat. We would stop off in town at lunchrooms and, seated on tall stools before the counter, we would devour ham-and-egg sandwiches, hot hamburgers red and pungent at their cores with coarse spicy sanguinary beef, coffee, glasses of foaming milk, and doughnuts, and then go home to eat up everything in sight upon the breakfast table.

## Suggestions for Study

1. Judging from this short essay, what qualities of writing would you expect to find in Thomas Wolfe's writing? In what ways is his prose like poetry?

2. Thomas Wolfe has said, " A man must use the material and experience of his own life if he is to create anything that has substantial value." Cite details from this essay which illustrate this principle.

3. In what ways does this glimpse into circus life change your preconceived ideas about circus people? What other people have you had wrong notions about before you became acquainted with them?

4. Try to put down on paper your own feelings when you first went to a circus.

5. Vocabulary: sporadic, exultant, receding, tawny, instancy, fidelity, sanguinary.

## For Your Vocabulary

WORD DISCRIMINATION. One of Wolfe's distinctions is the way he makes physical sensations vivid. Three words he uses of smell are richly descriptive. The " pungent (pŭn'jĕnt) odor of jungle animals " (page 153) is piercing and strong. A pungent odor may be pleasant or unpleasant, but it is always stimulating. The acrid (ăk'rĭd) smell of smoke (page 153) is sharp and penetrating, too strong, rather unpleasant. Acrid is often used of sharp and unpleasant remarks. Savor (page 155) is used of the smell of foods, and it has an appetite-stirring quality. For savor (sā'vẽr) is always pleasant, promising delicious tastes. The succulence (sŭk'ṵ-lĕns) of food (page 155) appeals to feeling, for it means juiciness. A bit of gossip, as well as food, can be succulent.

## Christopher Morley      1890–

As an essayist Christopher Morley has achieved high eminence among modern American writers. In maintaining the standard of the traditional informal literary essay no living author surpasses him.

Morley is an American in whom the English tradition is strong. Not only were his parents both born in England, but he himself was a Rhodes scholar at New College, Oxford.

Upon his return to America he variously connected with well-known publishing houses, magazines, and newspapers. For years he conducted " The Bowling Green " column in the New York Evening Post, thus linking himself with the professional humorists. In recent years he has devoted himself to independent writing, and it must not be forgotten that he has produced distinctive novels, short stories, plays and verse, as well as many volumes of essays. He has even ventured into the field of play production, having put on some old-fashioned melodramas with details carried out in the manner of a century ago.

## THE WOUNDED OYSTER

Two of Christopher Morley's earlier novels, *Parnassus on Wheels* and *The Haunted Bookshop*, established him not only as an author who knows and loves books, but also as one who knows sympathetically the problems of the bookseller. The touch of warmth with which he portrays the attractions of the second-hand bookshop has turned many a reader into a devotee of old bookstores. " The Wounded Oyster," a typical Morley essay, illustrates this particular characteristic of the many-sided Morley.

It was odd that of all those thousands of people streaming by, we were the only ones who stopped in to explore the dingy second-hand bookshop. Never before had so big a crowd gone past it. As we stood trying to see what classification, if any, existed along the grimy shelves we could hear the throng tramping past. There had been a world's championship prize fight near there, and sixty thousand spectators. Rather than fight for places in busses, taxis, and trolleys, about half of them preferred to walk back to the ferries.

There was pathos in the puzzled look of the old bookseller. He had emerged from his dusty little burrow at the back and stood at the open door watching the crowd press by. As Edna took off her smart white gloves and slipped them into my pocket, I saw that shadow of wistfulness that troubles her when we both feel the same thing but don't quite know how to communicate it. The hot summer afternoon, the impure air of the book-stuffed shop, the feeling of finality one has when a long-anticipated event is suddenly over, some dim awareness of all the tender and troubled secrets hidden in these masses of abandoned volumes, and the contrast of the voices and movement outside, life going by so fierce and random. . . . I could see in Edna's face that she wanted me to buy something, even if only to encourage the old bookseller. And it must be just the right thing, too. Edna has a queer way of putting one on his mettle, in niceties of sentiment.

Devotees of old bookstores are not nice about dirt, but I've never seen one sootier than that. There must be some secret symbolism in the affinity between books and dust. Second-hand bookshops that are much frequented keep fairly clean because the patrons carry away so much of the dust on their clothes. But I'm afraid this place had few customers. It was well-stocked: I saw at once several things that tempted me. As I worked my way deeper into the store I heard Edna amiably duetting with the old gentleman. She is always rather at the mercy of talkative people; she is not skillful at amputating conversations.

Perhaps because I had just lost a small wager on the fight I was feeling thrifty. But while I was glancing at a volume of Emerson's Essays I had a sudden impulse. Unobserved, I slipped a clean five-dollar bill into the book, at the first page of the essay on Compensation. I put the volume carefully back in its place on the shelf. Farther along the same row I found a copy of *Ethics of the Dust,* which I thought would be an appropriate souvenir of our visit. It was marked forty cents. I could see that Edna thought this hardly a large enough purchase, but I gave her our special signal which means " Come along and don't argue; something important is happening."

Every now and then, when Edna and I had a chance to lunch together, we used to slip across the river to revisit the bookshop. While she engaged the old man in conversation I would peep stealthily between the pages of Emerson. But always the bill was still there. In one or two hard-up spells I was almost tempted to replevin it myself. I suppose there's not much demand for Emerson in that region of docks and factories, but I was a little disappointed that my stratagem had had no effect. I even read the essay on Compensation aloud to Edna one evening; we found it a trifle solemn.

THE ROMANCE OF THE BOOKSHOP. Every city has its musty secondhand bookstore, tucked away on a back street. (Keystone-Underwood)

The following autumn, after a considerable interim, we visited the shop again. What a change! It had been painted, the books rearranged, and the old bibliophile showed signs of animation.

"Well," he said, "a mighty queer thing happened. Just before school opened there was a young woman in here, a teacher, looking for a copy of Emerson's Essays. She got it off the shelf, and then she says, ' Why, there's some money in it! ' Sure enough, there was a five-dollar bill in the book, what do you think of that? She might just as well kept it, I had no idea it was there, but she wouldn't. Said it didn't belong to her. Well, it didn't belong to me neither, but finally we agreed to split it. After she'd gone, I got to thinking. That was one of a lot I bought from an estate in Plainfield, an eccentric old

gentleman: maybe there might be more money in some of those books. Besides I was sort of scared, thought it might be some kind of a plant to get me in wrong somehow, or to pass off bad bills on me; you never know who might want to do you dirt. I went through all the shelves on that side of the store, just to see. I didn't find any money, but I like to suffocate with the dust. That started me cleaning up. This place was too dirty to get decent folks to come in. That schoolteacher was so excited about finding that bill she come in again and bought a lot more, and she sent all her pupils in here to buy their textbooks. Then the local paper got hold of it and wrote it up. Business has been grand. But say, that was a queer thing, hey? I'm going to put up this sign in the window."

He pointed to a placard, which read:

> YOU MAY FIND MONEY
> IN THESE BOOKS

As we went back in the ferry Edna looked at me with a special luster in her eyes. " The wounded oyster," she said, " mends his shell with pearl." That, I ought to explain, is a line from the essay on Compensation.

I really must get around to reading *Ethics of the Dust*. I have a feeling there are messages in it for me.

## Suggestions for Study

1. What is the meaning of the title of this essay?

2. To what extent have you developed skill in " amputating conversation "? What other well-worded phrases did you find in this essay?

3. Relate to the class some incident in which you were unable to communicate your feelings.

4. Vocabulary: affinity, replevin, stratagem, bibliophile.

## E. B. White        1899–

Since the birth of the *New Yorker* in 1926 and its rapid rise as one of our wittiest magazines of general comment, the name of E. B. White has stamped itself vividly on the public mind. (The E. B. serves to conceal the name of Elwyn Brooks.) He says that he became an " orderly " on the magazine, meaning that he did any job that needed to be done, from reviews to tag lines, even cover designs on occasion. He built up " The Talk of the Town " column, which gave him the right outlet for his versatility and originality. He could not work by set patterns. He tells how the *Seattle Times* had previously parted company with him because of his " uninhibited journalese."

In 1932 he married another member of the *New Yorker* staff, and he and his wife, Katharine S. White, have edited *A Sub-Treasury of American Humor*, an excellent and entertaining anthology. One of his most interesting books is *Stuart Little*, a delightful fantasy for young and old about the Littles' second son, who looked and acted like a mouse.

## ONCE MORE TO THE LAKE

For five years Mr. White contributed to *Harper's Magazine* a monthly record of his life on his Maine farm, under the title " One Man's Meat." These essays, published as a book with the same title, were awarded The Limited Editions Club's Gold Medal as " the book which is considered most nearly to attain the stature of a classic."

The following essay is from " One Man's Meat." It was written in August, 1941 — just four months before America entered World War II. But you will find the peace and tranquillity of the Maine woods far removed from world conflict and atomic bombs.

One summer, along about 1904, my father rented a camp on a lake in Maine and took us all there for the month of August. We all got ringworm from some kittens and had to rub Pond's Extract on our arms and legs night and morning, and my father rolled over in a canoe with all his clothes on; but outside of that the vacation was a success and from then on none of us ever thought there was any place in the world like that lake in Maine. We returned summer after summer — always on August 1 for one month. I have since become a salt-water man, but sometimes in summer there are days when the restlessness of the tides and the fearful cold of the sea water and the incessant wind which blows across the afternoon and into the evening make me wish for the placidity of a lake in the woods. A few weeks ago this feeling got so strong I bought myself a couple of bass hooks and a spinner and returned to the lake where we used to go, for a week's fishing and to revisit old haunts.

I took along my son, who had never had any fresh water up his nose and who had seen lily pads only from train windows. On the journey over to the lake I began to wonder what it would be like. I wondered how time would have marred this unique, this holy spot — the coves and streams, the hills that the sun set behind, the camps and the paths behind the camps. I was sure that the tarred road would have found it out and I wondered in what other ways it would be desolated. It is strange how much you can remember about places like that once you allow your mind to return into the grooves which lead back. You remember one thing, and that suddenly reminds you of another thing. I guess I remembered clearest of all the early mornings, when the lake was cool and motionless, remembered how the bedroom smelled of the lumber it was made of and of the wet woods whose scent entered through the screen. The partitions in the camp were thin and did not extend clear to the top of the rooms, and as I was always the first up I would dress softly so as not to wake the others, and sneak out into the sweet outdoors and start out in the canoe, keeping close along the shore in the long shadows of the pines. I remembered being very careful never to rub my paddle against the thwart for fear of disturbing the stillness of the cathedral.

The lake had never been what you would call a wild lake. There were cottages sprinkled around the shores, and it was in farming country, although the shores of the lake were quite heavily wooded. Some of the cottages were owned by near-by farmers, and you would live at the shore and eat your meals at the farmhouse. That's what our family did. But although it wasn't wild, it was a fairly large and undisturbed lake and there were places in it which, to a child at least, seemed infinitely remote and primeval.

I was right about the tar: it led to within half a mile of the shore. But when I got back there, with my boy, and we settled into a camp near a farmhouse and into the kind of summertime I had known, I could tell that it was going to be pretty much the same as it had been before — I knew it, lying in bed the first morning, smelling the bedroom, and hearing the boy sneak quietly out and go off along the shore in a boat. I began to sustain the illusion that he was I, and therefore, by simple transposition, that I was my father. This sensation persisted, kept cropping up all the time we were there. It was not an entirely new feeling, but in this setting it grew much stronger. I seemed to be living a dual existence. I would be in the middle of some simple act, I would be picking up a bait box or laying down a table fork, or I would be saying something, and suddenly it would be not I but my father who was saying the words or making the gesture. It gave me a creepy sensation.

We went fishing the first morning. I felt the same damp moss covering the worms in the bait can, and saw the dragonfly alight on the tip of my rod as it hovered a few inches from the surface of the water. It was the arrival of this fly that convinced me beyond any doubt that everything was as it always had been, that the years were a mirage and there had been no years. The small waves were the same, chucking the rowboat under the chin as we fished at anchor, and the boat was the same boat, the same color green and the ribs broken in the same places, and under the floorboards the same fresh-water leavings and débris — the dead helgramite, the wisps of moss, the rusty discarded fishhook, the dried blood from yesterday's catch. We stared silently at the tips of our rods, at the dragonflies that came and went. I lowered the tip of mine into the water, tentatively, pensively dislodging the fly, which darted two feet away, poised, darted two feet back, and came to rest again a little farther up the rod. There had been no years between the ducking of this dragonfly and the other one — the one that was part of memory. I looked at the boy, who was silently watching his fly, and it was my hands that held his rod, my eyes watching. I felt dizzy and didn't know which rod I was at the end of.

We caught two bass, hauling them in briskly as though they were mackerel, pulling them over the side of the boat in a businesslike manner without any landing net, and stunning them with a blow on the back of the head. When we got back for a swim before lunch, the lake was exactly where we had left it, the same number of inches from the dock, and there was only the merest suggestion of a breeze. This seemed an utterly enchanted sea, this lake you could leave to its own devices for a few hours and come back to, and find that it had not stirred, this constant and trustworthy body of water. In the shallows, the dark, water-soaked sticks and twigs, smooth and old, were undulating in clusters on the bottom against the clean ribbed sand, and the track of the mussel was plain. A school of minnows swam by, each minnow with its small individual shadow, doubling the attendance, so clear and sharp in the sunlight. Some of the other campers were in swimming, along the shore, one of them with a cake of soap, and the water felt thin and clear and unsubstantial. Over the years there had been this person with the cake of soap, this cultist, and here he was. There had been no years.

Up to the farmhouse to dinner through the teeming, dusty field, the road under our sneakers was only a two-track road. The middle track was missing, the one with the marks of the hoofs and the splotches of dried, flaky manure. There had always been three tracks to choose from in choosing which track to walk in; now the choice was narrowed down to two. For a moment I missed terribly the middle alternative. But the way led past the tennis court, and something about the way it lay there in the sun reassured me; the tape had loosened along the backline, the alleys were green with plantains and other weeds, and the net (installed in June and removed in September) sagged in the dry noon, and the whole place steamed with midday heat and hunger and emptiness. There was a choice of pie for dessert, and one was blueberry and one was apple, and the waitresses were the same country girls, there having been no passage of time, only the illusion of it as in a dropped curtain — the waitresses were still fifteen; their hair had been washed, that was the only difference — they had been to the movies and seen the pretty girls with the clean hair.

Summertime, oh, summertime, pattern of life indelible, the fadeproof lake, the woods unshatterable, the pasture with the sweetfern and the juniper forever and ever, summer without end; this was the background, and the life along the shore was the design, the cottagers with their innocent and tranquil design, their tiny docks with the flagpole and the American flag floating against the white clouds in the blue sky, the little paths over the roots of the trees leading from camp to camp and the paths leading back to the outhouse and the can of lime for sprinkling, and at the souvenir counters at the store the miniature birch-bark canoes and the post cards that showed things looking a little better than they looked.

It seemed to me, as I kept remembering all this, that those times and those summers had been infinitely precious and worth saving. There had been jollity and peace and goodness. The arriving (at the beginning of August) had been so big a business in itself, at the railway station the farm wagon drawn up, the first smell of the pine-laden air, the first glimpse of the smiling farmer, and the great importance of the trunks and your father's enormous authority in such matters, and the feel of the wagon under you for the long ten-mile haul, and at the top of the last long hill catching the first view of the lake after eleven months of not seeing this cherished body of water. The shouts and cries of the other campers when they saw you, and the trunks to be unpacked, to give up their rich burden. (Arriving was less exciting nowadays, when you sneaked up in your car and parked it under a tree near the camp and took out the bags and in five minutes it was all over, no fuss, no loud wonderful fuss about trunks.)

Peace and goodness and jollity. The only thing that was wrong now, really, was the sound of the place, an unfamiliar nervous sound of the outboard motors. This was the note that jarred, the one thing that would sometimes break the illusion and set the years moving. In those other summertimes all motors were inboard; and when they were at a little distance, the noise they made was a sedative, an ingredient of summer sleep. They were one-cylinder and two-cylinder engines, and some were make-and-break and some were jump-spark, but they

ONCE MORE TO THE LAKE. " The early mornings when the lake was cool and motion-less." (Saunders from Monkemeyer)

all made a sleepy sound across the lake. The one-lungers throbbed and fluttered, and the twin-cylinder ones purred and purred, and that was a quiet sound too. But now the campers all had outboards. In the daytime, in the hot mornings, these motors made a petulant, irritable sound; at night, in the still evening when the afterglow lit the water, they whined about one's ears like mosquitoes. My boy loved our rented outboard, and his great desire was to achieve singlehanded mastery over it, and authority, and he soon learned the trick of choking it a little (but not too much), and the adjustment of the needle valve. Watching him I would remember the things you could do with the old one-cylinder engine with the heavy flywheel, how you could have it eating out of your hand if you got really close to it spiritually. Motorboats in those days didn't have clutches, and you would make a landing by shutting off the motor at the proper time and coasting in with a dead rudder. But there was a way of reversing them, if you learned the trick, by cutting the switch and putting it on again exactly on the final dying revolution of the flywheel, so that it would kick back against compression and begin reversing. Approaching a dock in a strong following breeze, it was difficult to slow up sufficiently by the ordinary coasting method, and if a boy felt he had complete mastery over his motor, he was tempted to keep it running beyond its time and then reverse it a few feet from the dock. It took a cool nerve, because if you threw the switch a twentieth of a second too soon you would catch the flywheel when it still had speed enough to go up past center, and the boat would leap ahead, charging bull-fashion at the dock.

We had a good week at the camp. The bass were biting well and the sun shone endlessly, day after day. We would be tired at night and lie down in the accumulated heat of the little bedrooms after the long hot day and the breeze would stir almost imperceptibly outside and the smell of the swamp drift in through the rusty screens. Sleep would come easily, and in the morning the red squirrel would be on the roof, tapping out his gay routine. I kept remembering everything, lying in bed in the mornings — the small steamboat that had a long rounded stern like the lip of a Ubangi,[1] and how quietly she ran on the moonlight sails, when the older boys played their mandolins and the girls sang and we ate doughnuts dipped in sugar, and how sweet the music was on the water in the shining night, and what it had felt like to think about girls then. After breakfast we would go up to the store and the things were in the same place — the minnows in a bottle, the plugs and spinners disarranged and pawed over by the youngsters from the boys' camp, the fig newtons and the Beeman's gum. Outside, the road was tarred and cars stood in front of the store. Inside, all was just as it had always been, except there was more Coca Cola and not so much Moxie and root beer and birch beer and sarsaparilla. We would walk out with a bottle of pop apiece and sometimes the pop would backfire up our noses and hurt. We explored the streams, quietly, where the turtles slid off the sunny logs and dug their way into the soft bottom; and we lay on the town wharf and fed worms to the tame bass. Everywhere we went I had trouble making out which was I, the one walking at my side, the one walking in my pants.

One afternoon while we were there at that lake a thunderstorm came up. It was like the revival of an old melodrama that I had seen long ago with childish awe. The second-act climax of the drama of the electrical disturbance over a lake in America had not changed in any important respect. This was the big scene, still the big scene. The whole thing was so familiar, the first feeling of oppression and heat and a general air around camp of not wanting to go very far away. In midafternoon (it was all the same) a curious darkening of the sky, and a lull in everything that had made life tick; and then the way the boats suddenly swung

[1] **lip of a Ubangi:** Some of the natives living on the Ubangi River in Africa distend their lower lips to fantastic proportions by inserting wooden disks.

the other way at their moorings with the coming of a breeze out of the new quarter, and the premonitory rumble. Then the kettledrum, then the snare, then the bass drum and cymbals, then crackling light against the dark, and the gods grinning and licking their chops in the hills. Afterward the calm, the rain steadily rustling in the calm lake, the return of light and hope and spirits, and the campers running out in joy and relief to go swimming in the rain, their bright cries perpetuating the deathless joke about how they were getting simply drenched, and the children screaming with delight at the new sensation of bathing in the rain, and the joke about getting drenched linking the generations in a strong indestructible chain. And the comedian who waded in carrying an umbrella.

When the others went swimming my son said he was going in too. He pulled his dripping trunks from the line where they had hung all through the shower, and wrung them out. Languidly, and with no thought of going in, I watched him, his hard little body, skinny and bare, saw him wince slightly as he pulled up around his vitals the small, soggy, icy garment. As he buckled the swollen belt suddenly my groin felt the chill of death.

## Suggestions for Study

1. What does the last sentence mean? What is the main theme of this essay?

2. Tell the class of some place familiar to you as a young child and revisited recently. What changes did you find? Try to describe your feelings accurately.

3. Many American essayists write about nature and the outdoor life. You would doubtless find enjoyment in some of the essays of Audubon, Burroughs, Muir, D. L. Sharp, Thoreau, and Stewart Edward White. (See Reading List, page 175.)

4. Vocabulary: placidity, primeval, illusion, image, debris, helgramite, petulant.

## For Your Vocabulary

WORD POWER. Some words that we use frequently have a richer, fuller meaning than most people realize. It is in the full sense that the essayist uses *constant* to describe the lake (page 161). *Constant* means not only continuous, but continuing to be always the same. A *constant* friend may be relied on to show unchanging friendship. Love poems often complain of the loved one's *inconstancy*, changeable, unreliable affection, or complete change of attitude. Another word used in this sketch that from lack of full understanding is often misused is *unique* (ū-nēk'), which means much more than unusual. Anything *unique* is without a like or equal anywhere. That is what White means when he calls his lake *unique* (page 159). To speak of anything as "more unique" or "most unique" is an error that reveals imperfect understanding of the meaning of the word.

## Paul de Kruif                1890–

A bacteriologist with marked individuality of expression is in a position to give deserved publicity to a group of men too little known to the world as compared with the generals, authors, statesmen, and prize fighters. These are the scientists. Such a man is Paul de Kruif,[1] who in *Microbe Hunters* can hold one spellbound with the drama of the world known only through the microscope, or show how the thrills of hunting invisible microbes in Africa may exceed those of hunting big game. The success of this book led him to write three other series of biographical essays: *Hunger Fighters, Seven Iron Men,* and *Men against Death.* He has also ventured into the field of drama by collaborating with Sidney Howard in writing *Yellow Jack,* a play based on the story of Walter Reed. His latest volumes are concerned with current problems of public health. *Why Keep Them Alive?* shows the plight of underprivileged children, while *The Fight for Life* leads us along the concerted firing line against disease of recent years.

### WALTER REED

The following selection from *Microbe Hunters* concerns the fight made by Walter Reed against yellow fever. It is a combination of the biographical essay, the scientific essay, and the lively narrative — hard to classify but fasci-

[1] de Kruif: dĕ Krīf.

nating to read. Once you get into it, you will not care by what name it is called — you will just read on and on.

Everybody is agreed that Walter Reed — head of the Yellow Fever Commission — was a courteous man and a blameless one, that he was a mild man and a logical: there is not one particle of doubt he had to risk human lives; animals simply will not catch yellow fever!

Then it is certain that the ex-lumberjack, James Carroll, was perfectly ready to let go his own life to prove Reed's point, and he was not too sentimental about the lives of others when *he* needed to prove a point — which might and might not be what you would call a major point.

All Cubans (who were on the spot and ought to know) are agreed that those American soldiers who volunteered for the fate of guinea pigs were brave beyond imagining. All Americans who were then in Cuba are sure that those Spanish immigrants who volunteered for the fate of guinea pigs were not brave, but money-loving — for didn't each one of them get two hundred dollars?

Of course you might protest that fate hit Jesse Lazear [1] a hard knock — but it was his own fault; why didn't he brush that mosquito off the back of his hand instead of letting her drink her fill? Then, too, fate has been kind to his memory; the United States Government named a Battery in Baltimore Harbor in his honor! And that same government has been more than kind to his wife: the widow Lazear gets a pension of fifteen hundred dollars a year! You see, there are no arguments — and that makes it fun to tell this story of yellow fever. And aside from the pleasure, it has to be told: this history is absolutely necessary to the book of *Microbe Hunters*. It vindicates Pasteur! [2] At last Pasteur, from his handsome tomb in that basement in Paris, can

tell the world, " I told you so! " Because, in 1926, there is hardly enough of the poison of yellow fever left in the world to put on the points of six pins; in a few years there may not be a single speck of that virus left on earth — it will be as completely extinct as the dinosaurs — unless there is a catch in the fine gruesome experiments of Reed and his Spanish immigrants and American soldiers.

It was a grand co-operative fight, that scotching of the yellow jack. It was fought by a strange crew, and the fight was begun by a curious old man, with enviable muttonchop whiskers — his name was Doctor Carlos Finlay — who made an amazingly right guess, who was a terrible muddler at experiments, who was considered by all good Cubans and wise doctors to be a Theorizing Old Fool. What a crazy crank is Finlay, said everybody.

For everybody knew just how to fight that most panic-striking plague, yellow fever; everybody had a different idea of just how to combat it. You should fumigate silks and satins and possessions of folk before they *left* yellow-fever towns — no! that is not enough: you should burn them. You should bury, burn, and utterly destroy these silks and satins and possessions before they *come into* yellow-fever towns. It was wise not to shake hands with friends whose families were dying of yellow fever; it was perfectly safe to shake hands with them. It was best to burn down houses where yellow fever had lurked — no! it was enough to smoke them out with sulphur. But there was one thing nearly everybody in North, Central, and South America had been agreed upon for nearly two hundred years, and that was this: when folks of a town began to turn yellow and hiccup and vomit black, by scores, by hundreds, every day — the only thing to do was to get up and get out of that town. Because the yellow murderer had a way of crawling through walls and slithering along the ground and popping around corners — it could even pass through fires! — it could die and rise from the dead, that yellow murderer; and after

[1] **Jesse Lazear** (jĕs'ê lȧ-zēr'). [2] **Pasteur** (päs-tûr'): Louis Pasteur (1822–1895), French chemist who made extensive studies in the theory of germs, inoculation, and sterilization. The process of producing pasteurized milk is named for him. His work is described in earlier chapters of *Microbe Hunters*.

everybody (including the very best physicians) had fought it by doing as many contrary things as they could think of as frankly as they could do them — the yellow jack kept on killing, until suddenly it got fed up with killing. In North America that always came with the frosts in the fall.

This was the state of scientific knowledge about yellow fever up to the year 1900. But from between his muttonchop whiskers Carlos Finlay of Havana howled in a scornful wilderness, " You are all wrong — yellow fever is caused by a mosquito! "

There was a bad state of affairs in San Cristóbal de Habana in Cuba in 1900. The yellow jack had killed thousands more American soldiers than the bullets of the Spaniards had killed. And it wasn't like most diseases, which considerately pounce upon poor dirty people — it had killed more than one-third of the officers of General Leonard Wood's staff, and staff officers — as all soldiers know — are the cleanest of all officers and the best protected. General Wood had thundered orders; Havana had been scrubbed; happy dirty Cubans had been made into unhappy clean Cubans — " No stone had been left unturned " — in vain! There was more yellow fever in Havana than there had been in twenty years!

Cablegrams from Havana to Washington, and on June 25 of 1900 Major Walter Reed came to Quemados in Cuba with orders to " give special attention to questions relating to the cause and prevention of yellow fever." It was a big order. Considering who the man Walter Reed was, it was altogether too big an order. Pasteur had tried it! Of course, in certain ways — though you would say they had nothing to do with hunting microbes — Walter Reed had qualifications. He was the best of soldiers; fourteen years and more he had served on the western plains and mountains; he had been a brave angel flying through blizzards to the bedsides of sick settlers — he had shunned the dangers of beer and bottle pool in the officers' mess and resisted the seductions of poker. He had a strong moral nature. He was gentle. But it will take a genius to dig out this microbe of the yellow jack, you say — and are geniuses gentle? Just the same, you will see that this job needed particularly a strong moral nature, and then, besides, since 1891 Walter Reed *had* been doing a bit of microbe hunting. He had done some odd jobs of searching at the very best medical school under the most eminent professor of microbe hunting in America — and that professor had known Robert Koch [1] intimately.

So Walter Reed came to Quemados, and as he went into the yellow-fever hospital there, more than enough young American soldiers passed him, going out, on their backs, feet first. There were going to be plenty of cases to work on all right — fatal cases! Dr. James Carroll was with Walter Reed, and he was not what you would call gentle, but you will see in a moment what a soldier-searcher James Carroll was. And Reed found Jesse Lazear waiting for him — Lazear was a European-trained microbe hunter, aged thirty-four, with a wife and two babies in the States, and with doom in his eyes. Finally there was Aristides Agramonte [2] (who was a Cuban) — it was to be his job to cut up the dead bodies, and very well he did that job, though he never became famous because he had had yellow fever already and so ran no risks. These four were the Yellow Fever Commission.

The first thing the commission did was to fail to find any microbe whatever in the first eighteen cases of yellow fever that they probed into. There were many severe cases in those eighteen; there were four of those eighteen cases who died; there was not one of those eighteen cases that they didn't claw through from stem to gudgeon, so to speak, drawing blood, making cultures, cutting up the dead ones, making endless careful cultures — and not one bacillus [3] did they find. All the time — it was July and the very worst time for yellow fever — the sol-

[1] **Robert Koch** (kôĸ): a German doctor (1843–1910) who discovered the germs of tuberculosis and cholera. His work is described in an earlier chapter of *Microbe Hunters*. [2] **Aristides Agramonte** (ăr-ĭs-tī'dēz ä-grä-mōn'tȧ). [3] **bacillus:** a type of bacteria; here, a disease germ.

diers were coming out of the hospital of Las Animas feet first. The commission failed absolutely to find any cause, but that failure put them on the right track. That is one of the humors of microbe hunting — the way men make their finds! Theobald Smith [1] found out about those ticks because he had faith in certain farmers; Ronald Ross [2] found out the doings of those gray mosquitoes because Patrick Manson told him to; Grassi [3] discovered the *zanzarone* carrying malaria because he was patriotic. And now Walter Reed had failed in the very first part — anybody would say it was the most important part — of his work. What to do? There was nothing to do. And so Reed had time to hear the voice of that Theorizing Old Fool, Dr. Carlos Finlay, of Havana, shouting, " Yellow fever is caused by a *mosquito!* "

The commission went to call on Dr. Finlay, and that old gentleman — everybody had laughed at him; nobody had listened to him — was very glad to explain his fool theory to the commission. He told them the ingenious but vague reasons why he thought it was mosquitoes carried yellow fever; he showed them records of those awful experiments, which would convince nobody; he gave them some little black eggs shaped like cigars and said, " Those are the eggs of the criminal! " And Walter Reed took those eggs, and gave them to Lazear, who had been in Italy and knew a thing or two about mosquitoes, and Lazear put the eggs into a warm place to hatch into wigglers, which presently wiggled themselves into extremely pretty mosquitoes, with silver markings on their backs — markings that looked like a lyre. Now Walter Reed had failed, but you have to give him credit for being a sharp-

eyed man with plenty of common sense — and then, too, as you will see, he was extraordinarily lucky. While he was failing to find bacilli, even in the dreadful cases, with bloodshot eyes and chests yellow as gold, with hiccups and with those prophetic retchings — while he was failing, Walter Reed noticed that the nurses who handled those cases, were soiled by those cases, never got yellow fever! They were non-immunes too, those nurses, but they didn't get yellow fever.

" If this disease were caused by a bacillus, like cholera, or plague, some of those nurses certainly should get it," argued Walter Reed to his commission.

Then all kinds of strange tricks of yellow fever struck Walter Reed. He watched cases of the disease pop up most weirdly in Quemados. A man in a house in 102 Real Street came down with it; then it jumped around the corner to 20 General Lee Street, and from there it hopped across the road — and not one of these families had anything to do with each other, hadn't seen each other, even!

" That smells like something carrying the disease through the air to those houses," said Reed. There were various other exceedingly strange things about yellow fever — they had been discovered by an American, Carter. A man came down with yellow fever in a house. For two or three weeks nothing more happened — the man might die, he might have got better and gone away, but at the end of that two weeks, bang! a bunch of other cases broke out in that house. " That two weeks makes it look as if the virus were taking time to grow in some insect," said Reed to his commission, who thought it was silly; but they were soldiers.

" So we will try Finlay's notion about mosquitoes," said Walter Reed, for all of the just-mentioned reasons, but particularly because there was nothing else for the commission to do.

That was easy to say, but how to go on with it? Everybody knew perfectly well that you cannot give yellow fever to any

---

[1] **Theobald Smith:** an American physician who discovered how Texas fever is spread among cattle by ticks. [2] **Ronald Ross:** a medical officer of the English army in India, who studied the mosquito as a carrier of malaria germs. [3] **Grassi:** Battista Grassi, an Italian scientist who also studied the transmission of malaria germs. There was considerable controversy between these two men as to which was entitled to the discovery. Accounts of the works of the three men here mentioned are given in *Microbe Hunters*.

animal — not even to a monkey or an ape. To make any kind of experiment to prove mosquitoes carry yellow fever you *must* have experimental animals, and that meant nothing more nor less than human animals. But give human beings yellow fever! In some epidemics — there were records of them! — eighty-five men out of a hundred died of it, in some fifty out of every hundred — almost never less than twenty out of every hundred. It would be murder! But that is where the strong moral nature of Walter Reed came to help him. Here was a blameless man, a Christian man, and a man — though he was mild — who was mad to help his fellow men. And if you could *prove* that yellow fever was *only* carried by mosquitoes!

So, on one hot night after a day among dying men at Pinar del Río,[1] he faced his commission. " If the members of the commission take the risk first — if they let themselves be bitten by mosquitoes that have fed on yellow-fever cases, that will set an example to American soldiers, and then — " Reed looked at Lazear, and then at James Carroll.

" I am ready to take a bite," said Jesse Lazear, who had a wife and two small children.

" You can count on me, sir," said James Carroll, whose total assets were his searcher's brain, and his miserable pay as an assistant surgeon in the army. (His liabilities were a wife and five children.)

Then Walter Reed (he had been called home to Washington to make a report on work done in the Spanish War) gave elaborate instructions to Carroll and Lazear and Agramonte. They were secret instructions, and savage instructions when you consider the mild man he was. It was an immoral business — it was a breach of discipline in its way, for Walter Reed then had no permission from the high military authorities to start it. So Reed left for Washington, and Lazear and Carroll set off on the wildest, most daring journey any two microbe hunt-

[1] **Pinar del Río** (pĕ-när′ dĕl rē′ō).

ers had ever taken. Lazear? You could not see the doom in his eyes — the gleam of the searcher outshone it. Carroll? That was a soldier who cared neither for death nor courts-martial — Carroll was a microbe hunter of the great line.

Lazear went down between the rows of beds on which lay men, doomed men with faces yellow as the leaves of autumn, delirious men with bloodshot eyes. He bit those men with his silver-striped she-mosquitoes; carefully he carried these blood-filled beasts back to their glass homes, in which were little saucers of water and little lumps of sugar. Here the she-mosquitoes digested their meal of yellow-fever blood, and buzzed a little, and waited for the test.

" We should remember malaria," Reed had told Lazear and Carroll. " In that disease it takes two or three weeks for the mosquito to become dangerous — maybe it's the same here."

But look at the bold face of Jesse Lazear, and tell me if that was a patient man! Not he. Somehow he collected seven volunteers, who so far as I can find have remained nameless, since the test was done in dark secrecy. To these seven men — whom for all I know he may have shanghaied — but first of all to himself Lazear applied those mosquitoes who a few days before had fed on men who now were dead.

But alas, they all stayed as fit as fiddles, and that discouraged Lazear.

But there was James Carroll. For years he had been the right-hand man of Walter Reed. He had come into the army as a buck private and had been a corporal and a sergeant for years — obeying orders was burned into his very bones — and Major Reed had said, " Try mosquitoes! " What is more, what Major Reed thought was right, James Carroll thought was right, too, and Major Reed thought there was something in the notion of that Old Theorizing Fool. But in the army, thoughts are secondary — Major Reed had left them saying, " Try mosquitoes! "

So James Carroll reminded the discouraged Lazear, " I am ready! " He told Lazear to bring out the most dangerous mosquito in his collection — not one that had bitten only a single case, but he must use a mosquito that had bitten many cases — and they must be bad cases — of yellow fever. That mosquito must be as dangerous as possible! On the twenty-seventh of August, Jesse Lazear picked out what he thought to be his champion mosquito, and this creature, which had fed on four cases of yellow fever, two of them severe ones, settled down on the arm of James Carroll.

That soldier watched her while she felt around with her stinger. What did he think as he watched her swell into a bright balloon with his blood? Nobody knows. But he could think, what everybody knows, " I am forty-six years old, and in yellow fever the older the fewer — get better." He was forty-six years old. He had a wife and five children, but that evening James Carroll wrote to Walter Reed:

" If there is anything in the mosquito theory, I should get a good dose of yellow fever! " He did.

Two days later he felt tired and didn't want to visit patients in the yellow-fever ward. Two days after that he was really sick. " I must have malaria! " he cried, and went to the laboratory under his own power, to squint at his own blood under the microscope. But no malaria. That night his eyes were bloodshot, his face a dusky red. The next morning Lazear packed Carroll off to the yellow-fever wards; and there he lay, near to death for days and days. There was one minute when he thought his heart had stopped . . . and that, as you will see, was a bad minute for Assistant Surgeon Carroll.

He always said those were the proudest days of his life. " I was the first case to come down with yellow fever after the experimental bite of a mosquito! " said Carroll.

Then there was that American private soldier they called " X.Y." — these outlaw searchers called him " X.Y.," though he was really William Dean, of Grand Rapids, Michigan. While James Carroll was having his first headaches, they bit this X.Y. with four mosquitoes — the one that nearly killed Carroll, and then three other silver-striped beauties besides, who had fed on six men that were fairly sick, and four men that were very sick with yellow fever, and two men that died.

Now everything was fine with the experiments of Quemados. Eight men had been bitten, it is true, and were fit as fiddles — but the last two, James Carroll and X.Y., they were real experimental guinea pigs, those two; they had both got yellow fever — and James Carroll's heart had nearly stopped, but now they were both getting better, and Carroll was on the heights, writing to Walter Reed, waiting proudly for his chief to come back — to show him the records. Only Jesse Lazear was a little cynical about these two cases, because Lazear was a fine experimenter, a tight one, a man who had to have every condition just so, like a real searcher — and, thought Lazear, " It is too bad, seeing the nerve of Carroll and X.Y. — but both of them exposed themselves in dangerous zones once or twice, before they came down. It wasn't an absolutely perfect experiment — it isn't sure that *my* mosquitoes gave them yellow fever! " So Lazear was skeptical; but orders were orders, and every afternoon he went to those rows of beds at Las Animas, in the room with the faint strange smell, and here he turned his test tubes upside down on the arms of boys with bloodshot eyes, and let his she-mosquitoes suck their fill. But September 13 was a bad day, it was an unlucky day, for Jesse Lazear; for while he was at this silly job of feeding his mosquitoes, a stray mosquito settled down on the back of his hand. " Oh! that's nothing! " he thought. " That wouldn't be the right kind of mosquito anyway! " he muttered, and he let the mosquito drink her fill — though, mind you, she was a stray beast that lived in this ward where men were dying!

That was September 13.

" On the evening of September 18 Dr. Lazear complained of feeling out of sorts, and had a chill at 8 P.M.," says a hospital record at Las Animas.

"September 19: Twelve o'clock noon," goes on that laconic record, "temperature 102.4 degrees, pulse 112. Eyes injected, face suffused." (That means bloodshot and red.) "6 P.M. temperature 103.8 degrees, pulse 106. Jaundice appeared on the third day. The subsequent history of this case was one of progressive and fatal yellow fever" (and the record softens a little), "the death of our lamented colleague having occurred on the evening of September 25, 1900."

Then Reed came back to Cuba, and Carroll met him with enthusiasm, and Walter Reed was sad for Lazear, but very happy about those two successful cases of Carroll and X.Y. — and then, and then (brushing aside tears for Lazear) even in that there was the Hand of God, there was something for Science. "As Dr. Lazear was bitten by a mosquito while present in the wards of a yellow-fever hospital," wrote Walter Reed, "one must, at least, admit the possibility of this insect's contamination by a previous bite of a yellow-fever patient. This case of accidental infection therefore *cannot fail to be of interest*."

"Now it is my turn to take the bite!" said Walter Reed, but he was fifty years old, and they persuaded him not to. "But we *must* prove it!" he insisted, so gently, that, hearing his musical voice and looking at his chin that did not stick out like the chin of a he-man, you might think Walter Reed was wavering (after all, here was one man dead out of three).

"But we must prove it," said that soft voice, and Reed went to General Leonard Wood, and told him the exciting events that had happened. Who could be less of a mollycoddle than this Wood? And he gave Walter Reed permission to go as far as he liked. He gave him money to build a camp of seven tents and two little houses — to say nothing of a flagpole — but what was best of all, Wood gave him money to buy men, who would get handsomely paid for taking a sure one chance out of five of never hav-

ing a chance to spend that money! So Walter Reed said, "Thank you, General," and one mile from Quemados they pitched seven tents and raised a flagpole, and flew an American flag and called that place Camp Lazear (three cheers for Lazear!), and you will see what glorious things occurred there.

Now, nothing is more sure than this: that every man of the great line of microbe hunters is different from every other man of them, but every man jack of them has one thing in common: they are original. They were all original, excepting Walter Reed — who you cannot say would be shot for his originality, seeing that this business of mosquitoes and various bugs and ticks carrying diseases was very much in the air in those last ten years of the nineteenth century. It was natural for a man to think of that! But he was by all odds the most moral of the great line of microbe hunters — aside from being a very thorough clean-cut experimenter — and now that Walter Reed's moral nature told him, "You must kill men to save them!" he set out to plan a series of airtight tests — never was there a good man who thought of more hellish and dastardly tests!

And he was exact. Every man about to be bit by a mosquito must stay locked up for days and days and weeks, in that sunbaked Camp Lazear — to keep him away from all danger of accidental contact with yellow fever. There would be no catch in these experiments! And then Walter Reed let it be known, to the American soldiers in Cuba, that there was another war on, a war for the saving of men — were there men who would volunteer? Before the ink was dry on the announcements Private Kissenger of Ohio stepped into his office, and with him came John J. Moran, who wasn't even a soldier — he was a civilian clerk in the office of General Fitzhugh Lee. "You can try it on us, sir!" they told him.

Walter Reed was a thoroughly conscientious man. "But, men, do you realize the danger?" And he told them of the headaches and the hiccups and the black vomit

— and he told them of fearful epidemics in which not a man had lived to carry news or tell the horrors.

" We know," said Private Kissenger and John J. Moran of Ohio; " we volunteer solely for the cause of humanity and in the interest of science."

Then Walter Reed told them of the generosity of General Wood. A handsome sum of money they would get — two hundred, maybe three hundred dollars, if the silver-striped she-mosquitoes did things to them that would give them one chance out of five not to spend that money.

" The one condition on which we volunteer, sir," said Private Kissenger and civilian clerk John J. Moran of Ohio, " is that we get no compensation for it."

To the tip of his cap went the hand of Walter Reed (who was a major), " Gentlemen, I salute you! " And that day Kissenger and John J. Moran went into the preparatory quarantine, that would make them first-class, unquestionable guinea pigs, above suspicion and beyond reproach. On the fifth of December Kissenger furnished nice full meals for five mosquitoes — two of them had bitten fatal cases fifteen days and nineteen days before. Presto! Five days later he had the devil of a backache, two days more and he was turning yellow — it was a perfect case, and in his quarters Walter Reed thanked God, for Kissenger got better! Then great days came to Reed and Carroll and Agramonte — for, if they weren't exactly overrun with young Americans who were ready to throw away their lives in the interest of science and for humanity, still there were ignorant people, just come to Cuba from Spain, who could very well use two hundred dollars. There were five of these mercenary fellows — whom I shall simply have to call " Spanish immigrants," or I could call them Man 1, 2, 3, and 4 — just as microbe hunters often mark animals " Rabbit 1, 2, 3, and 4 — " anyway, they were bitten, carefully, by mosquitoes who, when you take averages, were much more dangerous than machine-gun bullets. They earned their two hundred

dollars — for four out of five of them had nice typical (doctors would look scientific and call them beautiful) cases of yellow fever! It was a triumph! It was sure! Not one of these men had been anywhere near yellow fever — like so many mice they had been kept in their screened tents at Quemados. If they hadn't been ignorant immigrants — hardly more intelligent than animals, you might say — they might have been bored, because nothing had happened to them excepting — the stabs of silver-striped she-mosquitoes.

" Rejoice with me, sweetheart," Walter Reed wrote to his wife, " as, aside from the antitoxin of diphtheria and Koch's discovery of the tubercle bacillus, it will be regarded as the most important piece of work, scientifically, during the nineteenth century."

Walter Reed was so thorough that you can call him original, as original as any of the microbe hunters of the great line — for he was certainly original in his thoroughness. He might have called it a day — you would swear he was tempted to call it a day: eight men had got yellow fever from mosquito bites, and only one — what amazing luck! — had died.

" But can yellow fever be carried in any other way? " asked Reed.

Everybody believed that clothing and bedding and possessions of yellow-fever victims were deadly — millions of dollars' worth of clothing and bedding had been destroyed; the Surgeon General believed it; every eminent physician in America, North, South, and Central (excepting that old fool Finlay) believed it. " But can it? " asked Reed, and while he was being so joyfully successful with Kissenger and Spaniards 1, 2, 3, and 4, carpenters came, and built two ugly little houses in Camp Lazear. House No. 1 was the nastier of these two little houses. It was fourteen feet by twenty, it had two doors cleverly arranged one back of the other so no mosquitoes could get into it, it had two windows looking south — they were on the same side as the door, so no draft could blow through that little house. Then it was furnished with a nice stove, to keep the temperature well above ninety, and there were tubs of water in the house — to keep the air as choky as the hold of a ship in the tropics. So you see it was an uninhabitable little house — under the best of conditions — but now, on the thirtieth of November in 1900, sweating soldiers carried several tightly nailed suspicious-looking boxes, that came from the yellow-fever wards of Las Animas — to make the house altogether cursed.

That night, of the thirtieth of November, Walter Reed and James Carroll were the witnesses of a miracle of bravery, for into this House No. 1 walked a young American doctor named Cooke, and two American soldiers, whose names — where are their monuments? — were Folk and Jernegan.

Those three men opened the tightly nailed, suspicious-looking boxes. They opened those boxes inside that house, in air already too sticky for proper breathing.

Phew! There were cursings, there were holdings of noses.

But they went on opening those boxes, and out of them Cooke and Folk and Jernegan took pillows, soiled with the black vomit of men dead of yellow fever; out of them they took sheets and blankets, dirty with the discharges of dying men past helping themselves. They beat those pillows and shook those sheets and blankets — " you must see the yellow-fever poison is well spread around that room! " Walter Reed had told them. Then Cooke and Folk and Jernegan made up their little army cots with those pillows and blankets and sheets. They undressed. They lay down on those filthy beds. They tried to sleep — in that room fouler than the dankest of medieval dungeons. And Walter Reed and James Carroll guarded that little house, so tenderly, to see no mosquito got into it, and Folk and Cooke and Jernegan had the very best of food, you may be sure.

Night after night those three lay in that house, wondering perhaps about the welfare of the souls of their predecessors in those sheets and blankets. They lay there, won-

dering whether anything else besides mosquitoes (though mosquitoes hadn't even been proved to carry it then!) carried yellow fever. Then Walter Reed, who was a moral man and a thorough man, and James Carroll, who was a grim man, came to make their test a little more thorough. More boxes came to them from Las Animas — and when Cooke and Jernegan and Folk unpacked them, they had to rush out of their little house, it was so dreadful.

But they went back in, and they went to sleep.

For twenty nights — where are their monuments? — these three men stayed there, and then they were quarantined in a nice airy tent, to wait for their attack of yellow fever. But they gained weight. They felt fit as fiddles. They made vast jokes about their dirty house and their perilous sheets and blankets. They were happy as so many schoolboys when they heard Kissenger and those Spaniards (1, 2, 3, and 4) had really got the yellow jack after the mosquito bites. What a marvelous proof, you will say, but what a dastardly experiment — but for the insanely scientific Walter Reed that most dastardly experiment was not marvelous enough! Three more American boys went in there, and for twenty nights slept in new unspeakable sheets and blankets — with this little refinement of the experiment: they slept in the very pajamas in which yellow-fever victims had died. And then for twenty more nights three other American lads went into House No. 1, and slept that way — with this additional little refinement of the experiment: they slept on pillows covered with towels soaked with the blood of men whom the yellow jack had killed.

But they all stayed fit as fiddles! Not a soul of these nine men had so much as a touch of yellow fever! How wonderful is science, thought Walter Reed. " So," he wrote, " the bubble of the belief that clothing can transmit yellow fever was pricked by the first touch of human experimentation." Walter Reed was right. It is true, science is wonderful. But science is cruel, microbe hunting can be heartless, and that relentless devil that was the experimenter in Walter Reed kept asking, " But is your experiment really sound? " None of those men who slept in House No. 1 got yellow fever, that is true — but how do you know they were *susceptible* to yellow fever? Maybe they were naturally immune! Then Reed and Carroll, who had already asked as much of Folk and Jernegan as any captain has ever asked of any soldier — so it was that Reed and Carroll now shot virulent yellow-fever blood under the skin of Jernegan, so it was they bit Folk with mosquitoes who had fed on fatal cases of yellow fever. They both came down with wracking pains and flushed faces and bloodshot eyes. They both came through their Valley of the Shadow. " Thank God," murmured Reed — but especially Walter Reed thanked God he had proved those two boys were not immune during those twenty hot stinking nights in House No. 1.

For these deeds Warren Gladsden Jernegan and Levi E. Folk were generously rewarded with a purse of three hundred dollars — which in those days was a lot of money.

While these tests were going on John J. Moran, that civilian clerk from Ohio, whom Walter Reed had paid the honor of a salute, was a very disappointed man. He had absolutely refused to be paid; he had volunteered in " the interest of science and for the cause of humanity "; he had been bitten by those silver-striped Stegomyia [1] mosquitoes (the bug experts just then thought this was the proper name for that mosquito) — he had been stabbed several times by several choice poisonous ones, but he hadn't come down with yellow fever, alas; he stayed fit as a fiddle. What to do with John J. Moran?

" I have it! " said Walter Reed. " This to do with John J. Moran! "

So there was built, close by that detestable little House No. 1, another little house, called House No. 2. That was a comfortable house! It had windows on the side opposite

[1] **Stegomyia** (stĕg-ŏ-mī′yá).

WALTER REED, head of the Yellow Fever Commission in 1900, and discoverer of the cause of this most deadly tropical disease. (Keystone View)

to its door, so that a fine trade wind played through it. It was cool. It had a nice clean cot in it, with steam-disinfected bedding. It would have been an excellent house for a consumptive to get better in. It was a thoroughly sanitary little house. Halfway across the inside of it was a screen, from top to bottom, a fine-meshed screen that the tiniest mosquito found it impossible to fly through. At twelve o'clock noon on the twenty-first of December in 1900, this John J. Moran (who was a hog for these tests) " clad only in a nightshirt and fresh from a bath," walked into this healthy little house. Five minutes before, Reed and Carroll had opened a glass jar in that room, and out of that jar flew fifteen she-mosquitoes, thirsty for blood, whining for a meal of blood, and each and every one of those fifteen mosquitoes had fed, on various days before — on the blood of yellow-faced boys in the hospital of Las Animas.

Clad only in a nightshirt and fresh from a bath, Moran — who knows of him now?

— walked into the healthy little room and lay down on his clean cot. In a minute that frightful buzzing started round his head, in two minutes he was bitten, in the thirty minutes he lay there he was stabbed seven times — without even the satisfaction of smashing those mosquitoes. You remember Mr. Sola, whom Grassi tortured — he probably had his worried moments — but all Mr. Sola had to look forward to was a little attack of malaria and a good dose of curative quinine to get him out of it. But Moran? But John J. Moran was a hog for such tests! He was back there at four-thirty the same afternoon, to be bitten again, and once more the next day — to satisfy the rest of the hungry she-mosquitoes who hadn't found him the first day. In the other room of this house, with only a fine-meshed but perfect wire screen between them and Moran — and the mosquitoes — lay two other boys, and those two boys slept in that house safely for eighteen nights.

But Moran?

On Christmas morning of 1900 there was a fine present waiting for him — in his head, how that thumped — in his eyes, how red they were and how the light hurt them — in his bones, how tired they were! A nasty knock those mosquitoes had hit him and he came within a hair of dying but (thank God! murmured Walter Reed) he was saved, this Moran, to live the rest of his life in an obscurity he didn't deserve. So Moran had his wish — in the interest of science, and for humanity! So he, with Folk and Jernegan and Cooke, and all those others, proved that the dirty pesthole of a house (with no mosquitoes) was safe; and that the clean house (but with mosquitoes) was dangerous, so dangerous! So at last Walter Reed had every answer to his diabolical questions, and he wrote, in that old-fashioned prose of his, " The essential factor in the infection of a building with yellow fever is the presence therein of mosquitoes that have bitten cases of yellow fever."

It was so simple. It was true. That was all. That was that. And Walter Reed wrote to his wife:

" The prayer that has been mine for twenty years, that I might be permitted in some way or at some time to do something to alleviate human suffering has been granted! A thousand Happy New Years. . . . Hark, there go the twenty-four buglers in concert, all sounding taps for the old year! "

They were sounding taps, were those buglers, for the searcher that was Jesse Lazear, and for the scourge of yellow fever that could now be wiped from the earth.

## Suggestions for Study

1. There are three outstanding features of interest in this essay: the human element, the scientific element, and the lively style of the author. Cite one particularly good example of each.

2. Of all the persons involved in the experiments, which ones did you find most interesting? Why?

3. What other great scientific discoveries that are of universal benefit to mankind can you name?

4. Read other chapters from *Microbe Hunters* and tell the class about them. Which discoveries were the most dramatic? the most valuable to mankind?

5. Report to the class other great scientific discoveries which have affected modern life. (See page 184 for Dr. Carver's work.)

## For Your Vocabulary

SPECIALIZED VOCABULARY. De Kruif has a good vocabulary for use in talking of disease and its treatment, and some of his most expressive words are used of other subjects as well. *Alleviate* (ă-lē′vĭ-āt) means to lighten, and is kin to the word *levity* for lighthearted manner or behavior. Walter Reed's aim was to *alleviate* human suffering (page 174). Much treatment of illness is intended only to *alleviate* the patient's sufferings — as distinguished from *curative* (kŭr′à-tĭv) treatment, which fights the disease directly. De Kruif speaks of taking " a *curative* dose of quinine " for malaria (page 174). *Virus* (vī′rŭs), the word for the poison of a disease, gives us the adjective *virulent* (vĭr′ů-lĕnt) in the phrase " virulent yellow-fever blood " (page 173). *Virulent* is used of bitter (or poisonous) attitudes and behavior as well as of the infections of disease.

# For Further Reading of Essays

## COMMENTS ON LIFE AND LITERATURE

Adamic, Louis: *My America; A Nation of Nations*

Allen, F. L.: *Only Yesterday; Since Yesterday*

Benchley, Robert C.: *After 1903 — What?; Inside Benchley*

Broun, Heywood: *Seeing Things at Night; Pieces of Hate; It Seems to Me*

Crothers, S. M.: *Among Friends; The Cheerful Giver; The Dame School of Experience; The Gentle Reader; By the Christmas Fire*

Day, Clarence: *Life with Father; Life with Mother; God and My Father*

Dodds, Harold W.: *Out of This Nettle, Danger*

Edman, Irwin: *Philosopher's Holiday*

Grayson, David (Ray Stannard Baker): *Adventures in Contentment; Adventures in Friendship; The Friendly Road; Great Possessions*

Holliday, R. C.: *Broome Street Straws; Turns about Town; Walking-Stick Papers; Men, Books, and Cities*

Keller, Helen: *The World I Live in; Optimism*

Leacock, Stephen: *Literary Lapses; The Iron Man and the Tin Woman; Too Much College; Laugh Parade*

McKinney, Ruth: *My Sister Eileen*

Morley, Christopher: *Mince Pie; Forty-four Essays*

Newton, A. E.: *The Amenities of Book Collecting*

Palmer, G. H.: *Self-Cultivation in English; Trades and Professions*

Phelps, W. L.: *As I Like It; Essays on Modern Novelists; Essays on Modern Dramatists; Happiness; Human Nature in the Bible*

Repplier, Agnes: *Americans and Others; Essays in Miniature; In Our Convent Days; Points of Friction*

Roosevelt, Theodore: *American Ideals; The Strenuous Life; The Winning of the West; African Game Trails*

Ross, Leonard Q.: *The Education of Hyman Kaplan*

Skinner, Cornelia Otis: *Excuse It, Please!; Our Hearts Were Young and Gay*

Smith, C. A.: *What Can Literature Do for Me?*

Thurber, James: *The Thurber Carnival*

Van Dyke, Henry: *Fisherman's Luck*

Warner, F. L.: *Endicott and I; Life's Minor Collisions; Surprising the Family and Other Peradventures*

Woollcott, Alexander: *While Rome Burns*

## NATURE AND SCIENCE

Beebe, William: *Zaca Venture; Nonsuch*

Burroughs, John: *Afoot and Afloat; Birds and Bees; Locusts and Wild Honey; Sharp Eyes; Wake-Robin; The Last Harvest*

Muir, John: *Our National Parks; Steep Trails; Travels in Alaska; My First Summer in the Sierra*

Olcott, W. T.: *The Book of the Stars for Young People*

Peattie, D. C.: *Flowering Earth*

Roberts, C. G. D.: *Kindred of the Wild; Hunters of the Silences; Watchers of the Trail*

Sharp, D. L.: *The Hills of Hingham; Roof and Meadow; The Whole Year Through; The Face of the Fields; A Watcher in the Woods; The Spirit of the Hive*

Slosson, E. E.: *Creative Chemistry; Chats on Science; Snapshots of Science*

Van Loon, Hendrik: *Ancient Man; Van Loon's Geography; The Story of Mankind; Ships*

White, S. E.: *The Cabin; The Forest; The Mountains; African Camp Fires; The Land of Footprints*

Yates, R. F.: *The Art of Inventing and What to Invent*

## TRAVEL AND ADVENTURE

Adamic, Louis: *The Native's Return*

Allen, Hervey, ed.: *The Rivers of America* (a series of excellent books)

Brooks, C. S.: *Journeys to Bagdad; There's Pippins and Cheese to Come; Chimney-Pot Papers; Hints to Pilgrims; A Thread of English Road; Roundabout to Canterbury; Roads to the North*

Caldwell, Erskine, ed.: *American Folkways*

Carmer, Carl: *Stars Fell on Alabama; The Hudson*

Chase, M. E.: *This England*

Chase, Stuart: *Mexico*

Collier, Price: *England and the English from an American Point of View*

Daniels, Jonathan: *A Southerner Discovers the South*

Fergusson, Harvey: *Rio Grande*

Flandrau, C. M.: *Viva Mexico*

Franck, H. A.: *Four Months Afoot in Spain; A Vagabond Journey around the World*

Gilfillan, Lauren: *I Went to Pit College*

Halliburton, Richard: *The Royal Road to Romance; The Glorious Adventure; The Magic Carpet*

Halsey, Margaret: *With Malice toward Some*

Hearn, Lafcadio: *Glimpses of Unfamiliar Japan; Kokoro; Out of the East; Fantastics and Other Fancies*

Irwin, Will: *Highlights of Manhattan*

Johnson, Osa: *I Married Adventure*

Kent, Rockwell: *The Wilderness*

London, Jack: *The Cruise of the Snark*

Seitz, D. C.: *Famous American Duels*

Smith, F. H.: *Gondola Days; In Dickens's Land; A White Umbrella in Mexico*

Stockton, F. R.: *Buccaneers and Pirates of Our Coast*

Street, Julian: *Abroad at Home*

Taylor, Bayard; *Views Afoot*

Vestal, Stanley, *pseud.: Old Santa Fe Trail*

Villiers, A. J.: *The Last of the Wind Ships; The Sea in Ships*

Waln, Nora: *Reaching for the Stars*

Ybarra, T. R.: *America Faces South*

COLLECTIONS OF ESSAYS

*Atlantic Classics* — First and second series

Brown, Sharon: *Essays of Our Times*

Chamberlain, Essie: *Essays Old and New*

Hastings, W. T.: *Contemporary Essays*

Heydrick, B. A.: *Types of the Essay*

Johnson, Burgess: *Essaying the Essay*

Knickerbocker, E. V.: *Present-Day Essays*

Law, F. H.: *Modern Essays and Stories; Modern Life and Thought; Science in Literature*

Lester, John A.: *Essays of Yesterday and Tomorrow*

McCullough, B. W. and Burgum, E. B.: *A Book of Modern Essays*

Morley, Christopher: *Modern Essays for Schools*

Tanner, W. M.: *Essays and Essay Writing; Modern Familiar Essays*

Walter, E. A.: *Essay Annual* (a series beginning in 1933)

Wood, W. W.: *Fact and Opinion*

# THE MAGAZINE AND NEWSPAPER ARTICLE

Our earliest essays were fathered by the colonial periodicals, and today the magazine of America continues to be the foster parent of the essay, giving it protection and nourishment. But, while in such magazines as *Harper's* and the *Atlantic Monthly* there is still a place for the familiar or personal essay written with literary distinction, most of the nonfiction material in our modern popular magazines consists of the informational or critical " article."

The typical magazine article presents information on science, current events, contemporary personalities; or it discusses current problems, books, the theater, or what not. Many — indeed, most — of these are purely popular and temporary in their appeal, and most of them are written with no great pretention of literary style. But they are nevertheless worth reading if we wish to be informed, alert citizens of twentieth-

century America. Indeed, one of the most valuable reading habits we can cultivate is the regular perusal of several good magazines.

Among the most popular of our periodicals are the *Saturday Evening Post* and *Collier's,* two weeklies which offer in every number an attractive combination of stories and articles, many of which are of exceedingly high quality.

For current events it is profitable to check the articles in our daily newspapers by reading *Time* or *Newsweek* regularly. *Life,* also, though mostly pictures, has some good articles each week.

The *American Magazine* and *Coronet* are two monthly magazines whose articles are interesting and informative.

*Harper's* and the *Atlantic Monthly* are two of our very best " quality " magazines. Their articles are superior. *Fortune,* also, is one of our best monthly periodicals. The *New Yorker,* a weekly, is noted for its cartoons, but it contains reading matter which many consider second to none. The *Yale Review* and the *American Scholar* are good examples of the dignified and scholarly " quarterlies," which are published four times a year and contain top-ranking articles.

The first three articles in the following section are typical of the great mass of material published in our modern periodicals. These are followed by two short selections from daily newspapers; for newspapers, as well as magazines, are publishing today many articles of timely comment — and occasionally even of literary distinction.

## J. Frank Dobie          1888–

J. Frank Dobie has dedicated his literary career to preserving the lore and legends of the Southwest. His own words give us some insight into his devotion to his chosen work: " I was born and reared far down the Nueces River in Texas. I grew up among cowmen, cowboys, Mexicans. I knew the life of the ranch, of cattle, of the cotton field. The prickly pear and the mesquite are yet to me as dear as the heather to the Scotchman or 'The Yellow Violet ' to William Cullen Bryant. But no one in all my school life ever directed me to a piece of literature in which one factor of that life down the Nueces River was revealed. Many times did I hear of Cotton Mather and Jonathan Edwards. Gladly do I acknowledge my debt ' both to Greek and to barbarian ' — but not to Cotton Mather and Jonathan Edwards. I am but one of thousands. The time is at hand when we shall no longer have to starve for a picture, a tale, a song that tells of the life out of which we have sprung." And truly, since Dobie began to publish his works, no one need starve for a taste of the Southwest in literature. He has brought to his writing finished literary craftsmanship and unparalleled knowledge of his own country. On his vacations from the University of Texas, where he is a professor of English, he roams the Southwest, a welcome visitor at big ranch house or cattle camp out on the range, at home in the shacks of Mexican laborers no less than in the company of scholars, talking, listening, making his gleanings into books that have won a following all over America.

The legends of the lost gold and silver mines of the Spaniards, and of the men who even today spend their lives with an old chart and a pickax in pursuit of buried treasure, are retold in *Coronado's Children,* which was a Literary Guild selection in 1931. *A Vaquero of the Brush Country* recounts the life of one of the great early cattlemen of South Texas, where a thick growth of mesquite, chaparral, and cactus made ranching a very different business from what it was out on the open plains. In 1939 Dobie published another collection of lost mine lore, *Apache Gold and Yaqui Silver,* made up of fact and legend about still more rich treasure once seen and forever after sought in vain. In addition to these and other books Dobie writes many essays about the life and, as he likes to call it, the " flavor " of his beloved Southwest. During World War II he went to Oxford University in England where he gave lectures on American literature to English soldiers and lectures on English literature to American soldiers stationed near by. His recent book, *A Texan in England,* records these experiences.

## THE HERALDRY OF THE RANGE

Out of his rich knowledge of the life of the cattle country Dobie writes this article on brands and the part they have played in ranch life. This article first appeared in the *Saturday Evening Post.*

The other day a ranchman out in West Texas whose brand is T Half Circle announced that the United States Patent Office had registered it as a trade-mark. Since many cattle raisers nowadays sell their product by mail, the owner's brand on an animal being a guaranty of its standard breeding, other cowmen are likely to have their brands registered as trade-marks. A brand is just that — a trade-mark — though it is also much more, and to it is attached all the sentiment and connotation once borne by coats of arms.

Primarily it is a means of identification, whether against thieves or among honest men, on the owner's home range or far away. If names and addresses were not so long, they would be branded on cattle. A brand is a seal that stands for a name; and somewhere, with name and address, every legal brand is recorded, just as with the purchaser's name are recorded the make and engine number of every automobile, somewhere.

Just when brands were introduced into the world it would be difficult to say. The claim has often been made that Cortes, conqueror of Mexico, originated branding in America. At Thebes, so it is said, a tomb twenty-five hundred years old has been uncovered bearing among other mural decorations the representation of a cow tied down and a man branding her with a geometric design. The tomb must have been that of an Egyptian cattle king. When Chaucer's pilgrims set out on their immortal journey from London to Canterbury more than five hundred years ago, some of them probably rode on rented horses. At least, horses kept for rent at that time were, says the great historian Jusserand — who cites authority for the statement — " branded in a prominent manner, so that unscrupulous travelers should not be tempted to quit the road and appropriate the steeds." In 1643, before the cattle industry in the Southwest was born, the New Haven, Connecticut, code stipulated how horses should be branded in order to prevent trouble between rival claimants of " horses running together in the woods."

But nowhere have brands been so important to people or so interwoven with their lives as on the ranges of western America. A ranchboy often learns the language of brands earlier than he learns the language of books.

When George Asa was a very small boy living on a big ranch near the Rio Grande, his father began one day to teach him the letters of the alphabet, drawing them on paper with a pencil. He drew A, and George Asa learned it; then B, and George Asa learned it. But when he drew a C and called it, George Asa refused to accept it as a letter.

" Aw, Daddy," he exclaimed, " you're trying to tease me now! That's not a letter at all. That's Mr. Cox's brand."

Mr. Cox was a neighboring ranchman whose brand, a big C, was familiar to George Asa before he knew one letter from another. As a ranchboy he was learning to read brands before he learned his A B C's.

At a one-teacher school out in the mesquite the Friday-afternoon session usually closed with recitations. A frequent recitation began with the well-known injunction to the little star:

> Twinkle, twinkle, little star!
> How I wonder what you are,
> Up above the world so high
> Like a diamond in the sky.

One of the school urchins was the son of a rancher who ran the Diamond P brand — ⟨P⟩. That was the only diamond the lad knew, and he confesses now that he used to study the stars by the hour, trying to catch one of them assuming the diamond shape so familiar to him on the sides of cows and at the hot end of a branding iron. He knew the language of brands better than he knew the language of jewels and poetry.

The brand gives its name to everything on the ranch. The chuck wagon of the Olmos — Elms — Ranch is seldom called the Olmos wagon, but is almost invariably referred to as the " A Dot wagon," Ⱥ being the ranch brand. The " cow crowd " working on the Withers range is customarily referred to not as the Withers outfit but as the " Pig Pen outfit "; the Pig Pen — made thus, ⊞ — being the Withers brand. A cowboy rides a " Double Circle horse," which is branded ◎. Another cowboy is " one of the Rocking Chair hands " because he works on the Rocking Chair — ⌐L — Ranch.

A ranch may be named for its owner, as the Kokernut Ranch; it may be named after a creek that runs through it, as the San Francisco Ranch; it may take its name from some other feature of nature, as the Seven Oaks Ranch. But the greater number of ranches by far take their names simply from the ranch brand: the J A Ranch —

𝒜 — the Pitchfork — Ψ — the Hundred and One — |○|. Sometimes after a brand is no longer in use some feature of the land keeps its name; although the great 7D outfit has quitted the Pecos forever, 7D Mountain keeps the brand as part of the language of the country.

The very owner of a ranch sometimes loses his name in his brand. There is " Diamond and a Half Hud " of the plains, who signs his checks as W. D. Hudson and gives ◊ as his brand. Colonel B. H. Campbell, a prominent cowman of the Indian Territory who for a time managed the great XIT Ranch of Texas, gave for his brand B̄Q̄. It was read as " Barbeque," and " Barbeque Campbell " became known where B. H. Campbell had never been heard of.

As a means of identification the brand envelops all things else on the range. An incident related by Walter Billingsley, an old trail driver, well illustrates this fact.

In 1884 [he says] I took a herd of King Ranch steers from South Texas to Cheyenne, Wyoming. Everything went all right until we crossed the South Platte and reached Fort Sidney, Nebraska. While we held the herd a few miles out from town, I let a bunch of the boys go in to see the sights. Five of them laid out and did not report for work next morning. I rode in, found them, and fired them on the spot. I owed them one hundred and twenty dollars apiece. I had no money to pay them off, and I did not know a soul in Sidney.

My first move was to see the banker. Says I to him: " I'm trail boss for the King Ranch, owned by Captain Richard King and known from Canada to the Rio Grande. I've fired five of the sorriest cowboys that ever rode out of Texas. They are due six hundred dollars, and when they get it they will make you fine citizens and spend it all right here. I want to leave them with you, and I want to draw on Wright and Beverley at Dodge City for the six hundred dollars. Will you cash my draft? "

" Well," says the banker, " you look all right and I am satisfied you are all right, but can't you get someone to identify you? "

" I'm where I never was before and where I never expect to be again," I replied, " and I don't see a soul in town that I know."

The banker seemed awful anxious to accommodate me, and I sure did not want to hire those cowboys back just because I couldn't pay them off. I just wasn't going to give them the whip hand over me that way.

" Suppose you look around a little and see if you can't strike somebody you know," the banker concluded, " and then come back."

I went out. My mind was made up. I rounded up the men I'd fired and said, " Follow me and get your money."

We galloped to camp. " Load up and hitch up," I says to the cook, " and follow me."

Then I called the horse wrangler. " Drive up that *remuda* [1] of saddle horses," I says to him, " and follow the chuck wagon."

When we were all ready we struck a high trot for town, and a sight we must have made — me in the lead, those five sorry cowboys swinging after me, then the chuck wagon with six mules hitched to it, and then one hundred and fifty saddle horses with the *remudero* and a couple of other hands driving them. I drew up at the bank and the outfit halted.

" Come here! " I yelled to the banker, who was already at the door. " Come out here and look at my identification! "

He came a-laughing.

" Now," says I, " I guess you know what the King Ranch brand is — Running W on the side and K on the jaw. Well, there's one hundred and fifty saddles horses branded K W. There's a wagon with K W branded on the sideboards, branded on the chuck box, branded all over everything. Look at the cook's saddle on that near wheel mule, and you'll see K W on it. In fact, everything and everybody in this outfit is branded K W."

The banker was impressed all right. He shelled out the six hundred dollars right away. I paid off the quitters; they unsaddled right there, turned their horses into the *remuda*, took their bedding out of the wagon, and the Running W outfit rolled its tail on for Cheyenne.

The average cow hand is so conscious of brands that in season and out of season, appropriately and inappropriately, consciously and unconsciously, he brands whatever he comes across. He whittles brands on sticks; he burns them into the planks of branding chutes, on pasture gates, on the

---

[1] **remuda** (rĕ-mū'dȧ): all of the saddle horses belonging to the outfit.

anchor posts of windmill towers. He smears them with axle grease across the doors of barns and garages. He paints them with charcoal on the rock walls of canyons in which he has made a campfire. He carves them into his spur traps, leggings, and saddle — above all, into his boot tops. More pistols were etched with cattle brands than were ever notched for dead victims. Many a cook has stenciled the ranch coat of arms into the top crust of that gala-day treat — a wild-plum cobbler. Ranchboys are incorrigible when it comes to carving brands on their desks at school. They play ranch, and with bailing wire for running irons brand oak balls, the sawed-off tips of horns, spools, and other objects used to represent cattle and horses.

An old-time, dyed-in-the-wool cowman took pride in nothing more than in his memory for brands, and good cowmen still take the same pride. There are hotel clerks who never forget a face, scholars who never falter on a date, and automobile salesmen who hold in mind the engine number of every car sold or inspected. One must marvel with Mark Twain at the memory of a trained Mississippi River steamboat pilot. But the memory of a top brandman surpasses any other kind of memory I have ever met or heard of. It is more than memory; it is an instinct for cattle. Still riding the range are men who can count a hundred head of mixed cattle as they string along, and then from memory classify them and give every brand correctly.

Some of the cattle inspectors operating today in stockyards and on the range can recognize, with only an occasional reference to their brand books, literally thousands of brands. They say that Lod Calohan, head inspector for the Texas and Southwestern Cattle Raisers' Association at the Kansas City stockyards, can tell what brand an animal had on it by tasting the beef.

Deciphering and remembering the letters, figures, curves, and other configurations that make up brands is not enough. The thoroughgoing rangeman is a master of brand nomenclature, on the esoteric principles of which somebody ought to write a grammar. Generally, be it said, brands read from top to bottom and from left to right. A majority of the cattle brands in use are so simple that nearly anyone, once he has mastered a few principles, can " call " them properly. The brand H4 can be nothing else than " H Four "; H⊳ will easily be conceived to be the " H Triangle." But only the initiated denominate ⊥ as " Lazy H," or Ɛ as " Crazy Three." Any letter " too tired to stand up " is " lazy "; though if it is merely in an oblique position and not on its back, it is " tumbling." ⊤ or ⊤ is " Tumbling T."

A letter with curves at the end is often said to be " running." The most noted illustration of this principle is the " Running W " brand ⌐∿∿ — of the million-acre King Ranch. A letter or figure with " wings " to it is " flying " — thus, W is the " Flying W."

Brands " walk," " drag," " swing," and " rock " as well as they " run " or " fly." Ⅼ is the " Walking F " and Λ is the " Walking A." The projection at the bottom of the figure makes Ƶ the " Drag Seven." L suspended from a curve — ⌐Ⅼ — becomes the " Swinging L." Many brands are on rockers, as the " Rocking H " — ⏝H. But if the rocker is unjoined, then it is a half or quarter circle; so ⏝H is " H Half Circle." One of the most historic brands of the West is the " Rocking Chair " — ⏝⊓.

Sometimes a brand rests on a " bench," as Y⏌, the " Y Bench." V-shaped prongs attached to some part of a letter make it forked. ⊱S is " Forked S," but ⫫N is not " Forked N "; it is " Forked Lightning."

A straight mark is usually called a " bar "; but if it is very long or leaning at an angle to the normal horizontal position, it is apt to be called a " slash." The \⫽ is called " Cut and Slash." ⊢— is " Bradded Dash." John Chisum, noted cowman of the Pecos, branded twenty thousand calves each year with a straight line running from shoulder to tail, and that " bar " was known all

CATTLE BRANDING is one of the dusty but exciting jobs that fall to the lot of the cowboy. (Meisel from Monkemeyer)

over the cattle country as the "Fence Rail." A brand burner added to it thus ▬o▬ , and the result was known both as "Knot on the Rail" and "Bug on the Rail." o▬o might be "O Bar O," but it isn't. It is "Hobble O," for it resembles a pair of horse hobbles.

One time a rancher started a new brand made thus, ◖). Somebody asked him what he called it. "*Quien sabe?*" ("Who knows?") he replied. And as the "Quien Sabe" brand it was known ever afterward and was placed on tens of thousands of cattle. Looking through a mixed herd of cattle or a brand book, one might note many brands of apparently a *quien sabe* nature; but somehow the rangemen have usually found a name for the most nameless device.

Fanciful designs frequently have fanciful names that could never be guessed even by good cowmen not familiar with the local interpretation of the brand. For instance, ᜊ was known on the Colorado River

in Texas as "Pot Hooks." When the owners moved their cattle to a new ranch several hundred miles to the southwest, the brand took the name of "Straddle Bug." A well-known brand was the "Gourd and Vine." It was run in this manner ᜉᜎ, so as to cover the whole side of an animal; and while everybody called it "Gourd and Vine," no stranger would at first sight of it ever guess the name.

Many owners use their initials in brands and sometimes even spell out their names. John M. Doak took **DOK** for his brand. With elegant simplicity Mrs. Katie Barr spelled out her whole name in **KT̲**, "KT Bar." Jack Barber approached the sound of his last name with **B̅R̅**. Pete Coffin had both his jest and his name in Ⓟ. A man by the name of Hightower used **HⓘⓇ**. Napoleon Daniel embodied in a brand his nickname — **BONY**. Ingenious but a little puzzling was Mr. Float's brand — ⅂ᴾ, which does spell FLOT.

Instead of telling the owner's name, a brand may suggest something of his biography. J. C. Studer was a blacksmith working for the Santa Fe Railroad when it was built across the Texas Panhandle. He fell in love with the country, invested his savings in land and cattle, and out of respect for his trade adopted an anvil — ⤳ — as his brand. One of the sea captains who used to sail in the Gulf of Mexico quit the sea for ranching; but he could not forget the old seafaring life, and his " Ship's Anchor " brand — ⚓ — was a tribute to the memory.

There are legendary tales about brands, as there are about everything else with which man has had a vital connection. One of the most widely known of these legends tells how the " Four Sixes " — 6666 — originated.

Back in the early days a young cowboy by the name of Burk Burnett, who was just getting his start in cattle, rode into the village of Fort Worth one morning bent on indulging his skill in the favorite game of the range — poker. At one of the many gaming tables, then wide open to the public, he invested in a sombrero full of chips. At first he lost heavily; then the game became variable; about midnight his luck had changed, and by daylight he had a barrelful of money.

One of his opponents was desperate. " Burk," he said, " I'm broke, but I'll play my ranch and cattle against your pile." " You've made a bet," was the reply.

On the deal Burk Burnett drew two sixes. He discarded three other cards, keeping the pair. Then he drew two more sixes. The four sixes won the ranch. Immediately, the story goes on, Burnett rebranded the cattle he had won with his lucky number — 6666. In time he increased his holdings until he had three hundred thousand acres in the Indian Territory stocked with Four Sixes cattle, besides an enormous ranch in North Texas. An oil field came in on his land and a boom city named Burkburnett sprang up. When his widow died, only a few years ago, she left several million dollars to Texas Christian University — probably the best poker hand that a Christian institution ever drew.

Whatever the facts, the poker story has fastened itself upon the imagination of thousands of recounters and will live for a long time.

No account of brands would be complete without consideration of the art of burning out brands. It was an art that reached the height of development during the days of open range, but it is by no means lost yet. Before the practice of counter-branding went out, a thief might void a brand by running a bar through it or by counterbranding the animal — as if it had been legitimately sold — and then putting his own brand on it. Again, he might rub out the owner's brand by taking a hot smoothing iron and burning all that part of an animal's hide covered by a brand. This was called blotching, or blotting. The result would be an enormous scar or blotch, through which the original lines were apt still to be visible. In any case, the blotch was evidence that the animal had been stolen, though not always could it be ascertained from whom stolen.

The most common practice by far was, and is yet, to run the original brand into something else.

One of the oldest chestnuts in the cow country is the " I See You Too " story. A ranchman somewhere started the **IC** brand. Before long he noticed that certain cattle in his herd wore the brand **ICU** Not to be outdone, he did a little doctoring himself, and then the whole herd wore the **ICU2** brand. Then there was the fellow who started with **B4** for a brand. A Longhorn neighbor presently claimed that cattle branded **B4U** were his. The king of brand alterers then rode in, and presently nobody could find on the range anything that was not branded **B4U2**.

If brands could always be added to so easily and if they could be subtracted from as well as added to, the problem of the brand burner would be much simpler; but in brands, as in Scripture, what is writ is writ. In addition to adding a fresh figure or mark to an old device, the brand burner must try to cover up his alterations. For instance, one cattle company gave ⅂P — "Seven P" — for a brand. A thief ran it into ⅂P — "Seven Up." But expert rangemen can usually detect such mutilations. The new part never has the same look as the old part that has been reburned.

The classic story of brand burning has, fittingly, to do with the largest ranch the United States of America has known, the XIT, the three million acres of which were granted by the State of Texas to the Capitol Syndicate in exchange for the present granite capitol building at Austin. Wherever men talk of brands — and that is wherever range cattle graze — the story of the "Star Cross burn" is told.

Range rustlers had tried and tried to figure out a way to turn XIT into another brand that would not give itself away. At last, so the yarn goes, a clever range rider solved the problem. He revealed his secret to no one; he never blurred a brand. He was an artist. Nevertheless, he was finally brought to trial. The evidence was conclusive that he had built up from nothing a herd of cattle branded "Star Cross" —

— but the prosecuting attorney was unable to inform the jury how XIT could be altered into that symbol. So the rustler was freed. The XIT people were helpless. They offered him five thousand dollars if he would tell them how he achieved the Star Cross and would quit burning it on their cattle. Then the legendary rustler told his secret.

Among the thousands of calves branded each year on the XIT Ranch many of them had one or more of the letters imperfectly placed. The rustler looked for animals on which the T was slanting. When he found

X⟩⟩ he easily ran it into ⋇.

Many brand burners have been clever, but probably not one of them ever gained anything by his cleverness. After all, a great majority of the rangemen have always been honest men, and among them brands on cattle have served well the purpose for which they were designed; that is, to identify and maintain ownership. On ranches cattle are branded today by the millions, just as they were branded during the days of the open range.

If branding could be avoided it would be avoided. Humane societies have protested against the practice; experiments have been conducted with chemical compositions purporting to make an indelible but painless mark. But no substitute has been found for branding. Anyhow, branding is not unduly cruel, and the resultant pain is of short duration. As long as there are ranches, there will be brands — and that will be until millions and millions of acres of rocks and arid soil are made fertile and moist. The heraldry of the range is not obsolete; it is not even obsolescent.

## Suggestions for Study

1. To understand better the meaning of the phrase "The Heraldry of the Range," look up heraldry and find some examples of coats of arms containing references to events or objects important in the history of the family.

2. Brands have been used as decorative motifs in modern buildings and furnishings in the Southwest. If you live in that region, see how many such uses you can think of. If you have never seen them used, pick out some of the brands that you think would make good decorative motifs.

3. What other professions does Dobie compare with that of "brandman" in its development of memory? Can you think of professions in your own neighborhood that rely as heavily on trained memory?

4. *Fortune* magazine for December, 1933, contains an article on the King Ranch, whose trail boss used the ranch brand for identification to cash a draft. Reading it, you can find out how justifiable is the comparison of the brand with a nobleman's coat of arms, and also how the modern ranch differs from the old-time one.

5. Besides the books by Dobie mentioned in the introduction, you would enjoy *Tongues of the Monte* and *The Flavor of Texas*. Some of his good articles are "The Last of the Grizzly Hunters," "The Saga of the Saddle," "Outlaws of the Brush," "Spanish Cow Pony," and "In the Brush Country."

## For Your Vocabulary

BASE-WORD. The Latin word *nomen,* name, is the basis of many English words. Dobie uses two which at first glance show little resemblance. *Nomenclature* (nō'měn-klā-tûr) means the system of naming in a particular branch of knowledge or art — as in saying that a man was a master of brand *nomenclature,* calling the right names of brands (page 180). *Denominate* (dě-nŏm'ĭ-nāt) means to give a certain name to. Can you draw the brand *denominated* "Lazy H" (page 180)? The noun *denomination* is used for a group gathered under one name, as Episcopalians. An interesting derivative of *nomen* is the adjective *nominal* (nŏm'ĭ-năl), which means in name but not in fact — as the King of England is the *nominal* head of the government; the Prime Minister, the actual head. Can you add to the list of words using this stem?

## James Saxon Childers   1899–

Except for his student days at Oberlin College, James Childers [1] has been identified with the South all his life. He was born in Birmingham, Alabama, was sent to Oxford as a Rhodes scholar from Atlanta, Georgia, and spent most of his later life as professor of English at Birmingham Southern College and literary editor of the Birmingham *News.* Having been an air-force pilot in World War I, he returned to that service in World War II with the rank of colonel. He has published fourteen volumes of both fiction and nonfiction. His latest book, *War Eagles,* is an account of the American Army Air Forces abroad.

### A BOY WHO WAS TRADED
### FOR A HORSE

Many magazine articles, like "The Heraldry of the Range," give the reader information on some interesting phase of life; others, like the following article from the *American Magazine,* acquaint the reader with some interesting personality. This is a good example of the interview, one of the most popular forms to be found in modern periodicals.

The "boy who was traded for a horse" was

[1] **Childers** (chĭl'dērz).

George Washington Carver, later director of the experimental station and head of the extension service of Tuskegee Institute, the famous Negro school founded by Booker T. Washington. A great chemist, a great horticulturist, a great researcher, Dr. Carver, beginning in the most humble way more than forty years ago, revolutionized the life of the agricultural Negro and buttressed the whole economy of the South. When he died in 1943, all America mourned the passing of one of her greatest and best-loved citizens.

The stooped old Negro shuffled along through the dust of an Alabama road at a curiously rapid rate. He was carrying an armful of sticks and wild flowers.

The sticks I could understand — he would use them for kindling — but I had never before seen an old black man ambling along a road at nine o'clock in the morning with swamp roses, wild geranium, and creeping buttercups mingled with a lot of dry sticks.

When I got a little closer to him I saw that he was wearing a saggy coat which originally might have been a green alpaca, but which the sun had faded until I couldn't be sure about the color; there were so many patches that I couldn't even be certain about the material.

The old man was walking toward a large brick building, one of the buildings of Tuskegee Institute, the famous school for Negroes at Tuskegee, Alabama. His thin body bent by the years, his hair white beneath a ragged cap, he seemed pathetically lost on the campus of a great modern educational institution.

At the entrance of the building toward which we were both walking, the old Negro turned in. "He's probably the janitor," I told myself, "and I'm sincerely glad that they've given him a job of some kind."

I stepped into the hallway. I saw a trim little secretary hurry toward the bent old Negro. I heard her say to him, "That delegation from Washington is waiting for you, Dr. Carver."

Dr. George Washington Carver, the very man I had come to see! Fantastic and unbelievable as it seemed, this old man with his armful of sticks and wild flowers was none other than the distinguished Negro scientist of Tuskegee Institute — a discoverer renowned far and wide for his chemical wizardry in creating useful new products from such stuff as peanut shells and fallen leaves, which most of us waste and throw away.

That saggy alpaca coat covered a Bachelor of Science, Master of Science, Honorary Doctor of Science; winner of the Spingarn Medal for Negro achievement; member of the Royal Society for the Encouragement of Arts, Manufactures, and Commerce of Great Britain.

Yet as I looked at him, studied his kindly face, and recalled what I had heard of the story of his life, I saw that the figure of the man himself was not half so fantastic or unbelievable as is the record of his achievement.

Dr. George Washington Carver started with nothing. He never had anything. Yet out of nothing he has created inestimable wealth for fellow human beings, to whom he has devoted his life.

Born a slave child, he began life without even so much as a name. He never knew his father. He never knew his mother. To this day he doesn't know just when he was born, though he figures his age at somewhere close to seventy. Without a red cent he worked out his own early schooling, then his higher college education, then the post-graduate work for his Master of Science degree. All his life he has been joyously at work with common, everyday things, making something out of nothing or next to nothing. During the thirty-six years in which he has been director of agricultural research at Tuskegee Institute, that has been his work. And out of it have come scientific marvels:

From wood shavings he has made synthetic marble.

From peanut shells he has made insulating walls for houses.

From the muck of swamps and the leaves of the forest floor he has made valuable fertilizers.

From cow dung he has made paint.

From the common, ordinary peanut he has made 285 useful products, including milk, butter, cheese, candies, instant coffee, pickles, sauces, oils, shaving lotions, wood stains, dyes, lard, linoleum, flour, breakfast foods, soap, stock foods, face powder, tan remover, shampoo, printer's ink, and even axle grease!

From the lowly sweet potato he has made 118 products, among them flour, meal, starch, library paste, vinegar, shoe blacking, ginger, ink, rubber compound, chocolate compound, dyes, molasses, wood filler, caramels.

From clays of the earth he has made nonfading paints and pigments.

From worn-out, sandy soil he has produced paying crops.

Something from nothing. And this is only a portion of his work. Experts say that he has probably done more than any other living man to rehabilitate agriculture in the South.

And more still. Dr. Carver is also an artist, especially skilled in painting flowers. His paintings have been exhibited at world fairs, and at least one is going to the Luxembourg Gallery in Paris after his death. He makes all his own paints, using Alabama clays. The paper he paints on he makes from peanut shells, and the frames for his pictures he makes out of cornhusks. His work in embroidery and crochet has won prizes in various exhibits. He has woven gorgeous rugs with fibers he had made from cotton stalks. He is a skilled musician, too — once he toured the Middle West as a concert pianist. And last, but not least, he is an expert cook. His recipes are used today in some of the leading hotels of the country.

All this does sound a bit incredible, doesn't it? I confess that when I set out for Tuskegee to see and talk with Dr. Carver I was more than skeptical of many of the stories I had heard about him. And so, after he had entertained the visiting delegations from Washington, I returned to see him, in his office in the big brick building, with many doubts lingering in my mind.

GEORGE WASHINGTON CARVER, at work in his laboratory at Tuskegee Institute. (Acme)

He was sitting behind a desk cluttered inches high with letters and papers. On top of the papers were the sticks and wild flowers that I had seen him carrying that morning. As I went in, he was looking through a microscope at the stem of a wild rose.

" I beg your pardon," I said.

The old man raised his head and looked at me; then, taking hold of the edge of the desk to steady himself, he pushed himself up from his squeaky swivel chair. He wore a long canvas apron that was splotched and stained. His gold-rimmed spectacles rested far down on his nose. Standing there so tall despite his noticeable stoop, he peered over the tops of his spectacles and smiled at me.

" Good morning," he said, and the quiet tone of his voice blended with the gentle sincerity of his smile.

In slight confusion, then, I explained why I had called on him.

" Do you mind if I stay here awhile? " I asked. " I'd like to very much — that is, if I won't trouble you."

" It will be a pleasure, sir, a very great pleasure to me."

I was touched by his gentleness, and by an unmistakable spiritual quality in the glow of his face. Frankly, I was confused. To open the conversation, I remarked on the numerous Maxfield Parrish paintings that hang on his office walls. " Somehow they seem a little out of place in the office of a scientist," I said lamely.

" But can't a scientist be a lover of the beautiful? " he asked. " There is no one of the moderns who uses blue half so well as Maxfield Parrish uses it."

And then he was off. For forty-five minutes he shuffled about his office, showing me how Maxfield Parrish uses blue, and telling how the ancients used the color. Quietly, even humbly, he told how the Egyptians loved it, how they had adorned their homes and tombs with it.

Then he led me from his office across the hall into his laboratory, a room about thirty by twenty feet. It was filled with racks and shelves and tables, bottles and tubes and retorts. He picked up a jar and carried it to the window. " See " — and he held it to the sun.

And I saw the richest, the purest blue that I have ever seen.

Dr. Carver was talking quietly as he tilted the jar one way and the other, giving the sun its full chance to mate with the glorious color. " I believe," he went on, " that it's a rediscovery of the old Egyptian blue. A number of chemists have come to see it, and they agree with me. At present I'm working on the Egyptian purple; I believe that soon we shall have that too.

" I get my dyes," the old man continued, " from Alabama clays. You remember what the Bible says " — Dr. Carver has built his life on what the Bible says — " you remember that the Bible says, ' Look to the hills from whence cometh your help.' I did it; I

looked to these Alabama hills, and I made these dyes from the clays that I found there. All these dyes and paints " — he waved toward thirty-six boards, each of which was colored differently — " all of them were made from Alabama clay — all," he added, " except this one; it was made from rotten sweet potatoes; and this one, which was made from cow dung; and this one, a much finer paint, was made from horse dung."

After I had been an hour in Dr. Carver's laboratory, after I had seen rope made from okra fiber; baskets from wistaria; and dyes from the dandelion, black oak, wood ashes, sweet gum, swamp maple, sweet potato, pomegranate, peanut, Osage orange, muscadine grape, onion, velvet bean, and tomato vine — after I had seen those discoveries, among a few hundred others, I was willing to believe almost anything possible to this kindly man to whom apparently bricks without straw [1] would be a simple problem.

" When you do the common things of life in an uncommon way," Dr. Carver once said to his students, " you will command the attention of the world." In that sentence lies the secret of his own achievement.

He was born in a rude slave cabin on the farm of Moses Carver near Diamond Grove, Missouri. Moses Carver owned his mother, and a neighbor owned his father. When he was a baby six months old, night riders swooped down on his master's plantation and carried away a number of slaves, among them the baby and his mother.

In their flight, the raiders took no care of the child; he developed whooping cough and was dying when emissaries sent out by Moses Carver arrived from Missouri to buy back the stolen slaves.

But the mother had already been disposed of; no one ever learned what became of her. Indeed, there is only one thing of hers that is left: in Doctor Carver's room in one of the dormitories at Tuskegee is a

---

[1] **bricks without straw:** When the Israelites were held as slaves by the Egyptians, they were commanded to make bricks without straw. The fifth chapter of Exodus tells the whole story.

battered old spinning wheel on which his mother spun flax when she was a slave. A friend of Doctor Carver's said to me, " I've seen him touch that wheel; he touches it like a priest reverently touching an altar. I sometimes feel that if I could be in his room when he retires, I should hear the old man say ' Good night ' to that wheel."

The emissaries sent to ransom the stolen slaves finally struck a bargain with the night riders. The baby was evaluated and traded back to his owner; he was traded for a broken-down race horse worth about $300!

## Suggestions for Study

1. Point out all the things about Dr. Carver's life and work that are unusual. Why are his experiments and discoveries of especial value to the nation as a whole?

2. What other new products have been developed by chemical experimentation in recent years? Discuss vocational opportunities in the field of chemistry.

3. Name other outstanding Negroes. A series of oral reports would provide an interesting class hour. Perhaps these reports can be given in the form of a " Who Am I? " radio program.

4. Mrs. Rackham Holt's *George Washington Carver*, written after his death, has aroused a great deal of interest in recent years.

5. Read the life story of another great Negro educator, Booker T. Washington. His autobiography is *Up From Slavery*.

6. Go as a reporter to have an interview with some interesting person in your school or town. Write the interview as you would for a newspaper or magazine. Make the person " come alive " to your readers.

## Walter Lippmann    1899–

Among modern writers on politics and current problems, Walter Lippmann occupies a distinguished position. The magazines and newspapers to which he has been a regular contributor include the *New Republic*, the New York *World*, and the New York *Herald Tribune;* and today his articles, published by a large newspaper syndicate, are of considerable importance in forming public opinion on many economic and political questions.

## THE PARADOX OF POVERTY AND PLENTY

In the following article Mr. Lippmann discusses the bewildering fact that periodically millions of Americans are forced to live in abject poverty despite the equally obvious fact that we Americans are capable of producing an abundance of food, clothing, and all the other necessities — and even luxuries — of life.

Can this problem be solved by the same rugged individualism which produced our abundance? Or must we submit to more and more government control in order to secure the distribution of purchasing power necessary to keep the wheels of industry turning? Mr. Lippmann is not discouraged by the problem; he accepts it as an inspiring challenge to the adventurous spirit of modern man.

Everyone is aware of the paradox at the heart of all the present-day suffering — the sensational and the intolerable paradox of want in the midst of abundance, of poverty in the midst of plenty. This is the first great economic depression [1] in which every thinking person has been conscious of such a paradox.

It is often said that this depression is not unlike the great depressions after 1837 and 1873. There are, indeed, many common elements; and if our knowledge of these other crises were more reliable than it is, we should probably have more practical wisdom at hand for meeting our problem. But in the mentality of the people there is a profound difference between this crisis and all its predecessors. This is the first time when it is altogether evident that man's power to produce wealth has reached a point when it is clearly unnecessary that millions in a country like the United States should be in want. In all previous crises there was some doubt as to whether the wealth of the nation was sufficient. That doubt no longer exists.

Man has invented and organized the power to produce wealth on a scale which allows us to say that the most ancient of hu-

[1] **This . . . depression:** This article was written during the great depression of the nineteen-thirties.

" The Paradox of Poverty and Plenty," from *Interpretations 1931-32*, by Walter Lippmann. Reprinted by permission of The Macmillan Company, publishers.

man problems — the problem of scarcity — has been solved. It has not been solved in all parts of the globe. It has not been solved in China or in India and not yet, I think, in Russia. There men are still under the dominion of scarcity; the wealth, no matter how fairly it may be distributed, does not exist, to liberate the peoples from the menace of want. There the problem is still the ancient problem — the problem of scarcity, of famine due to the shortage of food and other goods.

But in our Western world, and above all in the United States, this problem is solved. Not only do we know how to produce all the wealth needed for a decent standard of life for everybody, we actually do produce it in great abundance.

It has taken about three hundred years to arrive at the point where we can definitely say that the problem of scarcity is solved. It has required the development of modern science, the overthrow of feudalism, the liberation of personal energies through the democratic destruction of caste, and the widespread popularization of knowledge to accomplish the result. But it has been done. It is in any large perspective a great achievement.

We who stand at the culmination of this epoch can see today that in order to reap the results of this achievement, in order to translate the power we possess into a secure and ordered civilization, we have to do something which is extremely difficult. We have to tamper with the motives which made the achievement possible. For if we are realistic we must acknowledge that the moving force behind the stupendous material work of the nineteenth century was the acquisitive instinct stimulated to tremendous energy by the prospect of enormous personal profits and personal power. The supreme social problem of the twentieth century, and perhaps for a longer time than that, is to find energies as powerful and as persistent as the acquisitive and the competitive which are disinterested and co-operative in their effect.

If I read correctly the recent experience of Russia, it is being demonstrated there how difficult it is to solve that problem. For the Russian system starts with the premise that the acquisitive motive shall be outlawed. But the Russian experience seems to show, not only that the acquisitive motive is difficult to suppress, but that without it the energies of men to produce wealth are at present insufficient. That is why the Russians, when they find the output of wealth insufficient, are compelled, temporarily at least, to mitigate their pure doctrine and make concessions to private acquisitiveness.

I mention this, not by way of criticism, but because it seems to me to show the essential difficulty met by men who are making the most radical experiment with a problem which confronts all mankind. Their experiment shows thus far, it seems to me, that a technology for the production of wealth brought into being under the stimulus of strong acquisitiveness will not easily be maintained and mastered by disinterested and co-operative motives alone.

It seems probable, therefore — indeed, I think we may say it is certain — that as it took several centuries to solve the problem of scarcity so it will take long generations to solve what we may call the problem of the management of plenty. The solution of that problem depends upon changes in human motives as great as those which distinguish a feudal peasant from the modern businessman. I do not say this in the spirit of those who tell us that nothing is possible because human nature is unchangeable. Human nature is changeable in the sense that the informed idealist has in mind. The change that has come over human nature in the West since the fifteenth century has made possible the capitalist system. The modern businessman is the descendant of peasants, and if his human nature is unchanged from that of his ancestors, the motives which actuate him and the energies which he shows are at least a radical rearrangement and displacement of the ancient pattern. If the descendants of the modern businessman are to operate a social order in which personal initiative is to be combined with public responsibility, his motives will have to change as radically in the next centuries as they have in the past.

We are not, however, able to wait until human motives have been transformed. The pressure of events compels us to make experiments in the management of human affairs, for which, in fact, we lack adequate human material. We do not have the wisdom and disinterestedness to manage with any assurance the volume of credit which determines the rhythm of economic enterprise. We do not have the wisdom and disinterestedness to make the world secure against war. We do not have the wisdom and disinterestedness to plan and arrange the growth of our cities or the future of agriculture or the balance between agriculture and industry. Nevertheless, we have to attempt all these things, and many more besides, for which we are unprepared and inadequate. For the world in which we live, the world which our achievement in production has created, is a world which is so complicated, so dependent upon agreements and upon foresight that a policy of *laissez faire* [1] has become utterly impossible. We have to attempt the management of it, though we know so little how to manage it. We have to learn by trial and error, since the whole truth is not revealed to us and we cannot spin it a priori [2] out of our minds.

Therefore, the Ages of Discovery are not over. We are entering a new one in which the problems are as fascinating and the issues as momentous as any with which man has dealt. The voyage of Columbus opened up a new world to the European spirit, and within those widened horizons men accomplished miracles of invention and human organization. The solution of the problem of scarcity is a discovery like that of Columbus. It has opened a new world in which the human spirit can and will expand with hopes and energies and invincible ambitions for a better order of life than men have ever known before.

[1] laissez faire (lĕ′sä fâr′): French for "let alone." In economics, unrestricted competition.
[2] a priori (ā prĭ-ō′rī): from reason rather than experience; literally, "from what is before."

## Suggestions for Study

1. What is the problem of scarcity? To what human motive does Mr. Lippmann attribute the solution of this problem?

2. What is the problem now confronting the Western world? What motives will have to be developed to solve this problem? What must we do while these motives are being developed?

3. Name some of the differences in human motives between a feudal peasant and a modern businessman, between a modern businessman and a businessman in a system of successful " management of plenty."

4. In what ways do you believe human nature can, and cannot, be changed?

5. What is the difference between disinterestedness and lack of interest?

## For Your Vocabulary

WORD POWER. To get the full force of the opening statements in this article, you must know exactly what a *paradox* (păr′ȧ-dŏks) is — a statement or situation containing apparent contradictions. Many popular riddles are built on *paradoxes;* for example, " The more it dries, the wetter it gets. What is it? " [1] A *paradoxical* statement is often a mere play on words, but a paradoxical situation usually displays striking contrasts, as in Lippmann's *paradox* of poverty in the midst of plenty. Another word in the article much used in discussion of social and political theories is *premise* (prĕm′ĭs), which means a statement regarded as true and made the basis of other statements or beliefs. Find the *premise* which the author says is the basis of Russian political thinking (page 189). What are some of the premises on which our American thinking is based?

## William Allen White   1868–1944

If ever a literary man was identified through his whole life with a single town, that man was William Allen White, and the town was Emporia, Kansas. His birth, his schooling, and his long career as owner and editor of the Emporia *Gazette* forged such a strong link between his name and that of the town that one hardly thinks of the one without the other. Through Mr. White's grasp of public affairs and penetrating editorials, his newspaper attained an

[1] a towel.

unusual reputation throughout the country. He also wrote essays, biographies, short stories, and novels. His two best-known pieces of fiction are *The Court of Boyville* and *A Certain Rich Man.* But today his biographies of Woodrow Wilson and of Calvin Coolidge and his *Autobiography,* published posthumously in 1946, are more widely read than his fiction.

## MARY WHITE

It is not, however, as a publicist or novelist that we see him in this editorial, but as a father. Probably no such remarkable obituary has ever appeared in a newspaper as the one he wrote for his own daughter. Composed when her loss was still fresh enough to have overwhelmed an ordinary man, it nevertheless reveals a self-command and depth of affection which rise above ordinary expressions of grief and give to Mary White a lease of life far beyond her mortal years.

The Associated Press reports carrying the news of Mary White's death declared that it came as the result of a fall from a horse. How she would have hooted at that! She never fell from a horse in her life. Horses have fallen on her and with her — " I'm always trying to hold 'em in my lap," she used to say. But she was proud of few things, and one was that she could ride anything that had four legs and hair. Her death resulted not from a fall, but from a blow on the head which fractured her skull, and the blow came from the limb of an overhanging tree on the parking.

The last hour of her life was typical of its happiness. She came home from a day's work at school, topped off by a hard grind with the copy on the high-school *Annual,* and felt that a ride would refresh her. She climbed into her khakis, chattering to her mother about the work she was doing, and hurried to get her horse and be out on the dirt roads for the country air and the radiant fields of the spring. As she rode through the town on an easy gallop she kept waving at passers-by. She knew everyone in town. For a decade the little figure with the long pigtail and the red hair ribbon has been familiar on the streets of Emporia, and

WILLIAM ALLEN WHITE, for almost fifty years author, editor, and owner of the Emporia *Gazette.*

she got in the way of speaking to those who nodded at her. She passed the Kerrs, walking the horse, in front of the Normal Library, and waved at them; passed another friend a few hundred feet farther on, and waved at her. The horse was walking, and as she turned into North Merchant Street she took off her cowboy hat, and the horse swung into a lope. She passed the Tripletts and waved her cowboy hat at them, still moving gaily north on Merchant Street. A *Gazette* carrier passed — a high-school boy friend — and she waved at him, but with her bridle hand; the horse veered quickly, plunged into the parking where the low-hanging limb faced her, and, while she still looked back, waving, the blow came. But she did not fall from the horse; she slipped off, dazed a bit, staggered, and fell in a faint. She never quite recovered consciousness.

But she did not fall from the horse, neither was she riding fast. A year or so ago she used to go like the wind. But that habit was broken, and she used the horse to get into the open to get fresh, hard exercise, and to work off a certain surplus energy that welled up in her and needed a physical outlet. That need has been in her heart for years. It was back of the impulse that kept the dauntless little brown-clad figure on the streets and country roads of this community and built into a strong, muscular body what had been a frail and sickly frame during the first years of her life. But the riding gave her more than a body. It released a gay and hardy soul. She was the happiest thing in the world. And she was happy because she was enlarging her horizon. She came to know all sorts and conditions of men. Charley O'Brien, the traffic cop, was one of her best friends. W. L. Holtz, the Latin teacher, was another. Tom O'Connor, farmer-politician, and Rev. J. H. J. Rice, preacher and police judge, and Frank Beach, music master, were her special friends, and all the girls, black and white, above the track and below the track, in Pepville and Stringtown, were among her acquaintances. And she brought home riotous stories of her adventures. She loved to rollick; persiflage was her natural expression at home. Her humor was a continual bubble of joy. She seemed to think in hyperbole and metaphor. She was mischievous without malice, as full of faults as an old shoe. No angel was Mary White, but an easy girl to live with, for she never nursed a grouch five minutes in her life.

With all her eagerness for the out-of-doors, she loved books. On her table when she left her room were a book by Conrad, one by Galsworthy, *Creative Chemistry* by E. E. Slosson, and a Kipling book. She read Mark Twain, Dickens, and Kipling before she was ten — all of their writings. Wells and Arnold Bennett particularly amused and diverted her. She was entered as a student in Wellesley in 1922; was assistant editor of the high-school *Annual* this year, and in line for election to the editorship of the *Annual* next year. She was a member of the executive committee of the high-school Y. W. C. A.

Within the last two years she had begun to be moved by an ambition to draw. She began as most children do by scribbling, in her schoolbooks, funny pictures. She bought cartoon magazines and took a course — rather casually, naturally, for she was, after all, a child with no strong purposes — and this year she tasted the first fruits of success by having her pictures accepted by the high-school *Annual*. But the thrill of delight she got when Mr. Ecord, of the Normal *Annual*, asked her to do the cartooning for that book this spring, was too beautiful for words. She fell to her work with all her enthusiastic heart. Her drawings were accepted, and her pride — always repressed by a lively sense of the ridiculousness of the figure she was cutting — was a really gorgeous thing to see. No successful artist ever drank a deeper draft of satisfaction than she took from the little fame her work was getting among her schoolfellows. In her glory, she almost forgot her horse — but never her car.

For she used the car as a jitney bus. It was her social life. She never had a " party " in all her nearly seventeen years — wouldn't have one; but she never drove a block in the car in her life that she didn't begin to fill the car with pickups! Everybody rode with Mary White — white and black, old and young, rich and poor, men and women. She liked nothing better than to fill the car full of long-legged high-school boys and an occasional girl, and parade the town. She never had a " date," nor went to a dance, except once with her brother Bill, and the " boy proposition " didn't interest her — yet. But young people — great spring-breaking, varnish-cracking, fender-bending, door-sagging carloads of " kids " — gave her great pleasure. Her zests were keen. But the most fun she ever had in her life was acting as chairman of the committee that got up the big turkey dinner for the poor folks at the county home; scores of pies, gallons of slaw; jam, cakes, preserves, oranges, and a wilderness of turkey were loaded in the car and taken to the county home. And, being of a practical turn of mind, she risked her own Christmas dinner by staying to see that the poor folks actually got it all. Not that she was a cynic; she just disliked to tempt folks. While there, she found a blind colored uncle, very old, who could do nothing but make rag rugs, and she rustled up from her school friends rags enough to keep him busy for a season. The last engagement she tried to make was to take the guests at the county home out for a car ride. And the last endeavor of her life was to try to get a rest room for colored girls in the high school. She found one girl reading in the toilet, because there was no better place for a colored girl to loaf, and it inflamed her sense of injustice and she became a nagging Harpy to those who, she thought, could remedy the evil. The poor she had always with her and was glad of it. She hungered and thirsted for righteousness; and was the most impious creature in the world. She joined the Congregational Church without consulting her parents; not particularly for her soul's good. She never had a thrill of piety in her life, and would have hooted at a " testimony." But even as a little child she felt the church was an agency for helping people to more of life's abundance, and she wanted to help. She never wanted help for herself. Clothes meant little to her. It was a fight to get a new rig on her; but eventually a harder fight to get it off. She never wore a jewel and had no ring but her high-school class ring, and never asked for anything but a wrist watch. She refused to have her hair up, though she was nearly seventeen. " Mother," she protested, " you don't know how much I get by with, in my braided pigtails, that I could not with my hair up." Above every other passion of her life was her passion not to grow up, to be a child. The tomboy in her, which was big, seemed to loathe to be put away forever in skirts. She was Peter Pan, who refused to grow up.

Her funeral yesterday at the Congregational Church was as she would have wished it; no singing, no flowers save the big bunch of roses from her brother Bill's Harvard classmen — heavens, how proud that would have made her! — and the red roses from the *Gazette* force — in vases at her head and feet. A short prayer, Paul's beautiful essay on " Love " from the thirteenth chapter of First Corinthians, some remarks about her democratic spirit by her friend, John H. J. Rice, pastor and police judge, which she would have deprecated if she could, a prayer sent down for her by her friend, Carl Nau, and, opening the service, the slow, poignant movement from Beethoven's " Moonlight Sonata," which she loved, and, closing the service, a cutting from the joyously melancholy first movement of Tschaikowsky's *Pathetic Symphony,* which she liked to hear in certain moods on the phonograph; then the Lord's Prayer by her friends in the high school.

That was all.

For her pallbearers only her friends were chosen: her Latin teacher, W. L. Holtz; her high-school principal, Rice Brown; her doctor, Frank Foncannon; her friend, W. W. Finney; her pal at the *Gazette* office, Walter Hughes; and her brother Bill. It would have made her smile to know that her friend, Charley O'Brien, the traffic cop, had been transferred from Sixth and Commercial to the corner near the church to direct her friends who came to bid her good-by.

A rift in the clouds in a gray day threw a shaft of sunlight upon her coffin as her nervous, energetic little body sank to its last sleep. But the soul of her, the glowing, gorgeous, fervent soul of her, surely was flaming in eager joy upon some other dawn.

## Suggestions for Study

1. Give some of the details of Mary White's appearance and actions which make her seem like a real girl and not an idealized figure.

2. Would you have liked Mary as a classmate? Point out specific reasons for your answer. To what general type of high-school girl would you say she belonged?

3. How do her favorite authors match up with your own?

4. What was particularly appropriate about her funeral service?

5. Try writing a portrayal of one of your classmates in which vividness is achieved by intimate detail.

## For Your Vocabulary

WORD GROUP. Cynic (sĭn´ĭk) is one of those valuable words for which we have no substitute except to explain the whole idea. A *cynic* is a person who doubts the worth, truth, or virtue of what other people have genuine faith in. Why does the writer pause to assure the reader that Mary was not a *cynic* (page 193)? *Cynicism* (sĭn´ĭ-sĭsm) is the attitude of mocking other people's faith in right and goodness, or doubting the honor and trustworthiness of human nature. It is *cynical*, for example, to deny that those who are good are happy.

## Howard Vincent O'Brien     1888–

Among newspaper columns, Howard Vincent O'Brien's "All Things Considered" in the Chicago *Daily News* holds an honorable position.

### SO LONG, SON

In this column in January, 1942, Mr. O'Brien wrote the following farewell to his youngest boy, off to the war. Since publication, it has been reprinted twice in the *Reader's Digest*, and many times elsewhere, and has been broadcast over every network.

Later pieces by Mr. O'Brien followed his boy through his training and his departure for overseas. Then came the red-starred telegram: " The Secretary of War wishes to express his deep regret. . . ."

A little book entitled *So Long, Son* contains the whole story, tender and heartbreaking, but also inspiring in its revelation of the dignity and strength of the human spirit.

It was a few weeks after Pearl Harbor.

There was no band, no flags, no ceremonial. It wasn't dramatic — the beginning of this story. A car honked outside and he said, " Well, I guess that's for me."

He picked up his little bag, and his mother said: " You haven't forgotten your gloves? "

He kissed his mother and held out his hand to me. " Well, so long," he said. I took his hand but all I could say was, " Good luck."

The door slammed and that was that — another boy gone to war.

I had advised waiting for the draft — waiting at least until he was required to register. I had pointed out that he was not yet of age. He had smiled at that and assured me that his mind was made up. He wanted peace, he said. Without peace, what good was living?

There was finality in the way he said this — a finality at once grim and gentle. I said no more about waiting.

After the door closed behind him I went upstairs. I went to what had been his room. It was in worse chaos than usual. His bureau was littered — an incredible collection of things . . . letters, keys, invitations to parties he would not attend.

Clothing was scattered about — dancing pumps, a tennis racket; his precious collection of phonograph records; his trumpet, gleaming in its case.

I went then to my room. On the wall was a picture of a little boy, his toothless grin framed in tawny curls — the same boy who had just taken my hand and said: " Well, so long."

Not much time, I thought, between the making of that picture and the slamming of the front door. Not much more than a decade.

Suddenly, a queer thing happened. Objects came alive, whispering to me. The house was full of soft voices. They led me up to the attic — to a box of toy soldiers, a broken music rack, a football helmet, a homemade guitar, schoolbooks, class pictures, a stamp album, a penny bank with the lid pried off . . . ancient history, long hidden under dust.

The voices led me to a filing case and a folder stuffed with papers — report cards, letters — among them the wail of an exasperated teacher, " Though he looks like an angel . . ." — telegrams, passports, a baptismal certificate, a ribbon won in a track meet, faded photographs — one taken on the memorable first day of long pants — a bit of golden hair.

I sat down and thought how time had flown. Why, it was only yesterday when I had held him in my arms. That, somehow, made me remember all the scoldings I had given him, the preachments, the exhortation to a virtue and wisdom I did not myself possess.

I thought, too, of that last inarticulate " good luck," that last perfunctory handclasp; and I wished that I had somehow been able to tell him how much I really loved him. Had he perhaps penetrated my brusque reserve? Had he perhaps guessed what was in my heart?

And then I thought: what fools we are with our children — always plotting what we shall make of them; always planning for a future that never comes; always intent on what they *may* be — never accepting what they *are*.

Well, curlyhead — you're a man now, bearing your bright new shield and spear. I hated to see you go out of my house and close the door behind you; but I think I would not have halted you if I could. I salute you, sir. I cannot pretend that I am not sad; but I am proud, too.

So long.

## Suggestions for Study

1. What is your attitude toward the publication of such intimate incidents as this article records?
2. Bring to class specimens of the work of as many columnists as you can find. Try to characterize each.

# THE BOOK REVIEW

The book-review column of a good magazine or newspaper is like a map to guide you over unfamiliar ground. You cannot possibly read all the new books that come out. You don't wish to waste your time reading books that will not appeal to you in subject matter or books that are poorly written. Sometimes you don't care to read a certain book, but you wish to know something about it because everyone is talking about it. Sometimes you are looking for guidance in selecting books for another person. Sometimes, after you have read a book, you wish to find out whether you and the reviewer agree or disagree on it. Sometimes pure curiosity about what new books are on the horizon leads you to the reviewer's column. These are all legitimate reasons for reading book reviews. There is only one illegitimate one: to try to give the impression that you have read a book when all you have read is a review.

Since the book review is a form of writing which students are often called upon to employ in literature classes, and since book reviews are an interesting part of magazine literature, three good examples from recent periodicals are here presented for your enjoyment.

The first two are from two of our best magazines devoted exclusively to comment on literature. Both are by well-known writers: William Rose Benét is a leading poet, and Eudora Welty is one of our most prominent novel and short-story writers.

The third review is from *Time*, whose reviews are always anonymous. The " Books " section of *Time* is perhaps the very best place for you to start your book-review reading. The reviews in *Time* are intelligent and popular, and the magazine is readily obtainable.

Of the three books reviewed, two are recent nonfiction best sellers. The third is a collector's item, an interesting bit of Americana.

"Just gimme a coupla aspirin. I already got a Purple Heart."

# William Rose Benét     1886–

## UP FRONT

### BY BILL MAULDIN

A book review from the
*Saturday Review of Literature*

Bill Mauldin is the best cartoonist of the American foot soldier in this war, just as Bruce Bairnsfather was of the English

Tommy in the last one. But Bairnsfather had the comic-paper and music-hall touch. Mauldin is far more the realist. The Englishman's "Old Bill," "Fragments from France," "The Better 'Ole," etc., conveyed the tedium of the trench warfare of that time. Mauldin deals with a war no less tedious, if more in the open. There is no music-hall touch about his work, but much humor of a typically American kind. There is the truth of the mud, blood, dirt, and sweat, and of the intolerable boredom. Mauldin's Willie and Joe are even more real than the British Old Bill, Bert, and Alf. And now, in this book, Mauldin has written thirty thousand words to accompany his pictures, words that show him as uncompromising a truth-teller with the typewriter as with the pencil. His text has the same biting humor that has gone into his drawings of weary, unshaven, sardonic dogfaces. It makes the whole a " must " book of the war.

Mauldin is for the Joes, and not so partial to the high brass; though he did his job well and got along with everybody. He knows the daily life of the men intimately and thoroughly. He writes without sentimentality, and, on the other hand, without false " toughness." And that's the way he draws. He was everywhere the doughfoots went in Italy, and studied his material at first hand and under fire. Particularly for the doughfoot, war is a dirty business, literally and figuratively. You could call Mauldin the doughfoot's Homer, only he isn't a bit like Homer. Neither was Anzio a bit like encrimsoned Scamander, though there has been more sheer heroism all along the line in this war, if you come to that, than there ever was on " the ringing plains of windy Troy."

It is interesting to note that in Bill Mauldin's cartoons and prose the common denominator of war, the genuine lowdown, the glazed-eyed comment of the fed-up and barrage-drunk footslogger, conveys that heroism. It isn't a thing of oratory or drama. It's a thing of heavy, grousing patience and stunned acceptance of a bogged-down and mud-plastered situation. The ambush of two Joes who see a German go by with a bottle, and tell each other not to startle him because the bottle is nearly full, is the sardonic side of the medal. But in the picture of two doggies sitting under a mudbank, up to their posteriors in water, with mines exploding back of them and bullets whining over them, you get the real pay-off. The caption reads, " Wisht I could stand up an' git

some sleep." That is the unadulterated McCoy.

You get to know exactly how the front line regards the rear echelon; and how the battered veterans at a café table, for a change, look with a dead eye upon the swagger of those who don't yet really know what war is. You find them commenting upon the eupeptic appearance of a replacement right before his face. You find out just how they have what it takes, and also how they have absolutely no illusions concerning it. There is a wealth of evidence in this book. It will entertain you; but more, it will instruct you. It will show you just why, in the words of the late Wilfred Owen, the English poet and company commander killed on the Western Front in the last war, those who have not been through it are, in comparison with the ordinary G. I.'s who have borne the burden and heat — and mud and wet — of the day, " not worth their merriment." Personally, for his straight shooting, I'd give Bill Mauldin the Congressional Medal of Honor!

## Eudora Welty          1909–

### NAMES ON THE LAND

BY GEORGE R. STEWART

*A book review from The New York Times Book Review, May 6, 1945*

Outlaws X-Roads, Shiloh, Schenectady, Santa Fe — how did we get these names? And when?

The record of our place names is of course the skeleton story of our nation; in that array the intrinsic and underlying structure shows. Exploration and claiming — Cape Fear, Louisiana; colonization — Jamestown; immigration — New Rochelle; revolution—Lafayette; expansion—Deadman's Gulch. Our names tell us everything if we can read them. But every name has a name behind that — a one more story, a sea change.[1] The ambition of this book is

[1] **sea change:** a change wrought by the sea, as in the formation of a pearl; hence, a marked transformation.

staggering — like a demonstration of our national character in itself. Mr. Stewart uses the X-ray method on his material, but he has the zest of a Forty-niner, and what he makes is not a case, but a strike, and his book is a beauty. Only a passionate lover of facts, of facts rooted in the country and the people and the history of the land, could have written it. Mr. Stewart of course has written a meteorological novel (*Storm*) and a factual account of the Donner party. But what facts are closer to people, more revealing of people's hearts, than the names they bestow?

The scope here is so large, and the details so minute — taking in the whole country from the beginning on (with a nod at the Ice Age) and from one end to the other — that the story would collapse under its own weight in the hands of a man less deft at organizing it — a problem which was only one to tempt Mr. Stewart, one imagines, and lead him on. The lay reader such as the present reviewer has no way of knowing what degree of accuracy the work reaches, but will bet that it is good and high. Mr. Stewart has a reputation for getting data. In dealing with this material there must be guesswork and deduction in addition to the mountainous research; indeed, part of the fascination of the book lies in its ingenuity. A knowledge of languages including the Algonquin, a familiarity with American history from the earliest times on, a clear geographical grasp of the country from all four corners, a knowledge of law and land grants, miner's slang, Indian beliefs, agricultural developments, Mormon saints, and weather — a sizable background appears behind this book.

In the United States (Mr. Stewart does deplore that makeshift name for our country) are places named for battles, for a lost comrade, for the day of a saint, for a homesick moment, for a lure to bring neighbors, for kings and queens; places named for the namer, for a dead pony, for Lafayette, for a tavern sign, for a future wife, for a murder, for a deer in the creek, for a night of bad cards, for a rock that looked like the bosom of a lady, for a cockfight, for a poem in Scotland. Tradition, hope, love, pride, delight in the romantic, the bawdy, the beautiful, hope of gain, a keen and seeing eye, and likely a strutting fancy — these went into the naming of places in America. All Europe and Asia gave us names — and Puritans, Huguenots, Mormons and Quakers, miners, missionaries, outlaws, fishermen, scholars, traders, trappers, surveyors, priests, and planters' wives.

The astonishing variety of our names is to be expected, Mr. Stewart holds — after all, four centuries of changing peoples and changing aspirations went into the naming. Variety comes, too, because in giving names to places we cherished their strong link with actual persons and events — gave names " which seem to have stories of life and death behind them." " Variety also sprang from democracy — that stubborn local pride in the local name, and the feeling that I have just as much right to give and keep a name as you have." Chicken Bristle, or die. So we have Lexington and Union, and also Sweetwater, Marked Tree, Gunsight Hills, Cape Disappointment, Broken Bow, Roaring Run, Massacre Lake. And we have always loved a revolutionary, Mr. Stewart points out, and honored him, no further questions asked, with a town name — Kossuth, Kosciusko, even Ypsilanti did not stop us.

In the beginning the French were hunting a passage to the South Sea; the Spanish were looking for treasure in a fabulous kingdom and the elixir of life; the British were nosing for present holdings; the Dutch seeking trade. In all these pursuits, naming a place was an important point, a gain on the rivals. The differences in naming were clear-cut from the start. The Spanish always named places after the saint's day on which they found them, so that their maps are really calendars on which voyages can be read like diaries. The Dutch gave a practical name to each little kill and hook of the river they settled on, but they never did name the Hudson — it was simply " the river " — the English reproached them. The English of course drew upon courts and houses in England, gained favors or obeyed the king.

Ranging over four centuries, with pages packed with names and events, the book remains clear in trend, felicitous in pictures of the times which build along the way. We see the whole complexity and confusion of that early time when Joliet and Père Marquette with their boatmen, in two birch-bark canoes, set off down the Mississippi:

At last, near the middle of June in 1673, they came to the great river, which was already known by name. They wrote the word as Mississippi. But Marquette, it would seem, called it also Conception, and Joliet called it Buade, after the family name of Count Frontenac, the Governor. Thus all at once the river had three names — an Indian name for the boatmen, a religious name for the priest, and a political name for the officer.

In all the conglomeration of detail, the major design is not lost sight of, and we are shown panoramas of the nation as a whole at a given time, as:

. . . in the reign of Charles II, new great names arose, until twelve colonies and the Province of Maine were well established. In addition some cities and all the great rivers and capes and bays and islands of that coast had their names. Inland, the French had scattered names as far as Lake Superior and Kansas and Arkansas, and the Spaniards even further to the southwest. Since 1607 almost every year had seen the establishment of some new great name. In 1681 La Salle first used Louisiane; within a year Pennsylvania and Philadelphia were established; about the same time the Spaniards were beginning to use Texas. But the next two generations of men were to give few great names; instead they would fill in with thousands of little names, and establish new habits.

As he proceeds, the author shows how habit of life determined the kind of name. In the Virginia colonies, towns took the names of plantations, of little private chapels and churches, which were often named with Elizabethan fancy (Orphan's Gift, Chapel Hill, Chaplin's Choice, Jordan's Journey, Flower dieu Hundred). In the middle colonies, especially in Pennsylvania, towns took the names of the tavern signs, whose pictures survived as village names (Bird-in-Hand, Broad Axe, King of Prussia, Red Lion). When the Mormons went west they had a whole private holy book to draw names from and their own population of saints, and needed no dim-memoried dragon killer to name a town St. George after. When the Forty-niners went West they were in such a hurry that big things like mountains and rivers got names that were simple pinning-down affairs, the explicit " West Fork of the South Fork of the North Fork of the San Joaquin," so they could be found again. It was in the naming of their mining camps that they gave vent to their real enthusiasm and high spirits, for " No censorship restrained them; society was of men only. Most of them looked upon their sojourn in California . . . as temporary and riotous adventure. . . . Doubtless the more sophisticated often invented the most outlandish names; two Harvard men named Shirt-tail Canyon." . . .

The book deals constantly with the Indians, of course, and manages to correct many an error about Indian names. Transference, translation, and false etymology are the three ways in which a place name can be passed from language to language, Mr. Stewart points out. So the Indian names enduring as such are of course not the actual, original Indian names — they are what the French priests wrote down, what the Spanish thought they sounded like, what the English thought they undoubtedly meant, what the Dutch made sound as nearly Dutch as they could. Schenectady, for instance, is an anglicized form of the Dutch conception of a New York State Indian word. Mr. Stewart points out the important difference in the ways an Indian and a white man named a river. The European conception of a river was of a stream with a source, to which it and all its branches could and should be traced, and it had a single name. " What is the name of this river? " excited explorers would ask the

Indians. " Big Rock," the Indians would answer, pointing to a big rock in front of them. " Big Rock " was the name of the river *there*. At the bend it would be named " Little Bend." Mississippi, a French version of an Algonquin word, probably means " big river," but could never mean " Father of Waters " as the geography books told us — an abstract term no clear-headed Indian would ever give a river for a name. In the same way, the Indians running out to greet the white man in the southwest yelled " Techas! Techas! " This meant simply " Friends! " The Spaniards immediately thought the Indians were referring to some wonderful kingdom lying just back of them — Texas. But the Indians were hardly ever referring to anything except what was up at the moment. . . .

This book is a labor of love, such as few people would have had the energies, much less the abilities, or the pure courage, to undertake — and finish. The whole is written with a grace and engaging humor belying the work behind it. The nation from Seldom Seen to Possum Glory, Hog Eye to Bug Tustle, does owe Mr. Stewart a debt of gratitude for getting the tremendous material here between the covers of a book. " As the train announcer calls out the stations for a Philadelphia local, half the past of the nation unfolds." " It is a rich and poetic heritage," indeed.

## The Editors of *Time* Magazine

### STRUGGLING UPWARD AND OTHER WORKS

#### BY HORATIO ALGER, JR.

A book review from *Time,* August 13, 1945

Nothing recedes like success. In the field of juvenile literature, Horatio Alger, Jr., four of whose novels have just been reissued in this volume, was once regarded as the most successful writer who ever lived. Directly or indirectly he influenced the life of every United States town boy born between 1870 and 1900. Farm boys had less time and money for fiction, but if they did read stories, they read Alger; thousands of them imitated his heroes by going to Manhattan to seek their fortunes. But Alger's books lost most of their public during World War I and the rest of it during the '20s. In the Capone or quick-money era, boys were not attracted by titles like *Plan and Prosper, Slow and Sure, Work and Win.*

Until *Struggling Upward and Other Works* reappeared this week, the Alger books had completely vanished from the bookstores. They had also vanished from the circulation departments of public libraries, from Sunday schools where they were formerly given as prizes, from newsboys' homes of which Alger used to be a patron saint, and from the bookshelves of forward-looking children. Of the man and author, little was remembered except his name, around which had gathered a series of misconceptions. Some of them:

Alger wrote about poor boys who became millionaires. (His heroes rose from poverty to riches but by contemporary standards they did not rise to the top — their fortunes usually averaged ten thousand dollars.)

Alger heroes acquired their wealth by honesty, enterprise, and patience. (They acquired it chiefly by meeting kind old merchants who became their guardians or adoptive fathers.)

Alger himself made a fortune by the mass production of novels. (Never a shrewd businessman, Alger sold most of his works outright at moderate prices. At the height of his reputation, he had to piece out his literary earnings by tutoring schoolboys in French and Latin. One of his pupils: the future Supreme Court Justice Benjamin N. Cardozo.)

Alger was " the most widely read author of the ages " — according to his only biographer, Herbert R. Mayes (*Time,* May 7, 1928). (Not one of Alger's novels ever appeared near the top of any best-seller list.)

Alger was the most prolific writer who

ever lived. (He published about 130 books for boys, at least two novels for girls, and several books of bad poetry, besides some earlier pamphlets. But most of the books were short, averaging fifty-five thousand words by actual count; his total production was about seven million words. Frederick Dey, author of most of the " Nick Carter " series, ground out more than twenty-one million words.)

SUCCESSFUL FAILURE. Although he was a great success by popular standards, the real Alger was a failure by his own and his father's rules. Horatio, Sr., a Unitarian clergyman in Chelsea, Massachusetts, wanted his oldest son to become a great Boston preacher like Dr. William Channing or Edward Everett Hale. He made the boy read Plato [1] and Josephus [2] (in translation) at the age of eight, and taught him Latin at nine. When parishioners called, Father Alger would ask, " What are you going to be, Horatio? " Horatio, Jr., would stutter: " I shall be a t-teacher of the ways of God, a p-preacher of His commandments, a wiberal thinker, a woyal citizen." Schoolmates called him " Holy Horatio."

At Harvard, Horatio was the smallest man (five feet, two) in the class of 1852, ranked eighth in his studies, and wrote the class ode. As a senior, Horatio noted in his diary: " Am reading *Moby Dick,* and find it exciting. What a thrilling life the literary must be! . . . Would it be desirable for me to take up writing as a lifework? The satisfaction resulting from a beautiful story must be inspiring — a story that rouses readers to a new sense of the fine things of life." From that moment his ambition was fixed: he would write the great American novel.

FATHER COMPLEX. Horatio Alger never even wrote an outline for the novel, although he was still dreaming about it when he died (1899). In fact, Alger never succeeded in freeing himself from his father's domination, never quite grew up. At the age of fifty, he still liked to play with blocks. He sometimes disguised himself in a long cape and

[1] **Plato:** a Greek philosopher (427-347 B.C.).
[2] **Josephus:** a Jewish historian (37-96? A.D.).

a tousled wig and went wandering through Manhattan's streets — in search of material, he said. He preferred the company of bootblacks and match boys to that of adults. He liked to beat the big drum in the band that was organized at the Newsboys' Lodging House, where he spent most of his leisure hours.

LOOKING FOR FATHER. Every popular novel retells some ancient fairy tales. The Alger novel for boys, which is really one book with 130 different titles, is no exception. But the fairy story it repeats is not *Jack the Giant Killer,* which Alger read in his own boyhood — the eternal fable of the bright boy who made good. It is the Greek myth of Telemachus, the supposed orphan who found his father (Ulysses) and thus came into his kingdom.

Horatio's hero is always a prince in disguise, playing the part of a fiddler, a bootblack, a hired boy, but with attractive, cheerful, and resolute features under the dirt. His mother, always a widow, is tormented by the village squire, who plays the joint role of Penelope's suitors.[3] The hero meets a stranger and rescues his child from drowning (or from a mad dog or a runaway horse). The stranger turns out to be a rich merchant, who gives the boy new clothes, then sends him on a mission, a sort of knightly quest. On his triumphant return, the merchant adopts him as a son or ward, discomfits the wicked suitor, and settles a little fortune on the hero. Moralists used to complain that this fortune was gained by pure luck. On the contrary, it was gained by the hero's discovery of the place and parentage that were his by right.

PUNISHING PAPA. Alger, who was never freed from emotional bondage to his own fa-

[3] **Penelope's** (pē-nĕl'ō-pē) **suitors:** this is a reference to the faithful wife of Odysseus, or Ulysses, one of the Greek heroes of the Trojan War. During her husband's long absence, Penelope was besieged by a great many suitors. She promised to decide amongst them when she had finished weaving a funeral pall for her father-in-law. Since she unraveled every night what she had woven during the day she was able to delay her decision until Odysseus returned, disguised as a stranger, and, with the aid of their son, Telemachus, (tĕ-lĕm'à-kŭs) slew the wicked suitors.

ther, found a sort of compensation in telling this one story over and over. In each of his novels he punished his father three times. He killed him before the story opened by making the hero an orphan; he gave Horatio, Sr.'s worst traits to the villainous squire; and finally he provided the hero with a new father to cherish him.

*Struggling Upward,* which gives its name to the present volume, is the absolute dead mean and average of all the Alger books. It contains his stock characters, settings, and incidents, leading to his stock conclusion. " You need be under no anxiety about Luke and his prospects," says the rich merchant to the hero's widowed mother. " I shall make over to him ten thousand dollars at once, constituting myself his guardian, and will see that he is well started in business."

*Ragged Dick,* the second of the four novels now reprinted, was the first of Alger's books (1868) to reach a wide public. It is a moral but lively story dealing with the rise to respectability of a homeless bootblack.

*Phil, the Fiddler* is a memorial to a successful crusade that Alger led against the padrone system, by which hundreds of little street musicians, brought to Manhattan from Italy, were kept as virtual slaves. The story deals with one boy who escaped and was adopted by a rich doctor.

*Jed, the Poorhouse Boy* also was written with a purpose — to help the paupers — and its early chapters bear a secondhand resemblance to *Oliver Twist.*

## Suggestions for Study of Book Reviews

1. Which of these reviews is the most interesting to read in itself? Which book do you feel most impelled to read after seeing the review? Is there any that you would definitely not want to read? Why not? Does any review give you a different impression of the book from what you had obtained from reading or hearsay?

2. Do you find adverse criticism in these reviews? If so, where? Discuss the effects of adverse criticism in a magazine or in a class review. What would happen if adverse criticism were suppressed? Formulate some general advice to reviewers as to the handling of adverse criticism.

3. Turn to pages 138–139 and read again the directions for reviewing a novel. Then write a review of one book of fiction.

4. Write for some member of your family a review of a book he has been too busy to read. Have him read and criticize your review as to its general interest and helpfulness. What alterations would you make if you were giving it before a club where some had read the book?

5. As a class project, assemble as many magazines with good book-review sections as you can. Look these over and decide which section is most attractive to you. Then begin to form the habit (if you have not already done so) of reading one or more good book-review columns regularly. After a month or two decide whether you have gained greater interest in good reading as a result.

6. Vocabulary: sardonic, echelon, eupeptic, intrinsic, elixir, felicitous, conglomeration, etymology, prolific.

# REPORTAGE

The " stories " we read in newspapers seldom have much literary flavor. They are not intended to have. Originally the stories may have been written by a reporter who got his information firsthand, but the story may have been much altered by " rewrite

men " and editors before it finally appears. The writer's name is unknown.

There is another kind of news writing that has developed since the middle thirties. This news writing, too, is based on eyewitness accounts or other firsthand evidence.

It is carefully written, often attaining the quality of true literature. It is almost always narrative. The name of the writer is given. Sometimes this news writing appears in newspapers, sometimes in magazines, sometimes in books. Because it is different not only from other news writing but from other nonfiction, it has been given its own name — reportage.

The three pieces of reportage which follow are examples of the best of this kind of writing.

## William L. Shirer    1904–

Before our entrance into World War II no radio commentator stationed in Europe was listened to more eagerly than William L. Shirer. In 1941 he published his notes as *Berlin Diary*, a running account of European events since 1934.

### THE ARMISTICE IS SIGNED

#### June 21, 1940

The following account of Hitler's dictated peace to the defeated French is typical of this very interesting book and of Mr. Shirer's reportage.

*Paris, June 21, 1940*

On the exact spot in the little clearing in the Forest of Compiègne where at 5:00 A.M. on November 11, 1918 the armistice which ended the World War was signed, Adolph Hitler today handed his armistice terms to France. To make German revenge complete, the meeting of the German and French plenipotentiaries took place in Marshal Foch's private car, in which Foch laid down the armistice terms to Germany twenty-two years ago. Even the same table in the rickety old *wagon-lit* [1] car was used. And through the windows we saw Hitler occupying the very seat on which Foch had sat at that table when he dictated the other armistice.

[1] **wagon-lit** (và'gôn-lē'): French for sleeping-car.

The humiliation of France, of the French, was complete. And yet in the preamble to the armistice terms Hitler told the French that he had not chosen this spot at Compiègne out of revenge; merely to right an old wrong. From the demeanor of the French delegates I gathered that they did not appreciate the difference.

The armistice negotiations began at 3:15 P.M. A warm June sun beat down on the great elm and pine trees, and cast pleasant shadows on the wooded avenues as Hitler, with the German plenipotentiaries at his side, appeared. He alighted from his car in front of the French monument to Alsace-Lorraine which stands at the end of an avenue about two hundred yards from the clearing where the armistice car waits on exactly the same spot it occupied twenty-two years ago.

The Alsace-Lorraine statue, I noted, was covered with German war flags so that you could not see its sculptured work nor read its inscription. But I had seen it some years before — the large sword representing the sword of the Allies, and its point sticking into a large, limp eagle, representing the old Empire of the Kaiser. And the inscription underneath in French saying: TO THE HEROIC SOLDIERS OF FRANCE . . . DEFENDERS OF THE COUNTRY AND OF RIGHT . . . GLORIOUS LIBERATORS OF ALSACE-LORRAINE.

Through my glasses I saw the Führer stop, glance at the monument, observe the Reich flags with their big swastikas in the center. Then he strode slowly toward us, toward the little clearing in the woods. I observed his face. It was grave, solemn, yet brimming with revenge. There was also in it, as in his springy step, a note of the triumphant conqueror, the defier of the world. There was something else, difficult to describe, in his expression, a sort of scornful, inner joy at being present at this great reversal of fate — a reversal he himself had wrought.

Now he reaches the little opening in the woods. He pauses and looks slowly around. The clearing is in the form of a circle some two hundred yards in diameter and laid out like a park. Cypress trees line it all round — and behind them, the great elms and oaks of the forest. This has been one of France's national shrines for twenty-two years. From a discreet position on the perimeter of the circle we watch.

Hitler pauses, and gazes slowly around. In a group just behind him are the other German plenipotentiaries: Göring, grasping his field-marshal's baton in one hand. He wears the sky-blue uniform of the Air Force. All the Germans are in uniform, Hitler in a double-breasted gray uniform, with the Iron Cross hanging from his left breast pocket. Next to Göring are the two German Army chiefs — General Keitel, Chief of the Supreme Command, and General von Brauchitsch, Commander-in-Chief of the German Army. Both are just approaching sixty, but look younger, especially Keitel, who has a dapper appearance with his cap slightly cocked on one side.

Then there is Erich Raeder, Grand Admiral of the German Fleet, in his blue naval uniform and the invariable upturned collar which German naval officers usually wear. There are two nonmilitary men in Hitler's suite — his Foreign Minister, Joachim von Ribbentrop, in the field-gray uniform of the Foreign Office; and Rudolph Hess, Hitler's deputy, in a gray party uniform.

The time is now 3:18 P.M. Hitler's personal flag is run up on a small standard in the center of the opening.

Also in the center is a great granite block which stands some three feet above the ground. Hitler, followed by the others, walks slowly over to it, steps up, and reads the inscription engraved in great high letters on that block. It says: HERE ON THE ELEVENTH OF NOVEMBER 1918 SUCCUMBED THE CRIMINAL PRIDE OF THE GERMAN EMPIRE . . . VANQUISHED BY THE FREE PEOPLES WHICH IT TRIED TO ENSLAVE.

Hitler reads it and Göring reads it. They all read it, standing there in the June sun and the silence. I looked for the expression on Hitler's face. I am but fifty yards from him and see him through my glasses as though

he were directly in front of me. I have seen that face many times at the great moments of his life. But today! It is afire with scorn, anger, hate, revenge, triumph. He steps off the monument and contrives to make even this gesture a masterpiece of contempt. He glances back at it, contemptuous, angry — angry, you almost feel, because he cannot wipe out the awful, provoking lettering with one sweep of his high Prussian boot. He glances slowly around the clearing, and now, as his eyes meet ours, you grasp the depth of his hatred. But there is triumph there too — revengeful, triumphant hate. Suddenly, as though his face were not giving quite complete expression to his feelings, he throws his whole body into harmony with his mood. He swiftly snaps his hands on his hips, arches his shoulders, plants his feet wide apart. It is a magnificent gesture of defiance, of burning contempt for this place now and all that it has stood for in the twenty-two years since it witnessed the humbling of the German Empire.

Finally Hitler leads his party over to another granite stone, a smaller one fifty yards to one side. Here it was that the railroad car in which the German plenipotentiaries stayed during the 1918 armistice was placed — from November 8 to 11. Hitler merely glances at the inscription, which reads: " The German Plenipotentiaries." The stone itself, I notice, is set between a pair of rusty old railroad tracks, the ones on which the German car stood twenty-two years ago. Off to one side along the edge of the clearing is a large statue in white stone of Marshal Foch as he looked when he stepped out of the armistice car on the morning of November 11, 1918. Hitler skips it; does not appear to see it.

It is now 3:23 P.M. and the Germans stride over to the armistice car. For a moment or two they stand in the sunlight outside the car, chatting. Then Hitler steps up into the car, followed by the others. We can see nicely through the car windows. Hitler takes the place occupied by Marshal Foch when the 1918 armistice terms were signed. The others spread themselves around him.

WORLD WAR I OR II? The interior of the railroad car showing the table at which both Foch and Hitler laid down armistice terms. (Keystone View)

Four chairs on the opposite side of the table from Hitler remain empty. The French have not yet appeared. But we do not wait long. Exactly at 3:30 P.M. they alight from a car. They have flown up from Bordeaux to a near-by landing field. They too glance at the Alsace-Lorraine memorial, but it's a swift glance. Then they walk down the avenue flanked by three German officers. We see them now as they come into the sunlight of the clearing.

General Huntziger, wearing a bleached khaki uniform, Air General Bergeret and Vice-Admiral Le Luc, both in dark blue uniforms, and then, almost buried in the uniforms, M. Noël, French Ambassador to Poland. The German guard of honor, drawn up at the entrance to the clearing, snaps to attention for the French as they pass, but it does not present arms.

It is a grave hour in the life of France. The Frenchmen keep their eyes straight ahead. Their faces are solemn, drawn. They are the picture of tragic dignity.

They walk stiffly to the car, where they are met by two German officers, Lieutenant General Tippelskirch, Quartermaster General, and Colonel Thomas, chief of the Füh rer's headquarters. The Germans salute. The French salute. The atmosphere is what Europeans call "correct." There are salutes, but no handshakes.

Now we get our picture through the dusty windows of that old *wagon-lit* car. Hitler and the other German leaders rise as the French enter the drawing room. Hitler gives the Nazi salute, the arm raised. Ribbentrop and Hess do the same. I cannot see M. Noël to notice whether he salutes or not.

Hitler, as far as we can see through the windows, does not say a word to the French or to anybody else. He nods to General Keitel at his side. We see General Keitel adjusting his papers. Then he starts to read. He is reading the preamble to the German armistice terms. The French sit there with marblelike faces and listen intently. Hitler and Göring glance at the green table-top.

The reading of the preamble lasts but a few minutes. Hitler, we soon observe, has no intention of remaining very long, of listening to the reading of the armistice terms themselves. At 3:42 P.M., twelve minutes after the French arrive, we see Hitler stand up, salute stiffly, and then stride out of the drawing room, followed by Göring, Brauchitsch, Raeder, Hess, and Ribbentrop. The French, like figures of stone, remain at the green-topped table. General Keitel remains with them. He starts to read them the detailed conditions of the armistice.

Hitler and his aides stride down the avenue toward the Alsace-Lorraine monument, where their cars are waiting. As they pass the guard of honor, the German band strikes up the two national anthems, *Deutschland, Deutschland über Alles* and the *Horst Wessel* song. The whole ceremony in which Hitler has reached a new pinnacle in his meteoric career and Germany avenged the 1918 defeat is over in a quarter of an hour.

I know that the Germans have hidden microphones in the armistice car. I seek out a sound truck in the woods. No one stops me and so I pause to listen. It is just before the armistice is signed. I hear General Huntziger's voice, strained, quivering. I note down his exact words in French. They come out slowly, with great effort, one at a time. He says: " I declare the French government has ordered me to sign these terms of armistice. I desire to read a personal declaration. Forced by the fate of arms to cease the struggle in which we were engaged on the side of the Allies, France sees imposed on her very hard conditions. France has the right to expect in the future negotiations that Germany show a spirit which will permit the two great neighboring countries to live and work peacefully."

Then I hear the scratching of pens, a few muffled remarks from the French. Later someone, watching through the window, tells me Admiral Le Luc fights back the tears as the document is signed. Then the deep voice of Keitel: " I request all members of the German and French delegations to rise in order to fulfill a duty which the brave German and French soldiers have merited. Let us honor by rising from our seats all those who have bled for their fatherland and all those who have died for their country."

There is a minute of silence as they all stand.

As he finished speaking into the microphone, a drop of rain fell on my forehead. Down the road, through the woods, I could see the refugees, slowly, tiredly, filing by — on weary feet, on bicycles, on carts, a few on trucks, an endless line. They were exhausted and dazed, those walking were footsore, and they did not know yet that an armistice had been signed and that the fighting would be over very soon now.

I walked out to the clearing. The sky was overcast and rain was coming on. An army of German engineers, shouting lustily, had already started to move the armistice car. " Where to? " I asked.

" To Berlin," they said.

## For Your Vocabulary

BASE-WORDS. Shirer refers a number of times to the German *plenipotentiaries*. *Plenipotentiary* (plĕn-ĭ-pŏ-tĕn′shĭ-ĕ-rĭ) is a standard term for a diplomatic or military agent empowered to act with full authority for his nation. There is irony in its use for anyone but Hitler at this scene. General MacArthur had *plenipotentiary* authority to accept Japan's surrender for all the Allied nations. The word is built of *plen,* full, and *potent,* power. You often meet the word *replenish,* to fill again. *Plenty* comes from the same base-word. *Potent* is also a frequently used base-word. Boaz Negro in " Footfalls " was held motionless by the " curious *impotence* (ĭm′pŏ-tĕns) of the spectator " (page 75), complete lack of power to act. A *potent* argument or weapon is a powerful one. An interesting variation is the word *potential,* meaning having powers not in use. A *potentially* great man may never achieve greatness.

## Ernie Pyle 1900–1945

The most famous and best-loved correspondent in World War II was Ernie Pyle. His daily accounts of the life of G. I. Joe probably constitute the best body of reportage of World War II. When Ernie Pyle was killed April 18, 1945 by a Japanese machine-gun bullet on the Pacific island called Ie Jima, the whole nation mourned his passing.

## BREAK–THROUGH
## IN NORMANDY

### July 25, 1944

Many of Ernie Pyle's best stories have been collected in the books *Here Is Your War* and *Brave Men*. The following story, one of the most vivid — and perhaps the most tragic — of the whole war, is from the latter.

Surely history will give a name to the battle that sent us boiling out of Normandy, some name comparable with Saint-Mihiel or Meuse-Argonne of the last war. But to us there on the spot at the time it was known simply as the "break-through." We correspondents could sense that a big drive was coming. There are many little ways you can tell without actually being told, if you are experienced in war. And then one evening Lieutenant General Omar Bradley, commanding all American troops in France, came to our camp and briefed us on the coming operation. It would start, he said, on the first day we had three hours of good flying weather in the forenoon.

We were all glad to hear the news. There wasn't a correspondent over there, or soldier, or officer I ever heard of who hadn't complete and utter faith in General Bradley. If he felt we were ready for the push, that was good enough for us. The general told us the attack would cover a segment of the German line west of Saint-Lo, about five miles wide. In that narrow segment we would have three infantry divisions, side by side. Right behind them would be another infantry and two armored divisions. Once a hole was broken, the armored divisions would slam through several miles beyond, then turn right toward the sea behind the Germans in that sector in the hope of cutting them off and trapping them. The remainder of our line on both sides of the attack would keep the pressure on to hold the Germans in front of them so they couldn't send reinforcements against our main push.

The attack was to open with a gigantic two-hour air bombardment of 1,800 planes — the biggest ever attempted by air in direct support of ground troops. It would start with dive bombers, then great four-motored heavies would come, and then mediums, then dive bombers again, and then the ground troops would kick off, with air fighters continuing to work ahead of them. It was a thrilling plan to listen to. General Bradley didn't tell us that it was the big thing, but other officers gave us the word. They said, "This is no limited-objective drive. This is it. This is the big break-through."

In war everybody contributes something no matter how small or how far removed he may be. But on the front line the break-through was accomplished by four fighting branches of the services and I don't see truly how one can be given credit above another. None of the four could have done the job without the other three. The way they worked together was beautiful and precision-like, showering credit upon themselves and General Bradley's planning. The four branches were: Air Force, Tanks, Artillery, and Infantry.

I went with the infantry because it is my old love, and because I suspected the tanks, being spectacular, might smother the credit due the infantry. I teamed up with the Fourth Infantry Division since it was in the middle of the forward three, and spearheading the attack. The first night behind the front lines I slept comfortably on a cot in a tent at the division command post, and met for the first time the Fourth's commander — Major General Raymond O. Barton, a fatherly, kindly, thoughtful, good soldier. The second night I spent on the dirty floor of a rickety French farmhouse, far up in the lines, with the nauseating odor of dead cows keeping me awake half the night. The third night I slept on the ground in an orchard even farther up, snugly dug in behind a hedgerow so the 88's couldn't get at me so easily. And on the next day the weather cleared, and the attack was on. It was July 25.

If you don't have July 25 pasted in your hat I would advise you to put it there immediately. At least paste it in your mind. For I have a hunch that July 25 of the year

1944 will be one of the great historic pinnacles of this war. It was the day we began a mighty surge out of our confined Normandy spaces, the day we stopped calling our area the beachhead and knew we were fighting a war across the whole expanse of France. From that day onward all dread possibilities and fears for disaster to our invasion were behind us. No longer was there any possibility of our getting kicked off. No longer would it be possible for fate, or weather, or enemy to wound us fatally; from that day onward the future could hold nothing for us but growing strength and eventual victory.

For the five days and nights during that historic period I stayed at the front with our troops. The great attack began in the bright light of midday, not at the zero hour of a bleak and mysterious dawn as attacks are supposed to start in books. The attack had been delayed from day to day because of poor flying weather, and on the final day we hadn't known for sure till after breakfast whether it was on or off again. When the word came that it was on, the various battalion staffs of our regiment were called in from their command posts for a final review of the battle plan. Each one was given a mimeographed sketch of the frontline area, showing exactly where and when each type of bomber was to hammer the German lines ahead of them. Another mimeographed page was filled with specific orders for the grand attack to follow.

Officers stood or squatted in a circle in a little apple orchard behind a ramshackle stone farmhouse of a poor French family who had left before us. The stone wall in the front yard had been knocked down by shelling, and through the orchards there were shell craters and tree limbs knocked off and trunks sliced by bullets. Some enlisted men, sleeping the night before in the attic of the house, got the shock of their lives when the thin floor collapsed and they fell down into the cowshed below. Chickens and tame rabbits still scampered around the farmyard. Dead cows lay all around in the fields.

The regimental colonel stood in the center of the officers and went over the orders in detail. Battalion commanders took down notes in little books. The colonel said, " Ernie Pyle is with the regiment for this attack and will be with one of the battalions, so you'll be seeing him." The officers looked at me and smiled and I felt embarrassed.

Then General Barton arrived. The colonel called " Attention! " and everybody stood rigid until the general gave them " Carry on." An enlisted man ran to the mess truck and got a folding canvas stool for the general to sit on. He sat listening intently while the colonel wound up his instructions. Then the general stepped into the center of the circle. He stood at a slouch on one foot with the other leg far out like a brace. He looked all around him as he talked. He didn't talk long. He said something like this: " This is one of the finest regiments in the American Army. It was the last regiment out of France in the last war. It was the first regiment into France in this war. It has spearheaded every one of the division's attacks in Normandy. It will spearhead this one. For many years this was my regiment and I feel very close to you, and very proud."

The general's lined face was a study in emotion. Sincerity and deep sentiment were in every contour and they shone from his eyes. General Barton was a man of deep affections. The tragedy of war, both personal and impersonal, hurt him. At the end his voice almost broke, and I for one had a lump in my throat. He ended: " That's all. God bless you and good luck."

Then we broke up and I went with one of the battalion commanders. By field telephone, radio, and liaison men, word was passed down to the very smallest unit of troops that the attack was on. There was still an hour before the bombers, and three hours before the infantry were to move. There was nothing for the infantry to do but dig a little deeper and wait. A cessation of motion seemed to come over the countryside and all its brown-clad inhabitants, a sense of last-minute sitting in silence before the holocaust.

The first planes of the mass onslaught came over a little before 10 A.M. They were the fighters and dive bombers. The main road, running crosswise in front of us, was their bomb line. They were to bomb only on the far side of that road. Our kickoff infantry had been pulled back a few hundred yards from the near side of the road. Everyone in the area had been given the strictest orders to be in foxholes, for high-level bombers can, and do quite excusably, make mistakes.

We were still in country so level and with hedgerows so tall there simply was no high spot — neither hill nor building — from which we could get a grandstand view of the bombing as we used to do in Sicily and Italy. So one place was as good as another unless we went right up and sat on the bomb line. Having been caught too close to these things before, I compromised and picked a farmyard about eight hundred yards back of the kickoff line. And before the next two hours had passed I would have given every penny, every desire, every hope I ever had, to have been just another eight hundred yards farther back.

Our front lines were marked by long strips of colored cloth laid on the ground, and with colored smoke to guide our airmen during the mass bombing. Dive bombers hit it just right. We stood and watched them barrel nearly straight down out of the sky. They were bombing about half a mile ahead of where we stood. They came in groups, diving from every direction, perfectly timed, one right after another. Everywhere we looked separate groups of planes were on the way down, or on the way back up, or slanting over for a dive, or circling, circling, circling over our heads, waiting for their turn.

The air was full of sharp and distinct sounds of cracking bombs and the heavy rips of the planes' machine guns and the splitting screams of diving wings. It was all fast and furious, yet distinct. And then a new sound gradually droned into our ears, a sound deep and all-encompassing with no notes in it — just a gigantic faraway surge of doomlike sound. It was the heavies. They came from directly beind us. At first they were the merest dots in the sky. We could see clots of them against the far heavens, too tiny to count individually. They came on with a terrible slowness. They came in flights of twelve, three flights to a group, and in groups stretched out across the sky. They came in " families " of about seventy planes each. Maybe those gigantic waves were two miles apart, maybe they were ten miles, I don't know. But I do know they came in a constant procession and I thought it would never end. What the Germans must have thought is beyond comprehension.

The flight across the sky was slow and studied. I've never known a storm, or a machine, or any resolve of man that had about it the aura of such a ghastly relentlessness. I had the feeling that even had God appeared beseechingly before them in the sky, with palms outstretched to persuade them back, they would not have had within them the power to turn from their irresistible course.

I stood with a little group of men, ranging from colonels to privates, back of the stone farmhouse. Slit trenches were all around the edges of the farmyard and a dugout with a tin roof was nearby. But we were so fascinated by the spectacle overhead that it never occurred to us that we might need the foxholes.

The first huge flight passed directly overhead and others followed. We spread our feet and leaned far back trying to look straight up, until our steel helmets fell off. We'd cup our fingers around our eyes, like field glasses, for a clearer view. And then the bombs came. They began like the crackle of popcorn and almost instantly swelled into a monstrous fury of noise that seemed surely to destroy all the world ahead of us. From then on for an hour and a half that had in it the agonies of centuries, the bombs came down. A wall of smoke and dust erected by them grew high in the sky. It filtered along the ground back through our orchards. It

sifted around us and into our noses. The
bright day grew slowly dark from it. By
now everything was an indescribable caldron of sounds. Individual noises did not
exist. The thundering of the motors in the
sky and the roar of bombs ahead filled all
the space for noise on earth. Our own heavy
artillery was crashing all around us, yet
we could hardly hear it.

The Germans began to shoot heavy, high
ack-ack. Great black puffs of it by the score
speckled the sky until it was hard to distinguish smoke puffs from planes. And then
someone shouted that one of the planes was
smoking. Yes, we could all see it. A long
faint line of black smoke stretched straight
for a mile behind one of them. And as we
watched there was a gigantic sweep of
flame over the plane. From nose to tail it
disappeared in flame, and it slanted slowly
down and banked around the sky in great
wide curves, this way and that way, as
rhythmically and gracefully as in a slow-
motion waltz. Then suddenly it seemed to
change its mind and it swept upward, steeper
and steeper and ever slower until finally it
seemed poised motionless on its own black
pillar of smoke. And then just as slowly it
turned over and dived for the earth — a
golden spearhead on the straight black shaft
of its own creation — and disappeared behind the treetops. But before it was down
there were more cries of, " There's another
one smoking — and there's a third one
now." Chutes came out of some of the
planes. Out of some came no chutes at all.
One of white silk caught on the tail of a
plane. Men with binoculars could see him
fighting to get loose until flames swept over
him, and then a tiny black dot fell through
space, all alone.

And all that time the great flat ceiling of
the sky was roofed by all the other planes
that didn't go down, plowing their way forward as if there were no turmoil in the
world. Nothing deviated them by the
slightest. They stalked on, slowly and with
a dreadful pall of sound, as though they
were seeing only something at a great distance and nothing existed between. God,
how we admired those men up there and
sickened for the ones who fell.

It is possible to become so enthralled by
some of the spectacles of war that a man is
momentarily captivated away from his own
danger. That's what happened to our little
group of soldiers as we stood watching the
nightly bombing. But that benign state
didn't last long. As we watched, there crept
into our consciousness a realization that the
windrows of exploding bombs were easing
back toward us, flight by flight, instead of
gradually forward, as the plan called for.
Then we were horrified by the suspicion
that those machines, high in the sky and
completely detached from us, were aiming
their bombs at the smoke line on the ground
— and a gentle breeze was drifting the
smoke line back over us! An indescribable
kind of panic came over us. We stood tensed
in muscle and frozen in intellect, watching
each flight approach and pass over, feeling
trapped and completely helpless. And then
all of an instant the universe became filled
with a gigantic rattling as of huge ripe seeds
in a mammoth dry gourd. I doubt that any
of us had ever heard that sound before, but
instinct told us what it was. It was bombs
by the hundred, hurtling down through the
air above us.

Many times I've heard bombs whistle or
swish or rustle, but never before had I heard
bombs rattle. I still don't know the explanation of it. But it is an awful sound. We
dived. Some got into a dugout. Others made
foxholes and ditches and some got behind
a garden wall — although which side would
be " behind " was anybody's guess. I was
too late for the dugout. The nearest place
was a wagon shed which formed one end
of the stone house. The rattle was right
down upon us. I remember hitting the
ground flat, all spread out like the cartoons
of people flattened by steam rollers, and
then squirming like an eel to get under one
of the heavy wagons in the shed.

An officer whom I didn't know was wriggling beside me. We stopped at the same
time, simultaneously feeling it was hopeless to move farther. The bombs were al-

ready crashing around us. We lay with our heads slightly up — like two snakes — staring at each other. I know it was in both our minds and in our eyes, asking each other what to do. Neither of us knew. We said nothing. We just lay sprawled, gaping at each other in a futile appeal, our faces about a foot apart, until it was over.

There is no description of the sound and fury of those bombs except to say it was chaos, and a waiting for darkness. The feeling of the blast was sensational. The air struck us in hundreds of continuing flutters. Our ears drummed and rang. We could feel quick little waves of concussion on the chest and in the eyes.

At last the sound died down and we looked at each other in disbelief. Gradually we left the foxholes and sprawling places and came out to see what the sky had in store for us. As far as we could see other waves were approaching from behind. When a wave would pass a little to the side of us we were garrulously grateful, for most of them flew directly overhead. Time and again the rattle came down over us. Bombs struck in the orchard to our left. They struck in orchards ahead of us. They struck as far as half a mile behind us. Everything about us was shaken, but our group came through unhurt.

I can't record what any of us actually felt or thought during those horrible climaxes. I believe a person's feelings at such times are kaleidoscopic and indefinable. He just waits, that's all — with an inhuman tenseness of muscle and nerves. An hour or so later I began to get sore all over, and by midafternoon my back and shoulders ached as though I'd been beaten with a club. It was simply the result of muscles tensing themselves too tight for too long against anticipated shock. And I remember worrying about War Correspondent Ken Crawford, a friend from back in the old Washington days, who was several hundred yards ahead of me. As far as I knew, he and I were the only two correspondents with the Fourth Division. I didn't know who might be with the divisions on either side — which also

were being hit, as we could see. It was not until three days later, back at camp, that I learned that Lieutenant General McNair and AP Photographer Bede Irvin had been killed in this same bombing and that Ken was safe.

When we came out of our ignominious sprawling and stood up again to watch, we knew that the error had been caught and checked. The bombs again were falling where they were intended, a mile or so ahead. Even at a mile away a thousand bombs hitting within a few seconds can shake the earth and shatter the air. There was still a dread in our hearts, but it gradually eased as the tumult and destruction moved slowly forward.

Two Mustang fighters, flying like a pair of doves, patrolled back and forth, back and forth, just in front of each oncoming wave of bombers, as if to shout to them by their mere presence that here was not the place to drop — wait a few seconds, wait a few more seconds. And then we could see a flare come out of the belly of one plane in each flight, just after they had passed over our heads. The flare shot forward, leaving smoke behind it in a vivid line, and then began a graceful, downward curve that was one of the most beautiful things I've ever seen. It was like an invisible crayon drawing a rapid line across the canvas of the sky, saying in a gesture for all to see: " Here! Here is where to drop. Follow me." And each succeeding flight of oncoming bombers obeyed, and in turn dropped its own hurtling marker to guide those behind.

Long before, the German ack-ack guns had gone out of existence. The ack-ack gunners either took to their holes or were annihilated. How many waves of heavy bombers we put over I have no idea. I had counted well above 400 planes when personal distraction obliterated any capacity or desire to count. I only knew that 400 was just the beginning. There were supposed to be 1,800 planes that day, and I believe it was announced later that there were more than 3,000. It seems incredible to me that any German could have come out of that bombardment with his sanity. When it was over even I was grateful, in a chastened way that I had never experienced before, for just being alive.

I thought an attack by our troops was impossible then, for it is an unnerving thing to be bombed by your own planes. During the bad part a colonel I had known a long time was walking up and down behind the farmhouse, snapping his fingers.

And I said, " There can't be any attack now, can there? " And he said " No," and began walking again, snapping his fingers and tossing his arm as though he were throwing rocks at the ground.

The leading company of our battalion was to spearhead the attack forty minutes after our heavy bombing ceased. The company had been hit directly by our bombs. Their casualties, including casualties in shock, were heavy. Men went to pieces and had to be sent back. The company was shattered and shaken. And yet Company B attacked — and on time, to the minute! They attacked, and within an hour they sent word back that they had advanced eight hundred yards through German territory and were still going. Around our farmyard men with stars on their shoulders almost wept when the word came over the portable radio. The American soldier can be majestic when he needs to be.

I'm sure that back in England that night other men — bomber crews — almost wept, and maybe they did really, in the awful knowledge that they had killed our own American troops. But the chaos and the bitterness there in the orchards and between the hedgerows that afternoon soon passed. After the bitterness came the sober remembrance that the Air Force was the strong right arm in front of us. Not only at the beginning, but ceaselessly and everlastingly, every moment of the faintest daylight, the Air Force was up there banging away ahead of us.

Anybody makes mistakes. The enemy made them just the same as we did. The smoke and confusion of battle bewildered us on the ground as well as in the air. And in this case the percentage of error was really very small compared with the colossal storm of bombs that fell upon the enemy. The Air Force was wonderful throughout the invasion, and the men on the ground appreciated it.

## For Your Vocabulary

WORD DISCRIMINATION. The awful power of the heavy bombers seemed to Pyle to be able to wipe out completely any opposition. He felt sure that they had *annihilated* (ă-nī′hĭ-lāt-ĕd) the enemy's antiaircraft batteries (page 211), reduced them to nothingness. The rootword, *nihil*, means *nothing*. The swelling thunder of the bombers *obliterated* (ŏb-lĭt′ĕr-āt-ĕd) such conscious activity as counting them as they passed over (page 211), wiped out every trace of it. Their bombs could *obliterate* impressive fortifications. Another word that means to destroy completely is *exterminate* (ĕks-tûr′mĭ-nāt), but it is nearly always used of living creatures. You will find it used twice of the *extermination* of the Indians in the Eastern part of the country (pages 423 and 489). What is the most familiar current use of *exterminator?*

## Daniel Lang

Daniel Lang is one of the group of clever and sophisticated writers who make up the staff of the *New Yorker,* a magazine of varied comment, designed primarily to entertain. As a roving reporter, Lang has developed a style typical of the concise and informative writing to be found in this magazine.

### THE ATOMIC CITY
#### September 20, 1945

Among the many interesting articles in each *New Yorker* there is a regular feature called " Reporter at Large." This account of a visit to the famous community at Oak Ridge, Tennessee, illustrates the excellent reportage which is found each week in this stimulating magazine.

The community of Oak Ridge, Tennessee, is less than three years old, but it already has a tradition: secretiveness. Even now, a stranger in town like myself, casually mentioning U-235 or plutonium or any of the other obnoxious terms I never heard of until this summer, is likely to receive a stare fit for an Axis agent. I recently got acquainted with one of the more persistent starers, a physicist, and, after pointing out that the atom bomb had become a widely known matter, asked him to explain his suspicious looks. " Two years' worth of being told and warned and ordered not to talk about the project," he said. " I remember I was working the night shift August fifth, and the next day a friend of mine woke me up with a phone call. ' President Truman says it's an atom,' he told me. I hung up quick. I thought my friend had cracked." The physicist gave what seemed a slightly demented giggle. " I still don't see how my job ties up with the bomb," he said, " and I certainly don't know any more than you do just from reading the papers. I wouldn't know what to say even if I did open my mouth, but I'm going around not talking."

The higher-ranking Army officers here are cautious, too, but, being in positions of authority, they will unbend to the extent of reminiscing and imparting scattered, unrelated information. Unlike the science columnists, these officers say they haven't any idea how close our race with the Axis was, but they suspect that we got off to a later start than the Germans. The Manhattan Engineer District, I was told, set up, back in 1942, a long-range timetable for the production of the bomb, and kept so close to schedule that its horrible product was dropped practically on time; that is, only a few weeks late. Looking back on the project, the officers regard it as quite a calculated risk, to use the Army term, and one hell of a nervous strain, to use plain English. In addition to the distracting knowledge that Goebbels wasn't necessarily just yapping propaganda when he talked about a secret weapon, there were other worries. For one thing, the scientists weren't certain that they would be able to split atoms on a large enough scale to use in the war. However, at any given moment, a majority of

the men in charge — the majority wasn't always the same men — were in a sufficiently confident mood to keep things going full tilt. But their uncertainty dogged them right into 1945, when they were well over the hump and knew that they could soon turn out atom bombs. " That was the period," an anonymous colonel recalled, " when we began to sweat out the idea that the Germans might develop a terrific short cut. Maybe, we thought, one of those Nazis would wake up one morning and produce U-235 or plutonium right in his bathtub." Even after the Germans, who seem to have worried the Army much more than the Japs, surrendered, one fear remained. " Supposing," the colonel said, " we hadn't been able to make the bomb before the war ended. Why, we'd have been called a two-billion-dollar boon-doggle."

It is still impossible to learn from the authorities how many bombs we've manufactured or just how they are stored. However, the officers will go as far as to say that the Manhattan Engineer District is still turning out U-235 and plutonium to make atomic bombs. Also, they will disclose that we are still trying to figure out whether U-235 or plutonium is the more effective, and a few of them will venture the guess that the final form atomic power will take may be a blend of the two. Whatever the form, a certain amount of it will probably be available for limited public use, according to these cautious gentlemen, by 1960. There is no restriction, either, on the information that the entire processing, measured from the time the ore is dug out of the earth, takes a matter of many months. The preliminary refining of the ore is done in various spots outside Oak Ridge, but well over half the processing goes on here. The Army, incidentally, is holding on to its accumulating store of uranium from which U-235 and plutonium have been extracted and is going to give the stuff a second going-over sometime in the future in an effort to determine possible additional uses. After the uranium, which is brought into Oak Ridge in cardboard boxes and cylindrical

"ATOMIC CITY." Oak Ridge, Tennessee, where the greatest secret of the war was developed. (Acme)

metal containers, is refined, it is sent to New Mexico for what the Army calls " the utilization phase."

There are several plants in Oak Ridge, and they are widely separated. It takes thirty-five miles of circuitous driving — a trip I made in the company of a civilian official and a young Tennessee country girl, who was our chauffeur — to see what they all look like. The names of the plants sound like the combination to a safe — X-10, Y-12, S-50, and K-25. All the plants except X-10, a plutonium research laboratory, perform the same function — extracting U-235 from U-238 — but each unit has its own method. At S-50, what is termed a liquid thermal-diffusion process is employed. " Before Hiroshima," the official told me, " we called that place the Fox Farm — a cover term. A colonel by the name of Fox was in charge." At Y-12 an electromagnetic process is applied, and at K-25 — for all the difference it makes to a layman — the process is gaseous diffusion.

Each plant consists of a number of buildings. K-25, while not the biggest plant, does include the biggest building in Oak Ridge. Twelve thousand employees work in it day and night seven days a week. There are three shifts, starting at 7 A.M., 3 P.M., and 11 P.M. The night shift was on when we got there. A high ridge forms a backdrop for K-25, and beside the plant there is a small hill. We drove up the hill to look down at its immense, sprawling structure. The windows were brilliantly lit by thousands of bulbs, and its white cement-asbestos exterior added to the brightness. I listened closely for any sounds, but I could hear nothing. I mentioned this to the official, and he said, " Oh, there's one floor where you can hear motors turning over if you're inside, but it's really a pretty quiet place. No big compressors stamping anything. Nice and clean, too. No grease to speak of. An awful lot of piping. Just miles of pipes. The equipment's like nothing you've ever seen. Right out of Rube Goldberg. Nothing standard about it one bit. Nothing like it ever built before."

" Who's in there? " I asked.

" Mechanics to keep equipment in condition," he said. " Electrical and chemical and other kinds of engineers. Foremen who ride bikes to get from one part of a floor to another to check operations. Fitters and men who bring in uranium to feed the apparatus. Girls out of college supervising girls out of high school who stand in front of a dial watching to see if a needle jumps from zero to ten. Ph.D.'s who turn knobs."

We hung around a few minutes staring at the silent, glowing mass below us. " Doesn't anything come out of that place? " I asked the official after a while. " Man," he said pleasantly, " they're not making anything in there. They're just extracting." Several hundred lights suddenly and inexplicably illuminated a corner of the building that I hadn't noticed was dark. The girl chauffeur ah'd at that. " Bright lights," she said in her slow Southern voice. " Tennessee's got the bright lights now, just like Broadway."

To set in motion the mystifying manufacture of a mystifying product, the sudden town of Oak Ridge, population 75,000, has come into being. It takes up 59,000 acres of Roane and Anderson Counties, and is completely fenced in. The plants are off by themselves, in doubly restricted zones, anywhere from three to eleven miles from the center of town, and away from residential districts. The houses are scattered, too, but at intervals there are clusters of shops, movie houses, and ice-cream parlors that the people here like to refer to as " neighborhoods." Villages disappeared to make way for Oak Ridge. Scarboro, Wheat, and Robertsville are the names of vanished places where the hill folk of this region went in for what amounted to nonprofit farming — some tobacco planting, a couple of hogs, some poultry, perhaps a head or two of cattle, and a little moonshine-making. The Army forced them to sell their land, and they hated to do it. A small percentage of them have taken jobs with the project, but most of them have migrated to new farms. However, the Army lets them return, whenever they want, to visit their cemeteries. It was the second time some of them had become displaced persons; they had been evicted from other sites several years ago by the TVA, when it bought up land not far from Oak Ridge. One tough old gentleman, whose farm was in a particularly remote corner of this great acreage, decided to stay where he was as long as he could. He managed to hide out on the Army's top-secret reservation for a full year before a Piper Cub pilot, on patrol duty, spotted him feeding his chickens.

The natives of this Bible Belt country maintain that God is responsible for the picking of this particular spot as the setting for the Army's diabolical factories. The Manhattan Engineer District, however, offers some man-made reasons. Electric power, which is used in large quantities, is supplied by TVA. The Clinch River, which skirts the area, provides water for the inhabitants of Oak Ridge. The land was low-priced, selling, on the average, at forty dollars an acre. Knoxville, only eighteen miles east, was considered an uncritical labor area by the War Manpower Commission, and the Army figured it could hire a fair amount of civilian personnel there. Transportation facilities in Knoxville, both rail and air, were adequate for bringing in supplies. High ridges surrounding the plants made things hard for snoopers. Finally, the Luftwaffe would have had to penetrate well past the Atlantic coast to raid the plants.

The Army engineers and contractors arrived on the scene late in 1942 and went to work on the scrubby, unattractive, practically roadless terrain. Quail roamed the place then, and the guards picked off skunks with their rifles. The guards also had to shoo away curious people who turned up at the entrance gates. Among them was a bearded old fellow, a religious fanatic, who said he understood that a Vatican was being built here. He told the guards he wanted to have a go at being the American Pope and asked them where to apply for the job. " Beat it," the guards told him. " We don't know what's getting built here." The old man couldn't be brushed off that easily. " Well," he asked the watchmen, " if you don't know what's being built, how do you know it isn't a Vatican? "

One of the things that complicated the project was that the Army frequently changed its plans. The first blueprints didn't provide for the mammoth plants that have since been erected. As for housing, no more than three hundred dwellings were planned at the start, though eventually there were over fifteen thousand. " All we wanted to do," an Army lieutenant told me, " was take care of the long-hairs. You can't expect a high-powered scientific joe like Dr. Compton to sleep with ants." The approach to atom-splitting was to try every conceivable method that might work, and to try it in a hurry. The scientists kept thinking up new ideas, with the result that Oak Ridge went through a series of expansions. The summer of 1944, when construction reached its peak, must have been something. Last Christmas the children here didn't ask for electric trains but wanted toy bulldozers and roadscrapers. A certain amount of building is still going on, but no one thinks about it much; by now it is perfectly clear that another of those American construction feats that most of us are tired of marveling at has been brought off. Today there are good roads, bus lines, taxicabs, and lots of neon lights here. You can play pinball, roller-skate in a rink, and watch night baseball games. According to a mimeographed Army handout, Oak Ridge has thirteen supermarkets, seven movie houses, and nine drugstores, and I have no reason to doubt that these counts are entirely accurate.

The dominant architectural note of the town is something that might be called Early Alphabetical Cemesto. Thousands of the houses here are of Cemesto Board, a trade name for a mixture of cement and asbestos rolled into sheets that can be thrown together in a great hurry. There are six types of Cemesto homes — " A-House,"

" B-House," and so on. " F-House," the largest of the models, has six rooms and rents for seventy-three dollars a month. Many people live in prefabricated plywood houses (they're called " A-1," " B-1," and so on), and even more live in trailers which the Army scrounged from the TVA, the Federal Public Housing Authority, and other government agencies. There is also a gadget known as the " Efficiency Apartment," but I won't go into that. Visitors permitted on the reservation, such as scientists and journalists, are put up at the Guest House, a rudimentary but comfortable enough hostelry. Most of the trade at the Guest House, where I have been staying, seems quite definitely to be scientists. I have been addressed as Dr. Lang by the lady desk clerks since the afternoon I checked in. A few days ago I asked one of them to forget the " Dr." She took to my suggestion at once. " O.K., Doc," she said.

The city, for all its newness, is fairly cosmopolitan in character. People with all sorts of backgrounds have come from every state to work for the Manhattan Engineer District. There are men here who come from towns in which it is perfectly all right to hold crap games in the street, and they have continued to roll the dice openly here, too, amazed that anyone should stop and stare at them. And there are fellows who have been boosters all their lives and are now boosting Oak Ridge. They have attached small metal signs to their automobile license plates that say, " Oak Ridge: The Atomic City." A man named Bill Feldman has organized a Junior Chamber of Commerce. " I want to see this town beautified," he told me. " I see the day when the Lions, the Elks, Rotary, and Kiwanis will be holding luncheons in Oak Ridge." There is also quite a concentration of Ph.D.'s, as well as other educated folk, who in their off hours play chamber music, study foreign languages, and sit around their B-Houses discussing the more technical aspects of nuclear energy. These different groups keep pretty much to themselves, but their offspring are thrown together in school. There the children from rural districts blink with bewilderment when precocious metropolitan brats, fresh from progressive education, agitate for more student control over this or that and tell their teachers, " That's not the way we learned long division at Dalton."

The residents of Oak Ridge have no voting say about how their town is run. The Army runs it. This isn't quite as bad as it may sound; at least for the moment, the Army doesn't want its civilian employees, who were assembled with great difficulty, to pick up and return to the more comfortable communities from which they came, so its policy is one of considerable solicitude. The lieutenant colonel who administers the community, a pleasant, unwarlike individual, thinks it is probably a simpler proposition to be mayor of an ordinary city. " Then," he says, " all you have to do, if you want to be re-elected, is to try and please fifty-one per cent of the people. But I have to worry about one hundred per cent. If somebody complains that her neighbor's dog barks too much, I have to go out and ask the dog to stop barking."

The Army may not know it, but it is operating Oak Ridge on a downright radical principle. Only Manhattan Engineer District employees, and their families, are allowed to live in the area. Consequently, Oak Ridge is possibly the one American city in which there is full employment, a situation that ought to bring Senator Taft charging down here with an investigating committee. I've done a little investigating myself, and I herewith submit a few findings. The Oak Ridge crime rate is one of the lowest in the country. There have been only three homicides since the project was started. There hasn't been one decent robbery, and what thieving goes on involves shirts, cigarette lighters, and Parker 51's. Needless to say, there are no panhandlers. Everybody has enough money to invest in a group medical plan, and it is excellently managed. For an annual forty-eight dollars, a worker and his family can count on thirty

days' hospitalization, if necessary, and the worker himself can get medical treatment any time he feels like visiting his doctor. As a result, the population, despite the somewhat elementary nature of living conditions, is extraordinarily healthy. The schoolteachers here have had to work hard to get their educational system under way, but there is one thing they haven't had to worry about. " This is the first place I've taught," a primary schoolteacher told me, " where I haven't had to handle relief cases — youngsters who have to be helped out financially to buy their books and pencils and lunches. You try to keep the other kids from finding out such matters, but they always do and then you have a problem on your hands to stop them from teasing their classmates who aren't well off. Conditions here make teaching a little easier."

Some of the people around here who are up on their Lenin say that Oak Ridge is one of the better tries at a classless society. Both extreme wealth and poverty are nonexistent. A number of construction workers live in crowded trailer camps, but the issue is blurred because a good many of these workers are among the highest-paid men on the reservation. Certain members of the community have private incomes and are therefore better-heeled than others, but money can't buy much here. " Supposing you decide to splurge and get yourself a mansion to live in," an electrician transplanted from Chicago said to me. " So you look around and discover that an F-House is the best they've got in stock. And you can't get that unless you apply to the Housing Section and prove that you have a big enough family to fill up the rooms. And if you have, they tell you a lot of other people who can also afford seventy-three dollars a month are already in line in front of you."

Nobody knows what lies ahead for Oak Ridge. The city is waiting to see what Congress decides. Some people, confident that the project will be made permanent, have started small flower gardens in front of their homes. Others, more dubious, have let the weeds grow tall. In the meantime, K-25 and the other plants continue to produce U-235 and to ship the stuff out to New Mexico to increase America's stockpile of atomic bombs, now that peace has come.

## Suggestions for Study of Reportage

1. What is meant by " reportage "? How is it distinguished from the typical magazine article?

2. Bring to class examples of good reportage from the papers and magazines available to you. Make a list of the correspondents who are given " by-lines." Choose a reporter and follow his work for a week or two.

3. What does it mean to say that reportage should be " objective "? What is meant by the statement that certain newspapers editorialize the news? Name some newspapers that have a good national reputation for being particularly objective in their news columns. Do you know any which are particularly notorious for editorializing their news stories?

4. Try to write a bit of absolutely objective reporting. Then rewrite your story as a bit of propaganda to further some opinion.

# BIOGRAPHY

The increase in the number and quality of biographies produced in America during the twentieth century indicates that this type of literature has today reached a place of importance never attained before. From the time, two thousand years ago, when Plutarch wrote his famous *Lives* until recent years only an occasional volume of biography by sheer excellence pushed itself into public favor in competition with the more popular poetry, drama, or novel. But today biography is one of our most widely read forms of literature.

### THE OLDER CONCEPTION OF BIOGRAPHY

Present-day biography is different from the older biography, and in that difference lies the reason for its new popularity. Except for the few brilliant books that still loom up from past centuries, the older biographies were usually of two kinds, either purely informational records in which numerous details were presented in an uninspired style discouraging to the general reader, or flattering " official " biographies which tended to leave out the defects of great men and gloss over their weaknesses. The authors of this second type accepted wholeheartedly Longfellow's dictum:

Lives of great men all remind us
We can make our lives sublime,

and assumed that such reminders could come only from heroic figures stripped of all human frailities.

### THE NEW CONCEPTION OF BIOGRAPHY

But there has been a reaction to these methods — largely the result of the realistic and scientific spirit which has entered into all types of literature. A biographer of today knows that he must write with vigor and deftness if he is to win readers, and that he must present an honest, all-round picture of a person if he would retain the respect of his readers. As to inspiration, the modern biographer realizes that if his " great man " is set on too high a pedestal the reader is likely to be discouraged or repelled, whereas a true portrayal of the struggles of a human being may lead the reader to try for some laurels of his own.

The desire to improve the readability of biography has led to the introduction of many elements of good fiction, such as vivid description, sprightly conversation, suspense, and climax. Since the novel has come to deal more with the ordinary course of human lives than with elaborately constructed plots, it is evident that fiction and biography are coming more and more to resemble each other. Some novels are thinly disguised biographies, and some biographies are almost novels about actual people.

Taken on the whole, the new methods, when not carried to extremes, have greatly improved biography as a type of literature and have resulted in a great stream of excellent writing in that field.

### CLIMBING TO THE LEVELS OF THE GREAT THROUGH BIOGRAPHY

Why do we read biography? Our first thought is probably " to know the lives of great men." Many biographies are stories of high achievement, and we read to find out how it was done. What manner of human being was able to rise above his fellows and stamp his name upon the memory of the nation? In whatever field of enterprise our prime interest lies we may find recorded lives to point the way toward the crown of accomplishment. And this intimate association with greatness makes us feel temporarily on the same high footing. We, too, are lifted out of the commonplace into the heroic. Our pulses quicken; our resolves strengthen; we envision our own future as building on a powerful past.

### BIOGRAPHY OFTEN CLARIFIES HISTORY

But the value of reading biography is not limited to the inspiration that comes from acquaintance with the careers of great men. Biography may, for instance, be an excellent approach to the study of history. Thomas Carlyle, the famous English historian, declares in his *Heroes and Hero Worship,* " Universal history is at bottom the history of the great men who have worked here." As we read about the men, we see them acting before a background of public events, and we come to a better understanding of their times and the movements in which they were involved. Often biographies of this sort make the past living and real to us in a way that an ordinary history book never does.

### REMOVING PREJUDICE THROUGH BIOGRAPHY

Still another reason for reading biography is to enlarge our human sympathy and rid ourselves of unreasonable prejudices.

Often we dislike persons or whole classes of people just because we do not know them. Acquaintance brings understanding. Read Booker T. Washington's *Up from Slavery* and come to a better appreciation of the American Negro; read Edna Ferber's *A Peculiar Treasure* and learn to sympathize with the problems of a Jewish family in this country. If you are a Northerner with any traces of " Civil War " bitterness, read Thomas Nelson Page's *Robert E. Lee, Man and Soldier* to revere a true American who sorrowfully fought against the flag he loved because he considered it his duty. If you are a Southerner, read Lloyd Lewis's *Sherman, Fighting Prophet* to see how this general hated the measures to which military necessity drove him. If you find yourself becoming anti any group, read a good biography of one of its leaders. You will learn that " there are two sides to every question "; and you will grow into a much broader-minded, more intelligent, more useful man or woman.

### BIOGRAPHY OFFERS VOCATIONAL GUIDANCE

A fourth reason for reading biography is to find help in choosing a career. A boy who thinks he would like to be a doctor can find many excellent biographies and autobiographies of physicians. From these he may obtain a real insight into the ups and downs of a doctor's life and either be strengthened in his desire to follow this profession or perhaps decide that for him such a choice would be a mistake. Even if one has made no decision as to his lifework, just random reading of biographies often opens up the possibilities of some attractive vocation. Many a soldier, statesman, teacher, nurse has been led to choose his career — and later to achieve success in it — through the chance reading of some interesting biography.

### RUBBING ELBOWS WITH INTERESTING PERSONALITIES

Perhaps the pleasantest feature of reading biography is that while it is inspiring us to higher achievement, leading us into the study of history, enlarging our sympathies, or helping us to choose a career it is also making us acquainted with interesting personalities. Sam Houston's life may or may not arouse our latent capacity for leadership, but acquaintance with the man Houston certainly adds spice to life. We may or may not care for the study of history as such, but Lincoln, Cleveland, and Theodore Roosevelt are worth-while friends to have at one's side throughout life. We may or may not shed prejudices through the reading of biography, but we cannot help enjoying broadening our acquaintance among other races, nationalities, and social classes. Interesting people! That is the center of biography. Buffalo Bill, P. T. Barnum, Mark Twain, George Papashvily! Clara Barton, Helen Keller, Jane Addams, Malvina Hoffman! John James Audubon, Lincoln Steffens, Thomas Edison, Oliver Wendell Holmes! Actors, authors, pioneers, scientists! The list is endless.

## M. R. Werner          1897–

The chapter which follows is taken from *Barnum* by M. R. Werner. Mr. Werner has proved himself one of our especially able modern biographers. His attention has gone to picturesque personalities, such as Brigham Young and William Jennings Bryan, or to men in business and politics.

## BARNUM'S AMERICAN MUSEUM

Barnum was the most amazing showman our country has produced. From the point of view of biography one is tempted to apply to the man himself the title he gave his circus, " The Greatest Show on Earth."

He was born in Bethel, Connecticut, where his father was a tavernkeeper. The boy early showed a gift for salesmanship and for capitalizing on the gullibility of his fellow men. His first major enterprise in showmanship was to buy an old Negro woman, the reputed nurse of George Washington, and take her about the countryside with great profit to himself. The autopsy at her death, however, proved her age to be a fraud. The museum which made him a

national figure is described in the following selection. Later he brought Jenny Lind, the " Swedish Nightingale," to this country and is said to have taken in $700,000 for her concerts alone. After he had gone bankrupt on a clock factory and lost two museums by fire, he established his circus, which perpetuated his name after his death. Mingling in politics, he was four times elected to the Connecticut legislature, but was defeated for Congress. His *Autobiography* and his later books of a personal nature have given us a vivid picture of the man; for though they are exaggerated and sometimes untruthful in detail, they show through that very fault the essential core of the man's personality. His colorful career has lent itself to the making of a successful movie — a suitable immortality for the tireless showman.

At thirty-two Barnum described himself as being " at the foot of fortune's ladder," with a wife and two children to support. Scudder's American Museum in New York was for sale for fifteen thousand dollars. Barnum told a friend that he proposed to buy it with " brass — for silver and gold have I none." How his native " brass " succeeded is a long tale, but he eventually gained possession of the museum and entered upon an amazing career of entertaining and often hoodwinking the public.

Besides his notorious curiosities, Barnum enlarged the lecture room of the museum, and presented regular dramatic performances there. He felt that what he called the " moral drama " would pay better than anything that was attractively immoral; and the " moral drama " was more palatable to his own conscience, for from childhood until his last year he had a sincere religious fear of impropriety in public presentation. The greatest manifestation of Barnum's genius for theatrical management in this country was his instinctive realization that the largest part of the community is eminently respectable in public, and it was what, more than anything else, contributed to his financial success, that Barnum catered to the reputable who still retained vestiges of curiosity. Many persons who would not be seen in a theater visited regularly the museum lecture room — Barnum would never consent to calling it a theater — where the moral dramas of *Joseph and His Brethren, Moses,* and *The Drunkard* were performed. One afternoon a New England lady walked into Barnum's office and sat down on the sofa. She examined Barnum curiously for a minute, and then remarked that he looked " much like other common folks, after all."

" Mr. Barnum," she said, " I never went to any museum before, nor to any place of amusement or public entertainment, except our school exhibitions; and I have sometimes felt that they even may be wicked, because some parts of the dialogue seemed frivolous; but I have heard so much of your ' moral dramas,' and the great good you are doing for the rising generation, that I thought I must come here and see for myself."

At that moment the gong announcing the beginning of the show in the lecture room rang. The lady jumped from the sofa. " Are the services about to commence? " she asked anxiously.

There was the noise of shuffling feet as the crowd hurried to the seats. " Yes," said Barnum, " the congregation is now going up." Barnum wrote concerning his moral performances: " I resolved, as far as possible, to elevate and refine such amusements as I dispensed. Even Shakespeare's dramas were shorn of their objectionable features when placed upon my stage."

E. A. Sothern, Tony Pastor, and Barney Williams received their first stage training on the stage of Barnum's lecture room. On holidays performances were given every hour throughout the afternoon and evening, and Barnum is given credit in histories of the theater for originating the continuous performance, which has since proved so popular in vaudeville.

These continuous programs on holidays were very popular, and on the first Fourth of July of Barnum's management of the museum so many people visited the building that the sale of tickets was stopped. This Barnum described as " exceedingly harrowing to my feelings." He noted sadly that thousands were waiting outside to purchase tickets, and that those inside did not

seem in a hurry to leave. Barnum ordered his carpenter to build a temporary flight of stairs at the rear of the building, which opened out in Ann Street. At three o'clock that afternoon this exit was opened, but much money had been lost. When, on the next St. Patrick's Day, Barnum was informed in advance that the Irish population intended to visit the museum in large numbers, he opened the rear exit again. Before noon the museum was crowded, and the sale of tickets had to be stopped. Barnum rushed to the rear exit and asked how many hundreds had passed out that way. He was told that three persons had used it during the whole morning, for the visitors had brought their dinners and intended to remain in the museum all day and night. Barnum hurriedly called his sign painter and ordered a sign in large letters:

TO THE EGRESS

This was nailed over the rear door. Some of the Irish visitors spelled out the sign, " To the Aigress," and many remarked, " Sure, that's an animal we haven't seen," and found themselves on Ann Street, with no chance of re-entering the museum.

It was on his first Fourth of July in the museum that Barnum exhibited another instance of his ingenuity in the face of a difficulty. In order to make the most of the holiday by utilizing the publicity value of the American flag, Barnum fastened a string of large flags across Broadway, tying one end to the museum and the other to a tree in St. Paul's churchyard. Several days before Independence Day, Barnum had visited the vestrymen of St. Paul's and requested permission to use the tree in the churchyard, but they called his request insulting and talked of sacrilege. On the Fourth of July he gave orders for the flags to be attached, as he had originally planned. . . . The flags attracted huge crowds, and at half-past nine in the morning two indignant vestrymen entered Barnum's office and demanded that they be detached from their church immediately. Barnum answered pleasantly that he would go into the street with them and see what could be done. He looked at the flags and remarked solemnly that they were a beautiful sight. He argued with the vestrymen that he always had stopped his Free Music for the Million when they held their services, and he merely requested this favor in return. One of the vestrymen lost patience and shouted that unless Barnum took down the flags within ten minutes he would cut them down. The crowd was attracted by the angry gestures. Barnum suddenly took off his coat, rolled up his shirt sleeves, and shouted in his sonorous voice, tinged with anger, loudly enough for all in the crowd to overhear, " I should like to see you dare to cut down the American flag on the Fourth of July; you must be a Britisher to make such a threat, but I'll show you a thousand pairs of Yankee hands in two minutes, if you dare to take down the stars and stripes on this great birthday of American freedom." In a moment the vestrymen were surrounded by several heavy, angry men, who threatened varied punishment. The poor bewildered vestrymen disappeared quietly from the crowd, and Barnum with obsequious smiles enjoyed his triumph.

Barnum was apparently indefatigable in his personal interest in the museum and in his personal efforts to make it ever more popular. He often appeared before his audiences with stunts or speeches, because he knew he could entertain them, and because he liked to think that they were interested in him. When Peale, of Peale's Museum, presented an actor who pretended to conduct experiments in mesmerism, Barnum personally conducted his own experiments in animal magnetism from the stage of the moral lecture room. A young girl, carefully trained in advance, sat on the stage. Barnum made a few passes with his hand in front of her, and she was then under his control; she raised her hands when he requested her to do so, grimaced when he put tobacco in his mouth, and smiled when

he ate candy. Then it was his practice to turn to the audience and offer to forfeit fifty dollars if he could not put any member of the audience in the same state within five minutes. At the end of three minutes the volunteer was, of course, wide awake. Barnum would look at his watch, remark that he had two minutes, which was plenty of time, and offer to demonstrate to the audience that a person mesmerized was a person insensible to pain, by cutting off one of the fingers of the small girl, who was still asleep. He would take out his knife, feel the sharp edge, and turn toward the girl, who had meanwhile fled behind the scenes in a fright that delighted the audience. Barnum would say in an astonished tone of voice, " Then she was wide awake, was she? "

His volunteer from the audience usually answered, " Of course she was, she was wide awake all the time."

" I suppose so," was Barnum's answer, " and, my dear sir, I promised that you should be ' in the same state ' at the end of five minutes, and as I believe you are so, I do not forfeit fifty dollars." This type of trick never seemed to anger, rather than to amuse, the audiences.

No such trickery was too much for Barnum, and he carried out a similar deception on a public scale with no harm to his reputation and no qualms of conscience. In June of 1843 he attended the Bunker Hill celebration, where Daniel Webster delivered a stirring oration, but Barnum was just as interested in an old canvas tent near the Bunker Hill Monument as he was in the ceremonies of the day. He found in that tent a herd of fifteen one-year-old calf buffaloes, which he immediately purchased for seven hundred dollars; a scheme by which he could utilize these buffaloes had hatched in his mind almost as soon as he saw them. The animals were docile and tired, for they had been driven east from the Western plains. At Barnum's order they were brought to New York and then transported to a New Jersey barn near Hoboken. Barnum hired their former owner, C. D. French, to take care of the animals for thirty dollars per month, because French understood the lasso. The newspapers shortly afterward announced that a herd of wild buffaloes, captured in the Rocky Mountains, was passing through New York soon on its way to Europe, in charge of the very men who had captured the animals, and during the next few days suggestions appeared in the newspapers that it would be a fine thing for New York if the owners of these buffaloes could be induced to present a buffalo chase on a racecourse near New York, demonstrating to the Eastern population the use of the lasso and the ferocity of the buffalo. One of the correspondents expressed it as his sincere opinion that it would be worth a dollar to see such a sight, and that he for one would be willing to pay that amount. Another estimated that no less than fifty thousand persons would be interested in a buffalo chase without the danger but with the thrills, and other obliging correspondents suggested places for the hunt, including the racecourse at Hoboken, New Jersey. Before long advertisements appeared in all the newspapers, and handbills were circulated throughout New York announcing that there would be a

Grand Buffalo Hunt, Free of Charge — At Hoboken, on Thursday, August 31, at 3, 4, and 5 o'clock P.M. Mr. C. D. French, one of the most daring and experienced hunters of the West, has arrived thus far on his way to Europe with a herd of buffaloes, captured by himself, near Santa Fe. He will exhibit a method of hunting the wild buffaloes, and throwing the lasso, by which the animals were captured in their most wild and untamed state. This is perhaps one of the most exciting and difficult feats that can be performed, requiring at the same time the most expert horsemanship and greatest skill and dexterity. Every man, woman, and child can here witness the wild sports of the Western prairies, as the exhibition is to be free to all, and will take place on the extensive grounds and racecourse of Messrs. Stevens, within a few rods of the Hoboken ferry.

The public was further assured that " no possible danger need be apprehended, as a double railing has been put around the whole course, to prevent the possibility of the buffaloes approaching the multitude."

These announcements mystified and delighted New York. Who was the city's anonymous benefactor? Who supplied such entertainment free of charge and kept modestly in the background? Barnum meanwhile had purchased the rights to the receipts of all the ferryboats which crossed between New York and Hoboken on August 31, 1843, and extra ferryboats were provided for the day. The weather was clear, and the boats, under the administration of Captain Barnum, were crowded to the railings with adventurers. Twenty-four thousand people went to Hoboken that day. They stood on the railings and clutched the awnings to support themselves, and each paid six and a quarter cents going and the same to return.

When the crowds arrived in Hoboken, they waited in the arena for the wild buffaloes, who finally appeared in reluctant and tame parade of their alleged ferocity. The animals were thin and pale from lack of nourishment during their first master's patronage, and although they had been crammed with extra rations of oats for several days they refused at the outset to be wild. C. D. French, " one of the most daring and experienced hunters of the West," dressed and painted as an Indian, poked his wild buffaloes with a goad, but the most they would do for the twenty-four thousand interested spectators was to trot. There was much laughter and shouting at their recalcitrance, and the noise made by the crowd frightened the nervous buffaloes so much that they galloped from the inclosure in terror and threw the spectators, who believed that they had actually grown wild, into a panic. The buffaloes took refuge from their oppressors in a nearby swamp, and all that C. D. French could do would not persuade them to return to the racecourse. He finally lassoed one of them, and entertained the crowd with this beast, and with exhibitions of lassoing on horses and horsemen. No one suspected the ferryboat arrangement, and no one suspected Barnum. It was after midnight when the last of the crowds succeeded in getting home from Hoboken, but, apparently, a good time was had by all, for there were no riots, and the receipts of the ferryboats turned over to Barnum amounted to $3,500. After the exhibition Barnum sent his buffaloes to Camden, New Jersey, where they attracted Philadelphia crowds in the same manner. Some of the herd then went to England and were sold, while the others were fattened on a farm and sold for buffalo steak in Fulton Market at fifty cents per pound. In order that the museum might profit by the advertisement, Barnum made public his responsibility for the Great Buffalo Hunt.

Sometime after his success with the buffaloes, Barnum presented the first Wild West Show New York had seen. He engaged a band of Indians from Iowa, among whom were impressive men, beautiful squaws, and two or three papooses. The Indians appeared on the stage of the moral lecture room in real war dances, which they performed with all the vigor and realistic interpretation of their savage origin. In fact, it was necessary to rope them in, for fear that in their frenzy toward the end of a dance they might forget that they were merely players, and make for members of the audience; for Barnum's Indians had never before seen a railroad or a steamboat, and scalps were not yet obsolete in their minds. They seemed thoroughly under the impression that they were not acting but living, which in one particular caused the proprietor of the American Museum some expense. After a week of war dances, Barnum suggested a change of program, including an Indian wedding dance. The interpreter explained, and the chief agreed. On Monday afternoon when the first change to the wedding dance was to take place, Barnum was informed by the chief that he must supply a red woolen blanket as a wedding present for the bridegroom to give to the father of the bride, an inviolable Indian custom. After each performance the chief

insisted that he must have another new blanket for the next performance, and when Barnum attempted to explain that the wedding was only " make believe," the chief gave forth an ugly " Ugh! " terrifying Barnum into spending $120 for twelve red woolen blankets for the rest of the week.

These special exhibitions were supplemented by flower shows, dog shows, and poultry shows at the museum, and Barnum, soon after he became manager, decided that he must have a baby show. He organized such an exhibition with graduated scales of prizes for triplets, the fattest baby, the most beautiful baby, and the handsomest twins. The main prize of one hundred dollars for the most perfect baby was a source of considerable difficulty. Barnum thought that it would be a fine thing for him to award this prize himself, a fine thing in publicity for himself, and also for the baby, who could say in later years that he had been personally selected as unique by P. T. Barnum. In later years he did meet many men and women who claimed that honor, but at the time of the awards the defeated mothers stormed about Barnum, and their indignation could not be appeased until he announced that he would award a second prize of one hundred dollars to the baby selected by a committee of mothers. Whereupon each mother became the enemy of every other, and Barnum's one hundred dollars was safe. In deciding future baby contests, however, he sent in written reports and was not to be disturbed for the rest of the day.

In November, 1842, Barnum stopped one night at the Franklin Hotel in Bridgeport, Connecticut, which was kept by his brother, Philo F. Barnum. His brother mentioned that there was a dwarf in Bridgeport, who played daily in the streets and was accepted by the rest of the population as a natural curiosity. Barnum asked his brother to bring the child to the Franklin Hotel, and as soon as he saw this dwarf he realized that here was a natural curiosity who could be transformed by instruction and publicity into a unique and profitable one. The child was the smallest Barnum had ever seen, and was in excellent health, without any deformities. He was two feet, one inch in height and weighed fifteen pounds. His hair was flaxen, and his eyes dark; his cheeks were pink and his whole appearance gave the impression of health, symmetry, and whimsical charm on a lovely, diminutive scale. He was very bashful, and Barnum only learned after difficulty that his name was Charles S. Stratton, and that he was five years old. Barnum visited Mr. and Mrs. Sherwood E. Stratton, the child's parents, and after some persuasion they consented to exhibit their son at Barnum's museum for three dollars per week and board for himself and his mother. Barnum hired him for four weeks only, because at the time he was doubtful whether a five-year-old child who was only two feet in height might not grow before long to a normality that would make him mediocre.

The dwarf and his mother arrived in New York on Thanksgiving Day, 1842, and Barnum had something to be thankful for that day. Mrs. Stratton was astonished and somewhat annoyed when she noticed that her son was announced in large handbills as " General Tom Thumb," a dwarf eleven years of age, " just arrived from England." The " just arrived from England " was the first instance of a method Barnum often repeated. He realized early in his career the love of the American mind for an importation, and he never advertised anything as domestic if he could possibly deceive his patrons into believing that he had incurred much trouble and expense by importing it from abroad, where its popularity was always stupendous. He hoped, patriotically, in his autobiography that such deception might check " our disgraceful preference for foreigners."

Barnum made his dwarf eleven years old for fear that the public might not believe that a child five years old would not grow beyond his present height. In the various pamphlets concerning the life of General Tom Thumb, which were sold at his exhi-

bitions, it is recorded that when he was born he weighed nine pounds, two ounces, more than the average weight of a newborn baby, and that at five months he had ceased to grow and weighed only fifteen pounds. His weight of fifteen pounds and his height of two feet, one inch, were said to have remained unchanged from the age of five months until the age of five years and for many years thereafter.

The change of name from Charles S. Stratton to General Tom Thumb was a stroke of Barnum's inspiration, and it contributed largely to the General's subsequent success. Tom Thumb is the most appropriate name a dwarf ever had, and, besides, it possessed the advantage of some familiarity from the story of the legendary Tom Thumb, of whom it will be remembered:

> In Arthur's court Tom Thumb did live,
>   A man of mickle might,
> The best of all the table round,
>   And eke a doughty knight;
> His stature but an inch in height,
>   Or quarter of a span;
> Then think you not this little knight
>   Was prov'd a valiant man?

According to nursery lore, the legendary Tom Thumb was swallowed by a cow when he crossed the cow's blade of grass but was soon delivered up again from the cow's stomach, only to meet his death by a bumblebee after a series of valiant adventures. Barnum's addition of " General " to Tom Thumb enriched the name by a pompous mockery that was more valuable because of its incongruity.

General Tom Thumb was soon domesticated to the ways of public exhibition. Barnum taught his pupil day and night new jokes and old roles, which he learned quickly, for the child, according to Barnum, had a love of the ludicrous and a humorous charm. When he was ready to make his debut, Barnum took General Tom Thumb first on a tour of the newspaper offices, and even invaded the home of one newspaper editor, who happened to be eating dinner. Tom Thumb danced between

P. T. BARNUM with General and Mrs. Tom Thumb (center). Barnum eventually gathered together a small troop of dwarfs, including Commodore Nutt (left) and Minnie Warren (right), who were best man and maid of honor in Tom Thumb's wedding. (Westervelt Collection)

the tumblers and hopped over the roast. James Gordon Bennett wrote in the *Herald* on December 15, 1842: " We were visited yesterday by the comical little gentleman who is at present holding nightly levees at the American Museum. He is certainly the smallest specimen of a man we have ever seen."

The General's popularity was immediate, and after the first four weeks' engagement was finished, Barnum re-engaged him for one year at seven dollars a week, with a bonus of fifty dollars at the end of the engagement. It is clear that neither General Tom Thumb nor his father had any idea of the value of a dwarf, and Barnum took

advantage of the age of the boy and the ignorance of his father. Barnum also retained the privilege of sending the General on a tour of the country. Before the end of the year Barnum increased Tom Thumb's salary to twenty-five dollars per week, and he assures us that the General deserved the raise. Besides exhibiting frequently at the museum, where he sang songs, danced, and told stories in the pert and saucy manner of people who are too small to be slapped, General Tom Thumb was sent to other cities, where he made money for Barnum and advertised the American Museum.

At the same time as the exhibition of General Tom Thumb in New York, Barnum presented at the museum two famous giants, M. Bihin, the tall, thin French giant, and Colonel Goshen, a portly Arab. The giants were amiable enough, but jealous of each other's success, and quarreled furiously one day by engaging in a glorious bout of name-calling. They seized clubs and medieval swords on exhibition in cases, and made for each other, until Barnum interfered. He informed them that he had no objection to their fighting, maiming, or killing each other, but they were both under engagement to him, and if there was to be a duel, it must be duly advertised and take place on the stage of the lecture room. " No performance of yours would be a greater attraction, and if you kill each other, our engagement can end with your duel," Barnum assured them. The giants enjoyed the humor of the situation, and lived in peace until the end of their engagement.

After the contract with General Tom Thumb expired, Barnum engaged him for another year at fifty dollars per week and all his expenses, with the right to exhibit him in Europe. The museum was so successful and operating with so little friction after less than three years that Barnum was looking for new worlds to conquer, and he took his General under his arm and went to Europe. Passage was booked on the packet ship *Yorkshire* for Liverpool, and General Tom Thumb, his father and mother, the General's tutor, Professor Guillaudeu, and Barnum made ready to sail on January 18, 1844. Barnum made use of the General at the museum until the last moment before sailing. Advertisements appeared in the newspapers of the day announcing that the opportunity to see General Tom Thumb was rapidly slipping away. When the boat was delayed by adverse winds and tides, the General remained another day at the museum, and thousands of people visited him in a desperate attempt to get a last look. The *Evening Post* announced as an item of news on January 16, 1844:

A few hours more remain for General Tom Thumb to be seen at the American Museum, as the packet in which he has engaged passage to England does not sail today, in consequence of the easterly winds now prevailing. He may be seen throughout the entire day and evening; and at three and seven o'clock P.M. there will be grand performances; at each of which the General appears on the stage in the same characters which have excited so much admiration and applause of late.

The next day the weather was still bad, and people stormed the museum. On the day of the sailing, January 19, General Tom Thumb was on exhibition until eleven o'clock in the morning; the boat sailed at noon. He was escorted to the dock by the municipal brass band, and more than ten thousand persons saw him off. It was estimated that more than eighty thousand persons had visited General Tom Thumb at the museum.

## Suggestions for Study

1. List the various characteristics of Barnum you can discover from this selection. Are his motives admirable or not? Do you consider him dishonest? Discuss the ethics of his various schemes; also their ingenuity.

2. What do we have at present comparable to Barnum's museum? to his method of advertising?

3. Is the public as easily fooled today as in Barnum's time? Do people enjoy being fooled?

4. Barnum is an interesting person to follow up. You would enjoy reading Barnum's own version of his career in his autobiography, *Struggles and Triumphs*. The rest of Werner's account is fascinating, and H. W. Root's *Boy's Life of Barnum* is easy reading. Musically inclined students would enjoy reading the chapter on Jenny Lind and Barnum in Richard Aldrich's *Musical Discourses*.

5. Composition: (a) Write up some experience of your childhood in taking part in a circus or show as if it were a chapter in your autobiography. (b) Describe some museum, circus, or fair you have visited. (c) Report orally or in writing on the career of Jenny Lind.

## For Your Vocabulary

WORD HISTORY. Have you ever used the dictionary to discover odd and picturesque origins of words? According to modern usage, the *vestiges* (vĕs'tĭ-jĕz) of curiosity Barnum's customers retained (page 220) were merely faint traces. But the original meaning of *vestige* was a footprint or track. When you look up a word in the dictionary, notice the original meaning given first, and you will find many such curious developments in meaning. When anything reaches such a stage of disuse that only *vestiges* of it remain, it is *obsolete* (ŏb'sŏ-lēt). What does the author mean when he says that scalps were not yet *obsolete* in the minds of Barnum's Indians (page 224)? Words, customs, or laws that have passed out of active use are said to be *obsolete*. Does Frank Dobie think cattle brands are *obsolete*? (See page 183.)

## George and Helen Papashvily

In 1923, 700,000 immigrants were admitted to the United States. One of these was George Papashvily,[1] a penniless Russian from the province of Georgia, who had crossed the ocean as a steerage passenger on a Greek freighter. "In your position, frankly," said a Turkish shipmate, "I would kill myself."

But George Papashvily was too busy exploring the wonders of America to contemplate suicide. In quick succession he found jobs in a restaurant, a silk mill, a garage, a statue factory, a glue factory, a railway yard. In 1929 he sought to escape the depression by moving with his Russian friends to California.

[1] **Papashvily** (på-påsh'vē-lē).

GEORGE AND HELEN PAPASHVILY
have proved that "anything can happen"
to people with imagination, humor, and a
talent for living.

In California this immigrant met and married Helen Waite, descendant of a long line of Vermonters. Although friends of both the bride and groom doubted the wisdom of their marrying, the marriage has proved very successful. Perhaps Mrs. Papashvily has contributed to this success by following the advice of one of George's Russian friends: "At least once a day say to your husband, 'I love you.' And whenever you set a table for Georgians, remember — only too much is ever enough."

George and Helen Papashvily now live in an old Dutch farmhouse in Pennsylvania. George has raised successively chickens, goats, bees, corn, sheep, pigs, flax, and tomatoes. Helen manages the Moby Dick Bookshop in near-by Allentown.

## IT'S CALIFORNIA

Under the suggestive title *Anything Can Happen* Helen Papashvily has set down the merry, moving story of George's adventures in America. She has written the story as George would tell it, and as a result the book, like George, is "happy and full of prance." The following excerpt relates the hilarious adventures of George and his friends on their journey from Detroit to California in 1932 when America was sunk in the awful depths of our worst depression.

It's a heart-tearing sight to watch a person sicken and grow thin but oh so worse to see a city die before your eyes. Yet that's what happened to Detroit the winter of 1932. The city, so bright before and full of living, died.

First the factories went and then one by one the little shops, where somebody made his few pennies, closed and left the empty windows staring like dead eyes into deserted streets. The new houses and office buildings stood half finished because everywhere the money was running out like blood draining away.

Came each pay, more and more men found the pink slip that means don't come back again, clipped to their checks. I watched so many, when it was their turn, and saw them pale like men who feel the first chill of typhus. Because it was a kind of typhus, this depression, only the dying was slower.

And why did all this happen? Nobody knew. A stock market in New York? That's what some people thought. But then like others said, "How can a stock market thousands of miles away, never saw me, reach out and take away my piece of bread here in Detroit?"

For my part I didn't know the answer, if there was one. Only it seemed a shame to keep my job longer when men with families needed it, so I quit. With a coupla hundred dollars more I had saved by this time, I started a wrecking business to buy old cars, scrap them, and sell the parts and metal for what I could get.

In the house where I lived, things were going bad with them too. Every night when I came in from work Anna Feodorovna sat in her dining room drinking tea, and every night drinking with a longer and longer face.

Friday I stopped to pay my rent. "Be pleased to sit down, Giorgi Ivanitch." She poured a glass of tea for me. "Terrible times. Awful times. Your friend Vallodia lost now his job. And Madame Greshkin, she has no pupils at all."

" Have to expect," I said. " Nobody likes to make music, tra la la, when they hungry."

" Even Ermak and your old Persian gentleman move on Monday. Leaves me this whole big house with only you paying rent. What to do? "

" Maybe times get better," I told her.

" No, I don't expect," she said. " Frankly in my experience they usually get worse. And I thought America was rich. A place with everything enough."

" It's hard to believe it," I said, " but they can be poor here, too. Like any place else."

Her father, His Excellency, came in and sat down. Anna Feodorovna cut the cake. " Be pleased to take a piece, Giorgi Ivanitch. Today is my father's name day. But who knows if he lives to see another anniversary, my papasha? Or if any of us do. In fact is it any use to struggle more? Often I ask myself. Perhaps to die now is the best thing to do."

" Well," I said, " depends. Maybe you wouldn't enjoy that any better either. Once you tried."

" We have to do something." His Excellency made a big stirring in his tea. " This isn't right how things are going. They promised in America was jobs for everybody, didn't they? "

Why he cares I don't know. He never worked a day in his life. But no use to go into that.

" But what? " Anna Feodorovna asked. " What can we do? "

" Go somewhere else," His Excellency said. " And for that at least I have to admit America is good. No matter where you was already, is always left another place still to go."

" Let it be a place with jobs then, Papasha. Like America was before. And if we go quick, very quick maybe we escape this curse," she crossed herself, " is on Detroit."

" Takes time for deciding," His Excel-

lency said. " To examine the problem thoroughly." He put his hand over his eyes and started to think.

Luba, Anna Feodorovna's daughter, came in. She was little kid about fifteen, sixteen years old this time with angel blue eyes, pinky cheeks, and curls, yellow as baby duck feathers, all over her head. And to go with all this she had a disposition would fit a pack camel, stubborn, balky, turn a grudge until it was worn sharp, and if screaming didn't bring what she liked to have she wasn't too proud to bite. I was sorry for her brother, Artash, nice little kid, twelve years old. Often I wondered if he would manage to live through it to grow up.

" Hello, Luba," I told. " What did you learn today in school? "

" Don't call me Luba," she stamped her feets. " I told you a hundred times. You're doing it on purpose. Luba! Luba! I have name now of Lucette."

" Zdravstuite, Lucette Petrovna," I said. " How you do, Miss Lucette? Glad to know you. Better? "

" Besides I don't go in school more. I quit. I work."

" Doing what? "

" Usher in the movies."

" You leaved school," I said, " for a thing like that? How much it pays? "

" I see now every movie, three, four, five, how many times I want, free. That's my pay."

" The theater," Anna Feodorovna said. " Ah, the theater. I can't blame her. Truly she has it from me. The theater. How I loved. In Petrograd [1] we had a box — "

His Excellency gave a loud cough to show he's caught up on his thinking. " So we agree," he said. " Next thing — "

Artash opened the door and rolled in on his skates, pulled a chair over where Luba can't reach to pinch him, and sat down.

" What we agree? " he asked.

" Before I was interrupted," His Excellency said, " I was going to say we agree we're going someplace. Now the mistake we made when we came in U.S.A. was that

[1] **Petrograd:** now Leningrad.

we chose a place where nobody was speaking our language. So we don't do that again. This time we go where everybody is speaking Russian. We go in Alaska."

"Alaska. That be good," Artash said. He skated over to sideboard to get himself plate. "But who teached the Eskimos?"

"The result of an American education," His Excellency said to Anna Feodorovna. "I hope you're satisfied. My boy," he turned to Artash. "I have the honor to inform you Alaska was a possession of His Late Gracious Majesty Czar Nicolai Alexandrovitch. Naturally everybody there is speaking Russian and take off those skates."

"Czar sold to the U.S.A." I said.

"Gossip. Nothing but gossip."

"To pay his card debts was the way I heard it."

"Lies," he pounded the table. "His Imperial Highness would never have done a thing like that and not told peoples. All lies. So we go in Alaska."

"Yes. Yes." Anna Feodorovna closed her eyes. "To Alaska and the thick quiet snow will fall and fall, frosting over the houses and the churches like little cakes. The bells will ring. And we shall see again the shining faces of our peasants. Yes. We all go."

"But my junk yard," I said. "Why should I throw that away? It brings me a living."

Anna Feodorovna opened her eyes and came back in this world. "Wait, Giorgi Ivanitch. For myself I ask nothing. For me a crust bread, a cup of water is enough. But my childrens? You forget my childrens. Surely they deserve a future?"

"I don't deny it. But still I don't want to go in Alaska."

"Pardon." His Excellency interrupted me. "One question. Was you ever in Alaska?"

"Certainly I wasn't."

"Exactly my point. Then how do you know you don't like to go?"

"Besides," Anna Feodorovna said, "to go alone is impossible. A woman, weak, helpless on the road alone with childrens, two little childrens."

Luba cut a slice of *torte* and began to eat.

"Polar bears," Artash said, "and whales. And seals, Giorgi Ivanitch. Seals that clap their hands. I gonna steal a geography book from school tomorrow and bring home to show you."

"But I can see all that for ten cent fare to Belle Isle Park. In the zoo."

"The hand of God rest heavy on the widow." Anna Feodorovna began to cry, her tears spattering down like summer rain. "If you refuse us where I can turn?"

"Don't cry in your glass, Mamasha." Artash patted her hand. "Makes your tea weak. I gonna take you riding on my dog team when we get there. We gonna have dog teams, me and you, Giorgi Ivanitch, run like wind." He started to drive the table with his feet. "Mush, Mush. I'm carrying the serum through to Nome. Mush!"

Luba took again cake.

"Gold," His Excellency said. "It jumped my mind entirely, the gold. Any amount of it there once we catch on the places where to look for it."

"Walruses, too," Artash said, "like seals only with mustaches, Giorgi Ivanitch. I know you like."

"O.K., O.K." I said. "Don't cry more please, Anna Feodorovna. I go."

Luba finished last cake on plate and licked her fingers. "Only we not going in Alaska," she said. "I have an intention to be a movie star. So I decided we're going in Hollywood."

This starts a new argument. Alaska or California? But for once I was on Luba's side. If I have to go any place I prefer California. Uncle John had moved there about six months before and he was always writing me to come. Besides, from talking to Americans, I arrived at the conclusion California was a very highly valued place. Anyway there wouldn't be any snow.

And now began preparations for our journey. I went in my scrap yard and put together a car from best parts I had on hand. Was something like station wagon but then again resembled a hearse, too. "But we need truck besides," Anna Feodorovna said immediately I drove my invention home to show it off.

"Why? Goes you, His Excellency, the kids, and me. Five will fit good in here with even a place left over."

"But I persuaded Madame Greshkin, she'll enjoy the trip," Anna Feodorovna said, "and Ermak thinks he like to come, too."

"But the truck. What's that for?"

"My furniture naturally."

"Anna Feodorovna," I said, "you surely don't mean we're gonna carry your furniture to California? You don't mean that?"

But she did mean.

So finally I found a truck for $150, a pretty good job, one and half ton Ford. We started to load it.

Beds, tables, chairs, carpets — I didn't say anything but then we had to make a crate for the rubber tree, the rubber tree's going in California, and a fifty pound bag of feathers, too.

"Feathers from the dowry of my own great-grandmother," Anna Feodorovna said. "I have a sacred duty to save them for Luba's trousseau."

"Better Luba finds a husband first," I suggested.

Her only answer was to give me a bird cage to fit in. A big bird cage but the bird died coming from Russia.

"You couldn't leave the cage here I suppose?"

"Please," Anna Feodorovna said. "Why you deny me? So simple my pleasures and so few. Why you make me leave here my bird's cage? Kill in my heart all hope I'll have again some day a sweet canary to sing me songs."

I put it on. Canary's house is all aboard for California, too. And finally after they loaded a harness with bells for a three-horse sleigh and hive of bees Artash kept in the back yard I saw it was hopeless to say any more. Let them do how they want.

"I completed the final plans now for our expedition," His Excellency said one morning at breakfast. He unstrapped his big portfolio and took out a slip of paper. "In the car rides my daughter, the childrens, Madame Greshkin, and Ermak for their protector. And in truck goes me and you, Giorgi Ivanitch. We lead the way."

"We must follow each other and keep together. That's the main thing," Anna Feodorovna said. "If we be lost, I know we meet only in heaven."

"But how can we manage?" I said. "I can't read maps. When you see it on paper it looks all flat, but when you get there it goes up and down hills and turns corners, crosses over brooks. It never seems same."

"That will be my department," His Excellency promised. "I give the directions. I have a lifetime's experience in travel. I been from Transbaikal to Turkey, from Petrograd to Vladivostok. Don't worry more."

So now was ready everybody for the start?

But no, still Anna Feodorovna needed time to prepare food. For whole next week I smelled baking cookies and the tables were full with stuffed chickens and boiled hams and jars of salad and beets and pickles and whenever you sat had to watch that your sitting was not down on a cake.

"Anna Feodorovna, you make me curious," I said. "What you doing? Maybe you expect to meet Easter on the way someplace?"

"Please, please." Anna Feodorovna had no time. "Don't bother me. It's no joke to pack a lunch for seven people that reaches to California."

"But I expected we'll stop and eat in the restaurants," I said.

His Excellency put his head out the pantry where he was sampling *piroshkis*, that's a kind of crispy little pies filled with chopped meat and hard-boiled eggs. Very easy to eat. "My poor boy," he said, "you really expect to find meals ready for your eating when you stop? That shows you don't have any experience in travel. Maybe in a railroad station, yes, we can buy hot water to make tea. But we're poor people. Who can we send to ride on ahead and order the meals prepared for our coming?"

Well, to argue with His Excellency was like arguing with wind. I kept still.

So at last one day in October, on a bright morning, the air stickling and prickling like champagne bubbles, everything was ready and we began our travels.

Twenty-five, thirty of Anna Feodorovna's lady friends came to say the farewells and most of the men from His Excellency's club and a few boys I knew and a lot of the little kids were in school with Artash and Luba. They all gathered to watch us with round eyes. Truck is packed, gas and oil in the car. Now are we ready to start?

" No," Anna Feodorovna said. " No." She got out of the car. " To go like this. Impossible. To leave our friends with only the memory of a cold house. No. It's too cruel. Let them remember from Anna Feodorovna that she gave with both hands. Let them say she offered on the last day with same heart as on the first day. Unpack the samovar."

So we got it out from underneath the sewing machine and took the spoons out from the sawdust where they was put to don't get scratched and Artash ran to store for a sack of charcoal and Anna Feodorovna laid out most of the lunch to get at cakes. My job was to pass tea and listen to all the ladies tell the details of every trip they took in their lives. And mostly these were trips with very unhappy experiences in them.

By noon everybody finished eating and crying and we washed up the glasses, packed the truck again and this time we're really gone. Good-by! Good-by! Good-by!

Now His Excellency took command. " Turn right; turn left; straight," and got us out on crooked dirt road, one car wide. " Number Twelve Highway runs out of Detroit," I said. " Why don't we use that? "

" My boy. My boy." His Excellency shook his head. " You'll never learn. Experienced travelers always take the back roads. That way you avoid bandits and hold-uppers. You don't have to pay tolls, either."

So we ride, ride. Sometimes through mud; sometimes across cornfields; we by-passed around cows and detoured through blackberry patches. Night came, we stopped and made a camp in a churchyard. Next morning early we pulled on again. As far as I'm concerned California can't be too soon for me.

By suppertime that second day the lunch was all ate up. Thank God for that. Now we can go in a restaurant like humans. And no matter what His Excellency thought, I saw restaurants plenty, as many as we left in Detroit, every place we passed through.

So we picked out a nice clean diner and we all went in and sat down at a table and ordered. But my curiosity was itching. How far have we come on our way? So I went up by the front counter.

" Be so kind," I said, to the man frying sausage in the window, " to tell me what city I'm in? "

" Youngstown."

" Youngstown? What state is it usually considered to be in, Youngstown? "

" Ohio."

This was Ohio! Terrible shock to me. I'm positive I went through Ohio on my way from Pittsburgh to Detroit. It means we're in exactly the wrong direction.

" You'll excuse me," I said, " if I bother you with one more personal question. In your opinion which way from here would be California? "

He pointed toward the gentlemen's washroom. " West," he said.

I went out that way through the kitchen and into the back yard and sat down on a garbage can. I watched the sky for hour until I got the directions clear in my head from the stars, and then I went back in and ate how they call in English a " blue plate," it means only what is served on it. The plate, naturally, I gave back to the waiter.

Next morning I took charge. " Two days wasted," I said. " Two days that we'll never get back in this world. Spread out the maps. Now, Artash, you lay a stick down straight to California. O.K. Write me down states it goes across."

Artash put them nicely in order on a piece of paper, Ohio, Indiana, Illinois, Missouri, Kansas, Colorado —

" Now," I said, starting up the truck, " follow me, everybody. Straight ahead. I'm on the right track and where the sun goes down we'll find California waiting."

And now for me began one of the best times in my life, day by day I rode along and watched this wide beautiful country open before me. Day by day I found another new coin to add to my bag of gold that was America.

It was so big, this place. Every mile I discovered that all over again. So big. So big. So big. All the wheels in America sang the tune. The automobiles going so whizzing past; the proud motorcycles; the turning tractor treads. Even the locomotives — for a long, long time after they disappeared over the earth's curve, I could hear the rails still humming — So big. So big. So-o-o-o big.

And the people. Wherever we stopped they were glad to make friends and to talk with me. I met Mennonites out of Russia and Bohemians from Prague and Irishmen smelling of good whisky and strong tobaccos off the section gangs, anxious to spend their money, and Welsh slate miners whose voices rose and fell like singing birds. And in little white painted homes in Iowa were what they called " first settlers' " families that was pioneers from Ohio and before that from Vermont and even longer before that? — From England? Now I didn't feel bad about my broken language any more or my stranger ways. I saw everybody is a foreigner. Only difference, some came early and some came late.

I wished I was alone. I could have stayed a week, a month, a year in a hundred places. Only Luba wanted to hurry, hurry so she don't waste a minute to be a movie star, and nothing suited His Excellency: too hot, too cold, too crowded, too lonesome. Anna Feodorovna was weeping, weeping that she ever left Detroit and dropping things and mislaying our travel money that she carried, and every place we stopped she left something behind: her teeth, the silver holder for her tea glass, her special sleeping pillow.

" Personally, Anna Feodorovna," I said — it was the day we had to go from Canton back to Peoria because she forgot her icon hanging in the corner of the tourist cabin — " I don't know how you ever got from Petrograd to Detroit, unless somebody carried you in a bag."

Only Artash had brains to look out the windows and watch America unroll out before us like a carpet from heaven's best weaving.

Illinois, we went through there, riding miles and miles between forests of corn, heavy for harvest; and Missouri, in a town near the river we ate a kind of American food, fried chicken, in our hands without no forks or plates to interrupt its flavor, and hot golden biscuits, too, so melting good with honey and butter that anywhere else in the world they would have called them cake.

Nebraska I liked extra good because one day just at sundown we stopped at a place to see if we could get some milk. An old, old farmer, he had a beard as long and white as God's, took me out to the barn and he named me his every cow and showed me his big combine, patting its painted side like was a good horse. And what kind of stories he told me! How he walked all the way to Nebraska and lived first in a house made of mud where buffaloes ran in herds past his door.

" Pretty proud I was," he said, " when I got my first team, yep, Dolly and Rachel, and saw my first furrow turn. Yep. And knew," his voice dropped down almost to a whisper, " and knew no plow afore mine ever broke this ground since the world began."

Of course, I saw things I didn't like, too. In this world what place is perfect? But is a cheap kind of loving that can't admit the faults. I saw the poors in sagging houses with funny papers pasted on their walls, and the men waiting with such sad patience by the factory gates that didn't need them more. I saw them all.

Before my heart would have broke with this, but now since I traveled America, I was comforted because I knew there was enough for everybody. Only problem was to share it even.

So on we went without trouble until we were about a day into Colorado when His Excellency said he would take the wheel, give me little rest for a while. So I closed my eyes and as soon as I opened them again, we're miles off the main road, parked at the edge of a river bed. True there was only a trickle of water in it, but the sides were steep and there wasn't any bridge for crossing over.

" The way this happened," His Excellency began, " was — "

" I don't doubt it," I said, " whatever it was. O.K. Ermak, you got the lightest car. I'll pull around and you go first. If you get across, I'll come after."

" If I get stuck? " Ermak said.

" Still be easier to pull you out than me."

" No. No. You go this way. I go that way — " Ermak is the kind of man the minute you say black, he has to say white. " If I go here — "

" No time for the philosophy of crossing rivers," I said. " Be dark pretty soon. If you won't go, I have to." So I started over. Of course, in the center I got stuck, and immediately my wheels started to disappear in the sand. I was sinking.

" My furnitures. Help! " Anna Feodorovna stood on the bank and wrung her hands to the sky. " Help! They're going! " Truck sagged another inch.

" Don't worry, Anna Feodorovna," I got out and looked at my axle. I was so mad I could chew on knives. " Don't worry. Only a matter of time until I come out in China. I deliver your furnitures back in Vladivostok."

Everybody screamed and they came out and started carrying off the things, one by one, up on the far bank. Truck stopped settling then, but I still couldn't move it. I got out and went downstream to see if I could find some pieces of wood. In the distance I saw a lot of men coming toward us with horses and wagons and so much dust it must

be they were moving sheep. I went out to meet them.

" Give me hand, Boys," I said. " I'm stuck in the river."

But it seemed they didn't understand me. They made Ho-Ho-How-How among themselves and finally one young fellow rode up from the back and asked me in English what I wanted.

" What nationality you folks are anyway? " I asked him. " I'm stuck in the mud. Maybe you can help me? "

" We're Navahos. Wait. I ask and see what we can do."

" Nava Whos? "

" Nava Hoes. Indians."

" Glad to meet you," I said. " I often heard about you fellows, but I never expected to have the good luck to see."

So he rode to the back and talked with an old man. Meantime I told my party, " It's Indians."

Anna Feodorovna went on her knees, crossed herself, and started to pray out loud. His Excellency jumped off the unpacked sofa where he's resting and started throwing fire tongs and walking canes and pokers around like a crazy man. " Where's my sword? My sword! My sword! "

Ermak turned the kitchen table over, piled the chairs up, and crouched down behind it. " Don't be afraid," he said to Madame Greshkin, " before I die I try to shoot you and Luba, too, but if God wills overwise — " he opened a drawer in his barricade and pulled out a butcher knife, " use this, but don't ever let them take you alive."

" Shut up," Luba said. She tipped the mirror in the bureau, patted her curls in place, and put on a second coat of face. " Come on, Artash," she took his hand. " Sister's gonna take you to see the Indians."

" I take myself," Artash said. " Let go my arm."

Meantime Indian came back. " All right," he said. He waved his arms and the rest followed after him, and they drove their horses and wagons down into the water.

" Hi-ya. Hi."

" Hi," another one yells. And one, two,

three, truck was out, and next they pulled the car across.

"I guess you're like a village," I said to young Indian when all this was over, "so I like to meet your headman."

He took me to an old Indian that made me Ow-Ow-Ow sounds. I don't know what it meant but for politeness I did the same back to him. We was sitting quiet for a few minutes after that, both of us figuring out, I guess, what kind of man the other was. Finally I asked the young fellow how much they wanted for their work.

They talked some more together and at last he said, "Nothing."

I expected maybe it was gonna happen like this, so I prepared myself on the way over to them. I had a five-dollar bill ready, and so it doesn't look like pay, I wrapped it up in a nice red silk handkerchief I had.

I offered it to the old Indian. He looked over the money and the handkerchief on every side, and then he said something and pretty soon another Indian brought a good belt up and handed it to me. Few minutes more passed and then the young Indian came back and gave me a five-dollar gold piece.

So now it looked like we were good friends.

I asked the young Indian if he would sell me a sheep. After some more talk they brought one up.

"Now," I told them, "I'd like to invite all you boys to a party. I cook you a sheep how we do it in my country. Agreeable?"

I killed and skinned and cleaned it, and then I cut broiling sticks, and Artash and two little Indian kids built me fire, and I made *shashlik*.

They're funny people, Indians. Soon I started to make my way they killed another sheep and cooked too. Only different from me.

After about two hours passed, it was all ready. I called my party, but they wouldn't come.

"Certainly not," Anna Feodorovna said, "my childrens might catch something from them. Look at their clothes."

"No, no." His Excellency had found his sword and buckled it on. "No, Ermak and me stay on guard here. For your own protection, Giorgi Ivanitch. They might turn on you any time."

Luba wouldn't even answer me. She was sulking in a corner like a cat got its tail stepped on.

So only Artash came along. I started with old headman and passed a good smoking hot stickful of meat to everyone, about twenty or twenty-five of them altogether in the order what I guessed their ages was.

I don't know if they liked it or not, but anyway they was eating with loud sounds.

When we were all finished the young Indian, the one does all my talking for me, came up. He said, "My grandfather likes the way you kill sheep and clean and cook. He wants to know what tribe you come from. How many sheep you have? Is good hunting there?"

"I'm Georgian," I said, "from the other side of the world. In our village was about two hundred sheep last time I knew. If we kill with care, our hunting is enough for all."

Young Indian gave me a little piece of thing from stone, and I didn't have much left except a combination corkscrew knife so I made him present of that. We shaked hands, and they all rode away.

"I think they the most filthy disgusting people in the world," Anna Feodorovna said. "They smell." We got the furniture all loaded on and were ready to start off again.

"And ugly, too," Luba said. "Hideous."

"They're savages," His Excellency said, packing his sword back in the umbrella stand. "Can't expect more. Wild savages."

"Served you right, all of you, if they left you in the river," I said. "For my part I think they knew how to act like men, and they did."

Being stuck in the river bed didn't do my truck any good, but I went limping across Colorado and down through Arizona trying to keep up with them in the other car.

My two rear wheels were giving me

trouble. The old hard rubber tires started to spin loose and I patched them up best I could but it meant I had to stop so often the others were getting restless. So finally they decided they better go on ahead and we meet all in California.

When we started the trip we each put thirty dollars travel money in the pot and Anna Feodorovna kept this in her charge and from it she was gonna pay for gas and our sleeping and what food we bought and the post cards and so on.

Now if we separate we have to divide up our cash. Anna Feodorovna opened her purse. Well! Nobody is more surprised than her to find only $8.75 left.

" Good lord," Ermak said, " What happened to the rest? " We all listening to hear the answer to this.

Anna Feodorovna looked through everything again. Shook the lining, emptied her cardcase; thumbed through her papers. " I know," she said at last. " I know exactly what happened. I spent it." She started to cry. " I'm a thief."

" Stop crying," I said. " Can't do anything now. Scrape your pockets, everybody, and let's see how we stand."

Ermak turned his inside out. Empty. Artash had three dollars he was saving this long time to buy an automobile. Madame Greshkin asked us if we please be so kind to all get out of the car. We did and she pulled down the window shades. We stood on the road. Five, ten minutes passed. At last she snapped up the curtains, opened the door, and gave us a five dollar bill. His Excellency added $1.25 to that. If Luba had anything she didn't tell. Now put all together with fifteen dollars I had, we got thirty-three dollars exactly and California still six hundred miles away.

After a lot of talk they decided they take twenty-five dollars and go all in the car to Hollywood. I keep the other eight dollars and try to get to Yuma.

" You wait there," His Excellency said, " and inquire at the post office and in a coupla days we send you the money to come the rest of the way."

" Where you expect to get it from? "

" I have a nephew, my sister's oldest son, he came through Siberia to Los Angeles. He lends me."

" You know where he lives? "

" Certainly I know. He's my nephew, isn't he? "

" I make one more suggestion," I said. " And after that I save my words and sell to a dictionary. Let's go in the next town and whatever they offer for truck and furnitures we take it and go all in California."

Anna Feodorovna was in tears again. It was like talking to a wet sponge.

" All right," I said. " All right." So they take their suitcases and off they go. " And be sure you call at the general delivery in Yuma," His Excellency hollered out the back, last thing, " for your money."

I drove on past Gila Bend, past Sentinel, and even with no money, living on chili beans and soda crackers, I liked this part of the trip.

Soon as the sun went down I made a camp beside my truck and cooked whatever I had. Sometimes I talked to the men passing on the road. Sad men carrying blanket rolls like humps on their backs. That wouldn't be a life for me, I decided as I watched them walking, walking, walking. Walking to nowhere. If you're not father or husband, son or brother, neighbor or friend to somebody, who are you then to yourself?

And after in a minute night would come and the colors of the desert fade until nothing was left except maybe from a far-off cabin a lonesome light would poke a hole in the dark.

Best of all I liked when I could stop near tracks and all through the night wake up to see the trains go flashing back and forth like threaded needles lacing America together. No wonder in this country they save their most beautiful names to paint on the freight cars: the Atchison, Topeka and Santa Fe; the Delaware Lackawanna, Route of Rockets, Detroit and Mackinac, Huttig, Mansfield and Nacogdoches, Black Diamond and Nickel Plate.

So on I went and about ten miles outside

Yuma just when I'm congratulating myself everything gonna be O.K. my right rear tire whipped off and curled and uncurled itself across the sand like a big snake.

One look and I knew that was finished. I sat and waited almost the whole afternoon for somebody to pass and give me a lift into town. Not a single car. Then I tried to see if I could make it on the rim. Mile of that and I was riding on a square wheel.

So I pulled over and made myself comfortable. Looked like this be my home for some time. Next morning I managed to get into Yuma. No letter so I shopped around in all the junk yards and at last I found a good Ford wheel — but for $10. I had $4.50. I waited for afternoon mail. Again nothing.

Back to my truck. Next day I went after my letter again. Not yet. So almost a week passed this way and once every day, at least, I went in town and I got to know that road and every bush and cow skulleton and tin can and old piece of wreck beside it like the inside of my own hand.

And at last one morning I went in the post office, man knew me by now. " Here's your letter," he said.

But it wasn't a letter. It was a post card. Picture of palm trees on one side, " Main Street looking east " the printing said. I don't care which direction he looks. I turned over. His Excellency's hand. " We come in here O.K. Thanks be to God. Weather is fine. We was twice on the beach. Artash saw a movie star in the fish market." Few more lines. Gave their address. Down at bottom was P.S., " I didn't find my nephew yet, but don't worry. I keep looking."

I went out on the steps of the post office and sat down to think. Finally I made up my mind what I'm going to do. I went back in the junk yard. Will he give me Ford wheel for four dollars cash and I send him the rest? No. For four dollars cash and my camera? No. Four dollars cash, my camera, and my cuff links? No.

" I guess it wouldn't be any use to throw my head in either then," I said.

I went out. At the gate I stopped. " How much for this? " I asked him. It was an old Nash wheel lying in the grass . . . but all of a sudden it gave me idea.

" A dollar and stay out of my yard."

So I paid him and I started off rolling my wheel ahead of me. About mile out of town a car stopped and an American fellow gave me a lift. He didn't say nothing to me so I did the same to him until he came near the bend and then I asked him if he minded to stop a minute I want to pick up an old wreck battery I saw lying there. He pulled up. " Are you a junkman? " he said.

" No," I told him. " My car, Ford truck, broke down and I lost my wheel and I'm going to put this wheel on instead."

He turned and looked back at it. " That's a Nash wheel," he said. " Somebody stung you."

" I know is a Nash wheel, but I'm gonna use anyway."

" Won't fit."

" I make fit."

" Can't."

" I can try." Just then I remembered something about Americans. This is gonna get me to California, I thought to myself. " Sure I can," I said out loud. " I know I can. I bet you twenty bucks I put on and my truck runs."

We was up to my truck now. I had all the furniture unloaded off and the frame braced with some wood. He got out and looked it all over. " Twenty bucks it don't run." He sat down on the running board to watch me what I'm gonna do next.

I gathered twigs and started a fire with scraps of paper on a piece of old tin and when it got going good I threw the battery on. Meantime I raised my truck a little higher with the jack and took the wheel off. I tried the Nash wheel on the Ford hub. Fitted pretty loose. By this time man got so interested he was gathering brushes to keep the battery burning. Finally the lead I wanted melted out from the battery on to the tin and I poured a little into the wheel and hub joint and filled up the holes and worked it into shape until it fitted good. Then I put the wheel on and drove a few hundred feet.

Everything O.K. Only my truck looked now like he came back from the wars with one leg shorter than the other.

" Son of a gun! " man said. " I never believed it if I didn't see. Lucky thing for you that you remembered that old battery."

" No," I said, " the lucky thing was I remembered Americans always ready to bet on anything."

He peeled off two ten-dollar bills. " You win. But you're wasting your time on automobiles." He got in his car. " Try the horses."

I was thinking over that while I loaded the furnitures on again. Some kind of joke he meant, because even I know is impossible to change horses' legs around. If they break one, have to shoot.

So I'm back in Yuma with twenty dollars cash and I buy the Ford wheel and put on, eat a nice supper, and I'm ready to start.

So I rode along. I didn't have too much money, but I ate slim and I managed. The last night I was almost there so I decided not to sleep but just keep going and about midnight I pulled into Los Angeles. I found address His Excellency wrote me, but they weren't living there any more. " No," landlady said. " They moved all in Hollywood." She gave me another address.

I kept going. All kinds of curved streets and up and down roads, but at last I came to place. I rang and rang until I woke them up and they all came tumbling down the stairs, His Excellency still in his nightcap with the red tassel.

They turned on the lights. Quite a place they rented. Sofa made out of pipes and blue leather chairs and glass tables. Looked like good, dollar-a-haircut barber shop.

" Well, here is I am," I said. " I thought I never make it. I went — " Luba came trailing down the stairs in some kind of thing made out of pink fur, be interesting to see the animal that fur came off of —

" And now, Anna Feodorovna," I finished my story, " your worries are over. We unload the furnitures right now and you can tell us where to put it."

" Put it? " Luba said. " What we care

where you put it, that old junk. We bought this. Put it in the scrap heap." She turned up her nose like a bulldog. " I'm in the movies now."

## Suggestions for Study

1. Do you think the poor English adds to or detracts from the story? Explain.

2. Describe the character of the person who you think was most effectively characterized.

3. In what ways were these Russians different from most people you know?

4. What did you think was the funniest incident in the selection?

5. Mention some shrewd bits of wisdom you remember, such as, " I saw everybody is a foreigner."

6. Describe a foreign dish which you have tasted. Did you like it?

7. Vocabulary: samovar, icon.

## Lincoln Steffens     1866–1936

During the first decade of this century everyone was reading Lincoln Steffens' exposures of political corruption, which appeared first in *McClure's Magazine* and later in book form. These set the style for a great period of " muckraking." But when a history professor addressed Steffens as the first of the " muckrakers," he replied that the prophets of the Old Testament were ahead of him, and pointed out that President Theodore Roosevelt had taken the term from Bunyan's *Pilgrim's Progress*. The details of these exposures are matters of the past, but the experiences of a man who has probed into the substrata of political and economic intrigue are of permanent interest. When Lincoln Steffens' *Autobiography* appeared in 1931, it captured the fancy of the public at once and was hailed as one of the great American autobiographies. The author's long journalistic experience enabled him to write with an easy yet exciting style. It is the kind of book that is as fascinating as a novel, and at the same time opens up innumerable problems of our modern life. The frankness of treatment which made his early articles breathtaking is characteristic of this book also, whether he is discussing himself or others. One chapter is characteristically called " Muckraking Myself — a Little."

## I BECOME A REPORTER

Born into a well-to-do family of San Francisco, Steffens in his early life was typical of the young American with money and family protection behind him. But the following chapter shows him suddenly thrown upon his own resources at the end of an expensive education. In some measure Steffens' problem is that of a large proportion of American youth today: " After college — what? "

When my ship sailed into New York harbor, my father's agent brought down to quarantine a letter which I still remember, word perfect, I think.

MY DEAR SON: When you finished school you wanted to go to college. I sent you to Berkeley. When you got through there, you did not care to go into my business; so I sold out. You preferred to continue your studies in Berlin. I let you. After Berlin it was Heidelberg; after that Leipzig. And after the German university you wanted to study at the French universities in Paris. I consented, and after a year with the French, you had to have half a year of the British Museum in London. All right. You had that too.

By now you must know about all there is to know of the theory of life, but there's a practical side as well. It's worth knowing. I suggest that you learn it, and the way to study it, I think, is to stay in New York and hustle.

Enclosed please find one hundred dollars, which should keep you till you can find a job and support yourself.

This letter made me feel as if the ship were sinking under me; I had to swim. I did not know how, not in those waters, but it was not fear that hit me so hard. Nor disappointment. I had no plans to be disturbed. My vague idea was to go home to California and " see " what chance there was, say, at some college, to teach or lecture on the theories of ethics while making a study of morals: the professional ethics and the actual conduct of men in business, politics, and the professions. I could get no academic position in the East, where I was not known, but I might carry on my research as an insider in business just as well

LINCOLN STEFFENS' autobiography is one of the books of permanent worth in the twentieth century. He was the most skilful interviewer in American journalism.

as I could as an observer. My wife asked me how I was going to go about getting a job in business and how meanwhile we were to live. For the first time, I think, I realized that I was expected to support my wife and that meanwhile my wife expected my father to help us. And my father would have done it. He said afterward that if he had known that I was married, he would not have thrown me off as he did — for my good, " just to see what you could do for yourself," he said. My wife was for telling him then and there, but I could not. I declared that I would never ask my father for another cent, and I didn't. The next money transaction between us was a loan I made to him.

No, my father was putting me to a test, I said, and I would show him. And my mother-in-law, Mrs. Bontecou, backed me up. She said she would see us through with her little money. Josephine was angry, and, in brief, ours was a gloomy landing party.

I alone was cheerful, secretly; I had an idea. I would write.

At the small hotel Josephine knew, I took pencil and paper and I wrote a short story, " Sweet Punch." That was a Saturday. I did it that day and rewrote and finished it on Sunday. Louis Loeb called that night. He was illustrating for *Harper's Magazine,* and he said he would offer them my story the next day. He sold it to them for fifty dollars. I sat me down to calculate. That story was done and sold in three days. Call it a week. I could make fifty dollars a week, which multiplied by fifty-two was, say, twenty-five hundred dollars a year. Enough to live on. But I didn't do another story that week nor the next. Too busy looking for a job, I excused; but the fact was that I couldn't do another for a month, and then the second story was rejected. It was years before I got into the magazines again.

It was weeks before I found a job. I was amazed at the difficulty. There I was, all dressed up in my beautiful morning coat with top hat, answering ads, any ads for anything, from an editorship to errand boy. Literally. The juvenile literature I had read as a boy, about lads who began at the bottom and worked up, had stuck. Here I was, what I had once grieved that I was not, a poor but willing young fellow, without parents, friends, or money, seeking a start in life, just a foothold on the first rung of the ladder; I would, like my boy heroes, attend to the rest. And I couldn't get the chance! I couldn't understand it.

The most urgent ads came from the water front, and I would go into one of those shabby little dirty, dark shops, where they dealt in ship furnishings or produce — dressed like a dude, remember; especially careful to be in my best to make a good first impression — and showing the clipping from the paper, ask for an opening. The shopkeeper would throw himself back in his chair and stare at me and sputter, " But — but do you think you can do the work? It's hard work and — and — are you — qualified? What has been your experience? " And I answered that I had

studied at Berkeley, Berlin, Heidelberg, the Sorbonne! And for some reason that seemed to end it.

Those were the days when businessmen were prejudiced against a college education. My father's partners had the prejudice. They warned him that his course with me would ruin me, and I think that it was they who advised him to drop me in New York and see who was right, he or they. Businessmen have learned since that college does not unfit average young men for anything but an intellectual career; they take them on and will tell you that the colleges are the best source in the world for cheap labor. But in my day, next to my clothes and general beautifulness, the heaviest handicap I had was my claim to a college education, and not only one college, but — five. Some employers dropped their hands and jaw and stared me silently out of their sight; others pushed me out, and others again — two I remember vividly — called in all hands to " see this college graduate that wants to clean the windows and run errands."

My father was right. As I went home to my wife and mother-in-law to describe life as I found it and businessmen as they found me, I had to confess that I was learning something, that life wasn't what I had expected from my reading. My money was all gone, all the one hundred and also the fifty dollars, and I was paying for myself alone. Mrs. Bontecou paid for her daughter, and soon she was paying for her son-in-law too. I became desperate. My father had given me a letter from the supervising editor of all the Southern Pacific Railroad publications, the monthly magazines, weeklies, and daily newspapers that " the Road " owned or subsidized, to an editor of the *Century Magazine.* I had not used it, because I preferred not to apply " pull." I was for getting my start in life on merit alone. Mrs. Bontecou was with me on that; Josephine was impatient and practical. She pressed me to deliver the letter of introduction, and I did. I asked Mr. Robert Underwood Johnson to give me an editorial position on the *Century.*

He read the letter, pondered, asked me questions, and sized me up. Seeing through my clothes and my story, I guess, he very cautiously asked me if I would be willing to start — just for the practice — to begin my editorial career as — a — reporter. Would I? I certainly would; I would have laid off my top hat to be a copy boy. That cleared the air for him; maybe it stripped off my English clothes. Anyway he offered to get me on either the *Tribune* or the *Evening Post,* and I went home, happy and proud, to discuss with my family the choice I had between those two New York papers.

I can't recall what decided us, but I think it was only that the *Evening Post* was an evening paper; I could be home at night and so have time to do some literary work. However it was, I took a note from Mr. Johnson to Joseph B. Bishop, an editorial writer on the *Post*. Bishop frowned, but he led me out to the city room and introduced me to Henry J. Wright, the city editor, who looked helplessly at me and, I thought, resentfully at Bishop.

" I don't need any more reporters," he said to Bishop, " but," to me, " you can come in next Monday and sit down out there with the reporters, and as I get a chance, I'll try you out — on space."

I didn't know what that meant, but I didn't care. I had a job. As I described it to my wife and her mother, Josephine was not elated as her mother was, and the next Monday when I sat out there in the city room, ignored, while all the world seemed to be in a whirl, I was not elated either. The next day I saw " Larry " Godkin, the editor who wrote the leaders I read and reread, admiring; he passed by the city door. Bishop nodded to me once, but neither Wright nor the other reporters looked my way. Interesting fellows they seemed to be; they must know all the mysteries of a great city. They did not talk much, but I overheard enough to infer that they were familiar and bored with sport, politics, finance, and society. I was awed by the way they would, upon a few words from the city editor, dart or loaf out of the room, be

gone an hour or so, come in, report briefly, and then sit down, write, turn in their copy carelessly, and lie back and read, idly read, newspapers.

One afternoon about one o'clock Mr. Wright came into the room, and seeing no one there but me, exclaimed impatiently and went out. A moment later he came back and right up to me.

"See here," he said, " there's a member of a stockbrokerage firm missing. Disappeared utterly. Something wrong. Go and see his partner and find out why the man is gone, whether there's funds missing too."

He handed me a memorandum giving the firm name and address in Wall Street. An assignment! I was to report. I darted out of the office into the elevator, and asking anybody for directions, found my way to Wall Street — Wall Street! — and the office of the lost broker. His partner rebuffed me. " No, I don't know why he skipped. No idea. No, nothing missing. How should there be? " But I wasn't going to fail on my first chance; so I persisted, asking questions, all about the missing man, his character, antecedents, habits, and when that caused only irritation, I asked about Wall Street. The broker soon was talking; we moved into his private office, sat down, and I told him the story of my life; he told me his, and I was thinking all the time how I could write something interesting about the ethics of a stockbroker; I had long since been convinced that the missing broker was innocent of anything more than a drink or an escapade with a woman, when all of a sudden the partner sprang up and said:

"Well, you are the most persistent son of a gun I ever met in all my life, and you win. I'll give you what you seem so sure of anyhow. My partner has not only skipped, I don't know where; he has taken every cent there was in the office, in the banks, and — then some." He named the amount, and I, astonished by the revelation, but satisfied that I had a front-page sensation, ran back to the office, where I astonished my city editor.

" Really? " he said. " You are sure? It's

libel, you know, if it's wrong. He told you himself, the partner did? Sure? Umh— Well, write it, and we'll see."

I had pencils all sharpened — sharpened every day — ready for this moment, and I went to work. It was easy enough to report the facts, but I felt I must write this big news as the news was written. That I had studied in my idle hours, the newspaper style, and that was not easy. I labored till the city editor darted out to see what I was doing; he saw; he read over my shoulder the writes and rewrites of my first paragraph, and picking up one, said, " This is enough." And away he went with it. All I had to do was to lie back in a chair and wait to read my stuff in print, a long wait, perhaps half an hour, till three o'clock, when the last edition went to press, and then twenty minutes before the paper came down. And then when it came down, the damp, smelly paper, my paragraph wasn't in it! I searched again and again, with anxiety, hope, dread. I did not care for the money; the space was too short to count, but I felt that my standing as a reporter was at stake, and so, when I was at last convinced that my " story " was left out, I got up and dragged home, defeated and in despair. I told Mrs. Bontecou about it, not my wife, and was comforted some. If I failed at journalism, the old lady argued, there still was literature.

The facts of my story appeared in the morning newspapers, but they were better, more neatly, briefly stated, than I had put them; perhaps I had failed, not as a reporter, but as a writer. And this conclusion was confirmed at the office, where the city editor said " Good morning " to me and, after all the other reporters were gone out, gave me an assignment to ask the superintendent of schools something. One more chance.

Braced to make the most of it, I gave that official a bad hour. He had to answer, not only the question the city editor asked, but others, many others. He found himself telling me all about the schools, education and its problems, and his policy. I had some ideas on that subject, and he got them; and he had to accept or refute them. He became so interested that, when he had to break off, I was invited to come back another day to " continue our conversation." Good. I returned to the office and wrote a column interview, beginning with the city editor's question and the answer. This time, when the paper came out it had my story, but cut down to the first question and answer, rewritten as an authoritative statement of fact. My reporting was all right; my writing was not. The next day, a Friday, I had to go out, confirm a reported suicide, and telephone the news, which another reporter took down and wrote.

That afternoon I saw reporters clipping from the cut files of the *Post*. I asked what it was for, and one of them said he was making up his bill. He cut out his own stories, stuck them together in a long strip, and measuring them with a foot rule, reckoned up the amount of space and charged for it so much a column. I did the same, and my poor little bill of earnings for my first week of practical life was something like two dollars and ten cents. And I was not ashamed of it; I was reassured, if not proud.

Nor was that all. As I was finishing this task the city editor called me up to his desk and bade me rewrite as a separate story for the Saturday paper the interview I had had with the superintendent of schools during the week. He suggested the idea or theme to write it around, and I, elated, stayed there in the office till closing time, grinding out my first long " story." And the next day I had the deep gratification of reading it at full length, the whole thing as I had written it. I measured it, secretly, and it came to four dollars plus — a fine start for my next week.

That Sunday was a bore; I could hardly wait for Monday to go on with my reporting, and talking with my wife and her mother, I developed ideas and plans. There were several promising questions to put to the superintendent of schools; the news suggested other men to see and talk to, and no doubt now the city editor himself would ask me to do more. When I walked into the office on Monday morning, eager and confident, I was dashed by the way I was ignored. No greetings from anybody, and as the morning wore on and the other reporters were sent off on assignments, I realized heavily that I was not to be used. I took my hat and told the city editor I would like to go out on a quest of my own. He nodded consent, and I went and had with the superintendent of schools a long interview which I wrote and handed in. It did not appear in the paper, and for two days I was ignored and got nothing out of my assignments. The men I tried to see were not in or would not see me. I had the experience so common for reporters of being defeated, and in an obscure way, too. Toward the end of the week I was sent out to see a rapid-transit commissioner and got some news which pleased the city editor: a formal, printed statement, which was printed. That was all. My space bill was about six dollars. But on Saturday, too late to be included, appeared my interview with the superintendent of schools.

With this to start with again, I could live over Sunday and was ready to dive on Monday into my journalism. I had to be my own city editor, but I could be, now. I got another school story, which was printed; it was news; and another which was held, I knew now, for Saturday. I called again on the rapid-transit commissioner, and he gave me a brief interview which I used to tempt the other commissioners to answer. That was news and appeared right away. So was a statement by the mayor which I went for all by myself. Somebody had said something in print that was critical in a small way of some department, and his office being open to the public I walked in and talked to him about it. My bill that week was something like fifteen dollars.

My system was working, and, I learned afterward, was amusing the staff and interesting the city editor, who described it as I could not have described it. It was a follow-up system, well known in journalism but unknown to me as a method. Every

time I was sent to or met a man in a position to furnish news, I cultivated him as a source and went back repeatedly to him for more news or more general views on the news. If there was a news story in the papers, and not too big, I would read it through for some angle overlooked and slip out to the persons involved and ask some questions. My contribution often appeared as a part of some other reporter's story, usually at the end, but several times as the lead. And always there were school-news articles from my superintendent, who was talking policy to me weekly and letting me visit and write about schools. These articles brought letters to the editor, which showed that we were tapping a field of interest. I had a free hand here till, later, there was an education department which included the universities and private schools, and so brought in advertising. But there was the art museum, too, to " cover " and report; rapid transit with its plans, not only for transportation in the city, but for real estate, park, and street development. Every time the city editor sent me into a field for a bit of news I got what he wanted and went back for more general reports. He used me very little, however, leaving me to my own devices; and his reason came out when, after a few months, my bills were running up to fifty, sixty, and more dollars a week, and the other reporters were taking rather unfriendly notice of me.

One Friday, as I was making out my bill, William G. Sirrene, a fine Southern boy who was one of the star reporters, looked over my shoulder and exclaimed, " What's that? Seventy-two dollars! Why, that's nearly three times what I'm getting on salary."

He called out to the others the amount of my bill, and when they also exclaimed, he explained, " Why, you are the best-paid man on the staff! "

I felt like exclaiming myself. It was news to me. I had no knowledge of salaries or earnings on the paper; all I knew was that I was supporting myself and my wife at last, saving a little each week, and driving on for more, and more. And I would have given it all to be a regular reporter like Sirrene or the others, and that is what I was asked to do. I think now that some of the reporters, not Sirrene, " kicked " to the city editor that I, a new man, was being paid more than they were, the veterans. Anyway he sent for me and, explaining that my bills were running too high, asked me if I would be changed from space to a salary, the best salary they paid the ordinary reporter, thirty-five dollars a week.

" Then," he said, " I can use you more myself on more important news."

I not only consented, I was dazed with the implication of my triumph. All became clear in that short talk with my chief. I had not been sent off on assignments because I was making too much money on my own and I had " made good." Even my first disappointment, the failure to print my news of the defalcation of the missing broker, was to my credit. The city editor did not dare print the report, by a new and untried man, of a piece of libelous news; he had sent an old reporter down to confirm it, and the broker who had talked to me not only repeated what he told me; he had spoken well of me; but by the time the confirmation was delivered, it was too late. The paper was gone to press, I was " reliable, quick, and resourceful," the city editor said, as he made me a regular reporter.

In a word I was a success, and though I have never since had such a victory and have come to have some doubt of the success of success, I have never since failed to understand successful men; I know, as I see them, how they feel inside.

## Suggestions for Study

1. Point out details of Mr. Steffens' search for a job which a young person of today might experience. Which are somewhat different from the average experience of today?

2. What new impression of the inside of newspaper life do you gain from this chapter? Does it attract or repel you? How do the experiences of reporters on your school paper compare with this?

3. Characterize Mr. Steffens, his wife, and his mother-in-law. How does the last compare with the stock conception of mothers-in-law?

4. Point out examples of Mr. Steffens' frankness in writing both of himself and of the people who had some part in his life.

5. Select good examples of Mr. Steffens' vivid style, his use of short clinching sentences, of suspense, of climax.

6. You will enjoy reading other parts of this *Autobiography*, especially Part I, leading up to the chapter you have read, which opens Part II.

7. Write an account, from your own experience if possible, of looking for a job, reporting for the school paper, or something else suggested by this chapter.

## For Your Vocabulary

CONTEXT. The meaning of the legal term *libel* (li'bĕl), which played an important part in the handling of Steffens' first news story, should be quite clear from context. *Libel* is the printing or public pronouncement of damaging opinions or facts, and the injured person may take legal action to collect damages. You often read in the papers of people or publishing firms being sued for *libel*. The word is used generally, too, of damaging remarks less formally made, as in saying that much gossip is *libel*.

SPECIALIZED VOCABULARY. You will come across many other legal terms that are used generally in a sense less formal than the official meaning. Soon you will find *indictment* (ĭn-dīt'mĕnt) used in the legal sense of a formal charge of wrongdoing. Any clear statement of an existing evil or wrong idea supported by explanation and facts may be called an *indictment*. A novel that pictures clearly a bad condition is often called an *indictment* of that evil. In contrast, an *allegation* (ăl-ē-gā'shŭn) is an unproved, often unsupported charge. One party in a lawsuit may *allege* (ă-lĕj') something that cannot be proved. So to call a statement an *allegation* is to throw doubt on its truth. Still another legal term you will encounter is *arraign* (ă-rān'), to call before a court on a formal charge of wrongdoing. When you come to Mark Twain's statement (page 684) that he could not remember hearing the institution of slavery *arraigned*, you will have a good example of the way these legal terms have passed into the general language.

# Marquis James · 1891–

Marquis James, who won a Pulitzer prize in 1930 for his life of Houston, *The Raven,* was a successful journalist before he became a biographer. Working with the historian's care for accuracy and with the journalist's flair for interesting narrative, he has made his books read like novels while faithfully recreating true happenings. Since *The Raven* he has again won the Pulitzer prize, this time with a two-volume biography of another great frontier warrior and statesman who was a close friend of Houston's — Andrew Jackson. James's latest — and many think his best — book is *The Cherokee Strip,* the story of his own boyhood in Oklahoma.

## SAM HOUSTON AT SAN JACINTO

The story of Sam Houston reads like an epic. His was an epic background, stretching from the nation's capital to the Indian territory on the west and into the shadow of Spain in the southwest. He knew the life of the frontier community, of the military camp, of state and national capitals, and of the Indian tribe. He was governor of two states, member of Congress from one and of the United States Senate from the other, and President of the Republic of Texas. In the intervals of his public career he lived as a member of the tribe with the Cherokee Indians, who had adopted him as a boy and had given him the name of " The Raven." After his first spectacular rise to fame collapsed with his resignation as Governor of Tennessee, he returned to his Indian friends; and from the Cherokees he went on to his second great achievement in leading Texas to independence. But Fortune, though she smiled often and brightly on Houston, was never constant to him. After his brilliant success in Texas as general, President, and Senator, he was forced from the governor's chair in 1861 when he bitterly opposed secession. To Houston, bringing Texas into the United States was his greatest triumph; and it was in the shadow of defeat that he died in 1863, before he could know that the union was to be preserved. His biographer spoke truth in saying that his " finger tips had touched the stars and felt them change to dust."

Just before the battle of San Jacinto (St. Hyacinth) the affairs of Texas were in perilous condition. One brave force had been wiped out in the disaster at the Alamo; and during the retreat in process at the beginning of this narrative Houston received news that the best-trained army of the Texans had been trapped at Goliad and after surrender had been treacherously slaughtered. Texans were fleeing in droves toward the safety of the United States beyond the Sabine. Nor was the precarious military situation Houston's only worry. The hastily organized government of the young republic was proving more hindrance than help to its one able commander left in the field. As you read, you will see that Houston was as busy keeping his little army together as he was planning his campaign against Santa Anna, the Mexican President and commander.

Word that Santa Anna had abruptly abandoned his attempt to cross at San Felipe found Houston in a buoyant mood. He had just received his long-awaited guns — two iron six-pounders, the gift of friends in Cincinnati. Clad in a worn leather jacket, he was watching the camp blacksmith cut up old horseshoes for artillery ammunition, when a young soldier said that the lock on his rifle would not work. " All right, son," said General Houston, " set her down and call around in an hour." The boy came back, stammering an apology. He was a recruit, he said, and did not know that the man pointed out to him as a blacksmith was the commander in chief. " My friend, he told you right. I am a very good blacksmith," replied Houston, taking up the gun and snapping the lock. " She is in order now."

The next two days Houston devoted to moving his army across the Brazos, while Santa Anna crossed near Fort Bend. The Texans encamped on the premises of a well-to-do settler named Donahoe, who demanded that Houston stop the men from cutting his timber for firewood. General Houston reprimanded the wood gatherers. Under no circumstances, he said, should they lay ax to another of Citizen Donahoe's trees. Could they not see that Citizen Donahoe's rail fence would afford the fuel required? That night the army gallants scraped up an acquaintance with some girls in a refugee camp, turned Mr. Donahoe out of house, and held a dance.

When the army left Donahoe's at dawn Moseley Baker [1] demanded to know whether Houston intended to intercept Santa Anna at Harrisburg [2] or to retreat to the Sabine. The general declined to answer. Seventeen miles from Donahoe's the road forked, the left branch leading to Nacogdoches and the Sabine, the right branch to Harrisburg. If Houston should attempt to take the left road, Captain Baker proclaimed that he would " then and there be deposed from command." Rain slowed the march, however, and only by borrowing draft oxen from Mrs. Mann of a refugee band that followed the army did the troops by nightfall reach Sam McCurley's, a mile short of the cross-roads.

Next morning a torrential rain failed to extinguish the excitement in the ranks. Which road would Houston take? The menacing Baker thundered warnings, but the Sabine route had its partisans among the troops. All of the refugees favored it. The commander in chief treated the commotion as if it did not exist and without comment sent the advance guard over the Harrisburg Road.

A wail arose from the refugees. There was a halt and a wrangle which Houston terminated by ordering Wily Martin to escort the refugees and watch for Indian hostilities to the eastward. The commander in chief thought this cleared the path for his pursuit of Santa Anna, but he had reckoned without Mrs. Mann. She demanded the return of her oxen. Wagon Master Rohrer, a giant in buckskin with a voice like a bull, brushed the protest aside as too trivial for the attention of a man of affairs, and cracking his long whip, addressed the oxen in the sparkling idiom of the trail. Whereupon

Mrs. Mann produced from beneath her apron a pistol and, if rightly overheard, addressed Mr. Rohrer in terms equally exhilarating. General Houston arrived in time to compose the difficulty with his usual courtly deference to the wishes of a lady.

Three or four hundred men followed Martin, or departed independently, leaving Houston with less than a thousand to follow Santa Anna, who rode with a magnificent suite at the head of a picked force of veterans. But Santa Anna was now the pursued and Houston the pursuer. General Santa Anna commanded the center of three armies. The rains, however, had fought on Houston's side, and there was a chance that by fast marching he might catch the Mexican commander in chief out of reach of his co-operating columns. Another factor in Houston's favor was the Sabine retreat story. Houston had never intended to fall back to the Sabine, but the report was so persistently circulated and never denied that the Mexicans included it in their strategic calculations.

Over the boggy prairie path, by courtesy the Harrisburg Road, Houston drove the little column fearfully. Nothing delayed the advance. Wagons were carried over quagmires on the backs of the men. The greatest trial was the guns. In camp the enthusiastic soldiers had christened them the " Twin Sisters," but now they thought of other names.

On the morning of April 18 the army reached the Buffalo Bayou, opposite Harrisburg, having covered fifty-five miles in two and a half days. Mounts and men were dead beat. Houston had never been in this part of the country before. He spent his nights in constant touch with the scouts and in the study of a crude map, covered with cabalistic pencilings of his own.

The army rested. Harrisburg was in ashes; Santa Anna had come and gone. Deaf Smith [3] swam the bayou and toward evening returned with two prisoners, a Mexican scout and a courier. The courier's sad-

---

[1] **Baker:** one of the discontented followers who, with the Wily Martin mentioned a little later, had already tried to stir up mutiny against Houston. [2] **Harrisburg:** The capital of the Republic had been transferred only a few days earlier from Washington on the Brazos to Harrisburg as a place of greater safety. Harrisburg is at the edge of the present city of Houston.

[3] **Deaf Smith:** a famous scout, for whom a county in Texas was named.

dlebag bore the name of W. B. Travis [1] —
souvenir of the Alamo. It contained useful
information. Santa Anna had dashed upon
Harrisburg with eight hundred troops in an
effort to capture President Burnet, leaving
Cos to follow. But the raid netted only three
printers who had stuck to their cases in the
office of Gail Borden's *Texas Telegraph*.
Editor Borden and the government had fled
to Galveston Island in the nick of time,
with Santa Anna racing in futile pursuit to
take them before they left the mainland.
On his soiled map Houston traced the situation of his quarry, not ten miles away,
groping among the unfamiliar marshes that
indented Galveston Bay and the estuary of
a certain nebulous Rio San Jacinto. Sending his army to bed, the commander in
chief continued to pore over the chart. Two
hours before dawn he slept a little.

After the daybreak stand-to, General
Houston delivered a speech. The " ascending eloquence and earnestness " put one
impressionable young soldier in mind of
" the halo encircling the brow of our Sa-
vior." " Victory is certain! " Sam Houston
said. " Trust in God and fear not! And
remember the Alamo! Remember the
Alamo! "

" Remember the Alamo! " the ranks
roared back. They had a battle cry.

There was just time for a short letter to
Anna Raguet's [2] father: " This morning we
are in preparation to meet Santa Anna. . . .
It is wisdom growing out of necessity."

The pick of the army advanced, leaving
the sick and the wagons with a rear guard.
After a swift march Houston made a perilous crossing of Buffalo Bayou, using the
floor torn from a cabin as a raft. The column hid in a wood until dark, and then
advanced warily, encircled by the scouts
under Deaf Smith and Henry Karnes. At a
narrow bridge over a stream — Vince's

SAM HOUSTON, leading the Texans at
San Jacinto, when " Remember the Alamo "
became the victorious battle cry. (Culver)

bridge over Vince's Bayou, men who knew
the country said — the column trampled
the cold ashes of Santa Anna's campfires.
The night was black and the advance painfully slow. Equipment had been muffled so
as to make no sound. A low-spoken order
passed from rank to rank to be ready on the
instant to attack. Rifles were clutched a little closer. One mile, two miles beyond the
bridge, down a steep ravine and stealthily
up the other side crept the column.

At two o'clock in the morning the word
came to break ranks. In the damp grass the
men dropped beside their arms. With the
salt of the sea in their nostrils they slept
for an hour; then formed up and stumbled
on until daybreak, when their general concealed them in a patch of timber.

Some of the Vince brothers' cows were
grazing in this wood. The army had a commissary! Throats were noiselessly cut and
General Houston had given permission to
build fires when a party of scouts dashed
up. They had driven off a Mexican patrol

---

[1] **W. B. Travis:** commander of the garrison at
the Alamo when it was annihilated by the Mexicans. It was this massacre which furnished the
Texan battle cry, "Remember the Alamo!" [2] **Anna
Raguet** (rȧ-gĕ′): a young lady of Nacogdoches to
whom Houston was very attentive at this time.

and learned that Santa Anna was on the road to Lynch's Ferry. The butchers were called from their delectable task and the fires pulled apart. The men fell in to the banging of muskets and the clank of ramrods as old charges were fired [1] and fresh ones sent home. The breakfastless army headed for Lynch's Ferry, three miles eastward. Santa Anna approached the ferry from the south, with five miles to go.

From the crest of a grass-grown slope Houston's army got its first view of Lynch's Ferry, lying at the tip of a point of lowland where Buffalo Bayou flowed into the San Jacinto River. On the farther side of the river was a scattering of unpainted houses — the town of Lynchburg. Behind the town bulged a round hill, the side of which was covered with people who gazed for a moment at the column filing down the slope, and then melted away. They were Texas Tories waiting to pilot Santa Anna toward the Sabine.

Having the choice of positions, Houston established himself in a wood of great oak trees, curtained with Spanish moss, that skirted the bayou just above its junction with the San Jacinto. He posted the infantry and cavalry in order of battle within the thick shelter, and placed the Twin Sisters on the edge of the trees so as to command the swelling savanna that lay in front of the woods. This semitropical prairie extended to the front for nearly a mile, thick with waving green grass, half as high as wheat. A wood bounded the prairie on the left, screening a treacherous swamp that bordered the San Jacinto. Swamp and river swung to the right, half enclosing the prairie and giving it a background of green a tone darker than the active young grass. Over this prairie Santa Anna must pass to gain the ferry.

The Texans were prepared to fight, but the presence of cows in the grass revealed the force of Napoleon's famous maxim.[2]

Again the fires crackled, and this time steaks were sizzling on the spits when the scouts came galloping across the plain. They said that Santa Anna was advancing just beyond a rise. The Twin Sisters were wheeled out a little piece on the prairie. The infantry crept to the edge of the woods.

Santa Anna's bugles blared beyond the swell. A dotted line of skirmishers bobbed into view, and behind it marched parallel columns of infantry and of cavalry with slender lances gleaming. Between the columns Santa Anna advanced a gun. The skirmishers parted to let the clattering artillerymen through.

The Twin Sisters were primed and loaded with broken horseshoes. General Houston, on a great white stallion, rode up and down the front of his infantry. Under partial cover of a clump of trees, three hundred yards from the Texan lines, the Mexican gun wheeled into position.

Joe Neill, commanding the Twin Sisters, gave the word for one gun to fire. *Crash* went the first shot by Sam Houston's artillery in the war. There had been no powder for practice rounds. Through the ragged smoke the Texans could see Mexican horses down and men working frantically at their piece. Their captain had been wounded and the gun carriage disabled.

*Crash!* The second Twin cut loose, and the Mexican gun replied. Its shot tore through the branches of the trees above the Texans' heads, causing a shower of twigs.

*Rat-tat!* The Mexican skirmishers opened fire, and plumes of black dirt jumped in front of the Texas infantry. A ball glanced from a metal trimming on General Houston's bridle. Colonel Neill dropped with a broken hip.

The Texan infantrymen had held their beads on the dotted line for so long that their faces ached. Every dot was covered by ten rifles, for no Texan had to be told when he shot to shoot *at* something. A row of flaming orange jets rushed from the woods and expired in air; the dotted gray line sagged into the grass and did not reappear.

---

[1] **old charges were fired:** so as to have fresh powder in the guns when the battle commenced.
[2] **Napoleon's famous maxim:** that an army travels on its stomach.

The Twin Sisters whanged away and the Mexican gun barked back, but the state of its carriage made accurate aim impossible. Santa Anna decided not to bring on a general engagement, and sent a detachment of dragoons to haul off the crippled gun. Dashing Sidney Sherman begged to take the cavalry and capture the Mexican fieldpiece, and finally Houston consented. Sherman lost two men and several horses, but failed to get the gun. General Houston gave him a dressing-down that should have withered the leaves on the trees. A private by the conquering name of Mirabeau Buonaparte Lamar [1] who had borne himself courageously was promoted to command the cavalry regiment, numbering fifty-three.

Sherman was considerable of a camp hero just the same — he and Deaf Smith, who had captured the ferryboat loaded with Mexican flour. Dough, rolled on sticks and baked by the fire, made the postponed meal notable, after which the men spread blankets by the fires and talked themselves to sleep over the big fight that was to take place in the morning. Less than a mile away, under the watchful eyes of Houston's scouts, flickered the campfires of the enemy.

On the twenty-first of April, 1836, reveille rolled at the usual hour of four, but a strange hand [2] tapped the drum. The commander in chief was asleep, with a coil of rope under his head. He had left instructions not to be disturbed. It was evident that the anticipated dawn attack would not take place. The ranks silently stood to until daylight, precisely as they had done every other morning, except that the commander in chief slept through it all. Nor did the soldier hum of breakfast time arouse him. It was full day when Sam Houston opened his eyes — after his first sleep of more than three hours in six weeks. He lay on his back, studying the sky. An eagle wheeled before the flawless blue. The commander in chief sprang to his feet. " The

sun of Austerlitz," [3] he said, " has risen again."

An eagle over the Cumberland [4] on that awful April night — an eagle over the muddier Rubicon [5] — an eagle above the plain of St. Hyacinth. Did these symbolic birds exist, or were they simply reflections of a mind drenched with Indian lore? The eagle was Sam Houston's medicine animal. When profoundly moved it was from the Indian part of his being and not the white-man part that unbidden prayers ascended.

The camp was in a fidget to attack. It could not fathom a commander who sauntered aimlessly under the trees in the sheer enjoyment, he said, of a good night's sleep. Deaf Smith rode up and dismounted. The lines of the old plainsman's leathery face were deep. His short square frame moved with a heavy tread. The scout was very weary. Night and day he and Henry Karnes had been the eyes of the army; and considering the tax of the other faculties that deafness imposed upon a scout, the achievements of Smith elude rational explanation.

" Santa Anna is getting reinforcements," he said in his high-pitched voice. And surely enough a line of pack mules was just visible beyond the swell in the prairie. " They've just come over our track. I'm going to tell the general he ought to burn Vince's bridge before any more come up."

After a talk with Smith, Houston told his commissary general, John Forbes, to find two sharp axes, and then strolled past a gathering of soldiers remarking that it

---

[3] **Austerlitz:** a famous battle of Napoleon, in which both the relative numbers of men and the location of the forces resembled the situation at San Jacinto. [4] **Cumberland:** When he was fleeing Tennessee after the mysterious break with his first wife and his resignation as Governor of Tennessee, an eagle swooping over the river boat cheered him with the thought that a great destiny awaited him in the West. [5] **muddier Rubicon:** Julius Caesar's first step toward gaining control of the government in Rome was to lead his army back from Gaul across the border stream in defiance of the civil authorities. Since that time, "crossing the Rubicon" has meant committing oneself to a momentous enterprise. In coming to Texas, Houston called the Red River, the boundary, his "muddier Rubicon."

---

[1] **Lamar:** later President of the Republic of Texas. [2] **strange hand:** Houston usually beat tattoo and reveille himself.

wasn't often Deaf Smith could be fooled by a trick like that — Santa Anna marching men around and around to make it look like a reinforcement. Smith returned from another gallop on to the prairie. " The General was right," he announced loudly. " It's all a humbug." But privately he informed Houston that the reinforcement numbered five hundred and forty men under Cos, which raised Santa Anna's force to the neighborhood of thirteen hundred and fifty. Houston's strength was slightly above eight hundred.

Houston later told Santa Anna that his reason for waiting for Cos was to avoid making " two bites of one cherry." But he did not care to see Filísola, who might turn up at any time with two or three thousand Mexicans. Handing the axes to Smith, Houston told him to destroy Vince's bridge. " And come back like eagles, or you will be too late for the day."

Unaware of these preparations, the camp was working itself into a state. To all appearance the general was wasting good time, and jealous officers were only too eager to place this construction on the situation. At noon John A. Wharton, the adjutant general, with whom the commander in chief was not on the most cordial terms, went from mess to mess, stirring up the men. " Boys, there is no other word today, but fight, fight! " Moseley Baker harangued his company. They must neither give nor ask quarter, he said. Resting on his saddle horn, Houston narrowly observed the Baker proceedings. He rode on to a mess that Wharton had just addressed. Everyone was boiling for a fight. " All right," observed the general. " Fight and be damned."

Houston called a council of war — the first and last, but one, of his career. The question he proposed was, " Shall we attack the enemy or wait his attack upon us? " There was a sharp division of ideas. Houston expressed no opinion, and when the others had wrangled themselves into a thorough disagreement he dismissed the council.

At three-thirty o'clock the commander in chief abruptly formed his army for attack.

At four o'clock he lifted his sword. A drum and fife raised the air of a love song, " Come to the Bower," and the last army of the Republic moved from the woods and slowly up the sloping plain of San Jacinto. The left of the line was covered by the swamp, the right by the Twin Sisters, Millard's forty-eight regulars, and Lamar's fifty cavalry. A company from Newport, Kentucky, displayed a white silk flag, embroidered with an amateurish figure of Liberty. (The Lone Star emblem was a later creation.) A glove of the first lieutenant's sweetheart bobbed from the staff. On the big white stallion Sam Houston rode up and down the front.

" Hold your fire, men. Hold your fire. Hold your fire."

The mastery of a continent was in contention between the champions of two civilizations — racial rivals and hereditary enemies, so divergent in idea and method that suggestion of compromise was an affront. On an obscure meadow of bright grass, nursed by a watercourse named on hardly any map, wet steel would decide which civilization should prevail on these shores and which submit in the clash of men and symbols impending — the conquistador and the frontiersman, the Inquisition [1] and the Magna Charta,[2] the rosary and the rifle.[3]

For ten of the longest minutes that a man ever lives, the single line poked through the grass. In front lay a barricade of Mexican packsaddles and camp impedimenta, inert in the oblique rays of the sun.

" Hold your fire, men. Hold your fire."

Behind the Mexican line a bugle rang. A sketchy string of orange dots glowed from the packsaddles and a ragged rattle of musketry roused up a scolding swarm of birds from the trees on the Texan's left. A few

---

[1] **Inquisition:** medieval Spanish court of investigation famous for its severity. [2] **Magna Charta:** medieval English bill of rights, a contrasting symbol to the Inquisition. [3] **the rosary and the rifle:** Catholic missionaries were the vanguard of the growing Spanish empire in America, while the American penetration was led by frontiersmen and hunters.

Texans raised their rifles and let go at the dots.

" Hold your fire! Damn you, hold your fire! " General Houston spurred the white stallion to a gallop.

The orange dots continued to wink and die. The white stallion fell. Throwing himself upon a cavalryman's pony, Houston resumed his patrol of the line.

" Fight for your lives! Vince's bridge has been cut down! " It was Deaf Smith on a lathered mustang. Rather inaccurately, the soldiers understood Vince's bridge to be their sole avenue of retreat.

Twenty yards from the works, Houston made a signal with his hat. A blast of horseshoes from the Twin Sisters laid a section of the fragile breastwork flat. The infantrymen roared a volley and lunged forward drawing their hunting knives. " Remember the Alamo! Remember the Alamo! "

They swept over the torn barricade as if it had not been there. Shouts and yells and the pounding of hoofs smote their ears. Through keyholes in a pungent wall of smoke they saw gray-clad little figures, with chin straps awry, running back, kneeling and firing, and running back — toward some tents where greater masses of men were veering this way and that. The Texans pursued them. The pungent wall melted; the firing was not so heavy now, as the Texans were using their knives and the bayonets of Mexican guns. The surprise lacked nothing. Santa Anna had thought Houston would not, could not, attack. In his carpeted marquee, he was enjoying a siesta when a drowsy sentinel on the barricade descried the Texan advance. Cos's men were sleeping off the fatigue of their night march. Cavalrymen were riding bareback to and from water. Others were cooking and cutting wood. Arms were stacked.

When the barrier was overrun, a general of brigade rallied a handful of men about a fieldpiece; all fell before the Texans' knives. An infantry colonel got together a following under cover of some trees; a Texas sharpshooter killed him, and the following scattered. Almonte, the chief of staff,

rounded up four hundred men and succeeded in retreating out of the panic zone. Santa Anna rushed from his tent commanding everyone to lie down. A moment later he vaulted on a black horse and disappeared.

General Houston rode among the wreckage of the Mexican camp. He was on his third horse, and his right boot was full of blood. " A hundred steady men," he said, " could wipe us out." Except for a handful of regulars, the army had escaped control of its officers, and was pursuing, clubbing, knifing, shooting Mexicans wherever they were found. Fugitives plunged into the swamp and scattered over the prairie. " Me no Alamo! Me no Alamo! " Some cavalry bolted for bridgeless Vince's Bayou. The Texans rushed them down a vertical bank. A hundred men and a hundred horses, inextricably tangled, perished in the water.

Houston glanced over the prairie. A gray-clad column, marching with the swing of veterans, bore toward the scene of battle. After a long look the general lowered his field glass with a thankful sigh. Almonte and his four hundred were surrendering in a body.

As the sun of Austerlitz set, General Houston fainted in Hockley's arms. His right leg was shattered above the ankle. The other Texan casualties were six killed and twenty-four wounded. According to Texan figures the Mexicans lost 630 killed, 208 wounded, and 730 prisoners, making a total of 1,568 accounted for. This seems to be about two hundred more men than Santa Anna had with him.

The battle proper had lasted perhaps twenty minutes. The rest was in remembrance of the Alamo. This pursuit and slaughter continued into the night. The prisoners were herded in the center of a circle of bright fires. " Santa Anna? Santa Anna? " the Texans demanded until officers began to pull off their shoulder straps. But no Santa Anna was found.

After a night of pain General Houston propped himself against a tree; and Surgeon Ewing redressed his wound, which was more serious than had been supposed. While the surgeon probed fragments of bone from the mangled flesh, the patient fashioned a garland of leaves and tastefully inscribed a card " To Miss Anna Raguet, Nacogdoches, Texas: These are laurels I send you from the battlefield of San Jacinto. Thine. HOUSTON."

The commander in chief also penciled a note which was borne as fast as horseflesh could take it to the hands of one who deserved his own share of the laurels — Andrew Jackson.

All day bands of scared prisoners were brought in. But no Santa Anna, no Cos. This was more than vexing. The Texans wished simply to kill Cos for violation of parole, but Santa Anna might escape to Filísola and return with thrice the army Houston had just defeated. With the President of Mexico in his hands, however, Houston could rest assured that he had won the war, not merely a battle.

Toward evening a patrol of five men rode into camp. Mounted behind Joel Robison was a bedraggled little figure in a blue cotton smock and red felt slippers. The patrol had found him near the ruined Vince's Bayou bridge seated on a stump, the living picture of dejection. He said he had found his ridiculous clothes in a deserted house. He looked hardly worth bothering to take five miles to camp and would have been dispatched on the spot but for Robison, who was a good-hearted boy, and spoke Spanish. Robison and his prisoner chatted on the ride. How many men did the Americans have? Robison said less than eight hundred, and the prisoner said that surely there were more than that. Robison asked the captive if he had left a family behind. " Sí, señor." " Do you expect to see them again? " The little Mexican shrugged his shoulders. " Why did you come and fight us? " Robison wished to know. " A private soldier, señor, has little choice in such matters."

Robison had taken a liking to the polite little fellow and was about to turn him loose without ceremony among the herd of prisoners when the captives began to raise their hats.

" *El presidente! El presidente!* "

An officer of the guard ran up and, with an air that left the Texan flat, the prisoner asked to be conducted to General Houston.

Sam Houston was lying on a blanket under the oak tree, his eyes closed and his face drawn with pain. The little man was brought up by Hockley and Ben Fort Smith. He stepped forward and bowed gracefully.

" I am General Antonio López de Santa Anna, President of Mexico, Commander in Chief of the Army of Operations. I place myself at the disposal of the brave General Houston."

This much-unexpected Spanish was almost too great a strain upon the pupil of Miss Anna Raguet. Raising himself on one elbow, Houston replied as words came to him.

" General Santa Anna! Ah, indeed! Take a seat, general. I am glad to see you. Take a seat! "

The host waved his arm toward a black box, and asked for an interpreter. Zavala [1] came up. Santa Anna recognized him.

" Oh! My friend, the son of my *early* friend! "

The young patrician bowed coldly. Santa Anna turned to General Houston.

" That man may consider himself born to no common destiny who has conquered Napoleon of the West; and it now remains for him to be generous to the vanquished."

" You should have remembered that at the Alamo," Houston replied.

General Santa Anna made a bland Latin answer that loses much in translation. Houston pressed the point. What excuse for the massacre of Fannin's men? Another Latin answer. Another blunt interrogation, and for the first time in his amazing life

---

[1] **Zavala** (sà-vá′là): a Mexican, but a patriotic Texan and vice-president of the provisional government. His father had been a leader in the war that won Mexican independence from Spain; but he repudiated Santa Anna and fled to Texas, where he joined another struggle for independence.

Santa Anna's power of self-command deserted him. He raised a nervous hand to his pale face and glanced behind him. A ring of savage Texans had pressed around, with ominous looks on their faces and ominous stains on their knives. Santa Anna murmured something about a passing indisposition and requested a piece of opium.

The drug restored the prisoner's poise, and formal negotiations were begun. Santa Anna was deft and shrewd; but Houston declined to discuss terms of peace, saying that was a government matter not within the province of a military commander. Santa Anna proposed an armistice, which Houston accepted, dictating the terms which provided for the immediate evacuation of Texas by the Mexican armies. Santa Anna wrote marching orders for Filísola and the other generals. Houston beckoned to Deaf Smith, and the orders were on their way.

Houston had Santa Anna's marquee erected within a few yards of the tree under which the Texas general lay, and restored the captive's personal baggage to him. Santa Anna retired to change his clothes, and General Houston produced an ear of corn from beneath his blanket and began to nibble it. A soldier picked up a kernel and said he was going to take it home and plant it. A genius had opened his lips!

Houston's great voice summoned the men from their cordial discussion of the mode of General Santa Anna's execution. "My brave fellows," he said, scattering corn by the handful, "take this along with you to your own fields, where I hope you may long cultivate the arts of peace as you have shown yourselves masters of the art of war."

Irresistible. "We'll call it Houston corn!" they shouted.

"Not Houston corn," their general said gravely, "but San Jacinto Corn!"

And thousands of tasseled Texas acres today boast pedigrees that trace back to the San Jacinto ear.

## Suggestions for Study

1. James describes Houston to us with actions, not adjectives. Find incidents that show his bravery, his shrewdness, his kindliness, his leadership, his gallantry.

2. Show why Houston's followers would be sometimes suspicious of his leadership, and sometimes enthusiastic.

3. Why was Santa Anna so confident of victory? What part did this overconfidence play in his defeat?

4. What purpose did Houston have in calling the council of war? Why did his purpose make the council ironic?

5. Notice how in the exciting narrative of the battle James uses verbs to make the happenings vivid. Pick out some sentences in which the verb gives the statement added spirit.

6. Investigate and discuss heroes and happenings in the past history of your own state, or others in which you are especially interested. A group of students might work up a map of the United States with the greatest local heroes of each state indicated by name or picture.

7. Incidents in Houston's life have been recently dramatized over the radio. Make up your own radio program to present effectively the incidents of this chapter or others in the life of Houston. Consider this as a possible project for the other persons represented in this section. Such a method is particularly good for a small group of students to present to the rest of the class a more complete account of a person's life than is possible to get from a single chapter. These biographical programs are popular on the radio nowadays, and you can easily listen to examples to show you how to proceed.

## For Your Vocabulary

FIGURATIVE USE OF WORDS. Often the figurative use of a word is so expressive that the figurative meaning becomes a regular definition. That is the history of *buoyant* (boo'-yănt), derived from the buoys, or floating signals, that mark channels for mariners. Since the literal meaning is "rising above a heavier surrounding element," you can see how exactly the word describes Houston's mood when he at last foresees victory (page 245).

WORD GROUP. Another expressive word for dealing with high spirits is *exhilarating* (ĕg-zĭl'á-rāt-ĭng). There is a sly humor in the remark that Mrs. Mann's language in demanding the return of her oxen was *exhilarating* (page 246). For *exhilarating* means provoking merriment and is related to *hilarious* (hĭ-lâr′ĭ-ŭs) and *hilarity* (hĭ-lâr′ĭ-tĭ), words that deal with noisy good cheer. We often use *exhilarating* to mean creating high spirits, as when we call tennis and horseback riding *exhilarating* sports.

## Carl Sandburg 1878–

Carl Sandburg first made his reputation as a poet, and details of his life are therefore given in the Poetry section, page 299. Later, through his great interest in Abraham Lincoln, he turned to biography and won equal distinction in that field. In 1926 he published *Abraham Lincoln: The Prairie Years,* in two volumes, and in 1939 *Abraham Lincoln: The War Years,* in four volumes. Together, these volumes present, in the opinion of many critics, the truest, most intimate, most sympathetic biography of the most American of all Americans.

### LINCOLN SPEAKS AT GETTYSBURG

#### NOVEMBER 19, 1863

Probably no speech of so few words has ever become so celebrated as Lincoln's " Gettysburg Address," or aroused such dispute as to how it was written, delivered, and received. Many persons gain their impression of the circumstances of this speech from Mary Raymond Shipman Andrews' story *The Perfect Tribute,* but unfortunately that story is fiction and many of its details are not historically true. The following account shows exactly what did take place.

A printed invitation came to Lincoln's hands notifying him that on Thursday, November 19, 1863, exercises would be held for the dedication of a National Soldiers' Cemetery at Gettysburg. The same circular invitation had been mailed to Senators, Congressmen, the governors of Northern states, members of the cabinet, by the commission of Pennsylvanians who had organized a corporation through which Maine, New Hampshire, Vermont, Massachusetts, Rhode Island, Maryland, Connecticut, New York, New Jersey, Pennsylvania, Delaware, West Virginia, Ohio, Indiana, Illinois, Michigan, Wisconsin, and Minnesota were to share the cost of a decent burying ground for the dust and bones of the Union and Confederate dead.

In the helpless onrush of the war, it was known, too many of the fallen had lain as neglected cadavers rotting in the open fields or thrust into so shallow a resting place that a common farm plow caught in their bones. Now by order of Governor Curtin of Pennsylvania seventeen acres had been purchased on Cemetery Hill, where the Union center stood its colors on the second and third of July, and plots of soil had been allotted each state for its graves.

The sacred and delicate duties of orator of the day had fallen on Edward Everett. An eminent cultural figure, perhaps foremost of all distinguished American classical orators, he was born in 1794, had been United States Senator, Governor of Massachusetts, member of Congress, Secretary of State under Fillmore, minister to Great Britain, Phi Beta Kappa poet at Harvard, professor of Greek at Harvard, president of Harvard.

The Union of States was a holy concept to Everett, and the slavery issue secondary, though when president of Harvard from 1846 to 1849 he refused to draw the color line, saying in the case of a Negro applicant, Beverley Williams, that admission to Harvard College depended on examinations. " If this boy passes the examinations, he will be admitted; and if the white students choose to withdraw, all the income of the college will be devoted to his education." Not often was he so provocative.

Serene, suave, handsomely venerable in his sixty-ninth year, a prominent specimen of Northern upper-class distinction, Everett was a natural choice of the Pennsylvania commissioners, who sought an orator for a solemn national occasion. When in September they notified him that the date of the occasion would be October 23, he replied that he would need more time for preparation, and the dedication was postponed till November 19.

Lincoln meanwhile, in reply to the printed circular invitation, sent word to the commissioners that he would be present at the ceremonies. This made it necessary for the commissioners to consider whether the President should be asked to deliver an address when present. Clark E. Carr, of Galesburg, Illinois, representing his state on the Board of Commissioners, noted that the decision of the board to invite Lincoln to speak was an afterthought.

The question was raised as to his ability to speak upon such a grave and solemn occasion. Besides, it was said that, with his important duties and responsibilities, he could not possibly have the leisure to prepare an address. In answer it was urged that he himself, better than anyone else, could determine as to these questions, and that, if he were invited to speak, he was sure to do what, under the circumstances, would be right and proper.

And so on November 2 David Wills of Gettysburg, as the special agent of Governor Curtin and also acting for the several states, by letter informed Lincoln that the several states having soldiers in the Army of the Potomac who were killed, or had since died at hospitals in the vicinity, had procured grounds for a cemetery and proper burial of their dead.

These grounds will be consecrated and set apart to this sacred purpose by appropriate ceremonies on Thursday, the 19th instant. I am authorized by the Governors of the various States to invite you to be present and participate in these ceremonies, which will doubtless be very imposing and solemnly impressive. It is the desire that after the oration, you, as Chief Executive of the nation, formally set apart these grounds to their sacred use by a few appropriate remarks.

Mr. Wills proceeded farther as to the solemnity of the occasion, and when Lincoln had finished reading the letter he understood definitely that the event called for no humor and that a long speech was not expected of him.

The invitation [wrote Clark E. Carr] was not settled upon and sent to Mr. Lincoln until the second of November, more than six weeks after Mr. Everett had been invited to speak, and but little more than two weeks before the exercises were held.

On the second Sunday before the Gettysburg ceremonies were to take place Lincoln went to the studio of the photographer Gardner for a long-delayed sitting. Noah Brooks walked with him, and he carefully explained to Brooks that he could not go to the photographer on any other day without interfering with the public business and the photographer's business, to say nothing of his liability to be hindered en route by curiosity seekers " and other seekers." On the White House stairs Lincoln had paused, turned, walked back to his office, and rejoined Brooks with a long envelope in his hand, an advance copy of Edward Everett's address to be delivered at the Gettysburg dedication. It was thoughtful of Everett to take care they should not cover the same ground in their speeches, he remarked to Brooks, who exclaimed over the length of the Everett address, covering nearly two sides of a one-page supplement of a Boston newspaper. Lincoln quoted a line he said he had read somewhere from Daniel Webster: " Solid men of Boston, make no long orations." There was no danger that he should get upon the lines of Mr. Everett's oration, he told Brooks, for what he had ready to say was very short, or as Brooks recalled his emphasis, " short, short, short." He had hoped to read the Everett address between sittings, but the photographer worked fast, Lincoln got interested in talk, and did not open the advance sheets while at Gardner's. In the photograph which Lincoln later gave to Brooks an envelope lay next to Lincoln's right arm resting on a table. In one other photograph made by Gardner that Sunday the envelope was still on the table. The chief difference between the two pictures was that in one Lincoln had his knees crossed and in the other the ankles.

Lamon noted that Lincoln wrote part of his intended Gettysburg address at Wash-

ABRAHAM LINCOLN. This rare photograph is one of the two taken by Alexander Gardner on the Sunday before the Gettysburg Address. The envelope on the table contains Dr. Everett's oration, which Lincoln had planned to read, but didn't while at the photographer's. (Meserve Collection)

ington, covered a sheet of foolscap paper with a memorandum of it, and before taking it out of his hat and reading it to Lamon he said that it was not at all satisfactory to him, that he was afraid he would not do himself credit nor come up to public expectation. He had been too busy to give it the time he would like to.

Various definite motives besides vague intuitions may have guided Lincoln in his decision to attend and speak even though half his cabinet had sent formal declinations in response to the printed circular invitations they had all received. Though the Gettysburg dedication was to be under interstate auspices, it had tremendous national significance for Lincoln because on the platform would be the state governors whose cooperation with him was of vast importance. Also a slander and a libel had been widely mouthed and printed that on his visit to the battlefield of Antietam nearly a year before he had laughed obscenely at his own funny stories and called on Lamon to sing a cheap comic song. Perhaps he might go to Gettysburg and let it be seen how he demeaned himself on a somber landscape of sacrifice.

His personal touch with Gettysburg, by telegraph, mail, courier, and by a throng of associations, made it a place of great realities to him. Just after the battle there, a woman had come to his office, the doorman saying she had been " crying and taking on " for several days trying to see the President. Her husband and three sons were in the army. On part of her husband's pay she had lived for a time, till money from him stopped coming. She was hard put to scrape a living and needed one of her boys to help. The President listened to her, standing at a fireplace, hands behind him, head bowed, motionless. The woman finished her plea for one of her three sons in the army. He spoke. Slowly and almost as if talking to himself alone the words came and only those words:

" I have two, and you have none."

He crossed the room, wrote an order for the military discharge of one of her sons. On a special sheet of paper he wrote full and detailed instructions where to go and what to say in order to get her boy back.

In a few days the doorman told the President that the same woman was again on hand crying and taking on. " Let her in," was the word. She had found doors opening to her and officials ready to help on seeing the President's written words she carried. She had located her boy, camp, regiment, company. She had found him, yes, wounded at Gettysburg, dying in a hospital, and had followed him to the grave. And, she begged, would the President now give her the next of her boys?

As before he stood at the fireplace, hands behind him, head bent low, motionless. Slowly and almost as if talking to himself alone the words came and as before only those words:

" I have two, and you have none."

He crossed the room to his desk and began writing. As though nothing else was to do she followed, stood by his chair as he wrote, put her hand on the President's head, smoothed his thick and disorderly hair with motherly fingers. He signed an order giving her the next of her boys, stood up, put the priceless paper in her hands as he choked out the one word, " There! " and with long quick steps was gone from the room with her sobs and cries of thanks in his ears.

Thus the Kentuckian, James Speed, gathered the incident and told it. By many strange ways Gettysburg was to Lincoln a fact in crimson mist.

When Lincoln boarded the train for Gettysburg on November 18, his best chum in the world, Tad, lay sick abed and the doctors were not sure what ailed him. The mother still remembered Willie [1] and was hysterical about Tad. But the President felt imperative duty called him to Gettysburg.

Provost Marshal General James B. Fry as a War Department escort came to the White House, but the President was late in getting into the carriage for the drive to the station. They had no time to lose, Fry remarked. Lincoln said he felt like an Illi-

[1] **Willie:** a son who had died in 1862.

nois man who was going to be hanged and as the man passed along the road on the way to the gallows the crowds kept pushing into the way and blocking passage. The condemned man at last called out, " Boys, you needn't be in such a hurry to get ahead; there won't be any fun till I get there."

Flags and red-white-and-blue bunting decorated the four-car special train. Aboard were the three cabinet members, Nicolay and Hay, army and navy representatives, newspapermen, the French and Italian ministers and attachés. The rear third of the last coach had a drawing room, where from time to time the President talked with nearly everyone aboard as they came and went. Henry Clay Cochrane, lieutenant of marines, noted:

I happened to have a New York *Herald* and offered it to Mr. Lincoln. He took it and thanked me, saying, " I like to see what they say about us." The news was about Burnside at Knoxville, Grant and Sherman at Chattanooga, and Meade on the Rapidan, all expecting trouble. He read for a little while and then began to laugh at some wild guesses of the paper about pending movements. It was pleasant to see his sad face lighted up. He was looking sallow, sunken-eyed, thin, careworn, and very quiet. He returned the paper, remarking among other things that when he had first passed over that road on his way to Congress in 1847 he noticed square-rigged vessels up the Patapsco river as far as the Relay House and now there seemed to be only small craft.

At the Calvert Street Station, Secretary Seward began to get uneasy as we approached Baltimore. Upon reaching the Calvert Street Station in Baltimore all was quiet, less than two hundred people assembled, among them women with children in arms. They called for the President. He took two or three of the babies up and kissed them, which greatly pleased the mothers. General Schenck and staff joined us and soon after the President went forward in the car and seated himself with a party of choice spirits, among whom was Major Frederick W. Lincoln of Boston, not a kinsman. They told stories for an hour or so, Mr. Lincoln taking his turn and enjoying it. Approaching Hanover Junction, he arose and said, " Gentlemen, this is all very pleasant, but the people will expect me to say something to

them tomorrow, and I must give the matter some thought." He then returned to the rear room of the car.

At sundown the train pulled into Gettysburg and Lincoln was driven to the Wills residence, Seward to the Harper home fronting on the public square. A sleepy little country town of 3,500 was overflowing with human pulses again. Private homes were filled with notables and nondescripts. Hundreds slept on the floors of hotels. Military bands blared till late in the night serenading whomsoever. The weather was mild and the moon up for those who chose to go a-roaming. When serenaders called on the President for the speech, he made again one of those little addresses saying there was nothing to say. " In my position it is sometimes important that I should not say foolish things. [A voice: " If you can help it."] It very often happens that the only way to help it is to say nothing at all. Believing that is my present condition this evening, I must beg of you to excuse me from addressing you further."

The crowd didn't feel it was much of a speech. They went next door with the band and blared for Seward. He spoke so low that Hay could not hear him, but he opened the stopgaps of patriotic sentiment, saying in part, " I thank my God for the hope that this is the last fratricidal war which will fall upon the country which is vouchsafed to us by Heaven — the richest, the broadest, the most beautiful, the most magnificent, and capable of a greater destiny than has ever been given to any part of the human race." What more could a holiday crowd ask for on a fair night of moonlit November? Seward gave them more and closed: " Fellow citizens, good night." It was good night for him but not for them. They serenaded five other speakers.

At dinner in the Wills home that evening Lincoln met Edward Everett, a guest under the same roof, and Governor Curtin and others. About ten o'clock he was in his room, with paper and pencil ready to write, when he sent a colored servant down for Judge Wills to come up. Still later, about eleven o'clock, he sent the colored servant down again for Judge Wills, who came up and heard Lincoln request to see Mr. Seward. Judge Wills offered to go and bring Seward from next door at the Harpers'. "No, I'll go and see him," said Lincoln, who gathered his sheets of paper and went for a half-hour with his Secretary of State.

Whether Seward made slight or material alterations in the text on the sheets was known only to Lincoln and Seward. It was midnight or later that Lincoln went to sleep, probably perfectly clear in his mind as to what his speech would be the next day. The one certainty was that his " few appropriate remarks," good or bad, would go to an immense audience. Also he slept better for having a telegram from Stanton reporting there was no real war news and " On inquiry Mrs. Lincoln informs me that your son is better this evening."

Fifteen thousand, some said thirty thousand or fifty thousand people were on Cemetery Hill for the exercises the next day when the procession from Gettysburg arrived afoot and horseback representing the United States Government, the army and navy, governors of states, mayors of cities, a regiment of troops, hospital corps, telegraph-company representatives, Knights Templar, Masonic Fraternity, Odd Fellows, and other benevolent associations, the press, fire departments, citizens of Pennsylvania and other states. They were scheduled to start at ten o'clock, and at that hour on the clock Lincoln in a black suit, high silk hat, and white gloves came out of the Wills residence and mounted a horse. A crowd was on hand and he held a reception on horseback. At eleven the parade began to move. The President's horse seemed small for him, as some looked at it. Clark E. Carr, just behind the President, believed he noticed that the President sat erect and looked majestic to begin with and then got to thinking so that his body leaned forward, his arms hung limp, and his head bent far down.

A long telegram sent by Stanton at ten o'clock from Washington had been handed him. Burnside seemed safe though threat-

ened at Knoxville, Grant was starting a big battle at Chattanooga, and " Mrs. Lincoln reports your son's health as a great deal better and he will be out today."

The march of the procession of military and civic bodies began. " Mr. Lincoln was mounted upon a young and beautiful chestnut horse, the largest horse, the largest in the Cumberland Valley," wrote Lieutenant Cochrane. This seemed the first occasion that anyone had looked at the President mounted with a feeling that just the right horse had been picked to match his physical length. " His towering figure surmounted by a high silk hat made the rest of us look small," thought Cochrane.

Minute guns spoke while the procession moved along Baltimore Street to the Emmittsburg Road, then by way of the Taneytown Road to the cemetery, where troop lines stood in salute to the President.

The march was over in fifteen minutes. But Mr. Everett, the orator of the day, had not arrived. Bands played till noon. Mr. Everett arrived.

The United States House chaplain, the Reverend Thomas H. Stockton, offered a prayer while the thousands stood with uncovered heads.

Benjamin B. French, officer in charge of buildings in Washington, introduced the Honorable Edward Everett, orator of the day, who rose, bowed low to Lincoln, saying, " Mr. President." Lincoln responded, " Mr. Everett."

The orator of the day then stood in silence before a crowd that stretched to limits that would test his voice. Beyond and around were the wheat fields, the meadows, the peach orchards, long slopes of land, and five and seven miles farther the contemplative blue ridge of a low mountain range. His eyes could sweep them as he faced the audience. He had taken note of it in his prepared and rehearsed address.

Overlooking these broad fields now reposing from the labors of the waning year, the mighty Alleghenies dimly towering before us, the graves of our brethren beneath our feet, it is with hesitation that I raise my poor voice to break the eloquent silence of God and Nature. But the duty to which you have called me must be performed; — grant me, I pray you, your indulgence and your sympathy. [Everett proceeded] It was appointed by law in Athens [and gave an extended sketch of the manner in which the Greeks cared for their dead who fell in battle. He spoke of the citizens assembled to consecrate the day.] As my eye ranges over the fields whose sods were so lately moistened by the blood of gallant and loyal men, I feel, as never before, how truly it was said of old that it is sweet and becoming to die for one's country.

Northern cities would have been trampled in conquest but for " those who sleep beneath our feet," said the orator. He gave an outline of how the war began, traversed decisive features of the three days' battles at Gettysburg, discussed the doctrine of state sovereignty and denounced it, drew parallels from European history, and came to his peroration quoting Pericles on dead patriots: " The whole earth is the sepulcher of illustrious men." The men of nineteen sister states had stood side by side on the perilous ridges. " Seminary Ridge, the Peach Orchard, Cemetery, Culp, and Wolf Hill, Round Top, Little Round Top, humble names, henceforward dear and famous — no lapse of time, no distance of space, shall cause you to be forgotten." He had spoken for an hour and fifty-seven minutes, some said a trifle over two hours, repeating almost word for word an address that occupied nearly two newspaper pages, as he had written it and as it had gone in advance sheets to many newspapers.

Everett came to his closing sentence without a faltering voice: " Down to the latest period of recorded time, in the glorious annals of our common country there will be no brighter page than that which relates THE BATTLES OF GETTYSBURG." It was the effort of his life and embodied the perfections of the school of oratory in which he had spent his career. His erect form and sturdy shoulders, his white hair and flung-back head at dramatic points, his voice, his poise, and chiefly some quality of inside

goodheartedness, held most of his audience to him, though the people in the front rows had taken their seats three hours before his oration closed.

The Baltimore Glee Club sang an ode written for the occasion by Benjamin B. French, who had introduced Everett to the audience. The poets Longfellow, Bryant, Whittier, Lowell, George Boker, had been requested but none found time to respond with a piece to be set to music. The two closing verses of the ode by French immediately preceded the introduction of the President to the audience.

Having read Everett's address, Lincoln knew when the moment drew near for him to speak. He took out his own manuscript from a coat pocket, put on his steel-bowed glasses, stirred in his chair, looked over the manuscript, and put it back in his pocket. The Baltimore Glee Club finished singing the ode by French. Ward Hill Lamon introduced the President of the United States. He rose, and holding in one hand the two sheets of paper at which he occasionally glanced, he delivered the address in his high-pitched and clear-carrying voice. The Cincinnati *Commercial* reporter wrote: " The President rises slowly, draws from his pocket a paper, and, when commotion subsides, in a sharp, unmusical treble voice, reads the brief and pithy remarks." Hay wrote in his diary: " The President, in a firm, free way, with more grace than is his wont, said his half dozen words of consecration." Charles Hale of the Boston *Advertiser*, also officially representing Governor Andrew of Massachusetts, had notebook and pencil in hand, took down the slow-spoken words of the President, as follows: [1]

*Fourscore and seven years ago, our fathers brought forth upon this continent a new nation, conceived in liberty and dedicated to the proposition that all men are created equal.*

[1] The speech as here recorded has some slight variations in wording from the standard version, which appears among the Lincoln writings on page 673.

*Now we are engaged in a great civil war,
testing whether that nation — or any nation, so conceived and so dedicated — can
long endure.*

*We are met on a great battlefield of that
war. We are met to dedicate a portion of it
as the final resting place of those who have
given their lives that that nation might live.*

*It is altogether fitting and proper that we
should do this.*

*But, in a larger sense, we cannot dedicate,
we cannot consecrate, we cannot hallow,
this ground. The brave men, living and
dead, who struggled here, have consecrated
it, far above our power to add or to detract.*

*The world will very little note nor long
remember what we say here; but it can
never forget what they did here.*

*It is for us, the living, rather, to be dedi-
cated, here, to the unfinished work that they
have thus far so nobly carried on. It is
rather for us to be here dedicated to the
great task remaining before us; that from
these honored dead we take increased devotion to that cause for which they here
gave the last full measure of devotion; that
we here highly resolve that these dead shall
not have died in vain; that the nation shall,
under God, have a new birth of freedom,
and that government of the people, by the
people, for the people, shall not perish from
the earth.*

In a speech to serenaders just before the
battle of Gettysburg four and a half months
before, Lincoln had referred to the founding
of the republic as taking place " eighty odd
years since." Then he had hunted up the
exact date, which was eighty-seven years
since, and phrased it " Fourscore and seven
years ago " instead of " Eighty-seven years
since."

In the written copy of his speech from
which he read, Lincoln used the phrase " our
poor power." In other copies of the speech
which he wrote out later, he again used the
phrase " our poor power." So it was evident
that he meant to use the word " poor " when
speaking to his audience, but it escaped him.
Also in the copy held in his hands while
facing the audience he had not written the
words " under God," though he did include
those words in later copies which he wrote.
Therefore, the words " under God " were
decided upon after he wrote the text the
night before at the Wills residence.

The New York *Tribune* and many other
newspapers indicated " [Applause] " at
five places in the address and " [Long continued applause] " at the end. The applause,
however, according to most of the responsible witnesses, was formal and perfunctory,
a tribute to the occasion, to the high office,
to the array of important men of the nation
on the platform, by persons who had sat as
an audience for three hours. Nine sentences
had been spoken in five minutes, and some
were surprised that it should end before the
orator had really begun to get his outdoor
voice.

A photographer had made ready to record
a great historic moment, had bustled about
with his dry plates, his black box on a tri-
pod, and before he had his head under the
hood for an exposure, the President had
said " by the people, for the people " and
the nick of time was past for a photograph.

The New York *Times* reporter gave his
summary of the program by writing:

The opening prayer by Reverend Mr. Stockton was touching and beautiful, and produced
quite as much effect upon the audience as the
classic sentences of the orator of the day. President Lincoln's address was delivered in a clear
loud tone of voice, which could be distinctly
heard at the extreme limits of the large assemblage. It was delivered (or rather read from a
sheet of paper which the speaker held in his
hand) in a very deliberate manner, with strong
emphasis, and with a most businesslike air.

The Philadelphia *Press* man, John Russell Young, privately felt that Everett's
speech was the performance of a great actor
whose art was too evident, that it was
" beautiful but cold as ice." The New York
*Times* man noted:

Even while Mr. Everett was delivering his
splendid oration, there were as many people

wandering about the fields, made memorable by the fierce struggles of July, as stood around the stand listening to his eloquent periods. They seemed to have considered, with President Lincoln, that it was not what was *said* here, but what was *done* here, that deserved their attention. In wandering about these battlefields, one is astonished and indignant to find at almost every step of his progress the carcasses of dead horses which breed pestilence in the atmosphere. I am told that more than a score of deaths have resulted from this neglect in the village of Gettysburg the past summer; in the house in which I was compelled to seek lodgings, there are now two boys sick with typhoid fever attributed to this cause. Within a stone's throw of the whitewashed hut occupied as the headquarters of General Meade, I counted yesterday no less than ten carcasses of dead horses, lying on the ground where they were struck by the shells of the enemy.

The audience had expected, as the printed program stipulated, " Dedicatory Remarks, by the President of the United States." No eloquence was promised. Where eloquence is in flow the orator must have time to get tuned up, to expatiate and expand while building toward his climaxes, it was supposed. The New York *Tribune* man and other like observers merely reported the words of the address, with the one preceding sentence: " The dedicatory remarks were then delivered by the President." These reporters felt no urge to inform their readers about how Lincoln stood; what he did with his hands; how he moved, vocalized; or whether he emphasized or subdued any parts of the address. Strictly, no address as such was on the program for him. He was down for just a few perfunctory " dedicatory remarks."

According to Lamon, Lincoln himself felt that about all he had given the audience was ordinary garden-variety dedicatory remarks, for Lamon wrote that Lincoln told him just after delivering the speech that he had regret over not having prepared it with greater care. " Lamon, that speech won't *scour*. It is a flat failure and the people are disappointed." On the farms where Lincoln grew up as a boy, when wet soil stuck to the moldboard of a plow they said it didn't " scour."

The near-by *Patriot and Union* of Harrisburg took its fling:

The President succeeded on this occasion because he acted without sense and without constraint in a panorama that was gotten up more for the benefit of his party than for the glory of the nation and the honor of the dead. We pass over the silly remarks of the President; for the credit of the nation we are willing that the veil of oblivion shall be dropped over them and that they shall no more be repeated or thought of.

Everett's opinion of the speech he heard Lincoln deliver was written in a note to Lincoln the next day and was more than mere courtesy: " I should be glad if I could flatter myself that I came as near to the central idea of the occasion in two hours as you did in two minutes." Lincoln's immediate reply was: " In our respective parts yesterday, you could not have been excused to make a short address, nor I a long one. I am pleased to know that, in your judgment, the little I did say was not entirely a failure."

The ride to Washington took until midnight. Lincoln was weary, talked little, stretched out on one of the side seats in the drawing room, and had a wet towel laid across his eyes and forehead.

He had stood that day, the world's foremost spokesman of popular government, saying that democracy was yet worth fighting for. He had spoken as one in mist who might head on deeper yet into mist. He incarnated the assurances and pretenses of popular government, implied that it could and might perish from the earth. What he meant by " a new birth of freedom " for the nation could have a thousand interpretations. The taller riddles of democracy stood up out of the address. It had the dream touch of vast and furious events epitomized for any foreteller to read what was to come. He did not assume that the drafted soldiers, substitutes, and bounty-paid privates had died willingly under Lee's shot and shell, in deliberate consecration of themselves to the

Union cause. His cadences sang the ancient song that where there is freedom men have fought and sacrificed for it, and that freedom is worth men's dying for. For the first time since he became President he had on a dramatic occasion declaimed, howsoever it might be read, Jefferson's proposition which had been a slogan of the Revolutionary War — " All men are created equal " — leaving no other inference than that he regarded the Negro slave as a man. His outwardly smooth sentences were inside of them gnarled and tough with the enigmas of the American experiment.

Back at Gettysburg the blue haze of the Cumberland Mountains had dimmed till it was a blur in a nocturne. The moon was up and fell with a bland golden benevolence on the new-made graves of soldiers, on the sepulchers of old settlers, on the horse carcasses of which the onrush of war had not yet permitted removal. The New York *Herald* man walked amid them and ended the story he sent his paper: " The air, the trees, the graves are silent. Even the relic hunters are gone now. And the soldiers here never wake to the sound of reveille."

In many a country cottage over the land, a tall old clock in a quiet corner told time in a ticktock deliberation. Whether the orchard branches hung with pink-spray blossoms or icicles of sleet, whether the outside news was seedtime or harvest, rain or drouth, births or deaths, the swing of the pendulum was right and left and right and left in a ticktock deliberation.

The face and dial of the clock had known the eyes of a boy who listened to its ticktock and learned to read its minute and hour hands. And the boy had seen years measured off by the swinging pendulum, and grown to man size, had gone away. And the people in the cottage knew that the clock would stand there and the boy never again come into the room and look at the clock with the query, " What is the time? "

In a row of graves the unidentified boy would sleep long in the dedicated final resting place at Gettysburg. Why he had gone away and why he would never come back

had roots in some mystery of flags and drums, of national fate in which individuals sink as in a deep sea, of men swallowed and vanished in a man-made storm of smoke and steel.

The mystery deepened and moved with ancient music and inviolable consolation because a solemn Man of Authority had stood at the graves of the unidentified and spoken the words " We cannot consecrate — we cannot hallow — this ground. The brave men, living and dead, who struggled here, have consecrated it far above our poor power to add or detract. . . . From these honored dead we take increased devotion to that cause for which they gave the last full measure of devotion."

To the backward and forward pendulum swing of a tall old clock in a quiet corner they might read those cadenced words while outside the windows the first flurry of snow blew across the orchard and down over the meadow, the beginnings of winter in a gun-metal gloaming to be later arched with a star-flung sky.

## Suggestions for Study

1. Contrast the style of Lincoln's address with that of Everett's as indicated by the few excerpts included here.

2. Make a list of adjectives which might be applied to Lincoln because of his actions as recorded here; for example, modest, kind-hearted.

3. What is added to the account by the inclusion of the story of the woman who had lost her two sons?

4. In what details does the text of the " Gettysburg Address " printed here differ from the one generally used? Why did Sandburg use this one?

5. What details in this account indicate that its author is a poet?

6. Vocabulary: cadavers, suave, fratricidal, expatiate, nocturne.

7. What recent criticisms of public men seem to you to be as unwarranted as the Harrisburg *Patriot and Union's* criticism of Lincoln's remarks? Bring newspaper clippings to class to illustrate your point.

8. The class might find it interesting to

dramatize the commissioners' discussion of the question of asking Lincoln to speak at the ceremonies. Try to bring out the various attitudes toward Lincoln suggested by Sandburg.

## For Your Vocabulary

WORD POWER. Part of Lincoln's deserved popularity grew out of the feeling that he stood for much that was dear to the hearts of Americans. The lasting appeal of his utterances is due in large part to his power to express clearly what was vague but important to many others. In his closing comments Sandburg well expresses these traits when he says that Lincoln *incarnated* (ĭn-kär′năt-ed), or embodied in human flesh, the utterances of democracy, and that his words at Gettysburg epitomized (ĕ-pĭt′ŏ-mīz′d) the "vast and furious" events of his day. An *epitome* (ĕ-pĭt′ŏ-mē) is a brief but accurate statement of a whole case or cause. The word is also used of a man who is representative of his whole group, as "the *epitome* of aristocracy" or "the *epitome* of suffering humanity." *Incarnation* is similarly used, as in saying that a man is the *incarnation* of some quality such as vanity or generosity. The base-word is *carn*, meaning flesh, which occurs interestingly in *carnival* (*carne vale*, farewell to the flesh), originally used for the celebration that preceded the days of Lent, when the flesh was to be denied its usual indulgences.

WORD ANALYSIS. Analyze *nondescript* (nŏn′-dĕ-scrĭpt). This one takes a little imagination, since the base-word usually appears with a suffix that is absent this time. The context is also helpful (page 258).

## Catherine Drinker Bowen
### 1897–

The son of the Autocrat of the Breakfast Table, a hero of the War between the States, professor at Harvard University, Chief Justice of the Supreme Court of Massachusetts, Associate Justice of the Supreme Court of the United States — Oliver Wendell Holmes had a long, full life.

Of her biography of Justice Holmes, *Yankee from Olympus*, Catherine Drinker Bowen says that it is "an attempt to bring Justice Holmes

out of legal terms into human terms." This she accomplishes by assuming the role of novelist. Not only for the Justice himself, but for his father, the famous poet and essayist, and even for his grandfather, Mrs. Bowen creates details of action, conversation, and even their unspoken thoughts. Of this presumption Mrs. Bowen admits frankly, "I disapprove intensely of the kind of biography I write. But without the scenes I have to create, my biographies read like children's notebooks." Certainly from such resort to the device of fiction comes much of the compelling power of her book. As one critic says, "Justice Holmes lives in these pages in all his genuine nobility of mind, in all his fierce integrity of spirit, in all his salty, tolerant, practical wisdom."

Catherine Drinker Bowen is no novice as a biographer. In 1935 she wrote *Beloved Friend*, a sympathetic account of the troubled life of Tchaikovsky, and in 1939 in *Free Artist* she won more fame with another musical biography, this time about the two Rubinsteins.

## JUSTICE AND MRS. HOLMES MOVE TO WASHINGTON

This selection is Chapter 32 in *Yankee from Olympus*. The earlier chapters tell about Wendell's grandfather, Abiel Holmes, a solemn Puritan preacher who married wealthy Sally Wendell and thus established the Holmeses in comfortable circumstances for ever after. These chapters also describe Wendell's father and the inability of the quiet son to understand the wisecracking Autocrat. ("Don't take it so hard, Wendell," his Uncle John once told him. "You will get used to your father. I did, long ago.") Mrs. Bowen follows young Oliver Wendell Holmes through Harvard, through the War between the States, through Law School, through marriage with Fanny Dixwell (who, he said, for over fifty years made life poetry for him), and through twenty years on the Massachusetts Supreme Court. Now it is 1902, Oliver Wendell Holmes has been appointed to the United States Supreme Court by President Theodore Roosevelt, and the Holmeses are preparing to move to Washington.

On Friday morning, December 5, 1902, Holmes stepped off the Federal Express into the Pennsylvania station in Washington. Behind him, carrying his bag, was James Doherty the Irishman, for many years his clerk and messenger in the Massachusetts Court. Mrs. Holmes was not there; she was to follow in a week with the maids and the rest of the household.

The train barn was cold, noisy with steam and echoing voices. Inside the gates a stout, elderly, intensely respectable-looking colored man approached, cap in hand. " I am John Craig, sir," he said. " Your messenger in the Supreme Court. I was with Justice Gray twenty years. Justice Horace Gray from Boston, your predecessor, sir. Yessir, we always meets the new Justices when they comes to town. Will you go straight to your hotel, sir, or will you call first at the White House like the other Justices does? "

Holmes was astonished. He had been Chief Justice of Massachusetts, now he felt like a new boy at school. He grinned, turning to Doherty, who stood looking on with a slightly hostile air. " James," he said, " John here seems to know the ropes. I think I shall just follow his advice. You go on to the New Willard with my things. You know how to find the house. Ten, Lafayette Square — it's right across from the north gate to the White House. If you have any trouble at the coal company, show them my official card. It may not be easy to get coal; the strike is barely over. I'll come round later."

Holmes paused, smiled briefly at the colored man. " I'm going to call on the President," he said, and, turning, walked out of the station.

In the wide bright morning streets, trolleys clanged, cabs threaded in and out among the traffic, horses slipped in the wet December streets. Far up Pennsylvania Avenue the Capitol rose against a sky astoundingly blue. Holmes was conscious of a feeling of adventure. Here in this sprawling city he was a stranger, embarking, at sixty-one, upon a new life, with a name still to make in a new court, a new city. At home he had wondered if he would be slow in learning the court routine, if his colleagues

would be friendly. Sometimes in the dark hours, doubt had assailed him; would he be equal to this larger task? He was a scholar in the law, he had practiced law and taught law; he had had twenty years' experience on the bench. But in this National Court he might well be confronted with an element strange to him, an element he had, indeed, always avoided. Call it politics or call it statesmanship, if it reared its head, no amount of scholarship or mere local experience equipped a man to meet it.

Holmes had thought of these things — but concerning the city of Washington and his arrangements for living, he had thought little. Custom is strong; this was a man who had lived a lifetime among people who knew him and his father before him. It had made things very easy, all the mechanics of life had been smoothed by this familiarity.

It was lunch time before Holmes had paid his respects at the White House, stopped for a moment at the Cabot Lodges', and got round to 10 Lafayette Square. The shutters were closed, Doherty nowhere to be seen. Holmes walked back to the New Willard. Late that afternoon Doherty came to the hotel room looking crestfallen. He held out Holmes's card, soiled and battered. He had been to three coal companies. They wanted to know if this judge was to be a regular customer. They had never heard of Oliver Wendell Holmes and coal was thirty dollars a ton. . . . Did the Judge, Doherty asked wearily, think of putting in coke maybe? There surely was a bunch of cussers in this town. He missed the Boston Irish.

Holmes laughed. Obviously, no favors awaited him in this new life. They might as well let the thing lie over until Monday, after he was sworn in at Court. Would Doherty like to come to the Capitol and see the ceremony? Then they could go together to tackle those rascals and get the house opened on Lafayette Square.

On Monday, December 8, Holmes, dressed in his heavy long black gown, stood in the old Courtroom in the Capitol building and laid his hand on the great Bible before him. On this Bible, John Marshall had been sworn in, Taney and Story. Around him in niches on the wall, Justices in marble looked down; overhead the red, white, and blue shield gleamed. . . .

Holmes felt himself profoundly moved. This was more than adventure, now. Here in this ancient room, heavy and quiet with tradition, he was to be part of the highest court in the land, the court of last resort. Behind him in the Courtroom, spectators stood up, and the lawyers whose cases were to be heard that day. Mrs. Theodore Roosevelt was there, Mrs. Henry Cabot Lodge, and Henry Adams. . . .

Chief Justice Fuller made a sign; Holmes's voice rose clearly in the quiet room:

" *I, Oliver Wendell Holmes, do solemnly swear that I will administer justice without respect to persons, and do equal right to the poor and to the rich, and that I will faithfully and impartially discharge and perform all the duties incumbent on me as Associate Justice of the Supreme Court of the United States according to the best of my abilities and understanding, agreeably to the Constitution and laws of the United States, so help me God.*"

Afterward, walking the streets of Washington with his long stride, Doherty trotting beside him, Holmes looked eagerly about. The excitement of the ceremony had moved him, made him doubly conscious of all his surroundings. These wide avenues, the flamboyant statues of generals and statesmen, crowded suddenly by a block of tumbledown Negro shacks . . . the White House with its iron fence and bare wintry trees . . .

Turning the corner from H Street and coming suddenly upon the historic square that was to be his home, Holmes halted. How well he remembered this square! Here, some forty years ago, tired soldiers had bivouacked; the grass of the park had been trampled into mire. But how tall and sturdy the trees were now, and how orderly it looked with the painted benches, the fat pigeons pecking where the ground was wet. Only the statue of General Jackson was the same, prancing forever on its bronze rock-

ing horse, waving its cocked hat in a gesture ridiculous and touching.

" Doherty! " Holmes said. " The last time I walked here, I was ankle deep in mud. There were signs along the street: ' *Undertaker. Bodies embalmed while you wait.*' . . . And now I'm an elderly judge, and it's nineteen hundred and two, and there's been a coal strike. And how the devil, Doherty, are we to get coal into 10 Lafayette Square before Mrs. Holmes arrives on Thursday? "

But when Mrs. Holmes did arrive, late Thursday afternoon, she found the house warm, the furnace started, the rooms in hideous disorder, and Doherty upstairs in the study unpacking the last crate of books, putting them slowly on the shelves, each volume with meticulous care. Coming quietly up the long stairs, Mrs. Holmes heard her husband's voice, roaring at Doherty: " Doherty — no! Not on that shelf! What did you put those books on that shelf for? I told you I wanted them here, where I can reach them from the desk."

Standing in the doorway, Fanny Holmes surveyed the scene. Always, when these thousands of books were in order, her husband considered the household was settled. " Well! " Fanny said. " Well, Wendell! "

For an hour, Holmes followed his wife around the house, showing her the rooms, relating his adventures of the week. " Doherty went to three coal companies. Thirty dollars a ton, and they wouldn't sell him any. In the fourth place they asked if we were to be regular customers, and said who the devil was Oliver Wendell Holmes anyway."

Fanny sat down suddenly on a packing box. She was sixty-two and hideously tired, but for the moment fatigue left her; she felt lightsome, gay. A profound sigh escaped her. *Who the devil is Oliver Wendell Holmes!* . . . She smiled up at her husband. " After sixty years, Wendell, we have achieved a life where your father's name is of no significance, except as you make it so."

Wendell Holmes did not smile. He went quickly to his wife, took her hand, lifted it to his lips in a gesture fervent and courtly. Then he sat down and began to talk. Fanny must come to Court. Right away. Tomorrow, if she could. It was amazing. The old Senate chamber where they sat was beautiful, with its light gray walls, the bright shield of the Union, the eagle snarling, the red canopy over the Chief Justice's chair. All it needed, to make a perfect Guido Reni,[1] was a fellow at each end of the Bench with a brace of wolfhounds. . . . The very incongruity of things, here in Washington, was somehow exhilarating. That first day, when he was sworn in, for instance . . .

" We had our robes on," Holmes said. " I had already taken the first oath in the robing room and the judges had started across the hall. I was at the end of the line, of course. They go very slowly. There is always a crowd hanging round the Capitol corridors. Just as I started across the hall, a man spoke out very distinctly, in a sort of awed whisper. ' Lord! ' he said. ' What dignity! ' "

Fanny gasped. No, Holmes said quickly. The man wasn't joking. Let Fanny come to Court and find out for herself. The whole scene was extraordinary, the feeling of tradition behind it. And the questions that came up . . . from Arkansas, from Wisconsin and Texas — questions for statesmen, not lawyers. The whole thing was *big*. A man had no need to search within himself, to find his sense of the infinite. The infinite was right there, in that old Courtroom. . . .

Fanny Holmes looked around her, at the furniture, half unpacked. Newspapers littered the floor. In the hallway she heard Annie, the maid who had been with them since Dr. Holmes's time, complaining bitterly that the place was a shambles. What had Doherty been doing for six mortal days, the Irish voice demanded. Why hadn't he got the kitchen clean instead of playing up here with them books?

It would take weeks to get this house in order. . . . Come to Court tomorrow? Fanny looked at her husband. He had got

up and was pacing the room, his hands in his pockets like a college boy, talking nineteen to the dozen about an opinion he was hoping the Chief would assign to him. . . .

" Why, yes, Wendell," Fanny said. " I'll come to Court with you tomorrow. Can we drive there? Have you been able to hire a hack for every day? "

On Friday morning, in the chamber of the Supreme Court, Fanny Holmes watched the hands of the round clock above the Chief Justice's chair move toward noon. She had sat there for half an hour; the spell of the old room had settled upon her. Light came benignly from the domed ceiling, Justices in marble looked down from their pedestals. It was all as Wendell had described: overhead on the red, white, and blue shield, the stars were only twenty-six. Fanny counted them. . . . Why, John Quincy Adams had been President then! This room had been in continuous use ever since, first by the Senate. Just before the Civil War it was taken over by the Supreme Court.

On a raised dais, nine tall black leather chairs faced the chamber. In that center chair, under the red canopy, Justice Taney had sat at eighty-seven, reviled and mistrusted by a country he had served for half a century. Daniel Webster had debated here, and Calhoun. It was an awesome sight for the wife of any Justice, this quiet room with the round clock ticking above the eagle. In one of those great chairs, Wendell Holmes would sit, his gray hair outlined against the cushions. . . .

There was a stir to the left; in a long black line the Justices came slowly in: Chief Justice Fuller, hale and hearty at sixty-nine, his white hair worn long, after the Western fashion. How tiny he was, in front of Harlan! John Marshall Harlan of Kentucky, the giant who had been in the Court since '77. Last of the tobacco-spitting judges, Holmes called him. Next to Harlan was White of Louisiana, the sugar planter, veteran of the Rebel army, dark-haired, with a square, stubborn head.

Slowly the nine walked to their places.

[1] **Guido Reni** (gwē′dō rā′nĕ): Italian painter (1575–1642), famous for his use of deep, rich colors.

OLIVER WENDELL HOLMES as justice of the Supreme Court of the United States. (Keystone View)

Brewer of Kansas, Brown of Michigan. The Justice next to Brown was Peckham of New York, then came somebody Fanny could not place, and then, standing next to Wendell, was a man with a face like Lincoln's, whiskers all round under his chin. That was McKenna of California, the only McKinley appointee.

"*Oyez! Oyez! Oyez! . . . God Save the United States and This Honorable Court!*"

Fanny Holmes, looking up at her husband, was swept with sudden, deep emotion. It was not only that Wendell was so handsome, standing there straight and tall in his robes. But they had done right to come. Whatever might arrive, whatever fate had in store for him — and for her, in this sprawling city of strangers — they had done right to come. They had done right to leave home, break away, cut off the associations of a lifetime. Fanny Holmes had always felt it. But now she knew it and rejoiced.

Gazing up at her husband from under her prim dotted veil, Fanny felt tears surge to her eyes, hot and overflowing.

Washington in 1903 was the most exuberant place on the civilized earth. And in the center of it, in the midst of all this ferment of a new century, a new era, Theodore Roosevelt stirred the mixture with his Big Stick,[1] busting the trusts, curbing monopoly, shaking his fist, grinning from newspaper cartoons, one eye on the matter in hand, one on the Presidential convention next year in Chicago. . . .

Newspapermen had never had a President who was such copy. Everything he did was spectacular. The Sunday afternoon hikes through Rock Creek Park, with the French Ambassador panting behind in lavender kid gloves. "*Pour l'honneur de la France,*" the Ambassador had remarked resignedly, throwing off his clothes preparatory to swimming the Creek after the President.

"America," John Morley wrote home to London, "has two extraordinary spectacles: Niagara Falls and Theodore Roosevelt." In all its history, the country had never had such a noisy man in the White House. In the corridors upstairs, Archie and Quentin rode bronco on their father's back, and in cities from Maryland to Oregon, bands played "Alice, Where Art Thou," and the people noted the skirts of the President's delightful daughter, worn daringly short, almost to her boot tops.

The country liked it — the plain people especially. The West, almost forgetting Bryan, was glad of a leader who was not afraid of Wall Street. But the captains of industry, captains of railroads and captains in Wall Street, looked with anger and apprehension upon the Dude Cowboy who had promised to continue unchanged the policies of his predecessor, McKinley. . . . Theodore Roosevelt was not continuing anything; he was initiating, inaugurating, changing,

[1] **Big Stick:** a policy of using a show of force, then persuasion. The term comes from Roosevelt's famous statement, "We must speak softly, but carry a big stick."

reforming. His manner of settling the coal strike, for instance, had been completely out of line. Swiftly and without precedent he had taken the public into his confidence by publishing in the newspapers the owners' refusal to meet with the miners. The public, furious, had compelled the owners to arbitrate.

It was the first time the public had been consulted in an industrial dispute; the result was immediate and significant. Henceforth a Commodore Vanderbilt would not flaunt his scorn so arrogantly . . . " The public be damned." Henceforth an E. H. Harriman would not boast so openly concerning his power to buy both legislators and courts. The public conscience was aroused — and T. R. suited the public conscience perfectly. In the big new magazines, *McClure's, Collier's, Everybody's,* the muckrakers exposed the packers, the sweatshop proprietors. Lincoln Steffens was writing *The Shame of the Cities.* People read Frank Norris — *The Octopus, The Pit.* Upton Sinclair, Ida Tarbell, prepared their indictments.

Here in the White House was a man who the public knew would stand behind it. When Theodore Roosevelt did not like a thing, he set about instantly to legislate it out of existence. To him the legal and political viewpoint were one and the same; it did not occur to him that there were men — among them a new Court appointee from Massachusetts — who looked upon the thing far differently.

" What the boys like about Roosevelt," a Senator said, " is that he doesn't care a hoot for the law." Neither did the country. What the country desired just now was neither legality nor reason, but revenge. Let T. R. smash somebody *big,* make an example of him — a meat packer, the sugar trust, anybody or anything so long as there was action.

The country had not long to wait. Looking round, Roosevelt seized upon the biggest, newest railroad merger of them all — the Northern Securities Company — asked his Attorney General to investigate its legality under the Sherman Act. Knox went ahead, and in February, 1902, suit against the Northern Securities Company burst upon the captains of industry like a declaration of war.

The stock market plunged downward. " Doesn't your friend," a railroad man asked Owen Wister in Philadelphia, " ever *think?* " In Washington, Henry Adams answered the question. Roosevelt, he said, from head to foot was *pure act.* . . . And on the other side of Lafayette Square, the new Justice from Massachusetts watched a trifle sardonically while his President wielded the Big Stick. The Sherman Anti-Trust Act, obviously, was going to be Roosevelt's favorite weapon . . . and Holmes had always disliked the Act. " The Sherman Act isn't fair," he said often. " It won't let the strong man win the race." Besides, mere bigness didn't make a merger illegal. How it behaved, what it did, determined its legality. Very possibly the Northern Securities case would never reach the Supreme Court; with John G. Johnson as counsel, Morgan and Jim Hill might win their case in the lower courts. Suit was brought in St. Paul; as weeks passed, the public forgot it and turned to other matters.

Meanwhile, in Washington, Justice and Mrs. Holmes took their place in society — rather to their surprise, among the inmost circle of the Roosevelt Familiars. It was a natural affinity. The Cabot Lodges, Henry Adams, Owen Wister, Roosevelt, Holmes . . . Harvard men, with a like background and like tastes. Brilliant men, vigorous, good talkers who were ready to give an opinion on any subject on earth. Holmes had known them all in Boston except the President.

Mrs. Henry Adams was dead; Adams lived alone in the big beautiful house around the corner from the Holmeses. Adams still retained his pose of the old cardinal, turning life to dust and ashes. But underneath he was kinder, Holmes suspected, than his brother Brooks. And he was always interesting. Very often they dined informally at the White House. John Hay joined them, or the Jusserands, and they went afterward to the theater with Mrs. Roosevelt. Holmes's fervent joy in the play gave the others enormous pleasure. He was like a great boy. " Oh my lord! " he would cry out. " If only I could act like that! " On January 8, 1903, Wister records one such intimate dinner at the White House, when the talk bubbled over and the President, leaning his hands on the table, burst out suddenly in sheer joy, " Oh, *aren't* we having a good time! "

The Holmeses had been in Washington less than a month when this dinner party took place. To Holmes the whole situation was natural and pleasant. He took it easily; good company was relaxation after a hard day's work. But for Fanny Holmes, this association with presidents and ambassadors burst like a storm of lightning, like a tornado threatening to engulf her. That first function at the White House had not been intimate at all. It was a big formal dinner, to introduce the new Justice from Massachusetts. Fanny had approached it with trembling, a secret horror. She had dressed in silence and in silence had stepped into the cab. How magnificent Wendell looked in tails and white tie, his silk hat under his arm. *Tails and white satin . . . ambassadors will kiss your hand.*

Fanny had not worn white satin at all, to that first ordeal. She had worn gray silk; her long stiff skirt had rustled behind her as she entered the White House. At her bosom were her favorite flowers, violets from Wendell; from under her *décolletage* rose the white net guimpe, well boned to the ears. Her gray, straight hair swept backward to its tightly braided knot, white gloves reached above her elbows.

In the Green Room, filled with chattering, laughing people, the President himself came forward, greeting Mrs. Holmes as an old friend. He had heard about her, he said genially, from the Lodges, Owen Wister; at Harvard he had, indeed, boarded for a year in a little frame house not very far from the Dixwells. . . . How uncompromising she was and how distinguished, with her look of New England, her straight back like a ramrod, her extraordinary head with the bones showing in her cheeks like a mask.

The President spoke to her kindly, making conversation. Had she seen much of Washington in this first fortnight since her arrival? Had she been to Congress, met many people?

Quite a number of Congressmen's wives had called on her, Fanny replied politely. There was a veiled note in her voice that caused the President to look up, sharply. " You found the ladies pleasant? "

" Washington," Mrs. Holmes replied blandly, " is full of famous men and the women they married when they were young."

The President roared with laughter. Around them people turned inquiring heads. Mrs. Roosevelt came forward, greeting Mrs. Holmes warmly. Dinner was announced. Supreme Court Justices, of course, take precedence over everyone but ambassadors, and there were no ambassadors present. The President bowed to Fanny. Without so much as a look at her husband, moving across long carpets, under crystal chandeliers, Fanny Dixwell Holmes of Garden Street, Cambridge, laid her hand on the arm of the President of the United States and led the company in to dinner.

She was seated, of course, at the President's right. Wendell was a mile away, at the other end of the table. Roosevelt turned to Mrs. Holmes immediately, asked a question. Fanny's reply was quick. The President laughed. From across the table Fanny was aware once more of heads turned in her direction. . . .

She felt suddenly light, as free as air. Why, this was not difficult at all, this company! She could say anything, anything at all, or just sit and listen to the President. This was not a matter of trailing through brilliant rooms in the wake of a brilliant husband. In this company she was first by order of ceremony. Among all these women, so beautifully dressed and so charming, she need wait for no one to speak, for no one but her hostess to make a move.

The knowledge gave her sudden deep assurance. Fanny had always got on well with men. But here, even the women seemed eager to know her, eager to hear what she said that so amused her host. Whether they were friendly or hostile did not really matter. She was first anyway. . . . Why, one could feel at home here, could feel happy, exhilarated! It was as different from Beacon Street as heaven from hell.

All evening, Holmes watched his wife. But Fanny was marvelous! She was a huge success. This sparkling creature, easy, quick — this was the woman who for some thirty years had made life amusing, made life crackle and leap for him. Now for the first time in company he saw her let herself go, be herself, the self that never failed to fascinate.

Late that evening in the cab, leaving the White House portico, Holmes leaned forward in the darkness, tried to see his wife's face. " Fanny," he said. " You were magnificent. You captivated them all." He reached out, laid his hand over hers. " Are you happy? Fanny — tell me."

Fanny turned to her husband. Her face was grave, composed, and very tired. They rolled through the White House gates, light flashed into the carriage and was gone. " I think we shall be very much at home here, Wendell," she said. " I — find it somehow easier to go in to dinner at the head of all the company."

## Suggestions for Study

1. What characteristics of Oliver Wendell Holmes did you learn from this selection? of Fanny Holmes?

2. What suggestions did you discover of the attitude of either Fanny or Wendell to Oliver Wendell Holmes, Sr.?

3. Explain the difference between Holmes and Roosevelt in their attitude toward the law.

4. What details in this account have been created by the imagination of the biographer? Do you approve of this kind of biographical writing?

5. If you have ever had to adjust yourself to new surroundings, tell the class some amusing incident which was part of the adjustment.

6. Vocabulary: flamboyant, meticulous, sardonically.

## For Further Reading of Biography

FAMOUS MEN AND WOMEN OF THE PAST

AGASSIZ. Robinson, M. L.: *Runner of the Mountaintops, Louis Agassiz*

ALCOTT. Meigs, Cornelia: *Invincible Louisa*

AUDUBON. Peattie, D. C.: *Singing in the Wilderness;* Rourke, Constance: *Audubon*

BARTON. Epler, E. P.: *Life of Clara Barton*

BELL. Mackenzie, Catherine: *Alexander Graham Bell*

BOK. Bok, E. W.: *The Americanization of Edward Bok*

BOONE. Lives of Daniel Boone by John Bakeless, Flora Seymour, and S. E. White

BURROUGHS. Barrus, Clara: *John Burroughs, Boy and Man;* Sharp, D. L.: *A Boy's Life of John Burroughs*

CLEMENS. Proudfit, I. B.: *River Boy*

CODY (" Buffalo Bill "). Cody, W. F.: *Autobiography of Buffalo Bill;* Garst, D. S.: *Story of Buffalo Bill*

CUSTER. Custer, Mrs. E. B.: *Boots and Saddles*

EDISON. Meadowcroft, W. H.: *A Boy's Life of Edison*

GRANT. Grant, U. S.: *Personal Memoirs;* Hill, F. T.: *On the Trail of Grant and Lee;* Nicolay, Helen: *The Boy's Life of Ulysses S. Grant*

HUDSON. Powys, Llewelyn: *Henry Hudson*

JACKSON. James, Marquis: *Andrew Jackson*

JEFFERSON, JOSEPH. Jefferson, Joseph: *Autobiography*

JEFFERSON, THOMAS. Bowers, C. G.: *Young Jefferson*

JONES. Russell, Phillips: *John Paul Jones, Man of Action*

KEMBLE. Armstrong, Margaret: *Fanny Kemble*

LYON. Gilchrist, B. B.: *Life of Mary Lyon*

MUIR. Muir, John: *The Story of My Boyhood and Youth*

PAGE. Hendrick, B. J.: *Life and Letters of Walter H. Page; The Training of an American* (Page's youth)

PALMER. Palmer, G. H.: *The Life of Alice Freeman Palmer*

REVERE. Forbes, E.: *Paul Revere*

RIIS. Riis, Jacob: *The Making of an American*

SHERMAN. Lewis, Lloyd: *Sherman, Fighting Prophet*

SKINNER. Skinner, Otis: *Footlights and Spotlights*

# Modern American Poetry

POETRY is fairly easy to recognize but next to impossible to define. Even such good definition makers as encyclopedias admit the difficulty; one of them opens a long sentence full of abstract words with the apology, " Without attempting to define poetry — " The poets themselves (who should know, if anybody does) have tried to express this unexplainable quality of poetry. One says, " Poetry is the opening and closing of a door, leaving those who look through to guess what is seen during a moment." (Carl Sandburg) Another puts it this way, " Poetry is a language that tells us, through a more or less emotional reaction, something that cannot be said." (Edwin Arlington Robinson) Indefinable as poetry may be, it has elements that are commonly recognized. The first is the stirring of our emotions. " The right reader of a good poem can tell the moment it strikes him that he has taken an immortal wound — that he will never get over it." (Robert Frost) And again, " If I read a book and it makes my whole body so cold no fire can ever warm me, I know that it is poetry. If I feel physically as if the top of my head were taken off, I know that it is poetry. These are the only ways I know it. Are there any other ways? " (Emily Dickinson) These two statements sound rather appalling, but what the poets meant was that poetry in its best sense is something intensely personal and definitely individual. Even more than the short story, the essay, and biography, poetry is not just a type of literature but also a frame of mind, a point of view, a scent in the air, a fleeting memory, a hidden force of nature which, like electricity, flashes into light when given the right contacts. If something is poetry to you, it sends an invigorating current through your blood; if it leaves you unmoved, it is not poetry to you. One essence of poetry, then, is emotional appeal.

What stimulates the emotions? So far as poetry is concerned it is largely the imagination. The poet may start out with the rough clay of ordinary things seen every day; but before he has finished molding it, mental vision has far outstripped the merely physical. He has touched the imagination. With the magic spell of words he has clothed an idea with beauty. To realize this, we need only take some poem that really moves us, state the idea in plain prose, and compare the two. Shorn of its wings, the prose version simply confronts us with a fact or a principle; it has lost its power to thrill or sway or uplift us.

Now since most of us, however much capacity we may have for responding to beauty, can only express ourselves in plain prose and probably have difficulty even with that, the poet performs a real service for us by releasing into adequate words vague ideas and emotions that have seethed within us. For the moment we are saying those words from our own hearts, from our own experience. We are " mute, inglorious Miltons " suddenly given a voice. It is the sense of identification with the poet, as well as the mere pleasing sound of the words, which often makes us want to memorize a poem in order that we may in the fullest sense " possess " it.

But in addition to this release which the poet brings us, he may also lead us to new perceptions, new feelings of which we had not even been aware. The observations of

Pix

ROBERT FROST         ELINOR WYLIE         CARL SANDBURG

our eyes are directed by the interests of
our minds. Two persons walking together
down a street may be noticing entirely different details, according to their mental
slant. Now the poet lends us his eyes or his
ears to enable us to sense things previously
unnoticed — new tints brought by the rain,
overtones heard above the city's traffic, a
fleeting expression on a human face. Or, in
the world of thought, he leads us to new
perceptions of human values or new interpretations of divine power. A great poet not
only creates poems; he may also create new
people out of his readers.

Granting that emotion and the imagination are two of the essentials to poetry, what
more is there? Besides mere words, how
does the poet secure the final effect that he
desires? Again a direct answer eludes us,
but we may say that without *rhythm* there
can be no poetry. In a general way we all
know what the word means. Its Greek original meant " measured motion," and in English poetry this is to a large extent produced
by the more or less regular recurrence of
accented and unaccented syllables. Ideas
expressed in rhythmical language that stimulates the imagination and stirs the emotions constitute the essentials of poetry.

## GUIDE TO THE STUDY OF POETRY

Though poetry is almost impossible to
define satisfactorily, its elements are neither numerous nor difficult to identify. You
can never take a poem apart and tell exactly what makes its splendid total effect,
but you can greatly increase your enjoyment if you understand something about
the poet's art. *What* the poet has to tell you
will be either thought or imagery, often a
mingling of both. *How* he tells it accounts
for the music of the poem. Blending of the
thought and imagery and music creates the
*mood,* or general emotional effect, which is
often the very soul of poetry.[1]

### THOUGHT AND IMAGERY

To identify the general subject of a poem
is a mere fraction of grasping its thought.
Think of the thousands of poems that have
been written about nature, death, or love.
You must go farther and discover just what
the poet has to say about the subject. You
have probably had experience in writing a

[1] Definitions of types of poetry, meters, and
common figures of speech appear for reference
at the end of this section, page 341.

*Elliott and Fry*

T. S. ELIOT      EDNA ST. VINCENT MILLAY      STEPHEN V. BENÉT

précis, or one-sentence summary of the central thought of a poem. Reducing a thought from its sparkling expression in poetry to a simple statement in everyday language may destroy much of its beauty or force, but the process will also give you a clear understanding of the thought so that the poet's own words will mean more to you. Moreover, once the thought is in simple terms, you can readily tell whether it owes its value to being a genuinely new idea or to being a fine expression of a common human experience or of a lasting truth.

Only a part of the thought of a poem is actually expressed. What a poem never says but makes you think for yourself is often even more interesting. Read " Richard Cory," on page 282, to see how much material for thought a poem can give you, even when all that it *says* is immediately clear.

But in what the poet does express, he shows that his senses are unusually keen. He not only sees, feels, or hears in a certain way at a given moment, but he also remembers other experiences of seeing, feeling, or hearing that have something in common with this experience. By bringing the immediate and the indirect experiences together in an unexpected phrase, he has made us also have a richer experience and a fuller grasp of what he was trying to tell us. This power to report what he sees and hears so that his words carry the impression vividly to another produces *imagery*. Imagery stimulates our imagination to re-create the impression the poet caught. You can turn through the pages of poetry in this book, just dipping in here and there, never reading a whole poem, and soon find many of these vivid, short word pictures that have a charm all their own.

## THE MUSIC OF POETRY

The music of poetry, like all other music, is created by rhythm and melody, often combined in a repeated pattern.

Remember that the original Greek word from which we get the term *rhythm* meant " measured motion." In English poetry, rhythm is the feeling of movement created by the pattern of light and heavy syllables in the line, the alternation of one or several unaccented syllables with the accented ones. The more light syllables between accents, the faster the line seems to run. A skillful poet takes advantage of this means of varying the music of his lines to fit his thought or mood. So when Vachel Lindsay wishes to create a serious mood, he begins a poem:

It is portentous and a thing of state
That here at midnight in our little town
A mourning figure walks and will not rest,
Near the old courthouse pacing up and down.

But when Stephen Benét describes a fiddling contest, he uses a livelier meter:

He could fiddle all the bugs off a sweet potato vine.
He could fiddle down a possum from a mile-high tree,
He could fiddle up a whale from the bottom of the sea.

Remember that a rigid rhythm is as deadly dull in poetry as in the music of a mechanical piano. A good poet will vary the pattern of syllables and give his rhythm life. As you read poetry aloud, be careful not to make all the words in a line fall into the jog-trot pattern ridiculed in

You'd *scarce* ex*pect* one *of* my *age*
To *speak* in *public* on *the stage.*

When you catch yourself bearing down hard on a preposition like *of* or *on,* you are probably butchering the rhythm the poet created. True rhythm emphasizes, rather than confuses, the meaning of the lines.

Most of the melody in poetry, as in music, is created by skillful repetition of sounds — *refrain, rhyme, alliteration,* and *assonance.* You already know *refrain,* the repetition of whole phrases, and *rhyme,* the repetition of the end sounds of words at fixed intervals, usually at the ends of lines. You probably know *alliteration,* the repetition of the initial sounds of words, for it is a great favorite used in nursery rhymes like " Peter Piper picked a peck of pickled peppers," and in advertising slogans, as well as in fine poetry where the repetitions are less obvious. More subtle but more important in setting the tone of melody is *assonance,* the repetition

of vowel sounds. In Poe's poem " The Bells " (page 520) we have really an exercise in assonance and melody as the poet piles up repeated vowel sounds in each stanza not only to suggest the tone of each kind of bell, but also to suggest the mood associated with it. In any poem that has rich melody you will find not one but several of these melodic repetitions.

Pattern in poetry is based on rhythm, rhyme scheme, line length, and the number of lines in a stanza. Individual patterns, like the sonnet, can best be learned as you come to examples of them, but some of the terms used in describing patterns will be useful all through your study of poetry. The simplest and shortest stanza is the *couplet,* two lines rhyming together. The most common is the *quatrain,* of four lines. It may rhyme in many different ways, but usually in couplets or in the alternate rhyme, the third line rhyming with the first and the fourth line rhyming with the second. Skip through the pages of poetry following, looking at the quatrains, and you will soon see that different combinations of line lengths, rhythms, and rhyme schemes make possible a great variety in this simple verse form. One pattern that you should learn early to identify is *blank verse,* the fine unrhymed form in which most long English poems are written. It must not be confused with *free verse,* which follows no regular pattern, for blank verse follows two requirements of pattern — a regular line length of five accents, and a rhythm pattern of alternate light and heavy syllables, making up the line called *iambic pentameter.* Look at the blank verse on pages 293 and 294 and then at the free verse on pages 300–304 to see how a mere glance will often reveal the difference between these two forms.

These terms are given, not because they are of great importance in themselves, but because it is easier to talk about poetry if you have them at your command, just as it is easier to talk to a mechanic about repairs on an automobile if you know what to call the various mechanisms under the hood.

## MOOD IN POETRY

Every poem has a mood, an emotional tone, or perhaps a series of changing moods. Mood is closely related to thought, but thought alone can seldom create the strong emotional effect that can be achieved by harmonious use of several of the elements of poetry. Imagery is of great importance in mood, not only for the pictures the poet presents, but also for the comparisons he uses. A scarlet tulip may look like a carnival balloon or like a " thin, clear bubble of blood," according to the mood of the observer. Even single words have their own emotional connotation, or suggested associations, so that you can run through a poem and pick out the words that help to build up the dominant feeling. Assonance can have a great share in building up mood, for some vowel sounds are light and gay, while others are harsh, and still others are melancholy. Poe claims that he deliberately used a great number of long o's in " The Raven " (page 522) because he considered that the most mournful sound in human speech. Rhythm, too, contributes to the general emotional effect, for in general the slow, steady rhythms are most harmonious with serious or solemn thought, while the rapid ones lend themselves to lighter moods, though a faster, swinging rhythm is sometimes used to give greater intensity and vigor to serious moods. In any poem with a strong mood, you can soon discover which of these means the poet uses to get his effect.

### THE POET'S INDIVIDUALITY

As in other literary types, style is a good key to the author's individuality. The qualities of style that you have noticed in prose are just as marked in poetry — the writer's choice of words, his personal or impersonal tone, his dignity, or his humor. You will find that some poets like to invert the order of their sentences to gain greater emphasis or to bring the right word out at the end of the line for rhyme, while others, particularly in recent years, keep the natural order of simple speech. Similarly, some poets have a fondness for unusual and picturesque words, while others, chiefly among the moderns, favor simplicity in diction. Add what you can observe of a poet's style to his favorite subjects and ideas, his tendency to excel in imagery or melody or rhythm, and his favorite patterns, and you will be able to sum up the poet for yourself without depending on the critics and historians to tell you what to think and say about him.

## THE BACKGROUND OF MODERN AMERICAN POETRY

Fashions come and go in poems as well as in clothes. Every century seems to produce a different style of writing. Moreover, poetry, like the sea, has its high and low tides. A great wave of poetry is likely to be followed by a period of diminishing interest, and then suddenly poetry again billows up, bringing on its crest young writers with fresh ways of saying things — and thus a new style in poetry is born.

In Part II you will study the poetry of an earlier day and see how it differs from that of the twentieth century. However, there is one point that should be clear to your mind before you begin listening to the voices of the modern world. American poetry was riding at the crest of the wave during the first half of the nineteenth century. The voluminous verse of that period was usually romantic, sometimes overly sentimental and moralistic, often commonplace in its expression, and almost always following the rules of regular meter. This does not mean that the poetry of the nineteenth century was poor. On the contrary, much great poetry was produced. It simply means that styles tended in those directions and were bound to shift before long.

To understand how changes came about, it is necessary to know something of Walt Whitman, who was responsible for many of them. You will study him in greater detail in Part II where he appears among his contemporaries. But Whitman's face was set toward the future rather than the past. His own generation failed for many years to appreciate him. He had no noteworthy

 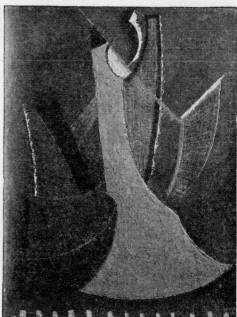

Modern American painting has developed along lines parallel with twentieth century poetry. Each of the five paintings on these pages illustrates one or more of the six points in the creed of the imagist poets (see page 280).

Morgan Russell's " Eidos 23 " (upper left) creates new rhythms and expresses new moods. Painting of this type, having no recognizable subject matter, is the " free verse " of visual art.

" Mime " by Man Ray (upper right) exhibits absolute freedom in the choice of subject. The witty treatment of the " image " suggests to the discerning eye the shallow, sophisticated character of the girl portrayed here.

Georgia O'Keeffe's " White Barn " in the medium of paint is " poetry that is hard and clear, never blurred or indefinite." It is a brilliant illustration of the effectiveness of extremely simple subject matter drawn from everyday life.

Charles Sheeler in "Church Street El" (above) concentrates on a minimum of lines and color areas to give us the "essence" of his impression of this city scene. Notice that his forms are clean-cut and exact, that they build up a strong composition without being in any respect "merely decorative."

"Chilmark" (right) by Thomas Benton illustrates pictorially all six imagist tenets for poetry. Its powerful emotional appeal is achieved through the repetition of the billowing forms of hills, trees, and clouds.

disciples during his life, but when the time was ripe new poets looked back to him as their master.

Whitman was an individualist who broke away from all tradition. He knew no difference between a supposedly poetic and an unpoetic subject but felt at liberty to write upon any subject he wished in a free swinging sort of chant that ignored the prescribed metrical laws. To many ears this was not poetry at all, but prose printed in lines of varying length. However, when poetry again came flowing back after its low ebb at the end of the nineteenth and beginning of the twentieth century, it was evident beyond denial that the new world had something to say in " free verse." Eventually, after a long fight for life, free verse became established as a recognized sister of metrical verse.

## TWENTIETH CENTURY BRINGS " THE NEW POETRY "

In 1912 there was established a little magazine of verse called *Poetry*. Poets hitherto unknown found encouragement between its covers. Strange kinds of poetry were fostered and began to develop. In the next few years volume after volume of poetry appeared on the market and, what was more, found a sale. " The new poetry " became a topic of general conversation, like the weather and baseball. People had a hard time deciding whether the new poetry *was* poetry, and then whether or not they liked it. But upon all this controversy the new poetry thrived, and now it seems neither new nor startling — just part of our heritage of poetry, just the voice of our modern America speaking to us. Those poets who thirty years ago seemed dangerous revolutionists are now our accepted and established artists.

It is hard to know which of these new poets to put first in point of time. The very fact that Masters, Robinson, Amy Lowell, Frost, Sandburg, and Lindsay broke almost simultaneously upon the shore of poetry added to the effectiveness of all of them. In the five years between 1912 and our entrance into World War I in 1917, each of them had published a significant volume which set the pace for what was to follow. Each of the six has his own clearly marked individuality. Robinson and Frost hold to traditional verse forms but picture a new New England with startling insight.

## THE IMAGISTS WIELD INFLUENCE

Amy Lowell pioneered in new verse forms and allied herself with the Imagists, a band of Englishmen and Americans who had distinct theories of poetry. Since the six tenets of the Imagists have had such widespread influence upon modern poetry and really sum up many of the important differences between nineteenth- and twentieth-century poetry even in the latter's more conservative forms, it is well to quote their creed:

1. To use the language of common speech; to employ always the *exact* word, not the merely decorative word.

2. To create new rhythms as the expression of new moods. We do not insist upon " free verse " as the only method of writing poetry. . . . We do believe that the individuality of a poet may often be better expressed in free verse than in conventional forms.

3. To allow absolute freedom in the choice of subject.

4. To present an image [hence the name " Imagist "]. We are not a school of painters; but we believe that poetry should render particulars exactly and not deal in vague generalities, however magnificent and sonorous.

5. To produce poetry that is hard and clear, never blurred or indefinite.

6. Finally, most of us believe that concentration is the very essence of poetry.

Many of these principles are illustrated also by Masters and Sandburg, both Illinois poets, who have made effective use of free verse, the crisp figure, startling epithet, and the unlimited selection of subject matter in their interpretations of the town, the city, and the plain. Lindsay, also a native of Illinois, is entirely different in his method, using a highly marked rhythm and numerous unusual devices to produce an intensely emotional musical effect.

These six were the most distinguished of

our older poets of the present century. Three of them are now dead.

## POETRY BETWEEN TWO WARS

After these six the choice becomes more difficult. You will find in this section six more poets, children of the eighties, who were the young poets of World War I and the years following it. Four of these six are now dead. Then follow four poets born in the nineties. Of these Edna St. Vincent Millay and Stephen Vincent Benét were the youthful prodigies of their generation. Fortunately the promise of their early years was fulfilled by continued publication of vigorous and individual poems. Benét's early death in 1943 enabled the world to evaluate his work as a whole, and he has already taken his place as a major poet of the twentieth century. Edna Millay is unchallenged as the leading woman poet living today. Archibald MacLeish won recognition later in life than the other two and is still actively producing new work.

## POETRY TODAY LESS FLOURISHING

While much good poetry is being written at present by an everspreading group of youthful poets, there seems to be no one among them who is universally hailed as a candidate to step into the shoes of those who are now far from young. Poetry seems to be again at the ebb. But a great war has just taken place, and a war sometimes brings great poetry in its wake. We have been told that there was an amazing interest in the writing of poetry among the men at the front — that they seemed to feel release and satisfaction in thus expressing themselves. From the ranks of the veterans may emerge the writers who will carry on the tradition of vigorous and original American poetry.

# Edwin Arlington Robinson
## 1869–1935

Edwin Arlington Robinson may be styled a portrait painter in poetry. A whole gallery of men is revealed to our eye and, better yet, to

our imagination as we turn the pages of Robinson's books. Sometimes their whole souls are laid open to us; sometimes we catch only a suggestion beneath a suave exterior. Sometimes they are treated earnestly, sometimes half cynically, sometimes with whimsical tenderness. In every case they are made very real, very human.

Robinson came from Maine, attended Harvard, and, though he lived most of the time in New York, was distinctly associated with New England, where the "Tilbury Town" and the "Town down the River" of his poems are located. He thrice won the Pulitzer prize, and many consider him the greatest recent American poet. Besides studying modern men he turned his attention to the Arthurian legends and in his long poems, *Merlin, Lancelot,* and *Tristram,* did the most extensive work based on these stories since Tennyson, though differing widely in treatment from the earlier poet. All the poems below will be found in the 1930 edition of his *Collected Poems.*

## MINIVER CHEEVY

Miniver Cheevy, child of scorn,
  Grew lean while he assailed the seasons;
He wept that he was ever born,
  And he had reasons.

Miniver loved the days of old    5
  When swords were bright and steeds were
    prancing;
The vision of a warrior bold
  Would set him dancing.

Miniver sighed for what was not,
  And dreamed, and rested from his labors;
He dreamed of Thebes° and Camelot,°  11
  And Priam's° neighbors.

Miniver mourned the ripe renown
  That made so many a name so fragrant;
He mourned Romance, now on the town,
  And Art, a vagrant.  16

11. **Thebes** (thēbz): a famous city of ancient Greece. (Notice the circle after the word *Thebes.* This sign is used in the poetry sections of this book to call your attention to each word which is explained in a footnote.) 11. **Camelot** (kăm′ĕ-lŏt): the city of King Arthur and the Knights of the Round Table. 12. **Priam** (prī′ăm): the king of Troy during the time the Greeks were besieging it.

Miniver loved the Medici,°
  Albeit he had never seen one;
He would have sinned incessantly
  Could he have been one.          20

Miniver cursed the commonplace
  And eyed a khaki suit with loathing;
He missed the medieval grace
  Of iron clothing.

Miniver scorned the gold he sought,          25
  But sore annoyed was he without it;
Miniver thought, and thought, and thought,
  And thought about it.

Miniver Cheevy, born too late,
  Scratched his head and kept on think-
     ing;          30
Miniver coughed, and called it fate,
  And kept on drinking.

17. **Medici** (měd′ê-chē): a highly cultivated
but often unprincipled family of Florence, Italy,
in the fifteenth and sixteenth centuries.

## RICHARD CORY

"Richard Cory" represents almost the reverse of "Miniver Cheevy." Richard Cory
seemed to be everything that anyone could
wish; Miniver Cheevy just took it out in wishing. He lived his dream life and "kept on
drinking," while Richard Cory went home one
night and —

Whenever Richard Cory went downtown,
  We people on the pavement looked at
    him:
He was a gentleman from sole to crown,
  Clean-favored, and imperially slim.

And he was always quietly arrayed,          5
  And he was always human when he
    talked;
But still he fluttered pulses when he said,
  "Good morning," and he glittered when
    he walked.

And he was rich — yes, richer than a king —
  And admirably schooled in every grace:

In fine, we thought that he was everything          11
  To make us wish that we were in his
  place.

So on we worked, and waited for the light,
  And went without the meat, and cursed
    the bread;          14
And Richard Cory, one calm summer night,
  Went home and put a bullet through his
  head.

## BEWICK FINZER

Bewick Finzer is a failure in a different way
from Miniver Cheevy and Richard Cory. He
is a sad picture of the man who had achieved
his dream, that of wealth, and cracked under
the strain when he lost it.

Time was when his half-million drew
  The breath of six per cent;
But soon the worm of what-was-not
  Fed hard on his content;
And something crumbled in his brain          5
  When his half-million went.

Time passed, and filled along with his
  The place of many more;
Time came, and hardly one of us
  Had credence to restore,          10
From what appeared one day, the man
  Whom we had known before.

The broken voice, the withered neck,
  The coat worn out with care,
The cleanliness of indigence,          15
  The brilliance of despair,
The fond imponderable dreams
  Of affluence — all were there.

Poor Finzer, with his dreams and schemes,
  Fares hard now in the race,          20
With heart and eye that have a task
  When he looks in the face
Of one who might so easily
  Have been in Finzer's place.

He comes unfailing for the loan 25
   We give and then forget;
He comes, and probably for years
   Will he be coming yet —
Familiar as an old mistake,
   And futile as regret. 30

## AN OLD STORY

This poem is not clearly a portrait as the three preceding poems are. Instead it describes a certain relationship between two persons. The poem appeals to the mind rather than to the eye. The clue to the speaker's jealousy of his friend lies in the second stanza. Do not be misled by the simple words into thinking this is an easy sentence to understand. As in many of Robinson's poems, the thought may require several rereadings. It will become clear if you will start at the end of the stanza and work back.

Strange that I did not know him then,
   That friend of mine!
I did not even show him then
   One friendly sign;

But cursed him for the ways he had 5
   To make me see
My envy of the praise he had
   For praising me.

I would have rid the earth of him
   Once in my pride! . . . 10
I never knew the worth of him
   Until he died.

## THE HOUSE ON THE HILL

In the preceding poems Robinson pictures people. This one is the exact converse — a picture of the absence of human beings. How the insistent loneliness of the deserted house is brought out through the repetition! Our curiosity about this house is stimulated, but not satisfied. What kind of people once lived there? Perhaps a Richard Cory or a Bewick Finzer?

They are all gone away,
   The house is shut and still,
There is nothing more to say.

Through broken walls and gray
   The wind blows bleak and shrill: 5
They are all gone away.

Nor is there one today
   To speak them good or ill:
There is nothing more to say.

Why is it then we stray 10
   Around the sunken sill?
They are all gone away.

And our poor fancy-play
   For them is wasted skill:
There is nothing more to say. 15

There is ruin and decay
   In the house on the hill:
They are all gone away,
There is nothing more to say.

## Suggestions for Study of Robinson

### MINIVER CHEEVY

1. In what spirit does the poet present Miniver? How does he make you feel about him? Indicate lines to prove your points. Notice how the name is repeated at the beginning of each stanza.

2. Did you ever know anyone like this? Would you call him a common type?

### RICHARD CORY

3. Why does one gasp on reading the last two lines for the first time? What suppositions flock to your mind as to possible causes for Richard's deed?

4. Is such a situation possible in life? Is it common? What bit of philosophy about life does it suggest to your mind?

5. What verbs in the second stanza have unusual force and originality? Explain them.

6. How do you explain the first two lines of the last stanza?

### BEWICK FINZER

7. How do you interpret "the worm of what-was-not"? Put into simple words just what happened to Finzer in the first stanza.

8. How do the people of the town regard Finzer now?

9. Which of the three men portrayed in these three poems do you consider most pathetic? Why?

AN OLD STORY

10. What is the significance of the title " An Old Story "?

11. State in your own words the reason for the speaker's jealousy. Does it seem to you a common or uncommon cause of jealousy? What shows that the speaker must be a man and not a woman?

12. Why did the death of the friend change the speaker's attitude toward him?

THE HOUSE ON THE HILL

13. Show how the poet makes every word count in his picture of complete desolation.

14. This poem is written in an old French form called a *villanelle*, which we do not often see in American poetry. By studying the poem first, try to discover what the characteristics of a villanelle are. Then check yourself by referring to the dictionary. Try writing a villanelle of your own. Does it seem an easy or difficult form to write?

SPECIAL ASSIGNMENTS

15. If you like to draw, try making sketches to show the differences in personality of the three men who are named in the first three poems. Or draw a sketch of some deserted house in your community, bringing out its desolation as Robinson does in the last poem. Why is " An Old Story " almost impossible to illustrate with a drawing?

16. Write brief stories or dialogues in which you bring out the personalities of one or more of the men described in the poems. Can " An Old Story " be better clarified by a dialogue than by a sketch? Why?

17. Write an account of conditions in modern life that tend to produce men like those in the first three poems.

18. Write a sketch or story based on some deserted house in your community. See the opening of Poe's " Fall of the House of Usher " for suggestions on creating a desolate atmosphere.

## For Your Vocabulary

ANTONYMS. We can often get a clearer conception of the meaning of a word by comparing it with its opposite. Words of opposite meaning are called *antonyms* (ăn′tŏ-nĭmz) — opposing names, as contrasted with synonyms — names meaning very nearly the same. In the third stanza of " Bewick Finzer " the poet uses two good terms for the contrasting states in which Finzer found himself, *indigence* (ĭn′-dĭ-jĕns) and *affluence* (ăf′lōō-ĕns). *Indigence* is simply a state of being in need. Care of the *indigent* has become a serious problem in modern society. *Affluence* is a state of abundance, with riches flowing in. What are the simplest synonyms for *indigent* and *affluent?* These two words will necessarily be antonyms for each other.

FIGURATIVE USE OF WORDS. When Robinson says, in " Richard Cory," that people *on the pavement* went without the *meat* and cursed the *bread,* he uses symbols. A symbol is something that stands for something else. *People on the pavement* or *in the street* is a symbol for " people in general " or the average man. *Meat* and *bread* are often used as symbols for food in general. Here *meat* stands for the more desirable things of life, as *bread* stands for bare necessities. Think of other ways in which both can be used symbolically. Try transferring the ideas into other symbols. If we use *velvet* to symbolize luxuries, what would symbolize bare necessities? What would symbolize actual want?

## Amy Lowell    1874–1925

You will probably like Amy Lowell either tremendously or not at all. She seldom leaves her readers lukewarm. She belonged to the same renowned Lowell family of Cambridge as James Russell Lowell, who was a cousin of her grandfather. One of her brothers was a distinguished astronomer, and another was president of Harvard University. Miss Lowell's education was entirely individual, through tutoring, extensive travel, and her own determined study of literature and verse technique after she decided at twenty-eight to become a poet. She did not try to rush into print, but laid careful foundations for herself and issued her first volume ten years after she had come to this decision. It was not, however, until her second volume, *Sword Blades and Poppy Seed* (1914), that her individual style was evident. She became the chief exponent of the Imagists and the promoter of " polyphonic prose."

Like other innovators, Miss Lowell became the target for both witticism and abuse, which gradually diminished as the public became more accustomed to her manner and realized that when she wished she could be a master of the regular rhythms as well as of " free verse." Finally, when her death came unexpectedly, through a paralytic stroke, the press was overflowing with praise of her great contributions to American literature.

In addition to her original verse, Miss Lowell made detailed studies of foreign literatures. Her English versions of Chinese poems, her critical essays on French poets, and her two-volume study of John Keats are notable. Following the footsteps of her famous poet-relative she wrote *A Critical Fable* as a sequel to his *Fable for Critics*. Her *Tendencies in Modern American Poetry* presents six of our modern poets in a style which high-school students can enjoy reading.

Here are two poems about persons, both from *Sword Blades and Poppy Seed*. Note how different they are from the pictures given us by Robinson — no names attached, no probing into their past histories or their present characters; simply the impression upon the poetic imagination made by these opposite types.

## A LADY

You are beautiful and faded
Like an old opera tune
Played upon a harpsichord;
Or like the sun-flooded silks
Of an eighteenth-century boudoir.          5
In your eyes
Smolder the fallen roses of outlived minutes,
And the perfume of your soul
Is vague and suffusing,
With the pungence of sealed spice jars.   10
Your half tones delight me,
And I grow mad with gazing
At your blent colors.
My vigor is a new-minted penny,
Which I cast at your feet.                  15
Gather it up from the dust,
That its sparkle may amuse you.

## MUSIC

The neighbor sits in his window and plays the flute.
From my bed I can hear him,
And the round notes flutter and tap about the room,
And hit against each other,
Blurring to unexpected chords.             5
It is very beautiful,
With the little flute notes all about me,
In the darkness.

In the daytime,
The neighbor eats bread and onions with one hand          10
And copies music with the other.
He is fat and has a bald head,

So I do not look at him,
But run quickly past his window.
There is always the sky to look at,        15
Or the water in the well!

But when night comes and he plays his flute,
I think of him as a young man,
With gold seals hanging from his watch,
And a blue coat with silver buttons.       20

As I lie in my bed
The flute notes push against my ears and lips,
And I go to sleep, dreaming.

## PATTERNS

" Patterns," from *Men, Women, and Ghosts*, is a lyric poem — deeply emotional and personal, as a good lyric should be. There is more than a touch of the romantic in both the setting and the story; but the poet is not merely describing a woman in a beautiful garden, thinking of her lover, nor is she merely telling a story, although both of these elements are present. These are part of the " pattern "; that is, the woman of the poem is presented as being and doing what a highly sensitive and cultured person might be expected to do under the circumstances. Through it all, the poet is also expressing an attitude toward life; and that is the most important of all.

I walk down the garden paths,
And all the daffodils
Are blowing, and the bright blue squills.
I walk down the patterned garden paths
In my stiff brocaded gown.                 5
With my powdered hair and jeweled fan,

I too am a rare
Pattern. As I wander down
The garden paths.

My dress is richly figured,                10
And the train
Makes a pink and silver stain
On the gravel, and the thrift
Of the borders.
Just a plate of current fashion,           15
Tripping by in high-heeled, ribboned shoes.
Not a softness anywhere about me,
Only whalebone and brocade.
And I sink on a seat in the shade
Of a lime tree. For my passion             20
Wars against the stiff brocade.
The daffodils and squills
Flutter in the breeze
As they please.
And I weep;                                25
For the lime tree is in blossom
And one small flower has dropped upon my
    bosom.

And the plashing of water drops
In the marble fountain
Comes down the garden paths.               30
The dripping never stops.
Underneath my stiffened gown
Is the softness of a woman bathing in a mar-
    ble basin,
A basin in the midst of hedges grown
So thick, she cannot see her lover hiding,
But she guesses he is near,                36
And the sliding of the water
Seems the stroking of a dear
Hand upon her.                             39
What is summer in a fine brocaded gown!
I should like to see it lying in a heap upon
    the ground.
All the pink and silver crumpled up on the
    ground.

I would be the pink and silver as I ran along
    the paths,
And he would stumble after,
Bewildered by my laughter.                 45
I should see the sun flashing from his sword
    hilt and the buckles on his shoes.
I would choose

To lead him in a maze along the patterned
    paths,
A bright and laughing maze for my heavy-
    booted lover.
Till he caught me in the shade,            50
And the buttons of his waistcoat bruised
    my body as he clasped me,
Aching, melting, unafraid.
With the shadows of the leaves and the sun
    drops,
And the plopping of the water drops,
All about us in the open afternoon —       55
I am very like to swoon
With the weight of this brocade,
For the sun sifts through the shade.

Underneath the fallen blossom
In my bosom,                               60
Is a letter I have hid.
It was brought to me this morning by a
    rider from the duke.
" Madam, we regret to inform you that Lord
    Hartwell
Died in action Thursday se'nnight." '
As I read it in the white morning sunlight,
The letters squirmed like snakes.          66
" Any answer, Madam? " said my footman.
" No," I told him.
" See that the messenger takes some refresh-
    ment.
No, no answer."                            70
And I walked into the garden,
Up and down the patterned paths,
In my stiff, correct brocade.
The blue and yellow flowers stood up
    proudly in the sun,
Each one.                                  75
I stood upright too,
Held rigid to the pattern
By the stiffness of my gown.
Up and down I walked
Up and down.                               80

In a month he would have been my hus-
    band.
In a month, here, underneath this lime,
We would have broke the pattern;
He for me, and I for him,
He as colonel, I as lady,                  85
On this shady seat.

He had a whim
That sunlight carried blessing.
And I answered, " It shall be as you have
    said."
Now he is dead.                                        90

In summer and in winter I shall walk
Up and down
The patterned garden paths
In my stiff brocaded gown.
The squills and daffodils                              95
Will give place to pillared roses, and to
    asters, and to snow.
I shall go
Up and down,
In my gown.
Gorgeously arrayed,                                    100
Boned and stayed.
And the softness of my body will be guarded
    from embrace
By each button, hook, and lace.
For the man who should loose me is dead,
Fighting with the Duke in Flanders,        105
In a pattern called a war.
Christ! What are patterns for?

## Suggestions for Study of Lowell

1. In the first two short poems point out the
contrast between the writer and the person observed. What kind of person is suggested by
the " new-minted penny "? Is Amy Lowell
speaking in her own person in these two poems
or is she speaking in the person of an entirely
imaginary character?

2. Find evidence in both these poems that
the writer likes antique things; that she follows
the principles of the Imagists. (See page 280
for their program.)

3. How many different kinds of " patterns "
can you find in the poem by that name? Look
up " pattern " in the dictionary and find out
how it fits the idea of the poem.

4. Notice some of the careful details of description and how they add to the picture.
What details suggest a certain country and
certain century for the story?

5. Tell briefly the story back of the picture.
How does the lady's manner of receiving the
fatal news fit into the pattern idea?

6. This poem is typical of the best so-called
" free verse." Comment on the rhythm, the
irregularity of the line lengths, the rhyme or
lack of it, and the general effect of it all.

7. What is meant by the last line? What
values do " patterns " have in life? When are
we likely to rebel against them?

8. Draw illustrations of the Lowell characters. Are they more or less easy to represent
than the Robinson characters?

9. Read her poem " Bombardment " and see
if you can find a difference between this " polyphonic prose " and free verse. This is an excellent poem for a good reader to present orally
to the class. Write a description of a modern
air raid in this style.

10. Read some of the interesting accounts
of Miss Lowell's unique personality and report
to the class. There is a good account in Louis
Untermeyer's autobiography, *From Another
World*.

## Robert Frost                        1875–

Strange that a poet who represents the very
essence of New England farm life and who
never writes of anything else should have spent
the first ten years of his life in San Francisco
and have been named after the Southern general Robert E. Lee! Yet Robert Frost was a
genuine New Englander by ancestry and disposition, and those first ten years before the
death of his father and his return East with
his mother seem to have left little impression
on his poetry. Neither did the mill town of
Lawrence, Massachusetts, where he went to
school and later worked as bobbin boy in a
mill. It was always the country that charmed
him. Spasmodic attempts at a college education both at Dartmouth and at Harvard were
given up through lack of interest. He supported his family by various temporary jobs,
teaching, cobbling, editing, and the like. Finally
his grandfather bought him a farm in New
Hampshire where, for a number of years, he
worked and wrote but was unable to get much
published. The sale of the farm enabled him
to move his family to England and it was
there, strange to say, that his distinctly American volumes, *A Boy's Will* and *North of Boston*, were published and received acclamation.
He returned to America with his literary reputation established, but with no desire to give
up farming in the New England hills. Intervals
of lecturing and of teaching at Amherst, the

University of Michigan, and other places are the only breaks in his peaceful farm life.

More than any other living poet, Frost gives us, not the artificial picture of country life viewed from a classical library, but the simple, genuine life he knows, expressed in the idiom of daily speech. It is the combination of this familiar speech with the rhythm of blank verse which marks the distinctive style of Robert Frost's poetry. His subject matter is sometimes the minutely observed details of nature interpreted through human experience, sometimes the exploration of the minds of his farm people with their instincts, their terrors, their griefs, and often their dumb inertia.

## THE PASTURE

" The Pasture " was printed as a motto at the beginning of *North of Boston* and may well serve as an invitation to become acquainted with the work of Robert Frost.

I'm going out to clean the pasture spring;
I'll only stop to rake the leaves away
(And wait to watch the water clear, I may):
I shan't be gone long — You come too.

I'm going out to fetch the little calf
That's standing by the mother. It's so young,
It totters when she licks it with her tongue.
I shan't be gone long — You come too.

## BIRCHES

Birch trees are fairly common in many parts of the country, and many boys besides Robert Frost have no doubt swung on them; but to the poet who in later life sees the birches and recalls his boyhood delight in swinging on them they suggest some of the most fundamental problems of life. That sounds as though you were about to read something difficult and involved, but such is far from being the case. Just as the birch tree is an everyday sight, so is the language of the poet that of everyday. Frost writes in a way that seems conversational, as though he were talking to a group of friends by a fireside, and that is one of the charms of his poetry.

When I see birches bend to left and right
Across the line of straighter darker trees,
I like to think some boy's been swinging them.
But swinging doesn't bend them down to stay.
Ice storms do that. Often you must have seen them           5
Loaded with ice a sunny winter morning
After a rain. They click upon themselves
As the breeze rises, and turn many-colored
As the stir cracks and crazes their enamel.
Soon the sun's warmth makes them shed crystal shells           10
Shattering and avalanching on the snow crust —
Such heaps of broken glass to sweep away
You'd think the inner dome of heaven had fallen.
They are dragged to the withered bracken by the load,
And they seem not to break; though, once they are bowed           15
So low for long, they never right themselves:
You may see their trunks arching in the woods
Years afterward, trailing their leaves on the ground
Like girls on hands and knees that throw their hair
Before them over their heads to dry in the sun.           20
But I was going to say when Truth broke in
With all her matter of fact about the ice storm
(Now am I free to be poetical?)
I should prefer to have some boy bend them
As he went out and in to fetch the cows —
Some boy too far from town to learn baseball,           26
Whose only play was what he found himself,
Summer or winter, and could play alone.
One by one he subdued his father's trees
By riding them down over and over again
Until he took the stiffness out of them,           31
And not one but hung limp, not one was left
For him to conquer. He learned all there was
To learn about not launching out too soon
And so not carrying the tree away           35

" Birches bend to left and right
Across the line of straighter, darker trees."

Clear to the ground. He always kept his poise
To the top branches, climbing carefully
With the same pains you use to fill a cup
Up to the brim, and even above the brim.
Then he flung outward, feet first, with a swish,    40
Kicking his way down through the air to the ground.
So was I once myself a swinger of birches;
And so I dream of going back to be.
It's when I'm weary of considerations,
And life is too much like a pathless wood
Where your face burns and tickles with the cobwebs    46
Broken across it, and one eye is weeping
From a twig's having lashed across it open.
I'd like to get away from earth awhile    49
And then come back to it and begin over.
May no fate willfully misunderstand me
And half grant what I wish and snatch me away
Not to return. Earth's the right place for love:
I don't know where it's likely to go better.
I'd like to go by climbing a birch tree,    55
And climb black branches up a snow-white trunk
*Toward* heaven, till the tree could bear no more,
But dipped its top and set me down again.
That would be good both going and coming back.
One could do worse than be a swinger of birches.    60

## STOPPING BY WOODS ON A SNOWY EVENING

As the title suggests, this poem is mainly a picture or, perhaps, an episode set within the picture. But to the poet there was much more, as you will see from the last three lines.

Whose woods these are I think I know.
His house is in the village though;
He will not see me stopping here
To watch his woods fill up with snow.

My little horse must think it queer    5
To stop without a farmhouse near
Between the woods and frozen lake
The darkest evening of the year.

He gives his harness bells a shake
To ask if there is some mistake.    10
The only other sound's the sweep
Of easy wind and downy flake.

The woods are lovely, dark, and deep,
But I have promises to keep,
And miles to go before I sleep,    15
And miles to go before I sleep.

## MENDING WALL

The poetry back of commonplace labor is evident to the imagination of Robert Frost. Here we have an ordinary enough task in New England, where low stone walls are the common boundaries between property. Two farmers move along either side of the wall repairing the winter's ravages. One is a practical, unimaginative man who thinks only conventionally as he has been taught in the past. The other has a lively fancy and a questioning mind. There is something fresh and flavorful in his mental approach even to this simple job. He is a poet.

Something there is that doesn't love a wall,
That sends the frozen ground swell under it,
And spills the upper boulders in the sun;
And makes gaps even two can pass abreast.
The work of hunters is another thing:    5
I have come after them and made repair
Where they have left not one stone on a stone,
But they would have the rabbit out of hiding,
To please the yelping dogs. The gaps I mean,
No one has seen them made or heard them made,    10
But at spring mending time we find them there.
I let my neighbor know beyond the hill;
And on a day we meet to walk the line
And set the wall between us once again.
We keep the wall between us as we go.    15

To each the boulders that have fallen to
each.
And some are loaves and some so nearly
balls
We have to use a spell to make them bal-
ance:
" Stay where you are until our backs are
turned! "
We wear our fingers rough with handling
them.                                          20
Oh, just another kind of outdoor game,
One on a side. It comes to little more:
There where it is we do not need the wall:
He is all pine and I am apple orchard.
My apple trees will never get across    25
And eat the cones under his pines, I tell
him.
He only says, " Good fences make good
neighbors."
Spring is the mischief in me, and I wonder
If I could put a notion in his head:
" *Why* do they make good neighbors? Isn't
it                                             30
Where there are cows? But here there are
no cows.
Before I built a wall I'd ask to know
What I was walling in or walling out,
And to whom I was like to give offense.
Something there is that doesn't love a wall,
That wants it down." I could say " Elves "
to him,                                        36
But it's not elves exactly, and I'd rather
He said it for himself. I see him there
Bringing a stone grasped firmly by the top
In each hand, like an old stone savage
armed.                                         40
He moves in darkness as it seems to me,
Not of woods only and the shade of trees.
He will not go behind his father's saying,
And he likes having thought of it so well
He says again, " Good fences make good
neighbors."                                    45

## A MINOR BIRD

What a lot of food for thought is packed in
the last two couplets of this apparently simple
little poem!

I have wished a bird would fly away,
And not sing by my house all day;

Have clapped my hands at him from the
door
When it seemed as if I could bear no more.

The fault must partly have been in me.
The bird was not to blame for his key.

And of course there must be something
wrong
In wanting to silence any song.

## THE ROAD NOT TAKEN

All the mystery of how fate affects human
lives is suggested in this little episode of a
walk in the woods. Frost does not put a
" moral tag " at the end of his poems as the
older writers were inclined to do. That is, he
does not say bluntly: " This is the lesson to be
found here." Instead, his whole poem becomes
a symbol of a great truth. The reader must
make out what the symbol stands for and follow up the idea in his own mind.

Two roads diverged in a yellow wood,
And sorry I could not travel both
And be one traveler, long I stood
And looked down one as far as I could
To where it bent in the undergrowth;    5

Then took the other, as just as fair,
And having perhaps the better claim,
Because it was grassy and wanted wear;
Though as for that the passing there
Had worn them really about the same,  10

And both that morning equally lay
In leaves no step had trodden black.
Oh, I kept the first for another day!
Yet knowing how way leads on to way,
I doubted if I should ever come back.  15

I shall be telling this with a sigh
Somewhere ages and ages hence:
Two roads diverged in a wood, and I —
I took the one less traveled by,
And that has made all the difference.  20

## A CONSIDERABLE SPECK

Humorous as this little incident is, it has the flavor of gentleness and tolerance so typical of Robert Frost's whole attitude toward life. Notice, too, the genial implication about human beings in the last lines. The poem appears in one of his latest volumes, *Come In.*

A speck that would have been beneath my sight
On any but a paper sheet so white
Set off across what I had written there.
And I had idly poised my pen in air
To stop it with a period of ink
When something strange about it made me think.
This was no dust speck by my breathing blown,
But unmistakably a living mite
With inclinations it could call its own.
It paused as with suspicion of my pen,
And then came racing wildly on again
To where my manuscript was not yet dry;
Then paused again and either drank or smelt —
With loathing, for again it turned to fly.
Plainly with an intelligence I dealt.
It seemed too tiny to have room for feet,
Yet must have had a set of them complete
To express how much it didn't want to die.
It ran with terror and with cunning crept.
It faltered; I could see it hesitate;
Then in the middle of the open sheet
Cower down in desperation to accept
Whatever I accorded it of fate.

I have none of the tenderer-than-thou
Collectivistic regimenting love
With which the modern world is being swept.
But this poor microscopic item now!
Since it was nothing I knew evil of
I let it lie there till I hoped it slept.

I have a mind myself and recognize
Mind when I meet with it in any guise.
No one can know how glad I am to find
On any sheet the least display of mind.

## THE DEATH OF THE HIRED MAN

This is the best of Frost's longer narrative poems. While it tells a story, definite and tragic, there is no action; merely a conversation between a New England farmer and his wife. As always in Frost's work, there are graphic pictures which enhance the setting and in this poem help to soften the sting of the tragedy. Frost, although so much of his poetry concerns the Yankee farmer, never uses dialect to create a rustic effect.

Mary sat musing on the lamp flame at the table,
Waiting for Warren. When she heard his step,
She ran on tiptoe down the darkened passage
To meet him in the doorway with the news
And put him on his guard. " Silas is back."        5
She pushed him outward with her through the door
And shut it after her. " Be kind," she said.
She took the market things from Warren's arms
And set them on the porch, then drew him down
To sit beside her on the wooden steps.    10

" When was I ever anything but kind to him?
But I'll not have the fellow back," he said.
" I told him so last haying, didn't I?
' If he left then,' I said, ' that ended it.'
What good is he? Who else will harbor him        15
At his age for the little he can do?
What help he is there's no depending on.
Off he goes always when I need him most.
' He thinks he ought to earn a little pay,
Enough at least to buy tobacco with,    20
So he won't have to beg and be beholden.'
' All right,' I say, ' I can't afford to pay
Any fixed wages, though I wish I could.'
' Someone else can.' ' Then someone else will have to.'
I shouldn't mind his bettering himself    25
If that was what it was. You can be certain,

When he begins like that, there's someone
  at him
Trying to coax him off with pocket
  money —
In haying time, when any help is scarce.
In winter he comes back to us. I'm
  done."                                          30

" Sh! not so loud: he'll hear you," Mary
  said.

" I want him to: he'll have to soon or late."

" He's worn out. He's asleep beside the
  stove.
When I came up from Rowe's I found him
  here,                                           34
Huddled against the barn door fast asleep,
A miserable sight, and frightening, too —
You needn't smile — I didn't recognize
  him —
I wasn't looking for him — and he's
  changed.
Wait till you see."

        " Where did you say he'd been? "

" He didn't say. I dragged him to the
  house,                                          40
And gave him tea, and tried to make him
  smoke.
I tried to make him talk about his travels,
Nothing would do: he just kept nodding
  off."

" What did he say? Did he say anything? "

" But little."

        " Anything? Mary, confess          45
He said he'd come to ditch the meadow for
  me."

" Warren! "

        " But did he? I just want to know."

" Of course he did. What would you have
  him say?

Surely you wouldn't grudge the poor old
  man
Some humble way to save his self-respect.
He added, if you really care to know,    51
He meant to clear the upper pasture, too.
That sounds like something you have heard
  before?
Warren, I wish you could have heard the
  way                                            54
He jumbled everything. I stopped to look
Two or three times — he made me feel so
  queer —
To see if he was talking in his sleep.
He ran on Harold Wilson — you remem-
  ber —
The boy you had in haying four years since.
He's finished school, and teaching in his
  college.                                       60
Silas declares you'll have to get him back.
He says they two will make a team for
  work:
Between them they will lay this farm as
  smooth!
The way he mixed that in with other things.
He thinks young Wilson a likely lad, though
  daft                                           65
On education — you know how they fought
All through July under the blazing sun,
Silas up on the cart to build the load,
Harold along beside to pitch it on."

" Yes, I took care to keep well out of ear-
  shot."                                         70

" Well, those days trouble Silas like a
  dream.
You wouldn't think they would. How some
  things linger!
Harold's young college boy's assurance
  piqued him.
After so many years he still keeps finding
Good arguments he sees he might have
  used.                                          75
I sympathize. I know just how it feels
To think of the right thing to say too late.
Harold's associated in his mind with Latin.
He asked me what I thought of Harold's
  saying
He studied Latin like the violin            80
Because he liked it — that an argument!

He said he couldn't make the boy believe
He could find water with a hazel prong° —
Which showed how much good school had
    ever done him.
He wanted to go over that. But most of
    all                   85
He thinks if he could have another chance
To teach him how to build a load of hay — "

" I know, that's Silas' one accomplishment.
He bundles every forkful in its place,
And tags and numbers it for future refer-
    ence,                 90
So he can find and easily dislodge it
In the unloading. Silas does that well.
He takes it out in bunches like big birds'
    nests.
You never see him standing on the hay
He's trying to lift, straining to lift him-
    self."                95

" He thinks if he could teach him that, he'd
    be
Some good perhaps to someone in the world.
He hates to see a boy the fool of books.
Poor Silas, so concerned for other folk,
And nothing to look backward to with
    pride,              100
And nothing to look forward to with hope,
So now and never any different."

Part of a moon was falling down the west,
Dragging the whole sky with it to the hills,
Its light poured softly in her lap. She
    saw              105
And spread her apron to it. She put out her
    hand
Among the harplike morning-glory strings,
Taut with the dew from garden bed to eaves,
As if she played unheard the tenderness
That wrought on him beside her in the
    night.             110
" Warren," she said, " he has come home to
    die:
You needn't be afraid he'll leave you this
    time."

83. **find water with a hazel prong:** a farm
superstition that a proper location for a well can
be ascertained by walking around holding a
branch in front of one. The branch is supposed
to bend down at the point where water is to be
found under the surface.

" Home," he mocked gently.

      " Yes, what else but home?
It all depends on what you mean by home.
Of course he's nothing to us, any more  115
Than was the hound that came a stranger
    to us
Out of the woods, worn out upon the trail."

" Home is the place where, when you have
    to go there,
They have to take you in."

          " I should have called it
Something you somehow haven't to de-
    serve."            120

Warren leaned out and took a step or two,
Picked up a little stick, and brought it back
And broke it in his hand and tossed it by.
" Silas has better claim on us, you think,
Than on his brother? Thirteen little miles
As the road winds would bring him to his
    door.            126
Silas has walked that far no doubt today.
Why didn't he go there? His brother's rich,
A somebody — director in the bank."

" He never told us that."

          " We know it though."  130

" I think his brother ought to help, of
    course.
I'll see to that if there is need. He ought of
    right
To take him in, and might be willing to —
He may be better than appearances.
But have some pity on Silas. Do you think
If he'd had any pride in claiming kin  136
Or anything he looked for from his brother,
He'd keep so still about him all this time? "

" I wonder what's between them."

          " I can tell you.
Silas is what he is — we wouldn't mind
    him —           140
But just the kind that kinsfolk can't abide.
He never did a thing so very bad.

He don't know why he isn't quite as good
As anyone. He won't be made ashamed
To please his brother, worthless though he
    is."                    145

" *I* can't think Si ever hurt anyone."

" No, but he hurt my heart the way he lay
And rolled his old head on that sharp-edged
    chair back.
He wouldn't let me put him on the lounge.
You must go in and see what you can
    do.                    150
I made the bed up for him there tonight.
You'll be surprised at him — how much he's
    broken.
His working days are done; I'm sure of it."

" I'd not be in a hurry to say that."

" I haven't been. Go, look, see for your-
    self.                  155
But, Warren, please remember how it is:
He's come to help you ditch the meadow.
He has a plan. You mustn't laugh at him.
He may not speak of it, and then he may.
I'll sit and see if that small sailing cloud
Will hit or miss the moon."        161

               It hit the moon.
Then there were three, making a dim row,
The moon, the little silver cloud, and she.

Warren returned — too soon, it seemed to
    her,
Slipped to her side, caught up her hand and
    waited.              165

" Warren? " she questioned.

       " Dead," was all he answered.

## Suggestions for Study of Frost

### SHORT POEMS

1. In " Birches " point out words and details
that make the description of the trees especially vivid. Have you seen ice storms such as
Frost describes? Which makes the more beautiful transformation of the world, an ice storm

or a snowstorm? What application to his own
life does the poet make at the end?

2. In " Stopping by Woods on a Snowy
Evening " what is the significance back of the
apparently simple incident? What effect does
the repetition of the last line have?

3. In " Mending Wall " how do you interpret the saying, " Good fences make good
neighbors "? Discuss the different personalities
of the two farmers as shown by their attitude
toward the wall. With which do you agree?

4. Apply the ideas of the two men in
" Mending Wall " to the international situation. Write a short dialogue between two nations in regard to the " wall " between them.

5. Summarize the meaning of " The Road
Not Taken." In what way did Frost take the
less frequently traveled road in his own life?
How do you think it made a difference?

6. You would enjoy reading the treatment
of a similar theme in O. Henry's story " Roads
of Destiny."

7. How does " A Considerable Speck " differ in general style from the rest of the short
poems? Consider both mood and vocabulary in
your answer.

8. How does Frost's method of linking his
observations to some great truth of human life
differ from the " moral tag " of the earlier New
England poets?

### THE DEATH OF THE HIRED MAN

9. Notice how simple the vocabulary of this
poem is. See whether you can find a single
word in it with which you are unfamiliar.

10. In the second stanza, lines 11–30, remember that Warren is saying all this to his
wife. Between whom is the conversation he is
quoting?

11. What points of contrast do you find between Silas and Harold Wilson? Are these differences principally between youth and age, or
between two kinds of background and education?

12. Study the two definitions of home (lines
118–20). Which do you prefer?

13. What does the discussion about the rich
brother (lines 124–45) add to our understanding of Silas?

14. What do you learn of the character of
Warren and Mary from their conversation?

15. What makes the end of the poem especially impressive?

16. Let two well-qualified students drama-

tize "The Death of the Hired Man" before the class. Be careful not to spoil the quiet pathos of the poem.

17. Study the meter of Frost's poetry. How many of his poems are in blank verse? Compare with passages of blank verse in Shakespeare and other poets. Try to find out what makes it have such a different sound and general effect upon the reader.

## Edgar Lee Masters    1869–

Imagine a book of poetry being a "best seller," shouldering out all the love stories, detective stories, travel books, and other kinds of prose which usually appear in that class. Yet that is what happened in 1915 when the *Spoon River Anthology* appeared in the bookshops. So original in its conception, so enticing in its varied pictures, so provocative of thought and discussion did it prove to be that everyone had to read it. Edgar Lee Masters was an Illinois lawyer-poet who had been writing for years without creating a ripple of excitement. Too much of his verse had been merely a poor imitation of the English poets whom he had studied. Finally at the suggestion of his friend, William Marion Reedy, editor of *Reedy's Mirror*, he turned his attention to his own surroundings and produced a masterpiece. Through the reading of the *Greek Anthology*, a collection of ancient poems, he conceived the idea of a series of epitaphs on the inhabitants of a fictitious Illinois town, written by the dead themselves.

Reading this book is like being present at the Day of Judgment, when the dead arise and the truth about their lives is set free. All the experiences of village life are here represented, the good and the bad crowded together, the joys and hopes recorded, the bitternesses and ironies, the misunderstandings and mysteries revealed. Robert Littell has well summarized the impression left after reading the book: "Their faces, less distinct than the gossip, detective work, and idealistic generalization in which they swam, have long since disappeared. There were no characters, and what we mistook for such were case histories in the clinic of life's hospital, with Mr. Masters as surgeon rather than artist."

The names of the men and women one indeed forgets, but can one ever look again upon a cemetery in a small town, or even the town itself, without repeopling it in imagination with many of these lives?

Anne Rutledge is the only actual historical character among those which follow. She will be remembered as the sweetheart of Lincoln's early life, lost to him through death.

## ANNE RUTLEDGE

Out of me unworthy and unknown
The vibrations of deathless music:
"With malice toward none, with charity
    for all."
Out of me the forgiveness of millions to-
    ward millions,
And the beneficent face of a nation     5
Shining with justice and truth.
I am Anne Rutledge who sleep beneath these
    weeds,
Beloved in life of Abraham Lincoln,
Wedded to him, not through union,
But through separation.     10
Bloom forever, O Republic,
From the dust of my bosom!

## JOHN HORACE BURLESON

I won the prize essay at school
Here in the village,
And published a novel before I was twenty-
    five.
I went to the city for themes and to enrich
    my art;
There married the banker's daughter,     5
And later became president of the bank —
Always looking forward to some leisure
To write an epic novel of the war.
Meanwhile friend of the great, and lover of
    letters,
And host to Matthew Arnold° and to Emer-
    son.     10
An after-dinner speaker, writing essays
For local clubs. At last brought here —
My boyhood home, you know —
Not even a little tablet in Chicago
To keep my name alive.     15

10. **Matthew Arnold:** a noted English writer and lecturer, much entertained in America.

How great it is to write the single line:
" Roll on, thou deep and dark blue Ocean,
   roll! "°

17. **"Roll on . . . roll":** one of the most frequently quoted lines written by the English poet
Lord Byron.

## MRS. GEORGE REECE

To this generation I would say:
Memorize some bit of verse of truth or
   beauty.
It may serve a turn in your life.
My husband had nothing to do
With the fall of the bank — he was only
   cashier.                                5
The wreck was due to the president,
   Thomas Rhodes,
And his vain, unscrupulous son.
Yet my husband was sent to prison,
And I was left with the children,
To feed and clothe and school them.    10
And I did it, and sent them forth
Into the world all clean and strong,
And all through the wisdom of Pope, the
   poet:
" Act well your part, there all the honor
   lies."

## GEORGE GRAY

I have studied many times
The marble which was chiseled for me —
A boat with a furled sail at rest in a harbor.
In truth it pictures not my destination
But my life.                               5
For love was offered me, and I shrank from
   its disillusionment;
Sorrow knocked at my door, but I was
   afraid;
Ambition called to me, but I dreaded the
   chances.
Yet all the while I hungered for meaning
   in my life
And now I know that we must lift the sail
And catch the winds of destiny         11
Wherever they drive the boat.
To put meaning in one's life may end in
   madness,

But life without meaning is the torture
Of restlessness and vague desire —    15
It is a boat longing for the sea and yet
   afraid.

## LUCINDA MATLOCK

I went to the dances at Chandlerville,
And played snap-out at Winchester.
One time we changed partners,
Driving home in the moonlight of middle
   June,
And then I found Davis.                  5
We were married and lived together for
   seventy years,
Enjoying, working, raising the twelve chil-
   dren,
Eight of whom we lost
Ere I had reached the age of sixty.
I spun, I wove, I kept the house, I nursed
   the sick,                            10
I made the garden, and for holiday
Rambled over the fields where sang the
   larks,
And by Spoon River gathering many a shell,
And many a flower and medicinal weed —
Shouting to the wooded hills, singing to the
   green valleys.                       15
At ninety-six I had lived enough, that is all,
And passed to a sweet repose.
What is this I hear of sorrow and weariness,
Anger, discontent, and drooping hopes?
Degenerate sons and daughters,         20
Life is too strong for you —
It takes life to love Life.

## SILENCE

None of the many volumes of poetry which
Masters published after the *Spoon River Anthology* was as powerful, but in *Songs and
Satires* (1916) is to be found one poem which
ranks with his best. It is one of those impressive meditations which one doesn't wish to talk
about after reading, but just think over in
silence.

I have known the silence of the stars and
   of the sea,
And the silence of the city when it pauses,
And the silence of a man and a maid,

And the silence for which music alone finds
    the word,
And the silence of the woods before the
    winds of spring begin,      5
And the silence of the sick
When their eyes roam about the room.
And I ask: For the depths
Of what use is language?
A beast of the field moans a few times   10
When death takes its young:
And we are voiceless in the presence of
    realities —
We cannot speak.

A curious boy asks an old soldier
Sitting in front of the grocery store,   15
" How did you lose your leg? "
And the old soldier is struck with silence,
Or his mind flies away
Because he cannot concentrate it on Gettys-
    burg.
It comes back jocosely   20
And he says, " A bear bit it off."
And the boy wonders, while the old soldier
Dumbly, feebly, lives over
The flashes of guns, the thunder of cannon,
The shrieks of the slain,   25
And himself lying on the ground,
And the hospital surgeons, the knives,
And the long days in bed.
But if he could describe it all
He would be an artist.   30
But if he were an artist there would be
    deeper wounds
Which he could not describe.

There is the silence of a great hatred,
And the silence of a great love,
And the silence of a deep peace of mind,   35
And the silence of an embittered friendship.
There is the silence of a spiritual crisis,
Through which your soul, exquisitely tor-
    tured,
Comes with visions not to be uttered
Into a realm of higher life,   40
And the silence of the gods who understand
    each other without speech.
There is the silence of defeat.
There is the silence of those unjustly pun-
    ished;

And the silence of the dying whose hand
Suddenly grips yours.   45
There is the silence between father and son,
When the father cannot explain his life,
Even though he be misunderstood for it.

There is the silence that comes between hus-
    band and wife,
There is the silence of those who have
    failed;   50
And the vast silence that covers
Broken nations and vanquished leaders.
There is the silence of Lincoln,
Thinking of the poverty of his youth.
And the silence of Napoleon   55
After Waterloo.
And the silence of Jeanne d'Arc
Saying amid the flames, " Blessèd Jesus " —
Revealing in two words all sorrow, all hope.
And there is the silence of age,   60
Too full of wisdom for the tongue to utter it
In words intelligible to those who have not
    lived
The great range of life.

And there is the silence of the dead.
If we who are in life cannot speak   65
Of profound experiences,
Why do you marvel that the dead
Do not tell you of death?
Their silence shall be interpreted
As we approach them.   70

## Suggestions for Study of Masters

1. Which of these persons represent the following things in life: apparent failure, but real success; apparent success, but hidden failure; courage; cowardice; a full and satisfying experience; a meager experience? Which do you admire the most? the least?

2. Under what circumstances did Lincoln say the third line in " Anne Rutledge "? (See page 675.) What is the significance of introducing this quotation here?

3. Although the three women have totally different lives, what one point do they all have in common?

4. In " Silence," the poet gives many illustrations of moments of silence. Can you add others? What is meant by lines 31 and 32? What does he say of " the silence of the dead "?

5. Try writing an epitaph for yourself or someone else in the manner of the *Spoon River Anthology*.

6. To get more satisfaction and better understanding out of *Spoon River Anthology* you should read other epitaphs. Some that you would enjoy are: "Dorcas Gustine," the outspoken woman; "Theodore the Poet" and "Petit the Poet," two opposite types who could be made to represent different types of poets in this book; "Jacob Goodpasture," who lost his son in the War between the States; "Hod Putt," who "went into bankruptcy" in an unusual way; "Emily Sparks," the devoted teacher; "Albert Scherding," the failure, whose children were all successful; "Isaiah Beethoven," who had three months to live; "Fiddler Jones," whose fiddling gave him no time to plow; "Griffy the Cooper," who saw us all living in tubs. Perhaps the most impressive one in the book is "Harry Wilmans," whose experience in the Philippine War is a terrible arraignment against war.

## Carl Sandburg 1878–

If Masters can be said to have immortalized the small town, another Illinois poet, Carl Sandburg, has shown that poetry can express the spirit of the great ungainly city with its sharp contrasts of beauty and ugliness. Just as many of the eastern poets were fitted at Harvard or Yale for their literary careers, so Carl Sandburg was fitted to become poet laureate of industrialism at the College of Hard Work, where he took courses in being a barbershop porter, a sceneshifter, a truck handler, a potter's apprentice, a hotel dishwasher, a construction worker on a railroad, a harvest hand, a soldier, and a janitor. Incidentally, he did go to a small Illinois college for a time; but that was not his real education. Naturally his product turned out to be quite different from that of poets schooled in tradition. From the beginning Whitman had been his master. From him Sandburg learned complete freedom of poetic form, and that vital facing of life which neither discards nor blinds itself to anything. He glosses over nothing in singing of his Chicago, but, like an ancient bard, glorifies ruthless deeds of his hero. One can almost imagine the chants intoned to the chords of a crude harp. Sandburg does, indeed, sing to the accompaniment of his guitar many of the folk songs he has collected in *The American Songbag*.

When *Chicago Poems* was published in 1916, it created much violent opposition. Many people felt about it as an earlier critic had in defining Whitman's poetry as "huge raw collops slashed from the rump of poetry, and never mind gristle." But as Louis Untermeyer pointed out, "Sandburg was only brutal when dealing with brutality; beneath his toughness he was one of the tenderest of living poets." As successive volumes of his poems appeared, the public became used to his style; its individuality became more appreciated and criticism grew less militant. Titles of some of these volumes suggest their dominant themes: *Cornhuskers* (1918), the expanse of the prairies; *Smoke and Steel* (1920), again the city with its overmastering industrialism; *The People, Yes* (1936), the multiple voice of democracy.

Today Carl Sandburg is regarded as one of the deans of American poetry, and those who have come face to face with his generous and warmly understanding personality can only smile to think that he was once regarded as a crude literary radical.

Recently Sandburg has devoted himself primarily to writing biography and his reputation in this field is unquestioned (see page 254).

## CHICAGO

The title piece in *Chicago Poems* was first published in *Poetry, a Magazine of Verse*. At that time it won a prize of two hundred dollars as "the best poem written by a citizen of the United States during the year." It was the foundation stone of Sandburg's fame.

Hog Butcher for the World,
Toolmaker, Stacker of Wheat,
Player with Railroads and the Nation's Freight Handler;
Stormy, husky, brawling,
City of the Big Shoulders:

*Keystone View*

" Stormy, husky, brawling,
      City of Big Shoulders: "

They tell me you are wicked and I believe them, for I have seen your painted women
     under the gas lamps luring the farmboys.
And they tell you you are crooked and I answer: Yes, it is true I have seen the gunman
     kill and go free to kill again.
And they tell me you are brutal and my reply is: On the faces of women and children
     I have seen the marks of wanton hunger.
And having answered so I turn once more to those who sneer at this my city, and I give
     them back the sneer and say to them:
Come and show me another city with lifted head singing so proud to be alive and coarse
     and strong and cunning.                                                        10
Flinging magnetic curses amid the toil of piling job on job, here is a tall bold slugger set
     vivid against the little soft cities;
Fierce as a dog with tongue lapping for action, cunning as a savage pitted against the
     wilderness,
          Bareheaded,
          Shoveling,
          Wrecking,                                                                 15
          Planning,
          Building, breaking, rebuilding,
Under the smoke, dust all over his mouth, laughing with white teeth,
Under the terrible burden of destiny laughing as a young man laughs,
Laughing even as an ignorant fighter laughs who has never lost a battle,             20

Bragging and laughing that under his wrist is the pulse, and under his ribs the heart
    of the people,
Laughing!
Laughing the stormy, husky, brawling laughter of Youth, half-naked, sweating, proud
    to be Hog Butcher, Toolmaker, Stacker of Wheat, Player with Railroads, and
    Freight Handler to the Nation.

## FOG

In contrast to " Chicago " are the next two short poems, which show the poet's ability to treat a subject with delicacy and beauty. Striking figures of speech are to be found in both.

The fog comes
on little cat feet.

It sits looking
over harbor and city
on silent haunches
and then moves on.

## NIGHT STUFF

Listen a while, the moon is a lovely woman,
    a lonely woman, lost in a silver dress,
    lost in a circus rider's silver dress.

Listen a while, the lake by night is a lonely woman,
    a lovely woman, circled with birches and pines,
    mixing their green and white among stars
    shattered in spray clear nights.

I know the moon and lake have twisted the roots under my heart
    the same as a lonely woman, a lovely woman,
    in a silver dress, in a circus rider's silver dress.

## BUTTONS

The effect of this, as in so many of Sandburg's poems, lies in a single sharp contrast, the parenthesis startling one like a flash back in a moving picture. The scene is, of course, during World War I, but the poet's mental picture was probably reinforced by memories of his own experiences as a soldier in Puerto Rico during the Spanish-American War.

I have been watching the war map slammed up for advertising in front of the news-
    paper office.
Buttons — red and yellow buttons — blue and black buttons — are shoved back and
    forth across the map.

A laughing young man, sunny with freckles,
Climbs a ladder, yells a joke to somebody in the crowd,

And then fixes a yellow button one inch west
And follows the yellow button with a black button one inch west.
(Ten thousand men and boys twist on their bodies in a red soak along a river edge,
Gasping of wounds, calling for water, some rattling death in their throats.)
Who would guess what it cost to move two buttons one inch on the war map here in
     front of the newspaper office where the freckle-faced young man is laughing to us?


## GRASS

As a companion picture to the preceding poem we have this one showing the healing power of nature over war. Note the unique way in which this idea is suggested. The five battles mentioned were those involving the greatest loss of human life in the Napoleonic wars, the War between the States, and World War I.

> Pile the bodies high at Austerlitz and Waterloo.
> Shovel them under and let me work —
>      I am the grass; I cover all.
>
> And pile them high at Gettysburg
> And pile them high at Ypres and Verdun.
> Shovel them under and let me work.
> Two years, ten years, and passengers ask the conductor:
>      What place is this?
>      Where are we now?
>
> I am the grass.
> Let me work.


## A FENCE

The first three lines of the following poem suggest only the average man's resentment of being shut out; the last line lifts it into the realm of imagination. This poem, as well as the next two poems, has a Chicago background.

Now the stone house on the lake front is finished and the workmen are beginning the
     fence.
The palings are made of iron bars with steel points that can stab the life out of any man
     who falls on them.
As a fence, it is a masterpiece, and will shut off the rabble and all vagabonds and hungry
     men and all wandering children looking for a place to play.
Passing through the bars and over the steel points will go nothing except Death and
     the Rain and Tomorrow.


## CLEAN CURTAINS

New neighbors came to the corner house at Congress and Green Streets.

The look of their clean white curtains was the same as the rim of a nun's bonnet.

One way was an oyster-pail factory, one way they made candy, one way paper boxes,
     strawboard cartons.

The warehouse trucks shook the dust of the ways loose and the wheels whirled dust —
there was dust of hoof and wagon wheel and rubber tire — dust of police and fire
wagons — dust of the winds that circled at midnight and noon listening to no
prayers.

" O mother, I know the heart of you," I sang passing the rim of a nun's bonnet — O
white curtains — and people clean as the prayers of Jesus here in the faded ramshackle at Congress and Green.

Dust and the thundering trucks won — the barrages of the street wheels and the lawless wind took their way — was it five weeks or six the little mother, the new neighbors, battled and then took away the white prayers in the windows?


## PRAYERS OF STEEL

Lay me on an anvil, O God.
Beat me and hammer me into a crowbar.
Let me pry loose old walls.
Let me lift and loosen old foundations.

Lay me on an anvil, O God.
Beat me and hammer me into a steel spike.
Drive me into the girders that hold a skyscraper together.
Take red-hot rivets and fasten me into the central girders.
Let me be the great nail holding a skyscraper through blue nights into white stars.


## THE PEOPLE, YES

Carl Sandburg's volume of poetry *The People, Yes* (1936) is a unique compilation. It opens with a modern version of the story of the Tower of Babel in the Bible, and the rest of the book is really the babel of voices arising from all parts of our nation and from all conditions of people. The reading of this book gives one somewhat the same sensations as turning the dial of a radio and hearing different voices come from hither and yon out of the air. The verse is without set form; the units of thought have no names, only numbers; there is no continuity of thought. But the total impression is that one has heard the rich vernacular, the reiterated sayings, the significant phrases, the underlying interpretations — in a word, the composite voice of America.

3

In the long flat panhandle of Texas
far off on the grassland of the cattle country
near noon they sight a rider coming toward them
and the sky may be a cold never-changing gray
or the sky may be changing its numbers
back and forth all day even and odd numbers

5

and the afternoon slides away somewhere
and they see their rider is alive yet
their rider is coming nearer yet
and they expect what happens and it happens again     10
he and his horse ride in late for supper
yet not too late
and night is on and the stars are out
and night too slides away somewhere
night too has even and odd numbers.     15

The wind brings " a norther "
to the long flat panhandle
and in the shivering cold they say:
    " Between Amarillo and the North Pole
    is only a barbwire fence,"     20
which they give a twist:
    " Out here the only windbreak
    is the North Star."

### 51

The copperfaces, the red men, handed us tobacco,
the weed for the pipe of friendship,
also the bah-tah-to, the potato, the spud.
Sunflowers came from Peruvians in ponchos.
Early Italians taught us of chestnuts,     5
walnuts and peaches being Persian mementos,
Siberians finding for us what rye might do,
Hindus coming through with the cucumber,
Egyptians giving us the onion, the pea,
Arabians handing advice with one gift:     10
" Some like it, some say it's just spinach."
    To the Chinese we have given
    kerosene, bullets, Bibles
    and they have given us radishes, soy beans, silk,
    poems, paintings, proverbs, porcelain, egg foo yong,     15
    gunpowder, Fourth of July firecrackers, fireworks,
    and labor gangs for the first Pacific railways.
      Now we may thank these people
      or reserve our thanks
      and speak of them as outsiders     20
      and imply the request,
" Would you just as soon get off the earth? "
holding ourselves aloof in pride of distinction
saying to ourselves this costs us nothing
as though hate has no cost     25
as though hate ever grew anything worth growing.
Yes we may say this trash is beneath our notice
or we may hold them in respect and affection
as fellow creepers on a commodious planet
saying, " Yes you too you too are people."     30

## Suggestions for Study of Sandburg

1. Point out all the poems in this group in which Sandburg makes use of striking contrast.

2. In which poems has he used a common object as a symbol of some deeper truth of life?

3. Where do you find examples of his " brutal " use of language? where of delicacy of language?

4. On the whole, does Sandburg seem to be more concerned with giving us external pictures of industrial life or interpretations of its underlying significance?

5. In the selections from *The People, Yes* point out examples of humorous exaggeration, irony, modern slang, the folly of race prejudice, the complexity of American life. How many things can you find mentioned that played little or no part in life a century ago?

6. Sandburg is the great poet of industrial life. By reading in his volumes: *Chicago; Smoke and Steel; Good Morning, America;* and *The People, Yes,* collect what you consider his most significant poems on this general subject. Discuss them and read some of the best to the class. Since modern art is also concerned with this subject, a set of illustrations to accompany your collection would add greatly to it. If you are interested in photography and live in a large city, you have opportunity for some fine illustrative shots.

7. Let a group of students interested in folk music prepare a program from the material in Sandburg's *The American Songbag.* Part of it might be a radio effect with different unidentified speaking voices contributing parts of *The People, Yes.* Choral reading of passages from the latter would also add to a program.

8. If you have had an opportunity to hear over the radio or on the phonograph *A Ballad for Americans* by John La Touche and Earl Robinson, compare its method of using different voice rhythms to interpret a nation with Sandburg's method in *The People, Yes.*

## Vachel Lindsay     1879–1931

Nicholas Vachel Lindsay was our modern American troubadour. He believed that poetry is made not for the eye, but for the ear; and he spent some of his life journeying up and down the land singing his songs, much as did the ballad singers in the days of knights and feudal castles. Sometimes he made dignified tours from city to city or college to college, appearing quite properly on lecture platform or at college chapel. But he sometimes threw convention to the winds, and set off boldly afoot across country with nothing to pay his way except his little pamphlet, *Rhymes to Be Traded for Bread.* Because Lindsay was essentially a singer, his poems must be chanted aloud in the Lindsay manner, or much of their appeal is lost. To help the reader, in many of his longer poems the poet printed directions for reading by the side of his verses.

After graduating from high school in Springfield, Illinois, Vachel Lindsay attended Hiram College and art schools in Chicago and New York. Shortly he was back in his home town, preaching his gospel of beauty and campaigning against civic unrighteousness and ugliness in his privately printed weekly *War Bulletin.* " Ugliness," he said, " is a kind of misgovernment." He continued ever after preaching to a materialistic and cynical age the Americanism of Walt Whitman and the beauty and art of Edgar Allan Poe.

Lindsay wrote many beautiful rhymes for children. He developed " poem games " to which children dance, needing no other instrument to beat the rhythm except the human voice. He sang songs about movie stars, and wrote one whole prose volume on *The Art of the Motion Picture.* He brought forth a Southern challenge to the New Englanders in his " The Virginians Are Coming Again." He set to word music the lives of picturesque and vivid Americans — Old Andrew Jackson, William Jennings Bryan, John Brown, Johnny Appleseed, Alexander Campbell. But his poetry is too various to be divided into neat little pigeonholes. The best of it has given him an international reputation as the modern American minstrel. All the poems given below will be found in his *Collected Poems.*

## ABRAHAM LINCOLN WALKS AT MIDNIGHT

### (IN SPRINGFIELD, ILLINOIS)

All three of the group of contemporary Illinois poets have written about Abraham Lin-

"Abraham Lincoln Walks at Midnight," from *Collected Poems,* by Vachel Lindsay. Reprinted by permission of The Macmillan Company, publishers.

coln in some form. Lindsay felt an especially close bond because he was brought up in Springfield, Lincoln's home town, and the Lincoln family was close to his own family traditions. The following poem, written during World War I, has become one of the most familiar of the many poems of that day. Since an assured peace has not yet come to the world, it still has its significant message.

It is portentous, and a thing of state
That here at midnight, in our little town
A mourning figure walks, and will not rest,
Near the old courthouse pacing up and
 down,    4

Or by his homestead, or in shadowed yards
He lingers where his children used to play,
Or through the market, on the well-worn
 stones
He stalks until the dawn stars burn away.

A bronzed, lank man! His suit of ancient
 black,
A famous high top hat and plain worn
 shawl    10
Make him the quaint great figure that men
 love,
The prairie lawyer, master of us all.

He cannot sleep upon his hillside now.
He is among us: — as in times before!
And we who toss and lie awake for long 15
Breathe deep, and start, to see him pass the
 door.

His head is bowed. He thinks on men and
 kings.
Yea, when the sick world cries, how can he
 sleep?
Too many peasants fight, they know not
 why,    19
Too many homesteads in black terror weep.

The sins of all the war lords burn his heart.
He sees the dreadnoughts scouring every
 main.
He carries on his shawl-wrapped shoulders
 now
The bitterness, the folly, and the pain.

He cannot rest until a spirit dawn  25
Shall come; — the shining hope of Europe
 free:
The league of sober folk, the workers' earth,
Bringing long peace to Cornland, Alp, and
 Sea.

It breaks his heart that kings must murder
 still,    29
That all his hours of travail here for men
Seem yet in vain. And who will bring white
 peace
That he may sleep upon his hill again?

## ON THE BUILDING OF SPRINGFIELD

Lindsay hoped profoundly that in its development his own town of Springfield would heed the call of beauty and satisfy the needs of the intellect and the spirit. His repeated preachments against mere materialism were given scant attention by his fellow townsmen during his lifetime. In recent years, however, Springfield has awakened to its possibilities as a national shrine because of its association with Lincoln's life, and great projects for beautifying the town have been completed. In July, 1935, a large artificial lake just outside the town was formally dedicated. The beautiful many-arched bridge which spans it was officially named the Vachel Lindsay Bridge. At one end of it stands a bust of the poet.

Let not our town be large, remembering
 That little Athens was the Muses' home;
That Oxford rules the heart of London still,
 That Florence gave the Renaissance to
  Rome.    4

Record it for the grandson of your son —
 A city is not builded in a day:
Our little town cannot complete her soul
 Till countless generations pass away.

Now let each child be joined as to a church
 To her perpetual hopes, each man or-
  dained;    10
Let every street be made a reverent aisle
 Where Music grows, and Beauty is un-
  chained.

"On the Building of Springfield," from *Collected Poems*, by Vachel Lindsay. Reprinted by permission of The Macmillan Company, publishers.

Let Science and Machinery and Trade
  Be slaves of her, and make her all in all —
Building against our blatant restless time
  An unseen, skillful, medieval wall.   16

Let every citizen be rich toward God.
  Let Christ, the beggar, teach divinity —
Let no man rule who holds his money dear.
  Let this, our city, be our luxury.   20

We should build parks that students from
    afar
  Would choose to starve in, rather than go
    home,
Fair little squares, with Phidian° ornament,
  Food for the spirit, milk and honeycomb.

Songs shall be sung by us in that good day—
  Songs we have written — blood within
    the rhyme   26
Beating, as when old England still was glad,
  The purple, rich, Elizabethan° time.

  •   •   •   •   •   •   •

Say, is my prophecy too fair and far?   29
  I only know, unless her faith be high,
The soul of this our Nineveh° is doomed,
  Our little Babylon° will surely die.

23. **Phidian** (fĭd′ĭ-ăn): Phidias was the greatest
of the ancient Greek sculptors. 28. **Elizabethan**
(ĕ-lĭz-ȧ-bē′thăn): pertaining to the flourishing of
poetry and drama during the reign of Queen Elizabeth of England in the late sixteenth century.

Some city on the breast of Illinois
  No wiser and no better at the start,
By faith shall rise redeemed, by faith shall
    rise   35
  Bearing the Western glory in her heart.

The genius of the Maple, Elm, and Oak,
  The secret hidden in each grain of corn,
The glory that the prairie angels sing
  At night when sons of Life and Love are
    born,   40

Born but to struggle, squalid and alone,
  Broken and wandering in their early
    years.
When will they make our dusty streets their
    goal,
  Within our attics hide their sacred tears?

When will they start our vulgar blood
    athrill   45
  With living language — words that set
    us free?
When will they make a path of beauty clear
  Between our riches and our liberty?

We must have many Lincoln-hearted men.
  A city is not builded in a day.   50
And they must do their work, and come
    and go
  While countless generations pass away.

31. **Nineveh** (nĭn′ĕ-vĕ): capital of ancient Assyr-
ia, which finally fell before the conquering Persians.
32. **Babylon** (băb′ĭ-lŏn): capital of Babylonia,
which suffered a fate similar to that of Nineveh.

## THE EAGLE THAT IS FORGOTTEN

Lindsay's admiration for a champion of the
unfortunate and submerged is warmly expressed in this poem. The "eagle" is John
Peter Altgeld (1847–1902), a judge and later
governor of Illinois, who was instrumental in
promoting prison reform and other measures
to right injustice. The fact that no statue, portrait, or commemorative tablet perpetuated his
name led Lindsay to write this poem with its
memorable last lines.

Sleep softly . . . eagle forgotten . . . under the stone,
Time has its way with you there, and the clay has its own.
"We have buried him now," thought your foes, and in secret rejoiced.
They made a brave show of their mourning, their hatred unvoiced.

They had snarled at you, barked at you, foamed at you, day after day,   5
Now you were ended. They praised you, . . . and laid you away.

The others that mourned you in silence and terror and truth,
The widow bereft of her pittance, the boy without youth,
The mocked and the scorned and the wounded, the lame and the poor
That should have remembered forever, . . . remember no more.　　10

Where are those lovers of yours, on what name do they call,
The lost, that in armies wept over your funeral pall?
They call on the names of a hundred high-valiant ones,
A hundred white eagles have risen, the sons of your sons,
The zeal in their wings is a zeal that your dreaming began,　　15
The valor that wore out your soul in the service of man.

Sleep softly, . . . eagle forgotten, . . . under the stone,
Time has its way with you there, and the clay has its own.
Sleep on, O brave-hearted, O wise man, that kindled the flame —
To live in mankind is far more than to live in a name,　　20
To live in mankind, far, far more . . . than to live in a name.

## GENERAL WILLIAM BOOTH ENTERS INTO HEAVEN

This astonishing poem, picturing General Booth, head of the Salvation Army, marching into heaven followed by his converts, is an excellent example of Lindsay's use of sound effects. The steady roll of the drum, the blatancy of the trumpets, the uneven tramping of the riffraff, with the motif of the hymn tune running through all, combine to make a sound-experience comparable to that produced in music by Stravinsky and other modern composers. When this poem was first published, some thought Lindsay was ridiculing the Salvation Army; but he explained that he meant it as a genuine tribute to the work of the great " General." The idea for the poem came to him during one of his troubadour journeys about the country selling rhymes for bread. One night when the rhymes had failed to produce enough for a lodging, he was about to sleep on the steps of a post office when he was invited to the Salvation Army quarters. His experience with the organization gave him great respect for its service to humanity.

[To be sung to the tune of " The Blood of the Lamb " with indicated instrument]

I

*[Bass drum beaten loudly]*

Booth led boldly with his big bass drum —
(Are you washed in the blood of the Lamb?)

The Saints smiled gravely and they said,
  " He's come."
(Are you washed in the blood of the Lamb?)
Walking lepers followed, rank on rank,　5
Lurching bravos from the ditches dank,
Drabs from the alleyways and drug fiends
  pale —
Minds still passion-ridden, soul powers
  frail: —
Vermin-eaten saints with moldy breath,
Unwashed legions with the ways of
  Death —　　10
(Are you washed in the blood of the Lamb?)
  *[Banjos]*
Every slum had sent its half a score
The round world over. (Booth had groaned
  for more.)
Every banner that the wide world flies　14
Bloomed with glory and transcendent dyes.
Big-voiced lasses made their banjos bang,
Tranced, fanatical, they shrieked and
  sang: —
" Are you washed in the blood of the
  Lamb? "
Hallelujah! It was queer to see
Bull-necked convicts with that land make
  free.　　20
Loons with trumpets blew a blare, blare,
  blare
On, on upward thro' the golden air!
(Are you washed in the blood of the Lamb?)

"General William Booth Enters into Heaven," from *Collected Poems*, by Vachel Lindsay. Reprinted by permission of The Macmillan Company, publishers.

II

*[Bass drum slower and softer]*

Booth died blind and still by Faith he trod,
Eyes still dazzled by the ways of God.   25
Booth led boldly, and he looked the chief,
Eagle countenance in sharp relief,
Beard a-flying, air of high command
Unabated in that holy land.   29

*[Sweet flute music]*

Jesus came from out the courthouse door,
Stretched his hands above the passing poor.
Booth saw not, but led his queer ones there
Round and round the mighty courthouse
   square.
Yet in an instant all that blear review   34
Marched on spotless, clad in raiment new.
The lame were straightened, withered
   limbs uncurled
And blind eyes opened on a new, sweet
   world.

*[Bass drum louder]*

Drabs and vixens in a flash made whole!
Gone was the weasel head, the snout, the
   jowl!   39

Sages and sibyls now, and athletes clean,
Rulers of empires, and of forests green!

*[Grand chorus of all instruments. Tam-
   bourines to the foreground]*

The hosts were sandaled, and their wings
   were fire!
(Are you washed in the blood of the Lamb?)
But their noise played havoc with the angel
   choir.   44
(Are you washed in the blood of the Lamb?)
O, shout Salvation! It was good to see
Kings and princes by the Lamb set free.
The banjos rattled and the tambourines
Jing-jing-jingled in the hands of queens.

*[Reverently sung, no instruments]*

And when Booth halted by the curb for
   prayer   50
He saw his Master thro' the flag-filled air.
Christ came gently with a robe and crown
For Booth the soldier, while the throng
   knelt down.
He saw King Jesus. They were face to
   face,   54
And he knelt a-weeping in that holy place.
Are you washed in the blood of the Lamb?

## THE SANTA FE TRAIL

### A HUMORESQUE

One of Lindsay's prose books is called *Adventures While Preaching the Gospel of Beauty*. It relates his experience while tramping across country from Springfield, Illinois, to the Southwest by way of Kansas. " The Santa Fe Trail " is a souvenir of that trip. The poet-tramp sits on a milestone by the side of the road while, in the form of cars labeled with the city pennants popular around 1912, " the United States goes by."

This time Lindsay gives the reader full directions. If you follow them, this poem will bring to the class a whole day of color and sound, beginning with sunrise and the first faint horn in the east, moving on through screaming cars and freight trains, and ending with the evening whispers of the prairie fairies hidden in the corn and grass. It is a poem of sharp contrasts and demands oral rendition, utilizing the full range of the voice.

*I asked the old Negro, " What is that bird that sings so well? " He
answered, " That is the Rachel-Jane." " Hasn't it another name
— lark, or thrush, or the like? " " No. Jus' Rachel-Jane."*

#### I. IN WHICH A RACING AUTO COMES FROM THE EAST

This is the order of the music of the morning: —
First, from the far East comes but a crooning.
The crooning turns to a sunrise singing.

*To be sung
delicately, to an
improvised tune.*

"The Santa Fe Trail," from *Collected Poems*, by Vachel Lindsay, Reprinted by permission of The Macmillan Company, publishers

Hark to the *calm*-horn, *balm*-horn, *psalm*-horn.
Hark to the *faint*-horn, *quaint*-horn, *saint*-horn. . . .      5
Hark to the *pace*-horn, *chase*-horn, *race*-horn.

*To be sung or read with great speed.*

And the holy veil of the dawn has gone.
Swiftly the brazen car comes on.
It burns in the east as the sunrise burns.
I see great flashes where the far trail turns.      10
Its eyes are lamps like the eyes of dragons.
It drinks gasoline from big red flagons.
Butting through the delicate mists of the morning,
It comes like lightning, goes past roaring.
It will hail all the windmills, taunting, ringing,      15
Dodge the cyclones,
Count the milestones,
On through the ranges the prairie dog tills —
Scooting past the cattle on the thousand hills. . . .
Ho for the *tear*-horn, *scare*-horn, *dare*-horn,      20
Ho for the *gay*-horn, *bark*-horn, *bay*-horn.

*To be read or sung in a rolling bass, with some deliberation.*

*Ho for Kansas, land that restores us*
*When houses choke us, and great books bore us!*
*Sunrise Kansas, harvesters' Kansas,*
*A million men have found you before us.*      25
*A million men have found you before us.*

## II. IN WHICH MANY AUTOS PASS WESTWARD

I want live things in their pride to remain.

*In an even, deliberate, narrative manner.*

I will not kill one grasshopper vain
Though he eats a hole in my shirt like a door.
I let him out, give him one chance more.      30
Perhaps, while he gnaws my hat in his whim,
Grasshopper lyrics occur to him.

I am a tramp by the long trail's border,
Given to squalor, rags, and disorder.
I nap and amble and yawn and look,      35
Write fool thoughts in my grubby book,
Recite to the children, explore at my ease,
Work when I work, beg when I please,
Give crank drawings, that make folks stare
To the half-grown boys in the sunset glare,      40
And get me a place to sleep in the hay
At the end of a live-and-let-live day.

I find in the stubble of the new-cut weeds
A whisper and a feasting, all one needs:
The whisper of the strawberries, white and red      45
Here where the new-cut weeds lie dead.

But I would not walk all alone till I die
Without some life-drunk horns going by.

Up round this apple earth they come
Blasting the whispers of the morning dumb: —                    50
Cars in a plain realistic row.
And fair dreams fade
When the raw horns blow.

On each snapping pennant
A big black name: —                                             55
The careering city
Whence each car came.
They tour from Memphis, Atlanta, Savannah,            *Like a train caller in*
Tallahassee and Texarkana.                            *a union depot.*
They tour from St. Louis, Columbus, Manistee,                   60
They tour from Peoria, Davenport, Kankakee.
Cars from Concord, Niagara, Boston,
Cars from Topeka, Emporia, and Austin.
Cars from Chicago, Hannibal, Cairo.
Cars from Alton, Oswego, Toledo.                                65
Cars from Buffalo, Kokomo, Delphi,
Cars from Lodi, Carmi, Loami.
Ho for Kansas, land that restores us
When houses choke us, and great books bore us!
While I watch the highroad                                      70
And look at the sky,
While I watch the clouds in amazing grandeur
Roll their legions without rain
Over the blistering Kansas plain —
While I sit by the milestone                                    75
And watch the sky,
The United States
Goes by.

Listen to the iron-horns, ripping, racking.          *To be given very*
Listen to the quack-horns, slack and clacking.        80  *harshly, with a*
Way down the road, trilling like a toad,              *snapping explo-*
Here comes the *dice*-horn, here comes the *vice*-horn,   *siveness.*
Here comes the *snarl*-horn, *brawl*-horn, *lewd*-horn,
Followed by the *prude*-horn, bleak and squeaking: —
(Some of them from Kansas, some of them from Kansas.)           85
Here comes the *hod*-horn, *plod*-horn, *sod*-horn,
Nevermore-to-*roam*-horn, *loam*-horn, *home*-horn.
(Some of them from Kansas, some of them from Kansas.)
    Far away the Rachel-Jane               *To be read or sung*
    Not defeated by the horns               *well-nigh in a*
    Sings amid a hedge of thorns: —    90    *whisper.*
    " Love and life,
    Eternal youth —
    Sweet, sweet, sweet, sweet,
    Dew and glory,                          95
    Love and truth,
    Sweet, sweet, sweet, sweet."

WHILE SMOKE-BLACK FREIGHTS ON THE DOUBLE-TRACKED RAILROAD,     *Louder and louder,*
DRIVEN AS THOUGH BY THE FOUL FIEND'S OXGOAD,     *faster and faster.*
SCREAMING TO THE WEST COAST, SCREAMING TO THE EAST,     100
CARRY OFF A HARVEST, BRING BACK A FEAST,
HARVESTING MACHINERY AND HARNESS FOR THE BEAST.
THE HAND CARS WHIZ, AND RATTLE ON THE RAILS,
THE SUNLIGHT FLASHES ON THE TIN DINNER PAILS.
And then in an instant,     105     *In a rolling bass,*
Ye modern men,     *with increasing*
Behold the procession once again,     *deliberation.*
The United States goes by.
Listen to the iron-horns, ripping, racking,
Listen to the *wise*-horn, desperate-to-*advise*-horn,     110     *With a snapping*
Listen to the *fast*-horn, *kill*-horn, *blast*-horn. . . .     *explosiveness.*
    Far away the Rachel-Jane
    Not defeated by the horns     *To be sung or read*
    Sings amid a hedge of thorns: —     *well-nigh in a*
    *whisper.*
    " Love and life,     115
    Eternal youth,
    Sweet, sweet, sweet, sweet,
    Dew and glory,
    Love and truth.
    Sweet, sweet, sweet, sweet."     120     *To be brawled in the*
The mufflers open on a score of cars     *beginning with a*
With wonderful thunder,     *snapping explosive-*
CRACK, CRACK, CRACK,     *ness, ending in a*
CRACK-CRACK, CRACK-CRACK,     *languorous chant.*
CRACK, CRACK, CRACK,     125
Listen to the gold-horn . . .
Old-horn . . .
Cold-horn . . .
And all of the tunes, till the night comes down
On haystack, and anthill, and wind-bitten town.     130
Then far in the west, as in the beginning,     *To be sung to*
Dim in the distance, sweet in retreating,     *exactly the same*
Hark to the faint-horn, quaint-horn, saint-horn,     *whispered tune as*
Hark to the calm-horn, balm-horn, psalm horn. . . .     *the first five lines.*

They are hunting the goals that they understand: —     135     *This section*
San Francisco and the brown sea sand.     *beginning*
My goal is the mystery the beggars win.     *sonorously, ending*
I am caught in the web the night winds spin.     *in a languorous*
The edge of the wheat ridge speaks to me.     *whisper.*
I talk with the leaves of the mulberry tree.     140
And now I hear, as I sit all alone
In the dusk, by another big Santa Fe stone,
The souls of the tall corn gathering round
And the gay little souls of the grass in the ground.
Listen to the tale the cottonwood tells.     145
Listen to the windmills, singing o'er the wells.

Listen to the whistling flutes without price
Of myriad prophets out of paradise.
Harken to the wonder
That the night air carries. . . .                                    150
Listen . . . to . . . the . . . whisper . . .
Of . . . the . . . prairie . . . fairies
    Singing o'er the fairy plain: —
    " Sweet, sweet, sweet, sweet.          *To the same*
    Love and glory,                    155    *whispered tune as*
    Stars and rain,                           *the Rachel-Jane*
    Sweet, sweet, sweet, sweet. . . ."        *song — but very*
                                                *slowly.*

## Suggestions for Study of Lindsay

1. How many of the causes for Lincoln's unrest in " Abraham Lincoln Walks at Midnight " still exist in the world? Give specific instances. What other legends have you heard of great leaders returning to earth in spirit form when their work was unfinished?

2. Why does Lindsay think it is not necessary for a town to be large in order to be important in its influence? Can you name other comparatively small towns in this country which have attained national reputation or influence through some field of intellectual interest or some special beauty?

3. Make a list of the things Lindsay would like to have in Springfield. Comment on this list. Would you add or omit any points for your ideal town? How many things on this list are to be found in your town? What does this poem suggest to you as possible improvements for your town?

4. What similarity is there between " The Eagle That Is Forgotten " and " General William Booth Enters Heaven "? What experiences in Lindsay's own life contributed to his interest in the " underdogs " and his sympathetic understanding of their champions?

5. Is it true that those who have worked slowly and constructively for the betterment of humanity have had less recognition than warriors and other types of public characters? Clarify your discussion with specific examples.

6. In both " General William Booth " and " The Santa Fe Trail " study the sound effects. In which passages do you think Lindsay has been particularly clever in suiting the words to the sound effect desired? Where do you find definite onomatopoeic words; that is, words whose meaning is dependent on their sound?

7. How do both these poems reflect experiences in the author's life? What attitude toward human beings do you find in both poems? Where do you find suggestions that he was interested in pictorial as well as musical art?

8. What other poems do you know that emphasize the rhythmic qualities of place names? Give examples. Select some place names you know that have rhythmic possibilities for a poem. How many of the places in " The Santa Fe Trail " could you locate on a map?

9. What is the meaning of the " Rachel-Jane's " message? Is there anything in " General William Booth " that affords a like contrast to the main tone of the poem?

10. Since the effect of these poems can be obtained only by oral reading, practice reading them aloud, forgetting yourself completely in the swing and mood of the different parts. Don't be afraid to exaggerate; the poet did in his own readings, for which he was famous.

11. No better material can be found for effective choral reading than the poems of Lindsay. They have unusual variation of sound effects and build up to dramatic climaxes. Besides, he has given the reading directions himself. Before trying choral reading, separate the high, low, and medium voice groups so that the leader can use them much as the director of a choir uses the singing voices. It might be well for a small interested group to practice separately on the main part of the poems, letting the class as a whole come in only on the grand chorus of " General William Booth " or on certain climactic lines of " The Santa Fe Trail " (such as 25–26, 77–78, 98–104, 123–25). In the latter poem there is wonderful opportunity for contrast in single voices in the names of the cities (58–67) and the different horns (4–5, 82–87, 109–11); and, of course, the Rachel-Jane should be a single high, sweet voice.

## For Your Vocabulary

The English 'anguage has such a great variety of suffixes that it is helpful to learn to recognize those which are related. The noun *squalor* (skwŏl'ēr) in " The Santa Fe Trail " (line 34), means a dirty, filthy condition, and the related adjective is *squalid* (skwŏl'ĭd) in " On the Building of Springfield " (line 41). These are typical of a group of words in which the nouns end in -*or* and adjectives in -*id*. You have already had *pallor* (page 86), unnatural paleness, and will find *pallid* a favorite of Poe's. *Fervor* (page 592), a word for intense emotional enthusiasm, has its adjective *fervid*. (*Fervent* on page 324 describes a milder warmth of feeling.) *Languor* (lăng'gēr), a droopy state without energy or interest, is perhaps less used than its adjective *languid*. *Stupor* and *rigor* are two more common members of the same series.

## James Weldon Johnson
### 1871–1938

An unusually varied career marked the life of the Negro poet, James Weldon Johnson. He was born in Jacksonville, Florida. After receiving his Master's degree from Atlanta University, he was principal of a high school, studied and practiced law, collaborated with his brother in writing light opera, spent seven years in Venezuela and Nicaragua as United States Consul, and translated a Spanish grand opera, *Goyescas*, which was produced at the Metropolitan Opera House in New York. From 1916 to 1930 he was secretary of the National Association for the Advancement of Colored People. After 1915 he gave his time largely to writing and to lecturing at Fisk University, New York University, and others on creative writing. His collections of Negro poetry and Negro spirituals were influential in arousing public appreciation of these rich veins of literature. Among his own writings *God's Trombones* (1927), from which the following poem is taken, has always made an especial appeal. Supposedly a series of seven Negro sermons in verse, these poems are deeply imbued with the vigorous rhythm and colorful imagery which give Negro literature its distinctive quality. *Black Manhattan* followed in 1930, and in 1933 his autobiography, *Along This Way*, a significant picture of modern life.

## THE CREATION

### A NEGRO SERMON

And God stepped out on space,
And He looked around and said,
" *I'm lonely —*
*I'll make me a world.*"
As far as the eye of God could see          5
Darkness covered everything,
Blacker than a hundred midnights
Down in a cypress swamp.

Then God smiled,
And the light broke,          10
And the darkness rolled up on one side,
And the light stood shining on the other,
And God said, " *That's good!* "

Then God reached out and took the light in
His hands,
And God rolled the light around in His
hands,          15
Until He made the sun;
And He set that sun a-blazing in the
heavens.
And the light that was left from making
the sun
God gathered up in a shining ball
And flung against the darkness,          20
Spangling the night with the moon and
stars.
Then down between
The darkness and the light
He hurled the world;
And God said, " *That's good!* "          25

Then God himself stepped down —
And the sun was on His right hand,
And the moon was on His left;
The stars were clustered about His head,
And the earth was under His feet.          30
And God walked, and where He trod
His footsteps hollowed the valleys out
And bulged the mountains up.

Then He stopped and looked and saw
That the earth was hot and barren.          35
So God stepped over to the edge of the world
And He spat out the seven seas;

He batted His eyes and the lightnings
    flashed;
He clapped His hands and the thunders
    rolled;
And the waters above the earth came down,
The cooling waters came down.          41

Then the green grass sprouted,
And the little red flowers blossomed,
The pine tree pointed his finger to the sky,
And the oak spread out his arms;          45
The lakes cuddled down in the hollows of
    the ground,
And the rivers ran down to the sea;
And God smiled again,
And the rainbow appeared,
And curled itself around His shoulder.   50

Then God raised His arm and He waved
    His hand
Over the sea and over the land,
And He said, " Bring forth! Bring forth! "
And quicker than God could drop His hand,
Fishes and fowls                          55
And beasts and birds
Swam the rivers and the seas,
Roamed the forests and the woods,
And split the air with their wings,
And God said, " That's good! "            60

Then God walked around
And God looked around
On all that He had made.
He looked at His sun,
He looked at His moon,                    65
And He looked at His little stars;
He looked on His world
With all its living things,
And God said, " I'm lonely still."

Then God sat down                         70
On the side of a hill where He could think;
By a deep, wide river He sat down;
With His head in His hands,
God thought and thought,
Till He thought, " I'll make me a man! "

Up from the bed of the river             76
God scooped the clay;
And by the bank of the river

He kneeled Him down;
And there the great God Almighty,         80
Who lit the sun and fixed it in the sky,
Who flung the stars to the most far corner
    of the night,
Who rounded the earth in the middle of His
    hand —
This Great God,
Like a mammy bending over her baby,       85
Kneeled down in the dust
Toiling over a lump of clay
Hill He shaped it in His own image;
Then into it He blew the breath of life,
And man became a living soul.             90
Amen. Amen.

## Suggestions for Study

1. Pick out words and phrases which give
an especially poetic quality to the story of
creation. Compare this with the first chapter
of Genesis to find likenesses and differences.

2. By what means does the poet give God
a marked personality? If you have read or
have seen the play Green Pastures, compare
the picturing of God and the universe in the
two pieces of literature.

3. What essential differences in form and
purpose do you see between this " sermon "
and a spiritual? Would the sermon lend itself
to a musical setting? If so, how would the music itself have to differ from that of the spiritual?

4. Do you see any resemblance between the
poetry of Johnson and that of Lindsay? If so,
what?

## Sara Teasdale                1884–1933

The chronicle of outward actions in the life
of Sara Teasdale is of little importance compared with the inner action of thought and
imagination. That she was born and educated
in St. Louis, Missouri, traveled extensively,
and later lived in New York City becomes a
matter of interest only in the sense of pinning
down a lovely butterfly and identifying it with
scientific tags. Her best volumes are Love
Songs (1917), Flame and Shadow (1920),
Country House (1932), and Strange Victory
(1933). Stars Tonight is a collection for boys
and girls. All her volumes are filled with deli-

cate bits like the following samples — elusive little flashes of emotion caught and molded for us like tiny figures in ivory. They are little coins for the memory such as she here describes.

## THE COIN

Into my heart's treasury
   I slipped a coin
That time cannot take
   Nor a thief purloin —
Oh, better than the minting
   Of a gold-crowned king
Is the safe-kept memory
   Of a lovely thing.

## BARTER

Life has loveliness to sell —
   All beautiful and splendid things,
Blue waves whitened on a cliff,
   Climbing fire that sways and sings,
And children's faces looking up     5
Holding wonder like a cup.

Life has loveliness to sell —
   Music like a curve of gold,
Scent of pine trees in the rain,
   Eyes that love you, arms that hold,   10
And for your spirit's still delight,
   Holy thoughts that star the night.

Spend all you have for loveliness,
   Buy it and never count the cost,
For one white singing hour of peace   15
   Count many a year of strife well lost,
And for a breath of ecstasy
Give all you have been or could be.

## NIGHT SONG AT AMALFI *

I asked the heaven of stars
   What I should give my love —
It answered me with silence,
   Silence above.

* **Amalfi** (ä-mäl′fē): a picturesque old town near Salerno on the southwest coast of Italy.

I asked the darkened sea     5
   Down where the fishermen go —
It answered me with silence,
   Silence below.

Oh, I could give him weeping,
   Or I could give him song —   10
But how can I give silence
   My whole life long?

## THE LONG HILL

I must have passed the crest a while ago
   And now I am going down —
Strange to have crossed the crest and not to know,
   But the brambles were always catching the hem of my gown.

All the morning I thought how proud I should be   5
   To stand there straight as a queen,
Wrapped in the wind and the sun with the world under me —
   But the air was dull; there was little I could have seen.

It was nearly level along the beaten track
   And the brambles caught in my gown —   10
But it's no use now to think of turning back,
   The rest of the way will be only going down.

## LEAVES

One by one, like leaves from a tree,
All my faiths have forsaken me;
But the stars above my head
Burn in white and delicate red,
And beneath my feet the earth   5
Brings the sturdy grass to birth.
I who was content to be
But a silken-singing tree,
But a rustle of delight
In the wistful heart of night —   10
I have lost the leaves that knew
Touch of rain and weight of dew.
Blinded by a leafy crown

I looked neither up nor down —
But the leaves that fall and die          15
Have left me room to see the sky;
Now for the first time I know
Stars above and earth below.

## THE LAMP

If I can bear your love like a lamp before
     me,
When I go down the long steep Road of
     Darkness,
I shall not fear the everlasting shadows,
          Nor cry in terror.

If I can find out God, then I shall find Him,
If none can find Him, then I shall sleep
     soundly,
Knowing how well on earth your love suf-
     ficed me,
          A lamp in darkness.

## Suggestions for Study of Teasdale

1. What contrasting moods do you find in
this group of poems? What great satisfactions
in life does the poet voice? Where do you find
sadness or wistfulness?

2. In " Barter " does the line, " Spend all
you have for loveliness," mean to spend money
or something else? Justify your answer from
the rest of the poem.

3. How do you interpret " Night Song at
Amalfi " if considered a serious poem? if considered a whimsical or semihumorous poem?

4. " The Long Hill " and " Leaves " are little allegories. What do the hill and the leaves
represent in life? What situations can you
imagine calling forth the feeling expressed in
these and other poems in the group?

5. Observe that " The Lamp," though a
lyric, has no rhyme. How do you think this
affects the mood of the poem? With what kind
of spirit does the poet approach death?

## Elinor Wylie          1885–1928

Elinor Wylie (Mrs. William Rose Benét)
was almost as distinguished a writer of prose
as of verse, but she was primarily thought of
as a poet. Her first volume, *Nets to Catch the*

*Wind* (1921), established her reputation, and
her three succeeding volumes more than bore
out the promise of the first. The four volumes
are now published together as *Collected Poems*.
Within the short span of five years, when she
was producing her last three volumes of poems,
she also wrote three outstanding novels, *Jenni-
fer Lorn* (1923), *The Venetian Glass Nephew*
(1925), and *The Orphan Angel* (1926). This
last novel pictures certain imaginary passages
in the life of Shelley, a poet who had profoundly influenced her; and, like Shelley, she
possessed the greatest delicacy and sensitive-
ness to beauty. Her work is always highly finished technically and yet deeply emotional as
well as personal. She seems to be groping for
some means of escape from the heavy problems of existence. This little group of poems
shows both the gay agility of her mind and
the elusiveness of much of her poetry. The
meaning is lying there just under the surface,
but often neatly hidden from the prosaic mind.
" Sea Lullaby " has the quality of cruelty that
nature sometimes manifests. The " Nonsense
Rhyme " is quite the opposite of its title. " Velvet Shoes " and " Pretty Words " show the
artist's highly developed senses of touch and
hearing as well as of sight. " Atavism " touches
on the mysteries of subconscious fear. Elinor
Wylie is truly an artist of great individuality.

## SEA LULLABY

The old moon is tarnished
With smoke of the flood,
The dead leaves are varnished
With color like blood,

A treacherous smiler          5
With teeth white as milk,
A savage beguiler
In sheathings of silk,

The sea creeps to pillage,
She leaps on her prey;          10
A child of the village
Was murdered today.

She came up to meet him
In a smooth golden cloak,
She choked him and beat him          15
To death, for a joke.

Her bright locks were tangled,
She shouted for joy,
With one hand she strangled
A strong little boy.                                        20

Now in silence she lingers
Beside him all night
To wash her long fingers
In silvery light.

## NONSENSE RHYME

Whatever's good or bad or both
Is surely better than the none;
There's grace in either love or loathe;
Sunlight, or freckles on the sun.

The worst and best are both inclined     5
To snap like vixens at the truth;
But O beware the middle mind
That purrs and never shows a tooth!

Beware the smooth ambiguous smile
That never pulls the lips apart;          10
Salt of pure and pepper of vile
Must season the extremer heart.

A pinch of fair, a pinch of foul,
And bad and good make best of all;
Beware the moderated soul               15
That climbs no fractional inch to fall.

Reason's a rabbit in a hutch,
And ecstasy's a werewolf's ghost;
But, O, beware the nothing-much
And welcome madness and the most!       20

## VELVET SHOES

Let us walk in the white snow
In a soundless space;
With footsteps quiet and slow,
At a tranquil pace,
Under veils of white lace.                 5

I shall go shod in silk,
And you in wool,
White as a white cow's milk,
More beautiful
Than the breast of a gull.                 10

We shall walk through the still town
In a windless peace;
We shall step upon white down,
Upon silver fleece,
Upon softer than these.                   15

We shall walk in velvet shoes:
Wherever we go
Silence will fall like dews
On white silence below.
We shall walk in the snow.                 20

## PRETTY WORDS

Poets make pets of pretty, docile words:
I love smooth words, like gold-enameled
  fish
Which circle slowly with a silken swish,
And tender ones, like downy-feathered
  birds:
Words shy and dappled, deep-eyed deer in
  herds,                                    5
Come to my hand, and playful if I wish,
Or purring softly at a silver dish,
Blue Persian kittens, fed on cream and
  curds.

I love bright words, words up and singing
  early;
Words that are luminous in the dark, and
  sing;                                     10
Warm lazy words, white cattle under trees;
I love words opalescent, cool, and pearly,
Like midsummer moths, and honeyed words
  like bees,
Gilded and sticky, with a little sting.

## ATAVISM *

I always was afraid of Somes's Pond:
Not the little pond by which the willow
  stands,
Where laughing boys catch alewives in their
  hands
In brown, bright shallows; but the one beyond.

* **Atavism** (ăt′à-vĭz′m): the recurrence in a
descendant of characteristics of a remote ancestor.

There, when the frost makes all the birches
   burn        5
Yellow as cow lilies, and the pale sky shines
Like a polished shell between black spruce
   and pines,
Some strange thing tracks us, turning where
   we turn.

You'll say I dream it, being the true daugh-
   ter
Of those who in old times endured this
   dread.        10
Look! Where the lily stems are showing red
A silent paddle moves below the water,
A sliding shape has stirred them like a
   breath;
Tall plumes surmount a painted mask of
   death.

## Suggestions for Study of Wylie

1. Select phrases or figures of speech which show the poet's unexpectedness, her love of the fantastic image, her appeal to the senses, especially of sound and touch.

2. Why does the picture of the sea seem more sinister than if she had described a destructive storm?

3. Explain the " sense " of the " Nonsense Rhyme." Do you agree with her choice between the extremes and the middle course? An informal debate on the subject might be of interest.

4. Can you find words in any of these poems which illustrate the kind she professes to love in " Pretty Words," especially in the last line?

5. Show the application of the title " Atavism " to the poem. How does she suggest the locality and experience of her ancestors without stating them in plain terms? Have you ever felt perfectly groundless fears similar to the poet's?

6. " Pretty Words " and " Atavism " are sonnets (see page 344 for definition). What other modern sonnets can you find? Why do you think this is a popular form with poets?

## For Your Vocabulary

FIGURATIVE USE OF WORDS. Freshness and vividness are two of Elinor Wylie's marked traits, and both are associated with figures of speech. " Sea Lullaby " is an excellent ex-ample of imaginative personification, with the sea spoken of as a person, yet vividly described. Turn over in your own mind the following descriptive bits, noting how they personify the sea and then how clearly they picture the real sea. Start off with " creeps to pillage . . . leaps on her prey." Can you see the varying movement of water along the shore? Now try the others:

" in a smooth golden cloak "
" choked him and beat him to death "
" Her bright locks were tangled "
" She shouted for joy "
" to wash her long fingers in silvery light "

The other poems abound in figurative use of language. See how many bits you can locate. Give the full attention of your imagination to each word or phrase, and you will get the meaning vividly, as if you had turned a spotlight on it for a moment.

WORD ANALYSIS. The ending -escent in opalescent (ō-păl-ĕs'ĕnt) in line 12 of " Pretty Words " is a reliable one that always means becoming, or beginning to be. You know it in adolescent, beginning to be an adult. You will come across senescent (sĕn-ĕs'ĕnt), becoming old. What is a convalescent person beginning to be? The shortest definition of opalescent is iridescent (ĭr-ĭ-dĕs'ĕnt), built on the base-word iris, the rainbow. What does an opal have in common with the rainbow?

## Robinson Jeffers        1887–

A tall, bronzed man, reserved in manner and living almost the life of a recluse, is Robinson Jeffers. His boyhood was spent in Pittsburgh, but from twelve to fifteen he attended school in Switzerland. Here he and his father, a man of scholarly tastes, took long walking trips in the Alps. When the family moved to California, Robinson had his college education at Occidental College, Los Angeles. Fortunately for his literary career, a legacy from an uncle left him free to live as he chose. He and his wife built a house on the top of a bluff overlooking the Pacific near Carmel, California. Not far from the house, Jeffers himself built a three-story stone tower. The first floor was for their twin sons born in 1916, the second floor was a sitting room for Mrs. Jeffers, and the top, a tiny room with a table and chair, was the poet's study. From this tower have come many volumes of singularly haunting poetry.

## JOY

Though joy is better than sorrow, joy is not great;
Peace is great, strength is great.
Not for joy the stars burn, not for joy the vulture
Spreads her gray sails on the air
Over the mountain; not for joy the worn mountain          5
Stands, while years like water
Trench his long sides. " I am neither mountain nor bird
Nor star; and I seek joy."
The weakness of your breed: yet at length quietness
Will cover those wistful eyes.          10

## TO THE STONE–CUTTERS

Stone-cutters fighting time with marble, you foredefeated
Challengers of oblivion
Eat cynical earnings, knowing rocks splits, records fall down,
The square-limbed Roman letters
Scale in the thaws, wear in the rain. The poet as well          5
Builds his monument mockingly;
For man will be blotted out, the blithe earth die, the brave sun
Die blind and blacken to the heart:
Yet stones have stood for a thousand years, and pained thoughts found
The honey of peace in old poems.          10

## HURT HAWKS

### I

The broken pillar of the wing jags from the clotted shoulder,
The wing trails like a banner in defeat,
No more to use the sky forever but live with famine
And pain a few days: cat nor coyote
Will shorten the week of waiting for death, there is game without talons.          5
He stands under the oak bush and waits
The lame feet of salvation; at night he remembers freedom
And flies in a dream; the dawns ruin it.
He is strong and pain is worse to the strong, incapacity is worse.
The curs of the day come and torment him          10
At distance, no one but death the redeemer will humble that head,
The intrepid readiness, the terrible eyes.
The wild God of the world is sometimes merciful to those
That ask mercy, not often to the arrogant.
You do not know him, you communal people, or you have forgotten him;          15
Intemperate and savage, the hawk remembers him;
Beautiful and wild, the hawks, and men that are dying, remember him.

### II

I'd sooner, except the penalties, kill a man than a hawk; but the great redtail
Had nothing left but unable misery

From the bone too shattered for mending, the wing that trailed under his talons when
    he moved.     20
We had fed him six weeks, I gave him freedom,
He wandered over the foreland hill and returned in the evening asking for death,
Not like a beggar, still eyed with the old
Implacable arrogance. I gave him the lead gift in the twilight. What fell was relaxed,
Owl, downy, soft feminine feathers; but what     25
Soared: the fierce rush: the night herons by the flooded river cried fear at its rising
Before it was quite unsheathed from reality.

## Suggestions for Study of Jeffers

1. In what way are peace and strength greater than joy? How do the poet's illustrations help you to see the answer? Who is speaking in lines 7–8? What do you think the poet means by the last two lines?

2. Why are stone-cutters defeated at the outset in trying to fight time? What is a poet's monument? Why is it built mockingly? What is the consolation for both stone-cutter and poet? In connection with this poem Shelley's famous sonnet " Ozymandias " would be worth reading as giving a concrete picture of time's triumph over stone records.

3. In " Hurt Hawks " point out details which give the impression of strength in the hawk, even though dying. Show how the hawk is almost given the personality of a human being. Explain the last two lines.

4. Observe how in the last lines of each poem the author challenges the reader with a thought that requires some rereading and deliberation before it is fully understood.

## Alan Seeger     1888–1916

### I HAVE A RENDEZVOUS
### WITH DEATH

Among soldiers, some, more gifted than their fellows — more sensitive perhaps, or at least more articulate — succeed in recording in prose or poetry the thrill and horror of their experience, and their personal reflections about war. Three such young men, who wrote memorable war poetry in the few brief months before they lost their lives in World War I, can well be mentioned together. The first is Rupert Brooke, gifted English poet; the second is a Canadian, John McCrae, author of " In Flanders Fields "; the third is the American poet, Alan Seeger.

Like many other foreign students who loved France, he enlisted in the Foreign Legion, which saw almost continuous service throughout the long struggle. Alan Seeger died in action in July, 1916, fulfilling the prophecy expressed in this, his best-known poem.

I have a rendezvous with Death
At some disputed barricade,
When Spring comes back with rustling shade
And apple blossoms fill the air —
I have a rendezvous with Death     5
When Spring brings back blue days and fair.

It may be he shall take my hand
And lead me into his dark land
And close my eyes and quench my breath —
It may be I shall pass him still.     10
I have a rendezvous with Death
On some scarred slope of battered hill,
When Spring comes round again this year
And the first meadow flowers appear.

God knows 'twere better to be deep     15
Pillowed in silk and scented down,
Where Love throbs out in blissful sleep,
Pulse nigh to pulse and breath to breath,
Where hushed awakenings are dear. . . .
But I've a rendezvous with Death     20
At midnight in some flaming town,
When Spring trips north again this year,
And I to my pledged word am true,
I shall not fail that rendezvous.

## Suggestions for Study

1. Be sure you know what the word " rendezvous " means.

2. Name the three places where Seeger thinks the rendezvous may have to be kept.

3. Why would it be particularly tragic for a poet to have to die in spring? Point out some proof of this from the poem.

4. Read other poems written by young soldiers of the two World Wars. See page 347 for
names of collections of these poems.

## T. S. Eliot        1888–

Though born the same year as Alan Seeger,
Thomas Stearns Eliot (he is usually known by
his initials) seems much more modern. Seeger's name lives in one poignant poem, borne
out by tragic experience. Eliot's is synonymous
with a new kind of poetry which has aroused
great controversy — almost as great as that
of earlier days centering around Whitman's
*Leaves of Grass* and the advent of the free-
versifiers. Eliot has inspired a devoted band
of followers and imitators, so that he has been
one of the most influential of the living poets
upon the world of literature.

Eliot was born in St. Louis, Missouri, but all
the background of his family connections and
his own interests drew him toward the older
civilization of the East. He studied at Harvard
and the Sorbonne, and became a Rhodes scholar
at Oxford. After 1913 he considered London
his home, and in 1927 he became a naturalized
British subject.

There is nothing stereotyped about Eliot.
Whether he writes biting, cynical verse as he
did in his earlier volumes, or great poetic
drama as in *Murder in the Cathedral* (1935),
based on a famous episode in English history,
or a sense-picture like " Prelude " or a whimsi-
cality like " The Naming of Cats," you may
know that Eliot follows his own poetic genius
and is never an imitator.

## PRELUDE

The winter evening settles down
With smell of steaks in passageways.
Six o'clock.
The burnt-out ends of smoky days.
And now a gusty shower wraps        5
The grimy scraps
Of withered leaves about your feet
And newspapers from vacant lots;
The showers beat
On broken blinds and chimney pots,        10
And at the corner of the street
A lonely cab horse steams and stamps.
And then the lighting of the lamps.

## THE HOLLOW MEN

We are the hollow men
We are the stuffed men
Leaning together
Headpieces filled with straw. Alas!
Our dried voices, when        5
We whisper together
Are quiet and meaningless
As wind in dry grass
Or rat's feet over broken glass
In our dry cellar;        10

Shape without form, shade without color,
Paralyzed force, gesture without motion;

Those who have crossed
With direct eyes, to death's other Kingdom
Remember us — if at all — not as lost        15
Violent souls, but only
As the hollow men
The stuffed men.

## THE NAMING OF CATS

The Naming of Cats is a difficult matter,
    It isn't just one of your holiday games;
You may think at first I'm as mad as a hatter
When I tell you, a cat must have THREE
    DIFFERENT NAMES.
First of all, there's the name that the family
    use daily,        5
    Such as Peter, Augustus, Alonzo, or
    James,
Such as Victor or Jonathan, George or Bill
    Bailey —
    All of them sensible everyday names.
There are fancier names if you think they
    sound sweeter,
    Some for the gentlemen, some for the
    dames:        10
Such as Plato, Admetus, Electra, Dem-
    eter —
    But all of them sensible everyday names.
But I tell you a cat needs a name that's par-
    ticular,
    A name that's peculiar and more digni-
    fied,
    Else how can he keep up his tail perpen-
    dicular,        15

Or spread out his whiskers or cherish his
    pride?
Of names of this kind I can give you a
    quorum,
Such as Munkustrap, Quaxo, or Corico-
    pat,
Such as Bombalurina, or else Jellylorum —
    Names that never belong to more than
    one cat.          20
But above and beyond there's still one name
    left over,
And that is the name that you never will
    guess;
The name that no human research can dis-
    cover —
But the CAT HIMSELF KNOWS, and will
    never confess.
When you notice a cat in profound medita-
    tion,          25
The reason, I tell you, is always the same:
His mind is engaged in a rapt contemplation
Of the thought, of the thought, of the
    thought of his name:
    His ineffable effable
    Effanineffable          30
Deep and inscrutable singular Name.

## Suggestions for Study of Eliot

1. In " Prelude," which details might be descriptive of almost any city? Which suggest a
certain specific city and a particular kind of
locality in that city?

2. How do you interpret " The Hollow
Men "? Can you give any examples from history or public life of the present century that
would illustrate " hollow " men?

3. What qualities of the cat are amusingly
illustrated by the necessity for its having three
names? How do the names mentioned add to
the humor of the poem? How does the author
work up to a climax of comic dignity?

# Stephen Vincent Benét
## 1898–1943

Stephen Vincent Benét was born in Bethlehem, Pennsylvania, but his family was stationed there only temporarily, and much of his
boyhood was spent in California and Georgia.
He belonged to a remarkably literary family.

His brother, William Rose Benét, is a well-
known critic and poet; his sister, Laura, is a
novelist. His wife, Rosemary, collaborated
with him on *A Book of Americans*, amusing
light-verse portrayals of famous men; Elinor
Wylie was his sister-in-law.

He attended Yale at a time when literary
activity was at its height among the students.
Among his contemporaries there, Archibald
MacLeish and Thornton Wilder have made outstanding reputations in the field of letters. Before leaving college, Stephen Benét had published two volumes, and within ten years after
graduation he had won both the *Nation's* poetry prize and the Pulitzer prize, the latter for
*John Brown's Body*. Preparation for writing
this great poem of the War between the States
had come through his long-standing interest in
old battles and campaigns in books handed
down from several West Point graduates in
his own family. Then, too, the wide geographic
spread of his own experience from North to
South gave him sympathetic insight into the
lives of those on both sides of the great conflict.

The vigor of Stephen Benét's poetic style
also showed itself in his ballads, revealing
different facets of American life. Shortly before his death he wrote another long poem
somewhat in the style of *John Brown's Body*,
with flashing pictures and episodes of the early
settlement of America. This was published
posthumously under the title *Western Star*.
The richness, variety, and originality of Stephen Benét's poetry put him by general consent in the front rank of our younger poets,
and his too early death was mourned as a real
calamity to American letters. It must not be
forgotten that he showed equal ability in fiction (see page 96) and thus won a kind of
bilateral distinction that reminds one of Poe.

## MARY LOU WINGATE

### FROM JOHN BROWN'S BODY

When *John Brown's Body* was published in
1928, it attained that unusual distinction for
a book of poetry — appearance on the best-
seller lists. It is truly a remarkable book, the
first serious attempt in poetry to present an
impartial view of the War between the States.
It is epic in its all-inclusiveness, yet it lacks
the unified form of the typical epic. Instead
of telling his story in a continuous narrative

the author has taken a number of representative characters, some real, some fictional, and has placed them in scenes that were significant of the trend of the war. The scene shifts rapidly from one group to another, but a connected thread of plot within each group maintains the reader's interest throughout. The metrical form also shifts. Some parts are in blank verse, some in free verse, some in pure lyrical form, while this sketch of Mary Lou Wingate, the lady of the plantation, is presented with the firm vigor and occasional satirical flash of rhymed couplet.

Mary Lou Wingate, as slightly made
And as hard to break as a rapier blade.
Bristol's daughter and Wingate's bride,
Never well since the last child died
But staring at pain with courteous eyes.    5
When the pain outwits it, the body dies,
Meanwhile the body bears the pain.
She loved her hands and they made her vain,
The tiny hands of her generation
That gathered the reins of the whole plantation;    10
The velvet sheathing the steel demurely
In the trained, light grip that holds so surely.

She was at work by candlelight,
She was at work in the dead of night,    14
Smoothing out troubles and healing schisms
And doctoring phthisics and rheumatisms,
Guiding the cooking and watching the baking,
The sewing, the soap- and candle-making,
The brewing, the darning, the lady-daughters,
The births and deaths in the Negro quarters,    20
Seeing that Suke had some new, strong shoes
And Joe got a week in the calaboose,
While Dicey's Jacob escaped a whipping
And the jelly bag dripped with its proper dripping,
And the shirts and estrangements were neatly mended,    25
And all of the tasks that never ended.

Her manner was gracious but hardly fervent
And she seldom raised her voice to a servant.

She was often mistaken, not often blind;
And she knew the whole duty of womankind,    30
To take the burden and have the power
And seem like the well-protected flower,
To manage a dozen industries
With a casual gesture in scraps of ease,
To hate the sin and to love the sinner    35
And to see that the gentlemen got their dinner
Ready and plenty and piping-hot
Whether you wanted to eat or not.
And always, always, to have the charm    39
That makes the gentlemen take your arm
But never the bright, unseemly spell
That makes strange gentlemen love too well,
Once you were married and settled down
With a suitable gentleman of your own.

And when that happened, and you had bred    45
The requisite children, living and dead,
To pity the fool and comfort the weak
And always let the gentlemen speak,
To succor your love from deep-struck roots
When gentlemen went to bed in their boots,    50
And manage a gentleman's whole plantation
In the manner befitting your female station.

This was the creed that her mother taught her
And the creed that she taught to every daughter.
She knew her Bible — and how to flirt    55
With a swansdown fan and a brocade skirt.
For she trusted in God but she liked formalities
And the world and heaven were both realities.
— In heaven, of course, we should all be equal,
But, until we came to that golden sequel,    60
Gentility must keep to gentility
Where God and breeding had made things stable,
While the rest of the cosmos deserved civility
But dined in its boots at the second table.

This view may be reckoned a trifle nar-
row, 65
But it had the driving force of an arrow,
And it helped Mary Lou to stand up
straight,
For she was gentle, but she could hate
And she hated the North with the hate of
Jael°
When the dry hot hands went seeking the
nail, 70
The terrible hate of women's ire,
The smoky, the long-consuming fire.
The Yankees were devils, and she could
pray,
For devils, no doubt, upon Judgment Day,
But now in the world, she would hate them
still 75
And send the gentlemen out to kill.

The gentlemen killed and the gentlemen
died,
But she was the South's incarnate pride
That mended the broken gentlemen
And sent them out to the war again, 80
That kept the house with the man away
And baked the bricks where there was no
clay,
Made courage from terror and bread from
bran
And propped the South on a swansdown fan
Through four long years of ruin and
stress, 85
The pride — and the deadly bitterness.

69. **Jael:** a woman of ancient Biblical times
who killed the captain of the Canaanites by
driving a nail through his forehead while he slept
(see Judges 4:15–22).

## THE MOUNTAIN
## WHIPPOORWILL

(*Or, How Hillbilly Jim Won the Great
Fiddlers' Prize*)

### A GEORGIA ROMANCE

Up in the mountains, it's lonesome all the
time,
(Sof' win' slewin' thu' the sweet-potato
vine).

Up in the mountains, it's lonesome for a
child,
(Whippoorwills a-callin' when the sap runs
wild).

Up in the mountains, mountains in the
fog, 5
Everythin's as lazy as an old houn' dog.

Born in the mountains, never raised a pet,
Don't want nuthin' an' never got it yet.

Born in the mountains, lonesome-born,
Raised runnin' ragged thu' the cockleburrs
and corn. 10

Never knew my pappy, mebbe never should.
Think he was a fiddle made of mountain-
laurel wood.

Never had a mammy to teach me pretty-
please.
Think she was a whippoorwill, a-skitin' thu'
the trees.

Never had a brother ner a whole pair of
pants, 15
But when I start to fiddle, why, yuh got to
start to dance!

*Listen to my fiddle — Kingdom Come —
Kingdom Come!
Hear the frogs a-chunkin' " Jug o' rum,
Jug o' rum! "
Hear that mountan whippoorwill be lone-
some in the air,
An' I'll tell yuh how I traveled to the Essex
County Fair.* 20

Essex County has a mighty pretty fair,
All the smarty fiddlers from the South come
there.

Elbows flyin' as they rosin up the bow
For the First Prize Contest in the Georgia
Fiddlers' Show.

Old Dan Wheeling, with his whiskers in his
ears, 25
Kingpin fiddler for nearly twenty years.

Big Tom Sargent, with his blue walleye,
An' Little Jimmy Weezer that can make a
    fiddle cry.

*All sittin' roun', spittin' high an' struttin'*
    *proud,*
*(Listen, little whippoorwill, yuh better bug*
    *yore eyes!)* 30
*Tun-a-tun-a-tunin' while the jedges told the*
    *crowd*
*Them that got the mostest claps 'd win the*
    *bestest prize.*

Everybody waitin' for the first tweedle-dee,
When in comes a-stumblin' — hillbilly me!

Bowed right pretty to the jedges an' the
    rest, 35
Took a silver dollar from a hole inside my
    vest,

Plunked it on the table an' said, " There's
    my callin' card!
An' anyone that licks me — well, he's got
    to fiddle hard! "

Old Dan Wheeling, he was laughin' fit to
    holler,
Little Jimmy Weezer said, " There's one
    dead dollar! " 40

Big Tom Sargent had a yaller-toothy grin,
But I tucked my little whippoorwill spang
    underneath my chin,
An' petted it an' tuned it till the jedges
    said, " Begin! "

Big Tom Sargent was the first in line;
He could fiddle all the bugs off a sweet-
    potato vine. 45
He could fiddle down a possum from a mile-
    high tree,
He could fiddle up a whale from the bottom
    of the sea.

Yuh could hear hands spankin' till they
    spanked each other raw,
When he finished variations on " Turkey in
    the Straw."

Little Jimmy Weezer was the next to
    play; 50
He could fiddle all night, he could fiddle all
    day.

He could fiddle chills, he could fiddle fever,
He could make a fiddle rustle like a low-
    land river.

He could make a fiddle croon like a lovin'
    woman.
An' they clapped like thunder when he'd
    finished strummin'. 55

Then came the ruck of the bobtailed fiddlers,
The let's-go-easies, the fair-to-middlers.

They got their claps an' they lost their
    bicker,°
An' they all settled back for some more corn
    licker.

An' the crowd was tired of their no-'count
    squealing, 60
When out in the center steps Old Dan
    Wheeling.

*He fiddled high and he fiddled low,*
*(Listen, little whippoorwill; yuh got to*
    *spread yore wings!)*
*He fiddled and fiddled with a cherry wood*
    *bow.*
*(Old Dan Wheeling's got bee honey in his*
    *strings.)* 65

He fiddled the wind by the lonesome moon,
He fiddled a most almighty tune.

He started fiddling like a ghost.
He ended fiddling like a host.

He fiddled north an' he fiddled south, 70
He fiddled the heart right out of yore mouth.

He fiddled here an' he fiddled there.
He fiddled salvation everywhere.

*When he was finished, the crowd cut loose.*
*(Whippoorwill, they's rain on yore breast.)*
    58. **lost their bicker:** failed.

*An' I sat there wonderin' "What's the
    use?"* 76
(*Whippoorwill, fly home to yore nest.*)

But I stood up pert an' I took my bow,
An' my fiddle went to my shoulder, so.

An' — they wasn't no crowd to get me
    fazed° — 80
But I was alone where I was raised.

Up in the mountains, so still it makes yuh
    skeered.
Where God lies sleepin' in his big white
    beard.

An' I heard the sound of the squirrel in
    the pine,
An' I heard the earth a-breathin' thu' the
    long nighttime. 85

They've fiddled the rose, and they've fiddled
    the thorn,
But they haven't fiddled the mountain corn.

They've fiddled sinful an' fiddled moral,
But they haven't fiddled the breshwood
    laurel.

They've fiddled loud, and they've fiddled
    still, 90
But they haven't fiddled the whippoorwill.

I started off with a *dump-diddle-dump*,
(*Oh, hell's broke loose in Georgia!*)
Skunk cabbage growin' by the bee-gum
    stump,
(*Whippoorwill, yo're singin' now!*) 95

My mother was a whippoorwill pert,
My father, he was lazy,
But I'm hell broke loose in a new store shirt
To fiddle all Georgia crazy.

Swing yore partners — up an' down the
    middle! 100

80. **fazed:** embarrassed.

Sashay now — oh, listen to that fiddle!
Flapjacks flippin' on a red-hot griddle,
An' hell broke loose,
Hell broke loose,
Fire on the mountains — snakes in the
    grass. 105
Satan's here a-bilin' — oh, Lordy, let him
    pass!
Go down Moses, set my people free;
Pop goes the weasel thu' the old Red Sea!
Jonah sittin' on a hickory bough,
Up jumps a whale — an' where's yore
    prophet now? 110
Rabbit in the pea patch, possum in the
    pot,
Try an' stop my fiddle, now my fiddle's get-
    tin' hot!
Whippoorwill, singin' thu' the mountain
    hush,
Whippoorwill, shoutin' from the burnin'
    bush, 114
Whippoorwill, cryin' in the stable door,
Sing tonight as yuh never sang before!
Hell's broke loose like a stompin' mountain
    shoat,
Sing till yuh bust the gold in yore throat!
Hell's broke loose for forty miles aroun'
Bound to stop yore music if yuh don't sing
    it down. 120
Sing on the mountains, little whippoorwill,
Sing to the valleys, an' slap 'em with a hill,
For I'm struttin' high as an eagle's quill,
An' hell's broke loose,
Hell's broke loose, 125
Hell's broke loose in Georgia!

They wasn't a sound when I stopped bowin',
(*Whippoorwill, yuh can sing no more*).
But, somewhere or other, the dawn was
    growin',
(*Oh, mountain whippoorwill!*) 130

An' I thought, " I've fiddled all night an'
    lost,
Yo're a good hillbilly, but yuh've been
    bossed."

So I went to congratulate old man Dan,
— But he puts his fiddle into my han' —
An' then the noise of the crowd began! 135

## THE BALLAD OF
## WILLIAM SYCAMORE

### (1790–1871)

My father, he was a mountaineer,
His fist was a knotty hammer;
He was quick on his feet as a running deer,
And he spoke with a Yankee stammer.

My mother, she was merry and brave,     5
And so she came to her labor,
With a tall green fir for her doctor grave
And a stream for her comforting neighbor.

And some are wrapped in the linen fine,
And some like a godling's scion;      10
But I was cradled on twigs of pine
In the skin of a mountain lion.

And some remember a white, starched lap
And a ewer with silver handles;
But I remember a coonskin cap      15
And the smell of bayberry candles.

The cabin logs, with the bark still rough,
And my mother who laughed at trifles,
And the tall, lank visitors, brown as snuff,
With their long, straight squirrel rifles.   20

I can hear them dance, like a foggy song,
Through the deepest one of my slumbers,
The fiddle squeaking the boots along
And my father calling the numbers.

The quick feet shaking the puncheon
    floor,      25
And the fiddle squealing and squealing,
Till the dried herbs rattled above the door
And the dust went up to the ceiling.

There are children lucky from dawn to dusk,
But never a child so lucky!      30
For I cut my teeth on " Money Musk "
In the Bloody Ground of Kentucky!

When I grew tall as the Indian corn,
My father had little to lend me,
But he gave me his great, old powder
    horn      35
And his woodsman's skill to befriend me.

With a leather shirt to cover my back,
And a redskin nose to unravel
Each forest sign, I carried my pack
As far as a scout could travel.      40

Till I lost my boyhood and found my wife,
A girl like a Salem clipper°!
A woman straight as a hunting knife
With eyes as bright as the Dipper!

We cleared our camp where the buffalo
    feed,      45
Unheard-of streams were our flagons;
And I sowed my sons like the apple-seed
On the trail of the Western wagons.

They were right, tight boys, never sulky or
    slow,
A fruitful, a goodly muster.      50
The eldest died at the Alamo.°
The youngest fell with Custer.°

The letter that told it burned my hand.
Yet we smiled and said, " So be it! "
But I could not live when they fenced the
    land,      55
For it broke my heart to see it.

I saddled a red, unbroken colt
And rode him into the day there;
And he threw me down like a thunderbolt
And rolled on me as I lay there.      60

The hunter's whistle hummed in my ear
As the city men tried to move me,
And I died in my boots like a pioneer
With the whole wide sky above me.

Now I lie in the heart of the fat, black
    soil,      65
Like the seed of a prairie thistle;

42. **Salem clipper:** Salem, Massachusetts, was
one of the chief seaports in the days of the clipper
ships. 51. **Alamo** (ăl'á-mō): an old Spanish mission, later used as a fort when in 1836 a garrison
of Texans were slaughtered by the Mexicans.
For later developments see "Sam Houston at
San Jacinto" (page 245). 52. **Custer:** General
George Custer, famous Indian fighter, who between 1866 and 1876 was sent to quell uprisings
in various parts of the West.

It has washed my bones with honey and oil
And picked them clean as a whistle.

And my youth returns, like the rains of
    Spring,
And my sons, like the wild geese flying;  70
And I lie and hear the meadowlark sing
And I have much content in my dying.

Go play with the towns you have built of
    blocks,
The towns where you would have bound me!
I sleep in my earth like a tired fox,     75
And my buffalo have found me.

## Suggestions for Study of Benét

MARY LOU WINGATE

1. Make a list of the main characteristics
of Mary Lou Wingate. Have you known anyone like her? Does she fit with your previous
idea of the lady of a plantation before the
war? If you have read *Gone with the Wind* or
have seen it in the movies, point out ways in
which Mary Lou and Scarlett O'Hara are alike
and unlike.

2. What elements of the old plantation life
have passed away forever? Which remain in
somewhat modified form?

THE MOUNTAIN WHIPPOORWILL

3. Picture in your own words the scene of
the story, the appearance of the characters,
and the speaker himself.

4. Why are certain lines put in italics?
Wherein does the story use the dramatic devices of contrast, suspense, climax? What gives
any public competition a dramatic flavor?
How does the method of judging this contest
compare with any you have witnessed or heard
on the radio? Is the outcome of the contest
more or less effective by being told so briefly?
Discuss " quick curtains " in general.

5. Where in the poem do you feel that the
poet is consciously building up sound effects?
How do they compare in manner and effectiveness with Vachel Lindsay's? Would this poem
lend itself to choral reading, as suggested for
Lindsay's poems?

6. By pointing out specific examples of
idioms, figures of speech, details of nature, con-
ceptions of Bible characters, superstitions, and
so forth, show how the poet creates the local
color of the unsophisticated mountain whites.

THE BALLAD OF WILLIAM SYCAMORE

7. Pick out details that show Sycamore to
have been a typical American in the early days
of the opening of the West.

8. Why is this poem called a ballad? (See
page 341 for definition.) Is it written in typical
ballad measure?

9. Point out some of the strikingly original
phrases in this poem, especially those relating
to Sycamore's death and burial.

10. A good description of how babies were
taken to dances in the early days is to be found
in Owen Wister's *The Virginian*.

11. Look up further details of the fight at
the Alamo and the exploits of Custer referred
to in this ballad.

12. Read others of Benét's excellent ballads
in *A Book of Americans* written in collaboration with his wife, Rosemary.

## Edna St. Vincent Millay
### 1892–

Edna St. Vincent Millay comes from a
poetry-writing family, for her mother and sister have also published volumes of verse. She
was born in Rockland, Maine, and her early
life was spent in New England. When she was
nineteen she wrote " Renascence," a poem so
remarkable that she was at once heralded as a
coming poet. This poem was the title piece in
her first volume, published in 1917, the same
year that she left Vassar College. Since then
she has published eight other slender but significant volumes of poetry; several short plays
in verse; and *The King's Henchman*, a libretto
to the opera by Deems Taylor. This is a notable attempt to establish the hitherto undeveloped form of grand opera in America. Aside
from its musical setting the libretto has taken
its own place as a splendid poetic drama. Miss
Millay's flowing melody is evident in her short
lyrics. In her earlier poems one finds often
exuberance of life; occasionally pertness; but
more frequently than either a kind of lyric
wistfulness. This is especially noticeable in
*The Harp-Weaver.* Observe the unusual rhyme
in the middle of each stanza of " The Spring
and the Fall," taken from this volume. In *The
Buck in the Snow*, from which " Dirge without Music " is taken, there is a growing bitterness at the injustices and tragedies of life. In
*Wine from These Grapes* (1934) she peers

into the dim past and into the dim future, seeking a unified pattern in human experience. " Autumn Daybreak " and " If Still Your Orchards Bear " are from this volume.

## LAMENT

The poignancy of this poem, from the volume *Second April*, lies in the twist of the last line, which comes like a cold shiver at the heart after the matter-of-fact tone of the first part.

Listen, children:
Your father is dead.
From his old coats
I'll make you little jackets;
I'll make you little trousers   5
From his old pants.
There'll be in his pockets
Things he used to put there,
Keys and pennies
Covered with tobacco;   10
Dan shall have the pennies
To save in his bank;
Anne shall have the keys
To make a pretty noise with.
Life must go on,   15
And the dead be forgotten;
Life must go on,
Though good men die;
Anne, eat your breakfast;
Dan, take your medicine;   20
Life must go on;
I forget just why.

## THE SPRING AND THE FALL

In the spring of the year, in the spring of
  the year,
I walked the road beside my dear.
The trees were black where the bark was
  wet.
I see them yet, in the spring of the year.
He broke me a bough of the blossoming
  peach   5
That was out of the way and hard to reach.

In the fall of the year, in the fall of the year,
I walked the road beside my dear.
The rooks went up with a raucous trill.
I hear them still, in the fall of the year.   10
He laughed at all I dared to praise,
And broke my heart, in little ways.

Year be springing or year be falling,
The bark will drip and the birds be calling.
There's much that's fine to see and hear   15
In the spring of a year, in the fall of a year.
'Tis not love's going hurts my days,
But that it went in little ways.

## DIRGE WITHOUT MUSIC

I am not resigned to the shutting away of loving hearts in the hard ground.
So it is, and so it will be, for so it has been time out of mind:
Into the darkness they go, the wise and the lovely. Crowned
With lilies and with laurel they go; but I am not resigned.

Lovers and thinkers, into the earth with you,   5
Be one with the dull, the indiscriminate dust.
A fragment of what you felt, of what you knew,
A formula, a phrase remains — but the best is lost.

The answers quick and keen, the honest look, the laughter, the love —
They are gone. They are gone to feed the roses. Elegant and curled   10
Is the blossom. Fragrant is the blossom. I know. But I do not approve.
More precious was the light in your eyes than all the roses of the world.

Down, down, down into the darkness of the grave
Gently they go, the beautiful, the tender, the kind;
Quietly they go, the intelligent, the witty, the brave.   15
I know. But I do not approve. And I am not resigned.

## AUTUMN DAYBREAK

Cold wind of autumn, blowing loud
At dawn, a fortnight overdue,
Jostling the doors, and tearing through
My bedroom to rejoin the cloud,

I know — for I can hear the hiss 5
And scrape of leaves along the floor —
How many boughs, lashed bare by this,
Will rake the cluttered sky once more.

Tardy, and somewhat south of east,
The sun will rise at length, made known 10
More by the meager light increased
Than by a disk in splendor shown;

When, having but to turn my head,
Through the stripped maple I shall see,
Bleak and remembered, patched with red,
The hill all summer hid from me. 16

## IF STILL YOUR ORCHARDS BEAR

Brother, that breathe the August air
   Ten thousand years from now,
And smell — if still your orchards bear
   Tart apples on the bough —

The early windfall under the tree 5
   And see the red fruit shine,
I cannot think your thoughts will be
   Much different from mine.

Should at that moment the full moon
   Step forth upon the hill, 10
And memories hard to bear at noon,
   By moonlight harder still,

Form in the shadows of the trees —
   Things that you could not spare
And live, or so you thought, yet these 15
   All gone, and you still there,

A man no longer what he was,
   Nor yet the thing he'd planned,
The chilly apple from the grass
   Warmed by your living hand — 20

I think you will have need of tears;
   I think they will not flow;
Supposing in ten thousand years
   Men ache, as they do now.

## Suggestions for Study of Millay

1. What similarity in the mood and situation do you find in "Lament" and "The Spring and the Fall"? What point of difference is there? Which do you find more poignant?

2. Explain the last two lines of "The Spring and the Fall." Do you get any hint of what these "little ways" were? Give some specific examples to illustrate what they might have been.

3. "Dirge without Music" is in strong contrast to Sara Teasdale's "The Lamp" (page 317). Summarize the attitude of each toward death. Notice how many of the modern poets have written of death in one form or another. Point out different angles from which the subject has been approached by each. In Part II you will find poems on death by earlier writers. Can you account for this being such a favorite subject with poets?

4. Compare "Autumn Daybreak" with Sara Teasdale's "Leaves" (see page 316). What point of similarity do you find in the two? Which of the two is more obviously an allegory of life? Could the other also be given an allegorical meaning?

5. Read Millay's "God's World," a well-known poem found in many collections, which also pictures autumn. What striking contrast is there in the mood of these two poems? Which mood does autumn more commonly arouse in you? Collect other poems on autumn.

6. In "If Still Your Orchards Bear" what unusual companionship in her loneliness does the author seek? In the same volume, *Wine from These Grapes*, Miss Millay writes a series of sonnets, called "Epitaph on the Race of Man," in which she traces the history of mankind through the ages. It is interesting to read these and compare them with this poem. They illustrate both the significance and the insignificance of time.

## Robert Peter Tristram Coffin
### 1892–

"My family has roots three hundred years deep in the New England soil and sea," Robert Coffin once said of himself, and this background is reflected in much of his poetry. He was born in Bowdoin, Maine, where he later attended the college famous for its earlier students, Longfellow and Hawthorne. He was sent to Oxford as Rhodes Scholar from Maine, and then spent two years in military service during World War I. After that interval he returned to academic life, and for thirteen years taught English at Wells College. Now he is professor of English at his Alma Mater, Bowdoin. His present home is close to his birthplace, and in a vein of sentiment he has purchased the little red schoolhouse of his boyhood. The strong hold of his background on his creative imagination is shown in two of his prose works, *Lost Paradise* (his own childhood) and *Portrait of an American* (his father).

Robert Coffin has published about twenty books in all. Nine of these are volumes of verse, and for one of them, *Strange Holiness,* he received the Pulitzer poetry prize in 1936. His latest volume (1945) stems from World War II, as shown by the title, *Poems for a Son with Wings.*

When asked to choose one of his poems for a collection of poetry for young people, he sent " Crystal Moment " as an example of the vividness with which an impression received in a fleeting moment of time can stamp itself upon the memory.

### CRYSTAL MOMENT

Once or twice this side of death
Things can make one hold his breath.

From my boyhood I remember
A crystal moment of September.

A wooded island rang with sounds          5
Of church bells in the throats of hounds.

A buck leaped out and took the tide
With jewels flowing past each side.

With his high head like a tree
He swam within a yard of me.          10

I saw the golden drop of light
In his eyes turned dark with fright.

I saw the forest's holiness
On him like a fierce caress.

Fear made him lovely past belief,          15
My heart was trembling like a leaf.

He leaned toward the land and life
With need upon him like a knife.

In his wake the hot hounds churned,
They stretched their muzzles out and
    yearned.          20

They bayed no more, but swam and
    throbbed,
Hunger drove them till they sobbed.

Pursued, pursuers reached the shore
And vanished. I saw nothing more.

So they passed, a pageant such          25
As only gods could witness much,

Life and death upon one tether
And running beautiful together.

## Suggestions for Study

1. What vivid details make this picture flash upon the eye of the reader as it did before the poet? What is the significance of the title?

2. Where else among the poets of this section have you seen intense sympathy with animal life? Would poets on the whole make good hunters? Discuss.

3. This poem has many figures of speech. Which do you think especially effective? Are any of them somewhat trite?

## Archibald MacLeish          1892–

Archibald MacLeish was born in Glencoe, Illinois, in what he describes as a wooden château overlooking Lake Michigan. He graduated from Yale and was in France during World War I, where his brother was killed in the air service. After the war MacLeish graduated from the Harvard Law School and practiced law for three years; but he finally gave it up in 1923, from which time he dates the real beginning of his life. He took his family to headquarters in France for five years, and they traveled as far as Persia. After 1928 he was back in this country living on a farm and writing poetry. In 1939 President Roosevelt appointed him head of the Library of Congress. Since then he has also served as an As-

"Crystal Moment," from *Yoke of Thunder,* by Robert P. T. Coffin. Reprinted by permission of The Macmillan Company, publishers.

sistant Secretary in the Department of State.

Six volumes of verse preceded *Conquistador,* which eventually brought him national reputation. Since then he has written radio dramas, of which *Air Raid* and *The Fall of the City* are the most famous. MacLeish has much to say and says it with originality and incisive force.

## ELEVEN

And summer mornings the mute child, rebellious,
Stupid, hating the words, the meanings, hating
The Think now, Think, the O but Think! would leave
On tiptoe the three chairs on the veranda
And crossing tree by tree the empty lawn                5
Push back the shed door and upon the sill
Stand pressing out the sunlight from his eyes
And enter and with outstretched fingers feel
The grindstone and behind it the bare wall
And turn and in the corner on the cool                 10
Hard earth sit listening. And one by one,
Out of the dazzled shadow in the room
The shapes would gather, the brown plowshare, spades,
Mattocks, the polished helves of picks, a scythe
Hung from the rafters, shovels, slender tines          15
Glinting across the curve of sickles — shapes
Older than men were, the wise tools, the iron
Friendly with earth. And sit there quiet, breathing
The harsh dry smell of withered bulbs, the faint
Odor of dung, the silence. And outside                 20
Beyond the half-shut door the blind leaves
And the corn moving. And at noon would come,
Up from the garden, his hard crooked hands
Gentle with earth, his knees still earth-stained, smelling
Of sun, of summer, the old gardener, like              25
A priest, like an interpreter, and bend
Over his baskets.
             And they would not speak:
They would say nothing. And the child would sit there
Happy as though he had no name, as though
He had been no one: like a leaf, a stem,               30
Like a root growing —

## IT IS A STRANGE THING — TO BE AN AMERICAN

### FROM AMERICAN LETTER

It is a strange thing — to be an American.
It is strange to sleep in the bare stars and to die
On an open land where few bury before us:
(From the new earth the dead return no more).
It is strange to be born of no race and no people.     5
In the old lands they are many together. They keep

The wise past and the words spoken in common.
They remember the dead with their hands, their mouths dumb.
They answer each other with two words in their meeting.
They live together in small things. They eat                                    10
The same dish, their drink is the same and their proverbs.
Their youth is like. They are like their ways of love.
They are many men. There are always others beside them.
Here it is one man and another and wide
On the darkening hills the faint smoke of the houses.                           15
Here it is one man and the wind in the boughs.

Therefore our hearts are sick for the south water.
The smell of the gorse comes back to our night thought.
We are sick at heart for the red roofs and the olives;
We are sick at heart for the voice and the footfall. . . .                      20

Therefore we will not go though the sea call us.

This, this is our land, this is our people,
This that is neither a land nor a race. We must reap
The wind here in the grass for our soul's harvest:
Here we must eat our salt or our bones starve.                                  25
Here we must live or live only as shadows.
This is our race, we that have none, that have had
Neither the old walls nor the voices around us,
This is our land, this is our ancient ground —
The raw earth, the mixed bloods and the strangers,                             30
The different eyes, the wind, and the heart's change.
These we will not leave though the old call us.
This is our country-earth, our blood, our kind.

### THE WESTERN SKY

Stand stand against the rising night
O freedom's land, O freedom's air:
Stand steep and keep the fading light
That eastward darkens everywhere.

Hold hold the golden light and lift                 5
Hill after hilltop, one by one —
Lift up America O lift
Green freedom to the evening sun.

Lift up your hills till conquered men
Look westward to their blazing height:              10
Lift freedom till its fire again
Kindles the countries of the night.

Be proud America to bear
The endless labor of the free —
To strike for freedom everywhere           15
And everywhere bear liberty.

Lift up O land O land lift clear
The lovely signal of your skies.
If freedom darkens eastward here
Here on the west let freedom rise.          20

## Suggestions for Study of MacLeish

1. Does the eleven-year-old boy seem real to you? What type of boy is he? Has your own experience echoed in any way the attitude of this boy? What is referred to in line 3?

2. Point out details in this poem which appeal to the various senses. Why is emphasis upon the senses especially appropriate to the idea back of the entire poem?

3. What similarity do you note between this poem and "The Death of the Hired Man" (page 292) in subject matter and meter? What contrast is there in the relations between the

old man and the youth in the two poems? Is this caused more by the difference in age between the boy and the young man, or by the difference in their personalities?

4. In " It Is a Strange Thing " what kinds of differences are brought out between America and Europe? What effect do these differences have upon the attitude of the American toward his country? Can you give specific examples to show that the tie of the new land is stronger·than the tie to the old home across the water?

5. In " The Western Sky " how does the poet use " east " and " west " — for parts of the United States or parts of the world? Justify your answer from the poem. What special application does this poem have to present-day conditions?

6. Look back over the poets in this section to see which ones have specifically expressed attachment to our country, or ideals and aspirations they wish for America? Where in the preceding prose selections do you find the same note? In Part II you will find the spirit of America voiced in the older literature, which helped to build in the minds of more recent writers the concept of what America stands for.

# LIGHT VERSE

For a mood of lighthearted gaiety the rhythm of verse and the snap of an unexpected rhyme are often more effective than prose. We have gradually accumulated in America a tremendous volume of light, humorous verse, some of which is so well written that it will probably go on amusing readers for generations to come. Many of our major poets have written light verse of great charm and wit; but there is another group of versifiers who do not pretend to be serious poets, but have a gift for turning a clever phrase and bringing a laugh. Many of them have been newspaper columnists with a following of daily readers. Others have built a wide reputation through repeated successes as magazine contributors.

In the following group of verses you will find great variety — hearty humor, clever " society verse," the surprise ending, the caricature, the humor based on a neat juggling of words or meters or even the absence of capitals and punctuation marks! There are no " Suggestions for Study " in this little section. Just enjoy the verses, and — if the spirit moves you — try the fun of writing some light verse of your own.

## Arthur Guiterman        1871–1943

Arthur Guiterman was undoubtedly one of our best writers of light humorous verse. The gay swing of his lines is always furthered by the neatness with which the right word falls into the right place. He is a master of the unexpected. Since there is often question as to the pronunciation of his name, he once wrote a little verse to remind those who are doubtful that his name rhymes not with " cuter man " or " brighter man," but with " fitter man."

Arthur Guiterman was born in Vienna, but his parents were Americans. After receiving his degree from the College of the City of New York, he served at various times on the staffs of the *Woman's Home Companion,* the *Literary Digest,* and other magazines. He spent much of his time on lecture tours, using different aspects of humor as his subject. His home was in New York City. Some of his many volumes of verse are *The Laughing Muse, The Mirthful Lyre,* and *Chips of Jade.*

### PERSHING AT THE FRONT

Every war, while tragic, has also had its humorous side. This is one of the best-known examples from World War I.

The General came in a new tin hat
To the shell-torn front where the war was at;
With a faithful Aide at his good right hand

He made his way toward No Man's Land,
And a tough Top Sergeant there they found,                5
And a Captain, too, to show them round.

Threading the ditch, their heads bent low,
Toward the lines of the watchful foe
They came through the murk and the powder stench
Till the Sergeant whispered, " Third-line trench! "       10
And the Captain whispered, " Third-line trench! "
And the Aide repeated, " Third-line trench! "
And Pershing answered — not in French —
" Yes, I see it. Third-line trench."

Again they marched with wary tread,                       15
Following on where the Sergeant led
Through the wet and the muck as well,
Till they came to another parallel.
They halted there in the mud and drench,
And the Sergeant whispered, " Second-line trench! "       20
And the Captain whispered, " Second-line trench! "
And the Aide repeated, " Second-line trench! "
And Pershing nodded: " Second-line trench! "

Yet on they went through mire like pitch
Till they came to a fine and spacious ditch               25
Well camouflaged from planes and Zeps
Where soldiers stood on firing steps
And a Major sat on a wooden bench;
And the Sergeant whispered, " First-line trench! "
And the Captain whispered, " First-line trench! "         30
And the Aide repeated, " First-line trench! "
And Pershing whispered, " Yes, I see.
How far off is the enemy? "
And the faithful Aide he asked, asked he,
" How far off is the enemy? "                             35
And the Captain breathed in a softer key,
" How far off is the enemy? "

The silence lay in heaps and piles
And the Sergeant whispered, " Just three miles."
And the Captain whispered, " Just three miles."           40
And the Aide repeated, " Just three miles."
" Just three miles! " the General swore,
" What in the hell are we whispering for? "
And the faithful Aide the message bore,
" What in the hell are we whispering for? "               45
And the Captain said in a gentle roar,
" What in the hell are we whispering for? "
" Whispering for? " the echo rolled;
And the Sergeant whispered, " I have a cold."

# Don Marquis 1878–1938

Is it any wonder that a man with a name like Donald Robert Perry Marquis and a humorous turn of mind should become Don Marquis permanently? Like so many of our other humorists, he was born in the Mississippi Valley. His birthplace was Walnut, Illinois, which he describes as " one of those towns that prop two cornfields apart." His young manhood was occupied with trying his hand at " almost all the trades and professions that flourished in Walnut and vicinity." This same pleasing variety was evident when he went to Washington, D. C., and combined a job in the census office with newspaper reporting and study in an art school. Later he assisted Joel Chandler Harris with *Uncle Remus' Magazine* in Atlanta, and finally settled down to a long career in New York newspaperdom, where his column, " The Sun Dial " in the New York *Sun,* made his reputation.

Like many of our humorists, Don Marquis has the gift of creating a vivid humorous character; but, unlike most of them, his fame rests on several widely differing types rather than on just one. One of his most amusing creations is " archy the cockroach " of the newspaper office. As a result of transmigration from a previous existence, archy has the soul of a free-verse poet. His innate longing for expression impels archy to use the typewriter at night to communicate to " the boss "; but as he cannot work the shift key, there are no capital letters and no punctuation marks in his effusions. He also has difficulty with the mechanism for making a new line and so his " poems " look most peculiar. Through the obvious satire on free verse and through the personalities of other creatures infesting the office, such as mehitabel the cat and freddy the rat, Marquis had a rich medium for amusing comment in his column.

## FREDDY THE RAT PERISHES

listen to me there have
been some doings here since last
i wrote there has been a battle
behind that rusty typewriter cover
in the corner                                   5
you remember freddy the rat well
freddy is no more but
he died game the other

day a stranger with a lot of
legs came into our little circle a tough looking kid                                        10
he was with a bad eye

who are you said a thousand legs
if I bite you once
said the stranger you won t ask
again he he° little poison tongue said     15
the thousand legs who gave you hydrophobia
i got it by biting myself said
the stranger i m bad keep away
from me where I step a weed dies
if i was to walk on your forehead it would
raise measles and if                           21
you give me any lip i ll do it

they mixed it then
and the thousand legs succumbed
well we found out this fellow              25
was a tarantula he had come up from
south america in a bunch of bananas
for days he bossed us life
was not worth living he would stand in
the middle of the floor and taunt       30
us ha ha he would say where i
step a weed dies do
you want any of my game i was
raised on red pepper and blood i am
so hot if you scratch me i will light    35
like a match you better
dodge me when i m feeling mean and
i don t feel any other way i was nursed
on a tabasco bottle if i was to slap
your wrist in kindness you                 40
would boil over like job° and heaven
help you if i get angry give me
room i feel a wicked spell coming on

last night he made a break at freddy
the rat keep your distance                45
little one said freddy i m not
feeling well myself somebody poisoned some
cheese for me i m as full of
death as a drugstore i

---

15. **he he:** derisive laughter, not a misprint as one might, at first glance, suppose. This "poem" makes one realize how much punctuation helps us understand the relationship between words. 41. **boil over like job:** Job in the Bible was affected with boils. See Job 2:7.

feel that i am going to die anyhow        50
come on little torpedo come on don t stop
to visit and search then they
went at it and both are no more please
throw a late edition on the floor i want to
keep up with china we dropped freddy        55
off the fire escape into the alley with
military honors

                                    archy

" with military honors "

*Illustration by George Harriman from* lives and times of Archy
and Mehitabel *by Don Marquis*

## Franklin P. Adams        1881–

Franklin Pierce Adams, usually known as
F. P. A., is another of our most able columnists. He got his impetus from Eugene Field,
had his first contributions published in
B. L. T.'s column in the Chicago *Tribune,*
and his first chance to write a column of his
own with the Chicago *Journal.* Later he went
to New York and after some experimental
work found his final place with the New York
*Tribune,* now the *Herald Tribune.* Here his
column, " The Conning Tower," established his
permanent reputation. Until 1941 it appeared
in the New York *Post.* Mr. Adams, beginning

in 1939, became one of the regulars on the
well-known radio program " Information
Please."

Mr. Adams maintains a high standard of humor and writes with the utmost sincerity. He
loves to play a joke on his reader by ending a
poem with an unexpectedly simple and naïve
conclusion. For instance, one of his poems describes how some may sing of the surging sea,
others of the open road, others of the bursting
bomb, and so on, leading the reader on to an-
ticipate that the climax will be the author's own
preference. But, instead, the last line is: " And
they all may sing of whatever they like, as far
as I'm concerned." In the following poem he
again plays a simple trick on the reader — or
does he?

## THOSE TWO BOYS

When Bill was a lad he was terribly bad.
    He worried his parents a lot;
He'd lie and he'd swear and pull little girls'
        hair;
    His boyhood was naught but a blot.

At play and in school he would fracture each
        rule —                                    5
    In mischief from autumn to spring;
And the villagers knew when to manhood he
        grew
    He would never amount to a thing.

When Jim was a child he was not very wild;
    He was known as a good little boy;        10
He was honest and bright and the teachers'
        delight —
    To his father and mother a joy.

All the neighbors were sure that his virtue'd
        endure,
    That his life would be free of a spot;
They were certain that Jim had a great head
        on him                                    15
    And that Jim would amount to a lot.

And Jim grew to manhood and honor and
        fame
    And bears a good name;
While Bill is shut up in a dark prison cell —
    You never can tell.                        20

## Dorothy Parker      1893–

In any discussion of modern American humorous verse writers there is one woman who cannot be omitted, and probably only one. Though women have a sense of humor, it usually runs to appreciation rather than creation. Dorothy Parker, however, has a gift for satirical verse that places her in a class by herself. She has been described as "a delicate little thing of great beauty and charm, who writes and says the most cutting things with a lamb-like air that would melt the heart of an iron statue." She is noted for her last lines, which are often like the pinprick to a toy balloon.

Mrs. Parker was born in New Jersey, and educated in private schools and a convent. Between 1916 and 1920 she was on the staff first of *Vogue*, then of *Vanity Fair*. Since 1920 she has been a free-lance writer, and half a dozen books have come from her pen. The best-known are *Enough Rope, Sunset Gun, Death and Taxes*. In 1929 she won the O. Henry Short Story award. In 1934 she turned to playwriting in collaboration with Elmer Rice, the result being *Close Harmony*. Her collection of short stories is called *Here Lies*.

### RÉSUMÉ

Suicide is no laughing matter, but even a serious-minded person could hardly forbear smiling at this succinct and oft-quoted bit, a satire on the literature of disillusionment so prevalent in the twenties.

> Razors pain you;
> Rivers are damp;
> Acids stain you;
> And drugs cause cramp.
> Guns aren't lawful;
> Nooses give;
> Gas smells awful;
> You might as well live.

## ONE PERFECT ROSE

A single flow'r he sent me, since we met.
All tenderly his messenger he chose;
Deephearted, pure, with scented dew still
   wet —
One perfect rose.

I knew the language of the floweret;    5
" My fragile leaves," it said, " his heart in-
  close."
Love long has taken for his amulet
One perfect rose.

Why is it no one ever sent me yet
One perfect limousine, do you suppose?   10
Ah no, it's always just my luck to get
One perfect rose.

### FOLK TUNE

Other lads, their ways are daring;
Other lads, they're not afraid;
Other lads, they show they're caring;
Other lads — they know a maid.
Wiser Jock than ever you were,      5
Will's with gayer spirit blest,
Robin's kindlier and truer —
Why should I love you the best?

Other lads, their eyes are bolder.
Young they are, and strong and slim,    10
Ned is straight and broad of shoulder,
Donald has a way with him,
David stands a head above you,
Dick's as brave as Lancelot —
Why, ah why, then, should I love you?   15
Naturally, I do not.

## Ogden Nash      1902–

If you see the *New Yorker* and the *Saturday Evening Post*, you have doubtless enjoyed many times the humorous verse of Ogden Nash. Although now a resident of Baltimore, he was born in Rye, New York. After St. George's School, Newport, Rhode Island, he went to Harvard for one year. His writing certainly gives the impression that he has had long prac-

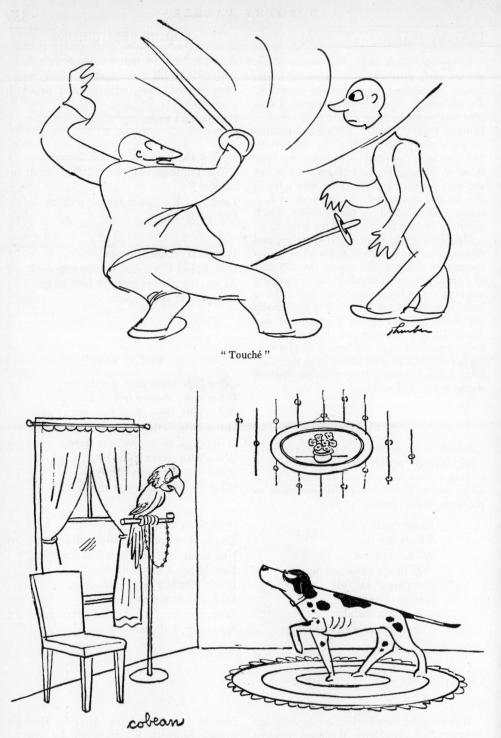

"Touché"

"Aw! Why don't you grow up?"

Cartoons are an expression of American humor. They make us laugh for many reasons. They may appeal to our sense of the ridiculous by overdrawing an existing custom or habit (as in the two cartoons at the left); they may give vent to a satirical comment on some phase of modern society (as in the drawing below); or they may poke fun at a totally serious situation (as does the cartoon at the right). Some of the outstanding cartoonists today besides these represented here are: Helen Hokinson, Robert Osborne, Peter Arno, Charles Adams, Robert Day, Sgt. George Baker, O. Soglow, and Whitney Darrow.

" Wisht I could stand up an' git some sleep."

" Yes, Rosemary does marry Doctor Bennett. Yes, Aunt Mildred recovers her missing jewels. Yes, little Bobby survives the difficult operation. Yes, I've been fired."

(*Permission Irwin Caplin and* The Saturday Evening Post)

tice at it, and that he writes with the greatest ease. His name is particularly associated with a certain irregular prose-poetry rhythm, which, like a ride over a rough road in a springless wagon, shakes a laugh out of you at unexpected moments. Another of Nash's characteristics is his original conception of the kinds of words and line lengths that can be made to rhyme with each other. The verses below are from his volume *The Face Is Familiar*.

## NATURE KNOWS BEST

People have been getting up for centuries,
They have been getting up in palaces and Pullmans and penitentiaries.
Yes, one fact for which every historian vouches,
Is that every morning in history began with people getting up off their couches.
The caveman had to get up before he could go out and track the brontosaurus,     5
Verdi had to get up before he could sit down and compose the Anvil Chorus,
Alexander had to get up before he could go around being dominant,
Even Rip Van Winkle had to get up from one sleep before he could climb the mountain
    and encounter the sleep that has made him prominent.
Some get up energetically and some in lassitude's throes,
And I myself happen to love a lassitude, a bonnie bonnie lassitude, but be that as it
    may, however they rose, they rose.     10
Well, birds are descended from birds and flowers are descended from flowers,
And human beings are descended from generation after generation of ancestors who
    got up at least once every twenty-four hours,
And since birds are descended from birds they don't have to be forced to sing like
    birds, instead of squeaking like rats,
And since flowers are descended from flowers they don't have to be forced to smell
    like flowers, instead of like burning rubber or the Jersey flats,
But you take human beings, why their countless generations of ancestors who were
    always arising might just as well have spent all their lives on their mattresses
    or pallets,     15
Because their descendants haven't inherited any talent for getting up at all, no, every
    morning they have to be forced to get up either by their own conscience or some-
    body else's, or alarm clocks or valets.
Well, there is one obvious conclusion that I have always held to,
Which is that if Nature had really intended human beings to get up, why they would
    get up naturally and wouldn't have to be compelled to.

## THIS IS GOING TO HURT JUST A LITTLE BIT

One thing I like less than most things is sitting in a dentist chair with my mouth wide
    open,
And that I will never have to do it again is a hope that I am against hope hopen.
Because some tortures are physical and some are mental,
But the one that is both is dental.     5
It is hard to be self-possessed
With your jaw digging into your chest,
So hard to retain your calm
When your fingernails are making serious alterations in your life line or love line or
    some other important line in your palm;
So hard to give your usual effect of cheery benignity

When you know your position is one of the two or three in life most lacking in
dignity.                                                                    10
And your mouth is like a section of road that is being worked on,
And it is all cluttered up with stone crushers and concrete mixers and drills and steam
rollers and there isn't a nerve of your head that you aren't being irked on.
Oh, some people are unfortunate enough to be strung up by thumbs,
And others have things done to their gums,
And your teeth are supposed to be being polished,                          15
But you have reason to believe they are being demolished,
And the circumstance that adds most to your terror
Is that it's all being done with a mirror,
Because the dentist may be a bear, or as the Romans used to say, only they were refer-
ring to a feminine bear when they said it, an *ursa*,
But all the same how can you be sure when he takes his crowbar in one hand and
mirror in the other, he won't get mixed up, the way you do when you try to tie
a bow tie with the aid of a mirror, and forget that left is right and *vice versa?*  20
And then at last he says That will be all; but it isn't because he then coats your mouth
from cellar to roof
With something that I suspect is generally used to put a shine on a horse's hoof,
And you totter to your feet and think, Well it's all over now and after all it was only
this once,
And he says come back in three monce.
And this, O Fate, is the most vicious circle that thou ever sentest,              25
That Man has to go continually to the dentist to keep his teeth in good condition when
the chief reason he wants his teeth in good condition is so that he won't have to
go to the dentist.

## TYPES OF POETRY

Poetry falls naturally into three great classes: narrative, dramatic, and lyric. The first two both tell stories, narrative resembling the short story or novel in its method, dramatic being a play or at least a dialogue in verse. Lyric poetry expresses thought or feeling. Though it may suggest a story, it does not tell it outright.

### KINDS OF NARRATIVE POETRY

THE EPIC. Narrative poetry has its subdivisions. The epic is a long narrative poem celebrating in dignified style the deeds of a hero. Among the European nations we find national epics which grew up in the early days before printing, by word-of-mouth transmission from one bard to another. American literature has nothing of that kind, but we have a few literary epics in which a specific author composes a poem based on the legends previously existing. Thus Longfellow's *The Song of Hiawatha* (page 582) is an epic of the Indians, and Neihardt's *The Song of Hugh Glass* of the hunters and trappers. Benét's *John Brown's Body* (page 323) has epic qualities, but does not center about any one hero.

METRICAL TALES. Shorter narrative poems corresponding to the prose short story, and called variously metrical romances, metrical tales, or idylls, abound in American literature, especially in the works of Longfellow and Whittier. Longfellow's *Tales of a Wayside Inn* are probably the best-known examples. In this book Lowell's " The Vision of Sir Launfal " (page 594) belongs to this class, though the preludes are distinctly lyrical. Benét's " The Mountain Whippoorwill " (page 325) is also a metrical tale.

BALLADS. Still shorter stories in verse with such marked singing quality that they are almost like lyrics are called ballads. Back in medieval times these grew up naturally like epics, and we may still see the process going on in our American folklore; but other ballads are definitely composed, such as Lowell's " The Courtin' " (page 590) and Benét's " The Ballad of William Sycamore " (page 328). Typical " ballad measure " is the four-line stanza with alternate rhymes, and three or four beats to a line. Variations of this pattern are, of course, found, and some ballads, like Whittier's " Skipper Ireson's Ride " (page 502), are in much longer stanzas.

DRAMATIC POETRY

Dramatic poetry has never flourished in America. Longfellow's " The Spanish Student " was a failure, and few of the older authors even attempted the form. In modern American poetry Edna Millay's *The King's Henchman* is almost unique in its vogue. Maxwell Anderson has used blank verse in his plays. Archibald MacLeish and others have experimented with dramatic poetry for the radio.

KINDS OF LYRIC POETRY

THE SONG. Lyric poetry is the form which has made itself most felt in America. Certain classifications can be made, but there are always lyrics which defy such labeling. The song is a simple little piece clearly intended for singing purposes. If of religious bent, it becomes a hymn. In Part II you will find Emerson's " The Concord Hymn " (page 560), Longfellow's " Hymn to the Night " (page 586), and Whittier's " The Eternal Goodness " (page 505).

THE ODE. The ode is a sustained poem of exalted mood, often irregular in metrical form. Timrod's " Ode " (page 676) is too short to be typical. Probably the two most famous odes in American literature (not included here because of their length and difficulty) are Lowell's " Commemoration Ode " and Moody's " Ode in Time of Hesitation."

THE ELEGY AND THE EPITAPH. The elegy is a mournful poem on death. Similar to it is the dirge, or funeral song. Edna Millay's " Dirge without Music " (page 330) is an example. It is questionable whether poems with the welcoming attitude toward death of Lanier's " The Stirrup Cup " (page 730) and Whitman's " The Carol of Death " (page 621) could properly be called elegies. Frost's " The Death of the Hired Man " (page 292) is an unusual type of elegy worked out through dialogue. Similar to the elegy and yet different is the epitaph, or inscription for the dead, of which Masters has made such surprising use in his *Spoon River Anthology* (page 296).

THE SONNET. The sonnet is the most restricted metrical form, being limited to fourteen lines. In the so-called Italian form there is a break in the thought between the first eight and the last six lines (called the *octave* and the *sestet*), a five-accent line, and an intricate rhyme scheme. The Shakespearean form is more flexible, usually in alternate rhyme, with a couplet at the end to clinch the idea. Perhaps because of this very challenge to ingenuity, the sonnet has been a great favorite with poets of all ages. Examples included in this book are Elinor Wylie's " Pretty Words " (page 318) and " Atavism " (page 318). The sonnet form is a favorite with Edna St. Vincent Millay.

## METRICAL TERMS

METER. Meter is an element of poetry which presents many possibilities of study. Of course, it is more important to enjoy the swing of a poem than to analyze it; but sometimes one has the same curiosity which prompts the small boy to take a clock apart to see what makes it tick. The meters described in the following pages may be called standard verse forms to distinguish them from free verse, which, as its name suggests, discards formal restrictions.

" FEET ": THE TROCHEE. Lines of poetry are divided into " feet " with one accented syllable to every " foot." The marching of soldiers illustrates one of the common forms of measure. In starting his men out together the sergeant emphasizes the left foot thus: " LEFT, right, LEFT, right," or perhaps just " LEFT . . . LEFT . . . LEFT " omitting the unaccented syllable entirely. An example of this kind of meter is found in Sara Teasdale's " Barter ":

> Life has loveliness to sell —
> Music like a curve of gold,
> Scent of pine trees in the rain,
> Eyes that love you, arms that hold.

There is a vigorous swing to this type of foot suggesting life and action. It is called the trochee, or trochaic foot.

THE IAMBIC FOOT. The reverse of this is the iambus, or iambic foot, in which the unaccented syllable comes first, followed by the accented syllable. Holmes's " Old Ironsides " illustrates it:

> Oh, better that her shattered hulk
> Should sink beneath the wave;
> Her thunders shook the mighty deep,
> And there should be her grave.

This is the most commonly used foot in English poetry.

THE DACTYL AND THE ANAPEST. Because of the alternate accents, the iambus and the trochee are marching feet, but there are others which are dancing feet. Could you imagine soldiers marching to waltz time? It couldn't be done. ONE, two, three, ONE, two, three. They would have to dance to it. By a queer twist of anatomy this foot is really a finger, for the Greeks called it a dactyl, or finger, because of the three bones in that part of the hand the first is long, the second and third short. When they wanted to reverse the accent and make it: one, two, THREE, one, two, THREE, they called it an anapest, which means striking back. In English poetry the dactyl is seldom found all by itself. Longfellow's *Evangeline* is one of the rare examples of prevailing dactylic measure:

> This is the forest primeval; but where are the
>     hearts that beneath it
> Leaped like the roe, when it hears in the wood-
>     land the voice of the huntsman?

Either the dactyl or the anapest, however, mixed with other feet, is frequently found, as in Edna Millay's

> In the spring of the year, in the spring of the
>     year,
> I walked the road beside my dear.

Prevailing three-syllable feet are used in poems about rides, to simulate horses' hoofbeats. Thus we find the three-syllable foot in " Paul Revere's Ride," " The Deacon's Masterpiece," " Sheridan's Ride," and in the English poems, " The Charge of the Light Brigade " and " How They Brought the Good News from Ghent to Aix." The anapest is more likely to be found in its pure form, as in Poe's " Ulalume ":

> It was night in the lonesome October
> Of my most immemorial year.

VARIOUS VERSE FORMS. In all but the most singsong of verse we come across variations in the prevailing form of foot. The poet is governed by the higher laws of his sensitive ear, rather than by the mechanical laws of mathematics. There must, however, be a real swing evident in the variations, else the lines mark the amateur poet by their " limping feet."

Sometimes we wish to indicate the number of feet to a line, and the ancient Greeks have again supplied us with some technical terms: one foot, *monometer;* two feet, *dimeter;* three, *trimeter;* four, *tetrameter;* five, *pentameter;* six, *hexameter;* seven, *heptameter;* eight, *octameter.* Fortunately for our memories, these terms, with the exception of pentameter, are seldom used.

" Iambic pentameter," however, is such a common term that we need to understand that, if no other. This dignified five-foot line is the basis of the sonnet, of blank verse (meaning unrhymed verse, not to be confused with free verse), and of many stanza forms. Frost's " Birches " is an example of blank verse. Robinson's " Richard Cory " shows a four-line stanza in iambic pentameter. Tetrameter is more often used than called by name. Millay's " Autumn Daybreak " is in iambic tetrameter; *Hiawatha* is in unrhymed trochaic tetrameter. Ballad measure alternates tetrameter and trimeter in a four-line stanza as in Whittier's " The

Eternal Goodness." Longfellow is almost unique among our poets for his use of the long and difficult hexameter, as in *Evangeline* and *The Courtship of Miles Standish*.

Knowledge of these matters is interesting and valuable after we have come to know and enjoy the poetry itself; but it can never be said to create a love for poetry, or in itself to make a poet. To illustrate this point read Master's " Petit the Poet " in *Spoon River Anthology*.

## FIGURES OF SPEECH

A figure of speech appeals directly to the imagination to create a mental picture or enrich an idea. It may use a concrete object to illuminate in a flash an abstract idea. It may employ the familiar experience as a guide to the unmapped realm of new experience. It may create an emotional reaction by associating ideas in fresh and vivid combinations.

It is more important to grasp the underlying significance of a figure of speech than to call it by a technical name; but since names are convenient handles in discussion, definitions of the most commonly found figures are here given. The illustrative examples are all from poems in this book. Figures, of course, are frequently used in prose, and supply the flavor to everyday conversation, particularly in the mood of humorous slang. But since figures are an especial part of the poet's working kit, we define them in this section.

The basis of the most frequently used figures in English is comparison between two things which are quite unlike in general but have some point of resemblance.

SIMILE: a comparison expressed by *like, as, such as, than*, or similar connecting word.

> One by one, like leaves from a tree,
> All my faiths have forsaken me.
> — " Leaves "

> The child would sit there
> Happy as though he had no name, as
> though

He had been no one: like a leaf, a stem,
Like a root growing.
> — " Eleven "

METAPHOR: a comparison assumed or implied.

> My father he was a mountaineer
> His fist was a knotty hammer.
> — " The Ballad of
>         William Sycamore "

> The harpies of the shore shall pluck
> The eagle of the sea.
> — " Old Ironsides "

ALLEGORY: a comparison extended to considerable length.

" The Road Not Taken," by Robert Frost; " The Chambered Nautilus," by Oliver Wendell Holmes; " The Long Hill," by Sara Teasdale.

PERSONIFICATION: a comparison of an object, an animal, or an idea to a human being by giving it either human emotions or speech.

Come and show me another city with lifted head singing so proud to be alive and coarse and strong and cunning. — " Chicago "

> When duty whispers low, *Thou must,*
> The youth replies, *I can.*
> — " Voluntaries III "

APOSTROPHE: a direct address to an idea or object as if it were a person; also to the dead or unborn as if living.

> O holy Night! from thee I learn to bear
> What man has borne before.
> — " Hymn to the Night "

> Brother, that breathe the August air
> Ten thousand years from now . . .
> I cannot think your thoughts will be
> Much different from mine.
> — " If Still Your Orchards Bear "

HYPERBOLE: an obvious exaggeration to produce a definite effect, such as impressiveness, terror, or humor.

> Here once the embattled farmers stood
> And fired the shot heard round the world.
> — " The Concord Hymn "

Ten days and nights, with sleepless eye
  I watched that wretched man,
And since, I never dare to write
  As funny as I can.
  — " The Height of the Ridiculous "

## For Further Reading of Poetry

The best way for high-school students to become acquainted with the many excellent poets of the present is to read widely in the anthologies here listed:

### COLLECTIONS OF POETRY

Bates, Herbert: *Modern Lyric Poetry*
Braithwaite, W. S. B.: *Anthology of Magazine Verse* (issued annually)
Broadhurst, Jean and Rhodes, C. L.: *Verse for Patriots*
Bryan, G. S.: *Poems of Country Life*
Clark, G. H.: *A Treasury of War Poetry*
Cunliffe, J. W.: *Poems of the Great War*
Daringer, H. F. and Eaton, A. T.: *The Poet's Craft*
Davis, M. G.: *The Girls' Book of Verse*
Drinkwater, John, Canby, H. S., and Benét, W. R.: *Twentieth Century Poetry*
Fish, H. D.: *The Boys' Book of Verse*
Gayley, C. M. and Flaherty, M. C.: *Poetry of the People*
Gordon, Marjory and King, M. B.: *Verse of Our Day*
Hohn, Max T.: *Stories in Verse*
Law, F. H.: *Selections from American Poetry*
Leonard, S. A.: *Poems of the War and Peace*
Lieberman, Elias: *Poems for Enjoyment*
Markham, Edwin: *The Book of Poetry* (Vol. I, *American*)
Mims, Edwin and Payne, B. R.: *Southern Prose and Poetry*
Monroe, Harriet and Henderson, A. C.: *The New Poetry*
Page, C. H.: *Chief American Poets*
Repplier, Agnes: *A Book of Famous Verse*
Richards, Mrs. Waldo: *The Melody of Earth; High-Tide; Star Points*
Rittenhouse, Jessie: *The Little Book of American Poets; The Little Book of Modern Verse* (3 vols.)
Sanders, G. DeW. and Nelson, J. H.: *Chief Modern Poets of England and America*
Schauffler, R. H.: *The Poetry Cure*
Stevenson, Burton: *Famous Single Poems; Home Book of Verse; Home Book of Verse for Young People*

Untermeyer, Louis: *Modern American Poetry; This Singing World; Yesterday and Today*
Wilkinson, Marguerite: *Contemporary Poetry; New Voices*

### LIGHT VERSE

Burdette, R. J.: *Chimes from a Jester's Bells; Smiles Yoked with Sighs; The Silver Trumpets*
Burgess, Gelett: *The Rubaiyat of Omar Cayenne; The Gaze of Youth*
Carryl, C. E.: *Davy and the Goblin; The Admiral's Caravan*
Carryl, G. W.: *Fables for the Frivolous; Grimm Tales Made Gay; Mother Goose for Grown-Ups*
Hay, John: *Pike County Ballads*
Lanigan, G. T.: *Canadian Ballads; Fables by G. Washington Aesop*
Montague, J. J.: *More Truth than Poetry*
Preston, Keith: *Splinters; Pot Shots from Pegasus; Types of Pan*
Robinson, E. M.: *Mere Melodies; Piping and Panning*
Roche, J. J.: *Songs and Satires*
Russell, Irwin: *Christmas Night in the Quarters, and Other Poems*
Taylor, B. L.: *Motley Measures; A Penny Whistle, together with the Babette Ballads*

Excellent humorous poems may be found among the *Collected Poems* of authors represented in other sections of this book, such as Oliver Wendell Holmes, James Russell Lowell, James Whitcomb Riley, Eugene Field, and Christopher Morley.

### COLLECTIONS OF LIGHT VERSE

Daly, T. A.: *A Little Book of American Humorous Verse*
Duffield, publisher: *A Book of American Humor in Prose and Verse*
French, J. L.: *Sixty Years of American Humor*
Herford, Oliver: *Poems from " Life "*
Knowles, F. L. (Paget, R. L., *pseud.*): *The Poetry of American Wit and Humor*
Morley, Christopher: *Bowling Green, an Anthology of Verse*
Preston, Keith: *Column Poets*
Stone & Co., publisher: *A Book of American Humorous Verse*
Wells, Carolyn: *A Nonsense Anthology* and eight other collections of light verse
White, E. B. and White, K. S.: *A Subtreasury of American Humor* (prose and verse)

LEADING ACTORS ON
THE MODERN AMERI-
CAN STAGE

Katharine Cornell

Ethel Barrymore

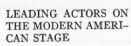

Orson Welles

John Barrymore

Frank Craven, in his role as
narrator in the first production of *Our Town*. (all pho-
tos, Vandamm)

# Modern American Drama

## THE DEVELOPMENT
## OF AMERICAN DRAMA

Americans have always been playgoers. Even in Colonial times, when life was busy and hard, regular theaters were established in New York, Philadelphia, Charleston, and Williamsburg. By 1800 even the misgivings of the Puritans had been conquered, and Boston opened a playhouse. In the early nation touring companies took the drama all up and down the country, often traveling by stagecoach. The comparative luxury of travel by water led to the building of theaters on river boats, so well described by Edna Ferber in her novel *Show Boat*.

As the network of railroads spread across the land, every town of any size had its theater or " opera house " where traveling stock companies put on brief theater seasons which most of the community attended. If your parents grew up in an average American town, they can remember the days when these small-town theaters were being converted for moving pictures. For not until the movies brought their own form of drama to town and village did the traveling companies of actors fade from the American scene. And today, when stage drama flourishes in the large cities as never before and motion-picture theaters are just around every corner, the popularity of radio drama shows that the American love of a play is not yet fully satisfied.

### EARLY AMERICAN PLAYS

The plays of colonial times, like nearly all the books, were imported from Europe. Even after the Revolution, when Americans began to write their own dramas, faraway places and times were represented on the stage much oftener than local scenes. But the American touch was usually present in some form or another. A poor young hero in a European play, for example, might win his happy ending by discovering that he was the long-lost son of a nobleman; but in an American play he would win out by native merit and natural nobility of character. Another native touch was to have a leading character break into a fine speech about democratic principles. That always brought rousing cheers, even if the character was a gladiator in ancient Rome.

But the favorite reminder of home was the stage Yankee. This type was introduced by Royall Tyler in the first truly American play, *The Contrast,* produced in New York in 1787. The contrast, as you may guess, was between a good homespun native American and a low grade of imported fop. That first Yankee was a serious character, but many a later stage Yankee brought shouts of laughter at his greenness before he brought cheers for the triumph of his commonsense and shrewdness over whatever evils or dangers opposed him. The late great national favorite, Will Rogers, presented in his stage personality a faithful echo of this early delight of theater-goers.

A popular story or novel of those earlier days was sure to be dramatized, just as nowadays all the best sellers are made into movies. *Rip Van Winkle* was presented on thousands of American stages, and a little later *Uncle Tom's Cabin* was such a mainstay of the theater that every company had to have a young actress who could play Little Eva and a " heavy " who made a convincing Simon Legree.

## THE SHIFT TO REALISM

Now all this time the fare of the theater had been either sentimental melodrama or melodramatic tragedy. But after the War between the States realism slowly gained in favor, in drama as in literature in general. Acting became quieter and more natural, and speaking less oratorical. Improved staging and theaters helped in the movement, for with good lighting a simple gesture was as easily seen as a sweeping flourish, and with good acoustics a natural voice carried more clearly than a shout. The characters represented behind the footlights grew to resemble more and more the people sitting out front. Plots included more and more situations such as the average American had to deal with. The drama was growing up.

Between 1890 and World War I three well-defined types of play developed in succession, and each produced dramatists of distinction. First to spring up was the local-color play, drawing its inspiration from the wave of local-color fiction which was presenting to the reading public the interesting peculiarities of the different sections of America. David Belasco (1853–1931) exploited the picturesque West in a series of plays, and the enthusiastic Augustus Thomas (1859–1934) planned to write a play about every state in the union.

But a new type of play, social comedy, soon took the spotlight away from local color. Clyde Fitch (1865–1909) wrote the best of the social comedies, and well he might, for he knew at first hand the society he pictured on the stage. His plays had the sparkle associated with social comedy, but they also had some fine characterizations and a somewhat somber study of the influence of money on social prestige. So he was well fitted to carry over into the third type, the problem play.

Dramatists decided that they should not be content just to entertain their audiences but should make them think about real life and its problems. The audiences discovered that these problems, dramatically presented, could be as absorbing as any light make-believe. All three of the dramatists named above and a number of others contributed to the development of the problem play, which more than any other type is associated with modern American drama.

## CONTEMPORARY DRAMA

Since the end of World War I American drama has come into a period of great variety and brilliance. Perhaps the most distinguished plays have been serious presentations of problems and ideas, but every imaginable type has been produced with success and acclaim. The two longest runs were piled up by *Tobacco Road,* a slice of sordid naturalism, and a dramatization of *Life with Father,* whose flavor you know from the selection in this book, a flavor very different from that of *Tobacco Road.* Musical comedy hits ranged from a satire on the presidential campaign of modern times, *Of Thee I Sing,* to a fresh and happy sketch of life in pioneer Oklahoma. Any theme, any time, seemed to be all right if the workmanship of the drama was good. It would be a man of narrow interests who did not find fare to his taste along Broadway these last two or three decades.

Many pessimists foresaw the decline of stage drama as a necessary result of the rise of motion pictures. Now it is evident that the opposite is true. Perhaps the movies are educating people to like all forms of drama. We no longer have traveling stock companies, but the major plays of Broadway, with their Broadway casts, now make tours of the chief cities and draw capacity houses everywhere, at Broadway prices. The real result of the movies on stage plays has been to free them from the rigid staging of earlier times, when action was gathered into three acts, often in the same setting. A new type of episodic play, with the action moving freely from place to place, is one of the major developments of recent years. Elaborate settings may be changed swiftly by electricity in a few moments of darkness onstage, or the producer may leave most of the shift to the imagination of the audience. Either way the drama has gained flexibility and variety.

## CONTEMPORARY DRAMATISTS

So many excellent dramatists are serving our stage today that it is difficult to select a few to introduce to you in a short sketch. Some are purely men of the theater, like Eugene O'Neill, still generally considered the greatest of our time, and George Kaufman, who has won his share of prizes as a playwright and is now trying his hand as a producer. Some have turned to the theater after winning their first success with novels or short stories, like Thornton Wilder and William Saroyan. A few can be counted on to produce a certain type, such as the sparkling social comedies of S. N. Behrman and Philip Barry, or the serious drama of ideas of Clifford Odets.

Others are unpredictable, like Maxwell Anderson, who began his career with the rowdy comedy *What Price Glory* about World War I and has written splendid blank-verse tragedies. One thing you can be sure of is that you have the good luck to live in a time when the drama of your nation is thriving, offering you excellent fare to see and hear — or to read.

## GUIDE TO DRAMA

A drama is any composition in prose or poetry which through dialogue and action tells a story. When action alone is employed, it is called pantomime. That thriving new branch of drama, the radio play, uses dialogue alone. If the lines are sung, a drama becomes opera. Ordinarily, however, the term " drama " is used for any production on the stage or screen in which actors present the words and deeds of the author's characters so as to create the impression that the story is actually taking place before the audience.

## TYPES OF THE DRAMA

In studying the drama it is helpful to be able to distinguish the various kinds of plays. From the classic Greek stage, which had only two distinct types of plays, drama inherited the broad division into comedy and tragedy. We still have tragedies, serious plays that end in death or disaster, and comedies, plays that are light in tone and end happily. But we also have plays that are too serious to be called comedy, and yet do not end in the sort of catastrophe that belongs to tragedy. Many critics call such plays merely " serious drama." Among the plays that fall into the two old classifications, modern drama has developed some definite subtypes. Two familiar kinds of comedy are farce and melodrama. In farce the action is hilariously exaggerated, often past all pretense of reality. Melodrama, too, is exaggerated past sober reality, but for emotional excitement rather than amusement. Sensational happenings, clearly contrasted heroes or heroines and villains, and a happy ending distinguish the typical melodrama. Nowadays the term is used slightingly for all sorts of cheap, overacted plays; but a well-plotted, well-written, well-acted melodrama can be a worthy product of dramatic art, because the basic appeal of drama lies in the emotional reaction of the audience to the people and happenings on the stage.

Still another type, long recognized as distinct from comedy and tragedy, is the chronicle play or dramatic history. Shakespeare did some of his finest writing in his chronicle plays, and modern American dramatists are finding inspiration for some of their best work in historical themes.

## THE PLEASURE OF READING PLAYS

Reading plays requires more imaginative activity than reading most other literary types, but it also offers richer rewards. Plays are written not for the library but for the stage. All that the actors and the stage setting do for the finished play in the theater, the reader's imagination must do for his private performance in his easy chair. But the fruit of alert reading of plays is a particularly vivid representation of active, moving life. The theater does not permit long rambling discussions and it does not permit dull summaries of parts of the action. Something is happening all the time. So even if you do not see many plays on the stage — and most people do not, aside from the motion pictures — you can have your own theater. Reading a play may even be an improvement over seeing a performance, because the reader is able to make his own version the way he thinks it should be by visualizing the characters, hearing them talk, and seeing them go through the action as they interpret the plot. This is certainly better than seeing a play poorly performed.

Drama is peculiar among the literary types, because it belongs primarily not to the field of literature but to the theater. Plays are written to be acted on a stage, and to be successful they must entertain audiences. Many a play, in former times as well as today, owed its success to purely theatrical values — to situations or lines that were highly entertaining or exciting, to timeliness, to the services of especially skillful actors, or even to effective stage presentation. To see and hear actors on a stage telling and acting a story, with all the trimmings that the art of dramatic production can supply, is often sufficient to carry a poor play to comparative success. But to stand the literary test of reading without such aids to the eye and ear, a play must have the same qualities that any other form of writing needs if it is to endure. The story must be basically true to life and human nature, the characters must seem real and alive, and the style must have distinction.

Along with these literary qualities, however, a play must meet successfully the peculiar demands of stage presentation of a story. Of these the most important are good dialogue, skillful handling of the problems of time and place, and getting over the idea behind the play.

GOOD DIALOGUE

It is obvious that dialogue is of tremendous importance in a play, because the play literally is dialogue and very little else. Not only the action, but the explanations and characterizations must be presented through conversation. Moreover, the limited time for a stage play requires that no lines be wasted. Dialogue must be more compact than real-life conversation, or the play will drag. Yet it must be very clear, for there is no time in the theater to go back over a puzzling remark. In apparently natural talk it must explain to the audience the situation that exists when the curtain rises and any important events that occurred before the beginning of the play. Dialogue must vary in tone and wording for the different speakers, or the characters will never come to life. It must reveal their emotions and conflicts so that the audience will not only know but feel their reactions. Any speech in a play is justified only if it explains the situation, reveals character, advances the story, or stimulates emotional response from the audience. You can tell for yourself as you read whether dialogue meets these tests. Do you get the explanations, which are called exposition, in the course of natural talk, or do you feel that they are dragged in for the benefit of the audience? Do you get a clear impression of each character from his first few lines, or does he remain an unknown quantity through half the play? Are emotional situations carried over clearly, or are you puzzled by the attitudes of the characters? Particularly, do you feel a thrill of response to the situation as you read certain lines? Good dialogue must meet all these requirements.

THE PROBLEM OF PLACE

Having to present his entire story on one stage makes the problem of place especially important to the dramatist. In the forty years just behind us dramatists focused their skill on bringing all the action to one place, or at most two or three, which staging could represent successfully for each act. Today this tyranny of mere place is being challenged, and dramatists move about from scene to scene, inspired perhaps by the flexibility of the motion picture. Sometimes they achieve the change of scene by a revolving stage and present a succession of scenes in accurate detail. Or they may use the barest suggestion of actual stage setting and call on the imagination of the audience to move with the action from place to place. One certainty remains. Whether the dramatist is trying to collect the action in one place or is trying to create an illusion that the same stage is successively many different places, his success in meeting the problem furnishes one of the most interesting clues to his dramatic technique. If he tries to collect the action, he has to exert his ingenuity to gather his characters. That is why house parties were so popular in plays that held firmly to the three-act tradition. If he wants the audience to believe that the same stage is a number of different places within a short time, even greater skill in writing (another job for the dialogue!) is required to make the illusion convincing. Shakespeare's poetry could make an audience watching a bare stage exposed to the full afternoon sun feel that they were in Juliet's moonlit garden. The modern experimental dramatist seldom breaks into lyrical description; but if he would preserve the illusion of reality, he must see to it that the dialogue makes up for any skimpiness of staging.

In checking up on the dramatist's handling of the problem of place you may ask, if he presents most of the action in one place: Does he select a place where most of the characters would naturally be gathered? Does he furnish adequate reason for the presence of each one? If he has given you many short scenes, you may ask: Is the arrangement of scenes a series of logical shifts in location of the happenings, so that your interest leads you from one to the other? Does each scene create some suspense to lead you naturally to the next? Are you sufficiently informed, by stage setting or by dialogue, of the change in location, so that you move easily with the action from one scene to another?

You will find in this book one play (*Where the Cross Is Made*) where the dramatist selects one place for all the action of his story, and another (*Our Town*) where the dramatist changes scene at will with little pretense at stage setting. You can soon realize that each method demands considerable skill of the playwright.

## THE PROBLEM OF TIME

Having to condense his entire story into a few hours creates another problem for the dramatist, although not such a serious one as that of place. The old tradition called for three, or at most five, continuous slices of action, with only the gaps between acts or an occasional briefly lowered curtain to indicate the passage of time. The playwright working in that system had to exert his powers to keep the action continuous, yet properly spaced and never dull. When he had to kill the time between two important parts of the action, he was aided by the common illusion of the theater that time is passing much more swiftly than the clock measures it. An audience will readily believe that half an hour elapses, while the play actually goes on for only ten or fifteen minutes. The modern experimental playwright can cut his action up into the smaller episodes that have real importance, and so avoid filling the gaps, but he must run the risk of breaking the illusion of reality between episodes. He must exercise his skill in knitting together his various incidents so that the audience follows him from one to another with no sense of interruption.

You will find that the questions that test the dramatist's handling of place frequently involve the successful handling of time. But you may also ask of plays in the three-act tradition. Is each act a smooth succession of incidents important to the play, or does the dramatist sometimes have to put in an interlude? If he has to fill in between two really important sections, does he give that bit of action and dialogue enough interest to keep up the tone of the play? The episodic play must meet other tests: Is the lapse of time between scenes indicated clearly enough by the dialogue for you to realize without effort the time relation between scenes? Does the dramatist make you feel that each scene is really the next important happening in the story he is telling, that he is skipping nothing you need to keep up with the story?

The same two plays that illustrate two

EUGENE O'NEILL, sketched by Mai-mai Sze, the Chinese artist.

contrasting methods of handling place will give you an opportunity to examine the effectiveness of the continuous play and of the episodic play, each handled by a master of his craft.

GETTING THE IDEA OVER

The drama is the only literary type in which the author has no opportunity to tell his ideas directly to a reader. In the short story, the novel, the essay, poetry, a writer can make comments that insure getting his own point of view clearly before his reader. But in the drama only the characters talk; and if the author wants to make sure that his own ideas carry over effectively, he must use those characters to make the impression. Sometimes he leaves the whole responsibility to the total effect of the action and dialogue. Sometimes he uses a character, called a commentator, to point out the significance of the happenings. Sometimes one remark in the dialogue sums up the main point the drama-

tist is making in the play. Such a remark is called a " tag." Because all effects in the drama must be immediately clear, you will probably recognize a " tag " as soon as you come to it. Do not expect one in every play, for action and conversation may be sufficient to present effectively the idea on which the play rests. The only requirement is that the dramatist must use these limited means so as to make that idea clear to his audience — or his reader.

## Eugene O'Neill　　1888–

Few men can retire from a field they have led for ten years and after ten inactive years still hold their laurels. That is Eugene O'Neill's achievement. He has been absent from Broadway since 1933. Yet his position as one of our greatest contemporary dramatists is still secure. His profoundly moving and highly individualized dramas have won him a wide audience in many European countries as well as in his own and gained for him in 1936 the international Nobel prize for literature. He it was who made the first effective attacks on the rigidly patterned drama that held our stage until 1920. His audiences may be puzzled by some of his attempts to probe beneath the surface of human life, but they are always moved by his intensity and force.

From childhood O'Neill knew the theater well, for his father, James O'Neill, was a great actor, and his son had often seen him play and had for a time been a member of his company presenting *The Count of Monte Cristo*, a great popular thriller. Behind the innovations of Eugene O'Neill's plays lies a sound knowledge of theatrical effectiveness. A second strong influence on O'Neill's development was two years of rough-and-ready life at sea and along water fronts in New York and Buenos Aires. He had tried a year at Princeton and a job in New York, but the beaten path suited him no better in his private life than it did on the stage. His seafaring days furnished him with the originals of many of the characters who later peopled his plays. During a period of enforced quiet living while he was in a sanatorium for tuberculosis, he decided that he wanted to write plays. He was already equipped with knowledge of both tools and materials for drama. After his recovery he enrolled in Professor Baker's famous playwriting course at Harvard and entered seriously upon his career as a dramatist.

At first he wrote one-act plays, based largely upon his experiences at sea, and brought the one-act form to an artistic level never before attained in this country. Of these plays the best known are *The Moon of the Caribbees, Ile, In the Zone, Bound East for Cardiff,* and the one you will read here, *Where the Cross Is Made.* In 1920 O'Neill reached Broadway with *Beyond the Horizon,* which won the first of the three Pulitzer prizes to his credit. This play was cast in the familiar three-act pattern which he deserted in most of his later work, but it shared with his other plays a tragic view of life in which fate and human failings are powerfully blended. In his next play, *The Emperor Jones* (1920), he deserted the old pattern for a series of shorter scenes, and introduced to a stage dominated by careful realism fantastic representations of fears and hallucinations.

Of the plays which O'Neill wrote during the twenties, *The Hairy Ape* (1922) is probably the clearest statement of a theme that constantly engaged his interest: the loneliness and defeat of an individual striving desperately to "belong" to a world in which he is not considered important. Of his technical innnovations the most interesting are the use of masks to represent the person the world sees rather than the real self, and the use of dialogue to represent the thoughts as well as the spoken words of the characters in *Strange Interlude* (1928).

Relaxing from his earlier intensity, O'Neill wrote in 1932 a comedy in a new and gentle vein, *Ah Wilderness!* Stage presentations in many different cities and an excellent screen version have enabled this sympathetically humorous story of an adolescent boy and his father to reach an exceptionally wide audience.

O'Neill's long absence from Broadway has not been idle. He is working on a cycle of nine plays dealing with the development of America. By the time you read this the Theater Guild may be presenting them to an eager public.

# WHERE THE CROSS IS MADE

O'Neill himself says of this play, "It was great fun to write, theatrically very thrilling,"

and disclaims any more serious interest in the play. Others have called it melodramatic, in the sense that it is exciting rather than significant. To you, that means that to lead off this group of American plays you have the least complex form of drama. For the one essential of drama is that it present people who seem real in action that is emotionally stirring. And this bit is from the pen of a master of dramatic craft.

## CHARACTERS

CAPTAIN ISAIAH BARTLETT
NAT BARTLETT, his son
SUE BARTLETT, his daughter
DOCTOR HIGGINS
SILAS HORNE, mate
CATES, bosun
JIMMY KANAKA,[1] harpooner
} of the schooner *Mary Allen*

SCENE. CAPTAIN BARTLETT'S " *cabin* "— *a room erected as a lookout post at the top of his house, situated on a high point of land on the California coast. The inside of the compartment is fitted up like the captain's cabin of a deep-sea sailing vessel. On the left, forward, a porthole. Farther back the stairs of the companionway. Still farther two more portholes. In the rear, left, a marble-topped sideboard with a ship's lantern on it. In the rear, center, a door opening on stairs which lead to the lower house. A cot with a blanket is placed against the wall to the right of the door. In the right wall five portholes. Directly under them a wooden bench. In front of the bench a long table with two straight-backed chairs, one in front, the other to the left of it. A cheap, dark-colored rug is on the floor. In the ceiling, midway from front to rear, a skylight, extending from opposite the door to above the left edge of the table. In the right extremity of the skylight is placed a floating ship's compass. The light from the binnacle sheds over this from above and seeps down into the room, casting a vague globular shadow of the compass on the floor.*

*The time is an early hour of a clear windy night in the fall of the year 1900. Moonlight, winnowed by the wind which moans in the stubborn angles of the old house,*

[1] **Kanaka** (kȧ-nȧk′ȧ).

*creeps wearily in through the portholes, and rests like tired dust in circular patches upon the floor and table. An insistent monotone of thundering surf, muffled and far off, is borne upward from the beach below.*

*After the curtain rises, the door in the rear is opened slowly and the head and shoulders of* NAT BARTLETT *appear over the sill. He casts a quick glance about the room and, seeing no one there, ascends the remaining steps and enters. He makes a sign to someone in the darkness beneath: " All right, Doctor."* DOCTOR HIGGINS *follows him into the room and, closing the door, stands looking with great curiosity around him. He is a slight, medium-sized, professional-looking man of about thirty-five.* NAT BARTLETT *is very tall, gaunt, and loose-framed. His right arm has been amputated at the shoulder, and the sleeve on that side of the heavy mackinaw he wears hangs flabbily or flaps against his body as he moves. He appears much older than his thirty years. His shoulders have a weary stoop as if worn down by the burden of his massive head with its heavy shock of tangled black hair. His face is long, bony, and sallow, with deep-set black eyes, a large aquiline nose, a wide, thin-lipped mouth shadowed by an unkempt bristle of mustache. His voice is low and deep with a penetrating, hollow, metallic quality. In addition to the mackinaw he wears corduroy trousers stuffed down into high laced boots.*

NAT. Can you see, Doctor?

HIGGINS (*in the too-casual tones which betray an inward uneasiness*). Yes — perfectly — don't trouble. The moonlight is so bright —

NAT. Luckily. (*Walking slowly toward the table*) He doesn't want any light — lately — only the one from the binnacle there.

HIGGINS. He? Ah — you mean your father?

NAT (*impatiently*). Who else?

HIGGINS (*a bit startled — gazing around him in embarrassment*). I suppose this is all meant to be like a ship's cabin?

NAT. Yes — as I warned you.

HIGGINS (*in surprise*). Warned me? Why, warned? I think it's very natural — and interesting — this whim of his.

NAT (*meaningly*). Interesting, it may be.

HIGGINS. And he lives up here, you said — never comes down?

NAT. Never — for the past three years. My sister brings his food up to him. (*He sits down in the chair to the left of the table.*) There's a lantern on the sideboard there, Doctor. Bring it over and sit down. We'll make a light. I'll ask your pardon for bringing you to this room on the roof — but — no one'll hear us here; and by seeing for yourself the mad way he lives — Understand that I want you to get all the facts — just that, facts! — and for that, light is necessary. Without that — they become dreams up here — dreams, Doctor.

HIGGINS (*with a relieved smile carries over the lantern*). It is a trifle spooky.

NAT (*not seeming to notice this remark*). He won't take any note of this light. His eyes are too busy — out there. (*He flings his left arm in a wide gesture seaward.*) And if he does notice — well, let him come down. You're bound to see him sooner or later. (*He scratches a match and lights the lantern.*)

HIGGINS. Where is — he?

NAT (*pointing upward*). Up on the poop. Sit down, man! He'll not come — yet awhile.

HIGGINS (*sitting gingerly on the chair in front of table*). Then he has the roof, too, rigged up like a ship?

NAT. I told you he had. Like a deck, yes. A wheel, compass, binnacle light, the companionway there (*he points*), a bridge to pace up and down on — *and keep watch.* If the wind wasn't so high you'd hear him now — back and forth — all the livelong night. (*With a sudden harshness*) Didn't I tell you he's mad?

HIGGINS (*with a professional air*). That was nothing new. I've heard that about him from all sides since I first came to the asylum yonder. You say he only walks at night — up there?

NAT. Only at night, yes. (*Grimly*) The things he wants to see can't be made out in daylight — dreams and such.

HIGGINS. But just what is he trying to see? Does anyone know? Does he tell?

NAT (*impatiently*). Why, everyone knows what Father looks for, man! The ship, of course.

HIGGINS. What ship?

NAT. His ship — the *Mary Allen* — named for my dead mother.

HIGGINS. But — I don't understand — Is the ship long overdue — or what?

NAT. Lost in a hurricane off the Celebes with all on board — three years ago!

HIGGINS (*wonderingly*). Ah. (*After a pause*) But your father still clings to a doubt —

NAT. There is no doubt for him or anyone else to cling to. She was sighted bottom up, a complete wreck, by the whaler *John Slocum*. That was two weeks after the storm. They sent a boat out to read her name.

HIGGINS. And hasn't your father ever heard —

NAT. He was the first to hear, naturally. Oh, he *knows* right enough, if that's what you're driving at. (*He bends toward the doctor — intensely.*) He *knows*, Doctor, he *knows* — but he won't *believe*. He can't — and keep living.

HIGGINS (*impatiently*). Come, Mr. Bartlett, let's get down to brass tacks. You didn't drag me up here to make things more obscure, did you? Let's have the facts you spoke of. I'll need them to give sympathetic treatment to his case when we get him to the asylum.

NAT (*anxiously — lowering his voice*). And you'll come to take him away tonight — for sure?

HIGGINS. Twenty minutes after I leave here I'll be back in the car. That's positive.

NAT. And you know your way through the house?

HIGGINS. Certainly, I remember — but I don't see —

NAT. The outside door will be left open for you. You must come right up. My sister and I will be here — with him. And you understand — Neither of us knows anything about this. The authorities have been complained to — not by us, mind — but by someone. He must never know —

HIGGINS. Yes, yes — but still I don't — Is he liable to prove violent?

NAT. No — no. He's quiet always — too quiet; but he might do something — anything — if he knows —

HIGGINS. Rely on me not to tell him, then; but I'll bring along two attendants in case — (*He breaks off, and continues in matter-of-fact tones.*) And now for the facts in this case, if you don't mind, Mr. Bartlett.

NAT (*shaking his head — moodily*). There are cases where facts — Well, here goes — the brass tacks. My father was a whaling captain as his father before him. The last trip he made was seven years ago. He expected to be gone two years. It was four before we saw him again. His ship had been wrecked in the Indian Ocean. He and six others managed to reach a small island on the fringe of the Archipelago — an island absolutely barren, Doctor — after seven days in an open boat. The rest of the whaling crew never were heard from again — gone to the sharks. Of the six who reached the island with my father only three were alive when a fleet of Malay canoes picked them up, mad from thirst and starvation, the four of them. These four men finally reached Frisco. (*With great emphasis*) They were my father; Silas Horne, the mate; Cates, the bosun; and Jimmy Kanaka, a Hawaiian harpooner. Those four! (*With a forced laugh*) There are facts for you. It was all in the papers at the time — my father's story.

HIGGINS. But what of the other three who were on the island?

NAT (*harshly*). Died of exposure, perhaps. Mad and jumped into the sea, perhaps. That was the told story. Another was whispered — killed and eaten, perhaps! But gone — vanished — that, undeniably. That was the fact. For the rest — who knows? And what does it matter?

HIGGINS (*with a shudder*). I should think it would matter — a lot.

NAT (*fiercely*). We're dealing with facts, Doctor! (*With a laugh*) And here are some more for you. My father brought the three down to this house with him — Horne and Cates and Jimmy Kanaka. We hardly recognized my father. He had been through hell and looked it. His hair was white. But you'll see for yourself — soon. And the others — they were all a bit queer, too — mad, if you will. (*He laughs again.*) So much for the facts, Doctor. They leave off there and the dreams begin.

HIGGINS (*doubtfully*). It would seem — the facts are enough.

NAT. Wait. (*He resumes deliberately.*) One day my father sent for me and in the presence of the others told me the dream. I was to be heir to the secret. Their second day on the island, he said, they discovered in a sheltered inlet the rotten, water-logged hulk of a Malay prau — a proper war prau such as the pirates used to use. She had been there rotting — God knows how long. The crew had vanished — God knows where, for there was no sign on the island that man had ever touched there. The Kanakas went over the prau — they're devils for staying under water, you know — and they found — in two chests — (*He leans back in his chair and smiles ironically.*) Guess what, Doctor?

HIGGINS (*with an answering smile*). Treasure, of course.

NAT (*leaning forward and pointing his finger accusingly at the other*). You see! The root of belief is in you, too! (*Then he leans back with a hollow chuckle.*) Why, yes. Treasure, to be sure. What else? They landed it and — you can guess the rest, too — diamonds, emeralds, gold ornaments — innumerable, of course. Why limit the stuff of dreams? Ha-ha! (*He laughs sardonically as if mocking himself.*)

HIGGINS (*deeply interested*). And then?

NAT. They began to go mad — hunger, thirst, and the rest — and they began to forget. Oh, they forgot a lot; and lucky for them they did, probably. But my father, realizing, as he told me, what was happening to them, insisted that while they still knew what they were doing they should — guess again now, Doctor. Ha-ha!

HIGGINS. Bury the treasure?

NAT (*ironically*). Simple, isn't it? Ha-ha. And then they made a map — the same old dream, you see — with a charred stick, and my father had care of it. They were picked up soon after, mad as hatters, as I have told you, by some Malays. (*He drops his mocking and adopts a calm, deliberate tone again.*) But the map isn't a dream, Doctor. We're coming back to facts again. (*He reaches into the pocket of his mackinaw and pulls out a crumpled paper.*) Here. (*He spreads it out on the table.*)

HIGGINS (*craning his neck eagerly*). This is interesting! The treasure, I suppose, is where —

NAT. Where the cross is made.

HIGGINS. And here are the signatures, I see. And that sign?

NAT. Jimmy Kanaka's. He couldn't write.

HIGGINS. And below? That's yours, isn't it?

NAT. As heir to the secret, yes. We all signed it here the morning the *Mary Allen*, the schooner my father had mortgaged this house to fit out, set sail to bring back the treasure. Ha-ha.

HIGGINS. The ship he's still looking for — that was lost three years ago?

NAT. The *Mary Allen*, yes. The other three men sailed away on her. Only father and the mate knew the approximate location of the island — and I — as heir. It's — (*He hesitates, frowning.*) No matter. I'll keep the mad secret. My father wanted to go with them — but my mother was dying. I dared not go either.

HIGGINS. Then you wanted to go? You believed in the treasure then?

NAT. Of course. Ha-ha. How could I help it? I believed until my mother's death. Then *he* became mad, entirely mad. He built this cabin — to wait in — and he suspected my growing doubt as time went on. So, as final proof, he gave me a thing he had kept hidden from them all — a sample of the richest of the treasure. Ha-ha. Behold! (*He takes from his pocket a heavy bracelet thickly studded with stones and throws it on the table near the lantern.*)

HIGGINS (*picking it up with eager curiosity — as if in spite of himself*). Real jewels?

NAT. Ha-ha! You want to believe, too. No — paste and brass — Malay ornaments.

HIGGINS. You had it looked over?

NAT. Like a fool, yes. (*He puts it back in his pocket and shakes his head as if throwing off a burden.*) Now you know why he's mad — waiting for that ship — and why in the end I had to ask you to take him away where he'll be safe. The mortgage — the price of that ship — is to be foreclosed. We have to move, my sister and I. We can't take him with us. She is to be married soon. Perhaps away from the sight of the sea he may —

HIGGINS (*perfunctorily*). Let's hope for the best. And I fully appreciate your position. (*He gets up, smiling.*) And thank you for the interesting story. I'll know how to humor him when he raves about treasure.

NAT (*somberly*). He is quiet always — too quiet. He only walks to and fro — watching —

HIGGINS. Well, I must go. You think it's best to take him tonight?

NAT (*persuasively*). Yes, Doctor. The neighbors — they're far away but — for my sister's sake — you understand.

HIGGINS. I see. It must be hard on her — this sort of thing — Well — (*He goes to the door, which NAT opens for him.*) I'll return presently. (*He starts to descend.*)

NAT (*urgently*). Don't fail us, Doctor. And come right up. He'll be here. (*He closes the door and tiptoes carefully to the companionway. He ascends it a few steps and remains for a moment listening for some sound from above. Then he goes over to the table, turning the lantern very low, and sits down, resting his elbow, his chin on his hand, staring somberly before him. The door in the rear is slowly opened. It creaks slightly and NAT jumps to his feet. . . . In a thick voice of terror*) Who's there?

[*The door swings wide open, revealing* SUE BARTLETT. *She ascends into the room*

*and shuts the door behind her. She is a tall, slender woman of twenty-five, with a pale, sad face framed in a mass of dark red hair. This hair furnishes the only touch of color about her. Her full lips are pale; the blue of her wistful wide eyes is fading into a twilight gray. Her voice is low and melancholy. She wears a dark wrapper and slippers.*]

SUE (*stands and looks at her brother accusingly*). It's only I. What are you afraid of?

NAT (*averts his eyes and sinks back on his chair again*). Nothing. I didn't know — I thought you were in your room.

SUE (*comes to the table*). I was reading. Then I heard someone come down the stairs and go out. Who was it? (*With sudden terror*) It wasn't — Father?

NAT. No. He's up there — watching — as he always is.

SUE (*sitting down — insistently*). Who was it?

NAT (*evasively*). A man — I know.

SUE. What man? What is he? You're holding something back. Tell me.

NAT (*raising his eyes defiantly*). A doctor.

SUE (*alarmed*). Oh! (*With quick intuition*) You brought him up here — so that I wouldn't know!

NAT (*doggedly*). No. I took him up here to see how things were — to ask him about Father.

SUE (*as if afraid of the answer she will get*). Is he one of them — from the asylum? Oh, Nat, you haven't —

NAT (*interrupting her — hoarsely*). No, no! Be still.

SUE. That would be — the last horror.

NAT (*defiantly*). Why? You always say that. What could be more horrible than things as they are? I believe — it would be better for him — away — where he couldn't see the sea. He'll forget his mad idea of waiting for a lost ship and a treasure that never was. (*As if trying to convince himself — vehemently*) I believe this!

SUE (*reproachfully*). You don't, Nat. You

know he'd die if he hadn't the sea to live with.

NAT (*bitterly*). And you know old Smith will foreclose the mortgage. Is that nothing? We cannot pay. He came yesterday and talked with me. He knows the place is his — to all purposes. He talked as if we were merely his tenants, curse him! And he swore he'd foreclose immediately unless —

SUE (*eagerly*). What?

NAT (*in a hard voice*). Unless we have — Father — taken away.

SUE (*in anguish*). Oh! But why, why? What is Father to him?

NAT. The value of the property — our home which is his, Smith's. The neighbors are afraid. They pass by on the road at night coming back to their farms from the town. They see *him* up there walking back and forth — waving his arms against the sky. They're afraid. They talk of a complaint. They say for his own good he must be taken away. They even whisper the house is haunted. Old Smith is afraid of his property. He thinks that *he* may set fire to the house — do anything —

SUE (*despairingly*). But you told him how foolish that was, didn't you? That Father is quiet, always quiet.

NAT. What's the use of telling — when they believe — when they're afraid? (SUE *hides her face in her hands — a pause.* NAT *whispers hoarsely.*) I've been afraid myself — at times.

SUE. Oh, Nat! Of what?

NAT (*violently*). Oh, him and the sea he calls to! Of the damned sea he forced me on as a boy — the sea that robbed me of my arm and made me the broken thing I am!

SUE (*pleadingly*). You can't blame Father — for your misfortune.

NAT. He took me from school and forced me on his ship, didn't he? What would I have been now but an ignorant sailor like him if he had had his way? No. It's the sea I should not blame, that foiled him by taking my arm and then throwing me ashore — another one of *his* wrecks!

SUE (*with a sob*). You're bitter, Nat —

and hard. It was so long ago. Why can't you forget?

NAT (*bitterly*). Forget! You can talk! When Tom comes home from this voyage, you'll be married and out of this with life before you — a captain's wife as our mother was. I wish you joy.

SUE (*supplicatingly*). And you'll come with us, Nat — and Father, too — and then —

NAT. Would you saddle your young husband with a madman and a cripple? (*Fiercely*) No, no, not I! (*Vindictively*) And not him, either! (*With sudden meaning — deliberately*) I've got to stay here. My book is three-fourths done — my book that will set me free! But I know, I feel, as sure as I stand here living before you, that I must finish it here. It could not live for me outside of this house where it was born. (*Staring at her fixedly*) So I will stay — I will, I tell you! (SUE *sobs hopelessly. After a pause he continues.*) Old Smith told me I could live here indefinitely without paying — as caretaker — if —

SUE (*fearfully — like a whispered echo*). If?

NAT (*staring at her — in a hard voice*). If I have *him* sent — where he'll no longer harm himself — nor others.

SUE (*with horrified dread*). No — no, Nat! For our dead mother's sake.

NAT (*struggling*). Did I say I had? Why do you look at me — like that?

SUE. Nat! Nat! For our mother's sake!

NAT (*in terror*). Stop! Stop! She's dead — and at peace. Would you bring her tired soul back to him again to be bruised and wounded?

SUE. Nat!

NAT (*clutching at his throat as though to strangle something within him — hoarsely*). Sue! Have mercy! (*His sister stares at him with dread foreboding.* NAT *calms himself with an effort and continues deliberately.*) Smith said he would give two thousand cash if I would sell the place to him — and he would let me stay, rent free, as caretaker.

SUE (*scornfully*). Two thousand! Why,

over and above the mortgage, it's worth —

NAT. It's not what it's worth. It's what one can get, cash — for my book — for freedom!

SUE. So that's why he wants Father sent away, the wretch! He must know the will Father made —

NAT. Gives the place to me. Yes, he knows. I told him.

SUE (*dully*). Ah, how vile men are!

NAT (*persuasively*). If it were to be done — if it were, I say — there'd be half for you for your wedding portion. That's fair.

SUE (*horrified*). Blood money! Do you think I could touch it?

NAT (*persuasively*). It would be only fair. I'd give it you.

SUE. My God, Nat, are you trying to bribe me?

NAT. No. It's yours in all fairness. (*With a twisted smile*) You forget I'm heir to the treasure, too, and can afford to be generous. Ha-ha.

SUE (*alarmed*). Nat! You're so strange. You're sick, Nat. You couldn't talk this way if you were yourself. Oh, we must go away from here — you and Father and I! Let Smith foreclose. There'll be something over the mortgage; and we'll move to some little house — by the sea so that Father —

NAT (*fiercely*). Can keep up his mad game with me — whispering dreams in my ear — pointing out to sea — mocking me with stuff like this! (*He takes the bracelet from his pocket. The sight of it infuriates him and he hurls it into a corner, exclaiming in a terrible voice*) No! No! It's too late for dreams now. It's too late! I've put them behind me tonight — forever!

SUE (*looks at him and suddenly understands that what she dreads has come to pass — letting her head fall on her outstretched arms with a long moan*). Then — you've done it! You've sold him! Oh, Nat, you're cursed!

NAT (*with a terrified glance at the roof above*). Ssshh! What are you saying? He'll be better off — away from the sea.

SUE (*dully*). You've sold him.

NAT (*wildly*). No! No! (*He takes the map from his pocket.*) Listen, Sue! For God's sake, listen to me! See! The map of the island. (*He spreads it out on the table.*) And the treasure — where the cross is made. (*He gulps and his words pour out incoherently.*) I've carried it about for years. Is that nothing? You don't know what it means. It stands between me and my book. It's stood between me and life — driving me mad! *He* taught me to wait and hope with him — wait and hope — day after day. He made me doubt my brain and give the lie to my eyes — when hope was dead — when I knew it was all a dream — I couldn't kill it! (*His eyes starting from his head*) God forgive me, I still believe! And that's mad — mad, do you hear?

SUE (*looking at him with horror*). And that is why — you hate him!

NAT. No, I don't — (*Then in a sudden frenzy*) Yes! I do hate him! He's stolen my brain! I've got to free myself, can't you see, from him — and his madness.

SUE (*terrified — appealingly*). Nat! Don't! You talk as if —

NAT (*with a wild laugh*). As if I were mad? You're right — but I'll be mad no more! See! (*He opens the lantern and sets fire to the map in his hand. When he shuts the lantern again it flickers and goes out. They watch the paper burn with fascinated eyes as he talks.*) See how I free myself and become sane. And now for facts, as the doctor said. I lied to you about him. He was a doctor from the asylum. See how it burns! It must all be destroyed — this poisonous madness. Yes, I lied to you — see — it's gone — the last speck — and the only other map is the one Silas Horne took to the bottom of the sea with him. (*He lets the ash fall to the floor and crushes it with his foot.*) Gone! I'm free of it — at last! (*His face is very pale, but he goes on calmly.*) Yes, I sold him, if you will — to save my soul. They're coming from the asylum to get him —

[*There is a loud, muffled cry from above, which sounds like "Sail-ho," and a stamping of feet. The slide to the companion-*

*way above is slid back with a bang. A gust of air tears down into the room.* NAT *and* SUE *have jumped to their feet and stand petrified.* CAPTAIN BARTLETT *tramps down the stairs.*]

(*With a shudder*) Did he hear?
SUE. Ssshh!

[CAPTAIN BARTLETT *comes into the room. He bears a striking resemblance to his son; but his face is more stern and formidable, his form more robust, erect, and muscular. His mass of hair is pure white, his bristly mustache the same, contrasting with the weather-beaten leather color of his furrowed face. Bushy gray brows overhang the obsessed glare of his fierce dark eyes. He wears a heavy, double-breasted blue coat, pants of the same material, and rubber boots turned down from the knee.*]

BARTLETT (*in a state of mad exultation strides toward his son and points an accusing finger at him.* NAT *shrinks backward a step.*) Bin thinkin' me mad, did ye? Thinkin' it for the past three years, ye bin — ever since them fools on the *Slocum* tattled their lie o' the *Mary Allen* bein' a wreck.

NAT (*swallowing hard — chokingly*). No — Father — I —

BARTLETT. Don't lie, ye whelp! You that I'd made my heir —aimin' to git me out o' the way! Aimin' to put me behind the bars o' the jail for mad folk!

SUE. Father — no!

BARTLETT (*waving his hand for her to be silent*). Not you, girl, not you. You're your mother.

NAT (*very pale*). Father — do you think — I —

BARTLETT (*fiercely*). A lie in your eyes! I bin-a-readin' 'em. My curse on you!

SUE. Father! Don't!

BARTLETT. Leave me be, girl. He believed, didn't he? And ain't he turned traitor — mockin' at me and sayin' it's all a lie — mockin' at himself, too, for bein' a fool to believe in dreams, as he calls 'em.

NAT (*placatingly*). You're wrong, Father. I do believe.

BARTLETT (*triumphantly*). Aye, now ye do! Who wouldn't credit their own eyes?

NAT (*mystified*). Eyes?

BARTLETT. Have ye not seen her, then? Did ye not hear me hail?

NAT (*confusedly*). Hail? I heard a shout. But — hail what? — seen what?

BARTLETT (*grimly*). Aye, now's your punishment, Judas. (*Explosively*) The *Mary Allen*, ye blind fool, come back from the Southern Seas — come back as I swore she must!

SUE (*trying to soothe him*). Father! Be quiet. It's nothing.

BARTLETT (*not heeding her — his eyes fixed hypnotically on his son's*). Turned the pint a half-hour back — the *Mary Allen* — loaded with gold as I swore she would be — carryin' her lowers — not a reef in 'em — makin' port, boy, as I swore she must — too late for traitors, boy, too late! — droppin' her anchor just when I hailed her.

NAT (*a haunted, fascinated look in his eyes, which are fixed immovably on his father's*). The *Mary Allen!* But how do you know?

BARTLETT. Not know my own ship! 'Tis you're mad!

NAT. But at night — some other schooner —

BARTLETT. No other, I say! The *Mary Allen* — clear in the moonlight. And heed this: D'you call to mind the signal I gave to Silas Horne if he made this port o' a night?

NAT (*slowly*). A red and a green light at the mainmasthead.

BARTLETT (*triumphantly*). Then look out if ye dare! (*He goes to the porthole, left forward.*) Ye can see it plain from here. (*Commandingly*) Will ye believe your eyes? Look — and then call me mad!

[NAT *peers through the porthole and starts back, a dumbfounded expression on his face.*]

NAT (*slowly*). A red and a green light at the mainmasthead. Yes — clear as day.

SUE (*with a worried look at him*). Let me see. (*She goes to the porthole.*)

BARTLETT (*to his son, with fierce satisfaction*). Aye, ye see now clear enough — too late for you.

[NAT *stares at him spellbound.*]

And from above I saw Horne and Cates and Jimmy Kanaka plain on the deck in the moonlight lookin' up at me. Come! (*He strides to the companionway, followed by NAT.*)

[*The two of them ascend.* SUE *turns from the porthole, an expression of frightened bewilderment on her face. She shakes her head sadly. A loud " Mary Allen, ahoy! " comes from above in* BARTLETT'S *voice, followed like an echo by the same hail from* NAT. SUE *covers her face with her hands, shuddering.* NAT *comes down the companionway, his eyes wild and exulting.*]

SUE (*brokenly*). He's bad tonight, Nat. You're right to humor him. It's the best thing.

NAT (*savagely*). Humor him? What do you mean?

SUE (*pointing to the porthole*). There's nothing there, Nat. There's not a ship in harbor.

NAT. You're a fool — or blind! The *Mary Allen's* there in plain sight of anyone, with the red and the green signal lights. Those fools lied about her being wrecked. And I've been a fool, too.

SUE. But, Nat, there's nothing. (*She goes over to the porthole again.*) Not a ship. See.

NAT. I saw, I tell you! From above it's all plain. (*He turns from her and goes back to his seat by the table.*)

SUE. (*following him — pleading frightenedly*). Nat! You mustn't let this — You're all excited and trembling, Nat. (*She puts a soothing hand on his forehead.*)

NAT. (*pushing her away from him roughly*). You blind fool!

[BARTLETT *comes down the steps of the companionway. His face is transfigured with the ecstasy of a dream come true.*]

BARTLETT. They've lowered a boat — the three — Horne and Cates and Jimmy Kanaka. They're a-rowin' ashore. I heard the oars in the locks. Listen!

[*A pause.*]

NAT. (*excitedly*). I hear!

SUE (*who has taken the chair by her brother — in a warning whisper*). It's the wind and sea you hear, Nat. Please!

BARTLETT (*suddenly*). Hark! They've landed. They're back on earth again as I swore they'd come back. They'll be a-comin' up the path now. (*He stands in an attitude of rigid attention.*)

[NAT *strains forward in his chair. The sound of the wind and sea suddenly ceases and there is a heavy silence. A dense green glow floods slowly in rhythmic waves like a liquid into the room — as of great depths of the sea faintly penetrated by light.*]

NAT (*catching at his sister's hand — chokingly*). See how the light changes! Green and gold! (*He shivers.*) Deep under the sea! I've been drowned for years! (*Hysterically*) Save me! Save me!

SUE (*patting his hand comfortingly*). Only the moonlight, Nat. It hasn't changed. Be quiet, dear, it's nothing.

[*The green light grows deeper and deeper.*]

BARTLETT (*in a crooning, monotonous tone*). They move slowly — slowly. They're heavy, I know, heavy — the two chests. Hark! They're below at the door. You hear?

NAT (*starting to his feet*). I hear! I left the door open.

BARTLETT. For them?

NAT. For them.

SUE (*shuddering*). Ssshh!

[*The sound of a door being heavily slammed is heard from way down in the house.*]

NAT (*to his sister — excitedly*). There! You hear?

SUE. A shutter in the wind.

NAT. There is no wind.

BARTLETT. Up they come! Up, bullies! They're heavy — heavy!

[*The padding of bare feet sounds from the floor below — then comes up the stairs.*]

NAT. You hear them now?

SUE. Only the rats running about. It's nothing, Nat.

BARTLETT (*rushing to the door and throwing it open*). Come in, lads, come in! — and welcome home!

[*The forms of* SILAS HORNE, CATES, *and* JIMMY KANAKA *rise noiselessly into the room from the stairs. The last two carry heavy inlaid chests.* HORNE *is a parrot-nosed, angular old man dressed in gray cotton trousers and a singlet torn open across his hairy chest.* JIMMY *is a tall, sinewy, bronzed young Kanaka. He wears only a breechcloth.* CATES *is squat and stout and is dressed in dungaree pants and a shredded white sailor's blouse, stained with iron rust. All are in their bare feet. Water drips from their soaked and rotten clothes. Their hair is matted, intertwined with slimy strands of seaweed. Their eyes, as they glide silently into the room, stare frightfully wide at nothing. Their flesh in the green light has the suggestion of decomposition. Their bodies sway limply, nervelessly, rhythmically as if to the pulse of long swells of the deep sea.*]

NAT (*making a step toward them*). See! (*Frenziedly*) Welcome home, boys!

SUE (*grabbing his arm*). Sit down, Nat. It's nothing. There's no one there. Father — sit down!

BARTLETT (*grinning at the three and putting his finger to his lips*). Not here, boys, not here — not before him. (*He points to his son.*) He has no right, now. Come. The treasure is ours only. We'll go away with it together. Come. (*He goes to the companionway. The three follow. At the foot of it* HORNE *puts a swaying hand on his shoulder and with the other holds out a piece of paper to him.* BARTLETT *takes it and chuckles exultantly.*) That's right — for him — that's right! (*He ascends. The figures sway up after him.*)

NAT (*frenziedly*). Wait! (*He struggles toward the companionway.*)

SUE (*trying to hold him back*). Nat — don't! Father — come back!

NAT. Father! (*He flings her away from him and rushes up the companionway. He pounds against the slide, which seems to have been shut down on him.*)

SUE (*hysterically — runs wildly to the door in rear*). Help! Help!

[*As she gets to the door* DOCTOR HIGGINS *appears, hurrying up the stairs.*]

HIGGINS (*excitedly*). Just a moment, Miss. What's the matter?

SUE (*with a gasp*). My father — up there!

HIGGINS. I can't see — where's my flash? Ah. (*He flashes it on her terror-stricken face, then quickly around the room. The green glow disappears. The wind and sea are heard again. Clear moonlight floods through the portholes.* HIGGINS *springs to the companionway.* NAT *is still pounding.*) Here, Bartlett. Let me try.

NAT (*coming down — looking dully at the doctor*). They've locked it. I can't get up.

HIGGINS (*looks up — in an astonished voice*). What's the matter, Bartlett? It's all open. (*He starts to ascend.*)

NAT (*in a voice of warning*). Look out, man! Look out for them!

HIGGINS (*calls down from above*). Them? Who? There's no one here. (*Suddenly — in alarm*) Come up! Lend me a hand here! He's fainted!

[NAT *goes up slowly,* SUE *goes over and lights the lantern, then hurries back to the foot of the companionway with it. There is a scuffling noise from above. They reappear, carrying* CAPTAIN BARTLETT'S *body.*]

Easy now!

*[They lay him on the couch in rear.* SUE *sets the lantern down by the couch.* HIG- GINS *bends and listens for a heartbeat. Then he rises, shaking his head.]*

I'm sorry —

SUE (*dully*). Dead?

HIGGINS (*nodding*). Heart failure, I should judge. (*With an attempt at conso- lation*) Perhaps it's better so, if —

NAT (*as if in a trance*). There was some- thing Horne handed him. Did you see?

SUE (*wringing her hands*). Oh, Nat, be still! He's dead. (*To* HIGGINS *with pitiful appeal*) Please go — go —

HIGGINS. There's nothing I can do?

SUE. Go — please —

*[*HIGGINS *bows stiffly and goes out.* NAT *moves slowly to his father's body, as if attracted by some irresistible fascina- tion.]*

NAT. Didn't you see? Horne handed him something.

SUE (*sobbing*). Nat! Nat! Come away! Don't touch him, Nat! Come away.

*[But her brother does not heed her. His gaze is fixed on his father's right hand, which hangs downward over the side of the couch. He pounces on it and, forcing the clenched fingers open with a great ef- fort, secures a crumpled ball of paper.]*

NAT (*flourishing it above his head with a shout of triumph*). See! (*He bends down and spreads it out in the light of the lan- tern.*) The map of the island! Look! It isn't lost for me after all! There's still a chance — *my* chance! (*With mad, solemn decision*) When the house is sold I'll go — and I'll find it! Look! It's written here in his handwriting: " The treasure is buried where the cross is made."

SUE (*covering her face with her hands — brokenly*). Oh! Come away, Nat! Come away!

[CURTAIN]

## Suggestions for Study

1. Why did O'Neill select this particular room for the setting of the play? Why did he have the action take place at night?

2. Notice the skillful handling of the expo- sition. How is the summary of previous hap- penings made natural? Why is Dr. Higgins in- stead of Sue with Nat at first? What is the first hint that Nat, too, is threatened with insanity?

3. The markings on the map are referred to in the title to call the attention of the audience to the map in the play. How does it high light the wavering of Nat's hold on sanity?

4. In the argument over putting the captain in the asylum, do you sympathize with Nat or with Sue? What are the strongest reasons on each side?

5. What is the climax of the excitement over the return of the *Mary Allen?* Why are the ghosts shown as real men and not just sug- gested by the dialogue?

6. Why does Sue hurry Dr. Higgins away at the end of the play? Is the ending fair to Nat? To Sue? Are you glad the old captain died? Why?

7. Emotional excitement is the whole pur- pose of the play. Find particular lines that re- veal situations or emotions so as to send a thrill through the audience.

8. Vocabulary: mainmasthead, companion- way, poop, binnacle, dungaree.

## For Your Vocabulary

WORD BUILDING. Comparison is the life of description — especially when you can make the comparison in a single word, as in the phrase " an aquiline (ăk'wĭ-lĭn) nose " (page 356). *Aquiline* means like an eagle and should give you a picture of a great beak of a nose. The ending *-ine* on adjectives means like or of the nature of. We have a whole series of ad- jectives formed from the Latin names of ani- mals with this suffix. *Leonine* (lē'ō-nīn), like a lion, is used of a head with a heavy " mane " of hair and a majestic look. Would the word be a good one to describe Nat? Do you know *feline* (fē'līn), the sophisticated word for catty, and *bovine* (bō'vĭn), or cowlike, used to indicate a dull, placid expression or disposi- tion? You do not need to know Latin to guess the meaning of *asinine* (ăs'ĭ-nīn).

# Thornton Wilder 1897–

Like Eugene O'Neill, Thornton Wilder scored a hit with his first play to reach Broadway. But he had already established an enviable reputation as a novelist before he turned dramatist; and he is the only writer to have won the Pulitzer prize in both fields, for the novel with *The Bridge of San Luis Rey* (1928) and for the drama with *Our Town* (1938). This full-length play was preceded by a group of very short plays, *The Angel That Troubled the Waters* (1928), and a number of excellent one-act plays published in the collection called *The Long Christmas Dinner* (1932).

In 1942 Wilder stirred a riot of discussion with the fantasy, *The Skin of Our Teeth,* which makes one family's life a parable of the struggle through the ages of the whole human race to learn more and make a better life. This play was stimulating, but it was also confusing and did not approach the popular success of *Our Town.*

Wilder's early life and education followed a winding trail. Born in Madison, Wisconsin, he started his schooling in California; continued it in China, where his father was stationed for eight years in government service; and attended college at Oberlin, in Ohio, and at Yale. During 1920 he was a graduate student at the American Academy in Rome. Of all these places, only Rome found its way into his writings — in his first novel, *The Cabala* (1926). His most successful novel, *The Bridge of San Luis Rey,* has its scene in early Peru, a country he has never visited, and his most successful play is about a small town in New Hampshire. But such is his skill at mastering and re-creating details and general mood that he seems to be writing from firsthand, intimate knowledge.

Wilder belongs to the group of dramatists who have broken with the old order. His methods are seldom realistic and he is responsible for some interesting technical innovations in drama, but his basic interest is a continuing search for what is real in human life and destiny.

## OUR TOWN [1]

In a day when new patterns and forms are the rule rather than the exception in the thea-ter, *Our Town* is notable for genuine originality. Its free and easy shifts of scenes; the liberties it takes with time, moving now forward, now backward; its independence of conventional scenery and stage properties, are smoothly knit together by the remarkable invention of the Stage Manager, who directs and explains the action, takes the part of a minor character here and there, sets up the simple substitutes for regular properties, takes over the usual responsibilities of the printed program, and regards the whole life of the little village with understanding and quiet humor. Wilder himself says that the Stage Manager is "a hangover from a novelist's technique," and critics say that he is a compound of the property man of Chinese drama and the chorus of Greek drama. But he is not fully explained by either explanation. He is the spirit, the genius, of his town; and he is a poet and a philosopher as well. Superhuman or not, he is most of the time simply one of the most genial and winning characters yet to appear on our stage.

But one novel character, or creation rather, could never have won America as this play has. It has been produced by professional and amateur groups all over the country, everywhere with great success and with a warmer response than any technical innovation could call forth. Coming at a time when most literature is critical and satirical or gloomy and pessimistic, when most of the theatrical fare offered the public is either sensational or over-sophisticated, this honest, warmhearted, cheering view of the satisfactions of simple living has won its thousands of admirers with plain goodness and wholesomeness. Do not look for excitement or for sentimentality. If you enter wholeheartedly into the dramatist's story and mood, you will find a deep satisfaction that is infinitely better.

*The entire play takes place in Grover's Corners, N. H., 1901 to 1913.*

## ACT I

*No curtain. No scenery. The audience, arriving, sees an empty stage in half-light.*

*Presently the* STAGE MANAGER, *hat on and pipe in mouth, enters and begins placing a table and several chairs downstage left, and a table and chairs downstage right. " Left " and " right " are from the point of view of the actor facing the audience." Up " is toward the back wall.*

*As the house lights go down, he has finished setting the stage and, leaning against the right proscenium pillar, watches the late arrivals in the audience. When the auditorium is in complete darkness, he speaks.*

STAGE MANAGER. This play is called *Our Town.* It was written by Thornton Wilder; produced and directed by A_____ [or: produced by A_____; directed by B_____]. In it you will see Miss C_____, Miss D_____, Miss E_____, and Mr. F_____, Mr. G_____, Mr. H_____, and many others.

The name of the town is Grover's Corners, New Hampshire — just across the Massachusetts line: longitude forty-two degrees, forty minutes; latitude seventy degrees, thirty-seven minutes.

The first act shows a day in our town. The day is May 7, 1901. The time is just before dawn.

[*A rooster crows.*]

The sky is beginning to show some streaks of light over in the east there, behind our mount'in. The morning star always gets wonderful bright the minute before it has to go. (*He stares at it for a moment, then goes upstage.*)

Well, I'd better show you how our town lies. Up here (*that is, parallel with the back wall*) is Main Street. Way back there is the railway station; tracks go that way. Polish Town's across the tracks and some Canuck familes. (*Toward the left*) Over there is the Congregational Church; across the street's the Presbyterian. Methodist and Unitarian are over there. Baptist is down in the holla' by the river. Catholic Church is over beyond the tracks.

Here's the Town Hall and Post Office combined; jail's in the basement. Bryan once made a speech from these steps here. Along here's a row of stores. Hitching posts and horse blocks in front of them. First automobile's going to come along in about five years — belonged to Banker Cartwright, our richest citizen . . . lives in the big white house up on the hill.

Here's the grocery store and here's Mr. Morgan's drugstore. Most everybody in town manages to look into those two stores once a day. Public school's over yonder. High school's still farther over. Quarter of nine mornings, noontimes, and three o'clock afternoons, the hull town can hear the yelling and screaming from those schoolyards. (*He approaches the table and chairs downstage right.*)

This is our doctor's house — Doc Gibbs's. This is the back door.

[*Two arched trellises are pushed out, one by each proscenium pillar.*]

There's some scenery for those who think they have to have scenery. There's a garden here. Corn . . . peas . . . beans . . . hollyhocks . . . heliotrope . . . and a lot of burdock. (*Crosses the stage.*)

In those days our newspaper come out twice a week — the Grover's Corners *Sentinel* — and this is Editor Webb's house. And this is Mrs. Webb's garden. Just like

Mrs. Gibbs's, only it's got a lot of sunflowers, too. Right here — big butternut tree.

[*He returns to his place by the right proscenium pillar and looks at the audience for a minute.*]

Nice town, y'know what I mean? Nobody very remarkable ever come out of it — s'far as we know. The earliest tombstones in the cemetery up there on the mountain say 1670, 1680 — they're Grovers and Cartwrights and Gibbses and Herseys — same names as are around here now.

Well, as I said, it's about dawn. The only lights on in town are in a cottage over by the tracks where a Polish mother's just had twins. And in the Joe Crowell house, where Joe Junior's getting up so as to deliver the paper. And in the depot, where Shorty Hawkins is gettin' ready to flag the five forty-five for Boston.

[*A train whistle is heard. The* STAGE MANAGER *takes out his watch and nods.*]

Naturally, out in the country — all around — they've been lights on for some time, what with milkin's and so on. But town people sleep late.

So — another day's begun. There's Doc Gibbs comin' down Main Street now, comin' back from that baby case. And here's his wife comin' downstairs to get breakfast. Doc Gibbs died in 1930. The new hospital's named after him. Mrs. Gibbs died first — long time ago, in fact. She went out to visit her daughter, Rebecca, who married an insurance man in Canton, Ohio, and died there — pneumonia — but her body was brought back here. She's up in the cemetery there now, in with a whole mess of Gibbses and Herseys — she was Julia Hersey 'fore she married Doc Gibbs in the Congregational Church over there.

In our town we like to know the facts about everybody. . . . That's Doc Gibbs. And there comes Joe Crowell, Jr., delivering Mr. Webb's *Sentinel*.

[DR. GIBBS *has been coming along Main Street from the left. At the point where he would turn to approach his house, he*

*stops, sets down his — imaginary — black bag, takes off his hat, and rubs his face with fatigue, using an enormous handkerchief.* MRS. GIBBS *has entered her kitchen, gone through the motions of putting wood into a stove, lighting it, and preparing breakfast. Suddenly,* JOE CROWELL, JR., *starts down Main Street from the right, hurling imaginary newspapers into doorways.*]

JOE CROWELL, JR. Morning, Doc Gibbs.

DR. GIBBS. Morning, Joe.

JOE CROWELL, JR. Somebody been sick, Doc?

DR. GIBBS. No. Just some twins born over in Polish Town.

JOE CROWELL, JR. Do you want your paper now?

DR. GIBBS. Yes, I'll take it. Anything serious goin' on in the world since Wednesday?

JOE CROWELL, JR. Yessir. My school teacher, Miss Foster, 's getting married to a fella over in Concord.

DR. GIBBS. I declare. How do you boys feel about that?

JOE CROWELL, JR. Well, of course, it's none of my business — but I think if a person starts out to be a teacher, she ought to stay one.

DR. GIBBS. How's your knee, Joe?

JOE CROWELL, JR. Fine, Doc. I never think about it at all. Only like you said, it always tells me when it's going to rain.

DR. GIBBS. What's it telling you today? Goin' to rain?

JOE CROWELL, JR. No, sir.

DR. GIBBS. Sure?

JOE CROWELL, JR. Yessir.

DR. GIBBS. Knee ever make a mistake?

JOE CROWELL. JR. No, sir.

[JOE *goes off.* DR. GIBBS *stands reading his paper.*]

STAGE MANAGER. Here comes Howie Newsome delivering the milk.

[HOWIE NEWSOME *comes along Main Street, passes* DR. GIBBS, *comes down the center of the stage, leaves some bottles at* MRS.

WEBB'S *back door, and crosses the stage to* MRS. GIBBS'S.]

HOWIE NEWSOME. Git-ap, Bessie. What's the matter with you? . . . Morning, Doc.

DR. GIBBS. Morning, Howie.

HOWIE NEWSOME. Somebody sick?

DR. GIBBS. Pair of twins over to Mrs. Goruslawski's.

HOWIE NEWSOME. Twins, eh? This town's gettin' bigger every year.

DR. GIBBS. Going to rain, Howie?

HOWIE NEWSOME. No, no. Fine day — that'll burn through. Come on, Bessie.

DR. GIBBS. Hello, Bessie. (*He strokes her.*) How old is she, Howie?

HOWIE NEWSOME. Going on seventeen. Bessie's all mixed up about the route ever since the Lockharts stopped takin' their quart of milk every day. She wants to leave 'em a quart just the same — keeps scolding me the hull trip.

[*He reaches* MRS. GIBBS'S *back door. She is waiting for him.*]

MRS. GIBBS. Good morning, Howie.

HOWIE NEWSOME. Morning, Mrs. Gibbs. Doc's just comin' down the street.

MRS. GIBBS. Is he? Seems like you're late today.

HOWIE NEWSOME. Yes. Somep'n went wrong with the separator. Don't know what 'twas.

[*He goes back to Main Street, clucks for Bessie, and goes off right.* DR. GIBBS *reaches his home and goes in.*]

MRS. GIBBS. Everything all right?

DR. GIBBS. Yes. I declare — easy as kittens.

MRS. GIBBS. Bacon'll be ready in a minute. Set down and drink your coffee. Child-*run!* Child-*run!* Time to get up. George! Rebecca! . . . You can catch a couple hours' sleep this morning, can't you?

DR. GIBBS. Hm! . . . Mrs. Wentworth's coming at eleven. Guess I know what it's about, too. Her stummick ain't what it ought to be.

MRS. GIBBS. All told, you won't get more'n three hours' sleep. Frank Gibbs, I don't know what's goin' to become of you. I do wish I could get you to go away some place and take a rest. I think it would do you good.

MRS. WEBB. Emileeee! Time to get up! Wally! Seven o'clock!

MRS. GIBBS. I declare, you got to speak to George. Seems like something's come over him lately. He's no help to me at all. I can't even get him to cut me some wood.

DR. GIBBS. Is he sassy to you?

MRS. GIBBS. No. He just whines! All he thinks about is that baseball — George! Rebecca! You'll be late for school.

DR. GIBBS. M-m-m. . . .

MRS. GIBBS. George!

DR. GIBBS. George, look sharp!

GEORGE'S VOICE. Yes, Pa!

DR. GIBBS (*as he goes off the stage*). Don't you hear your mother calling you?

MRS. WEBB. Walleee! Emilee! You'll be late for school! Walleee! You wash yourself good or I'll come up and do it myself.

REBECCA GIBBS'S VOICE. Ma! What dress shall I wear?

MRS. GIBBS. Don't make a noise. Your father's been out all night and needs his sleep. I washed and ironed the blue gingham for you special.

REBECCA. Ma, I hate that dress.

MRS. GIBBS. Oh, hush up with you.

REBECCA. Every day I go to school dressed like a sick turkey.

MRS. GIBBS. Now, Rebecca, don't be impossible. You always look *very* nice.

REBECCA. Mamma, George's throwing soap at me.

MRS. GIBBS. I'll come up and slap the both of you — that's what I'll do.

[*A factory whistle sounds. The children enter and take their places at the breakfast tables:* EMILY *and* WALLY WEBB; GEORGE *and* REBECCA GIBBS.]

STAGE MANAGER. We've got a factory in our town too — hear it? Makes blankets. Cartwrights own it and it brung 'em a fortune.

MRS. WEBB. Children! Now I won't have

it. Breakfast is just as good as any other meal and I won't have you gobbling like wolves. It'll stunt your growth — that's a fact. Put away your book, Wally.

WALLY. Aw, Ma!

MRS. WEBB. You know the rule's well as I do — no books at table. As for me, I'd rather have my children healthy than bright.

EMILY. I'm both, Mamma; you know I am. I'm the brightest girl in school for my age. I have a wonderful memory.

MRS. WEBB. Eat your breakfast.

WALLY. I'm bright, too, when I'm looking at my stamp collection.

MRS. GIBBS. I'll speak to your father about it when he's rested. Seems to me twenty-five cents a week's enough for a boy your age. I declare I don't know how you spend it all.

GEORGE. Aw, Ma — I gotta lotta things to buy.

MRS. GIBBS. Strawberry phosphates — that's what you spend it on.

GEORGE. I don't see how Rebecca comes to have so much money. She has more'n a dollar.

REBECCA (spoon in mouth, dreamily). I've been saving it up gradual.

MRS. GIBBS. Well, dear, I think it's a good thing every now and then to spend some.

REBECCA. Mamma, do you know what I love most in the world — do you? Money!

MRS. GIBBS. Eat your breakfast.

[The school bell is heard.]

THE CHILDREN. Mamma, there's first bell. . . . I gotta hurry. . . . I don't want any more.

MRS. WEBB. Walk fast, but you don't have to run. Wally, pull up your pants at the knee. Stand up straight, Emily.

MRS. GIBBS. Tell Miss Foster I send her my best congratulations. Can you remember that?

REBECCA. Yes, Ma.

MRS. GIBBS. You look real nice, Rebecca. Pick up your feet.

ALL. Good-by.

[The children from the two houses join at the center of the stage and go up to Main Street, then off left. MRS. GIBBS fills her apron with food for the chickens and comes down to the footlights.]

MRS. GIBBS. Here, chick, chick, chick, . . . No, go away, you. Go away. . . . Here, chick, chick, chick. What's the matter with you? Fight, fight, fight — that's all you do. Hm . . . you don't belong to me. Where'd you come from? (She shakes her apron.) Oh, don't be so scared. Nobody's going to hurt you.

[MRS. WEBB is sitting by her trellis, stringing beans.]

Good morning, Myrtle. How's your cold?

MRS. WEBB. Well, it's better; but I told Charles I didn't know as I'd go to choir practice tonight. Wouldn't be any use.

MRS. GIBBS. Just the same, you come to choir practice, Myrtle, and try it.

MRS. WEBB. Well, if I don't feel any worse than I do now I probably will. While I'm resting myself, I thought I'd string some of these beans.

MRS. GIBBS (rolling up her sleeves as she crosses the stage for a chat). Let me help you. Beans have been good this year.

MRS. WEBB. I've decided to put up forty quarts if it kills me. The children say they hate 'em, but I notice they're able to get 'em down all winter. (Pause)

MRS. GIBBS. Now, Myrtle. I've got to tell you something, because if I don't tell somebody I'll burst.

MRS. WEBB. Why, Julia Gibbs!

MRS. GIBBS. Here, give me some more of those beans. Myrtle, did one of those secondhand furniture men from Boston come to see you last Friday?

MRS. WEBB. No—o.

MRS. GIBBS. Well, he called on me. First I thought he was a patient wantin' to see Dr. Gibbs. 'N he wormed his way into my parlor, and, Myrtle Webb, he offered me three hundred and fifty dollars for Grandmother Wentworth's highboy, as I'm sitting here!

MRS. WEBB. Why, Julia Gibbs!

MRS. GIBBS. He did! That old thing! Why, it was so big I didn't know where to put it, and I almost give it to Cousin Hester Wilcox.

MRS. WEBB. Well, you're going to take it, aren't you?

MRS. GIBBS. I don't know.

MRS. WEBB. You don't know — three hundred and fifty dollars! What's come over you?

MRS. GIBBS. Well, if I could get the Doctor to take the money and go away some place on a real trip I'd sell it like that. Myrtle, ever since I was *that* high I've had the thought that I'd like to see Paris, France. I suppose I'm crazy.

MRS. WEBB. Oh, I know what you mean. How does the Doctor feel about it?

MRS. GIBBS. Well, I did beat about the bush a little and said that if I got a legacy — that's the way I put it — I'd make him take me somewhere.

MRS. WEBB. M-m-m. . . . What did he say?

MRS. GIBBS. You know how he is. I haven't heard a serious word out of him ever since I've known him. No, he said, it might make him discontented with Grover's Corners to go traipsin' about Europe; better let well enough alone, he says. Every two years he makes a trip to the battlefields of the Civil War; and that's enough treat for anybody, he says.

MRS. WEBB. Well, Mr. Webb just *admires* the way Dr. Gibbs knows everything about the Civil War. Mr. Webb's a good mind to give up Napoleon and move over to the Civil War, only Dr. Gibbs being one of the greatest experts in the country just makes him despair.

MRS. GIBBS. It's a fact! Dr. Gibbs is never so happy as when he's at Antietam or Gettysburg. The times I've walked over those hills, Myrtle, stopping at every bush and pacing it all out, like we was going to buy it.

MRS. WEBB. Well, if that secondhand man's really serious about buyin' it, Julia, you sell it. And then you'll get to see Paris, all right.

MRS. GIBBS. Oh, I'm sorry I mentioned it. Only it seems to me that once in your life before you die you ought to see a country where they don't talk and think in English and don't even want to.

[*The* STAGE MANAGER *returns to the center of the stage.*]

STAGE MANAGER. That'll do. That'll do. Thank you very much, ladies.

[MRS. GIBBS *and* MRS. WEBB *gather up their things, return into their homes, and disappear.*]

Now we're going to skip a few hours in the day at Grover's Corners. But before we go on, I want you to know some more things about the town — all kinds of things. So I've asked Professor Willard of our State University to come down here and sketch in a few details of our past history — kind of scientific account, you might say. Is Professor Willard here?

[PROFESSOR WILLARD, *a rural savant, pince-nez on a wide satin ribbon, enters from the right with some notes in his hand.*]

May I introduce Professor Willard of our university. A few brief notes, thank you, Professor — unfortunately our time is limited.

PROFESSOR WILLARD. Grover's Corners . . . let me see . . . Grover's Corners lies on the old Archeozoic granite [1] of the Appalachian range. I may say it's some of the oldest land in the world. We're very proud of that. A shelf of Devonian basalt [2] crosses it with vestiges of Mesozoic shale,[3] and some sandstone outcroppings; but that's all more recent: two hundred, three hundred, million years old. Some highly interesting fossils have been found — I may say unique fossils — two miles out of town, in Silas Peckham's cow pasture. They can be seen at the museum in our university at any time.

[1] **Archeozoic granite** (är-kē-ō-zō′ĭk): granite formed in the earliest era of geological history. [2] **Devonian basalt** (dĕ-vō′nĭ-ăn bȧ-sôlt′): very old rock of volcanic origin. [3] **Mesozoic shale** (mĕs-ō-zō′ĭk shāl): another type of rock formed very early in the world's history.

. . . Did you wish the meteorological conditions?

STAGE MANAGER. Thank you. We would.

PROFESSOR WILLARD. The mean precipitation is forty inches. The mean annual temperature is forty-three degrees, ranging between one hundred two degrees in the shade and thirty-eight degrees below zero in winter. The . . . the . . . uh . . .

STAGE MANAGER. Thank you, Professor. And have you Professor Gruber's notes on the history of human life here?

PROFESSOR WILLARD. Hm . . . yes . . . anthropological data. Early Amerindian stock. Cotahatchee [1] tribes . . . no evidence before the tenth century of this era . . . hm . . . now entirely disappeared . . . possible traces in three families. Migration toward the end of the seventeenth century of English brachycephalic [2] blue-eyed stock . . . for the most part. Since then some influx of Slav and Mediterranean types. . . .

STAGE MANAGER. And the population, Professor Willard?

PROFESSOR WILLARD. Within the town limits, 2,640. The postal district brings in 507 more. Mortality and birth rates are constant; by MacPherson's gauge, 6.032.

STAGE MANAGER. Thank you *very* much, Professor. We're all very much obliged to you, I'm sure.

PROFESSOR WILLARD. Not at all, sir; not at all.

STAGE MANAGER. This way, Professor, and thank you again.

[*Exit* PROFESSOR WILLARD.]

Now the political and social report: Editor Webb. . . . Oh, Mr. Webb?

[MRS. WEBB *appears at her back door.*]

MRS. WEBB. He'll be here in a minute. . . . He just cut his hand while he was eatin' an apple.

STAGE MANAGER. Thank you, Mrs. Webb.

MRS. WEBB. Charles! Everybody's waitin'. (*Exit.*)

STAGE MANAGER. Mr. Webb is publisher and editor of the Grover's Corners *Sentinel.* That's our local paper, y'know.

[MR. WEBB *enters from his house, pulling on his coat. His finger is bound in a handkerchief.*]

MR. WEBB. Hm. . . . I don't have to tell you that we're run here by a board of selectmen. All males vote at the age of twenty-one. Women vote indirect. We're lower middle-class, sprinkling of professional men . . . ten per cent illiterate laborers. Politically, we're eighty-six per cent Republicans; six per cent Democrats; four per cent Socialists; rest, indifferent. Religiously, we're eighty-five per cent Protestants; twelve per cent Catholics; rest, indifferent. Do you want the poverty and insanity statistics?

STAGE MANAGER. Thank you, no. Have you any comments, Mr. Webb?

MR. WEBB. Very ordinary town, if you ask me. Little better behaved than most. Probably a lot duller. But our young people here seem to like it well enough: ninety per cent of 'em graduating from high school settle down right here to live — even when they've been away to college.

STAGE MANAGER. Thank you, Mr. Webb. Now, is there anyone in the audience who would like to ask Editor Webb anything about the town?

WOMAN IN THE BALCONY. Is there much drinking in Grover's Corners?

MR. WEBB. Well, ma'am, I wouldn't know what you'd call *much.* Satiddy nights the farm hands meet down in Ellery Greenough's stable and holler some. Fourth of July I've been known to taste a drop myself — and Decoration Day, of course. We've got one or two town drunks, but they're always having remorses every time an evangelist comes to town. No, ma'am, I'd say likker ain't a regular thing in the home here, except in the medicine chest. Right good for snakebite, y'know — always was.

---

[1] **Cotahatchee** (kŏ-tà-hă′chĕ). [2] **brachycephalic** (brăk-ĭ-sĕ-făl′ĭk): short-headed, or broad-headed.

TALL MAN AT THE BACK OF AUDITORIUM. Is there no one in town aware of —

STAGE MANAGER. Come forward, will you, where we can all hear you — what were you saying?

TALL MAN. Is there no one in town aware of social injustice and industrial inequality?

MR. WEBB. Oh, yes, everybody is — somethin' terrible. Seems like they spend most of their time talking about who's rich and who's poor.

TALL MAN. Then why don't they do something about it?

MR. WEBB. Well, we're ready to listen to everybody's suggestion as to how you can see that the diligent and sensible'll rise to the top and the lazy and quarrelsome sink to the bottom. We'll listen to anybody. Meantime, until that's settled, we try to take care of those that can't help themselves, and those that can we leave alone. Are there any more questions?

LADY IN A BOX. Oh, Mr. Webb? Mr. Webb, is there any culture or love of beauty in Grover's Corners?

MR. WEBB. Well, ma'am, there ain't much — not in the sense you mean. Come to think of it, there's some girls that play the piano at high-school commencement; but they ain't happy about it. Yes, and I see where my daughter's been made to read *The Merchant of Venice* over to the school. Seems all pretty remote to 'em, y'know what I mean. No, ma'am, there isn't much culture; but maybe this is the place to tell you that we've got a lot of pleasures of a kind here: we like the sun comin' up over the mountain in the morning, and we all notice a good deal about the birds. We pay a lot of attention to them, and trees and plants. And we watch the change of the seasons: yes, everybody knows about them. But those other things — you're right, ma'am — there ain't much. *Robinson Crusoe* and the Bible; and Handel's " Largo," we all know that; and Whistler's " Mother " — those are just about as far as we go.

LADY IN A BOX. So I thought. Thank you, Mr. Webb.

STAGE MANAGER. All right! All right! Thank you, everybody.

[MR. WEBB *retires.*]

We'll go back to the town now. It's middle of the afternoon. All 2,642 have had their dinners, and all the dishes have been washed. There's an early-afternoon calm in our town: a buzzin' and a hummin' from the school buildings; only a few buggies on Main Street — the horses dozing at the hitching posts; you all remember what it's like. Doc Gibbs is in his office, tapping people and making them say " Ah." Mr. Webb's cuttin' his lawn over there; one man in ten thinks it's a privilege to push his own lawn mower.

No, sir. It's later than I thought. There are the children coming home from school already.

[EMILY WEBB *comes sedately down Main Street, carrying some schoolbooks. There are some signs that she is imagining herself to be a lady of striking elegance. Her father's movements to and fro with the lawn mower bring him into her vicinity.*]

EMILY. I *can't*, Lois. I've got to go home and help my mother. I *promised.*

MR. WEBB. Emily, walk simply. Who do you think you are today?

EMILY. Papa, you're terrible. One minute you tell me to stand up straight, and the next minute you call me names. I just don't listen to you. (*She gives him an abrupt kiss.*)

MR. WEBB. Golly, I never got a kiss from such a great lady before.

[He goes out of sight. EMILY *leans over and picks some flowers by the gate of her house.* GEORGE GIBBS *comes careening down Main Street. He is throwing a ball up to dizzy heights and waiting to catch it again. This sometimes requires his taking six steps backward.*]

GEORGE. Excuse me, Mrs. Forrest.

STAGE MANAGER (*as* MRS. FORREST). Go out and play in the fields, young man. You got no business playing baseball on Main Street.

GEORGE. Awfully sorry, Mrs. Forrest. . . . Hello, Emily.

EMILY. H'lo.

GEORGE. You made a fine speech in class.

EMILY. Well . . . I was really ready to make a speech about the Monroe Doctrine, but at the last minute Miss Corcoran made me talk about the Louisiana Purchase instead. I worked an awful long time on both of them.

GEORGE. Gee, it's funny, Emily. From my window up there I can just see your head nights when you're doing your homework over in your room.

EMILY. Why, can you?

GEORGE. You certainly do stick to it, Emily. I don't see how you can sit still that long. I guess you like school.

EMILY. Well, I always feel it's something you have to go through.

GEORGE. Yeah.

EMILY. I don't mind it really. It passes the time.

GEORGE. Yeah. . . . Emily, what do you think? We might work out a kinda telegraph from there to there; and once in a while you could give me a kinda hint or two about one of those algebra problems. I don't mean the answers, Emily, of course not . . . just some little hint. . . .

EMILY. Oh, I think *hints* are allowed. So-ah — if you get stuck, George, you whistle to me; and I'll give you some hints.

GEORGE. Emily, you're just naturally bright, I guess.

EMILY. I figure that it's just the way a person's born.

GEORGE. Yeah. But, you see, I want to be a farmer, and my Uncle Luke says whenever I'm ready I can come over and work on his farm and if I'm any good I can just gradually have it.

EMILY. You mean the house and everything?

[*Enter* MRS. WEBB.]

GEORGE. Yeah. Well, thanks. . . . I better be getting out to the baseball field.

Thanks for the talk, Emily. . . . Good afternoon, Mrs. Webb.

MRS. WEBB. Good afternoon, George.

GEORGE. So long, Emily.

EMILY. So long, George.

MRS. WEBB. Emily, come and help me string these beans for the winter. George Gibbs let himself have a real conversation, didn't he? Why, he's growing up. How old would George be?

EMILY. I don't know.

MRS. WEBB. Let's see. He must be almost sixteen.

EMILY. Mamma, I made a speech in class today and I was very good.

MRS. WEBB. You must recite it to your father at supper. What was it about?

EMILY. The Louisiana Purchase. It was like silk off a spool. I'm going to make speeches all my life. . . . Mamma, are these big enough?

MRS. WEBB. Try and get them a little bigger if you can.

EMILY. Mamma, will you answer me a question, serious?

MRS. WEBB. Seriously, dear — not serious.

EMILY. Seriously. Will you?

MRS. WEBB. Of course, I will.

EMILY. Mamma, am I good-looking?

MRS. WEBB. Yes, of course you are. All my children have got good features; I'd be ashamed if they hadn't.

EMILY. Oh, Mamma, that's not what I mean. What I mean is: Am I *pretty?*

MRS. WEBB. I've already told you, yes. Now that's enough of that. You have a nice, young, pretty face. I never heard of such foolishness.

EMILY. Oh, Mamma, you never tell us the truth about anything.

MRS. WEBB. I *am* telling you the truth.

EMILY. Mamma, were *you* pretty?

MRS. WEBB. Yes, I was, if I do say it. I was the prettiest girl in town next to Mamie Cartwright.

EMILY. But, Mamma, you've got to say *some*thing about me. Am I pretty enough . . . to get anybody . . . to get people interested in me?

MRS. WEBB. Emily, you make me tired. Now stop it. You're pretty enough for all normal purposes. Come along now and bring that bowl with you.

EMILY. But, Mamma, you're no help at all.

STAGE MANAGER. Thank you. Thank you! That'll do. We'll have to interrupt again here. Thank you, Mrs. Webb; thank you, Emily.

[MRS. WEBB *and* EMILY *withdraw.*]

There are some more things we've got to explore about this town. This time we're going to go about it in another way: we're going to look back on it from the future. I'm not going to tell you what became of these two families we're seeing most of, because the rest of the play will tell you about them. But take some of these others.

Take Joe Crowell, Junior. Joe was a very bright fellow. He graduated with honors and got a scholarship to Boston Tech — M.I.T., that is. But the war broke out, and Joe died in France. All that education for nothing.

Howie Newsome's still delivering milk at Grover's Corners. He's an old man now, has a lot of help; but he still delivers it himself. Says he gets the feel of the town that way. Carries all the accounts in his head; never has to write down a word.

Mr. Morgan's drugstore ain't the same — it's all citified. Mr. Morgan retired and went to live in San Diego, California, where his daughter married a real-estate man, name of Kerby. Mr. Morgan died there in 1935 and was buried in a lot of palm trees. Kinda lost his religion at the end and took up New Thought or something. They read some newfangled poetry over him and cremated him. The New Hampshire in him sort of broke down in him in that climate, seems like.

The Cartwrights got richer and richer. The house is closed most of the year. They're off eating big dinners in hotels now — in Virginia Hot Springs and Miami Beach. They say the winters are cold here. I see where they've become 'Piscopalians.

The Cartwright interests have just begun building a new bank in Grover's Corners — had to go to Vermont for the marble, sorry to say. And they've asked a friend of mine what they should put in the cornerstone for people to dig up a thousand years from now. Of course, they've put in a copy of the New York *Times* and a copy of Mr. Webb's *Sentinel*. We're kind of interested in this, because some scientific fellas have found a way of painting all that reading matter with a kind of glue — silicate glue — that'll make it keep a thousand, two thousand, years. We're putting in a Bible . . . and the Constitution of the United States and a copy of William Shakespeare's plays. What do you say, folks? What do you think? Y'know — Babylon once had two million people in it, and all we know about 'em is the names of the kings and some copies of wheat contracts and . . . the sales of slaves. Yes, every night all those families sat down to supper, and the father came home from his work, and the smoke went up the chimney — same as here. And even in Greece and Rome all we know about the real life of the people is what we can piece together out of the joking poems and the comedies they wrote for the theater back then. So I'm going to have a copy of this play put in the cornerstone and the people a thousand years from now'll know a few simple facts about us — more than the Treaty of Versailles and the Lindbergh flight. See what I mean?

Well — you people a thousand years from now — in the provinces north of New York at the beginning of the twentieth century, people et three times a day: soon after sunrise, at noon, and at sunset. Every seventh day, by law and by religion, was a day of rest, and all work came to a stop. The religion at that time was Christianity. I guess you have some other records about Christianity. The domestic setup was marriage: a binding relation between a male and one female that lasted for life. Christianity strictly forbade killing; but you were allowed to kill animals, and you were allowed to kill human beings in war and government punishings. I guess we don't have to tell you about the government and business forms, because that's the kind of thing people seem to hand down first of all. Let me see now if there's anything else. Oh, yes — at death people were buried in the ground just as they are.

So, friends, this is the way we were in our growing up and in our marrying and in our doctoring and in our living and in our dying. Now we'll return to our day in Grover's Corners: A lot of time has gone by. It's evening. You can hear choir practice going on in the Congregational Church. All the children are at home doing their schoolwork. The day is running down like a tired clock.

[*A choir partially concealed in the orchestra pit has begun singing " Blessed Be the Tie That Binds."* SIMON STIMSON *stands directing them. Two ladders have been pushed onto the stage; they serve as indication of the second story in the Gibbs and Webb houses.* GEORGE *and* EMILY *mount them, and apply themselves to their schoolwork.* DR. GIBBS *has entered and is seated in his kitchen, reading.*]

SIMON STIMSON. Now look here, everybody. Music come into the world to give pleasure. Softer! Softer! Get it out of your heads that music's only good when it's loud. You leave loudness to the Methodists. You couldn't beat 'em, even if you wanted to. Now again. Tenors!

GEORGE. Hssst! Emily!

EMILY. Hello.

GEORGE. Hello!

EMILY. I can't work at all. The moonlight's so *terrible.*

GEORGE. Emily, did you get the third problem?

EMILY. Which?

GEORGE. The *third?*

EMILY. Why, yes, George — that's the easiest of them all.

GEORGE. I don't see it. Emily, can you give me a hint?

EMILY. I'll tell you one thing: the answer's in yards.

GEORGE. In yards! How do mean?

EMILY. In *square* yards.

GEORGE. Oh . . . in square yards.

EMILY. Yes, George, don't you see?

GEORGE. Yeah.

EMILY. In square yards of *wallpaper.*

GEORGE. Wallpaper — oh, I see. Thanks a lot, Emily.

EMILY. You're welcome. My, isn't the moonlight *terrible?* And choir practice going on. I think if you hold your breath you can hear the train all the way to Contookuck. Hear it?

GEORGE. M-m-m. What do you know!

EMILY. Well, I guess I better go back and try to work.

GEORGE. Good night, Emily. And thanks.

EMILY. Good night, George.

SIMON STIMSON. Before I forget it: How many of you will be able to come in Tuesday afternoon and sing at Fred Hersey's wedding? Show your hands. That'll be fine; that'll be right nice. We'll do the same music we did for Jane Trowbridge's last month. . . . Now we'll do " Art thou weary; art thou languid? " It's a question, ladies and gentlemen, make it talk. Ready.

DR. GIBBS. Oh, George, can you come down a minute?

GEORGE. Yes, Pa. (*He descends the ladder.*)

DR. GIBBS. Make yourself comfortable, George; I'll only keep you a minute. George, how old are you?

GEORGE. I? I'm sixteen, almost seventeen.

DR. GIBBS. What do you want to do after school's over?

GEORGE. Why, you know, Pa, I want to be a farmer on Uncle Luke's farm.

DR. GIBBS. You'll be willing, will you, to get up early and milk and feed the stock . . . and you'll be able to hoe and hay all day?

GEORGE. Sure, I will. What are you . . . what do you mean, Pa?

DR. GIBBS. Well, George, while I was in my office today I heard a funny sound. . . . And what do you think it was? It was your mother chopping wood. There you see your mother — getting up early, cooking meals all day long, washing and ironing; and still she has to go out in the back yard and chop wood. I suppose she just got tired of asking you. She just gave up and decided it was easier to do it herself. And you eat her meals and put on the clothes she keeps nice for you, and you run off and play baseball — like she's some hired girl we keep around the house but that we don't like very much. Well, I knew all I had to do was call your attention to it. Here's a handkerchief, son. George, I've decided to raise your spending money twenty-five cents a week. Not, of course, for chopping wood for your mother, because that's a present you give her, but because you're getting older — and I imagine there are lots of things you must find to do with it.

GEORGE. Thanks, Pa.

DR. GIBBS. Let's see — tomorrow's pay-day. You can count on it. Hmm. Probably Rebecca'll feel she ought to have some more too. Wonder what could have happened to your mother. Choir practice never was as late as this before.

GEORGE. It's only half-past eight, Pa.

DR. GIBBS. I don't know why she's in that old choir. She hasn't any more voice than an old crow. . . . Traipsin' around the streets at this hour of the night. . . . Just about time you retired, don't you think?

GEORGE. Yes, Pa.

[GEORGE *mounts to his place on the ladder. Laughter and good nights can be heard on stage left and presently* MRS. GIBBS, MRS. SOAMES, *and* MRS. WEBB *come down Main Street. When they arrive at the center of the stage, they stop.*]

MRS. SOAMES. Good night, Martha. Good night, Mr. Foster.

MRS. WEBB. I'll tell Mr. Webb; I *know* he'll want to put it in the paper.

MRS. GIBBS. My, it's late!

MRS. SOAMES. Good night, Irma.

MRS. GIBBS. Real nice choir practice, wa'n't it? Myrtle Webb! Look at that moon, will you! Tsk-tsk-tsk. Potato weather, for sure.

MRS. SOAMES. Naturally I didn't want to say a word about it in front of those others, but now we're alone — really, it's the worst scandal that ever was in this town!

MRS. GIBBS. What?

MRS. SOAMES. Simon Stimson!

MRS. GIBBS. Now, Louella!

MRS. SOAMES. But, Julia! To have the organist of a church drink and drunk year after year. You know he was drunk tonight.

MRS. GIBBS. Now, Louella. We all know about Mr. Stimson, and we all know about the troubles he's been through, and Dr. Ferguson knows too; and if Dr. Ferguson keeps him on there in his job, the only thing the rest of us can do is just not to notice it.

MRS. SOAMES. Not to notice it! But it's getting worse.

MRS. WEBB. No, it isn't, Louella. It's getting better. I've been in that choir twice as long as you have. It doesn't happen anywhere near so often. . . . My, I hate to go to bed on a night like this. I better hurry. Those children'll be sitting up till all hours. Good night, Louella. (*She hurries downstage, enters her house, and disappears.*)

MRS. GIBBS. Can you get home safe, Louella?

MRS. SOAMES. It's as bright as day. I can see Mr. Soames scowling at the window now. You'd think we'd been to a dance the way the menfolk carry on.

[*Repeated good nights.* MRS. GIBBS *arrives at her home.*]

MRS. GIBBS. Well, we had a real good time.

DR. GIBBS. You're late enough.

MRS. GIBBS. Why, Frank, it ain't any later 'n usual.

DR. GIBBS. And you stopping at the corner to gossip with a lot of hens.

MRS. GIBBS. Now, Frank, don't be grouchy. Come out and smell my heliotrope in the moonlight.

[*They stroll out arm in arm along the footlights.*]

Isn't that wonderful? What did you do all the time I was away?

DR. GIBBS. Oh, I read — as usual. What were the girls gossiping about tonight?

MRS. GIBBS. Well, believe me, Frank — there is something to gossip about.

DR. GIBBS. Hmm! Simon Stimson far gone, was he?

MRS. GIBBS. Worst I've ever seen him. How'll that end, Frank? Dr. Ferguson can't forgive him forever.

DR. GIBBS. I guess I know more about Simon Stimson's affairs than anybody in this town. Some people ain't made for small-town life. I don't know how that'll end; but there's nothing we can do but just leave it alone. Come, get in.

MRS. GIBBS. No, not yet. . . . Oh, Frank, I'm worried about you.

DR. GIBBS. What are you worried about?

MRS. GIBBS. I think it's my duty to make plans for you to get a real rest and change. And if I get that legacy, well, I'm going to insist on it.

DR. GIBBS. Now, Julia, there's no sense in going over that again.

MRS. GIBBS. Frank, you're just *unreasonable!*

DR. GIBBS. Come on, Julia, it's getting late. First thing you know you'll catch cold. I gave George a piece of my mind tonight. I reckon you'll have your wood chopped for awhile anyway. No, no, start getting upstairs.

MRS. GIBBS. Oh, dear. There's always so many things to pick up, seems like. You know, Frank, Mrs. Fairchild always locks her front door every night. All those people up that part of town do.

DR. GIBBS. They're all getting citified, that's the trouble with them. They haven't got nothing fit to burgle and everybody knows it.

[*They disappear.* REBECCA *climbs up the ladder beside* GEORGE.]

GEORGE. Get out, Rebecca. There's only room for one at this window. You're always spoiling everything.

REBECCA. Well, let me look just a minute.

GEORGE. Use your own window.

REBECCA. I did; but there's no moon there.

. . . George, do you know what I think, do you? I think maybe the moon's getting nearer and nearer and there'll be a big 'splosion.

GEORGE. Rebecca, you don't know anything. If the moon were getting nearer, the guys that sit up all night with telescopes would see it first and they'd tell about it, and it'd be in all the newspapers.

REBECCA. George, is the moon shining on South America, Canada, and half the whole world?

GEORGE. Well — prob'ly is.

[*The* STAGE MANAGER *strolls on.*]

STAGE MANAGER. Nine-thirty. Most of the lights are out. No, there's Constable Warren trying a few doors on Main Street. And here comes Editor Webb, after putting his newspaper to bed.

MR. WEBB. Good evening, Bill.

CONSTABLE WARREN. Evenin', Mr. Webb.

MR. WEBB. Quite a moon!

CONSTABLE WARREN. Yepp.

MR. WEBB. All quiet tonight?

CONSTABLE WARREN. Simon Stimson is rollin' around a little. Just saw his wife movin' out to hunt for him, so I looked the other way — there he is now.

[SIMON STIMSON *comes down Main Street from the left, only a trace of unsteadiness in his walk.*]

MR. WEBB. Good evening, Simon. . . . Town seems to have settled down for the night pretty well. . . .

[SIMON STIMSON *comes up to him and pauses a moment.*]

Good evening. . . . Yes, most of the town's settled down for the night, Simon. . . . I guess we better do the same. Can I walk along a ways with you?

[SIMON STIMSON *continues on his way without a word and disappears at the right.*]

Good night.

CONSTABLE WARREN. I don't know how that's goin' to end, Mr. Webb.

MR. WEBB. Well, he's seen a peck of trouble, one thing after another. . . . Oh, Bill . . . if you see my boy smoking cigarettes, just give him a word, will you? He thinks a lot of you, Bill.

CONSTABLE WARREN. I don't think he smokes no cigarettes, Mr. Webb. Leastways, not more'n two or three a year. He don't belong to that crowd that hangs out down by the gully.

MR. WEBB. Hm. . . . I hope not. Well, good night, Bill.

CONSTABLE WARREN. Good night, Mr. Webb. (*Exit.*)

MR. WEBB. Who's that up there? Is that you, Myrtle?

EMILY. No, it's me, Papa.

MR. WEBB. Why aren't you in bed?

EMILY. I don't know. I just can't sleep yet, Papa. The moonlight's so *won*-derful. And the smell of Mrs. Gibbs's heliotrope. Can you smell it?

MR. WEBB. Hm. . . . Yes. Haven't any troubles on your mind, have you, Emily?

EMILY. *Troubles*, Papa. *No*.

MR. WEBB. Well, enjoy yourself, but don't let your mother catch you. Good night, Emily.

EMILY. Good night, Papa.

[MR. WEBB *crosses into the house, whistling " Blessed Be the Tie That Binds," and disappears.*]

REBECCA. I never told you about that letter Jane Crofut got from her minister when she was sick. The minister of her church in the town she was in before she came here. He wrote Jane a letter and on the envelope the address was like this. It said: Jane Crofut, The Crofut Farm, Grover's Corners, Sutton County, New Hampshire, United States of America.

GEORGE. What's funny about that?

REBECCA. But listen, it's not finished: the United States of America, Continent of North America, Western Hemisphere, the Earth, the Solar System, the Universe, the Mind of God — that's what it said on the envelope.

GEORGE. What do you know!

REBECCA. And the postman brought it just the same.

GEORGE. What do you know!

STAGE MANAGER. That's the end of the first act, friends. You can go and smoke now, those that smoke.

## Suggestions for Study of Act I

1. How soon do you realize that the Stage Manager is not an ordinary human being? What does he say that reveals the fact?

2. Compare the detailed description of the scene in *Where the Cross Is Made* with the suggestive description the Stage Manager uses to give the setting for this play. What advantages does each method have? What type of person would prefer Wilder's method? How is each method particularly suited to the type of play in which it is used?

3. Does the admission that Grover's Corners pays little attention to social injustice or to culture and beauty affect your attitude toward the town? Have you had personal experience with the " culture " Editor Webb lists as typical of what his town has?

4. Do you like the family relationships of the Webbs and the Gibbses? How do the parents handle their children's failings or foolishness? Why is " Blessed Be the Tie That Binds " a good song for the choir to be practicing?

5. Did you notice the quiet, not unkind humor in the accounts of the ways of the townfolk who went to California and to stylish resorts? In the references to Methodists and " 'Piscopalians "?

6. Why does Rebecca's little news item about the peculiarly addressed letter make a good ending for the first act?

## ACT II

*The tables and chairs of the two kitchens are still on the stage. The ladders have been withdrawn. The* STAGE MANAGER *has been at his accustomed place, watching the audience return to its seats.*

STAGE MANAGER. Three years have gone by. Yes, the sun's come up over a thousand times. Summers and winters have cracked the mountains a little bit more, and the rains have brought down some of the dirt. Some babies that weren't even born before have begun talking regular sentences already; and a number of people who thought they were right young and spry have noticed that they can't bound up a flight of stairs like they used to, without their heart fluttering a little. Some older sons are sitting at the head of the table, and some people I know are having their meat cut up for them.

All that can happen in a thousand days. Nature's been pushing and contriving in other ways, too: a number of young people fell in love and got married. Yes, the mountain got bit away a few fractions of an inch, millions of gallons of water went by the mill, and here and there a new home was set up under a roof. Almost everybody in the world gets married. You know what I mean? In our town there aren't hardly any exceptions. Most everybody in the world climbs into their graves married.

The first act was called " The Daily Life." This act is called " Love and Marriage." There's another act coming after this; I reckon you can guess what that's about.

So it's three years later. It's 1904. It's July 7, just after high-school commencement. That's the time most of our young people jump up and get married. Soon as they've passed their last examinations in solid geometry and Cicero's Orations, looks like they suddenly feel themselves fit to be married.

It's early morning. Only this time it's been raining. It's been pouring and thundering. Mrs. Gibbs's garden, and Mrs. Webb's here — drenched. All those bean poles and pea vines — drenched. All yesterday over there on Main Street the rain looked like curtains being blown along. Hm . . . it may begin again any minute.

There! You can hear the five-forty-five for Boston. And here comes Howie Newsome delivering the milk. And there's Si Crowell delivering the papers like his brother before him. You remember about his brother — all that education he's going to get and that'll be wasted? And there's Mrs. Gibbs and Mrs. Webb come down to make breakfast, just as though it were an ordinary day. I don't have to point out to the women in my audience that those ladies they see before them, both those ladies cooked three meals a day — one of 'em for twenty years, the other for forty — and no summer vacation. They brought up two children apiece, washed, cleaned the house — and never a nervous breakdown. Never thought themselves hard-used, either.

It's like what one of those Middle West poets said: You've got to love life to have life, and you've got to have life to love life.[1] . . . It's what they call a vicious circle.

[SI CROWELL *has entered, hurling imaginary newspapers into doorways.* HOWIE NEWSOME *has come along Main Street with* BESSIE.]

HOWIE NEWSOME. Git-ap, Bessie.

SI CROWELL. Morning, Howie.

HOWIE NEWSOME. Morning, Si. Anything in the papers I ought to know?

SI CROWELL. Nothing much, except we're losing about the best baseball pitcher Grover's Corners ever had.

HOWIE NEWSOME. Reckon he was. He's been standing off the whole of south New Hampshire singlehanded, looks like.

SI CROWELL. He could hit and run bases, too.

HOWIE NEWSOME. Yep. Mighty fine ball player. . . . Bessie! I guess I can stop and talk if I've a mind to!

SI CROWELL. I don't see how he could give up a thing like that just to get married. Would you, Howie?

HOWIE NEWSOME. Can't tell, Si. Never had no talent that way.

[CONSTABLE WARREN *enters. They exchange good mornings.*]

You're up early, Bill.

CONSTABLE WARREN. Seein' if there's anything I can do to prevent a flood. River's been risin' all night.

HOWIE NEWSOME. Si Crowell's all worked up here about George Gibbs's retiring from baseball.

[1] See "Lucinda Matlock," page 297.

CONSTABLE WARREN. Yes, sir; that's the way it goes. Back in eighty-four we had a player, Si — even George Gibbs couldn't touch him. Name of Hank Todd. Went down to Maine and become a parson. Wonderful ball player. . . . Howie, how did the weather look to you?

HOWIE NEWSOME. No, 'tain't bad. Think maybe it'll clear up for good.

[CONSTABLE WARREN *and* SI CROWELL *continue on their way.* HOWIE NEWSOME *brings the milk first to* MRS. GIBBS's *house. She meets him by the trellis.*]

MRS. GIBBS. Good morning, Howie. Do you think it's going to rain again?

HOWIE NEWSOME. Morning, Mrs. Gibbs. It rained so heavy, I think maybe it'll clear up.

MRS. GIBBS. Certainly hope it will.

HOWIE NEWSOME. How much did you want today?

MRS. GIBBS. I guess I'll need three-a-milk and two-a-cream, Howie. I'm going to have a house full of relations.

HOWIE NEWSOME. My wife says to tell you we both hope they'll be very happy, Mrs. Gibbs. Know they *will*.

MRS. GIBBS. Thanks a lot, Howie. Tell your wife I hope she gits there to the wedding.

HOWIE NEWSOME. Yes, she'll be there; she'll be there if she kin. (*He crosses to* MRS. WEBB's *house.*) Morning, Mrs. Webb.

MRS. WEBB. Oh, good morning, Mr. Newsome. I told you four quarts of milk, but I hope you can spare me another.

HOWIE NEWSOME. Yes'm . . . and the two of cream.

MRS. WEBB. Will it rain all day, Mr. Newsome?

HOWIE NEWSOME. No'm. Just sayin' to Mrs. Gibbs as how it may lighten up. Mrs. Newsome told me to tell you as how we hope they'll both be very happy, Mrs. Webb. Know they *will*.

MRS. WEBB. Thank you, and thank Mrs. Newsome; and we hope to see you all at the wedding.

HOWIE NEWSOME. Yes, Mrs. Webb. We hope to git there. Couldn't miss that. Chck! Bessie!

[*Exit* HOWIE NEWSOME. DR. GIBBS *descends in his shirt sleeves, and sits down at his breakfast table.*]

DR. GIBBS. Well, Ma, the day has come. You're losin' one of your chicks.

MRS. GIBBS. Frank Gibbs, don't you say another word. I feel like crying every minute. Sit down and drink your coffee.

DR. GIBBS. The groom's up shaving himself. Whistling and singing, like he's glad to leave us. Every now and then he says " I do " to the mirror, but it don't sound convincing to me.

MRS. GIBBS. I declare I don't know how he'll get along. I've arranged his clothes and seen to it he's put warm things on — Frank, they're too young! Emily won't think of such things. He'll catch his death of cold within a week. . . . Here's something I made for you.

DR. GIBBS. Why, Julia Hersey! French toast!

MRS. GIBBS. 'Tain't hard to make, and I had to do something.

DR. GIBBS. I remember my wedding morning, Julia.

MRS. GIBBS. Now don't start that, Frank Gibbs. I tell you I can't stand it.

DR. GIBBS. I was the scaredest young fella in the State of New Hampshire. I thought I'd made a mistake for sure. And when I saw you comin' down that aisle I thought you were the prettiest girl I'd ever seen, but the only trouble was that I'd never seen you before. There I was in the Congregational Church marryin' a total stranger.

MRS. GIBBS. And how do you think I felt! . . . Did you hear Rebecca stirring about upstairs?

DR. GIBBS. Only morning in the year she hasn't been managing everybody's business. She's shut up in her room. I got the impression that maybe she's crying.

MRS. GIBBS. Good Lord! This has got to stop. . . . Rebecca! Rebecca! Everything's getting cold down here.

[GEORGE *comes rattling down the stairs, very brisk.*]

GEORGE. Good morning, everybody. Only five more hours to live. (*Makes the gesture of cutting his throat.*)

MRS. GIBBS. Where are you going?

GEORGE. Just stepping across the grass to see my girl.

MRS. GIBBS. Now, George! You take an umbrella, or I won't let you out of this house.

GEORGE. Aw, Ma. It's just a *step!*

MRS. GIBBS. From tomorrow on you can kill yourself in all weathers; but while you're in my house you live wisely, thank you. There are your overshoes right there in the hall. And here's an umbrella.

GEORGE. Aw, Ma!

MRS. GIBBS. Maybe Mrs. Webb isn't used to callers at seven in the morning. Take a cup-a-coffee first.

GEORGE. Be back in a minute. (*He crosses the stage, leaping over the puddles.*) Good morning, Mother Webb.

MRS. WEBB. Goodness! You frightened me! Now, George, you can come in a minute out of the wet, but you know I can't ask you in.

GEORGE. Why not?

MRS. WEBB. George, you know's well as I do: the groom can't see his bride on his wedding day, not until he sees her in church.

GEORGE. Aw! That's just a superstition.

[*Enter* MR. WEBB.]

MR. WEBB. Good morning, George.

GEORGE. Mr. Webb, you don't believe in that superstition, do you?

MR. WEBB. There's a lot of common sense in some superstitions, George.

MRS. WEBB. Millions have folla'd it, George, and you don't want to be the first to fly in the face of custom.

GEORGE. How is Emily?

MRS. WEBB. She hasn't waked up yet. I haven't heard a sound out of her.

GEORGE. Emily's *asleep!*

MRS. WEBB. No wonder! We were up till all hours, sewing and packing. I'll tell you what I'll do; you set down here a minute with Mr. Webb and drink this cup of coffee, and I'll go upstairs and see she doesn't come down and surprise you. There's some bacon, too; but don't be long about it.

[*Exit* MRS. WEBB. *Embarrassed silence.*]

MR. WEBB. Well, George, how are you?

GEORGE. Oh, fine. I'm fine. (*Pause*) Mr. Webb, what sense could there be in a superstition like that?

MR. WEBB. Well, you see, on her wedding morning a girl's head's apt to be full of . . . clothes and things like that. Don't you think that's probably it?

GEORGE. Ye-e-s. I never thought of that.

MR. WEBB. A girl's apt to be a mite nervous on her wedding day. (*Pause*)

GEORGE. I wish a fellow could get married without all that marching up and down.

MR. WEBB. Well, every man that's ever lived has felt that way about it, George; but it hasn't done much good. It's the women that have built up weddings, my boy. From now on they have it pretty much as they like. . . . All those good women standing shoulder to shoulder making sure that the knot's tied in a mighty public way.

GEORGE. But . . . you *believe* in it, don't you, Mr. Webb?

MR. WEBB. Oh, yes; oh, yes. Don't you misunderstand me, my boy. Marriage is a wonderful thing — wonderful thing. And don't you forget that, George.

GEORGE. No, sir. Mr. Webb, how old were you when you got married?

MR. WEBB. Well, you see, I'd been to college and I'd taken a little time to get settled. But Mrs. Webb — she wasn't much older than what Emily is. Oh, age hasn't much to do with it, George — not compared to other things.

GEORGE. What were you going to say, Mr. Webb?

MR. WEBB. Oh, I don't know — was I going to say something? (*Pause*) George, I was thinking the other night of some advice my father gave me when I got married. Charles, he said, Charles, start out early showing who's boss, he said. Best thing to do is to give an order, even if it don't make sense; just so she'll learn to obey. And he said: If anything about your wife irritates you — her conversation, or anything — just get up and leave the house. That'll make it clear to her, he said. And, ah, yes! he said never, *never* let your wife know how much money you have, never.

GEORGE. Well, Mr. Webb . . . I don't think I could . . .

MR. WEBB. So I took the opposite of my father's advice and I've been happy ever since. And let that be a lesson to you, George, never to ask advice on personal matters. . . . George, are you going to raise chickens on your farm?

GEORGE. What?

MR. WEBB. Are you going to raise chickens on your farm?

GEORGE. Uncle Luke's never been much interested, but I thought —

MR. WEBB. A book came into my office the other day, George, on the Philo System of raising chickens. I want you to read it. I'm thinking of beginning in a small way in the back yard, and I'm going to put an incubator in the cellar —

[*Enter* MRS. WEBB.]

MRS. WEBB. Charles, are you talking about that old incubator again? I thought you two'd be talking about things worth while.

MR. WEBB. Well, Myrtle, if you want to give the boy some good advice, I'll go upstairs and leave you alone with him.

MRS. WEBB. Now, George, I'm sorry, but I've got to send you away so that Emily can come down and get some breakfast. She told me to tell you that she sends you her love, but that she doesn't want to lay eyes on you. So good-by, George.

[GEORGE *crosses the stage to his own home and disappears.*]

MR. WEBB. Myrtle, I guess you don't know about that older superstition.

MRS. WEBB. What do you mean, Charles?

MR. WEBB. Since the cave men: the groom shouldn't be left alone with his father-in-law on the day of the wedding, or near it. Now don't forget that!

STAGE MANAGER. Thank you. Thank you, everybody. Now I have to interrupt again here. You see, we want to know how all this began — this wedding, this plan to spend a lifetime together. I'm awfully interested in how big things like that begin. You know how it is. You're twenty-one or twenty-two, and you make some decisions; then whissssh! you're seventy. You've been a lawyer for fifty years, and that white-haired lady at your side has eaten over fifty thousand meals with you. How do such things begin?

George and Emily are going to show you now the conversation they had when they first knew that . . . that . . . as the saying goes . . . they were meant for one another. But before they do it I want you to try and remember what it was like when you were young, when you were fifteen or sixteen. For some reason it is very hard to do: those days when even the little things in life could be almost too exciting to bear. And particularly the days when you were first in love; when you were like a person sleep-walking, and you didn't quite see the street you were in and didn't quite hear everything that was said to you. You're just a little bit crazy. Will you remember that, please?

Now they'll be coming out of high school at three o'clock. George has just been elected president of the junior class; and, as it's June, that means he'll be president of the senior class all next year. And Emily's just been elected secretary and treasurer. I don't have to tell you how important that is. (*He places a board across the backs of two chairs, parallel to the footlights, and places two high stools behind it. This is the counter of* MR. MORGAN's *drugstore.*) All ready!

[EMILY, *carrying an armful of imaginary schoolbooks, comes along Main Street from the left.*]

EMILY. I can't, Louise. I've got to go home. Good-by. . . . Oh, Earnestine! Earnestine! Can you come over tonight and do algebra? I did the first and third in study hall. No, they're not hard. But, Earnestine, that Caesar's awful hard. I don't see why we have to do a thing like that. Come over about seven. Tell your mother you *have* to. G'by. . . . G'by, Helen. G'by, Fred.

[GEORGE, *also carrying books, catches up with her.*]

GEORGE. Can I carry your books home for you, Emily?

EMILY (*coldly*). Thank you. (*She gives them to him.*)

GEORGE. Excuse me a minute, Emily. . . . Say, Bob, get everything ready. I'll be there in a quarter of an hour. If I'm a little late, start practice anyway. And give Herb some long high ones. His eye needs a lot of practice. Seeya later.

EMILY. Good-by, Lizzy.

GEORGE. Good-by, Lizzy. . . . I'm awfully glad you were elected, too, Emily.

EMILY. Thank you.

[*They have been standing on Main Street, almost against the back wall.* GEORGE *is about to take the first steps toward the audience when he stops again.*]

GEORGE. Emily, why are you mad at me?

EMILY. I'm not mad at you.

GEORGE. You . . . you treat me so funny.

EMILY. Well, I might as well say it right out, George. I don't like the whole change that's come over you in the last year. I'm sorry if that hurts your feelings, but I've just got to tell the truth and shame the devil.

GEORGE. I'm awfully sorry, Emily. Wha-a-what do you mean?

EMILY. Well, up to a year ago I used to like you a lot. And I used to watch you as you did everything . . . because we'd been friends so long . . . and then you began spending all your time at baseball . . . and you never even spoke to anybody any more; not even to your own family you didn't . . . and, George, it's a fact, you've got awful conceited and stuck-up, and all the girls say so. They may not say so to your face, but that's what they say about you behind your back; and it hurts me to hear them say it, but I've got to agree with them a little. I'm sorry if it hurts your feelings . . . but I can't be sorry I said it.

GEORGE. I . . . I'm glad you said it, Em-

ily. I never thought that such a thing was happening to me. I guess it's hard for a fella not to have faults creep into his character.

[*They take a step or two in silence, then stand still in misery.*]

EMILY. I always expect a man to be perfect, and I think he should be.

GEORGE. Oh . . . I don't think it's possible to be perfect, Emily.

EMILY. Well, my father is and, as far as I can see, your father is. There's no reason on earth why you shouldn't be, too.

GEORGE. Well, Emily . . . I feel it's the other way round. That men aren't naturally good, but girls are. Like you and your mother and my mother.

EMILY. Well, you might as well know right now that I'm not perfect. It's not as easy for a girl to be perfect as a man, because we girls are more nervous. Now I'm sorry I said all that about you. I don't know what made me say it.

GEORGE. No, no — I guess if it's the truth you ought to say it. You stick to it, Emily.

EMILY. I don't know if it's the truth or not. And I suddenly feel that it isn't important at all.

GEORGE. Emily, would you like an ice-cream soda, or something, before you go home?

EMILY. Well, thank you. . . . I would.

[*They come into the drugstore and seat themselves on the stools.*]

STAGE MANAGER (*as* MR. MORGAN). Hello, George. Hello, Emily. What'll you have? Why, Emily Webb, what've you been crying about?

GEORGE (*groping for an explanation*). She . . . she just got an awful scare, Mr. Morgan. She almost got run over by that hardware-store wagon. Everybody always says that Tom Huckins drives like a crazy man.

STAGE MANAGER. Here, take a drink of water, Emily. You look all shook up. . . . There! Now, what'll you have?

EMILY. I'll have a strawberry phosphate, thank you, Mr. Morgan.

OUR TOWN is brought to life by skilled actors on a bare stage with the merest suggestion of properties. The bare plank represents the drugstore fountain at which George and Emily settle their future. (VanDamm)

GEORGE. No, no. You go and have an ice-cream soda with me, Emily. Two strawberry ice-cream sodas, Mr. Morgan.

STAGE MANAGER (*working the faucets*). Yes, sir. I tell you, you've got to look both ways before you cross Main Street these days. Gets worse every year. There are a hundred and twenty-five horses in Grover's Corners this minute I'm talking to you. State inspector was in here yesterday. And now they're bringing in these auto-mobiles, the best thing to do is to just stay home. Why, I can remember the time when a dog could lie down all day in the middle of Main Street and nothing would come to disturb him. . . . Yes, Miss Ellis; be with you in a minute. . . . Here are your sodas. Enjoy 'em. (*He goes off.*)

EMILY. They're so expensive.

GEORGE. No, no — don't you think of that. We're celebrating. First, we're celebrating our election. And then do you know what else I'm celebrating?

EMILY. No.

GEORGE. I'm celebrating because I've got a friend who tells me all the things that ought to be told me.

EMILY. George, *please* don't think of that.

I don't know why I said it. It's not true. You're —

GEORGE. No, you stick to it, Emily. I'm glad you spoke to me like you did. But you'll see: I'm going to change so quick — you bet I'm going to change. And, Emily, I want to ask you a favor.

EMILY. What?

GEORGE. Emily, if I go away to State Agriculture College next year, will you write me a letter once in a while?

EMILY. I certainly will. I certainly will, George. (*Pause*) It certainly seems like being away three years you'd get out of touch with things.

GEORGE. No, no. I mustn't do that. You see, I'm not only going to be just a farmer. After awhile, maybe, I'll run for something to get elected. So your letters'll be very important to me; you know, telling me what's going on here and everything. . . .

EMILY. Just the same, three years is a long time. Maybe letters from Grover's Corners wouldn't be so interesting after a while. Grover's Corners isn't a very important place when you think of all New Hampshire; but I think it's a very nice town.

GEORGE. The day wouldn't come when I

wouldn't want to know everything that's happening here. I know *that's* true, Emily.

EMILY. Well, I'll try to make my letters interesting. (*Pause*)

GEORGE. Y'know, Emily, whenever I meet a farmer I ask him if he thinks it's important to go to agricultural school to be a good farmer.

EMILY. Why, George —

GEORGE. Yeah, and some of them say that it's even a waste of time. You can get all those things, anyway, out of the pamphlets the government sends out. And Uncle Luke's getting old — he's about ready for me to start in taking over his farm tomorrow, if I could.

EMILY. My!

GEORGE. And, like you say, being gone all that time . . . in other places and meeting other people . . . If anything like that can happen, I don't want to go away. I guess new people aren't any better than old ones. I'll bet they almost never are. Emily, I feel that you're as good a friend as I've got. I don't need to go and meet the people in other towns.

EMILY. But, George, maybe it's very important for you to go and learn all that about cattle judging and soils and those things. And if you're going into politics, maybe you ought to meet people from other parts of the state . . . of course, I don't know.

GEORGE (*after a pause*). Emily, I'm going to make up my mind right now. I won't go. I'll tell Pa about it tonight.

EMILY. Why, George, I don't see why you have to decide right now. It's a whole year away.

GEORGE. Emily, I'm glad you spoke to me about that . . . that fault in my character. And what you said was right; but there was *one* thing wrong in it, and that was when you said that for a year I wasn't noticing people, and . . . you, for instance. Listen, Emily . . . you say you were watching me when I did everything. . . . Why, I was doing the same about you all the time. Why, sure — I always thought about you as one of the chief people I thought about. I al-

ways made sure where you were sitting on the bleachers, and who you were with. And we've always had lots of talks . . . and joking, in the halls; and they always meant a lot to me. Of course, they weren't as good as the talk we're having now. Lately I'd been noticing that you'd been acting kind of funny to me; and for three days I've been trying to walk home with you, but something's always got in the way. Yesterday I was standing over against the wall waiting for you, and you walked home with Miss Corcoran.

EMILY. George! . . . Life's awful funny! How could I have known that? Why, I thought —

GEORGE. Listen, Emily, I'm going to tell you why I'm not going to agricultural school. I think that once you've found a person that you're very fond of . . . I mean a person who's fond of you, too — at least enough to be interested in your character . . . Well, I think that's just as important as college is, and even more so. That's what I think.

EMILY. I think it's awfully important, too.

GEORGE. Emily.

EMILY. Yes, George.

GEORGE. Emily, if I improve and make a big change . . . would you be . . . I mean, *could* you be . . .

EMILY. I . . . I am now; I always have been. (*Pause*)

GEORGE. So I guess this is an important talk we've been having.

EMILY. Yes.

GEORGE (*taking a deep breath and straightening his back*). Wait just a minute and I'll take you home. (*He rises and goes to the* STAGE MANAGER, *who appears and comes toward him.*) Mr. Morgan, I'll have to go home and get the money to pay you for this. It'll only take me a minute.

STAGE MANAGER. What's that? George Gibbs, do you mean to tell me —

GEORGE. Yes, but I had reasons, Mr. Morgan. Look, here's my gold watch to keep until I come back with the money.

STAGE MANAGER. That's all right. Keep your watch. I'll trust you.

GEORGE. I'll be back in five minutes.

STAGE MANAGER. I'll trust you ten years, George — not a day more. . . . Got all over your shock, Emily?

EMILY. Yes, thank you, Mr. Morgan. It was nothing.

GEORGE (*taking up the books from the counter*). I'm ready.

[*They walk in grave silence down the stage, turn, and pass through the trellis at the Webbs' back door and disappear.*]

STAGE MANAGER. Thank you, Emily. Thank you, George. . . . Now before we go on to the wedding, there are still some more things we ought to know about this — about this marriage. I want to know some more about how the parents took it; but what I want to know most of all is — oh, you know what I mean — what Grover's Corners thought about marriage, anyway. You know's well as I do: people are never able to say right out what they think of money, or death, or fame, or marriage. You've got to catch it between the lines; you've got to *over*hear it.

Oh, Doctor! Mrs. Gibbs!

[*They appear at their side of the stage and exchange a glance of understanding with him. The* STAGE MANAGER *lays across two chairs the same plank that served as a drugstore counter, and it has now become* MRS. GIBBS's *ironing board.* DR. GIBBS *sits down in a rocker and smokes.* MRS. GIBBS *irons a moment in silence, then goes to the foot of the stairs.*]

MRS. GIBBS (*calling*). Rebecca! It's time you turned out your light and went to sleep. George, you'd better get some sleep, too.

REBECCA'S VOICE. Ma, I haven't finished my English.

MRS. GIBBS. What? Well, I bet you haven't been working, Rebecca. You've been reading that Sears, Roebuck catalogue, that's what you've been doing. All right, I'll give you ten more minutes. If you haven't finished by then, you'll just have to fail the course and be a disgrace to your father and me. . . . George, what are you doing?

GEORGE'S VOICE (*hurt*). I'm doing history.

MRS. GIBBS. Well, you'd better go to bed. You're probably sleeping at the desk as it is. (*She casts an amused eye at her husband and returns to her ironing.*)

DR. GIBBS. I had a long talk with the boy today.

MRS. GIBBS. Did you?

DR. GIBBS. I tell you, Mrs. G., there's nothing so terrifying in the world as a son. The relation of a father to a son is the confounded awkwardest — I always come away feeling like a soggy sponge of hypocrisy.

MRS. GIBBS. Well, a mother and a daughter's no picnic, let me tell you.

DR. GIBBS. George is set on it: he wants to marry Emily soon as school's out and take her right on to the farm. (*Pause*) He says he can sit up nights and learn agriculture from government pamphlets, without going to college for it.

MRS. GIBBS. He always was crazy about farming. Gets that from my people.

DR. GIBBS. At a pinch I guess he could start in farming; but I swear I think he's too young to get married. Julia, he's just a green half-grown kid. He isn't ready to be a family man.

MRS. GIBBS. No, he ain't. You're right. But he's a good boy and I wouldn't like to think of him being alone out there . . . coming into town Satiddy nights, like any old farm hand, tuckered out from work and looking for excitement. He might get into bad ways. It wouldn't be enough fun for him to come and sit by our stove, and holding hands with Emily for a year mightn't be enough either. He might lose interest in her.

DR. GIBBS. Hm.

MRS. GIBBS. Frank, I been watching her. George is a lucky boy when you think of all the silly girls in the world.

DR. GIBBS. But, Julia, George *married*. That great, gangling, selfish nincompoop.

MRS. GIBBS. Yes, I know. (*She takes up a collar and examines it.*) Frank, what do you do to your collars? Do you gnaw 'em? I never saw such a man for collars.

DR. GIBBS. Julia, when I married you, do you know what one of my terrors was in getting married?

MRS. GIBBS. Pshaw! Go on with you!

DR. GIBBS. I was afraid we weren't going to have material for conversation more'n'ld last us a few weeks. I was afraid we'd run out and eat our meals in silence. That's a fact. You and I've been conversing for twenty years now without any noticeable barren spells.

MRS. GIBBS. Well, good weather, bad weather, 'tain't very choice but I always manage to find something to say. (*Pause*)

DR. GIBBS. What do you think? What do you think, Julia? Shall we tell the boy he can go ahead and get married?

MRS. GIBBS. Seems like it's up to us to decide. Myrtle and Charles Webb are willing. They think it's a good idea to throw the young people into the sea and let'm sink or swim, as soon as they're ready.

DR. GIBBS. What does that mean? Must we decide right now? This minute?

MRS. GIBBS. There you go putting the responsibility on me!

DR. GIBBS. Here it is, almost April. . . . I'll go up and say a word to him right now before he goes to bed. (*He rises.*) You're sure, Julia? You've nothing more to add?

MRS. GIBBS (*stops ironing a moment*). I don't know what to say. Seems like it's too much to ask, for a big outdoor boy like that to go and get shut up in classrooms for three years. And once he's on the farm he might just as well have a companion, seeing he's found a fine girl like Emily. . . . People are meant to live two-by-two in this world. . . . Yes, Frank, go up and tell him it's all right.

[DR. GIBBS *crosses and is about to call when* MRS. GIBBS, *her hands on her cheeks, staring into the audience, speaks in sharp alarm.*]

Wait a minute! Wait a minute! (*Then, resuming her ironing*) No — go and tell him.

DR. GIBBS. Why did you stop then, Julia?

MRS. GIBBS. Oh, you know: I thought of all those times we went through in the first years when George and Rebecca were babies — you walking up and down with them at three in the morning, the whooping cough, the time George fell off the porch. You and I were twenty-five years old, and more. It's wonderful how one forgets one's troubles, like that. . . . Yes, Frank, go upstairs and tell him. It's worth it.

DR. GIBBS. Yes, they'll have a lot of troubles, but that's none of our business. Let'm. Everybody has a right to his own troubles. You ought to be present, Julia — important occasion like that. I'll call him. . . . George! Oh, George!

GEORGE'S VOICE. Yes, Pa.

DR. GIBBS. Can you come down a minute? Your mother and I want to speak to you.

GEORGE. Yeah, sure.

MRS. GIBBS (*putting her arm through her husband's*). Lord, what fool I am; I'm trembling all over. There's nothing to tremble about.

STAGE MANAGER. Thank you! Thank you! . . . Now we're ready to go on with the wedding.

[*While he talks, the actors remove the chairs and tables and trellises from the Gibbs and Webb homes. They arrange the pews for the church in the back of the stage. The congregation will sit facing the back wall. The aisle of the church is in the middle of the scene. A small platform is placed against the back wall; on this the* STAGE MANAGER *as minister can stand.*]

There are a lot of things to be said about a wedding; there are a lot of thoughts that go on during a wedding. We can't get them all into one wedding, naturally, and especially not into a wedding at Grover's Corners, where they're awfully plain and short. In this wedding I play the minister. That gives me the right to say a few more things about it.

For a while now, the play gets pretty serious. Y'see, some churches say that marriage is a sacrament. I don't quite know what that means, but I can guess. Like Mrs. Gibbs said a few minutes ago: People were made to live two-by-two. This is a good wedding, but people are so put together that even at a good wedding there's a lot of confusion way down deep in people's minds; and we thought that that ought to be in our play, too.

The real hero of this scene isn't on the stage at all, and you know who that is. It's like what one of those European fellas said: Every child born into the world is nature's attempt to make a perfect human being. Well, we've seen nature pushing and contriving for some time now. We all know that nature's interested in quantity; but I think she's interested in quality, too — that's why I'm in the ministry. Maybe she's trying to make another good governor for New Hampshire. And don't forget the other witnesses at this wedding — the ancestors. Millions of them. Most of them set out to live two-by-two, also. Millions of them.

Well, that's all my sermon. 'Twan't very long, anyway.

[*The organ starts playing Handel's " Largo." The congregation streams into the church and sits in silence.* MRS. WEBB, *on the way to her place, turns back and speaks to the audience.*]

MRS. WEBB. I don't know why on earth I should be crying. I suppose there's nothing to cry about. It came over me at breakfast this morning; there was Emily eating her breakfast as she's done for seventeen years, and now she's going off to eat it in someone else's house. I suppose that's it. And Emily! She suddenly said: I can't eat another mouthful, and she put her head down on the table and *she* cried.

[*The choir starts singing " Love Divine, All Love Excelling."* GEORGE *has reached the stage. He stares at the congregation a moment, then takes a few steps of withdrawal toward the right proscenium pillar.*]

GEORGE (*darkly, to himself*). I wish I were back at school. . . . I don't want to get married.

[*His mother has left her seat and come toward him. She stops, looking at him anxiously.*]

MRS. GIBBS. George, what's the matter?

GEORGE. Ma, I don't want to grow *old*. Why's everybody pushing me so?

MRS. GIBBS. Why, George . . . you wanted it.

GEORGE. Why do I have to get married at all? Listen, Ma, for the last time I ask you —

MRS. GIBBS. No, no, George . . . you're a man now.

GEORGE. Listen, Ma, you never listen to me. All I want to do is to be a fella. Why do —

MRS. GIBBS. George! If anyone should hear you! Now stop. Why, I'm ashamed of you!

GEORGE (*passing his hand over his forehead*). What's the matter? I've been dreaming. Where's Emily?

MRS. GIBBS. Gracious! You gave me such a turn.

GEORGE. Cheer up, Ma. What are you looking so funny for? Cheer up; I'm getting married.

MRS. GIBBS. Let me catch my breath a minute.

GEORGE. Now, Ma, you save Thursday nights. Emily and I are coming over to dinner every Thursday night . . . you'll see. Ma, what are you crying for? Come on, we've got to get ready for this.

[*In the meantime* EMILY, *in white and wearing her wedding veil, has come through the audience and mounted on to the stage. She, too, draws back when she sees the congregation in the church. The choir begins " Blessed Be the Tie That Binds."*]

EMILY. I never felt so alone in my whole life. And George over there, looking so . . . I *hate* him. I wish I were dead. Papa! Papa!

MR. WEBB (*leaving his seat in the pews and coming toward her anxiously*). Emily! Emily! Now don't get upset.

EMILY. But, Papa, I don't want to get married.

MR. WEBB. Sh-sh — Emily. Everything's all right.

EMILY. Why can't I stay for a while just as I am? Let's go away.———

MR. WEBB. No, no, Emily. Now stop and think.

EMILY. Don't you remember that you used to say — all the time you used to say that I was *your* girl. There must be lots of places we can go to. Let's go away. I'll work for you. I could keep house.

MR. WEBB. Sh. . . . You mustn't think of such things. You're just nervous, Emily. Now, now — you're marrying the best young fellow in the world. George is a fine fellow.

EMILY. But, Papa —

MR. WEBB. George! George!

[MRS. GIBBS *returns to her seat.* GEORGE *hears* MR. WEBB *and looks up.* MR. WEBB *beckons to him. They move to the center of the stage.*]

I'm giving away my daughter, George. Do you think you can take care of her?

GEORGE. Mr. Webb, I want to . . . I want to try. Emily, I'm going to do my best. I love you, Emily. I need you.

EMILY. Well, if you love me, help me. All I want is someone to love me.

GEORGE. I will, Emily.

EMILY. If ever I'm sick or in trouble, that's what I mean.

GEORGE. Emily, I'll try. I'll try.

EMILY. And I mean for ever. Do you hear? For ever and ever.

[*They fall into each other's arms. The March from* Lohengrin *is heard.*]

MR. WEBB. Come, they're waiting for us. Now you know it'll be all right. Come, quick.

[GEORGE *slips away and takes his place beside the* STAGE MANAGER-CLERGYMAN. EMILY *proceeds up the aisle on her father's arm.*]

STAGE MANAGER. Do you, George, take this woman. Emily, to be your wedded wife, to have . . .

[MRS. SOAMES *has been sitting in the last row of the congregation. She now turns to her neighbors and speaks in a shrill voice.*]

MRS. SOAMES. Perfectly lovely wedding! Loveliest wedding I ever saw. Oh, I do love a good wedding, don't you? Doesn't she make a lovely bride?

GEORGE. I do.

STAGE MANAGER. Do you, Emily, take this man, George, to be your wedded husband . . .

MRS. SOAMES. Don't know *when* I've seen such a lovely wedding. But I always cry. Don't know why it is, but I always cry. I just like to see young people happy, don't you? Oh, I think it's lovely.

[*The ring. The kiss. The stage is suddenly arrested into silent tableau.*]

STAGE MANAGER (*his eyes on the distance, says to the audience*). I've married two hundred couples in my day. Do I believe in it? I don't know. M____ marries N____. Millions of them. The cottage, the gocart, the Sunday afternoon drives in the Ford, the first rheumatism, the grandchildren, the second rheumatism, the deathbed, the reading of the will — Once in a thousand times it's interesting. Well, let's have Mendelssohn's " Wedding March "!

[*The organ picks up the March. The bride and groom come down the aisle, radiant but trying to be very dignified.*]

MRS. SOAMES. Aren't they a lovely couple? Oh, I've never been to such a nice wedding. I'm sure they'll be happy. I always say *happiness,* that's the great thing! The important thing is to be happy.

[*The bride and groom reach the steps leading into the audience. A bright light is thrown upon them. They descend into the auditorium and run up the aisle joyously.*]

STAGE MANAGER. That's all the second act. Ten minutes' intermission, folks.

## Suggestions for Study of Act II

1. What effect does the dramatist get by having the second act open with the same people and the same activities as the first?

2. Do you attach any importance to the fact that the wedding day was a rainy one?

3. Does the conversation between Emily and George after school help you to understand " how all this began," as the Stage Manager says? Why had Emily resented George's spending all his time at baseball? Do they seem to realize what a serious step they are approaching? Find lines that show that they do realize it, and others that make the two of them sound young and inexperienced. What are some of the things they keep saying are " important "?

4. Why do both the parents and the young couple have spells of reluctance to go on with the wedding? What had been Dr. Gibbs's own terror about getting married? What do you think of his statement that " everybody has a right to his own troubles "?

5. What does Mrs. Soames stand for in the wedding scene? Did you like her, or think she was silly? Notice whether you change your opinion of her any in the last act. She has one definite virtue. See if you can tell what it is.

6. Why does the Stage Manager say that this is a " good " wedding? What does he say every child born into the world is?

## ACT III

*During the intermission the audience has seen the actors arranging the stage. On the right-hand side, a little right of the center, ten or twelve ordinary chairs have been placed in three openly spaced rows facing the audience. These are graves in the cemetery.*

*Toward the end of the intermission the actors enter and take their places. The front row contains, toward the center of the stage, an empty chair; then* MRS. GIBBS *and* SIMON STIMSON. *The second row contains, among others,* MRS. SOAMES. *The third row has* WALLY WEBB. *The dead sit in a quiet without stiffness and in a patience without listlessness.*

*The* STAGE MANAGER *takes his accustomed place and waits for the house lights to go down.*

STAGE MANAGER. This time nine years have gone by, friends — summer, 1913. Gradual changes in Grover's Corners. Horses are getting rarer. Farmers coming into town in Fords. Chief difference is in the young people, far as I can see. They want to go to the moving pictures all the time. They want to wear clothes like they see there . . . want to be citified. Everybody locks their house doors now at night. Ain't seen any burglars in town yet, but everybody's heard about 'em. But you'd be surprised, though — on the whole, things don't change much at Grover's Corners.

Guess you want to know what all these chairs are here fur. Smarter ones have guessed it already. I don't know how you feel about such things, but this certainly is a beautiful place. It's on a hilltop — a windy hilltop — lots of sky, lots of clouds, often lots of sun and moon and stars. You come up here on a fine afternoon and you can see range on range of hills — awful blue they are — up there by Lake Sunapee and Lake Winnepesaukee . . . and way up, if you've got a glass, you can see the White Mountains and Mt. Washington — where North Conway and Conway is. And, of course, our favorite mountain, Mt. Monadnock's right here — and all around it lie these towns — Jaffrey, 'n East Jaffrey, 'n Peterborough, 'n Dublin; and (*then, pointing down in the audience*) there, quite a ways down, is Grover's Corners.

Yes, beautiful spot up here. Mountain laurel and li-lacks. I often wonder why people like to be buried in Woodlawn and Brooklyn when they might pass the same time up here in New Hampshire. Over in that corner (*pointing to stage left*) are the old stones — 1670, 1680. Strong-minded people that come a long way to be independent. Summer people walk around there laughing at the funny words on the tombstones . . . it don't do any harm. And genealogists come up from Boston — get paid by city people for looking up their an-

cestors. They want to make sure they're
Daughters of the American Revolution and
of the *Mayflower*. . . . Well, I guess that
don't do any harm, either. Wherever you
come near the human race, there's layers
and layers of nonsense.

Over there are some Civil War veterans
too. Iron flags on their graves. . . . New
Hampshire boys . . . had a notion that the
Union ought to be kept together, though
they'd never seen more than fifty miles of
it themselves. All they knew was the name,
friends — the United States of America.
The United States of America. And they
went and died about it.

This here is the new part of the cemetery.
Here's your friend, Mrs. Gibbs. 'N let me
see — Here's Mr. Stimson, organist at the
Congregational Church. And over there's
Mrs. Soames, who enjoyed the wedding so
— you remember? Oh, and a lot of others.
And Editor Webb's boy, Wallace, whose appendix burst while he was on a Boy Scout
trip to Crawford Notch. Yes, an awful lot
of sorrow has sort of quieted down up here.
People just wild with grief have brought
their relatives up to this hill. We all know
how it is. And then time . . . and sunny
days . . . and rainy days . . . 'n snow
. . . tz-tz-tz. We're all glad they're in a
beautiful place, and we're coming up here
ourselves when our fit's over. This certainly
is an important part of Grover's Corners.
A lot of thoughts come up here, night and
day, but there's no post office.

Now I'm going to tell you some things
you know already. You know'm as well as
I do, but you don't take'm out and look at'm
very often. I don't care what they say with
their mouths — everybody knows that
*something* is eternal. And it ain't houses,
and it ain't names, and it ain't earth, and it
ain't even the stars . . . everybody knows
in their bones that *something* is eternal, and
that something has to do with human beings. All the greatest people ever lived have
been telling us that for five thousand years,
and yet you'd be surprised how people are
always losing hold of it. There's something
way down deep that's eternal about every

human being. (*Pause*) You know as well as
I do that the dead don't stay interested in
us living people for very long. Gradually,
gradually, they let hold of the earth . . .
and the ambitions they had . . . and the
pleasures they had . . . and the things
they suffered . . . and the people they
loved. They get weaned away from earth.
That's the way I put it — weaned away.
Yes, they stay here while the earth part of
'em burns away, burns out; and all that
time they slowly get indifferent to what's
goin' on in Grover's Corners.

They're waitin'. They're waitin' for
something that they feel is comin'. Something important and great. Aren't they
waitin' for the eternal part in them to come
out clear? Some of the things they're going
to say maybe'll hurt your feelings — but
that's the way it is: mother 'n daughter . . .
husband 'n wife . . . enemy 'n enemy . . .
money 'n miser — all those terribly important things kind of grow pale around here.
And what's left? What's left when memory's gone, and your identity, Mrs. Smith?
(*He looks at the audience a minute, then
turns to the stage.*)

Well! There are some *living* people.
There's Joe Stoddard, our undertaker, supervising a new-made grave. And here
comes a Grover's Corners boy, that left
town to go out West.

[JOE STODDARD *has hovered about in the
background.* SAM CRAIG *enters left, wiping his forehead from the exertion. He
carries an umbrella and strolls front.*]

SAM CRAIG. Good afternoon, Joe Stoddard.

JOE STODDARD. Good afternoon, good afternoon. Let me see now: Do I know you?

SAM CRAIG. I'm Sam Craig.

JOE STODDARD. Gracious sakes' alive! Of
all people! I should'a knowed you'd be
back for the funeral. You've been away a
long time, Sam.

SAM CRAIG. Yes, I've been away over
twelve years. I'm in business out in Buffalo
now, Joe. But I was in the East when I got
news of my cousin's death, so I thought I'd

combine things a little and come and see the old home. You look well.

JOE STODDARD. Yes, yes, can't complain. Very sad, our journey today, Samuel.

SAM CRAIG. Yes.

JOE STODDARD. Yes, yes. I always say I hate to supervise when a young person is taken. I see you brought your umbrella. It's going to rain and make it sadder still, seems like. They'll be here in a few minutes now. I had to come here early today — my son's supervisin' at the home.

SAM CRAIG (*reading stones*). Old Farmer McCarty. I used to do chores for him — after school. He had the lumbago.

JOE STODDARD. Yes, we brought Farmer McCarty here a number of years ago now.

SAM CRAIG (*staring at* MRS. GIBBS's *knees*). Why, this is my Aunt Julia. . . . I'd forgotten that she'd . . . of course, of course.

JOE STODDARD. Yes, Doc Gibbs lost his wife two, three years ago . . . about this time. And today's another pretty bad blow for him, too.

MRS. GIBBS (*to* SIMON STIMSON, *in an even voice*). That's my sister Carey's boy, Sam — Sam Craig.

SIMON STIMSON. I'm always uncomfortable when *they're* around.

MRS. GIBBS. Simon.

SIMON STIMSON. They and their nonsense and their idiotic glee at being alive.

MRS. GIBBS. Simon, be patient.

SAM CRAIG. Do they choose their own verses much, Joe?

JOE STODDARD. No . . . not usual. Mostly the bereaved pick a verse.

SAM CRAIG. Doesn't sound like Aunt Julia. There aren't many of those Hersey sisters left now. Let me see. Where are — I wanted to look at my father's and mother's . . .

JOE STODDARD. Over there with the Craigs. . . . Avenue F.

SAM CRAIG (*reading* SIMON STIMSON'S *epitaph*). He was organist at church, wasn't he? Hm, drank a lot, we used to say.

JOE STODDARD. Nobody was supposed to know about it. He'd seen a peck of trouble.

Those musical fellas ain't like the rest of us, I reckon. (*Behind his hand*) Took his own life, y' know?

SAM CRAIG. Oh, did he?

JOE STODDARD. Hung himself in the attic. They tried to hush it up, but of course it got around. His wife's just married Senator Barstow. Many a time I've seen her, eleven o'clock at night, goin' around the streets huntin' for her husband. Think o' that! Now she's married to Senator Barstow over at Manchester. He chose his own epy-taph. You can see it there. It ain't a verse exactly.

SAM CRAIG. Why, it's just some notes of music! What is it?

JOE STODDARD. Oh, I wouldn't know. It was wrote up in the Boston papers at the time.

SAM CRAIG. Joe, what did she die of?

JOE STODDARD. Who?

SAM CRAIG. My cousin.

JOE STODDARD. Oh, didn't you know? Had some trouble bringing a baby into the world. Let's see, today's Friday — 'twas almost a week ago now.

SAM CRAIG (*putting up his umbrella*). Did the baby live?

JOE STODDARD (*raising his coat collar*). No. 'Twas her second, though. There's a little boy 'bout four years old.

SAM CRAIG. The grave's going to be over there?

JOE STODDARD. Yes, there ain't much more room over here among the Gibbses, so they're opening up a whole new Gibbs section over by Avenue B. You'll excuse me now. I see they're comin'.

THE DEAD (*not lugubrious, and strongly New England in accent*). Rain'll do a lot of good. . . . Yes, reckon things were gettin' downright parched. Don't look like it's goin' to last long, tho'. . . . Lemuel, you remember the floods of seventy-nine? Carried away all the bridges but one.

[*From left to right, at the back of the stage, comes a procession. Four men carry a casket, invisible to us. All the rest are under umbrellas. One can vaguely see* DR.

ANOTHER SCENE FROM THE STAGE PRODUCTION. Here we see Emily after her death curiously looking at the dead whom she is about to join. (VanDamm)

GIBBS, GEORGE, *the* WEBBS, *etc. They gather about a grave in the back center of the stage, a little to the left of center.*]

MRS. SOAMES. Who is it, Julia?

MRS. GIBBS (*without raising her eyes*). My daughter-in-law, Emily Webb.

MRS. SOAMES (*a little surprised, but no emotion*). Well, I declare! The road up here must have been awful muddy. What did she die of, Julia?

MRS. GIBBS. In childbirth.

MRS. SOAMES. Childbirth. (*Almost with a laugh*) I'd forgotten all about that! My, wasn't life awful (*with a sigh*) and wonderful.

SIMON STIMSON (*with a sideways glance*). Wonderful, was it?

MRS. GIBBS. Simon! Now, remember!

MRS. SOAMES. I remember Emily's wedding. Wasn't it a lovely wedding! And I remember her reading the class poem at graduation exercises. Emily was one of the brightest girls ever graduated from high school. I've heard Principal Wilkins say so time after time. I called on them at their new farm just before I died. Perfectly beautiful farm.

A WOMAN FROM AMONG THE DEAD. It's on the same road we lived on.

A MAN AMONG THE DEAD. Yes, just near the Elks' picnic grounds. Remember, Joe?

By the lake where we always used to go Fourth of July? Right smart farm.

[*They subside. The group by the grave start singing " Blessed Be the Tie That Binds."*]

A WOMAN AMONG THE DEAD. I always liked that hymn. I was hopin' they'd sing a hymn.

A MAN AMONG THE DEAD. My wife — my second wife — knows all the verses of about every hymn there is. It just beats the Dutch — she can go through them all by heart.

[*Pause. Suddenly* EMILY *appears from among the umbrellas. She is wearing a white dress. Her hair is down her back and tied by a white ribbon like a little girl's. She comes slowly, gazing wonderingly at* THE DEAD, *a little dazed. She stops halfway and smiles faintly.*]

EMILY. Hello.

VOICES AMONG THE DEAD. Hello, Emily. H'lo, M's. Gibbs.

EMILY. Hello, Mother Gibbs.

MRS. GIBBS. Emily.

EMILY. Hello. (*The hymn continues.* EMILY *looks back at the funeral. She says dreamily*) It's raining.

MRS. GIBBS. Yes. . . . They'll be gone soon, dear. Just rest yourself.

[EMILY *sits down in the empty chair by* MRS. GIBBS.]

EMILY. It seems thousands and thousands of years since I . . . How stupid they all look. They don't have to look like that!

MRS. GIBBS. Don't look at them now, dear. They'll be gone soon.

EMILY. Oh, I wish I'd been here a long time. I don't like being new here. . . . How do you do, Mr. Stimson?

SIMON STIMSON. How do you do, Emily.

[EMILY *continues to look about her with a wan and wondering smile, but for a moment her eyes do not return to the funeral group. As though to shut out from her mind the thought of that group, she starts speaking to* MRS. GIBBS. *with a touch of nervousness.*]

EMILY. Mother Gibbs, George and I have made that farm into just the best place you ever saw. We thought of you all the time. We wanted to show you the new barn and a great long ce-ment drinking fountain for the stock. We bought that out of the money you left us.

MRS. GIBBS. I did?

EMILY. Don't you remember, Mother Gibbs — the legacy you left us? Why, it was over three hundred and fifty dollars.

MRS. GIBBS. Yes, yes, Emily.

EMILY. Well, there's a patent device on this drinking fountain so that it never overflows, Mother Gibbs, and it never sinks below a certain mark they have there. It's fine. (*Her voice trails off, and her eyes return to the funeral group.*) It won't be the same to George without me, but it's a lovely farm. (*Suddenly she looks directly at* MRS. GIBBS.) Live people don't understand, do they?

MRS. GIBBS. No, dear — not very much.

EMILY. They're sort of shut up in little boxes, aren't they? I feel as though I knew them last a thousand years ago. . . . My boy is spending the day at Mrs. Carter's. (*She sees* MR. CARTER *among* THE DEAD.) Oh, Mr. Carter, my little boy is spending the day at your house.

MR. CARTER. Is he?

EMILY. Yes, he loves it there. . . . Mother Gibbs, we 'have a Ford, too. Never gives any trouble. I don't drive, though. Mother Gibbs, when does this feeling go away? Of being . . . one of *them?* How long does it . . .

MRS. GIBBS. Sh! dear. Just wait and be patient.

EMILY (*with a sigh*). I know. . . . Look, they're finished. They're going.

MRS. GIBBS. Sh. . . .

[*The umbrellas leave the stage.* DR. GIBBS *comes over to his wife's grave and stands before it a moment.* EMILY *looks up at his face.* MRS. GIBBS *does not raise her eyes.*]

EMILY. Look! Father Gibbs is bringing some of my flowers to you. He looks just like George, doesn't he? Oh, Mother Gibbs, I never realized before how troubled and how . . . how in the dark live persons are. From morning till night that's all they are — troubled.

[DR. GIBBS *goes off.*]

THE DEAD. Little cooler than it was. . . . Yes, that rain cooled it off a little. Those northeast winds always do the same thing, don't they? If it isn't a rain, it's a three-day blow. . . . Reckon it may clear up before night; often does.

[*A patient calm falls on the stage. The* STAGE MANAGER *appears at his proscenium pillar, smoking.* EMILY *sits up abruptly, with an idea.*]

EMILY. But, Mother Gibbs, one can go back; one can go back there again . . . into living. I feel it. I know it. Why, just then for a moment I was thinking about . . . about the farm . . . and for a minute I *was* there, and my baby was on my lap as plain as day.

MRS. GIBBS. Yes, of course you can.

EMILY. I can go back there and live all those days over again . . . why not?

MRS. GIBBS. All I can say is, Emily, don't.

EMILY (*taking a few steps toward the* STAGE MANAGER). But it's true, isn't it? I

can go and live . . . back there . . .
again.

STAGE MANAGER. Yes, some have tried —
but they soon come back here.

MRS. GIBBS. Don't do it, Emily.

MRS. SOAMES. Emily, don't. It's not what
you think it'd be.

EMILY. But I won't live over a sad day.
I'll choose a happy one — I'll choose the
day I first knew that I loved George. Why
should that be painful?

[*They are silent. Her question turns to the*
STAGE MANAGER.]

STAGE MANAGER. You not only live it, but
you watch yourself living it.

EMILY. Yes?

STAGE MANAGER. And as you watch it, you
see the thing that they — down there —
never know. You see the future. You know
what's going to happen afterward.

EMILY. But is that — painful? Why?

MRS. GIBBS. That's not the only reason
why you shouldn't do it, Emily. When
you've been here longer, you'll see that our
life here is our hope that soon we'll forget
all that, and think only of what's ahead,
and be ready for what's ahead. When you've
been here longer, you'll understand.

EMILY (*softly*). But, Mother Gibbs, how
can I ever forget that life? It's all I know.
It's all I had.

[MRS. GIBBS *does not answer.*]

Mr. Stimson, did you go back?

SIMON STIMSON (*sharply*). No.

EMILY. Did you, Mrs. Soames?

MRS. SOAMES. Oh, Emily. It isn't wise.
Really, it isn't. All we can do is just warn
you. It won't be what you expect.

EMILY (*slowly*). But it's a thing I must
know for myself. I'll choose a happy day,
anyway.

MRS. GIBBS. No. At least, choose an unimportant day. Choose the least important
day in your life. It will be important
enough.

EMILY (*to the* STAGE MANAGER). Then it
can't be since I was married, or since the
baby was born. I can choose a birthday at

least, can't I? . . . I choose my twelfth
birthday.

STAGE MANAGER. All right. February 11,
1899. A Tuesday. . . . Do you want any
special time of day?

EMILY. Oh, I want the whole day.

STAGE MANAGER. We'll begin at dawn.
You remember it had been snowing for several days; but it had stopped the night before, and they had begun clearing the roads.
The sun's coming up.

EMILY (*with a cry*). There's Main Street.
. . . Why, that's Mr. Morgan's drugstore
before he changed it! . . . And there's the
livery stable. (*She walks toward the back
of the stage.*)

STAGE MANAGER. Yes, it's 1899. This is
fourteen years ago.

EMILY. Oh, that's the town I knew as a
little girl. And, look, there's the old white
fence that used to be around our house. Oh,
I'd forgotten that! Oh, I love it so! Are
*they* inside?

STAGE MANAGER. Yes, your mother'll be
coming downstairs in a minute to make
breakfast.

EMILY (*softly*). Will she?

STAGE MANAGER. And you remember: your
father had been away for several days; he
came back on the early-morning train.

EMILY. No . . .

STAGE MANAGER. He'd been back to his
college to make a speech — in western New
York, at Clinton.

EMILY. Look! There's Howie Newsome.
There's our policeman. But he's *dead;* he
*died.*

[*The* STAGE MANAGER *retires to his corner.
The voices of* HOWIE NEWSOME, CONSTA-
BLE WARREN, *and* JOE CROWELL, JR., *are
heard at the left of the stage.*]

HOWIE NEWSOME. Whoa, Bessie! Bessie!
. . . Morning, Bill.

BILL. Morning, Howie.

HOWIE NEWSOME. You're up early.

BILL. Been rescuin' a party; darn near
froze to death, down by Polish Town thar.
Got drunk and lay out in the snowdrifts.
Thought he was in bed when I shook 'm.

EMILY. Why, there's Joe Crowell.

JOE CROWELL. Good morning, Mr. Warren. Morning, Howie.

[MRS. WEBB *has appeared in her kitchen, but* EMILY *does not see her until she calls.*]

MRS. WEBB. Chil-*dren!* Wally! Emily! . . . Time to get up.

EMILY. Mamma, here I am! Oh, how young Mamma looks! I didn't know Mamma was ever that young. Oh!

MRS. WEBB. You can come and dress by the kitchen fire, if you like; but hurry.

[HOWIE NEWSOME *has entered along Main Street and brings the milk to* MRS. WEBB'S *door.*]

Good morning, Mr. Newsome. Whhhh — it's cold.

HOWIE NEWSOME. Ten below by my barn, Mrs. Webb.

MRS. WEBB. Think of it! Keep yourself wrapped up. (*She takes her bottles in, shuddering.*)

EMILY (*with an effort*). Mamma, I can't find my blue hair ribbon anywhere.

MRS. WEBB. Just open your eyes, dear, that's all. I laid it out for you special — on the dresser, there. If it were a snake, it would bite you.

EMILY. Yes, yes. . . . (*She puts her hand on her heart.*)

[MR. WEBB *comes along Main Street, where he meets* CONSTABLE WARREN.]

MR. WEBB. Good morning, Bill.

BILL. Good morning, Mr. Webb. You're up early.

MR. WEBB. Yes, just been back to my old college in New York State. Been any trouble here?

BILL. Well, I was called up this mornin' to rescue a Polish fella — darn near froze to death he was.

MR. WEBB. We must get it in the paper.

BILL. 'Twan't much.

EMILY (*whispers*). Papa.

[MR. WEBB *shakes the snow off his feet and enters his house.*]

MR. WEBB. Good morning, Mother.

MRS. WEBB. How did it go, Charles?

MR. WEBB. Oh, fine, I guess. I told'm a few things.

MRS. WEBB. Did you sit up on the train all night?

MR. WEBB. Yes. Never could sleep on a Pullman anyway.

MRS. WEBB. Charles, seems to me — we're rich enough so that you could sleep in a train once in a while.

MR. WEBB. Everything all right here?

MRS. WEBB. Yes — can't think of anything that's happened, special. Been right cold. Howie Newsome says it's ten below over to his barn.

MR. WEBB. Yes? Well, it's colder than that at Hamilton College. Students' ears are falling off. It ain't Christian. . . . Paper have any mistakes in it?

MRS. WEBB. None that I noticed. Coffee's ready when you want it.

[*He starts upstairs.*]

Charles! Don't forget; it's Emily's birthday. Did you remember to get her something?

MR. WEBB (*patting his pocket*). Yes, I've got something here.

MRS. WEBB. Goodness sakes! I hope she likes what I got for her. I hunted hard enough for it. Child*ren!* Hurry up! Hurry up!

MR. WEBB. Where's my girl? Where's my birthday girl? (*He goes off left.*)

MRS. WEBB. Don't interrupt her now, Charles. You can see her at breakfast. She's slow enough as it is. Hurry up, children! It's seven o'clock. Now, I don't want to call you again.

EMILY (*softly, more in wonder than in grief*). I can't bear it. They're so young and beautiful. Why did they ever have to get old? Mama, I'm here. I'm grown up. I love you all, everything. . . . I can't look at everything hard enough. There's the butternut tree. (*She wanders up Main Street.*) There's Mr. Morgan's drugstore. And there's the high school, for ever and ever and ever. And there's the Congregational

Church, where I got married. Oh, dear. Oh, dear. Oh, dear!

[*The* STAGE MANAGER *beckons partially to her. He points to the house. She says a breathless " yes " and goes to the house.*]

Good morning, Mamma.

MRS. WEBB (*at the foot of the stairs, kissing her in a matter-of-fact way*). Well, now, dear, a very happy birthday to my girl and many happy returns. There are some surprises waiting for you on the kitchen table.

EMILY. Oh, Mamma, you *shouldn't* have. (*She throws an anguished glance at the* STAGE MANAGER.) I can't — I can't.

MRS. WEBB (*facing the audience, over her stove*). But birthday or no birthday, I want you to eat your breakfast good and slow. I want you to grow up and be a good strong girl. (*She goes to the stairs and calls.*) Wally! Wally, wash yourself good. Everything's getting cold down here. (*She returns to the stove with her back to* EMILY.)

[EMILY *opens her parcels.*]

That in the blue paper is from your Aunt Carrie, and I reckon you can guess who brought the post-card album. I found it on the doorstep when I brought in the milk. George Gibbs must have come over in the cold pretty early . . . right nice of him.

EMILY (*to herself*). Oh, George! I'd forgotten that.

MRS. WEBB. Chew that bacon slow. It'll help keep you warm on a cold day.

EMILY (*beginning softly but urgently*). Oh, Mamma, just look at me one minute as though you really saw me. Mamma, fourteen years have gone by. I'm dead. You're a grandmother, Mamma. I married George Gibbs, Mamma. Wally's dead, too. Mamma, his appendix burst on a camping trip to North Conway. We felt just terrible about it — don't you remember? But, just for a moment now we're all together. Mamma, just for a moment we're happy. Let's look at one another.

MRS. WEBB. That in the yellow paper is something I found in the attic among your grandmother's things. You're old enough to wear it now, and I thought you'd like it.

EMILY. And this is from you. Why, Mamma, it's just lovely and it's just what I wanted. It's beautiful! (*She flings her arms around her mother's neck.*)

[*Her mother goes on with her cooking, but is pleased.*]

MRS. WEBB. Well, I hoped you'd like it. Hunted all over. Your Aunt Norah couldn't find one in Concord, so I had to send all the way to Boston. (*Laughingly*) Wally has something for you, too. He made it at manual-training class, and he's very proud of it. Be sure you make a big fuss about it. Your father has a surprise for you, too; don't know what it is myself. Sh — here he comes.

MR. WEBB (*off stage*). Where's my girl? Where's my birthday girl?

EMILY (*in a loud voice to the* STAGE MANAGER). I can't. I can't go on. Oh! Oh. It goes so fast. We don't have time to look at one another. (*She breaks down, sobbing.*)

[*At a gesture from the* STAGE MANAGER, MRS. WEBB *disappears.*]

I didn't realize. So all that was going on and we never noticed. Take me back — up the hill — to my grave. But first — wait! One more look. Good-by, good-by, world. Good-by, Grover's Corners . . . Mamma and Papa. Good-by to clocks ticking . . . and Mamma's sunflowers. And food and coffee. And new-ironed dresses and hot baths . . . and sleeping and waking up. Oh, earth, you're too wonderful for anybody to realize you. (*She looks toward the* STAGE MANAGER *and asks, abruptly, through her tears*) Do any human beings ever realize life while they live it — every, every minute?

STAGE MANAGER. No. (*Pause*) The saints and poets, maybe — they do some.

EMILY. I'm ready to go back. (*She returns to her chair beside* MRS. GIBBS.) Mother Gibbs, I should have listened to you. Now I want to be quiet for a while. . . . Oh, Mother Gibbs, I saw it all. I saw your garden.

MRS. GIBBS. Did you, dear?

EMILY. That's all human beings are! Just blind people.

MRS. GIBBS. Look, it's clearing up. The stars are coming out.

EMILY. Oh, Mr. Stimson, I should have listened to them.

SIMON STIMSON (*with mounting violence; bitingly*). Yes, now you know. Now you know! That's what it was to be alive. To move about in a cloud of ignorance, to go up and down trampling on the feelings of those . . . of those about you. To spend and waste time as though you had a million years. To be always at the mercy of one self-centered passion or another. Now you know — that's the happy existence you wanted to go back and see. Did you shout to 'em? Did you call to 'em?

EMILY. Yes, I did.

SIMON STIMSON. Now you know them as they are: in ignorance and blindness.

MRS. GIBBS (*spiritedly*). Simon Stimson, that ain't the whole truth and you know it.

[THE DEAD *have begun to stir.*]

THE DEAD. Lemuel, wind's coming up, seems like. . . . Oh, dear, I keep remembering things tonight. . . . It's right cold for June, ain't it?

MRS. GIBBS. Look what you've done, you and your rebellious spirit stirring us up here. . . . Emily, look at that star. I forget its name.

THE DEAD. I'm getting to know them all, but I don't know their names. My boy, Joel, was a sailor — knew 'em all. He'd set on the porch evenings and tell 'em all by name. Yes, sir, it was wonderful. A star's mighty good company. Yes, yes. Yes, 'tis.

SIMON STIMSON. Here's one of *them* coming.

THE DEAD. That's funny. 'Tain't no time for one of them to be here. Goodness sakes.

EMILY. Mother Gibbs, it's George.

MRS. GIBBS. Sh, dear. You just rest yourself.

EMILY. It's George.

[GEORGE *enters from the left and slowly comes toward them.*]

A MAN FROM AMONG THE DEAD. And my boy, Joel, who knew the stars — he used to say it took millions of years for that speck o' light to git to the earth. Don't seem like a body could believe it, but that's what he used to say — millions of years.

ANOTHER. That's what they say.

[GEORGE *flings himself on* EMILY'S *grave.*]

THE DEAD. Goodness! That ain't no way to behave! He ought to be home.

EMILY. Mother Gibbs?

MRS. GIBBS. Yes, Emily?

EMILY. They don't understand much, do they?

MRS. GIBBS. No, dear, not very much.

[*The* STAGE MANAGER *appears at the right, one hand on a dark curtain which he slowly draws across the scene. In the distance a clock is heard striking the hour very faintly.*]

STAGE MANAGER. Most everybody's asleep in Grover's Corners. There are a few lights on. Shorty Hawkins, down at the depot, has just watched the Albany train go by. And at the livery stable somebody's setting up late and talking. . . . Yes, it's clearing up. There are the stars — doing their old, old crisscross journeys in the sky. Scholars haven't settled the matter yet, but they seem to think there are no living beings up there. They're just chalk . . . or fire. Only this one is straining away, straining away all the time to make something of itself. The strain's so bad that every sixteen hours everybody lies down and gets a rest. (*He winds his watch.*) Hm. . . . Eleven o'clock in Grover's Corners. . . . You get a good rest, too. Good night.

[THE END]

## Suggestions for Study of Act III

1. Would the last act, with the dead sitting in rows of chairs, have " gone over " as well if it had been first? Why does its place at the last make it less of a strain on the audience's imagination?

2. Have you ever thought that poetry about

death and immortality was unnecessarily obscure? Read the Stage Manager's speech on page 392 on this subject. Is the thought poetic? Does it lose anything from being simply expressed?

3. In a novel written earlier than *Our Town*, Wilder tells a short incident about a man who, like Emily, was given permission after his death to go back to earth for one day — the least eventful day in his life. But he soon begged to be allowed to rejoin the dead because he " saw that the living, too, are dead and that we can only be said to be alive in those moments when our hearts are conscious of our treasure." Is this the same effect as Emily's return had on her, or a different one? Find Emily's own sad comment on earthly life and compare the two. Do you think reading the play will make you a little more aware of the many little kindnesses, the unnoticed goodness in your own life?

4. Why are the Stage Manager's last gesture and last words a particularly appropriate ending for the play?

## Suggestions for Study of the Whole Play

1. Why has the dramatist limited the incidents he presents to simple happenings that occur frequently? Find a passage in the first act in which the Stage Manager explains exactly what he is trying to show.

2. The dialogue in this play is never intended to be new or original. It is not a surprise at something new but a chuckle over an old familiar saying that gives the play its flavor. Can you think of some remarks in the play that you have heard many, many times?

3. One writer in reviewing *Our Town* said, " In the day of great language in the theater, paint and canvas were missing. Great language cannot hold its own against the weight of papier-mâché. . . . It is because there are no painted houses that audiences see so clearly the beauty of [Wilder's] language. It is because there is no canvas hill on the stage that Mr. Wilder has the opportunity to give us eternity." Do you agree? Find passages of " great language " that take the place of paint and canvas.

4. The Stage Manager solves completely some of the problems of the dramatist, listed in " A Guide to Drama " (see pages

352–353), and he helps on all four. Can you tell how?

5. In Dickinson's *Chief Contemporary Dramatists*, second series, you can find a play in the Chinese tradition, *The Yellow Jacket*, by Hazelton and Benrimo. Get some of the class to read it and compare the Chinese property man with Wilder's Stage Manager. Other students can read about the chorus of Greek drama in the encyclopedia and see how the Stage Manager is akin to the chorus.

6. If you were to choose a " Stage Manager " on this pattern to supervise a play about your own home town or city, what sort of person would you select? Would Carl Sandburg make a good one for Chicago? Walter Winchell for New York?

7. Try your hand at writing an opening speech for the Stage Manager for your own home community, and let him describe briefly two families whose life would be typical of your community as the Webbs and Gibbses are typical of Grover's Corners.

8. Before writing *Our Town*, Wilder had tried out in short plays some of the dramatic experiments that give special interest to the long play. Let three different students read *The Long Christmas Dinner*, *Pullman Car Hiawatha*, and *The Happy Journey to Trenton and Camden* (all published in the volume *The Long Christmas Dinner*) to discover what experiments are carried over from these plays to *Our Town*.

9. If you have seen the screen production or heard the radio version of *Our Town*, compare them with the play as to use of " flash backs," " cut-ins," and other techniques. How were the endings different? Which of the three versions appealed to you most? Why?

10. You may have thought that sparkling, witty lines make the best dramatic dialogue. In fact, faithful realism is a surer source of enjoyment. Find lines that are entertaining primarily because they sound so much like real people talking. Then write up a bit of dramatic dialogue of your own about a happening that takes place every day. Listen to people as they talk, and catch their phrases and try to put them down on paper in as lifelike a manner as possible. Some of your friends or relatives may have the habit of greeting a situation with the same remark every time. Try to get in these typical bits. Then read the result in class and you will understand the appeal of good, handmade, realistic dialogue.

# RADIO DRAMA

The youngest member of the drama family is the radio play. But so active is radio that drama over the air has as much opportunity to grow and develop in a month as drama on the stage has in the richest full season. In the twenty years since radio first achieved a sizable audience, much has been learned about the peculiar problems — and possibilities — of its own type of drama.

The distinctive characteristics of radio drama stem from its complete dependence on sound. Radio depends on sound as completely as silent motion pictures depended on sight. Television may soon give radio another dimension, as the sound track did for the movies. But for the present the radio dramatist must tell with sound alone all that is shown to other audiences. Music and sound effects can help him, but without skillful use of words these aids are powerless to tell a story.

Since there is no stage and no scenery, radio drama can move about in time and place with a freedom unknown in other dramatic types. To be sure, the dramatist must take care that the shift is clear to his audience, and the shifts must be chosen for their value in telling the story. So both technical skill and dramatic judgment are called upon to keep the play moving smoothly.

The greatest demand made upon the radio dramatist is in characterization. The physical appearance of an actor, his bearing, and his gestures play their part in impressions of a character on the stage, no less than the words he speaks and his voice. Voice and words alone must give the impression over the radio. For that reason the language in a good radio play varies more for the different characters.

Another interesting quality of radio characters is the ease with which they can be made symbols for many people rather than simple individuals. Much less imagination is required to transform the voice of one man into the voice of many men than is needed to make one visible human being stand for his whole group or nation. So radio drama can easily give a wide significance to its narratives, and some of the most effective plays heard on the air take advantage of this distinctive power.

There is no denying that most radio plays are still mediocre. They are turned out in great quantity, with the expectation of a single performance, and they are designed to please a large audience rather than a discriminating one. But there are many signs of better days ahead. The large networks are featuring programs of individual plays written with care especially for radio by skilled craftsmen, and these programs are making impressive gains in popularity. Published collections of radio plays are becoming numerous — a sure sign that the product is winning recognition as literature. The surest sign of all is that the names of dramatists who write only for radio are becoming known and the announcement that a radio play is by Norman Corwin, or Arch Oboler, or Norman Rosten, carries a guarantee that the entertainment will reward attentive listening.

## Paul Gallico        1897–

Paul Gallico [1] is a versatile writer. Although he is not a writer of plays, his fine story *The Snow Goose* was the basis of the radio play you are about to read. After his graduation from Columbia University in 1921, Gallico spent almost fifteen years as a newspaper writer; he was successively movie critic, sports writer, and sports editor and columnist for the New York *Daily News*. In 1936 he left the newspaper field to become a free-lance fiction writer. He has contributed short stories to several magazines and his list of published works includes such diverse titles as *Farewell to Sport,* published in 1938, and *The Snow Goose,* published in 1941.

[1] **Gallico** (găl′ĭ-kō).

## THE SNOW GOOSE

*adapted for radio by William A. Bacher and Malcolm Meacham*

One of the finest series of dramatic radio performances America has known was developed not for the high pay radio offers, but simply for love of our country. In 1941 the Secretary of the Treasury asked radio leaders if they could help with the War Bond campaign. Almost overnight they had enlisted in the undertaking the best radio experts, the best writers and actors in the country. The series of short plays they produced was a splendid vote of confidence in the soundness of American patriotism. There was no plea to sign on the dotted line, little emphasis on the bitter price some young Americans were paying for our freedom. They sought only, for that quarter of an hour, to make some touch of the war on human lives vivid and human and real, and trusted Americans for the rest. Consequently, their plays were not the temporary sort of product that is usually turned out for a specific occasion, but true drama that will last as literature long after its echo has faded from the air.

"The Snow Goose" was one of the plays on the Treasury Star Parade. William A. Bacher, director of the program, collaborated with Malcolm Meacham to make the radio adaptation of Gallico's story. Jane Cowl and Fredric March read the major parts. As you read, take time to let your imagination create the full effect of the music. It takes the place of much of Gallico's descriptive writing in the story, and it is essential to the mood of the play.

### CHARACTERS

#### NARRATOR

| | |
|---|---|
| PHILIP RHAYADER [1] | BANDY |
| FRITHA | SMITHERS |
| PRIVATE POTTEN | ARTILLERYMAN |

[*Orchestra full into title theme and then down under.*]

NARRATOR. This is the story of a man — a lonely man — whose body was warped, but whose heart was filled with love for wild and hunted things. He was ugly to look upon, but he created great beauty. It is

[1] Rhayader (rā′á-dĕr).

about him, and a child who came to know him and see beyond the grotesque form that housed him to what lay within, that this story is told.

[*Orchestra swells slightly and modulates to theme of the marsh — low, cold, barren.*]

The Great Marsh lies on the Essex coast between the village of Chelmbury and the ancient Saxon fishing hamlet of Wickaeldroth.[2] It is one of the last wild places of England, desolate, utterly lonely, and made lonelier by the calls and cries of the wild fowl that make their homes in the marshlands and saltings.

[*Low effect held off mike . . . cries and calls of scattered wild fowl . . . hold clear a few seconds.*]

Hard by one of the winding arms of the little River Aelder [3] runs the embankment of an old sea wall. At low water, the ruins of an old abandoned lighthouse show above the wall.

[*Orchestra moods with effect of water washing up against the lighthouse . . . hold a few seconds.*]

In the late spring of 1930, young Philip Rhayader came to live at the lighthouse. He was a painter of birds and nature, who, for reason, had withdrawn from all human society. For he was a hunchback and his left arm was crippled, thin and bent at the wrist, like the claw of a bird . . . and he had found this a world in which he could not take part as other men.

[*Orchestra into mood from Sibelius' [4] "Swan of Tuonela".[5]*]

He was a friend to all things wild, and all wild things repaid him with their friendship. Each fall, the wild geese would come winging down the coast from Iceland and Spitsbergen in great skeins that darkened the sky and filled the air with the rushing noise of their passage . . . (*effect of joy-*

[2] **Wickaeldroth** (wĭk′äl-drŏth). [3] **Aelder** (äl′-dĕr). [4] **Sibelius** (sĭ-bā′lĭ-ŏŏs). [5] **Tuonela** (tŏŏ-ŏ-nä′lá).

*ous return of birds with record added*)
barking and whooping and honking in the
autumn sky, to circle the landmark of the
old light and drop to earth near by to be
his guests again — birds that he well remembered and recognized from the previous year.

This made Rhayader happy. And he did
not seem to mind so much that the natives
looked askance at his misshapen body and
dark visage.

But one November afternoon, three years
after Rhayader had come to the Great
Marsh, a child approached the lighthouse
studio by means of the sea wall. In her arms
she carried a burden. (*Orchestra in with
slender theme for the girl.*) She was no
more than twelve, slender, dirty, nervous
and timid as a bird, but beneath the grime
as eerily beautiful as a marsh faery. She was
desperately frightened of the ugly man she
had come to see, but greater than her fear
was the legend that this ogre who lived in
the lighthouse had magic that could heal
injured things. For in her arms was a large
white bird, and it was quite still . . . (*Orchestra mood changes.*) There were stains
of blood on its whiteness and on her kirtle
where she had held it to her . . .

RHAYADER (*deep, gentle*). What is it,
child? (*Orchestra softly out.*)

FRITHA. I found it, sir. It's hurted. I found
it in t' marsh where hunters had been. Can
'ee heal it, sir?

RHAYADER. Yes, yes — we will try. Come,
you shall help me.

NARRATOR. There were scissors and bandages and splints on a shelf, and he was marvelously deft. The child watched, fascinated.
He bandaged the wing close to the body,
and made a splint for the shattered leg. . . .

FRITHA. What — what is it, sir?

RHAYADER. It's a snow goose from Canada. Terrible storms must have driven her
far off her course. I have never seen one here
before. We will call her the " Lost Princess."
In a few days she will be feeling much better. See?

NARRATOR. He reached into his pocket
and produced a handful of grain. The snow

goose nibbled at it. (*Effect of laughter under
line.*) The child laughed with delight —
then suddenly caught her breath with alarm
as the full import of where she was pressed
in upon her, and, without a word, she turned
and fled out of the door. . . .

RHAYADER. Wait, wait!

NARRATOR. The girl was already fleeing
down the sea wall, but she paused at his
voice and looked back.

RHAYADER (*calling*). What is your name,
child?

FRITHA (*from a little distance*). Fritha
. . .

RHAYADER (*Calling*). Where do you live?

FRITHA. Wi' t' fisherfolk at Wickaeldroth.

RHAYADER. Will you come back tomorrow, or the next day, to see how the Princess is getting along?

[*Orchestra softly back to her theme.*]

NARRATOR. She paused, and Rhayader
thought of the wild water birds caught motionless in that split second of alarm before
they took their flight. But her thin voice
came back to him. . . .

FRITHA (*off*). Ay!

NARRATOR. And then she was gone, with
her fair hair streaming out behind her.

[*Orchestra swells to hold few seconds . . .
and fades out under.*]

The goose mended rapidly, and the child
Fritha became a frequent visitor. Until one
day in June, the snow goose, with the others,
answered the strong call of the breeding
grounds, climbed into the sky in ever widening circles, and vanished.

[*Into opening theme, cold and lonely.*]

With the departure of the snow goose
ended the visits of Fritha to the lighthouse.
And that summer, out of his memory Rhayader painted a picture of a slender, grime-
covered child, her fair hair blown by a
November storm, who bore in her arms a
wounded white bird. . . .

[*Orchestra swells slightly and then we hear
from distance the theme of the snow goose
fading in again.*]

But in mid-October, the miracle occurred. Above the sea and tide, he heard a clear high note (*bird call*) and saw a white-pinioned dream that circled the lighthouse once, then dropped to earth and came waddling forward importantly to be fed. It was the snow goose. When next Rhayader went to the village, he left a message with the postmistress:

RHAYADER. Tell Fritha, who lives with the fisherfolk at Wickaeldroth, that the Lost Princess has returned. . . .

NARRATOR. And three days later, Fritha, taller, still tousled and unkempt, came shyly to the lighthouse to visit the Lost Princess.

[*Orchestra into low music, distant, ominous.*]

Time passed. The world outside boiled and seethed and rumbled with the eruption that was soon to break forth. But it had not touched them. Every year, the snow goose would disappear in the spring — and with her, Fritha — for it seemed that when the snow goose was gone, some kind of a bar was up between them, and she did not come to the lighthouse. (*Orchestra out.*)

And then one fall, in answer to the message left for her with the postmistress, Fritha reappeared at the lighthouse, and Rhayader, with a shock, realized that she was a child no longer.

[*Orchestra swells into her theme developed.*]

In the spring of 1940, the birds migrated early from the Great Marsh. The whine and roar of the bombers and the thudding explosions frightened them. Fritha and Rhayader stood shoulder to shoulder on the sea wall and watched them go; she, tall, slender, free as air, and hauntingly beautiful; he, dark, grotesque, his massive bearded head raised to the sky, his glowing dark eyes watching the geese form their flight tracery . . . and suddenly . . .

FRITHA (*excitedly*). Look, Philip, look!

NARRATOR. Rhayader followed her eyes. The snow goose had taken flight, her giant wings spread, but she was flying low. Once,

twice, she circled the lighthouse . . . then dropped to earth again in the enclosure and commenced to feed. . . .

FRITHA (*marvelling*). She be'ent goin', Philip! The Princess be goin' to stay!

RHAYADER (*shaken*). Ay, she'll stay. She will never go away again. This is her home now — of her own free will.

NARRATOR. And Fritha was suddenly conscious of the fact that she was frightened . . . (*orchestra into minor treatment of love theme*) and the things that frightened her were in Rhayader's eyes — the longing and the loneliness — and the deep, welling unspoken things that he could not speak, because of what he felt himself to be — misshapen and grotesque.

And the woman in her bade her take flight from something she was not yet capable of understanding.

[*Orchestra swells softly and back to theme of the marsh.*]

It was more than three weeks before she returned to the lighthouse. She came back, she told herself, only to see the snow bird. But she found Philip loading supplies into his little sailboat, which she had often seen him handle with such skill — and a great fear, she knew not why, came into her heart.

[*Orchestra modulates to sea music with counterpoint of war music.*]

FRITHA (*terrified*). Philip — ye be goin' away?

NARRATOR. Forgotten was the snow goose. Rhayader paused in his work to greet her, and there was something in his face, a glow and a look, that she had never seen there before. . . .

RHAYADER (*great suppressed excitement*). Fritha! I am glad you came. . . . Yes, I must go away . . . a little trip. . . . I will come back.

FRITHA. Where must ye go?

NARRATOR. Words came tumbling from Rhayader now. He must go to Dunkirk. A hundred miles across the Channel. A British army was trapped there on the sands, awaiting destruction at the hands of the advancing Germans. The port was in flames. He had heard it in the village where he had gone for supplies. In answer to the Government's call, every tug and fishing boat or power launch that could propel itself was heading across the Channel, to haul the men off the beaches to the transports and destroyers that could not reach the shallows. His little boat could take six men at a time; in a pinch seven . . .

[*Orchestra softly out.*]

FRITHA (*terrified*). Philip! Must 'ee go? You'll not come back. Why must it be 'ee?

RHAYADER. I must, my dear, I must! Men are huddled on the beaches like hunted birds, Fritha, like the wounded and hunted birds we used to find and bring to the sanctuary. They are lost and storm-driven and harried like the Lost Princess you found and brought to me out of the marshes many years ago, and we healed her. They need help, as our wild creatures have needed help, and this is why I must go. It is something that I can do. Yes, I can. For once — for once I can be a man and play my part.

[*Orchestra back to her theme.*]

NARRATOR. And as Fritha stared at Rhayader he no longer seemed ugly or misshapen or grotesque, but very beautiful. Things were turmoiling in her own soul, crying to be said, and she did not know how to say them. . . .

FRITHA. I'll come with 'ee, Philip.

RHAYADER. No. Your place in the boat would cause a soldier to be left behind, and another and another. I must go alone. Will you look after the birds until I return, Fritha?

FRITHA. I will . . . and God speed you, Philip . . . (*So low we can hardly hear her*) God speed you.

[*Orchestra softly into theme of departure to slowly build.*]

NARRATOR. Fritha stood on the sea wall and watched the sail gliding into the sea.

[*Swan theme blends with departure theme.*]

Suddenly, from the darkness behind her, there came a rush of wings and something swept past her in the air. In the night she saw the flash of white wings and the thrust-forward head of the snow goose. It rose and cruised over the lighthouse once (*call of the snow goose*) then headed out toward where Rhayader's sail was slanting in the gaining breeze, and flew above him in slow, wide circles. . . . " Watch o'er him. Watch o'er him," Fritha whispered.

[*Orchestra up passionately and fades off with a last call of the snow goose far off.*]

NARRATOR. Now the story becomes fragmentary . . . it has been gathered from many sources and many people. Some of it comes from men who have looked upon strange and violent scenes.

[*Orchestra in softly; slight suggestion of war.*]

One of the fragments come in the words of a man on leave who told it in the public room of the Crown and Arrow, an East Chapel pub. . . .

PRIVATE POTTEN (*fading in*). A goose, a bloomin' goose, so 'elp me.

BANDY (*disbelieving*). Garn . . .

POTTEN. A goose it was. Jock 'ere, seen it same as me. It came flyin' down outa the muck an' stink an' smoke of Dunkirk that was over'ead. It was white, wiv black wings, an' it circles us like a bloomin' dive bomber. Jock, 'ere, 'e sez, " We're done for. It's the hangel of death a-come for us."

[*Orchestra quick swell to gradually develop into war theme.*]

SMITHERS. Garn, Hi sez, it's a ruddy goose, come over from 'ome wiv a message from Churchill, an' 'ow are we henjoying the bloomin' bathing. It's a omen, that's what it is, a bloomin' omen. We'll get out of this yet, my lad. . . .

[*Orchestra quick swell to war music and sound effects full and then down.*]

ARTILLERYMAN (*fading in over effect*). A goose . . . a bloomin' goose, so 'elp me. We was roastin' on the beach between Dunkirk and Lapanny, an' offshore is the *Kentish Maid*, a ruddy excursion scow, waitin' to take us off. When a Stuka dives on her . . . and a destroyer comes up an' says, " No, ye don't " to the Stuka with ack-acks and pom-poms, but another Jerry dives on the destroyer, and 'its 'er. Coo, did she go up! She burned before she sunk, an' the smokes come driftin' in, all yellow and black, an' out of it comes this bloomin' goose, a-circlin' around us, trapped on the beach. . . .

[*Call of goose fading in, leading* RHAYADER *theme in with it.*]

A bloomin' omen, I says! An' then 'e comes. . . .

BANDY. 'Oo comes? (RHAYADER'S *theme in full.*)

ARTILLERYMAN. 'Im — that saved the lot of us. Into the shallows 'e sailed, as cool as you please, in a bloomin' little sailboat . . . through a boil of machine-gun bullets and divin' Stukas, never givin' 'em no mind, 'e didn't . . . sailin' between the shells right past the burnin' destroyer, a little dark man wiv a beard, a bloomin' claw for a 'and, and a 'ump on 'is back.

[*War music . . . bombers . . . whining shells in strong behind . . . wash and splash of waves and through it all like an organpoint comes the repeated call of the snow goose.*]

RHAYADER (*through effect . . . slightly off*). I can take seven at a time!

ARTILLERYMAN. An' we waded out to where 'e was . . . the goose conkin' all the time . . . 'im at the tiller lookin' up an' grinnin' 'at 'er, like 'e knows 'er a lifetime. 'E brings us out to the *Kentish Maid* and turns around and goes back for another load. 'E makes trips all afternoon an' all night, too, because the bloody light of Dunkirk burnin' was light enough to see by.

[*Battle begins to let up.*]

I don't know how many trips 'e made, but 'e brought us all off that particular stretch of 'ell, without the loss of a man.

An then 'e sails back toward Dunkirk, an' the bird wiv 'im, flying around the boat like a white hangel against the smoke . . . (*Fades on line.*) .

[*Orchestra swells up full and then softly down to signify the end of the battle.*]

Hi never did find out what become of 'im, or 'oo 'e was — 'im wiv the 'ump an' 'is little sailboat. A bloomin' good man 'e was, that chap.

NARRATOR. Those were a few fragments of the story. There was just one more.

[*Orchestra swells softly and back to Fritha theme.*]

Fritha had remained alone at the lighthouse, wandering through the storerooms and examining the wonderful paintings within them. Among these, she found the picture that Rhayader had painted of her from memory so many years ago when she was still a child, and the things she saw in it stirred her as nothing ever had before, for much of Rhayader's soul had gone into it. She knew that Rhayader would not return.

[*Orchestra into snow goose theme coming in stronger and stronger and stronger under.*]

And so when she heard the high-pitched, well-remembered note of the snow goose cries from the heaven, it brought no instant of false hope to her heart . . . but the sight, the sound, and the solitude surrounding her broke the dam within her and released the surging, overwhelming truth of her love, let it well forth in tears.

[*The love theme comes up full and tragic but triumphant, built upon the snow goose theme.*]

But the snow goose did not come to earth this time. It only skimmed low, then soared up again, flew in a wide, graceful spiral around the old lighthouse, and then began to climb. But Fritha did not see the snow goose . . .

[*Chorus joins softly . . . ascending.*]

She saw the soul of Rhayader taking farewell of her before departing forever. She stretched her arms up into the sky and

SOUND EFFECTS in a radio drama take the place of description in a written narrative. They require close synchronizing, as this group well knows, in order to be convincing. (Columbia Broadcasting System)

stood on tiptoe, crying, " Godspeed! Godspeed! Philip! "

[*Orchestra and singers up full to finish. And then hold strings for epilogue.*]

NARRATOR (*almost like a commentator*). Early the next morning a German pilot on a dawn raid mistook the old abandoned lighthouse for an active military objective, dived on it, a screaming steel hawk, and blew it and all it contained into oblivion.

[*Orchestra sneaks into original bleak theme.*]

And the sea moved in to cover it over. (*Scattered cries of wild sea gulls*). And now nothing was left to break the utter desolation — nothing was left but the frightened gulls that wheeled and soared and mewed their plaint over the place that once had been.

[*Orchestra fades out leaving only the plaintive cries of the sea gulls . . . hold few seconds.*]

## Suggestions for Study

1. What makes this radio play read much like a short story? Why must it still be classed as drama?

2. How is the Narrator like the Stage Manager in *Our Town?* What is the chief difference between them? Which type do you prefer?

3. It may seem at first glance that radio drama has no problem in shifting scenes, because it has no scenery to change. Yet it faces the same old problem of moving the listener to the new scene, and perhaps new mood. How is the problem met in this play?

4. Music is not just an added attraction in the play, but part of the story. What does the music do that stage setting usually does? What does it do for the play that stage setting could not do? You can get a recording of " The Swan of Tuonela " used for the snow goose theme. What music would you suggest for Fritha's theme? for the marshes?

5. Why is this really the story of the snow goose, rather than of Fritha and Rhayader, or of Dunkirk? Check the many ways the goose is the real center of the story.

6. What did the snow goose bring to Rhayader that he had missed before? Why did he glory more than most men in the help he could give at Dunkirk?

7. Like poetry, this play leaves many mysteries unanswered for the listener (or reader) to wonder about. List some of them. Would you prefer to have them settled? You can find some of the mysteries solved in the short story from which the play was made.

8. Read other plays of this series in *Treasury Star Parade*, edited by William A. Bacher. It represents the work of many writers and is a fine introduction to a variety of types of radio drama.

## Pearl S. Buck     1892–

### WILL THIS EARTH HOLD?

The great possibilities of radio drama have attracted a number of writers who have already won their laurels in other literary fields, like Stephen Vincent Benét, Archibald MacLeish, and Pearl S. Buck. (For a full sketch of Mrs. Buck's literary career see page 83.) Mrs. Buck became so interested in radio that she enrolled incognito in a special course in radio writing at an eastern university and devoted a semester to concentrated study and practice in writing scripts. Then she used her new skill to serve the Office of War Information in building better understanding between China and America. During the war her early role as interpreter of China to Americans was reversed; she wrote plays about America to be translated into Chinese for broadcasts to encourage our hard-pressed ally. Now with the return of peace she again pictures the real China for her fellow Americans, continuing the great contribution to international understanding that won her the Nobel prize.

"Will This Earth Hold?" is the work of a real radio enthusiast. Mrs. Buck has said, "I feel enormously interested in radio. It seems to me that radio is the best dramatic medium writers can have." Now let your eyes be your ears, and discover for yourself how the new medium serves to tell a new story on her favorite subject.

MUSIC. *"America the Beautiful." It is being played by some horns and a drum,* *and being sung by mixed and garden variety voices, against which three voices are clearer than the rest. These three voices are Mrs. Broder's piercing one, supported by Mr. Broder's bass, which mumbles along in a monotone — and just at the end Mary Broder's clear high soprano, lifting the last line like a banner and flinging it out. There is a confusion of voices as the singing ends and calls of " Good night," " Glad you're home again, Johnny," and so on. A door shuts and there is silence.*

MR. BRODER. Take it easy, Johnny. Here, sit in my chair. It's comfortable.

JOHNNY. I'm all right. I don't have to coddle myself.

MRS. BRODER (*who has been warned through women's magazines against oversympathy for the returning wounded*). Sure, you're just fine. I can see it. I — I (*her voice breaks*) I smell the cake burning. (*Her feet running and a door slams.*)

MR. BRODER. Well, now, you mustn't mind mother, Johnny.

JOHNNY. I'm used to — to not walking very well. Plenty of others. You get used to it.

MR. BRODER (*too heartily*). Sure you do — sure you do —

MARY (*abruptly*). Johnny, you didn't sing!

JOHNNY. Didn't I?

MARY. No, I noticed it. You just stood there on the porch staring out over their heads as though you saw something.

JOHNNY. All of a sudden I remembered something. Funny the way you remember things — not like when you lived 'em day after day. When it's all done you see them in pieces all tossed together anyhow.

MARY. What did you see from the porch?

JOHNNY. Oh — just some people in China.

MARY. You haven't told us anything!

JOHNNY. Oh, I dunno — they weren't anybody, just a family I used to see over there. I dunno why I saw them, sort of, when the folks were singin'.

MARY. How funny, when you were lookin' at our own folks here in Clifton, Pennsylvania.

JOHNNY (*as though a stopper had been removed*). We was gettin' the big airfield, see? There had to be big airfields, naturally, for the B-29's to take off for Japan. They were goin' to be flown over the Hump [1] and there had to be somewhere for 'em to land. We had our orders to be ready for 'em. Well, over there in China there isn't such a thing as a lot of empty land. It's not like it is over here where you walk a mile and not see anybody. There's people everywhere over there, and villages, they call 'em. When it came to makin' the airfield you just naturally had to smooth off the farms and villages. The farms are little, five acres or so to one. We had to smooth off a lot of farms and villages, see? Well, naturally, it was hard on the people. Like it would be on us here, see?

MR. BRODER. Mary, I don't think you ought to have started this. John, you take it easy.

JOHNNY (*paying no attention*). Well, we had our orders. It had to be done. They sent Chinese fellows with us who could speak English so we could explain everything to the people, how we had to take their land for airfields, so we could take off with the bombers against Japan —

[*Music: Simple, not the usual Chinese imitation, fades down under.*]

CHINESE (*speaking a very pure English with a Harvard accent*). The people do not like to lose their ancestral homes, even though everything has been explained to them, sir. Yet this is not what disturbs them most.

JOHNNY (*his voice in China is very different from what it is in Clifton, Pa. In China it is loud, a little truculent, full of authority*). Don't they know there's a war on?

CHINESE (*roughly to the farmers*). You,

farmers, this is war; the foreign soldiers want your land for an airfield.

WONG (*very deep, quiet voice, without accent but not too cultivated*). These are the graves of our ancestors. I have told you.

JOHNNY. What does he say?

CHINESE (*returning to his politeness*). Sir, he says these are the graves of his ancestors. His own house he gladly gives, but he does not wish to disturb his ancestors.

JOHNNY. Tell him they've dug up plenty of graves in other countries.

CHINESE. Our graves are so old. Our ancestors have been buried so long — for four thousand years.

JOHNNY. Sorry, it's orders. (*His voice again from the living room of the Broder house, near and close*) Gosh, I did wish for a bulldozer. If we'd had a coupla bulldozers we could just have gone plowin' over the land and knockin' down the mud houses and it would have been over with quickly. But everything had to be done with people's hands. You can't get bulldozers over the Himalayas. Fifty thousand men and women and children came pourin' in from everywhere to work on that airfield. They had little short-handled hoes and spades and baskets slung on poles. They went pickin' at the graves, kind of gingerly, like they was afraid of ghosts. The Wong family — I got to know them by then — stood there in a little bunch, watchin' their ancestors' graves bein' dug up. Mrs. Wong cried quiet like she was sick. She made me think of Mom a little somehow.

[*The door opens . . . Mrs. Broder comes in.*]

MRS. BRODER (*brightly*). I made you a marble cake, Johnny. Look, I just poured on the icing and you'll have to eat it with a fork.

JOHNNY (*absently*). Gosh, that's wonderful, Mom —

MR. BRODER (*in a whisper*). He's talking, Mother.

MRS. BRODER (*half hushed*). Oh . . .

JOHNNY. Their graves weren't like ours

[1] **Hump:** airmen's name for the route over the Himalayas (hǐ-mä´lá-yàz), the high mountains over which all aid to China had to be transported by air from India.

here in the cemetery. They were right out in the middle of a field, maybe, in a circle of low mud wall. After a while I couldn't keep from seein' them the way the Wongs did. At the back was a high old grave that must have belonged to some great-grand-father Wong. Grandfather Wong was still alive. He came out of the house last of all. He was a little old man in a gray robe and a black wool cap over his ears and always a brass tobacco pipe in his hand. When the big grave was opened he tottered forward and bowed to the dust they were takin' out. Mr. Wong rushed up and took the dust himself. Everything was gone and it was only dust. He held out the end of his coat and they poured it in and then he let it fall slowly into a brown jar that Mrs. Wong held. It lay there in the bottom. The next grave was great-grandmother's, I reckon, and so they went, the Wong family bowin' before them all, old men and young men and women and their children. The last grave was the smallest and it had bones in it, the bones of a baby, and the women be-gan to cry out loud and Mrs. Wong held out her arms and took it — the little skele-ton.

MRS. BRODER. Oh, Johnny, the poor soul!

JOHNNY. It's funny how I remember that. I saw fellows blown to pieces the days the Japs came over us, and kep' right on eatin' my three square meals a day. When I think of those Wongs I — I can't even eat this cake, Mom.

MR. BRODER. Take it easy, Son.

JOHNNY. Funny thing, when I was over there I kept seein' home. I thought about Grandad and Gramma, here in the ceme-tery, and Aunt Mollie and little Jim that died before I was old enough even to go to school.

MRS. BRODER (weeping a little). Oh, Johnny . . .

JOHNNY. Funny, because now I'm home I keep thinkin' about the Wongs. I got to know them so well, see?

MARY. But they couldn't talk to you?

JOHNNY. It was funny, I got so I almost knew what they were sayin'. It was true

they minded the graves more than any-thing, though. We tore down the villages. Fifty thousand people workin' together — well, the Wong village was gone in no time. The bricks turn to dust easy.

MRS. BRODER. Where'd you put the Wongs?

JOHNNY. There wasn't any place to put 'em.

MRS. BRODER (her voice outraged). You mean to tell me you left those poor inno-cent people out in the weather without a roof over their heads? And little children, and that good old man?

JOHNNY. Mom, it was war. And we had our orders. We couldn't stop to build a lot of houses. The Wongs put their bedquilts up on some poles.

MARY (very quietly). Couldn't they have gone somewhere else?

JOHNNY. Well, there didn't seem to be any place for them to go. Anyway, they stayed. It wasn't too bad if it didn't rain. When it rained the earth was mud. They sat on their beds and tables and waited for it to clear off.

MR. BRODER (rather solemnly). How did Mr. Wong feed the family?

JOHNNY. They worked on the airfield. They all worked. I went out a couple of days after. They were workin' like every-body else, as though it wasn't their own land. Grandpa Wong sat on a coupla bricks and he had a little stone mallet like all the others and he was poundin' bricks to pieces — poundin' 'em back to dust. Maybe it was his own house. You couldn't tell. They were all there. They were all poundin', poundin' —

[As though at a distance the steady, rhyth-mic pounding of stone mallets upon earth, a dull, dry sound. Against it voices are muted.]

MRS. WONG. I cannot keep from grief. What will happen to us? We are homeless, living and dead; no home!

MR. WONG. What would happen to us if the enemy made us slaves? You must pound the bricks more small. They must be made into dust.

[*The mallets, with no voice, pounding in a rhythmic click, click, clickety clack . . . Fades out.*]

JOHNNY. It was done so quickly. You wouldn't believe it. It made you feel queer to look over the acres and acres of people sitting flat on the ground, the sun beating down on their black heads and on their thousands and thousands of hands rising and falling, rising and falling —

[*The mallets rise to a steady pitch, against which voices speak muted.*]

VOICES. Will this land come back to us? Never if we lose it to the enemy.
We work for victory when we pound this earth of ours, stone upon earth.
We offer up our land.
It has become sacred land.
Land where our fathers died.
Land of our children's pride.
Dust under the wheels and the wings of the bombers.
Winged harvest.

[*The mallets fade to finish.*]

JOHNNY. We lived all day with the sound of those beating mallets in our ears. Our blood ran to the beat. We talked against it, worked against it.

[*The mallets, steady, so rhythmic it drives you mad . . . Against it rough, irritable American voices.*]

VOICE. Here you, Joe, get on the job there. Don't let these Chinamen see you loafing!
SECOND VOICE. I want to go home —
FIRST VOICE. Shut up!

[*Sound fades out.*]

JOHNNY. The dust was into everything. It got into our clothes and our beds, into our food —

[*The mallets, and angry rough American voices against it.*]

VOICES. What's this — ashcake?

Naw, grits.
Darned if the sugar hasn't turned to mud. Coffee's mud, too.
JOHNNY. At night — the silence — it was so still it made you afraid. They stopped at dark, all at the same minute. Your blood had been racing along to the beat of the mallets and when they stopped your heart seemed to stop too. You were tired to death. You just leaned against anything. And you stared over the field where the silence was and lights flickered, tiny lantern lights. They were eating their rice and a handful of beans apiece. I used to go over and see the Wongs.
MR. WONG (*his voice remote as all the Chinese voices are*). Father, you haven't eaten your bowlful.
GRANDPA WONG. I cannot eat.
MR. WONG. You must not work so hard. You will die, and where shall we bury you?
GRANDPA WONG. I will not die until the land is given back to us. That will be my victory.
JOHNNY (*voice near and clear*). They sat there with their sticks of furniture under the quilts they had hung on poles for a tent. The jar of ashes was there, too, waiting. As soon as it was dawn the pounding began. It drove some of the fellows crazy. They began to worry about the field. When the B-29's flew in from the Himalayas, could they land or would the field just crumple up under them? Maybe the whole thing would be a flop.

[*Sound of the mallets.*]

AMERICAN VOICES. It won't hold up.
It's sheer waste of time.
A couple of steam rollers and we'd have —
You can't haul steam rollers over the Hump.
It ain't gonna do. You can't land them big bombers on a field that Chinks have pounded flat with little toy hammers.

[*Sound fades and out.*]

JOHNNY. Somehow or other they got to understand that we thought they weren't any good. Don't ask me how they knew.

They got to worryin'. They hadn't even seen a real bomber. They'd ask, with their hands, but we knew what they meant, how long B-29's were. Just for the hell of it, some of the fellows measured off a quarter of a mile or so. Then the whole lot of them would sit around at night and worry.

VOICES (*remote*). The Americans think we cannot make the earth hard enough for their bombers.

They don't know us.

They don't know our earth.

We know our earth. It can be rich as river land and hard as stone.

We make our earth into a battlefield for the wheels and the wings of our allies, and they will lift themselves from our earth. We have beaten our earth into the foundation for victory.

JOHNNY (*half sobbing*). They'd go back and begin to pound again and pound again and pound again —

MR. BRODER. Take it easy, Johnny.

JOHNNY. The Wongs grew as thin as laths. They'd never been fat. But they turned the color of the earth under that sun. We didn't have rain for days. The sun beat down on them like fire. Our fellows couldn't hardly stand it and we had sun helmets. The Chinese hadn't anything. A woman maybe would tie a piece of blue cloth over her head. Most of the time they didn't bother. The kids ran around with nothing much on, the little ones, and the big ones worked. The water dried up in the creeks and the wells got low. We began to get scared about water. None of the Chinese washed and we didn't let them see us wash even our hands and faces. They hung around with tin cans and took anything we threw out. I went by the Wongs' one night just to see how they were makin' it. Their faces were parched and their lips were all sores. But they had some incense stuck in a crack in the ground outside their make-shift tent and it was burnin' and the gray smoke curlin' up. I used to talk pretty good with my hands then —

MR. WONG (*his voice remote*). He wants to know why we are burning the incense.

GRANDPA WONG. I will explain it to him. (*He clears his throat.*)

WOMAN. Grandfather, he cannot understand you.

GRANDPA WONG (*reprovingly*). These foreigners understand more than you think, if you give them time, and speak slowly, and use your hands. See, I point to heaven —

JOHNNY. I made out they were burnin' incense to heaven to ask their gods to hold off on the rain. The field was nearly done. Another coupla weeks of that poundin' and it would be hard as cement. Then rain wouldn't hurt. But we didn't know if they could hold out.

VOICES (*against the incessant pounding*). Water — is there no water in the buckets?

At noon they will give us a cup apiece.

How long is it until noon?

The sun is halfway to the zenith.

[*A child wails.*]

MRS. BRODER. Wait a minute, Johnny, I'm goin' to fix a pitcher of lemonade.

JOHNNY. Mom, wait a minute.

MR. BRODER. Take it easy, take it easy.

JOHNNY. We'd had our orders to be done a certain day. Nobody knew if it was the big day or not. We'd talk about it — how it would look to see those big B-29's sailin' in out of the west. Nobody knew if it would be on that day. But the Chinese just took it for granted it would be. They began workin' nights. Then it was night and day. There wasn't a minute's silence. We all got strung up as tight as fiddle strings. Nobody talked. You couldn't. You just went around in a daze. Everything, everybody, doin' what you had to do, just listenin', listenin', not hearin' anything, not thinkin', just movin' and doin' what you had to do.

[*Sound of the mallets and Chinese voices.*]

VOICES. How many nights since you have slept, mother of my little son?

Can any of us sleep?

What if we fail? We have never made these floors before. We have only made our threshing floors.

What if the wings cannot rise?

They are foreign machines and we have never seen them.

What if we fail?

JOHNNY. We were all bettin', of course. (*He gives a strange excited laugh*). The odds were against us.

[*Sound of the mallets and American voices.*]

VOICES. Aw, it won't work.

What' ya bet?

You'd oughta see LaGuardia Field[1] at home. It's like a table, hard as stone, smooth as your hand.

Them big bombers —

The earth will crack like paper, I'll betcha.

What' ya bet?

You can't get steam rollers over the Hump.

JOHNNY. Funny thing, I was kind of bettin' on the Wongs. The old man was a shred by now. He made me think of old Mr. Haines. 'Member Mr. Haines, Mom? He died when I was a kid.

MRS. BRODER. He was ninety-six when he died. The last five years he couldn't walk. They had to carry him to the sofa while they made his bed up in the mornin'. He didn't weight more'n ninety pounds.

JOHNNY. Grandpa Wong tottered out every mornin' bright and early and took up his mallet. I could see his old claws of hands trembling. Mr. Wong kept near to kind of watch him.

[*The mallets, quicker now than before and voices against them.*]

MR. WONG. Father . . . go and rest, Father. We will finish the task.

GRANDPA WONG. Let me finish my work. You young men — you're so — so —

[*Sound dies out.*]

JOHNNY. They were pounding straight on the field now. Dust was pounded into stone, hard. They stopped one night and the field was done. Next day was the big

[1] **LaGuardia Field** (là-gwär′dê-à)· New York City's municipal airport.

day. We couldn't sleep. I guess nobody slept. The lights flickered all night long around the field, like fireflies. The Wongs didn't go to bed. They sat outside their tent, all of them, nobody talkin'. They had incense burnin' again. Everybody had incense burnin'. The air was fragrant with it, like flowers. I never knew how still it could be in the world, at night . . . And then at dawn —

[*Voices remote.*]

MR. WONG. They will come in from the western sky.

GRANDPA WONG. Eat, my son.

MR. WONG. I can't eat. What if the earth wrinkles like cloth under their wheels? I will kill myself.

GRANDPA WONG. Trust the earth. I tell you, I know our earth.

MR. WONG. But it has never been put to this great test. The bombers weigh —

GRANDPA WONG. Be quiet — you have said that a hundred times.

MR. WONG. I am going outside. I can't bear this roof. I must see the sky.

GRANDPA WONG (*chuckling*). Go on — go on — I want to eat.

JOHNNY (*his voice in the foreground always*). We did all the last little things all day. We thought they'd be in maybe around the middle of the afternoon. They didn't come. The sky lit up with such a sunset —

GRANDPA WONG. You see the heavens. They light the way. You see the earth how it waits.

MR. WONG. Father, father, look!

GRANDPA WONG. Where?

MR. WONG. There — where I point —

GRANDPA WONG. Eagles!

MR. WONG. No — the bombers — they come — they come —

[*His words are taken and tossed out by many voices — submerged. Sound of bombers approaching louder, to sudden finish.*]

JOHNNY. They came roarin' in out of the west. Nobody said a word when they began to come down. We were all watchin' that field under the wheels. The Wongs were in the front of the crowd, ol' Grandpa smilin'. But I saw the sweat pourin' down Mr. Wong's face. When the first bomber hit the ground I was watchin' him. There was a look on his face like the wheels were runnin' over his own body. Then he bust out laughin' —

MR. WONG. This earth holds!

GRANDPA WONG. What did I say?

JOHNNY. Yep, the earth held, like she was cement. The big beauties, they came down as light as feathers and hit and bounced a little and the earth acted like it had always been airfield.

MR. BRODER. Well, by heck —

MRS. BRODER (half dazed). It's queer how I see it all. I'd like to know those Wongs —

MARY. Johnny, Johnny, don't stop. What happened next?

JOHNNY. Funny thing, nothin' much. Of course we were awfully busy, but the Chinese just seemed to melt away. We thought they'd be trekkin' out that night — they'd all been paid off. But nobody went away. That night the lantern lights around the field were still just like fireflies. Everybody just sat waitin'. They waited that night and the next day and the next night — we began to get a hunch what they were waitin' for. They were waitin' to see the big bombers take off for Japan!

[Clatter of voices, Chinese and American, and fragmentary words.]

MR. WONG. We shall all stay to see if the land holds for their going. Who knows? It is more easy to come down than to go up.

GRANDPA WONG. You still do not trust our earth!

JOHNNY. The morning the boys took off — of course it was still nearly dark when we got the propellers spinnin'. I had a queer feeling, I remember, when I was workin'. I felt as though a crowd was watchin'. Then the sky split in the east, and light came through, and I saw them. They were all watchin', every one of those men,

women, and children, pressin' around the field, as near as they were allowed to come. I could see the Wongs and I waved to them.

MR. WONG. Now the Americans are in the machines. The wings quiver!

GRANDPA WONG. Be silent!

[There is an instant of silence, then the sound of the planes, and a loud medley of American and Chinese voices breaks out, the Americans shouting commands, the Chinese as below. This continues for a few seconds and then the confusion resolves itself by a transition that is almost like the precipitation of a chemical, so that out of the confusion a harmony forms. Mr. Wong's voice is the first clear resolution, at the end, then others join.]

VOICES. Look at the wings —
The wings, the wings!
But we laid the foundations.
They spring from our shoulders, these wings.
Our feet are upon the earth.
Our hands made the foundations.
From which our brothers fly into the heavens.
And over the seas.
All we have and all we are —
Victory!

MR. WONG (singing). " Arise, ye who refuse to be bondslaves! "

[The singing rises to a great chorus, continues for two seconds and recedes, not fading away so much as receding to a finish . . . Out of the silence, Johnny's voice.]

JOHNNY (very matter-of-fact). Well, I guess that's all, folks. They're usin' the field every day over there. It's a dandy.

## Suggestions for Study

1. There were many reasons why the Chinese so desperately wanted the airfield to be a success, the earth to hold under the weight of the B–29's. How many can you give? Why was their burning of incense to hold off rain so significant?

2. Why does Johnny's welcome home make

him think of the Wongs? Why is the story more impressive for being told in an American home? How do the different members of the family react to the story? Who is the best listener?

3. Grandpa Wong and his son show two different kinds of feeling that the Chinese had. What attitude did each take about the success of the airfield? Which man makes the better symbol for the Chinese as you understand them? If you have read Mrs. Buck's *The Good Earth* you can answer with confidence.

4. What special power of radio does this play make use of? How is the listener carried from one land to another?

5. What sound effects are used? Check each one to see what action it gets over to the listener. What is the "theme sound" for the play? Compare the use of music in this play with that in "The Snow Goose."

6. Mrs. Buck hopes to see real novels of literary merit written for radio. What special requirements would you set up for a high-grade radio novel? Think over your favorite continued stories on the radio. What makes you like them — characters, lively incidents, long-run suspense, or the kind of life pictured? Can you think of novels that would compete successfully with the "soap operas"?

## For Further Reading of Plays

### FULL-LENGTH PLAYS

Anderson, Maxwell: *Elizabeth the Queen; Mary of Scotland*
Austin, Mary: *The Arrowmaker*
Barry, Philip: *Holiday; You and I; The Youngest*
Beach, Lewis: *The Goose Hangs High*
Belasco, David: *The Return of Peter Grimm*
Connelly, Marc: *Green Pastures*
Craven, Frank: *The First Year; New Brooms*
Crothers, Rachel: *He and She; Mary the Third; Expressing Willie*
Fitch, Clyde: *Nathan Hale; Captain Jinks of the Horse Marines; The Climbers; The Truth; The Girl with the Green Eyes*
Gale, Zona: *Miss Lulu Bett*
Gillette, William: *Held by the Enemy; Secret Service*
Goldsmith, Clifford: *What a Life*
Goodrich, Arthur: *So This Is London; Mr. Grant*
Green, Paul: *The Field God; Johnny Johnson*

Howard, Bronson: *Shenandoah*
Howard, Sidney: *The Late Christopher Bean*
Howard, Sidney and De Kruif, Paul: *Yellow Jack*
Kaufman, G. S. and Connelly, Marc: *Dulcy; Merton of the Movies; Beggar on Horseback; To the Ladies*
Kaufman, G. S. and Ferber, Edna: *Minick; The Royal Family*
Kaufman, G. S. and Hart, Moss: *You Can't Take It with You; The American Way*
Klein, Charles: *The Lion and the Mouse*
MacKaye, Percy: *The Scarecrow; A Thousand Years Ago; Jeanne d'Arc; Washington, the Man Who Made Us; Yankee Fantasies*
Millay, E. St. V.: *The King's Henchman; The Lamp and the Bell*
Moody, W. V.: *The Great Divide; The Faith Healer*
Odets, Clifford: *Awake and Sing; Golden Boy*
Peabody, J. P.: *The Piper; The Wolf of Gubbio*
Pollock, Channing: *The Fool; The Enemy*
Sherwood, R. E.: *Abe Lincoln in Illinois*
Smith, H. J.: *A Tailor-Made Man; Mrs. Bumpstead-Leigh*
Thomas, Augustus: *The Witching Hour; The Copperhead; As a Man Thinks; In Mizzoura*

### PLAYS BY ENGLISHMEN ABOUT AMERICA

Drinkwater, John: *Abraham Lincoln; Robert E. Lee*
Zangwill, Israel: *The Melting Pot*

### COLLECTIONS OF FULL-LENGTH PLAYS

Baker, G. P.: *Modern American Plays*
Cerf, B. and Cartwell, V. H.: *S.R.O.* (*The Most Successful Plays in the History of the American Stage*); *Sixteen Famous American Plays*
Coe, Kathryn and Cordell, W. H.: *The Pulitzer Prize Plays 1918–1934*
Cohen, H. L.: *Longer Plays by Modern Authors*
Dickinson, T. H.: *Chief Contemporary Dramatists* (three series)
Gassner, John: *Twenty Best Plays of the Modern American Theater*
Halline, A. G.: *American Plays*
Hatcher, Harlan: *Contemporary American Dramas*
Moses, Montrose J.: *Representative American Dramas; Representative Plays by American Dramatists* (3 vols.)

Quinn, A. H.: *Contemporary American Plays; Representative American Plays*

Tucker, S. M.: *Modern American and British Plays*

COLLECTIONS OF ONE-ACT PLAYS

Baker, G. P.: *Yale One-Act Plays*

Clark, B. H. and Cook, T. R.: *One-Act Plays*

Clark, B. H. and Nicholson, K.: *The American Scene*

Cohen, H. L.: *One-Act Plays; More One-Act Plays*

Dickinson, T. H.: *Representative One-Act Plays*

French, S.: *One-Act Plays for Stage and Study* (series one to seven)

Galbraith, E. E.: *Plays without Footlights*

Goldstone, G. A.: *One-Act Plays*

Hughes, Glenn: *Short Plays for Modern Players*

Isaacs, E. J. R.: *Plays of American Life and Fantasy*

Johnson, Theodore: *Miniature Plays for Stage and Study; Plays in Miniature* (2 vols.); *Ten Fantasies for Stage and Study*

Knickerbocker, E. V.: *Short Plays; Twelve Plays; Plays for Classroom Interpretation*

Leonard, S. A.: *Atlantic Book of One-Act Plays*

Mayorga, Margaret: *Representative One-Act Plays by American Authors; The Best One-Act Plays of 1937* (and of each year thereafter); *Plays of Democracy*

Nicholson, Kathryn: *The Appleton Book of Short Plays* (series one to four)

Shay, Frank: *Twenty Contemporary One-Act Plays; Twenty-Five Short Plays*

Shay, Frank and Loving, R.: *Fifty Contemporary One-Act Plays; Fifty More Contemporary One-Act Plays*

Snook, L. O.: *The First Yearbook of Short Plays*

Thomas, C. S.: *Atlantic Book of Junior Plays*

Tucker, S. M.: *Twelve One-Act Plays for Study and Production*

Webber, J. P. and Webster, H. H.: *Short Plays for Junior and Senior High Schools; Short Plays for Young People; One-Act Plays for Secondary Schools*

Zachar, I. and Kimball, R. A.: *Plays as Experience*

COLLECTIONS OF RADIO PLAYS

Bacher, W. A.: *The Treasury Star Parade*

Barnouw, E.: *Radio Drama in Action*

Corwin, Norman: *Thirteen by Corwin*

Oboler, Arch: *Oboler Omnibus; Fourteen Radio Plays; This Freedom; Plays for Americans*

Oboler, A. and Longstreet, S.: *Free World Theater*

Wylie, Max: *Best Broadcasts of 1939–1940* (series continues annually)

# PART TWO

# The Growth of American

# Literature

HOME TO THANKSGIVING. A Currier and Ives engraving. (Culver)

CHURCH AT MILL RIVER, MASSACHUSETTS. The lives of the earliest settlers centered in their religion. This house of worship reflects the simple taste and sturdy faith of our colonial forebears. (Gregor from Monkemeyer)

# The Colonial Time

NO OTHER great country has ever had its beginnings so fully recorded. Two Icelandic sagas tell the story of Leif the Lucky. Columbus kept a full diary. We know how much he was paid — about three hundred dollars a year — and how much his first trip to America cost — about seven thousand dollars. We know it was a fine April morning when the Virginia colonists landed on the shores of Chesapeake Bay. The strawberries were uncommonly large and tasty, and the Indians came bringing gifts (although later they came with tomahawks and war cries). We know this because almost as soon as men landed in America they began to write books about it.

Actually, the first book written in America was in press (in England) less than fifteen months after the first permanent settlement at Jamestown in 1607. The first American printing press was operating only nine years after the settlement on Massachusetts Bay. Nothing could show more clearly one great difference between American literature and the literature of other great nations.

Not for hundreds of years after the beginnings of culture in England was the first English book written; and the history of England was recorded hundreds of years before the first famous English writer, Chaucer, was born. Chaucer's books had to be copied out painfully by hand and distributed in editions of one copy each! English literature, French, Latin, and Greek literatures, all began long before the printing press, and grew out of dim centuries. They began with folklore, and minstrel ballads, and child's rhymes. A few of the early writings were handed down by word of mouth from generation to generation to be recorded later. We do not know who wrote the *Iliad* and the *Odyssey*, which were composed when the Greeks had already reached a fairly high stage of civilization. Until Schliemann went to Asia Minor and excavated nine ancient Troys, one built on the ruins of another, we did not even know whether the story of the Trojan War was a fairy tale or based on truth.

But America and American literature were born in the glare of publicity. American literature was the first great national literature that began after the invention of mechanical printing. In the year 1300 it cost a prince three thousand dollars to have a book made as a gift for his fiancée. In 1608, the same amount of money printed a large edition of Captain John Smith's book on Virginia. Five hundred dollars would equip a print shop. Settlers came to America bringing with them the books of the world. They sent back notes on America to be put into other books. In effect, therefore, literature in America was a going concern from the hour of the first permanent settlement. The story of American literature is a story of how the new continent, the new people, and the doings of the people on that continent gradually changed a colonial literature into a literature that was not colonial at all, but national and American.

## WHY DID THE FIRST PEOPLE COME TO AMERICA?

There is a grim fact in some of our early records which we tend to forget in these days when airplanes span the ocean between dinner and breakfast: many a ship in those first years unloaded as many dead passengers as live ones! The trip was desperately hard. Journey's end had nothing more to offer than uncommon diseases, unprepared-for hardships, hostile savages, and whatever could be won, by hard work and co-operation, from a wilderness.

Let us ask first questions first. Why did anyone want to come to America?

The very first ones came for the same reasons that sent later Americans to explore the Arctic and the Antarctic. They wanted the thrill of exploration, the satisfaction of rolling back the frontiers of knowledge, the first chance at whatever rewards the new land might offer. Some were seeking a short route to India, or a northwest passage to China, or the seven fabulous cities of gold. Some were looking for empire — John Cabot was one of these, and when he claimed the whole continent of North America for Britain his grateful king gave him the handsome reward of forty dollars.

But what about the permanent settlers, the three quarters of a million Europeans who came to America to live before 1770? A good many of them came to get away from intolerable conditions in Europe. Many a European family stood at the seashore and looked west, imagining a land which the endless wars of the Old World could not disturb; a land where their husbands and sons would be free from the fear of being impressed into the army; a land where they would be free to work for themselves, rather than for someone else, with a fair chance of living comfortably; a land where they could worship freely in the way they felt they should; a land where they could live in friendship among people who believed as they did, and where they could freely speak and print and learn. In other words, the America of the Four Freedoms.

When you read Crèvecoeur,[1] you may think that only the poor of Europe came, but that is not true. Two thirds of the early settlers were able to pay all the costs of their coming. The other third had such special

[1] Crèvecoeur (krĕv-kûr′).

talents that other colonists thought it worth while to pay their way over and let them work off the debt. They were not uneducated, either. The American settlers were neither all university graduates nor all poorly educated. They had about the normal amount of education for the English middle class. No large percentage of them were political refugees or religious fanatics. What was it, then, that set these followers of the western star apart from those who stayed at home?

It is pleasant to think that the Europeans who came to America were those who were more daring, more adventurous, more willing to face unfamiliar problems and measure themselves against unknown opposition, more confident in themselves, and willing to risk more for what they wanted and believed. That was the kind of spirit that pushed the frontier back and settled the West. It must also have been the kind of spirit that settled the lonely bays on the eastern coast of the continent.

THE COLONIES THEY BUILT

The mark of the land is on Americans and their literature. If you have any doubt of that, consider what might have happened if the same Europeans who settled America had landed, instead, on a South Pacific island. Would they not have developed a quite different civilization from the one that grew up in America? What if our Southern colonists had landed in New England. Would they have been able to establish their large plantations, their leisurely way of life, in that cold climate and rocky, hilly country?

The Southern colonies were fated to develop as agricultural states. They were fertile and warm and level. They produced heavy crops of tobacco and rice, later indigo and cotton. Those were products that England needed. The colonists had no need to build an industrial system of their own; they could ship the raw produce abroad at a large and easy profit. Most of the Cavaliers who migrated from England settled in the South. The Cavaliers were the people who supported the King and the State Church against the Puritan revolution in England. The Puritans wanted certain fundamental changes made in the English Church, and in 1649 they gathered under the leadership of Oliver Cromwell and overthrew the King. The monarchy was restored after eleven years, however, and the Cavaliers came back into power. The Cavaliers were mostly substantial landholders in England. They laid out the fertile Southern colonies in large plantations, with the result that comparatively few cities developed in this part of the country.

New England, on the other hand, was poor farm land, and the crops it produced were mostly the same ones England produced. Settlers there could grow their own food, but in order to develop a foreign trade they had to make something to sell. Farms were small; farmers gathered into villages. When machinery came into wide use in the eighteenth century, factories and mercantile houses employed many persons; cities grew up around them. In centers like Boston, Providence, and New Haven, urban culture and universities flourished. That was the kind of life the English Puritans — who settled mostly in New England, as the Cavaliers settled in the South — were used to.

The Middle States had better farm land than New England, but they, too, grew about the same crops as the old country, and therefore were forced into manufacturing and selling. New York and Philadelphia were natural centers of trade. They soon outgrew Boston and far outstripped Charleston. You may be interested in knowing how large the cities in colonial America were. In 1690, sixty years after it was founded and eighty-three years after the first settlement, the greatest city in America was Boston, and it had seven thousand people. In 1774, on the eve of the Revolution, Philadelphia had forty thousand people and was the second largest city in the British Empire. In all of colonial America in 1690 there were only three hundred thousand people; in 1774, about two million.

## HOW THE COLONISTS LIVED

But let us look back for a moment to those first years when the colonial settlements clung to the shore between the sea and the deep forest. What did they look like? They were groups of huts, made of logs and clay, huddled in a clearing at the edge of the woods. The huts faced south, for warmth. They had one room, with a stone chimney at the end. When another room was built on, it was put on the other side of the chimney, so that the same fire could warm both rooms. At first many windows were of oiled paper. The first dwellings in Philadelphia were caves, and a law had to be passed to make men move into wood or brick houses. Not for a long time did the graceful plantation houses of the South, and the dignified " colonial " houses of New England rise out of the forests. But from the very first, one of the huts served as a church — even though it was without the white steeple we have come to associate with colonial churches.

Nine tenths of all the colonists lived on the land. They cleared away a section of woods or found a grassy meadow, turned the soil with handmade tools, and planted the food they needed to live on. They were busy people. They had to be. They had to watch out for Indians. They had to learn to be more self-sufficient than they had ever been in the old country. They were on their own — that made the great difference. They were not working for princes or lords now; they were working for themselves. Whether they were hungry or not depended mostly on their care with the crops, their skill with the rifle and the fishing net. Whether they were well clothed depended on their skill with the skinning knife, the spinning wheel, and the needle. Whether they were comfortably well to do depended on how well they managed, how sharp they were at selling and buying, not on how much the prince let them keep. Whether they were well governed depended more on them than ever before. They were on their own. They had freedom of opportunity but had to accept the responsibilities that went with it.

In the South, the planters and the merchants emerged as the dominant classes; in New England, the clergy, professional men, and merchants; in New York, the merchant, the professional man, the trader. In New England, hardy settlers pushed along the rivers until they found white water, and set up mill wheels to run the industries that were beginning to develop. In the South, the plantations grew larger, the manor houses farther apart, and more and more slaves and tenants were needed to take care of the fields. Manhattan Island began to fill up with counting houses and warehouses, and Philadelphia bustled with business and ideas.

Nothing could be farther wrong than to think of the early colonies as places of idyllic quiet and leisure. They were not. Every moment was potentially exciting. Inland, the forest was alive both with danger and opportunity. The soil had to be conquered, and homes had to be made with sheer strength and ingenuity from such raw materials as could be found. The sea was white with sails. Colony boats went to a dozen ports in Europe, to the West Indies, to Africa. Colonists worked hard, fought hard when they had to, played hard when they could. Do not be misled by the dark, plain-colored clothes you see in colonial pictures. Those were easier to get and more durable. Do not be put off the track by the name Puritan. The Puritan religion was one of the most colorful and exciting man has ever followed.

RELIGIOUS FREEDOM IN THE COLONIES

The first public building that went up, almost invariably in New England and often so in the South, was the church. Religion was important in colonial America. It was the reason why many settlers came, and one reason why the colonies developed as they did. And it was more than coincidence that a large proportion of the important books written in colonial America before 1750 were by the Puritan clergy.

Yet religious freedom, like every other freedom, was a hard-won right. There was more religious freedom in America than in any part of the Old World, but there was by no means complete tolerance in colonial times. If we understand that, we are in position to understand one of the great truths about history — that freedom does not suddenly come into existence; it cannot even be legislated; it has to develop, and be fought for and won.

A great many settlers came to America in those first years seeking religious freedom and finding it. But they were seeking freedom *for themselves* — not for all men! This is not surprising, because tolerance was almost unknown in Europe, and had been since the Roman Empire. The colonists had been brought up in the tradition of a state church. On the continent, and in the Middle Ages, it had been the Roman Catholic Church. In England, at the time when most of the English settlers migrated, it was the Church of England. A large part of them came to America because they did not like the state church. But as soon as they were settled in a place where they would be free from constraint and persecution, they wanted at once to make *their own religion* the state church of the new colony!

That was what happened in Massachusetts. The colonists there had separated from the Church of England, and established what they called the Congregational Church. That became the official church, and its members were highly intolerant of Quakers and other dissenters. A New World version of the Church of England became the official church of Virginia. For a long time the privilege of voting in some colonies depended upon whether one belonged to the right church. But in the colonies as a whole there was no single denomination with enough membership or power to dominate the others. By picking his place, a man could be sure of being able to worship as he believed.

Slowly, gradually, this freedom broadened. New York and New Jersey began to admit all varieties of Protestants. William

Penn invited all except unbelievers to Pennsylvania. The larger the colonies grew, the less inclined they became to police their immigrants on religious grounds. More and more islands of safety were found for minority groups. By the time we became a nation, the American people were willing to write into the first article of the Bill of Rights: " Congress shall make no law respecting an establishment of religion, or prohibiting the free exercise thereof." No one would contend that we have complete religious tolerance even now, but intolerance has become social and informal, rather than formal and legal. It was a long hard journey to this point of tolerance, but in the early decades even our weariest road seemed to persecution-ridden Europe like a pathway of shining gold.

### THE PURITANS

We know the Puritans by story and by picture. We know they wore plain, severe clothes, and long faces; the pictures show them that way. We know they listened to three-hour sermons, meditated for long periods on religion, hanged witches, and frightened their children with hell-fire. Those are the stories that come down to us. And yet those stories and those pictures must be something less than the whole truth, for no people like that would have been able to do all the Puritans did.

Let us look at the Puritans again. They were great fighters. More than one of their Indian wars ended with the complete extermination of the Indian tribe involved. They were brave and tough. The very fact that they settled in cold, rocky New England, rather than the warmer, more fertile colonies farther south, tells us something about them. They were hard-working. They had to be, to make a living off the land where they settled. They were shrewd businessmen. They found a wilderness in New England and built it up into a manufacturing center that competed with the old country. They built ships (remember the Yankee clippers?) and sailed them on the seven seas. The fame of Yankee traders spread wherever men bought or sold goods. These facts do not fit any picture of the Puritan as a retiring, unworldly, meditative man.

They were uncommonly literate. New England colonies were the first to develop adequate school systems. They founded the first college (Harvard, in 1636), the first printing press (in 1639), the first newspapers (*Publick Occurrences,* founded in 1690, was at once suppressed by the government; the Boston *News-Letter,* founded in 1704, lasted for seventy-two years). The first noteworthy colonial scientists were Puritans. The Puritan clergy were some of the most learned men in the world. One of them, Cotton Mather, published more than four hundred books.

Were they long-faced? They had a fine sense of humor. There was no humorist like Mark Twain among them, but Mark himself kept a long face when he told his funniest jokes. There was little time in the northern colonies for play. Whole families had to work to subdue that New England soil, keep watch on the Indians, build the houses, make the clothes, tend the sick, spin the cloth, grind the flour, trap the animals, work the wood and iron, build up business with the Old World and the other colonies. They worked. They were serious. They wanted to make their colony succeed. They threw out Thomas Morton, who raised the Maypole of Merry Mount, because they knew that only hard work would succeed; and Morton was a bad influence on their young people, perhaps an inciter of the Indians against them. They could enjoy themselves on the right occasion: read the account of their first Thanksgiving. The suspicion grows that the long-faced Puritans of our pictures wore the stern faces that come from competence and vigilance. Ask the Indians. Ask the people who traded with them.

How about the long sermons? They had them. There was no doubt of that. And ushers kept the children awake by tapping their heads with long poles wielded from the back of the church. That is true. But the question is, why did they want to have such long sermons? They were not compelled to. And that leads us to ask what the church meant to the Puritans.

The church had certain jobs in those days which have since been given to other institutions. For a while, it took the place of the newspaper. It was an occasion for men to pass on to others what they had heard and learned. Sometimes a town crier stood outside the church and shouted the news. The church was usually an educational center. It was also a government center. The ministers were the best educated men in the community. To their own knowledge they added the wisdom derived from scripture and meditation. The Puritans thought of their government as a kind of theocracy — the leadership of God — and the ministers had an influence and a power which few American religious leaders have had since their time. And judging by the growth of the Puritan colonies, they did a good job.

There was still another reason behind the long sermons and the private meditations. The Puritans believed that because of Adam's sin in the Garden of Eden, mankind was consigned to Hell. Jesus's sacrifice had modified and softened that sentence, so that only some persons were doomed. But those were doomed forever.

Hell was a very real thing to the Puritans, and a very exciting idea. Their writers and preachers described every level, almost every foot, of Hell — the fire and the ice and the tortures, and the men and women who were already suffering there. To put it in a way that would probably shock the Puritans, Hell was the most interesting subject matter they knew. A sermon like Jonathan Edwards' " Sinners in the Hands of an Angry God " was the most exciting experience of the week for them. It was more intense, more moving, than any play or movie you have ever seen. In a sense, it took the place of theater and moving picture; even of reading matter.

Then why did they meditate? Because they believed that God would let them know, sometime during their life, whether they were destined to go to Heaven or Hell. That was perhaps the most important question they had to ask.

If the Puritans had little sympathy for Thomas Morton's Maypole, there were good reasons for it. For one thing, they were too busy. For another, Maypoles seemed to them pretty small potatoes beside the kind of excitement they lived all the time in their religion.

## WHAT DID THEY WRITE?

We have talked for a long time about the Puritans, because they did a large share of the writing that has come to us from colonial times. We have talked a long time about the colonists and the colonies, rather than about their books, because those books are important chiefly in that they reflect and illuminate colonial America. For the most part, they are not great literature; they are the records of a young country.

What was written in the colonies?

Americans land on Guadalcanal Island. What do you want to know about it? Two things, probably — what is the island like, and what were the experiences of those who landed? That is exactly what Europeans wanted to know about America. At the very first, there were a number of accounts of the land. Captain John Smith's was one of the best sellers along that line. Sometimes the good captain was accurate, sometimes he yielded to the opportunity to tell a good story. As far as we can find out, his story of Pocahontas was pure imagination, especially since the princess would have been only twelve years old when the incident was supposed to have taken place. But it is a charming incident, and shows some of the attractions that were used to appeal to the folks at home in order to make them pull up stakes and come to the New World.

William Bradford's famous account of the settlement at Plymouth was in a more serious, factual vein. Many a colonist coming to the New World had a sense of the importance of what he was doing. Many of them made some record, for their children, for the folks back home, of what they did. Only a few of these records passed into literature. Bradford's first account came out only a year after the first settlement. A decade later he began his *History of Plymouth Plantation,* which he kept up to date till 1647. As the work of a distinguished pioneer who had been thirty times governor of Plymouth, it is our best source of information about the colony. If you were to read his account, you would understand more of the excitement that lay behind these matter-of-fact reports of what the first Puritan scouts saw when they landed on the new continent — the excitement of coming to a land where they could set up the church they believed in, and work and prosper according to what they deserved.

You will find on pages 427 and 428 a psalm in the form the Puritans sang it in church, and a selection from *The New England Primer.* This primer, the Bible, and the Psalter were for fifty years the only textbooks used in elementary schools in New England. The primer was one of the most widely sold and perhaps most influential of all American books; more than five million copies went into the hands of school children. More than five million school children began to learn their alphabet by memorizing the most fundamental of all truths to the Puritans: " In Adam's fall, we sinned all."

Some of the diaries that were preserved and later printed give us our best pictures of life in the colonies. You will read examples of two of these diaries in this book — one from New England, one from the South. The New Englander, Mrs. Sarah Kemble Knight, was herself an illustration of the freedom of opportunity which the New World stood for. She kept a shop in Boston and taught school. She knew enough about business to be called to New York to help settle an estate. She kept a vivid record of a horseback trip to New York in 1704. It is part of this trip that she is describing in the passage reprinted in this volume. The Southerner was an aristocrat, owner of a great estate, head of one of the most famous families of Virginia, the Byrds. Colonel

CAPTAIN JOHN SMITH was not only an adventurer but was one of the first and most persuasive promoters of the advantages of living in America. (Three Lions)

Byrd had come a long way from the log huts of Jamestown. He lived in a mansion at Westover, and had been educated in England. You will notice his polished style of writing, his references to Aesop, Chaucer, and the Bible, his easy use of Latin, his easy contempt of lower classes. All such generalizations are dangerous, but if you will read William Byrd and Sarah Knight together, you will get a pretty good picture of the difference between what was happening shortly after 1700 in New England and in the South.

THE LAST PURITAN

But perhaps the most interesting of all the selections from this early period of our literature is a part of a Puritan sermon, one of the most famous of all American sermons by one of the most famous of American preachers, Jonathan Edwards.

Edwards was the last of a famous group of Puritan preachers. The influence these men exerted on New England for a full hundred years is almost beyond belief. In the case of some of them, the least word from the pulpit became law. Hardly a sermon went by in some churches without at least one of the parishioners crying out in mortal fear, " What can I do to be saved? " The influence was almost as great in the political realm as in the spiritual. The first code of law in New England — significantly called " The Body of Liberties " — was drafted by a Puritan preacher. Increase Mather, the minister of Boston, became president of Harvard, ambassador from the Massachusetts Bay colony to the Court of St. James's, unquestioned spiritual and political leader of the colony. He wrote more than one hundred and fifty books. His son Cotton, the greatest prodigy of the colony, wrote more than four hundred. Cotton Mather was the most eloquent historian of the early colonies, the greatest American scientist of his time (a member of the Royal Society of London), the first American to practice inoculation for smallpox, a leader in the crusade against witchcraft, a powerful and learned preacher and fighter against sin. Yet he lived in the time when the influence of the preachers was dying. The witchcraft persecutions backfired; Increase was dismissed from the Harvard presidency, and Cotton was proposed twice but never elected. Even his best gifts to his fellow men, such as the smallpox inoculations, worked against him; someone threw a rock through his window, with this note attached: " Cotton Mather, you Dog! I'll inoculate you with this, with a pox to you." He and his father lived to see religious tolerance established by law in Massachusetts, and the authority of the clergy pass to civil officials.

There is a tradition in folk tales that the greatest hero is always the last of the line. So it was with Jonathan Edwards, who was born in 1703, when already the civil influence of the Puritan priests was nearly dead. He was a greater scientist than Cotton Mather; sometime you will enjoy reading his description of the flying spider, which was the most accurate observation of spiders up to that time. He was the greatest philosopher of the Puritans, and his long *Treatise on Freedom of the Will* won a world-wide reputation. No one could write more beautifully of God and holiness and righteous men; his description of his future wife and his personal narrative of mystical experiences, it has been said, are like the playing of harps and the blowing of trumpets. On the other hand, no one could preach more terrifyingly of hell. On Sundays when he gave sermons like " Sinners in the Hands of an Angry God," his congregation would shiver in terror, and strong men would cry, " Mr. Edwards, forbear! " But he came too late. A century earlier he might have been the greatest man in the colonies. As it was, he preached in a small community in western Massachusetts. Finally called to the presidency of Princeton, with a chance to mold that college along the lines of his thinking, he died of smallpox at the age of fifty-four — ironically of the very disease from which Cotton Mather could have saved him.

Edwards was born only three years before Benjamin Franklin, but Franklin lived on far past him. As Franklin might truly be called the first great American, so Edwards was the last great colonial preacher and writer. He was at the end of a century and a half of development, beginning with the first tentative and cautious landings on the eastern coast, described by Smith and Bradford. In that one hundred and fifty years, cities, schools, colleges, laws, courts, factories, and trades had grown up. In the colonies were merchants capable of holding their own with the traders in the old country; scientists, philosophers, and writers to whom the Old World listened. The colonies had developed greater freedom of worship and more freedom of opportunity than the mother country. Now their development was no longer in a colonial direction. Every step was toward independence.

## THE BAY PSALM BOOK

The first book off the American press, *The Bay Psalm Book* (1640), illustrates one of the great uses the Puritans made of literature: to aid in worship. The three ministers who edited this book wanted to adapt Psalms from the Bible to simple tunes which the congregation could sing. " God's altar needs not our polishings," they tell us in their preface, " for we have respected rather a plain translation, than to smooth our verses with the sweetness of any paraphrase, and so have attended con-science rather than elegance." It is well that they had the consolations of conscience, for indeed their versions have little elegance. The lack of real poetic feeling is all the more evident when one compares the doggerel of Psalm I in *The Bay Psalm Book* with the beautiful and dignified King James version.

| THE BAY PSALM BOOK | THE KING JAMES VERSION |
|---|---|
| O Blessed man, that in th' advice of wicked<br>    doeth not walk;<br>nor stand in sinners way, nor sit in chayre<br>    of scornfull folk, | 1. Blessed is the man that walketh not in<br>    the counsel of the ungodly, nor standeth<br>    in the way of sinners, nor sitteth in the<br>    seat of the scornful. |
| But in the law of Jehovah,<br>    is his longing delight:<br>and in his law doth meditate, by day and<br>    eke by night. | 2. But his delight is in the law of the Lord;<br>    and in his law doth he meditate day and<br>    night. |
| And he shall be like to a tree<br>    planted by water rivers:<br>that in his season yields his fruit,<br>    and his leaf never withers. | 3. And he shall be like a tree planted by<br>    the rivers of water, that bringeth forth<br>    his fruit in his season; his leaf also shall<br>    not wither; and whatsoever he doeth<br>    shall prosper. |
| And all he doth, shall prosper well,<br>    the wicked are not so:<br>but they are like unto the chaffe,<br>    which winde drives to and fro. | 4. The ungodly are not so: but are like the<br>    chaff which the wind driveth away. |
| Therefore shall not ungodly men,<br>    rise to stand in the doome,<br>nor shall the sinners with the just,<br>    in their assemblie come. | 5. Therefore the ungodly shall not stand in<br>    the judgment, nor sinners in the congregation of the righteous. |
| For of the righteous men, the Lord<br>    acknowledgeth the way:<br>but the way of ungodly men,<br>    shall utterly decay. | 6. For the Lord knoweth the way of the<br>    righteous: but the way of the ungodly<br>    shall perish. |

## THE NEW ENGLAND PRIMER

In early New England, religion was the center of all instruction. The function of the college was to train ministers, and the purpose of schooling was to teach children to read the Bible. For more than a hundred years *The New England Primer,* known as " The Little Bible," was the basic textbook in Puritan schools. Although we do not know exactly when it was first published, researchers think it was in existence by 1688 and that more than five million copies of its various editions were printed. School children committed the following alphabet to memory and chanted it piously in unison. This version is from the 1727 edition.

# Jonathan Edwards    1703–1758

## SINNERS IN THE HANDS OF AN ANGRY GOD

A local historian reports that when Jonathan Edwards, the last great Puritan minister, delivered the sermon from which this excerpt was taken, " there was heard such a breathing of distress and weeping, that the preacher was obliged to speak to the people and desire silence that he might be heard." Edwards's delivery is said to have been forceful, but not violent; and his other writings show him to have been of a gentle nature. It is Puritan theology rather than Edwards himself that speaks here, though the power of the language belongs to Edwards.

The God that holds you over the pit of hell much as one holds a spider or some loathsome insect over the fire, abhors you, and is dreadfully provoked; his wrath toward you burns like fire; he looks upon you as worthy of nothing else but to be cast into the fire; he is of purer eyes than to bear to have you in his sight; you are ten thousand times so abominable in his eyes as the most hateful and venomous serpent is in ours. You have offended him infinitely more than ever a stubborn rebel did his prince: and yet it is nothing but his hand that holds you from falling into the fire every moment. 'Tis ascribed to nothing else, that you did not go to hell the last night; that you was [1] suffered to awake again in this world after you closed your eyes to sleep and there is no other reason to be given why you have not dropped into hell since you arose in the morning, but that God's hand has held you up. There is no other reason to be given why you ha'n't gone to hell since you have sat here in the house of God, provoking his pure eyes by your sinful wicked manner of attending his solemn worship. Yea, there is nothing else that is to be given as a reason why you don't this very moment drop down into hell.

O sinner! Consider the fearful danger you are in. 'Tis a great furnace of wrath, a wide and bottomless pit, full of the fire of wrath, that you are held over in the hand of that God whose wrath is provoked and incensed as much against you as against many of the damned in hell. You hang by a slender thread, with the flames of divine wrath flashing about it, and ready every moment to singe it and burn it asunder; and you have no interest in any Mediator, and nothing to lay hold of to save yourself, nothing to keep off the flames of wrath, nothing of your own, nothing that you ever have done, nothing that you can do, to induce God to spare you one moment.

It is *everlasting* wrath. It would be dreadful to suffer this fierceness and wrath of Almighty God one moment; but you must suffer it to all eternity: there will be no end to this exquisite, horrible misery. When you look forward you shall see a long forever, a boundless duration before you, which will swallow up your thoughts and amaze your soul; and you will absolutely despair of ever having any deliverance, any end, any mitigation, any rest at all; you will know certainly that you must wear out long ages, millions of millions of ages, in wrestling and

[1] **you was:** often found in eighteenth-century writings for the singular, not then considered illiterate as it is now.

JONATHAN EDWARDS, preacher and writer, is considered to have had one of the most powerful intellects in American history. (Culver)

conflicting with this almighty, merciless vengeance; and then when you have so done, when so many ages have actually been spent by you in this manner, you will know that all is but a point to what remains. So that your punishment will indeed be infinite. Oh, who can express what the state of a soul in such circumstances is! All that we can possibly say about it gives but a very feeble, faint representation of it; it is inexpressible and inconceivable: for " who knows the power of God's anger? "

## THUNDER AND LIGHTNING

The many-sided Jonathan Edwards was also one of our earliest American scientific observers. From his *Notes on Natural Science,* this analysis of the causes of thunder and lightning shows his inquiring and penetrating mind. Perhaps his descriptions of the fires of hell were vivified by his careful observation of the fires of heaven. It is interesting, too, to note that while Edwards studied the principles of lightning, his contemporary, Benjamin Franklin, made his famous experiments with kite and key to bring lightning under man's control.

It is remarkable of thunder how long one part of the sound will be heard after another, when it is evident that the sound is made all in an instant by the lightning, which continues no longer. This arises from the length of the stream of lightning, whereby one part is a great deal farther from us than another, so that the sound is a great while coming successively. Hence it is that in claps of thunder that are near us, the first noise that we hear seems to be very near the earth, and then it seems to go further and further from us, and the last will be a murmuring up in the clouds; for although the noise that was made in the clouds, and the noise near the earth, was made[1] together as at an instant, yet that in the clouds is much farther, and therefore is longer coming, and is a much lower sound when it sounds.

The rapid vibration of the air jars and jumbles, breaks and condenses the bubbles of the cloud; whence it is that, soon after hard claps of thunder, rain falls in greater plenty.

I regard thunder as a meteor by far the most wonderful and least explicable of any whatsoever. . . .

Lightning seems to be this: An almost infinitely fine, combustible matter that floats in the air, that takes fire by a sudden and mighty fermentation that is some way promoted by the cool and moisture, and perhaps attraction, of the clouds. By this sudden agitation, this fine floating matter is driven forth with a mighty force one way or other, whichever way it is directed, by the circumstances and temperature of the circumjacent air; for cold and heat, density and rarity, moisture and dryness has almost an infinitely strong influence upon the fine particles of matter. This fluid matter, thus

[1] **was made:** This use of *was* with a plural subject was not considered incorrect in Edward's time; see also the similar use of *has* in paragraph 4.

projected, still fermenting to the same degree, divides the air as it goes, and every moment receives a new impulse by the continued fermentation; and as its motion received its direction, at first, from the different temperature of the air, on different sides, so its direction is changed, according to the temperature of the air it meets with, which renders the path of the lightning so crooked.

## Sarah Kemble Knight 1666–1727

### FROM HER JOURNAL

Nowadays swift airplanes make frequent round trips between Boston and New York. One can eat breakfast in Boston, attend to a full day's business in New York, and return home for dinner. But in 1704 when Mrs. Sarah Kemble Knight wished to make a similar business trip, it took her five months. There were no airplanes then, no railroad trains, not even stagecoaches. She traveled on horseback.

On every page of the journal she kept on this trip one finds evidence of her keen observation and lively imagination. Capable and energetic as she was, it is no wonder that she felt free to sit in judgment on less able fellow Americans she met along the way.

In these selections the author's original spelling and capitalization have been preserved.

#### STRANGE CUSTOMS OF CONNECTICUT

*Saturday, Oct. 7th,* wee sett out early in the Morning, and being something unaquainted with the way, having ask't it of some wee mett, they told us wee must Ride a mile or two and turne down a Lane on the Right hand; and by their Direction wee Rode on but not Yet comeing to the turning, we mett a Young fellow and ask't him how farr it was to the Lane which turn'd down towards Guilford. Hee said wee must Ride a little further, and turn down by the Corner of uncle Sams Lott. My Guide vented his Spleen at the Lubber; and we soon after came into the Rhode, and keeping still on, without any thing further Remarkebell, about two a clock afternoon we arrived at New Haven, where I was received with all Possible Respects and civility. Here I discharged Mr. Wheeler with a reward to his satisfaction, and took some time to rest after so long and toilsome a Journey; And Inform'd myselfe of the manners and customs of the place, and at the same time employed myselfe in the afair I went there upon.

They are Govern'd by the same Laws as wee in Boston, (or little differing,) thr'out this whole Colony of Connecticot, And much the same way of Church Government, and many of them good, Sociable people, and I hope Religious too: but a little too much Independant in their principalls, and, as I have been told, were formerly in their Zeal very Riggid in their Administrations towards such as their Lawes made Offenders, even to a harmless Kiss or Innocent merriment among Young People. Whipping being a frequent and counted an easy Punishment, about which, as other Crimes, the Judges were absolute in their Sentences. Their Diversions in this part of the Country are on Lecture days [1] and Training days mostly: on the former there is Riding from town to town.

And on training dayes The Youth divert themselves by Shooting at the Target, as they call it, (but it very much resembles a pillory,) where hee that hitts neerest the white has some yards of Red Ribbin presented him, which being tied to his hattband, the two ends streeming down his back, he is Led away in Triumph, with great applause, as the winners of the Olympiack Games.[2] They generally marry very young: the males oftener as I am told under twentie than above; they generally make public wedings, and have a way something singular (as they say) in some of them, viz. Just before Joyning hands the Bridegroom quitts the place, who is soon followed by the

Bridesmen, and as it were, dragg'd back to duty — being the reverse to the former practice among us, to steal Mrs. Bride.

There are great plenty of Oysters all along by the sea side, as farr as I Rode in the Collony, and those very good. And they Generally lived very well and comfortably in their famelies. But too Indulgent (especially the farmers) to their slaves: sufering too great familiarity from them, permitting them to sit at Table and eat with them, (as they say to save time,) and into the dish goes the black as freely as the white hand. They told me that there was a farmer lived nere the Town where I lodgd who had some difference with his slave, concerning something the master had promised him and did not punctualy perform; which caused some hard words between them; But at length they put the matter to Arbitration and Bound themselves to stand to the award of such as they named — which done, the Arbitrators Having heard the Allegations of both parties, Order the master to pay 40s to black face, and acknowledge his fault. And so the matter ended: the poor master very honestly standing to the award.

There are every where in the Towns as I passed, a Number of Indians the Natives of the Country, and are the most salvage of all the salvages of that kind that I had ever Seen: little or no care taken (as I heard upon enquiry) to make them otherwise. They have in some places Landes of their owne, and Govern'd by Law's of their own making; — they marry many wives and at pleasure put them away, and on the least dislike or fickle humor, on either side, saying *stand away* to one another is a sufficient Divorce. And indeed those uncomely *Stand aways* are too much in Vougue among the English in this [Indulgent Colony] as their Records plentifully prove, and that on very trivial matters, of which some have been told me, but are not proper to be Related by a Female pen, tho some of that foolish sex have had too large a share in the story.

If the natives committ any crime on their own precincts among themselves, the Eng-

---

[1] **Lecture days:** Thursdays were so called because of the regular midweek religious lecture.
[2] **Olympiack Games:** The Greeks held great athletic festivals every four years, beginning in 776 B.C., at Olympia. It is from these that the modern Olympic games take their name.

lish takes no Cognezens [1] of. But if on the English ground, they are punishable by our Laws. They mourn for their Dead by blacking their faces, and cutting their hair, after an Awkerd and frightfull manner; But can't bear You should mention the names of their dead Relations to them: they trade most for Rum, for which they'd hazzard their very lives; and the English fit them Generally as well, by seasoning it plentifully with water.

They give the title of merchant to every trader; who Rate their Goods according to the time and spetia [2] they pay in: viz. Pay, mony, Pay as mony, and trusting. *Pay* is Grain, Pork, Beef, &c. at prices sett by the General Court that Year; *mony* is pieces of Eight,[3] Ryalls,[4] or Boston or Bay shillings (as they call them,) or Good hard money, as sometimes silver coin is termed by them; also Wampom, vizt. Indian beads which serves for change. *Pay as mony* is provisions, as aforesaid one Third cheaper then as the Assembly or General Court sets it; and *Trust* as they and the merchant agree for time.

Now, when the buyer comes to ask for a comodity, sometimes before the merchant answers that he has it, he sais, *is Your pay redy?* Perhaps the Chap Reply's Yes: what do You pay in? say's the merchant. The buyer having answered, then the price is set; as suppose he wants a sixpenny knife, in pay it is 12*d* — in pay as money eight pence, and hard money its own price, viz. 6*d*. It seems a very Intricate way of trade and what Lex Mercatoria [5] had not thought of.

Being at a merchants house, in come a tall country fellow, with his alfogeos [6] full of Tobacco; for they seldom Loose their Cudd, but keep Chewing and Spitting as long as they're eyes are open, — he advanc't to the midle of the Room, makes an Awkward Nodd, and spitting a Large deal of Aromatick Tincture, he gave a scrape with his shovel like shoo, leaving a small shovel full of dirt on the floor, made a full stop, Hugging his own pretty Body with his hands under his arms, Stood staring rown'd him, like a Catt let out of a Baskett. At last, like the creature [7] Balamm Rode on, he opened his mouth and said: have You any Ribinen for Hatbands to sell I pray? The Questions and Answers about the pay being past, the Ribin is bro't and opened. Bumpkin Simpers, cryes its confounded Gay I vow; and beckning to the door, in comes Jone Tawdry [8] dropping about 50 curtsees, and stands by him: hee shows her the Ribin. *Law, You,* sais shee, *its right Gent,*[9] do You take it, *tis dreadfully pretty.* Then she enquires, *have you any hood silk I pray?* Which being brought and bought, *Have You any thred silk to sew it with* says shee, which being accommodated with they Departed. They Generaly stand after they come in a great while speachless, and sometimes dont say a word till they are askt what they want, which I impute to the Awe they stand in of the merchants, who they are constantly almost Indebted too; and must take what they bring without Liberty to choose for themselves; but they serve them as well, making the merchants stay long enough for their pay.

We may Observe here the great necessity and bennifitt both of Education and Conversation; for these people have as Large a portion of mother witt, and sometimes a Larger, than those who have bin brought up in Cities; But for want of emprovements, Render themselves almost Ridiculos, as above. I should be glad if they would leave such follies, and am sure all that Love Clean Houses (at least) would be glad on't too.

They are generaly very plain in their dress, throuout all the Colony, as I saw, and

---

[1] **Cognezens:** cognizance. In other words, the English pay no attention to these crimes. [2] **spetia:** specie; coin. [3] **pieces of Eight:** Spanish dollars containing eight reals, worth ninety-six cents. [4] **Ryalls:** reals, Spanish silver coins worth about twelve cents. [5] **Lex Mercatoria** (mŭr-kȧ-tō'rǐ-ȧ): the law of merchants. [6] **alfogeos** (ăl-fō'jǐ-ōs): Spanish saddlebags; here humorously used for cheeks.

[7] **creature:** a famous ass in the Bible, which could speak (Num. 22:21–33). [8] **Jone Tawdry:** humorous name for the country girl. [9] **Gent:** a rustic abbreviation for genteel or elegant.

follow one another in their modes; that You may know where they belong especially the women, meet them where you will.

Their Chief Red Letter day is St. Election,[1] which is annually Observed according to Charter, to choose their Govenr: a blessing[2] they can never be thankfull enough for, as they will find, if ever it be their hard fortune to loose it. The present Governor in Conecticott is the Honorable John Winthrop Esq. A Gentleman of an Ancient and Honourable Family, whose Father was Govenor here sometime before, and his Grand father had bin Govr of the Massachusetts. This gentleman is a very curteous and afable person, much Given to Hospitality, and has by his Good services Gain'd the affections of the people as much as any who had bin before him in that post.

### HARDSHIPS OF TRAVEL

*Decr. 6th.* Being by this time well Recruited and rested after my Journy, my business lying unfinished by some concerns at New York depending thereupon, my Kinsman, Mr. Thomas Trowbridge of New Haven, must needs take a Journy there before it could be accomplished, I resolved to go there in company with him, and a man of the town which I engaged to wait on me there. Accordingly, Dec. 6th we set out from New Haven, and about 11 the same morning came to Stratford ferry; which crossing, about two miles on the other side Baited our horses and would have eat a morsell ourselves, But the Pumpkin and Indian mixt Bred had such an Aspect, and the Barelegg'd Punch so awkerd or rather Awful a sound, that we left both, and proceeded forward, and about seven at night come to Fairfield, where we met with good entertainment and Lodg'd; and early next morning set forward to Norowalk, from its halfe Indian name *Northwalk,* when about 12 at noon we arrived, and Had a Dinner of Fryed Venison, very savoury. Landlady

wanting some pepper in the seasoning, bid the Girl hand her the spice in the little *Gay* cupp on the shelfe. From hence we Hasted towards Rye, walking and Leading our Horses neer a mile together, up a prodigios high Hill; and so Riding till about nine at night, and there arrived and took up our Lodgings at an ordinary,[3] which a French family kept. Here being very hungry, I desired a fricasee which the Frenchman undertakeing, mannaged so contrary to my notion of Cookery, that I hastned to Bed superless; And being shewd the way up a pair of stairs which had such a narrow passage that I had almost stopt by the Bulk of my Body; But arriving at my apartment found it to be a little Lento[4] Chamber furnisht amongst other Rubbish with a High Bedd and a Low one, a Long Table, a Bench and a Bottomless chair, — Little Miss went to scratch up my Kennell[5] which Russelled as if shee'd bin in the Barn amongst the Husks, and supose such was the contents of the tickin — nevertheless being exceedingly weary, down I laid my poor Carkes[6] (never more tired) and found my Covering as scanty as my Bed was hard. Annon I heard another Russelling noise in The Room — called to know the matter — Little miss said shee was making a bed for the men; who, when they were in Bed, complained their leggs lay out of it by reason of its shortness — my poor bones complained bitterly not being used to such Lodgings, and so did the man who was with us; and poor I made but one Grone, which was from the time I went to bed to the time I Riss, which was about three in the morning, Setting up by the Fire till Light, and having discharged our ordinary[7] which was as dear as if we had had far Better fare — wee took our leave of Monsieur and about seven in the morn come to New Rochell a french town, where we had a good Breakfast. And in the strength of that about an how'r before sunsett got to York. Here I

EARLY NEW ENGLAND HOME. Built in Duxbury, Massachusetts by Miles Standish's son in 1666 (the year Sarah Kemble Knight was born), this simple frame dwelling is typical of the functional style built by the settlers in the New England colonies. Having neither time nor money for the refinements of decoration, their chief concern was to erect substantial shelters against the northern climate. Note that the chimney is placed in the center to heat all the rooms in the house. The plan for this type of home was developed by carpenters in the colonies and may be said to be the first purely American architecture. (Brown Brothers)

applyd myself to Mr. Burroughs, a merchant to whom I was recommended by my Kinsman Capt. Prout, and received great Civilities from him and his spouse, who were now both Deaf but very agreeable in their Conversation, Diverting me with pleasant stories of their knowledge in Brittan from whence they both come.

## Colonel William Byrd 1674–1744

### A HISTORY OF THE DIVIDING LINE

Colonel William Byrd was one of the commissioners in charge of running the boundary line between the colonies of Virginia and Carolina, which is still the boundary between the states. He accompanied the expedition in person and watched over its activities, but he also observed the surrounding country and its in-habitants. He writes from the point of view of the aristocrat. Democracy was not yet established upon these shores; and as the colonies developed socially and economically, they naturally followed patterns of life they were accustomed to in England. Both the estate he inherited and his own distinguished service to the colony entitled Byrd to a place in the aristocracy. His background and wide reading also contributed to the development of a more polished style than is displayed by the other colonial keepers of journals. You can see this difference for yourself as you go with him along the new boundary line.

### CAMP LIFE

*March 12* [*1728*]. . . . Our landlord [1] had a tolerable good house and clean furniture, and yet we could not be tempted to lodge in it. We chose rather to lie in the open field, for fear of growing too tender. A clear sky, spangled with stars, was our

[1] **landlord:** a plantation owner named Balance.

EARLY SOUTHERN HOME. The Westover, Virginia, home of William Byrd reflects the more gracious life in the southern colonies in the late seventeenth century. In general, the southern colonists were wealthier and the climate kinder than in New England. Plans for Byrd's home, and for most houses in the South, were imported from England. (Culver)

canopy which, being the last thing we saw before we fell asleep, gave us magnificent dreams. The truth of it is, we took so much pleasure in that natural kind of lodging that I think at the foot of the account mankind are great losers by the luxury of feather beds and warm apartments.

The curiosity of beholding so new and withal so sweet a method of encamping, brought one of the senators of North Carolina to make us a midnight visit. But he was so very clamorous in his commendations of it that the sentinel, not seeing his quality, either through his habit or behavior, had like to have treated him roughly.

After excusing the unseasonableness of his visit, and letting us know he was a Parliament man, he swore he was so taken with our lodging that he would set fire to his house as soon as he got home and teach his wife and children to lie, like us, in the open field.

## THE DISMAL SWAMP

*March 14.* Before nine of the clock this morning, the provisions, bedding, and other necessaries were made up into packs for the men to carry on their shoulders into the Dismal. They were victualed for eight days at full allowance, nobody doubting but that would be abundantly sufficient to carry them through that inhospitable place; nor indeed was it possible for the poor fellows to stagger under more. As it was, their loads weighed from sixty to seventy pounds, in just proportion to the strength of those who were to bear them.

'Twould have been unconscionable to have saddled them with burthens heavier than that, when they were to lug them through a filthy bog which was hardly practicable with no burthen at all. Besides this luggage at their backs, they were obliged to measure the distance, mark the trees, and clear the way for the surveyors every step they went. It was really a pleasure to see with how much cheerfulness they undertook, and with how much spirit they went through all this drudgery. For their greater safety, the commissioners took care to furnish them with Peruvian bark, rhubarb, and hipocoacanah,[1] in case they might happen, in that wet journey, to be taken with fevers or fluxes.

Although there was no need of example to inflame persons already so cheerful, yet, to enter the people with better grace, the author and two more of the commissioners accompanied them half a mile into the Dismal. The skirts of it were thinly planted with dwarf reeds and gall bushes but, when we got into the Dismal itself, we found the reeds grew there much taller and closer and, to mend the matter, was [2] so interlaced with bamboo briars that there was no scuffling through them without the help of pioneers. At the same time, we found the ground moist and trembling under our feet like a quagmire, insomuch that it was an easy matter to run a ten-foot pole up to the head in it, without exerting any uncommon strength to do it.

Two of the men, whose burthens were the least cumbersome, had orders to march before with their tomahawks and clear the way, in order to make an opening for the surveyors. By their assistance we made a shift to push the line half a mile in three hours, and then reached a small piece of firm land about one hundred yards wide standing up above the rest like an island. Here the people were glad to lay down their loads and take a little refreshment, while the happy man whose lot it was to carry the jug of rum began already, like Aesop's bread-carriers,[3] to find it grow a good deal lighter.

After reposing about an hour, the commissioners recommended vigor and constancy to their fellow travelers, by whom they were answered with three cheerful huzzas in token of obedience. This ceremony was no sooner over but they took up their burthens and attended the motion of the surveyors who, though they worked with all their might, could reach but one mile farther, the same obstacles still attending them which they had met with in the morning.

However small this distance may seem to such as are used to travel at their ease, yet our poor men, who were obliged to work with an unwieldy load at their backs, had reason to think it a long way; especially in a bog where they had no firm footing, but every step made a deep impression, which was instantly filled with water. At the same time they were laboring with their hands to cut down the reeds, which were ten feet high, their legs were hampered with the briars. Besides, the weather happened to be very warm, and the tallness of the reeds kept off every friendly breeze from coming to refresh them. And, indeed, it was a little provoking to hear the wind whistling among the branches of the white cedars, which grew here and there amongst the reeds, and at the same time not have the comfort to feel the least breath of it.

In the meantime the three commissioners returned out of the Dismal the same way they went in and, having joined their brethren, proceeded that night as far as Mr. Wilson's.

This worthy person lives within sight of the Dismal, in the skirts whereof his stocks range and maintain themselves all the winter, and yet he knew as little of it as he did of *Terra Australis Incognita*.[4] He told us a Canterbury tale [5] of a North Briton whose curiosity spurred him a long way into this

---

[1] **hipocoacanah:** known today as ipecac. [2] **was:** See note on *was* as a plural verb (page 429.) [3] **Aesop's bread-carriers:** According to the fable the man who wanted the lightest burden on the journey was laughed at for choosing the bread, which was the heaviest; but by night the bread had all been distributed and he had only the empty basket to carry.

[4] **Terra Australis Incognita:** unknown southern land, such as Byrd's descendant has lately explored. [5] **Canterbury tale:** here an incredible tale. The *Canterbury Tales* were famous old stories recounted in verse by the first great English poet, Chaucer. The reference shows Byrd's literary education.

great desert, as he called it, near twenty years ago, but he having no compass, nor seeing the sun for several days together, wandered about till he was almost famished; but at last he bethought himself of a secret his countrymen make use of to pilot themselves in a dark day.

He took a fat louse out of his collar and exposed it to the open day on a piece of white paper which he brought along with him for his journal. The poor insect, having no eyelids, turned himself about till he found the darkest part of the heavens, and so made the best of his way toward the north. By this direction he steered himself safe out, and gave such a frightful account of the monsters he saw and the distresses he underwent, that no mortal since has been hardy enough to go upon the like dangerous discovery.

### NORTH CAROLINA PLANTATION LIFE

*March 25.* . . . In the mean time, we who stayed behind had nothing to do but to make the best observations we could upon that part of the country. The soil of our landlord's plantation, though none of the best, seemed more fertile than any thereabouts, where the ground is near as sandy as the deserts of Africa, and consequently barren. The road leading from thence to Edenton, being in distance about twenty-seven miles, lies upon a ridge called Sandy Ridge, which is so wretchedly poor that it will not bring potatoes.

The pines in this part of the country are of a different species from those that grow in Virginia: their bearded leaves are much longer and their cones much larger. Each cell contains a seed of the size and figure of a black-eyed pea, which, shedding in November, is very good mast for hogs, and fattens them in a short time.

The smallest of these pines are full of cones, which are eight or nine inches long, and each affords commonly sixty or seventy seeds. This kind of mast has the advantage of all other by being more constant, and less liable to be nipped by the frost or eaten by the caterpillars. The trees also abound more with turpentine, and consequently yield more tar than either the yellow or the white pine; and for the same reason make more durable timber for building. The inhabitants hereabouts pick up knots of lightwood in abundance, which they burn into tar, and then carry it to Norfolk or Nansimond for a market. The tar made in this method is the less valuable because it is said to burn the cordage, though it is full as good for all other uses as that made in Sweden and Muscovy.[1]

Surely there is no place in the world where the inhabitants live with less labor than in North Carolina. It approaches nearer to the description of Lubberland[2] than any other, by the great felicity of the climate, the easiness of raising provisions, and the slothfulness of the people.

Indian corn is of so great increase that a little pains will subsist a very large family with bread, and then they may have meat without any pains at all, by the help of low grounds, and the great variety of mast that grows on the high land. The men for their parts, just like the Indians, impose all the work upon the poor women. They make their wives rise out of their beds early in the morning, at the same time that they lie and snore till the sun has run one-third of his course and dispersed all the unwholesome damps. Then, after stretching and yawning for half an hour, they light their pipes, and, under the protection of a cloud of smoke, venture out into the open air; though, if it happens to be never so little cold, they quickly return shivering into the chimney corner. When the weather is mild, they stand leaning with both their arms upon the cornfield fence, and gravely consider whether they had best go and take a small heat at the hoe: but generally find reasons to put it off till another time.

Thus they loiter away their lives, like

[1] **Muscovy:** Russia. [2] **Lubberland:** a paradise for lazy fellows. The following comments on the natives show the antipathy between the aristocratic Virginians and the small farmers of North Carolina, who were largely former servants.

Solomon's sluggard [1] with their arms across, and at the winding up of the year scarcely have bread to eat.

To speak the truth, 'tis a thorough aversion to labor that makes people file off to North Carolina, where plenty and warm sun confirm them in their disposition to laziness for their whole lives.

## Suggestions for Study of Colonial Literature

1. What was the positive and valuable contribution of the Puritans to the American spirit? Point out places where you discover it in these selections. Are any Puritan attitudes still alive in your community?

2. In your own reading and writing, which do you prefer to have emphasized, " conscience " or " elegance "? If you had to give up either, which would you sacrifice? Which selection comes nearest combining the two?

3. What other famous American schoolbooks besides *The New England Primer* have you heard of? Do you know what most of the early readers had in common with the *Primer?*

4. Did you discover why Puritan theology was really exciting? Do you think you could go to sleep in church if Jonathan Edwards were preaching? Would he be an interesting preacher Sunday after Sunday? Why, or why not?

5. Does Edwards' explanation of thunder and lightning seem clear to you? Is it an acceptable explanation to a modern scientist? If you do not know, ask your physics teacher.

6. What conditions in Connecticut did Mistress Knight find inferior to those in Massachusetts, and what others did she find preferable? On the whole, would you consider her tolerant or intolerant? Discuss the difficulties of travel of her day. Have we any comparable difficulties today? If so, what?

7. You will find a modern account of Mistress Knight and her journey in *Dames and Daughters of Colonial Days* by Geraldine Brooks. Read this and tell the class more about this famous trip.

8. Find evidences of Byrd's energy, his sense of humor, his London education. What passage shows most clearly how far his own life had changed from pioneer conditions?

[1] **Solomon's sluggard:** King Solomon said, " Go to the ant, thou sluggard; consider her ways and be wise" (Prov. 6:6).

9. Each of the diarists shows that he feels superior to some of the people he encounters, but each has a different reason for this feeling. What is it, in each case?

10. Read Rear Admiral Richard E. Byrd's *Skyward* or *Little America* and see what similarities you can find in the adventures and personalities of William Byrd and his descendant.

## For Your Vocabulary

BASE-WORD. Jonathan Edwards says that " sinners in the hands of an angry God " must despair of any *mitigation* (mĭt-ĭ-gā'shŭn) of their hard lot (page 429), of that lot's ever becoming milder. We use several related words with the same base-word, which means mild, soft. More frequent than the verb *mitigate,* to make mild, is the participle *mitigating,* usually applied to circumstances. It would be a *mitigating* circumstance in a burglary, for example, if the offender was a man who stole only food to feed a starving family. What would be a *mitigating* circumstance in your failing to remember to do an errand for your mother? Offenses are described as *unmitigated* when there is no excuse for them, and qualities may also be *unmitigated,* as " *unmitigated* harshness."

## For Further Reading on the Colonial Time

### LITERATURE OF THE PERIOD

Cairns, W. B.: *Early American Writers* (anthology)

Hart, A. B. and Chapman, A. B.: *How Our Grandfathers Lived* (source material)

### BOOKS ABOUT THE PERIOD

Adams, R. G.: *Pilgrims, Indians, and Patriots*
Bailey, C. S.: *Pioneer Art in America*
Browne, G. W.: *Real Legends of New England*
Earle, A. M.: *Home Life in Colonial Days*
Eaton, J.: *Lone Journey* (Roger Williams)
Gray, E. J.: *Penn*
Hart, A. B. and Hazard, B. E.: *Colonial Children*
Hartman, Gertrude: *These United States and How They Came to Be*
Knowlton, D. C. and Gill, C. M.: *When We Were Colonies*

See also list of novels, page 141, and general works, page 784.

# The Making of a Nation

PHILIP FRENEAU, who has some right to be called the first real poet of America, once looked condescendingly down at the audience he was trying to write for. " Barbers cannot exist as such among people who have neither hair nor beards," he said. " How, then, can a poet hope for success in a city where there are not three persons possessed of elegant ideas? "

" Elegant ideas " of the kind Freneau meant were undoubtedly lacking in the colonies. People were too busy. They were subduing a wilderness. They were working at that most absorbing of all problems: Given a desert isle and all that you can remember and carry with you from civilization, what kind of life and culture and home will you build? They were absorbed in religious problems that seemed to them a good deal more important than elegant ideas. In the seventeen hundreds they became absorbed in political problems that were solved only by a bloody revolution and the making of a new nation. The real genius of colonial Americans went into the creative act of settling a continent, the building of agriculture and commerce, the raising up of some noble houses and public buildings, the maintaining of churches, and, above all, political planning, action, and writing. ·

Perhaps you have wondered why hardly a poem, story, or novel we are proud of has come down to us from America before 1800. The reason is that in the bustling colonies people had little occasion to use literature for anything other than a tool. Literature had to do a job — like the axe that cut the forest, or the clipper that carried the goods. It had to pay its way. It had to tell the people back home about the new world

(Captain John Smith). It had to preserve the record of these momentous years (Bradford and the diarists). It had to keep the people devout and God-fearing (the Puritan sermons). It had to tell the people when the governors were abusing political power; it had to rouse the people to revolt and fan the flames of revolution during cold winters and military defeat; finally it had to present and weigh all the conflicting ideas of how a new nation should be made, and reconcile them into documents which would last far into the future.

The best brains of the colonies were going into jobs like these — not into elegant ideas. But there is one shelf of these practical writings we would not trade for the most elegant poems or stories ever written on the continent. That is the shelf of political essays, speeches, and public documents written in America between 1750 and 1800. Perhaps the American talent is for politics and mechanics, rather than art; some people have said so. Whatever the reason, American talent, American thinking and American energy combined in those years to produce documents that were read with admiration by the whole world. Franklin, Adams, Paine, Jefferson, Washington — none of them except Franklin and Paine professional writers — became world figures in a way that few of our poets and novelists have. Perhaps the greatest tribute ever paid them was spoken on the floor of the very body they attacked most vigorously, the British Parliament. Lord Chatham said there:

When your Lordships look at the papers transmitted to us from America; when you consider their decency, firmness, and wisdom, you cannot but respect their cause and wish to make it your own. . . . For solidity of reasoning, force of sagacity, and wisdom of conclusion, under such a difficult body of circumstances, no nation or body of men can stand in preference to the general congress at Philadelphia.

Let us look at some of the circumstances that lay behind that shelf of political writing.

## WHY DID THE COLONISTS WANT POLITICAL INDEPENDENCE?

Why did it happen? Few men in the colonies wanted independence before the 1770's. Even after the first battle, many leaders thought the differences with England could still be reconciled. If war had depended on a popular vote it might never have happened, for, as Washington himself said, even during the fighting there were never more than a third of the colonists active in support of the revolution. A third were indifferent, another third unfavorable. And yet, from 1760 on, the Atlantic colonies moved as irresistibly as fate toward independence.

As we look back now, we see that war could have been avoided. If certain English statesmen had ever understood the colonies, it could have been avoided. If England had offered the colonies such a plan of federation as Canada and Australia now enjoy, all that the Americans wanted could probably have been achieved without separation. But England did not.

The trouble was a simple one. The colonies had grown up, and the mother country did not realize it. Many a mother thinks of her strapping son as still a baby. Many a country in those days thought of its colonies as always subordinate, always existing to contribute to the wealth and greatness of the mother country. Although men as brilliant and distinguished as Dr. Franklin came to Europe to represent the colonies, English society held blindly to the fiction that no colonial could be quite the equal of a Briton born. Although the colonies were

vastly larger in territory, richer in potential wealth, manpower, and energy, still the ruling class of England maintained the fiction that America was a small annex of England. A British colony, in the minds of the wealthy English ruling class and the statesmen they appointed, never grew up. When it was young, it should be financed, nursed, jollied; as soon as it was large enought to work it should go to work for the mother country. " Sir," said Dr. Johnson, " we do not put a calf into the plow, we wait until he is an ox."

It seems hard to believe now that so many signposts of trouble went unheeded in England. The colonies reproduced neither the single state church nor the English social system. They lopped off titles of nobility. They gave men a chance to speak for themselves in town meetings, and an even chance to work for themselves in the fields and businesses. How could the rulers of England fail to see that the colonies faced west as well as east? The colonies were land hungry; they sent Daniel Boone beyond the Alleghenies to look at the rich and unsettled territories. They had a taste of the wealth of the New World, now; there was no holding them back from it.

Why did England forbid settlement beyond the Alleghenies, try to force the colonies to look only eastward toward Europe? England must have seen, too, that colonial trade was outgrowing the colonial system. The colonies realized that they were becoming really trade rivals, rather than partners, of England. Every year they bought as much from England as England had sent to the whole world at the beginning of the century. They felt that they were no longer so dependent upon England as England was upon them and that their colonial relation to England was actually working against them.

Once they had needed England. That was when they were barely able to squeeze a living out of the soil of the new world. Now the wealth of a continent was within sight, and England, they felt, was holding them back, not only from the fertile West, but also from an immensely profitable world trade. (By the Trade Acts, colonists were forbidden to export such profitable commodities as tobacco, iron, rice, lumber, and furs to any country except England. By Royal Order, the king alone could dispose of lands in the West.) As one pamphleteer put it, once the American ship needed an anchor to hold it against the storm; now the storm was over, and the anchor held it against favorable winds.

The very nature of life in America encouraged a spirit of independence. The pioneer learned to rely on himself. He learned that his community was capable of organizing and governing itself, usually of defending itself. He had seen Braddock's regulars under fire in the Pennsylvania woods, and he knew that there were a good many things the colonial militia could do better than British regulars. When the French were expelled from Canada in 1760 and there was no longer any threat from the north, he saw no more need of redcoat troops on this side of the Atlantic. In fact, they were an irritation, just as the British Parliament and the British colonial office were irritations.

Here was the British Parliament, three thousand miles and several weeks away, passing laws for Massachusetts and Virginia as confidently as it passed them for London and Lancashire! Some of those laws read as though they were designed purposely to goad the high-spirited men on the Atlantic seaboard. Those men looked around them at prosperous cities, well-kept farms, a thriving commerce, and said: " All this we have built. All this we have carved out of the forest and won from savages. All this we have paid for in muscle, ideas, and sacrifice. And for what? For the counting houses of England? For colonial administrators who look down their noses at us? "

Into this explosive situation came books and ideas from Europe. Tom Paine and Sam Adams talked about those ideas a lot. They said that every man was born with certain rights — life, liberty, and the pursuit of happiness, Jefferson called them in

1776. No government had a right to get in the way of those rights. If it did, there was only one thing to do. If an absentee owner got in the way of America's destiny, that absentee owner had to go! Almost from the first ship that landed Englishmen on this shore, the idea had been growing that America had a special destiny, the hope of a great future among nations. And no parliament three thousand miles away was going to get in the way!

## WHAT IS AN AMERICAN:
### BENJAMIN FRANKLIN

John Smith, William Bradford, Increase Mather, William Byrd, and Jonathan Edwards were strong men, admirable men. But they were English colonials living on the continent of America. Ralph Waldo Emerson, Abraham Lincoln, Mark Twain, Thomas A. Edison, and William Allen White were likewise strong and admirable men, and anywhere in the world they would have been recognized as Americans. Somewhere between those groups of men the colonial fell away, the American type emerged. Exactly where and when we cannot tell, but we do know who it was that stood forth before all the world as the unmistakable representative of the new type, the American. He was Benjamin Franklin.

If England had thoroughly understood Franklin, it would have understood the colonies. If you know enough about Franklin, you will be a long way toward knowing how America grew from colonies into the United States.

Look at Franklin's life for a moment. He lived for eighty-four years. One of his contemporaries said it was a special dispensation of Providence that Dr. Franklin should be spared to the colonies for more than his allotted three score years and ten. If he had died at the age of seventy he would have been cut off before the Declaration of Independence, and the colonies would have lost their best ambassador and wisest elder statesman. When he was born, in 1706, there were not many more than three hundred thousand people in the colonies. They

HARVARD COLLEGE in 1739, exactly a century after it was founded. (Culver)

were stretched in a thin line along the coast. One finger of settlement stretched up the Hudson to Albany, another up the Connecticut into central Massachusetts. The Tidewater plain was settled in Virginia, but there was no settlement even as far west as the Shenandoah Valley. Roads were few and far between. Fifty Bostonians went to London for every one that came to New York; they could get there more easily. There were three colleges in all English America, and one newspaper — which struggled along with about 300 subscribers.

When Franklin died, in 1790, the population of the colonies had increased tenfold. Settlers had moved everywhere as far west as the Alleghenies, and in several favored places had broken through the mountains onto the midland plains. Seventy thousand settlers had already followed Daniel Boone's trail into Kentucky; thirty thousand had gone into Tennessee. The colonies, which in 1706 had been so miserably connected that each could deal with England more easily than with its neighbors, were now connected by postal service, transportation, and government. They were a federated republic, totally independent of England. They owned all the continent north of Florida and east of the Mississippi. Every colony had at least one newspaper; Boston alone had five. The united colonies had fought a war and produced distinguished political literature. To the freedom of religion they already had, they had added political freedom. All that, Franklin saw and had a part in.

Everything about Franklin's life was symbolic of what was happening in the colonies. He was born in Boston, the seat of the Mathers and the throne of Puritanism, but Puritan religion slipped easily from him. He believed devoutly in a God, but little in the formalities of religion he saw around him. The Puritans were always turning inward; he was turning outward.

The Puritans had a very personal and intimate religion; he held what we might call a social religion. The best way to serve God, Franklin said, is in doing good to His other children. He illustrates the change that was coming over the northern colonies. The Puritan, the typical New Englander of the seventeenth century, was passing off the stage; the Yankee, the shrewd, kindly, businessman, the typical New Englander of the eighteenth century, was replacing him. The New Englander always had been a good businessman. In the eighteenth century he shifted his weight from religion to business.

Franklin was a living example of freedom of opportunity. Born in the great educational center of the colonies, he sat in school probably not more than two years altogether. He got his schooling from business. When he was twelve he went to work as an apprentice in his brother's newspaper print shop. His choice of trade was itself prophetic, because the power of the press was just beginning to be felt; without it, there could have been no revolution in 1775; without it, the colonies could never have been ready for independent existence. The trade brought Franklin into contact with books, news, ideas. It took him to Philadelphia. It took him to England for two years when he was eighteen. That is a kind of symbol, too. William Byrd went to England for education; so did Increase Mather. But Franklin went for business. Business was his schoolmaster, and business gave him a great deal of incidental education. He came back from England, cosmopolitan and successful, at the age of twenty, and settled, not in Boston, the great theological town, but in Philadelphia, the great center of business. All the colonies were facing the same choice between theology and business.

Philadelphia later gave thanks for his choice. When he was barely twenty-one Franklin started a debating and social club called the Junto — the progenitor of all our businessmen's luncheon clubs. Most of its meetings were concerned with the good of Philadelphia, and from those meetings came many of the progressive ideas that

*Culver*

went into making Philadelphia a great city. The first public library in the colonies was one of them. Franklin was instrumental in founding the academy that grew into the University of Pennsylvania. No one did more than he to provide a good communication system for the colonists. As postmaster of Philadelphia, and later postmaster-general of all the colonies, he provided good mail service. He encouraged publishing, and himself issued books, newspapers, and magazines; the *Saturday Evening Post* traces its literary ancestry to one of his magazines. He had immense faith in science, which, he thought, was the weapon by which the New World could outstrip the old. Someone asked him what good the balloon, just invented, could possibly do. " What good is a newborn baby? " he asked. He became somewhat of a genius at adapting the newborn babies of science to practical use. He invented a better stove for the drafty colonial homes. He developed bifocal glasses. He drew lightning down from the skies along his kite string, and proved it no different from laboratory electricity. From this experiment, he developed the lightning rod.

It was inevitable that Franklin should be drawn into political service. When he was thirty, he was made clerk of the general assembly of Pennsylvania. The next year he was postmaster of Philadelphia. He became an assemblyman, and people looked toward him as the best practical intelligence in the colony. They began to push more and more jobs to him. " Get Franklin to do it," they would say. He took on the postmastership of all the colonies, the task of representing Pennsylvania at the inter-colonial congress, the job of trying to get redress for Pennsylvania's grievances at the English court. He had hardly come back when the situation grew worse again, and the clamor grew, " Call in Franklin." Back to England he went, for eleven years. At first he believed that the break could be mended, and worked manfully to explain the colonies to the crown. When he gave it up as a bad job, no force was stronger, no advice sounder, than Franklin's, back of the movement toward independence.

When the war came, they called in Franklin again, this time to return to Europe and get the aid of France and other countries unfriendly to England. No ambassador in Europe did a better job. Which would have been the greater loss — Franklin in Europe or Washington in the field — no man knows, but without either one of them the war might well have been lost. Franklin helped negotiate the peace treaty, came home to be president of Pennsylvania, and served, at the age of eighty-one, as his state's venerable delegate to the Constitutional Convention.

A remarkable record; perhaps no other American can equal it. An American record — but what were the qualities in it that made it so American? One was his extraordinary grasp of practical affairs, side by side with an idealism that never let him quit trusting in man or in the future of the colonies. That combination of practicality plus idealism goes all through American history from Franklin's time on. Franklin could be at once a shrewd businessman and a devoted public servant, a merchant and an artist, a hard bargainer and a generous friend. He was imaginative and progressive, but a careful speculator. He had little eye for the past, but an insatiable interest in the future. He had a typically American faith in and grasp of practical science. And he had an American sense of humor.

All the European countries noticed that. Later they picked out the same quality in Lincoln and Twain and many other Americans. It was a Western quality, they said. John Adams, from New England, did not like the way Franklin was acting as ambassador; he said that the duties of that job were too serious for levity. But the French loved it, and gave the smiling Franklin far more than the serious Adams. They blinked, then roared, when Franklin told them solemnly of the " great leap of the whale over Niagara." They liked him the more for chuckling at himself in his autobiography. They respected him for the wit with which he exploded every sentence of " Rules by Which a Great Empire May be Reduced to a Small One " like a whipcrack over the faces of the statesmen of England.

It is easy to forget, in the glory of his public achievement, that Franklin was a writer. If he had never been a scientist, or a statesman, or a public man, or a businessman, he would still get into histories as a writer. He was not the greatest of our literary men, but he was a good one. His *Autobiography* is one of the classics of our literature; you will read some of it in this book. His most popular writing in his own time was *Poor Richard's Almanac*. He published the first almanac when he was only twenty-six. The booklet represented to all the world America's homely wisdom, humor, and way with words. It was the first book from the colonies that seemed to the readers of Europe anything more than a colonial book. Its circulation was fabulous, and anyone who could read English was likely to be repeating, " Poor Richard Says,"

God helps them that help themselves.

Keep thy shop and thy shop will keep thee.

Early to bed, and early to rise,
Will make a man healthy, wealthy, and wise.

He wrote some essays and short magazine pieces, a series of witty and graceful bagatelles for the courtiers and ladies of France, some political documents, and a series of remarkable letters. One of the briefest of these you may remember. It was written in 1775 to an old friend in the English parliament.

MR. STRAHAN [it began]:
You are a Member of Parliament, and one of that Majority which has doomed my Country to Destruction. — You have begun to burn our Towns, and murder our People. — Look upon your Hands! They are stained with the Blood of your Relations! — You and I were long Friends: — You are now my Enemy, — and I am

Yours,<br>B. FRANKLIN

The French statesman, Turgot, composed a Latin epitaph on Franklin which was translated as " He snatched the lightning from the heavens and the scepter from the hands of tyrants." But there were better epitaphs. One was the way people in the great cities of Europe said, when the news came in 1790, " Dr. Franklin is dead." Another was spoken by one of his fellow townsmen: " From the day he came to Philadelphia, Dr. Franklin never let a year go by without doing some noteworthy service for all of us." Formally, they said: " His shadow lies heavier than any other man's on this young nation."

*When Franklin was born (1706) Puritan power was at its height, and Jonathan Edwards, greatest of the Puritan preachers, was only three years old. When Franklin died (1790), Edwards had been dead thirty-three years, Puritanism was dead as a political force, national independence had been won, and Washington was President.*

## WHAT IS AN AMERICAN: CRÈVECOEUR

Crèvecoeur's essay may tell you less about what is an American than will Franklin's life, but it will tell you much about what the common people of Europe thought of America. Crèvecoeur was born in France, came to New York colony in 1759, and in the next twenty years put together a series of letters on his impressions of the New World. Wonder lies heavy on them — wonder that man should be so free. The freedom he most especially picks out is freedom of opportunity. This is the message that went back to the tax-ridden, hungry, insecure people of Europe, the message that made them follow the western star, and, especially during the nineteenth century, that kept a steady stream of immigration flowing through our eastern ports to fill up the West. Crèvecoeur speaks the message for the New World in a passage not included in the selection on page 457:

Welcome to my shores, distressed European. If thou wilt work, I have bread for thee; if thou wilt be honest, sober, and industrious, I have greater rewards to confer on thee — ease and independence.

## THE VOICES OF THE REVOLUTION:
### PAINE, HENRY, JEFFERSON, OTHERS

In these days we have our choice of twelve thousand newspapers, six thousand magazines, and seventeen thousand moving-picture theaters. The latest news is never farther than our radio dial. We find it hard to imagine what America was like when all news had to come by word of mouth, and when there was no quick way to express an opinion to a number of people larger than the congregation of a church or the audience of a public speech. America was in that situation in 1700. The great change that occurred between 1700 and 1800 — the change that Franklin saw the need of and encouraged with every tool at his command — was the coming of mass communication to the colonies. Newspapers, magazines, broadsides, pamphlets, and publishing houses acquainted the colonies for the first time with each other, let them discuss their common needs and common grievances, and finally carried the burden of drawing them together in war and federation.

A thrilling thing happened to American writing. Lawyers, printers, newspaper reporters, farmers took advantage of the new means of communication to talk to their fellow colonials, and under the inspiration of the fight for freedom raised the level of their writing above the level of law brief, newspaper report, letter to the editor, and political speech — raised it to the level of important literature.

Serious trouble between the colonies and the mother country started in 1760, when the French were driven out of Canada and their Indian allies subdued. From that moment on, the colonies were feeling their strength and chafing against what seemed to them unjust restrictions and punishments on the part of the mother country. From 1760 until war's end, it seemed to England as though Isaiah, Jeremiah, and Ezekiel together had been let loose in the colonies. The voice of righteous indignation that rose from the papers and pamphlets of the Atlantic seaboard was like nothing so much as the voice of the Old Testament prophets.

We can mention only a few of them. There was James Otis, the lawyer who led the battle in Massachusetts against the first punitive measures taken by the British crown. Otis's particular aversion was the writs of assistance which enabled British officers to search any home they wished. A man's house is his castle, he argued, and he made that a symbol of the whole colonial relation to England.

There were John and Samuel Adams — John, the lawyer, orator, and writer of polished essays that appeared as frequently in London as in Boston; and Samuel, the tax-collector, politician, and pamphleteer. John wrote polite and dignified pieces. Samuel was unashamedly one of the great propagandists of his time. The papers were filled with his shrewd, angry arguments, usually under assumed names, but all de-signed as he said to " keep the enemy in the wrong," to encourage the colonists, and to give the budding revolutionary movement heart and fist.

There was John Dickinson, the Pennsylvania gentleman farmer, who was asked to write many of the most important documents of the continental congress, and who wrote a series of letters " from an American farmer in Pennsylvania to the inhabitants of the British colonies " which set forth with great dignity and persuasiveness the American arguments. An example of what mass communication meant to the colonies is the record of these letters — reprinted in most of the colonial newspapers, republished in booklet form eight times in America and twice in London, and translated into French.

Some men, like Patrick Henry, made their contribution in oratory, which the papers picked up and spread. Henry was a representative from western Virginia to the state assembly. He was a different type from the plantation aristocracy of the east, and men like William Byrd might have looked down on him. But men like Henry contributed much of the vigor and impetuosity to the colonial cause. Henry rose as early as 1765 to fight the Stamp Act. The act, of course, was an unfortunate mistake. It taxed legal documents, newspapers, pamphlets, and periodicals, and therefore irritated the most vocal men in the colonies, the lawyers, editors, pamphleteers. Henry told the house in his speech against that act: " Caesar had his Brutus; Charles the First, his Cromwell; and George the Third — may profit by their example! " Ten years later his words on liberty became a battle cry for the colonists.

But of all the penmen — and Franklin, too, whose satires against British rule were biting and effective — no writer had more to do with the Revolution than Thomas Paine. Paine was born in England and came to America only in 1774 — in time to help administer the final blow to the forces opposing revolution. These forces were considerable. Some of the greatest leaders in

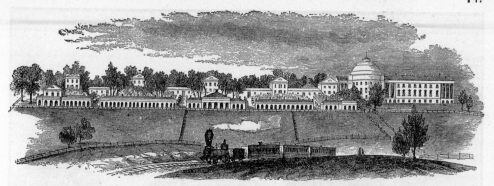

AN EARLY VIEW OF THE UNIVERSITY OF VIRGINIA, founded by Thomas Jefferson in 1818. (Culver)

the colonies hoped up to the last moment to avoid revolution. Washington, even after he had taken command of the army, expressed his abhorrence of revolution and his hope that it might still be avoided. Many of the colonists feared the rule of King Mob. Many of the aristocracy who felt their ties in England closer than their ties to the colonies sailed out of Charleston and Boston with the British troops and never came back; others made their way into Canada. Paine was a good man to deal with this kind of opposition. He came to America for one reason only: that he believed in the rights of man, as Jefferson stated them in the Declaration, and wanted to do everything possible to maintain and extend them. He was as nearly a professional revolutionary as the Americans had on their side. Furthermore, he could write so the people would read. His pen, they said, trailed fire and blood.

He wrote *Common Sense* in 1776. The time was past for appealing to Britain. The time had come to talk to the people of America and tell them plainly what they had to do. Nobody could do this better than Paine. You will see what an extraordinarily persuasive writer he is. He is appealing only to common sense, he says, but how carefully, how shrewdly!

*Common Sense* sold one hundred thousand copies inside three months. Paine believed what he wrote. He enlisted in the Continental army as a private. In the face of the first defeats, he wrote another piece, which he called simply *The Crisis*. He began with a sentence like a trumpet call: " These are the times that try men's souls." He went on, " The summer soldier and the sunshine patriot will, in this crisis, shrink from the service of their country. . . ." Washington read it with a stirring of heart, ordered it read to all his troops. The commanders said it was as good as a regiment.

But Thomas Jefferson, when he was only thirty-three, wrote the greatest piece of literature that came out of the Revolution, the Declaration of Independence. No document of such paramount importance could be written entirely by one man; Jefferson had suggestions from Franklin and others. The final product rang like a clarion. Yet it was simply written. The argument was that man had certain rights, which no government may interfere with; the British government had interfered with those rights in the cases listed; therefore, the only recourse of the colonies was to declare themselves independent of Britain and fight for independence if necessary. You will, of course, read the Declaration carefully. It is not only one of the great political documents of all time; it is the heart of the argument for political freedom.

In his later career, Jefferson stood before the country as the greatest champion of the right of the people to control government. " I am not one of those who fear the people," he told the Americans who talked about

WASHINGTON AND LAFAYETTE, pictured during the terrible winter at Valley Forge
when prospects of winning independence looked blackest. (Culver)

King Mob, and he said again and again in
one phrase or other, " I know no safe de-
pository of the ultimate powers of society
but the people themselves." In Jefferson's
thinking, political freedom was closely entwined with freedom to worship according
to conscience, and freedom to learn. Two of
his greatest achievements were bringing
about religious freedom in Virginia and the
founding of the University of Virginia, the
first state university in America. These were
the actions celebrated in the epitaph which
he himself composed for his gravestone:

HERE WAS BURIED
THOMAS JEFFERSON
AUTHOR OF THE DECLARATION
OF AMERICAN INDEPENDENCE,
OF THE STATUTE OF VIRGINIA
FOR RELIGIOUS FREEDOM,
AND FATHER OF THE UNIVERSITY
OF VIRGINIA

THE MAKING OF A NATION

The war dragged on. The Americans were
badly beaten on Long Island, on Manhattan Island, and in the South. Each year
they had to crawl into winter quarters and
lick their wounds. Sometimes Washington
had three thousand men; sometimes fifteen
thousand. In some actions, like Saratoga,
as many as twenty thousand militia appeared from the farms and the forests and
then went back. Saratoga was a great, perhaps a decisive, victory. When the un-
trained Americans surrounded and captured
Burgoyne they took almost half the King's
army out of the fight, and kept Burgoyne's
army from joining Howe's, which might
have been an unbeatable combination. But
Washington was beaten at Germantown
and retired to the horrible winter at Valley
Forge. In the South, the British were find-

ing out what guerrilla warfare meant. They won all the battles, but lost the campaign, for the American troops kept coming back again and again, and at last the British had to abandon Charleston. Franklin began sending over French aid — troops and the fleet — and with their aid Washington pinned Clinton in Yorktown, and took out the whole southern flank of the English armies. That left only the British garrison in New York, and by and by they too gave up the fight, and peace was made. The Americans got free title to all the country east of the Mississippi. Then they went to work to make a government equal to the potentialities of the new country.

That was the most dangerous period. The people had never been united behind the revolution. Some of the leaders did not even know the names of the leaders from the other colonies. Some of them were not in favor of uniting the colonies in single federation. There were wide differences of opinon even among federalists as to what kind of government should be formed to embody the new right of political freedom, so hard-earned. Europe watched the leaders of the young nation carefully, to see whether they would take the colonies farther apart or closer together. They saw the Constitutional Convention sit down together, subordinate their prejudices, argue their differences honestly, give and take in a spirit of high purpose and responsibility, and arrive at a system and a document which they could take back to their state legislatures for ratification.

What came out was a compromise. It had to be. But it was a plan designed to represent the people and forever shut out tyrants. There was to be a single government for all the colonies. There were to be three parts of the government, checking and balancing one another — executive, congress, and supreme court. There was a provision for popular vote. There was no bill of rights, and a number of the delegates thought there should be. One was added a few years later. But on the whole it was a good blueprint for government, as time has proved.

You ought to remember the name of one classic of political writing that was produced during the period when the new constitution was being discussed, the *Federalist* papers. They were a series of essays on the form that the new government should take, and a defense of the proposed constitution. Hamilton, Madison, and Jay collaborated in writing them, and they helped to focus the thinking of the colonists.

Washington, inevitably, was the first President. He could have been the first king, but he declined the crown. He served two terms, saw the country well started, and retired to Mount Vernon on the Potomac. When he left the capital, he wrote an address of kindly advice — as the father of his country might be expected to do. Part of it is reprinted in the following pages. As you read it over you will realize what a long road the country had walked in a century. How strange and inapplicable Washington's phrases would have sounded in 1696: " The unity of government . . . is a main pillar of your real independence. . . . The name of America, which belongs to you, in your national capacity. . . . The basis of our political systems is the right of the people to make and alter their constitutions of government. . . . The power and the right of the people to establish government."

It is undoubtedly true that the germ of political freedom was in the colonies from the moment the settlers began to come, but it is also true, as John Adams said, that the real revolution was in the minds of Americans rather than on the battlefield. Somewhere in the years before 1796, the American people came to hold such ideas of political freedom as Washington expressed. That was the revolution.

## Benjamin Franklin    1706–1790

Franklin's *Autobiography* is a full account of his life up to 1757, portraying his weakness frankly and his strength with no false modesty. The first section, written in the form of a letter to his son, is especially direct, simple, and interesting. So varied is the picture of the author's experience that it is hard to judge the whole by any one chapter. The following one, however, shows as clearly as any part the difference between the great disciple of common sense and his Puritan forebears. Whereas the devout New Englanders of earlier generations searched the Scriptures and listened anxiously to long sermons in the attempt to discover whether they were among the chosen of God, Franklin calmly decided for himself what virtues were desirable and with the coolest practical judgment laid out a daily course of action that would develop the qualities in himself. You will enjoy testing his list to decide whether these qualities are still desirable virtues and whether they can still be achieved by the procedure Franklin laid out.

## PROJECT OF ARRIVING AT MORAL PERFECTION

It was about this time I conceived the bold and arduous project of arriving at moral perfection. I wished to live without committing any fault at any time; I would conquer all that either natural inclination, custom, or company might lead me into. As I knew, or thought I knew, what was right and wrong, I did not see why I might not always do the one and avoid the other. But I soon found I had undertaken a task of more difficulty than I had imagined. While my care was employed in guarding against one fault, I was often surprised by another; habit took the advantage of inattention; inclination was sometimes too strong for reason. I concluded, at length, that the mere speculative conviction that it was our interest to be completely virtuous was not sufficient to prevent our slipping; and that the contrary habits must be broken, and good ones acquired and established, before we can have any dependence on a steady, uniform rectitude of conduct. For this purpose I therefore contrived the following method.

In the various enumerations of the moral virtues I had met with in my reading, I found the catalogue more or less numerous, as different writers included more or fewer ideas under the same name. Temperance, for example, was by some confined to eating and drinking, while by others it was extended to mean the moderating every other pleasure, appetite, inclination, or passion, bodily or mental, even to our avarice and ambition. I proposed to myself, for the sake of clearness, to use rather more names, with fewer ideas annexed to each, than a few names with more ideas; and I included under thirteen names of virtues all that at that time occurred to me as necessary or desirable, and annexed to each a short precept, which fully expressed the extent I gave to its meaning.

These names of virtues, with their precepts, were:

### 1. TEMPERANCE

Eat not to dullness; drink not to elevation.

### 2. SILENCE

Speak not but what may benefit others or yourself; avoid trifling conversation.

### 3. ORDER

Let all your things have their places; let each part of your business have its time.

### 4. RESOLUTION

Resolve to perform what you ought; perform without fail what you resolve.

### 5. FRUGALITY

Make no expense but to do good to others or yourself; i.e., waste nothing.

### 6. INDUSTRY

Lose no time; be always employed in something useful; cut off all unnecessary actions.

### 7. SINCERITY

Use no hurtful deceit; think innocently and justly; and, if you speak, speak accordingly.

### 8. JUSTICE

Wrong none by doing injuries, or omitting the benefits that are your duty.

### 9. MODERATION

Avoid extremes; forbear resenting injuries so much as you think they deserve.

### 10. CLEANLINESS

Tolerate no uncleanliness in body, clothes, or habitation.

### 11. TRANQUILLITY

Be not disturbed at trifles, or at accidents common or unavoidable.

### 12. CHASTITY

### 13. HUMILITY

Imitate Jesus and Socrates.

My intention being to acquire the *habitude* of all these virtues, I judged it would be well not to distract my attention by attempting the whole at once, but to fix it on one of them at a time; and, when I should be master of that, then to proceed to another, and so on, till I should have gone through the thirteen; and as the previous acquisition of some might facilitate the acquisition of certain others, I arranged them with that view, as they stand above. Temperance first, as it tends to procure that coolness and clearness of head, which is so necessary where constant vigilance was to be kept up, and guard maintained against the unremitting attraction of ancient habits and the force of perpetual temptations. This being acquired and established, Silence would be more easy; and my desire being to gain knowledge at the same time that I improved in virtue, and considering that in conversation it was obtained rather by the use of the ears than of the tongue, and therefore wishing to break a habit I was getting into of prattling, punning, and joking, which only made me acceptable to trifling company, I gave Silence the second place. This and the next, Order, I expected would allow me more time for attending to my project and my studies. Resolution, once become habitual, would keep me firm in my endeavors to obtain all the subsequent virtues; Frugality and Industry, freeing me from my remaining debt and producing affluence and independence, would make more easy the practice of Sincerity and Justice, etc., etc. Conceiving then, that, agreeably to the advice of Pythagoras [1] in his Golden Verses, daily examination would be necessary, I contrived the following method for conducting that examination.

I made a little book, in which I allotted a page for each of the virtues. I ruled each page with red ink, so as to have seven columns, one for each day of the week, marking each column with a letter for the day. I crossed these columns with thirteen red lines, marking the beginning of each line with the first letter of one of the virtues, on which line, and in its proper column, I might mark, by a little black spot, every fault I found upon examination to have been committed respecting that virtue upon that day.

I determined to give a week's strict attention to each of the virtues successively. Thus, in the first week, my great guard was to avoid even the least offense against Temperance, leaving the other virtues to their ordinary chance, only marking every evening the faults of the day. Thus, if in the first week I could keep my first line, marked T, clear of spots, I supposed the habit of that virtue so much strengthened, and its opposite weakened, that I might venture extending my attention to include the next, and for the following week keep both lines clear of spots. Proceeding thus to the last, I could go through a course complete in thirteen weeks, and four courses in a year. And like him who, having a garden to weed, does not attempt to eradicate all the bad herbs at once, which would exceed his reach and his strength, but works on one of the beds at a time, and, having accomplished the first, proceeds to a second, so I should have, I hoped, the encouraging pleasure of seeing on my pages the progress I made in virtue, by clearing successively my lines of their spots, till in the end, by a number of courses, I should be happy in viewing a

---

[1] **Pythagoras:** (pĭ-thăg′ô-răs): a famous Greek philosopher of the sixth century B.C.

*Forms of the Pages*

| TEMPERANCE | | | | | | | |
| --- | --- | --- | --- | --- | --- | --- | --- |
| EAT NOT TO DULLNESS; DRINK NOT TO ELEVATION. | | | | | | | |
|  | S. | M. | T. | W. | T. | F. | S. |
| T. |  |  |  |  |  |  |  |
| S. | * | * |  | * |  | * |  |
| O. | ** | * | * |  | * | * | * |
| R. |  |  | * |  |  | * |  |
| F. |  | * |  |  | * |  |  |
| I. |  |  | * |  |  |  |  |
| S. |  |  |  |  |  |  |  |
| J. |  |  |  |  |  |  |  |
| M. |  |  |  |  |  |  |  |
| C. |  |  |  |  |  |  |  |
| T. |  |  |  |  |  |  |  |
| C. |  |  |  |  |  |  |  |
| H. |  |  |  |  |  |  |  |

clean book, after a thirteen weeks' daily examination. . . .

The precept of Order requiring that *every part of my business should have its allotted time,* one page in my little book contained the following scheme of employment for the twenty-four hours of a natural day.

I entered upon the execution of this plan for self-examination, and continued it with occasional intermissions for some time. I was surprised to find myself so much fuller of faults than I had imagined; but I had the satisfaction of seeing them diminish. To avoid the trouble of renewing now and then my little book, which, by scraping out the marks on the paper of old faults to make room for new ones in a new course, became full of holes, I transferred my tables and precepts to the ivory leaves of a memorandum book, on which the lines were drawn with red ink, that made a durable stain, and on those lines I marked my faults with a black lead pencil, which marks I could easily wipe out with a wet sponge. After a while I went through one course only in a year, and afterward only one in several years, till at length I omitted them entirely, being employed in voyages and business abroad, with a multiplicity of affairs that interfered; but I always carried my little book with me.

My scheme of Order gave me the most trouble; and I found that, though it might be practicable where a man's business was such as to leave him the disposition of his time, that of a journeyman printer, for in-

| THE MORNING | 5 | Rise, wash, and address *Powerful* |
| | 6 | *Goodness!* Contrive day's business, |
| *Question.* What good shall I do | | and take the resolution of the day; |
| this day? | | prosecute the present study, and |
| | 7 | breakfast. |
| | 8 | |
| | 9 | Work. |
| | 10 | |
| | 11 | |
| NOON | 12 | Read, or overlook my accounts, |
| | 1 | and dine. |
| | 2 | |
| | 3 | Work. |
| | 4 | |
| | 5 | |
| EVENING | 6 | Put things in their places. Sup- |
| | 7 | per. Music or diversion, or conver- |
| *Question.* What good have I done | 8 | sation. Examination of the day. |
| today? | 9 | |
| | 10 | |
| | 11 | |
| | 12 | |
| NIGHT | 1 | Sleep. |
| | 2 | |
| | 3 | |
| | 4 | |

stance, it was not possible to be exactly observed by a master, who must mix with the world, and often receive people of business at their own hours. Order, too, with regard to places for things, papers, etc., I found extremely difficult to acquire. I had not been early accustomed to it, and, having an exceeding good memory, I was not so sensible of the inconvenience attending want of method. This article, therefore, cost me so much painful attention, and my faults in it vexed me so much, and I made so little progress in amendment, and had such frequent relapses, that I was almost ready to give up the attempt, and content myself with a faulty character in that respect, like the man who, in buying an ax of a smith, my neighbor, desired to have the whole of its surface as bright as the edge. The smith consented to grind it bright for him if he would turn the wheel; he turned, while the smith pressed the broad face of the ax hard and heavily on the stone, which made the turning of it very fatiguing. The man came every now and then from the wheel to see how the work went on, and at length would take his ax as it was, without further grinding. " No," said the smith, " turn on, turn on; we shall have it bright by and by; as yet, it is only speckled." " Yes," says the man, " *but I think I like a speckled ax best.*"

And I believe this may have been the case with many, who, having, for want of some such means as I employed, found the difficulty of obtaining good and breaking bad habits in other points of vice and virtue, have given up the struggle, and concluded that " *a speckled ax was best*"; for something that pretended to be reason was every now and then suggesting to me that such extreme nicety as I exacted of myself might be a kind of foppery in morals, which, if it were known, would make me ridiculous; that a perfect character might be attended with the inconvenience of being envied and hated; and that a benevolent man should allow a few faults in himself, to keep his friends in countenance.

In truth, I found myself incorrigible with respect to Order; and now I am grown old, and my memory bad, I feel very sensibly the want of it. But, on the whole, though I never arrived at the perfection I had been so ambitious of obtaining, but fell far short of it, yet I was, by the endeavor, a better and a happier man than I otherwise should have been if I had not attempted it; as those who aim at perfect writing by imitating the engraved copies, though they never reach the wished-for excellence of those copies, their hand is mended by the endeavor.

It may be well my posterity should be informed that to this little artifice, with the blessing of God, their ancestor owed the constant felicity of his life, down to his seventy-ninth year, in which this is written. What reverses may attend the remainder is in the hand of Providence; but, if they arrive, the reflection on past happiness enjoyed ought to help his bearing them with more resignation. To Temperance he ascribes his long-continued health, and what is still left to him of a good constitution; to Industry and Frugality, the early easiness of his circumstances and acquisition of his fortune, with all that knowledge that enabled him to be a useful citizen, and obtained for him some degree of reputation among the learned; to Sincerity and Justice, the confidence of his country, and the honorable employs it conferred upon him; and to the joint influence of the whole mass of the virtues, even in the imperfect state he was able to acquire them, all that evenness of temper, and that cheerfulness in conversation, which makes his company still sought for, and agreeable even to his younger acquaintance. I hope, therefore, that some of my descendants may follow the example and reap the benefit.

It will be remarked that, though my scheme was not wholly without religion, there was in it no mark of any of the distinguishing tenets of any particular sect. I had purposely avoided them; for, being fully persuaded of the utility and excellency of my method, and that it might be serviceable to people in all religions, and intending some time or other to publish it, I would not have anything in it that should prejudice anyone, of any sect, against it. I purposed writing a little comment on each virtue, in which I would have shown the advantages of possessing it, and the mischiefs attending its opposite vice; and I should have called my book *The Art of Virtue,* because it would have shown the means and manner of obtaining virtue, which would have distinguished it from mere exhortation to be good, that does not instruct and indicate the means, but is like the apostle's man of verbal charity, who, without showing to the naked and hungry how or where they might get clothes or victuals, only exhorted them to be fed and clothed. — James 2:15, 16.

But it so happened that my intention of writing and publishing this comment was never fulfilled. I did, indeed, from time to time, put down short hints of the sentiments, reasonings, etc., to be made use of in it, some of which I have still by me; but the necessary close attention to private business in the earlier part of my life, and public business since, have occasioned my postponing it; for, it being connected in my mind with *a great and extensive project* that required the whole man to execute, and which an unforseen succession of employs prevented my attending to, it has hitherto remained unfinished.

In this piece it was my design to explain and enforce this doctrine, that vicious actions are not hurtful because they are forbidden, but forbidden because they are hurtful, the nature of man alone considered; that it was, therefore, everyone's interest to be virtuous who wished to be happy even in this world; and I should, from this circumstance (there being always in the world a number of rich merchants, nobility, states, and princes, who have need of honest instruments for the management of their affairs, and such being so rare), have endeavored to convince young persons that no qualities were so likely to make a poor man's fortune as those of probity and integrity.

My list of virtues contained at first but twelve; but a Quaker friend having kindly informed me that I was generally thought proud; that my pride showed itself frequently in conversation; that I was not content with being in the right when discussing any point, but was overbearing and rather insolent, of which he convinced me by mentioning several instances; I determined endeavoring to cure myself, if I could, of this vice or folly among the rest, and I added Humility to my list.

I cannot boast of much success in acquiring the *reality* of this virtue, but I had a good deal with regard to the *appearance* of it. I made it a rule to forbear all direct contradiction to the sentiments of others, and all positive assertion of my own. I even forbade myself, agreeably to the old law of our Junto,[1] the use of every word or expression in the language that imported a fixed opinion, such as *certainly, undoubtedly,* etc., and I adopted, instead of them, *I conceive, I apprehend,* or *I imagine* a thing to be so or so; or it *so appears to me at present.* When another asserted something that I thought an error, I denied myself the pleasure of contradicting him abruptly, and of showing immediately some absurdity in his proposition; and in answering I began by observing that in certain cases or circumstances his opinion would be right, but in the present case there *appeared* or *seemed* to me some difference, etc. I soon found the advantage of this change in my manner; the conversations I engaged in went on more pleasantly. The modest way in which I proposed my opinions procured them a readier reception and less contradiction; I had less mortification when I was found to be in the wrong, and I more easily prevailed with others to give up their mistakes and join with me when I happened to be in the right.

And this mode, which I at first put on with some violence to natural inclination, became at length so easy and so habitual to me that perhaps for these fifty years past no one has ever heard a dogmatical expression escape me. And to this habit (after my character of integrity) I think it principally

[1] **Junto:** name of the debating society organized by Franklin.

owing that I had early so much weight with my fellow citizens when I proposed new institutions, or alterations in the old, and so much influence in public councils when I became a member; for I was but a bad speaker, never eloquent, subject to much hesitation in my choice of words, hardly correct in language, and yet I generally carried my points.

In reality, there is, perhaps, no one of our natural passions so hard to subdue as *pride.* Disguise it, struggle with it, beat it down, stifle it, mortify it as much as one pleases, it is still alive, and will every now and then peep out and show itself; you will see it, perhaps, often in this history; for, even if I could conceive that I had completely overcome it, I should probably be proud of my humility.

## SAYINGS OF POOR RICHARD

In 1732 (the year of Washington's birth) Franklin began his *Poor Richard's Almanac* by playing a practical joke on his only rival almanac maker, Titus Leads, a quack astrologer. Poor Richard prophesied the death of this man the following October, in accordance with the infallible stars. When Leads protested violently, Poor Richard replied that he must be dead because the stars could not lie and no living man would use such unchristian language or publish such an unworthy almanac. This trick had been played in England some years before by Jonathan Swift, author of *Gulliver's Travels,* but most Americans did not know about that and accepted the incident as a huge joke.

The almanac continued in popularity for twenty-five years, and many of its wise saws still live in American conversation. Franklin borrowed largely from the wisdom of the ages, but often rephrased the maxims or put them into fresh metaphors. His versions possess the neatness, the balance, and the clever contrasts which go with brevity to form the soul of wit. But these sayings illustrate more than Franklin's humor; they also reveal this great American's practical common sense, both its strength — a shrewd insight into human nature — and its weakness — a failure to emphasize spiritual and idealistic qualities.

Poor Richard, 1733.

AN

Almanack

For the Year of Christ

1733,

Being the First after LEAP YEAR:

And makes since the Creation    Years
By the Account of the Eastern Greeks   7241
By the Latin Church, when ⊙ ent ♈   6932
By the Computation of W.W.    5742
By the Roman Chronology    5682
By the Jewish Rabbies    5494

Wherein is contained

The Lunations, Eclipses, Judgment of the Weather, Spring Tides, Planets Motions & mutual Aspects, Sun and Moon's Rising and Setting. Length of Days. Time of High Water, Fairs, Courts, and observable Days

Fitted to the Latitude of Forty Degrees and a Meridian of Five Hours West from London, but may without sensible Error serve all the adjacent Places, even from Newfoundland to South-Carolina.

By RICHARD SAUNDERS, Philom.

PHILADELPHIA:
Printed and sold by B. FRANKLIN, at the New Printing-Office near the Market.

TITLE PAGE OF "Poor Richard's Almanack." (Culver)

1. Experience keeps a dear school, but a fool will learn in no other.

2. Hunger is the best pickle.

3. Love your neighbor; yet don't pull down your hedge.

4. If a man empties his purse into his head, no man can take it away from him. An investment in knowledge always pays the best interest.

5. Three may keep a secret if two of them are dead.

6. Tart words make no friends; a spoonful of honey will catch more flies than a gallon of vinegar.

7. Glass, china, and reputation are easily cracked and never well mended.

8. Fish and visitors smell in three days.

9. One today is worth two tomorrows.

10. A truly great man will neither trample on a worm nor sneak to an emperor.

11. He that riseth late must trot all day, and shall scarce overtake his business at night; while laziness travels so slowly that poverty soon overtakes him. Drive thy business. Let it not drive thee.

12. A little neglect may breed mischief; for want of a nail the shoe was lost; for want of a shoe the horse was lost; for want of a horse the rider was lost; for want of the rider the battle was lost.

13. If you would know the value of money, go and try to borrow some; he that goes a-borrowing goes a-sorrowing.

14. He that composes himself is wiser than he that composes books.

15. He that is of the opinion that money will do everything may well be suspected of doing everything for money.

16. If a man could have half his wishes he would double his troubles.

17. Creditors have better memories than debtors.

18. 'Tis hard for an empty bag to stand upright.

19. A lie stands on one leg, truth on two.

20. The sleeping fox catches no poultry.

21. A plowman on his legs is higher than a gentleman on his knees.

22. When the well's dry, we know the worth of water.

23. A small leak will sink a great ship.

24. 'Tis easier to build two chimneys than to keep one in fuel.

25. Now that I have a sheep and a cow everybody bids me good morrow.

26. Silks and satins, scarlet and velvet, put out the kitchen fire.

## Suggestions for Study of Franklin

PROJECT OF ARRIVING AT MORAL PERFECTION

1. What sort of Franklin does this chapter reveal to you? Would you have liked him as a friend? Why or why not?

2. Find out from a psychology book or from

your teacher some of the laws of habit forma-tion. Did Franklin understand these? Discuss the part habit plays in our lives.

3. Do you agree with Franklin that temper-ance is the virtue to be first striven for? Why? Just what is meant by " temperance "?

4. Which of Franklin's virtues seems to you the hardest to attain? the easiest? most worth while? least worth while? What is the chief de-fect of his virtues? Make your own list, with improvements if possible.

5. Why did humility come last on Franklin's list? How did it affect his method of carrying on an argument? How did this lesson affect his later career? Do you think his method is widely practiced? Listen to arguments, and collect evidence to support your answer.

6. Would the Puritans have approved Frank-lin's list of virtues? Why does the whole dis-cussion clearly belong to an age of common sense rather than to the late Puritan period?

SAYINGS OF POOR RICHARD

7. Be sure you understand the meaning of each of these sayings. The last nine are highly figurative. For each of these nine write a sen-tence that gives the literal meaning.

8. Make a list of all the virtues preached by these sayings, such as thrift, perseverance, and so on. What kind of virtues are emphasized? Do they properly belong to an age of common sense? What kinds of virtues are conspicuous by their absence? Does your list verify or con-tradict the comment at the end of the intro-ductory remarks?

9. Try your hand at writing some parodies on these sayings or some wise saws of your own which will apply to your school life.

## For Your Vocabulary

WORD POWER. Franklin draws a nice parallel when he compares the gardener's attempt to *eradicate* (ĕ-răd'ĭ-kāt) weeds to his own at-tempts to get rid of his faults (page 451), for *eradicate* means to get out by the roots, and so to get entirely rid of. The common word *radical* comes from the same stem, meaning root. A *radical* change is one which strikes at the very roots of an established order. Scien-tists are constantly at work to *eradicate* plant pests and diseases. Franklin's program to *erad-icate* his faults met with one defeat. Do you remember which endeavor convinced him that

he was *incorrigible* (ĭn-kŏr'ĭ-gĭ-b'l), or incapa-ble of being corrected (page 453)? One other trait, humility, he did not wholly achieve, but he acquired the appearance of it by curing him-self of making *dogmatical* statements (page 455). Nowadays we use the simplified form *dogmatic* (dŏg-măt'ĭk) to describe the state-ment of mere opinions as if they were proven facts, or to describe a person who has the habit of having an exaggerated regard for his own opinions. Do you think it is *dogmatic* to state that criminals are *incorrigible* and that it is impossible to *eradicate* crime?

## Jean de Crèvecoeur 1735-1813

### WHAT IS AN AMERICAN?

Although Crèvecoeur's *Letters from an American Farmer* were published in London in 1782, they are quite properly a part of American literature and furnish the most illu-minating picture we have of America just be-fore the Revolution. As you read the selection printed here, you can see for yourself how America differed from Europe and what de-votion it inspired. Perhaps Crèvecoeur's ad-miration for this country can even make you understand why he would have no part in the Revolution: he thought America already so much happier than any country in Europe that unnecessary strife was bitter folly.

I wish I could be acquainted with the feelings and thoughts which must agitate the heart and present themselves to the mind of an enlightened Englishman when he first lands on this continent. He must greatly rejoice that he lived at a time to see this fair country discovered and settled; he must necessarily feel a share of national pride when he views the chain of settle-ments which embellishes these extended shores. When he says to himself, " This is the work of my countrymen, who, when convulsed by factions, afflicted by a variety of miseries and wants, restless and impa-tient, took refuge here. They brought along with them their national genius, to which they principally owe what liberty they enjoy, and what substance they possess."

Here he sees the industry of his native country, displayed in a new manner, and traces in their works the embryos of all the arts, sciences, and ingenuity which flourish in Europe. Here he beholds fair cities, substantial villages, extensive fields, an immense country filled with decent houses, good roads, orchards, meadows, and bridges, where an hundred years ago all was wild, woody, and uncultivated!

What a train of pleasing ideas this fair spectacle must suggest! It is a prospect which must inspire a good citizen with the most heartfelt pleasure. The difficulty consists in the manner of viewing so extensive a scene. He is arrived on a new continent; a modern society offers itself to his contemplation, different from what he had hitherto seen. It is not composed, as in Europe, of great lords who possess everything, and of a herd of people who have nothing. Here are no aristocratical families, no courts, no kings, no bishops, no ecclesiastical dominion,[1] no invisible power giving to a few a very visible one; no great manufacturers employing thousands, no great refinements of luxury. The rich and the poor are not so far removed from each other as they are in Europe.

Some few towns excepted, we are tillers of the earth, from Nova Scotia to West Florida. We are a people of cultivators, scattered over an immense territory, communicating with each other by means of good roads and navigable rivers, united by the silken bands of mild government, all respecting the laws without dreading their power, because they are equitable. We are all animated with the spirit of industry, which is unfettered and unrestrained, because each person works for himself.

If he travels through our rural districts he views not the hostile castle and the haughty mansion, contrasted with the clay-built and miserable cabin, where cattle and men help to keep each other warm, and dwell in meanness, smoke, and indigence. A pleasing uniformity of decent competence appears throughout our habitations. The meanest of our log houses is a dry and comfortable habitation.

Lawyer or merchant are the fairest titles our towns afford; that of a farmer is the only appellation of the rural inhabitants of our country. It must take some time ere he can reconcile himself to our dictionary, which is but short in words of dignity and names of honor. There, on a Sunday, he sees a congregation of respectable farmers and their wives, all clad in neat homespun, well mounted, or riding in their own humble wagons. There is not among them an esquire, saving the unlettered magistrate. There he sees a parson as simple as his flock, a farmer who does not riot on the labor of others.

We have no princes, for whom we toil, starve, and bleed; we are the most perfect society now existing in the world. Here man is free as he ought to be; nor is this pleasing equality so transitory as many others are. Many ages will not see the shores of our great lakes replenished with inland nations, nor the unknown bounds of North America entirely peopled. Who can tell how far it extends? Who can tell the millions of men whom it will feed and contain? for no European foot has as yet traveled half the extent of this mighty continent!

The next wish of the traveler will be to know whence came all these people? They are a mixture of English, Scotch, Irish, French, Dutch, Germans, and Swedes. From this promiscuous breed, that race now called Americans have arisen. The eastern provinces[2] must indeed be excepted, as being unmixed descendants of Englishmen. I have heard many wish that they had been more intermixed also: for my part, I am no wisher; and think it much better as it has happened. They exhibit a most conspicuous figure in this great and variegated picture;

---

[1] **no bishops, no ecclesiastical dominion:** The American colonists had repudiated the European system of a state-established church.

[2] **eastern provinces:** "New Hampshire, Massachuset[t]s, Rhode-Island, Connecticut." (Note by Crèvecoeur.)

they too enter for a great share in the pleasing perspective displayed in these thirteen provinces. I know it is fashionable to reflect on them; but I respect them for what they have done; for the accuracy and wisdom with which they have settled their territory; for the decency of their manners; for their early love of letters; their ancient college,[1] the first in this hemisphere; for their industry, which to me who am but a farmer, is the criterion of everything. There never was a people, situated as they are, who with so ungrateful a soil have done more in so short a time. Do you think that the monarchial ingredients which are more prevalent in other governments have purged them from all foul stains? Their histories assert the contrary.

In this great American asylum, the poor of Europe have by some means met together, and in consequence of various causes; to what purpose should they ask one another what countrymen they are? Alas, two thirds of them had no country. Can a wretch who wanders about, who works and starves, whose life is a continual scene of sore affliction or pinching penury; can that man call England or any other kingdom his country? A country that had no bread for him, whose fields procured him no harvest, who met with nothing but the frowns of the rich, the severity of the laws, with jails and punishments; who owned not a single foot of the extensive surface of this planet? No! Urged by a variety of motives, here they came. Everything has tended to regenerate them; new laws, a new mode of living, a new social system. Here they are become men; in Europe they were as so many useless plants, wanting vegetative mold and refreshing showers; they whispered, and were mowed down by want, hunger, and war; but now, by the power of transplantation, like all other plants, they have taken root and flourished! Formerly they were not numbered in any civil list of their country, except in those of the poor; here they rank as citizens.

By what invisible power has this surprising metamorphosis been performed? By that of the laws and that of their industry. The laws, the indulgent laws, protect them as they arrive, stamping on them the symbol of adoption; they receive ample rewards for their labors; these accumulated rewards procure them lands; those lands confer on them the title of freemen; and to that title every benefit is affixed which men can possibly require. This is the great operation daily performed by our laws. From whence proceed these laws? From our government. Whence the government? It is derived from the original genius and strong desire of the people, ratified and confirmed by government. This is the great chain which links us all; this is the picture which every province exhibits, Nova Scotia [2] excepted. There the crown has done all; either there were no people who had genius, or it was not much attended to: the consequence is, that the province is very thinly inhabited indeed; the power of the crown, in conjunction with the mosquitoes, has prevented men from settling there. Yet some parts of it flourished once, and it contained a mild harmless set of people.[3] But for the fault of a few leaders, the whole were banished. The greatest political error the crown ever committed in America was to cut off men from a country which wanted nothing but men!

What attachment can a poor European emigrant have for a country where he had nothing? The knowledge of the language, the love of a few kindred as poor as himself, were the only cords that tied him: his country is now that which gives him land, bread, protection, and consequence: *Ubi panis ibi patria*,[4] is the motto of all emigrants.

What then is the American, this new man? He is either an European, or the descendant of an European; hence that strange mixture

---

[1] **ancient college:** Harvard College, founded 1636, opened 1640.

[2] **Nova Scotia:** ruled by military governors from its cession to England in 1713 to 1749; then granted a general assembly, but public indifference delayed its meeting for nine years. [3] **harmless set of people:** the Acadians. Their banishment is the subject of Longfellow's *Evangeline.* [4] **Ubi panis ibi patria:** Wherever bread is, there is my country.

of blood, which you will find in no other country. I could point out to you a family whose grandfather was an Englishman, whose wife was Dutch, whose son married a French woman, and whose present four sons have now four wives of different nations. *He* is an American, who, leaving behind him all ancient prejudices and manners, receives new ones from the new mode of life he has embraced, the new government he obeys, and the new rank he holds. He becomes an American by being received in the broad lap of our great *Alma Mater*.[1] Here individuals of all nations are melting into a new race of men, whose labors and posterity will one day cause great changes in the world. Americans are the western pilgrims, who are carrying along with them that great mass of arts, sciences, vigor, and industry, which began long since in the east; they will finish the great circle. The Americans were once scattered all over Europe; here they are incorporated into one of the finest systems of population which has ever appeared, and which will hereafter become distinct by the power of the different climates they inhabit. The American ought therefore to love this country much better than that wherein either he or his forefathers were born. Here the rewards of his industry follow with equal steps the progress of his labor; his labor is founded on the basis of nature, *self-interest;* can it want a stronger allurement? Wives and children, who before in vain demanded of him a morsel of bread, now, fat and frolicsome, gladly help their father to clear those fields whence exuberant crops are to arise to feed and to clothe them all without any part being claimed, either by a despotic prince, a rich abbot, or a mighty lord. Here religion demands but little of him; a small voluntary salary to the minister, and gratitude to God; can he refuse these? The American is a new man, who acts upon new principles; he must therefore entertain new ideas, and form

[1] **Alma Mater:** cherishing mother, phrase originally applied to Venus, here to the nation, but today most commonly to the college one has attended.

new opinions. From involuntary idleness, servile dependence, penury, and useless labor, he has passed to toils of a very different nature, rewarded by ample subsistence. — This is an American.

## Suggestions for Study

1. What idea of conditions in Europe during the eighteenth century do you get from this essay? What in this picture of America would not be true today?

2. What is your opinion of the claims often made by political factions that their way is the " American way," that theirs are true " American " principles, and that they are the real upholders of " Americanism "? What is the danger of such assumptions? Why are they often unwarranted?

3. Read Israel Zangwill's *The Melting Pot*, Mary Antin's *The Promised Land*, and Kaufman and Hart's *The American Way* for other presentations of the meaning of America to the European immigrant. What do you think it means to such people today? What other books presenting the point of view of the immigrant do you know?

4. Prepare a three-minute radio talk on " What It Means to Be an American Today."

## Patrick Henry            1736–1799

Patrick Henry was convinced that the colonists must resort to armed resistance. On March 23, 1775, he delivered the following speech before the Virginia House of Burgesses. This body had reassembled after being dissolved by the royal governor, and a resolution had been proposed that " Virginia be immediately put into a posture of defense." Against strong and influential opposition (the rich planters feared a popular uprising), Patrick Henry's impassioned appeal so moved the burgesses that the resolution was passed and rebellion became a reality.

Patrick Henry was a six-footer, raw-boned and slightly stoop-shouldered. His firm jaw, flashing blue eyes, and force of personality gained him eminence as lawyer, as Governor of Virginia, and as a power in the Virginia legislature.

## SPEECH IN THE VIRGINIA CONVENTION

*Mr. President:* —

No man thinks more highly than I do of the patriotism, as well as abilities, of the very worthy gentlemen who have just addressed the house. But different men often see the same subject in different lights; and, therefore, I hope it will not be thought disrespectful to those gentlemen, if, entertaining as I do opinions of a character very opposite to theirs, I shall speak forth my sentiments freely, and without reserve. This is no time for ceremony. The question before the house is one of awful moment to this country. For my own part, I consider it as nothing less than a question of freedom or slavery. And in proportion to the magnitude of the subject ought to be the freedom of the debate. It is only in this way that we can hope to arrive at truth, and fulfill the great responsibility which we hold to God and our country. Should I keep back my opinions at such a time, through fear of giving offense, I should consider myself as guilty of treason toward my country, and of an act of disloyalty toward the Majesty of Heaven, which I revere above all earthly kings.

Mr. President, it is natural to man to indulge in the illusions of hope. We are apt to shut our eyes against a painful truth, and listen to the song of that siren till she transforms us into beasts. Is this the part of wise men, engaged in a great and arduous struggle for liberty? Are we disposed to be of the number of those who having eyes see not, and having ears hear not, the things which so nearly concern their temporal salvation? For my part, whatever anguish of spirit it may cost, I am willing to know the whole truth; to know the worst and to provide for it.

I have but one lamp by which my feet are guided, and that is the lamp of experience. I know of no way of judging of the future but by the past. And judging by the past, I wish to know what there has been in the conduct of the British ministry for the last ten years to justify those hopes with which gentlemen have been pleased to solace themselves and the house? Is it that insidious smile with which our petition has been lately received? Trust it not, sir; it will prove a snare to your feet. Suffer not yourselves to be betrayed with a kiss. Ask yourselves how this gracious reception of our petition comports with those warlike preparations which cover our waters and darken our land. Are fleets and armies necessary to a work of love and reconciliation? Have we shown ourselves so unwilling to be reconciled that force must be called in to win back our love? Let us not deceive ourselves, sir. These are the implements of war and subjugation — the last arguments to which kings resort. I ask gentlemen, sir, what means this martial array, if its purpose be not to force us to submission? Can gentlemen assign any other possible motive for it? Has Great Britain any enemy in this quarter of the world, to call for all this accumulation of navies and armies? No, sir, she has none. They are meant for us: they can be meant for no other. They are sent over to bind and rivet upon us those chains which the British ministry have been so long forging. And what have we to oppose to them? Shall we try argument? Sir, we have been trying that for the last ten years. Have we anything new to offer upon the subject? Nothing. We have held the subject up in every light of which it is capable; but it has been all in vain. Shall we resort to entreaty and humble supplication? What terms shall we find which have not been already exhausted? Let us not, I beseech you, sir, deceive ourselves longer.

Sir, we have done everything that could be done to avert the storm which is now coming on. We have petitioned; we have remonstrated; we have supplicated; we have prostrated ourselves before the throne and have implored its interposition to arrest the tyrannical hands of the ministry and Parliament. Our petitions have been slighted; our remonstrances have produced additional violence and insult; our supplications have been disregarded; and we have been spurned with contempt from the foot

PATRICK HENRY reaches a stirring climax in his address to the Virginia assembly.
(Pictorial Archives from Three Lions)

of the throne! In vain, after these things, may we indulge the fond hope of peace and reconciliation. There is no longer any room for hope. If we wish to be free, if we mean to preserve inviolate those inestimable privileges for which we have been so long contending, if we mean not basely to abandon the noble struggle in which we have been so long engaged, and which we have pledged ourselves never to abandon until the glorious object of our contest shall be obtained — we must fight! I repeat it, sir, we must fight! An appeal to arms and to the God of Hosts is all that is left us!

They tell us, sir, that we are weak — unable to cope with so formidable an adversary. But when shall we be stronger? Will it be the next week, or the next year? Will it be when we are totally disarmed, and when a British guard shall be stationed in every house? Shall we gather strength by irresolution and inaction? Shall we acquire the means of effectual resistance by lying supinely on our backs, and hugging the delusive phantom of hope until our enemies shall have bound us hand and foot? Sir, we are not weak, if we make a proper use of those means which the God of nature hath placed in our power. Three millions of people, armed in the holy cause of liberty, and in such a country as that which we possess, are invincible by any force which our enemy can send against us. Besides, sir, we shall not fight our battles alone. There is a just God who presides over the destinies of nations, and who will raise up friends to fight our battles for us. The battle, sir, is not to the strong alone; it is to the vigilant, the active, the brave. Besides, sir, we have no election. If we were base enough to desire it, it is now too late to retire from the contest. There is no retreat but in submission and slavery! Our chains are forged! their clanking may be heard on the plains of Boston! The war is inevitable — and let it come! I repeat it, sir, let it come!

It is in vain, sir, to extenuate the matter. Gentlemen may cry, Peace, Peace — but there is no peace. The war is actually begun! The next gale that sweeps from the north will bring to our ears the clash of resounding arms! Our brethren are already in the field! Why stand we here idle? What is it that gentlemen wish? What would they have? Is life so dear, or peace so sweet, as to be purchased at the price of chains and slavery? Forbid it, Almighty God! I know not what course others may take; but as for me, give me liberty or give me death!

## Suggestions for Study

1. The best way to study this speech is to practice reading it aloud, reproducing as far as you are able the spirit in which it was originally delivered. Be careful to avoid an exaggeration which becomes mere ranting. It would be interesting for the class to elect one member to deliver the speech before the class, preliminary to discussion of it. Another entertaining plan is to dramatize the Virginia Convention with students assigned to prepare speeches of reluctant burgesses, to whom Patrick Henry may reply, concluding with a vote on the resolution. Let the objectors not forget to mention the usual internal results of revolution.

2. Some of the rhetorical devices with which this speech abounds are repetition, the question and the exclamation, the balanced sentence, the figure of speech, and the climax. Can you find good examples of all of them? There are several touches of Biblical language which are also interesting to look for.

3. John Randolph said of Patrick Henry that he was Shakespeare and Garrick combined. What did he mean by this?

## For Your Vocabulary

WORD HISTORY. Many of our words for abstract ideas have developed from other words with more definite meaning. Patrick Henry, in trying to stir his associates into active resistance, uses two which are almost taunts. *Supplication* (sŭp-lĭ-kā′shŭn), an attitude of humble entreaty, means bending under and is associated with kneeling in entreaty, not a position very acceptable to the proud burgesses of Virginia. The orator reminds them that they have already *supplicated* the throne in vain attempts to gain redress for their wrongs (page 461). Then he asks whether they will gain strength for resistance by "lying *supinely* on our backs" (page 462). Here he repeats to emphasize his point, for *supine* (sū-pīn′) means literally lying on one's back, and therefore abjectly submissive. The British aim, he warns them (page 461), is their *subjugation* (sŭb-jŭ-gā′shŭn), putting them under a yoke. The yoke was the ancient symbol, and often burden, of a slave. Small wonder that he aroused his audience, for the Virginia burgesses were well versed in the English language.

## Thomas Paine      1737–1809

Patrick Henry's oratory had its effect upon the Virginia House of Burgesses; but it was Thomas Paine, greatest of our pamphleteers, who most effectively persuaded men in all the colonies that they could no longer be Americans and, at the same time, British subjects.

His tract *Common Sense* effectively spread the plea to sever connections with the mother country; within six months of its publication the Declaration of Independence was signed. Then, when the first days of the war brought one discouragement after another to the Americans, Paine again fortified them with a stirring pamphlet *The Crisis*, part of which you may read here. The opening sentence has been quoted and requoted as our nation has faced later crises. It is one of the great phrases of our American tradition.

### THE TIMES THAT TRY MEN'S SOULS

These are the times that try men's souls. The summer soldier and the sunshine patriot will, in this crisis, shrink from the service of their country; but he that stands it *now*, deserves the love and thanks of man and woman. Tyranny, like hell, is not easily conquered; yet we have this consolation with us, that the harder the conflict, the more glorious the triumph. What we obtain too cheap, we esteem too lightly: it is dearness only that gives everything its value. Heaven knows how to put a proper price

THOMAS PAINE, "greatest of our pamphleteers." (Culver)

upon its goods, and it would be strange indeed if so celestial an article as *freedom* should not be highly rated. Britain, with an army to enforce her tyranny, has declared that she has a right, not only to *tax*, but " to *bind* us in *all cases whatsoever* "; and if being bound in that manner is not slavery, then there is not such a thing as slavery upon earth. Even the expression is impious, for so unlimited a power can belong only to God.

I have as little superstition in me as any man living, but my secret opinion has ever been, and still is, that God Almighty will not give up a people to military destruction, or leave them unsupportedly to perish, who have so earnestly and so repeatedly sought to avoid the calamities of war by every decent method which wisdom could invent. Neither have I so much of the infidel in me as to suppose that He has relinquished the government of the world and given us up to the care of devils; and, as I do not, I cannot see on what grounds the king of Britain can look up to heaven for help against us.

I once felt all that kind of anger which

a man ought to feel against the mean principles that are held by the Tories. A noted one, who kept a tavern at Amboy, was standing at his door, with as pretty a child in his hand, about eight or nine years old, as ever I saw, and after speaking his mind as freely as he thought was prudent, finished with this unfatherly expression. " Well! give me peace in my day." Not a man lives on the continent but fully believes that a separation must some time or other finally take place, and a generous parent should have said, " If there must be trouble, let it be in my day, that my child may have peace "; and this single reflection, well applied, is sufficient to awaken every man to duty. Not a place upon earth might be so happy as America. Her situation is remote from all the wrangling world, and she has nothing to do but to trade with them. A man can distinguish himself between temper and principle, and I am as confident as I am that God governs the world, that America will never be happy till she gets clear of foreign dominion. Wars, without ceasing, will break out till that period arrives, and the continent must in the end be conqueror; for though the flame of liberty may sometimes cease to shine, the coal can never expire.

The heart that feels not now, is dead; the blood of his children will curse his cowardice who shrinks back at a time when a little might have saved the whole and made them happy. I love the man that can smile in trouble, that can gather strength from distress and grow brave by reflection. 'Tis the business of little minds to shrink; but he whose heart is firm, and whose conscience approves his conduct, will pursue his principles unto death. My own line of reasoning is to myself as straight and clear as a ray of light. Not all the treasures of the world, so far as I believe, could have induced me to support an offensive war, for I think it murder; but if a thief breaks into my house, burns and destroys my property, and kills or threatens to kill me, or those that are in it, and to " bind me in all cases whatsoever " to his absolute will, am I to suffer it? What signifies it to me, whether he who does it is a king or a common man; my countryman or not my countryman; whether it be done by an individual villain or an army of them? If we reason to the root of things, we shall find no difference; neither can any just cause be assigned why we should punish in the one case and pardon in the other.

## Suggestions for Study

1. What does Paine mean by " the summer soldier and the sunshine patriot "?
2. What statement by the British government does he consider a clear example of tyranny?
3. What answer does Paine have for the timid person who is afraid of England's might? For the one who says, " Give me peace in my day "? For the one who believes all war is wrong?
4. If you had been an undecided citizen of that day, which would have moved you more strongly to action — Patrick Henry or Thomas Paine? Why?

## For Your Vocabulary

BASE-WORD. Paine gives us several clear examples of *fallacious* (fă-lā′shŭs) argument, deceptive or faulty reasoning. Such an argument or belief is called a *fallacy* (făl′à-sĭ). The stem, meaning to deceive or to fail, gives us our common words *fail, fault,* and *false.* Do you remember Father's *infallible* watch in Clarence Day's essay on the hard-rocking ship (see page 152)? It was incapable of error or failure.

## Thomas Jefferson    1743–1826

In June, 1776, a committee of the Second Continental Congress, consisting of Thomas Jefferson, John Adams, Benjamin Franklin, Roger Sherman, and Robert R. Livingston, was appointed to draft a declaration of independence. At the request of this committee Thomas Jefferson wrote the text, which, after a few changes by the committee, was presented to Congress on June 28. After several days of debate the Declaration of Independence was formally adopted on July 4, 1776. This document is remarkable for the clarity, dignity, and beauty of its language.

# THE DECLARATION OF INDEPENDENCE

When, in the course of human events, it becomes necessary for one people to dissolve the political bands which have connected them with another, and to assume among the powers of the earth the separate and equal station to which the laws of nature and of nature's God entitle them, a decent respect to the opinions of mankind requires that they should declare the causes which impel them to the separation.

We hold these truths to be self-evident: that all men are created equal, that they are endowed by their Creator with certain inalienable rights, that among these are life, liberty, and the pursuit of happiness. That to secure these rights, governments are instituted among men, deriving their just powers from the consent of the governed. That whenever any form of government becomes destructive of these ends it is the right of the people to alter or abolish it, and to institute a new government, laying its foundation on such principles, and organizing its powers in such form, as to them shall seem most likely to effect their safety and happiness. Prudence, indeed, will dictate that governments long established should not be changed for light and transient causes; and accordingly all experience hath shown that mankind are more disposed to suffer, while evils are sufferable, than to right themselves by abolishing the forms to which they are accustomed. But when a long train of abuses and usurpations, pursuing invariably the same object, evinces a design to reduce them under absolute despotism, it is their right, it is their duty, to throw off such government, and to provide new guards for their future security. Such has been the patient sufferance of these colonies; and such is now the necessity which constrains them to alter their former systems of government. The history of the present King of Great Britain is a history of repeated injuries and usurpations, all having in direct object the establishment of an absolute tyranny over these states.

DRAFTING THE DECLARATION OF INDEPENDENCE. The committee, Franklin, Jefferson, Adams, Livingston, and Sherman, from a painting by Chappel. (Culver)

To prove this, let facts be submitted to a candid world.

[Here are listed the many injustices suffered by the colonies.]

In every stage of these oppressions we have petitioned for redress in the most humble terms; our repeated petitions have been answered only by repeated injuries. A prince whose character is thus marked by every act which may define a tyrant is unfit to be the ruler of a free people.

Nor have we been wanting in attentions to our British brethren. We have warned them from time to time of attempts by their legislature to extend an unwarrantable jurisdiction over us. We have reminded them of the circumstances of our emigration and settlement here. We have appealed to their native justice and magnanimity and we have conjured them by the ties of our common kindred to disavow these usurpations, which would inevitably interrupt our connection and correspondence. They too have been deaf to the voice of justice and of consanguinity. We must, therefore, acquiesce in the necessity which denounces our separation and hold them, as we hold the rest of mankind, enemies in war, in peace, friends.

We, therefore, the representatives of the United States of America, in General Congress assembled, appealing to the Supreme Judge of the world for the rectitude of our intentions, do, in the name and by the authority of the good people of these colonies, solemnly publish and declare, that these united colonies are, and of right ought to be, free and independent states; that they are absolved from all allegiance to the British crown, and that all political connection between them and the State of Great Britain is, and ought to be, totally dissolved; and that, as free and independent states, they have full power to levy war, conclude peace, contract alliances, establish commerce, and to do all other acts and things which independent states may of right do.

And, for the support of this declaration, with a firm reliance on the protection of Divine Providence, we mutually pledge to

*Pictorial Archives from Three Lions*

each other our lives, our fortunes, and our sacred honor.

## Suggestions for Study

1. What oft-quoted phrases do you find here? In the popular mind the Declaration of Independence and the Constitution of the United States are sometimes confused. Do you find any phrases here which you had supposed were in the Constitution?

2. Is it true that all men are created entirely equal? In what sense did the writers of this document mean " equal "?

3. What part of this document might the Southern states have quoted to justify their secession from the Union?

4. What attitude is shown toward the British people?

5. What are some of the problems confronting the world today that have a direct connec-

tion with the self-evident truths expressed in the second paragraph?

6. Write a resolution declaring for safe driving, better English, or some phase of good citizenship in your school. Try to make your language as definite and impressive as Jefferson's.

## For Your Vocabulary

BASE-WORD. One great service of the Declaration was its success in presenting to all the world the *rectitude* (rĕk′tĭ-tûd) of our intentions (page 467), their rightness and integrity. The base-word *rect* means upright in a literal sense as it is used in mathematical terms like *rectangle*. In most of the general words like *correct* it means simply right, up to an established standard, as a clock or set of scales is *correct*. Be sure of your own standards before you start to *correct* others, to set them right according to your standards. *Rectify* is a more formal term for setting an error right.

## Francis Hopkinson     1737-1791

## THE BATTLE OF THE KEGS

As with other wars, the Revolution had its lighter side. The soldiers had their camp and marching songs, the most famous of which is " Yankee Doodle." Satire was a popular weapon of the literary men of the day, and they lost no opportunity to make the enemy appear ridiculous. Among these satirical poems, one of the most amusing is " The Battle of the Kegs." Its author was a Philadelphia lawyer who had signed the Declaration of Independence and helped to draft the Articles of Confederation.

Hopkinson's own note to this poem says: " The ballad was occasioned by a real incident. Certain machines, in the form of kegs, charged with gunpowder, were sent down the river to annoy the British shipping, then at Philadelphia. The danger of these machines being discovered, the British manned the wharfs and shipping, and discharged their small arms and cannons at everything they saw floating in the river during the ebb tide."

Gallants, attend, and hear a friend
  Trill forth harmonious ditty:
Strange things I'll tell, which late befell
  In Philadelphia city.

'Twas early day, as poets say,              5
  Just when the sun was rising,
A soldier stood on a log of wood
  And saw a thing surprising.

As in amaze he stood to gaze,
  The truth can't be denied, sir,         10
He spied a score of kegs or more
  Come floating down the tide, sir.

A sailor, too, in jerkin blue,
  This strange appearance viewing,        14
First damned his eyes, in great surprise,
  Then said, " Some mischief's brewing:

" These kegs, I'm told, the rebels hold,
  Packed up like pickled herring;
And they're come down to attack the town,
  In this new way of ferrying."           20

The soldier flew, the sailor too,
  And scared almost to death, sir,
Wore out their shoes to spread the news,
  And ran till out of breath, sir.

Now up and down throughout the town     25
  Most frantic scenes were acted;
And some ran here and others there,
  Like men almost distracted.

Some fire cried, which some denied,
  But said the earth had quakèd;          30
And girls and boys, with hideous noise,
  Ran through the streets half naked.

Sir William, he, snug as a flea,
  Lay all this time a-snoring,
Nor dreamed of harm, as he lay warm,      35
  [The Yankees quite ignoring].

Now in a fright he starts upright,
  Awaked by such a clatter;
He rubs his eyes and boldly cries,        39
  " For God's sake, what's the matter? "

At his bedside he then espied
  Sir Erskine at command, sir:
Upon one foot he had one boot,
  An t'other in his hand, sir.

" Arise, arise! " Sir Erskine cries;    45
  " The rebels, more's the pity,
Without a boat are all afloat
  And ranged before the city.

" The motley crew, in vessels new,
  With Satan for their guide, sir,    50
Packed up in bags, or wooden kegs,
  Come driving down the tide, sir,

" Therefore prepare for bloody war:
  These kegs must all be routed
Or surely we despised shall be,    55
  And British courage doubted."

The royal band now ready stand,
  All ranged in dread array, sir,
With stomachs stout, to see it out,
  And make a bloody day, sir.    60

The cannons roar from shore to shore,
  The small arms make a rattle;
Since wars began, I'm sure no man
  E'er saw so strange a battle.

The rebel dales, the rebel vales,    65
  With rebel trees surrounded,
The distant woods, the hills and floods,
  With rebel echoes sounded.

The fish below swam to and fro,
  Attacked from every quarter:    70
" Why, sure," thought they, " the devil's to pay
  'Mongst folks above the water."

The kegs, 'tis said, though strongly made
  Of rebel staves and hoops, sir,
Could not oppose their powerful foes,    75
  The conquering British troops, sir.

From morn till night these men of might
  Displayed amazing courage,
And when the sun was fairly down
  Retired to sup their porridge.    80

An hundred men, with each a pen,
  Or more, upon my word, sir,
It is most true would be too few
  Their valor to record, sir.

Such feats did they perform that day    85
  Against those wicked kegs, sir,
That years to come, if they get home,
  They'll make their boasts and brags, sir.

## Suggestions for Study

1. What is satire? How effective do you consider it as a weapon?
2. Where else in this volume have you encountered satire? Compare other examples with this as to general spirit. Would you call this a bitter or a light satire?
3. Write a bit of satire, in prose if you prefer, attacking something which you dislike.

## Alexander Hamilton    1757–1804

The following speech, one of many made by Hamilton in favor of ratification of the Constitution, was delivered on June 21, 1788, before the New York State Legislature. By the force of Hamilton's logic and oratory the sixty-five legislators, forty-six of whom were Antifederalists, were persuaded to ratify by a majority of three — a rare instance of the vote of a deliberative body changed by sheer argument. The speech answers the objection that the proposed Constitution did not prevent the rich and well-educated from gaining control of the government.

The sentiments expressed are typical of Hamilton's philosophy. In American thought the term " Hamiltonian " has come to characterize a belief in government by a selected group of the " best people," the more intelligent, the more wealthy, the more able, as contrasted with " Jeffersonian," which denotes faith in democratic government by the whole people. Jefferson was the liberal of his day; Hamilton, the conservative.

### SPEECH IN DEFENSE OF THE CONSTITUTION

Sir, we hear constantly a great deal which is rather calculated to awake our passions, and create prejudices, than to conduct us to

Culver

*A Hamilton*

the truth, and teach us our real interests. I do not suppose this to be the design of the gentlemen. Why, then, are we told so often of an aristocracy? For my part, I hardly know the meaning of this word, as it is applied. If all we hear be true, this government is really a very bad one. But who are the aristocracy among us? Where do we find men elevated to a perpetual rank above their fellow citizens, and possessing powers entirely independent of them? The arguments of the gentlemen only go to prove that there are men who are rich, men who are poor, some who are wise, and others who are not; that, indeed, every distinguished man is an aristocrat. This reminds me of a description of the aristocrats I have seen in a late publication styled the *Federal Farmer*. The author reckons in the aristocracy all governors of states, members of Congress, chief magistrates, and all officers of the militia. This description, I presume to say, is ridiculous. The image is a phantom. Does the new government render a rich man more eligible than a poor one? No.

It requires no such qualification. It is bottomed on the broad and equal principle of your state constitution.

Sir, if the people have it in their option to elect their most meritorious men, is this to be considered as an objection? Shall the Constitution oppose their wishes and abridge their most invaluable privilege? While property continues to be pretty equally divided, and a considerable share of information pervades the community, the tendency of the people's suffrages will be to elevate merit even from obscurity. As riches increase and accumulate in few hands, as luxury prevails in society, virtue will be in a greater degree considered as only a graceful appendage of wealth, and the tendency of things will be to depart from the republican standard. This is the real disposition of human nature: it is what neither the honorable member nor myself can correct; it is a common misfortune, that awaits our state constitution as well as all others.

There is an advantage incident to large districts of election, which perhaps the gentlemen, amidst all their apprehensions of influence and bribery, have not adverted to. In large districts, the corruption of the electors is much more difficult; combinations for the purposes of intrigue are less easily formed; factions and cabals are little known. In a small district, wealth will have a more complete influence, because the people in the vicinity of a great man are more immediately his dependents, and because this influence has fewer objects to act upon. It has been remarked, that it would be disagreeable to the middle class of men to go to the seat of the new government. If this be so, the difficulty will be enhanced by the gentleman's proposal. If his argument be true, it proves that the larger the representation is, the less will be your chance of having it filled. But it appears to me frivolous to bring forward such arguments as these. It has answered no other purpose than to induce me, by way of reply, to enter into discussion which I consider as useless and not applicable to our subject.

It is a harsh doctrine that men grow

wicked in proportion as they improve and enlighten their minds. Experience has by no means justified us in the supposition that there is more virtue in one class of men than in another. Look through the rich and the poor of the community, the learned and the ignorant. Where does virtue predominate? The difference indeed consists, not in the quantity, but kind, of vices which are incident to various classes; and here the advantage of character belongs to the wealthy. Their vices are probably more favorable to the prosperity of the state than those of the indigent, and partake less of moral depravity.

After all, sir, we must submit to this idea, that the true principle of a republic is, that the people should choose whom they please to govern them. Representation is imperfect in proportion as the current of popular favor is checked. This great source of free government, popular election, should be perfectly pure and the most unbounded liberty allowed. Where this principle is adhered to; where, in the organization of the government, the legislative, executive, and judicial branches are rendered distinct; where, again, the legislature is divided into separate houses, and the operations of each are controlled by various checks and balances, and, above all, by the vigilance and weight of the state governments — to talk of tyranny and the subversion of our liberties, is to speak the language of enthusiasm. This balance between the national and state governments ought to be dwelt on with peculiar attention, as it is of the utmost importance. It forms a double security to the people. If one encroaches on their rights, they will find a powerful protection in the other. Indeed, they will both be prevented from overpassing their constitutional limits, by a certain rivalship, which will ever subsist between them. I am persuaded that a firm union is as necessary to perpetuate our liberties as it is to make us respectable; and experience will probably prove that the national government will be as natural a guardian of our freedom as the state legislatures themselves.

## Suggestions for Study

1. With what parts of Hamilton's argument do you agree? With what parts do you disagree?

2. What two prophecies does Hamilton make in this speech? Have they come to pass?

3. Contrast the political philosophies of Hamilton and Jefferson. Which is more nearly embodied in the United States Constitution? Toward which has been the trend of the general nature of the amendments?

4. The Preamble to the Constitution is well worth memorizing: "We, the people of the United States, in order to form a more perfect Union, establish justice, insure domestic tranquility, provide for the common defense, promote the general welfare, and secure the blessings of liberty to ourselves and our posterity, do ordain and establish this Constitution for the United States of America."

5. Name three problems now facing our government, and state what you think would have been Hamilton's position in regard to each.

6. Read the Bill of Rights. What fundamental liberties are guaranteed in this part of the Constitution? Cite instances of recent attempts to deny these rights to individuals or groups.

## For Your Vocabulary

BASE-WORD. One of the most-used basewords in English is *vert,* meaning to turn. You already know many words of the family, *divert* (to turn from), *convert* (to turn with), *avert* (to turn away). Hamilton uses two less common forms, *advert* (page 470) and *subversion* (page 471). *Advert* (ăd-vûrt′) means to turn toward, and *subversion* (sŭb-vûr′shŭn) means turning under, or destroying completely. You will find George Washington, in his " Farewell Address," warning Americans against means by which unprincipled men can *subvert* the power of the people. All these verb forms ending in *-t* have noun forms ending in *-sion.* Two members of the *vert* family that we hear often are *introvert* and *extrovert,* nouns used to describe types of personality in which interest is turned inward upon one's own self (the *introvert*) or is turned outward on the world and affairs outside the individual (the *extrovert*).

What do we mean when we say that a person told his own *version* of a happening?

# George Washington     1732–1799

In the fall of 1796 Washington decided that the state of America, external as well as internal, justified him in returning to that retirement from which he had been reluctantly drawn to assume the presidency. To notify his fellow citizens of his resolution not to be a candidate for a third term, he published in a Philadelphia newspaper the famous document now known as "Washington's Farewell Address." It is said that no other state paper has been so frequently reprinted as this so-called address. Small wonder it is that the parting advice of one who had been the pre-eminent leader of military, economic, and political struggle should be sought again and again as successive questions of policy have arisen.

## FAREWELL ADDRESS

### TO THE PEOPLE OF THE UNITED STATES
### SEPTEMBER 17, 1796

Written in a formal and dignified style and employing a large and unusual vocabulary, this address presents considerable difficulty to the high-school student. However, since the modern American will frequently hear statesmen, politicians, and lecturers refer to this document, it is well to know and understand the principles enunciated in this famous message by the father of our country. In the following selected passages you will find, in Washington's own words, statements of these basic principles, which he himself designated as " some sentiments, which are the result of much reflection, of no inconsiderable observation, and which appear to me all-important to the permanency of your felicity as a people."

Perhaps some of you will care to look up and read the entire address. It is not easy reading, but it is a challenge to you to bring all the powers of your mind to bear on a worth-while message.

Since one of the prime difficulties is the vocabulary, look up the following words before you start reading: appellation, explicit, requisite, discountenance, specious, baneful, reciprocal, weal, usurpation, indispensable, vicissitudes, disinterested.

Interwoven as is the love of liberty with **every ligament of your hearts**, no recom-mendation of mine is necessary to fortify or confirm the attachment.

The unity of government, which constitutes you one people, is a main pillar of your real independence, the support of your tranquillity at home, your peace abroad; of your safety; of your prosperity; of that very liberty which you so highly prize. The name of America, which belongs to you, in your national capacity, must always exalt the just pride of patriotism, more than any appellation derived from local discriminations. One of the expedients of party to acquire influence, within particular districts, is to misrepresent the opinions and aims of other districts. You cannot shield yourselves too much against the jealousies and heartburnings which spring from these misrepresentations.

The basis of our political systems is the right of the people to make and to alter their constitutions of government. But the constitution which at any time exists, till changed by an explicit and authentic act of the whole people, is sacredly obligatory upon all. The very idea of the power and the right of the people to establish government presupposes the duty of every individual to obey the established government.

All combinations and associations, under whatever plausible character, with the real design to direct, control, counteract, or awe the regular deliberation and action of the constituted authorities are likely, in the course of time and things, to become potent engines, by which cunning, ambitious, and unprincipled men will be enabled to subvert the power of the people, and to usurp for themselves the reins of government.

Toward the preservation of your government, and the permanency of your present happy state, it is requisite, not only that you steadily discountenance irregular opposition to its acknowledged authority, but also that you resist with care the spirit of innovation upon its principles, however specious the pretexts. Remember that facility in changes, upon the credit of mere hypothesis and opinion. exposes to perpetual change, from the endless variety of hypothesis and opinion; and remember, especially, that, for the efficient management of your common interests, in a country so extensive as ours a government of as much vigor as is consistent with the perfect security of liberty is indispensable. Liberty itself will find in such a government, with powers properly distributed and adjusted, its surest guardian.

Let me warn you in the most solemn manner against the baneful effects of the spirit of party generally. The alternate domination of one faction over another, sharpened by the spirit of revenge natural to party dissension, is in itself a frightful despotism. The disorders and miseries which result gradually incline the minds of men to seek security and repose in the absolute power of an individual; and sooner or later the chief of some prevailing faction, more able or more fortunate than his competitors, turns this disposition to the purposes of his own elevation, on the ruins of public liberty.

The necessity of reciprocal checks in the exercise of political power, by dividing and distributing it into different depositories, and constituting each the guardian of the public weal against invasions by the others, has been evinced by experiments ancient and modern, some of them in our country and under our own eyes. To preserve them must be as necessary as to institute them. If, in the opinion of the people, the distribution or modification of the constitutional powers be in any particular wrong, let it be corrected by an amendment in the way which the Constitution designates. But let there be no change by usurpation.

Of all the dispositions and habits which lead to political prosperity, religion and morality are indispensable supports.

Promote, as an object of primary importance, institutions for the general diffusion of knowledge. In proportion as the structure of a government gives force to public opinion, it is essential that public opinion should be enlightened.

As a very important source of strength and security, cherish public credit.

Observe good faith and justice toward all

*Pictorial Archives from Three Lions*

nations; cultivate peace and harmony with all. The nation which indulges toward another an habitual hatred or an habitual fondness is in some degree a slave. It is a slave to its animosity or to its affection, either of which is sufficient to lead it astray from its duty and its interest.

The great rule of conduct for us, in regard to foreign nations, is, in extending our commercial relations, to have with them as little political connection as possible. Europe has a set of primary interests, which to us have none, or a remote relation. Hence she must be engaged in frequent controversies, the causes of which are essentially foreign to our concerns. Hence, therefore, it must be unwise in us to implicate ourselves by artificial ties, in the ordinary vicissitudes of her politics or the ordinary combinations and collisions of her friendships and enmities. Our detached and distant situation invites and enables us to pursue a different course. Why forego the advantages of so peculiar a situation? It is our true policy to steer clear of permanent alliances with any portion of the foreign world. Even our commercial policy should hold an equal and impartial hand; neither seeking nor granting exclusive favors or preferences, constantly keeping in view that it is folly in one nation to look for disinterested favors from another; that it must pay with a portion of its independence for whatever it may accept under that character.

## Suggestions for Study

1. In order to understand this address fully, you must be able to realize the difference between the United States in Washington's day and in ours. It would be well to have brief reports from members of the class on such matters as the boundaries, population, and political parties; conditions of commerce, manufacturing, and education; relationship with England, France, and other foreign nations; and the number of republics in the world at that time — comparing all of them with conditions in our own day.

2. The body of this address falls into two main parts: advice on home affairs and advice on foreign affairs. Make an outline of the points under each.

3. Washington warns emphatically against the dangers of long and decided affections or antipathies between nations. Give some striking examples of this in the world's history or among countries today.

4. Compare the style of this speech with the sharp, terse sentences of Patrick Henry (page 461) or the simplicity of Lincoln's phrasing (pages 671–675). How is the style of an address intended for oral delivery likely to differ from that of one intended to be read in print?

5. In the light of changed conditions, which parts of Washington's advice do you think apply today and which do not? This affords good subject matter for informal debates.

6. An interesting project for a class or committee would be the making of two small world maps, one for Washington's day, one for ours, to show the number of republics in the world. In both maps color absolute monarchies black, limited or constitutional monarchies gray, totalitarian states red, and leave republics white.

## For Your Vocabulary

WORD GROUP. Many of the difficult words in this "Address" are too formal to be used often in our informal times, but *expedient*

(page 472) is useful in any day. As a noun it means a course of action designed to achieve a desired end, whether noble or base, important or trifling. Did you ever pretend to be ill as an *expedient* (ĕks-pē′dĭ-ĕnt) to keep from going to school? As an adjective, *expedient* means suitable or advantageous to the end in view, often as opposed to what is strictly right or admirable. *Expediency* is the quality of working effectively toward a desired end, and practical men of affairs must often be guided by motives of *expediency*. They choose their course in order to *expedite* (ĕks′pĕ-dīt) the achievement of their aims. Does it make the word any clearer to know that it originally meant to get one's foot loose, ready to go places?

## For Further Reading on the Making of a Nation

### LITERATURE OF THE PERIOD

Hart, A. B. and Hill, Mabel: *Camps and Firesides of the Revolution* (source material)

Lawson, Robert: *Watchwords of Liberty* (famous slogans and the circumstances of their origin)

### BOOKS ABOUT THE PERIOD

#### Biography

ETHAN ALLEN. Dean, S. W.: *He Fought for Freedom*

AARON BURR. Carroll, Mary: *The Man Who Would Not Wait*

BENJAMIN FRANKLIN. Daugherty, J. H.: *Poor Richard;* Meadowcroft, E. L.: *Benjamin Franklin;* Nicolay, Helen: *Boys' Life of Benjamin Franklin*

ALEXANDER HAMILTON. Nicolay, Helen: *Boys' Life of Alexander Hamilton;* Smertenko, J. J.: *Alexander Hamilton, Man of Action*

THOMAS JEFFERSON. Daugherty, Sonia: *The Way of an Eagle;* Lisitsky, Gene: *Thomas Jefferson;* Nicolay, Helen: *Boys' Life of Thomas Jefferson;* Van Loon, H. W.: *Thomas Jefferson*

JOHN PAUL JONES. Ellsberg, Edward: *I Have Just Begun to Fight*

FRANCIS SCOTT KEY. Holland, R. S.: *Freedom's Flag*

LAFAYETTE. Eaton, Jeanette: *Young Lafayette;* Nicolay, Helen: *Boys' Life of Lafayette*

# THE FIRST TWO CENTURIES

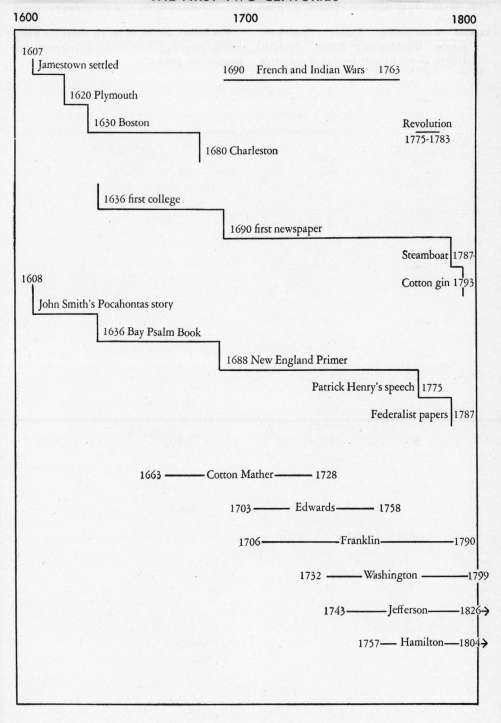

1600                         1700                         1800

1607
Jamestown settled                    1690    French and Indian Wars    1763

1620 Plymouth

1630 Boston                                              Revolution
                                                         1775-1783
1680 Charleston

1636 first college

1690 first newspaper

Steamboat 1787

Cotton gin 1793

1608
John Smith's Pocahontas story

1636 Bay Psalm Book

1688 New England Primer

Patrick Henry's speech 1775

Federalist papers 1787

1663 ———— Cotton Mather ———— 1728

1703 ———— Edwards ———— 1758

1706 ——————— Franklin ——————— 1790

1732 ——— Washington ——— 1799

1743 ——————— Jefferson ——— 1826→

1757 —— Hamilton —— 1804→

ISRAEL PUTNAM. Dean, L. W.: *Old Wolf*

PAUL REVERE. Rogers, F. and Beard, A.: *Paul Revere*

GEORGE WASHINGTON. Foster, Genevieve: *George Washington's World;* Nicolay, Helen: *Boys' Life of George Washington*

MARTHA WASHINGTON. Desmond, Alice: *Martha Washington, Our First Lady*

For fiction, see list of novels about the Revolution, page 141. For historical reference, see general list, page 784.

# The Flowering of the East

## PART ONE

"WHO READS an American book?" an English critic asked scornfully in an Edinburgh magazine. " Or goes to an American play? " he added. " Or looks at an American picture or statue? What does the world yet owe to American physicians or surgeons? What new substances have their chemists discovered? What constellations have been discovered by the telescopes of Americans? What have they done in mathematics? "

That was in 1820. Even then it was not a fair comment. Europe had paid attention to Ben Franklin when he had come over representing the colonies. Europe had listened to the revolutionary orators and pamphleteers. England had chuckled at Washington Irving's *Knickerbocker History* in 1809, and one editor had paid Bryant's " Thanatopsis " (1817) the tribute of saying that it was too good, too mature to have been written in America. Bryant must be a pen name for some Englishman, the editor said.

But by and large the English critic was right. Two hundred and thirteen years after the first permanent English settlement, there was yet no real American literature. The strength of America had not yet expressed itself in great artists; it had expressed itself in frontier scouts and statesmen and practical men of affairs. America had not created fine art; it had created at first strong colonies, and then a free nation.

The exciting thing about the American story, as we look back over it now, is how, in the hundred years after 1820, Ameri-

cans have made that English critic eat his words.

In 1820 there was very little to disprove him. Fifty years later there was already a long shelf of distinguished American books — Irving, Cooper, Bryant, Poe, Hawthorne, Whittier, Emerson, Thoreau, Lincoln, Longfellow, Holmes, Lowell, Prescott, Parkman, Melville, Whitman. Fifty years more, in 1920, and an American writer, Mark Twain, had received one of the greatest world-wide acclaims ever given any man of letters from any country. Europe was reading by American electric lights, flying in a device developed by the American Wright brothers, hiring a Johns Hopkins professor of surgery to be an Oxford professor, hearing about a new American device called radio broadcasting, and looking to an American President to lead the world to peace.

All that in one hundred years! How did it happen? We don't know exactly. If we knew how to make Edisons and Twains we would make more of them. But we can look back and see some reasons why American art and science suddenly flowered after 1800.

For one thing, Americans had time. There had been very little time for art and literature when the colonists were trying to hold on to a little strip of land between sea and forest, fighting Indians and hunger and distance. There had been very little time while they were fighting for political freedom and planning a constitution and government. Literature is not written on the frontier. There isn't time for it. There is time only to keep alive, and build, and plan for a fu-

THE LITERARY GIANTS OF THE MID–NINETEENTH CENTURY. The artist has assembled the following writers at this fictitious gathering in Washington Irving's study: Simms, Holmes, Halleck, Hawthorne, Longfellow, Willis, Prescott, Irving, Paulding, Emerson, Bryant, Kennedy, Cooper, and Bancroft. (Brown Brothers)

ture that will give later generations more time and opportunity.

But in the nineteenth century the frontier was rolling far to the West, pouring its riches back to the East. The East had to make the machinery to settle the West. The East had to put up the supplies for western migration. The East had to finance a transportation system for the whole country. And so, while the frontier pushed west, large cities and rich states grew on the eastern seaboard. There is something about a literary movement that seems to need cities, where men can gather and talk and argue, where theaters and museums and art galleries flourish, and where publishers and editors can have their headquarters. So in the nineteenth century, New York, Boston, and Charleston, South Carolina, became centers of literary and artistic production, with smaller centers all around them.

The time was ripe. The freedoms for which Americans had been fighting for two centuries had been won. The nation was in-

dependent, and was feeling its muscles proudly like an adolescent boy. A spirit of adventure and accomplishment was in the air. The feeling was something like the Elizabethan Age of England, when Drake had beaten back the Spanish Armada, English ships were sailing to every coast in the world and bringing back wealth and knowledge, and men like Shakespeare were writing in London. The States had won their first war, they were winning the West and sending out ships and goods to all the world, they were growing rich and powerful, and they were proud of being a nation, proud of being Americans. In fact, writers began to be as excited over literary freedom as other Americans had been over freedom of religion and political freedom. They said that American literature had been a colonial literature too long; now it should stand forth as a true national literature in its own right. American writers, too, should declare independence of Europe. They should write like Americans, not like Englishmen. Numbers

WASHINGTON IRVING'S NEW YORK. This is lower Broadway in 1831. At left is P. T. Barnum's American Museum (later torn down); at right is St. Paul's Church. (Brown Brothers)

of "American epics" began to appear. Greece and Rome had their epics, the writers said; the new nation was destined to be no less great than they; therefore, it was time for an American epic!

And so all the hard-won freedom, the new prosperity and leisure, the idealism, the new national pride, the vigor that had formerly been drained off by the fight for other freedoms — all this flowered in America's first great age of literature.

"We are the pioneers," Herman Melville said of Americans. "God has predestined, mankind expects, great things from our race; and great things we feel in our souls."

## 1. IRVING AND COOPER

### THE FLOWERING OF NEW YORK

The first flowering was in New York. From the very beginning, New York had been cosmopolitan. As early as 1643, a Dutch settler reported, eighteen languages were being spoken there. It was a natural port of entry, and, as industry grew around

it in the eighteenth century, it became the great funnel through which much of American export was poured into ships bound for Europe and Asia. Some parts of it looked like a little country town, with streets wandering on old cowpaths through what has now become the financial district, and pigs running wild over the lawns and roadways. But Broadway was straight and wide. And great things were being done. By 1800, a cabinet maker named Duncan Phyfe had a little shop near the foot of Broadway where he was making furniture that brings fabulous sums today and is often duplicated. By 1800, a fur-trader named John Jacob Astor was building a business that connected New York to every part of the continent. The town at the end of the Oregon Trail, where the Columbia River met the Pacific, was named after him, Astoria. From the beginning New York had good businessmen. The first evidence was the purchase of all of Manhattan Island from the Indians for twenty-four dollars.

In 1800, New York was a little brick town at the lower end of Manhattan Island, where men talked like eighteenth-century Englishmen and gathered in coffeehouses consciously patterned after London coffeehouses. But it was changing. It was becoming different from anything Europe had seen: a melting pot for the races of Europe, an example of the American qualities of shrewdness and enterprise, a center for American thinkers and writers.

## WASHINGTON IRVING

The first important writer born in New York was Washington Irving. His whole life is symbolic of what was happening. When he was still a lap baby, in 1783, the British troops moved out of New York and out of the States. He was not born to a professional or literary family, as so many European writers were; his father was a hardware merchant, and Washington was trained, like many another middle-class American boy, for law and business. If he had followed the road cut out for him, he might have continued as secretary to the governor of New York and perhaps gone into politics, or been the European manager of a hardware firm. But by one of the chances that make literature, he was never attracted by law enough to practice it; he was attracted more by a trip to Europe than by the further opportunities of New York politics, and when he got to Europe the hardware firm went bankrupt around him. So it was that the thing he liked to do but never thought of seriously as a money-making activity had to support him. He became a writer, one of the first professional writers in America.

As a writer, too, he was symbolic. American literature in his time had not yet declared full literary independence, though it was moving toward it. Irving looked toward Europe more than toward the West. He spent twenty of his first fifty years in Europe. His writing was not much different from the writing of the kindly, urbane humorists and essayists who wrote in England during the eighteenth century. Indeed, he was a curiosity to the English not because he wrote differently from them, but because an American could write so well. " It has been a matter of marvel to my European readers that a man from the wilds of America should express himself in tolerable English," he reported, with tongue in cheek. " I was looked upon as something new and strange in literature; a kind of demisavage with a feather in his hand instead of on his head; and there was a curiosity to hear what such a being had to say about civilized society."

Everybody liked the " demisavage." He was lovable, sociable, a good storyteller, playful, witty, fond of gay parties (his social life as a young man became something of a legend in New York), sentimental enough to be interested in anything old, anything strange or distant. He was a kind humorist, not a bitter one. He laughed with, rather than at, his subjects, and he wrote of experiences he was fond of and wanted to share with his readers.

As we look back over his life, we can see that he was profoundly moved by three geographical areas, three civilizations, of which only one was American. That was, of course, the New York where he grew up — the city that was growing from an old Dutch town into a melting-pot city, and the Hudson valley that was already so rich in memory and legend. As a matter of fact, Irving himself did a lot to hasten that change in New York city by writing one book, his first one, *A History of New York by Diedrich Knickerbocker*. It was a comic parody on a certain pompous history of the city. The original history has been forgotten, but Irving's parody lives on, and nobody dared be very pompous about the old Dutch settlers after Irving had set the whole English-speaking world chuckling at his hilarious caricatures of the solid Dutch burghers. Irving was like a little boy sticking pins into balloons. New Yorkers chuckled, too, amidst their embarrassment, for it was a kindly book, and Irving's love for the " Golden Reign of Wouter Van Twiller " and other chapters in the story of old New York was just as evident as his amusement.

Even more important than old New York to Irving was the old Hudson valley. He made his first trip up the valley in 1800 — that was a kind of symbol of the new century, too. On that trip he saw Sleepy Hollow and Rip Van Winkle's Catskills. Later he often went squirrel hunting in Sleepy Hollow. When he came back from his seventeen-year stay in Europe, he bought a house near Tarrytown, and was buried at last in Sleepy Hollow cemetery. Probably he loved no other place on earth so much as that Hudson valley country, and perhaps none of his writing will last longer than the stories he wrote about it — " Rip Van Winkle " and " The Legend of Sleepy Hollow."

But two parts of Europe competed with the Hudson valley for his affection. They were England and Spain. He went to England in 1815 (the first news he heard on shore was that Napoleon had been defeated). He traveled through England, France, and Italy like a pilgrim, reveling in the old buildings, the legends, the unfamiliar scenes, and the gracious living. He felt at home in this kind of life, much more at home certainly than he felt in most parts of America. As he traveled he kept a notebook of what he saw and heard. In 1820, the same year in which the *Edinburgh Review* had asked, "Who reads an American book? " he published the best of his notes in England as *The Sketch Book,* and even the *Edinburgh Review* hastened to pay tribute to it. For this book was as good as the best English travel sketches. It was graceful, genial, humorous, urbane. Not even the English had written better about their old inns and their countryside. There was very little about it, in fact, that stamped it as an American book; but the very fact that it was written by an American served notice to the world that talent might be expected in a new direction.

Irving's last, and in some respects greatest, love was Spain. He resurrected its romantic old history and legends in *The Conquest of Granada* and the tales of *The Alhambra,* and studied its records for his life of Columbus. He served four years as American minister to Spain, and was deeply fond of the Spanish country and the memories it held.

In his later years he tried to move in the direction of the American literature around him. He went to the West and wrote a journal of his trip over the great plains. He wrote, for the Astors, a book on Astoria. He wrote a vigorous reply to European criticism, called " English Writers on America." His last long work was a biography of Washington. But none of these was equal to *The Sketch Book,* the Hudson valley stories, or the tales of Spain. The center of his interest and sympathy was nearer England than Astoria. His place in our literary tradition was not as a leader of a new national literature, but as the first great exponent of polite literature in a new country. He opened European eyes to us, but he had no particular message. As he himself said, " I have attempted no lofty theme, nor sought to look wise and learned. . . . I have preferred addressing myself to the feeling and fancy of the reader, more than to his judgment." He was a gentleman in literature, a genial, kindly, dignified practitioner of the best informal prose we had learned from the old country.

*Irving was born at the end of the Revolution (1783), and died (1858) just before the War between the States. When he was born, only one major American writer was living — Franklin. When he died, all the great writers of the Eastern Flowering had published.*

## JAMES FENIMORE COOPER

Cooper was different. Nobody would have mistaken his novels for English books, and yet when we look at them today they seem to be a long way from the kind of American writing we have become used to in the works of indisputably American writers like Mark Twain.

In his own time, though, Cooper was a truer representative of the new country than Irving. For one thing, he learned different lessons from Europe and European books. Irving learned a graceful style, a respect for mellow humor, and a dilettante attitude. Cooper's style of writing was rough, sometimes crude. He was hardworking (thirty-two novels in twenty-nine years), intensely serious, sometimes too serious for his own good. A better sense of humor would have helped him through some of the troubles he got into in later life. Irving went to England as a pilgrim; Cooper went as a critic. And yet he learned his lessons too. He learned from novelists like Sir Walter Scott the excitement of telling a rousing adventure story. He learned from other Europeans a rather sentimental respect for the " noble Indian " and for nature and manners " unspoiled " by civilization.

His New York was not like Irving's New York, either. Irving's was the old Dutch city and the romantic Hudson. Cooper's was the finger-lake country of central New York State, where his father founded Cooperstown and lived as the master of many square miles of rich land. Cooperstown was the place where the first baseball game in the United States was played. In Cooper's time it was not very far from the frontier. The Iroquois lived thereabouts, and some of the first stories the boy Cooper heard were of the Indian wars and the pioneer scouts. As Irving " collected " old inns, cathedrals, and ghost stories, so Cooper gathered tales of the frontier and the sea and the making of America.

As Irving was brought up for business, so Cooper was expected to succeed his father as a gentleman farmer. But coincidences came to the rescue of American literature, even as they had in the case of Irving. Cooper's training did not develop as expected. He didn't like Yale, and Yale didn't like him; they parted company before graduation. Then he shipped to sea and would have made a career in the Navy if his father's death and his own marriage had not required his return to civilian life at Cooperstown. For eight years he did the work expected of him — caring for his father's estate. Then occurred the greatest happenstance of all. He decided, on a wager, to try to write a book. He said he could write one

as good as the English novel he was reading. The result was a novel, imitative and unoriginal, of which he was heartily ashamed later. But it did one priceless service for generations of Americans; it got Cooper interested in writing fiction.

That first experiment taught him another thing — that he should write about subject matter he knew. So he turned to the stories of the making of America he had heard since boyhood, to the stories of the frontier, and to his own experiences at sea. The first of these books came out only a year after the experimental novel. It was *The Spy,* an exciting novel of the Revolution, in which George Washington himself was a character. That was in 1821. In 1823 he published *The Pioneers,* a frontier novel, in which he introduced a character whom almost every young American knows — Natty Bumppo, or Leatherstocking, the scout modeled after Daniel Boone. The next year he published his first sea book, *The Pilot,* which he wrote to prove that a man who had been to sea could write about the ocean better than Sir Walter Scott, who was only a landsman. (Cooper was never one to avoid a controversy!) That was only four years after he had begun to write, and he had already produced three of the most exciting romances on American bookshelves. Now the critic in the *Edinburgh Review* might well reconsider his question, " Who reads an American book? " because throughout England readers were poring over the stories of Harvey Birch (*The Spy*), Leatherstocking (*The Pioneers*), and Long Tom Coffin (*The Pilot*). When *The Last of the Mohicans* came out in 1826, there could have been no doubt that American books were read.

His later novels fell into the three classes just named — the Leatherstocking frontier series, romances of American history like *The Spy,* and sea stories like *The Pilot.* The Leatherstocking series is the best known. These exciting romances show all of Cooper's strengths and weaknesses as a novelist. They are roughly written. The women in the books — Cooper usually calls them " females " — sometimes strike us as funny, because Cooper goes to such lengths to keep them socially proper and well groomed; a woman fleeing from Indians in the forest still maintains the manners of a Cooperstown drawing room. The historic characters, too, are more like statues than men. Sometimes we feel that he is too sentimental over " the poor Indian." But against those qualities we can name great and good ones. For one thing, the books are vital, real, exciting! The great characters are really great characters, and some of the scenes are really moving. What American boy or girl will ever forget the ending of *The Last of the Mohicans* or the character of Natty Bumppo, who said, " The only book I read, or care about reading, is the one which God has opened here before us, his creatures, in the noble forest, broad lakes, rolling rivers, blue skies, and the wind, and tempests, and sunshine, and other glorious marvels of the land."

In his late years Cooper spent much of his time in controversy. He had tried to mediate between European critics of America and American critics of Europe. The feeling was tense. In America men felt that they must have intellectual and artistic independence, as much as political. In Europe there was scorn and superciliousness. Cooper, never very graceful or adroit, managed to step on the toes of both sides. Europe refused to listen; American writers and editors heaped abuse on him for what they called disloyalty. He lost his temper, and spent a number of years answering accusations and suing editors for libel. It was an unfortunate last chapter for a man who was so intensely patriotic, so much concerned with putting his country into literature. But public affection for his books has long survived memory of the controversy.

*Cooper was born the year Washington became President (1789) and died in 1851, when Americans were streaming into California and when the Fugitive Slave Law was good for an argument almost anywhere in the country.*

## Washington Irving   1783–1859

### IN THE DAYS OF WOUTER VAN TWILLER

Washington Irving knew the value of arousing curiosity about a new product before putting it on the market. During the months of October and November, 1809, there appeared in the New York *Evening Post* a series of notices and letters concerning the disappearance of one Diedrich Knickerbocker, a small, elderly gentleman, who had left in his lodgings a " curious kind of written book." The landlord gave warning that he intended to publish this book in order to pay off the old gentleman's board bill in case of his nonappearance. A week later a publishing firm announced the approaching publication of *A History of New York* in two volumes, price three dollars, published to discharge the debts of the mysteriously vanished Mr. Diedrich Knickerbocker. The summary of its contents suggested a profound piece of scholarship " interspersed with philosophical speculations and moral precepts."

The book was prefaced by an account of the author from the pen of Seth Handaside, his landlord, and a statement by the author of the historical methods employed and of his own indebtedness to the New York Historical Society. After these solemn preliminaries, the book opened with an absurd description of the beginning of the world, and its readers soon realized that a hoax had been played on them. Reviewers hailed the book as " the wittiest our press has ever produced," but some members of the Historical Society and the old Dutch families were indignant at what they considered its ridicule of them. Forty years later Irving wrote an apology, for a later edition, showing how the term " Knickerbocker " had come to be used for everything from bread to insurance companies, and how the old Dutch families now prided themselves on being " genuine Knickerbockers." Irving truly contributed a new word to our language. The selection that follows is Chapter 4 of Book III.

In this dulcet period of my history, when the beauteous island of Manna-hata [1] presented a scene, the very counterpart of those

---

[1] **Manna-hata:** the Indian name for the island on which New York City is built.

glowing pictures drawn of the golden reign of Saturn,[1] there was, as I have before observed, a happy ignorance, an honest simplicity prevalent among its inhabitants, which, were I even able to depict, would be but little understood by the degenerate age for which I am doomed to write. Even the female sex, those arch innovators upon the tranquillity, the honesty, and graybeard customs of society, seemed for a while to conduct themselves with incredible sobriety and comeliness.

Their hair, untortured by the abominations of art, was scrupulously pomatumed back from their foreheads with a candle, and covered with a little cap of quilted calico, which fitted exactly to their heads. Their petticoats of linsey-woolsey[2] were striped with a variety of gorgeous dyes — though I must confess these gallant garments were rather short, scarce reaching below the knee; but then they made up in the number, which generally equalled that of the gentlemen's smallclothes; and what is still more praiseworthy, they were all of their own manufacture — of which circumstance, as may well be supposed, they were not a little vain.

These were the honest days in which every woman stayed at home, read the Bible, and wore pockets — ay, and that too of a goodly size, fashioned with patchwork into many curious devices, and ostentatiously worn on the outside. These, in fact, were convenient receptacles, where all good housewives carefully stored away such things as they wished to have at hand; by which means they often came to be incredibly crammed; and I remember there was a story current, when I was a boy, that the lady of Wouter Van Twiller once had occasion to empty her right pocket in search of a wooden ladle, when the contents filled a couple of corn baskets, and the utensil was discovered lying among some rubbish in one corner — but we must not give too much faith to all these stories, the anecdotes of those remote periods being very subject to exaggeration.

Besides these notable pockets, they likewise wore scissors and pincushions suspended from their girdles by red ribands, or, among the more opulent and showy classes, by brass, and even silver chains — indubitable tokens of thrifty housewives and industrious spinsters. I cannot say much in vindication of the shortness of the petticoats;[3] it doubtless was introduced for the purpose of giving the stockings a chance to be seen, which were generally of blue worsted, with magnificent red clocks — or, perhaps, to display a well-turned ankle, and a neat, though serviceable foot, set off by a high-heeled leathern shoe, with a large and splendid silver buckle. Thus we find that the gentle sex in all ages have shown the same disposition to infringe a little upon the laws of decorum, in order to betray a lurking beauty, or gratify an innocent love of finery.

From the sketch here given, it will be seen that our good grandmothers differed considerably in their ideas of a fine figure from their scantily dressed descendants of the present day. A fine lady, in those times, waddled under more clothes, even on a fair summer's day, than would have clad the whole bevy of a modern ballroom. Nor were they less admired by the gentlemen in consequence thereof. On the contrary, the greatness of a lover's passion seemed to increase in proportion to the magnitude of its object — and a voluminous damsel, arrayed in a dozen of petticoats, was declared by a Low-Dutch sonneteer of the province to be radiant as a sunflower, and luxuriant as a full-blown cabbage. Certain it is that in those days the heart of a lover could not contain more than one lady at a time; whereas the heart of a modern gallant has often room enough to accommodate half a dozen. The reason of which I conclude to be, that either the hearts of the gentlemen

---

[1] **Saturn:** the Roman god who was supposed to have taught the primitive people how to sow and harvest their grain. [2] **linsey-woolsey:** a cloth mixture of linen and wool.

[3] **shortness of the petticoats:** In Irving's day women wore skirts almost to the floor, cut on long, straight lines. It is this slim silhouette which he probably had in mind in speaking later of "their scantily dressed descendants."

have grown larger, or the persons of the ladies smaller: this, however, is a question for physiologists to determine.

But there was a secret charm in these petticoats, which, no doubt, entered into the consideration of the prudent gallants. The wardrobe of a lady was in those days her only fortune; and she who had a good stock of petticoats and stockings was as absolutely an heiress as is a Kamchatka [1] damsel with a store of bearskins, or a Lapland [2] belle with a plenty of reindeer. The ladies, therefore, were very anxious to display these powerful attractions to the greatest advantage; and the best rooms in the house, instead of being adorned with caricatures of Dame Nature, in watercolors and needlework, were always hung round with abundance of homespun garments, the manufacture and the property of the females — a piece of laudable ostentation that still prevails among the heiresses of our Dutch villages.

The gentlemen, in fact, who figured in the circles of the gay world in these ancient times, corresponded, in most particulars, with the beauteous damsels whose smiles they were ambitious to deserve. True it is, their merits would make but a very inconsiderable impression upon the heart of a modern fair: they neither drove their curricles,[3] nor sported their tandems,[4] for as yet those gaudy vehicles were not even dreamt of; neither did they distinguish themselves by their brilliancy at the table, and their consequent rencontres [5] with watchmen, for our forefathers were of too pacific a disposition to need those guardians of the night, every soul throughout the town being sound asleep before nine o'clock. Neither did they establish their claims to gentility at the expense of their tailors, for as yet those offenders against the pockets of society, and the tranquillity of all aspiring young gentle-

men, were unknown in New Amsterdam; every good housewife made the clothes of her husband and family, and even the goede vrouw [6] of Van Twiller himself thought it no disparagement to cut out her husband's linsey-woolsey galligaskins.[7]

Not but what there were some two or three youngsters who manifested the first dawning of what is called fire and spirit; who held all labor in contempt; skulked about docks and market places; loitered in the sunshine; squandered what little money they could procure at hustlecap [8] and chuck farthing; [9] swore, boxed, fought cocks, and raced their neighbors' horses; in short, who promised to be the wonder, the talk, and abomination of the town, had not their stylish career been unfortunately cut short by an affair of honor with a whipping-post.

Far other, however, was the truly fashionable gentleman of those days: his dress, which served for both morning and evening, street and drawing room, was a linsey-woolsey coat, made, perhaps, by the fair hands of the mistress of his affections, and gallantly bedecked with abundance of large brass buttons; half a score of breeches heightened the proportions of his figure; his shoes were decorated by enormous copper buckles; a low-crowned broad-rimmed hat overshadowed his burly visage; and his hair dangled down his back in a prodigious queue of eelskin.

Thus equipped, he would manfully sally forth, with pipe in mouth, to besiege some fair damsel's obdurate heart — not such a pipe, good reader, as that which Acis did sweetly tune in praise of his Galatea,[10] but one of true Delft [11] manufacture, and furnished with a charge of fragrant tobacco. With this would he resolutely set himself down before the fortress, and rarely failed,

[1] **Kamchatka** (kăm-chăt'kà): a peninsula of northeastern Asia. [2] **Lapland:** a region in the extreme north of Europe. [3] **curricles** (kûr'ĭ-k'lz): two-wheeled, two-horse carriages popular in Irving's day. [4] **tandems:** vehicles with two or more horses, one in front of the other [5] **rencontres** (rĕn-kŏn'tĕrz): encounters.

[6] **goede vrouw** (gū'dĕ vrou): Dutch for goodwife. [7] **galligaskins** (găl-ĭ-găs'kĭnz): long, loose breeches. [8] **hustlecap:** a game with coins somewhat like pitch and toss. [9] **chuck farthing:** another coin game, in which coins were thrown at a hole. [10] **Acis** (ā'kĭs) ... **Galatea** (găl-à-tē'à): lovers in Greek mythology. Acis' pipe was of course a reed, a musical instrument. [11] **Delft:** a town in Holland famous for glazed earthenware.

in the process of time, to smoke the fair enemy into a surrender, upon honorable terms.

Such was the happy reign of Wouter Van Twiller, celebrated in many a long-forgotten song as the real golden age, the rest being nothing but counterfeit copper-washed coin. In that delightful period a sweet and holy calm reigned over the whole province. The burgomaster smoked his pipe in peace; the substantial solace of his domestic cares, after her daily toils were done, sat soberly at the door, with her arms crossed over her apron of snowy white, without being insulted with ribald streetwalkers or vagabond boys — those unlucky urchins who do so infest our streets, displaying, under the roses of youth, the thorns and briers of iniquity. Then it was that the lover with ten breeches, and the damsel with petticoats of half a score, indulged in all the innocent endearments of virtuous love, without fear and without reproach; for what had that virtue to fear, which was defended by a shield of good linsey-woolseys, equal at least to the seven bullhides of the invincible Ajax? [1]

Ah, blissful and never to be forgotten age! when everything was better than it has ever been since, or ever will be again — when Buttermilk Channel [2] was quite dry at low water — when the shad in Hudson were all salmon — and when the moon shone with a pure and resplendent whiteness, instead of that melancholy yellow light which is the consequence of her sickening at the abominations she every night witnesses in this degenerate city!

Happy would it have been for New Amsterdam could it always have existed in this state of blissful ignorance and lowly simplicity; but, alas! the days of childhood are too sweet to last! Cities, like men, grow out of them in time, and are doomed alike to grow into the bustle, the cares, and miseries of the world. Let no man congrat-

[1] Ajax (ā′jăks): the most muscular Greek hero of the Trojan War. [2] Buttermilk Channel: a channel in New York harbor which separates Governor's Island from Brooklyn.

ulate himself, when he beholds the child of his bosom or the city of his birth increasing in magnitude and importance — let the history of his own life teach him the dangers of the one, and this excellent little history of Manna-hata convince him of the calamities of the other.

## THE DEVIL AND TOM WALKER

This story is included in *Tales of a Traveler* (1824).

Imagine yourself a guest at Sunnyside, Irving's home. You are near Sleepy Hollow, and from the windows you may look out over the Hudson River. You have just finished dinner, and before a blazing and crackling log fire you lean back in an easy chair and wait for your host to tell a story. There are no telephones, no radios to interrupt; no train will roar past toward Albany or New York City. In his charming old-school manner, pausing now and then to chuckle with you at some queer twist of the yarn, Irving weaves into his story the artistry of a master storyteller. Last night, perhaps, it was a colorful legend of old Spain with a little of the flavor of the Arabian Nights, but tonight he spins a story as American as are the characters of Rip Van Winkle and Ichabod Crane. He takes his time about the telling. Don't interrupt him or hurry him; a long, pleasant evening is before you.

A few miles from Boston in Massachusetts, there is a deep inlet, winding several miles into the interior of the country from Charles Bay, and terminating in a thickly wooded swamp or morass. On one side of this inlet is a beautiful dark grove; on the opposite side the land rises abruptly from the water's edge into a high ridge, on which grow a few scattered oaks of great age and immense size. Under one of these gigantic trees, according to old stories, there was a great amount of treasure buried by Kidd the pirate. The inlet allowed a facility to bring the money in a boat secretly and at night to the very foot of the hill; the elevation of the place permitted a good lookout to be kept that no one was at hand;

SUNNYSIDE, Washington Irving's home on the Hudson River, near Sleepy Hollow, where he spent the last twenty-seven years of his life. (Brown Brothers)

while the remarkable trees formed good landmarks by which the place might easily be found again. The old stories add, moreover, that the devil presided at the hiding of the money, and took it under his guardianship; but this, it is well known, he always does with buried treasure, particularly when it had been ill-gotten. Be that as it may, Kidd never returned to recover his wealth; being shortly after seized at Boston, sent out to England, and there hanged for a pirate.

About the year 1727, just at the time that earthquakes were prevalent in New England, and shook many tall sinners down upon their knees, there lived near this place a meager, miserly fellow, of the name of Tom Walker. He had a wife as miserly as himself: they were so miserly that they even conspired to cheat each other. Whatever the woman could lay hands on, she hid away; a hen could not cackle but she was on the alert to secure the new-laid egg. Her husband was continually prying about to detect her secret hoards, and many and fierce were the conflicts that took place about what ought to have been common property.

They lived in a forlorn-looking house that stood alone, and had an air of starvation. A few straggling savin [1] trees, emblems of sterility, grew near it; no smoke ever curled from its chimney; no traveler stopped at its door. A miserable horse, whose ribs were as articulate as the bars of a gridiron, stalked about a field where a thin carpet of moss, scarcely covering the ragged beds of pudding stone, tantalized and balked his hunger; and sometimes he would lean his head over the fence, look piteously at the passer-by, and seem to petition deliverance from this land of famine.

The house and its inmates had altogether a bad name. Tom's wife was a tall termagant, fierce of temper, loud of tongue, and strong of arm. Her voice was often heard in wordy warfare with her husband; and his face sometimes showed signs that their conflicts were not confined to words. No one ventured, however, to interfere between them. The lonely wayfarer shrunk within himself at the horrid clamor and clapper-clawing; eyed the den of discord askance;

[1] savin (săv'ĭn): a North American juniper or red cedar.

and hurried on his way, rejoicing, if a bachelor, in his celibacy.

One day that Tom Walker had been to a distant part of the neighborhood, he took what he considered a short cut homeward, through the swamp. Like most short cuts, it was an ill-chosen route. The swamp was thickly grown with great gloomy pines and hemlocks, some of them ninety feet high, which made it dark at noonday, and a retreat for all the owls of the neighborhood. It was full of pits and quagmires, partly covered with weeds and mosses, where the green surface often betrayed the traveler into a gulf of black, smothering mud; there were also dark and stagnant pools, the abodes of the tadpole, the bullfrog, and the water snake; where the trunks of pines and hemlocks lay half drowned, half rotting, looking like alligators sleeping in the mire.

Tom had long been picking his way cautiously through this treacherous forest; stepping from tuft to tuft of rushes and roots, which afforded precarious footholds among deep sloughs; or pacing carefully, like a cat, along the prostrate trunks of trees; startled now and then by the sudden screaming of the bittern, or the quacking of a wild duck rising on the wing from some solitary pool. At length he arrived at a firm piece of ground, which ran out like a peninsula into the deep bosom of the swamp. It had been one of the strongholds of the Indians during their wars with the first colonists. Here they had thrown up a kind of fort, which they had looked upon as almost impregnable, and had used as a place of refuge for their squaws and children. Nothing remained of the old Indian fort but a few embankments, gradually sinking to the level of the surrounding earth, and already overgrown in part by oaks and other forest trees, the foliage of which formed a contrast to the dark pines and hemlocks of the swamp.

It was late in the dusk of evening when Tom Walker reached the old fort, and he paused there awhile to rest himself. Anyone but he would have felt unwilling to linger in this lonely, melancholy place, for the common people had a bad opinion of it, from the stories handed down from the time of the Indian wars, when it was asserted that the savages held incantations here, and made sacrifices to the evil spirit.

Tom Walker, however, was not a man to be troubled with any fears of the kind. He reposed himself for some time on the trunk of a fallen hemlock, listening to the boding cry of the tree toad, and delving with his walking staff into a mound of black mold at his feet. As he turned up the soil unconsciously, his staff struck against something hard. He raked it out of the vegetable mold and lo! a cloven skull, with an Indian tomahawk buried deep in it, lay before him. The rust on the weapon showed the time that had elapsed since this death-blow had been given. It was a dreary memento of the fierce struggle that had taken place in this last foothold of the Indian warriors.

" Humph! " said Tom Walker, as he gave it a kick to shake the dirt from it.

" Let that skull alone! " said a gruff voice. Tom lifted up his eyes, and beheld a great black man seated directly opposite him, on the stump of a tree. He was exceedingly surprised, having neither heard nor seen anyone approach; and he was still more perplexed on observing, as well as the gathering gloom would permit, that the stranger was neither Negro nor Indian. It is true he was dressed in a rude half-Indian garb, and had a red belt or sash swathed round his body; but his face was neither black nor copper-color, but swarthy and dingy, and begrimed with soot, as if he had been accustomed to toil among fires and forges. He had a shock of coarse black hair, that stood out from his head in all directions, and bore an ax on his shoulder.

He scowled for a moment at Tom with a pair of great red eyes.

" What are you doing on my grounds? " said the black man, with a hoarse growling voice.

" Your grounds! " said Tom, with a sneer,

" no more your grounds than mine; they belong to Deacon Peabody."

" Deacon Peabody be d——d," said the stranger, " as I flatter myself he will be, if he does not look more to his own sins and less to those of his neighbors. Look yonder, and see how Deacon Peabody is faring."

Tom looked in the direction that the stranger pointed, and beheld one of the great trees, fair and flourishing without, but rotten at the core, and saw that it had been nearly hewn through, so that the first high wind was likely to blow it down. On the bark of the tree was scored the name of Deacon Peabody, an eminent man, who had waxed wealthy by driving shrewd bargains with the Indians. He now looked around, and found most of the tall trees marked with the name of some great man of the colony, and all more or less scored by the ax. The one on which he had been seated, and which had evidently just been hewn down, bore the name of Crowninshield; and he recollected a mighty rich man of that name, who made a vulgar display of wealth, which it was whispered he had acquired by buccaneering.

" He's just ready for burning! " said the black man, with a growl of triumph. " You see I am likely to have a good stock of firewood for winter."

" But what right have you," said Tom, " to cut down Deacon Peabody's timber? "

" The right of a prior claim," said the other. " This woodland belonged to me long before one of your white-faced race put foot upon the soil."

" And pray, who are you, if I may be so bold? " said Tom.

" Oh, I go by various names. I am the wild huntsman in some countries; the black miner in others. In this neighborhood I am known by the name of the black woodsman. I am he to whom the red men consecrated this spot, and in honor of whom they now and then roasted a white man, by way of sweet-smelling sacrifice. Since the red men have been exterminated by you white savages, I amuse myself by presiding at the persecutions of Quakers and Anabaptists; [1] I am the great patron and prompter of slave dealers, and the grand master of the Salem witches."

" The upshot of all which is that, if I mistake not," said Tom, sturdily, " you are he commonly called Old Scratch."

" The same, at your service! " replied the black man, with a half-civil nod.

Such was the opening of this interview, according to the old story; though it has almost too familiar an air to be credited. One would think that to meet with such a singular personage, in this wild, lonely place, would have shaken any man's nerves; but Tom was a hard-minded fellow, not easily daunted, and he had lived so long with a termagant wife that he did not even fear the devil.

It is said that after this commencement they had a long and earnest conversation together, as Tom returned homeward. The black man told him of great sums of money buried by Kidd the pirate, under the oak trees on the high ridge, not far from the morass. All these were under his command, and protected by his power, so that none could find them but such as propitiated his favor. These he offered to place within Tom Walker's reach, having conceived an especial kindness for him; but they were to be had only on certain conditions. What these conditions were may be easily surmised, though Tom never disclosed them publicly. They must have been very hard, for he required time to think of them, and he was not a man to stick at trifles when money was in view. When they had reached the edge of the swamp, the stranger paused. " What proof have I that all you have been telling me is true? " said Tom. " There's my signature," said the black man, pressing his finger on Tom's forehead. So saying, he turned off among the thickets of the swamp, and seemed, as Tom said, to go down, down, down, into the earth, until

[1] **Anabaptists:** a religious sect which arose in Switzerland in 1523. Its members were subject to persecution because of their opposition to infant baptism.

nothing but his head and shoulders could be seen, and so on, until he totally disappeared.

When Tom reached home, he found the black print of a finger burnt, as it were, into his forehead, which nothing could obliterate. The first news his wife had to tell him was the sudden death of Absalom Crowninshield, the rich buccaneer. It was announced in the papers with the usual flourish, that " a great man had fallen in Israel."

Tom recollected the tree which his black friend had just hewn down, and which was ready for burning. " Let the freebooter roast," said Tom, " who cares! " He now felt convinced that all he had heard and seen was no illusion.

He was not prone to let his wife into his confidence; but as this was an uneasy secret, he willingly shared it with her. All her avarice was awakened at the mention of hidden gold, and she urged her husband to comply with the black man's terms, and secure what would make them wealthy for life. However Tom might have felt disposed to sell himself to the devil, he was determined not to do so to oblige his wife; so he flatly refused, out of the mere spirit of contradiction. Many and bitter were the quarrels they had on the subject; but the more she talked, the more resolute was Tom not to be damned to please her.

At length she determined to drive the bargain on her own account and, if she succeeded, to keep all the gain to herself. Being of the same fearless temper as her husband, she set off for the old Indian fort toward the close of a summer's day. She was many hours absent. When she came back, she was reserved and sullen in her replies. She spoke something of a black man, whom she had met about twilight hewing at the root of a tall tree. He was sulky, however, and would not come to terms: she was to go again with a propitiatory offering, but what it was she forbore to say.

The next evening she set off for the swamp, with her apron heavily laden. Tom waited and waited for her, but in vain; midnight came, but she did not make her appearance: morning, noon, night returned, but still she did not come. Tom now grew uneasy for her safety, especially as he found she had carried off in her apron the silver teapot and spoons, and every portable article of value. Another night elapsed, another morning came, but no wife. In a word, she was never heard of more.

What was her real fate nobody knows, in consequence of so many pretending to know. It is one of those facts which have become confounded by a variety of historians. Some asserted that she lost her way among the tangled mazes of the swamp, and sank into some pit or slough; others, more uncharitable, hinted that she had eloped with the household booty, and made off to some other province; while others surmised that the tempter had decoyed her into a dismal quagmire, on the top of which her hat was found lying. In confirmation of this, it was said a great black man, with an ax on his shoulder, was seen late that very evening coming out of the swamp, carrying a bundle tied in a checked apron, with an air of surly triumph.

The most current and probable story, however, observes that Tom Walker grew so anxious about the fate of his wife and his property that he set out at length to seek them both at the Indian fort. During a long summer's afternoon he searched about the gloomy place, but no wife was to be seen. He called her name repeatedly, but she was nowhere to be heard. The bittern alone responded to his voice, as he flew screaming by; or the bullfrog croaked dolefully from a neighboring pool. At length, it is said, just in the brown hour of twilight, when the owls began to hoot, and the bats to flit about, his attention was attracted by the clamor of carrion crows hovering about a cypress tree. He looked up, and beheld a bundle tied in a checked apron and hanging in the branches of the tree, with a great vulture perched hard by, as if keeping watch upon it. He leaped with joy; for he recognized his wife's apron, and supposed it to contain the household valuables.

"Let us get hold of the property," said he, consolingly to himself, "and we will endeavor to do without the woman."

As he scrambled up the tree, the vulture spread its wide wings, and sailed off, screaming, into the deep shadows of the forest. Tom seized the checked apron, but, woeful sight! found nothing but a heart and liver tied up in it!

Such, according to this most authentic old story, was all that was to be found of Tom's wife. She had probably attempted to deal with the black man as she had been accustomed to deal with her husband; but though a female scold is generally considered a match for the devil, yet in this instance she appears to have had the worst of it. She must have died game, however; for it is said Tom noticed many prints of cloven feet deeply stamped about the tree, and found handfuls of hair, that looked as if they had been plucked from the coarse black shock of the woodman. Tom knew his wife's prowess by experience. He shrugged his shoulders, as he looked at the signs of a fierce clapperclawing. "Egad," said he to himself, "Old Scratch must have had a tough time of it!"

Tom consoled himself for the loss of his property with the loss of his wife, for he was a man of fortitude. He even felt something like gratitude toward the black woodman, who, he considered, had done him a kindness. He sought, therefore, to cultivate a further acquaintance with him, but for some time without success; the old blacklegs played shy, for, whatever people may think, he is not always to be had for calling for; he knows how to play his cards when pretty sure of his game.

At length, it is said, when delay had whetted Tom's eagerness to the quick, and prepared him to agree to anything rather than not gain the promised treasure, he met the black man one evening in his usual woodman's dress, with his ax on his shoulder, sauntering along the swamp, and humming a tune. He affected to receive Tom's advances with great indifference, made brief replies, and went on humming his tune.

By degrees, however, Tom brought him to business, and they began to haggle about the terms on which the former was to have the pirate's treasure. There was one condition which need not be mentioned, being generally understood in all cases where the devil grants favors; but there were others about which, though of less importance, he was inflexibly obstinate. He insisted that the money found through his means should be employed in his service. He proposed, therefore, that Tom should employ it in the black traffic; that is to say, that he should fit out a slave ship. This, however, Tom resolutely refused; he was bad enough in all conscience; but the devil himself could not tempt him to turn slave trader.

Finding Tom so squeamish on this point, he did not insist upon it, but proposed, instead, that he should turn usurer; the devil being extremely anxious for the increase of usurers, looking upon them as his peculiar people.

To this no objections were made, for it was just to Tom's taste.

"You shall open a broker's shop in Boston next month," said the black man.

"I'll do it tomorrow, if you wish," said Tom Walker.

"You shall lend money at two per cent a month."

"Egad, I'll charge four!" replied Tom Walker.

"You shall extort bonds, foreclose mortgages, drive the merchants to bankruptcy —"

"I'll drive them to the d——l," cried Tom Walker.

"You are the usurer for my money!" said blacklegs with delight. "When will you want the rhino?"[1]

"This very night."

"Done!" said the devil.

"Done!" said Tom Walker.

[1] **rhino:** money.

So they shook hands and struck a bargain.

A few days' time saw Tom Walker seated behind his desk in a countinghouse in Boston.

His reputation for a ready-moneyed man, who would lend money out for a good consideration, soon spread abroad. Everybody remembers the time of Governor Belcher,[1] when money was particularly scarce. It was a time of paper credit. The country had been deluged with government bills; the famous Land Bank [2] had been established; there had been a rage for speculating; the people had run mad with schemes for new settlements; for building cities in the wilderness; land jobbers went about with maps of grants, and townships, and El Dorados, lying nobody knew where, but which everybody was ready to purchase. In a word, the great speculating fever which breaks out every now and then in the country had raged to an alarming degree, and everybody was dreaming of making sudden fortunes from nothing. As usual the fever had subsided; the dream had gone off, and the imaginary fortunes with it; the patients were left in doleful plight, and the whole country resounded with the consequent cry of " hard times."

At this propitious time of public distress did Tom Walker set up as usurer in Boston. His door was soon thronged by customers. The needy and adventurous; the gambling speculator; the dreaming land jobber; the thriftless tradesman; the merchant with cracked credit; in short, everyone driven to raise money by desperate means and desperate sacrifices hurried to Tom Walker.

Thus Tom was the universal friend of the needy, and acted like a " friend in need "; that is to say, he always exacted good pay and good security. In proportion to the distress of the applicant was the highness of his terms. He accumulated bonds and mortgages, gradually squeezed his customers closer and closer: and sent them at length, dry as a sponge, from his door.

In this way he made money hand over hand; became a rich and mighty man, and exalted his cocked hat upon 'Change. He built himself, as usual, a vast house, out of ostentation; but left the greater part of it unfinished and unfurnished, out of parsimony. He even set up a carriage in the fullness of his vainglory, though he nearly starved the horses which drew it; and as the ungreased wheels groaned and screeched on the axletrees, you would have thought you heard the souls of the poor debtors he was squeezing.

As Tom waxed old, however, he grew thoughtful. Having secured the good things of this world, he began to feel anxious about those of the next. He thought with regret on the bargain he had made with his black friend, and set his wits to work to cheat him out of the conditions. He became, therefore, all of a sudden, a violent churchgoer. He prayed loudly and strenuously, as if heaven were to be taken by force of lungs. Indeed, one might always tell when he had sinned most during the week, by the clamor of his Sunday devotion. The quiet Christians who had been modestly and steadfastly traveling Zionward were struck with self-reproach at seeing themselves so suddenly outstripped in their career by this new-made convert. Tom was as rigid in religious as in money matters; he was a stern supervisor and censurer of his neighbors, and seemed to think every sin entered up to their account became a credit on his own side of the page. He even talked of the expediency of reviving the persecution of Quakers and Anabaptists. In a word, Tom's zeal became as notorious as his riches.

Still, in spite of all this strenuous attention to forms, Tom had a lurking dread that the devil, after all, would have his due. That he might not be taken unawares, therefore, it is said he always carried a small Bible in his coat pocket. He had also

---

[1] **Belcher:** Jonathan Belcher was governor of Massachusetts from 1730 to 1741. [2] **Land Bank:** a system by which the province advanced money on mortgages on land.

a great folio Bible on his countinghouse desk, and would frequently be found reading it when people called on business; on such occasions he would lay his green spectacles in the book, to mark the place, while he turned round to drive some usurious bargain.

Some say that Tom grew a little crackbrained in his old days, and that, fancying his end approaching, he had his horse newshod, saddled and bridled, and buried with his feet uppermost; because he supposed that at the last day the world would be turning upside down; in which case he should find his horse standing ready for mounting, and he was determined at the worst to give his old friend a run for it. This, however, is probably a mere old wives' fable. If he really did take such a precaution, it was totally superfluous; at least so says the authentic old legend, which closes this story in the following manner.

One hot summer afternoon in the dog days, just as a terrible black thunder-gust was coming up, Tom sat in his countinghouse, in his white linen cap and India silk morning gown. He was on the point of foreclosing a mortgage, by which he would complete the ruin of an unlucky land speculator for whom he had professed the greatest friendship. The poor land jobber begged him to grant a few months' indulgence. Tom had grown testy and irritated, and refused another day.

" My family will be ruined, and brought upon the parish," said the land jobber.

" Charity begins at home," replied Tom; " I must take care of myself in these hard times."

" You have made so much money out of me," said the speculator.

Tom lost his patience and his piety. " The devil take me," said he, " if I have made a farthing! "

Just then there were three loud knocks at the street door. He stepped out to see who was there. A black man was holding a black horse, which neighed and stamped with impatience.

" Tom, you're come for," said the black fellow, gruffly. Tom shrank back, but too late. He had left his little Bible at the bottom of his coat pocket, and his big Bible on the desk buried under the mortgage he was about to foreclose: never was sinner taken more unawares. The black man whisked him like a child into the saddle, gave the horse the lash, and away he galloped, with Tom on his back, in the midst of the thunderstorm. The clerks stuck their pens behind their ears, and stared after him from the windows. Away went Tom Walker, dashing down the streets; his white cap bobbing up and down; his morning gown fluttering in the wind, and his steed striking fire out of the pavement at every bound. When the clerks turned to look for the black man, he had disappeared.

Tom Walker never returned to foreclose the mortgage. A countryman, who lived on the border of the swamp, reported that in the height of the thunder-gust he had heard a great clattering of hoofs and a howling along the road, and running to the window caught sight of a figure, such as I have described, on a horse that galloped like mad across the fields, over the hills, and down into the black hemlock swamp toward the old Indian fort; and that shortly after a thunderbolt falling in that direction seemed to set the whole forest in a blaze.

The good people of Boston shook their heads and shrugged their shoulders, but had been so much accustomed to witches and goblins, and tricks of the devil, in all kinds of shapes, from the first settlement of the colony, that they were not so much horror-struck as might have been expected. Trustees were appointed to take charge of Tom's effects. There was nothing, however, to administer upon. On searching his coffers, all his bonds and mortgages were found reduced to cinders. In place of gold and silver, his iron chest was filled with chips and shavings; two skeletons lay in his stable instead of his half-starved horses, and the very next day his great house took fire and was burnt to the ground.

Such was the end of Tom Walker and his ill-gotten wealth. Let all griping money brokers lay this story to heart. The truth of it is not to be doubted. The very hole under the oak trees, whence he dug Kidd's money, is to be seen to this day; and the neighboring swamp and old Indian fort are often haunted in stormy nights by a figure on horseback, in morning gown and white cap, which is doubtless the troubled spirit of the usurer. In fact, the story has resolved itself into a proverb, and is the origin of that popular saying, so prevalent throughout New England, of " The Devil and Tom Walker."

## Suggestions for Study of Irving

### IN THE DAYS OF WOUTER VAN TWILLER

1. Be sure to have in mind a clear picture of the dress of men and women as described by Irving. Those who like to sketch can picture it graphically. Since the traditional Dutch costumes are still worn in remote parts of Holland, it is easy to find pictures of them to compare with Irving's description.

2. What hints do you find that Irving moved in the fashionable world of his day?

3. Point out places where Irving makes use of the humor of contrast.

4. Write or give orally a humorous contrast between the early days of your school or community and the present.

5. Write a composition in which you imagine a person a hundred years from now looking back at the present day and citing it as the era of true morality or the opposite.

6. Amusing details may be added to your picture of New Amsterdam by special reports: Chapter 1, on Van Twiller, and Chapter 3 on manners and customs (both in Book III).

### THE DEVIL AND TOM WALKER

7. Did this story make you laugh aloud or chuckle to yourself? How would you characterize Irving's humor? Give some examples.

8. In what spirit does Irving say, " Let all griping money brokers lay this story to heart "?

9. If you like this story, what reply have you for the realists of your class who did not like it " because it is so impossible and could never have happened "?

10. Count up the familiar expressions which Irving has made concrete in this story, such as " The devil would have his due."

11. Compare this story with " The Devil and Daniel Webster " (page 96) as to its point, its general tone, and the picture of " the devil." Compare also with the Faust legend, best known today through the story of Gounod's opera, Faust.

12. What other stories by Irving do you know in which the fantastic or supernatural play an important part? By reading several legends from The Sketch Book, The Alhambra, and Tales of a Traveler (see page 552), discover how Irving's characteristic use of the supernatural differs from that in the typical horror story.

## For Your Vocabulary

CONTEXT. In " The Devil and Tom Walker," whose mainspring is an unwholesome desire for wealth, you naturally find useful terms for dealing with that attitude, and the whole story serves as context to enrich their meaning. A usurer (ū′zhōō-rēr) is one who accumulates money by charging extravagantly high interest on loans. Most states now have laws against usury. To extort (ĕks-tôrt′) is to wring something out of a person by fear or threats. Blackmailers and kidnapers are modern extortioners. Who urged Tom to turn usurer and extort bonds (page 491)? Avarice (ăv′à-rĭs) is the greedy desire for money or gain which drove Tom's wife to her death (page 490). Parsimony (pär′sĭ-mō-nĭ) is extreme dislike of parting with the money, once gained — excessive economy in spending. The immediate context (page 492) illuminates this word beautifully. Compare parsimony with frugality (frōō-găl′-ĭ-tĭ), which Benjamin Franklin listed as a trait he wanted to acquire. What economies do you consider to be only frugal, not parsimonious?

## 2. BRYANT AND WHITTIER

### THE BEGINNINGS OF POETRY

#### IN AMERICA

There were American poets before Bryant. There was Anne Bradstreet, for instance, who came to Massachusetts with the first Boston colony in 1630, was the daughter of one governor of Massachusetts Bay and the wife of another. She wrote second-rate English poetry in America, and published a volume of it in 1650. Only scholars read it today. There was Michael Wigglesworth, who lived about the same time as Anne Bradstreet and wrote a long harrowing poem on " The Day of Doom." More important, there was Philip Freneau, who wrote some good poetry shortly after the Revolution and has some right to be called the first real American poet. But the real beginner was Bryant. As Irving had proved to European readers that grace and humor might be expected of American writing, and as Cooper had proved that Americans could write exciting fiction, so Bryant demonstrated that first-rate poetry might likewise be expected from the country of the coonskin cap and the wigwam.

## WILLIAM CULLEN BRYANT

Lyric poets are usually young men. When they grow older they often turn to writing philosophical or narrative poetry, or drama; but not many of them can prolong the lyric fire beyond forty. Bryant wrote his greatest poem when he was in his teens, and all his major poetry before he was forty.

The great poem was " Thanatopsis." The story of how it came to be published is still worth telling — how Bryant's father found it in his son's desk (the boy was just twenty-three, and had apparently written it some years before), and how he took it to the editor of the *North American Review,* who said in astonishment, " No one on this side of the Atlantic is capable of writing such verses." Proof was demanded and furnished; the poem was published in 1817.

Bryant rewrote the beginning and added the end of it later, but the central part of the poem stands now as it was written, by a teen-age boy in western Massachusetts. The *North American Review* asked for more poems. Bryant produced " To a Waterfowl," which he had written in 1815, when he was twenty-one.

What kind of young man wrote poetry like that? Bryant was born and grew up in the Berkshire Hills of N[...] sometimes prayed for th[...] to match the beauty of [...] Nature was always a gre[...] life. He was one of the [...] feel that violets and fi[...] other natural objects were [...] poetry. He was one of the first Americans to feel that they should write about *American* nature. Perhaps earlier poets had not looked carefully at their own birds and trees and flowers. Whatever the reason, they wrote about the same ones the English poets did. It took Bryant to get the skylark out of American poetry and American birds in!

Bryant was a thoughtful, meditative boy, brought up by parents who were of Puritan descent. He was disappointed deeply in not being able to afford to go to Yale. Suspected of being in ill-health, he tended toward melancholy and was fond of the more melancholy English poets. Nature usually stimulated him to reflect on life and death. He felt that God was closely identified with nature, and nature with goodness, so that when he wrote about flowers and trees he had no difficulty in changing the subject to ethics or morals or religion. That was the mood in which he wrote the austere and beautiful poem which the magazine editor said could have been written by no one this side of the Atlantic.

In these days of cities and radios and fast automobiles, it is sometimes hard for us to understand how these writers of the Eastern Flowering — Bryant, Whittier, Thoreau, Emerson, among others — felt about nature. We can understand how they liked to walk in the woods and fields, but it is hard for us to appreciate their feeling that living close to nature was much like living close to God, and that thinking about nature was much like thinking about religion. As one cynical critic has said, that view of nature is hidden today behind billboards.

Bryant read law in a lawyer's office instead of going to Yale. He practiced law in Massachusetts for ten years. Then, when his reputation as a poet had been established, he went to New York as writer and

WILLIAM CULLEN BRYANT wrote most of his lyric poetry as a young man. (Brown Brothers)

magazine editor, and soon became editor of the New York *Evening Post*. " Thanatopsis " and " To a Waterfowl " were in final shape for the volume of poems published in 1821; " To a Fringed Gentian " for the volume of 1832. He wrote a small amount of poetry during the rest of his life, but as his output of poetry decreased, so his influence as a vigorous and liberal editor grew. He started as a conservative, but came over soon to the side of " the common man " and supported Jackson. He opposed all financial and class legislation, and urged Lincoln to free the slaves sooner than he did. He made the *Post* a paper of high literary quality, and its editorial columns an example of the dignified public service a paper can render a democracy.

But every afternoon when he could get away from work he escaped from his office in the city to the open countryside where he could hear the bobolink, the rustle of cornfields, and the swish of American trees that poets seemed never to have heard before his time. And whether his mornings or his afternoons, the editorial work he did in maturity or the poetry he wrote as a young man, will ultimately be considered the greater contribution to the good of his countrymen, who can now say?

*Bryant was born* (1794) *just after the death of Franklin. He lived until 1878, when Edison was using electricity, in which Franklin had been so much interested, to light homes and cities.*

JOHN GREENLEAF WHITTIER

Bryant and Whittier were born and grew up within one hundred miles of each other in the hills of Massachusetts. Both were thought to be sickly as young men, but Bryant lived to be eighty-four, and Whittier eighty-five. Both had a deep feeling for the nature around them, wrote simple, dignified poetry, were editors, and held firm political convictions. But beyond that, their differences are more significant than their likenesses.

Bryant lived two thirds of his life in New York. Whittier was born in the house built by his first American ancestor, and bought a house for himself only a few miles away at Amesbury. All of Bryant's well-known poetry came early in life, most of Whittier's late. Although Bryant was only thirteen years older, his *last* important book of new poetry was published within one year of Whittier's *first*, and his best-known poem, " Thanatopsis," was actually published forty-nine years before Whittier's best-known poem, *Snow-Bound*. The two men reversed their life patterns. Bryant wrote his poetry first and then moved into journalism and politics; Whittier got his journalism and politics over first, and then concentrated on poetry.

Just as we know too little about Bryant the mature and influential editor, so we know too little of Whittier's younger and more active years. He was not always the venerable poet of *Snow-Bound*, "Maud Muller," "The Barefoot Boy," and "In School-Days." For two thirds of his life he was a fiery abolitionist who fought mobs, political opponents, intolerance, and poverty, and to whom poetry was only a pleasant avocation or a propaganda tool.

There is something very engaging about the picture of this young Quaker, saying "thee" and "thou," behaving with the sweetness and modesty characteristic of his sect, and yet burning with the inner hatred of slavery and willing to fight when aroused, with any weapons at hand, for what he believed. He wrote an anti-slavery pamphlet so vigorous that it closed the door on what had looked like a promising political career. (The abolitionist cause was not popular then even in the North.) As editor of the *Pennsylvania Freeman*, he aroused so much opposition with abolitionist editorials that a mob burned and sacked his office. He became a contributing editor of the journal that published *Uncle Tom's Cabin*. He wrote moving anti-slavery lyrics, and in one of the sternest poems in the language, "Ichabod," denounced Webster for compromising with the pro-slavery faction. Never wealthy, he actually suffered from poverty in early years, but still gave his money freely for the cause. That is the Whittier whose portrait seldom gets into the books — the man of civic indignations, the champion of the underdog, the flashing-eyed, firm-chinned reformer.

Yet his stature as a poet began to be evident even through the smoke screen of his political activity. He became a contributor to the *Atlantic Monthly*, along with Lowell, Emerson, Longfellow, Holmes, and the other great New Englanders. He was hailed by many as the best American balladist, for poems like "Skipper Ireson's Ride." And when the War between the States was over he lived quietly in the white frame house at Amesbury, grew his white beard, and wrote warm, reminiscent poems like *Snow-Bound*.

His house at Amesbury was something like his poetry — simple, unpretentious,

JOHN GREENLEAF WHITTIER wrote most of his lyric poetry in his later years. (Brown Brothers)

unaffected, in no way artificial. It was a real American house — like his subject matter; Whittier didn't have to be told that there were no skylarks in America. It was the kind of a house in which one might expect to see the warm, kind family life he so often writes about. Perhaps it is better for him to be remembered thus, for the purity and deep spiritual quality of his poetry and the sweetness of his nature, rather than for his turbulent early years. And yet you will never understand Whittier if you take only one side of him. You can quote him on that. Against his half-regretful admission that he had not always done his best by poetry —

And one there was, a dreamer born,
  Who with a mission to fulfil,
Had left the Muses' haunts to turn
  The crank of an opinion-mill. . . .

against that you can quote his defiant challenge: " I set a higher value on my name as appended to the Anti-Slavery Declaration of 1833 than on the title page of any book! " Both these are Whittier.

*Whittier was born (1807) the year Fulton's steamboat ran on the Hudson and died (1892) in the year that the long distance telephone came into use.*

# William Cullen Bryant
## 1794–1878

### THANATOPSIS *

This is the poem that Bryant wrote at seventeen (see page 495) — a poem that is usually considered the first to deserve a place among the great poems of America. The dignity of its blank verse and the power of its expression are truly remarkable, coming from so young a writer. In the restraint of his emotions and the balanced beauty of his language, Bryant has often been said to resemble the ancient Greeks.

To him who in the love of Nature holds
Communion with her visible forms, she
 speaks
A various language; for his gayer hours
She has a voice of gladness, and a smile
And eloquence of beauty, and she glides  5
Into his darker musings, with a mild
And healing sympathy, that steals away
Their sharpness, ere he is aware. When
 thoughts
Of the last bitter hour come like a blight
Over thy spirit, and sad images   10
Of the stern agony, and shroud, and pall,
And breathless darkness, and the narrow
 house,
Make thee to shudder and grow sick at
 heart —
Go forth, under the open sky, and list
To Nature's teachings, while from all
 around —   15

* **Thanatopsis** (thăn-à-tŏp′sĭs): a view of death (Greek).

Earth and her waters, and the depths of
 air —
Comes a still voice — Yet a few days,° and
 thee
The all-beholding sun shall see no more
In all his course; nor yet in the cold ground,
Where thy pale form was laid, with many
 tears,   20
Nor in the embrace of ocean, shall exist
Thy image. Earth, that nourished thee,
 shall claim
Thy growth, to be resolved to earth again,
And, lost each human trace, surrendering
 up
Thine individual being, shalt thou go  25
To mix forever with the elements,
To be a brother to the insensible rock
And to the sluggish clod, which the rude
 swain
Turns with his share, and treads upon. The
 oak
Shall send his roots abroad, and pierce thy
 mold.   30

 Yet not to thine eternal resting place
Shalt thou retire alone, nor couldst thou
 wish
Couch more magnificent. Thou shalt lie
 down
With patriarchs of the infant world — with
 kings,
The powerful of the earth — the wise, the
 good,   35
Fair forms, and hoary seers of ages past,
All in one mighty sepulcher. The hills
Rock-ribbed and ancient as the sun — the
 vales   38
Stretching in pensive quietness between;
The venerable woods — rivers that move
In majesty, and the complaining brooks
That make the meadows green; and, poured
 round all,
Old Ocean's gray and melancholy waste —
Are but the solemn decorations all
Of the great tomb of man. The golden
 sun,   45
The planets, all the infinite host of heaven,

17. **Yet a few days:** This is the first line to be retained from the original poem. The opening couplets of the earlier version were dropped.

Are shining on the sad abodes of death,
Through the still lapse of ages. All that
    tread
The globe are but a handful to the tribes
That slumber in its bosom — Take the
    wings                                          50
Of morning, pierce the Barcan° wilderness,
Or lose thyself in the continuous woods
Where rolls the Oregon,° and hears no
    sound,
Save his own dashings — yet the dead are
    there;                                         54
And millions in those solitudes, since first
The flight of years began, have laid them
    down
In their last sleep — the dead reign there
    alone.
So shalt thou rest, and what if thou with-
    draw
In silence from the living, and no friend
Take note of thy departure? All that
    breathe                                        60
Will share thy destiny. The gay will laugh
When thou art gone, the solemn brood of
    care
Plod on, and each one as before will chase
His favorite phantom; yet all these shall
    leave
Their mirth and their employments, and
    shall come                                     65
And make their bed with thee.° As the long
    train
Of ages glides away, the sons of men,
The youth in life's green spring, and he
    who goes
In the full strength of years, matron and
    maid,
The speechless babe, and the gray-headed
    man —                                          70
Shall one by one be gathered to thy side,
By those who in their turn shall follow
    them.

So live, that when thy summons comes
    to join

<hr>

51. **Barcan:** pertaining to Barca, a district in
North Africa on the Mediterranean coast.
53. **Oregon:** now known as the Columbia
River, between Oregon and Washington. 66. **And
make their bed with thee:** This was the end of the
original poem.

The innumerable caravan, which moves
To that mysterious realm, where each shall
    take                                           75
His chamber in the silent halls of death,
Thou go not, like the quarry slave at night,
Scourged to his dungeon, but, sustained and
    soothed
By an unfaltering trust, approach thy
    grave,
Like one who wraps the drapery of his
    couch                                          80
About him, and lies down to pleasant
    dreams.

## TO A WATERFOWL

When Bryant as a young man was licensed
to practice law, he was confronted by the
problem of where to open his office. One December day while tramping over the hills to
consider the town of Plainfield, Massachusetts, he felt particularly depressed by the
uncertainty of his future. As his biographer,
John Bigelow, describes it, " The sun had already set, leaving behind it one of those brilliant seas of chrysolite and opal which often
flood the New England skies, and while pausing to contemplate the rosy splendor with
rapt adoration, a solitary bird made its winged
way along the illuminated horizon. He watched
the lone wanderer until it was lost in the distance. He then went on with new strength and
courage. When he reached the house where he
was to stop for the night, he immediately sat
down and wrote the lines ' To a Waterfowl,'
the concluding verse of which will perpetuate
to future ages the lesson on faith which the
scene had impressed upon him."

Whither, midst falling dew,
While glow the heavens with the last steps
    of day,
Far, through their rosy depths, dost thou
    pursue
Thy solitary way?

Vainly the fowler's eye                            5
Might mark thy distant flight to do thee
    wrong,
As, darkly seen against the crimson sky,
Thy figure floats along.

Seek'st thou the plashy brink
Of weedy lake, or marge of river wide,   10
Or where the rocking billows rise and sink
    On the chafed oceanside?

There is a Power whose care
Teaches  thy  way  along  the  pathless
    coast —
The desert and illimitable air —        15
    Lone wandering, but not lost.

All day thy wings have fanned,
At that far height, the cold, thin atmos-
    phere,
Yet stoop not, weary, to the welcome land,
    Though the dark night is near.        20

And soon that toil shall end;
Soon shalt thou find a summer home, and
    rest,
And scream among thy fellows; reeds shall
    bend,
Soon, o'er thy sheltered nest.

Thou'rt gone, the abyss of heaven    25
Hath swallowed up thy form; yet, on my
    heart
Deeply hath sunk the lesson thou hast
    given,
And shall not soon depart.

He who, from zone to zone,
Guides through the boundless sky thy cer-
    tain flight,                          30
In the long way that I must tread alone,
    Will lead my steps aright.

## TO THE FRINGED GENTIAN

Simple as this little poem is, it is one of the
favorites among Bryant's poems. It illustrates
two of his marked characteristics. First he
brought to the poetry of English-speaking people the freshness of the American scene. No
one before him had written about gentians —
or goldenrod, or prairies, " for which," he said,
" the speech of England has no name." Second, he frequently put a short lesson at the
end of a poem — the moral tag, as it is often
called. This was the fashion of his day, much
frowned upon by the modern poet.

Thou blossom bright with autumn dew,
And colored with the heaven's own blue,
That openest when the quiet light
Succeeds the keen and frosty night,

Thou comest not when violets lean        5
O'er wandering brooks and springs unseen,
Or columbines, in purple dressed,
Nod o'er the ground-bird's hidden nest.

Thou waitest late and com'st alone,      9
When woods are bare and birds are flown,
And frosts and shortening days portend
The aged year is near his end.

Then doth thy sweet and quiet eye
Look through its fringes to the sky,
Blue — blue — as if that sky let fall    15
A flower from its cerulean° wall.

I would that thus, when I shall see
The hour of death draw near to me,
Hope, blossoming within my heart,
May look to heaven as I depart.          20

    16. **cerulean** (sĕ-rōō'lē-ăn): azure, blue.

## ABOLITION RIOTS

The other side of Bryant's writing may be
seen in this vigorous and courageous editorial
which appeared in the New York *Evening Post*
on August 8, 1836. Already the lines were being
drawn for the coming struggle over the slavery
question; already reason was yielding to force
on this great issue. Bryant understood the real
danger of mob violence to free institutions, and
in this editorial he courageously defended the
rights of the unpopular abolitionists to the
freedom of the press.

A meeting of the people of Cincinnati
have proclaimed the right of silencing the
expression of unpopular opinions by violence. We refer our readers to the proceedings of an anti-abolition meeting lately held
in that city. They will be found in another
part of this paper.

The Cincinnati meeting, in the concluding resolution offered by Wilson N. Brown
and adopted with the rest, declare in so
many words that, if they cannot put down

the abolitionist press by fair means, they will do it by foul; if they cannot silence it by remonstrance, they will silence it by violence; if they cannot persuade it to desist, they will stir up mobs against it, inflame them to madness, and turn their brutal rage against the dwellings, the property, the persons, the lives of the wretched abolitionists and their families. In announcing that they will put them down by force all this is included. Fire, robbery, and bloodshed are the common excesses of an enraged mob. There is no extreme of cruelty and destruction to which, in the drunkenness and delirium of its fury, it may not proceed. The commotions of the elements can as easily be appeased by appeals to the quality of mercy as these commotions of the human mind; the whirlwind and the lightning might as well be expected to pause and turn aside to spare the helpless and innocent as an infuriated multitude.

If the abolitionists must be put down, and if the community are of that opinion, there is no necessity of violence to effect the object. The community have the power in their own hands; the majority may make a law declaring the discussion of slavery in a certain manner to be a crime, and imposing penalties. The law may then be put in force against the offenders, and their mouths may be gagged in due form and with all the solemnities of justice.

What is the reason this is not done? The answer is ready. The community are for leaving the liberty of the press untrammeled; there is not a committee that can be raised in any of the state legislatures north of the Potomac who will report in favor of imposing penalties on those who declaim against slavery; there is not a legislature who would sanction such a report; there is not a single free state the people of which would sustain a legislature in so doing. These are facts, and the advocates of mob law know them to be so.

Who are the men that issue this invitation to silence the press by violence? Who but an insolent, brawling minority, a few noisy fanatics, who claim that their own opinions shall be the measure of freedom for the rest of the community, and who undertake to overawe a vast, pacific majority by threats of wanton outrage and plunder? These men are for erecting an oligarchy of their own and riding roughshod over the people and the people's rights. They claim a right to repeal the laws established by the majority in favor of the freedom of the press. They make new laws of their own, to which they require that the rest of the community shall submit, and, in case of a refusal, they threaten to execute them by the ministry of a mob. There is no tyranny or oppression exercised in any part of the world more absolute or more frightful than that which they would establish. So far as we are concerned, we are determined that this despotism shall neither be submitted to nor encouraged. In whatever form it makes its appearance, we shall raise our voice against it. We are resolved that the subject of slavery shall be as it ever has been — as free a subject of discussion and argument and declamation as the difference between whiggism and democracy, or the difference between the Arminians and the Calvinists.[1] If the press chooses to be silent on the subject, it shall be the silence of perfect free will, and not the silence of fear. We hold that this combination of the few to govern the many by the terror of illegal violence is as wicked and indefensible as a conspiracy to rob on the highway. We hold it to be the duty of good citizens to protest against it whenever and wherever it shows itself, and to resist it, if necessary, to the death.

## Suggestions for Study of Bryant

### THANATOPSIS

1. According to the first stanza, what different messages does nature have for us? Give some specific examples from your own experience of how nature has affected your mood.

2. Contrast the two views of death in lines 17–30 and 31–72. Does the idea of the com-

[1] **Arminians and Calvinists:** two groups of Protestants, followers of Arminius, a Hollander, and Calvin, a Swiss, who had different theological ideas.

panionship of the dead seem consoling to you? In what spirit does the poet think one should approach death?

3. Does this poem express belief in a life after death? Read carefully before answering; there has been considerable difference of opinion on this point.

4. Vocabulary: pall (11), hoary seers (36), sepulcher (37), venerable (40), scourged (78).

### TO A WATERFOWL

5. Point out the stanzas containing each of the three parts of the poem: the picture seen by the poet, his meditation about the bird, and his application to his own life.

6. In view of the circumstances under which the poem was written do you like or dislike the " moral tag "?

7. Vocabulary: plashy (9), marge (10), illimitable (15), abyss (25).

8. It is interesting to compare " To a Waterfowl " with " To a Mouse " by Robert Burns. Each poet comments on his own future, but with how different a note!

### TO THE FRINGED GENTIAN

9. If you had never seen a gentian, what details about it would you learn from this poem?

10. Find a scientific description of a gentian in an encyclopedia or botany text. What does a poem give that a scientific description fails to give, and vice versa? Show the function of each type in our understanding of nature.

11. If you are especially interested in nature poetry, now is a good time to start making a collection of some poems you especially like, for Bryant affords many examples. Perhaps you would like to specialize on bird or flower poetry. Some students have even been interested in collecting poems on death.

### ABOLITION RIOTS

12. Do you agree with Bryant on the dangers of mob violence? Do you think you could always withstand the invitation to join a mob? Discuss.

13. What instances of mob violence have you read about recently? Did editors and public officials uphold or condemn the mob? Which attitude took the greater courage?

14. What do you think of Bryant's implication that men resort to mob violence only when they cannot obtain laws to accomplish their purpose?

15. Bring to class an editorial from a current newspaper which strikes you as having persuasive power. Try to find one on the subject of freedom of speech or of the press. Compare the arguments with Bryant's.

## For Your Vocabulary

BASE-WORDS. When conflict and argument over government arise, men frequently employ words descriptive of types of government. You know some using the ending -cracy from the Greek word for rule or power — democracy, or rule by the people, and aristocracy, or rule by only the " best " people. Bryant expresses his alarm (page 501) at the threat of an oligarchy (ŏl′ĭ-gär-kĭ), rule by only a few and not necessarily the best. The ending -archy, like -cracy, means rule, but this word part occurs also at the beginning of words like archbishop, a bishop with special ruling powers. The term oligarchy is used most often in criticism or attack, aristocracy in approval or praise. You will find Henry W. Grady using the term oligarchs ironically of the Southern leaders, because it was so often hurled at them by the North. The same ending occurs in patriarchs (pā′trĭ-ärks) in " Thanatopsis " (line 34) for the fathers or older men who ruled early tribes. Do you know the exact meaning of more familiar terms built on these same basewords — plutocracy, autocracy, monarchy, anarchy?

## John Greenleaf Whittier
### 1807–1892

### SKIPPER IRESON'S RIDE

When Whittier was a young man at Haverhill Academy, a schoolmate from Marblehead told him the story of Skipper Ireson and the old song which had been derisively hurled at him by the women of Marblehead. Many years after, Whittier turned the story into the following ballad, published in the Atlantic Monthly in 1857. It has always been one of the most popular of the many ballads that the poet wrote on American legends or historical incidents. But more than twenty years after he had written it, Whittier discovered from a *History of Marblehead* that Ireson had really been an innocent victim. He had taken the punishment in silence rather than betray his mutinous crew, who refused to stop for the sinking ship lest their valuable catch of cod be spoiled. Whittier thanked the author of the history for clearing the matter up, saying, " I certainly would not do injustice to anyone, dead or living."

Of all the rides since the birth of time,
Told in story or sung in rhyme —
On Apuleius' Golden Ass,°
Or one-eyed Calendar's° horse of brass,
Witch astride of a human hack,    5
Islam's prophet on Al-Borák° —
The strangest ride that ever was sped
Was Ireson's, out from Marblehead!
   Old Floyd Ireson, for his hard heart,
   Tarred and feathered and carried in a
     cart    10
   By the women of Marblehead!

Body of turkey, head of owl,
Wings adroop like a rained-on fowl,
Feathered and ruffled in every part,
Skipper Ireson stood in the cart.    15
Scores of women, old and young,
Strong of muscle, and glib of tongue,
Pushed and pulled up the rocky lane,
Shouting and singing the shrill refrain:
   " Here's Flud Oirson, fur his horrd
     horrt,    20
   Torr'd an' futherr'd an' corr'd in a corrt
   By the women o' Morble'ead! "

Wrinkled scolds with hands on hips,
Girls in bloom of cheek and lips,
Wild-eyed, free-limbed, such as chase  25
Bacchus round some antique vase,
Brief of skirt, with ankles bare,
Loose of kerchief and loose of hair,

3. **Apuleius' Golden Ass** (ăp-ū-lē′yŭs): Apuleius, a Roman writer of the second century A.D., told the adventures of a young man turned into an ass. 4. **one-eyed Calendar:** Whittier's memory of the Arabian Nights was somewhat confused. The Calendar and the brass horse which could fly were in two different stories. 6. **Al-Borák:** the winged horse with human face that carried Mohammed to heaven.

With conch shells blowing and fish horns'
   twang,
Over and over the Maenads° sang:    30
   " Here's Flud Oirson, fur his horrd horrt,
   Torr'd an' futherr'd an' corr'd in a corrt
   By the women o' Morble'ead! "

Small pity for him! — He sailed away
From a leaking ship in Chaleur Bay° — 35
Sailed away from a sinking wreck,
With his own town's people on her deck!
" Lay by! lay by! " they called to him.
Back he answered, " Sink or swim!
Brag of your catch of fish again! "    40
And off he sailed through the fog and rain!
   Old Floyd Ireson, for his hard heart,
   Tarred and feathered and carried in a
     cart
   By the women of Marblehead!

Fathoms deep in dark Chaleur    45
That wreck shall lie forevermore.
Mother and sister, wife and maid,
Looked from the rocks of Marblehead
Over the moaning and rainy sea —
Looked for the coming that might
   not be!    50
What did the winds and the sea birds say
Of the cruel captain who sailed away? —
   Old Floyd Ireson, for his hard heart,
   Tarred and feathered and carried in a
     cart
   By the women of Marblehead.    55

Through the street, on either side,
Up flew windows, doors swung wide;
Sharp-tongued spinsters, old wives gray,
Treble lent the fish horn's bray.
Sea-worn grandsires, cripple-bound,    60
Hulks of old sailors run aground,
Shook head, and fist, and hat, and cane,
And cracked with curses the hoarse refrain:
   " Here's Flud Oirson, fur his horrd horrt,
   Torr'd an' futherr'd an' corr'd in a
     corrt    65
   By the women o' Morble'ead! "

30. **Maenads** (mē′nădz): followers of Bacchus, god of wine. 35. **Chaleur** (shȧl-ûr′) **Bay:** in the Gulf of St. Lawrence.

Sweetly along the Salem road
Bloom of orchard and lilac showed.
Little the wicked skipper knew
Of the fields so green and the sky so
    blue.                                          70
Riding there in his sorry trim,
Like an Indian idol glum and grim,
Scarcely he seemed the sound to hear
Of voices shouting far and near:
    " Here's Flud Oirson, fur his horrd
      horrt,                               75
    Torr'd an' futherr'd an' corr'd in a corrt
    By the women o' Morble'ead! "

" Hear me, neighbors! " at last he cried —
" What to me is this noisy ride?
What is the shame that clothes the skin  80
To the nameless horror that lives within?
Waking or sleeping, I see a wreck,
And hear a cry from a reeling deck!
Hate me and curse me — I only dread
The hand of God and the face of the
    dead! "                                    85
    Said old Floyd Ireson, for his hard heart,
    Tarred and feathered and carried in a
      cart
    By the women of Marblehead!

Then the wife of the skipper lost at sea
Said, " God has touched him! why should
    we! "                                      90
Said an old wife mourning her only son,
" Cut the rogue's tether and let him run! "
So with soft relentings and rude excuse,
Half scorn, half pity, they cut him loose,
And gave him a cloak to hide him in,   95
And left him alone with his shame and sin.
    Poor Floyd Ireson, for his hard heart,
    Tarred and feathered and carried in a
      cart
    By the women of Marblehead!

## ABRAHAM DAVENPORT

In *The Tent on the Beach* Whittier used a
slight thread of story to assemble a number of
his narrative poems. Four friends, a scholar,
a poet (Whittier himself), a traveler, and a
singer, who are spending a summer vacation
on the beach are exchanging stories and songs

in the evening. The following story is the last
one read by the poet. Just as he finishes it, the
moon rises out of the ocean, and all are silent
" before that sudden glory."

The tale is based on an actual occurrence to
be found in historical records. The poet tells
his friends before reading it to them that he
wrote the poem when the coming in of the
Asiatic plague was terrifying the country. You
will see the connection when you read it.

In the old days (a custom laid aside
With breeches and cocked hats) the people
    sent
Their wisest men to make the public laws.
And so, from a brown homestead, where
    the Sound°
Drinks the small tribute of the Mianas,°   5
Waved over by the woods of Rippowams,°
And hallowed by pure lives and tranquil
    deaths,
Stamford sent up to the councils of the state
Wisdom and grace in Abraham Davenport.

    'Twas on a May day of the far old
    year                                      10
Seventeen hundred eighty, that there fell
Over the bloom and sweet life of the spring,
Over the fresh earth and the heaven of
    noon,
A horror of great darkness, like the night
In day of which the Norland sagas
    tell —                                     15
The Twilight of the Gods.° The low-hung
    sky
Was black with ominous clouds, save where
    its rim
Was fringed with a dull glow, like that
    which climbs
The crater's sides from the red hell below.
Birds ceased to sing, and all the barnyard
    fowls                                      20
Roosted; the cattle at the pasture bars
Lowed, and looked homeward; bats on
    leathern wings

4. **Sound:** Long Island Sound, east of New
York City. 5. **Mianas** (mī'ăn-ăs): a little river
near **Stamford.** 5. **Mianas** (line 8), a town in southwestern
Connecticut. 6. **Rippowams** (rĭp'ô-wămz): another
river near Stamford. 16. **Twilight of the Gods:** in
Norse mythology the final darkness and destruction of everything. It is the subject of a famous
opera by Wagner.

Flitted abroad; the sounds of labor died;
Men prayed, and women wept; all ears
    grew sharp
To hear the doom blast of the trumpet°
    shatter                    25
The black sky, that the dreadful face of
    Christ
Might look from the rent clouds, not as he
    looked
A loving guest at Bethany, but stern
As Justice and inexorable Law.

    Meanwhile in the old Statehouse,° dim
    as ghosts,                 30
Sat the lawgivers of Connecticut,
Trembling beneath their legislative robes.
" It is the Lord's Great Day! Let us ad-
    journ,"
Some said; and then, as if with one accord,
All eyes were turned to Abraham Daven-
    port.                    35
He rose, slow cleaving with his steady voice
The intolerable hush. " This well may be
The Day of Judgment which the world
    awaits;
But be it so or not, I only know
My present duty, and my Lord's com-
    mand                 40
To occupy till He come. So at the post
Where He hath set me in His providence,
I choose, for one, to meet Him face to
    face —
No faithless servant frightened from my
    task,
But ready when the Lord of the harvest
    calls;                45
And therefore, with all reverence, I would
    say,
Let God do His work, we will see to ours.
Bring in the candles." And they brought
    them in.

    Then by the flaring lights the Speaker
    read,
Albeit with husky voice and shaking
    hands,                50

25. **the doom blast of the trumpet:** The Puritan teaching emphasized the Day of Judgment,
announced by an angel's trumpet, so that this was
a very real fear to people of that day. 30. **Statehouse:** at Hartford, the capital of Connecticut.

An act to amend an act to regulate
The shad and alewife fisheries. Whereupon
Wisely and well spake Abraham Daven-
    port,
Straight to the question, with no figures of
    speech               54
Save the ten Arab signs,° yet not without
The shrewd dry humor natural to the man:
His awe-struck colleagues listening all the
    while,
Between the pauses of his argument,
To hear the thunder of the wrath of God
Break from the hollow trumpet of the
    cloud.              60

    And there he stands in memory to this
    day,
Erect, self-poised, a rugged face, half seen
Against the background of unnatural dark,
A witness to the ages as they pass,
That simple duty hath no place for fear.  65

55. **ten Arab signs:** Our numerals are derived
from the Arabic. In other words, he quoted exact
figures in the problem.

## THE ETERNAL GOODNESS

    Written in 1865 just at the close of the War
between the States, this is generally considered
the finest of Whittier's religious poems. Simplicity, sincerity, and human kindness are evident throughout. It was addressed to those
who held the " iron creeds " of the Puritans
that God as a stern judge would severely punish the wicked, and was therefore to be feared.
Whittier believed that if hate and revenge were
wrong in human beings, they would also be
wrong in God. If God is good, He must therefore be a God of love and mercy.
    A few stanzas have been omitted.

O friends! with whom my feet have trod
    The quiet aisles of prayer,
Glad witness to your zeal for God
    And love of man I bear.

I trace your lines of argument;         5
    Your logic linked and strong
I weigh as one who dreads dissent,
    And fears a doubt as wrong.

But still my human hands are weak
 To hold your iron creeds:    10
Against the words ye bid me speak
 My heart within me pleads.

Who fathoms the Eternal Thought?
 Who talks of scheme and plan?
The Lord is God! He needeth not    15
 The poor device of man.

I walk with bare, hushed feet the ground
 Ye tread with boldness shod;
I dare not fix with mete and bound°
 The love and power of God.    20

Ye praise His justice; even such
 His pitying love I deem:
Ye seek a king; I fain would touch
 The robe that hath no seam.°

Ye see the curse which overbroods    25
 A world of pain and loss;
I hear our Lord's beatitudes°
 And prayer upon the cross.

More than your schoolmen teach, within
 Myself, alas! I know:    30
Too dark ye cannot paint the sin,
 Too small the merit show.

I bow my forehead to the dust,
 I veil mine eyes for shame,
And urge, in trembling self-distrust,    35
 A prayer without a claim.

I see the wrong that round me lies,
 I feel the guilt within;
I hear, with groan and travail-cries,
 The world confess its sin.    40

Yet, in the maddening maze of things,
 And tossed by storm and flood,
To one fixed trust my spirit clings;
 I know that God is good!

19. **mete and bound:** definite boundaries (legal term). 24. **the robe . . . no seam:** the robe worn by Christ just before his crucifixion. 27. **beatitudes** (bē-ăt′ĭ-tūdz): series of blessings given in Matt. 5:3–12.

Not mine to look where cherubim    45
 And seraphs may not see,
But nothing can be good in Him
 Which evil is in me.

The wrong that pains my soul below
 I dare not throne above;    50
I know not of His hate, — I know
 His goodness and His love. . . .

I long for household voices gone,
 For vanished smiles I long,
But God hath led my dear ones on,    55
 And He can do no wrong.

I know not what the future hath
 Of marvel or surprise,
Assured alone that life and death
 His mercy underlies. . . .    60

I know not where His islands lift
 Their fronded palms in air;
I only know I cannot drift
 Beyond His love and care. . . .

## SNOW–BOUND

### A WINTER IDYLL

After the close of the War between the States, with the question of slavery settled, Whittier's mind turned more toward personal reminiscence. Being a bachelor, he had lived in closer touch with the family of his boyhood than he might have otherwise, and these home ties had recently been broken by the death of his mother and elder sister, and later his younger sister, Elizabeth. No one was left now but his brother Matthew and himself. What more natural than that he should write a memorial poem dedicated to the old household? The poem was published in 1866 and was immediately hailed as the greatest American pastoral poem. It is printed here in a shortened version.

The sun that brief December day
Rose cheerless over hills of gray,
And, darkly circled, gave at noon
A sadder light than waning moon.
Slow tracing down the thickening sky    5
Its mute and ominous prophecy,
A portent seeming less than threat,

WHITTIER'S BIRTHPLACE AT HAVERHILL was the setting for *Snow-Bound*. This typical New England farmhouse, like Whittier's poetry, is simple, unpretentious, unaffected.

It sank from sight before it set.
A chill no coat, however stout,
Of homespun stuff could quite shut out, 10
A hard, dull bitterness of cold,
  That checked, mid-vein, the circling race
  Of lifeblood in the sharpened face,
The coming of the snowstorm told.
The wind blew east: we heard the roar  15
Of Ocean on his wintry shore,
And felt the strong pulse throbbing there
Beat with low rhythm our inland air.

Meanwhile we did our nightly chores —
Brought in the wood from out of doors,  20
Littered the stalls, and from the mows
Raked down the herd's-grass for the cows;
Heard the horse whinnying for his corn;
And, sharply clashing horn on horn,
Impatient down the stanchion rows  25
The cattle shake their walnut bows;
While, peering from his early perch
Upon the scaffold's pole of birch,
The cock his crested helmet bent
And down his querulous challenge sent.  30

Unwarmed by any sunset light
The gray day darkened into night,
A night made hoary with the swarm
And whirl-dance of the blinding storm,
As zigzag, wavering to and fro,  35
Crossed and recrossed the wingèd snow:
And ere the early bedtime came
The white drift piled the window frame,
And through the glass the clothesline posts
Looked in like tall and sheeted ghosts.  40

So all night long the storm roared on:
The morning broke without a sun;
In tiny spherule traced with lines
Of Nature's geometric signs,
In starry flake and pellicle,  45
All day the hoary meteor fell;
And, when the second morning shone,
We looked upon a world unknown,
On nothing we could call our own.
Around the glistening wonder bent  50
The blue walls of the firmament,
No cloud above, no earth below —
A universe of sky and snow!

The old familiar sights of ours
Took marvelous shapes; strange domes and
    towers    55
Rose up where sty or corncrib stood,
Or garden wall, or belt of wood;
A smooth white mound the brush pile
    showed,
A fenceless drift what once was road;
The bridle post an old man sat    60
With loose-flung coat and high cocked hat;
The wellcurb had a Chinese roof;°
And even the long sweep, high aloof,
In its slant splendor, seemed to tell
Of Pisa's leaning miracle.°    65

A prompt, decisive man, no breath
Our father wasted: " Boys, a path! "
Well pleased, (for when did farmer boy
Count such a summons less than joy?)
Our buskins° on our feet we drew;    70
    With mittened hands, and caps drawn
    low,
    To guard our necks and ears from snow,
We cut the solid whiteness through.
And, where the drift was deepest, made
A tunnel walled and overlaid    75
With dazzling crystal: we had read
Of rare Aladdin's° wondrous cave,
And to our own his name we gave,
With many a wish the luck were ours
To test his lamp's supernal powers.    80
We reached the barn with merry din,
And roused the prisoned brutes within.
The old horse thrust his long head out,
And grave with wonder gazed about;
The cock his lusty greeting said,    85
And forth his speckled harem led;
The oxen lashed their tails, and hooked,
And mild reproach of hunger looked;
The hornèd patriarch of the sheep,

62. **wellcurb had a Chinese roof:** Whittier explained, when asked how this could be, that a board had been placed across the curb to hold the bucket and that this gave the roof effect. 65. **Pisa's** (pē′zàz) **leaning miracle:** a famous slanting tower in Pisa, Italy. 70. **buskins:** a name for heavy boots derived from the high-heeled boots worn by ancient Greek actors. 77. **Aladdin:** the youth in the Arabian Nights who discovered great treasure in a cave through the power of a magical lamp.

Like Egypt's Amun° roused from sleep,    90
Shook his sage head with gesture mute,
And emphasized with stamp of foot.

All day the gusty north wind bore
The loosening drift its breath before;
Low circling round its southern zone,    95
The sun through dazzling snow-mist shone.
No church bell lent its Christian tone
To the savage air, no social smoke
Curled over woods of snow-hung oak.
A solitude made more intense    100
By dreary-voicèd elements,
The shrieking of the mindless wind,
The moaning tree boughs swaying blind,
And on the glass the unmeaning beat
Of ghostly finger tips of sleet.    105
Beyond the circle of our hearth
No welcome sound of toil or mirth
Unbound the spell, and testified
Of human life and thought outside.
We minded that the sharpest ear    110
The buried brooklet could not hear,
The music of whose liquid lip
Had been to us companionship,
And, in our lonely life, had grown
To have an almost human tone.    115

As night drew on, and, from the crest
Of wooded knolls that ridged the west,
The sun, a snow-blown traveler, sank
From sight beneath the smothering bank,
We piled with care our nightly stack    120
Of wood against the chimney back —
The oaken log, green, huge, and thick,
And on its top the stout backstick;
The knotty forestick laid apart,
And filled between with curious art    125
The ragged brush; then, hovering near,
We watched the first red blaze appear,
Heard the sharp crackle, caught the gleam
On whitewashed wall and sagging beam,
Until the old, rude-furnished room    130
Burst, flowerlike, into rosy bloom;
While radiant with a mimic flame
Outside the sparkling drift became,
And through the bare-boughed lilac tree

90. **Egypt's Amun:** Egyptian god frequently represented with a ram's head, usually spelled Amon or Ammon.

Our own warm hearth seemed blazing
   free.    135
The crane and pendent trammels showed,
The Turks' heads° on the andirons glowed;
While childish fancy, prompt to tell
The meaning of the miracle,
Whispered the old rhyme: *" Under the*
   *tree*    140
*When fire outdoors burns merrily,*
*There the witches are making tea."*

The moon above the eastern wood
Shone at its full; the hill range stood
Transfigured in the silver flood,    145
Its blown snows flashing cold and keen,
Dead white, save where some sharp ravine
Took shadow, or the somber green
Of hemlocks turned to pitchy black
Against the whiteness at their back.    150
For such a world and such a night
Most fitting that unwarming light,
Which only seemed where'er it fell
To make the coldness visible.

Shut in from all the world without,    155
We sat the clean-winged hearth° about,
Content to let the north wind roar
In baffled rage at pane and door,
While the red logs before us beat
The frost line back with tropic heat;    160
And ever, when a louder blast
Shook beam and rafter as it passed,
The merrier up its roaring draft
The great throat of the chimney laughed;
The house dog on his paws outspread    165
Laid to the fire his drowsy head,
The cat's dark silhouette on the wall
A couchant tiger's seemed to fall;
And, for the winter fireside meet,
Between the andirons' straddling feet,    170
The mug of cider simmered slow,
The apples sputtered in a row,
And, close at hand, the basket stood
With nuts from brown October's wood.

What matter how the night behaved?    175
What matter how the north wind raved?

137. **Turks' heads:** the design of the top of
the andiron resembled a Turkish cap. 156. **clean-
winged hearth:** A turkey wing was used for a
hearth broom.

Blow high, blow low, not all its snow
Could quench our hearthfire's ruddy
   glow. . . .

We sped the time with stories old,
Wrought puzzles out, and riddles told,    180
Or stammered from our schoolbook lore
" The Chief of Gambia's golden
   shore."° . . .

Our father rode again his ride
On Memphremagog's° wooded side;
Sat down again to moose and samp    185
In trapper's hut and Indian camp;
Lived o'er the old idyllic ease
Beneath St. François'° hemlock trees. . . .

We shared the fishing off Boar's Head,°
   And round the rocky Isles of Shoals°    190
   The hake-broil° on the driftwood coals;
The chowder on the sand beach made,
Dipped by the hungry, steaming hot,
With spoons of clamshell from the pot.
We heard the tales of witchcraft old,    195
And dream and sign and marvel told
To sleepy listeners as they lay
Stretched idly on the salted hay,
Adrift along the winding shores,
When favoring breezes deigned to blow    200
The square sail of the gundalow,°
And idle lay the useless oars.

Our mother, while she turned her wheel
Or ran the new-knit stocking heel,    204
Told how the Indian hordes came down
At midnight on Cocheco° town,
And how her own great-uncle bore
His cruel scalp-mark to fourscore.
Recalling, in her fitting phrase,

182. **"The chief of Gambia's golden shore":**
a line from a popular poem of the day called
"The African Chief." This shows the interest in
antislavery in Whittier's boyhood. 225. **Memphremagog** (mĕm-frĕ-mā'gŏg): a lake between
Vermont and Canada. 229. **St. François** (săn frän-
swä'; pronounced frän'swä here for the rhythm):
a river in Quebec. 189, 190. **Boar's Head, Isles of
Shoals:** points along the coast north of Salisbury,
Massachusetts. 191. **hake-broil:** a hake is a fish
resembling the codfish. 201. **gundalow:** a variant
of gondola, a heavy, flat-bottomed barge or
boat. 206. **Cocheco** (kō-chē'kō): Indian name for
Dover, New Hampshire.

So rich and picturesque and free,          210
(The common unrhymed poetry
Of simple life and country ways,)
The story of her early days —
She made us welcome to her home;
Old hearths grew wide to give us room;     215
We stole with her a frightened look
At the gray wizard's conjuring-book,
The fame whereof went far and wide
Through all the simple countryside;
We heard the hawks at twilight play,       220
The boat horn on Piscataqua,°
The loon's weird laughter far away;
We fished her little trout brook, knew
What flowers in wood and meadow grew,
What sunny hillsides autumn-brown          225
She climbed to shake the ripe nuts down,
Saw where in sheltered cove and bay
The ducks' black squadron anchored lay,
And heard the wild geese calling loud
Beneath the gray November cloud....        230

Our uncle,° innocent of books,
Was rich in lore of fields and brooks,
The ancient teachers never dumb
Of Nature's unhoused lyceum.
In moons and tides and weather wise,       235
He read the clouds as prophecies,
And foul or fair could well divine,
By many an occult hint and sign,
Holding the cunning-warded keys°
To all the woodcraft mysteries;            240
Himself to Nature's heart so near
That all her voices in his ear
Of beast or bird had meanings clear. . . .
A simple, guileless, childlike man,
Content to live where life began;          245
Strong only on his native grounds,
The little world of sights and sounds
Whose girdle was the parish bounds. . . .

Next, the dear aunt,° whose smile of cheer
And voice in dreams I see and hear —       250

The sweetest woman ever Fate
Perverse denied a household mate,
Who, lonely, homeless, not the less
Found peace in love's unselfishness,
And welcome wheresoe'er she went,          255
A calm and gracious element,
Whose presence seemed the sweet income
And womanly atmosphere of home —
Called up her girlhood memories,
The huskings and the apple bees,           260
The sleigh rides and the summer sails,
Weaving through all the poor details
And homespun warp of circumstance
A golden woof-thread of romance. . . .

There, too, our elder sister° plied         265
Her evening task the stand beside;
A full, rich nature, free to trust,
Truthful and almost sternly just,
Impulsive, earnest, prompt to act,
And make her generous thought a fact,      270
Keeping with many a light disguise
The secret of self-sacrifice.
O heart sore tried! thou hast the best     273
That Heaven itself could give thee — rest,
Rest from all bitter thoughts and things!
  How many a poor one's blessing went
  With thee beneath the low green tent
Whose curtain never outward swings!

As one who held herself a part
Of all she saw, and let her heart          280
  Against the household bosom lean,
Upon the motley-braided mat
Our youngest° and our dearest sat. . . .

The chill weight of the winter snow
  For months upon her grave has lain;      285
And now, when summer south winds blow
  And brier and harebell bloom again,
I tread the pleasant paths we trod,
I see the violet-sprinkled sod             289
Whereon she leaned, too frail and weak

221. **Piscataqua** (pĭs-kăt'á-kwȧ): a river in
Maine. The rhyme shows that they gave it a
rustic pronunciation. 231. **Our uncle:** Moses, the
bachelor brother of Whittier's father. 239. **cunning-warded keys:** keys with notches nicely adjusted to fit different locks. 249. **the dear aunt:**
Aunt Mercy, his mother's sister, who always
made her home with the Whittiers.

265. **elder sister:** Mary, who died five years
before the poem was written. She was Mrs. Jacob
Caldwell of Haverhill. 283. **Our youngest:** Elizabeth, the unmarried sister, who kept house for
Whittier until she died about a year before the
poem was written. As she too possessed some
poetic gift, the brother and sister were most congenial, and the poet's mourning for her is feelingly expressed.

The hillside flowers she loved to seek,
Yet following me where'er I went
With dark eyes full of love's content.
The birds are glad; the brier rose fills
The air with sweetness; all the hills      295
Stretch green to June's unclouded sky;
But still I wait with ear and eye
For something gone which should be nigh,
A loss in all familiar things,
In flower that blooms, and bird that
      sings. . . .                          300

Brisk wielder of the birch and rule,°
The master of the district school
Held at the fire his favored place;
Its warm glow lit a laughing face
Fresh-hued and fair, where scarce appeared
The uncertain prophecy of beard.           306
He teased the mitten-blinded cat,
Played cross pins on my uncle's hat,
Sang songs, and told us what befalls
In classic Dartmouth's° college halls.     310
Born the wild Northern hills among,
From whence his yeoman father wrung
By patient toil subsistence scant,
Not competence and yet not want,
He early gained the power to pay           315
His cheerful, self-reliant way;
Could doff at ease his scholar's gown
To peddle wares from town to town;
Or through the long vacation's reach
In lonely lowland districts teach,         320
Where all the droll experience found
At stranger hearths in boarding round,
The moonlit skater's keen delight,
The sleigh drive through the frosty night,
The rustic party, with its rough           325
Accompaniment of blindman's buff,
And whirling plate, and forfeits paid,
His winter task a pastime made.
Happy the snow-locked homes wherein
He tuned his merry violin,                  330
Or played the athlete in the barn,
Or held the good dame's winding yarn,
Or mirth-provoking versions told
Of classic legends rare and old,
Wherein the scenes of Greece and Rome

Had all the commonplace of home,           336
And little seemed at best the odds
'Twixt Yankee peddlers and old gods. . . .

Another guest° that winter night          339
Flashed back from lustrous eyes the light.
Unmarked by time, and yet not young,
The honeyed music of her tongue
And words of meekness scarcely told
A nature passionate and bold,              344
Strong, self-concentered, spurning guide,
Its milder features dwarfed beside
Her unbent will's majestic pride.
She sat among us, at the best,
A not unfeared, half-welcome guest. . . .

At last the great logs, crumbling low,     350
Sent out a dull and duller glow,
The bull's-eye watch that hung in view,
Ticking its weary circuit through,
Pointed with mutely warning sign
Its black hand to the hour of nine.        355
That sign the pleasant circle broke:
My uncle ceased his pipe to smoke,
Knocked from its bowl the refuse gray
And laid it tenderly away;
Then roused himself to safely cover        360
The dull red brands with ashes over.
And while, with care, our mother laid
The work aside, her steps she stayed
One moment, seeking to express
Her grateful sense of happiness            365
For food and shelter, warmth and health,
And love's contentment more than wealth,
With simple wishes (not the weak,
Vain prayers which no fulfillment seek,
But such as warm the generous heart,       370
O'erprompt to do with Heaven its part)
That none might lack, that bitter night,
For bread and clothing, warmth and light.

Within our beds awhile we heard
The wind that round the gables roared,     375
With now and then a ruder shock,
Which made our very bedsteads rock.
We heard the loosened clapboards tost,
The board nails snapping in the frost;     379

301. **Brisk wielder of the birch and rule:**
George Haskell was his name. 310. **Dartmouth:**
a well-known New Hampshire college.

339. **Another guest:** Harriet Livermore, a
brilliant but eccentric woman, who went to
Palestine believing that the second coming of
Christ was near at hand.

And on us, through the unplastered wall,
Felt the light-sifted snowflakes fall.
But sleep stole on, as sleep will do
When hearts are light and life is new;
Faint and more faint the murmurs grew,
Till in the summerland of dreams    385
They softened to the sound of streams,
Low stir of leaves, and dip of oars,
And lapsing waves on quiet shores.

Next morn we wakened with the shout
Of merry voices high and clear;    390
And saw the teamsters drawing near
To break the drifted highways out.
Down the long hillside treading slow
We saw the half-buried oxen go,
Shaking the snow from heads uptost,    395
Their straining nostrils white with frost.
Before our door the straggling train
Drew up, an added team to gain.
The elders threshed their hands a-cold,
    Passed, with the cider mug, their jokes
    From lip to lip; the younger folks    401
Down the loose snowbanks, wrestling, rolled,
Then toiled again the cavalcade
    O'er windy hill, through clogged ravine,
    And woodland paths that wound be-
        tween    405
Low drooping pine boughs winter-weighed.
From every barn a team afoot,
At every house a new recruit,
Where, drawn by Nature's subtlest law,
Haply the watchful young men saw    410
Sweet doorway pictures of the curls
And curious eyes of merry girls,
Lifting their hands in mock defense
Against the snowball's compliments,
And reading in each missive tost    415
The charm with Eden never lost.

We heard once more the sleigh bells' sound;
    And, following where the teamsters led,
The wise old Doctor went his round,
Just pausing at our door to say,    420
In the brief autocratic way
Of one who, prompt at Duty's call,
Was free to urge her claim on all,
    That some poor neighbor sick abed
At night our mother's aid would need.    425
For, one in generous thought and deed,

What mattered in the sufferer's sight
    The Quaker matron's inward light,
The Doctor's mail of Calvin's creed?°
All hearts confess the saints elect    430
    Who, twain in faith, in love agree,
And melt not in an acid sect
    The Christian pearl of charity!

So days went on: a week had passed    434
Since the great world was heard from last.
The Almanac we studied o'er,
Read and reread our little store
Of books and pamphlets, scarce a score;
One harmless novel, mostly hid
From younger eyes, a book forbid,    440
And poetry, (or good or bad,
A single book was all we had,)
Where Ellwood's meek, drab-skirted Muse,°
    A stranger to the heathen Nine,°
    Sang, with a somewhat nasal whine,    445
The wars of David and the Jews.
At last the floundering carrier bore
The village paper to our door.
Lo! broadening outward as we read,
To warmer zones the horizon spread;    450
In panoramic length unrolled
We saw the marvels that it told. . . .

Welcome to us its week-old news,
Its corner for the rustic Muse,
    Its monthly gauge of snow and rain,    455
Its record, mingling in a breath
The wedding bell and dirge of death;
Jest, anecdote, and lovelorn tale,
The latest culprit sent to jail;
Its hue and cry of stolen and lost,    460
Its vendue° sales and goods at cost,
    And traffic calling loud for gain.
We felt the stir of hall and street,
The pulse of life that round us beat;
The chill embargo of the snow    465
Was melted in the genial glow;
Wide swung again our ice-locked door,
And all the world was ours once more! . . .

429. **Calvin's creed:** The doctor was a Presbyterian, or follower of Calvin, a Swiss reformer.
443. **Ellwood's meek, drab-skirted Muse:**
Thomas Ellwood was a Quaker poet; therefore
his muse was clothed in gray. 444. **the heathen
Nine:** the Greek Muses who presided over the
arts. 461. **vendue** (vĕn-dū′): auction.

## Suggestions for Study of Whittier

SKIPPER IRESON'S RIDE

1. What details make you feel the spirit of the women? Why did they finally let the skipper go? His speech is imaginary; in reality he said nothing during the ride. Does Whittier's change make a more effective poem? Why or why not?

2. Read a modern version in "The True Story of Skipper Ireson" by Charles Buxton Going (to be found in Hohn's *Stories in Verse*). Point out differences in the two versions. Which do you like better as a poem? Why?

3. If possible, show pictures of the quaint town of Marblehead or have a description given in class by someone who has been there.

4. Write up a legend or old settler's tale of the early days of your own community.

ABRAHAM DAVENPORT

5. What is the main point brought out by Davenport's character? What other examples can you give from literature, history, or your own experience, of persons who have done their duty in the face of great difficulties?

6. Write a brief story of cool, straightforward action in an emergency, such as a fire, a tornado, or an automobile accident.

THE ETERNAL GOODNESS

7. Sum up in a few sentences the main thought of the poem. Does it show in any way that Whittier was a Quaker?

8. What contrast is there between the thinking of Whittier and that of the "friends" addressed? With which side do you agree?

9. Select lines that are often quoted or that you think are well suited to quotation. Memorize some of these.

SNOW-BOUND

10. Point out some of the details which make the forecast of snow and the storm itself especially vivid. Select figures of speech that add to the imaginative quality of the description.

11. Debate the advantages and disadvantages of living in a snowy country.

12. Describe the various members of the group around the fire. Each character may be taken by a different student for description in class. Select the character best liked by the class. Which do you think Whittier described most sympathetically?

13. Compare the amusements of the evening with those which would probably entertain a modern family. How does the reading matter compare with that in your home?

14. Put the conversation around the fire into dramatic form that could be acted in class. A contrasting dramatization of the conversation of a modern family group might be put on as part of the same program.

15. Find other poems on snow and frost, such as "The Snow Storm," by Ralph W. Emerson; "A Snow Storm," by Henry van Dyke; "Snow Shower," by Bryant; "Snow Song," by Lucy Larcom; "An Arctic Night," by Fridtjof Nansen; "To a Snowflake," by Francis Thompson; "An Old-Fashioned Snow Storm," by Warner; "The Frost Spirit," by Whittier. How do these compare with *Snow-Bound* in effectiveness of description?

16. If you can obtain a picture of the interior of Whittier's boyhood home, study its details. How does this room differ from living rooms of today? Many modern homes are built in imitation of old New England farmhouses. What details of this room do you think are often imitated today?

## 3. POE, HAWTHORNE, MELVILLE

Sometimes you can tell a lot about a literary movement by noticing what its men wrote about. Recall what themes seemed to be most interesting to the writers we have so far talked about.

Irving loved to write of things that were old and unusual and strange — the castles of Spain, the inns and churches of England, the legends of the Hudson valley. Cooper liked to write about what was old and exciting — the adventures of frontier scouts, sea captains, Revolutionary War spies. His favorite theme was the battle between white and red men, and he had great sympathy for the Indians because he felt they were being "spoiled" by civilization. Bryant wrote about nature, in the way some men write about religion. Whittier wrote about nature, too, and the simple life, and old ballads, and freedom for slaves. When you come to read Poe and Hawthorne you will see another kind of theme that these men were interested in — magic; supernatural things; unexplainable things that send chills up your backbone.

There is no need to get caught up in literary names, especially since writers write what they feel like, anyway, and seldom realize that they are members of a literary movement. But you might remember that today we say these men who took part in the Flowering of the East were a part of the Romantic Movement in literature. And without trying to define that movement, remember two things about it. For one thing, the movement was not limited to America; European writers were interested in about the same things as American writers. And you might remember some of the things they were interested in: the old; the strange; romantic and unusual events; nature; natural men ("noble Indians" and other savages "unspoiled" by civilization; and simple people who lived close to nature) ; magic and the supernatural; sad and melancholy stories. Not all were interested in all these things. But pick them out as you read on.

EDGAR ALLAN POE

Poe was the first great writer who came out of the South. Why should a section of the country so cultivated and literate have produced no more literature than it did? The question is no easier to answer than the other question, why do men write great books? But in the case of the South we can guess that it had something to do with the way those states developed. There were few great cities to attract groups of artists and publishers. There was no Boston or Concord or New York in the South. It was a country of broad plantations, stately houses, and aristocratic landowners who administered the affairs of a subservient class. The arts of administration, law, and graceful living were encouraged more than the art of literature. "We produce men, rather than books," a Southerner once said, and pointed to the long and distinguished list of Southern statesmen, soldiers, and jurists, headed by Washington, Jefferson, Lee, and John Marshall.

"The great intellect with the sad heart," Edwin Markham called Poe. "The great talent with the sad life," would be another way to put it.

We need not spend too much time on the details of his life, because everyone who loves Poe's stories and poems knows something about his life and regrets that he could not have been happier and lived longer to write more. Poe was born in Boston of a Southern family who were in a traveling company of actors. Two years later his parents were dead. He was supported by a wealthy Richmond family, the Allans, who gave him his middle name. Attractive, brilliant, erratic, the young Poe never got along very well with anybody who imposed restraint on him. He often quarreled with his foster father. The Allans took him to England for five years, then sent him to the University of Virginia. He spent a wild year there, for he moved in a set where drinking and gambling were fashionable, and Poe never did anything by halves. When he lost twenty-five hundred dollars in a card game, he was taken out of the University and put into Mr. Allan's business. That didn't work either. He had an unhappy love affair and didn't like his job. He ran away. Later he tried Army life under an assumed name. Mr. Allan rescued him from that, had him appointed to West Point, but Poe got himself dismissed within a year. Thereafter he had to go it alone.

The rest of the story is not very pretty. He was a brilliant editor, and made the *Southern Literary Messenger* the outstanding magazine of the South, but lost his editorship as he lost so many other situations, because he drank too much and didn't keep schedules. He married his thirteen-year-old cousin, and thereafter lived mostly in Philadelphia and New York, fighting poverty, in and out of editorial jobs, taking care of his child wife when she developed tuberculosis, depending more and more upon drugs and drink to make him forget his troubles, but always writing brilliantly.

His wife died, only twenty-four years old. Two years later he himself was found dying in a Baltimore street. No one knew what had happened to him. But he was dead at forty, when most writers are ready to begin their solidest work.

What Poe did in his few years, though, in spite of some of the greatest handicaps ever set in the way of a man's writing, was more than most Americans have ever done in a full lifetime. Writers usually don't like to talk about genius because they know that writing is more hard work than inspiration, but when they look at Poe's career they are at a loss to explain it except in terms of genius.

Forget the life, for a moment. He didn't do very well on that. But add up his literary score: He wrote better poetry, better short stories, better criticism than had been written in America up to his time. Some people excelled during the period of the Flowering in one of these fields (like Bryant and Whittier in poetry, or Irving and Hawthorne in stories), and some in two (like Emerson and Lowell, in poetry and criticism), but nobody else was able to be a top man in *three*. And Poe did all this in twenty years, between 1829 and his death in 1849. Emerson, Longfellow, Lowell, Whittier, Bryant, Whitman had literary careers of nearly fifty years. Poe burned like a short candle, but no light burned brighter.

No other American of his time left so many stories that are still part of our common reading, part of our heritage, and part of the world's heritage, too — because the short story developed chiefly in America.

Some of his enduring stories are detective stories, like " The Gold Bug." Poe was the first great writer of mystery and detective stories, many years before Stevenson and Conan Doyle. He had a hard, sharp mind which would have made him a great lawyer or a great cryptographer if his interests had gone that way.

Others are stories of horror and magic, like " The Fall of the House of Usher " and " The Tell-Tale Heart." No one has ever succeeded in getting more cold chills into

a few thousand words than Poe. Poe built his stories like a modern streamlined airplane, with the very first sentence on the theme, and every other sentence pointed straight to the effect he wanted to make.

In both stories and poems you will notice an interesting characteristic of Poe — he was not " local." Bryant wrote about the flowers around him, Whittier about the people of Massachusetts, and Cooper about the American forest and frontier. Whitman spread American scenes and people through every paragraph he wrote. But Poe wrote often as though he had never seen Richmond or New York. He set most of his stories and poems in an unreal, imaginary world — " the misty mid-region of Weir " — where he could paint any kind of setting he wanted, or in Paris or a distant island where people couldn't check on the accuracy of his details. He didn't care about details of setting. He cared about what kind of emotional effect his stories had on the reader.

Those are the two sides of Poe — the hard, logical intellect that let him write the detective stories and made him a ruthless but brilliant critic, and the sense of unreality and magic that let him create a world of his own and write poetry in which sound was sometimes more important than sense.

For as he was an artist in the emotional effect of fiction, so he was an artist in the sound effect of verse. He could make the bells ring in words. He could make readers shiver from the very sound of a poem. He could put together words so that they had the beauty of a Persian tapestry, and merely to hear the words without thinking of their meaning was an aesthetic experience.

Poe had no particular message for his readers. He was not a moral writer, like Hawthorne or Bryant. As Lowell said, his heart " somehow seems all squeezed out by the mind." He was an artist for the sake of art — for the sake of making a beautiful poem or story, every word of which would be pointed toward a single effect on the reader. You will notice that his stories and poems usually deal with Love, Beauty, and

Death. Those were his three themes, and he used them over and over. He was not concerned with explaining them, advising about them, or discussing the social problems they created. He was concerned with the literary effect he could make out of them. That was the quality in which he was most different from his New England contemporaries.

In brilliant essays, he put forth his theory of criticism. The purpose of writing, he said, is "pleasure, not truth." The object of poetry is "the rhythmical creation of beauty." The well-made story or poem will have every word, every sound contributing to the effect the writer wants to achieve.

Almost alone among his great contemporaries, he did not hesitate to criticize contemporary writers. Great or small, he put them under the microscope. He gave them such an examination as writers had never before had from an American critic. In cutting out their bad spots, he was impersonal as a surgeon. He allowed no patriotism, no pleas or threats, to stand in the way of his judgment. "As for American letters," he said, "plain speaking about them is simply the one thing needed." He gave them what they needed.

*Poe was born in the year (1809) when Jefferson finished his term as President, and died in the year of the great gold rush (1849). No major American writer in the nineteenth century except Lanier lived a shorter life span.*

### NATHANIEL HAWTHORNE

It is interesting to look at Poe and Hawthorne together. They stand together as the greatest writers of the short story in their century, and they were both interested in the dark and mysterious places of life, the ways of magic and the mysteries of the supernatural. But their differences tell more about them than their similarities.

Poe was not at all local; Hawthorne was intensely local. New England was in everything he wrote. In fact, the origin of his dark temperament was local. He grew up in Salem, where the pictures of the great Puri-

tans still hung, and the witchcraft scare was still remembered. His house had an ancestral curse on it, and a ghost that was alleged to haunt the yard. His mother took to her room on the day she heard of her husband's death on a distant voyage in a Salem clipper, and there is a legend that she was never seen to emerge until the day she died, nor did anyone else enter the room. When Hawthorne graduated from Bowdoin, he came back home, and lived for twelve years like a recluse. So did all the Hawthornes in those years, staying in their rooms, having their meals left outside the door. In the evening, though, Nathaniel and one of his sisters would usually take a walk — alone and in opposite directions — through Salem.

No town was so full of dark legends as old Salem: skeletons in closets; blood on the walls; houses that poisoned their occupants; old wives living in darkness with the ghosts of their husbands; bodies that walked from graves; men condemned to wander the hills until doomsday; the devil himself meeting his faithful followers at midnight in the woods. In busy New York these stories would not have been heard. In Concord, men were too much outdoors to carry such tales, and the wind off Walden Pond would have blown away the mystery. But in dark old Salem people told them and half believed them; it was hard to tell where reality stopped and fancy started.

Those were the conditions under which Hawthorne served his twelve-year apprenticeship as a writer, sitting in his attic bedroom, looking out the window to see the ghost in the yard, walking through the old town, and writing all day at the stories suggested to him by the old legends and by his surroundings. It was not surprising that he did not grow up to be the kind of writer Bryant became in the Berkshire Hills, or Irving in the gay literary fellowship of New York and London.

He left Salem when he was thirty-five and lived away from it for most of the rest of his life. He was fortunate in his friends. George Bancroft, the historian, then in charge of the Boston customhouse, gave him

THE HOUSE OF SEVEN GABLES in Hawthorne's native Salem, made famous by his novel of that name. (Brown Brothers)

a job and made it possible for him to leave Salem. President Franklin Pierce, his old college mate, made him consul to Liverpool for a short time. He took his wife (a Salem girl who had imagined herself an invalid waiting for a magician to command her to rise from her couch) to the Old Manse in Concord, where his friends and neighbors were Emerson, Alcott, and Thoreau. His horizons broadened away from the gabled house in Salem with the ghost in the yard, but the atmosphere of the early years darkened his stories until he died.

When you have told about the Salem years, you have told almost everything important to know about the external facts of Hawthorne's life. What happened to him externally was not important; the important things were what happened to him inside,

what he was thinking and why. He wasn't a man of action; he was a man of thought.

And so were the men in his stories. Poe didn't care much about what his characters were thinking, about their struggles with guilt or society. Poe treated his people almost like puppets, moving them wherever he needed them to give the effect he wanted to get from the story. But to Hawthorne the most important part of the story was what his characters were thinking, how they worked out their moral problems, how they answered the questions he posed for them.

Another way to put that difference is to say that Poe was an artistic writer, Hawthorne a psychological writer. Poe wanted to make a perfect work of art; Hawthorne wanted to find out how his characters thought and what made them act as they did. Poe made more perfect stories, but Hawthorne made more complete stories. Poe showed the world how a story should be put together, but Hawthorne showed the world how to put real people into a story. Together they put the new country (" Who reads an American book? " the *Edinburgh Review* had asked only a few years earlier) far ahead of the rest of the world in the art of writing the short story.

Hawthorne's best stories refuse to stand on the shelves. They walk like people. We know his characters, and almost feel we should help them work out their problems. They are burdened down with problems, all of them. The darkness of old Salem hangs over them. The characters in his fine novel, *The Scarlet Letter* (which critics have sometimes called a perfect novel) are involved in a triangle situation which forces them to answer such questions as " What is sin? How can it be expiated? What happens when man takes it upon himself to punish sin? " One of his finest stories, " Ethan Brand," deals with a man's effort to discover the unpardonable sin. Even when he wrote *The Marble Faun,* a fantasy of a statue in Rome, it became a study of the effect of sin on one's conscience. He looked always inward. One of his best-known stories, " The Great Stone Face," is concerned with the effect of the stone face on the character of a boy who grew up near it. " Dr. Heidigger's Experiment " and " Rappaccini's Daughter " study the result when a scientist tries to alter the laws of nature. Even when he wrote stories of the Puritans he was trying to see what they were thinking, why they thought as they did.

In fact, as you read his stories, you will see that you are reading a better biography than could be written from the facts of his life. The problems in the stories are like his problems. The problem of sin and guilt and conscience is his heritage from the Puritans. His brooding, shy nature, his turning inward, his interest in the dark places of the human mind are his heritage from old Salem.

*Hawthorne was born (1804) in the year when Lewis and Clark started on their expedition into the unexplored Northwest. He died (1864) as the War between the States drew near a close.*

## HERMAN MELVILLE

To go from the books of Irving and Cooper to the books of Poe, Hawthorne, and Melville is like going from sunny roads to a dark, rocky ravine.

Something there was about those last three writers that led them always to seek the dark places of life. Poe's stories are like a dim and shadowy theater, in which supernatural events, crimes, and horrors fill the stage, and the only light is from an eerie, mysterious lantern. Hawthorne's stories are full of the dark legends of Salem, and of the author's own explorations into the inner mysteries of the human mind. But Melville went even further. If they were exciting, he could be more exciting. If they were intense and mysterious, he could be more so. If they lived extraordinary lives, he lived a still more extraordinary one. For there was never another man quite like Melville in American literature. And, to make his record still more unusual, it took critics three-quarters of a century to realize that he had written a great book.

He was born in New York and grew up in the Hudson valley — so far, like Irving and Cooper, but there the likeness ends. His boyhood was shadowed over by the declining fortunes of his family and the death of his father. He was unhappy, he was poor, he worried about his widowed mother and his five brothers. He went to work in a bank when he was seventeen, then tried school teaching, finally did what many a boy did in those days of clipper ships — ran away to sea.

It was a short trip, but thereafter he could never quite get the sea out of his blood or sea stories out of his mind. Three more years of school teaching, and then he went to sea again — this time on a whaler from one of those New England fishing ports from which, in those days, men departed almost daily for every corner of the earth. He sailed when he was only twenty-one. He came back when he was twenty-five. Into those years he packed enough adventure to last a lifetime.

When his slow ship reached the Marquesas Islands in the south central Pacific, he deserted. He wandered several days in a wilderness and came to a kind of tropical paradise which few white men had ever seen and which was yet hardly changed by civilization. He lived four months with the natives (whom he suspected of being cannibals), watched their dances and feasts, compared their primitive life with the civilization he had known. But he discovered that after a man had tasted " the fatal draught of civilization " he could never be wholly content even in those idyllic surroundings. An Australian whaling crew visited the cannibal islands. Melville sailed away with them.

It was 1844 when he came back to Boston harbor. He had left as a boy, come back a man. He had faced death, suffered, met with danger, seen and felt deep emotions, observed civilizations as different from his own as any could possibly be. Above all, he had come to know the sea.

He wrote a book called *Typee*. It was a picture of the life he had seen on the South Pacific islands. Some people thought parts of it were indecent, but it was truthful. In his lifetime, it was his most popular book. It brought him the grand sum of four hundred dollars.

He wrote *Omoo* and several books about Pacific island life and whaling experiences. They were less popular than *Typee*. He had trouble making ends meet. In debt to his publishers, he still found money to take a little house in the Berkshire Hills of Massachusetts. There he moved his family, and settled down to write what he felt would be his great book.

Hawthorne was then living and writing in a near-by village. The two men saw each other frequently. " On the hither side of Pittsfield sits Herman Melville," Hawthorne wrote, " shaping out the gigantic conception of his ' White Whale,' while the gigantic shadow of Greylock looms upon him from his study window." There in the shadow of the great rocky hills, Melville wrote about the sea. He wrote as though this were his last book. He worked at his desk without eating until late afternoon, rose early again the next morning, walked and split firewood in the chilly dawn, hurried back to his desk and his manuscript.

He was writing a story of a great white whale named Moby Dick, and of Ahab, a sea captain who had lost a leg to the whale and had dedicated the rest of his life to hunting and killing Moby Dick. On that level *Moby Dick* is an exciting adventure story — the greatest whaling story ever written. But it is much more than that. The men on the ship are so real that a reader thinks of them as persons rather than characters. And the whale is no ordinary whale. It becomes a kind of symbol for natural forces, and the hunt is a kind of allegory for man's struggle with nature. A sense of mystery broods over the book — mysterious predictions, magical sights and sounds, strange and inexplicable happenings — as though Melville were trying to take his readers into the mystery of life itself. And through the whole book roars the sea. No American has ever put on paper so much of the feeling of the sea, its strength and mystery, poetry and beauty, danger and cruelty. Perhaps no American book ever written has in it so much sustained excitement, so much elemental terror and beauty. When critics write of it today they fall back on the words " symphony " or " epic," because it has the grandeur and freedom of music, and the sweep of heroic poetry.

It is unquestionably one of the great American books, but it fell flat on the readers of its own time. His next book was even less successful. He struggled for a while with poverty and ill health, then gave up writing as a career, and found a job in the New York customhouse. Not till long after he died was *Moby Dick* rediscovered. Then new editions were called for, people began to seek it on library shelves, and critics gave it the praise it deserved.

*Melville was born and died in the same years as Lowell (1819–1891). He was born in the year the first steamboat crossed the Atlantic. He died when trains had spanned the continent, the automobile had been patented, electric railways were in operation, and men were already working on ideas for airplanes.*

## Edgar Allan Poe    1809–1849

### TO HELEN

This is one of the earliest poems by Poe, inspired by his youthful admiration for Mrs. Jane Stith Stanard of Richmond, the mother of one of his school friends. He later identified her as "the first purely ideal love of my soul." Two lines of this poem are frequently quoted. Do you recognize them?

Helen, thy beauty is to me
　　Like those Nicean° barks of yore,
That gently, o'er a perfumed sea,
　　The weary, wayworn wanderer bore
　　To his own native shore.　　　　5

On desperate seas long wont to roam,
　　Thy hyacinth° hair, thy classic face,
Thy Naiad° airs have brought me home
　　To the glory that was Greece
　　And the grandeur that was Rome.　10

Lo! in yon brilliant window niche
How statuelike I see thee stand,

2. **Nicean** (nī-sē′ăn): pertaining to Nicea, a town of Asia Minor. Poe probably had no reason for referring to this town especially, but chose the word for its sound and its suggestion of a picturesque ancient ship. 7. **hyacinth:** a favorite adjective for hair in the old Greek epics was "hyacinthine," usually meaning beautiful and curling. 8. **Naiad** (nā′ăd): in Greek mythology, a water nymph.

The agate lamp within thy hand!
　　Ah, Psyche,° from the regions which
　　Are Holy Land!　　　　　　　15

14. **Psyche** (sī′kē): the Greek word for "soul" or "mind," derived from the myth of the Greek maiden beloved of Cupid. Poe uses the word again in "Ulalume," page 525.

### THE BELLS

This is as pure an example of a "sound" poem as there is in our language. Here Poe reproduces the tonal effects of the silver, golden, brazen, and iron bells, largely by choice of consonants combined with certain vowels. One of his favorite devices is onomatopoeia (ŏn-ō-măt-ō-pē′yȧ), the use of a word whose sound suggests its meaning, such as *tintinnabulation*.

It is interesting to note that the first version of this poem had only eighteen lines and included only the silver and iron bells, both meagerly described. During a period of almost two years Poe revised it several times before it reached its present complete state. This is a good illustration of the gradual growth of a poem in a poet's mind.

I

Hear the sledges with the bells,
　　Silver bells!
What a world of merriment their melody foretells!
　　How they tinkle, tinkle, tinkle,
　　　　In the icy air of night!　　　　5
　　While the stars, that oversprinkle
　　All the heavens, seem to twinkle
　　　　With a crystalline delight;
　　Keeping time, time, time,
　　　　In a sort of runic° rhyme,　　10
To the tintinnabulation that so musically wells
　　From the bells, bells, bells, bells,
　　　　Bells, bells, bells —
　　From the jingling and the tinkling of the bells.

10. **runic** (rōō′nĭk): pertaining to runes, letters in an ancient alphabet, used in the writing of ancient Teutonic poetry; hence, strange, magical.

II

Hear the mellow wedding bells, 15
　Golden bells!
What a world of happiness their harmony
　　foretells!
Through the balmy air of night
How they ring out their delight!
　From the molten-golden notes, 20
　And all in tune,
What a liquid ditty floats
To the turtledove that listens, while she
　　gloats
　On the moon!
Oh, from out the sounding cells, 25
What a gush of euphony voluminously
　　wells!
　How it swells!
　How it dwells
On the future! how it tells
Of the rapture that impels 30
To the swinging and the ringing
Of the bells, bells, bells,
Of the bells, bells, bells, bells,
　Bells, bells, bells —
To the rhyming and the chiming of the
　　bells! 35

III

Hear the loud alarum bells,
　Brazen bells!
What a tale of terror, now, their turbulency
　　tells!
In the startled ear of night
How they scream out their affright!
　Too much horrified to speak, 41
　They can only shriek, shriek,
　Out of tune,
In a clamorous appealing to the mercy of
　　the fire,
In a mad expostulation with the deaf and
　　frantic fire, 45
　Leaping higher, higher, higher,
　With a desperate desire,
And a resolute endeavor
Now — now to sit or never,
By the side of the pale-faced moon. 50
　Oh, the bells, bells, bells!
What a tale their terror tells
　Of despair!
How they clang, and clash, and roar!

What a horror they outpour 55
On the bosom of the palpitating air!
　Yet the ear it fully knows,
　　By the twanging
　　And the clanging,
　How the danger ebbs and flows;
Yet the ear distinctly tells, 61
　　In the jangling
　　And the wrangling,
How the danger sinks and swells —
By the sinking or the swelling in the anger
　　of the bells, 65
　Of the bells,
Of the bells, bells, bells, bells,
　Bells, bells, bells —
In the clamor and the clangor of the bells!

IV

Hear the tolling of the bells, 70
　Iron bells!
What a world of solemn thought their mon-
　　ody° compels!
In the silence of the night
How we shiver with affright
At the melancholy menace of their
　　tone! 75
For every sound that floats
From the rust within their throats
　Is a groan.
And the people — ah, the people,
They that dwell up in the steeple, 80
　All alone,
And who tolling, tolling, tolling
　In that muffled monotone,
Feel a glory in so rolling
　On the human heart a stone — 85
They are neither man nor woman,
They are neither brute nor human,
　They are ghouls:°
And their king it is who tolls;
And he rolls, rolls, rolls, 90
　Rolls
　A paean from the bells;
And his merry bosom swells
With the paean of the bells,

72. **monody** (mŏn′ô-dĭ): a type of music carried by one voice. In ancient Greek times a
monody was sung as a dirge or funeral song;
hence, the word suggests sorrow and tragedy.
88. **ghouls** (gōōlz): imaginary evil creatures
reputed to rob graves and eat the corpses.

And he dances, and he yells:    95
Keeping time, time, time,
In a sort of runic rhyme,
    To the paean of the bells,
    Of the bells:
Keeping time, time, time,    100
In a sort of runic rhyme,
    To the throbbing of the bells,
Of the bells, bells, bells —
    To the sobbing of the bells;

Keeping time, time, time,    105
    As he knells, knells, knells,
In a happy runic rhyme,
    To the rolling of the bells,
Of the bells, bells, bells:
    To the tolling of the bells,    110
Of the bells, bells, bells, bells,
    Bells, bells, bells —
To the moaning and the groaning of the
    bells.

## THE RAVEN

Poe had very definite beliefs as to the nature of poetry — that its essence should be beauty and that sadness was the mood most in keeping with poetic beauty. Therefore, he said there was no subject more fitting for poetry than the death of a beautiful woman. Uninformed persons have sometimes thought that this poem grew out of Poe's sorrow for the death of his own wife; but unfortunately for that theory, the poem was published almost two years before his wife died. Since she was an invalid for many years, however, there must have been a dread in Poe's mind of losing her which stamped its impress upon the quality of the poem. Many of the effects of the poem were built up quite deliberately, Poe tells us, by the use of sonorous words, alliteration, internal rhyme, and repetition.

Once upon a midnight dreary, while I pondered, weak and weary,
Over many a quaint and curious volume of forgotten lore —
While I nodded, nearly napping, suddenly there came a tapping,
As of someone gently rapping, rapping at my chamber door.
" 'Tis some visitor," I muttered, " tapping at my chamber door:    5
    Only this and nothing more."

Ah, distinctly I remember it was in the bleak December,
And each separate dying ember wrought its ghost upon the floor.
Eagerly I wished the morrow; — vainly I had sought to borrow
From my books surcease of sorrow — sorrow for the lost Lenore,    10
For the rare and radiant maiden whom the angels name Lenore:
    Nameless here forevermore.

And the silken sad uncertain rustling of each purple curtain
Thrilled me — filled me with fantastic terrors never felt before;
So that now, to still the beating of my heart, I stood repeating,    15
" 'Tis some visitor entreating entrance at my chamber door,
Some late visitor entreating entrance at my chamber door:
    This it is and nothing more."

Presently my soul grew stronger; hesitating then no longer,
" Sir," said I, " or Madam, truly your forgiveness I implore;    20
But the fact is I was napping, and so gently you came rapping,
And so faintly you came tapping, tapping at my chamber door,
That I scarce was sure I heard you " — here I opened wide the door —
    Darkness there and nothing more.

Deep into that darkness peering, long I stood there wondering, fearing,    25
Doubting, dreaming dreams no mortal ever dared to dream before;
But the silence was unbroken, and the stillness gave no token,
And the only word there spoken was the whispered word, " Lenore? "
This I whispered, and an echo murmured back the word, " Lenore ":
    Merely this and nothing more.    30

Back into the chamber turning, all my soul within me burning,
Soon again I heard a tapping somewhat louder than before.
" Surely," said I, " surely that is something at my window lattice;
Let me see, then, what thereat is, and this mystery explore:
Let my heart be still a moment and this mystery explore:    35
    'Tis the wind and nothing more."

Open here I flung the shutter, when, with many a flirt and flutter,
In there stepped a stately Raven of the saintly days of yore.
Not the least obeisance made he; not a minute stopped or stayed he;
But, with mien of lord or lady, perched above my chamber door,    40
Perched upon a bust of Pallas° just above my chamber door:
    Perched, and sat, and nothing more.

Then this ebony bird beguiling my sad fancy into smiling
By the grave and stern decorum of the countenance it wore —
" Though thy crest be shorn and shaven, thou," I said, " art sure no craven,    45
Ghastly grim and ancient Raven wandering from the nightly shore:
Tell me what thy lordly name is on the night's Plutonian° shore! "
    Quoth the Raven, " Nevermore."

Much I marveled this ungainly fowl to hear discourse so plainly,
Though its answer little meaning — little relevancy bore;    50
For we cannot help agreeing that no living human being
Ever yet was blessed with seeing bird above his chamber door,
Bird or beast upon the sculptured bust above his chamber door,
    With such name as " Nevermore."

But the Raven, sitting lonely on the placid bust, spoke only    55
That one word, as if his soul in that one word he did outpour.
Nothing further then he uttered, not a feather then he fluttered,
Till I scarcely more than muttered — " Other friends have flown before;
On the morrow *he* will leave me, as my hopes have flown before."
    Then the bird said, " Nevermore."    60

Startled at the stillness broken by reply so aptly spoken,
" Doubtless," said I, " what it utters is its only stock and store,
Caught from some unhappy master whom unmerciful disaster
Followed fast and followed faster till his songs one burden bore:
Till the dirges of his hope that melancholy burden bore    65
    Of ' Never — nevermore.' "

41. **Pallas** (păl′ăs): Pallas Athene, Greek goddess of wisdom, called Minerva by the Romans.
47. **Plutonian** (plōō-tō′nĭ-ăn): referring to Pluto, the god who in Greek mythology presided over the regions of the dead.

But the Raven still beguiling all my fancy into smiling,
Straight I wheeled a cushioned seat in front of bird and bust and door;
Then, upon the velvet sinking, I betook myself to linking
Fancy unto fancy, thinking what this ominous bird of yore,                    70
What this grim, ungainly, ghastly, gaunt, and ominous bird of yore
    Meant in croaking " Nevermore."

This I sat engaged in guessing, but no syllable expressing
To the fowl whose fiery eyes now burned into my bosom's core;
This and more I sat divining, with my head at ease reclining             75
On the cushion's velvet lining that the lamplight gloated o'er,
But whose velvet violet lining with the lamplight gloating o'er,
    *She* shall press, ah, nevermore!

Then, methought, the air grew denser, perfumed from an unseen censer
Swung by seraphim whose footfalls tinkled on the tufted floor.            80
" Wretch," I cried, " thy God hath lent thee — by these angels he hath sent thee
Respite — respite and nepenthe° from thy memories of Lenore!
Quaff, oh quaff this kind nepenthe, and forget this lost Lenore! "
    Quoth the Raven, " Nevermore."

" Prophet! " said I, " thing of evil — prophet still, if bird or devil!       85
Whether tempter sent, or whether tempest tossed thee here ashore,
Desolate yet all undaunted, on this desert land enchanted —
On this home by horror haunted — tell me truly, I implore:
Is there — *is* there balm in Gilead?° — tell me — tell me, I implore! "
    Quoth the Raven, " Nevermore."                                  90

" Prophet! " said I, " thing of evil — prophet still, if bird or devil!
By that heaven that bends above us, by that God we both adore,
Tell this soul with sorrow laden if, within the distant Aidenn,°
It shall clasp a sainted maiden whom the angels name Lenore:
Clasp a rare and radiant maiden whom the angels name Lenore! "               95
    Quoth the Raven, " Nevermore."

" Be that word our sign of parting, bird or fiend! " I shrieked, upstarting:
" Get thee back into the tempest and the night's Plutonian shore!
Leave no black plume as a token of that lie thy soul hath spoken!
Leave my loneliness unbroken! quit the bust above my door!                  100
Take thy beak from out my heart, and take thy form from off my door! "
    Quoth the Raven, " Nevermore."

And the Raven, never flitting, still is sitting, still is sitting
On the pallid bust of Pallas just above my chamber door;
And his eyes have all the seeming of a demon's that is dreaming,             105
And the lamplight o'er him streaming throws his shadow on the floor:
And my soul from out that shadow that lies floating on the floor
    Shall be lifted — nevermore!

---

82. nepenthe (nē-pĕn'thĕ): a drug that destroys pain and brings forgetfulness. 89. **balm in Gilead**
(gĭl'ē-ăd): a healing lotion made in Gilead, a part of ancient Palestine (Jer. 8:22). It has become
a common expression meaning relief for affliction. 93. **Aidenn** (ā'dĕn): from the Arabic for Eden.

## ULALUME *

Here is a poem that really did follow the death of Poe's wife, for it was published before the first anniversary of her loss after he had suffered a critical illness. It suggests a deeply despairing and almost disordered mind. Do not try to understand the exact meaning of every line, for it has baffled even the critics. Read it rather for the remarkable creation of a mood and the sonorous roll of the lines.

The skies they were ashen and sober;
  The leaves they were crispèd and sere —
  The leaves they were withering and
    sere;
It was night in the lonesome October
  Of my most immemorial year;   5
It was hard by the dim lake of Auber,°
  In the misty mid-region of Weir° —
It was down by the dank tarn of Auber,
  In the ghoul-haunted woodland of Weir.

Here once, through an alley Titanic°   10
  Of cypress,° I roamed with my Soul —
  Of cypress, with Psyche,° my Soul.
These were days when my heart was vol-
    canic
  As the scoriac rivers that roll —
  As the lavas that restlessly roll   15
Their sulphurous currents down Yaanek°
  In the ultimate climes of the pole,
That groan as they roll down Mount
    Yaanek
  In the realms of the boreal pole.

Our talk had been serious and sober,   20
  But our thoughts they were palsied and
    sere,
  Our memories were treacherous and sere,
For we knew not the month was October,
  And we marked not the night of the
    year —
  (Ah, night of all nights in the year!)   25

We noted not the dim lake of Auber
  (Though once we had journeyed down
    here),
Remembered not the dank tarn of Auber,
  Nor the ghoul-haunted woodland of
    Weir.

And now, as the night was senescent   30
  And star dials pointed to morn,
  As the star dials hinted of morn,
At the end of our path a liquescent
  And nebulous luster was born,
Out of which a miraculous crescent   35
  Arose with a duplicate horn —
Astarte's° bediamonded crescent
  Distinct with its duplicate horn.

And I said — " She is warmer than Dian:°
  She rolls through an ether of sighs,   40
  She revels in a region of sighs:
She has seen that the tears are not dry on
  These cheeks, where the worm never dies,
And has come past the star of the Lion°
  To point us the path to the skies —   45
  To the Lethean° peace of the skies:
Come up, in despite of the Lion,
  To shine on us with her bright eyes:
Come up through the lair of the Lion,
  With love in her luminous eyes."   50

But Psyche, uplifting her finger,
  Said — " Sadly this star I mistrust,
  Her pallor I strangely mistrust:
Oh, hasten! — oh, let us not linger!
  Oh, fly — let us fly! — for we must."
In terror she spoke, letting sink her   56
  Wings till they trailed in the dust;
In agony sobbed, letting sink her
  Plumes till they trailed in the dust,
  Till they sorrowfully trailed in the
    dust.   60

I replied — " This is nothing but dream-
    ing:
  Let us on by this tremulous light!

* Ulalume (ū-là-lōōm'). 6, 7, 16. Auber (ô'bēr) ... Weir (wēr) ... Yaanek (yä'nĕk): These are all imaginary names made up by Poe for their sound and suggestive effect. 10. Titanic (tī-tăn'ĭk): referring to the Titans, a race of giants in Greek mythology. Here it suggests vastness. 11. cypress: a tree symbolizing mourning because so frequently planted in graveyards. 12. Psyche (sī'kē): See note on page 520.

37. Astarte (ăs-tär'tē): the Phoenician goddess of the moon. 39. Dian: Diana, the Roman goddess of the moon. 44. Lion: a northern constellation pictured as a lion. 46. Lethean (lē'thē-ăn for the rhythm, but usually lē-thē'ăn): referring to Lethe, the river of forgetfulness in the Greek regions of the dead.

Let us bathe in this crystalline light!
Its sibyllic° splendor is beaming
  With hope and in beauty tonight:   65
  See, it flickers up the sky through the
    night!
Ah, we safely may trust to its gleaming,
  And be sure it will lead us aright:
We safely may trust to a gleaming
  That cannot but guide us aright,   70
  Since it flickers up to heaven through the
    night."

Thus I pacified Psyche and kissed her,
  And tempted her out of her gloom,
  And conquered her scruples and gloom;
And we passed to the end of the vista,  75
  But were stopped by the door of a tomb,
  By the door of a legended tomb;
And I said — "What is written, sweet
    sister,
  On the door of this legended tomb? "
  She replied — " Ulalume — Ulalume —
  'Tis the vault of thy lost Ulalume! "  81

Then my heart it grew ashen and sober
  As the leaves that were crispèd and sere,
  As the leaves that were withering and
    sere,
And I cried — " It was surely October  85
  On *this* very night of last year
  That I journeyed — I journeyed down
    here,
  That I brought a dread burden down
    here:
  On this night of all nights in the year,
  Ah, what demon has tempted me here?
Well I know, now, this dim lake of
    Auber —   91
  This misty mid-region of Weir —
Well I know, now, this dank tarn of Auber,
  This ghoul-haunted woodland of Weir."

64. **sibyllic** (sĭ-bĭl'ĭk): pertaining to a sibyl,
in Greek mythology a prophetess.

## ANNABEL LEE

This and " The Raven " are probably the
two best known poems by Poe. One of his last
writings, it probably refers to his wife. This
poem has rhythmic beauty and the simplicity

of true sorrow, and therefore makes a more
general appeal than the tantalizing confusions
of " Ulalume."

It was many and many a year ago,
  In a kingdom by the sea,
That a maiden there lived whom you may
    know
  By the name of Annabel Lee;
And this maiden she lived with no other
    thought   5
  Than to love and be loved by me.

*She* was a child and *I* was a child,
  In this kingdom by the sea;
But we loved with a love that was more than
    love,
  I and my Annabel Lee;   10
With a love that the wingèd seraphs of
    heaven
  Coveted her and me.

And this was the reason that, long ago,
  In this kingdom by the sea,
A wind blew out of a cloud, chilling   15
  My beautiful Annabel Lee;
So that her highborn kinsmen came
  And bore her away from me,
To shut her up in a sepulcher
  In this kingdom by the sea.   20

The angels, not half so happy in heaven,
  Went envying her and me;
Yes, that was the reason (as all men know,
  In this kingdom by the sea)
That the wind came out of the cloud by
    night,   25
  Chilling and killing my Annabel Lee.

But our love it was stronger by far than
    the love
  Of those who were older than we,
  Of many far wiser than we;
And neither the angels in heaven above,
  Nor the demons down under the sea,  31
Can ever dissever my soul from the soul
  Of the beautiful Annabel Lee:

For the moon never beams, without bring-
    ing me dreams
  Of the beautiful Annabel Lee;   35
And the stars never rise, but I feel the
    bright eyes

Of the beautiful Annabel Lee;
And so, all the night-tide, I lie down by the
  side
Of my darling, my darling, my life and my
  bride
  In her sepulcher there by the sea,    40
  In her tomb by the sounding sea.

## ELDORADO

"Eldorado" was one of the last poems written by Poe, and strikes a more vigorous note than the preceding ones. He had once more made severe resolutions about his habits and was planning to be married a second time. It is possible that he may have had definite visions of an ideal toward which he was striving.

        Gaily bedight,
        A gallant knight,
    In sunshine and in shadow,
        Had journey long,
        Singing a song,                5
    In search of Eldorado.

        But he grew old,
        This knight so bold,
    And o'er his heart a shadow
        Fell as he found             10
        No spot of ground
    That looked like Eldorado.

        And, as his strength
        Failed him at length,
    He met a pilgrim shadow;         15
        "Shadow," said he,
        "Where can it be,
    This land of Eldorado?"

        "Over the Mountains
        Of the Moon,                 20
    Down the Valley of the Shadow,
        Ride, boldly ride,"
        The shade replied,
    "If you seek for Eldorado!"

6. **Eldorado** (ĕl-dō-rä′dŏ; in this poem may be pronounced to rhyme with *shadow*): literally, "the gilded," an imaginary place abounding in gold, supposed by the sixteenth-century Spaniards to be located in America. It has come to stand for any place abounding in wealth and opportunity.

## Suggestions for Study
## of Poe's Poems

THE BELLS

1. Since this is pre-eminently a sound poem, the best way to study it is to read it aloud. Reading it with the eye alone is like reading a piece of sheet music in the same way.

2. Observe carefully the use of the liquid consonants — *l*, *m*, *n*. What other consonants appear with notable frequency? What difference can you note in the use of the vowels for the different bells? How does this selection of vowels and consonants affect the general mood and sound of the four different sections?

3. Find good examples of assonance, alliteration, onomatopoeic words, many-syllabled words, effective repetition of words and phrases.

4. Vocabulary: crystalline (8), tintinnabulation (11), euphony (26), expostulation (45), palpitating (55).

THE RAVEN

5. What atmosphere and mood are established at the very beginning of the poem?

6. From the few effective details given, picture to yourself the kind of room in which this story is set. Contrast this with the bare cottage at Fordham where Poe's own wife died two years later.

7. What in the Raven's behavior makes the poem unusually gruesome and depressing? Of what in life is the Raven a symbol?

8. Find striking examples throughout of Poe's devices: internal rhyme, alliteration, and repetition.

9. Vocabulary: surcease (10), fantastic (14), obeisance (39), mien (40), decorum (44), relevancy (50), ominous (70), censer (79), seraphim (80), pallid (104).

ULALUME

10. How do the time of the year, the time of the night, and the surroundings of nature all contribute to the mood of the poem? How does the moonlight betray the false hope that the poet had placed in it? What warning had he that the place was not a good one to be in?

11. What mood is suggested by the very sound of the name Ulalume? Look up the word *ululate* in the dictionary to find its present meaning and derivation. Does this throw any added light on Poe's choice of the name?

12. Select lines or passages in which the

sound particularly appeals to you. For melodious flow and sound effects how do you think it compares with " The Bells," " The Raven," and " Annabel Lee "?

13. Vocabulary: sere (2), immemorial (5), dank tarn (8), volcanic (13), scoriac (14), ultimate (17), boreal (19), senescent (30), liquescent (33), nebulous (34), luminous (50).

### ANNABEL LEE

14. Compare this with the other two poems on the death of a beautiful woman — " The Raven " and " Ulalume " — as to emotional appeal, simplicity of style, and use of sound effects. Which of the three do you prefer? Why?

15. This poem was printed more than two years after the death of Poe's wife, and most critics think it refers to her. It was also claimed, however, by Elmira Shelton, a sweetheart of Poe's youth, whose family had broken up their early love affair. Poe was engaged to her again just before he died. What lines in the poem would have different interpretations according to each of these two possibilities?

### ELDORADO

16. If this little tale is applied to life, what might Eldorado stand for?

17. There are three possible interpretations of this poem: (a) You can never reach Eldorado, for there is no such place; (b) whether you find it or not, live courageously; (c) the only way you can find it is by living courageously. The first is cynical; the second, brave; the third, inspirational. Which do you prefer?

## Choral Reading

Poe's poems lend themselves particularly well to choral reading by the class or part of the class. If you wish to try this, here are a few simple directions: Divide your voices according to high, medium, and low voices, somewhat as in a singing choir. Vary the effects of the reading by having certain passages read by a single voice or a single range of voices in contrast to passages read by the entire group. " The Bells " is especially good to begin with as the differences are so obvious, beginning with the high voices and dropping to the low voices. Vary the volume as well as the pitch. Some passages may be read lightly; others, with the emphasis of the entire chorus.

Have a leader direct the reading, and see what interesting voice music you can produce.

See also the suggestions for choral reading of Lindsay's poems (page 313).

## For Your Vocabulary

CONNOTATION. An interesting part of word study is connotation, the secondary meanings or associations a word has, in addition to its essential or simplest meaning. Poe uses two words for songs which have very different connotation, *dirge* in " The Raven " (line 65) and *paean* in " The Bells " (line 92). A *dirge* (dûrj) is a funeral song, a wail for the dead. A *paean* (pē'ăn) is a triumphant song of exultation or praise. Look at the connotation of other words for songs in this book. O. Henry's Soapy was moved to reform by listening to an *anthem*, a hymn of praise, devotion, or patriotism. We have religious *anthems* and a national *anthem*. The light ballad " The Battle of the Kegs " is called a *ditty* (line 2). You will find Thoreau speaking of a *requiem* (rē'kwĭ-ĕm), a hymn in honor of the dead, as compared with the wail of the *dirge*. Walt Whitman calls a poem " The Carol of Death," though a *carol* is a happy, joyous song, like a Christmas carol, because he is presenting death as a bringer of peace and rest, not as a sorrow, and it is the paradoxical (remember that one?) connotations of *carol* and *death* that make the title striking.

## THE PIT AND THE PENDULUM

Poe had definite ideas about how a short story should be written, and these he practiced consistently. He said that a literary artist deliberately conceives " a certain unique or single effect to be wrought out " and " then combines such incidents as may best aid him in establishing his preconceived effect." He believed that a story should be short because " during the hour of perusal the soul of the reader is at the writer's control." He thought that an author had failed in his first step " if his very initial sentence tend not to the outbringing of this effect." These are Poe's great contributions to the development of the American short story: brevity of treatment and the single effect maintained from the opening sentence to the end. Observe how Poe carries out his ideas in the two following stories.

The first is a story of the days of the Spanish Inquisition, a court renowned for cruel and unrelenting pursuit of any who differed in religious or political belief from those in power. Poe has found in this situation the elements of horror. He is not concerned with informing us about the historical facts of the Inquisition, or of the accusations against the prisoner, or any other introduction such as an earlier writer might have used. He thrusts us at once into the mind of the prisoner as he hears his death sentence pronounced. Never throughout the story do we leave that mind, and so we actually *feel* the horror of what happens to him.

I was sick — sick unto death with that long agony; and when they at length unbound me, and I was permitted to sit, I felt that my senses were leaving me. The sentence — the dread sentence of death — was the last of distinct accentuation which reached my ears. After that, the sound of the inquisitorial voices seemed merged in one dreamy indeterminate hum. It conveyed to my soul the idea of *revolution* — perhaps from its association in fancy with the burr of a mill-wheel. This only for a brief period; for presently I heard no more. Yet, for a while, I saw; but with how terrible an exaggeration! I saw the lips of the black-robed judges. They appeared to me white — whiter than the sheet upon which I trace these words — and thin even to grotesqueness; thin with the intensity of their expression of firmness — of immovable resolution — of stern contempt of human torture. I saw that the decrees of what to me was fate were still issuing from those lips. I saw them writhe with a deadly locution. I saw them fashion the syllables of my name; and I shuddered because no sound succeeded. I saw, too, for a few moments of delirious horror, the soft and nearly imperceptible waving of the sable draperies which enwrapped the walls of the apartment. And then my vision fell upon the seven tall candles upon the table. At first they wore the aspect of charity, and seemed white slender angels who would save me; but then, all at once, there came a most deadly nausea over my spirit, and I felt

EDGAR ALLAN POE. In his short life he wrote better poetry, better short stories, better criticism than had been written in America up to his time. (Brown Brothers)

every fiber in my frame thrill as if I had touched the wire of a galvanic battery, while the angel forms became meaningless specters, with heads of flame, and I saw that from them there would be no help. And then there stole into my fancy, like a rich musical note, the thought of what sweet rest there must be in the grave. The thought came gently and stealthily, and it seemed long before it attained full appreciation; but just as my spirit came at length properly to feel and entertain it, the figures of the judges vanished, as if magically, from before me; the tall candles sank into nothingness; their flames went out utterly; the blackness of darkness supervened; all sensations appeared swallowed up in a mad rushing descent as of the soul into Hades. Then silence, and stillness, and night were the universe.

I had swooned; but still will not say that all of consciousness was lost. What of it there remained I will not attempt to define, or even to describe; yet all was not lost. In the deepest slumber — no! In delirium — no! In a swoon — no! In death — no! even in the grave all *is not* lost. Else there is no immortality for man. . . .

These shadows of memory tell, indistinctly, of tall figures that lifted and bore me in silence down — down — still down — till a hideous dizziness oppressed me at the mere idea of the interminableness of the descent. They tell also of a vague horror at my heart, on account of that heart's unnatural stillness. Then comes a sense of sudden motionlessness throughout all things; as if those who bore me (a ghastly train!) had outrun, in their descent, the limits of the limitless, and paused from the wearisomeness of their toil. After this I call to mind flatness and dampness; and then all is *madness* — the madness of a memory which busies itself among forbidden things.

Very suddenly there came back to my soul motion and sound — the tumultuous motion of the heart, and, in my ears, the sound of its beating. Then a pause in which all is blank. Then again sound, and motion, and touch — a tingling sensation pervading my frame. Then the mere consciousness of existence, without thought — a condition which lasted long. Then, very suddenly, *thought,* and shuddering terror, and earnest endeavor to comprehend my true state. Then a strong desire to lapse into insensibility. Then a rushing revival of soul and a successful effort to move. And now a full memory of the trial, of the judges, of the sable draperies, of the sentence, of the sickness, of the swoon. Then entire forgetfulness of all that followed; of all that a later day and much earnestness of endeavor have enabled me vaguely to recall.

So far, I had not opened my eyes. I felt that I lay upon my back, unbound. I reached out my hand, and it fell heavily upon something damp and hard. There I suffered it to remain for many minutes, while I strove to imagine where and *what* I could be. I longed, yet dared not to employ my vision. I dreaded the first glance at objects around me. It was not that I feared to look upon things horrible, but that I grew aghast lest there should be *nothing* to see. At length, with a wild desperation at heart, I quickly unclosed my eyes. My worst thoughts, then, were confirmed. The blackness of eternal night encompassed me. I struggled for breath. The intensity of the darkness seemed to oppress and stifle me. The atmosphere was intolerably close. I still lay quietly, and made effort to exercise my reason. I brought to mind the inquisitorial proceedings, and attempted from that point to deduce my real condition. The sentence had passed; and it appeared to me that a very long interval of time had since elapsed. Yet not for a moment did I suppose myself actually dead. Such a supposition, notwithstanding what we read in fiction, is altogether inconsistent with real existence — but where and in what state was I? The condemned to death, I knew, perished usually at the *autos-da-fé*,[1] and one of these had been held on the very night of the day of my trial. Had I been remanded to my dungeon, to await the next sacrifice, which would not take place for many months? This I at once saw could not be. Victims had been in immediate demand. Moreover, my dungeon, as well as all the condemned cells at Toledo, had stone floors, and light was not altogether excluded.

A fearful idea now suddenly drove the blood in torrents upon my heart, and for a brief period, I once more relapsed into insensibility. Upon recovering, I at once started to my feet, trembling convulsively in every fiber. I thrust my arms wildly above and around me in all directions. I felt nothing; yet dreaded to move a step, lest I should be impeded by the walls of a *tomb*. Perspiration burst from every pore, and stood in cold big beads upon my forehead. The agony of suspense grew at length intolerable, and I cautiously moved forward, with my arms extended, and my eyes straining from their sockets, in the hope of catching

[1] **autos-da-fé** (ô'tŏz-dȧ-fāʹ): literally, acts of faith; a term used during the Inquisition for the execution or burning of heretics.

some faint ray of light. I proceeded for many paces; but still all was blackness and vacancy. I breathed more freely. It seemed evident that mine was not, at least, the most hideous of fates.

And now, as I still continued to step cautiously onward, there came thronging upon my recollection a thousand vague rumors of the horrors of Toledo. Of the dungeons there had been strange things narrated — fables I had always deemed them — but yet strange, and too ghastly to repeat, save in a whisper. Was I left to perish of starvation in this subterranean world of darkness; or what fate, perhaps even more fearful, awaited me? That the result would be death, and a death of more than customary bitterness, I knew too well the character of my judges to doubt. The mode and the hour were all that occupied or distracted me.

My outstretched hands at length encountered some solid obstruction. It was a wall, seemingly of stone masonry — very smooth, slimy, and cold. I followed it up; stepping with all the careful distrust with which certain antique narratives had inspired me. This process, however, afforded me no means of ascertaining the dimensions of my dungeon; as I might make its circuit, and return to the point whence I set out, without being aware of the fact, so perfectly uniform seemed the wall. I therefore sought the knife which had been in my pocket, when led into the inquisitorial chamber; but it was gone; my clothes had been exchanged for a wrapper of coarse serge. I had thought of forcing the blade in some minute crevice of the masonry, so as to identify my point of departure. The difficulty, nevertheless, was but trivial; although, in the disorder of my fancy, it seemed at first insuperable. I tore a part of the hem from the robe and placed the fragment at full length, and at right angles to the wall. In groping my way around the prison, I could not fail to encounter this rag upon completing the circuit. So, at least, I thought; but I had not counted upon the extent of the dungeon, or upon my own weakness.

The ground was moist and slippery. I staggered onward for some time, when I stumbled and fell. My excessive fatigue induced me to remain prostrate; and sleep soon overtook me as I lay.

Upon awaking, and stretching forth an arm, I found beside me a loaf and a pitcher with water. I was too much exhausted to reflect upon this circumstance, but ate and drank with avidity. Shortly afterward, I resumed my tour around the prison, and with much toil, came at last upon the fragment of the serge. Up to the period when I fell I had counted fifty-two paces, and upon resuming my walk, I had counted forty-eight more — when I arrived at the rag. There were in all, then, a hundred paces; and, admitting two paces to the yard, I presumed the dungeon to be fifty yards in circuit. I had met, however, with many angles in the wall, and thus I could form no guess at the shape of the vault; for vault I could not help supposing it to be.

I had little object — certainly no hope — in these researches; but a vague curiosity prompted me to continue them. Quitting the wall, I resolved to cross the area of the enclosure. At first I proceeded with extreme caution, for the floor, although seemingly of solid material, was treacherous with slime. At length, however, I took courage, and did not hesitate to step firmly; endeavoring to cross in as direct a line as possible. I had advanced some ten or twelve paces in this manner, when the remnant of the torn hem of my robe became entangled between my legs. I stepped on it, and fell violently on my face.

In the confusion attending my fall, I did not immediately apprehend a somewhat startling circumstance, which yet, in a few seconds afterward, and while I still lay prostrate, arrested my attention. It was this: my chin rested upon the floor of the prison, but my lips and the upper portion of my head, although seemingly at a less elevation than the chin, touched nothing. At the same time my forehead seemed bathed in a clammy vapor, and the peculiar smell of decayed fungus arose to my nostrils. I put forward my arm, and shuddered to find that I had fallen at the very brink of a circular pit, whose extent, of course, I had no means of ascertaining at the moment. Groping about the masonry just below the margin, I succeeded in dislodging a small fragment, and let it fall into the abyss. For many seconds I hearkened to its reverberations as it dashed against the sides of the chasm in its descent; at length there was a sullen plunge into water, succeeded by loud echoes. At the same moment there came a sound resembling the quick opening, and as rapid closing of a door overhead, while a faint gleam of light flashed suddenly through the gloom, and as suddenly faded away.

I saw clearly the doom which had been prepared for me, and congratulated myself upon the timely accident by which I had escaped. Another step before my fall, and the world had seen me no more. And the death just avoided was of that very character which I had regarded as fabulous and frivolous in the tales respecting the Inquisition. To the victims of its tyranny, there was the choice of death with its direst physical agonies, or death with its most hideous moral horrors. I had been reserved for the latter. By long suffering my nerves had been unstrung, until I trembled at the sound of my own voice, and had become in every respect a fitting subject for the species of torture which awaited me.

Shaking in every limb, I groped my way back to the wall; resolving there to perish rather than risk the terrors of the wells, of which my imagination now pictured many in various positions about the dungeon. In other conditions of mind I might have had courage to end my misery at once by a plunge into one of these abysses; but now I was the veriest of cowards. Neither could I forget what I had read of these pits — that the *sudden* extinction of life formed no part of their most horrible plan.

Agitation of spirit kept me awake for many long hours; but at length I again slumbered. Upon arousing, I found by my side, as before, a loaf and a pitcher of water. A burning thirst consumed me, and I emptied the vessel at a draught. It must have been drugged; for scarcely had I drunk, before I became irresistibly drowsy. A deep sleep fell upon me — a sleep like that of death. How long it lasted, of course, I know not; but when, once again, I unclosed my eyes, the objects around me were visible. By a wild sulphurous luster, the origin of which I could not at first determine, I was enabled to see the extent and aspect of the prison.

In its size I had been greatly mistaken. The whole circuit of its walls did not exceed twenty-five yards. For some minutes this fact occasioned me a world of vain trouble; vain indeed! for what could be of less importance, under the terrible circumstances which environed me, than the mere dimensions of my dungeon? But my soul took a wild interest in trifles, and I busied myself in endeavors to account for the error I had committed in my measurement. The truth at length flashed upon me. In my first attempt at exploration I had counted fifty-two paces, up to the period when I fell; I must then have been within a pace or two of the fragment of serge; in fact, I had nearly performed the circuit of the vault. I then slept, and upon awaking, I must have returned upon my steps — thus supposing the circuit nearly double what it actually was. My confusion of mind prevented me from observing that I began my tour with the wall to the left, and ended it with the wall to the right.

I had been deceived, too, in respect to the shape of the enclosure. In feeling my way I had found many angles, and thus deduced an idea of great irregularity; so potent is the effect of total darkness upon one arousing from lethargy or sleep! The angles were simply those of a few slight depressions, or niches, at odd intervals. The general shape of the prison was square. What I had taken for masonry seemed now to be iron, or some other metal, in huge plates, whose sutures or joints occasioned the depression. The entire surface of this metallic enclosure was rudely daubed in all the hideous and repulsive devices to which the charnel superstition of the monks has given rise. The figures of fiends in aspects of menace, with skeleton forms, and other more really fearful images, overspread and disfigured the walls. I observed that the outlines of these monstrosities were sufficiently distinct, but that the colors seemed faded and blurred, as if from the effects of a damp atmosphere. I now noticed the floor, too, which was of stone. In the center yawned the circular pit from whose jaws I had escaped; but it was the only one in the dungeon.

All this I saw indistinctly and by much effort: for my personal condition had been greatly changed during slumber. I now lay upon my back, and at full length, on a species of low framework of wood. To this I was securely bound by a long strap resembling a surcingle.[1] It passed in many convolutions about my limbs and body, leaving at liberty only my head and my left arm to such extent that I could, by dint of much exertion, supply myself with food from an earthen dish which lay by my side on the floor. I saw, to my horror, that the pitcher had been removed. I say to my horror; for I was consumed with intolerable thirst. This thirst it appeared to be the design of my persecutors to stimulate. for the food in the dish was meat pungently seasoned.

Looking upward, I surveyed the ceiling of my prison. It was some thirty or forty feet overhead, and constructed much as the side walls. In one of its panels a very singular figure riveted my whole attention. It was the painted figure of Time as he is commonly represented, save that, in lieu of a scythe, he held what, at a casual glance, I supposed to be the pictured image of a huge pendulum such as we see on antique clocks. There was something, however, in the appearance of this machine which caused me to regard it more attentively. While I gazed directly upward at it (for its position was immediately over my own) I fancied that I saw it in motion. In an instant

afterward the fancy was confirmed. Its sweep was brief, and of course slow. I watched it for some minutes, somewhat in fear, but more in wonder. Wearied at length with observing its dull movement, I turned my eyes upon the other objects in the cell.

A slight noise attracted my notice, and, looking to the floor, I saw several enormous rats traversing it. They had issued from the well, which lay just within view to my right. Even then, while I gazed, they came up in troops, hurriedly, with ravenous eyes, allured by the scent of the meat. From this it required much effort and attention to scare them away.

It might have been half an hour, perhaps even an hour (for I could take but imperfect note of time), before I again cast my eyes upward. What I then saw confounded and amazed me. The sweep of the pendulum had increased in extent by nearly a yard. As a natural consequence, its velocity was also much greater. But what mainly disturbed me was the idea that it had perceptibly *descended*. I now observed — with what horror it is needless to say — that its nether extremity was formed of a crescent of glittering steel, about a foot in length from horn to horn; the horns upward, and the under edge evidently as keen as that of a razor. Like a razor also, it seemed massy and heavy, tapering from the edge into a solid and broad structure above. It was appended to a weighty rod of brass, and the whole *hissed* as it swung through the air.

I could no longer doubt the doom prepared for me by monkish ingenuity in torture. My cognizance of the pit had become known to the inquisitorial agents — *the pit* whose horrors had been destined for so bold a recusant [2] as myself — *the pit*, typical of hell, and regarded by rumor as the Ultima Thule [3] of all their punishments. The plunge into this pit I had avoided by the merest of accidents, and I knew that surprise, or en-

---

[1] surcingle (sûr′sĭng-g'l): a belt or girth used to fasten something to a horse's back.

[2] recusant (rĕk′ū-zănt): one who refuses to comply with some established regulation. [3] Ultima Thule (ŭl′tĭ-má thū′lĕ): the northernmost part of the habitable world; hence, most extreme example.

trapment into torment, formed an important portion of all the grotesquerie of these dungeon deaths. Having failed to fall, it was no part of the demon plan to hurl me into the abyss; and thus (there being no alternative) a different and a milder destruction awaited me. Milder! I half smiled in my agony as I thought of such application of such a term.

What boots it to tell of the long, long hours of horror more than mortal, during which I counted the rushing vibrations of the steel! Inch by inch — line by line — with a descent only appreciable at intervals that seemed ages — down and still down it came! Days passed — it might have been that many days passed — ere it swept so closely over me as to fan me with its acrid breath. The odor of the sharp steel forced itself into my nostrils. I prayed — I wearied heaven with my prayer for its more speedy descent. I grew frantically mad, and struggled to force myself upward against the sweep of the fearful scimitar. And then I fell suddenly calm, and lay smiling at the glittering death, as a child at some rare bauble.

There was another interval of utter insensibility; it was brief; for, upon again lapsing into life there had been no perceptible descent in the pendulum. But it might have been long; for I knew there were demons who took note of my swoon, and who could have arrested the vibration at pleasure. Upon my recovery, too, I felt very — oh, inexpressibly sick and weak, as if through long inanition. Even amid the agonies of that period, the human nature craved food. With painful effort I outstretched my left arm as far as my bonds permitted, and took possession of the small remnant which had been spared me by the rats. As I put a portion of it within my lips, there rushed to my mind a half-formed thought of joy — of hope. Yet what business had *I* with hope? It was, as I say, a half-formed thought — man has many such which are never completed. I felt that it was of joy — of hope; but I felt also that it had perished in its formation. In vain I struggled to perfect — to

regain it. Long suffering had nearly annihilated all my ordinary powers of mind. I was an imbecile — an idiot.

The vibration of the pendulum was at right angles to my length. I saw that the crescent was designed to cross the region of the heart. It would fray the serge of my robe — it would return and repeat its operations — again — and again. Notwithstanding its terrifically wide sweep (some thirty feet or more) and the hissing vigor of its descent, sufficient to sunder these very walls of iron, still the fraying of my robe would be all that, for several minutes, it would accomplish. And at this thought I paused. I dared not go farther than this reflection. I dwelt upon it with a pertinacity of attention — as if, in so dwelling, I could arrest *here* the descent of the steel. I forced myself to ponder upon the sound of the crescent as it should pass across the garment — upon the peculiar thrilling sensation which the friction of cloth produces on the nerves. I pondered upon all this frivolity until my teeth were on edge.

Down — steadily down it crept. I took a frenzied pleasure in contrasting its downward with its lateral velocity. To the right — to the left — far and wide — with the shriek of a damned spirit; to my heart with the stealthy pace of the tiger! I alternately laughed and howled as the one or the other idea grew predominant.

Down — certainly, relentlessly down! It vibrated within three inches of my bosom! I struggled violently, furiously, to free my left arm. This was free only from the elbow to the hand. I could reach the latter, from the platter beside me, to my mouth, with great effort, but no farther. Could I have broken the fastenings above the elbow, I would have seized and attempted to arrest the pendulum. I might as well have attempted to arrest an avalanche!

Down — still unceasingly — still inevitably down! I gasped and struggled at each vibration. I shrunk convulsively at its every sweep. My eyes followed its outward or upward whirls with the eagerness of the most unmeaning despair; they closed themselves spasmodically at the descent, although death would have been a relief, oh! how unspeakable! Still I quivered in every nerve to think how slight a sinking of the machinery would precipitate that keen, glistening ax upon my bosom. It was *hope* that prompted the nerve to quiver — the frame to shrink. It was *hope* — the hope that triumphs on the rack — that whispers to the death-condemned even in the dungeons of the Inquisition.

I saw that some ten or twelve vibrations would bring the steel in actual contact with my robe, and with this observation there suddenly came over my spirit all the keen, collected calmness of despair. For the first time during many hours — or perhaps days — I *thought*. It now occurred to me that the bandage, or surcingle, which enveloped me, was *unique*. I was tied by no separate cord. The first stroke of the razor-like crescent athwart any portion of the band, would so detach it that it might be unwound from my person by means of my left hand. But how fearful, in that case, the proximity of the steel! The result of the slightest struggle how deadly! Was it likely, moreover, that the minions of the torturer had not foreseen and provided for this possibility? Was it probable that the bandage crossed my bosom in the track of the pendulum? Dreading to find my faint, and, as it seemed, my last hope frustrated, I so far elevated my head as to obtain a distinct view of my breast. The surcingle enveloped my limbs and body close in all directions — *save in the path of the destroying crescent*.

Scarcely had I dropped my head back into its original position, when there flashed upon my mind what I cannot better describe than as the unformed half of that idea of deliverance to which I have previously alluded, and of which a moiety only floated indeterminately through my brain when I raised food to my burning lips. The whole thought was now present — feeble, scarcely sane, scarcely definite — but still entire. I proceeded at once, with the nervous energy of despair, to attempt its execution.

For many hours the immediate vicinity of the low framework upon which I lay, had been literally swarming with rats. They were wild, bold, ravenous; their red eyes glaring upon me as if they waited but for motionlessness on my part to make me their prey. " To what food," I thought, " have they been accustomed in the well? "

They had devoured, in spite of all my efforts to prevent them, all but a small remnant of the contents of the dish. I had fallen into an habitual seesaw, or wave of the hand about the platter: and, at length, the unconscious uniformity of the movement deprived it of effect. In their voracity the vermin frequently fastened their sharp fangs in my fingers. With the particles of the oily and spicy viand which now remained, I thoroughly rubbed the bandage wherever I could reach it; then, raising my hand from the floor, I lay breathlessly still.

At first the ravenous animals were startled and terrified at the change — at the cessation of movement. They shrank alarmedly back; many sought the well. But this was only for a moment. I had not counted in vain upon their voracity. Observing that I remained without motion, one or two of the boldest leaped upon the framework, and smelt at the surcingle. This seemed the signal for a general rush. Forth from the well they hurried in fresh troops. They clung to the wood — they overran it, and leaped in hundreds upon my person. The measured movement of the pendulum disturbed them not at all. Avoiding its strokes they busied themselves with the anointed bandage. They pressed — they swarmed upon me in ever accumulating heaps. They writhed upon my throat; their cold lips sought my own; I was half stifled by their thronging pressure; disgust, for which the world has no name, swelled my bosom, and chilled, with a heavy clamminess, my heart. Yet one minute, and I felt that the struggle would be over. Plainly I perceived the loosening of the bandage. I knew that in more than one place it must be already severed. With a more than human resolution I lay *still*.

Nor had I erred in my calculations — nor had I endured in vain. I at length felt that I was *free*. The surcingle hung in ribands from my body. But the stroke of the pendulum already pressed upon my bosom. It had divided the serge of the robe. It had cut through the linen beneath. Twice again it swung, and a sharp sense of pain shot through every nerve. But the moment of escape had arrived. At a wave of my hand my deliverers hurried tumultuously away. With a steady movement — cautious, sidelong, shrinking, and slow — I slid from the embrace of the bandage and beyond the reach of the scimitar. For the moment, at least, *I was free.*

Free! — and in the grasp of the Inquisition! I had scarcely stepped from my wooden bed of horror upon the stone floor of the prison, when the motion of the hellish machine ceased and I beheld it drawn up, by some invisible force, through the ceiling. This was a lesson which I took desperately to heart. My every motion was undoubtedly watched. Free! — I had but escaped death in one form of agony, to be delivered unto worse than death in some other. With that thought I rolled my eyes nervously around on the barriers of iron that hemmed me in. Something unusual — some change which, at first, I could not appreciate distinctly — it was obvious, had taken place in the apartment. For many minutes of a dreamy and trembling abstraction, I busied myself in vain, unconnected conjecture. During this period, I became aware, for the first time, of the origin of the sulphurous light which illumined the cell. It proceeded from a fissure, about half an inch in width, extending entirely around the prison at the base of the walls, which thus appeared, and were, completely separated from the floor. I endeavored, but of course in vain, to look through the aperture.

As I arose from the attempt, the mystery of the alteration in the chamber broke at once upon my understanding. I have observed that, although the outlines of the figures upon the walls were sufficiently distinct, yet the colors seemed blurred and indefinite. These colors had now assumed, and were momentarily assuming, a startling and most intense brilliancy, that gave to the spectral and fiendish portraitures an aspect that might have thrilled even firmer nerves than my own. Demon eyes, of a wild and ghastly vivacity, glared upon me in a thousand directions, where none had been visible before, and gleamed with the lurid luster of a fire that I could not force my imagination to regard as unreal.

*Unreal!* — Even while I breathed there came to my nostrils the breath of the vapor of heated iron! A suffocating odor pervaded the prison! A deeper glow settled each moment in the eyes that glared at my agonies! A richer tint of crimson diffused itself over the pictured horrors of blood. I panted! I gasped for breath! There could be no doubt of the design of my tormentors — oh! most unrelenting! oh! most demoniac of men! I shrank from the glowing metal to the center of the cell. Amid the thought of the fiery destruction that impended, the idea of the coolness of the well came over my soul like balm. I rushed to its deadly brink. I threw my straining vision below. The glare from the enkindled roof illumined its inmost recesses. Yet, for a wild moment, did my spirit refuse to comprehend the meaning of what I saw. At length it forced — it wrestled its way into my soul — it burned itself in upon my shuddering reason. — Oh! for a voice to speak! — oh! horror! — oh! any horror but this! With a shriek, I rushed from the margin, and buried my face in my hands — weeping bitterly.

The heat rapidly increased, and once again I looked up, shuddering as with a fit of the ague. There had been a second change in the cell — and now the change was obviously in the *form*. As before, it was in vain that I, at first, endeavored to appreciate or understand what was taking place. But not long was I left in doubt. The Inquisitorial vengeance had been hurried by my twofold escape, and there was to be no more dallying with the King of Terrors. The room had been square. I saw that two of its iron angles were now acute — two, consequently, obtuse. The fearful difference quickly increased with a low rumbling or moaning sound. In an instant the apartment had shifted its form into that of a lozenge.[1] But the alteration stopped not here — I neither hoped nor desired it to stop. I could have clasped the red walls to my bosom as a garment of eternal peace. " Death," I said, " any death but that of the pit! " Fool! might I have not known that *into the pit* it was the object of the burning iron to urge me? Could I resist its glow? or, if even that, could I withstand its pressure? And now, flatter and flatter grew the lozenge, with a rapidity that left me no time for contemplation. Its center, and of course, its greatest width, came just over the yawning gulf. I shrank back — but the closing walls pressed me resistlessly onward. At length for my seared and writhing body there was no longer an inch of foothold on the firm floor of the prison. I struggled no more, but the agony of my soul found vent in one loud, long, and final scream of despair. I felt that I tottered upon the brink — I averted my eyes —

There was a discordant hum of human voices! There was a loud blast as of many trumpets! There was a harsh grating as of a thousand thunders! The fiery walls rushed back! An outstretched arm caught my own as I fell, fainting, into the abyss. It was that of General Lasalle.

The French army had entered Toledo. The Inquisition was in the hands of its enemies.

## THE TELL-TALE HEART

This story is shorter than " The Pit and the Pendulum " but an even greater test of Poe's skill, for the cause of the horror comes from *within* the man's mind rather than being imposed from the outside. You can read this story in less than half an hour. Choose a time when you are sure to be free from interruption. Breaking into the story would be as unfair to Poe as an interruption to a violinist who is building up the emotional power of a beautiful sonata. Each requires your complete and unbroken attention to accomplish his purpose. This is no story for a nervous person to read at night. Poe is trying to make you feel horror at the insanity which leads to murder.

[1] lozenge (lŏz'ĕnj): a diamond-shaped figure.

Notice how the *first* sentence gives you a hint. Gradually you become more and more certain that the speaker is a maniac. Finally in a climax of frenzy he drives himself to confession.

True! — nervous — very, very dreadfully nervous I had been and am; but why *will* you say that I am mad? The disease had sharpened my senses — not destroyed — not dulled them. Above all was the sense of hearing acute. I heard all things in the heaven and in the earth. I heard many things in hell. How, then, am I mad? Hearken! and observe how healthily — how calmly I can tell you the whole story.

It is impossible to say how first the idea entered my brain; but once conceived, it haunted me day and night. Object there was none. Passion there was none. I loved the old man. He had never wronged me. He had never given me insult. For his gold I had no desire. I think it was his eye! yes, it was this! He had the eye of a vulture — a pale blue eye, with a film over it. Whenever it fell upon me, my blood ran cold; and so by degrees — very gradually — I made up my mind to take the life of the old man, and thus rid myself of the eye forever.

Now this is the point. You fancy me mad. Madmen know nothing. But you should have seen *me.* You should have seen how wisely I proceeded — with what caution — with what foresight — with what dissimulation I went to work! I was never kinder to the old man than during the whole week before I killed him. And every night, about midnight, I turned the latch of his door and opened it — ah, so gently! And then, when I had made an opening sufficient for my head, I put in a dark lantern, all closed, closed, so that no light shone out, and then I thrust in my head. Oh, you would have laughed to see how cunningly I thrust it in! I moved it slowly — very, very slowly, so that I might not disturb the old man's sleep. It took me an hour to place my whole head within the opening so far that I could see him as he lay upon his bed. Ha! — would a madman have been so wise as this? And then, when my head was well in the room, I undid the lantern cautiously — oh, so cautiously — cautiously (for the hinges creaked) — I undid it just so much that a single thin ray fell upon the vulture eye. And this I did for seven long nights — every night just at midnight — but I found the eye always closed; and so it was impossible to do the work; for it was not the old man who vexed me, but his Evil Eye. And every morning, when the day broke, I went boldly into the chamber, and spoke courageously to him, calling him by name in a hearty tone, and inquiring how he had passed the night. So you see he would have been a very profound old man, indeed, to suspect that every night, just at twelve, I looked in upon him while he slept.

Upon the eighth night I was more than usually cautious in opening the door. A watch's minute hand moves more quickly than did mine. Never, before that night, had I *felt* the extent of my own powers — of my sagacity. I could scarcely contain my feelings of triumph. To think that there I was, opening the door, little by little, and he not even to dream of my secret deeds or thoughts. I fairly chuckled at the idea; and perhaps he heard me; for he moved on the bed suddenly, as if startled. Now you may think that I drew back — but no. His room was as black as pitch with the thick darkness (for the shutters were close fastened, through fear of robbers), and so I knew that he could not see the opening of the door, and I kept pushing it on steadily, steadily.

I had my head in, and was about to open the lantern, when my thumb slipped upon the tin fastening, and the old man sprang up in bed, crying out, "Who's there?"

I kept quite still and said nothing. For a whole hour I did not move a muscle, and in the meantime I did not hear him lie down. He was still sitting up in the bed listening — just as I have done, night after night, hearkening to the death watches [1] in the wall.

Presently I heard a slight groan, and I knew it was the groan of mortal terror. It was not a groan of pain or of grief — oh, no! — it was the low stifled sound that arises from the bottom of the soul when overcharged with awe. I knew the sound well. Many a night, just at midnight, when all the world slept, it has welled up from my own bosom, deepening, with its dreadful echo, the terrors that distracted me. I say I knew it well. I knew what the old man felt, and pitied him, although I chuckled at heart. I knew that he had been lying awake ever since the first slight noise, when he had turned in the bed. His fears had been ever since growing upon him. He had been trying to fancy them causeless, but could not. He had been saying to himself — "It is nothing but the wind in the chimney — it is only a mouse crossing the floor," or "It is merely a cricket which has made a single chirp." Yes, he had been trying to comfort himself with these suppositions: but he had found all in vain. *All in vain;* because Death, in approaching him, had stalked with his black shadow before him, and enveloped the victim. And it was the mournful influence of the unperceived shadow that caused him to feel — although he neither saw nor heard — to *feel* the presence of my head within the room.

When I had waited a long time, very patiently, without hearing him lie down, I resolved to open a little — a very, very little crevice in the lantern. So I opened it — you cannot imagine how stealthily, stealthily — until at length a single dim ray, like the thread of the spider, shot from out the crevice and fell full upon the vulture eye.

It was open — wide, wide open — and I grew furious as I gazed upon it. I saw it with perfect distinctness — all a dull blue, with a hideous veil over it that chilled the very marrow in my bones; but I could see nothing else of the old man's face or person: for I had directed the ray as if by instinct, precisely upon the damned spot.

And have I not told you that what you mistake for madness is but over-acuteness of the senses? — now, I say, there came to my ears a low, dull, quick sound, such as a watch makes when enveloped in cotton. I

---

[1] **death watches:** insects that make a ticking sound, regarded by the superstitious as prophesying death.

knew *that* sound well, too. It was the beating of the old man's heart. It increased my fury, as the beating of a drum stimulates the soldier into courage.

But even yet I refrained and kept still. I scarcely breathed. I held the lantern motionless. I tried how steadily I could maintain the ray upon the eye. Meantime the hellish tattoo of the heart increased. It grew quicker and quicker, and louder and louder every instant. The old man's terror *must* have been extreme! It grew louder, I say, louder every moment! — do you mark me well? I have told you that I am nervous: so I am. And now at the dead hour of the night, amid the dreadful silence of that old house, so strange a noise as this excited me to uncontrollable terror. Yet, for some minutes longer I refrained and stood still. But the beating grew louder, louder! I thought the heart must burst. And now a new anxiety seized me — the sound would be heard by a neighbor! The old man's hour had come! With a loud yell, I threw open the lantern and leaped into the room. He shrieked once — once only. In an instant I dragged him to the floor, and pulled the heavy bed over him. I then smiled gaily, to find the deed so far done. But, for many minutes, the heart beat on with a muffled sound. This, however, did not vex me; it would not be heard through the wall. At length it ceased. The old man was dead. I removed the bed and examined the corpse. Yes, he was stone, stone dead. I placed my hand upon the heart and held it there many minutes. There was no pulsation. He was stone dead. His eye would trouble me no more.

If still you think me mad, you will think so no longer when I describe the wise precautions I took for the concealment of the body. The night waned, and I worked hastily, but in silence. First of all I dismembered the corpse. I cut off the head and the arms and the legs.

I then took up three planks from the flooring of the chamber, and deposited all between the scantlings. I then replaced the boards so cleverly, so cunningly, that no human eye — not even *his* — could have detected anything wrong. There was nothing to wash out — no stain of any kind — no blood spot whatever. I had been too wary for that. A tub had caught all — ha! ha!

When I had made an end of these labors, it was four o'clock — still dark as midnight. As the bell sounded the hour, there came a knocking at the street door. I went down to open it with a light heart — for what had I *now* to fear? There entered three men, who introduced themselves, with perfect suavity, as officers of the police. A shriek had been heard by a neighbor during the night; suspicion of foul play had been aroused; information had been lodged at the police office, and they (the officers) had been deputed to search the premises.

I smiled — for *what* had I to fear? I bade the gentlemen welcome. The shriek, I said, was my own in a dream. The old man, I mentioned, was absent in the country. I took my visitors all over the house. I bade them search — search *well*. I led them, at length, to *his* chamber. I showed them his treasures, secure, undisturbed. In the enthusiasm of my confidence, I brought chairs into the room, and desired them *here* to rest from their fatigues, while I myself, in the wild audacity of my perfect triumph, placed my own seat upon the very spot beneath which reposed the corpse of the victim.

The officers were satisfied. My *manner* had convinced them. I was singularly at ease. They sat, and while I answered cheerily, they chatted of familiar things. But, erelong, I felt myself getting pale and wished them gone. My head ached, and I fancied a ringing in my ears: but still they sat and still chatted. The ringing became more distinct — it continued and became more distinct; I talked more freely to get rid of the feeling; but it continued and gained definiteness — until, at length, I found that the noise was *not* within my ears.

No doubt I now grew *very* pale — but I talked more fluently, and with a heightened voice. Yet the sound increased — and what could I do? It was *a low, dull, quick sound — much such a sound as a watch makes when enveloped in cotton.* I gasped for breath — and yet the officers heard it not. I talked more quickly — more vehemently; but the noise steadily increased. I arose and argued about trifles, in a high key and with violent gesticulations; but the noise steadily increased. Why *would* they not be gone? I paced the floor to and fro with heavy strides, as if excited to fury by the observations of the men — but the noise steadily increased. Oh, God! what *could* I do? I foamed — I raved — I swore! I swung the chair upon which I had been sitting, and grated it upon the boards, but the noise arose over all and continually increased. It grew louder — louder — *louder!* And still the men chatted pleasantly, and smiled. Was it possible they heard not? Almighty God! — no, no! They heard! — they suspected! — they *knew!* — they were making a mockery of my horror! — this I thought, and this I think. But anything was better than this agony! Anything was more tolerable than this derision! I could bear those hypocritical smiles no longer! I felt that I must scream or die! and now — again! — hark! louder! louder! louder! *louder!*

"Villains!" I shrieked, "dissemble no more! I admit the deed! — tear up the planks! here, here! — it is the beating of his hideous heart!"

## Suggestions for Study of Poe's Stories

### THE PIT AND THE PENDULUM

1. How does Poe make the prisoner's period of unconsciousness seem especially real? Compare it with any experience of your own in fainting or only falling asleep, and returning to consciousness.

2. Describe the changes that took place in the method of torture. How do they illustrate the point made in the story that the inquisitors practiced mental as well as physical tortures?

3. What evidence was there that the prisoner was being watched by his tormentors?

4. Suggest situations you have read about in World War II which would make good backgrounds for a horror story. What differences would you find in the way these conditions would be described in a newspaper account and in a short story as Poe would have written it?

### THE TELL-TALE HEART

5. Did you feel the horror Poe expected you to feel? If not, for you the story was a failure.

6. Point out details by which Poe builds up the feeling of horror to a climax.

7. How do the two opposing forces in this story differ from those in "The Pit and the Pendulum"?

8. Have you learned anything about human nature from reading these two stories? If so, what? Was it worth learning?

## For Further Reading

To see other sides of Poe's skill read a tale based on reasoning, such as "The Gold Bug" or "The Purloined Letter." Stories of strange uncanny beauty are "The Masque of the Red Death" and "Ligeia." Other masterpieces depicting mental unbalance are "The Cask of Amontillado" and "The Black Cat."

## For Your Vocabulary

BASE-WORD. One word part that appears in two different forms, *loqu* and *locu* (to speak), is worth learning because it occurs in so many useful words. *Locution* (lṓ-kū′shŭn), a formal word for speaking (page 529), has the same root as the more familiar *eloquent. Elocution* is the noun for *eloquent* speaking. All the talking that made the young Italian in "Ring around a Rosy" homesick for Germany seemed only *loquacious* (lṓ-kwā′shŭs), or overtalkative, idleness to the scientific-minded Helmuth (page 67). You will find a *soliloquy* (sṓ-lĭl′ṓ-kwĭ) mentioned later (page 690) and can figure it out if you do not know it already. And you will find an *interlocutor* (ĭn-tẽr-lŏk′ṓ-tẽr) asking questions to bring out a story (page 739). The master of ceremonies in a minstrel show, who asks the questions that lead to the jokes, is called the *Interlocutor.* Language that is acceptable in conversation but not in formal writing is called *colloquial* (kŏ-lō′kwĭ-ăl), suitable for talking with people. Can you name two stories in this book that are written in a *colloquial* style, as if one of the characters were talking to you?

# Nathaniel Hawthorne 1804–1864

## DR. HEIDEGGER'S EXPERIMENT

This story appeared in the volume *Twice-Told Tales,* and, interestingly enough, it was in his review of this book that Poe stated his philosophy of short-story writing.

" Dr. Heidegger's Experiment " is a fantasy built around the idea of the Fountain of Youth, thought by early Spanish explorers to be located in Florida. By reading it you can observe in short space some of the ideas with which Hawthorne is concerned in many of his other stories. There is the idea of scientific experiment, which took strong hold of popular fancy in that dawn of a century of marvelous scientific discovery. There is also the problem of the effect of sin in its various forms upon human nature. Binding everything together there is a philosophical question, which in this story might be stated thus: If we had our lives to live over again would we profit by experience? You can easily see that Hawthorne was studying right and wrong in human conduct, while Poe was interested in artistic effects without moral implication.

That very singular man, old Dr. Heidegger, once invited four venerable friends to meet him in his study. There were three white-bearded gentlemen, Mr. Medbourne, Colonel Killigrew, and Mr. Gascoigne, and a withered gentlewoman, whose name was the Widow Wycherly. They were all melancholy old creatures, who had been unfortunate in life, and whose greatest misfortune it was that they were not long ago in their graves. Mr. Medbourne, in the vigor of his age, had been a prosperous merchant, but had lost his all by a frantic speculation, and was now little better than a mendicant. Colonel Killigrew had wasted his best years, and his health and substance, in the pursuit of sinful pleasures, which had given birth to a brood of pains, such as the gout, and divers other torments of soul and body. Mr. Gascoigne was a ruined politician, a man of evil fame, or at least had been so till time had buried him from the knowledge of the present generation, and made him obscure instead of infamous. As for the Widow

*Culver*

Wycherly, tradition tells us that she was a great beauty in her day; but, for a long while past, she had lived in deep seclusion, on account of certain scandalous stories which had prejudiced the gentry of the town against her. It is a circumstance worth mentioning that each of these three old gentlemen, Mr. Medbourne, Colonel Killigrew, and Mr. Gascoigne, were early lovers of the Widow Wycherly, and had once been on the point of cutting each other's throats for her sake. And, before proceeding further, I will merely hint that Dr. Heidegger and all his four guests were sometimes thought to be a little beside themselves — as is not unfrequently the case with old people, when worried either by present troubles or woeful recollections.

" My dear old friends," said Dr. Heidegger, motioning them to be seated, " I am desirous of your assistance in one of those little experiments with which I amuse myself here in my study."

If all stories were true, Dr. Heidegger's study must have been a very curious place. It was a dim, old-fashioned chamber, festooned with cobwebs, and besprinkled with antique dust. Around the walls stood several oaken bookcases, the lower shelves of which were filled with rows of gigantic folios and black-letter quartos, and the upper with little parchment-covered duodeci-mos.[1] Over the central bookcase was a bronze bust of Hippocrates,[2] with which, according to some authorities, Dr. Heidegger was accustomed to hold consultations in all difficult cases of his practice. In the obscurest corner of the room stood a tall and narrow oaken closet, with its door ajar, within which doubtfully appeared a skeleton. Between two of the bookcases hung a looking glass, presenting its high and dusty plate within a tarnished gilt frame. Among many wonderful stories related of this mirror, it was fabled that the spirits of all the doctor's deceased patients dwelt within its verge, and would stare him in the face whenever he looked thitherward. The opposite side of the chamber was ornamented with the full-length portrait of a young lady, arrayed in the faded magnificence of silk, satin, and brocade, and with a visage as faded as her dress. Above half a century ago, Dr. Heidegger had been on the point of marriage with this young lady; but, being affected with some slight disorder, she had swallowed one of her lover's prescriptions, and died on the bridal evening. The greatest curiosity of the study remains to be mentioned; it was a ponderous folio volume, bound in black leather, with massive silver clasps. There were no letters on the back, and nobody could tell the title of the book. But it was well known to be a book of magic; and once, when a chambermaid had lifted it, merely to brush away the dust, the skeleton had rattled in its closet, the picture of the young lady had stepped one foot upon the floor, and several ghastly faces had peeped forth from the mirror; while the brazen head of Hippocrates frowned, and said, " Forbear! "

Such was Dr. Heidegger's study. On the summer afternoon of our tale a small round table, as black as ebony, stood in the center of the room, sustaining a cut-glass vase of beautiful form and elaborate workman-ship. The sunshine came through the window, between the heavy festoons of two faded damask curtains, and fell directly across this vase; so that a mild splendor was reflected from it on the ashen visages of the five old people who sat around. Four champagne glasses were also on the table.

" My dear old friends," repeated Dr. Heidegger, " may I reckon on your aid in performing an exceedingly curious experiment? "

Now Dr. Heidegger was a very strange old gentleman, whose eccentricity had become the nucleus for a thousand fantastic stories. Some of these fables, to my shame be it spoken, might possibly be traced back to my own veracious self; and if any passages of the present tale should startle the reader's faith, I must be content to bear the stigma of a fiction monger.

When the doctor's four guests heard him talk of his proposed experiment, they anticipated nothing more wonderful than the murder of a mouse in an air pump, or the examination of a cobweb by the microscope, or some similar nonsense, with which he was constantly in the habit of pestering his intimates. But, without waiting for a reply, Dr. Heidegger hobbled across the chamber and returned with the same ponderous folio, bound in black leather, which common report affirmed to be a book of magic. Undoing the silver clasps, he opened the volume and took from among its black-letter pages a rose, or what was once a rose, though now the green leaves and crimson petals had assumed one brownish hue, and the ancient flower seemed ready to crumble to dust in the doctor's hands.

" This rose," said Dr. Heidegger, with a sigh, " this same withered and crumbling flower, blossomed five and fifty years ago. It was given me by Sylvia Ward, whose portrait hangs yonder; and I meant to wear it in my bosom at our wedding. Five and fifty years it has been treasured between the leaves of this old volume. Now, would you deem it possible that this rose of half a century could ever bloom again? "

---

[1] **duodecimos** (dū-ŏ-dĕs′ĭ-mōz): small volumes, about five by eight inches. [2] **Hippocrates** (hĭ-pŏk-rȧ-tēz): an ancient Greek physician (460–377? B.C.), often called the father of medicine.

" Nonsense! " said the Widow Wycherly, with a peevish toss of her head. " You might as well ask whether an old woman's wrinkled face could ever bloom again."

" See! " answered Dr. Heidegger.

He uncovered the vase and threw the faded rose into the water which it contained. At first, it lay lightly on the surface of the fluid, appearing to imbibe none of its moisture. Soon, however, a singular change began to be visible. The crushed and dried petals stirred and assumed a deepening tinge of crimson, as if the flower were reviving from a deathlike slumber; the slender stalk and twigs of foliage became green; and there was the rose of half a century, looking as fresh as when Sylvia Ward had first given it to her lover. It was scarcely full blown; for some of its delicate red leaves curled modestly around its moist bosom, within which two or three dewdrops were sparkling.

" That is certainly a very pretty deception," said the doctor's friends; carelessly, however, for they had witnessed greater miracles at a conjurer's show; " pray how was it effected? "

" Did you never hear of the ' Fountain of Youth '? " asked Dr. Heidegger, " which Ponce de Leon,[1] the Spanish adventurer, went in search of two or three centuries ago? "

" But did Ponce de Leon ever find it? " said the Widow Wycherly.

" No," answered Dr. Heidegger, " for he never sought it in the right place. The famous Fountain of Youth, if I am rightly informed, is situated in the southern part of the Floridian peninsula, not far from Lake Macaco. Its source is overshadowed by several gigantic magnolias, which, though numberless centuries old, have been kept as fresh as violets by the virtues of this wonderful water. An acquaintance of mine, knowing my curiosity in such matters, has sent me what you see in the vase."

" Ahem! " said Colonel Killigrew, who

believed not a word of the doctor's story; " and what may be the effect of this fluid on the human frame? "

" You shall judge for yourself, my dear colonel," replied Dr. Heidegger; " and all of you, my respected friends, are welcome to so much of this admirable fluid as may restore to you the bloom of youth. For my own part, having had much trouble in growing old, I am in no hurry to grow young again. With your permission, therefore, I will merely watch the progress of the experiment."

While he spoke, Dr. Heidegger had been filling the four champagne glasses with the water of the Fountain of Youth. It was apparently impregnated with an effervescent gas, for little bubbles were continually ascending from the depths of the glasses, and bursting in silvery spray at the surface. As the liquor diffused a pleasant perfume, the old people doubted not that it possessed cordial and comfortable properties; and though utter skeptics as to its rejuvenescent power, they were inclined to swallow it at once. But Dr. Heidegger besought them to stay a moment.

" Before you drink, my respectable old friends," said he, " it would be well that, with the experience of a lifetime to direct you, you should draw up a few general rules for your guidance, in passing a second time through the perils of youth. Think what a sin and shame it would be, if, with your peculiar advantages, you should not become patterns of virtue and wisdom to all the young people of the age! "

The doctor's four venerable friends made him no answer, except by a feeble and tremulous laugh; so very ridiculous was the idea that, knowing how closely repentance treads behind the steps of error, they should ever go astray again.

" Drink, then," said the doctor, bowing. " I rejoice that I have so well selected the subjects of my experiment."

With palsied hands, they raised the glasses to their lips. The liquor, if it really possessed such virtues as Dr. Heidegger imputed to it, could not have been bestowed

[1] **Ponce de Leon** (Spanish, pŏn'thä dā lā-ōn'; Anglicized, pŏns dē lē'ŭn): Spanish discoverer of Florida (1460?–1521).

on four human beings who needed it more woefully. They looked as if they had never known what youth or pleasure was, but had been the offspring of Nature's dotage, and always the gray, decrepit, sapless, miserable creatures who now sat stooping round the doctor's table, without life enough in their souls or bodies to be animated even by the prospect of growing young again. They drank off the water, and replaced their glasses on the table.

Assuredly there was an almost immediate improvement in the aspect of the party, not unlike what might have been produced by a glass of generous wine, together with a sudden glow of cheerful sunshine brightening over all their visages at once. There was a healthful suffusion on their cheeks, instead of the ashen hue that had made them look so corpselike. They gazed at one another and fancied that some magic power had really begun to smooth away the deep and sad inscriptions which Father Time had been so long engraving on their brows. The Widow Wycherly adjusted her cap, for she felt almost like a woman again.

" Give us more of this wondrous water! " cried they, eagerly. " We are younger — but we are still too old! Quick — give us more! "

" Patience, patience! " quoth Dr. Heidegger, who sat watching the experiment with philosophic coolness. " You have been a long time growing old. Surely, you might be content to grow young in half an hour! But the water is at your service."

Again he filled their glasses with the liquor of youth, enough of which still remained in the vase to turn half the old people in the city to the age of their own grandchildren. While the bubbles were yet sparkling on the brim, the doctor's four guests snatched their glasses from the table, and swallowed the contents at a single gulp. Was it delusion? Even while the draught was passing down their throats, it seemed to have wrought a change on their whole systems. Their eyes grew clear and bright; a dark shade deepened among their silvery locks, they sat around the table, three gen-

tlemen of middle age, and a woman, hardly beyond her buxom prime.

" My dear widow, you are charming! " cried Colonel Killigrew, whose eyes had been fixed upon her face, while the shadows of age were flitting from it like darkness from the crimson daybreak.

The fair widow knew, of old, that Colonel Killigrew's compliments were not always measured by sober truth; so she started up and ran to the mirror, still dreading that the ugly visage of an old woman would meet her gaze. Meanwhile, the three gentlemen behaved in such a manner as proved that the water of the Fountain of Youth possessed some intoxicating qualities; unless, indeed, their exhilaration of spirits were merely a lightsome dizziness caused by the sudden removal of the weight of years. Mr. Gascoigne's mind seemed to run on political topics, but whether relating to the past, present, or future could not easily be determined, since the same ideas and phrases have been in vogue these fifty years. Now he rattled forth full-throated sentences about patriotism, national glory, and the people's right; now he muttered some perilous stuff or other, in a sly and doubtful whisper, so cautiously that even his own conscience could scarcely catch the secret; and now, again, he spoke in measured accents, and a deeply deferential tone, as if a royal ear were listening to his well-turned periods. Colonel Killigrew all this time had been trolling forth a jolly bottle song, and ringing his glass in symphony with the chorus, while his eyes wandered toward the buxom figure of the Widow Wycherly. On the other side of the table, Mr. Medbourne was involved in a calculation of dollars and cents, with which was strangely intermingled a project for supplying the East Indies with ice, by harnessing a team of whales to the polar icebergs.

As for the Widow Wycherly, she stood before the mirror curtsying and simpering to her own image, and greeting it as the friend whom she loved better than all the world beside. She thrust her face close to the glass, to see whether some long-remembered wrinkle or crow's-foot had indeed vanished. She examined whether the snow had so entirely melted from her hair that the venerable cap could be safely thrown aside. At last, turning briskly away, she came with a sort of dancing step to the table.

" My dear old doctor," cried she, " pray favor me with another glass! "

" Certainly, my dear madam, certainly! " replied the complaisant doctor; " see! I have already filled the glasses."

There, in fact, stood the four glasses, brimful of this wonderful water, the delicate spray of which, as it effervesced from the surface, resembled the tremulous glitter of diamonds. It was now so nearly sunset that the chamber had grown duskier than ever; but a mild and moonlike splendor gleamed from within the vase, and rested alike on the four guests and on the doctor's venerable figure. He sat in a high-backed, elaborately-carved oaken armchair, with a gray dignity of aspect that might have well befitted that very Father Time, whose power had never been disputed, save by this fortunate company. Even while quaffing the third draught of the Fountain of Youth, they were almost awed by the expression of his mysterious visage.

But, the next moment, the exhilarating gush of young life shot through their veins. They were now in the happy prime of youth. Age, with its miserable train of cares and sorrows and diseases, was remembered only as the trouble of a dream, from which they had joyously awaked. The fresh gloss of the soul, so early lost, and without which the world's successive scenes had been but a gallery of faded pictures, again threw its enchantment over all their prospects. They felt like new-created beings in a new-created universe.

" We are young! We are young! " they cried exultingly.

Youth, like the extremity of age, had effaced the strongly-marked characteristics of middle life, and mutually assimilated them all. They were a group of merry youngsters, almost maddened with the exuberant frolicsomeness of their years. The most singular effect of their gaiety was an impulse to mock the infirmity and decrepitude of which they had so lately been the victims. They laughed loudly at their old-fashioned attire, the wide-skirted coats and flapped waistcoats of the young men, and the ancient cap and gown of the blooming girl. One limped across the floor like a gouty grandfather; one set a pair of spectacles astride of his nose, and pretended to pore over the black-letter pages of the book of magic; a third seated himself in an armchair, and strove to imitate the venerable dignity of Dr. Heidegger. Then all shouted mirthfully, and leaped about the room. The Widow Wycherly — if so fresh a damsel could be called a widow — tripped up to the doctor's chair, with a mischievous merriment in her rosy face.

" Doctor, you dear old soul," cried she, " get up and dance with me! " And then the four young people laughed louder than ever, to think what a queer figure the poor old doctor would cut.

" Pray excuse me," answered the doctor quietly. " I am old and rheumatic, and my dancing days were over long ago. But either of these gay young gentlemen will be glad of so pretty a partner."

" Dance with me, Clara! " cried Colonel Killigrew.

" No, no, I will be her partner! " shouted Mr. Gascoigne.

" She promised me her hand, fifty years ago! " exclaimed Mr. Medbourne.

They all gathered round her. One caught both her hands in his passionate grasp — another threw his arm about her waist — the third buried his hand among the glossy curls that clustered beneath the widow's cap. Blushing, panting, struggling, chiding, laughing, her warm breath fanning each of their faces by turns, she strove to disengage herself, yet still remained in their triple embrace. Never was there a livelier picture of youthful rivalship, with bewitching beauty for the prize. Yet, by a strange deception, owing to the duskiness of the chamber, and the antique dresses which they still wore, the tall mirror is said to have reflected the figures of the three old, gray, withered grandsires ridiculously contending for the skinny ugliness of a shriveled grandam.

But they were young: their burning passions proved them so. Inflamed to madness by the coquetry of the girl-widow, who neither granted nor quite withheld her favors, the three rivals began to interchange threatening glances. Still keeping hold of the fair prize, they grappled fiercely at one another's throats. As they struggled to and fro, the table was overturned, and the vase dashed into a thousand fragments. The precious Water of Youth flowed in a bright stream across the floor, moistening the wings of a butterfly, which, grown old in the decline of summer, had alighted there to die. The insect fluttered lightly through the chamber, and settled on the snowy head of Dr. Heidegger.

" Come, come, gentlemen! — come, Madam Wycherly," exclaimed the doctor, " I really must protest against this riot."

They stood still and shivered; for it seemed as if gray Time were calling them back from their sunny youth, far down into the chill and darksome vale of years. They looked at old Dr. Heidegger, who sat in his carved armchair, holding the rose of half a century, which he had rescued from among the fragments of the shattered vase. At the motion of his hand, the four rioters resumed their seats; the more readily, because their violent exertions had wearied them, youthful though they were.

" My poor Sylvia's rose! " ejaculated Dr. Heidegger, holding it in the light of the sunset clouds; " it appears to be fading again."

And so it was. Even while the party were looking at it, the flower continued to shrivel up, till it became as dry and fragile as when the doctor had first thrown it into the vase. He shook off the few drops of moisture which clung to its petals.

" I love it as well thus as in its dewy freshness," observed he, pressing the withered rose to his withered lips. While he spoke, the butterfly fluttered down from the doctor's snowy head, and fell upon the floor.

His guests shivered again. A strange chillness, whether of the body or spirit they could not tell, was creeping gradually over them all. They gazed at one another, and fancied that each fleeting moment snatched away a charm, and left a deepening furrow where none had been before. Was it an illusion? Had the changes of a lifetime been crowded into so brief a space, and were they now four aged people, sitting with their old friend, Dr. Heidegger?

" Are we grown old again, so soon? " cried they, dolefully.

In truth they had. The Water of Youth possessed merely a virtue more transient than that of wine. The delirium which it created had effervesced away. Yes! they were old again. With a shuddering impulse, that showed her a woman still, the widow clasped her skinny hands before her face, and wished that the coffin lid were over it, since it could be no longer beautiful.

" Yes, friends, ye are old again," said Dr. Heidegger, " and lo! the Water of Youth is all lavished on the ground. Well — I bemoan it not; for if the fountain gushed at my very doorstep, I would not stoop to bathe my lips in it — no, though its delirium were for years instead of moments. Such is the lesson ye have taught me! "

But the doctor's four friends had taught no such lesson to themselves. They resolved forthwith to make a pilgrimage to Florida, and quaff at morning, noon, and night, from the Fountain of Youth.

## THE AMBITIOUS GUEST

Here we see how Hawthorne could take an actual incident and give it deeper meaning by the philosophical content he put into it. The account of the avalanche and the strange fate of the escaping family he read in *Historical Relics of the White Mountains* by J. H. Spaulding. It happened in 1826. But the characters were his own creation; their ambitions, their fears, and their fancies add poignancy to the final tragedy.

One September night a family had gathered round their hearth, and piled it high with the driftwood of mountain streams, the dry cones of the pine, and the splintered ruins of great trees that had come crashing down the precipice. Up the chimney roared the fire, and brightened the room with its broad blaze. The faces of the father and mother had a sober gladness; the children laughed; the eldest daughter was the image of Happiness at seventeen; and the aged grandmother, who sat knitting in the warmest place, was the image of Happiness grown old. They had found the "herb, heart's-ease," in the bleakest spot of all New England. This family was situated in the Notch of the White Hills, where the wind was sharp throughout the year, and pitilessly cold in the winter — giving their cottage all its fresh inclemency before it descended on the valley of the Saco. They dwelt in a cold spot and a dangerous one; for a mountain towered above their heads, so steep that the stones would often rumble down its sides and startle them at midnight.

The daughter had just uttered some simple jest that filled them all with mirth, when the wind came through the Notch and seemed to pause before their cottage — rattling the door, with a sound of wailing and lamentation, before it passed into the valley. For a moment it saddened them, though there was nothing unusual in the tones. But the family were glad again when they perceived that the latch was lifted by some traveler, whose footsteps had been unheard amid the dreary blast which heralded his approach, and wailed as he was entering, and went moaning away from the door.

Though they dwelt in such a solitude, these people held daily converse with the world. The romantic pass of the Notch is a great artery, through which the lifeblood of internal commerce is continually throbbing between Maine, on one side, and the Green Mountains and the shores of the St. Lawrence, on the other. The stagecoach always drew up before the door of the cottage. The wayfarer, with no companion but his staff, paused here to exchange a word, that the sense of loneliness might not utterly overcome him ere he could pass through the cleft of the mountain, or reach the first house in the valley. And here the teamster, on his way to Portland market, would put up for the night; and, if a bachelor, might sit an hour beyond the usual bedtime, and steal a kiss from the mountain maid at parting. It was one of those primitive taverns where the traveler pays only for food and lodging, but meets with a homely kindness beyond all price. When the footsteps were heard, therefore, between the outer door and the inner one, the whole family rose up, grandmother, children, and all, as if about to welcome some one who belonged to them, and whose fate was linked with theirs.

The door was opened by a young man. His face at first wore the melancholy expression, almost despondency, of one who travels a wild and bleak road, at nightfall and alone, but soon brightened up when he saw the kindly warmth of his reception. He felt his heart spring forward to meet them all, from the old woman, who wiped a chair with her apron, to the little child that held out its arms to him. One glance and smile placed the stranger on a footing of innocent familiarity with the eldest daughter.

"Ah, this fire is the right thing!" cried he; "especially when there is such a pleasant circle round it. I am quite benumbed; for the Notch is just like the pipe of a great pair of bellows; it has blown a terrible blast in my face all the way from Bartlett."

"Then you are going toward Vermont?" said the master of the house, as he helped to take a light knapsack off the young man's shoulders.

"Yes; to Burlington, and far enough beyond," replied he. "I meant to have been at Ethan Crawford's tonight; but a pedestrian lingers along such a road as this. It is no matter; for, when I saw this good fire, and all your cheerful faces, I felt as if you had kindled it on purpose for me, and were waiting my arrival. So I shall sit down among you, and make myself at home."

The frank-hearted stranger had just drawn his chair to the fire when something like a heavy footstep was heard without, rushing down the steep side of the mountain, as with long and rapid strides, and taking such a leap in passing the cottage as to strike the opposite precipice. The family held their breath, because they knew the sound, and their guest held his by instinct.

"The old mountain has thrown a stone at us, for fear we should forget him," said the landlord, recovering himself. "He sometimes nods his head and threatens to come down; but we are old neighbors, and agree together pretty well on the whole. Besides, we have a sure place of refuge hard by if he should be coming in good earnest."

Let us now suppose the stranger to have finished his supper of bear's meat; and, by his natural felicity of manner, to have placed himself on a footing of kindness with the whole family, so that they talked as freely together as if he belonged to their mountain brood. He was of a proud, yet gentle spirit — haughty and reserved among the rich and great; but ever ready to stoop his head to the lowly cottage door, and be like a brother or a son at the poor man's fireside. In the household of the Notch he found warmth and simplicity of feeling, the pervading intelligence of New England, and a poetry of native growth, which they had gathered when they little thought of it from the mountain peaks and chasms, and at the very threshold of their romantic and dangerous abode. He had traveled far and alone; his whole life, indeed, had been a solitary path; for, with the lofty caution of his nature, he had kept himself apart from those who might otherwise have been his companions. The family, too, though so kind and hospitable, had that consciousness of unity among themselves, and separation from the world at large which, in every domestic circle, should still keep a holy place where no stranger may intrude. But this evening a prophetic sympathy impelled the refined and educated youth to pour out his heart before the simple mountaineers, and constrained them to answer him with the same free confidence. And thus it should have been. Is not the kindred of a common fate a closer tie than that of birth?

The secret of the young man's character was a high and abstracted ambition. He could have borne to live an undistinguished life, but not to be forgotten in the grave. Yearning desire had been transformed to hope: and hope, long cherished, had become like certainty, that, obscurely as he journeyed now, a glory was to beam on all his pathway — though not, perhaps, while he was treading it. But when posterity should gaze back into the gloom of what was now the present, they would trace the brightness of his footsteps, brightening as meaner glories faded, and confess that a gifted one had passed from his cradle to his tomb with none to recognize him.

"As yet," cried the stranger — his cheek glowing and his eye flashing with enthusiasm — "as yet, I have done nothing. Were I to vanish from the earth tomorrow, none would know so much of me as you; that a nameless youth came up at nightfall from the valley of Saco, and opened his heart to you in the evening, and passed through the Notch by sunrise, and was seen no more. Not a soul would ask, 'Who was he? Whither did the wanderer go?' But I cannot die till I have achieved my destiny. Then, let death come! I shall have built my monument!"

There was a continual flow of natural emotion, gushing forth amid abstracted reverie, which enabled the family to understand this young man's sentiments, though so foreign from their own. With quick sensibility of the ludicrous, he blushed at the ardor into which he had been betrayed.

"You laugh at me," said he, taking the eldest daughter's hand, and laughing himself. "You think my ambition as nonsensical as if I were to freeze myself to death on the top of Mount Washington, only that people might spy at me from the country round about. And, truly, that would be a noble pedestal for a man's statue!"

"It is better to sit here by this fire," answered the girl, blushing, "and be comfortable and contented, though nobody thinks about us."

" I suppose," said her father, after a fit of musing, " there is something natural in what the young man says; and if my mind had been turned that way, I might have felt just the same. It is strange, wife, how his talk has set my head running on things that are pretty certain never to come to pass."

" Perhaps they may," observed the wife. " Is the man thinking what he will do when he is a widower? "

" No, no! " cried he, repelling the idea with reproachful kindness. " When I think of your death, Esther, I think of mine, too. But I was wishing we had a good farm in Bartlett, or Bethlehem, or Littleton, or some other township round the White Mountains; but not where they could tumble on our heads. I should want to stand well with my neighbors and be called Squire, and sent to General Court for a term or two; for a plain, honest man may do as much good there as a lawyer. And when I should be grown quite an old man, and you an old woman, so as not to be long apart, I might die happy enough in my bed, and leave you all crying around me. A slate gravestone would suit me as well as a marble one — with just my name and age, and a verse of a hymn, and something to let people know that I lived an honest man and died a Christian."

" There, now! " exclaimed the stranger; " it is our nature to desire a monument, be it slate or marble, or a pillar of granite, or a glorious memory in the universal heart of man."

" We're in a strange way tonight," said the wife, with tears in her eyes. " They say it's a sign of something, when folks' minds go a-wandering so. Hark to the children! "

They listened accordingly. The younger children had been put to bed in another room, but with an open door between, so that they could be heard talking busily among themselves. One and all seemed to have caught the infection from the fireside circle, and were outvying each other in wild wishes, and childish projects of what they would do when they came to be men and women. At length a little boy, instead of addressing his brothers and sisters, called out to his mother.

" I'll tell you what I wish, mother," cried he. " I want you and father and grandma'm, and all of us, and the stranger, too, to start right away, and go and take a drink out of the basin of the Flume! "

Nobody could help laughing at the child's notion of leaving a warm bed, and dragging them from a cheerful fire, to visit the basin of the Flume — a brook which tumbles over the precipice, deep within the Notch. The boy had hardly spoken when a wagon rattled along the road, and stopped a moment before the door. It appeared to contain two or three men who were cheering their hearts with the rough chorus of a song, which resounded in broken notes between the cliffs, while the singers hesitated whether to continue their journey or put up here for the night.

" Father," said the girl, " they are calling you by name."

But the good man doubted whether they had really called him, and was unwilling to show himself too solicitous of gain by inviting people to patronize his house. He therefore did not hurry to the door; and the lash being soon applied, the travelers plunged into the Notch, still singing and laughing, though their music and mirth came back drearily from the heart of the mountain.

" There, mother! " cried the boy, again. " They'd have given us a ride to the Flume."

Again they laughed at the child's pertinacious fancy for a night ramble. But it happened that a light cloud passed over the daughter's spirit; she looked gravely into the fire, and drew a breath that was almost a sigh. It forced its way, in spite of a little struggle to repress it. Then starting and blushing, she looked quickly round the circle, as if they had caught a glimpse into her bosom. The stranger asked what she had been thinking of.

" Nothing," answered she, with a downcast smile. " Only I felt lonesome just then."

" Oh, I have always had a gift of feeling what is in other people's hearts," said he,

THE OLD MANSE still stands in Concord, rich in literary associations. Both Emerson and Hawthorne lived and wrote here. (Brown Brothers)

half seriously. " Shall I tell the secrets of yours? For I know what to think when a young girl shivers by a warm hearth, and complains of lonesomeness at her mother's side. Shall I put these feelings into words? "

" They would not be a girl's feelings any longer if they could be put into words," replied the mountain nymph, laughing, but avoiding his eye.

All this was said apart. Perhaps a germ of love was springing in their hearts, so pure that it might blossom in Paradise, since it could not be matured on earth; for women worship such gentle dignity as his; and the proud, contemplative, yet kindly soul is oftenest captivated by simplicity like hers. But while they spoke softly, and he was watching the happy sadness, the lightsome shadows, the shy yearnings of a maiden's nature, the wind through the Notch took a deeper and drearier sound. It seemed, as the fanciful stranger said, like the choral strain of the spirits of the blast, who in old Indian times had their dwelling among these mountains, and made their heights and recesses a sacred region. There was a wail along the road, as if a funeral were passing. To chase away the gloom, the family threw pine branches on their fire, till the dry leaves crackled and the flame arose, discovering once again a scene of peace and humble happiness. The light hovered about them fondly, and caressed them all. There were the little faces of the children, peeping from their bed apart, and here the father's frame of strength, the mother's subdued and careful mien, the high-browed youth, the budding girl, and the good old grandma, still knitting in the warmest place. The aged woman looked up from her task, and, with fingers ever busy, was the next to speak.

" Old folks have their notions," said she, " as well as young ones. You've been wishing and planning, and letting your heads run on one thing and another, till you've set my mind a-wandering too. Now what should an old woman wish for, when she can go but a step or two before she comes to her grave? Children, it will haunt me night and day till I tell you."

" What is it, mother? " cried the husband and wife at once.

Then the old woman, with an air of mystery which drew the circle closer round the fire, informed them that she had provided her graveclothes some years before — a nice linen shroud, a cap with a muslin ruff, and everything of a finer sort than she had worn since her wedding day. But this evening an old superstition had strangely recurred to her. It used to be said, in her younger days, that if anything were amiss with a corpse, if only the ruff were not smooth, or the cap did not set right, the corpse in the coffin and beneath the clods would strive to put up its cold hands and arrange it. The bare thought made her nervous.

" Don't talk so, grandmother! " said the girl, shuddering.

" Now," continued the old woman, with singular earnestness, yet smiling strangely at her own folly, " I want one of you, my children — when your mother is dressed and in the coffin — I want one of you to hold a looking glass over my face. Who knows but I may take a glimpse at myself, and see whether all's right? "

" Old and young, we dream of graves and monuments," murmured the stranger youth. " I wonder how mariners feel when the ship is sinking, and they, unknown and undistinguished, are to be buried together in the ocean — that wide and nameless sepulcher? "

For a moment, the old woman's ghastly conception so engrossed the minds of her hearers that a sound abroad in the night, rising like the roar of a blast, had grown broad, deep, and terrible, before the fated group were conscious of it. The house and all within it trembled; the foundations of the earth seemed to be shaken, as if this awful sound were the peal of the last trump. Young and old exchanged one wild glance, and remained an instant, pale, affrighted, without utterance, or power to move. Then the same shriek burst simultaneously from all their lips.

" The slide! The slide! "

The simplest words must intimate, but not portray, the unutterable horror of the catastrophe. The victims rushed from their cottage, and sought refuge in what they deemed a safer spot — where, in contempla-tion of such an emergency, a sort of barrier had been reared. Alas! they had quitted their security, and fled right into the pathway of destruction. Down came the whole side of the mountain, in a cataract of ruin. Just before it reached the house, the stream broke into two branches — shivered not a window there, but overwhelmed the whole vicinity, blocked up the road, and annihilated everything in its dreadful course. Long ere the thunder of the great slide had ceased to roar among the mountains, the mortal agony had been endured, and the victims were at peace. Their bodies were never found.

The next morning, the light smoke was seen stealing from the cottage chimney up the mountain side. Within, the fire was yet smoldering on the hearth, and the chairs in a circle round it, as if the inhabitants had but gone forth to view the devastation of the slide, and would shortly return, to thank Heaven for their miraculous escape. All had left separate tokens, by which those who had known the family were made to shed a tear for each. Who has not heard their name? The story has been told far and wide, and will forever be a legend of these mountains. Poets have sung their fate.

There were circumstances which led some to suppose that a stranger had been received into the cottage on this awful night, and had shared the catastrophe of all its inmates. Others denied that there were sufficient grounds for such a conjecture. Woe for the high-souled youth, with his dream of earthly immortality! His name and person utterly unknown; his history, his way of life, his plans, a mystery never to be solved, his death and his existence equally a doubt! Whose was the agony of that death moment?

## Suggestions for Study of Hawthorne

### DR. HEIDEGGER'S EXPERIMENT

1. Why did the characters have to be the kind that one could not admire?

2. Did their actions after drinking the magic

liquid impress you as funny or sad? Explain your answer.

3. What is Hawthorne's answer to the question on which the story hinges: Would we live our lives differently if we could live them over? Do you agree with his conclusion? What value is there in considering a question which could not happen in actual life?

4. Vocabulary: mendicant, eccentricity, veracious, stigma, impregnated, effervescent, rejuvenescent, complaisant.

5. Special report: Read James M. Barrie's play *Dear Brutus,* which hinges on the same idea. How does Barrie's answer to the question of reliving one's life compare with Hawthorne's?

### THE AMBITIOUS GUEST

6. This story is marked by strong contrasts. Point out those between the interior and exterior, between the family and the stranger, the nature of their conversation and the strange fate that overtook them.

7. What similarities do you find to the situation in *Snow-Bound?* Are the two families alike or different? Prove by details.

8. Do the ambitions of the stranger seem natural ones to you? How do they affect the other members of the family?

9. What terrible irony is there in the final fate of the family?

10. How many questions on the meaning and value of human life can you find involved in this story?

## For Your Vocabulary

CONTEXT. Dr. Heidegger's little party is remarkable in the advanced age of the entire group. By taking the full account of their actions and characters for context, you can master some richly descriptive words to deal with old age. The guests are *palsied* (pôl'zǐd), or trembling and shaking from age and weakness (page 543). They are *decrepit* (dē-krĕp'ĭt), weak and feeble with age (page 544). They are in their *dotage* (dōt'åj), growing feeble of mind as well as body (page 544). But the good doctor himself, who has grown old gracefully, deserves the term *venerable* (vĕn'-ĕr-à-b'l) applied ironically to the whole group (page 541). He is worthy of admiration and respect for the wisdom and good sense he has acquired with his years. Bryant found the woods in " Thanatopsis " *venerable,* and the

respected main speaker at Gettysburg was described with the same word (page 254).

## For Further Reading on the Flowering of the East, Part One

### LITERATURE OF THE PERIOD
#### Fiction

Irving, Washington: *The Sketch Book:* " Rip Van Winkle," " The Spectre Bridegroom," " The Legend of Sleepy Hollow." *Bracebridge Hall:* " The Stout Gentleman." *The Alhambra:* " The Legend of the Moor's Legacy," " The Legend of the Two Discreet Statues," " The Legend of the Three Beautiful Princesses." *Tales of a Traveler:* " The Adventure of My Uncle," " The Bold Dragoon "

Cooper, James Fenimore: *The Spy, The Pilot, The Deerslayer, The Last of the Mohicans*

Poe, Edgar Allan: " The Black Cat," " A Descent into the Maelstrom," " The Fall of the House of Usher," " The Gold Bug," " MS. Found in a Bottle," " The Masque of the Red Death," " Murders in the Rue Morgue," " The Purloined Letter," " A Cask of Amontillado "

Hawthorne, Nathaniel: *Twice-Told Tales:* " The Gray Champion," " Mr. Higginbotham's Catastrophe," " Lady Eleanore's Mantle," " The Wedding Knell," " The Minister's Black Veil." *Mosses from an Old Manse:* " The Birthmark," " Drowne's Wooden Image," " Rappaccini's Daughter." *The Snow Image:* " The Great Stone Face," " Ethan Brand "

Melville, Herman: *Moby Dick*

#### Poetry

Bryant, William Cullen: " Robert of Lincoln," " The Death of the Flowers," " A Forest Hymn," " June," " The Yellow Violet," " Song of Marion's Men," " The Battlefield," " Hymn of the City," " Abraham Lincoln "

Whittier, John Greenleaf: " Maud Muller," " Barbara Frietchie," " Barclay of Ury," " The Angels of Buena Vista," " The Pipes of Lucknow," " The Trailing Arbutus," " Laus Deo," " Dear Lord and Father of Mankind "

Poe, Edgar Allan: "To One in Paradise," "Lenore," "The Haunted Palace"

### Nonfiction

Irving, Washington: *The Sketch Book:* "English Writers on America," "Rural Life in England," "Five Christmas Sketches," "Stratford-on-Avon." *Bracebridge Hall:* "Family Servants," "An Old Soldier," "May-Day Customs," "Popular Superstitions." *The Alhambra:* "The Palace of the Alhambra," "The Hall of Ambassadors," "The Court of Lions," "A Fête in the Alhambra"

### BOOKS ABOUT THE PERIOD

Brenner, Rica: *Twelve American Poets before 1900*
Brooks, Van Wyck: *The World of Washington Irving; The Flowering of New England*
Macy, John, ed.: *American Literature by American Authors* (thirty-seven essays)
Ticknor, Caroline: *Glimpses of Authors*

### On Individual Authors

IRVING. Benét, Laura: *Washington Irving, Explorer of American Legend*
POE. Allen, Hervey: *Israfel;* Benét, Laura: *Young Edgar Allan Poe;* Quinn, A. H.: *Edgar Allan Poe*
HAWTHORNE. Hawthorne, Hildegarde: *A Romantic Rebel* (by his granddaughter)

Detailed biographies of these authors are to be found by numerous writers of an earlier day, and in series such as American Men of Letters, American Writers, etc.

RALPH WALDO EMERSON, one of America's truly great men. He had the ability to make everyone with whom he came into contact think — harder, more deeply, more clearly. (Brown Brothers)

# The Flowering of the East

## PART TWO

### 1. *EMERSON AND THOREAU*

THE FLOWERING OF CONCORD

You drive out twenty miles from Boston, and there it is. " The rude bridge that arched the flood " spans a gentle stream; if you live west of the Hudson you might call it a creek instead of a river. Here where the Statue of the Minuteman now stands, the minutemen themselves stood in 1776 and " fired the shot heard round the world." And on the banks of the river Concord stretches out in quiet streets and broad lawns.

Forget the grocery stores and tourist signs; they weren't there a hundred years ago. But the Old Manse stands hard by the bridge. Emerson's grandfather lived there, and Emerson himself before he built his own home, and then Hawthorne while he was writing *Mosses from an Old Manse.* Walk across the town. It is a town now; it was a country village when Hawthorne lived there. Here is Hawthorne's later home, and the house where Bronson Alcott lived and taught school and which Louisa May Alcott described in *Little Women.* And here is Emerson's own home — square, white, colonial, neither a mansion nor a cottage, but a dignified comfortable house with an avenue of hemlocks Emerson himself planted.

Someone will tell you what lane to follow, and a few minutes' walk will bring you to Walden Pond. There are summer cottages on its banks now, and a public amusement park, but forget those, too. Think of the Indian path that was still visible around the lake when Emerson and Thoreau went there, and go see the cove where Thoreau built his cabin.

There is nothing remarkable about the town. It lies in low hills. Its church spires rise out of avenues of trees. It has a common, and its houses are simple and dignified and white. It is not unlike most New England towns near a large city. And yet, by chance or by design, this town for a generation was such a center of high thinking and good talk and writing as few towns have been, anywhere, at any time.

One hundred years ago there was a lyceum in Concord, and the speakers were all local residents. Anybody who had something to say gave a lecture. That included Emerson, Thoreau, Alcott, Margaret Fuller, and many others. Why should they go outside for speakers? In almost any house in town you could hear good talk. So famous was the Concord talk that tickets were sometimes sold for " Conversations," as for a lecture, and people came from afar to hear two or three of the town's eminent citizens sit on a stage and talk with each other about anything that happened to be on their minds. *The Dial,* perhaps the most intellectual magazine in America, was edited in Concord. Almost any week might bring another essay by Emerson, another tale by Hawthorne, one of Thoreau's nature descriptions, another group of Alcott's orphic sayings. Any week might bring a batch of new poems by one of the numerous minor artists who lived in Concord. Any week

IN THE CHAPEL AT CONCORD Bronson Alcott, a leading member of the Concord group, delivers a lecture before interested townsfolk. (Culver)

might bring distinguished visitors from this country or abroad to see the great men of Concord. Perhaps nowhere in America did men quite equal the combination of leisurely, contemplative living and white-hot intellectual excitement which was Concord at its best.

In Concord, men were always trying something new. A few miles away were Brook Farm and Fruitlands, two of our most interesting experiments in building ideal communities. Alcott was forever trying something new in education. Thoreau was trying to find a new way to live by nature's laws. No one had ever written stories of the kind Hawthorne wrote. The poets were trying to find a new way to write poetry. And Emerson — everything he looked at took on a new shape and fresh color and meaning. In Concord, one of its men said, the world was new every morning, and sometimes impatient philosophers had it renewed several times a day.

But if you ask what Concord had to deserve this flowering, the answer must be that Concord had no more than a dozen other country villages near Boston. It was indeed important that Concord was near Boston, which was the cultural center, the wellspring. But Concord was made by the men who lived there. Concord was great because of the accident that great men settled there. And for a generation it was great indeed.

RALPH WALDO EMERSON

The greatest man in Concord, one of the greatest men in America, was Emerson. He was different from any literary man we have met so far in this account of American writers. He was a poet, and a good one, but his influence did not rest on his poetry, as did Whittier's, for instance. He was an essayist, and a good one, but we remember him today not for entire essays so much as for striking quotations from them. He was chiefly an intellectual and spiritual force, a man who had the ability to make everyone with whom he came into contact *think* — harder, more deeply, more clearly. Matthew Arnold put it best. Emerson, he said, was " friend and aider to those who would live in the spirit."

How does a man rise to that kind of position among his fellow men? In Emerson's case it took thirty years before he got the idea he needed. Thirty years of study, thought, travel, trying this and that, rejecting everything that did not fit, always seeking the new approach, the new idea. He found it finally when he was thirty.

Thousands of New England youngsters spent their first twenty years almost exactly as Emerson spent his. He was born in Boston, of a preacher's family. Boston was a country town, too; he used to lead the family cow to pasture on Boston Common. He went to Harvard, graduated just below the middle of his class, gave his classmates the impression of being retiring, not socially inclined, calm and restrained, but " a man in quest of something."

In quest of something he was. He tried school teaching for a few years, then changed over to the family profession and entered divinity school. At twenty-six he was pastor of one of the most famous churches in Boston, the same pulpit from which the Mathers had preached hell-fire and damnation. But that was not the answer either; he found he could not believe in the ritual of the church, and resigned. He read deeply in the great books, sought out famous thinkers and scholars. He wanted their answer to the riddle of the universe; he wanted to find out what he could really believe — what was truth and how to arrive at truth. And the more he consulted other men, the more he read books, the more he became convinced that no one could help him, that he had to find the road himself.

But he saved a little money and went to Europe, met Carlyle (who became a life-long friend) and Wordsworth, and in Paris, one July day in 1833, found the idea he needed. He was in the museum of natural history, looking at the ferns and flowers.

Suddenly a feeling he had often had when walking through the woods or beside Walden came back to him, but clearer than ever before: it was simply that all living things are related, that there is some common element in man and in all nature. And in that instant, he said, he felt for the first time that the world was one piece and he had the tool to understand it.

It seems a very little thing, but on that experience Emerson built his philosophy. He stated it more clearly when he came back to Concord and went to live in the house with the row of hemlocks. He called the common force which he perceived in all living things the Oversoul. Other people might have called it God. To Emerson it was the same as life, goodness, and truth. Emerson explained it with a little parable. He said the Oversoul was like the sea. When the tide went out it left puddles on the beach; these were like the little bits of Oversoul in all living things. When they died, when the tide came in, their parts of the Oversoul went back to the great sea.

If he had lived a little later, he might have described the Oversoul as an electric current. All living things draw their currents from this central source. When a poet plugs in, the current flows through him as poetry. When a philosopher plugs in, it flows through him as wisdom. In the hands of an artist it is the source of beauty.

Every man since the beginning of time has been connected with this same current — Homer, Plato, the prophets of the Bible, the wise men of western Europe. But the same current that flowed in Plato's time also flows today. And if the ancient philosophers had access to it, men of today have just as good access. That was the idea Emerson needed. For he now saw clearly that it was no longer necessary to go to other times or other countries for wisdom or truth. It was no longer necessary for Americans to humble themselves before the great traditions of Europe, the great names of distant places or past ages. For the truth is here today! The truth is free for the seeking! The truth is within man, and within nature — if man will only have the good sense to perceive it.

That was Emerson's message. He put it in ringing phrases that men still remember and quote. " The sun shines today also! " he said, and " Build therefore your own world! " and " Trust thyself: every heart vibrates to that iron string! " In all these he meant simply that every man has access to truth and strength, that he can be his own boss and his own prophet, and does not need to kowtow to anyone, past or present. It was an optimistic point of view, a good point of view for the America that was winning the West. It avoided the sense of guilt that lay over men like Hawthorne, and encouraged a generation of already self-reliant men to deepen and spiritualize their self-reliance.

The rest of Emerson's story is very simple: he preached that belief to ever widening circles. He lived in Concord, but lectured widely. Three times he crossed the frozen Mississippi on foot to lecture, and late in life he gave a series of talks in California. He published a number of books of essays. He made little money; in fact, he is said never to have received a royalty check for a book of his until he was past fifty. But he had enough income to live in Concord. He had friends, great friends, good enough friends to rebuild his house for him when it burned down. And he had the satisfaction of shocking many of his countrymen into wiser thinking, as for instance the day when he stood on the platform in Harvard's main auditorium to speak on the subject of " The American Scholar," and told his audience: " We have listened too long to the courtly muses of Europe. . . . We will walk on our own feet; . . . we will speak our own minds." Some of the scholars in his audience were shocked, and some of the ministers thought he was preaching blasphemy, but the younger men went away feeling, as later critics felt, that they had heard a declaration of American intellectual independence comparable to Jefferson's declaration of political independence. He had satisfactions like these, and he had the satisfaction of helping young men in whom he

believed start their careers — Thoreau, for instance, and Whitman. Before he died his ringing phrases and his thin, serene, intelligent face became known all over America as a prophet's.

*Emerson was born (1803) three years after Washington's death, and died (1882) in the year of Franklin Roosevelt's birth. In the year of Emerson's birth, Jefferson bought the Mississippi valley from France. By the time of his death, that purchased land — three quarters of a million square miles — was almost entirely settled.*

### HENRY DAVID THOREAU

The picture we remember of Thoreau is the one Emerson painted. " He knew the country like a fox or a bird, and passed through it as freely by paths of his own," Emerson said. " Under his arm he carried an old music book to press plants; in his pocket, his diary and pencil, a spyglass for birds, microscope, jackknife and twine. He wore a straw hat, stout shoes, strong gray trousers, to brave scrub oaks and smilax, and to climb a tree for a hawk's or a squirrel's nest. He waded into the pool for the water plants, and his strong legs were no insignificant part of his armor."

It is a true picture, according to all we can find out. That is the Thoreau who built a ten- by fifteen-foot hut beside Walden Pond for twenty-nine dollars, and managed to live off the soil at an annual cost of eight dollars. That is the Thoreau who paddled up and down the Concord and Merrimac rivers and kept a delightful journal of what he saw and heard. That is the Thoreau who knew every bird and flower, who always knew where to find an Indian arrowhead, who introduced the citybred Emerson to the names and habits of wild things. It is the Thoreau who loved nature and went to school to it, and let its inspiration blow through him like the wind through an Aeolian harp.

But it is not the whole Thoreau. It is not the Thoreau who was described by his neighbors as " a very stubborn and opinionated young man." For among the Concord men, Thoreau was the great arguer, the great dissenter. He argued against the eating of meat, the drinking of alcoholic liquor, the institution of marriage, and the established church. But most of all, he argued against the government.

There is no inconsistency between the Thoreau who loved nature and the Thoreau who refused to pay some of his taxes. Thoreau believed in the simple life. He felt that business and government and civilized institutions got in the way of simple living. While at Harvard, he upheld the thesis that man should really work only the seventh day, and keep the other six free for a real " Sabbath of the soul," for getting close to nature and for thinking. He was especially irritated when the government asked him to pay money for activities of which he did not approve — the Mexican war, for instance, and the enforcement of slavery. He went to jail for that refusal, and when Emerson asked him, " Henry, what are you doing in there? " he looked sternly out through the bars and replied, " What are you doing *out there?* "

Emerson used to amuse himself with thoughts of the mutual condescension with which Thoreau and a rich Boston banker would look on each other, the banker pitying Thoreau for his poverty and rather disgusted with him for what seemed to be a lack of ambition and lack of respect for established institutions; Thoreau pitying the banker because he was working only to pile up rather useless pieces of gold and silver and disgusted with him because his ideals of thrift made him struggle to retain the useless possessions.

But Thoreau rarely came into contact with bankers he might have converted. In fact, his ideas had little impact in his own time. The quality that made Emerson a preacher or teacher in all his lectures and writings was somehow left out of Thoreau. He cared little what others believed, and was content with his own problems, his own code, and his own studies of nature. Other men might have been lonely, but Thoreau

HENRY DAVID THOREAU. Because he believed that business and government and the institutions of civilization got in the way of the simple life, he became the great arguer, the great dissenter. (Culver)

was never lonely with nature. Other men might have felt the obligation to reform their fellow men or at least to share their discoveries, but Thoreau said, " I came into the world, not chiefly to make this a good place to live in, but to live in it, be it good or bad."

He wrote with little eye to publication, piled up journals and notes and essays which were never seen until he died. Nobody has ever written a more delightful book about the simple life than *Walden*. Nobody has ever written more vividly of such natural scenes as his famous " Battle of the Ants." Nobody has ever written more explosive documents than his essay on " Civil Disobedience," in which he argued, in effect, for individual secession whenever a citizen found himself hampered by his government or not in agreement with it. But the dynamite was hidden during his lifetime, and the challenge of his ideas was not widely known until he died.

Thoreau came from Harvard College to Concord village and lived there except for brief intervals until he died — at the age of forty-four, of the old New England scourge, tuberculosis. He seldom felt the need to travel, the urge for wider experience, the attraction of a more complex and ancient society. He had the open book of nature to study, the Harvard College library, when necessary, and the society of the good men of Concord. " I have traveled much," he said, " — in Concord! "

*Thoreau was born (1817) just before the first steamship crossed the Atlantic, and died (1862) shortly after the first Atlantic cable had been laid. When he was born, only Irving of the great Easterners had published. When he died, all of them were well known, but Mark Twain, the first great writer of the West, had not yet published.*

# Ralph Waldo Emerson
## 1803–1882

## THE CONCORD HYMN

This poem was written for the dedication on July 4, 1837, of the monument to the minutemen of the Battle of Concord, which opened the American Revolution. Oliver Wendell Holmes thought it the most complete and faultless of Emerson's poems. Today it is regarded as one of the classics of American literature.

Remember that Emerson's grandfather, a minister of that town, had watched the battle from the Old Manse, only a stone's throw from the bridge. Today the bronze minuteman may be seen through a leafy vista on the far side of the new stone arch which has replaced the original bridge of rough wood. On the base of the statue is inscribed the first stanza of the poem.

By the rude bridge that arched the flood,
   Their flag to April's breeze unfurled,
Here once the embattled farmers stood,
   And fired the shot heard round the world.

The foe long since in silence slept;     5
   Alike the conqueror silent sleeps;
And Time the ruined bridge has swept
   Down the dark stream which seaward creeps.

On this green bank, by this soft stream,
   We set today a votive stone;     10
That memory may their deed redeem,
   When, like our sires, our sons are gone.

Spirit, that made those heroes dare
   To die and leave their children free,
Bid Time and Nature gently spare     15
   The shaft we raise to them and thee.

## THE RHODORA *
### ON BEING ASKED, WHENCE IS THE FLOWER?

In his essay on " Nature " Emerson says that the " love of Beauty " is one of the nobler wants of man. While the beauty of nature and its form delights the eye, the appreciation of beauty is also necessary for spiritual perfection. This thought of Emerson is strikingly similar to the theories of Wordsworth, expressed in many poems on flowers, and to Keats's famous line, " Beauty is truth, truth beauty."

In May, when sea winds pierced our solitudes,
I found the fresh rhodora in the woods,
Spreading its leafless blooms in a damp nook,
To please the desert and the sluggish brook.
The purple petals, fallen in the pool,     5
Made the black water with their beauty gay;

* **Rhodora** (rŏ-dō′rȧ): a shrub commonly found in New England, having large clusters of pink flowers shading into purple, which come out before the leaves in early spring. The original Greek meaning of the word was "rose."

Here might the redbird come his plumes
  to cool,
And court the flower that cheapens his
  array.
Rhodora! if the sages ask thee why    9
This charm is wasted on the earth and sky,
Tell them, dear, that if eyes were made for
  seeing,
Then Beauty is its own excuse for being.
Why thou wert there, O rival of the rose!
I never thought to ask, I never knew:
But, in my simple ignorance, suppose   15
The selfsame Power that brought me there
  brought you.

## COMPENSATION

Emerson wrote two short poems and one
long essay on this subject (see page 567). The
idea of balance in human life was a favorite
of his. In the first stanza, when he is gay,
others are silent; in the second it is the reverse.

Why should I keep holiday
  When other men have none?
Why but because, when these are gay,
  I sit and mourn alone?

And why, when mirth unseals all tongues,
  Should mine alone be dumb?
Ah! late I spoke to silent throngs,
  And now their hour is come.

## FORBEARANCE

Hast thou named all the birds without a
  gun?
Loved the wood rose, and left it on its stalk?
At rich men's tables eaten bread and pulse?°
Unarmed, faced danger with a heart of
  trust?

And loved so well a high behavior,
In man or maid, that thou from speech re-
  frained,
Nobility more nobly to repay?
O, be my friend, and teach me to be thine!

3. **pulse:** the seeds of peas, beans, or similar
vegetables.

## VOLUNTARIES III

The long poem " Voluntaries " contains five
disconnected stanzas, each treating of some act
of the will in relation to the struggles of life.
The third one of these is the most easily understood and the best known. It sounds as if it
had been written during our recent World War
II. The last four lines are frequently quoted.

In an age of fops and toys,
Wanting wisdom, void of right,
Who shall nerve heroic boys
To hazard all in Freedom's fight —
Break sharply off their jolly games,   5
Forsake their comrades gay
And quit proud homes and youthful dames
For famine, toil, and fray?
Yet on the nimble air benign
Speed nimbler messages,   10
That waft the breath of grace divine
To hearts in sloth and ease.
So nigh is grandeur to our dust,
So near is God to man,
When duty whispers low, *Thou must,*   15
The youth replies, *I can.*

## EACH AND ALL

That each person or thing is dependent on
all that surrounds it is the theme of this poem.
First the poet shows how unaware we may be
of our effect upon others. Then he builds up
his idea of the importance of environment by
showing changes that take place when things
are removed from their original setting. He
closes with the idea that one cannot escape
from the spell of complete beauty.

Little thinks, in the field, yon red-cloaked
  clown,
Of thee from the hilltop looking down;
The heifer that lows in the upland farm,
Far-heard, lows not thine ear to charm;
The sexton, tolling his bell at noon,   5
Deems not that great Napoleon
Stops his horse, and lists with delight,
Whilst his files sweep round yon Alpine
  height;
Nor knowest thou what argument   9
Thy life to thy neighbor's creed has lent.

All are needed by each one;
Nothing is fair or good alone.
I thought the sparrow's note from heaven,
Singing at dawn on the alder bough;     14
I brought him home, in his nest, at even;
He sings the song, but it cheers not now,
For I did not bring home the river and
    sky —
He sang to my ear — they sang to my eye.


The delicate shells lay on the shore;
The bubbles of the latest wave     20
Fresh pearls to their enamel gave,
And the bellowing of the savage sea
Greeted their safe escape to me.
I wiped away the weeds and foam,
I fetched my sea-born treasures home;     25
But the poor, unsightly, noisome things
Had left their beauty on the shore
With the sun and the sand and the wild
    uproar.


The lover watched his graceful maid,
As 'mid the virgin train she strayed,     30
Nor knew her beauty's best attire
Was woven still by the snow-white choir.
At last she came to his hermitage,
Like the bird from the woodlands to the
    cage —
The gay enchantment was undone,     35
A gentle wife, but fairy none.


Then I said, " I covet truth;
Beauty is unripe childhood's cheat;
I leave it behind with the games of
    youth " —
As I spoke, beneath my feet     40
The ground pine curled its pretty wreath,
Running over the club-moss burrs;
I inhaled the violet's breath;
Around me stood the oaks and firs;     44
Pine cones and acorns lay on the ground;
Over me soared the eternal sky,
Full of light and of deity;
Again I saw, again I heard,
The rolling river, the morning bird —
Beauty through my senses stole;     50
I yielded myself to the perfect whole.

## Suggestions for Study of Emerson's Poems

1. For each poem write a good sentence or two to show the point Emerson wished to make. In general, how do these poems differ from Poe's?

2. In " The Concord Hymn " what is meant by " the shot heard round the world "? What appeal is made in the last stanza? Why is *hymn* a suitable word to describe this poem?

3. Report to the class interesting details about the Battle of Concord and its results. In this connection read Longfellow's " Paul Revere's Ride."

4. Compare " The Concord Hymn " with Lincoln's " Gettysburg Address " (see page 260). What similarities and differences were there in the occasion? in the appeal made at the end?

5. What evidence can you find in these poems that Emerson, as well as Bryant, was a lover of nature? Which two poems of this group discuss the meaning of beauty? Is there any difference in the point about beauty made in them?

6. If you are collecting poems on flowers, compare the ideas that different flowers have suggested to different poets: the rhodora to Emerson, the fringed gentian to Bryant, the honeysuckle to Freneau, the daffodil to Wordsworth, the dandelion to Lowell, and so on.

7. As you observe your own life and that of others, do you find compensation such as Emerson describes? other kinds of compensation?

8. Why do you think Emerson admired a person who displayed the qualities found in " Forbearance "? Are these some of the qualities you would seek in a friend? If not, make your own list of qualities.

9. What does " Voluntaries III " show of Emerson's attitude toward youth? How was youth's response illustrated in World War II? What examples can you give of sacrifice of self to duty in time of peace? (See in this connection " Walter Reed," page 164.)

10. What does " Each and All " say about the unconscious influence of one person on another, especially in lines 9 and 10? Point out examples of loss of charm through loss of environment. Can you give examples from your own experience? Does this poem contradict Emerson's plea for self-reliance?

## GIFTS

You have seen that Emerson's poems were like little essays in verse, because he was usually trying to convey some thought or bit of philosophy. His essays were lectures originally, and so are somewhat different from the essay not intended for oral delivery. More profoundly than most essays they deal with interpretations of life and abstract thought. A swift glance at the titles will show this. " Friendship," " Love," " Self-Reliance," " Heroism," " Character," " Manners," " Compensation " — each treats of some quality of human life with a sincerity and wisdom which have won for their author such titles as seer, sage, and prophet.

It will help you in reading Emerson to understand that his unit of thought is generally the sentence — not the paragraph, as with most writers. You must, therefore, read slowly and let the complete meaning of each sentence sink in.

> Gifts of one who loved me —
> 'Twas high time they came;
> When he ceased to love me,
> Time they stopped for shame.

It is said that the world is in a state of bankruptcy, that the world owes the world more than the world can pay, and ought to go into chancery, and be sold. I do not think this general insolvency, which involves in some sort all the population, to be the reason of the difficulty experienced at Christmas and New Year, and other times, in bestowing gifts; since it is always so pleasant to be generous, though very vexatious to pay debts. But the impediment lies in the choosing. If, at any time, it comes into my head that a present is due from me to somebody, I am puzzled what to give, until the opportunity is gone. Flowers and fruits are always fit presents — flowers, because they are a proud assertion that a ray of beauty outvalues all the utilities of the world. These gay natures contrast with the somewhat stern countenance of ordinary nature; they are like music heard out of a workhouse. Nature does not cocker [1] us; we are children, not pets; she

[1] **cocker:** spoil, coddle.

is not fond [2]; everything is dealt to us without fear or flavor, after severe universal laws. Yet these delicate flowers look like the frolic and interference of love and beauty. Men used to tell us that we love flattery, even though we are not deceived by it, because it shows that we are of importance enough to be courted. Something like that pleasure, the flowers give us: what am I to whom these sweet hints are addressed?' Fruits are acceptable gifts, because they are the flower of commodities, and admit of fantastic values being attached to them. If a man should send to me to come a hundred miles to visit him, and should set before me a basket of fine summer fruit, I should think there was some proportion between the labor and the reward.

For common gifts, necessity makes pertinences and beauty every day, and one is glad when an imperative leaves him no option, since if the man at the door has no shoes you have not to consider whether you could procure him a paintbox. And as it is always pleasing to see a man eat bread, drink water, in the house or out of doors, so it is always a great satisfaction to supply these first wants. Necessity does everything well. In our condition of universal dependence, it seems heroic to let the petitioner be the judge of his necessity, and to give all that is asked, though at great inconvenience. If it be a fantastic desire, it is better to leave to others the office of punishing him. I can think of many parts I should prefer playing to that of the Furies.[3]

Next to things of necessity, the rule for a gift, which one of my friends prescribed, is, that we might convey to some person that which properly belonged to his character, and was easily associated with him in thought. But our tokens of compliment and love are for the most part barbarous. Rings and other jewels are not gifts, but apologies for gifts. The only gift is a portion of thyself. Thou must bleed for me. Therefore

[2] **fond:** in the sense of foolishly tender. [3] **Furies:** in Greek mythology, beings who punished the wicked.

the poet brings his poem; the shepherd, his lamb; the farmer, corn; the miner, a gem; the sailor, coral and shells; the painter, his picture; the girl, a handkerchief of her own sewing. This is right and pleasing, for it restores society in so far to its primary basis, when a man's biography is conveyed in his gift, and every man's wealth is an index of his merit. But it is a cold, lifeless business when you go to the shops to buy me something which does not represent your life and talent, but a goldsmith's. This is fit for kings, and rich men who represent kings, and a false state of property, to make presents of gold and silver stuffs, as a kind of symbolical sin-offering, or payment of blackmail.

The law of benefits is a difficult channel, which requires careful sailing, or rude boats. It is not the office of a man to receive gifts. How dare you give them? We wish to be self-sustained. We do not quite forgive a giver. The hand that feeds us is in some danger of being bitten. We can receive anything from love, for that is a way of receiving it from ourselves; but not from anyone who assumes to bestow. We sometimes hate the meat which we eat, because there seems something of degrading dependence in living by it.

Brother, if Jove to thee a present make,
Take heed that from his hands thou nothing take.

We ask the whole. Nothing less will content us. We arraign society, if it do not give us, besides earth and fire and water, opportunity, love, reverence, and objects of veneration.

He is a good man who can receive a gift well. We are either glad or sorry at a gift, and both emotions are unbecoming. Some violence, I think, is done, some degradation borne, when I rejoice or grieve at a gift. I am sorry when my independence is invaded, or when a gift comes from such as do not know my spirit, and so the act is not supported; and if the gift pleases me overmuch, then I should be ashamed that the donor should read my heart, and see that I love his commodity and not him. The gift, to be true, must be the flowing of the giver unto me, correspondent to my flowing unto him. When the waters are at a level, then my goods pass to him, and his to me. All his are mine, all mine his. I say to him, " How can you give me this pot of oil, or this flagon of wine, when all your oil and wine is mine? " which belief of mine this gift seems to deny. Hence the fitness of beautiful, not useful things for gifts. This giving is flat usurpation, and therefore when the beneficiary is ungrateful, as all beneficiaries hate all Timons,[1] not at all considering the value of the gift, but looking back to the greater store it was taken from, I rather sympathize with the beneficiary than with the anger of my lord Timon. For the expectation of gratitude is mean, and is continually punished by the total insensibility of the obliged person. It is a great happiness to get off without injury and heartburning from one who has had the ill luck to be served by you. It is a very onerous business, this of being served, and the debtor naturally wishes to give you a slap. A golden text for these gentlemen is that which I so admire in the Buddhist, who never thanks, and who says, " Do not flatter your benefactors."

The reason of these discords I conceive to be that there is no commensurability between a man and any gift. You cannot give anything to a magnanimous person. After you have served him, he at once puts you in debt by his magnanimity. The service a man renders his friend is trivial and selfish, compared with the service he knows his friend stood in readiness to yield him, alike before he had begun to serve his friend, and now also. Compared with that good will I bear my friend, the benefit it is in my power to render him seems small. Besides, our action on each other, good as well as evil, is so incidental and at random, that we can seldom hear the ac-

[1] **Timon:** the leading character in Shakespeare's play *Timon of Athens*, who spent his entire fortune on lavish gifts and was then spurned by those who had flattered him.

knowledgments of any person who would thank us for a benefit without some shame and humiliation. We can rarely strike a direct stroke, but must be content with an oblique one; we seldom have the satisfaction of yielding a direct benefit, which is directly received. But rectitude scatters favors on every side without knowing it, and receives with wonder the thanks of all people.

I fear to breathe any treason against the majesty of love, which is the genius and god of gifts, and to whom we must not affect to prescribe. Let him give kingdoms or flower leaves indifferently. There are persons from whom we always expect fairy tokens; let us not cease to expect them. This is prerogative, and not to be limited by our municipal rules. For the rest, I like to see that we cannot be bought and sold. The best of hospitality and of generosity is also not in the will, but in fate. I find that I am not much to you; you do not need me; you do not feel me; then am I thrust out of doors, though you proffer me house and lands. No services are of any value, but only likeness. When I have attempted to join myself to others by services, it proved an intellectual trick — no more. They eat your service like apples, and leave you out. But love them, and they feel you, and delight in you all the time.

# Selections from Other Emerson Essays

Since Emerson's essays are rather rambling in construction, one can gain from quotations here and there an idea of his point of view, and a vivid impression of the great thoughts which have stirred the minds of men and women for a century.

## FROM "NATURE"

It seems as if the day was not wholly profane in which we have given heed to some natural object. The fall of snowflakes in a still air, preserving to each crystal its perfect form; the blowing of sleet over a wide sheet of water, and over plains; the waving rye field; the mimic waving of acres of houstonia,[1] whose innumerable florets whiten and ripple before the eye; the reflections of trees and flowers in glassy lakes; the musical steaming odorous south wind, which converts all trees to wind harps; the crackling and spurting of hemlock in the flames; or of pine logs, which yield glory to the walls and faces in the sitting room — these are the music and pictures of the most ancient religion. . . . We can find these enchantments without visiting the Como Lake, or the Madeira Islands. . . . In every landscape, the point of astonishment is the meeting of the sky and the earth, and that is seen from the first hillock as well as from the top of the Alleghenies. The stars at night stoop down over the brownest, homeliest common with all the spiritual magnificence which they shed on the Campagna, or on the marble deserts of Egypt. . . . The difference between landscape and landscape is small, but there is great difference in the beholders. . . . Nature cannot be surprised in undress. Beauty breaks in everywhere.

## FROM "MANNERS"

The gentleman is a man of truth, lord of his own actions, and expressing that lordship in his behavior, not in any manner dependent and servile either on persons, or opinions, or possessions. Beyond this fact of truth and real force, the word denotes good nature or benevolence; manhood first and then gentleness. The popular notion certainly adds a condition of ease and fortune; but that is a natural result of personal force and love, that they should possess and dispense the goods of the world. In times of violence every eminent person must fall in with many opportunities to approve[2] his stoutness and worth; therefore every man's name that emerged at all from the mass in the feudal ages, rattles in our

[1] **houstonia** (hōōs-tō′nĭ-à) : a low, slender plant named for Dr. Houston, a naturalist. [2] **approve:** prove.

ear like a flourish of trumpets. But personal force never goes out of fashion. That is still paramount today, and in the moving crowd of good society, the men of valor and reality are known, and rise to their natural place. The competition is transferred from war to politics and trade, but the personal force appears readily enough in these new arenas. . . . My gentleman gives the law where he is; he will outpray saints in chapel, outgeneral veterans in the field, and outshine all courtesy in the hall. He is good company for pirates, and good with academicians.

## FROM " FRIENDSHIP "

A friend is a person with whom I may be sincere. Before him I may think aloud. I am arrived at last in the presence of a man so real and equal that I may drop even those undermost garments of dissimulation, courtesy, and second thought, which men never put off, and may deal with him with the simplicity and wholeness with which one chemical atom meets another. Sincerity is the luxury allowed, like diadems and authority, only to the highest rank, *that* being permitted to speak truth, as having none above it to court or conform unto. Every man alone is sincere. At the entrance of a second person, hypocrisy begins. We parry and fend the approach of our fellow man by compliments, by gossip, by amusements, by affairs. We cover up our thought from him under a hundred folds. . . . Almost every man we meet requires some civility, requires to be humored — he has some fame, some talent, some whim of religion or philanthropy in his head that is not to be questioned, and which spoils all conversation with him. But a friend is a sane man who exercises not my ingenuity but me. My friend gives me entertainment without requiring me to stoop, or to lisp, or to mask myself. A friend therefore is a sort of paradox in nature. I who alone am, I who see nothing in nature whose existence I can affirm with equal evidence to my own, behold now the semblance of my being, in all its height, variety, and curiosity, reiterated in a foreign form; so that a friend may well be reckoned the masterpiece of nature.

## FROM " COMPENSATION "

The same dualism underlies the nature and condition of man. Every excess causes a defect; every defect an excess. Every sweet hath its sour; every evil its good. Every faculty which is a receiver of pleasure has an equal penalty for its abuse. It is to answer for its moderation with its life. For every grain of wit there is a grain of folly. For everything you have missed, you have gained something else; and for everything you gain, you lose something. If riches increase, they are increased that use them. If the gatherer gathers too much, nature takes out of the man what she puts into his chest; swells the estate, but kills the owner. Nature hates monopolies and exceptions. The waves of the sea do not more speedily seek a level from their loftiest tossing than the varieties of condition tend to equalize themselves. There is always some leveling circumstance that puts down the overbearing, the strong, the rich, the fortunate, substantially on the same ground with all others. . . .

The farmer imagines power and place are fine things. But the President has paid dear for his White House. It has commonly cost him all his peace, and the best of his manly attributes. To preserve for a short time so conspicuous an appearance before the world, he is content to eat dust before the real masters who stand erect behind the throne. Or do men desire the more substantial and permanent grandeur of genius? Neither has this an immunity. He who by force of will or of thought is great and overlooks thousands, has the responsibility of overlooking. With every influx of light comes new danger. Has he light? He must bear witness to the light, and always outrun that sympathy which gives him such keen satisfaction, by his fidelity to new revelations of the incessant soul.

## FROM " SELF–RELIANCE "

There is a time in every man's education when he arrives at the conviction that envy is ignorance; that imitation is suicide; that he must take himself for better, for worse, as his portion; that though the wide universe is full of good, no kernel of nourishing corn can come to him but through his toil bestowed on that plot of ground which is given him to till. The power which resides in him is new in nature, and none but he knows what he can do, nor does he know until he has tried. . . .

Society everywhere is in conspiracy against the manhood of every one of its members. Society is a joint-stock company, in which the members agree, for the better securing of his bread to each shareholder, to surrender the liberty and culture of the eater. The virtue in most request is conformity. Self-reliance is its aversion. It loves not realities and creators, but names and customs.

Whoso would be a man must be a nonconformist. He who would gather immortal palms must not be hindered by the name of goodness, but must explore if it be goodness. Nothing is at last sacred but the integrity of your own mind. . . .

A foolish consistency is the hobgoblin of little minds, adored by little statesmen and philosophers and divines. With consistency a great soul has simply nothing to do. He may as well concern himself with his shadow on the wall. Speak what you think now in hard words, and tomorrow speak what tomorrow thinks in hard words again, though it contradict everything you said today. " Ah, so you shall be sure to be misunderstood." Is it so bad, then, to be misunderstood? Pythagoras was misunderstood, and Socrates, and Jesus, and Luther, and Copernicus, and Galileo, and Newton, and every pure and wise spirit that ever took flesh. To be great is to be misunderstood. . . .

The civilized man has built a coach, but has lost the use of his feet. He is supported on crutches, but lacks so much support of muscle. He has got a fine Geneva watch, but he has lost the skill to tell the hour by the sun. A Greenwich nautical almanac he has, and so, being sure of the information when he wants it, the man in the street does not know a star in the sky. The solstice he does not observe; the equinox he knows as little; and the whole bright calendar of the year is without a dial in his mind. His notebooks impair his memory; his libraries overload his wit; the insurance office increases the number of accidents; and it may be a question whether machinery does not encumber; whether we have not lost by refinement some energy, by a Christianity intrenched in establishments and forms some vigor of wild virtue. For every Stoic was a Stoic; but in Christendom, where is the Christian?

## FAMOUS QUOTATIONS
## FROM EMERSON

Like Franklin, Emerson has contributed many wise sayings that have passed into our common stock of quotations. But the essential difference between the two men is easily seen when one rereads the Sayings of Poor Richard on page 456, and then turns immediately to these which follow. Emerson supplies the qualities of idealism and high aspiration which were lacking in Franklin's plain common sense.

1. Hitch your wagon to a star. — " Civilization "

2. 'Tis man's perdition to be safe, when for the truth he ought to die. — " Sacrifice "

3. For what avail the plow or sail,
   Or land or life, if freedom fail.
   — " Boston "

4. Nothing great was ever achieved without enthusiasm. — " Circles "

5. The reward of a thing well done is to have done it. — " New England Reformers "

6. The true test of a civilization is, not the census, nor the size of cities, nor the crops — no, but the kind of man the country turns out. — " Civilization "

7. The ornament of a house is the friends who frequent it. — " Domestic Life "

8. What you *are* stands over you the while, and thunders so that I cannot hear what you say to the contrary. — " Social Aims "

9. Great men are they who see that spiritual is stronger than any material force, that thoughts rule the world. — " Progress of Culture "

10. [One of the most popular quotations attributed to Emerson is, oddly enough, not to be found among his printed writings in the form it commonly takes, but the *idea* behind it appears in his Journals. Here is the quotation as found in print:]

I trust a good deal to common fame as we all must. If a man has good corn, or wood, or boards, or pigs to sell, or can make better chairs or knives, crucibles or church organs than anybody else, you will find a broad, hard-beaten road to his house, though it be in the woods.

[And here it is in briefer form as you have probably heard it:]

If you write a better book, or preach a better sermon, or build a better mousetrap than your neighbor, the world will make a beaten track to your door.

## Suggestions for Study of Emerson's Essays

GIFTS

1. Why does Emerson think that flowers and fruits are always fit presents? Does he approve of giving necessaries? jewelry? handkerchiefs? Under what circumstances do you think he would approve or disapprove of the following as gifts: a check, winter underwear, a gold bracelet, a photograph, an embroidered lunch cloth, a corsage bouquet, a book of poetry, a necktie?

2. What difficulties does he see in receiving gifts? In the light of this essay what criticisms can you make of some of our common practices in Christmas giving? Do you disagree with Emerson on any point? If so, what?

SELECTIONS FROM OTHER ESSAYS

3. How many ideas expressed in Emerson's poems do you find echoed in his essays?

4. Name two or three persons prominent in public life today who you think could be called gentlemen according to Emerson's definition. Name two or three who could not. Defend your answers.

5. What difference is there between a friend as Emerson defines one and a friend in the common use of the word as an acquaintance? Do you think that most school friendships stand the test of Emerson's definition?

6. Give examples from your own experience to illustrate some of the general statements made about compensation. Would you agree with Emerson that there are *always* compensations in life? Give illustrations to prove your point. (See poem " Compensation," page 562.)

7. By what kind of people is Emerson's message of self-reliance most needed? Do you feel that it is needed in your high school? Is it needed generally in the country today? Prove your points by examples.

8. What dangers would there be to society if Emerson's words on self-reliance were taken too literally? From what you know of Emerson do you think he is approving lawbreaking? Why or why not?

9. Look up the lives of the great men mentioned in the selection from " Self-Reliance " to find out in what ways they were misunderstood. Suggest other names of great men in history today who have been misunderstood.

10. Discuss the meanings of the famous quotations, and whether or not you think they are borne out in your experience. What single sentences do you find in any of the paragraphs from his essays which might be added to the list of famous quotations? From the entire group memorize those you think particularly valuable.

11. Write a short contrast between Franklin and Emerson illustrating their differences in subject matter and point of view as shown in the quotations from each writer.

12. Consider, not necessarily for class discussion, but in your own mind, ways in which any of Emerson's ideas might enter into your own attitudes or actions.

13. If you have found the paragraphs from the essays challenging, try reading the essays in their complete form. Others which might interest you are " Experience," " Character,"

"Politics," "Heroism," "Love," "The American Scholar." If you find the essays too difficult, you might enjoy *The Heart of Emerson's Journals,* where you will find bits of his philosophy interspersed with the daily happenings of his life.

## For Your Vocabulary

BASE-WORDS. This is a good time to review the word part *bene,* good. Emerson uses three words built on it – *benign* (bĕ-nīn'), good in the sense of kindly and gracious (page 562); *beneficiary* (bĕn-ĕ-fĭsh'ĭ-ĕr-ĭ), the one who *benefits* (page 565); and *benevolence* (bĕ-nĕv'ō-lĕns), the quality of wishing others good fortune (page 566). A *benevolent* person may take action as a *benefactor* to make the good come to pass. Parallel words with *male-* at the beginning substitute evil for good. When you meet the characters in "The Outcasts of Poker Flat," notice that some of them deal in both *malevolence* and *malediction.* (Do you know exactly what a *benediction* is?) A *malign* person, wishing evil to others, is little better than the *malefactor* who does evil to others.

CONTEXT. Check *insolvency* (ĭn-sŏl'vĕn-sĭ) in context (page 564). The preceding sentence states the idea clearly. The *in-* here means *not.* Then what is a *solvent* business firm?

WORD ANALYSIS. Analyze *insensibility* (page 565), *nonconformist* (page 568), and *intrenched* (page 568). *Insensibility* uses a stricter meaning of *sensible* than our everyday one. Take the literal meaning of *sense* and apply it to *sensible* to get the meaning exactly stated.

# Henry David Thoreau 1817–1862

## WALDEN

Man's struggle to get possession of *things* to make life easier and pleasanter is as old as the human race. The struggle to keep things from swamping him is almost as old. We all know women who are so busy keeping their houses in beautiful order that they find no pleasure in them, or men who are so occupied in making money that they never have time to enjoy what their money can buy. These people have lost the struggle. The medieval hermits withdrew from the comparatively simple world of their time to escape the tyranny of things and to have time to think, time to be themselves. They won the struggle. But we do not want to be hermits any more than we want to be the woman ruled by her house or the man ruled by his money.

The happy middle path is not easy to find. The world we live in pulls hard for things. Every newspaper or magazine we open, every lull on the radio, tempts us with new things skillfully presented to make us want them. But we can turn to great books and find support for the human element in life, for keeping an interest in living rather than in material possessions. Many great writers down through the ages have warned us that the surest way to have an empty life is to fill it with *things.* When you are young and still want many things, this warning is not so impressive. It is only when the edge is worn off the delight of possession and the possessions take up more and more of your time and attention that you begin to see the charms of the simple life.

*Walden* is one of the greatest accounts in literature of an experiment with the simple life. It was only an experiment. Thoreau was no hermit. He learned what he wanted to know — what is real living? — and went back to his usual village life, wiser and happier.

What Thoreau enthusiasts cherish most is not whole passages of description and narrative but brilliant short statements that catch and hold a truth as if in the beam of a spotlight. Here are some of them. If you think them through, you may achieve the happy compromise and never be hedged in by your material possessions, but taste the flavor of each day as you live it. Or, fifteen or twenty years from now, when you find things closing in on you until you cannot tell whether you are living at all, some short observation of Thoreau's can work like a charm to bring balance and sanity back into your life. That is why Thoreau has grown steadily in popularity as life has grown more complex.

Most of the luxuries, and many of the so-called comforts of life are not only not indispensable, but positive hindrances to the elevation of mankind.

Every morning was a cheerful invitation to make my life of equal simplicity, and I may say innocence, with Nature herself.

THOREAU'S HUT at Walden Pond. (Culver)

I have been as sincere a worshiper of Aurora [1] as the Greeks. I got up early and bathed in the pond; that was a religious exercise, and one of the best things which I did.

To him whose elastic and vigorous thought keeps pace with the sun, the day is a perpetual morning. It matters not what the clocks say or the attitudes and labors of men. Morning is when I am awake and there is a dawn in me. Moral reform is the effort to throw off sleep. Why is it that men give so poor an account of their day if they have not been slumbering? They are not such poor calculators. If they had not been overcome with drowsiness, they would have performed something. The millions are awake enough for physical labor; but only one in a million is awake enough for effective intellectual exertion, only one in a hundred millions to a poetic or divine life. To be awake is to be alive. I have never yet met a man who was quite awake. How could I have looked him in the face?

[1] **Aurora:** the goddess of morning; the personification of dawn.

I went to the woods because I wished to live deliberately, to front only the essential facts of life, and see if I could not learn what it had to teach, and not, when I came to die, discover that I had not lived. I did not wish to live what was not life, living is so dear; nor did I wish to practice resignation, unless it was quite necessary. I wanted to live deep and suck out all the marrow of life, to live so sturdily and Spartanlike as to put to rout all that was not life, to cut a broad swath and shave close, to drive life into a corner and reduce it to its lowest terms, and, if it proved to be mean, why then to get the whole and genuine meanness of it and publish its meanness to the world; or, if it were sublime, to know it by experience and be able to give a true account of it in my next excursion.

Still we live meanly, like ants; though the fable tells us that we were long ago changed into men; like pygmies we fight with cranes; it is error upon error, and clout upon clout, and our best virtue has for its occasion a superfluous and evitable wretchedness. Our life is frittered away by detail.

Simplify, simplify. Instead of three meals a day, if it be necessary eat but one; instead of a hundred dishes, five; and reduce other things in proportion.

Why should we live with such hurry and waste of life? We are determined to be starved before we are hungry. Men say that a stitch in time saves nine, and so they take a thousand stitches today to save nine tomorrow. As for *work*, we haven't any of any consequence. We have the Saint Vitus's dance, and cannot possibly keep our heads still.

When we are unhurried and wise, we perceive that only great and worthy things have any permanent and absolute existence, that petty fears and petty pleasures are but the shadow of the reality. This is always exhilarating and sublime.

Let us spend one day as deliberately as Nature, and not be thrown off the track by every nutshell and mosquito's wing that falls on the rails. Let us rise early and fast, or break fast, gently and without perturbation; let company come and let company go, let the bells ring and the children cry — determined to make a day of it.

Time is but the stream I go a-fishing in. I drink at it; but while I drink I see the sandy bottom and detect how shallow it is. Its thin current slides away, but eternity remains.

If the day and the night are such that you greet them with joy, and life emits a fragrance like flowers and sweet-scented herbs, is more elastic, more starry, more immortal — that is your success.

## BRUTE NEIGHBORS

With both time and desire to observe nature in all her forms, Thoreau made good use of his life in the woods to watch and record the animal life about him. Except for Audubon, the student of birds, he was the first of a large group of American nature writers. Not quite a scientific naturalist like many of his successors, Thoreau enlivened his accounts with bits of philosophy and humor. One of the best known parts of *Walden* is the vividly told battle of the ants in this selection.

It is remarkable how many creatures live wild and free though secret in the woods, and still sustain themselves in the neighborhood of towns, suspected by hunters only. How retired the otter manages to live here! He grows to be four feet long, as big as a small boy, perhaps without any human being getting a glimpse of him. I formerly saw the raccoon in the woods behind where my house is built, and probably still heard their whinnering at night. Commonly I rested an hour or two in the shade at noon, after planting, and ate my lunch, and read a little by a spring which was the source of a swamp and of a brook, oozing from under

Brister's Hill, half a mile from my field. The approach to this was through a succession of descending grassy hollows, full of young pitch pines, into a larger wood about the swamp. There, in a very secluded and shaded spot, under a spreading white pine, there was yet a clean, firm sward to sit on. I had dug out the spring and made a well of clear gray water, where I could dip up a pailful without roiling it, and thither I went for this purpose almost every day in midsummer, when the pond was warmest. Thither, too, the woodcock led her brood, to probe the mud for worms, flying but a foot above them down the bank, while they ran in a troop beneath; but at last, spying me, she would leave her young and circle round and round me, nearer and nearer till within four or five feet, pretending broken wings and legs, to attract my attention, and get off her young, who would already have taken up their march, with faint, wiry peep, single file through the swamp, as she directed. Or I heard the peep of the young when I could not see the parent bird. There too the turtledoves sat over the spring, or fluttered from bough to bough of the soft white pines over my head; or the red squirrel, coursing down the nearest bough, was particularly familiar and inquisitive. You only need sit still long enough in some attractive spot in the woods that all its inhabitants may exhibit themselves to you by turns.

I was witness to events of a less peaceful character. One day when I went out to my woodpile, or rather my pile of stumps, I observed two large ants, the one red, the other much larger, nearly half an inch long, and black, fiercely contending with one another. Having once got hold they never let go, but struggled and wrestled and rolled on the chips incessantly. Looking farther, I was surprised to find that the chips were covered with such combatants, that it was not a *duellum*[1] but a *bellum*,[2] a war between two races of ants, the red always pitted against the black, and frequently two red ones to one black. The legions of these

[1] **duellum:** duel. [2] **bellum:** war.

Myrmidons [1] covered all the hills and vales in my woodyard, and the ground was already strewn with the dead and dying, both red and black. It was the only battle which I have ever witnessed, the only battlefield I ever trod while the battle was raging; internecine war; the red republicans on the one hand, and the black imperialists on the other. On every side they were engaged in deadly combat, yet without any noise that I could hear, and human soldiers never fought so resolutely. I watched a couple that were fast locked in each other's embraces in a little sunny valley amid the chips, now at noonday prepared to fight till the sun went down, or life went out. The smaller red champion had fastened himself like a vise to his adversary's front, and through all the tumblings on that field never for an instant ceased to gnaw at one of his feelers near the root, having already caused the other to go by the board; while the stronger black one dashed him from side to side, and, as I saw on looking nearer, had already divested him of several of his members. They fought with more pertinacity than bulldogs. Neither manifested the least disposition to retreat. It was evident that their battle cry was " Conquer or die." In the meanwhile there came along a single red ant on the hillside of this valley, evidently full of excitement, who either had dispatched his foe, or had not yet taken part in the battle; probably the latter, for he had lost none of his limbs; whose mother had charged him to return with his shield or upon it. Or perchance he was some Achilles,[2] who had nourished his wrath apart, and had now come to avenge or rescue his Patroclus. He saw this unequal combat from afar — for the blacks were nearly twice the size of the red — he drew near with rapid pace till he stood on his guard within half an inch of the combat-

ants; then, watching his opportunity, he sprang upon the black warrior, and commenced his operations near the root of his right foreleg, leaving the foe to select among his own members; and so there were three united for life, as if a new kind of attraction had been invented which put all other locks and cements to shame. I should not have wondered by this time to find that they had their respective musical bands stationed on some eminent chip, and playing their national airs the while, to excite the slow and cheer the dying combatants. I was myself excited somewhat even as if they had been men. The more you think of it, the less the difference. And certainly there is not the fight recorded in Concord history, at least, if in the history of America, that will bear a moment's comparison with this, whether for the numbers engaged in it, or for the patriotism and heroism displayed. For numbers and for carnage it was an Austerlitz or Dresden.[3] Concord Fight! [4] Two killed on the patriots' side, and Luther Blanchard wounded! Why, here every ant was a Buttrick — " Fire! for God's sake, fire! " — and thousands shared the fate of Davis and Hosmer.[5] There was not one hireling there. I have no doubt that it was a principle they fought for, as much as our ancestors, and not to avoid a threepenny tax on their tea; and the results of this battle will be as important and memorable to those whom it concerns as those of the battle of Bunker Hill, at least.

I took up the chip on which the three I have particularly described were struggling, carried it into my house, and placed it under a tumbler on my window sill, in order to see the issue. Holding a microscope to the first-mentioned red ant, I saw that, though he was assiduously gnawing at the near foreleg of his enemy, having severed

[1] **Myrmidons:** followers of Achilles in the Trojan War. The word originally meant "ant-men." [2] **Achilles:** Greek hero, represented in the *Iliad* as sulking in his tent over a hurt to his pride; but when his best friend, Patroclus, is killed, he forgets his wrath and re-enters the battle in his desire for vengeance.

[3] **Austerlitz, Dresden:** battles of Napoleon, attended by terrible loss of life. In the former, 42,000 were killed; in the latter, between 7,000 and 8,000. [4] **Concord Fight:** the Battle of Concord, which with that of Lexington opened the American Revolution. [5] **Blanchard, Buttrick, Davis, Hosmer:** natives of Concord participating in the fight, the last two being the only ones killed.

his remaining feeler, his own breast was all torn away, exposing what vitals he had there to the jaws of the black warrior, whose breastplate was apparently too thick for him to pierce; and the dark carbuncles of the sufferer's eyes shone with ferocity such as war only could excite. They struggled half an hour longer under the tumbler, and when I looked again the black soldier had severed the heads of his foes from their bodies, and the still living heads were hanging on either side of him like ghastly trophies at his saddlebow, still apparently as firmly fastened as ever, and he was endeavoring with feeble struggles, being without feelers and with only the remnant of a leg, and I know not how many other wounds, to divest himself of them; which at length, after half an hour more, he accomplished. I raised the glass, and he went off over the window sill in that crippled state. Whether he finally survived that combat, and spent the remainder of his days in some Hôtel des Invalides,[1] I do not know; but I thought that his industry would not be worth much thereafter. I never learned which party was victorious, nor the cause of the war; but I felt for the rest of that day as if I had had my feelings excited and harrowed by witnessing the struggle, the ferocity and carnage, of a human battle before my door.

Kirby and Spence[2] tell us that the battles of ants have long been celebrated and the dates of them recorded, though they say that Huber is the only modern author who appears to have witnessed them. "Aeneas Sylvius," say they, "after giving a very circumstantial account of one contested with great obstinacy by a great and small species on the trunk of a pear tree, adds that 'this action was fought in the pontificate of Eugenius the Fourth, in the presence of Nicholas Pistoriensis, an eminent lawyer, who related the whole history of the battle with the greatest fidelity.' A similar engagement between great and small ants is recorded by Olaus Magnus, in which the small ones, being victorious, are said to have buried the bodies of their own soldiers, but left those of their giant enemies a prey to the birds. This event happened previous to the expulsion of the tyrant Christiern the Second from Sweden." The battle which I witnessed took place in the Presidency of Polk, five years before the passage of Webster's Fugitive Slave Bill.

Many a village Bose, fit only to course a mud turtle in a victualing cellar, sported his heavy quarters in the woods, without the knowledge of his master, and ineffectually smelled at old fox burrows and woodchucks' holes; led perchance by some slight cur which nimbly threaded the wood, and might still inspire a natural terror in its denizens — now far behind his guide, barking like a canine bull toward some small squirrel which had treed itself for scrutiny, then, cantering off, bending the bushes with his weight, imagining that he is on the track of some stray member of the jerbilla family. Once I was surprised to see a cat walking along the stony shore of the pond, for they rarely wander so far from home. The surprise was mutual. Nevertheless the most domestic cat, which has lain on a rug all her days, appears quite at home in the woods, and, by her sly and stealthy behavior, proves herself more native there than the regular inhabitants. Once, when berrying, I met with a cat with young kittens in the woods, quite wild, and they all, like their mother, had their backs up and were fiercely spitting at me. A few years before I lived in the woods there was what was called a "winged cat" in one of the farmhouses in Lincoln nearest the pond, Mr. Gilian Baker's. When I called to see her in June, 1842, she was gone a-hunting in the woods, as was her wont (I am not sure whether it was a male or female, and so use the more common pronoun), but her mistress told me that she came into the neighborhood a little more than a year be-

[1] Hôtel des Invalides: famous veterans' hospital in Paris. [2] Kirby and Spence: English naturalists of the early nineteenth century. Huber was a Swiss naturalist of the same time. The other names given are of persons who lived in the fifteenth century.

fore, in April, and was finally taken into their house; that she was of a dark brownish-gray color, with a white spot on her throat, and white feet, and had a large bushy tail like a fox; that in the winter the fur grew thick and flatted out along her sides, forming strips ten or twelve inches long by two and a half wide, and her chin like a muff, the upper side loose, the under matted like felt, and in the spring these appendages dropped off. They gave me a pair of her " wings," which I keep still. There is no appearance of a membrane about them. Some thought it was part flying squirrel or some other wild animal, which is not impossible, for, according to naturalists, prolific hybrids have been produced by the union of the marten and domestic cat. This would have been the right kind of cat for me to keep, if I had kept any; for why should not a poet's cat be winged as well as his horse?

In the fall the loon (*Colymbus glacialis*) came, as usual, to molt and bathe in the pond, making the woods ring with his wild laughter before I had risen. At rumor of his arrival all the Milldam sportsmen are on the alert, in gigs and on foot, two by two and three by three, with patent rifles and conical balls and spyglasses. They come rustling through the woods like autumn leaves, at least ten men to one loon. Some station themselves on this side of the pond, some on that, for the poor bird cannot be omnipresent; if he dive here he must come up there. But now the kind October wind rises, rustling the leaves and rippling the surface of the water, so that no loon can be heard or seen, though his foes sweep the pond with spyglasses, and make the woods resound with their discharges. The waves generously rise and dash angrily, taking sides with all waterfowl, and our sportsmen must beat a retreat to town and shop and unfinished jobs. But they were too often successful. When I went to get a pail of water early in the morning I frequently saw this stately bird sailing out of my cove within a few rods. If I endeavored to overtake him in a boat, in order to see how he would maneuver, he would dive and be completely lost, so that I did not discover him again, sometimes, till the latter part of the day. But I was more than a match for him on the surface. He commonly went off in a rain.

As I was paddling along the north shore one very calm October afternoon, for such days especially they settle onto the lakes, like the milkweed down, having looked in vain over the pond for a loon, suddenly one, sailing out from the shore toward the middle a few rods in front of me, set up his wild laugh and betrayed himself. I pursued with a paddle and he dived, but when he came up I was nearer than before. He dived again, but I miscalculated the direction he would take, and we were fifty rods apart when he came to the surface this time, for I had helped to widen the interval; and again he laughed long and loud, and with more reason than before. He maneuvered so cunningly that I could not get within half a dozen rods of him. Each time, when he came to the surface, turning his head this way and that, he coolly surveyed the water and the land, and apparently chose his course so that he might come up where there was the widest expanse of water and at the greatest distance from the boat. It was surprising how quickly he made up his mind and put his resolve into execution. He led me at once to the widest part of the pond, and could not be driven from it. While he was thinking one thing in his brain, I was endeavoring to divine his thought in mine. It was a pretty game, played on the smooth surface of the pond, a man against a loon. Suddenly your adversary's checker disappears beneath the board, and the problem is to place yours nearest to where his will appear again. Sometimes he would come up unexpectedly on the opposite side of me, having apparently passed directly under the boat. So long-winded was he and so unweariable, that when he had swum farthest he would immediately plunge again, nevertheless; and then no wit could divine where in the deep pond, beneath the smooth surface, he might be speeding his way like a fish, for he had time and ability to visit the bottom of the pond in its deepest part. It is said that loons have been caught in the New York lakes eighty feet beneath the surface, with hooks set for trout — though Walden is deeper than that. How surprised must the fishes be to see this ungainly visitor from another sphere speeding his way amid their schools! Yet he appeared to know his course as surely under water as on the surface, and swam much faster there. Once or twice I saw a ripple where he approached the surface, just put his head out to reconnoiter, and instantly dived again. I found that it was as well for me to rest on my oars and wait his reappearing as to endeavor to calculate where he would rise; for again and again, when I was straining my eyes over the surface one way, I would suddenly be startled by his unearthly laugh behind me. But why, after displaying so much cunning, did he invariably betray himself the moment he came up by that loud laugh? Did not his white breast enough betray him? He was indeed a silly loon, I thought. I could commonly hear the plash of the water when he came up, and so also detected him. But after an hour he seemed as fresh as ever, dived as willingly, and swam yet farther than at first. It was surprising to see how serenely he sailed off with unruffled breast when he came to the surface, doing all the work with his webbed feet beneath. His usual note was this demoniac laughter, yet somewhat like that of a waterfowl; but occasionally, when he had balked me most successfully and come up a long way off, he uttered a long-drawn unearthly howl, probably more like that of a wolf than any bird; as when a beast puts his muzzle to the ground and deliberately howls. This was his looning — perhaps the wildest sound that is ever heard here, making the woods ring far and wide. I concluded that he laughed in derision of my efforts, confident of his own resources. Though the sky was by this time overcast, the pond was so smooth that I could see where he broke the surface when I did not

hear him. His white breast, the stillness of the air, and the smoothness of the water were all against him. At length, having come up fifty rods off, he uttered one of those prolonged howls, as if calling on the god of loons to aid him, and immediately there came a wind from the east and rippled the surface, and filled the whole air with misty rain, and I was impressed as if it were the prayer of the loon answered, and his god was angry with me; and so I left him disappearing far away on the tumultuous surface.

For hours, in fall days, I watched the ducks cunningly tack and veer and hold the middle of the pond, far from the sportsman; tricks which they will have less need to practice in Louisiana bayous. When compelled to rise they would sometimes circle round and round and over the pond at a considerable height, from which they could easily see to other ponds and the river, like black motes in the sky; and, when I thought they had gone off thither long since, they would settle down by a slanting flight of a quarter of a mile onto a distant part which was left free; but what beside safety they got by sailing in the middle of Walden I do not know, unless they love its water for the same reason that I do.

## Suggestions for Study

1. Why did Thoreau go to the woods to live? Find the paragraph where he explains his purpose clearly. Read it aloud. Pick out the statement that you think gives the best reason for his experiment.

2. What are some of Thoreau's objections to the way most people live? What reason does he usually give for his objections? Which objections do you agree with? disagree with? Can you understand your personal reasons for some disagreements? Can you imagine yourself reaching a stage in life when you would agree with him on the same points? Think of your own favorite ways of passing time away. Which ones simply pass the time? Which ones involve growth in understanding and enjoyment of life?

3. You are an unusual high-school student

if you read all of *Walden*. But if you grow up to be a thoughtful sort of person, interested in understanding and savoring life, you will then enjoy the whole book — reading it as Thoreau lived, in a leisurely fashion with time to stop and think over anything you come to that particularly interests you.

4. Make a list of all the different living creatures which Thoreau has observed as indicated in " Brute Neighbors." Do his observations seem to you wide or limited?

5. In the battle of the ants, how does the author make the ants seem human? How does he show his familiarity with history? with writings on natural science?

6. What evidence do you find of his attitude toward the hunters who came to Walden Pond? It would be interesting to have an informal class debate as to whether hunting for sport is justifiable.

7. When Thoreau records so exactly the time of his observation of the battle of the ants, do you think he is being serious or facetious?

8. For a clever description of the changed appearance of Walden today, see E. B. White's "One Man's Meat " in *Harper's Magazine*, August, 1939.

9. To know more about Thoreau himself consult *The Heart of Thoreau's Journals*, edited by Odell Shepard, and the recent biography *Thoreau* by H. S. Canby. Emerson, Lowell, John Burroughs, and many others have written essays on him.

10. What other American nature writers can you name? A day spent on oral reports about different nature writers would be valuable. Some of the recent biographies of Audubon have been illustrated by excellent reproductions of his famous paintings of birds. See lists on pages 175 and 271.

## For Your Vocabulary

When Thoreau speaks of the loon's *demoniac* (dĕ-mō'nĭ-ăk) laughter, page 576, he is stressing its unearthly quality as well as the evil nature associated with demons. Such laughter sounds as if it could come from the throat of no earthly creature; it is weird and frenzied and sends shivers through the listener. From different languages we get a whole series of adjectives built on words for a superhuman evil creature: *fiendish* (fēnd'ĭsh), from Anglo-Saxon, which implies great cruelty; *devilish* (dĕv''l-ĭsh), also from Anglo-Saxon, which is used of wickedness in general, sometimes rather lightly; and *diabolical* (dī-à-bŏl'ĭ-kăl), from Greek by way of French, which implies coldly calculating evil designs. Here is an example of the way English has enriched itself from its various parent languages.

## 2. LONGFELLOW, LOWELL, HOLMES, PARKMAN

### THE FLOWERING OF BOSTON

" How do you endure this constant praise of Boston? " a New Yorker once asked a prominent Bostonian about 1850. The Bostonian answered modestly and candidly: " Because we suspect it is true."

Maybe it was. Boston was what the historians call the " culture town " of the Eastern Flowering. It was the source of ideas, the gathering place of thinkers and writers, the point of highest specific gravity in all the intense intellectual life of New England. Include with Boston its suburban Cambridge and its close neighbor Concord, and you have a center which for high thinking and good writing was never equaled again in America.

You could tell the difference between the men who lived in those three towns. The men of Concord were the ones who liked the meadows and the woods and the sunshine, like Emerson and Thoreau. The men of Cambridge were the men of books, the Harvard teachers and scholars, like Longfellow and Lowell. The men of Boston itself were the businessmen, the bankers, the publishers, the club men, the men of family and position whose houses rose on Beacon Hill and along the extension of Beacon Street. Parkman lived in the family home on the Hill. Holmes moved from Cambridge to a house on Beacon Street.

Boston was a flourishing business center gathered around the harbor and the Hill. Clippers from all over the world came into the harbor, and the countinghouses and stores stood on narrow, twisting streets around the harbor. On the Hill stood the gold-domed statehouse as a symbol of the

LOOKING DOWN BEACON HILL. This part of Boston looks the same today as it did when Oliver Wendell Holmes called the city "the thinking center of the continent." (Monkemeyer)

ordered freedom for which Massachusetts Bay had always stood. Cambridge was a few miles away across the Charles River — a little country town with graceful homes and Harvard College. Concord was a little country town on the Boston turnpike, with its men clustered around Emerson.

But where else in America could you find a club like the Saturday Club, which numbered among its members Emerson, Lowell, Longfellow, Holmes, Whittier, Prescott and Motley the historians, Hawthorne and Dana, Agassiz the naturalist and Pierce the astronomer, Whipple and Norton the critics, and, a little later, Henry James and Charles Sumner? Where else could you find so much real literary activity? Visitors who came to Boston and the towns around it wrote back home that everyone seemed to be writing a book! Where else could you walk a few miles with the feeling that you had certainly passed houses where classics were being written — Parkman's histories, Longfellow's epic poem, Emerson's new essay? Where could you get a more genial and better informed argument — and even without going to Alcott or Thoreau for it? Where could you find a section of the country that gave birth to so many reform movements, so many social experiments? People now sometimes go to Massachusetts to see *old* Boston — Fanueil Hall and Bunker Hill and Paul Revere's shop and the houses of great men. In those days people went to see *new* Boston, although it was already two hundred years old; they went for new ideas, the new books, the new magazine, the new star on the literary horizon.

Culture towns, the historians tell us, go through seasons like the earth. They have a springtime, like Boston in the 1840's, when everything was new and fresh and vigorous. They have a summer, like Boston in the 1850's, when the town was most productive and sure of itself. They have an autumn, like Boston after the War between the States, when some of the early vigor was gone and new ideas were more likely to come from New York or the West.

But forget the Boston of your picture books, the venerable Boston of the old houses and long history, and think of the live Boston which existed in the middle of the nineteenth century.

## HENRY WADSWORTH LONGFELLOW

It was Longfellow who finally answered the question, " Who reads an American book? " His books sold in the millions during his lifetime. Every school child who knew English knew some of Professor Longfellow's poetry. In Europe, Poe was more highly praised and followed, but Longfellow was more read. No other American poet has been so much translated as he.

He was a Portland boy, a Bowdoin graduate and classmate of Hawthorne. On commencement day he had a singular piece of good luck. His college gave him a six hundred dollar fellowship, told him to go to Europe and prepare himself to teach modern languages. That was the first of a number of trips abroad, and it was the first step in his path toward the distinguished Harvard professorship of modern languages, to which he succeeded in 1836, at the phenomenal age of twenty-nine.

He was a good teacher. For eighteen years he made the great books of Europe live for Harvard undergraduates. Then he resigned his professorship to have more time for the musical and polished poetry which the whole world was beginning to read.

There isn't much to say about his life. He had two great personal sorrows, when his young wife died suddenly, and when his second wife burned to death. Europe was probably the greatest thing that happened to him. He went there frequently and read its literature always. He lived in beautiful Craigie House in Cambridge, which had been Washington's headquarters during part of the Revolution. He lived quietly and serenely, surrounded by good and literary friends, and by the most literate community he could have found to live in. As a man and as a poet he was widely beloved and honored, and his death at seventy-five was mourned by both the Old World and the New.

Longfellow left a great deal of poetry, probably more than any other American. It is not all top-notch; it is not all as good as his admirers in his own time said it was. Poetic reputations have a way of going by extremes. In Longfellow's time he was extravagantly praised; after he died, his reputation snapped back like a rubber band, and it became fashionable to be scornful about his poems. Now we are beginning to reach an equilibrium again, and we can see that he wrote some very fine poetry indeed, and that he left a number of poems which will be in our poetic heritage for as long as we can foresee.

How can one describe Longfellow's poetry? It was, for one thing, always perfectly smoothed and finished and joined, in the same loving way a fine sculptor works over a statue. It was musical and melodious. It had a twilight shade, a mood of melancholy, wistfulness, a longing toward the past. It was poetry of peace and serenity, rather than of war and change. It was poetry which sometimes echoed European writers, and could only have been written by a man who had read widely and well.

But perhaps the best way to describe it is to remind ourselves of some of the poems he left:

Poems of the simple life and homely ethics, like " The Village Blacksmith," " The Psalm of Life," " Excelsior," " The Arrow and the Song," and " The Children's Hour."

Melodious lyrics, like " Hymn to the Night," " The Day Is Done," " The Tide Rises, the Tide Falls," and " My Lost Youth."

Thoughtful and challenging poems, like " The Arsenal at Springfield," " The Jewish Cemetery at Newport," " Morituri Salutamus," and " The Building of the Ship."

Historical tales and ballads, like " Paul Revere's Ride " and " The Wreck of the Hesperus."

Some of the best poetic translations ever made, like the " Wanderer's Night Songs," which he translated from Goethe.

A number of fine sonnets, like the one in this book.

Some vigorous anti-slavery poems.

A series of poetic stories patterned after old

HENRY WADSWORTH LONGFELLOW as a young man. His poems were best sellers throughout the nineteenth century. (Culver)

legends, which he called *Tales of a Wayside Inn.*

Some of the best long narrative poetry written by an American — *The Song of Hiawatha,* his free rendering of Indian legends and history; *Evangeline,* the story of the Acadians told in epic verse; and *The Courtship of Miles Standish,* a chapter out of New England history which he retold with perception and loving care.

*Longfellow was born (1807) in the same year as Whittier, and died (1882) in the same year as Emerson. When he was born, the exciting new invention was the steam engine. When he died, the exciting new development was the use of electricity.*

## JAMES RUSSELL LOWELL

Lowell succeeded Longfellow as professor of modern languages at Harvard. He lived all his life in Cambridge near Longfellow's Craigie House, in the beautiful ancestral home of the Lowells called Elmwood. He traveled widely and was as well read as Longfellow in French, Spanish, German, and Italian literature. His library was quite as well lined as Longfellow's. But if you try to describe him in terms of book-lined studies and college professorships, you will go far astray. For Lowell was a man of public affairs with a civic conscience.

He described himself with uncanny insight in *A Fable for Critics:*

There is Lowell, who's striving Parnassus to
    climb
With a whole bale of *isms* tied together with
    rhyme. . . .
The top of the hill he will ne'er come nigh
    reaching
Till he learns the distinction 'twixt singing and
    preaching.

The truth is, he simply had too many interests to give the kind of attention to poetry that Longfellow gave. There is an interesting thing about the three poems of his which you will read in this book; they were all published in book form in the same year, 1848, when Lowell was not quite thirty. It was not until the 60's that he again challenged people with his poetry on the War between the States, culminating with the noble "Harvard Commemoration Ode."

So while Longfellow was singing himself into the hearts of people with his melodious poems, Lowell was addressing himself to their minds on a series of public questions. He was a vigorous abolitionist, whose lines, " Truth forever on the scaffold, Wrong forever on the throne," were quoted by many an anti-slavery orator. He campaigned for temperance and woman suffrage. He had his say about the Mexican War and the War between the States in *The Biglow Papers*. He wrote about politics and foreign affairs, and was his country's representative at the courts of Spain and England. In fact, he was not chiefly a poet at all. As Longfellow was the poet of the Cambridge group, so Lowell was the critic.

His literary criticism filled a number of volumes and included essays on many of the great writers of the world. It was urbane, suave, based on wide reading, sensible. Often it was based on his lectures, and always it gave the impression that Lowell was trying to arbitrate among the pre-vious critics, trying to find the middle road, trying to show his readers a safe, well-rounded viewpoint. As a critic, Poe was more brilliant, more erratic, more original; Lowell was safer. Poe was more penetrating; Lowell, broader.

But even as literary critic, Lowell was interested in the contemporary affairs of his country, for he became the first editor of the *Atlantic Monthly*, founded in 1857, in the midsummer of literary New England, to carry the finest fruits of the literary flowering. Perhaps no magazine attracted more distinguished contributors in its first years — Emerson, Thoreau, Holmes, Lowell, Longfellow, Parkman, and all the rest of that Boston-Concord group. Later Lowell became editor of the *North American Review*, and his service to American writers in these two editorships was great.

As a social critic, Lowell put his roots down into a part of New England that Longfellow never reached. That was the robust humor, the homely common sense of the Yankee. Franklin was a master of this Yankee humor, and Emerson captured it in some of his pithy sayings, but the influence of Europe crowded out the Yankee in Longfellow. People read *The Biglow Papers* — the alleged work of a shrewd, little-schooled New England farmer named Hosea Biglow — in somewhat the same spirit as they had read *Poor Richard*. And under this literary mask, Lowell managed to say a lot of homespun wisdom about what the government was and was not doing.

Perhaps Lowell scattered his energies too much. Perhaps he could never decide — as he suggested in *A Fable for Critics* — whether to be a poet or a reformer. But he was a good citizen and a good writer, and one of the best informed and most versatile men in the whole remarkable New England group.

*Lowell was born (1819) two years later than Thoreau, four years before Parkman. He died (1891) two years before Parkman, twenty-nine years after Thoreau. The frontier was between the Alleghenies and the*

*Mississippi when he was born. When he died there was no longer any open frontier.*

## OLIVER WENDELL HOLMES

We sometimes forget that Holmes was a physician and a professor of medicine at Harvard. Yet he practiced medicine from the day he hung out his shingle at the age of twenty-seven (saying, so he later claimed, " the smallest fevers gratefully received ") and taught at Harvard until he was seventy-four. In his own time he was known as the author of an important medical article on puerperal fever, which saved many lives, and as the author of fiction which applied medical knowledge to social problems.

The picture we remember is the Holmes who took things less seriously than Holmes the doctor and lecturer on medicine. It is the Holmes who lived in the gracious house on Beacon Street beside the Charles River, the gay, laughing Holmes, the witty Holmes who was the favorite guest at all the best Boston dinners, the Holmes who was as interested in horse races and prize fights as in lectures and music, the Holmes who was a loyal friend of all the Boston writers and many others, and above all the Holmes who would come to a dinner or a meeting with an appropriate poem written for the occasion.

When he graduated from Harvard (Samuel Smith, author of " America," was a classmate) Holmes was asked to give the class poem. It was a kind of foreshadowing of what was to come, for after that came an endless series of class poems, alumni poems, dinner poems, commemorative poems. No one could do this kind of thing quite so well as Holmes; no one would do it so gladly and graciously and with such a light touch. So throughout his life he was in demand as a writer of occasional verses. He had no equal in that field in Europe or America.

A few times he dropped the playful mood and wrote out of deep and sincere feeling. That was how we got " Old Ironsides " and " The Chambered Nautilus." Sometimes his light touch went deeper than most of the banquet poems, as for instance when he wrote " My Aunt " or " The Last Leaf " or " The Boys " in which he looked back sentimentally on the old days. And sometimes his humor was just the right touch for an important subject, as for instance in " The Deacon's Masterpiece," which described the breakdown of the old Puritan order in New England.

Even more than as a poet or a physician, Holmes was renowned in Boston as a conversationalist — the man whose presence would make any dinner a success, the man whose talk crackled with electric sparks, or as Lowell said,

A Leyden jar always fully charged, from which flit
The electrical tingles of hit after hit.

It is hard for us to preserve that talent of Holmes. The nearest we can come to it is to read some of the conversational essays he published in the *Atlantic Monthly* and in book form as *The Autocrat at the Breakfast Table.* A sampling of it is in this book — his own words on the art of conversation.

*Holmes was born (1809) about the same time as Whittier, Longfellow, and Poe, but outlived them all (dying in 1894). During his lifetime the country grew from around five million to about seventy million people.*

## FRANCIS PARKMAN AND THE
### NEW ENGLAND HISTORIANS

At least four of New England's historians wrote books that were as widely read as novels and books of verse. George Bancroft wrote an exciting and emotional history of the United States; John Lothrop Motley wrote the dramatic history of Holland in its fight with Spain; William Hickling Prescott wrote the glamorous story of early Spanish conquests in the New World; and Francis Parkman wrote a monumental series of books on the long battle of England and France for North America.

Of these four, it is Parkman who stands

FRANCIS PARKMAN proved to all later generations that historical writing could be both reliable and dramatic. (Brown Brothers)

through thousands of pages of documents, many of them in manuscript, many in French or Spanish. When his eyes were unequal to the task, he had to get somebody to read to him. The reader was usually a high-school girl who knew no foreign language and pronounced all the words like English. Poor Parkman had therefore to guess what the words really were, and then to remember the points and references he wanted to use, and finally to dictate his own book, often without the use of notes or text. The fact that he triumphed over these obstacles and successfully completed one of the biggest jobs a historian ever tackled bears witness to the toughness of New England fiber and the strength of the literary devotion which men held in those great years of the Eastern Flowering.

*Parkman was born (1823) when men were still trying to perfect the steam engine for factory and transportation use. When he died (1893) the automobile, phonograph, telephone, and electric light had been invented.*

out now from the others, and you might well remember some things about him. He was Boston born, Harvard educated. His first great interest was the frontier and Indians, and in 1846 he took a trip over the Oregon Trail to see what the West looked like and how the red man really lived. He wrote a memorable book about this trip (*The Oregon Trail*). But he began to have a wider view of his job. The real story of the American forest and frontier before the Revolution, he decided, was the story of the battle of France and England for the continent. No one before Parkman had ever seen the history of the continent in such a dramatic focus. No one had ever written so dramatically of the forest battles involving both savage tribes and grenadiers from Europe.

Parkman proved to all later generations that history might be both scholarly and dramatic. He proved it the hard way. For almost all his adult life he was a semi-invalid and nearly blind. He had to go

# Henry Wadsworth Longfellow
## 1807–1882

### HIAWATHA'S WOOING *

Though *The Song of Hiawatha* was the last to be written of the Longfellow poems here included, it is a good one with which to begin your reading. Perhaps you have known parts of this poem since you were a child, for children love its swinging meter, its personification of animals, and its Indian lore. But *Hiawatha* is more than a child's poem. It has a unique place in American literature which cannot be overlooked. It comes close to being an American national epic. However, it cannot quite qualify for that title because it was composed by a single author rather than developed through generations of retold stories, as the European

* **Hiawatha** (hē-á-wä′thá or hǐ-á-wä′thá). Longfellow is said to have preferred the first pronunciation.

national epics grew. The Indians had no written literature, but their oral legends have been passed down to us by many collectors. Longfellow, after reading various volumes of Indian lore by Henry Schoolcraft, longed to preserve the spirit of these stories in a form comparable to the European epics. As a professor of comparative literature he had had wide experience with such poems, and he chose to follow the lively meter of the Finnish epic *Kalevala*. He tried also to give his poem the naïve quality of primitive literature.

The most romantic episode of the story is Hiawatha's wooing of Minnehaha, which is supposed to have taken place by the beautiful little waterfall of that name, now part of the city of Minneapolis, Minnesota. There today one may see the life-size bronze figures of the two lovers near the head of the falls; street names echo the names in the poem; there is even a replica of Longfellow's Cambridge house near by. The poet's spirit still haunts the place, though he never saw it in actual life.

" As unto the bow the cord is,
So unto the man is woman,
Though she bends him, she obeys him,
Though she draws him, yet she follows,
Useless each without the other! "    5
   Thus the youthful Hiawatha
Said within himself and pondered,
Much perplexed by various feelings,
Listless, longing, hoping, fearing,
Dreaming still of Minnehaha,    10
Of the lovely Laughing Water,
In the land of the Dacotahs.
   " Wed a maiden of your people,"
Warning said the old Nokomis;°
" Go not eastward, go not westward,    15
For a stranger, whom we know not!
Like a fire upon the hearthstone
Is a neighbor's homely daughter,
Like the starlight or the moonlight
Is the handsomest of strangers! "    20
   Thus dissuading spake Nokomis,
And my Hiawatha answered
Only this: " Dear old Nokomis,
Very pleasant is the firelight,
But I like the starlight better,    25
Better do I like the moonlight! "

14. **Nokomis** (nŏ-kō′mĭs): Hiawatha's grandmother.

   Gravely then said old Nokomis:
" Bring not here an idle maiden,
Bring not here a useless woman,
Hands unskillful, feet unwilling;    30
Bring a wife with nimble fingers,
Heart and hand that move together,
Feet that run on willing errands! "
   Smiling answered Hiawatha:
" In the land of the Dacotahs    35
Lives the Arrow-maker's daughter,
Minnehaha, Laughing Water,
Handsomest of all the women.
I will bring her to your wigwam,
She shall run upon your errands,    40
Be your starlight, moonlight, firelight,
Be the sunlight of my people! "
   Still dissuading said Nokomis:
" Bring not to my lodge a stranger
From the land of the Dacotahs!    45
Very fierce are the Dacotahs.
Often is there war between us,
There are feuds yet unforgotten,
Wounds that ache and still may open! "
   Laughing answered Hiawatha:    50
" For that reason, if no other,
Would I wed the fair Dacotah,
That our tribes might be united,
That old feuds might be forgotten,
And old wounds be healed forever! "    55
   Thus departed Hiawatha
To the land of the Dacotahs,
To the land of handsome women;
Striding over moor and meadow,
Through interminable forests,    60
Through uninterrupted silence.
   With his moccasins of magic,
At each stride a mile he measured;
Yet the way seemed long before him,
And his heart outran his footsteps;    65
And he journeyed without resting,
Till he heard the cataract's laughter,
Heard the Falls of Minnehaha
Calling to him through the silence.
" Pleasant is the sound! " he murmured,
" Pleasant is the voice that calls me! "    71
   On the outskirts of the forest,
'Twixt the shadow and the sunshine,
Herds of fallow deer were feeding,
But they saw not Hiawatha;    75
To his bow he whispered, " Fail not! "

To his arrow whispered, " Swerve not! "
Sent it singing on its errand,
To the red heart of the roebuck;
Threw the deer across his shoulder,    80
And sped forward without pausing.

At the doorway of his wigwam
Sat the ancient Arrow-maker,
In the land of the Dacotahs,
Making arrow-heads of jasper,    85
Arrow-heads of chalcedony.°
At his side, in all her beauty,
Sat the lovely Minnehaha,
Sat his daughter, Laughing Water,
Plaiting mats of flags and rushes;    90
Of the past the old man's thoughts were,
And the maiden's of the future.

He was thinking, as he sat there,
Of the days when with such arrows
On the Muskoday,° the meadow,    95
He had struck the deer and bison,
Shot the wild goose, flying southward,
On the wing, the clamorous Wawa;°
Thinking of the great war-parties,
How they came to buy his arrows,    100
Could not fight without his arrows.
Ah, no more such noble warriors
Could be found on earth as they were!
Now the men were all like women,
Only used their tongues for weapons!    105

She was thinking of a hunter,
From another tribe and country,
Young and tall and very handsome,
Who one morning, in the Springtime,
Came to buy her father's arrows,    110
Sat and rested in the wigwam,
Lingered long about the doorway,
Looking back as he departed.
She had heard her father praise him,
Praise his courage and his wisdom;    115
Would he come again for arrows
To the Falls of Minnehaha?
On the mat her hands lay idle,
And her eyes were very dreamy.

Through their thoughts they heard a
    foostep,    120
Heard a rustling in the branches,

And with glowing cheeks and forehead,
With the deer upon his shoulders,
Suddenly from out the woodlands
Hiawatha stood before them.    125
Straight the ancient Arrow-maker
Looked up gravely from his labor,
Laid aside the unfinished arrow,
Bade him enter at the doorway,
Saying, as he rose to meet him,    130
" Hiawatha, you are welcome! "

At the feet of Laughing Water
Hiawatha laid his burden,
Threw the red deer from his shoulders;
And the maiden looked up at him,    135
Looked up from her mat of rushes,
Said with gentle look and accent,
" You are welcome, Hiawatha! "

Very spacious was the wigwam,    139
Made of deerskin dressed and whitened,
With the Gods of the Dacotahs
Drawn and painted on its curtains,
And so tall the doorway, hardly
Hiawatha stooped to enter,
Hardly touched his eagle feathers    145
As he entered at the doorway.

Then uprose the Laughing Water,
From the ground fair Minnehaha,
Laid aside her mat unfinished,    149
Brought forth food and set before them,
Water brought them from the brooklet,
Gave them food in earthen vessels,
Gave them drink in bowls of basswood,
Listened while the guest was speaking,
Listened while her father answered,    155
But not once her lips she opened,
Not a single word she uttered.

Yes, as in a dream she listened
To the words of Hiawatha,
As he talked of old Nokomis,    160
Who had nursed him in his childhood,
As he told of his companions,
Chibiabos,° the musician,
And the very strong man, Kwasind,°
And of happiness and plenty    165
In the land of the Ojibways,°
In the pleasant land and peaceful.

" After many years of warfare,
Many years of strife and bloodshed,

---

86. chalcedony (kăl-sĕd′ŏ-nĭ, or, as here,
kăl′sĕ-dŏ-nĭ). A variety of pale blue or gray
stone with a soft luster. 95. Muskoday (mŭs′kō-
dā). 98. Wawa (wä′wä).

163. Chibiabos (chĭb-ĭ-ä′bōs). 164. Kwasind
(kwä′sĭnd). 166. Ojibways (ŏ-jĭb′wāz).

There is peace between the Ojibways 170
And the tribe of the Dacotahs."
Thus continued Hiawatha,
And then added, speaking slowly,
" That this peace may last forever,
And our hands be clasped more closely, 175
And our hearts be more united,
Give me as my wife this maiden,
Minnehaha, Laughing Water,
Loveliest of Dacotah women! "
    And the ancient Arrow-maker 180
Paused a moment ere he answered,
Smoked a little while in silence,
Looked at Hiawatha proudly,
Fondly looked at Laughing Water,
And made answer very gravely: 185
" Yes, if Minnehaha wishes;
Let your heart speak, Minnehaha! "
    And the lovely Laughing Water
Seemed more lovely, as she stood there,
Neither willing nor reluctant, 190
As she went to Hiawatha.
Softly took the seat beside him,
While she said, and blushed to say it,
" I will follow you, my husband! "
    This was Hiawatha's wooing! 195
Thus it was he won the daughter
Of the ancient Arrow-maker,
In the land of the Dacotahs!
    From the wigwam he departed,
Leading with him Laughing Water; 200
Hand in hand they went together,
Through the woodland and the meadow,
Left the old man standing lonely
At the doorway of his wigwam,
Heard the Falls of Minnehaha 205
Calling to them from the distance,
Crying to them from afar off,
" Fare thee well, O Minnehaha! "
    And the ancient Arrow-maker
Turned again unto his labor, 210
Sat down by his sunny doorway,
Murmuring to himself, and saying:
" Thus it is our daughters leave us,
Those we love, and those who love us!
Just when they have learned to help us, 215
When we are old and lean upon them,
Comes a youth with flaunting feathers,
With his flute of reeds, a stranger
Wanders piping through the village,

Beckons to the fairest maiden, 220
And she follows where he leads her,
Leaving all things for the stranger! "
    Pleasant was the journey homeward,
Through interminable forests,
Over meadow, over mountain, 225
Over river, hill, and hollow.
Short it seemed to Hiawatha,
Though they journeyed very slowly,
Though his pace he checked and slackened
To the steps of Laughing Water. 230
    Over wide and rushing rivers
In his arms he bore the maiden;
Light he thought her as a feather,
As the plume upon his headgear;
Cleared the tangled pathway for her, 235
Bent aside the swaying branches,
Made at night a lodge of branches,
And a bed with boughs of hemlock,
And a fire before the doorway
With the dry cones of the pine tree. 240
    All the traveling winds went with them,
O'er the meadow, through the forest:
All the stars of night looked at them,
Watched with sleepless eyes their slumber;
From his ambush in the oak tree 245
Peeped the squirrel, Adjidaumo,°
Watched with eager eyes the lovers;
And the rabbit, the Wabasso,°
Scampered from the path before them,
Peering, peeping from his burrow, 250
Sat erect upon his haunches,
Watched with curious eyes the lovers.
    Pleasant was the journey homeward!
All the birds sang loud and sweetly
Songs of happiness and heart's-ease; 255
Sang the. bluebird, the Owaissa,°
" Happy are you, Hiawatha,
Having such a wife to love you! "
Sang the robin, the Opechee,°
" Happy are you, Laughing Water, 260
Having such a noble husband! "
    From the sky the sun benignant
Looked upon them through the branches,
Saying to them, " O my children,
Love is sunshine, hate is shadow, 265
Life is checkered shade and sunshine,

246. **Adjidaumo** (ăj-ĭ-dô′mō). 248. **Wabasso**
(wȧ-băs′ō). 256. **Owaissa** (ō-wä′sȧ). 259. **Opechee**
(ō-pē′chē).

Rule by love, O Hiawatha! "
From the sky the moon looked at them,
Filled the lodge with mystic splendors,
Whispered to them, " O my children,    270
Day is restless, night is quiet,
Man imperious, woman feeble;
Half is mine, although I follow;
Rule by patience, Laughing Water! "
Thus it was they journeyed homeward;
Thus it was that Hiawatha    276
To the lodge of old Nokomis
Brought the moonlight, starlight, firelight,
Brought the sunshine of his people,
Minnehaha, Laughing Water,    280
Handsomest of all the women
In the land of the Dacotahs,
In the land of handsome women.

## HYMN TO THE NIGHT

This poem appeared in the volume *Voices of
the Night*, published four years after the death
of Longfellow's first wife. It shows the kind of
consolation which came to him in this period
of sadness.

'Ασπασίη, τρίλλιστος *

I heard the trailing garments of the Night
    Sweep through her marble halls!
I saw her sable skirts all fringed with light
    From the celestial walls!

I felt her presence, by its spell of might,    5
    Stoop o'er me from above;
The calm, majestic presence of the Night,
    As of the one I love.

I heard the sounds of sorrow and delight,
    The manifold, soft chimes,    10
That fill the haunted chambers of the Night,
    Like some old poet's rhymes.

From the cool cisterns of the midnight air
    My spirit drank repose;
The fountain of perpetual peace flows
        there —    15
    From those deep cisterns flows.

* 'Ασπασίη, τρίλλιστος (ăs-pȧ-zē'ā, trĭl'ĭs-tŏs):
"Welcome, thrice prayed for . . ." *Iliad*, viii.,
488.

O holy Night! from thee I learn to bear
    What man has borne before!
Thou layest thy finger on the lips of Care,
    And they complain no more.    20

Peace! Peace! Orestes-like° I breathe this
        prayer!
    Descend with broad-winged flight,
The welcome, the thrice-prayed for, the
        most fair,
    The best-beloved Night!

21. **Orestes-like:** Orestes (ŏ-rĕs'tēz) was a
youth in Greek literature who prayed to Athena
for peace from the pursuit of the Furies.

## THE TIDE RISES, THE TIDE FALLS

The fascination that the sea held for Longfellow in his boyhood expressed itself throughout his life in many ways. In fact, he is America's greatest poet of the sea. Observe the
smooth-flowing rhythm and the sense of fate
that are perfectly adapted to the thought of
the inevitable tide of the ocean.

The tide rises, the tide falls,
The twilight darkens, the curlew calls;
Along the sea sands damp and brown
The traveler hastens toward the town,
    And the tide rises, the tide falls.    5

Darkness settles on roofs and walls,
But the sea, the sea in the darkness calls;
The little waves, with their soft white hands,
Efface the footprints in the sands,
    And the tide rises, the tide falls.    10

The morning breaks; the steeds in their
        stalls
Stamp and neigh as the hostler calls;
The day returns, but nevermore
Returns the traveler to the shore,
    And the tide rises, the tide falls.    15

## THE TWO RIVERS

More than any other of our nineteenth-
century poets, Longfellow was successful with
the sonnet form, which plays such an impor-

LONGFELLOW IN HIS STUDY at Cambridge, where his young daughters used to come at "the children's hour" to listen to stories. (Culver)

tant part in all English literature. His sonnets, though not so well known as many of his lyrics, are among the best of his mature poems. In this one he writes on a favorite theme — the passing of time. Here we find the same emphasis on the great rhythms of life as in the preceding poem.

To understand the octave of this sonnet we must realize that the poet is looking at one of those old-fashioned grandfather's clocks (now so prized by collectors) which has above the dial a picture of a ship riding the waves to the beat of the pendulum (see Clarence Day's clock, page 151). The hour is struck by a miniature watchman emerging from his tower. The sestet meditates upon the significance of midnight as the dividing line between two rivers of time, one flowing back into the past, the other flowing forward into the future.

Slowly the hour-hand of the clock moves
  round;
So slowly that no human eye hath power
To see it move! Slowly in shine or shower
The painted ship above it homeward bound,

Sails but seems motionless as if aground; 5
Yet both arrive at last; and in his tower
The slumberous watchman wakes and
  strikes the hour,
A mellow, measured, melancholy sound.

Midnight! the outpost of advancing day!
The frontier town and citadel of night! 10
The watershed of Time, from which the
  streams
Of Yesterday and Tomorrow take their way,
One to the land of promise and of light,
One to the land of darkness and of dreams.

## THE ARSENAL AT SPRINGFIELD

This impressive plea for peace was written long before the War between the States. In the light of the great struggles through which our country has passed since then, and of the efforts to establish world peace during the twentieth century, this poem has a real message for the modern world.

This is the Arsenal.° From the floor to ceiling,
Like a huge organ, rise the burnished arms;
But from their silent pipes no anthem pealing
Startles the villages with strange alarms.
Ah! what a sound will rise, how wild and dreary,    5
When the death angel touches those swift keys!
What loud lament and dismal Miserere°
Will mingle with their awful symphonies!

I hear even now the infinite fierce chorus,
The cries of agony, the endless groan,
Which, through the ages that have gone before us,    11
In long reverberations reach our own.

On helm and harness rings the Saxon hammer,
Through Cimbric° forest roars the Norseman's song,
And loud, amid the universal clamor,    15
O'er distant deserts sounds the Tatar° gong.

I hear the Florentine,° who from his palace
Wheels out his battle bell with dreadful din,
And Aztec° priests upon their teocallis°
Beat the wild war drums made of serpent's skin;    20

The tumult of each sacked and burning village ;

The shout that every prayer for mercy drowns;
The soldiers' revels in the midst of pillage;
The wail of famine in beleaguered towns;

The bursting shell, the gateway wrenched asunder,    25
The rattling musketry, the clashing blade;
And ever and anon, in tones of thunder,
The diapason of the cannonade.

Is it, O man, with such discordant noises,
With such accursèd instruments as these,
Thou drownest Nature's sweet and kindly voices,    31
And jarrest the celestial harmonies?

Were half the power, that fills the world with terror,
Were half the wealth bestowed on camps and courts,
Given to redeem the human mind from error,    35
There were no need of arsenals nor forts:

The warrior's name would be a name abhorrèd!
And every nation, that should lift again
Its hand against a brother, on its forehead
Would wear forevermore the curse of Cain!°    40

Down the dark future, through long generations,
The echoing sounds grow fainter and then cease;
And like a bell, with solemn, sweet vibrations,
I hear once more the voice of Christ say,
" Peace! "

Peace! and no longer from its brazen portals
The blast of War's great organ shakes the skies!    46
But beautiful as songs of the immortals,
The holy melodies of love arise.

1. **Arsenal** (är'sĕ-năl): a building where weapons are stored. This one is in Springfield, Massachusetts. 7. **Miserere** (mĭz-ĕ-rē'rĕ): the first word in the Latin version of the Psalm beginning "Have mercy upon me, O Lord!" 14. **Cimbric** (sĭm'brĭk): referring to the Cimbri, a tribe of Norsemen destroyed by the Romans. 16. **Tatar** (tä'tĕr): The Tatars, a race of savage Orientals, swept over Asia and most of Europe in the thirteenth century. 17. **Florentine** (flŏr'ĕn-tēn): The soldiers of Florence, Italy, in medieval times actually wheeled a great bell out into the battle field. 19. **Aztec:** a native race of Mexicans, found and later practically exterminated by the Spaniards. 19. **teocallis** (tē-ō-kăl'ĭz): flat-topped pyramids of worship.

40. **Cain:** a son of Adam and Eve who was cursed because he slew his brother Abel (Genesis, Chapter 4).

## THE SHIP OF STATE

The closing lines of "The Building of the Ship" have become part of the body of patriotic literature which should be known by every citizen of the United States. In this long poem the author describes the careful building of a great sailing vessel to be named the *Union* because on the day of its completion the old master builder will give his daughter in marriage to the young craftsman. The conclusion of the poem follows the launching of the ship and the wedding ceremony with this extension of the analogy to the Ship of State. In 1849, when the poem was published, the Union of States had already been threatened by dissension between the North and the South. There is still significance for the present generation in this solemn dedication to the Union.

Thou, too, sail on, O Ship of State!
Sail on, O *Union*, strong and great!
Humanity with all its fears,
With all the hopes of future years,
Is hanging breathless on thy fate!   5
We know what Master laid thy keel,
What Workmen wrought thy ribs of steel,
Who made each mast, and sail, and rope,
What anvils rang, what hammers beat,
In what a forge, and what a heat   10
Were shaped the anchors of thy hope!
Fear not each sudden sound and shock,
'Tis of the wave and not the rock;
'Tis but the flapping of the sail,
And not a rent made by the gale!   15
In spite of rock and tempest's roar,
In spite of false lights on the shore,
Sail on, nor fear to breast the sea!
Our hearts, our hopes, are all with thee,
Our hearts, our hopes, our prayers, our
  tears,   20
Our faith triumphant o'er our fears,
Are all with thee — are all with thee!

## Suggestions for Study of Longfellow

1. Point out details in the episode of "Hiawatha's Wooing" that show it to be a romantic, legendary picture of Indian life rather than a realistic account of it. By what means does Longfellow make the poem sound simple and primitive?

2. Review the definition of an epic poem (page 341). Does *Hiawatha* fulfill all the requirements? As a special assignment read John G. Neihardt's *Song of the Indian Wars,* another example of an epic about the Indians. Which of the two poems seems to you to meet the definition more fully? Which gives the clearer picture of Indian life? What difference do you find in the meter of the two?

3. Identify the meter of *Hiawatha* by the definitions on pages 344–345. Do you consider this an easy meter to write? Test your answer by writing a short original passage. Can you name any other poems in this same meter?

4. In "Hymn to the Night" point out words or lines which seem to refer to the poet's recent bereavement, those which have a soothing effect upon the spirit, those which show his knowledge of ancient literature. Special assignment: Read "Footsteps of Angels" and compare it with this poem as to the consolation the poet felt in the spirit of his dead wife.

5. In "The Tide Rises, the Tide Falls" what is the mood of the poem? What effect does the refrain have upon you? What is suggested by the lines:

"The day returns, but nevermore
  Returns the traveler to the shore."

What other sea poems do you know? What different aspects of the sea do they bring out?

6. Write a short summary of "The Two Rivers" to show that you understand its meaning. Describe any interesting old clocks you have seen which have animated symbols or figures. Special assignment: This sonnet is the first in a series of four under the heading "The Two Rivers." Read the others to see how Longfellow carries out the idea of Yesterday and Tomorrow. An easier poem by the same author is "The Old Clock on the Stairs" — a good one to compare with the first sonnet.

7. Review the form of the sonnet (page 344). What other poets can you name who have written successful sonnets? In what way is the form of the sonnet a greater challenge to the poet than the metrical form of *Hiawatha?*

8. In "The Arsenal at Springfield" show how the idea of sound or music is carried through the entire poem. In what two ways is the organ the most fitting instrument to which to compare the arsenal? What different ages and parts of the world are brought into the

survey of war sounds? How does this strengthen Longfellow's point? What great plea does he make for peace? Special assignments: Write an additional stanza describing modern aerial warfare to follow line 28. Sum up the various attempts to establish world peace since Longfellow's day. What is the outlook at present?

9. In "The Ship of State" explain what you think is meant by the Master and the Workmen. Give some examples from American history of what the poet might have had in mind to represent the anvils, hammers, forge, etc. What events just prior to 1849, when the poem was published, might have been referred to in "sudden sound and shock," "rock and tempest's roar," "false lights on the shore"? The entire passage is a fine example of analogy. Explain the meaning of this word. Compare the dedication at the end with that at the conclusion of Lincoln's "Gettysburg Address" (page 261). The entire stanza deserves memorization.

10. Longfellow's many narrative poems and easily understood lyrics make him especially well suited to home reading. If you have never read *The Courtship of Miles Standish, Evangeline,* and *Tales of a Wayside Inn,* or the rest of *Hiawatha* and "The Building of the Ship," now is a good time to begin.

# James Russell Lowell 1819–1891

## THE COURTIN'

Lowell was one of the first American poets to write successfully in dialect. He created Hosea Biglow, an illiterate but shrewd New England farmer, to give vent to his feelings on the Mexican War situation in 1848. *The Biglow Papers* have immortalized the Yankee twang. To add to the humor, the papers were supposed to have been edited by a minister, Homerus Wilbur, Esq., in whose elaborate footnotes Lowell satirized pedantic learning. A second series of *The Biglow Papers* during the War between the States expressed in homely fashion the ideas of New Englanders concerning the progress of the war. Many parts of *The Biglow Papers* are crowded with references unintelligible to readers of today, but some of the verses will continue to delight young people for years to come. Among these "The Courtin'" is usually the favorite.

Zekle crep' up, quite unbeknown,
    An' peeked in thru the winder,
An' there sot Huldy all alone,
    'ith no one nigh to hender.

Agin' the chimbly crooknecks hung,   5
    An' in amongst 'em rusted
The ole queen's-arm° thet gran'ther Young
    Fetched back frum Concord busted.

The wannut logs shot sparkles out
    Towards the pootiest, bless her!   10
An' leetle fires danced all about
    The chiny on the dresser.

The very room, coz she wuz in,
    Looked warm frum floor to ceilin',
An' she looked full ez rosy agin   15
    Ez th' apples she wuz peelin'.

She heerd a foot an' knowed it, tu,
    A-raspin' on the scraper —
All ways to once her feelin's flew
    Like sparks in burnt-up paper.   20

He kin' o' l'itered on the mat,
    Some doutfle o' the sekle;
His heart kep' goin' pitypat,
    But hern went pity Zekle.

An' yit she gin her cheer a jerk   25
    Ez though she wished him furder,
An' on her apples kep' to work,
    Parin' away like murder.

"You want to see my Pa, I s'pose?"
    "Wal, no; I come designin' — "   30
"To see my Ma? She's sprinklin' clo'es
    Agin tomorrer's i'nin'."

He stood a spell on one foot fust,
    Then stood a spell on t'other.
An' on which one he felt the wust   35
    He couldn't ha' told ye, nuther.

Sez he, "I'd better call agin";
    Sez she, "Think likely, *Mister*";

7. **ole queen's-arm:** old musket.

The last word pricked him like a pin,
 An' — wal, he up an' kist her.    40

When Ma bimeby upon 'em slips,
 Huldy sot pale ez ashes,
All kind o' smily round the lips
 An' teary round the lashes.

Her blood riz quick, though, like the tide
 Down to the Bay o' Fundy,    46
An' all I know is they wuz cried°
 In meetin', come nex' Sunday.

47. **they wuz cried:** The banns (that is, the announcement of their approaching marriage) were read in church.

## A FABLE FOR CRITICS

Lowell's skill as a literary critic, which found its serious expression in long and learned essays, here takes him into lively couplets, supposedly describing to Apollo the American writers of his day. The witty lines have behind them a keen perception of the strength and weakness of the authors described. Lowell even points out his own vulnerable spot. From this selection you can realize Lowell's mental acumen without being confused by the many literary allusions and involved sentences of his essays. Except for Cooper, whom you doubtless have read, all the authors described in this selection are represented in this volume.

[*Emerson*] There comes Emerson first, whose rich words, every one,
Are like gold nails in temples to hang trophies on,
Whose prose is grand verse, while his verse, the Lord knows,
Is some of it pr———. No, 'tis not even prose;
I'm speaking of meters; some poems have welled    5
From those rare depths of soul that have ne'er been excelled.
They're not epics, but that doesn't matter a pin,
In creating, the only hard thing's to begin;
A grass blade's no easier to make than an oak,
If you've once found the way, you've achieved the grand stroke. . . .    10

[*Bryant*] There is Bryant, as quiet, as cool, and as dignified,
As a smooth silent iceberg, that never is ignified,
Save when by reflection 'tis kindled o' nights
With a semblance of flame by the chill northern lights.
He may rank (Griswold° says so) first bard of your nation,    15
(There's no doubt that he stands in supreme iceolation,)
Your topmost Parnassus° he may set his heel on,
But no warm applauses come, peal following peal on —
He's too smooth and too polished to hang any zeal on. . . .
If he stir you at all, it is just, on my soul,    20
Like being stirred up with the very North Pole. . . .

[*Whittier*] There is Whittier, whose swelling and vehement heart
Strains the strait-breasted drab of the Quaker apart,
And reveals the live man, still supreme and erect,
Underneath the bemummying wrappers of sect;    25
There was ne'er a man born who had more of the swing
Of the true lyric bard and all that kind of thing;
And his failures arise (though he seems not to know it)

15. **Griswold:** American critic and editor of Lowell's day who was represented in the poem as leading the poets up to Apollo. 17. **Parnassus** (pär-năs′ŭs): mountain in Greece, home of Apollo and the Muses.

From the very same cause that has made him a poet —
A fervor of mind which knows no separation                    30
'Twixt simple excitement and pure inspiration. . . .
Then his grammar's not always correct, nor his rhymes,
And he's prone to repeat his own lyrics sometimes,      ˎ
Not his best, though, for those are struck off at white heats
When the heart in his breast like a trip hammer beats,        35
And can ne'er be repeated again any more
Than they could have been carefully plotted before. . . .

[*Hawthorne*] There is Hawthorne, with genius so shrinking and rare
That you hardly at first see the strength that is there;
A frame so robust, with a nature so sweet,                    40
So earnest, so graceful, so solid, so fleet,
Is worth a descent from Olympus° to meet;
'Tis as if a rough oak that for ages had stood,
With his gnarled bony branches like ribs of the wood,
Should bloom after cycles of struggle and scathe,°            45
With a single anemone trembly and rathe.°. . . .
When Nature was shaping him, clay was not granted
For making so full-sized a man as she wanted,
So, to fill out her model, a little she spared
From some finer-grained stuff for a woman prepared,          50
And she could not have hit a more excellent plan
For making him fully and perfectly man. . . .

[*Cooper*] Here's Cooper, who's written six volumes to show
He's as good as a lord: well, let's grant that he's so;
If a person prefer that description of praise,               55
Why, a coronet's certainly cheaper than bays;°
But he need take no pains to convince us he's not
(As his enemies say) the American Scott.
Choose any twelve men, and let C. read aloud
That one of his novels of which he's most proud,            60
And I'll lay any bet that, without ever quitting
Their box, they'd be all, to a man, for acquitting.
He has drawn you one character, though, that is new,
One wild flower he's plucked that is wet with the dew
Of this fresh Western world, and, the thing not to mince,   65
He has done naught but copy it ill ever since;
His Indians, with proper respect be it said,
Are just Natty Bumppo° daubed over with red. . . .
And the women he draws from one model don't vary,
All sappy as maples and flat as a prairie. . . .           70
Don't suppose I would underrate Cooper's abilities,
If I thought you'd do that I should feel very ill at ease;
The men who have given to *one* character life

42. **Olympus**: mountain in Greece, home of the gods. 45. **scathe**: misfortune. 46. **rathe**: early
in the season. 56. **bays**: In ancient Greece successful writers were crowned with bay leaves (laurel).
68. **Natty Bumppo**: the famous scout, whose nickname "Leatherstocking" designates the series of
tales about his life.

And objective existence, are not very rife,
You may number them all, both prose writers and singers,                    75
Without overrunning the bounds of your fingers. . . .

[*Poe and Longfellow*] There comes Poe, with his raven, like Barnaby Rudge,°
Three fifths of him genius and two fifths sheer fudge,
Who talks like a book of iambs and pentameters,°
In a way to make people of common sense damn meters,                        80
Who has written some things quite the best of their kind,
But the heart somehow seems all squeezed out by the mind,
Who — but heyday! What's this? Messieurs Mathews° and Poe,
You mustn't fling mud balls at Longfellow so,
Does it make a man worse that his character's such                          85
As to make his friends love him (as you think) too much?
Why, there is not a bard at this moment alive
More willing than he that his fellows should thrive;
While you are abusing him thus, even now
He would help either one of you out of a slough;                            90
You may say that he's smooth and all that till you're hoarse,
But remember that elegance also is force;
After polishing granite as much as you will,
The heart keeps its tough old persistency still;
Deduct all you can, *that* still keeps you at bay;                          95
Why, he'll live till men weary of Collins and Gray.°. . .

[*Irving*] What? Irving? Thrice welcome, warm heart and fine brain,
You bring back the happiest spirit from Spain,°
And the gravest sweet humor, that ever were there
Since Cervantes° met death in his gentle despair. . . .                     100
But allow me to speak what I honestly feel —
To a true poet heart add the fun of Dick Steele,°
Throw in all of Addison,° *minus* the chill,
With the whole of that partnership's stock and good will,
Mix well, and while stirring, hum o'er as a spell,                          105
The fine *old* English gentleman, simmer it well,
Sweeten just to your own private liking, then strain,
That only the finest and clearest remain,
Let it stand out of doors till a soul it receives
From the warm lazy sun loitering down through green leaves,                 110
And you'll find a choice nature, not wholly deserving
A name either English or Yankee — just Irving. . . .

[*Holmes*] There's Holmes, who is matchless among you for wit,
A Leyden jar° always full charged, from which flit

77. **Barnaby Rudge:** a crazed youth in Dickens's novel of that name, who had a pet raven; Poe had his poem "The Raven." 79. **iambs and pentameters:** See pages 344–345, for explanation of these meters. 83. **Mathews:** an editor and critic of the time who, like Poe, wrote severe criticism of Longfellow. 96. **Collins and Gray:** well-known English poets of the eighteenth century. 98. **from Spain:** Irving had just returned from a long sojourn as American minister to Spain. 100. **Cervantes** (sĕr-vän′tēz): (1547–1616), author of *Don Quixote.* 102, 103. **Steele . . . Addison:** famous essayists of eighteenth-century England, who together wrote the *Tatler* and *Spectator* papers. 114. **Leyden** (lī′dĕn) **jar:** an electricity condenser which can give strong shocks.

The electrical tingles of hit after hit;                                              115
In long poems 'tis painful sometimes, and invites
A thought of the way the new telegraph writes,
Which pricks down its little sharp sentences spitefully,
As if you'd got more than you'd title to rightfully,
And you find yourself hoping its wild father lightning                                120
Would flame in for a second and give you a fright'ning. . . .

[*Lowell*] There is Lowell, who's striving Parnassus to climb
With a whole bale of *isms* tied together with rhyme;
He might get on alone, spite of brambles and boulders,
But he can't with that bundle he has on his shoulders.                                125
The top of the hill he will ne'er come nigh reaching
Till he learns the distinction 'twixt singing and preaching;
His lyre has some chords that would ring pretty well,
But he'd rather by half make a drum of the shell,
And rattle away till he's old as Methusalem,°                                         130
At the head of a march to the last new Jerusalem.

130. **Methusalem**(mĕ-thū′zĕ-lĕm): Methuselah, oldest man in the Bible (Gen. 5:27).

# THE VISION OF SIR LAUNFAL

Published the same year as the first series of *The Biglow Papers*, yet entirely different from them in treatment, is *The Vision of Sir Launfal*, probably the best-known and most-quoted poem by Lowell. In it may be traced the influence of his wife, Maria White, to whom he had been married only a few years when he wrote this. She, too, was a poet and so ardent a believer in the brotherhood of man that she had succeeded in winning Lowell over from his scoffing attitude toward the abolitionists.

The author's own note of explanation is helpful: " According to the mythology of the romancers, the San Greal, or Holy Grail, was the cup out of which Jesus partook of the Last Supper with his disciples. It was brought into England by Joseph of Arimathea, and remained there, an object of pilgrimage and adoration, for many years in the keeping of his lineal descendants. It was incumbent upon those who had charge of it to be chaste in thought, word, and deed; but one of the keepers having broken this condition, the Holy Grail disappeared. From that time it was a favorite enterprise of the knights of Arthur's court to go in search of it. Sir Galahad was at last successful in finding it, as may be read in the seventeenth book of the *Romance of King Arthur*. Tennyson has made Sir Galahad the subject of one of the most exquisite of his poems. The plot (if I may

give that name to anything so slight) of the following poem is my own, and to serve its purposes, I have enlarged the circle of competition in search of the miraculous cup in such a manner as to include, not only other persons than the heroes of the Round Table, but also a period of time subsequent to the supposed date of King Arthur's reign."

### PRELUDE TO PART FIRST

Over his keys the musing organist,
  Beginning doubtfully and far away,
First lets his fingers wander as they list,
  And builds a bridge from Dreamland for
    his lay:
Then, as the touch of his loved instru-
    ment                                              5
  Gives hope and fervor, nearer draws his
    theme,
First guessed by faint, auroral flushes sent
  Along the wavering vista of his dream.

Not only around our infancy°                                9
Doth Heaven with all its splendors lie;
Daily, with souls that cringe and plot,

9. **Not . . . infancy:** The English poet, Wordsworth, had written, "Heaven lies about us in our infancy." Lowell disagreed that Heaven was limited to our infancy.

We Sinais° climb and know it not.
Over our manhood bend the skies;
 Against our fallen and traitor lives
The great winds utter prophecies;    15
 With our faint hearts the mountain
  strives;
Its arms outstretched, the druid° wood
 Waits with its benedicite;°
And to our age's drowsy blood
 Still shouts the inspiring sea.    20

Earth gets its price for what Earth gives
  us;
 The beggar is taxed for a corner to die in,
The priest hath his fee who comes and
  shrives us,
 We bargain for the graves we lie in;
At the devil's booth are all things sold,   25
Each ounce of dross costs its ounce of gold;
 For a cap and bells° our lives we pay,
Bubbles we buy with a whole soul's tasking:
'Tis Heaven alone that is given away,
'Tis only God may be had for the ask-
  ing;    30
No price is set on the lavish summer;
June may be had by the poorest comer.

And what is so rare as a day in June?
 Then, if ever, come perfect days;    34
Then Heaven tries earth if it be in tune,
 And over it softly her warm ear lays;
Whether we look, or whether we listen,
We hear life murmur, or see it glisten;
Every clod feels a stir of might,
 An instinct within it that reaches and
  towers,    40
And groping blindly above it for light,
 Climbs to a soul in grass and flowers.
The flush of life may well be seen
 Thrilling back over hills and valleys;
The cowslip startles in meadows green,   45
 The buttercup catches the sun in its
  chalice,

12. **Sinais** (sī'nȧ-īz): Mount Sinai was the
place where God gave Moses the Ten Commandments (Exodus, Chapter 19). Here it
symbolizes communion with Heaven. 17. **druid:**
ancient Celtic priest who held the oak sacred
and worshiped in the woods. 18. **benedicite** (běn-
ê-dĭs'ĭ-tê): blessing. 27. **cap and bells:** the jingling
headdress of a king's jester; in other words,
mere superficial pleasures.

And there's never a leaf or a blade too mean
 To be some happy creature's palace;
The little bird sits at his door in the sun,
 Atilt like a blossom among the leaves,
And lets his illumined being o'errun    51
 With the deluge of summer it receives;
His mate feels the eggs beneath her wings,
And the heart in her dumb breast flutters
  and sings;
He sings to the wide world, and she to her
  nest —    55
In the nice ear of Nature which song is the
  best?

Now is the high tide of the year,
 And whatever of life hath ebbed away
Comes flooding back with a ripply cheer
 Into every bare inlet and creek and bay;
Now the heart is so full that a drop over-
  fills it;    61
We are happy now because God wills it;
No matter how barren the past may have
  been,
'Tis enough for us now that the leaves are
  green;
We sit in the warm shade and feel right
  well    65
How the sap creeps up and the blossoms
  swell;
We may shut our eyes, but we cannot help
  knowing
That skies are clear and grass is growing.
The breeze comes whispering in our ear
That dandelions are blossoming near,   70
 That maize has sprouted, that streams
  are flowing,
That the river is bluer than the sky,
That the robin is plastering his house hard
  by;
And if the breeze kept the good news back,
For other couriers we should not lack;   75
 We could guess it all by yon heifer's low-
  ing —
And hark! how clear bold chanticleer,
Warmed with the new wine of the year,
 Tells all in his lusty crowing!

Joy comes, grief goes, we know not how;
Everything is happy now,    81
 Everything is upward striving;

'Tis as easy now for the heart to be true
As for grass to be green or skies to be
blue —
   'Tis the natural way of living.    85
Who knows whither the clouds have fled?
   In the unscarred heaven they leave no
     wake;
And the eyes forget the tears they have
     shed,
   The heart forgets its sorrow and ache;
The soul partakes the season's youth,    90
   And the sulphurous rifts of passion and
     woe
Lie deep 'neath a silence pure and smooth,
   Like burnt-out craters healed with snow.
What wonder if Sir Launfal now
Remembered the keeping of his vow?    95

### PART FIRST

#### I

" My golden spurs now bring to me,
   And bring to me my richest mail,
For tomorrow I go over land and sea
   In search of the Holy Grail.
Shall never a bed for me be spread,    100
Nor shall a pillow be under my head,
   Till I begin my vow to keep;
Here on the rushes° will I sleep,
And perchance there may come a vision
    true
Ere day create the world anew."    105
   Slowly Sir Launfal's eyes grew dim;
   Slumber fell like a cloud on him,
And into his soul the vision flew.

#### II

The crows flapped over by twos and threes;°
In the pool drowsed the cattle up to their
    knees;    110
   The little birds sang as if it were
   The one day of summer in all the year;
And the very leaves seemed to sing on the
    trees;
The castle alone in the landscape lay    114
Like an outpost of winter, dull and gray;

103. **rushes:** This is inside the castle, not outside. The floors were covered with rushes.
109. **The crows ... threes:** This is the beginning of the vision, which ends with line 327 of
Part Second.

'Twas the proudest hall in the North Coun-
    tree,
And never its gates might opened be
Save to lord or lady of high degree;
Summer besieged it on every side,
But the churlish stone her assaults de-
   fied;    120
She could not scale the chilly wall,
Though around it for leagues her pavilions
    tall
Stretched left and right,
Over the hills and out of sight.
   Green and broad was every tent,    125
   And out of each a murmur went
Till the breeze fell off at night.

#### III

The drawbridge dropped with a surly clang,
And through the dark arch a charger
    sprang,    129
Bearing Sir Launfal, the maiden knight,°
In his gilded mail, that flamed so bright
It seemed the dark castle had gathered all
Those shafts the fierce sun had shot over its
    wall
   In his siege of three hundred summers
    long,
And, binding them all in one blazing
    sheaf,    135
   Had cast them forth; so, young and
    strong,
And lightsome as a locust leaf,
Sir Launfal flashed forth in his unscarred
    mail,
To seek in all climes for the Holy Grail.

#### IV

It was morning on hill and stream and
    tree,    140
   And morning in the young knight's heart;
Only the castle moodily
Rebuffed the gifts of the sunshine free,
   And gloomed by itself apart;    144
The season brimmed all other things up
Full as the rain fills the pitcher plant's cup.

#### V

As Sir Launfal made morn through the
    darksome gate,

130. **maiden knight:** one who has not been in
battle.

He was 'ware of a leper, crouched by the same,
Who begged with his hand and moaned as he sate;                    149
And a loathing over Sir Launfal came.
The sunshine went out of his soul with a thrill,
The flesh 'neath his armor 'gan shrink and crawl,
And midway its leap his heart stood still
Like a frozen waterfall;                    154
For this man, so foul and bent of stature,
Rasped harshly against his dainty nature,
And seemed the one blot on the summer morn —
So he tossed him a piece of gold in scorn.

### VI

The leper raised not the gold from the dust:
" Better to me the poor man's crust,   160
Better the blessing of the poor,
Though I turn me empty from his door;
That is no true alms which the hand can hold;
He gives nothing but worthless gold
    Who gives from a sense of duty;   165
But he who gives but a slender mite,
And gives to that which is out of sight,
    That thread of the all-sustaining Beauty
Which runs through all and doth all unite —
The hand cannot clasp the whole of his alms,                    170
The heart outstretches its eager palms,
For a god goes with it and makes it store
To the soul that was starving in darkness before."

### PRELUDE TO PART SECOND

Down swept the chill wind from the mountain peak,
From the snow five thousand summers old;                    175
On open wold and hilltop bleak
    It had gathered all the cold,
And whirled it like sleet on the wanderer's cheek;
It carried a shiver everywhere

From the unleafed boughs and pastures bare;                    180
The little brook heard it and built a roof
'Neath which he could house him, winter-proof;
All night by the white stars' frosty gleams
He groined his arches and matched his beams;                    184
Slender and clear were his crystal spars
As the lashes of light that trim the stars;
He sculptured every summer delight
In his halls and chambers out of sight;
Sometimes his tinkling waters slipped
Down through a frost-leaved forest crypt,
Long, sparkling aisles of steel-stemmed trees                    191
Bending to counterfeit a breeze;
Sometimes the roof no fretwork knew
But silvery mosses that downward grew;
Sometimes it was carved in sharp relief                    195
With quaint arabesques of ice-fern leaf;
Sometimes it was simply smooth and clear
For the gladness of heaven to shine through, and here
He had caught the nodding bulrush tops
And hung them thickly with diamond drops,                    200
That crystaled the beams of moon and sun,
And made a star of every one.
No mortal builder's most rare device
Could match this winter palace of ice;
'Twas as if every image that mirrored lay                    205
In his depths serene through the summer day,
Each fleeting shadow of earth and sky,
    Lest the happy model should be lost,
Had been mimicked in fairy masonry
    By the elfin builders of the frost.   210

Within the hall are song and laughter;
    The cheeks of Christmas glow red and jolly;
And sprouting is every corbel° and rafter
    With lightsome green of ivy and holly;
Through the deep gulf of the chimney wide                    215

213. **corbel** (kôr'bĕl): bracket.

Wallows the Yule log's roaring tide;
The broad flame pennons droop and flap
  And belly and tug as a flag in the wind;
Like a locust shrills the imprisoned sap,
  Hunted to death in its galleries blind;
And swift little troops of silent sparks,
Now pausing, now scattering away as in
  fear,                                    222
Go threading the soot forest's tangled darks
Like herds of startled deer.
But the wind without was eager and
  sharp;                                   225
Of Sir Launfal's gray hair it makes a harp,
  And rattles and wrings
  The icy strings,
  Singing, in dreary monotone,
  A Christmas carol of its own,            230
  Whose burden still, as he might guess,
  Was " Shelterless, shelterless, shelter-
  less! "
The voice of the seneschal° flared like a
  torch
As he shouted the wanderer away from the
  porch,
And he sat in the gateway and saw all
  night                                    235
  The great hall fire, so cheery and bold,
  Through the window slits of the castle
  old,
Build out its piers of ruddy light
Against the drift of the cold.


### PART SECOND

#### I

There was never a leaf on bush or
  tree,                                    240
The bare boughs rattled shudderingly;
The river was dumb and could not speak,
  For the weaver Winter its shroud had
  spun;
A single crow on the treetop bleak
  From his shining feathers shed off the
  cold sun;                               245
Again it was morning, but shrunk and cold,
As if her veins were sapless and old,
And she rose up decrepitly
For a last dim look at earth and sea.

233. **seneschal** (sĕn'ĕ-shăl): steward.

#### II

Sir Launfal turned from his own hard
  gate,                                    250
For another heir in his earldom sate;
An old, bent man, worn out and frail,
He came back from seeking the Holy Grail;
Little he recked of his earldom's loss;
No more on his surcoat was blazoned the
  cross,                                   255
But deep in his soul the sign he wore,
The badge of the suffering and the poor.

#### III

Sir Launfal's raiment thin and spare
Was idle mail 'gainst the barbèd air,
For it was just at the Christmas time;   260
So he mused, as he sat, of a sunnier clime,
And sought for a shelter from cold and
  snow
In the light and warmth of long ago;
He sees the snakelike caravan crawl
O'er the edge of the desert, black and
  small,                                   265
Then nearer and nearer, till, one by one,
He can count the camels in the sun,
As over the red-hot sands they pass
To where, in its slender necklace of grass,
The little spring laughed and leaped in the
  shade,                                   270
And with its own self like an infant played,
And waved its signal of palms.

#### IV

" For Christ's sweet sake, I beg an
  alms " —
The happy camels may reach the spring,
But Sir Launfal sees naught save the grue-
  some thing,                             275
The leper, lank as the rain-blanched bone,
That cowers beside him, a thing as lone
And white as the ice isles of Northern seas
In the desolate horror of his disease.

#### V

And Sir Launfal said, " I behold in
  thee                                     280
An image of Him who died on the tree.
Thou also hast had thy crown of thorns,
Thou also hast had the world's buffets and
  scorns,

And to thy life were not denied
The wounds in the hands and feet and
    side.         285
Mild Mary's Son, acknowledge me;
Behold, through him, I give to Thee! "

### VI

Then the soul of the leper stood up in his
    eyes
    And looked at Sir Launfal, and straight-
        way he
Remembered in what a haughtier guise
    He had flung an alms to leprosie,   291
When he girt his young life up in gilded
    mail
And set forth in search of the Holy Grail.
The heart within him was ashes and dust;
He parted in twain his single crust,   295
He broke the ice on the streamlet's brink,
And gave the leper to eat and drink.
'Twas a moldy crust of coarse, brown bread,
'Twas water out of a wooden bowl —
Yet with fine wheaten bread was the leper
    fed,         300
    And 'twas red wine he drank with his
    thirsty soul.

### VII

As Sir Launfal mused with a downcast face,
A light shone round about the place;
The leper no longer crouched at his side,
But stood before him glorified,   305
Shining and tall and fair and straight
As the pillar that stood by the Beautiful
    Gate° —
Himself the Gate° whereby men can
Enter the temple of God and Man.

### VIII

His words were shed softer than leaves from
    the pine,       310
And they fell on Sir Launfal as snows on
    the brine,
That mingle their softness and quiet in one

With the shaggy unrest they float down
    upon;
And the voice that was calmer than silence
    said,
" Lo, it is I, be not afraid!    315
In many climes, without avail,
Thou has spent thy life for the Holy Grail;
Behold, it is here — this cup which thou
Didst fill at the streamlet for Me but now;
This crust is My body broken for thee;
This water His blood that died on the
    tree;      321
The Holy Supper° is kept, indeed,
In whatso we share with another's need;
Not what we give, but what we share,
For the gift without the giver is bare;  325
Who gives himself with his alms feeds three,
Himself, his hungering neighbor, and Me."

### IX

Sir Launfal awoke as from a swound;
" The Grail in my castle here is found!
Hang my idle armor up on the wall;  330
Let it be the spider's banquet hall;
He must be fenced with stronger mail
Who would seek and find the Holy Grail."

### X

The castle gate stands open now,
    And the wanderer is welcome to the
    hall      335
As the hangbird is to the elm-tree bough;
    No longer scowl the turrets tall,
The Summer's long siege at last is o'er;
When the first poor outcast went in at the
    door,
She entered with him in disguise,  340
And mastered the fortress by surprise;
There is no spot she loves so well on ground,
She lingers and smiles there the whole year
    round;
The meanest serf on Sir Launfal's land
Has hall and bower at his command;  345
And there's no poor man in the North
    Countree
But is lord of the earldom as much as he.

307. **the Beautiful Gate:** a gate of the temple at Jerusalem (Acts 3:2). 308. **Himself the Gate:** Christ said, "I am the door." The leper had become the Christ.

322. **Holy Supper:** the Last Supper of Christ and His disciples, commemorated in the communion service of Christian churches.

## Suggestions for Study of Lowell

### THE COURTIN'

1. Be sure that you understand the dialect. Any words or phrases that are not clear should be restated in standard English. What does a dialect poem lose when translated into standard English?

2. Point out details that are typical of an old-fashioned New England kitchen. If possible, find pictures of such kitchens with their open fireplaces.

3. Point out bits of humor either in the actions of the characters or in the poet's choice of words.

### A FABLE FOR CRITICS

4. The most natural way to study *A Fable for Critics* is to discuss whether Lowell's comments seem justified from what you have been able to read by these individual authors. If you disagree with his impression of any of them, try to discover whether he was wrong or whether you have not yet read enough by that author to judge his work as a whole.

5. Point out good examples of Lowell's wit. Are there lines that make you laugh audibly, or do they just give you mental amusement? Find some examples of puns. Can you justify the use of puns in this type of poem? Where does exaggerated rhyme add to the humor?

6. Are the authors on the whole treated sympathetically, or satirically? If you had been any of these men, would you have felt angry at Lowell's comments on you? Discuss individual cases.

7. The manner of this poem is not hard to parody. Try writing " A Fable for Teachers," " A Fable for Students," or another type of humorous brief comments on persons or types with which you are familiar.

### THE VISION OF SIR LAUNFAL

#### Prelude to Part First

8. How does the organist compare with the poet approaching his theme? with yourself writing a theme for school? Why are the first ideas called " auroral flushes "?

9. What proof does the poet give that we have contacts with Heaven all through our lives? What kind of things must we pay for and what things are given away in this world?

10. In the famous description of the June day, pick out the details that suggest awakening and teeming life. How would you answer the question in line 56? What is the effect of such a day upon a person?

#### Part First

11. Look up the part played by the vigil in the training of a knight (E. M. Tappan, *When Knights Were Bold*).

12. Beginning with stanza II, the rest of the poem to Part Second, stanza IX, is the vision Sir Launfal had on the night of his vigil. Describe the way he appears in the vision as he goes forth on his quest. You would enjoy reading a similar description of Sir Lancelot in Tennyson's " The Lady of Shalott," Part III.

13. Why did the leper reject Sir Launfal's gift? Have you read any other works in which lepers figure? *Ben Hur* by Lew Wallace and Stevenson's " Father Damien " are notable examples.

#### Prelude to Part Second

14. Mark the words and phrases you think especially vivid in the famous description of winter. Give examples from your own observation of how the frost mimics the images of summer.

15. Explain the tradition of the Yule log and other medieval Christmas customs which have come down to our own day. See Irving's " Christmas Sketches " in *The Sketch Book*.

16. Point out the various figures of speech the poet uses in describing the great hall fire.

#### Part Second

17. Part Second is in direct contrast to Part First. See how many points of contrast you can find.

18. Why does the leper accept Sir Launfal's gift this time? What miraculous transformation takes place? Explain the speech of the transformed leper in your own words. Henry van Dyke's *The Story of the Other Wise Man* expresses a similar idea. Have you read it?

19. What effect did the vision have on Sir Launfal?

## For Your Vocabulary

FIGURATIVE USE OF WORDS. The contrast of summer and winter in *The Vision of Sir Launfal* is created by listing details of summer and winter scenes. But the impression of the inhospitable castle is achieved by figurative use of words that usually name unlikable human

A RECENT PICTURE OF THE CONSTITUTION. "Old Ironsides" has been preserved in its original form as a national memorial at the Charlestown Navy Yard, Charlestown, Massachusetts. (Ewing Galloway)

traits. The *churlish* (chûr'lĭsh) stone defied the assaults of the summer (line 120). A *churl* is a rude, bad-tempered person. The drawbridge dropped with a *surly* clang (line 128). *Surly* is used particularly of an ill-humored manner or tone of voice in dealings with other people. The castle *moodily rebuffed* the gifts of summer (lines 142–143), refused bluntly to meet a friendly advance. After Sir Launfal has learned sympathy for his fellowmen, the turrets "no longer *scowl*." By such metaphoric use of single words the castle is given as definite a personality as a human being and not a likable being, either. With this good example of the method fresh in your mind, try writing a brief paragraph, such as would be used in a story, describing a house that has a distinctive feeling — a simple but friendly, happy house; or a stiffly formal house. Think of words to describe the personality you want to give it, and then use them figuratively as you give factual details. Try to get some verbs, some nouns, and some adjectives among your key words.

# Oliver Wendell Holmes

## 1809–1894

## OLD IRONSIDES

When Holmes was just twenty-one, he gained for himself permanent fame, and for the United States the preservation of a historic relic, by writing "Old Ironsides." This poem was a vigorous protest against the destruction of the frigate *Constitution*, which had defeated the *Guerrière* in the War of 1812. At first published in the Boston *Advertiser*, the verses were later copied in newspapers and scattered on broadsides all over the country. Such indignation was aroused that the ship was saved and became an object of great interest in the Charlestown Navy Yard, just outside of Boston. In 1928, because of its rotting timbers, it was taken apart and restored to its original form to be kept as a national memorial.

Ay, tear her tattered ensign down!
  Long has it waved on high,
And many an eye has danced to see
  That banner in the sky;
Beneath it rung the battle shout,      5
  And burst the cannon's roar —
The meteor of the ocean air
  Shall sweep the clouds no more.

Her decks, once red with heroes' blood,
  Where knelt the vanquished foe,    10
When winds were hurrying o'er the flood,
  And waves were white below,
No more shall feel the victor's tread,
  Or know the conquered knee —
The harpies of the shore shall pluck    15
  The eagle of the sea!

Oh, better that her shattered hulk
  Should sink beneath the wave;
Her thunders shook the mighty deep,
  And there should be her grave;      20
Nail to the mast her holy flag,
  Set every threadbare sail,
And give her to the god of storms,
  The lightning and the gale!

## MY AUNT

This and the next poem, "The Last Leaf,"
were first published when Holmes was twenty-
two years old. In both of them youth smiles
at the older generation.

My aunt! my dear unmarried aunt!
  Long years have o'er her flown;
Yet still she strains the aching clasp
  That binds her virgin zone;
I know it hurts her — though she looks  5
  As cheerful as she can;
Her waist is ampler than her life,
  For life is but a span.

My aunt! my poor deluded aunt!
  Her hair is almost gray;            10
Why will she train that winter curl
  In such a springlike way?
How can she lay her glasses down,
  And say she reads as well,
When through a double convex lens     15
  She just makes out to spell?

Her father — Grandpapa! forgive
  This erring lip its smiles —
Vowed she should make the finest girl
  Within a hundred miles;             20
He sent her to a stylish school;
  'Twas in her thirteenth June;
And with her, as the rules required,
  "Two towels and a spoon."

They braced my aunt against a board,  25
  To make her straight and tall;
They laced her up, they starved her down,
  To make her light and small;
They pinched her feet, they singed her hair,
  They screwed it up with pins —      30
O never mortal suffered more
  In penance for her sins.

But when my precious aunt was done,
  My grandsire brought her back;
(By daylight, lest some rabid youth   35
  Might follow on the track;)
" Ah! " said my grandsire, as he shook
  Some powder in his pan,°
" What could this lovely creature do
  Against a desperate man! "          40

Alas! nor chariot, nor barouche,
  Nor bandit cavalcade,
Tore from the trembling father's arms
  His all-accomplished maid.
For her how happy had it been!        45
  And Heaven had spared to me
To see one sad, ungathered rose
  On my ancestral tree.

38. **powder in his pan:** gunpowder in the hollow lock by which old guns were primed.

## THE LAST LEAF

This poem was suggested to Holmes by the
appearance of old Major Thomas Melville,
grandfather of Herman Melville, author of
*Moby Dick*. It is interesting to know that the
portrait of the old man and the suit of clothes
described in the poem are both preserved in
the Old Boston Statehouse museum.

I saw him once before,
As he passed by the door,
  And again
The pavement stones resound
As he totters o'er the ground        5
  With his cane.

They say that in his prime,
Ere the pruning knife of Time
  Cut him down,
Not a better man was found        10
By the crier on his round
  Through the town.

But now he walks the streets,
And he looks at all he meets
  Sad and wan,        15
And he shakes his feeble head,
That it seems as if he said,
  " They are gone."

The mossy marbles rest
On the lips that he has prest        20
  In their bloom,
And the names he loved to hear
Have been carved for many a year
  On the tomb.

My grandmamma has said —        25
Poor old lady, she is dead
  Long ago —
That he had a Roman nose,
And his cheek was like a rose
  In the snow.        30

But now his nose is thin,
And it rests upon his chin
  Like a staff,
And a crook is in his back,
And a melancholy crack        35
  In his laugh.

I know it is a sin
For me to sit and grin
  At him here;
But the old three-cornered hat,        40
And the breeches, and all that,
  Are so queer!

And if I should live to be
The last leaf upon the tree
  In the spring,        45
Let them smile, as I do now,
At the old forsaken bough
  Where I cling.

## THE BOYS

Dr. Holmes's wit and engaging personality made him highly popular in Boston as an after-dinner speaker and writer of poems for special occasions. Probably the best known of these poems is " The Boys," written for the thirtieth reunion of his own Harvard class of 1829, a class famous for the notable men it produced.

Has there any old fellow got mixed with the boys?
If there has, take him out, without making a noise.
Hang the almanac's cheat and the catalogue's spite!
Old time is a liar! We're twenty tonight!

We're twenty! We're twenty! Who says we are more?        5
He's tipsy — young jackanapes! — show him the door!
" Gray temples at twenty? " — Yes! *white* if we please;
Where the snowflakes fall thickest there's nothing can freeze!

Was it snowing I spoke of? Excuse the mistake!
Look close — you will not see a sign of a flake!        10
We want some new garlands for those we have shed —
And these are white roses in place of the red.

We've a trick, we young fellows, you may have been told,
Of talking (in public) as if we were old —
That boy we call " Doctor," and this we call " Judge ";        15
It's a neat little fiction — of course it's all fudge.

That fellow's the " Speaker " — the one on the right;
" Mr. Mayor," my young one, how are you tonight?
That's our " Member of Congress," we say when we chaff;
There's the " Reverend " What's his name? — don't make me laugh.     20

That boy with the grave mathematical look
Made believe he had written a wonderful book,
And the Royal Society thought it was *true!*
So they chose him right in; a good joke it was, too!

There's a boy, we pretend, with a three-decker brain,     25
That could harness a team with a logical chain;
When he spoke for our manhood in syllabled fire,
We called him " The Justice," but now he's " The Squire."

And there's a nice youngster of excellent pith —
Fate tried to conceal him by naming him Smith;°     30
But he shouted a song for the brave and the free —
Just read on his medal, " My country," " of thee! "

You hear that boy laughing? — You think he's all fun;
But the angels laugh, too, at the good he has done;
The children laugh loud as they troop to his call,     35
And the poor man that knows him laughs loudest of all!

Yes, we're boys — always playing with tongue or with pen —
And I sometimes have asked — Shall we ever be men?
Shall we always be youthful, and laughing, and gay,
Till the last dear companion drops smiling away?     40

Then here's to our boyhood, its gold and its gray!
The stars of its winter, the dews of its May!
And when we have done with our life-lasting toys,
Dear Father, take care of thy children, *the boys!*

30. **Smith:** Samuel Francis Smith, author of "America." Note that this is the only one called by name; and he is probably the only one whose name has ever been heard by the average high-school student of today. Anyone who is curious to identify the others can find them listed in the footnotes of the Cambridge edition of Holmes's poems.

## THE HEIGHT OF THE RIDICULOUS

Here is indeed the climax of a humorist's life, with a neat little alibi in the last two lines. Be sure you catch the pun in line 16.

I wrote some lines once on a time
  In wondrous merry mood,
And thought, as usual, men would say
  They were exceeding good.

They were so queer, so very queer,     5
  I laughed as I would die;
Albeit, in the general way,
  A sober man am I.

I called my servant, and he came;
  How kind it was of him     10
To mind a slender man like me,
  He of the mighty limb!

" These to the printer," I exclaimed,
 And, in my humorous way,
I added (as a trifling jest),   15
 " There'll be the devil to pay."

He took the paper, and I watched,
 And saw him peep within;
At the first line he read, his face
 Was all upon the grin.   20

He read the next; the grin grew broad,
 And shot from ear to ear;
He read the third; a chuckling noise
 I now began to hear.

The fourth; he broke into a roar; 25
 The fifth; his waistband split;
The sixth; he burst five buttons off,
 And tumbled in a fit.

Ten days and nights, with sleepless eye,
 I watched that wretched man, 30
And since, I never dare to write
 As funny as I can.

## THE CHAMBERED NAUTILUS

 You must not think of Dr. Holmes as merely " a funny man." This poem, which he preferred above all his writings and by which he hoped to be remembered, is one of the best-loved poems of aspiration in our national literature. He caught his idea from the shell of the nautilus, of which he had several specimens. In *The Autocrat of the Breakfast Table*, where this poem was originally published, the author describes " the ship of pearl " as " a series of enlarging compartments successively dwelt in by the animal that inhabits the shell, which is built in a widening spiral." The name " nautilus," meaning sailor, grew out of the old belief that the little creature sailed by the gauzy wings which are really its tentacles.

This is the ship of pearl, which, poets feign,
 Sails the unshadowed main —
 The venturous bark that flings
On the sweet summer wind its purpled wings

In gulfs enchanted, where the Siren° sings,
 And coral reefs lie bare,   6
Where the cold sea maids rise to sun their
 streaming hair.

Its webs of living gauze no more unfurl;
 Wrecked is the ship of pearl!
 And every chambered cell,  10
Where its dim dreaming life was wont to
 dwell,
As the frail tenant shaped his growing shell,
 Before thee lies revealed —
Its irised ceiling rent, its sunless crypt unsealed!

Year after year beheld the silent toil 15
 That spread his lustrous coil;
 Still, as the spiral grew,
He left the past year's dwelling for the new,
Stole with soft step its shining archway
 through,
 Built up its idle door,   20
Stretched in his last-found home, and knew
 the old no more.

Thanks for the heavenly message brought
 by thee,
 Child of the wandering sea,
 Cast from her lap, forlorn!  24
From thy dead lips a clearer note is born
Than ever Triton° blew from wreathèd
 horn!
 While on mine ears it rings,
Through the deep caves of thought I hear
 a voice that sings:

Build thee more stately mansions, O my
 soul,
 As the swift seasons roll!  30
 Leave thy low-vaulted past!
Let each new temple, nobler than the last,
Shut thee from heaven with a dome more
 vast,
 Till thou at length art free,
Leaving thine outgrown shell by life's unresting sea!   35

 5. **Siren:** in classical mythology the sirens were sea nymphs near the west coast of Italy who lured mariners to their death by their enchanting songs. 26. **Triton** (trī'tŏn): ancient sea god whose lower part resembled a fish. He is usually represented as blowing a trumpet made of a sea shell.

## ON CONVERSATION

Holmes's great contribution to prose is *The Autocrat of the Breakfast Table* series written for early numbers of the *Atlantic Monthly* at the request of his friend Lowell, its first editor. *The Autocrat* was followed by *The Professor* and later *The Poet at the Breakfast Table*. These papers are usually designated as essays, but they have no real counterpart. They represent a series of conversations, or rather a monologue — for the persons around a boardinghouse breakfast table, though distinct characters, figure largely as background for the autocrat's remarks. Disconnected, indeed, these conversations are, but surprising in the variety of topics and brilliance of language. The following extract from Part I of *The Autocrat* is a good example.

This business of conversation is a very serious matter. There are men whom it weakens one to talk with an hour more than a day's fasting would do. Mark this which I am going to say, for it is as good as a working professional man's advice, and costs you nothing: It is better to lose a pint of blood from your veins than to have a nerve tapped. Nobody measures your nervous force as it runs away, nor bandages your brain and marrow after the operation.

There are men of *esprit* [1] who are excessively exhausting to some people. They are the talkers who have what may be called *jerky* minds. Their thoughts do not run in the natural order of sequence. They say bright things on all possible subjects, but their zigzags rack you to death. After a jolting half-hour with one of these jerky companions, talking with a dull friend affords great relief. It is like taking the cat in your lap after holding a squirrel.

What a comfort a dull but kindly person is, to be sure, at times! A ground-glass shade over a gas lamp does not bring more solace to our dazzled eyes than such a one to our minds.

" Do not dull people bore you? " said one of the lady boarders — the same who sent me her autograph book last week with a request for a few original stanzas, not re-membering that the *Pactolian* pays me five dollars a line for everything I write in its columns.

" Madam," said I (she and the century were in their teens together), " all men are bores, except when we want them. There never was but one man whom I would trust with my latchkey."

" Who might that favored person be? "

" Zimmerman." [2]

The men of genius that I fancy most have erectile heads like the cobra de capello. [3] You remember what they tell of William Pinckney, the great pleader, how in his eloquent paroxysms the veins of his neck would swell and his face flush and his eyes glitter, until he seemed on the verge of apoplexy. The hydraulic arrangements for supplying the brain with blood are only second in importance to its own organization. The bulbous-headed fellows who steam well when they are at work are the men that draw big audiences and give us marrowy books and pictures. It is a good sign to have one's feet grow cold when he is writing. A great writer and speaker once told me that he often wrote with his feet in hot water; but for this, *all* his blood would have run into his head, as the mercury sometimes withdraws into the ball of a thermometer.

You don't suppose that my remarks made at this table are like so many postage stamps, do you — each to be only once uttered? If you do, you are mistaken. He must be a poor creature who does not often repeat himself. Imagine the author of the excellent piece of advice " Know thyself " never alluding to that sentiment again during the course of a protracted existence! Why, the truths a man carries about with him are his

---

[1] **esprit** (ĕs-prē'): sprightly wit (French).

[2] The *Treatise on Solitude* is not so frequently seen lying about on library tables as in our younger days. I remember that I always respected the title and let the book alone. [Author's note.] [3] **cobra de capello** (kō'bra̍ dē ka̍-pĕl'ō): literally, serpent of the hood; a poisonous snake of Asia and Africa which, when excited, expands its neck into a broad hood.

tools; and do you think a carpenter is bound to use the same plane but once to smooth a knotty board with, or to hang up his hammer after it has driven its first nail? I shall never repeat a conversation, but an idea often. I shall use the same types when I like, but not commonly the same stereotypes.[1] A thought is often original, though you have uttered it a hundred times. It has come to you over a new route, by a new and express train of associations.

Sometimes, but rarely, one may be caught making the same speech twice over, and yet be held blameless. Thus, a certain lecturer, after performing in an inland city, where dwells a *littératrice*[2] of note, was invited to meet her and others over the social teacup. She pleasantly referred to his many wanderings in his new occupation. " Yes," he replied, " I am like the Huma, the bird that never lights, being always in the cars, as he is always on the wing." Years elapsed. The lecturer visited the same place once more for the same purpose. Another social cup after the lecture, and a second meeting with the distinguished lady. " You are constantly going from place to place," she said. " Yes," he answered, " I am like the Huma " — and finished the sentence as before.

What horrors, when it flashed over him that he had made this fine speech, word for word, twice over! Yet it was not true, as the lady might perhaps have fairly inferred, that he had embellished his conversation with the Huma daily during that whole interval of years. On the contrary, he had never once thought of the odious fowl until the recurrence of precisely the same circumstances brought up precisely the same idea. He ought to have been proud of the accuracy of his mental adjustments. Given certain factors, and a sound brain should always evolve the same fixed product

with the certainly of Babbage's calculating machine.

What a satire, by the way, is that machine on the mere mathematician! A Frankenstein[3] monster, a thing without brains and without heart, too stupid to make a blunder; which turns out results like a corn sheller, and never grows any wiser or better, though it grind a thousand bushels of them!

I have an immense respect for a man of talents *plus* " the mathematics." But the calculating power alone should seem to be the least human of qualities, and to have the smallest amount of reason in it; since a machine can be made to do the work of three or four calculators, and better than any one of them. Sometimes I have been troubled that I had not a deeper intuitive apprehension of the relations of numbers. But the triumph of the ciphering hand organ has consoled me. I always fancy I can hear the wheels clicking in a calculator's brain. The power of dealing with numbers is a kind of " detached lever " arrangement, which may be put into a mighty poor watch. I suppose it is about as common as the power of moving the ears voluntarily which is a moderately rare endowment.

Little localized powers and little narrow streaks of specialized knowledge are things men are very apt to be conceited about. Nature is very wise; but for this encouraging principle how many small talents and little accomplishments would be neglected! Talk about conceit as much as you like, it is to human character what salt is to the ocean; it keeps it sweet, and renders it endurable. Say rather it is like the natural unguent of the seafowl's plumage, which enables him to shed the rain that falls on him and the wave in which he dips. When one has had *all* his conceit taken out of him, when he has lost *all* his illusions, his feathers will soon soak through, and he will fly no more.

" So you admire conceited people, do

---

[1] **stereotypes** (stĕr'ĕ-ō-tīps): casts or plates used in printing. Here it means the exact unchangeable form. [2] **littératrice** (lē-tä-rà-trēs'): a literary woman. This incident actually occurred to Holmes at Hartford, Connecticut. The lady was Mrs. Sigourney, a well-known writer of that day.

[3] **Frankenstein** (frăngk'ĕn-stīn): the hero of a novel by Mary Godwin Shelley. He created a human monster who committed horrible crimes and who finally destroyed him.

you? " said the young lady who has come to the city to be finished off for — the duties of life.

I am afraid you do not study logic at your school, my dear. It does not follow that I wish to be pickled in brine because I like a salt-water plunge at Nahant.[1] I say that conceit is just as natural a thing to human minds as a center is to a circle. But little-minded people's thoughts move in such a small circle that five minutes' conversation gives you an arc long enough to determine their whole curve. An arc in the movement of a large intellect does not sensibly differ from a straight line. Even if it have the third vowel as its center, it does not soon betray it. The highest thought, that is, is the most seemingly impersonal; it does not obviously imply any individual center.

Audacious self-esteem, with good ground for it, is always imposing. What resplendent beauty that must have been which could have authorized Phryne[2] to " peel " in the way she did! What fine speeches are those two: " *Non omnis moriar,*"[3] and " I have taken all knowledge to be my province "![4] Even in common people, conceit has the virtue of making them cheerful; the man who thinks his wife, his baby, his house, his horse, his dog, and himself severally un-equalled is almost sure to be a good-humored person, though liable to be tedious at times.

What are the great faults of conversation? Want of ideas, want of words, want of manners, are the principal ones, I suppose you think. I don't doubt it, but I will tell you what I have found spoil more good talks than anything else — long arguments on special points between people who differ on the fundamental principles upon which

these points depend. No men can have sat-isfactory relations with each other until they have agreed on certain ultimata[5] of belief not to be disturbed in ordinary con-versation, and unless they have sense enough to trace the secondary questions de-pending upon these ultimate beliefs to their source. In short, just as a written constitu-tion is essential to the best social order, so a code of finalities is a necessary condition of profitable talk between two persons. Talking is like playing on the harp; there is as much in laying the hand on the strings to stop their vibrations as in twanging them to bring out their music.

## Suggestions for Study of Holmes

POEMS

1. Why was the nickname " Old Ironsides " given to the *Constitution?* Who were the " harpies of the shore "? Compare the three possible fates of the vessel: the proposed dis-mantling, which called forth the poem; the fate preferred by Holmes; and what has actu-ally happened to the ship. Which do you think the best fate?

2. Look up the history of the *Constitution,* especially its fight with the *Guerrière,* and find out whether you think Holmes was justified in his indignation. Study the picture on page 601 and other pictures of old fighting vessels. How do they differ from modern armed ships?

3. " My Aunt " and " The Last Leaf " may be looked upon as companion pieces. What clearly indicates that they were written in Holmes's youth? What is similar in the tone of the two poems? Is either character treated more sympathetically than the other? Do the poems seem disrespectful? What general com-ments on the relations between youth and age do they open up to you?

4. How did the education of " my aunt " differ from that of a girl today? What change has come about in the position and interests of unmarried women since Holmes's day? As-semble pictures of ladies' costumes of the late eighteenth century, when " my aunt " was a girl, and of the eighteen-thirties, when Holmes was observing his aunt's appearance. *Godey's Lady's Book* is especially good for the latter.

---

[1] **Nahant** (nȧ-hănt'): a coast town in Massa-chusetts. [2] **Phryne** (frī'nē): a famous Greek wom-an who before many people stripped off all her garments and plunged into the sea, suggesting to Apelles his famous picture of " Aphrodite Anadyomene." [3] **Non . . . moriar** (nōn ŏm'nĭs mō'-rĭ-är): " I shall not wholly die," a quotation from Horace. [4] **I . . . province:** a famous statement by Francis Bacon.

[5] **ultimata** (ŭl-tĭ-mā'tȧ): final or fundamental matters.

5. Assemble pictures of men's costumes of the Revolutionary War and of the eighteen-thirties to see the difference in appearance between Holmes and the old man.

6. Find out whether Holmes's semiprophecy at the end of " The Last Leaf " was fulfilled by consulting the time chart on page 626, to see whether he outlived other writers of his generation.

7. Pick out from the humorous poems words, phrases, or rhymes which seem to snap into the right place with the suddenness and appropriateness that we call wit.

8. In the vein of " The Boys " write a prophecy for your class thirty years hence, or write reminiscences of your present school life as if you were looking back on it for a thirtieth reunion.

9. Class project: Imagine that your class is having its thirtieth reunion banquet. Identify different members with the characters of " The Boys." Let each make a few remarks appropriate to his character. Then let a student who has memorized the poem recite it as the climax of the program.

10. Point out phrases or lines in " The Chambered Nautilus " that show the delicate beauty of the shell. If possible bring a picture, or better yet, a specimen of a nautilus shell to class to see just how it is formed. Express in your own words the comparison made by the poet between the shell and man's life.

11. Compare the idea of " The Chambered Nautilus " with Longfellow's " The Ladder of St. Augustine " and " Excelsior," and with the first stanza of Tennyson's " In Memoriam." Which of these four figures of speech for man's aspiration appeals to you most strongly?

12. " The Chambered Nautilus " has been made into a beautiful cantata by John S. Fearis. It is not too hard for high-school glee clubs. Have you heard it?

ON CONVERSATION

13. Be sure you understand the difference between " autocrat " and " aristocrat." Both apply to Holmes, but not with the same meaning. Find examples in this selection which show in what sense he is an autocrat.

14. Do you agree with his opinion on mathematicians, conceit, or conversational faults? Notice the variety of subjects discussed in this short selection. How many do you find in all?

15. Write a short essay suggested to you by this selection, such as:

a. A monologue on your views or prejudices

b. Breakfast-table conversation as you have observed it

c. " The Automat of the Breakfast Table " (if you have ever eaten in an automat)

16. If you enjoyed this selection from *The Autocrat of the Breakfast Table,* Chapters VII and XI are recommended for reading.

# Francis Parkman     1823–1893

Most of the early writing about the Indians was colored either by the hostility of those who fought them on the frontier or by the romantic notions of those who lived at a safe distance. Parkman escaped from both exaggerations. He said of the writing of history that " the narrator must seek to imbue himself with the life and spirit of the times." Because he held such views, he felt that he must find the life and spirit of the seventeenth-century American frontier — the scene of the historical events he planned to record in his great work on France and England in America. In 1846 he found in the broad plateau between Missouri and Dakota the frontier conditions he was seeking. Here he spent most of the summer studying the contradictory character of the American Indian. His famous account of this adventurous summer is *The Oregon Trail.* The hardships he endured so enfeebled Parkman that he remained an invalid the rest of his life, and the great history which is his lifework is not only a historical and literary masterpiece but an inspiring triumph of the human will over physical weakness and suffering.

## THE OGILLALLAH [1] VILLAGE

This is hardly the place for portraying the mental features of the Indians. The same picture, slightly changed in shade and coloring, would serve with very few exceptions for all the tribes north of the Mexican territories. But with this similarity in their modes of thought, the tribes of the lake and ocean shores, of the forests and of the plains, differ greatly in their manner of

[1] **Ogillallah** (ō-gĭl-lä′là).

life. Having been domesticated for several weeks among one of the wildest of the hordes that roam over the remote prairies, I had unusual opportunities of observing them and flatter myself that a sketch of the scenes that passed daily before my eyes may not be devoid of interest. They were thorough savages. Neither their manners nor their ideas were in the slightest degree modified by contact with civilization. They knew nothing of the power and real character of the white men, and their children would scream in terror when they saw me. Their religion, superstitions, and prejudices were the same handed down to them from immemorial time. They fought with the weapons that their fathers fought with, and wore the same garments of skins. They were living representatives of the " stone age "; for though their lances and arrows were tipped with iron procured from the traders, they still used the rude stone mallet of the primeval world.

Great changes are at hand in that region. With the stream of emigration to Oregon and California, the buffalo will dwindle away and the large wandering communities who depend on them for support must be broken and scattered. The Indians will soon be abased by whisky and overawed by military posts; so that within a few years the traveler may pass in tolerable security through their country. Its danger and its charm will have disappeared together.

As soon as Raymond and I discovered the village from the gap in the hills, we were seen in our turn; keen eyes were constantly on the watch. As we rode down upon the plain, the side of the village nearest us was darkened with a crowd of naked figures. Several men came forward to meet us. I could distinguish among them the green blanket of the Frenchman Reynal. When we came up, the ceremony of shaking hands had to be gone through in due form; and then all were eager to know what had become of the rest of my party. I satisfied them on this point and we all moved together toward the village.

" You've missed it," said Reynal; " if you'd been here day before yesterday, you'd have found the whole prairie over yonder black with buffalo as far as you could see. There were no cows, though; nothings but bulls. We made a ' surround ' every day till yesterday. See the village there; don't that look like good living? "

In fact, I could see, even at that distance, long cords stretched from lodge to lodge, over which the meat, cut by the squaws into thin sheets, was hanging to dry in the sun. I noticed, too, that the village was somewhat smaller than when I had last seen it, and I asked Reynal the cause. He said that old Le Borgne had felt too weak to pass over the mountains, and so had remained behind with all his relations, including Mahto-Tatonka and his brothers. The Whirlwind, too, had been unwilling to come so far, because, as Reynal said, he was afraid. Only half a dozen lodges had adhered to him, the main body of the village setting their chief's authority at naught and taking the course most agreeable to their inclinations.

" What chiefs are there in the village now? " asked I.

" Well," said Reynal, " there's old Red Water, and the Eagle Feather, and the Big Crow, and the Mad Wolf, and the Panther, and the White Shield, and — what's his name? — the half-breed Shienne." [1]

By this time we were close to the village, and I observed that, while the greater part of the lodges were very large and neat in their appearance, there was at one side a cluster of squalid, miserable huts. I looked toward them, and made some remark about their wretched appearance. But I was touching upon delicate ground.

" My squaw's relations live in those lodges," said Reynal, very warmly; " and there isn't a better set in the whole village."

" Are there any chiefs among them? "

" Chiefs? " said Reynal. " Yes, plenty! "

" What are their names? "

" Their names? Why, there's the Arrow-Head. If he isn't a chief, he ought to be one. And there's the Hail-Storm. He's nothing

[1] Shienne (shĭ-ĕn'): Parkman's spelling of Cheyenne.

but a boy, to be sure; but he's bound to be a chief one of these days."

Just then we passed between two of the lodges, and entered the great area of the village. Superb, naked figures stood silently gazing on us.

" Where's the Bad Wound's lodge? " said I to Reynal.

" There you've missed it again! The Bad Wound is away with the Whirlwind. If you could have found him here, and gone to live in his lodge, he would have treated you better than any man in the village. But there's the Big Crow's lodge yonder, next to old Red Water's. He's a good Indian for the whites, and I advise you to go and live with him."

" Are there many squaws and children in his lodge? " said I.

" No; only one squaw and two or three children. He keeps the rest in a separate lodge by themselves."

So, still followed by a crowd of Indians, Raymond and I rode up to the entrance of Big Crow's lodge. A squaw came out immediately and took our horses. I put aside the leather flap that covered the low opening and, stooping, entered the Big Crow's dwelling. There I could see the chief in the dim light, seated at one side on a pile of buffalo robes. He greeted me with a guttural " How, Colà! " I requested Reynal to tell him that Raymond and I were come to live with him. The Big Crow gave another low exclamation. The announcement may seem intrusive, but, in fact, every Indian in the village would have deemed himself honored that white men should give such preference to his hospitality.

The squaw spread a buffalo robe for us in the guest's place at the head of the lodge. Our saddles were brought in, and scarcely were we seated upon them before the place was thronged with Indians, crowding to see us. The Big Crow produced his pipe and filled it with a mixture of tobacco and *shongsasha*, or red willow bark. Round and round it passed, and a lively conversation went forward. Meanwhile a squaw placed before the two guests a wooden bowl

of boiled buffalo meat; but unhappily this was not the only banquet destined to be inflicted on us. One after another, boys and young squaws thrust their heads in at the opening, to invite us to various feasts in different parts of the village. For half an hour or more we were actively engaged in passing from lodge to lodge, in each tasting of the bowl of meat set before us and inhaling a whiff or two from our entertainer's pipe. A thunderstorm that had been threatening for some time now began in good earnest. We crossed over to Reynal's lodge, though it hardly deserved the name, for it consisted only of a few old buffalo robes, supported on poles, and was quite open on one side. Here we sat down, and the Indians gathered round us.

" What is it," said I, " that makes the thunder? "

" It's my belief," said Reynal, " that it's a big stone rolling over the sky."

" Very likely," I replied; " but I want to know what the Indians think about it."

So he interpreted my question, which produced some debate. There was a difference of opinion. At last old Mene-Seela, or Red Water, who sat by himself at one side, looked up with his withered face and said he had always known what the thunder was. It was a great black bird; and once he had seen it, in a dream, swooping down from the Black Hills, with its loud roaring wings; and when it flapped them over a lake, they struck lightning from the water.

" The thunder is bad," said another old man, who sat muffled in his buffalo robe; " he killed my brother last summer."

Reynal, at my request, asked for an explanation; but the old man remained doggedly silent and would not look up. Some time after, I learned how the accident occurred. The man who was killed belonged to an association which, among other mystic functions, claimed the exclusive power and privilege of fighting the thunder. Whenever a storm which they wished to avert was threatening, the thunder fighters would take their bows and arrows, their guns, their magic drum, and a sort of whistle made out of the wing bone of the war eagle, and, thus equipped, run out and fire at the rising cloud — whooping, yelling, whistling, and beating their drum, to frighten it down again. One afternoon, a heavy black cloud was coming up; and they repaired to the top of a hill, where they brought all their magic artillery into play against it. But the undaunted thunder, refusing to be terrified, darted out a bright flash, which struck one of the party dead as he was in the very act of shaking his long iron-pointed lance against it. The rest scattered and ran yelling in an ecstasy of superstitious terror back to their lodges.

The lodge of my host, Kongra-Tonga, or the Big Crow, presented a picturesque spectacle that evening. A score or more of Indians were seated around it in a circle, their dark naked forms just visible by the dull light of the smoldering fire in the middle. The pipe glowed brightly in the gloom as it passed from hand to hand. Then a squaw would drop a piece of buffalo fat on the dull embers. Instantly a bright flame would leap up, darting its light to the very apex of the tall conical structure, where the tops of the slender poles that supported the covering of hide were gathered together. It gilded the features of the Indians, as with animated gestures they sat around it, telling their endless stories of war and hunting, and displayed rude garments of skins that hung around the lodge; the bow, quiver, and lance, suspended over the resting place of the chief, and the rifles and powder horns of the two white guests. For a moment all would be bright as day; then the flames would die out, fitful flashes from the embers would illumine the lodge and then leave it in darkness. Then the light would wholly fade, and the lodge and all within it be involved again in obscurity.

As I left the lodge next morning, I was saluted by howling and yelping all around the village; and half its canine population rushed forth to the attack. Being as cowardly as they were clamorous, they kept jumping about me at the distance of a few yards, only one little cur, about ten inches long, having spirit enough to make a direct assault. He dashed valiantly at the leather tassel which in the Dahcotah fashion was trailing behind the heel of my moccasin, and kept his hold, growling and snarling all the while, though every step I made almost jerked him over on his back. As I knew that the eyes of the whole village were on the watch to see if I showed any sign of fear, I walked forward without looking to the right or left, surrounded wherever I went by this magic circle of dogs. When I came to Reynal's lodge I sat down by it, on which the dogs dispersed, growling, to their respective quarters. Only one large white one remained, running about before me and showing his teeth. I called him, but he only growled the more. I looked at him well. He was fat and sleek; just such a dog as I wanted. " My friend," thought I, " you shall pay for this! I will have you eaten this very morning! "

I intended that day to give the Indians a feast, by way of conveying a favorable impression of my character and dignity; and a white dog is the dish which the customs of the Dahcotah prescribe for all occasions of formality and importance. I consulted Reynal; he soon discovered that an old woman in the next lodge was owner of the white dog. I took a gaudy cotton handkerchief, and, laying it on the ground, arranged some vermilion, beads, and other trinkets upon it. Then the old squaw was summoned. I pointed to the dog and to the handkerchief. She gave a scream of delight, snatched up the prize, and vanished with it into her lodge. For a few more trifles I engaged the services of two other squaws, each of whom took the white dog by one of his paws and led him away behind the lodges. Having killed him, they threw him into a fire to singe; then chopped him up and put him into two large kettles to boil. Meanwhile I told Raymond to fry in buffalo fat what little flour we had left, and also to make a kettle of tea as an additional luxury.

The Big Crow's squaw was briskly at work sweeping out the lodge for the approaching festivity. I confided to my host himself the task of inviting the guests, thinking that I might thereby shift from my own shoulders the odium of neglect and oversight.

When feasting is in question, one hour of the day serves an Indian as well as another. My entertainment came off at about eleven o'clock. At that hour Reynal and Raymond walked across the area of the village, to the admiration of the inhabitants, carrying the two kettles of dog meat slung on a pole between them. These they placed in the center of the lodge, and then went back for the bread and the tea. Meanwhile I had put on a pair of brilliant moccasins, and substituted for my old buckskin frock a coat which I had brought with me in view of such public occasions. I also made careful use of the razor, an operation which no man will neglect who desires to gain the good opinion of Indians. Thus attired, I seated myself between Reynal and Raymond at the head of the lodge. Only a few minutes elapsed before all the guests had come in and were seated on the ground, wedged together in a close circle. Each brought with him a wooden bowl to hold his share of the repast. When all were assembled, two of the officials called " soldiers " by the white men came forward with ladles made of the horn of the Rocky Mountain sheep and began to distribute the feast, assigning a double share to old men and chiefs. The dog vanished with astonishing celerity, and each guest turned his dish bottom upward to show that all was gone. Then the bread was distributed in its turn, and finally the tea. As the " soldiers " poured it out into the same wooden bowls that had served for the substantial part of the meal, I thought it had a particularly curious and uninviting color.

" Oh," said Reynal, " there was not tea enough, so I stirred some soot in the kettle to make it look strong."

Fortunately an Indian's palate is not very discriminating. The tea was well sweetened, and that was all they cared for.

Now, the feast being over, the time for speechmaking was come. The Big Crow produced a flat piece of wood on which he cut up tobacco and *shongsasha,* and mixed them in due proportions. The pipes were filled and passed from hand to hand around the company. Then I began my speech, each sentence being interpreted by Reynal as I went on, and echoed by the whole audience with the usual exclamations of assent and approval. As nearly as I can recollect, it was as follows:

" I had come," I told them, " from a country so far distant, that at the rate they travel they could not reach it in a year."

" How! how! "

" There the Meneaska [1] were more numerous than the blades of grass on the prairie. The squaws were far more beautiful than any they had ever seen, and all the men were brave warriors."

" How! how! how! "

I was assailed by twinges of conscience as I uttered these last words. But I recovered myself and began again.

" While I was living in the Meneaska lodges, I had heard of the Ogillallah, how great and brave a nation they were, how they loved the whites, and how well they could hunt the buffalo and strike their enemies. I resolved to come and see if all that I heard was true."

" How! how! how! how! "

" As I had come on horseback through the mountains, I had been able to bring them only a very few presents."

" How! "

" But I had enough tobacco to give them all a small piece. They might smoke it and see how much better it was than the tobacco which they got from the traders."

" How! how! how! "

" I had plenty of powder, lead, knives, and tobacco at Fort Laramie. These I was anxious to give them; and if any of them should come to the fort before I went away, I would make them handsome presents."

" How! how! how! how! "

Raymond then cut up and distributed

[1] **Meneaska** (mē-nē-ăs′kȧ): the Indian name for white men.

among them two or three pounds of tobacco, and old Mene-Seela began to make a reply. It was long, but the following was the pith of it:

" He had always loved the whites. They were the wisest people on earth. He believed they could do anything, and he was always glad when any of them came to live in Ogillallah lodges. It was true I had not made them many presents, but the reason of it was plain. It was clear that I liked them, or I never should have come so far to find their village."

Several other speeches of similar import followed, and then, this more serious matter being disposed of, there was an interval of smoking, laughing, and conversation. Old Mene-Seela suddenly interrupted it with a loud voice:

" Now is a good time," he said, " when all the old men and chiefs are here together, to decide what the people shall do. We came over the mountains to make our lodges for next year. Our old ones are good for nothing; they are rotten and worn out. But we have been disappointed. We have killed buffalo bulls enough, but we have found no herds of cows, and the skins of bulls are too thick and heavy for our squaws to make lodges of. There must be plenty of cows about the Medicine Bow Mountain. We ought to go there. To be sure, it is farther westward than we have ever been before; and perhaps the Snakes will attack us, for those hunting grounds belong to them. But we must have new lodges at any rate; our old ones will not serve for another year. We ought not to be afraid of the Snakes. Our warriors are brave, and they are all ready for war. Besides, we have three white men with their rifles to help us! "

This speech produced a good deal of debate. As Reynal did not interpret what was said, I could only judge of the meaning by the features and gestures of the speakers. At the end of it, however, the greater number seemed to have fallen in with Mene-Seela's opinion. A short silence followed; and then the old man struck up a discordant chant, which I was told was a song of thanks

for the entertainment I had given them. " Now," said he, " let us go and give the white men a chance to breathe."

So the company all dispersed into the open air; and for some time the old chief was walking round the village, singing his song in praise of the feast, after the custom of the nation.

At last the day drew to a close; and as the sun went down, the horses came trooping from the surrounding plains to be picketed before the dwellings of the respective masters. Soon within the great circle of lodges appeared another concentric circle of restless horses; and here and there fires glowed and flickered amid the gloom, on the dusky figures around them. I went over and sat by the lodge of Reynal. The Eagle Feather, who was a son of Mene-Seela and brother of my host the Big Crow, was seated there already; and I asked him if the village would move in the morning. He shook his head, and said that nobody could tell; for since old Mahto-Tatonka had died, the people had been like children that did not know their own minds. They were no better than a body without a head. So I, as well as the Indians themselves, fell asleep that night without knowing whether we should set out in the morning toward the country of the Snakes.

## Suggestions for Study

1. What characteristics of the Indian do you discover in this account?

2. How do Parkman's Indians differ from Cooper's? from Longfellow's? Which do you think come nearer to being a true characterization?

3. What other Indian superstitions besides the one about thunder do you know? What other explanations of thunder and lightning can you recall? (Remember Rip Van Winkle!)

4. To what extent do you think the white man was justified in taking the American continent away from the Indian as he did? Do you consider any portions of the world still so lacking in civilization that the more civilized nations would be justified in seizing them?

5. In Parkman's *France and England in North America* and *The Conspiracy of Pon-*

*tiac* you will find other entertaining stories of life on the frontier. If you have enjoyed recent novels of the Westward Movement, read a few chapters in these histories.

## 3. WALT WHITMAN

In this account of the literary flowering of the east, we have saved for last the chief nonconformist of the group.

You could go on for pages counting up the contradictions in Walt Whitman's life. He was born on Long Island and spent all his adult years in New York or Washington, yet was proud of his westernness and called himself " a great wild buffalo, with much hair." By experience he was more Eastern than any of the other Eastern writers, and yet all his life he was in revolution against the kind of poetry they wrote. Of all the Eastern writers, he was the one that tried hardest to write of and for the masses of people, and yet he had no more than one reader for Longfellow's ten. His first recognition came from writers in the Boston vicinity, yet his chief book was banned in Boston. He was presented to the world as " The Good Gray Poet," and yet was dismissed from a federal job because his poems were thought to be immoral. In his own time there was some question whether he was a poet at all and whether what he wrote was poetry, but of all the Eastern group he has had the most influence on later poets.

He was born on a farm, but moved into Brooklyn when he was very young. Unlike most of the Eastern writers he did not have the advantage of four years at Harvard or Yale. In fact he left school at twelve, and thereafter was his own schoolmaster and gave himself a hard course.

He began with a print shop — like Mark Twain and many other American writers. Newspapers attracted him because they gave him a chance to write and, more important, a chance to meet and observe people. He worked for several papers, tried country schoolteaching a little while, came back to the newspaper business, and once got to be editor of the Brooklyn *Eagle*. He had decided that the chief subject in his self-taught school would have to be people — he wanted to understand people, see how they live, talk to them, see how they think and feel. If he could understand people he could come nearer understanding himself, and the chief purpose of all education, he felt, was to understand oneself. So he spent many an afternoon and holiday in New York wandering through the harbor district and the markets, talking to anyone who wanted to talk to him, watching and learning. He rode the Fulton Street ferry again and again, because that gave a good cross section of human beings. He tried to put his ideas together in some of the editorials he wrote for the *Eagle*. But he got into trouble with the publisher. The publisher said he was too radical and muddled. No straight-thinking man, said the publisher, could support both abolition and pacifism. That was Whitman's position. He was fired.

He agreed cheerfully enough that he hadn't straightened out his own ideas yet. He hadn't learned enough. His self-organized schooling was still inadequate. He read Shakespeare, Dante, and the great books of the ancient world. He decided he didn't know enough about people and places outside New York, and so went to New Orleans by stage, railroad, and steamboat. This gave him his first taste of the West. He came back, tried running a bookshop and a print shop, tried building and selling houses, earned enough to keep alive while he kept on schooling himself, training himself. For he realized now what it was he was preparing for. He was getting ready to write.

None of the Easterners had ever learned to write that way. They had gone to the university, read the great books, gone to Europe, associated with the great literary men. But Whitman had hardly seen a university or a literary man. He was getting ready by learning all about ordinary men, by talking to sailors on the docks, by riding the Fulton Street ferry, by listening to the life stories of tramps and derelicts.

And then in 1855 he printed a book called *Leaves of Grass*. He said it was poetry, but some people were dubious. It had very few rhymes and none of the elegance and niceties of the regular verse which respectable poets like Longfellow, Holmes, and Lowell wrote. It had long free-verse lines, which might have sounded all right as chants or declamations, but looked very queer in print. And then — such subject matter!

It was certainly the most unusual book of poetry published in America in the nineteenth century. Bronson Alcott's cryptic "Orphic Sayings" or Stephen Crane's poems printed on dark gray paper were nothing compared to this. Whitman himself said:

Camerado, this is no book;
Who touches this, touches a man.

There was nothing literary, nothing traditional about the book. It *was* a man. It was a man's thoughts and feelings. It was a glorification of man. Not of a Greek god, not of an ideal man, but of an ordinary average man. Not of man in a dress suit, but man in overalls at work. Be proud of your muscles, your health, your vigor, said Whitman. Be strong, be natural. You are just as much a part of nature as a leaf of grass.

Not many people read the book. Of those who did, more than half were not interested or didn't understand, and most of the others were a little shocked. But a few of the readers of the book were excited. Emerson got a free copy and wrote Whitman, "I greet you at the beginning of a great career!" Whitman was a newspaper man and knew the value of advertising; he used Emerson's sentence to advertise his book. Then Emerson backtracked on his endorsement, but he sent Thoreau to see Whitman, and gradually a little circle of live minds began to gather around this unusual poet.

The literary history of Whitman is the history of *Leaves of Grass*. All his life he wrote that one book over. It grew in length, changed in contents, mellowed, but still was the same book, the result of a man's self-schooling in the university of life. That schooling went on as long as Whitman lived. The War between the States was a great university for him. Whitman worked in the hospitals during that war, taking care of the wounded. His experiences moved him deeply, added deep and solemn notes to his writing. Two of his best poems dealt with the death of Lincoln. But long after the war, the learning process continued. He wrote other books, some of them very good. He never made much money; in fact, he was sometimes in want. But he went on reading, listening, walking the docks and the slum streets, talking long hours with his good friends — and rewriting *Leaves of Grass*.

We have become used to free verse now and know that Whitman's verse is not barbarous, as some of his contemporaries said it was. We know that he wrote some ordinary verse and some of the truest poetry ever written in America. And we remember him for two messages he put over and over again into his poems and his criticism.

One of these we have already mentioned: Be in love with life. Don't be afraid of it; don't be ashamed of being a part of nature. Be strong, be natural. Be proud that you are related to every living thing, and don't set yourself apart from other living things because you use a fork and eat off a plate.

The other was somewhat like Emerson's: "The sun shines today also." The past is dead, said Whitman. You can get some of it from books. But don't mourn the past; live today! The best way to wisdom is to study the people around you, the common people, the poor people. Don't be highbrow; don't scorn the average man around you. For these average men here in America have the "fullest potential known to history." There is no limit to what can be done in America if Americans will only stop worshiping the past and Europe, and believe in themselves and their country.

*Walt Whitman was born (1819) in the same year as Lowell and two years after Thoreau, and died (1892) in the same year as Whittier. When he was born, Irving was beginning to publish "The Sketch Book." When he died, Rudyard Kipling was beginning to publish his poems.*

## Walt Whitman          1819–1892

You cannot read Whitman with indifference. You will be either powerfully drawn or violently repelled by his utterances. Some of you will not even grant him the title of poet; some will find an impelling rhythm in his uneven lines. You will have your ideas of poetry challenged; you will be moved to argument; but you cannot go to sleep over Whitman. It is well to know before reading him just what his poetic principles are. He intentionally throws out "the entire stock in trade of rhyme-talking heroes and heroines and all the lovesick plots of customary poetry, and constructs his verse in a loose and free meter of his own." The rhythm is not like the regular beat of waves on the shore, but rather like the impetuous gusts of wind in March. As Edgar Lee Masters said, "Whitman roared in the pines." Though it took many years for his power to be widely recognized, Whitman is now securely placed among such original and distinctly *American* personalities as Emerson, Mark Twain, and Lincoln.

WALT WHITMAN, one of the most controversial poets in American literature. Today he is regarded as the father of modern poetry. (Culver)

## I HEAR AMERICA SINGING

This poem is often cited as one of the best to voice in condensed form the spirit of America. It suggests Whitman's varied and democratic contacts with life.

I hear America singing, the varied carols I hear,
Those of mechanics, each one singing his as it should be blithe and strong,
The carpenter singing his as he measures his plank or beam,
The mason singing his as he makes ready for work, or leaves off work,
The boatman singing what belongs to him in his boat, the deck hand singing on the
    steamboat deck,                                                                                               5
The shoemaker singing as he sits on his bench, the hatter singing as he stands,
The woodcutter's song, the plowboy's on his way in the morning, or at noon inter-
    mission or at sundown,
The delicious singing of the mother, or of the young wife at work, or of the girl sewing
    or washing,
Each singing what belongs to him or her and to none else,
The day what belongs to the day — at night the party of young fellows, robust,
    friendly,                                                                                                          10
Singing with open mouths their strong melodious songs.

## MANNAHATTA

Whitman loved the old Indian names. His native Long Island he preferred to call Paumanok, and his exuberant affection for his city, New York, needed Mannahatta to express it. The name is, of course, perpetuated in Manhattan Island, which forms the core of the city today. In *Sands at Seventy* Whitman printed a three-line poem with the same title.

I was asking for something specific and perfect for my city,
Whereupon lo! upsprang the aboriginal name.

Now I see what there is in a name, a word, liquid, sane, unruly, musical, self-sufficient,
I see that the word of my city is that word from of old,
Because I see that word nested in nests of water bays, superb,      5
Rich, hemmed thick all around with sailships and steamships, an island sixteen miles
     long, solid-founded,
Numberless crowded streets, high growths of iron, slender, strong, light, splendidly
     uprising toward clear skies,
Tides swift and ample, well loved by me, toward sundown,
The flowing sea-currents, the little islands, larger adjoining islands, the heights, the
     villas,
The countless masts, the white shore-steamers, the lighters, the ferryboats, the black
     sea-steamers well modeled,      10
The downtown streets, the jobbers' houses of business, the houses of business of the
     ship merchants and money brokers, the river streets,
Immigrants arriving, fifteen or twenty thousand in a week,
The carts hauling goods, the manly race of drivers of horses, the brown-faced sailors,
The summer air, the bright sun shining, and the sailing clouds aloft,
The winter snows, the sleigh bells, the broken ice in the river, passing along up or
     down with the flood tide or ebb tide,      15
The mechanics of the city, the masters, well formed, beautiful-faced, looking you
     straight in the eyes,
Trottoirs° thronged, vehicles, Broadway, the women, the shops and shows,
A million people — manners free and superb — open voices — hospitality — the most
     courageous and friendly young men,
City of hurried and sparkling waters! city of spires and masts!
City nested in bays! my city!      20

17. **trottoirs** (trŏ-twär′): French for sidewalks.

## SONG OF MYSELF

This very long poem, of which only part is here given, forms the core of *Leaves of Grass*. After many revisions in different editions it now stands as Whitman's declaration of independence of man as an individual, the product of all that has preceded him, the epitome of everything in the world. It is not easy reading, but will amply repay thoughtful rereading.

1

I celebrate myself, and sing myself,
And what I assume you shall assume,
For every atom belonging to me as good belongs to you.

I loaf and invite my soul,
I lean and loaf at my ease observing a spear of summer grass.                    5
My tongue, every atom of my blood, formed from this soil, this air,
Born here of parents born here from parents the same, and their parents the same,
I, now thirty-seven years old in perfect health, begin,
Hoping to cease not till death.

Creeds and schools in abeyance,                                                 10
Retiring back awhile sufficed at what they are, but never forgotten,
I harbor for good or bad, I permit to speak at every hazard,
Nature without check with original energy. . . .

VI

A child said, *What is the grass?* fetching it to me with full hands;
How could I answer the child? I do not know what it is any more than he.       15

I guess it must be the flag of my disposition, out of hopeful green stuff woven.

Or I guess it is the handkerchief of the Lord,
A scented gift and remembrancer designedly dropt,
Bearing the owner's name someway in the corners, that we may see and remark, and
  say *Whose?*

Or I guess the grass is itself a child, the produced babe of the vegetation.    20

Or I guess it is a uniform hieroglyphic,
And it means, Sprouting alike in broad zones and narrow zones,
Growing among black folks as among white,
Kanuck,° Tuckahoe,° Congressman, Cuff,° I give them the same, I receive them
  the same.

And now it seems to me the beautiful uncut hair of graves.                      25

Tenderly will I use you, curling grass,
It may be you transpire from the breasts of young men,
It may be if I had known them I would have loved them,
It may be you are from old people, or from offspring taken soon out of their mothers'
  laps,
And here you are the mothers' laps.                                             30

This grass is very dark to be from the white heads of old mothers,
Darker than the colorless beards of old men,
Dark to come from under the faint red roofs of mouths.

O I perceive after all so many uttering tongues,
And I perceive they do not come from the roofs of mouths for nothing.           35

I wish I could translate the hints about the dead young men and women,
And the hints about old men and mothers, and the offspring taken soon out of their laps.

24. **Kanuck, Tuckahoe, Cuff:** colloquial terms for Canadian, Virginian, Negro, respectively.

What do you think has become of the young and old men?
And what do you think has become of the women and children?

They are alive and well somewhere,                                                            40
The smallest sprout shows there is really no death,
And if ever there was it led forward life, and does not wait at the end to arrest it,
And ceased the moment life appeared.

All goes onward and outward, nothing collapses,
And to die is different from what anyone supposed, and luckier. . . .                         45


## BEAT! BEAT! DRUMS!

The terrific upheaval that war brings into civilian life has never been more vividly pictured than in this poem. Here the irregularity of the meter serves to emphasize the general chaos, with the throb of the drums running throughout.

Whitman had more direct contact with the War between the States than did the other writers included in this chapter. When his younger brother was wounded, he went to Washington as a volunteer nurse, and ministered with the greatest affection and tenderness to hundreds of soldiers in the army hospital until he became infected with blood poisoning from dressing a wound. He suffered a long illness before regaining his customary abundant health. Whitman knew what war could do to a man's life.

Beat! beat! drums! — blow! bugles! blow!
Through the windows — through doors — burst like a ruthless force,
Into the solemn church, and scatter the congregation,
Into the school where the scholar is studying;
Leave not the bridegroom quiet — no happiness must he have now with his bride,    5
Nor the peaceful farmer any peace, plowing his field or gathering his grain,
So fierce you whir and pound, you drums — so shrill you bugles blow.

Beat! beat! drums! — blow! bugles! blow!
Over the traffic of cities — over the rumble of wheels in the streets;
Are beds prepared for sleepers at night in the houses? no sleepers must sleep in those
    beds,                                                                                      10
No bargainers' bargains by day — no brokers or speculators — would they continue?
Would the talkers be talking? would the singer attempt to sing?
Would the lawyer rise in the court to state his case before the judge?
Then rattle quicker, heavier drums — you bugles wilder blow.

Beat! beat! drums! — blow! bugles! blow!                                                       15
Make no parley — stop for no expostulation,
Mind not the timid — mind not the weeper or prayer,
Mind not the old man beseeching the young man,
Let not the child's voice be heard, nor the mother's entreaties,
Make even the trestles to shake the dead where they lie awaiting the hearses,     20
So strong you thump O terrible drums — so loud you bugles blow.

## THE CAROL OF DEATH

It is natural that a man of Whitman's elemental vigor should have been greatly attracted by the personality of Abraham Lincoln. Of all the poets who have paid tribute to him none has sounded so feelingly the note of personal grief at his death as Whitman. When the news of the assassination came to the poet, he was at home with his mother. He tells us, "Not a mouthful was eaten all day by either of us. We each drank half a cup of coffee; that was all. Little was said. We got every newspaper, morning and evening, and the frequent extras of that period and passed them silently to each other."

You have doubtless known for many years that poem by Whitman so universally loved, "O Captain, My Captain!" A full and complete expression of his grief was given in the long poem "When Lilacs Last in the Dooryard Bloomed." In this he pictures himself as finding consolation in the following carol of a "gray-brown bird" among "the ghostly pines." "And the voice of my spirit tallied the song of the bird."

Come lovely and soothing death,
Undulate round the world, serenely arriving, arriving,
In the day, in the night, to all, to each,
Sooner or later delicate death.

Praised be the fathomless universe,                                   5
For life and joy, and for object and knowledge curious,
And for love, sweet love — but praise! praise! praise!
For the sure-enwinding arms of cool-enfolding death.

Dark mother always gliding near with soft feet,
Have none chanted for thee a chant of fullest welcome?                 10
Then I chant it for thee, I glorify thee above all,
I bring thee a song that when thou must indeed come, come unfalteringly.

Approach strong deliveress,
When it is so, when thou hast taken them I joyously sing the dead,
Lost in the loving floating ocean of thee,                            15
Laved in the flood of thy bliss O death.

From me to thee glad serenades,
Dances for thee I propose saluting thee, adornments and feastings for thee,
And the sights of the open landscape and the high-spread sky are fitting,
And life and the fields, and the huge and thoughtful night.           20

The night in silence under many a star,
The ocean shore and the husky whispering wave whose voice I know,
And the soul turning to thee O vast and well-veiled death,
And the body gratefully nestling close to thee.

Over the treetops I float thee a song,                                25
Over the rising and sinking waves, over the myriad fields and the prairies wide,
Over the dense-packed cities all and the teeming wharves and ways,
I float this carol with joy, with joy to thee O death.

## GIVE ME THE SPLENDID SILENT SUN

The following poem expresses the conflict in the poet's mind between his longing for the peace of nature and his love of pulsing life in the city even though it be during the horrors of wartime. Which conquers? The repetitions and exclamations throughout are highly typical of Whitman's mode of expression.

I

Give me the splendid silent sun with all his beams full-dazzling,
Give me juicy autumnal fruit ripe and red from the orchard,
Give me a field where the unmowed grass grows,
Give me an arbor, give me the trellised grape,
Give me fresh corn and wheat, give me serene-moving animals teaching content,    5
Give me nights perfectly quiet as on high plateaus west of the Mississippi, and I
    looking up at the stars,
Give me odorous at sunrise a garden of beautiful flowers where I can walk undisturbed,
Give me for marriage a sweet-breathed woman of whom I should never tire,
Give me a perfect child, give me away aside from the noise of the world a rural
    domestic life,
Give me to warble spontaneous songs recluse by myself, for my own ears only,    10
Give me solitude, give me Nature, give me again O Nature your primal sanities!

These demanding to have them (tired with ceaseless excitement, and racked by the
    war strife),
These to procure incessantly asking, rising in cries from my heart,
While yet incessantly asking still I adhere to my city,
Day upon day and year upon year O city, walking your streets,    15
Where you hold me enchained a certain time refusing to give me up,
Yet giving to make me glutted, enriched of soul, you give me forever faces;
(O I see what I sought to escape, confronting, reversing my cries,
I see my own soul trampling down what it asked for).

II

Keep your splendid silent sun,    20
Keep your woods O Nature, and the quiet places by the woods,
Keep your fields of clover and timothy, and your cornfields and orchards,
Keep the blossoming buckwheat fields where the Ninth-month° bees hum;
Give me faces and streets — give me these phantoms incessant and endless along the
    trottoirs!
Give me interminable eyes — give me women — give me comrades and lovers by the
    thousand!    25
Let me see new ones every day — let me hold new ones by the hand every day!
Give me such shows — give me the streets of Manhattan!
Give me Broadway, with the soldiers marching — give me the sound of the trumpets
    and drums!
(The soldiers in companies or regiments — some starting away, flushed and reckless,
Some, their time up, returning with thinned ranks, young, yet very old, worn, marching,
    noticing nothing);    30
Give me the shores and wharves heavy-fringed with black ships!

    23. **Ninth-month:** September (the Quaker name).

O such for me! O an intense life, full to repletion and varied!
The life of the theater, barroom, huge hotel, for me!
The saloon of the steamer! the crowded excursion for me! the torchlight procession!
The dense brigade bound for the war, with high piled military wagons following;   35
People, endless, streaming, with strong voices, passions, pageants,
Manhattan streets with their powerful throbs, with beating drums as now,
The endless and noisy chorus, the rustle and clang of muskets (even the sight of the
    wounded)
Manhattan crowds, with their turbulent musical chorus!
Manhattan faces and eyes forever for me.                                    40

## A NOISELESS PATIENT SPIDER

This poem represents the deeper spiritual quality of Whitman's later poetry. It suggests the longings, the gropings, of the soul for some-thing beyond itself. Keep in mind that this is the poet of "Song of Myself," where he is seeking solidarity with mankind.

A noiseless patient spider,
I marked where on a little promontory it stood isolated,
Marked how to explore the vacant vast surrounding,
It launched forth filament, filament, filament, out of itself,
Ever unreeling them, ever tirelessly speeding them.                          5

And you O my soul where you stand,
Surrounded, detached, in measureless oceans of space,
Ceaselessly musing, venturing, throwing, seeking the spheres to connect them,
Till the bridge you will need be formed, till the ductile anchor hold,
Till the gossamer thread you fling catch somewhere, O my soul.              10

## WHEN I HEARD THE LEARN'D ASTRONOMER

Whitman's intense feeling for nature is caught in this poem and in "Miracles," which follows. The quiet solemnity of the first is in contrast with the exuberance of the second.

When I heard the learn'd astronomer,
When the proofs, the figures, were ranged in columns before me,
When I was shown the charts and diagrams, to add, divide, and measure them,
When I sitting heard the astronomer where he lectured with much applause in the
    lecture room,
How soon unaccountable I became tired and sick,
Till rising and gliding out I wandered off by myself,
In the mystical moist night air, and from time to time,
Looked up in perfect silence at the stars.

## MIRACLES

Why, who makes much of a miracle?
As to me I know of nothing else but miracles,
Whether I walk the streets of Manhattan,
Or dart my sight over the roofs of houses toward the sky,

Or wade with naked feet along the beach just in the edge of the water,　5
Or stand under trees in the woods,
Or talk by day with anyone I love, or sleep in the bed at night with anyone I love,
Or sit at table at dinner with the rest,
Or look at strangers opposite me riding in the car,
Or watch honeybees busy around the hive of a summer forenoon,　10
Or animals feeding in the fields,
Or birds, or the wonderfulness of insects in the air,
Or the wonderfulness of the sundown, or of stars shining so quiet and bright,
Or the exquisite delicate curve of the new moon in spring;
These with the rest, one and all, are to me miracles,　15
The whole referring, yet each distinct and in its place.


To me every hour of the night and dark is a miracle,
Every cubic inch of space is a miracle,
Every square yard of the surface of the earth is spread with the same,
Every foot of the interior swarms with the same.　20


To me the sea is a continual miracle,
The fishes that swim — the rocks — the motion of the waves — the ships with men in them,
What stranger miracles are there?


## DAREST THOU NOW O SOUL

Darest thou now O soul,
Walk out with me toward the unknown region,
Where neither ground is for the feet nor any path to follow?


No map there, nor guide,
Nor voice sounding, nor touch of human hand,　5
Nor face with blooming flesh, nor lips, nor eyes, are in that land.


I know it not O soul,
Nor dost thou; all is a blank before us,
All waits undreamed of in that region, that inaccessible land.


Till when the ties loosen,　10
All but the ties eternal, Time and Space,
Nor darkness, gravitation, sense, nor any bounds bounding us.


Then we burst forth, we float,
In Time and Space O soul, prepared for them,
Equal, equipped at last (O joy! O fruit of all!) them to fulfill O soul.　15

## Suggestions for Study of Whitman

1. How does each of the first three poems show Whitman's democratic interest in all types of people? Where does he describe them objectively and where identify himself with their lives more fully?

2. Does his picture of American life in the first poem give a cross section of all types of society, or would you add any types of singing to give a more complete picture?

3. Compare his picture of New York with the cities in which you have lived or traveled. Does he make you feel the spirit of city life in contrast to that of the small town or country? How does his "cataloguing" method of listing details add to the general effect? Try writing a similar picture of your own city or town.

4. In "Song of Myself" point out lines or passages in which Whitman regards himself as part of nature, as part of the history of mankind, as part of the present experience of man, as an independent being. What in this poem do you think would have pleased Emerson? displeased the other New England poets? Does this poem bring you a new understanding or appreciation of human values? If so, how?

5. Which three poems are based on experiences connected with the War between the States? In "Beat! Beat! Drums!" what effects of war upon civilian life are especially emphasized? Which of the effects mentioned seem to you the most devastating? Could this poem be used as an argument against war in general? In what way is the irregular meter appropriate to the subject?

6. Is the tone of "The Carol of Death" prevailingly mournful or consoling? How does this picture of death compare with those given by Bryant in "Thanatopsis" (page 498) and Edna St. Vincent Millay (page 330)? with other poems on death you have read? Would you like to read this poem after a death had occurred in your family? Why or why not? Reread Whitman's "O Captain, My Captain!" — which you doubtless know. What marked difference do you find in the whole treatment of the death of Lincoln in these two poems?

7. In what way does "Give Me the Splendid Silent Sun" reflect Whitman's war experience? What definite change in mood is found in the middle of the poem? How does the second mood resemble the first three poems by Whitman? Have you experienced both these moods yourself? Which is your prevailing mood?

8. How do the last four poems show that Whitman has become more concerned with the spirit and less with the material world than in most of his earlier poems? Which again strike the note of profound interest in everything about him? Where do you find the note of courage? of simplicity? of reverence for nature? of wonder about eternity?

9. Considering all that you have read of Whitman, list the main themes which you have found him treating, and the various peculiarities of his poetic style. What is your own reaction to his poetry? What do you now think of the suitability of Masters' phrase, "Whitman roared in the pines"?

10. If there is disagreement in a class as to whether Whitman deserved the name of "poet," an informal debate on the subject will bring out varying points of view and open up the whole subject of "What is poetry?"

11. Where in these poems can you find evidence of a loose sort of pattern based on parallels and repetition? Can you find similar patterns in the Psalms?

## For Your Vocabulary

BASE-WORDS. Whitman distrusted the complexity of modern life and sought for simple realities. Sometimes he searched for the earliest facts, as when he found the *aboriginal* (ăb-ŏ-rĭj'ĭ-năl) name for Manhattan (page 618). *Aborigines* (ăb-ŏ-rĭj'ĭ-nēz) are those who live in a place first, or originally. *Aboriginal* ways and names belong to the first known inhabitants. Watch for Jedediah Smith (page 641) to discover signs written on the rock walls of a canyon by *aboriginal* people. He found also *primitive* (prĭm'ĭ-tĭv) candy manufactories. *Primitive* connotes rude, unskilled workmanship, and is used most often of things and customs; while *primal* means of first rank or importance and is used of principles and truths. Whitman asks for nature's *primal* (prī'măl) sanities, the first, the essential truths of life. Parkman found the Ogillallahs using the *primitive* tools of the *primeval* world (page 610), the earliest life of which we have knowledge.

WORD ANALYSIS. Analyze *unfalteringly* (page 621), *incessantly* (page 622), and *interminable* (page 622). Don't let a hasty glance at the last word deceive you about the prefix. The base-word is *termin,* meaning boundary or end.

# THE FLOWERING OF THE EAST

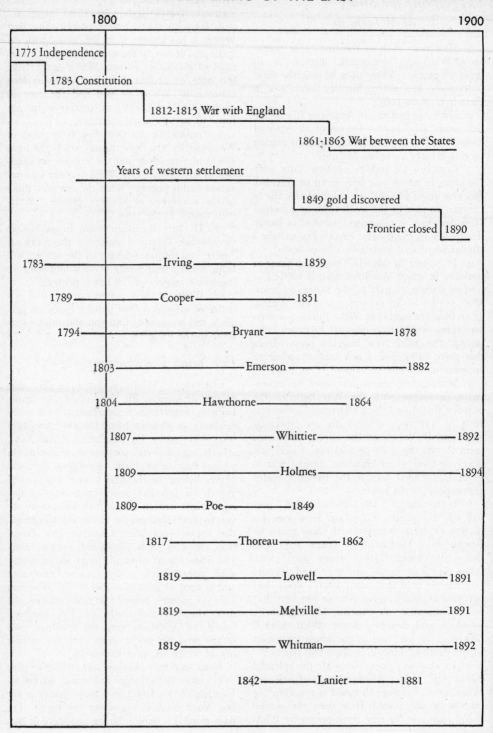

1800                                                                     1900

1775 Independence

1783 Constitution

1812-1815 War with England

1861-1865 War between the States

Years of western settlement

1849 gold discovered

Frontier closed | 1890

1783 ——————————— Irving ——————— 1859

1789 ——————————— Cooper ——————— 1851

1794 ——————————————— Bryant ——————————————— 1878

1803 ——————————————— Emerson ————————————— 1882

1804 ——————————— Hawthorne ——————— 1864

1807 ——————————————— Whittier ——————————————— 1892

1809 ——————————————— Holmes ——————————————— 1894

1809 ——————————— Poe ——————— 1849

1817 ——————————— Thoreau ——————— 1862

1819 ——————————————— Lowell ——————————————— 1891

1819 ——————————————— Melville ——————————————— 1891

1819 ——————————————— Whitman ——————————————— 1892

1842 ——————————— Lanier ——————— 1881

# For Further Reading on the Flowering of the East, Part Two

## LITERATURE OF THE PERIOD

### Poetry

Emerson, Ralph Waldo: " The Humblebee," " The Snowstorm," " The Romany Girl," " The Problem," " The Test," " A Fable "

Thoreau, Henry David: " A Prayer," " Independence "

Longfellow, Henry Wadsworth: " My Lost Youth," " The Psalm of Life," " The Wreck of the Hesperus," " The Skeleton in Armor," " The Old Clock on the Stairs," " The Discoverer of the North Cape," *Evangeline, The Courtship of Miles Standish, The Tales of a Wayside Inn*

Lowell, James Russell: " The First Snowfall," " She Came and Went," " The Changeling," " To a Dandelion," " The Fatherland," " Stanzas on Freedom," " The Present Crisis," " Commemoration Ode " (especially Stanza VI on Lincoln)

Holmes, Oliver Wendell: " The Deacon's Masterpiece," " How the Old Horse Won the Bet," " To an Insect," " The Voiceless," " Dorothy Q.," " Homesick in Heaven "

Whitman, Walt: " Crossing Brooklyn Ferry," " I Saw in Louisiana a Live Oak Growing," " For You, O Democracy," " Pioneers, O Pioneers," " Cavalry Crossing a Ford," " Come Up from the Fields, Father," " Hushed Be the Camps Today," " Old Salt Kossabone," " O Captain, My Captain "

### Nonfiction

Emerson, Ralph Waldo: See study suggestions, pages 568–569

Thoreau, Henry David: *Walden*

Parkman, Francis: *The Oregon Trail, Pioneers of France in the New World, La Salle and the Discovery of the Great West, Montcalm and Wolfe, A Half Century of Conflict*

## BOOKS ABOUT THE PERIOD

See general titles under The Flowering of the East, Part One, page 553.

### On Individual Authors

EMERSON. Brooks, Van Wyck: *Life of Emerson;* Hawthorne, Hildegarde: *Youth's Captain*

THOREAU. Canby, H. S.: *Thoreau;* Emerson, E. W.: *Henry Thoreau as Remembered by a Young Friend;* Emerson, R. W.: *Biographical Sketch of Thoreau;* Hawthorne, Hildegarde: *Concord's Happy Rebel*

LONGFELLOW. Thompson, L. R.: *Young Longfellow;* Hawthorne, Hildegarde: *The Poet of Craigie House*

LOWELL. Beatty, R. C.: *James R. Lowell*

HOLMES. Bowen, Catherine: *Yankee from Olympus;* Hawthorne, Hildegarde: *The Happy Autocrat*

PARKMAN. Wade, M.: *Francis Parkman, Heroic Historian*

Detailed biographies of these authors are to be found by numerous writers of an earlier day, and in series such as American Men of Letters, American Writers, etc.

THE GREAT WEST

A NINTEENTH CENTURY POSTER pictures the West as a land of brightest opportunity. The prospects of more of everything for everybody drew settlers by the thousands to make the hazardous trip across the plains. (Culver)

# The Westward Movement

## I. *THE ADVANCING FRONTIER*

A great newspaper editor in New York, Horace Greeley, was giving his readers some good advice. " Go West, young man," he said.

And how the young men went! They bought themselves coonskin caps, and oiled their flintlock guns, and rode Indian ponies out to seek adventure. Or they bought a Conestoga wagon with the canvas top looking so much like a sail that people began to call it a prairie schooner. They traded guns and flour and big silver coins for a pair of oxen, and rumbled off in their big Conestogas to find a homestead.

And not only the young men. Their wives and babies rode along in the Conestoga. Their big boys walked along beside the oxen or cantered up and down on a pony, looking for buffalo. Their mothers and grandmothers came along west, hardly complaining when the wagon jiggled on the rough trail and made them drop a stitch in their knitting or patching. Whole families, whole communities moved west. Whole churches moved west, stopping morning and evening for their pastor to hold divine services. There were a dozen places in the country where travelers could write a message on the rock cliffs in perfect confidence that friends and relatives from the home town would see it. *Everybody* seemed to be coming west!

The nineteenth century was the Western century. The great books were being written in the East, but the great history was being made in the West. The footsteps of Western immigrants on the Wilderness Road and the Oregon Trail were echoing in every corner of the land. " It is now plain," Lyman Beecher, the great pulpit orator, told his congregation in 1835, " that the destiny of our nation is being decided in the West! "

At the end of the Revolution, the United States owned the country as far west as the Mississippi, but Maine was still a frontier. Land speculators had bought millions of acres in western New York, hoping that would be the next frontier. A few thousand immigrants had followed Daniel Boone over the Wilderness Road into central Kentucky, and were hanging on perilously there, a far western outpost of civilization. The Allegheny mountains stood like a huge dam, a few hundred miles from the seacoast, holding the tide of settlement from flowing west.

And then the dam broke! When the last shot was fired at the redcoats, it seemed as though the whole country turned its back on Europe and climbed up the Alleghenies for a look at the West. They cut ribbons of clear land through the thick Allegheny forests. They streamed over Daniel Boone's road into Kentucky, keeping a sharp eye open for Indians behind the trees. They made an ox road over the Pennsylvania mountains to Fort Pitt, where they built barges and sailed away into the fertile plain country, singing " Hi-O, away we go, Floating down the river on the O-hi-O! " They dug the Erie Canal and sailed along the Great Lakes to what looked like good farm land. The whole irresistible tide of human migration burst through the dam and rolled toward the Mississippi.

Just in time, Thomas Jefferson found that he could do real estate business with France. He bought Louisiana. That included the whole western half of the Mis-

PRAIRIE WAR. This scene from the movie "The Covered Wagon" occurs during one of the frequent attacks by the Indians on the wagon train of the pioneers. (Brown Brothers)

sissippi valley, as far north as the border of Canada, as far west — well, there was some argument about that. He bought all that land for about as much as it would cost to buy a single block now in the heart of one of our great cities. And the frontier jumped the Mississippi.

Jefferson sent Lewis and Clark to see what lay in the mysterious distances to the west. Zebulon Pike (his name is on Pike's Peak) went to look at the upper Mississippi and the mountain country of the Southwest. Jedediah Smith found a way over the dry lands and the desert to the southwest. They came back with stories of snowy mountains, herds of buffalo, boiling geysers, and rich soil. And hardly were their reports in the newspapers when covered wagons began to follow the trails they had blazed.

This was not like traveling through the plains country east of the Mississippi. As soon as a caravan left the Missouri River it was in a high dry plain, which was as boundless and markerless as the sea, and on which the six-foot prairie grass blew in waves like sea water. In fact, the prairies reminded people of the sea, and storms were

like sea storms, and starting on the trail was like sailing out of port. Once out, a man was on his own. Civilization fell away. It was man against nature. He had to protect himself, feed himself, find his way. He even had to navigate, sometimes, as though he were at sea. Farther west, he had to face, first wild animals, and then deserts where the temperature went up to one hundred and thirty and there was no water for sixty miles. From the Missouri to the good western land was about four months, if the caravan was lucky. Many a caravan never got there. Many a settler, many a child, ended his trip in a shallow grave just far enough off the trail so that wagons would not run over it.

A party of fur traders made a discovery — a natural gateway through the Rockies at South Pass in Wyoming. And then, in 1848, men began to whisper a wild rumor that had supposedly started in California. Gold had been found at Sutter's Mill!

In 1849 the human tide that flowed west was like a Mississippi flood. In the late 40's and the 50's, the Oregon Trail was worn smooth for half a mile wide, in some places, and even today you can see where the trail ran because the land was so pounded down by the feet of oxen that even prairie grass and prickly pear will hardly grow there. In those years, so many people, so many families, went to the West that there was an almost constant cloud of dust above the trail.

The men in Washington who keep our census records marked carefully on the map where the frontier seemed to be from year to year. They followed it through Ohio, Indiana, and Illinois, into Iowa and Missouri in the 30's, then on its big jump across the dry plains to the western slopes. They put down a neat row of figures:

| YEAR | SIZE OF COUNTRY IN SQ. MI. | POPULATION | PEOPLE PER SQ. MI. |
|------|---------|------------|--------|
| 1790 | 867,980 | 3,929,881 | 4.5 |
| 1850 | 2,944,337 | 23,191,876 | 7.9 |
| 1900 | 2,974,159 | 75,994,575 | 25.6 |

They figured that in 1900 there were more than eight times as many people in the West alone as had been in the whole country in 1800. They calculated that in some decades toward the end of the century more people had come to this country from Europe than had been in the whole United States at the beginning of the century.

They said it was the greatest mass migration in history. When it began, there were thirteen colonies clinging precariously to national existence between the sea and the first mountains. A hundred years later, states reached from sea to sea. The central prairies that had been blank were covered with checkerboard farms and smoking factories. The distant western slopes, that no colonist had ever seen in 1800, were dark with cities and cultivation. Lines of steel ran from border to border like a spider web, and the bays and harbors on three sides of the continent were filled with ships.

But the real story is men, not numbers. The American people found trails that had once been buffalo paths to the salt licks. Indians had used those trails. And then the white scouts came cautiously over them.

Fur traders came, hard on the heels of the scouts. And close behind them came the settlers, the great wave of brave adventurous people from the East and from Europe. They carried their pots and pans and household furniture and Kentucky long rifles, and drove the oxen they hoped to use for plowing. Along the whole length of the continent they left a line of graves beside the trails. But into the wilderness they brought the church, the law, the newspaper, trade and manufacturing, and all the precious freedoms won along the Atlantic seaboard. In a hundred years they took the bare face of a continent, three million square miles, and built a nation on it.

## WHAT THE FRONTIER MEANT TO AMERICA

The westward-rolling frontier, more than anything else, made Americans different from Europeans. And since books are made by men, it helped make American books different from European books.

Here are some of the characteristics the frontier developed in men. Check these against what you would call " typically American " characteristics.

Frontiersmen were *self-reliant*. They had to be. There were no garages, repairmen, doctors, advisers to consult.

They were *adventurous, willing to try new things, ready to improvise, resourceful*. There was only one Edison, but every frontiersman, in his small way, had to be an inventor. He had to invent new ways of doing what had to be done, new tools to do the work of machines that were not available. He had to take new roads, and gamble on untried things.

They were *practical* and *ingenious*. Every frontiersman had to be, or he didn't last long. Even today Americans are better at practical than abstract problems. When surprised Europeans called the Americans who invaded Normandy " an army of mechanics " they were paying tribute to the same practicality Americans learned on the frontier.

CALIFORNIA 1850. The prospect of gold lured thousands to the West Coast to filter the streams for the precious metal. Perhaps these men got rich — some did — but many more were disappointed. (Brown Brothers)

They were *idealistic* and *optimistic*. They were looking toward the future, not the past; making history, not reading it. They could always get a new start in the West when they needed. They were masters of their own destiny in a way that a man could never be in Europe. In the American West a man might own as much land as a baron in the old country, if he were willing to clear it and put up a log cabin. He might find, in one afternoon, in some mountain ledge, the equivalent of a prince's patrimony. He might settle in the shadow of mountains, beside a lake, on a prairie where the black soil was twelve feet deep, or beside the sea, or deep in the forest — he could choose. He could dream ahead to a better world because he had a chance to make one.

They were *confident,* sometimes *cocky.* They were doing great things and seeing great things done all around them.

They had a *sense of humor.* They liked to throw back their heads and laugh loudly.

They were *liberal,* rather than conservative. Change was in the air. They came to the West not to preserve what was, but to make a new world.

They were *individualistic.* The individual was important on the frontier. He carved out his own land and ruled it. He made his own decisions, defended his own property, made his own little center of civilization. He had his own ideas, and nobody was going to make up his mind for him.

And they were *democratic.* No other political philosophy except democracy could possibly have come out of the American frontier. The frontiersman was used to doing a lot of his own governing. He didn't want to turn over his vote and his voice. He wanted to be heard.

It was noticed in the East that the frontier roughened manners. But it was also noticed that out of the West came a great vitality and freshness and strength, which went into American thinking and writing. Out of the frontier land came the most " American " things we have in our heritage.

## THE LITERATURE OF THE FRONTIER

Great writers, great books, did not come at once from the frontier. Great novels and poems come from the eddies, not the main streams of history. There isn't time in the midst of a great event to write great fiction or poetry about it. Sometime later, when history has passed by, writers have time to think about what has happened and leisure to write about it. Meanwhile, the subject matter has been gathering richness. That is the process of writing Wordsworth called " emotion recollected in tranquillity."

Frontiersmen didn't have time to write. They were too busy clearing their acres, keeping night watches against the Indians, setting traps in the mountains. Later, when the frontier had passed, men like Mark Twain soaked themselves in it and went east to write.

When frontiersmen did write, it was usually letters or a diary, or a record to help other travelers (like Josiah Gregg's *Commerce of the Prairies*). Sometimes an Easterner like Francis Parkman came out to the frontier and went home to write an excellent piece of reportage about it (like *The Oregon Trail*). The sea was a frontier, too, and one Easterner, Richard Henry Dana, Jr., sailing for his health, caught the spirit of that frontier in a book called *Two Years before the Mast*. Mostly, though, the records of the frontiersmen have had to be restudied and retold as literature in our own times by men like Stanley Vestal and Maurice Sullivan.

The frontiersman's real contribution to literature was his kind of humor. Sitting around the campfire he loved to spin tales. He would keep a straight face, but his stories were as incredible as the Western country, his imagination as boundless as the prairie, his subject matter as fantastic as the boiling springs in which a man could cook a trout twenty feet from the icy stream where he caught it. The stories were not modest, they were often slapstick, and they did not use drawing-room language. Language itself bowed to the demands of Western storytellers. When ordinary words were not sufficient, the frontiersman coined new ones — " tetotaciously," " exfluncted," " obfliscated," " bodayciously." Nothing was ordinary about these tall tales — any more than the West was ordinary. The men could " walk like an ox, run like a fox, swim like an eel, make love like a mad bull " — that was Davy Crockett's boast. Paul Bunyan could carry water for the Minnesota lakes, build the Black Hills, and use a full-grown pine tree for a toothpick.

Such stories had to wait to be considered good literature until after Mark Twain had given prestige to the " tall tale." But a group of professional " Western humorists " picked up the method and made the East familiar with it. One of these was Artemus Ward, who was born in Maine, and worked in Cleveland, and told side-splitting tales in the most outrageous spelling ever devised by man. The spelling was part of his pose. He pretended to be the proprietor of a wax-figure show, and the droll deadpan stories of his adventures were as exaggerated as the best frontier storyteller could have wished. President Lincoln used to startle his cabinet and his visitors by reading Artemus Ward aloud to them. It was his way to relax and break the almost unbearable tension of the war years.

## Indian Folk Literature

All too often we forget that the first Americans were the Indians. You will see as you read about life on the western frontier that their culture was varied. Some tribes led a desperate, hand-to-mouth existence little better than that of the animals around them. But among the proud mounted Indians of the plains and the pueblo-dwellers of the Southwest a better life gave time for the development of legends and songs of real charm. Here are two bits of folk literature from two of the more advanced tribes.

## SONG OF THE HORSE

### NAVAJO INDIAN SONG

In the songs of the American Indians, vivid characterizations of the gods who represent the powers of nature are a prevailing element. The " Song of the Horse " is a hymn of praise to the Turquoise Horse, which the Sun God rides across the sky on fair days when the sky is blue. The " precious hides " on which he stands are the clouds. Each detail in the song adds to the metaphor.

How joyous his neigh!
Lo, the Turquoise Horse of Johano-ai,°
How joyous his neigh,
There on precious hides outspread standeth he;
How joyous his neigh,                         5
There on tips of fair fresh flowers feedeth he;
How joyous his neigh,
There of mingled waters holy drinketh he;
How joyous his neigh,
There he spurneth dust of glittering grains;
How joyous his neigh,                        11
There in midst of sacred pollen hidden, all hidden he;
How joyous his neigh,
There his offspring many grow and thrive for evermore;
How joyous his neigh!                        15
        *Natalie Curtis Burlin, Translator*

2. **Johano-ai** (jŏ-hä′nŏ-ā).


## THE SHARPENED LEG

Although most of the stories prevalent among the American Indians are either religious or heroic, there are a number that at least verge on the humorous. Among these tales of tricksters " The Sharpened Leg " is a good example of those that involve the undoing of " White Man." This legend came from the Cheyenne Indians.

There was a man whose leg was pointed, so that by running and jumping against trees he could stick in them. By saying " naiwatoutawa," he brought himself back to the ground. On a hot day he would stick himself against a tree for greater shade and coolness. However, he could not do this trick more than four times. Once while he was doing this, White Man came to him, crying, and said, " Brother, sharpen my leg! " The man replied, " That is not very hard. I can sharpen your leg." White Man stood on a large log, and the other, with an ax, sharpened his leg, telling him to hold still bravely. The pain caused the tears to come from his eyes.

When the man had sharpened his leg, he told him to do the trick only four times a day and to keep count in order not to exceed this number. White Man went down toward the river, singing. Near the bank was a large tree; toward this he ran, then jumped and stuck in it. Then he called himself back to the ground. Again he jumped, this time against another tree; but now he counted one, thinking in this way to get the better of the other man. The third time, he counted two. The fourth time, birds and animals stood by; and he was proud to show his ability, and jumped high, and pushed his leg in up to the knee. Then coyotes, wolves, and other animals came to see him; some of them asked how he came to know the trick and begged him to teach it to them, so they could stick to trees at night.

He was still prouder now; and for the fifth time he ran and jumped as high as he could, and half his thigh entered the tree. Then he counted four. Then he called to get to the ground again. But he stuck. He called out all day; he tried to send the animals to the man who had taught him. He was fast in the tree for many days, until he starved to death.


## Suggestions for Study

1. Does this sample of their folklore change your former impression of Indians? What is your reaction to " White Man " in their story?
2. Were these tribes more or less advanced than the Ogillallahs Parkman visited? Do you

see any resemblance in the ideas about weather?

3. Can you find out from history or local old-timers what Indians lived in your locality before the white men came? How advanced was their way of life?

4. You can read more of the Indian songs in *The Path of the Rainbow,* edited by George Cronin, and more narratives in *Pueblo Indian Folk Stories,* collected by Charles F. Loomis. Both are good reading, as well as enlightening.

## Stanley Vestal          1887–

### JOHN COLTER'S RACE FOR LIFE

First of all the westward-pushing Americans to come in contact with the Indians were the trappers and fur traders. The best way to realize what courage and quickwittedness and stamina were demanded of these men on that outer fringe of the frontier is to follow an actual incident. One of the most famous encounters of the trappers, or " mountain men," was John Colter's foot race with the Blackfeet. Here it is, retold by a man who knows as much about those early days as anyone now living. Stanley Vestal grew up in western Oklahoma amid the tribes who were the antagonists of the trappers in the Rockies, and his stepfather knew intimately many of their old chiefs and heard their own versions of such happenings as Colter's brush with the Blackfeet. The boy filled his head with tales gathered from the Indians; and when he was grown he became a professor of history at the University of Oklahoma and also a writer, combining his knowledge from both the white man's libraries and the Indian's legends to give us some of the richest narratives we have about the early frontier. This account is from *Mountain Men* (1937), a book which will introduce you to more of the fur traders and their exploits.

John Colter caused the mountain men more trouble than any other one man living. For hostile Injuns gave the trappers more trouble than all other things combined, and of all the hostiles on the Missouri the Blackfeet were the worst. That is why Colter may be said to have caused the mountain

men so much trouble. He it was who made the Blackfeet hostile!

It happened in this way: Manuel Lisa,[1] that old fox of the fur trade, was burning up with eagerness to trade with the Blackfeet. All traders were, for that matter, because the Blackfeet had a magnificent range, rich in fur and game of all kinds, and utterly unspoiled — since they allowed no white trappers in their country. Lisa had talked with some Blackfeet at his fort at the mouth of the Big Horn, and had found them friendly. He rubbed his greedy hands, and made up his mind to send a man to the Three Forks of the Missouri to fix things up with the chiefs.

John Colter was the best man Lisa had. John Colter was the man to go. And because old Lisa was so greedy, he sent Colter also to the camps of the Crow Nation — then on the Upper Wind River, near Jackson's Hole.

It was five hundred miles to the Crow camp. But Colter, a veteran of the Lewis and Clark expedition, who had already spent several winters trapping on the Upper Missouri, simply filled his shot pouch and powder horn, slung a thirty-pound pack on his shoulders, picked up his long rifle, and hit the trail alone. Five hundred miles was nothing to John Colter. Before he was through, he walked five thousand.

He found the Crows on Wind River, and informed them that Lisa was coming to trade. Then he asked the chiefs to send a man to guide him over the mountains to the headwaters of the Missouri. No white man had ever gone that way before.

That request made the chiefs grunt and stare. They knew that no Crow living was bold enough to venture alone into the country of the hostile Blackfeet. For ages those two tribes had been deadly enemies. Old Lisa's packs couldn't hold enough vermilion,[2] gunpowder, or butcher knives to pay for a risk like that. They didn't like to admit that, but it was true. And so they merely stared and grunted.

[1] **Lisa** (lē′så).  [2] **vermilion** (ver-mĭl′yŭn): for use as war paint.

TETON PASS. John Colter traveled over this wild terrain to open fur-trading with the savage Blackfeet Indians. (Ewing Galloway)

But Colter insisted, and at last, after conferring among themselves, the chiefs agreed to guide him through.

"Good," said Colter. "Who will go with me?"

The oldest chief grinned at the fearless white man. "We *all* go," he said grimly.

Then Colter and a heap of Crows headed west through that wild, rugged country, crossed the Wind River Mountains by Two-gwo-tee Pass and the Teton [1] Range by Teton Pass. That brought them to the Teton Basin, known in old times as Pierre's Hole.

That lovely valley was dangerous country — a battleground of warring tribes. The Blackfeet and their allies, the Gros Ventres [2] of the prairies, claimed the Hole as

their hunting grounds. No spot in the mountains held more peril for the mountain men.

One afternoon, as the colorful cavalcade strung down into the broad valley, Colter suddenly halted. Up ahead, behind a clump of sagebrush, he had seen somebody moving. But now that he had halted he saw nothing. There was not a sound to be heard.

Then, suddenly, a man sprang up and tossed a double handful of dust into the air, as an angry buffalo bull paws up the earth before he charges. The wind caught the dust and spread it into a broad tawny banner — the Injun call to battle. At the same moment the war whoop chattered in Colter's ears, raising prickles along his spine: *Wah-ah-ah-ah-ah!*

"Blackfeet!" yelled the Crow chief, pulling the buckskin cover from his fusil. [3]

[1] **Teton** (tē′tŏn). [2] **Gros Ventres** (grō vän′tr′): French for "big stomachs" from their greediness.

[3] **fusil** (fū′sĭl): a light flintlock musket.

Blackfeet — or Gros Ventres — they certainly were, and on the warpath! A hundred of them suddenly rose from the ground like magic, and came plunging pell-mell out of the ravine and across the open. On they came at the dead run on their spotted ponies, with motley ornaments and arms, splendid war bonnets of lustrous black-and-white eagle feathers swinging about their heads, half-naked, painted, yelling at the top of their lungs, brandishing their bows and lances.

The Crow chief rode back and forth, yelling at his men. They were all in confusion, stripping off their buffalo robes, jerking the covers from their shields, unlimbering their bows, yelling and singing war songs to make their hearts strong. Looking at them, Colter almost wished he had come alone.

He sat still in his saddle. He had no wish to fight the Crows' battles. He had come there to smoke with the Blackfeet.

But already the battle had been joined. The foremost Blackfeet were upon the Crows, charging them confidently with all the advantage of superior numbers, surprise, and the fierce momentum of attack. They circled along the Crow front, waging a hit-and-run warfare, pushing the disorganized Crows back. Every moment the Crows gave ground. Colter found himself out in front, alone.

The Blackfeet charged past him like swallows or swooping hawks. The first to pass tapped him smartly over the head with his bow. The second stung his left leg with an arrow, which passed through, pinning him to his pony's ribs. The horse reared and shook his head, fighting the bit, as the third Injun dashed up and tried to split Colter's skull with a hatchet.

Then Colter went into action. His rifle lay across the pommel of his saddle. Without raising it, he yanked back the hammer, pulled the trigger, and dropped the nearest of his enemies. Then he swung his rifle in one hand and knocked the second from his saddle. The third he caught by his long hair, pulled him backward across his own horse, and stabbed him in the ear.

That was enough for the Blackfeet. The others sheered off from Colter, and gave him time to gain control of his plunging horse, cut off the shaft of the arrow through his leg, dismount, and reload.

Then the Crows, seeing their lone ally victorious, rallied. And as they swarmed back toward him, Colter threw himself prone, leveled his rifle, and picked off another painted enemy. His third shot killed the Blackfoot chief's horse. At that, the Blackfeet galloped away out of range, the chief hanging on to the tail of one of the Blackfoot ponies.

From that safe distance they made insulting gestures at the Crows and called to them in the Blackfoot language, which Colter understood well enough. " The white man saved you," they jeered." Wait! " they yelled. " We have friends with guns, too. Stay where you are, and tomorrow we will rub you out to the last man."

The Crows skirmished with the Blackfeet until sundown. Then the Blackfeet rode away.

Colter dressed his wounded leg as best he could. His leg was sore; but his heart was sorer than his leg, for he knew that this chance fight had made his mission a failure. The Blackfeet had seen him, knew him for a white man, blamed their defeat upon him. Probably they would recognize him if they saw him again. He dared not venture farther into their country after that. His only consolation was that it wasn't his fault.

That night the Crows did not make camp in the Hole. They hit the trail for their camp on Wind River.

Colter protested, but the Crows covered their ears. Their chief said blandly, " You asked us to bring you over the mountains. We have done it. Now we go home." And away they went.

Colter refused to go with them. He remained in the Hole with his wounded leg. But not for long. He mounted, rode on the trail of the Crows until he found a place where he could diverge from it and cover his trail. Then he struck into the pines and rode for Lisa's fort at the mouth of the Big

Horn. That unexplored route took him across what is now Yellowstone Park. It was the summer of 1807.

Thus Colter was the first white man to behold the wonders of the Yellowstone, to see the Three Tetons, Pierre's Hole, and the headwaters of Snake River. At last he got back to the fort, where he passed the winter. His leg healed nicely, and he had little to do but grow a beard.

Old Lisa was deeply disappointed. But he could not give up his dream of trade with the Blackfeet. In the spring he ordered Colter to go and visit them again! This time a man named Potts went along.

The two of them made headquarters on the Jefferson Fork of the Missouri and set their traps, waiting for Injuns to show up. They had not long to wait.

Neither of these men was very eager to meet the Blackfeet. They set their traps by night, and took them up again before sunrise. One morning very early the two of them were paddling silently up a small creek on the Jefferson Fork, examining their traps from their canoe. All at once they heard a great noise, as of a herd of horses or buffalo. The banks of the little stream were too high for them to see what caused the racket.

Colter whispered to his comrade, " Injuns. Let's cache! "

" You must be scairt, for sartain," Potts sneered. " Them's buffaloes."

Colter might have argued the matter. But before he could say anything the Indians came in sight, hundreds of them — and on both sides of the creek. They signaled the white men to come ashore.

The trappers had no choice. They paddled to the bank. The moment the canoe touched the bank, the nearest Indian grabbed Potts's rifle. But Colter, who was a big man and as strong as he was brave, wrested it from the redskin and handed it back to Potts. Colter stepped ashore. But Potts, now thoroughly frightened, stayed in the canoe and shoved off into the water.

That move ended all pretense of friendship. One of the Indians shot an arrow at Potts. The man in the canoe called out, " Colter, I'm wounded! "

" Come on back, you fool! " Colter yelled. " You cain't get away now."

But Potts, losing his head again, raised his rifle, took aim at the mass of Indians, and fired. One of the redskins dropped, dead as a nail. Immediately the air was filled with arrows; and Potts collapsed in the canoe, stuck full of feathered shafts. As Colter said, " He was made a riddle of."

The folly of Potts had put poor Colter in terrible jeopardy. The Indians grabbed him, tore off his clothing, held him fast. Then they began to talk and gesture, arguing as to the method by which he should be put to death. He waited, helpless, naked as a jay bird, while his executioners coolly discussed the method of his slaying.

Most of them favored setting him up as a target for their arrows. But one of the chiefs, wishing to show his authority, differed from the rest. Going up to Colter, he took hold of him by his shoulder, shook him, and demanded to know how fast he could run.

During his stay with the Crows, Colter had made it a point to learn some Blackfoot words. Their language was commonly understood by their neighbors. Colter knew what the chief was saying. He knew that he had a chance to make " the Injun run."

The trapper was a swift runner, and he infinitely preferred a run for his life to being tied up and slowly tortured to death with arrows. Therefore, he cunningly replied that he was a very bad runner. " No good," he answered. " Heap no good."

The chief grinned grimly. Taking Colter from his captors, he led him out on the prairie some three hundred yards from the horde of redskins. Then, turning the white man loose, he said, " Run, then, and save yourself, if you *can!* "

The chief beckoned to his followers. They yelped the war whoop. Colter sprang forward, and ran so fast that he surprised himself.

Before him stretched the open prairie. Beyond it, six miles away, lay the Jefferson

Fork. He ran for that, and for three miles he did not look back.

No wonder. The plain was thick with prickly pear, and Colter's feet were bare. Soon the soles of his feet were filled with the spines of the cactus. But Colter did not let that slow him down. He preferred cactus spines to arrows in his body. He ran like a deer. And when he did look back over his shoulder, he took courage. Most of the Indians were far behind. Only one — a long-legged fellow armed with a lance — was nearer than a hundred yards.

For the first time Colter began to hope that he might escape. He put everything he had into the race, and sprinted so hard that a torrent of blood burst from his nostrils and covered his chest and belly. That almost finished him, but he labored on, though he knew that the man with the lance was gaining.

The river was only a mile off now. But suddenly he heard the thud of his enemy's feet coming up behind. Every moment he expected to feel the spearhead strike his naked back. He looked over his shoulder — the warrior was not twenty paces back! He knew that it would not be long now.

Colter was a fighter; he had no intention of being stabbed from behind without a struggle. And so, unarmed, bleeding, and naked as he was, he suddenly stopped, faced about, and spread out his arms.

The warrior, startled at this sudden move and at Colter's body all covered with blood, tried to stop, and raised his lance to strike the white man. But he was tired also, and stumbled as he threw the lance. The point struck the earth and lodged there; the shaft broke in his hand. The Blackfoot went down.

Colter snatched up the lance head, stabbed the redskin before he could get up. Then he ran on. When the foremost Indians reached their dying comrade, they halted; and all at once began to wail and yell.

But Colter, gasping and exhausted as he was, never faltered. He plunged on to the river bottoms, rushed through the fringe of stately cottonwoods, and plunged into the cool waters of the river. The current swept him down, half-fainting.

Not far below lay an island; and about it a great clutter of drift timber had piled up, making a sort of raft above the island. Colter dived under these interlocked logs and, coming to the surface, bumped his head several times upon them. Finally, when his lungs were ready to burst, he managed to find a space among the trunks above water — and rested there, drawing deep breaths in the darkness. His hiding place was covered with small drift, leaves, and sticks — a layer several feet deep.

From that refuge he heard the Blackfeet come running down the bank, screeching like so many devils. All that day they poked about the pile of driftwood. Sometimes he could see them through the chinks of his hiding place. But whenever he thought they might see him, he pulled himself entirely under water. He began to think he had saved his life, until it came to his mind that they might set the wood on fire.

So he remained, torn with anxiety, until at last night came. Then, hearing nothing of the Blackfeet, he dived out from under the ruck of logs, and floated down-river until he thought all danger of discovery was ended. Then he swam ashore, and hurried overland toward Lisa's fort all night.

He was fully seven days' journey from the fort. He was starving, and had no means of killing meat. He was naked and exposed to the rays of the summer sun. His feet were full of spines, swollen and sore. But it was the season when the tipsin ripens, and Colter fed himself on this root as he went along. Somehow or other he reached the fort at last.

Such was John Colter.

## Suggestions for Study

1. What incident shows Colter to be cooler in his judgment than the other trappers? How does his endurance compare with that developed by modern athletes? Do any of his actions here narrated show unusual courage? Which ones?

2. This narrative, like many others of its period, shows that chance played a large part in determining whether the Indians were to be friends or enemies. What chance turned the tide against Colter on two different occasions?

3. Colter told many tales of the wonders he saw in the Yellowstone Park region, but they were taken for pure tall tales. Look up Yellowstone in an encyclopedia and find out how many years passed before people believed that the geysers and hot springs really existed. Perhaps you will find the nickname the section long bore, harking back to Colter's tales.

4. Many other adventures of the early trappers are recounted in *Mountain Men*. John G. Neihardt has told some of the same stories in *The Song of Hugh Glass* and *The Song of the Three Friends*. Read some from both to see which manner of storytelling you like better.


Maurice Sullivan          1893–1935

## JEDEDIAH SMITH EXPLORES THE FAR WEST

Most of the fur traders did their exploring incidentally. They followed the track of the beaver and were not too pleased when their trails were plain enough for pioneer settlers to follow. Settlers were bad for the trapping business. But one of the "mountain men," Jedediah[1] Smith, felt a potent challenge in the unknown lands beyond and blazed the trails over which Americans a generation later would cross the Rockies and the great desert to reach the coast. This stalwart young Yankee from New York State landed in St. Louis in 1822 when he was only twenty years old. Before he was thirty he had to his credit an impressive list of discoveries and achievements. Promptly entering the fur trade, he worked far into the Rockies with such enterprise and success that he soon became a partner in the largest fur-trading company in St. Louis. Then as leader of the trading parties he pushed farther and farther into new country. He led the party that discovered the great South Pass through which the Oregon Trail later crossed the Rockies. You will read here of the expedition on which he reached California, the first American to make the trip overland.

[1] Jedediah (jĕd-ē-dī′á).

On the twenty-second of August, 1826, Jedediah Smith and his seventeen men struck out with the cavallard[2] of the Southwest expedition.

Captain Smith, a clean-shaven, sharp-eyed, commanding figure, led the procession into the land of mystery. Single file behind him were his mountain men, each leading one or more horses or mules. Harrison Rogers, like Smith a person of piety, brought up the rear.

The first large encampment of Indians encountered by Captain Smith was that of the Uta Nation at Utah Lake. Proud, equestrian chiefs of a far-roving people greeted Jedediah as a friend and readily made a treaty of alliance with him. With liberality he distributed presents among them; and when he left, the women of the chief men were bright with "foofaraw."[3]

A towering mountain chain on his left and low foothills on the right, southward through rolling hills the pathfinder went — pushing on to the Sevier[4] River.

The Sevier is a peculiar stream in a land of picture-book colors. It rises in high mountains and flows northward between two ranges, brightly tinted with red, yellow, and purple. After long journeying it seems suddenly to tire of the north, turns, breaks westward through the hills, and sets out for the south again.

There were marks of the beaver here; but the time was bad for fur, and Jedediah did not tarry. This was an important new discovery, though, and Jedediah named it Ashley River in honor of the general.[5]

Upstream among the bright-colored mountains went Jedediah's cavallard. He traversed numerous meadowlands, but never a sign of buffalo did he find; nor was there any indication that hoofs of any horses save his own had struck this virgin grass.

On the Sevier River, near the branch called San Pete, Captain Smith came upon

[2] cavallard (kăv′ăl-yärd): a procession on horseback. [3] "foofaraw" (fōō-fá-rô′): trinkets and finery. [4] Sevier (sē-vēr′). [5] the general: William H. Ashley, organizer and early head of the Rocky Mountain Fur Company.

a nation of Indians, who, he understood, called themselves Sampatch. They were the Sanpets, a tribe related to the Utes but inferior to the bold horsemen of mountain and prairie. Though the summer was scarcely past, they wore robes made of rabbit skins.

The Sanpets were friendly, and Jedediah traded for a little dried rabbit meat and the edible roots which supplied the scanty fare of these natives.

The cavallard crossed the Sevier above the mouth of Clear Creek and here, in a bright red setting, came upon jet boulders evidently sprayed in the dim past from some spouting volcano. Farther on, the canyon of the creek was all of an ashen gray; and there were thousands of cabalistic writings on rocks, not the work of civilized men but of an aboriginal and perhaps unremembered people. Truly this was a mysterious land in which no one could guess what lay before.

At the head of Clear Creek, Captain Smith ascended a mountain range and, coming down on the west side, saw before him, as far as the eye could reach, a desert of sand and barren hills. Here, certainly, there could be little game or peltry.

Onward, nevertheless, he urged his company, until he struck a river which, from the size of its bed, appeared to have been a considerable stream. Now under the blaze of summer heat there were only a few pools of water in its course, and Jedediah named it Lost River — a name which itself has been lost, for on modern maps it is called the Beaver.

On Lost River he saw numerous Indians; but they fled like coyotes at the apparition of strange, bearded humans with four legs, who killed hares by pointing a long stick and making a noise like thunder.

With all the signs of peace at his command, Jedediah tried to approach these wild creatures and make friends; but they hid from him. To prove his pacific intention he left a knife and other attractive presents lying on the ground in the Indian camp.

Across Lost River and still southward down to the Virgin went the cavallard, leaving skeletons of horses behind them. It seemed to Jedediah a pitiful thing to fire a bullet into the head of a faltering animal, no longer able to carry a pack though willing and wistful to follow its human master; but lack of grass and water had worn the poor beasts down, and lack of game made them a sacrifice, tough and unwholesome, to the men's starvation.

Along the red-walled, shallow Virgin the party traveled, pursuing a southwest course. Jedediah now encountered numerous groups of natives whom he called Pautches.[1]

Fearsome, skulking Indians were the Piutes,[2] though many of them lived within sight of some of the most striking grandeur in creation. From time to time, standing on high places, Jedediah caught glimpses of the marvels of Zion Canyon, cathedral domes and towers glistening in the rarefied air. It was a scene of inspiring sublimity; but here in the valleys of the Virgin and the Santa Clara rivers human beings lived in rounded, brush shelters, more like kennels or lairs than lodges, so poorly made they barely shielded the inhabitants from the fierce beat of the sun. Like the Sanpets, the Piutes wore rabbitskin robes. Both the fur and their own hairy adornment were homes for myriad vermin, with which the simple natives had a reciprocal arrangement: the lodgers obtained their sustenance from the hides of the Indians, and the Piutes ate their guests.

They had pleasanter, better fare though. On the Santa Clara River Jedediah found growing corn, and he therefore named the stream Corn Creek. There were, too, primitive candy manufactories, with stone vessels in which cane grass was pounded to pulp, then boiled with water until a thick sugar was extracted.

In the bed of the Virgin River, through a deep, narrow gorge with perpendicular walls, Jedediah marched his cavalcade. Gloom and foreboding took possession of the courageous fellows who had enlisted for romance and high adventure. The sinister aspect of this quiet place appalled them.

[1] **Pautches** (pä-ōō'chĕz).　[2] **Piutes** (pī'ūts).

When at last, with infinite toil, they managed the passage of the narrows, they emerged into the worst desert any of them had ever seen.

The young commander urged them on. To the men in file this journey was trifling with death, but to Jedediah Smith it was the pattern of his dream. At night they brooded at the fire, imagined that before them to the edge of the world lay desert, and saw in their mind's eye skeletons of forgotten men bleaching in the sun. Jedediah Smith wrote in his journal, recording with satisfaction places and things of which neither he nor any of his company had ever heard before; and he read his books and knelt often to pray. Too, he gathered souvenirs — a marble pipe, a knife of flint, and other curiosities to be sent back to civilization.

Fifty horses and mules when they started. Soon forty-five, then forty, thirty-five, thirty, twenty-nine, twenty-eight . . . they dropped one by one as their feeble strength, taxed with the burdens of other fallen, failed to make the passage of the badlands.

Still Jedediah would not turn back; indeed, even if he wished to return now, an attempt to do so might be fatal unless some means should be found for getting provisions. He promised they should soon come upon a superior Indian nation or a Spanish settlement.

[After six days of hardship they reached a village of Mojave Indians where they were able to get food, rest, and fresh horses.]

With two Indian guides leading the way, Jedediah turned directly to the westward and into a barren country even worse than the one in which they had lost their horses.

This was the white-heart Mojave,[1] the passive protector of the California settlements.

Years before, a war party of Indians, accustomed to travel for days at a time without food and much of the time without water, crossed this desert, descended upon a mission rancho, and ran off a band of horses. But when they tried to drive the animals across that fearsome land, they found the beasts could not endure the waterless journey. Horses withered in the flame of the sun, and thenceforth Californians felt secure in the belief that invasion from the east was impossible.

Into the fire of the Mojave, in the face of the sun, rode the tall young Yankee and his ragged cavalcade.

Mirages mocked them as they traveled sometimes from dawn to dark without finding a spring. The hoofs of their horses broke through the surface at every step as for a whole day they passed over a crust of beautiful white salt, now called Soda Lake, or the Mojave Sink, at the dry mouth of the Mojave River.

A curious river Jedediah found the Mojave. As if to avoid the sucking terror of the sun, it had disappeared into the ground; and only at rare intervals along its course did the explorer find water. Inconstant River is the name he gave it, and Inconstant River it appears on the new maps his discoveries inspired.

The heat at length became unbearable, and the captain ordered holes dug into the sand so that the men might rest and cool their bodies. Refreshed by this device, they pursued their way through pricking cactus and a sparse forest of fantastic yuccas rising leafless from the grayish sand. They saw no animate thing at which to shoot; hunger allied itself with thirst in grisly attempt to halt this presumptuous violation of the desert barrier. But Jedediah Smith marched on.

He followed the ancient Indian trail along the bend of the dry river until he came to a place where the guides pointed out a gap in the snow-crowned mountains to the southward. The trail led up a steep, cool, pine-grown canyon, through which the white men harried their laboring beasts.

With infinite toil Captain Smith attained the snow-covered summit of the range now called the San Bernardino[2] Mountains. Cold air struck his flesh through the rents in his

---

[1] Mojave (mṓ-hä′vå): a desert in southern California.

[2] San Bernardino (săn bûr-nàr-dē′nŏ).

ragged shirt as he rode aside from the trail to a rocky point from which he could look down into what seemed like a promised land.

Back of him was the seared, barren desert, with delusion dancing in the sun. Before him was a green valley, restfully, lusciously green from early rains, soothing to eyes tortured by fifteen days of maddening brilliance. No mocking mirage, this view. It was unmistakably, vividly real.

To the southeast and the west there were magnificent, white-capped peaks; far to the south, lower mountains. Down in the valley there was a wide, tree-bordered wash, with water running in abundance in its channel and everywhere immense herds of cattle and horses.

His eye traveled westward through the clear November air, following the pointing finger of the younger of the two guides.

" San Gabriel! " said the Indian, indicating that somewhere near the limits of that lovely land was the Spanish settlement of that name.

Jedediah Smith looked far, far away to the horizon. The land ended; there was water, and an island in a vast ocean.

Down into the valley of San Bernardino, in the last week of November, 1826, rode the ragged, half-starved expedition.

A native *vaquero*,[1] amazed at this apparition of men of a strange, white nation descending a ridge of the mountains, galloped into the headquarters of the major-domo, or overseer, at the Indian village of Guachama, ten miles southeast of the pass. From there a messenger rushed with the tidings to Mission San Gabriel, sixty miles to the westward.

As they watered their horses at the foot of the range, Jedediah Smith and his men, according to the habit of hunters, turned to examine the trail for guiding landmarks.

Suddenly someone cried " Look! " and pointed.

High on the side of the mountains was an almost unbelievable thing: an enormous, perfectly shaped arrowhead, outlined in

[1] vaquero (vä-kä'rō): cowpuncher.

bare rock against the dark background of the chaparral.

Taking the plainly marked road to the westward, he and his hunters kept their rifles ready. " Spanyards " were given a sinister reputation in the one-sided literature of English-speaking people, because it is the way of men, writing of conflict with folk of different manners, customs, and beliefs, to impute much villainy to them.

Through great herds of cattle, sheep, and horses the strange cavalcade made its way along the south side of the San Bernardino and San Gabriel mountains. An Indian, who spoke Spanish, appeared; then soldiers approached on prancing, gaily ornamented horses, but there was nothing of menace about them. Instead, they were polite; and seeing the hungry look of Jedediah's men, they killed a fat cow and sent back to the mission for corn meal. Soon there was joyful feasting, and for the first time in many weeks Captain Smith looked upon a contented encampment.

Jedediah rode into San Gabriel with the military commandant, while Harrison Rogers stayed in charge of the company. At the door of the mission the captain was greeted by a pleasant, gray-haired friar, Father José Bernardo Sánchez.[2]

We are indebted to the diary of Harrison Rogers for an account of the reception given the invaders from the East. For more than eighty years this record of Rogers remained hidden, while writers of history, having no facts at hand, told indignantly of the grievous imprisonment of Jedediah Smith by the cruel Spanish.

Mr. S. [the clerk recorded] wrote me a note in the morning, stating that he was received as a gentleman and treated as such. I arrived late in the evening, was received very politely and showed into a room and my arms taken from me. About 10 o'clock at night supper was served, and Mr. S. and myself sent for. I was introduced to the 2 priests over a glass of good old whisky, and found them to be very jovial, friendly gentlemen. The supper consisted of a

[2] José Bernardo Sánchez (hŏ-zā' bĕr-när'dō sän'chĕs).

number of different dishes, served different from any table I ever was at. Plenty of good wine during supper. Before the cloth was removed cigars was introduced.

There was difficulty in conversation until a visitor who knew a little English came from Los Angeles. Now the missionaries expressed their wonder at this journey. They had heard something of the big salt lake far to the northeast. The American captain traveled with horses and goods all the way from St. Louis on the Mississippi River to the salt sea, and from the salt sea to California? This was indeed a marvel.

What was the country like? He drew maps for them. What manner of gentiles [1] lived in this great wilderness? He told them of the Blackfeet, the Snakes, the Crows, the Piutes. What were the laws of the American States? He mentioned those which most impressed him.

Jedediah later wrote that to achieve his purpose he had deprived himself of " the privilege of society and the satisfaction of the converse of friends." These were among the things which the Franciscan padres, men of cultured families, reared in civilized Spain, gave up when they entered the service of the Indians. So now, far from home, they found pleasure in the company of the Methodist Smith and the Calvinist Rogers and let the civil authorities, the Mexicans, worry about the political aspect of the visit.

Jedediah wrote to the Governor of the Department of California, then at San Diego, to the southward, announcing his arrival. Meanwhile he continued to enjoy the hospitality of the mission.

Still at the mansion [wrote Rogers, meaning mission]. We was sent for about sunrise to drink a cup of tea, and eat some bread and cheese. They all appear friendly and treat us well. Although they are Catholicks by profession, they allow us liberty of conscience and treat us as they do their own countrymen or brethren.

[1] **gentiles:** used by Christians to mean heathen.

At dinner " everything went on in style," according to the diarist. Their hosts were merry; and, he recorded, " they all appear to be gentlemen of the first class, both in manners and habits."

There was a grand wedding, then, to which people traveled from settlements many miles away. Smith and Rogers were invited and were made welcome at " an elegant dinner."

The " booshway " [2] and the little " booshway " of the wild mountain men felt somewhat diffident among the leading people of that part of the province. Frankly Rogers admitted he and his commander were very dirty; their clothing was tattered and soiled with the sweat of months; and they " acted quite independent," not knowing the language of the other guests at the table. Their excuses were waved aside, though, and the diners were as courteous to them as if they were clothed in fine garments.

While Smith and Rogers lived with the missionaries, the other members of the expedition had an apartment to themselves, with cooking utensils and an abundance of provisions. They were not contented, however, and Captain Smith was obliged to prove that piety is not incompatible with physical prowess.

James Read, a husky blacksmith, was a chronic maker of trouble. His impertinence in the end brought him a flogging from his captain, and for the rest of that day, as Rogers noted, he " appeared more complasant than usual." This same Read, while under the domination of strong waters, later engaged in a fist fight with another member of the party, and further ingratiated himself by invading the dining room during a meal and making himself somewhat objectionable.

In the company of Abraham LaPlant, whose companionship he seems to have favored, Jedediah went down to the pueblo of Los Angeles and there met a certain Fran-

[2] **"booshway"** (bo͞osh-wā′): usual "mountain" term for the leader of a trapping expedition, the little "booshway" being his lieutenant. The word developed from the French *bourgeois*.

cisco Martinez,[1] who promised to provide as many horses and mules as he wished for his journey.

On Sunday, December 6, Mass was at six o'clock in the morning.

They poured into the church from all quarters, men, women and children. There was none of us invited, therefore we all remained at our lodgings. The Indians play bandy [shinny, or field hockey] with sticks, it being the only game I have seen as yet among them. They play before the priest's door. [And, Rogers added] I am told they dance, both Spanyards and Inds., in the course of the evening.

The next day Father Sánchez gave Smith sixty-four yards of material so that he and his men could make shirts for themselves. A couple of days later Rogers made Father Sánchez a present of his buffalo robe — doubtless a great sacrifice on the part of Rogers, considering the condition of the company. The ever-generous padre accepted the gift, but gave in return an unusually large blanket.

Smith in the meantime began to grow impatient because he had received no reply from the Governor of the province. He was having his first experience of the celebrated José María de Echeandía,[2] whose vacillations later drove the American almost to distraction.

Don José considered himself a harassed man even before the problem of Smith, J. S., burst upon him with so little warning.

To begin with, Don José was none too well. He lacked vitality, and the energy of such men as Smith depressed him. When he established his capital at San Diego, because he thought the climate better suited to his poor health, he grievously outraged the feelings of the inhabitants of Monterey.

Further, his excellency was not on the best of terms with the Spanish missionaries, who had little liking for the Mexican Republic and the recent revolution. Don José and his political friends had in mind what

one historian calls " an enlightened scheme of secularization " for the chain of missions which extended from Lower California northward to San Francisco. This and similar schemes were looked upon by the padres with a non-co-operative eye.

Within the span of a generation the Franciscans had succeeded in Christianizing the Indians of the coast territory. They had found them a multitude of miserable, warring tribes, living on roots, acorns, vermin, and such small game as they could snare or kill. They seemed, as Jedediah Smith remarked of gentile Indians of the north, the connecting link between man and brute creation, rising from their beds of earth, like the animals around them, to eat that day or to go hungry as fortune favored them.

Now they were settled peacefully around the missions, producing by agriculture and stock raising a variety of food, working at the mechanical arts then common among civilized men. Their herds had multiplied, and their improved economic condition caused inland tribes to ask for missions.

When the San Gabriel missionaries questioned Jedediah Smith about the desert country to the eastward, they had in mind their plan for reaching the wild Indians of the interior with another chain of missions. It was their intent that when they had completed the spiritual conquest of the Spanish territory they should organize the Christians into pueblos and allow them to govern themselves.

This was a noble plan; but it did not appeal to the practical men, the politicians. It seemed to them, as their own situation seemed later to the invading Americans, to be much too good for inferior folk. Hence it is that eight years after Smith arrived in California one finds the mission lands and other properties falling into the hands of the " right people," and the Indians either bewildered or returning to savage life.

[A long passage describes Smith's difficulties in obtaining passports from the Governor, his final success, and his return to the mission on January 10.]

---

[1] **Martinez** (mär-tēn′ĕs).   [2] **José María de Encheandía** (hŏ-zā′ mä-rē′à dä ā-chä-än-dē′à).

Jedediah Smith doubtless was relieved to get away from the Governor, who seemed, according to Smith, to have been placed in power to perplex him and those over whom he was called to govern. Doubtless, too. Echeandía was glad to be rid of Smith, for there is evidence that Jedediah, despite the danger of imprisonment in a foreign land, was stubbornly determined to do as he pleased.

He acceded, though, to the official refusal to allow him to travel up the seacoast toward the Russian colony at Bodega, above San Francisco. He was ordered to leave the country by a route which would avoid the settlements. In the middle of January the party finally got under way, with sixty-eight horses — some very wild. From the first camping place, four miles from the mission, Smith and Rogers returned to have a farewell supper with Father Sánchez.

" The old Father has given a great deal to Mr. Smith, and some of the men, and continues giving," Rogers had written. Now, as the American leader and his clerk were leaving, Father Sánchez presented parting gifts: cheese, a gourdful of brandy, and blankets. Besides, Smith obtained an order on the major-domo at San Bernardino, who was instructed to let him have whatever supplies he might need for his journey. This crowning act of generosity so affected Rogers that he panegyrized:

Old Father Sánchez has been the greatest friend that I ever met with in all my travels. He is worthy of being called a Christian as he possesses charity in the highest degree, and a friend to the poor and distressed. I ever shall hold him as a man of God, taking us in when in distress, feeding and clothing us, and may God prosper him and all such men.

At San Bernardino, Smith and his men killed some cattle and dried the meat. The order on the major-domo was complied with immediately, and they obtained corn, peas, parched meal, and wheat flour.

It was the later part of January, and Rogers observed with satisfaction that the weather still was mild. Doubtless he thought of the trappers in the mountains, or on the Upper Missouri, holed up for the winter or moving about amid ice, snow, and bitter winds. " This country," he wrote, " in many respects is the most desirable part of the world I ever was in; the climate so regular and beautiful. The thermometer stands daily from 65 to 70 degrees."

Back to the desert the little party went about February 1, crossing the mountains north of San Bernardino. Then, ignoring Mexican governors and their absurd objections, Smith continued his exploration of California and its resources.

He took a northwest course, heading toward the Tulare [1] Lake region, where, he had heard, there were beaver. He passed many naked, short-haired Indians, living on fish, acorns, and grass.

Northward from the Spanish *Río de los Santos Reyes* [2] — now Kings River — which Smith named Wim-mul-che because he found a friendly tribe of that name living there, the Americans found good hunting and settin' for their traps.

They followed the San Joaquin,[3] taking beaver from its tributaries. Between the streams now called the Stanislaus [4] and the Mokélumne [5] they encountered friendly and useful natives in the Apelamenes [6] and Mokélumnes, on whom Jedediah bestowed evanescent honor by giving to the Stanislaus and the Calaveras [7] the names Appelamminy and Mackalumbry.

The calm indifference of Captain Smith and his men to the authority of Mexico has its amusing aspect. One wonders what would have happened to a band of Mexicans riding into Missouri on horses stolen from the Missourians, showing by their manner that they were contemptuous of the Missourians; fraternizing with the native enemies of the settlers; renaming the rivers; insisting on choosing their own course through the territory; and, as they went,

---

[1] Tulare (tōō-lár'å). [2] Río de los Santos Reyes (rē'ô dä lōs sän'tōs rä'ås): Spanish, River of the Holy Kings. [3] San Joaquin (săn wä-kēn'). [4] Stanislaus (stăn-ĭs-lou'). [5] Mokélumne (mô-kå-lōōm'-nå). [6] Apelamenes (ä-på-lå-mä'nås). [7] Calaveras (kăl-á-vä'rås).

gathering the natural wealth of the country. Certainly the Missourians would have been less indulgent than the " jealous Spaniard."

In the end this tolerance of invasion lost the magnificent empire of the Pacific slope. Jedediah Smith had opened the gate, and Mexico was never able to close it.

## Suggestions for Study

1. List some of the hardships Smith and his men encountered on the way to California. Do you think the achievement was worth the suffering?

2. How did the Indians whom Smith encountered on this trip differ from the usual idea of the Indian? What did the land have to do with the way the Indians lived? West of the plains country, what was the chief use the Indians had for horses?

3. What incident first showed that Smith's expedition was to be received kindly by the Californians? What further kindnesses were shown the Americans?

4. What details show that the Californians were used to more luxuries than were the American frontiersmen?

5. Do you get a clear impression of Jedediah Smith's character from this narrative? What were his most marked traits? You can know Jedediah much better, and also the life along the farthest edge of the frontier, if you read all of the biography from which this selection was taken.

6. Vocabulary: cabalistic, peltry, chaparral, panegyrized, evanescent.

## Josiah Gregg      1806–1850

### ON THE SANTA FE TRAIL

The men who braved the early West had a streak of the adventurer in them, but they also had a streak of Yankee. They liked a little excitement, they were jaunty about hardships, and they all hoped to make their fortunes on the frontier. One venture that guaranteed the excitement and hardships also gave glowing promise of fortune. That was the trade with the upper Mexican provinces that flowed over the Santa Fe Trail. Unlike most of the sagas of the West, this one had its own contemporary historian, and a good one. Josiah Gregg's *Commerce of the Prairies,* first published in 1844, ran through six editions in little more than ten years and is still the prime source of information on the Santa Fe Trail. In this selection you start out with Gregg on his first trip over the Trail, but he later became a regular trader and followed the route many times. Notice how he mingles excitement over adventure with shrewd observation of practical details.

I

People who reside at a distance, and especially at the North, have generally considered St. Louis as the emporium of the Santa Fe trade; but that city, in truth, has never been a place of rendezvous, nor even of outfit, except for a small portion of the traders who have started from its immediate vicinity.

As Independence is a point of convenient access (the Missouri River being navigable at all times from March till November), it has become the general port of embarkation for every part of the great western and northern " prairie ocean." Besides the Santa Fe caravans, most of the Rocky Mountain traders and trappers, as well as emigrants to Oregon, take this town in their route. During the season of departure, therefore, it is a place of much bustle and active business.

Among the concourse of travelers at this starting point, besides traders and tourists a number of pale-faced invalids are generally to be met with. The prairies have, in fact, become very celebrated for their sanative effects — more justly so, no doubt, than the more fashionable watering places of the North. Most chronic diseases, particularly liver complaints, dyspepsias, and similar affections, are often radically cured; owing, no doubt, to the peculiarities of diet and the regular exercise incident to prairie life, as well as to the purity of the atmosphere of those elevated unembarrassed regions. An invalid myself, I can answer for the efficacy of the remedy, at least in my own case.

Though, like other valetudinarians,[1] I was disposed to provide an ample supply of such commodities as I deemed necessary for my comfort and health, I was not long upon the prairies before I discovered that most of such extra preparations were unnecessary, or at least quite dispensable. A few knickknacks, as a little tea, rice, fruits, crackers, etc., suffice very well for the first fortnight, after which the invalid is generally able to take the fare of the hunter and teamster. Though I set out myself in a carriage, before the close of the first week I saddled my pony; and when we reached the buffalo range I was not only as eager for the chase as the sturdiest of my companions, but I enjoyed far more exquisitely my share of the buffalo than all the delicacies which were ever devised to provoke the most fastidious appetite.

The ordinary supplies for each man's consumption during the journey are about fifty pounds of flour, as many more of bacon, ten of coffee and twenty of sugar, and a little salt. Beans, crackers, and trifles of that description are comfortable appendages, but being looked upon as dispensable luxuries, are seldom to be found in any of the stores on the road. The buffalo is chiefly depended upon for fresh meat, and great is the joy of the traveler when that noble animal first appears in sight.

The wagons now most in use upon the prairies are manufactured in Pittsburgh; and are usually drawn by eight mules or the same number of oxen. Of late years, however, I have seen much larger vehicles employed, with ten or twelve mules harnessed to each and a cargo of goods of about five thousand pounds in weight. At an early period the horse was more frequently in use, as mules were not found in great abundance; but as soon as the means for procuring these animals increased, the horse was gradually and finally discarded, except occasionally for riding and the chase.

Oxen having been employed by Major

Riley for the baggage wagons of the escort which was furnished the caravan of 1829, they were found, to the surprise of the traders, to perform almost equal to mules. Since that time, upon an average about half the wagons in these expeditions have been drawn by oxen. They possess many advantages, such as pulling heavier loads than the same number of mules, particularly through muddy or sandy places; but they generally fall off in strength as the prairie grass becomes drier and shorter, and often arrive at their destination in a most shocking plight. In this condition I have seen them sacrificed at Santa Fe for ten dollars the pair; though in more favorable seasons they sometimes remain strong enough to be driven back to the United States the same fall. Therefore, although the original cost of a team of mules is much greater, the loss ultimately sustained by them is usually less, to say nothing of the comfort of being able to travel faster and more at ease. . . .

The supplies being at length procured and all necessary preliminaries systematically gone through, the trader begins the difficult task of loading his wagons. Those who understand their business take every precaution so to stow away their packages that no jolting on the road can afterward disturb the order in which they had been disposed. The ingenuity displayed on these occasions has frequently been such that after a tedious journey of eight hundred miles the goods have been found to have sustained much less injury than they would have experienced on a turnpike road, or from the ordinary handling of property upon our western steamboats.

At last all are fairly launched upon the broad prairie — the miseries of preparation are over — the thousand anxieties occasioned by wearisome consultations and delays are felt no more. The charioteer as he smacks his whip feels a bounding elasticity of soul within him, which he finds it impossible to restrain; even the mules prick up their ears with a peculiarly conceited air, as if in anticipation of that change of scene

[1] valetudinarians (văl-ê-tū-dĭ-nâr'ĭ-ănz): weak or sickly persons, especially those whose chief concern is their ill-health.

THE ARRIVAL OF THE CARAVAN AT SANTA FE was an event of tremendous excitement. It meant the end of long weary months of difficult and dangerous travel. (Brown Brothers)

which will presently follow. Harmony and good feeling prevail everywhere. The hilarious song, the *bon mot*,[1] and the witty repartee go round in quick succession; and before people have had leisure to take cognizance of the fact, the lovely village of Independence with its multitude of associations is already lost to the eye.

It was on the fifteenth of May, 1831, and one of the brightest and most lovely of all the days in the calendar, that our little party set out from Independence. The general rendezvous at Council Grove was our immediate destination. It is usual for the traders to travel thus far in detached parties, and to assemble there for mutual security and defense during the remainder of the journey. It was from thence that the formation of the caravan was to be dated and the chief interest of our journey to commence: therefore, to this point we all looked forward with great anxiety. The intermediate travel was marked by very few events of any interest. As the wagons had gone before us and

we were riding in a light carriage, we were able to reach the Round Grove, about thirty-five miles distant, on the first day, where we joined the rear division of the caravan, comprising about thirty wagons.

On the following day we had a foretaste of those protracted, drizzling spells of rain, which at this season of the year so much infest the frontier prairies. It began sprinkling about dark and continued pouring without let or hindrance for forty-eight hours in succession; and as the rain was accompanied by a heavy northwester and our camp was pitched in the open prairie without a stick of available timber within a mile of us, it must be allowed that the whole formed a prelude anything but flattering to valetudinarians. For my own part, finding the dearborn[2] carriage in which I had a berth not exactly waterproof, I rolled myself in a blanket and lay snugly coiled upon a tier of boxes and bales, under cover of a wagon, and thus managed to escape a very severe drenching.

[1] **bon mot** (bôɴ mō'): a witty remark.

[2] **dearborn** (dēr'bŭrn): four-wheeled carriage with curtained sides.

The mischief of the storm did not exhaust itself, however, upon our persons. The loose animals sought shelter in the groves at a considerable distance from the encampment, and the wagoners being loth to turn out in search of them during the rain, not a few, of course, when applied for were missing. This, however, is no uncommon occurrence. Travelers generally experience far more annoyance from the straying of cattle during the first hundred miles than at any time afterward; because, apprehending no danger from the wild Indians (who rarely approach within two hundred miles of the border) they seldom keep any watch, although that is the very time when a cattle guard is most needed. It is only after some weeks' travel that the animals begin to feel attached to the caravan, which they then consider about as much their home as the stockyard of a dairy farm.

After leaving this spot the troubles and vicissitudes of our journey began in good earnest; for on reaching the narrow ridge which separates the Osage and Kansas waters (known as the Narrows), we encountered a region of very troublesome quagmires. On such occasions it is quite common for a wagon to sink to the hubs in mud while the surface of the soil all around would appear perfectly dry and smooth. To extricate each other's wagons we had frequently to employ double and triple teams, with all hands to the wheels in addition — often led by the proprietors themselves up to the waist in mud and water.

Three or four days after this and while crossing the head branches of the Osage River we experienced a momentary alarm. Conspicuously elevated upon a rod by the roadside we found a paper purporting to have been written by the Kansas agent, stating that a band of Pawnees were said to be lurking in the vicinity! The first excitement over, however, the majority of our party came to the conclusion that it was either a hoax of some of the company in advance or else a stratagem of the Kaws (or Kansas Indians), who, as well as the Osages, prowl about those prairies and steal

from the caravans during the passage, when they entertain the slightest hope that their maraudings will be laid to others. They seldom venture further, however, than to seize upon an occasional stray animal, which they frequently do with the view alone of obtaining a reward from its owner for its return. As to the Pawnees, the most experienced traders were well aware that they had not been known to frequent those latitudes since the commencement of the Santa Fe trade. But what contributed as much as anything else to lull the fears of the timid was an accession to our forces of seventeen wagons which we overtook the same evening.

Early on the twenty-sixth of May we reached the long looked-for rendezvous of Council Grove, where we joined the main body of the caravan. Lest this imposing title suggest to the reader a snug and thriving village, it should be observed that on the day of our departure from Independence we passed the last human abode upon our route; therefore, from the borders of Missouri to those of New Mexico not even an Indian settlement greeted our eyes. . . .

The designation of Council Grove, after all, is perhaps the most appropriate that could be given to this place; for *we* there held a grand council, at which the respective claims of the different aspirants to office were considered, leaders selected, and a system of government agreed upon, as is the standing custom of these promiscuous caravans. One would have supposed that electioneering and party spirit would hardly have penetrated so far into the wilderness; but so it was. Even in our little community we had our office seekers and their political adherents, as earnest and as devoted as any of the modern school of politicians in the midst of civilization. After a great deal of bickering and wordy warfare, however, all the candidates found it expedient to decline, and a gentleman by the name of Stanley, without seeking or even desiring the office, was unanimously proclaimed captain of the caravan. The powers of this officer were undefined by any constitutional provision, and consequently vague and uncertain: orders being only viewed as mere requests, they are often obeyed or neglected at the caprice of the subordinates. It is necessary to observe, however, that the captain is expected to direct the order of travel during the day and to designate the camping ground at night; with many other functions of a general character, in the exercise of which the company find it convenient to acquiesce. . . .

But after this comes the principal task of organizing. The proprietors are first notified by proclamation to furnish a list of their men and wagons. The latter are generally apportioned into four divisions, particularly when the company is large — and ours consisted of nearly a hundred wagons, besides a dozen of dearborns and other small vehicles and two small cannons (a four and six pounder), each mounted upon a carriage. To each of these divisions a lieutenant was appointed, whose duty it was to inspect every ravine and creek on the route, select the best crossings, and superintend what is called in prairie parlance the " forming " of each encampment.

Upon the calling of the roll we were found to muster an efficient force of nearly two hundred men, without counting invalids or other disabled bodies, who, as a matter of course, are exempt from duty. There is nothing so much dreaded by inexperienced travelers as the ordeal of guard duty. But no matter what the condition or employment of the individual may be, no one has the smallest chance of evading the common law of the prairies. The amateur tourist and the listless loafer are precisely in the same wholesome predicament — they must all take their regular turn at the watch. There is usually a set of genteel idlers attached to every caravan, whose wits are forever at work in devising schemes for whiling away their irksome hours at the expense of others. By embarking in these trips of pleasure they are enabled to live without expense; for the hospitable traders seldom refuse to accommodate even a loafing companion with a berth at their mess without charge. But then these lounging attachés are expected at least to do good service by way of guard duty. None are even permitted to furnish a substitute, as is frequently done in military expeditions, for he that would undertake to stand the tour of another besides his own would scarcely be watchful enough for the dangers of the prairies. Even the invalid must be able to produce unequivocal proofs of his inability, or it is a chance if the plea is admitted. For my own part, although I started on the sick list, and though the prairie sentinel must stand fast and brook the severest storm (for then it is that the strictest watch is necessary), I do not remember ever having missed my post but once during the whole journey.

The usual number of watches is eight, each standing a fourth of every alternate night. When the party is small the number is greatly reduced, while in the case of very small bands they are sometimes compelled for safety's sake to keep one watch on duty half the night. With large caravans the captain usually appoints eight sergeants of the guard, each of whom takes an equal portion of men under his command.

The wild and motley aspect of the caravan can be but imperfectly conceived without an idea of the costumes of its various members. The most fashionable prairie dress is the fustian frock of the city-bred merchant furnished with a multitude of pockets capable of accommodating a variety of extra tackling. Then there is the backwoodsman with his linsey or leather hunting shirt — the farmer with his blue-jean coat — the wagoner with his flannel-sleeve vest — besides an assortment of other costumes which go to fill up the picture.

In the article of firearms there is also an equally interesting medley. The frontier hunter sticks to his rifle, as nothing could induce him to carry what he terms in derision " the scatter-gun." The sportsman from the interior flourishes his double-barreled fowling piece with equal confidence in its superiority. The latter is certainly the most convenient description of gun that can be carried on this journey; as a charge of buckshot in night attacks (which are the most common) will of course be more likely to do execution than a single rifle-ball fired at random. The repeating arms have lately been brought into use upon the prairies and they are certainly very formidable weapons, particularly when used against an ignorant savage foe. A great many were furnished besides with a bountiful supply of pistols and knives of every description, so that the party made altogether a very brigandlike appearance.

During our delay at the Council Grove the laborers were employed in procuring timber for axletrees and other wagon repairs, of which a supply is always laid in before leaving this region of substantial growths; for henceforward there is no wood on the route fit for these purposes; not even in the mountains of Santa Fe do we meet with any serviceable timber. The supply procured here is generally lashed under the wagons, in which way a log is not unfrequently carried to Santa Fe, and even sometimes back again.

## II

Although the usual hour of starting with the prairie caravans is after an early breakfast, yet on this occasion we were hindered till in the afternoon. The familiar note of preparation, " Catch up! Catch up! " was now sounded from the captain's camp, and re-echoed from every division and scattered group along the valley. On such occasions a scene of confusion ensues which must be seen to be appreciated. The woods and dales resound with the gleeful yells of the lighthearted wagoners, who, weary of inaction and filled with joy at the prospect of getting under way, become clamorous in the extreme. Scarcely does the jockey on the racecourse ply his whip more promptly at that magic word, " Go," than do these emulous wagoners fly to harnessing their mules at the spirit-stirring sound of " Catch up." Each teamster vies with his fellows who shall be soonest ready; and it is a mat-

ter of boastful pride to be the first to cry out, " All's set! "

The uproarious bustle which follows — the hallooing of those in pursuit of animals — the exclamations which the unruly brutes call forth from their wrathful drivers; together with the clatter of bells — the rattle of yokes and harness — the jingle of chains — all conspire to produce a clamorous confusion which would be altogether incomprehensible without the assistance of the eyes; while these alone would hardly suffice to unravel the labyrinthian maneuvers and hurly-burly of this precipitate breaking-up. It is sometimes amusing to observe the athletic wagoner hurrying an animal to its post — to see him heave upon the halter of a stubborn mule, while the brute as obstinately sets back, determined not to move a peg till his own good pleasure thinks it proper to do so — his whole manner seeming to say, " Wait till your hurry's over! " I have more than once seen a driver hitch a harnessed animal to the halter and by that process haul " his mulishness " forward, while each of his four projected feet would leave a furrow behind; until at last the perplexed master would wrathfully exclaim, " A mule will be a mule anyway you can fix it! "

" All's set! " is finally heard from some teamster — " All's set " is directly responded from every quarter. " Stretch out! " immediately vociferates the captain. Then the " Heps! " of drivers — the cracking of whips — the trampling of feet — the occasional creak of wheels — the rumbling of wagons — form a new scene of exquisite confusion, which I shall not attempt further to describe.

Our route lay through uninterrupted prairie for about forty miles — in fact, I may say, for five hundred miles, excepting the very narrow fringes of timber along the borders of the streams.

Our hopes of game were destined soon to be realized; for early on the second day after leaving Cottonwood (a few miles beyond the principal Turkey Creek) our eyes were greeted with the sight of a herd amounting to nearly a hundred head of buffalo quietly grazing in the distance before us. The fleetest of the pursuers were soon in the midst of the game, which scattered in all directions, like a flock of birds upon the descent of a hawk.

A few beeves were killed during the chase; and as soon as our camp was pitched, the bustle of kindling fires and preparing for supper commenced. The new adventurers were curious to taste this prairie luxury; while we all had been so long upon salt provisions — now nearly a month — that our appetites were in exquisite condition to relish fresh meat. The fires had scarcely been kindled when the fumes of broiling meat pervaded the surrounding atmosphere; while all huddled about anxiously watching their cookeries and regaling their senses in anticipation upon the savory odors which issued from them.

For the edification of the reader, who has, no doubt, some curiosity on the subject, I will briefly mention that the kitchen- and tablewares of the traders usually consist of a skillet, a frying pan, a sheet-iron camp kettle, a coffeepot, and each man with his tin cup and a butcher's knife. The culinary operations being finished, the pan and kettle are set upon the grassy turf, around which all take a lowly seat and crack their gleesome jokes while from their greasy hands they swallow their savory viands — all with a relish rarely experienced at the well-spread tables of the most fashionable and wealthy.

The insatiable appetite acquired by travelers upon the prairies is almost incredible, and the quantity of coffee drunk is still more so. It is an unfailing and apparently indispensable beverage, served at every meal — even under the broiling noonday sun the wagoner will rarely fail to replenish a second time his huge tin cup.

A few days before the caravan had reached this place, a Mr. Broadus, in attempting to draw his rifle from a wagon muzzle foremost, discharged its contents into his arm. The bone being dreadfully shattered, the unfortunate man was advised to submit to an amputation at once; otherwise, it being in the month of August and excessively warm, mortification would soon ensue. But Broadus obstinately refused to consent to this course till death began to stare him in the face. By this time, however, the whole arm had become gangrened, some spots having already appeared above the place where the operation should have been performed. The invalid's case was therefore considered perfectly hopeless and he was given up by all his comrades, who thought of little else than to consign him to the grave.

But being unwilling to resign himself to the fate which appeared frowning over him without a last effort, he obtained the consent of two or three of the party who undertook to amputate his arm merely to gratify the wishes of the dying man; for in such a light they viewed him. Their only case of instruments consisted of a handsaw, a butcher's knife, and a large iron bolt. The teeth of the saw being considered too coarse, they went to work and soon had a set of fine teeth filed on the back. The knife having been whetted keen and the iron bolt laid upon the fire, they commenced the operation, and in less time than it takes to tell it the arm was opened round to the bone, which was almost in an instant sawed off; and with the whizzing hot iron the whole stump was so effactually seared as to close the arteries completely. Bandages were now applied and the company proceeded on their journey as though nothing had occurred. The arm commenced healing rapidly and in a few weeks the patient was sound and well.

We encamped at Ash Creek, where we again experienced sundry alarms in consequence of " Indian sign " that was discovered in the creek valley, such as unextinguished fires, about which were found some old moccasins — a sure indication of the recent retreat of savages from the vicinity. These constant alarms, however, although too frequently the result of groundless and unmanly fears, are not without their salutary effects upon the party. They serve to keep one constantly on the alert and to sharpen those faculties of observation which would otherwise become blunted or inactive. Thus far, also, we had marched in two lines only; but after crossing the Pawnee Fork each of the four divisions drove on in a separate file, which became henceforth the order of march till we reached the border of the mountains. By moving in long lines as we did before, the march is continually interrupted; for every accident which delays a wagon ahead stops all those behind. By marching four abreast this difficulty is partially obviated, and the wagons can also be thrown more readily into a condition of defense in case of attack.

Upon encamping, the wagons are formed into a hollow square (each division to a side), constituting at once an enclosure (or *corral*) for the animals when needed, and a fortification against the Indians. Not to embarrass this cattle pen, the campfires are all lighted outside of the wagons. Outside of the wagons, also, the travelers spread their beds, which consist, for the most part, of buffalo rugs and blankets. Many content themselves with a single Mackinaw; but a pair constitutes the most regular pallet; and he that is provided with a buffalo rug into the bargain is deemed luxuriously supplied. It is most usual to sleep out in the open air, as well to be at hand in case of attack as, indeed, for comfort; for the serene sky of the prairies affords the most agreeable and wholesome canopy. That deleterious attribute of night air and dews so dangerous in other climates is but little experienced upon the high plains: on the contrary, the serene evening air seems to affect the health rather favorably than otherwise. Tents are so rare on these expeditions that in a caravan of two hundred men I have not seen a dozen. In time of rain the traveler resorts to his wagon, which affords a far more secure shelter than a tent; for if the latter is not beaten down by the storms which so often accompany rain upon the prairies, the ground underneath is at least apt to be flooded. During dry weather, however, even the invalid prefers the open air.

## Suggestions for Study

1. Would you recommend a trip over the Santa Fe Trail for an invalid? Why do you think it had such a reputation for cures? What sorts of ailments was it particularly good for?

2. What equipment and supplies made up a good kit for one about to take the Trail? Can you see the usefulness of each item? Which side do you take in the shotgun-rifle controversy?

3. How was the caravan organized? Why was the night watch so important? Describe the layout of a night encampment.

4. How does the attitude of these traders toward Indians differ from Jedediah Smith's attitude toward them? There is a reason for the difference which you can figure out.

5. What incident impresses you most with hardships of life on the Trail? What reason do you discover for the fascination the Trail had, in spite of these hardships?

6. You can get the whole story of the Trail from two good books published recently, *The Old Santa Fe Trail*, by Stanley Vestal, who told the story of John Colter's race with the Indians, and *The Santa Fe Trail*, by R. L. Duffus.

7. Vocabulary: emporium, rendezvous, efficacy, vicissitudes, emulous, vociferates, salutary, deleterious.

## For Your Vocabulary

WORD DISCRIMINATION. The party decided that the warning about the Pawnees was either a *hoax* (hōks) of another company of traders (page 650), or a *stratagem* (străt'ă-jĕm) of another Indian tribe (page 650). There is a nice difference, though both are intended to deceive. The *hoax* would be a mischievous deception, just for the fun of alarming the next party to come along. But a *stratagem* is deception used against an enemy for later advantage. Gregg explains what the advantage would be in this case. Military *strategy* is this type of deception. Robert E. Lee was a notable *strategist*.

WORD ANALYSIS. Simple English words form the basis of *apportioned* (page 651) and *indispensable* (page 653). But the meaning of *mortification* (môr-tĭ-fĭ-kā'shŭn) as it is used here (page 653) brings in a bit of interesting word history. The root is *mort,* death, and the word literally means to make like death. The part of the trader's arm affected by the wound had really become dead flesh. This original meaning makes clearer a frequent figure of speech used by a *mortified* person, " I could have died."

# Richard Henry Dana, Jr.
## 1815–1882

## FROM THE FORECASTLE

It seems to have been quite the fashion in the early 1800's for an invalid to try the strenuous life. Richard Henry Dana, Jr., had to leave Harvard because of failing eyesight, and when his physician recommended a long sea voyage, Richard shipped as an ordinary sailor on a vessel bound from Boston around Cape Horn to California and back. After his return he wrote the famous *Two Years before the Mast* (1840) with the avowed purpose of telling of life at sea not from the point of view of the officers, as had formerly been done, but " from the forecastle " — from the point of view of the common sailor. He was greatly concerned over the tyranny and brutal treatment which sailors had to endure, as you can see from his account of the captain's behavior in this selection. The book had important influence on maritime legislation; but it also became one of the best-loved adventure stories America has produced. The pioneers on land had no more hardships than those on sea, as you can soon realize. We find the young gentleman-sailor suffering from a badly infected tooth, as well as the usual rigors of the weather and the captain's despotism.

*Friday, July 1.* We were now nearly up to the latitude of Cape Horn; and having over forty degrees of easting to make, we squared away the yards before a strong westerly gale, shook a reef out of the fore topsail, and stood on our way, east by south, with the prospect of being up with the cape in a week or ten days. As for myself, I had had no sleep for forty-eight hours; and the want of rest, together with constant wet and cold, had increased the swelling, so that my face was nearly as large as two, and I found

it impossible to get my mouth open wide enough to eat. In this state the steward applied to the captain for some rice to boil for me, but he only got a — " No! d—— you! Tell him to eat salt junk and hard bread, like the rest of them." This was, in truth, what I expected. However, I did not starve; for Mr. Brown, who was a man as well as a sailor and had always been a good friend to me, smuggled a pan of rice into the galley, and told the cook to boil it for me, and not let the " old man " see it. Had it been fine weather, or in port, I should have gone below and lain by until my face got well; but in such weather as this, and shorthanded as we were, it was not for me to desert my post; so I kept on deck, and stood my watch and did my duty as well as I could.

*Monday, July 4.* This was " Independence Day " in Boston. What firing of guns, and ringing of bells, and rejoicings of all sorts, in every part of our country! The ladies (who have not gone down to Nahant for a breath of cool air and sight of the ocean) walking the streets with parasols over their heads, and the dandies in their white pantaloons and silk stockings! What quantities of ice cream have been eaten, and how many loads of ice brought into the city from a distance and sold out by the lump and the pound!

The smallest of the islands which we saw today would have made the fortune of poor Jack, if he had had it in Boston; and I dare say he would have had no objection to being there with it. This, to be sure, was no place to keep the Fourth of July. To keep ourselves warm, and the ship out of the ice, was as much as we could do. Yet no one forgot the day; and many were the wishes and conjectures and comparisons, both serious and ludicrous, which were made among all hands. The sun shone bright as long as it was up, only that a scud of black clouds was ever and anon driving across it. At noon we were in latitude 54° 27′ S., and longitude 85° 5′ W., having made a good deal of easting, but having lost in our latitude by the heading off of the wind. Between daylight we saw thirty-four ice islands of various sizes; some no bigger than the hull of our vessel, and others apparently nearly as large as the one that we first saw.

At 4:00 P.M. (it was then quite dark) all hands were called, and sent aloft, in a violent squall of hail and rain, to take in sail. We had now all got on our " Cape Horn rig," thick boots, southwesters coming down over our necks and ears, thick trousers and jackets, and some with oil-cloth suits over all. Mittens, too, we wore on deck; but it would not do to go aloft with them, as, being wet and stiff, they might let a man slip overboard, for all the hold he could get upon a rope: so we were obliged to work with bare hands, which, as well as our faces, were often cut with the hailstones, which fell thick and large. Our ship was now all cased with ice — hull, spars, and standing rigging; and the running rigging so stiff that we could hardly bend it so as to belay it, or, still less, take a knot with it; and the sails frozen. One at a time (for it was a long piece of work and required many hands) we furled the courses, mizzen topsail, and fore-topmast staysail; and close-reefed the fore and main topsails; and hove the ship to under the fore, with the main hauled up by the clew-lines and buntlines and ready to be sheeted home if we found it necessary to make sail to get the windward of an ice island. A regular lookout was then set, and kept by each night. It blew hard the whole time, and there was an almost constant driving of either rain, hail, or snow. In addition to this, it was " as thick as muck " and the ice was all about us.

The captain was on deck nearly the whole night, and kept the cook in the galley, with a roaring fire, to make coffee for him, which he took every few hours, and once or twice gave a little to his officers; but not a drop of anything was there for the crew. The captain, who sleeps all the daytime and comes and goes at night as he chooses, can have his brandy and water in the cabin, and his hot coffee at the galley; while Jack, who has to stand through everything and work in wet and cold, can have nothing to wet his lips or warm his stomach. This was a " temperance ship," by her articles, and, like too many such ships, the temperance was all in the forecastle. The sailor, who only takes his one glass as it is dealt out to him, is in danger of being drunk; while the captain, upon whose self-possession and cool judgment the lives of all depend, may be trusted with any amount to drink at his will.

But this is not doubling Cape Horn. Eight hours of the night our watch was on deck, and during the whole of that time we kept a bright lookout: one man on each bow, another in the bunt of the foreyard, the third mate on the scuttle, one man on each quarter, and another always standing by the wheel. The chief mate was everywhere, and commanded the ship when the captain was below. When a large piece of ice was seen in our way, or drifting near us, the word was passed along, and the ship's head turned one way and another; and sometimes the yards squared or braced up. There was little else to do than to look out, and we had the sharpest eyes in the ship on the forecastle. The only variety was the monotonous voice of the lookout forward — " Another island! " — " Ice ahead! " — " Ice on the lee bow! " — " Hard up the helm! " — " Keep her off a little! " — " Stead-y! "

In the meantime the wet and cold had brought my face into such a state that I could neither eat nor sleep; and though I stood it out all night, yet, when it became light, I was in such a state that all hands told me I must go below, and lie by for a day or two, or I should be laid up for a long time. When the watch was changed I went into the steerage, and took off my hat and comforter, and showed my face to the mate, who told me to go below at once, and stay in my berth until the swelling went down, and gave the cook orders to make a poultice for me, and said he would speak to the captain.

I went below and turned in, covering myself over with blankets and jackets, and lay in my berth nearly twenty-four hours, half asleep and half awake, stupid from the dull pain.

It was a dreadful night for those on deck. A watch of eighteen hours, with wet and cold and constant anxiety, nearly wore them out; and when they came below at nine o'clock for breakfast, they almost dropped asleep on their chests, and some of them were so stiff that they could with difficulty sit down. Not a drop of anything had been given them during the whole time (though the captain, as on the night that I was on deck, had his coffee every four hours), except that the mate stole a potful of coffee for two men to drink behind the galley, while he kept a lookout for the captain. Every man had his station and was not allowed to leave it; and nothing happened to break the monotony of the night, except once setting the main topsail to run clear of a large island to leeward which they were drifting fast upon. Some of the boys got so sleepy and stupefied that they actually fell asleep at their posts; and the young third mate, Mr. Hatch, whose post was the exposed one of standing on the fore scuttle, was so stiff, when he was relieved, that he could not bend his knees to get down. By a constant lookout and a quick shifting of the helm, as the islands and pieces came in sight, the ship went clear of everything but a few small pieces, though daylight showed the ocean covered for miles.

At daybreak it fell a dead calm; and with the sun the fog cleared a little and a breeze sprung up from the westward, which soon grew into a gale. We had now a fair wind, daylight, and comparatively clear weather; yet, to the surprise of everyone, the ship continued hove-to. " Why does not he run? " " What is the captain about? " was asked by everyone; and from questions it soon grew into complaints and murmurings. When the daylight was so short, it was too bad to lose it, and a fair wind, too, which everyone had been praying for. As hour followed hour, and the captain showed no sign of making sail, the crew became impatient, and there was a good deal of talking and consultation together on the forecastle.

They had been beaten out with the exposure and hardship, and impatient to get out of it; and this unaccountable delay was more than they could bear in quietness, in their excited and restless state. Some said the captain was frightened — completely cowed by the dangers and difficulties that surrounded us, and was afraid to make sail — while others said that in his anxiety and suspense he had made a free use of brandy and opium, and was unfit for his duty.

The carpenter, who was an intelligent man, and a thorough seaman, and had great influence with the crew, came down into the forecastle and tried to induce them to go aft and ask the captain why he did not run, or request him, in the name of all hands, to make sail. This appeared to be a very reasonable request, and the crew agreed that if he did not make sail before noon they would go aft. Noon came, and no sail was made. A consultation was held again; and it was proposed to take the ship from the captain and give the command of her to the mate, who had been heard to say that if he could have his way the ship would have been half the distance to the cape before night — ice or no ice. And so irritated and impatient had the crew become that even this proposition, which was open mutiny, was entertained; and the carpenter went to his berth, leaving it tacitly understood that something serious would be done if things remained as they were many hours longer. When the carpenter left, we talked it all over and I gave my advice strongly against it. Another of the men, too, who had known something of the kind attempted in another ship by a crew who were dissatisfied with their captain, and which was followed with serious consequences, was opposed to it. Stimson, who soon came down, joined us, and we determined to have nothing to do with it. By these means the crew were soon induced to give it up for the present, though they said they would not lie where they were much longer without knowing the reason.

I still remained in my berth, fast recovering, yet not well enough to go safely on deck. And I should have been perfectly useless; for, from having eaten nothing for nearly a week, except a little rice which I forced into my mouth the last day or two, I was as weak as an infant. To be sick in a forecastle is miserable indeed. It is the worst part of a dog's life, especially in bad weather. The forecastle, shut up tight to keep out the water and cold air; the watch either on deck or asleep in their berths; no one to speak to; the pale light of the single lamp, swinging to and fro from the beam, so dim that one can scarcely see, much less read, by it; the water dropping from the beams and carlines and running down the sides, and the forecastle so wet and dark and cheerless, and so lumbered up with chests and wet clothes, that sitting up is worse than lying in the berth. These are some of the evils. Fortunately I needed no help from anyone, and no medicine; and if I had needed help, I don't know where I should have found it. Sailors are willing enough; but it is true, as is often said, no one ships for nurse on board a vessel. Our merchant ships are always undermanned; and if one man is lost by sickness, they cannot spare another to take care of him. A sailor is always presumed to be well, and if he's sick he's a poor dog. One has to stand his wheel, and another his lookout; and the sooner he gets on deck again the better.

Accordingly, as soon as I could possibly go back to my duty, I put on my thick clothes and boots and southwester and made my appearance on deck. I had been but a few days below, yet everything looked strangely enough. The ship was cased in ice — decks, sides, masts, yards, and rigging. Two close-reefed topsails were all the sail she had on, and every sail and rope was frozen so stiff in its place that it seemed as though it would be impossible to start anything. Reduced, too, to her topmasts, she had altogether a most forlorn and crippled appearance. The sun had come up brightly; the snow was swept off the decks and ashes thrown upon them so that we could walk, for they had been as slippery as glass. It was, of course, too cold to carry on any ship's work, and we had only to walk the deck and keep ourselves warm. The wind was still ahead, and the whole ocean, to the eastward, covered with islands and field ice.

At four bells the order was given to square away the yards, and the man who came from the helm said that the captain had kept her off to N.N.E. What could this mean? The wildest rumors got adrift. Some said that he was going to run out of the ice and cross the Pacific, and go home round the Cape of Good Hope. Soon, however, it leaked out, and we found that we were running for the Straits of Magellan. The news soon spread through the ship, and all tongues were at work talking about it. No one on board had been through the straits; but I had in my chest an account of the passage of the ship *A. J. Donelson,* of New York, through those straits a few years before. The account was given by the captain, and the representation was as favorable as possible. It was soon read by everyone on board, and various opinions pronounced. The determination of our captain had at least this good effect: it gave us something to think and talk about, made a break in our life, and diverted our minds from the monotonous dreariness of the prospect before us. Having made a fair wind of it, we were going off at a good rate and leaving the thickest of the ice behind us. This, at least, was something.

Having been long enough below to get my hands well warmed and softened, the first handling of the ropes was rather tough; but a few days hardened them. And as soon as I got my mouth open wide enough to take in a piece of salt beef and hard bread, I was all right again.

## Suggestions for Study

1. What evidence does Dana cite to prove that the distinction between captain and crew was exaggerated and unfair? Do you think this captain was worse than most?

2. What details does Dana give that make you feel keenly the bitter cold in which the sailors worked? What part did the sailors' hatred of the cold play in the drama aboard ship?

What recollections of life at home intensify the unhappy situation of the sailors?

3. Some people feel that the romance of ships died when the sailing vessels gave way to steamships. Then the sailors did the heavy work; now the stokers do it. Had you rather be a sailor, even in the winter near Cape Horn, than a stoker on a modern steamship? Judging by your own answer, what kind of a pioneer would you have made?

4. For more information about the actual life of a sailor, read further in *Two Years before the Mast*. For a masterly story of whaling at about the same time, read Herman Melville's *Moby Dick* — the other great American classic of the sea in the days of the sailing vessels.

5. Vocabulary: topsail, galley, hull, spars, belay, rigging, furled, hove-to, leeward.

## Artemus[1] Ward    1834–1867

### A BUSINESS LETTER

Close behind the advancing trappers and traders came the horde of settlers building up pioneer communities. The frontier, not the East, was the major concern of these settlements, and when they set up their newspapers, the West had a voice. The columnists who were most popular, far from echoing the seaboard journals, made capital of the crude vernacular of the frontier. Many wrote in dialect. Artemus Ward (as Charles Farrar Browne signed his column), one of the most widely popular, went further and used outrageous misspelling as an additional source of fun. The audience he addressed was not in the parlors of Boston but in the circle sitting on crackerboxes around the stove in country stores. The group of humorists he represents is called "The Crackerbox Philosophers." They deserve the full title, for along with fun, they served up shrewd observation on their communities. You can see the Yankee keenness on getting on in the world in this advance letter. The "moral show" was all a fiction which Ward carried on in his column in the Cleveland *Plain Dealer*.

[1] **Artemus** (är′tĕ-mŭs).

To the Editor of the —

Sir. — I'm movin' along — slowly along — down tords your place. My show at present consists of three moral Bares, a Kangaroo (a amoozin little Raskal — 'twould make you larf yerself to deth to see the little cuss jump up and squeal), wax figgers of G. Washington, Gen. Taylor, John Bunyan, Capt. Kidd, and Dr. Webster in the act of killin' Dr. Parkman, besides several miscellanyus moral wax statoots of celebrated piruts & murderers, &c., ekalled by few & exceld by none. Now, Mr. Editor, scratch orf a few lines sayin' how is the show bizness down to your place. I shall have my hanbills dun at your offiss. Depend upon it. I want you should git my hanbills up in flamin' stile. Also, git up a tremenjus excitement in yr. paper 'bowt my onparaleld Show. We must fetch the public somhow. We must wurk on their feelins. Cum the moral on 'em strong. If it's a temperance community, tell 'em I sined the pledge fifteen minutes arter Ise born, but on the contery, ef your peple take their tods, say Mister Ward is as Jenial a feller as we ever met, full of conwivIality, & the life an sole of the Soshul Bored. Take, don't you? If you say anythin' abowt my show, say my snaiks is as harmliss as the newborn Babe. What a interestin' study it is to see a zewolOgical animil like a snaik under perfeck subjection! My Kangaroo is the most larfable little cuss I ever saw. All for 15 cents. I am anxyus to skewer your infloounce. I repeet in regard to them hanbills, that I shall git 'em struck orf up to your printin' offiss. My perliteral sentiments agree with yourn exactly. I know thay do, becawz I never saw a man whoos didn't.

Respectively yures,

A. Ward.

P.S. — You scratch my back & Ile scratch your back.

## Suggestions for Study

1. In what way is this letter a satire on advertising? On the intelligence of the public?

2. How does the spelling add to the humor-

ous effect? What words are so spelled as to convey a backwoods pronunciation?

3. What in this letter do you think would especially appeal to Abraham Lincoln?

## 2. THE WAR BETWEEN THE STATES

Not much of the literature we read today came out of the years between 1861 and 1865 when the eyes of the world turned away from the rushing frontier to the battlefields where the Northern and Southern states settled an old problem. Not much great literature is ever written in the midst of a war. But the War between the States has entered into our feeling and thinking, and become a part of our heritage, in a way that few other events have. It has been the subject of many books and poems since 1865, and in a sense it has gone into every book written in America since then, because it has become a part of every American. Therefore, let us remind ourselves what happened.

WHY DID THEY FIGHT?

Now it seems inevitable. As we read back over the newspapers and the records, it seems to us that the war drums were beating for decades before the guns began to shoot; in fact, that the die was cast for war from the first year when the Northern and Southern colonies began to develop in different directions. But never was a war undertaken with less willingness or with heavier hearts. This was a war between states that had fought side by side for independence. This was brother against brother.

Many Northerners believed sincerely that slavery was morally wrong and degrading, and were infuriated that " the land of the free " should also be the land of slavery. Many Southerners believed just as sincerely that slavery was necessary to the best way of life; they pointed to the achievements of Greece when Athens had four slaves to every freeman; and they were infuriated at the thought that Northerners should set themselves up as judges over the South.

But the issue was older and deeper than that. From the first, the South had developed into a country of broad plantations owned by a leisurely, cultivated aristocracy. There were few factories, few large cities. The country lived on what it grew and the cotton it sent abroad for sale. The North, on the other hand, early developed cities, manufacturing centers, financiers. Its agriculture was in farms, rather than plantations; the owner and his family tilled the farm; and the hired workers, if any, sat at the family table and were called " help." These two sections naturally came to feel differently about political questions and to have different needs. The North wanted a strong central government and a high tariff to protect its manufactures and its wage scale; the South preferred a localized government, and a low tariff which would encourage trade and make the most of its cheap labor.

But it was the West that really pushed the older sections into war. We have come to see now that the War between the States was really one chapter in the settling of the West. Both sections needed the wealth of the West. The North did not want the slave lands extended. The South felt it should not be excluded from a part of the continent it had helped to gain. When the South talked secession, the northern Mississippi states talked union because they did not want customhouses blocking their outlet to the Gulf of Mexico. The statesmen of the East arranged compromise after compromise — one slave state for one free state, one free state for one slave state. But the situation grew more and more explosive. Some of the Western states began to take things into their own hands — Kansas with John Brown, for example, and California, which announced calmly that it was going to be a free state regardless of what anybody else said. It became apparent, as Lincoln said, that " The union cannot permanently exist half slave and half free." The election of 1860 laid the fire, and the attack on Sumter supplied the spark. The South seceded, and the North went to war.

THE BATTLE OF GETTYSBURG (with Cemetery Hill, right background). This was the turning point in the struggle between the Northern and Confederate armies — one of the decisive battles of history. (Brown Brothers)

They were finally fighting over the right to secede, rather than over slavery. We realize now that slavery was like a wolf which the South held by the ears, and could neither hold indefinitely nor let go. We realize also that emancipation did not solve the racial problem underlying slavery, and that emancipation and the war together ruined the South and kept it poor for decades. Some men in 1860 and 1861 were merely hotheaded. Others, like Lincoln, saw the gravity of the problem and foresaw some of the results. They went to war sadly and with foreboding.

### THE WAR AND ITS LITERATURE

The fight was not even. The North had two and one half times as many people. New York State alone manufactured twice as much as the whole South. The North could make its own materials of war; the South had to import its guns and ammunition through the Northern blockade. The North had a lion's share of the wealth, and most of the railroads.

On the other hand, the South had a fighting tradition and some great generals like Robert E. Lee and Stonewall Jackson. The South could fight a defensive war, because it was fighting merely for the right to live its own life, not for conquest. It could fight on its own land and near its own supplies. But there was too much weight on the other side.

The capitals of the two sections were less than one hundred miles apart, and for four years the tide of battle moved back and forth in that hundred miles, now threatening Washington, now Richmond. The North had the larger army, but the South had Lee and Jackson. If it had not been for two other theaters of battle, the war would have been a stalemate, equivalent to a Southern victory.

The first of these theaters was the sea. The North had the federal navy. The South put together what it could, including the first armored ship, the *Merrimac.* But the North developed its own ironclad, the *Monitor,* and soon clamped a starving blockade on the Atlantic coast. Farragut sailed into the mouth of the Mississippi and captured the South's greatest city, New Orleans. Later he took Mobile, and the South was cut off from European aid.

But the West was the decisive theater. The West developed a general capable of using the great material advantages of the North. He was U. S. Grant, less brilliant and imaginative than Lee, but tenacious as a bulldog. " I can't spare this man," said Lincoln. " He fights! " Under Grant the Northern armies cleared the Mississippi, cut off the South from the rich lands of Texas and Arkansas, started Sherman on his trail of burned farmhouses and pillaged stores from Chattanooga to the Georgia seacoast. When Lee saw what was happening in the West, he made one supreme effort to take Washington and end the stalemate. That was in the summer of 1863. He pushed into Pennsylvania as far as Gettysburg, and for two days the issue of the war hung in the balance. But the Northern troops were too strongly entrenched. Lee ordered one final charge. Pickett's men moved across a mile of open ground through a rain of cannonballs. A few of the men reached the Northern lines on the next hill, and for a brief moment the stars and bars waved above the Northern ramparts. Then the flag fell, the few survivors staggered back, and the cause of the Confederacy was lost. Lee retreated into Virginia. The Northern army was too shattered to follow. But almost exactly at the same time, Grant captured Vicksburg, and we know now that the war was decided on that day.

Sherman marched to the sea. Sheridan put the torch to the fertile Shenandoah valley so ruthlessly that " a crow flying over would have to carry his own rations." Lee kept Grant away from Richmond as long as he could, fighting gallantly and brilliantly, losing fewer men than the Northerners, maneuvering his tired little force until it seemed three times as big as it was.

But the end could not be postponed indefinitely. Lee surrendered at Appomattox in 1865.

No chapter in our national history has so wrung our hearts, so deeply moved and stirred us. And yet there was surprisingly little important literature written about the war until much later. There were some great songs, like " The Battle Hymn of the Republic." A little later there were fine poems, like Lowell's " Commemoration Ode," Timrod's " Ode," and Father Ryan's poem " The Conquered Banner." But great chapters of history do not make great books until later; they make great men!

*The War between the States (1861–65) came, on the average, about two thirds through the careers of Emerson, Longfellow, Lowell, Whittier, and Holmes. Poe and Irving were already dead. Thoreau and Hawthorne died during the war. Whitman had just begun his career. Mark Twain had not yet published.*

## TWO GREAT AMERICANS

The War between the States gave us at least two men who are among our greatest.

One of them was a soldier, born of a soldier's family, father of soldiers. When the war began, he was offered the command of the Northern army, but he stayed with his state and his South. He was more than a general; he was a great leader. He represented all the chivalry of the South, all the daring and bravery and resourcefulness that Europe had learned to expect of Americans, all the humanity and regard for his men that might be expected of any greathearted Christian gentleman. He was not a great writer, but when the time came to admit that the war was lost and say farewell to his troops he said it with a restrained dignity that hid heartbreak, signed " Robert E. Lee " in firm letters, and turned all his energies to helping the Southern states return to the American family of states, bury their bitterness, and look ahead, not back. That last order to the Army of Northern Virginia is reprinted in this book, and with it

Culver

a later historian's account of General Lee. Historians have disagreed on some of the details, but they have agreed that he was one of the greatest of Americans, one of the finest products of the civilization that made Washington and Jefferson.

The other man of the war was the product of a different civilization, and important to us not only because of his greatness but because he represents a new kind of American and a new America. He was a Westerner, and could have come from no other part of the country. He had been a poor boy and a rail-splitter and he had lived on the frontier. He was lean and awkward, ill at ease with a teacup or small talk. His second Secretary of War called him a " gorilla," although later the Secretary changed his mind and said that the President was the greatest and kindest of leaders. He had been a lawyer in the back country, and had a way of saying things shrewdly, briefly, and cutting right to the point. He had an exuberant sense of humor, although he was a sad man, and he loved to drive home a point with a story. In the tensest moments of the war he could read a Western humorist and chuckle and relax from stress that would have killed a softer man. He was warmhearted and kindly, but tough — in doing what he believed in. He was practical and earthy and homespun, and yet could write sentences that shouted and sang. He was the first great American out of the West. And as the Yankee Franklin was the typical American of the eighteenth century, and Ralph Waldo Emerson of Concord was the greatest thinker of the Eastern Flowering, so Abraham Lincoln stood forth to all the world as the man of this new America that was growing behind the frontier.

He was a great writer as well as a great man. Or perhaps it was that the greatness of the man transferred itself to many of the speeches, state papers, letters he wrote. Some of them are in this book: his solemn, modest farewell to his home-town friends when he left to be inaugurated as President; his masterly constructive rebuke to General Hooker; his letter of sympathy to the woman who had given her sons in battle; his address at Gettysburg which was so short that almost nobody who heard it realized he had heard one of the great masterpieces of all oratory; and his second inaugural address, looking forward to the tasks of reuniting the country, which an assassin's bullet kept him from undertaking. In another section of the book you will find Carl Sandburg's description of the dedication ceremonies at Gettysburg, during which Lincoln gave his brief but thrilling speech.

In Lincoln the West flowered as the seaboard had flowered in Franklin, Washington, Jefferson, and Lee. But the time of literary flowering of the West, corresponding to the literary flowering of the seaboard, was yet to come.

*Abraham Lincoln was born (1809) in the same year as Poe, and just after Emerson, Hawthorne, and Longfellow. He was killed (1865) one year after Hawthorne's death, seventeen years before Emerson and Longfellow died.*

*When Lincoln was born, Jefferson was still President, the country was about 1,700,000 square miles in area, and had seventeen states. When he died, the area was over three million square miles, and the states numbered thirty-six.*

# Negro Spirituals

Out of the dark days of his slavery, the Negro wrought one of the richest groups of songs in all American music. Into his religious songs he poured his troubles in this world and his hope for happiness in the next. The mellow harmonies and the moving sincerity of his spirituals have won them a high place in popular favor and in the repertory of great concert singers. You can best appreciate the great beauty of these songs by listening to recordings such as Marian Anderson's. But you can make them most real by imagining, as you read, the slaves picking cotton in the fields, or loading the heavy bales on barges, with one rich voice singing out the varying lines and the whole company coming in on the repeated ones. Then you will understand why Moses was a favorite hero, and why the troubles of this life, "this heavy load," come into the songs so often.

## LET MY PEOPLE GO!

When Is-rael was in E-gypt's land Let my peo-ple go, Oppressed so hard they could not stand, Let my peo-ple go.

Go down Mos-es, 'Way down in E-gypt's land,—— Tell ole— Pha - - raoh, To let my peo-ple go. O let my peo-ple go.——

2. "When spoke the Lord," bold Moses said,
   "Let my people go!
   If not I'll smite your first-born dead;
   Let my people go!"

3. No more shall they in bondage toil,
   Let my people go!
   Let them come out with Egypt's spoil,
   Let my people go!

## NOBODY KNOWS DE TROUBLE I SEE

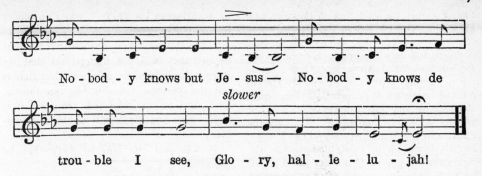

No - bod - y knows but Je - sus — No - bod - y knows de

*slower*

trou - ble I see, Glo - ry, hal - le - lu - jah!

(Both of these spirituals have additional stanzas.)

## Suggestions for Study

1. Do you know other spirituals that are mournful recitations of the troubles of this world? Why was the story of Joshua bringing down the walls of Jericho a favorite with the Negroes?

2. What is the theme of most of the spirituals that have a more hopeful mood? " Deep River " and " Swing Low, Sweet Chariot " can give you a clue.

## Robert E. Lee      1807–1870

### FAREWELL TO HIS ARMY

HEADQUARTERS ARMY OF NORTHERN VIRGINIA (APRIL 10, 1865)

The military leader of the South was not a literary man. We have little from his pen except letters. In his military papers, however, we have brief passages even more valuable for revealing glimpses of the man than for their historical importance. Here is his last order to his defeated but passionately loyal troops. One of his greatest assets was the capacity for arousing the utmost devotion of the soldiers who served under him. Can you sense, as you read, the personal qualities that inspired such devotion?

After four years of arduous service marked by unsurpassed courage and fortitude, the Army of Northern Virginia has been compelled to yield to overwhelming numbers and resources.

I need not tell the survivors of so many hard-fought battles who have remained steadfast to the last that I have consented to this result from no distrust of them; but feeling that valor and devotion could accomplish nothing that would compensate for the loss that must have attended the continuance of the contest, I determined to avoid the useless sacrifice of those whose past services have endeared them to their countrymen. By the terms of the agreement, officers and men can return to their homes and remain until exchanged.

You may take with you the satisfaction that proceeds from the consciousness of duty faithfully performed, and I earnestly pray that a merciful God will extend to you His blessing and protection.

With an unceasing admiration of your constancy and devotion to your country, and a grateful remembrance of your kind and generous consideration of myself, I bid you all an affectionate farewell.

R. E. LEE, *General*

## Thomas Nelson Page      1853–1922

### LEE IN DEFEAT

It is typical of Lee that, to learn to know him, we must turn to others. His modesty never permitted him to set down any record of the most outstanding fact of his life: the great admiration and devotion that surrounded him. For that we must turn to the men who knew him. Thomas Nelson Page, from whose *Robert E. Lee, Man and Soldier,* this account is taken, was only a lad of twelve years when Lee surrendered at Appomattox, but he grew up in Virginia, where Lee was widely known, and he attended Washington College (now Washington and Lee University) when Lee was its president. You will feel not only the reaction of troops and populace to Lee in 1865, but also some of the great admiration of the writer for his subject. This is not just a record of happenings but a sample of an attitude that spread in widening circles to establish such a place for Lee among his country's great that his statue stands today in the Capitol at Washington — in Confederate uniform.

And now, having endeavored to picture Lee during those glorious campaigns which must, to the future student of military skill, place him among the first captains of history, I shall not invite attention further to Lee the soldier — to Lee the strategist — to Lee the victorious, but to a greater Lee — to Lee the defeated.

As glorious as were these campaigns, it is on the last act of the drama — the retreat from Petersburg, the surrender at Appomattox, and the dark period that followed that surrender — that we must look to see him at his best. His every act, his every word, showed how completely he had surrendered himself to Duty, and with what implicit obedience he followed the command of that " stern daughter of the voice of God."

" Are you sanguine of the result of the war? " asked Bishop Wilmer of him in the closing days of the struggle. His reply was:

" At present I am not concerned with results. God's will ought to be our aim, and I am quite contented that His designs should be accomplished and not mine."

On that last morning when his handful of worn and starving veterans had made their last charge, to find themselves shut in by ranks of serried steel, hemmed in by Grant's entire army, he faced the decree of Fate with as much constancy as though that decree were success, not doom.

" What will history say of the surrender of an army in the field? " asked an officer of his staff in passionate grief.

" Yes, I know they will say hard things of us; they will not understand that we were overwhelmed by numbers; but that is not the question, colonel. The question is, is it right to surrender this army? If it is right, then I will take all of the responsibility."

It was ever the note of duty that he sounded.

" You will take with you," he said to his army in his farewell address, " the satisfaction that proceeds from the consciousness of duty faithfully performed."

" We are conscious that we have humbly tried to do our duty," he said, a year or more after the war, when the clouds hung heavy over the South; " we may, therefore, with calm satisfaction trust in God and leave results to Him."

The sun which has shone in the morning, but has become obscured by clouds in the afternoon, sometimes breaks forth and at its setting shines with a greater splendor than it knew even at high noon.

So here. Sheathing his stainless sword, surrendering in the field the remnant of an army that had once been the most redoubtable body of fighting men of the century, the greatest captain, the noblest gentleman of our time, expecting to slip into the darkness of oblivion, suddenly stepped forth from the gloom of defeat into the splendor of perpetual fame.

I love to think of Grant as he appeared that April day at Appomattox: the simple soldier, the strenuous fighter who, though thrashed, was always ready to fight again; who now, though he had achieved the prize for which he had fought so hard and had paid so dearly, was so modest and so unassuming that but for his shoulder straps and that yet better mark of rank, his generosity, he might not have been known as the victor. Southerners generally have long forgiven Grant all else for the magnanimity that he showed that day to Lee. By his orders no salutes of joy were fired, no public marks of exultation over his fallen foe were

THE SURRENDER AT APPOMATOX, from a painting by Chappel showing General Grant and General Lee and their aides. (Culver)

allowed. History contains no finer example of greatness. Not Alexander in his generous youth excelled him.

Yet, it is not more to the victor that Posterity will turn her gaze than to the vanquished, her admiration at the glory of the conqueror well-nigh lost in amazement at the dignity of the conquered.

Men who saw the defeated general when he came forth from the chamber where he had signed the articles of capitulation saw that he paused a moment as his eyes rested once more on the Virginia hills, smote his hands together as though in some excess of inward agony, then mounted his gray horse, Traveler, and rode calmly away.

If that was the very Gethsemane of his trials, yet he must have had then one moment of supreme, if chastened, joy. As he rode quietly down the lane leading from the scene of capitulation, he passed into view of his men — of such as remained of them. The news of the surrender had got abroad and they were waiting, griefstricken and dejected, upon the hillsides, when they caught sight of their old commander on the gray horse. Then occurred one of the most notable scenes in the history of war. In an instant they were about him, bareheaded, with tear-wet faces; thronging him, kissing his hand, his boots, his saddle; weeping; cheering him amid their tears; shouting his name to the very skies. He said, " Men, we have fought through the war together. I have done my best for you. My heart is too full to say more."

The cheers were heard afar off over the hills where the victorious army lay encamped, and awakened some anxiety. It was a sound they well knew:

The voice once heard through Shiloh's woods,
　And Chickamauga's solitudes,
The fierce South cheering on her sons.

It was reported in some of the Northern papers that it was the sound of jubilation at the surrender. But it was not. It was the voice of jubilation, yet not for surrender, but for the captain who had surrendered their muskets but was still the commander of their hearts.

This is Lee's final victory and the highest tribute to the South: that the devotion of the South to him was greater in the hour of defeat than in that of victory. It is said that Napoleon was adored by the men of France, but hated by the women. It was not so with Lee. No victor ever came home to receive more signal evidences of devotion than this defeated general.

Richmond was in mourning. Since the Union army had entered her gates, every house had been closed as though it were the house of death. One afternoon, a few days after the surrender, Lee, on his gray horse, Traveler, attended by two or three officers, crossed the James and rode quietly up the street to his home on Franklin Street, where he dismounted. That evening it was noised abroad that General Lee had arrived; he had been seen to enter his house. Next morning the houses were open as usual; life began to flow in its accustomed channels. Those who were there have said that when General Lee returned they felt as safe as if he had had his whole army at his back.

His first recorded words on his arrival were a tribute to his successful opponent. " General Grant has acted with magnanimity," he said to some who spoke of the victor with bitterness. It was the keynote to his afterlife.

Indeed, from this record a few facts stand forth beyond all others: Lee's nobility and genius; the fortitude of the Southern people; Grant's resolution and magnanimity; and the infinite valor of the American soldier.

Over forty years have gone by since that day in April when Lee, to avoid further useless sacrifice of life, surrendered himself and all that remained of the Army of Northern Virginia and gave his *parole*

*d'honneur* [1] to bear arms no more against the United States. To him, who with prescient mind had long borne in his bosom knowledge of the exhausted resources of the Confederacy, and had seen his redoubtable army, under the " policy of attrition," dwindle away to a mere ghost of its former self, it might well appear that he had failed, and, if he ever thought of his personal reputation, that he had lost the soldier's dearest prize; that Fame had turned her back and Fate usurped her place. Thenceforth he who had been the leader of armies, whose glorious achievements had filled the world, who had been the prop of a highhearted nation's hope, was to walk the narrow byway of private life, defeated, impoverished, and possibly misunderstood.

But to us who have survived for the space of more than a generation, how different it appears. We know that Time, the redresser of wrongs, is steadily righting the act of unkind Fate; and Fame, firmly established in her high seat, is ever replacing a richer laurel on his brow.

Yea, ride away, thou defeated general! Ride through the broken fragments of thy shattered army, ride through thy warwasted land, amid thy desolate and stricken people. But know that thou art riding on Fame's highest way:

This day shall see
Thy head wear sunlight and thy feet touch
  stars.

## Suggestions for Study

1. Consideration for others is said to be the distinguishing mark of a gentleman. How does Lee's farewell to his troops show this trait? For whom does he show concern in this order? What false impressions does he particularly try to forestall? Pick out phrases in which he commends the record of his troops. What is the only expression of personal feeling?

2. Do you think it was respect for the South or for Lee that moved Grant to his generous attitude at the meeting for surrender? How did Lee prove his gratitude?

[1] **parole d'honneur** (pȧ-rôl′ d'ŏn-ûr′): word of honor.

3. One element of Lee's leadership was his ability to remain calm and dignified in times of stress. What evidence do you find of this quality? What is the one sign Page records of the feeling beneath the calm?

4. One writer has said that the fact that Lee has become a national rather than a Confederate hero is an even greater compliment to the spirit of the American people than to Lee. Do you agree?

5. Vocabulary: implicit, sanguine, serried, redoubtable, magnanimity, prescient, redresser.

# Abraham Lincoln 1809–1865

It would be difficult to imagine a greater contrast in background than we find between Lee and Lincoln. Lee grew up in the cultured setting of a Virginia plantation, won honors at West Point, and went into an assured military career. Lincoln grew up in the backwoods, struggled to educate himself by the light from an open fireplace, and knew hard days in the beginning of his law practice in Illinois. Both received the highest confidence and honor, first of their own sections and finally of the whole nation. It takes both these men to represent the America of their day. It was Lincoln who set down in simple words the truest statement America has of the trials and griefs and triumphant faiths of the time. These brief selections from his writings show his gift for speaking simply, honestly, and yet with the profound wisdom and nobility of a truly great nature.

## FAREWELL AT SPRINGFIELD

When Lincoln left Springfield, Illinois, in 1861, to take up his duties as President in Washington, he seemed to realize that Fate might never let him return. The scene of his departure has been vividly described by Carl Sandburg in his *Abraham Lincoln: the Prairie Years:* " A cold drizzle of rain was falling on the morning of February 11 when Lincoln and his party of fifteen were to leave Springfield on the eight-o'clock at the Great Western Railway station. Chilly gray mist hung the circle of the prairie horizon. A short little locomotive with a flat-topped smokestack stood puffing with a baggage car and special passenger car hitched on; a railroad president and superintendent were on board. A thousand people crowded in and around the brick station, inside of which Lincoln was standing, and one by one came hundreds of old friends, shaking hands, wishing him luck and Godspeed, all faces solemn. Even Judge David Davis, weighing 350 pounds, wearing a new white silk hat, was a serious figure.

" A path was made for Lincoln from the station to his car; hands stretched out for one last handshake. He hadn't intended to make a speech; but on the platform of the car, as he turned and saw his home people, he took off his hat, stood perfectly still, and looked almost as he had at the Bowling Green burial services when tears had to take the place of words. He raised a hand for silence. They stood with hats off. Then he said slowly, amid the soft gray drizzle from the sky:

" Friends, no one who has never been placed in a like position can understand my feelings at this hour nor the impressive sadness I feel at this parting. For more than a quarter of a century I have lived among you, and during all that time I have received nothing but kindness at your hands. Here I have lived from my youth till now I am an old man. Here the most sacred trusts of earth were assumed; here all my children were born and one of them lies buried. To you, dear friends, I owe all that I have, all that I am. All the strange checkered past seems to crowd now upon my mind. Today I leave you; I go to assume a task more difficult than that which devolved upon General Washington. Unless the great God who assisted him shall be with and aid me, I must fail. But if the same omniscient mind and the same Almighty arm that directed and protected him shall guide and support me, I shall not fail; I shall succeed. Let us all pray that the God of our fathers may not forsake us now. To Him I commend you all. Permit me to ask that with equal sincerity and faith you will all invoke His wisdom and guidance for me. With these few words I must leave you — for how long I know not. Friends, one and all, I must now bid you an affectionate farewell."

Mr. Sandburg continues:

"Bells rang, there was a grinding of wheels, and the train moved and carried Lincoln away from Springfield. The tears were not yet dry on some faces when the train had faded into the gray to the east.

"Some of the crowd said afterward that Lincoln, too, was in tears, that tears ran down his face as he spoke that morning.

"And one of the crowd said there were no tears on Lincoln's face. 'But he had a face with dry tears,' said this one. 'He was a man who often had dry tears.'"

## LETTER TO
## GENERAL JOSEPH HOOKER

During 1862 the Northern army had suffered several defeats and Lincoln had had to remove both General McClellan and General Burnside. The man that he put in command of the Army of the Potomac over the protests of Secretary Stanton and General Halleck was General Joseph Hooker, who had served under both of his predecessors and had criticized both with great frankness. The day after the appointment Lincoln sent General Hooker this remarkable letter, which shows his directness, fearlessness, and understanding of men. It administers a rebuke at the same time that it shows confidence and encouragement.

I have placed you at the head of the Army of the Potomac. Of course I have done this upon what appear to me to be sufficient reasons, and yet I think it best for you to know that there are some things in regard to which I am not quite satisfied with you. I believe you to be a brave and skillful soldier, which, of course, I like. I also believe you do not mix politics with your profession, in which you are right. You have confidence in yourself, which is a valuable, if not an indispensable, quality. You are ambitious, which, within reasonable bounds, does good rather than harm; but I think that during General Burnside's command of the army you have taken counsel of your ambition, and thwarted him as much as you could, in which you did a great wrong to the country and to a most meritorious and honorable brother officer. I have heard, in

such way as to believe it, of your recently saying that both the army and the government needed a dictator. Of course it was not for this, but in spite of it, that I have given you the command. Only those generals who gain successes can set up dictatorships. What I now ask of you is military success, and I will risk the dictatorship. The government will support you to the utmost of its ability, which is neither more nor less than it has done and will do for all commanders. I much fear that the spirit which you have aided to infuse into the army, of criticizing their commander and withholding confidence from him, will now turn upon you. I shall assist you as far as I can to put it down. Neither you nor Napoleon, if he were alive again, could get any good out of an army while such a spirit prevails in it. And now, beware of rashness, but with energy and sleepless vigilance go forward and give us victories.

## LETTER TO MRS. BIXBY

It is characteristic of Lincoln that he found time amid his care and heavy responsibility to write this personal letter to a mother mourning her sons lost for the cause of the Union. Characteristic, too, is the fact that he expressed in the letter feelings many people had experienced but few had found words for.

I have been shown in the files of the War Department a statement of the Adjutant-General of Massachusetts that you are the mother of five sons who have died gloriously on the field of battle. I feel how weak and fruitless must be any words of mine which should attempt to beguile you from the grief of a loss so overwhelming. But I cannot refrain from tendering to you the consolation that may be found in the thanks of the Republic they died to save. I pray that our heavenly Father may assuage the anguish of your bereavement, and leave you only the cherished memory of the loved and lost, and the solemn pride that must be yours to have laid so costly a sacrifice upon the altar of freedom.

**THE GRAVES OF THE DEAD AT GETTYSBURG,** eternally commemorated by Lincoln's brief address. (Brown Brothers)

## GETTYSBURG ADDRESS

Carl Sandburg has given you a full account (page 254) of the circumstances under which this brief address was first given. You read it then to place it in its original setting. Read it now to fill in your understanding of the man and his way of thinking.

Four score and seven years ago our fathers brought forth on this continent a new nation, conceived in liberty, and dedicated to the proposition that all men are created equal.

Now we are engaged in a great civil war, testing whether that nation, or any nation so conceived and so dedicated, can long endure. We are met on a great battlefield of that war. We have come to dedicate a portion of that field as a final resting place for those who here gave their lives that that nation might live. It is altogether fitting and proper that we should do this.

But in a larger sense we cannot dedicate, we cannot consecrate, we cannot hallow this ground. The brave men, living and dead, who struggled here have consecrated it far above our poor power to add or detract. The world will little note nor long remember what we say here, but it can never forget what they did here. It is for us, the living, rather, to be dedicated here to the unfinished work which they who fought here have thus far so nobly advanced. It is rather for us to be here dedicated to the great task remaining before us — that from these honored dead we take increased devotion to that cause for which they gave the last full measure of devotion; that we here highly resolve that these dead shall not have died in vain; that this nation, under God, shall have a new birth of freedom; and that government of the people, by the people, and for the people, shall not perish from the earth.

## SECOND INAUGURAL ADDRESS

### MARCH 4, 1865

The morning of Lincoln's second inauguration was cold and stormy, but at noon the sun came out as the procession moved with dignity from the White House. Numbers of wounded soldiers were conspicuous in the great throng. The following comment upon the address was made by the London *Spectator* after the President's death: " We cannot read it without a renewed conviction that it is the noblest political document known to history, and should have for the nation and the statesmen he left behind him something of a sacred and almost prophetic character." This speech and the " Gettysburg Address " are inscribed on opposite walls of the beautiful Lincoln Memorial at Washington.

FELLOW COUNTRYMEN: At this second appearing to take the oath of the presidential office, there is less occasion for an extended address than there was at the first. Then a statement, somewhat in detail, of a course to be pursued, seemed fitting and proper. Now, at the expiration of four years, during which public declarations have been constantly called forth on every point and phase of the great contest which still absorbs the attention and engrosses the energies of the nation, little that is new could be presented. The progress of our arms, upon which all else chiefly depends, is as well known to the public as to myself; and it is, I trust, reasonably satisfactory and encouraging to all. With high hope for the future, no prediction in regard to it is ventured.

On the occasion corresponding to this four years ago, all thoughts were anxiously directed to an impending civil war. All dreaded it — all sought to avert it. While the inaugural address was being delivered from this place, devoted altogether to saving the Union without war, insurgent agents were in the city seeking to destroy it without war — seeking to dissolve the Union, and divide effects, by negotiation. Both parties deprecated war; but one of them would make war rather than let the nation survive; and the other would accept war rather than let it perish. And the war came.

One eighth of the whole population were colored slaves, not distributed generally over the Union, but localized in the southern part of it. These slaves constituted a peculiar and powerful interest. All knew that this interest was, somehow, the cause of the war. To strengthen, perpetuate, and extend this interest was the object for which the insurgents would rend the Union, even by war; while the government claimed no right to do more than to restrict the territorial enlargement of it.

Neither party expected for the war the magnitude or the duration which it has already attained. Neither anticipated that the cause of the conflict might cease with, or even before, the conflict itself should cease. Each looked for an easier triumph and a result less fundamental and astounding. Both read the same Bible, and pray to the same God; and each invokes His aid against the other. It may seem strange that any men should dare to ask a just God's assistance in wringing their bread from the sweat of other men's faces; but let us judge not, that we be not judged.[1] The prayers of both could not be answered — that of neither has been answered fully.

The Almighty has his own purposes. " Woe unto the world because of offenses! for it must needs be that offenses come; but woe to the man by whom the offense cometh." [2] If we shall suppose that American slavery is one of those offenses.which, in the province of God, must needs come, but which, having continued through His appointed time, He now wills to remove, and that He gives to both North and South this terrible war, as the woe due to those by whom the offense came, shall we discern therein any departure from those divine attributes which the believers in a living God

[1] judge not . . . judged: Matt. 7:1. [2] woe . . . cometh: Matt. 18:7.

always ascribe to Him? Fondly do we hope — fervently do we pray — that this mighty scourge of war may speedily pass away. Yet, if God wills that it continue until all the wealth piled by the bondman's two hundred and fifty years of unrequited toil shall be sunk, and until every drop of blood drawn with the lash shall be paid by another drawn with the sword, as was said three thousand years ago, still it must be said, " The judgments of the Lord are true and righteous altogether." [1]

With malice toward none; with charity for all; with firmness in the right, as God gives us to see the right, let us strive on to finish the work we are in; to bind up the nation's wounds; to care for him who shall have borne the battle, and for his widow and his orphan — to do all which may achieve and cherish a just and lasting peace among ourselves, and with all nations.

## Suggestions for Study
## of Abraham Lincoln

1. Many qualities of Lincoln are reflected in this series of brief utterances. Find passages that show his humility; his consideration of others; his insistence on the right; his devoutness; his heavy sense of responsibility as commander-in-chief.

2. It is now recognized that Lincoln's death was an even greater loss to the South than to the North. Where does he indicate the course he would have taken with the defeated Confederacy? Which of his ideals for reunion was imperfectly achieved?

3. One of Lincoln's gifts was the ability to put into simple words the profound feelings that often defeat attempts at expression. Find passages that have become part of the creed of our nation.

4. Do you find any points of resemblance between Lincoln and Lee? What was the greatest difference between the two men? If their backgrounds had been reversed, would Lee have enjoyed the humor of Artemus Ward? Would Lincoln have made a fine college president?

[1] The judgments . . . altogether: Ps. 19:9.

Abram J. Ryan        1839–1886

### THE CONQUERED BANNER

Most of the poetry of the war went into songs or solemn and dignified rejoicing that the Union was saved. We have only a few pieces like this one, simply expressing emotion at its height. It was written by a Roman Catholic priest who served in the Confederate army as a chaplain. The lines ring with the hopeless grief of defeat and fierce pride in the comrades who served with him under the banner he bids farewell.

Furl that banner, for 'tis weary;
Round its staff 'tis drooping dreary:
   Furl it, fold it — it is best;
For there's not a man to wave it,
And there's not a sword to save it,    5
And there's not one left to lave it
In the blood which heroes gave it,
And its foes now scorn and brave it:
   Furl it, hide it — let it rest!

Take that banner down! 'tis tattered;  10
Broken is its staff and shattered;
And the valiant hosts are scattered,
   Over whom it floated high.
Oh, 'tis hard for us to fold it,
Hard to think there's none to hold it,  15
Hard that those that once unrolled it
   Now must furl it with a sigh!

Furl that banner — furl it sadly!
Once ten thousands hailed it gladly,
And ten thousands wildly, madly, ·  20
   Swore it should forever wave;
Swore that foeman's sword should never
Hearts like theirs entwined dissever,
Till that flag should float forever
   O'er their freedom or their grave!  25

Furl it! for the hands that grasped it,
And the hearts that fondly clasped it,
   Cold and dead are lying low;
And that banner — it is trailing,
While around it sounds the wailing  30
   Of its people in their woe.

For, though conquered, they adore it —
Love the cold, dead hands that bore it,
Weep for those who fell before it,
Pardon those who trailed and tore it;    35
And oh, wildly they deplore it,
   Now to furl and fold it so!

Furl that banner! True, 'tis gory,
Yet 'tis wreathed around with glory,
And 'twill live in song and story    40
   Though its folds are in the dust!
For its fame on brightest pages,
Penned by poets and by sages,
Shall go sounding down the ages —
   Furl its folds though now we must.    45

Furl that banner, softly, slowly!
Treat it gently — it is holy,
   For it droops above the dead.
Touch it not — unfold it never;
Let it droop there, furled forever —    50
   For its people's hopes are fled!

## Suggestions for Study

1. Do you think this poem was written soon
after the end of the war, or later? Can you
explain why?

2. In what spirit does the poet meet defeat? Compare his attitude with that shown
by Lee. How is the feeling of each one appropriate to the part the man played in the war?

3. Pick out words and phrases that give the
poem its strong emotional tone. Does the list
you collect give the same emotional impression as the poem as a whole? Does this selection fit Wordsworth's definition of poetry,
" emotion recollected in tranquillity "?

# Henry Timrod    1829–1867

## ODE

SUNG AT THE OCCASION OF DECORATING THE
GRAVES OF THE CONFEDERATE DEAD, AT
MAGNOLIA CEMETERY, CHARLESTON, S. C.,
1867

You have read Lincoln's tribute to the
Northern dead buried at Gettysburg. Here is
the best of the tributes to the Southern dead,

first pronounced, like the Gettysburg Address,
above the graves of those it honored. The author, a gifted poet, was himself one of the
casualities of war. Though he survived the
struggle, he died soon after of tuberculosis
contracted during the exposure and under-
nourishment of the war.

Sleep sweetly in your humble graves,
   Sleep, martyrs of a fallen cause;
Though yet no marble column° craves
   The pilgrim here to pause.

In seeds of laurel in the earth    5
   The blossom of your fame is blown,
And somewhere, waiting for its birth,
   The shaft is in the stone!

Meanwhile, behalf the tardy years
   Which keep in trust your storied° tombs,
Behold! your sisters bring their tears,    11
   And these memorial blooms.

Small tributes! but your shades will smile
   More proudly on these wreaths today,
Than when some cannon-molded pile°    15
   Shall overlook this bay.

Stoop, angels, hither from the skies!
   There is no holier spot of ground
Than where defeated valor lies,
   By mourning beauty crowned!    20

3. **marble column:** Today there is a marble
and bronze monument in this cemetery in honor
of the fallen soldiers. 10. **storied:** suggesting stories of valor. 15. **cannon-molded pile:** Monuments
to soldiers are often made from melted cannon.

## Suggestions for Study

1. How did the occasion for this poem differ
from the one for which Lincoln composed his
Gettysburg Address? Is the poetic form more
appropriate for this one? Why would poetry
have been inappropriate at Gettysburg?

2. Two emotions mark this poem. Is bitterness over the defeat one? Is there any echo of
the issues for which the war was fought?

3. The poets of the North celebrated their
victory with moving poems. Read Whittier's
" Laus Deo " and Lowell's " Commemoration
Ode " to see what poets on the other side had
to say.

A FRONTIER TOWN, typical of the boisterous settlements that were springing up all over the West in the late nineteenth century. (Culver)

## 3. THE SETTLEMENT OF THE WEST

The West's first great writer came out of the years after the war, when the country beyond the Mississippi was filling up with what an amazed French traveler, De Tocqueville, called "a deluge of men."

In 1865 the South was bankrupt and pillaged, the East was weary and drained, but the West was more than ever a land of opportunity. The Homestead Law had done away with even the trifling cost — $1.25 an acre — for which western land had formerly been sold. There was still gold in California, and new deposits were being found in Colorado and South Dakota. Silver was being found in large quantities throughout the mountain states. Petroleum, "black gold," was being pumped out of the ground in western Pennsylvania. The railroads were racing across the continent. In 1869 a golden spike joined the rails of the Union Pacific and the Central Pacific at Promontory Point, Utah, in the first cross-continent line to the west coast. Posters, advertisements, and personal letters were dispatched to the hopeful people of Europe offering freedom, fortune, and a fresh start in the American West!

And how they poured in! Half a million came in one year — later, a million. Those who could not speak English tied tags on their coats and allowed themselves to be shipped and unloaded like baggage. Miners explored the mountains and sieved the creek sand. Cattlemen sought out the water holes. Farmers crowded the cattlemen. By 1890, settlements were so close together that the census bureau could no longer chart a frontier line. The 1890 census solemnly reported that the frontier was at an end.

But by that time the century of Western settlement had put the blood of every race into the American melting pot. It had given the characteristics of its life to American customs and American thinking. And it had breathed its vigor into a few writers like Mark Twain.

THE WEST'S FIRST GREAT WRITER

Mark Twain blew into American literature like a fresh wind off the prairies. As Lincoln had brought the spirit of the West into our statesmanship, so Mark Twain put it into our books.

There were many things alike in those two Westerners. They both came out of log cabins, frontier experiences, and boyhood years sparse with education. They were simple men, and unaffected. They came awkwardly, bashfully to the cultured East, and they had the same ability first to inspire ridicule (Lincoln was called a gorilla, and Mark Twain a ruffian) and then to inspire love. Both were fond of a good story, and told it well. They had the same boisterous Western humor, covering up the same thoughtful sadness. They were both intensely American. Europeans had marveled at how much like cultured Europeans were Longfellow and Lowell, but they exclaimed at how unlike Europeans, how American, were Lincoln and Mark Twain. As Lowell called Lincoln

New birth of our new soil,
The first American!

so a later historian wrote of Mark Twain: "Here at last was an authentic American — a native writer thinking his own thoughts, using his own eyes, speaking his own dialect — everything European fallen away." But the path of one of these Americans led to the White House and death at fifty-six when his real greatness was just beginning to be understood; and the path of the other led through a series of adventures to a series of triumphs which made him one of the best-known, best-loved men alive; and when he died at seventy-five the whole world mourned.

His real name was Samuel Clemens, and he grew up at Hannibal, Missouri, on the west bank of the Mississippi. In those days a pageant of the frontier passed up and down the river, and every steamboat carried men who came from great events and exciting adventures, and men who were going to such adventures. Sam Clemens lived the boyhood of Tom Sawyer and Huck Finn, playing pranks, swimming in the river, exploring the cave in the hill, listening to the slaves, the pilots, the frontiersmen. When he was old enough, he learned to set type in his brother's print shop, and helped put out a weekly newspaper. But the river life was more glamorous, and he apprenticed himself to one of the most famous pilots on the river. Five hundred dollars was the fee he was to pay from his first salary as a pilot, and in return he got such a course in river navigation as would have driven an open-water navigator to drink. He had to learn every foot of a constantly changing river, by day and by night, from St. Louis to New Orleans. He tells about it in one of the selections in this book.

He learned to be a pilot and a good one, in the days when pilots were highly paid and envied. But the war closed down the river trade. He enlisted in the militia, and served a few weeks. What happened to him shouldn't have happened to a comic opera soldier. Before his little squad could even find the Confederate army, he had sprained his ankle, gone hungry awhile, and been nearly captured by U. S. Grant. That was enough war. When his older brother was named Secretary to the new Territory of Nevada, Sam Clemens piled into the overland stage and went along as his assistant.

That was a new kind of frontier for him. He had soaked up the legends and the color of the river frontier, but this wild and woolly Far West was a different thing. He loved it. He prospected for silver, and came within an hour of owning one of the biggest lodes in Nevada. He wrote for the rough and ready newspapers of the silver frontier, and got so well into the spirit of things that he had to leave suddenly for California with a two-gun man looking all over Nevada for him. In San Francisco he became a star reporter and a peerless storyteller. He spent many an evening swapping stories with Artemus Ward; and San Franciscans still prize legends of the parties Clemens, Ward, and their hearty friends used to have,

THE "IRON HORSE" drove the buffalo herds from the prairie in the years after the war. (Brown Brothers)

usually ending near dawn with Clemens leading the rest in a game of follow-the-leader, jumping from roof to roof down the steep hills of San Francisco.

That was in the 1860's. Toward the end of that decade three things happened that changed the whole course of young Clemens's life. In the first place, he sent a story to a New York magazine. It was a story he had heard from prospectors in California, called "The Jumping Frog." He sent it off, and never expected to hear of it again, but Easterners read it and chuckled and then laughed broadly, and sent a hurry call to find out who was this Westerner, Clemens. That was the first thing. The second was an assignment from one of the San Francisco papers to go to the Hawaiian Islands (Sandwich Islands, they were called then) and write signed articles on what he saw. When he returned, some of his cronies persuaded him to give a public lecture on his experi-

ences. The articles had been good, but the lecture was like nothing else ever heard in San Francisco. The audience held its sides and rolled in the aisles. The very walls shook with the laughter. The echoes traveled as far as the eastern seaboard, and invitations came addressed to "a man named Clemens" inviting him to come east and lecture on the Sandwich Islands.

And so those two events helped make the third. Samuel Clemens went east with his slow Western drawl, his inimitable art of storytelling, his long mustaches and his stock of Western anecdotes, and got a chance to go on a cruise to Europe and the Mediterranean. He was to write back letters to American newspapers. A publisher gathered them together under the title *Innocents Abroad*, and Samuel Clemens signed the good strong pen name derived from his experience as a pilot, Mark Twain. The book swept America, just as the story and the

MARK TWAIN at ease at his desk. (Culver)

lectures had. This was something new, something fresh. Most Americans had gone to Europe as pilgrims to marvel; Mark Twain had gone to Europe with the Western "show me" attitude. He poked fun alike at the traditions of ancient Europe and the gullibility of American tourists. He played pranks in Rome, and bet money with Egyptians on foot races up the pyramids. He forgot to be sentimental and had an uproarious time, and wrote a best seller.

From that time on, Mark Twain's career was patterned. He married an Eastern girl, and lived most of his writing years in the East. He wrote successful book after successful book. He became a bosom friend of Eastern writers like Aldrich and Howells. He made a lot of money, and lived in great houses. But he remained always as unaffectedly Western, as impulsive and lovable as he had ever been. Once he went to see General Grant, and found him near death and penniless, working on his memoirs. He gave the old man $75,000, and published his memoirs for him. Altogether, the General and his widow made $400,000 from

that book, through Mark Twain. But Mark Twain himself was not so lucky. He lost a good deal of money in publishing, a good deal more in trying to perfect a typesetting machine which printers had urgently needed ever since Gutenberg. If he had backed the Mergenthaler Linotype, he might have become a millionaire. But he backed the wrong inventor, and his firm went bankrupt. He refused to take advantage of the bankruptcy laws, assumed the entire debt himself, and set off, at the age of sixty, on a world-wide lecture tour and a three-year program of writing to repay the debt. He paid it all, and lived fifteen years more, honored in his own country and abroad, his flowing white hair, drooping white mustaches, and bright blue eyes better known all over the world than the face of many a king.

He lived and wrote in the East, yet wrote like a Westerner and usually of the West. *Tom Sawyer* and *Huckleberry Finn* are novels based on his own boyhood. *Life on the Mississippi* is about his river and his days as a pilot. *Roughing It* is about his years in the Far West. *A Connecticut Yankee* is about King Arthur's Court, but it is a burlesque in the lighthearted style of *Innocents Abroad. Personal Recollections of Joan of Arc* was one of his own favorites. In his last ten years he produced a different kind of book, a book that many people could not believe Mark Twain had written. The laughing Mark Twain had become a bitter, satirical Mark Twain, and they couldn't believe it. But as Mark Twain himself said in early years, that was merely the other side of the coin. Scratch a humorist, and you find a sad man. In those last years, Mark Twain put into books some of the disillusionment he had hidden under his boisterous laughter. That is why *The Man Who Corrupted Hadleyburg, The Mysterious Stranger,* and *What Is Man?* come as a shock after the earlier and more famous books.

By the time he wrote those late books the temper of the West was changing. Some of the optimism had gone. Most of the good land was settled, the mines were appropriated, and many men were finding that they had settled on land too dry for good farming. It was the end of the frontier, the natural reaction after a period of great optimism and hope, and Mark Twain reflected some of the change.

But the earlier, happier books are the ones by which we are likely to remember him. In a sense which would not be true of many other American authors, those books *are* Mark Twain. There was very little artifice in them. As Howells said, " Of all the literary men I have ever known, he was the most unliterary . . ." The books are the man. They are his slow Western drawl, his wholesomeness and health and lack of affectation, his manner of bringing realities and absurdities together and then keeping a straight face as though he had not the slightest idea that anything he said might be convulsing readers from New York to Calcutta.

*When Mark Twain was born (1835) Andrew Jackson was President. When he died (1910), Theodore Roosevelt had just gone out of office. When he was born, Emerson had not yet published. When he died, E. A. Robinson had already been publishing for ten years.*

### THE SPIRIT OF THE WEST

There were few first-rate Western writers, even in Mark Twain's time. Most of the material had to be saved up and retold or reprinted later. Examples were the songs of the cattlemen, such as " The Cowboy's Lament," the pioneer ballads like " The Little Old Sod Shanty," and the legends of that typically Western doer of great deeds, Paul Bunyan. Another kind of material saved by later telling is represented by the selection from O. E. Rölvaag's *Giants in the Earth*. Rölvaag wrote the book in the 1920's, but he came early to South Dakota from his native Norway, saw some of the problems of immigration and settlement, and heard his fellow settlers tell many tales of the earlier frontier. When he came

to write about it, therefore, he wrote in a soberer key. He had heard of the loneliness and hardships of the pioneer women, the horrors of drought and prairie cyclones, the sadness of parting from friends in the old country. Therefore, he wrote of the West after the frontier had passed by, and before cities and hard roads and radios came. His description of the West is a good corrective to the optimism of the early explorers and settlers who still had free land and a farther West to go to if necessary.

### BRET HARTE AND LOCAL COLOR

The difference between Bret Harte and Mark Twain shows something that was happening to American writing in the last third of the nineteenth century.

Harte was an Easterner who came to California and dug literary gold out of the hills. He learned the customs, the language, the setting, the adventures of the Western miners and prospectors, and then put them into fiction. He wrote half a dozen memorable stories, and went back east, with a guarantee of $10,000 a year, to write for the *Atlantic Monthly*.

Harte wrote about the quaint and interesting aspects of the West, the ways in which it was different from other parts of the country. Mark Twain wrote about the West without trying to show its quaintness or its differences — but merely because he had been brought up in it and was a part of it. Harte was more like a reporter covering an assignment; Mark Twain was more like a man writing his autobiography.

The fact that Harte wrote of the West as he did shows that the West was losing something it had once had — its boisterous humor, its young spirit, its lack of sophistication. It was coming to the stage where it was self-conscious. It began to look at itself in mirrors, and to be aware that it was not like the other sections. In earlier years, it hadn't cared whether it was or was not like any other section.

All over the country there was this same interest in localities — what was quaint or interesting or different about this place as compared to others? In New Orleans, George W. Cable was discovering the Creoles. In Virginia, Thomas Nelson Page was writing about the romance of the old plantation mansions. In Georgia, Joel Chandler Harris was retelling the charming folklore of the Negro. In Tennessee, Mary Murfree had discovered the mountaineers. In New England, Sarah Orne Jewett and Mary Wilkins Freeman; in Kentucky, James Lane Allen; in the Middle West, Edward Eggleston — all these recorded the quaint and distinctive " local color " of their regions.

Local color was a healthy sign because it showed that writers wanted to put a real America into literature. In the time of Poe, that hadn't bothered writers much. Poe himself preferred to write about a mysterious land that never existed outside imagination. But these writers were trying to put down the record of a real country. The country was huge and diverse, and so they began with the sections they knew. And therefore local color was a step toward the realism which began with William Dean Howells and Henry James, and which has been the favorite tone of American literature ever since.

## Mark Twain                1835–1910

### BOYHOOD

Here you will find not only Mark Twain remembering the carefree days of his boyhood, but a picture of life in a family in comfortable circumstances in a country that was past the roughness of the frontier, yet still simple in its ways. If you know Tom Sawyer and Huckleberry Finn you already know this setting and some of the people.

My parents removed to Missouri in the early thirties; I do not remember just when, for I was not born then and cared nothing for such things. It was a long journey in those days, and must have been a rough and tiresome one. The home was made in the wee village of Florida, in Monroe County, and I was born there in 1835. The village contained a hundred people and I increased the population by one per cent. It is more than many of the best men in history could have done for a town. It may not be modest in me to refer to this but it is true. There is no record of a person doing as much — not even Shakespeare. But I did it for Florida, and it shows I could have done it for any place — even London, I suppose.

Recently someone in Missouri has sent me a picture of the house I was born in. Heretofore I have always stated that it was a palace, but I shall be more guarded now.

I used to remember my brother Henry walking into a fire outdoors when he was a week old. It was remarkable in me to remember a thing like that, and it was still more remarkable that I should cling to the delusion, for thirty years, that I *did* remember it — for of course it never happened; he would not have been able to walk at that age. If I had stopped to reflect, I should not have burdened my memory with that impossible rubbish so long. It is believed by many people that an impression deposited in a child's memory within the first two years of its life cannot remain there five years, but that is an error. For many years I believed that I remembered helping my grandfather drink his whisky toddy when I was six weeks old, but I do not tell about that any more, now; I am grown old and my memory is not as active as it used to be. When I was younger I could remember anything, whether it had happened or not; but my faculties are decaying now, and soon I shall be so that I cannot remember any but the things that never happened. It is sad to go to pieces like this, but we all have to do it.

My uncle, John A. Quarles, was a farmer, and his place was in the country, four miles from Florida. He had eight children and fifteen or twenty Negroes, and was also fortunate in other ways, particularly in his character. I have not come across a better man than he was. I was his guest for two or three months every year, from the fourth year after we removed to Hannibal till I was eleven or twelve years old. I have never consciously used him or his wife in a book, but his farm has come very handy to me in literature once or twice. In *Huck Finn* and in *Tom Sawyer, Detective* I moved it down to Arkansas. It was all of six hundred miles, but it was no trouble; it was not a very large farm — five hundred acres, perhaps — but I could have done it if it had been twice as large. And as for the morality of it, I cared nothing for that; I would move a state if the exigencies of literature required it.

It was a heavenly place for a boy, that farm of my Uncle John's. The house was a double log one, with a spacious floor (roofed in) connecting it with the kitchen. In the summer the table was set in the middle of that shady and breezy floor, and the sumptuous meals — well, it makes me cry to think of them. Fried chicken, roast pig; wild and tame turkeys, duck, geese; venison just killed; squirrels, rabbits, pheasants, partridges, prairie chickens; biscuits, hot battercakes, hot buckwheat cakes, hot " wheat bread," hot rolls, hot corn pone; fresh corn boiled on the ear, succotash, butter beans, string beans, tomatoes, peas, Irish potatoes, sweet potatoes; buttermilk, sweet milk, " clabber "; watermelons, muskmelons, cantaloupes — all fresh from the garden; apple pie, peach pie, pumpkin pie, apple dumplings, peach cobbler — I can't remember the rest. The way that the things were cooked was perhaps the main splendor — particularly a certain few of the dishes. For instance, the corn bread, the hot biscuits, and wheat bread, and the fried chicken. These things have never been properly cooked in the North — in fact, no one there is able to learn the art, so far as my experience goes. The North thinks it knows how to make corn bread, but this is mere superstition. Perhaps no bread in the world is quite so good as Southern corn bread, and perhaps no bread in the world is quite so bad as the Northern imitation of it. The North seldom tries to fry chicken, and this is

well; the art cannot be learned north of the line of Mason and Dixon, nor anywhere in Europe.

[The author here goes into a long digression on European cooking.]

The farmhouse stood in the middle of a very large yard, and the yard was fenced on three sides with rails and on the rear side with high palings; against these stood the smokehouse; beyond the palings was the orchard; beyond the orchard were the Negro quarters and the tobacco fields. The front yard was entered over a stile made of sawed-off logs of graduated heights; I do not remember any gate. In a corner of the front yard were a dozen lofty hickory trees and a dozen black walnuts, and in the nutting season riches were to be gathered there.

Down a piece, abreast the house, stood a little log cabin against the rail fence; and there the woody hill fell sharply away past the barns, the corncrib, the stables, and the tobacco-curing house, to a limpid brook which sang along over its gravelly bed and curved and frisked in and out and here and there and yonder in the deep shade of overhanging foliage and vines — a divine place for wading, and it had swimming pools, too, which were forbidden to us and therefore much frequented by us. For we were little Christian children and had early been taught the value of forbidden fruit.

All the Negroes were friends of ours, and with those of our own age we were in effect comrades. I say in effect, using the phrase as a modification. We were comrades, and yet not comrades; color and condition interposed a subtle line which both parties were conscious of and which rendered complete fusion impossible. We had a faithful and affectionate good friend, ally, and adviser in " Uncle Dan'l," a middle-aged slave whose head was the best one in the Negro quarter, whose sympathies were wide and warm, and whose heart was honest and simple and knew no guile. He has served me well these many, many years. I have not seen him for more than half a century, and yet spiritually I have had his welcome company a good part of that time, and have staged him in books under his own name and as " Jim," and carted him all around — to Hannibal, down the Mississippi on a raft, and even across the Desert of Sahara in a balloon — and he has endured it all with the patience and friendliness and loyalty which were his birthright. It was on the farm that I got my strong liking for his race and my appreciation of certain of its fine qualities. This feeling and this estimate have stood the test of sixty years and more, and have suffered no impairment. The black face is as welcome to me now as it was then.

In my schoolboy days I had no aversion to slavery. I was not aware that there was anything wrong about it. No one arraigned it in my hearing; the local papers said nothing against it; the local pulpit taught us that God approved it, that it was a holy thing, and that the doubter need only to look in the Bible if he wished to settle his mind — and then the texts were read aloud to us to make the matter sure; if the slaves themselves had an aversion to slavery, they were wise and said nothing. In Hannibal we seldom saw a slave misused; on the farm, never.

There was, however, one small incident of my boyhood days which touched this matter, and it must have meant a good deal to me or it would not have stayed in my memory, clear and sharp, vivid and shadowless, all these slow-drifting years. We had a little slave boy whom we had hired from someone, there in Hannibal. He was from the eastern shore of Maryland, and had been brought away from his family and his friends, halfway across the American continent, and sold. He was a cheery spirit, innocent and gentle, and the noisiest creature that ever was, perhaps. All day long he was singing, whistling, yelling, whooping, laughing — it was maddening, devastating, unendurable. At last, one day, I lost all my temper, and went raging to my mother and said Sandy had been singing for an hour without a single break, and I

couldn't stand it, and *wouldn't* she please shut him up. The tears came into her eyes and her lips trembled, and she said something like this:

" Poor thing, when he sings it shows that he is not remembering, and that comforts me; but when he is still I am afraid he is thinking, and I cannot bear it. He will never see his mother again; if he can sing, I must not hinder it, but be thankful for it. If you were older, you would understand me; then that friendless child's noise would make you glad."

It was a simple speech and made up of small words, but it went home, and Sandy's noise was not a trouble to me any more. She never used large words, but she had a natural gift for making small ones do effective work. She lived to reach the neighborhood of ninety years and was capable with her tongue to the last — especially when a meanness or an injustice roused her spirit. She has come handy to me several times in my books, where she figures as Tom Sawyer's Aunt Polly. I fitted her out with a dialect and tried to think up other improvements for her, but did not find any. I used Sandy once, also; it was in *Tom Sawyer*. I tried to get him to whitewash the fence, but it did not work. I do not remember what name I called him by in the book.

I can see the farm yet, with perfect clearness. I can see all its belongings, all its details; the family room of the house, with a " trundle " bed in one corner and a spinning wheel in another — a wheel whose rising and falling wail, heard from a distance, was the mournfulest of all sounds to me, and made me homesick and low-spirited, and filled my atmosphere with the wandering spirits of the dead; the vast fireplace, piled high, on winter nights, with flaming hickory logs from whose ends a sugary sap bubbled out, but did not go to waste, for we scraped it off and ate it; the lazy cat spread out on the rough hearthstones; the drowsy dogs braced against the jambs and blinking; my aunt in one chimney corner, knitting; my uncle in the other, smoking his corncob pipe; the slick and carpetless oak floor faintly mirroring the dancing flame tongues and freckled with black indentations where fire coals had popped out and died a leisurely death; half a dozen children romping in the background twilight; " split "-bottomed chairs here and there, some with rockers; a cradle — out of service, but waiting, with confidence; in the early cold mornings a snuggle of children, in shirts and chemises, occupying the hearthstone and procrastinating — they could not bear to leave that comfortable place and go out on the windswept floor space between the house and kitchen where the general tin basin stood, and wash.

Along outside of the front fence ran the country road, dusty in the summertime, and a good place for snakes — they liked to lie in it and sun themselves; when they were rattlesnakes or puff adders, we killed them; when they were black snakes, or racers, or belonged to the fabled " hoop " breed, we fled, without shame; when they were " house snakes," or " garters," we carried them home and put them in Aunt Patsy's workbasket for a surprise; for she was prejudiced against snakes, and always when she took the basket in her lap and they began to climb out of it it disordered her mind. She never could seem to get used to them; her opportunities went for nothing. And she was always cold toward bats, too, and could not bear them; and yet I think a bat is as friendly a bird as there is. My mother was Aunt Patsy's sister and had the same wild superstitions. A bat is beautifully soft and silky; I do not know any creature that is pleasanter to the touch or is more grateful for caressings, if offered in the right spirit. I know all about these coleoptera,[1] because our great cave, three miles below Hannibal, was multitudinously stocked with them, and often I brought them home to amuse my mother with. It was easy to manage if it was a school day, because then I had ostensibly been to school and hadn't any bats. She was not a

[1] coleoptera (kō-lḗ-ŏp'tḗ-rȧ): beetles. The inaccurate scientific term is used humorously.

suspicious person, but full of trust and confidence; and when I said, " There's something in my coat pocket for you," she would put her hand in. But she always took it out again, herself. I didn't have to tell her. It was remarkable the way she couldn't learn to like private bats. The more experience she had, the more she could not change her views.

I think she was never in the cave in her life; but everybody else went there. Many excursion parties came from considerable distances up and down the river to visit the cave. It was miles in extent and was a tangled wilderness of narrow and lofty clefts and passages. It was an easy place to get lost in; anybody could do it — including the bats. I got lost in it myself, along with a lady, and our last candle burned down to almost nothing before we glimpsed the search party's lights winding about in the distance.

" Injun Joe," the half-breed, got lost in there once, and would have starved to death if the bats had run short. But there was no chance of that; there were myriads of them. He told me all his story. In the book called *Tom Sawyer* I starved him entirely to death in the cave, but that was in the interest of art; it never happened. " General " Gaines, who was our first town drunkard before Jimmy Finn got the place, was lost in there for the space of a week, and finally pushed his handkerchief out of a hole in a hilltop near Saverton, several miles down the river from the cave's mouth, and somebody saw it and dug him out. There is nothing the matter with his statistics except the handkerchief. I knew him for years and he hadn't any. But it could have been his nose. That would attract attention.

The cave was an uncanny place, for it contained a corpse — the corpse of a young girl of fourteen. It was in a glass cylinder inclosed in a copper one which was suspended from a rail which bridged a narrow passage. The body was preserved in alcohol, and it was said that loafers and rowdies used to drag it up by the hair and look at the dead face. The girl was the daughter of a St. Louis surgeon of extraordinary ability and wide celebrity. He was an eccentric man and did many strange things. He put the poor thing in that forlorn place himself.

Beyond the road where the snakes sunned themselves was a dense young thicket, and through it a dim-lighted path led a quarter of a mile; then out of the dimness one emerged abruptly upon a level great prairie which was covered with wild strawberry plants, vividly starred with prairie pinks, and walled in on all sides by forests. The strawberries were fragrant and fine, and in the season we were generally there in the crisp freshness of the early morning, while the dew beads still sparkled upon the grass and the woods were ringing with the first songs of the birds.

Down the forest slopes to the left were the swings. They were made of bark stripped from hickory saplings. When they became dry they were dangerous. They usually broke when a child was forty feet in the air, and this was why so many bones had to be mended every year. I had no ill luck myself, but none of my cousins escaped. There were eight of them, and at one time and another they broke fourteen arms among them. But it cost next to nothing, for the doctor worked by the year — twenty-five dollars for the whole family. I remember two of the Florida doctors, Chowning and Meredith. They not only tended an entire family for twenty-five dollars a year, but furnished the medicines themselves. Good measure, too. Only the largest persons could hold a whole dose. Castor oil was the principal beverage. The dose was half a dipperful, with half a dipperful of New Orleans molasses added to help it down and make it taste good, which it never did.

I was always told that I was a sickly and precarious and tiresome and uncertain child, and lived mainly on allopathic medicines during the first seven years of my life. I asked my mother about this, in her old

age — she was in her eighty-eighth year — and said:

" I suppose that during all that time you were uneasy about me? "

" Yes, the whole time."

" Afraid I wouldn't live? "

After a reflective pause — ostensibly to think out the facts — " No — afraid you would."

## A LIGHTNING PILOT

When we join the young apprentice in the following selection from *Life on the Mississippi,* he has already made one trip up the river in training to become a pilot, jotting down notes on all the landmarks a pilot had to know if he was to bring his boat through in safety. Those notes are in the " book " he refers to. Mr. Bixby is the master pilot who has agreed to " teach him the river " for a fee of five hundred dollars. The price may not seem too high when you see Mr. Bixby in action and realize the quality of training it went for.

When I returned to the pilothouse St. Louis was gone, and I was lost. Here was a piece of river which was all down in my book, but I could make neither head nor tail of it: you understand, it was turned around. I had seen it when coming upstream, but I had never faced about to see how it looked when it was behind me. My heart broke again, for it was plain that I had got to learn this troublesome river *both ways*.

The pilothouse was full of pilots, going down to " look at the river." What is called the " upper river " (the two hundred miles between St. Louis and Cairo, where the Ohio comes in) was low; and the Mississippi changes its channel so constantly that the pilots used to always find it necessary to run down to Cairo to take a fresh look, when their boats were to lie in port a week; that is, when the water was at a low stage. A deal of this " looking at the river " was done by poor fellows who seldom had a berth and whose only hope of getting one lay in their being always freshly posted and therefore ready to drop into the shoes of

MISSISSIPPI RIVER TRAFFIC. This Currier and Ives print conveys something of the glamour and romance of life on the Mississippi. (Culver)

some reputable pilot, for a single trip, on account of such pilot's sudden illness or some other necessity. And a good many of them constantly ran up and down inspecting the river, not because they ever really hoped to get a berth, but because (they being guests of the boat) it was cheaper to " look at the river " than stay ashore and pay board. In time these fellows grew dainty in their tastes, and only infested boats that had an established reputation for setting good tables. All visiting pilots were useful, for they were always ready and willing, winter or summer, night or day, to go out in the yawl and help buoy the channel or assist the boat's pilots in any way they could. They were likewise welcomed because all pilots are tireless talkers, when gathered together, and as they talk only about the river they are always understood and are always interesting. Your true pilot cares nothing about anything on earth but the river, and his pride in his occupation surpasses the pride of kings.

We had a fine company of these river in-spectors along this trip. There were eight or ten, and there was abundance of room for them in our great pilothouse. Two or three of them wore polished silk hats, elaborate shirt fronts, diamond breastpins, kid gloves, and patent-leather boots. They were choice in their English, and bore themselves with a dignity proper to men of solid means and prodigious reputation as pilots. The others were more or less loosely clad, and wore upon their heads tall felt cones that were suggestive of the days of the Commonwealth.[1]

I was a cipher in this august company, and felt subdued, not to say torpid. I was not even of sufficient consequence to assist at the wheel when it was necessary to put the tiller hard down in a hurry; the guest that stood nearest did that when occasion required — and this was pretty much all the time, because of the crookedness of the channel and the scant water. I stood in a

[1] **Commonwealth:** the period 1649 to 1660 in English history when the King had been beheaded and the Puritans were in power.

corner, and the talk I listened to took the hope all out of me. One visitor said to another:

" Jim, how did you run Plum Point, coming up? "

" It was in the night, there, and I ran it the way one of the boys on the *Diana* told me; started out about fifty yards above the woodpile on the false point, and held on the cabin under Plum Point till I raised the reef — quarter less twain — then straightened up for the middle bar till I got well abreast the old one-limbed cottonwood in the bend, then got my stern on the cottonwood, and head on the low place above the point, and came through a-booming — nine and a half."

" Pretty square crossing, ain't it? "

" Yes, but the upper bar's working down fast."

Another pilot spoke up and said:

" I had better water than that, and ran it lower down; started out from the false point — mark twain [1] — raised the second reef abreast the big snag in the bend, and had quarter less twain."

One of the gorgeous ones remarked:

" I don't want to find fault with your leadsmen, but that's a good deal of water for Plum Point, it seems to me."

There was an approving nod all around as this quiet snub dropped on the boaster and " settled " him. And so they went on talk-talk-talking. Meantime the thing that was running in my mind was, " Now, if my ears hear aright, I have not only to get the names of all the towns and islands and bends, and so on, by heart, but I must even get up a warm personal acquaintanceship with every old snag and one-limbed cottonwood and obscure woodpile that ornaments the banks of this river for twelve hundred miles; and more than that, I must actually know where these things are in the dark, unless these guests are gifted with eyes that can pierce through two miles of solid blackness. I wish the piloting business was in Jericho and I had never thought of it."

[1] **mark twain:** the leadsman's cry for two fathoms of water, safe depth for the boat.

At dusk Mr. Bixby tapped the big bell three times (the signal to land), and the captain emerged from his drawing room in the forward end of the " texas " [2] and looked up inquiringly. Mr. Bixby said:

" We will lay up here all night, captain."

" Very well, sir."

That was all. The boat came to shore and was tied up for the night. It seemed to me a fine thing that the pilot could do as he pleased, without asking so grand a captain's permission. I took my supper and went immediately to bed, discouraged by my day's observations and experiences. My late voyage's notebooking was but a confusion of meaningless names. It had tangled me all up in a knot every time I had looked at it in the daytime. I now hoped for respite in sleep; but no, it reveled all through my head till sunrise again, a frantic and tireless nightmare.

Next morning I felt pretty rusty and low-spirited. We went booming along, taking a good many chances, for we were anxious to " get out of the river " (as getting out to Cairo was called) before night should overtake us. But Mr. Bixby's partner, the other pilot, presently grounded the boat, and we lost so much time getting her off that it was plain the darkness would overtake us a good long way above the mouth. This was a great misfortune, especially to certain of our visiting pilots, whose boats would have to wait for their return, no matter how long that might be. It sobered the pilothouse talk a good deal. Coming upstream, pilots did not mind low water or any kind of darkness; nothing stopped them but fog. But downstream work was different; a boat was too nearly helpless, with a stiff current pushing behind her; so it was not customary to run downstream at night in low water.

There seemed to be one small hope, however: if we could get through the intricate and dangerous Hat Island crossing before night, we could venture the rest; for we would have plainer sailing and better water.

[2] **"texas":** the structure at the front of the boat which housed the officers' quarters and the pilothouse.

But it would be insanity to attempt Hat Island at night. So there was a deal of looking at watches all the rest of the day, and a constant ciphering upon the speed we were making. Hat Island was the eternal subject; sometimes hope was high and sometimes we were delayed in a bad crossing, and down it went again. For hours all hands lay under the burden of this suppressed excitement; it was even communicated to me, and I got to feeling so solicitous about Hat Island, and under such an awful pressure of responsibility, that I wished I might have five minutes on shore to draw a good, full, relieving breath and start over again. We were standing no regular watches. Each of our pilots ran such portions of the river as he had run when coming upstream, because of his greater familiarity with it; but both remained in the pilothouse constantly.

An hour before sunset Mr. Bixby took the wheel, and Mr. W. stepped aside. For the next thirty minutes every man held his watch in his hand and was restless, silent, and uneasy. At last somebody said, with a doomful sigh:

" Well, yonder's Hat Island — and we can't make it."

All the watches closed with a snap; everybody sighed and muttered something about its being " too bad, too bad " — " ah, if we could *only* have got here half an hour sooner! " — and the place was thick with the atmosphere of disappointment. Some started to go out but loitered, hearing no bell tap to land. The sun dipped behind the horizon; the boat went on. Inquiring looks passed from one guest to another; and one who had his hand on the doorknob and had turned it waited, then presently took away his hand and let the knob turn back again. We bore steadily down the bend. More looks were exchanged, and nods of surprised admiration — but no words. Insensibly the men drew together behind Mr. Bixby, as the sky darkened and one or two dim stars came out. The dead silence and sense of waiting became oppressive. Mr. Bixby pulled the cord, and two deep, mellow notes from the big bell floated off on the night.

Then a pause, and one more note was struck. The watchman's voice followed, from the hurricane deck:

" Labboard lead, there! Stabboard [1] lead! "

The cries of the leadsmen began to rise out of the distance, and were gruffly repeated by the word passers on the hurricane deck.

" M-a-r-k three! M-a-r-k three! Quarter less three! Half twain! Quarter twain! M-a-r-k twain! Quarter less — "

Mr. Bixby pulled two bell ropes, and was answered by faint jinglings far below in the engine room, and our speed slackened. The steam began to whistle through the gauge cocks. The cries of the leadsmen went on — and it is a weird sound, always, in the night. Every pilot in the lot was watching now, with fixed eyes, and talking under his breath. Nobody was calm and easy but Mr. Bixby. He would put his wheel down and stand on a spoke, and as the steamer swung into her (to me) utterly invisible marks — for we seemed to be in the midst of a wide and gloomy sea — he would meet and fasten her there. Out of the murmur of half-audible talk, one caught a coherent sentence now and then — such as:

" There; she's over the first reef all right! "

After a pause, another subdued voice:

" Her stern's coming down just *exactly* right, by *George!* "

" Now she's in the marks; over she goes! "

Somebody else muttered:

" Oh, it was done beautiful — *beautiful!* "

Now the engines were stopped altogether, and we drifted with the current. Not that I could see the boat drift, for I could not, the stars being all gone by this time. This drifting was the dismalest work; it held one's heart still. Presently I discovered a blacker gloom than that which surrounded us. It was the head of the island. We were closing

---

[1] **"Labboard ... Stabboard"** (lä′bŏrd, stä′-bŏrd): larboard, or left, and starboard, or right. Calling for soundings on both sides of the boat showed that they were in a tight spot.

right down upon it. We entered its deeper shadow, and so imminent seemed the peril that I was likely to suffocate; and I had the strongest impulse to do *something,* anything, to save the vessel. But still Mr. Bixby stood by his wheel, silent, intent as a cat, and all the pilots stood shoulder to shoulder at his back.

" She'll not make it! " somebody whispered.

The water grew shoaler and shoaler, by the leadsman's cries, till it was down to:

" Eight and a half! E-i-g-h-t feet! E-i-g-h-t feet! Seven and — "

Mr. Bixby said warningly through his speaking tube to the engineer:

" Stand by, now! "

" Ay, ay, sir! "

" Seven and a half! Seven feet! *Six* and — "

We touched bottom! Instantly Mr. Bixby set a lot of bells ringing, shouted through the tube, " *Now,* let her have it — every ounce you've got! " then to his partner, " Put her hard down! Snatch her! Snatch her! " The boat rasped and ground her way through the sand, hung upon the apex of disaster a single tremendous instant, and then over she went! And such a shout as went up at Mr. Bixby's back never loosened the roof of a pilothouse before!

There was no more trouble after that. Mr. Bixby was a hero that night; and it was some little time, too, before his exploit ceased to be talked about by rivermen.

Fully to realize the marvelous precision required in laying the great steamer in her marks in that murky waste of water, one should know that not only must she pick her intricate way through snags and blind reefs, and then shave the head of the island so closely as to brush the overhanging foliage with her stern, but at one place she must pass almost within arm's reach of a sunken and invisible wreck that would snatch the hull timbers from under her if she should strike it, and destroy a quarter of a million dollars' worth of steamboat and cargo in five minutes, and maybe a hundred and fifty human lives into the bargain.

The last remark I heard that night was a compliment to Mr. Bixby, uttered in soliloquy and with unction by one of our guests. He said:

" By the Shadow of Death, but he's a lightning pilot! "

## ACROSS THE PLAINS BY STAGECOACH

You remember that the War between the States interrupted Mark Twain's career as a river pilot. Now we go with him on his journey to Nevada with his older brother, the newly appointed Secretary of that Territory. The statutes and unabridged dictionary that are so troublesome in the stagecoach are the new Secretary's equipment for his office. This trip was made in 1861, thirty years after Josiah Gregg first struck out across the prairies for Santa Fe. In *Roughing It,* from which this selection is taken, Mark Twain gives a rich picture of his experiences in the Far West.

By eight o'clock everything was ready, and we were on the other side of the river.[1] We jumped into the stage, the driver cracked his whip, and we bowled away and left " the States " behind us. It was a superb summer morning, and all the landscape was brilliant with sunshine. There was a freshness and breeziness, too, and an exhilarating sense of emancipation from all sorts of cares and responsibilities, that almost made us feel that the years we had spent in the close, hot city, toiling and slaving, had been wasted and thrown away. We were spinning along through Kansas, and in the course of an hour and a half we were fairly abroad on the great Plains. Just here the land was rolling — a grand sweep of regular elevations and depressions as far as the eye could reach — like the stately heave and swell of the ocean's bosom after a storm. And everywhere were cornfields, accenting with squares of deeper green this limitless expanse of grassy

[1] river: the Missouri. The fact that at this time the land west of the State of Missouri had not yet been admitted to statehood explains the next sentence.

land. But presently this sea upon dry ground was to lose its " rolling " character and stretch away for seven hundred miles as level as a floor!

Our coach was a great swaying and swinging stage, of the most sumptuous description — an imposing cradle on wheels. It was drawn by six handsome horses, and by the side of the driver sat the " conductor," the legitimate captain of the craft; for it was his business to take charge and care of the mails, baggage, express matter, and passengers.

We three were the only passengers this trip. We sat on the back seat, inside. About all the rest of the coach was full of mailbags — for we had three days delayed mails with us. Almost touching our knees, a perpendicular wall of mail matter rose up to the roof. There was a great pile of it strapped on top of the stage, and both the fore and hind boots [1] were full. We had twenty-seven hundred pounds of it aboard, the driver said — " a little for Brigham, and Carson, and 'Frisco, but the heft of it for the Injuns, which is powerful troublesome 'thout they get plenty of truck to read." But as he just then got up a fearful convulsion of his countenance which was suggestive of a wink being swallowed by an earthquake, we guessed that his remark was intended to be facetious, and to mean that we would unload the most of our mail matter somewhere on the Plains and leave it to the Indians, or whosoever wanted it.

We changed horses every ten miles, all day long, and fairly flew over the hard level road. We jumped out and stretched our legs every time the coach stopped, and so the night found us still vivacious and unfatigued. . . .

About an hour and a half before daylight we were bowling along smoothly over the road — so smoothly that our cradle only rocked in a gentle, lulling way that was gradually soothing us to sleep, and dulling our consciousness — when something gave

[1] **boots:** leather compartments for baggage at each end of the coach.

way under us. We were dimly aware of it, but indifferent to it. The coach stopped. We heard the driver and conductor talking together outside, and rummaging for a lantern, and swearing because they could not find it — but we had no interest in whatever had happened, and it only added to our comfort to think of those people out there at work in the murky night, and we snug in our nest with the curtains drawn. But presently, by the sounds, there seemed to be an examination going on, and then the driver's voice said:

" By George, the thorough brace is broke! "

This startled me broad awake — as an undefined sense of calamity is always apt to do. I said to myself: " Now, a thorough brace is probably part of a horse; and doubtless a vital part, too, from the dismay in the driver's voice. Leg, maybe, and yet how could he break his leg waltzing along such a road as this? No, it can't be his leg. That is impossible unless he was reaching for the driver. Now, what can be the thorough brace of a horse, I wonder? Well, whatever comes, I shall not air my ignorance in this crowd, anyway."

Just then the conductor's face appeared at a lifted curtain, and his lantern glared in on us and our wall of mail matter. He said:

" Gents, you'll have to turn out a spell. Thorough brace is broke."

We climbed out into a chill drizzle, and felt ever so homeless and dreary. When I found that the thing they called a " thorough brace " was the massive combination of belts and springs which the coach rocks itself in, I said to the driver:

" I never saw a thorough brace used up like that, before, that I can remember. How did it happen? "

" Why, it happened by trying to make one coach carry three days' mail — that's how it happened," said he. " And right here is the very direction [2] which is wrote on all the newspaper bags which was to be put out for the Injuns for to keep 'em quiet. It's most uncommon lucky becuz it's so nation

[2] **direction:** address.

dark I should 'a' gone by unbeknowns if that air thorough brace hadn't broke."

I knew that he was in labor with another of those winks of his, though I could not see his face, because he was bent down at work; and wishing him a safe delivery, I turned to and helped the rest get out the mail sacks. It made a great pyramid by the roadside when it was all out. When they had mended the thorough brace we filled the two boots again, but put no mail on top, and only half as much inside as there was before. The conductor bent all the seat backs down, and then filled the coach just half full of mail-bags from end to end. We objected loudly to this for it left us no seats. But the conductor was wiser than we, and said a bed was better than seats, and moreover this plan would protect his thorough braces. We never wanted any seats after that. The lazy bed was infinitely preferable. I had many an exciting day, subsequently, lying on it, reading the statutes and the dictionary, and wondering how the characters would turn out.

The conductor said he would send back a guard from the next station to take charge of the abandoned mailbags, and we drove on.

It was now just dawn; and as we stretched our cramped legs full length on the mail sacks, and gazed out through the windows across the wide wastes of greensward clad in cool powdery mist, to where there was an expectant look in the eastern horizon, our perfect enjoyment took the form of a tranquil and contented ecstasy. The stage whirled along at a spanking gait, the breeze flapping curtains and suspended coats in a most exhilarating way; the cradle swayed and swung luxuriously, the pattering of the horses' hoofs, the cracking of the driver's whip, and his " Hi-yi! g'lang! " were music; the spinning ground and the waltzing trees appeared to give us a mute hurrah as we went by, and then slack up and look after us with interest, or envy, or something; and as we lay and smoked the pipe of peace and compared all this luxury with the years of tiresome city life that had gone before it,

we felt that there was only one complete and satisfying happiness in the world and we had found it.

After breakfast, at some station whose name I have forgotten, we three climbed up on the seat behind the driver, and let the conductor have our bed for a nap. And by and by, when the sun made me drowsy, I lay down on my face on top of the coach, grasping the slender iron railing and slept for an hour or more. That will give one an appreciable idea of those matchless roads. Instinct will make a sleeping man grip a fast hold of the railing when the stage jolts, but when it only swings and sways, no grip is necessary. Overland drivers and conductors used to sit in their places and sleep thirty or forty minutes at a time, on good roads, while spinning along at the rate of eight or ten miles an hour. I saw them do it, often. There was no danger about it; a sleeping man *will* seize the irons in time when the coach jolts. These men were hard-worked, and it was not possible for them to stay awake all the time. . . .

As the sun went down and the evening chill came on, we made preparation for bed. We stirred up the hard leather letter sacks, and the knotty canvas bags of printed matter (knotty and uneven because of projecting ends and corners of magazines, boxes, and books). We stirred them up and redisposed them in such a way as to make our bed as level as possible. And we *did* improve it, too, though after all our work it had an upheaved and billowy look about it, like a little piece of a stormy sea. Next we hunted up our boots from odd nooks among the mail bags where they had settled, and put them on. Then we got down our coats, vests, pantaloons, and heavy woolen shirts, from the arm loops where they had been swinging all day, and clothed ourselves in them — for there being no ladies either at the stations or in the coach, and the weather being hot, we had looked to our comfort by stripping to our underclothing, at nine o'clock in the morning.

All things being now ready, we stowed

the uneasy dictionary where it would lie as quiet as possible, and placed the water canteen and pistols where we could find them in the dark. Then we smoked a final pipe, and swapped a final yarn; after which we put the pipes, tobacco, and bag of coin in snug holes and caves among the mail-bags, and then fastened down the coach curtains all around and made the place as " dark as the inside of a cow," as the conductor phrased it in his picturesque way. It was certainly as dark as any place could be — nothing was even dimly visible in it. And finally we rolled ourselves up like silkworms, each person in his own blanket, and sank peacefully to sleep.

Whenever the stage stopped to change horses, we would wake up, and try to recollect where we were — and succeed — and in a minute or two the stage would be off again, and we likewise. We began to get into country, now, threaded here and there with little streams. These had high steep banks on each side, and every time we flew down one bank and scrambled up the other, our party inside got mixed somewhat. First we would all be down in a pile at the forward end of the stage, nearly in a sitting posture, and in a second we would shoot to the other end, and stand on our heads. And we would sprawl and kick, too, and ward off corners and ends of mailbags that came lumbering over us and about us; and as the dust arose from the tumult, we would all sneeze in chorus, and the majority of us would grumble and probably say some hasty thing like: " Take your elbow out of my ribs! — Can't you quit crowding? "

Every time we avalanched from one end of the stage to the other, the unabridged dictionary would come too; and every time it came it damaged somebody. One trip it " barked " the Secretary's elbow; the next trip it hurt me in the stomach, and the third it tilted Bemis's nose up till he could look down his nostrils — he said. The pistols and coin soon settled to the bottom, but the pipes, pipestems, tobacco, and canteens clattered and floundered after the dictionary every time it made an assault upon us, and

aided and abetted the book by spilling tobacco in our eyes, and water down our backs.

Still, all things considered, it was a very comfortable night. It wore gradually away, and when at last a cold gray light was visible through the puckers and chinks in the curtains, we yawned and stretched with satisfaction, shed our cocoons, and felt that we had slept as much as was necessary. By and by as the sun rose up and warmed the world, we pulled off our clothes and got ready for breakfast. We were just pleasantly in time, for five minutes afterward the driver sent the weird music of his bugle winding over the grassy solitudes, and presently we detected a low hut or two in the distance. Then the rattling of the coach, the clatter of our six horses' hoofs, and the driver's crisp commands awoke to a louder and stronger emphasis, and we went sweeping down on the station at our smartest speed. It was fascinating — that old overland stagecoaching.

### THE PONY EXPRESS

In a little while all interest was taken up with stretching our necks and watching for the " pony-rider " — the fleet messenger who sped across the continent from St. Joe to Sacramento, carrying letters nineteen hundred miles in eight days! Think of that for perishable horse and human flesh and blood to do! The pony-rider was usually a little bit of a man, brimful of spirit and endurance. No matter what time of the day or night his watch came on, and no matter whether it was winter or summer, raining, snowing, hailing, or sleeting, or whether his " beat " was a level straight road or a crazy trail over mountain crags and precipices, or whether it led through peaceful regions or regions that swarmed with hostile Indians, he must be always ready to leap into the saddle and be off like the wind! There was no idling-time for a pony-rider on duty. He rode fifty miles without stopping, by daylight, moonlight, starlight, or through the blackness of darkness, just as it happened. He rode a splendid horse that was born for a racer and fed and lodged like a gentleman;

THE PONY EXPRESS rode a dangerous race against time and occasional marauders. It was, in its time, the fastest mail service on earth. (Brown Brothers)

kept him at his utmost speed for ten miles, and then as he came crashing up to the station where stood two men holding fast a fresh, impatient steed, the transfer of rider and mail-bag was made in the twinkling of an eye, and away flew the eager pair and were out of sight before the spectator could get hardly the ghost of a look.

Both rider and horse went " flying light." The rider's dress was thin, and fitted close; he wore a " roundabout " and a skullcap, and tucked his pantaloons into his boot-tops like a race-rider. He carried no arms — he carried nothing that was not absolutely necessary, for even the postage on his literary freight was worth *five dollars a letter*. He got but little frivolous correspondence to carry — his bag had business letters in it, mostly. His horse was stripped of all unnecessary weight, too. He wore a little wafer of a racing saddle, and no visible blanket. He wore light shoes, or none at all. The lit-

tle flat mail pockets strapped under the rider's thighs would each hold about the bulk of a child's primer. They held many and many an important business chapter and newspaper letter, but these were written on paper as airy and thin as gold leaf, nearly, and thus bulk and weight were economized. The stagecoach traveled about a hundred to a hundred and twenty-five miles a day (twenty-four hours), the pony-rider about two hundred and fifty. There were about eighty pony-riders in the saddle all the time, night and day, stretching in a long scattering procession from Missouri to California, forty flying eastward, and forty toward the west, and among them making four hundred gallant horses earn a stirring livelihood and see a deal of scenery every single day in the year.

We had had a consuming desire from the beginning, to see a pony-rider, but somehow or other all that passed us and all that met us managed to sneak by in the night, and so we heard only a whiz and a hail, and the swift phantom of the desert was gone before we could get our heads out of the windows. But now we were expecting one along every moment, and would see him in broad daylight. Presently the driver exclaims:

" *Here he comes!* "

Every neck is stretched further, and every eye strained wider. Away across the endless dead level of the prairie a black speck appears against the sky, and it is clear that it moves. Well, I should think so! In a second or two it becomes a horse and rider, rising and falling, rising and falling — sweeping toward us nearer and nearer — growing more and more distinct, more and more sharply defined — nearer and still nearer, and the flutter of the hoofs comes faintly to the ear — another instant a whoop and a hurrah from our upper deck, a wave of the rider's hand, but no reply, and man and horse burst past our excited faces and go swinging away like a belated fragment of a storm!

So sudden is it all, and so like a flash of unreal fancy, that but for the flake of white foam left quivering and perishing on a mail sack after the vision had flashed by and disappeared, we might have doubted whether we had seen any actual horse and man at all.

## TAMING A GUIDE

Some years after the stagecoach trip Sam Clemens had achieved a reputation as a reporter — " commentator " would describe him better — that resulted in his being sent on a luxury cruise to write back accounts of the experience for American newspapers. Here, at last, in *Innocents Abroad* Western humor collided with the culture of Europe. Perhaps the guides drew his fire particularly because their business was to hold fast to the wonders and shrines of the past, while Mark Twain's curiosity led him off on such contemporary subjects as the scarcity of soap and the novel mechanics of European windows.

In this place I may as well jot down a chapter concerning those necessary nuisances, European guides. Many a man has wished in his heart he could do without his guide; but knowing he could not, has wished he could get some amusement out of him as a remuneration for the affliction of his society. We accomplished this latter matter, and if our experience can be made useful to others they are welcome to it.

Guides know about enough English to tangle everything up so that a man can make neither head nor tail to it. They know their story by heart — the history of every statue, painting, cathedral, or other wonder they show you. They know it and tell it as a parrot would — and if you interrupt and throw them off the track, they have to go back and begin again. All their lives long they are employed in showing strange things to foreigners and listening to their bursts of admiration. It is human nature to take delight in exciting admiration. It is what prompts children to say " smart " things, and do absurd ones, and in other ways " show off " when company is present. It is what makes gossips turn out in rain and storm to go and be the first to tell a startling bit of news. Think, then, what a passion it becomes with a guide, whose privilege it is, every day, to show to strangers wonders that throw them into perfect ecstasies of admiration! He gets so that he could not by any possibility live in a soberer atmosphere. After we discovered this we *never* went into ecstasies any more — we never admired anything — we never showed any but impassible [1] faces and stupid indifference in the presence of the sublimest wonders a guide had to display. We had found their weak point. We have made good use of it ever since. We have made some of those people savage, at times, but we have never lost our own serenity.

The doctor asks the questions, generally, because he can keep his countenance, and look more like an inspired idiot, and throw more imbecility into the tone of his voice

[1] **impassible:** impassive, without expression.

than any man that lives. It comes natural to him.

The guides in Genoa are delighted to secure an American party, because Americans so much wonder, and deal so much in sentiment and emotion before any relic of Columbus. Our guide there fidgeted about as if he had swallowed a spring mattress. He was full of animation, full of impatience. He said:

" Come wis me, genteelmen! — come! I show you ze letter-writing by Christopher Colombo! — write it himself! — write it wis his own hand! — come! "

He took us to the municipal palace. After much impressive fumbling of keys and opening of locks, the stained and aged document was spread before us. The guide's eyes sparkled. He danced about us and tapped the parchment with his finger:

" What I tell you, genteelmen. Is it not so? See! handwriting Christopher Colombo! write it himself! "

We looked indifferent, unconcerned. The doctor examined the document very deliberately, during a painful pause. Then he said without any show of interest:

" Ah — Ferguson — what — what did you say was the name of the party who wrote this? "

" Christopher Colombo! ze great Christopher Colombo! "

Another deliberate examination.

" Ah — did he write it himself, or — or how? "

" He write it himself! — Christopher Colombo! he's own handwriting, write by himself! "

Then the doctor laid the document down and said:

" Why, I have seen boys in America only fourteen years old that could write better than that."

" But zis is ze great Christo — "

" I don't care who it is! It's the worst writing I ever saw. Now you mustn't think you can impose on us because we are strangers. We are not fools by a good deal. If you have got any specimens of penmanship of real merit, trot them out! — and if you haven't, drive on! "

We drove on. The guide was considerably shaken up, but he made one more venture. He had something which he thought would overcome us. He said:

" Ah, genteelmen, you come wis me! I show you beautiful, oh, magnificent bust of Christopher Colombo! — splendid, grand, magnificent."

He brought us before the beautiful bust — for it *was* beautiful — and sprang back and struck an attitude:

" Ah, look, genteelmen! — beautiful, grand — bust, Christopher Colombo! — beautiful bust, beautiful pedestal! "

The doctor put up his eyeglasses — procured for such occasions:

" Ah — what did you say this gentleman's name was? "

" Christopher Colombo! — ze great Christopher Colombo! "

" Christopher Colombo — the great Christopher Colombo. Well, what did *he* do? "

" Discover America! — discover America, oh, ze devil! "

" Discover America. No — that statement will hardly wash. We are just from America ourselves. We heard nothing about it. Christopher Colombo — pleasant name — is — is he dead? "

" Oh, *corpo di Baccho!* [1] — three hundred year! "

" What did he die of? "

" I do not know! — I cannot tell."

" Smallpox, think? "

" I do not know, genteelmen! — I do not know *what* he die of."

" Measles, likely? "

" Maybe — maybe — I do *not* know — I think he die of somethings."

" Parents living? "

" Im-posseeble! "

" Ah — which is the bust and which the pedestal? "

" Santa Maria! — *zis* ze bust! — *zis* ze pedestal! "

[1] corpo di Baccho (kôr'pỏ dē bä'kō): body of Bacchus, an exclamation of exasperation.

" Ah, I see, I see — happy combination — very happy combination indeed. Is — is this the first time this gentleman was ever on a bust? "[1]

That joke was lost on the foreigner — guides cannot master the subtleties of the American joke.

We have made it interesting for this Roman guide. Yesterday we spent three or four hours in the Vatican again, that wonderful world of curiosities. We came very near expressing interest, sometimes — even admiration — it was very hard to keep from it. We succeeded though. Nobody else ever did in the Vatican museums. The guide was bewildered — nonplussed. He walked his legs off, nearly, hunting up extraordinary things, and exhausted all his ingenuity on us, but it was a failure; we never showed any interest in anything. He had reserved what he considered his greatest wonder till the last — a royal Egyptian mummy, the best-preserved in the world, perhaps. He took us there. He felt so sure, this time, that some of his old enthusiasm came back to him:

" See, genteelmen! — Mummy! Mummy! "

The eyeglasses came up as calmly, as deliberately as ever.

" Ah, — Ferguson — what did I understand you to say the gentleman's name was? "

" Name? — he got no name! — Mummy! — 'Gyptian mummy! "

" Yes, yes. Born here? "

" No! 'Gyptian mummy! "

" Ah, just so. Frenchman, I presume? "

" No! — not Frenchman, not Roman! — born in Egypta! "

" Born in Egypta. Never heard of Egypta before. Foreign locality likely. Mummy — Mummy. How calm he is — how self-possessed. Is, ah — is he dead? "

" Oh, sacré bleu, been dead three thous' year! "

The doctor turned on him savagely:

" Here, now, what do you mean by such

[1] on a bust: slang for "on a spree."

conduct as this! Playing us for Chinamen because we are strangers and trying to learn! Trying to impose your vile, secondhand carcasses on us! — thunder and lightning, I've a notion to — to — if you've got a nice fresh corpse, fetch him out! — or, by George, we'll brain you! "

We make it exceedingly interesting for this Frenchman. However, he has paid us back, partly, without knowing it. He came to the hotel this morning to ask if we were up, and he endeavored as well as he could to describe us, so that the landlord would know which persons he meant. He finished with the casual remark that we were lunatics. The observation was so innocent and so honest that it amounted to a very good thing for a guide to say.

## Suggestions for Study of Mark Twain

### BOYHOOD

1. What sort of activities filled Sam's boyhood? Describe his home. What details impress you with the simplicity of life there? What was his mother like? Did she ever get even with Sam for his teasing?

2. How does Mark Twain feel about his youth and his family? Is he sentimental about the past? conceited? frank? Find evidence to support your answers.

3. What books and characters does he mention in recalling his use of scenes and people of his boyhood? Did your own reading of these books give you the same impression you get from this account?

4. Vocabulary: exigencies, arraigned, ostensibly (see page 47), eccentric, precarious, allopathic.

### A LIGHTNING PILOT

5. Can you understand why the apprentice pilot was discouraged at the outset? What does he say he had to learn? Why would both classes of visiting pilots add to his discouragement?

6. The pilot was the head of a busy team on a steamboat. Did you notice who worked constantly with him when the going became difficult? What part did each one play?

7. Make a chart showing the course Mr.

Bixby had to follow to bring his boat safely past the island. Some of the hazards are vaguely located, but most of them are very definite.

8. Why did Mark Twain quit a profession that so fascinated him? The answer lies in the year that he quit, 1860, and the location of the Mississippi River. Figure it out.

ACROSS THE PLAINS BY STAGECOACH

9. Describe the stagecoach in which the brothers made their trip, and the system of shifting horses and drivers. What was the "conductor's" job? How careful was the handling of the mail?

10. What were the chief hardships of the trip? Did the passengers seem to mind them? Why did they seem to enjoy the trip so much? What bit of comfort did they enjoy that passengers on modern transportation cannot indulge in?

11. Does any new achievement of today stir the wonder and interest the travelers showed in the pony express? What details of the rider's costume and equipment show the straining for all possible speed? Explain how the pony express system operated.

TAMING A GUIDE

12. What was the tourists' only real grudge against the guides? Can you see how the tourists would get worn out with the guides' spiels? Do you think many people would take the pains this group did to get a rise out of a guide? Why would most people not take this method? Do they get as much fun out of life as Mark Twain did?

13. What was the policy this group followed with the guides? Why was the doctor the spokesman? What passages reveal that Mark Twain actually was interested and appreciative?

14. If you like this sort of conversation, get *Tom Sawyer Abroad, and Other Stories* and read "Encounter with an Interviewer."

15. Imagine what the guides must have had to say about this party! Try writing the conversation in which one of them tells another guide, or perhaps his family when he gets home in the evening, about the "lunatics" he has been conducting about the city.

16. Now that you have sampled four of Mark Twain's books, pick out one and read it all. There is no American writer more worth knowing — or more fun to read.

## For Your Vocabulary

WORD POWER. The children *procrastinating* (prŏ-krăs′tĭ-nā-tĭng), putting off as long as possible leaving the warm fireside to go out in the cold to the washbasin (page 685), were indulging in a common human weakness. We are all prone to *procrastinate* when faced with an unpleasant duty. Hence the old saying: "*Procrastination* is the thief of time." The root of these words means tomorrow, but we do not use them so literally. We may *procrastinate* for an hour or a week. From the root *tempus,* time, we get a word of similar meaning, *temporize* (tĕm′pŏ-rīz), meaning to play for time deliberately rather than in the aimless way of the *procrastinator.*

FIGURATIVE USE OF WORDS. Any stagecoach trip was probably lively, and so was any trip with Mark Twain for a companion. But not every writer can get the effect over to a reader so well. One way Mark Twain gives you the feeling so clearly is by the figurative use of verbs. The lantern brought to the door of the coach *glared* in on the passengers. Two features of the landscape viewed from the moving stagecoach were the *spinning* ground and the *waltzing* trees. What made the trees seem to waltz? When they crossed streams with steep banks, the passengers *avalanched* (ăv′à-lăncht) from one end of the stage to the other. An *avalanche* is literally a landslide such as the one in "The Ambitious Guest." Do you remember a fateful *avalanche* of snow in "To Build a Fire"? Mark Twain uses other types of figurative language. Find some of the similes, expressed comparisons with *like* or *as.*

## Folk Literature of the Frontier

### THE COWBOY'S DREAM

COWBOY SONG, TO THE AIR OF
" MY BONNIE LIES OVER THE OCEAN "

The cowboys' songs were not just a diversion for idle hours around the chuck wagon or the bunkhouse. They learned early that singing kept the cattle quiet on their bedding grounds at night and helped to prevent stampedes. Other songs of the "Git along, little dogies" variety were sung to relieve the dusty job of prodding up the laggards, or "drags," at the end of the trail herd, the high points of the refrain coming up to a yell as a rope flicked at a slow calf: "Whoopee tí, yi yó, git a-lóng, little dó-gies."

The young American of today who gets his ideas of the cowboy from the typical Western movie has a very one-sided and distorted picture indeed. The songs of the cowboy, which have been collected by John A. Lomax into *Cowboy Songs and Other Frontier Ballads* and *Songs of the Cattle Trail and Cow Camp*, reveal the true cowboy to us. He was a hardworking fellow, different from the familiar movie hero, who seems never to have any real work to do but is always free to scour the country to rescue maidens in distress or rid the community of Eastern villains. Most of the songs were mournful, because the cowboy was often far from home and homesick — and also because slow, sad tunes seemed to soothe the cattle. The songs often touch on a simple religious faith reminiscent of their boyhood homes. Perhaps the outstanding qualities of the cowboy songs are their masculine vitality and direct, simple honesty, notable traits of their makers.

1. Last night as I lay on the prairie,
   And looked at the stars in the sky,
   I wondered if ever a cowboy
   Would drift to that sweet by and by.

*Chorus:*
   Roll on, roll on;                              5
   Roll on, little dogies, roll on, roll on,
   Roll on, roll on;
   Roll on, little dogies, roll on.

2. The road to that bright, happy region
   Is a dim, narrow trail, so they say;    10
   But the broad one that leads to perdition
   Is posted and blazed all the way.

3. They say there will be a great roundup,
   And cowboys, like dogies, will stand,
   To be marked by the Riders of Judgment                                      15
   Who are posted and know every brand.

4. I know there's many a stray cowboy
   Who'll be lost at the great, final sale,
   When he might have gone in the green pastures
   Had he known of the dim, narrow trail.

5. I wonder if ever a cowboy                 21
   Stood ready for that Judgment Day,
   And could say to the Boss of the Riders,
   "I'm ready, come drive me away."

6. For they, like the cows that are locoed,
   Stampede at the sight of a hand,         26
   Are dragged with a rope to the roundup,
   Or get marked with some crooked man's brand.

7. And I'm scared that I'll be a stray yearling —
   A maverick, unbranded on high —      30
   And get cut in the bunch with the "rusties"
   When the Boss of the Riders goes by.

8. For they tell of another big owner
   Who's ne'er overstocked, so they say,
   But who always makes room for the sinner                                      35
   Who drifts from the strait, narrow way.

9. They say he will never forget you,
   That he knows every action and look;
   So, for safety, you'd better get branded,
   Have your name in the great Tally Book.                                      40

## Suggestions for Study

1. What big event in life on the range is used for the basis of this song? How well does the comparison with the Judgment Day fit? Give details.

2. One cowboy usually sang a verse, and then all the group, if they were around the fire or in the bunkhouse, joined in the chorus. Sometimes each fellow in the circle took his turn at singing the stanzas. Try the song this way in class.

## For Your Vocabulary

FIGURATIVE USE OF WORDS. The cowboy expresses his wonderings about Judgment Day figuratively in terms he uses in his job. Since the cowboy has remained a favorite figure in American song and fiction, these words are widely used in their figurative sense. The *roundup* is not just a gathering, but a gathering for the specific purpose of checking over, sorting out, and branding with the proper brand. So the "last roundup" idea fits the meaning perfectly. *Dogies* (dō′gĭz) are motherless calves who require particular care. They always trailed along at the end of a herd, and that is why so many "get along" choruses are addressed to them. A *maverick* (măv′ĕr-ĭk) is different from a *dogie* in that it, though also separated from its mother, is usually older and able to take care of itself. The important fact is that *mavericks* are unbranded and no one knows what brand belongs on them. A human *maverick* is an individualist who is not easily labeled and classified, or one who has departed from the ways of his group. An independent in politics is often called a *maverick*. *Stampede* has carried over into general use for a movement caused by crowd psychology rather than good sense.

# THE LITTLE OLD SOD SHANTY

### PIONEER BALLAD

Wherever men go and however they live, sooner or later their country and their life crop out in their songs. Carl Sandburg printed in his *American Songbag* this ballad from the bare Western prairies, with this introduction:

"A little girl from western Nebraska, home again after a trip to the East, was asked, 'What is the East?' She answered, 'The East is where trees come between you and the sky.' Early settlers noticed log cabins were scarcer as timberland thinned out going farther west. On the windy, open prairies of the Great Plains, the best house to be had in short order was of sod. A cellar was dug first; long slices of turf were piled around the cellar lines; wooden crosspoles held the sod roof. Ceilings went high or low: tall men put roofs farther from the ground than short men did. In timber country farther east they sang 'The Little Old Log Cabin in the Lane'; its tune was familiar to the lonely 'sodbuster' who made this song about his dwelling — in a region where rivers are sometimes a half mile wide and a half inch deep."

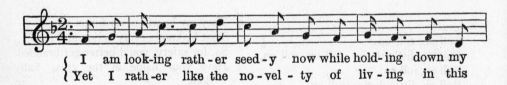

I am look-ing rath-er seed-y now while hold-ing down my
Yet I rath-er like the no-vel-ty of liv-ing in this

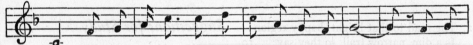

claim, And my vict-uals are not al-ways of the best; .. And the
way, Though my bill of fare is al-ways rath-er tame, . But I'm

mice play shy-ly round me as I nes-tle down to rest, In my
hap-py as a clam on the land of Un-cle Sam, In my

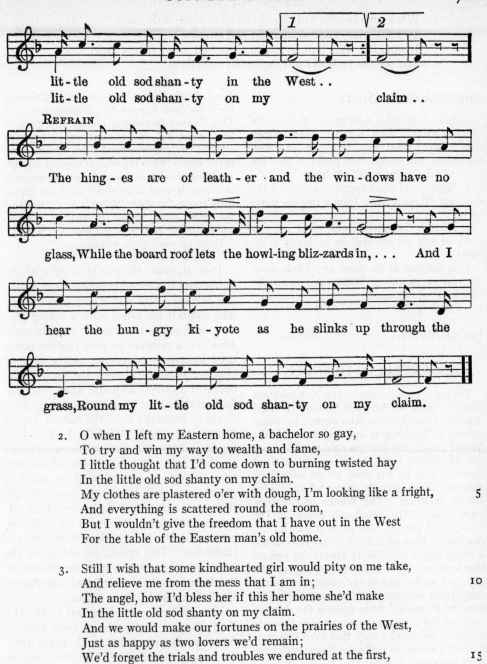

lit - tle old sod shan - ty in the West . .
lit - tle old sod shan - ty on my claim . .

REFRAIN

The hing - es are of leath - er · and the win - dows have no

glass, While the board roof lets the howl-ing bliz-zards in, . . . And I

hear the hun - gry ki - yote as he slinks up through the

grass, Round my lit - tle old sod shan - ty on my claim.

2. O when I left my Eastern home, a bachelor so gay,
   To try and win my way to wealth and fame,
   I little thought that I'd come down to burning twisted hay
   In the little old sod shanty on my claim.
   My clothes are plastered o'er with dough, I'm looking like a fright, 5
   And everything is scattered round the room,
   But I wouldn't give the freedom that I have out in the West
   For the table of the Eastern man's old home.

3. Still I wish that some kindhearted girl would pity on me take,
   And relieve me from the mess that I am in; 10
   The angel, how I'd bless her if this her home she'd make
   In the little old sod shanty on my claim.
   And we would make our fortunes on the prairies of the West,
   Just as happy as two lovers we'd remain;
   We'd forget the trials and troubles we endured at the first, 15
   In the little old sod shanty on our claim.

4. And if kindly fate should bless us with now and then an heir,
   To cheer our hearts with honest pride of fame,
   O then we'd be contented for the toil that we had spent
   In the little old sod shanty on our claim. 20

When time enough had lapsed and all of those little brats
To noble man- and womanhood had grown,
It wouldn't seem half so lonely as around us we should look,
And see the little old sod shanty on our claim.

## Suggestions for Study

1. Give a detailed description of the little old sod shanty. What peculiar disadvantages does it have? What does the settler have with his shanty that makes him prefer it to " the table of the Eastern man's old home "?

2. What detail most impresses you with the fact that this song came from a treeless country?

3. What is the settler's one wish? Do you think he will get it? Will he be happy if he does?

4. Is the tone of the poem as a whole more cheerful or plaintive? What effect does the tune have on the mood?

## James Stevens          1892–

### AN AMERICAN HERCULES

The great contribution of the Northwestern lumber camps to American folklore is Paul Bunyan. James Stevens, who worked for many months in Washington and Oregon and Idaho lumber camps, was just the right person to put into permanent form the adventures of Paul Bunyan. This he has done in his book *Paul Bunyan,* which records many of the lively stories, including " The Winter of the Blue Snow " and " The Sourdough Drive." " The Black Duck Dinner," the greatest yarn of all, describes a feast so satisfying that after it not a single logger was able to appear for supper. One made an effort: at the call for supper " he appeared in the door of the bunkhouse, stared dully for a moment, and then staggered back into the darkness." After reading the descriptions of the groaning boards on this historic occasion, we wonder only that even one man had the courage to make the tiniest move toward more food that day.

In " An American Hercules " Mr. Stevens has written especially for *Adventures in American Literature* an account of the manner in which the Paul Bunyan legend has developed; he has followed this with a hitherto unrecorded yarn, almost, if not quite, the equal of " The

Black Duck Dinner." In the introduction to his book *Paul Bunyan* Mr. Stevens says: " A Paul Bunyan bunkhouse service is a glory to hear, when it is spontaneous and in a proper setting; preferably around a big heated stove in the winter, when the wind is howling through crackling boughs outside and the pungent smell of steaming wool drifts down from the drying lines above the stove. When a vasty spirit of the woods really moves the meeting, a noble and expansive ecstasy of the soul is exhibited."

Draw up your chair, stranger.

Paul Bunyan, the mythical hero of the lumberjacks, is the supreme figure of American folklore. Paul was a Herculean logger who combed his beard with a young pine tree; who skidded his timber with Babe the Blue Ox, a creature so vast that he measured forty-two ax handles and a plug of chewing tobacco between the horns; who operated a camp cookhouse where the flapjack griddle was greased by twenty-four Arabs — imported from the Sahara Desert because they could stand the heat — skating to and fro with slabs of bacon strapped to their feet; who tamed the Mississippi when it was young and wild by building river corrals and driving the river through their gates (the Great Lakes remain as evidence of this feat); who ruled the American country in the period when it was only a timberland. This epoch, according to the best authorities, began with the Winter of the Blue Snow and ended with the Spring the Rain Came Up from China.

Here, indeed, is a full-bodied myth. The Paul Bunyan stories have been told in American logging camps since 1840. They are unquestionably of Canadian origin. There was a Paul Bunyan who won fame in the Papineau Rebellion of 1837. There is no evidence that the beginnings of the stories are beyond him. The other materials and characters of the myth were developed out of the magic of bunkhouse nights; when the workday in the woods, or on the iced road, or on the drive, was done; when the camp men, isolated from all life but that of the woods, had no other outlet for their fancies than the creation of romances about their own life.

Thus Paul Bunyan; Babe the Blue Ox; Johnny Inkslinger, the timekeeper who figured with a fountain pen fed by hose lines from twenty-four barrels of ink; Hels Helson, the Big Swede and bull of the woods, who muddied the Missouri River forever with one spring bath; and many smaller characters — such as Hot Biscuit Slim, the cook; Shanty Boy, the bard; and Big Ole, the blacksmith — have been celebrated in logging camps from Bangor, Maine, to Portland, Oregon. The tall tale, the "whopper," is not confined, of course, to the lumber camps. It appears with the earliest accounts of the Appalachian pioneers. It is forever present in the best writings of Mark Twain. Other mythical heroes have won a certain fame, such as Tony Beaver of the Virginia mountains and Pecos Bill, the Southwestern *vaquero* [1] who once straddled a cyclone and rode it to a finish. But the myth of Paul Bunyan stands alone, possessing, as it does, its own time, place, and people.

The stories are told in this manner:

Supper is over in the logging camp, and the after-supper period of smoking and quiet is also done. A murmur of talk about the day's work rises from the gang around the heating stove. There is a strong smell of steaming wool from the drying lines. Blue pipe smoke drifts through the mellow light of the Rochester burners. A gust of frosty air blows in whenever the bunkhouse door is opened. Some logger ventures the opinion that this will be the hardest winter this part of the country has ever known. Weather talk runs on until someone states solemnly that "the weather ain't what she used to be. Gettin' old now, the weather is. Take the Year of the Two Winters, in Paul Bunyan's time. Yes, sir. Then. That year two winters come all at once. — "

[1] **vaquero** (vä-kä′rō): cowpuncher.

PAUL BUNYAN STATUE, a tremendous block of concrete cast in the hero's likeness by the townsfolk at Bemidji, Minnesota. (Brown Brothers)

Then there is a contest to see who can tell the tallest tale about cold weather in the day of Paul Bunyan.

Or it is a summer night, and the loggers are circling a smudge fire outside the bunkhouse. Mosquitoes swarm up from the swamp below camp. So mosquito stories are in order. Any man is free to invent new Paul Bunyan yarns himself, or he can repeat the stories heard from other bards. Occasionally some bard is so inspired that his creation is never forgotten, and becomes a permanent addition to the Paul Bunyan myth. Such is the story of the mammoth mosquitoes and their amazing experiences with Bum and Bill, Paul Bunyan's battling bees.

Here is the story.

It was in the Year of the Dry Summer that Paul Bunyan's loggers first encountered mosquitoes. That was the season Paul Bunyan invented thunder. Day after day, week after week, month after month, the great hero-leader of the loggers toiled through experiments with all the sounds he could imagine. Just as cows, pigs, dogs, hens, and ducks could be called, so could clouds be called, thought Paul Bunyan. Seventeen thousand various kinds of calls the great logger tried that summer before he hit on the sound of thunder. Then his labors were rewarded. Paul Bunyan had not thundered once before a stray cloud rolled up from the west. He thundered on, and by midnight so many clouds had gathered that the Dry Summer ended in a downpour that was a deluge instead of a rain. Ever since that parched season the weather has used the thunder which Paul Bunyan invented for it.

But Paul Bunyan had other troubles during this wretched summer. Time and again he had to quit his important labor of trying out sounds that would call up clouds, and attend to small bothers, plagues, and worries. The most troublesome of all these troubles was the invasion of mosquitoes.

The mammoth mosquitoes came from the Tall Wolf country. There the tribe had experienced a devastating famine. For the larger it grew, the smaller became the tribe of tall wolves, the mammoth mosquitoes' natural prey. Eventually the last tall wolf was gone, and only a small company of female mosquitoes was left from the once vast and powerful insect tribe. These females were forced by hunger into migration. They were ready to fall and perish from exhaustion when they reached Paul Bunyan's loggers, who, stripped to the waist, were at work even on this, the hottest of the Dry Summer's days.

Paul Bunyan was afar from his loggers at the moment, pondering deeply on the problem of calling up the clouds. He failed to notice when the ring of axes and the drone of saws were hushed. Not until agonizing yells arose from his loggers did the hero-leader realize that a new trouble had come to camp. Then he saw that his men were struggling for their lives all through the timber five miles away. Two strides and one leap, and Paul Bunyan was on the scene of battle.

Many of his loggers were already white and faint from loss of blood, and the others were hacking desperately with their axes at the dodging, diving mosquitoes. Two of the mammoth winged females were sprawled lifelessly over some pine logs. Others had paused in the fight to bind up their split bills. The battle raged on.

Paul Bunyan was so stirred with wrath at the sight that he unloosed a yell of astonishment and anger. The loggers, of course, were all lifted off their feet and then hurled to the ground by the force of that cyclonic voice; and the mammoth mosquitoes instantly took advantage of this and plunged on the loggers with bloodthirsty hums. Each one held down seven or more men at once and prepared to feast.

For a moment Paul Bunyan was in a panic. He thought of smashing the mosquitoes with smacks of his hand but that would have crushed the loggers underneath. With a mighty effort, the great logger collected his wits. He had to think fast, and he did. Paul Bunyan was that kind of man. And at once he acted.

What he did was to call for Babe the Blue Ox, whose ears were so far from his muzzle that he couldn't hear himself snort. As he approached, Babe saw what was needed for the emergency. He did not wait for orders. Without even a glance at Paul, the Blue Ox did a squads rightabout, halted, straightened out his tail, and began to flirt the mosquitoes off the prone loggers with swishes of his huge tail brush. In one minute every frustrated mosquito was humming angrily in the air and the saved loggers were galloping for the protection of the bunkhouses. There they remained. All night the ravenous mammoth mosquitoes maintained a deafening and ominous hum over the bunkhouses. Paul Bunyan listened. He figured and planned, the ideas for sounds to call clouds forgotten for the moment. At dawn Paul Bunyan had a satisfying idea. He called for Johnny Inkslinger, his timekeeper and man of science.

" Johnny," said Paul, " you need a vacation."

" Yes, sir, Mr. Bunyan," said Johnny, but not very enthusiastically; for if there was anything he hated it was to leave his figures, his grand fountain pen and ink barrels.

"A vacation," Paul Bunyan repeated firmly. "So a vacation you shall take. A hunting vacation, Johnny. I'm going to send you bee hunting."

"Mr. Bunyan," said Johnny Inkslinger, "I am a good hunter and I like to hunt. Why, once I found a moose who had died of old age, found his moldering bones, I did, and I tracked him to his birthplace. How's that for hunting, Mr. Bunyan?" said Johnny proudly. But then he looked doubtful. "I don't know about hunting bees, though, Mr. Bunyan."

"You must not only hunt bees, Johnny. You must trap 'em and tame 'em."

"Now, Mr. Bunyan, that's asking a lot," protested Johnny Inkslinger. "I never did claim to be a bee trapper, or a bee tamer, either. Why pick on me, Mr. Bunyan?"

"Don't question orders, Johnny," said Paul Bunyan, kindly but sternly. "You pack up now for a vacation in the Mastodonic Clover country. Once there, hunt, trap, and tame the two fightingest, savagest, irritablest, cantankerousest bees you can find. Then trot 'em home to camp."

"Trot 'em, Mr. Bunyan?"

"Trot 'em, Johnny. Trot the bees."

"Yes, sir," said Johnny; and with a will, for he was sentimental about obeying orders.

When Johnny Inkslinger was sent by Paul Bunyan to do anything, he did it. So he wasn't a day in the Mastodonic Clover country until he had hunted down, trapped, and tamed — as nearly as two such fighting, savage, irritable, and cantankerous bees could be tamed — the two famous battling bees, Bum and Bill. Johnny tamed the two bees so that they allowed him to chain their wings to their bodies. They also trusted him with their stingers, which he put in his knapsack. Then Johnny Inkslinger put calked boots on the bees' hind feet, trotted them out of the clover country, trotted them on over hill and dale, trotted them all the way to camp, just as Paul Bunyan had ordered.

Paul Bunyan had a great hive ready for the two warriors. When their wings were unchained, Bum and Bill took off their calked boots, stretched their legs, ate a hearty meal of lump sugar and turned in for a refreshing sleep. The next morning they buzzed for their stingers at sunup and showed in other ways that they were eager for battle. Paul Bunyan himself led them to the woods, for Johnny Inkslinger insisted on getting back to his figures at once.

Logging had been continued under the tail of Babe the Blue Ox. For three days he had been swishing the ravenous mammoth mosquitoes away from the loggers. He was so tail-weary that he welcomed Bum and Bill, the battling bees, with a joyful moo that shivered the timber for miles. The bees answered with buzzes of rage, and it required all of Paul Bunyan's bee-taming art to convince the fighting bees that Babe was a friend and not the enemy. Bum and Bill were still buzzing suspicion when they sighted the actual foe. Then, with a battle cry that sounded like the rasping roar of a band saw, Bum and Bill lit out in a beeline and charged in an irresistible attack. In seventeen seconds the bodies of seventeen mammoth mosquitoes crashed down into the timber, shattering scores of great pines into splinters. A thunderous hum of fear sounded from the survivors. They flew off in a panic. Pursued and pursuers vanished in the haze of the Dry Summer, which smothered the forest. Soon the hums of fear and the buzzes of rage were only faint murmurs among the far trees. Paul Bunyan's teeth shone through his beard in a smile of triumph.

"Yay, Babe!" he commanded the Blue Ox.

The logging went on.

Paul Bunyan brushed his hands and praised the saints that this mosquito trouble had been so easily ended. Then he returned to his great task of trying out sounds which would call up clouds. The labor engrossed the great logger to such a degree that the mosquito invasion vanished from his thoughts. He also forgot the two big battling bees who had driven the invaders from the logging camp. But Johnny Inkslinger did not forget. Often he raised his head from his books and held his fountain pen poised in the air, while the hose lines from the ink barrels gushed an inky flood to the office floor. This Johnny Inkslinger did not notice in such moments, for he was remembering his grand success as a bee hunter, a bee trapper, and a bee tamer. It was one of the proudest memories of his life.

And often Johnny Inkslinger wondered what had become of the bees he had tamed, what had happened to the female mammoth mosquitoes Bum and Bill had driven from the camp. Weeks had passed, and still there was not a hum from the mosquitoes or a buzz from the bees.

Then, during such a moment of wondering and remembering, Johnny Inkslinger heard a sound from the distance that was nothing but a buzz-hum. He ran out of the office and peered into the heat haze. A small, dark cloud seemed to be moving toward the camp. Johnny watched and waited. The cloud grew larger. As it approached the loggers in the woods, Johnny saw that the cloud was a vast swarm of giant insects. They hovered over the loggers for an instant, then dived without circling. And again agonizing yells rolled up from the timber and smote Paul Bunyan's ears.

"What's happened down there?" Paul Bunyan shouted.

"The mosquitoes have come back!" said Johnny Inkslinger.

"It's a new kind, then," said Paul Bunyan, coming on the run and calling Babe the Blue Ox. "Look at 'em. They're bees!"

"They're mosquitoes," said Johnny. "Look at their bills!"

"But look at their stingers!"

"Sure enough," said Johnny Inkslinger, almost dumb with astonishment. "Why — why — Mr. Bunyan — they — "

"Look at 'em!" yelled Paul Bunyan. "Why, they got bills in front and stingers behind, and they're getting the loggers going and coming! You know what's happened? Those two bees have married the mosquitoes, that's what! And these are the offspring! Bills in front and stingers behind! Yay, Babe!"

And on Paul galloped with Babe the Blue Ox, who soon got his tail brush to working and let the loggers escape to the bunkhouses. But these mammoth insects which were half mosquito and half bee wouldn't be denied. They attacked the bunkhouses. One would stick his bill under one side of a shake on a bunkhouse roof, and his stinger under the other side; and then he would flap his wings until he had ripped off the shake; and the loggers would have to stand guard with pike poles and peavies [1] to keep the savage insects from coming at them through the ripped roofs. Paul Bunyan saw that he needed to act quick. So he spent another night in figuring and planning. And, just as usual, he had a grand idea at daylight. He called for Johnny Inkslinger.

"Johnny," said Paul Bunyan, "we are going to carry sugar."

"Yes, Mr. Bunyan."

"We are going to throw some rafts together, Johnny, and then we are going to load the rafts with all the sugar in camp. After that we are going to rope the rafts together and have Babe the Blue Ox tow the whole raft fleet out into the middle of Lake Michigan."

Johnny Inkslinger never batted an eye. He knew the great logger too well to think that any of his ideas were foolish. So Johnny went to work without a word; and by noon the rafts were built, loaded, and roped together. Paul hitched Babe to the head raft of the fleet.

"Yay, Babe," he commanded.

And the Blue Ox bowed his neck, lumbered off, and straight to the center of Lake Michigan he towed the raftloads of sugar. Johnny Inkslinger stayed on shore. He watched and waited. Soon he saw all the mosquito-bees flying out over the lake after the rafts. Then Johnny Inkslinger realized what Paul Bunyan was up to.

"Oh, ain't he got a brain, though?" said Johnny Inkslinger worshipfully. "Oh, but ain't Paul Bunyan got a brain?"

[1] **peavies:** poles with iron points and movable iron hooks.

And a brain Paul Bunyan certainly had. For he had figured that the bee blood in the hybrid insects would send them after the sugar. And he had figured that their mosquito blood would make them fill their stomachs till they were stuffed. And Paul Bunyan knew the weight of sugar. . . .

Sure enough, the mosquito-bees glutted themselves on sugar till they could hardly fly. Then Paul Bunyan started Babe on a run for the shore. The stuffed insects tried to follow. But lower and lower they flew; and soon, with anguished buzz-hums, they all sank into the waters of the great lake; and that was the last of them.

The camp of Paul Bunyan was never again troubled by mammoth mosquitoes, or by mammoth mosquito-bees, either. Bum and Bill at last returned to camp, and gave every appearance of being ashamed of themselves. Paul Bunyan did not reproach them, but gave them a home in a furnished hive; and thereafter Bum and Bill occupied themselves solely with making honey for the loggers' flapjacks. Their fighting days were done.

History does not state the fate of the female mammoth mosquitoes. Some authorities advance the idea that they flew to Asia. They point to the elephant to prove their contention. The elephant, they assert, is descended from the mammoth mosquito of Paul Bunyan's time. Other authorities ridicule this idea, asserting that the elephant is too small to be a descendant of the mammoth mosquito.

All such ideas and contentions are guesswork, however. And guesswork has no place in the history of Paul Bunyan.

## Suggestions for Study

1. Can you understand why life on the frontier made "tall tales" especially popular there? Do you know other folk heroes of amazing power, like Pecos Bill the cowboy, and John Henry the railroad builder? Compare their exploits with Paul Bunyan's.

2. Even with the fun and exaggeration you can learn something about logging camps and how they operated from tales of Paul Bun-

yan. What real information did you pick up about the life?

3. Tall tales have always been a favorite diversion of Americans. Your own neighborhood has its pet "whoppers." Write out one of them — or make up a fresh one of your own. It is a good way to exercise your imagination.

4. If you like tall tales, take James Stevens's *Paul Bunyan*, J. C. Bowman's *Pecos Bill*, or Margaret Prescott Montague's *Tony Beaver* for one of your outside reading assignments. If you prefer short stories, try Mark Twain's great yarn, "The Jumping Frog."

# Ole E. Rölvaag [1]    1876–1931

## PRAIRIE DOOM

Along with the adventure and high-spirited fun of the frontier, it is well to have some simpler, darker details of the story. Ole Rölvaag came as a young man from Norway to join his uncle on a farm in North Dakota, where he heard tales of the early struggles of the pioneer settlers. Later he put them into the novel *Giants in the Earth* and its sequel *Peder Victorious*. The family in the novel consists of Per Hansa,[2] the father; Beret,[3] the mother; and their four children. At this point in the story they have completed their long journey from the East and are settled in a sod house in Dakota. But the great wave of settlers is constantly coming on from the East, and passing them for points farther west. Hardship and tragedy often ride with the caravans. Neighborliness and generosity are frequently called upon to help exhausted travelers. In those days every man's house had to be an inn. Along with independence and individualism, the pioneers had to develop the spirit of co-operation. Otherwise they could not have survived.

That summer many land seekers passed through the settlement on their way west. The arrival of a caravan was always an event of the greatest importance. How exciting they were, those little ships of the Great Plain! The prairie schooners, rigged with canvas tops which gleamed whitely in

[1] **Ole Rölvaag** (ō'lĕ rŭl'vôg). [2] **Per Hansa** (pĕr hän'sà). [3] **Beret** (bĕr'ĕt).

the shimmering light, first became visible as tiny specks against the eastern sky; one might almost imagine them to be sea gulls perched far, far away on an endless green meadow; but as one continued to watch, the white dots grew; they came drifting across the prairie like the day; after long waiting, they gradually floated out of the haze, distinct and clear; then, as they drew near, they proved to be veritable wagons, with horses hitched ahead, with folk and all their possessions inside, and a whole herd of cattle following behind.

The caravan would crawl slowly into the settlement and come to anchor in front of one of the sod houses; the moment it halted, people would swarm down and stretch themselves and begin to look after the teams; cattle would bellow; sheep would bleat as they ran about. Many queer races and costumes were to be seen in these caravans, and a babble of strange tongues shattered the air. Nut-brown youngsters, dressed only in a shirt and a pair of pants, would fly around between the huts, looking for other youngsters; an infant, its mother crooning softly to it, would sit securely perched in the fold of her arm; white-haired old men and women, who should have been living quietly at home, preparing for a different journey, were also to be seen in the group, running about like youngsters; the daily jogging from sky line to sky line had brightened their eyes and quickened their tongues. All were busy; each had a thousand questions to ask; every last one of them was in high spirits, though they knew no other home than the wagon and the blue skies above. . . . [1] The Lord only could tell whence all these people had come and whither they were going! . . .

The caravan usually intended to stop only long enough for the womenfolk to boil coffee and get a fresh supply of water; but the starting was always delayed, for the men had so many questions to ask. Once in a while during these halts a fiddler would bring out his fiddle and play a tune or two, and then there would be dancing. Such instances were rare, but good cheer and excitement invariably accompanied these visits.

Why not settle right here? the Spring Creek folk would ask the west movers. . . . There's plenty of good land left — nothing better to be found between here and the Pacific Ocean!

No, not yet. They weren't quite ready to settle; these parts looked fairly crowded. . . . The farther west, the better. . . . They guessed they would have to go on a way, though this really looked pretty good! . . .

And so the caravans would roll onward into the green stillness of the West. How strange — they vanished faster than they had appeared! The white sails grew smaller and smaller in the glow of the afternoon, until they had dwindled to nothing; the eye might seek them out there in the waning day, and search till it grew blurred, but all in vain — they were gone, and had left no trace! . . .

Foggy weather had now been hanging over the prairie for three whole days; a warm mist of rain mizzled continuously out of the low sky. Toward evening of the third day the fog lifted and clear sky again appeared; the setting sun burst through the cloud banks rolling up above the western horizon, and transformed them into marvelous fairy castles. . . . While this was going on, over to the northeast of the Solum boys' place a lonely wagon had crept into sight; it had almost reached the creek before anyone had noticed it, for the Solum boys were visiting among the Sognings, where there were many young people. But as Beret sat out in the yard, milking, the wagon crossed her view. When she brought in the milk, she remarked in her quiet manner that they were going to have company, at which tidings the rest of the family had to run out and see who might be coming at this time of day.

There was only one wagon, with two cows

---

[1] In this selection the dots do not represent something omitted, but are used by the author, as often in poetry, to suggest a thoughtful pause and produce a slow-moving, meditative style.

following behind; on the left side walked a brown-whiskered, stooping man — he was doing the driving; close behind him came a half-grown boy, dragging his feet heavily. The wagon at last crawled up the hill and came to a stop in Per Hansa's yard, where the whole family stood waiting.

"I don't suppose there are any Norwegians in this settlement? No, that would be too much to expect," said the man in a husky, wornout voice.

"If you're looking for Norwegians, you have found the right place, all right! We sift the people as they pass through here — keep our own, and let the others go!" . . . Per Hansa wanted to run on, for he felt in high spirits; but he checked himself, observing that the man looked as if he stood on the very brink of the grave.

Was there any chance of putting up here for the night?

"Certainly! certainly!" cried Per Hansa briskly, "provided they were willing to take things as they were."

The man didn't answer but walked, instead, to the wagon and spoke to someone inside.

"Kari,[1] now you must brace up and come down. Here we have found Norwegians at last!" As if fearing a contradiction, he added, "Ya, they are real Norwegians. I've talked with them."

On top of his words there came out of the wagon, first a puny boy with a hungry face, somewhat smaller than the other boy; then a girl of about the same size, but looking much older. She helped to get down another boy, about six years old, who evidently had been sleeping and looked cross and tired. That seemed to be all.

The man stepped closer to the wagon. "Aren't you coming, Kari?

A groan sounded within the canvas. The girl grabbed hold of her father's arm. "You must untie the rope! Can't you remember *anything?*" she whispered angrily.

"Ya, that's right! Wait a minute till I come and help you."

An irresistible curiosity took hold of Per

[1] **Kari** (kăr'ĭ).

Hansa; in two jumps he stood on the tongue of the wagon. The sight that met his eyes sent chills running down his spine. Inside sat a woman on a pile of clothes, with her back against a large immigrant chest; around her wrists and leading to the handles of the chest a strong rope was tied; her face was drawn and unnatural. Per Hansa trembled so violently that he had to catch hold of the wagon box, but inwardly he was swearing a steady stream. To him it looked as if the woman was crucified.

"For God's sake, man!" . . .

The stranger paid no attention; he was pottering about and pleading, "Come down now, Kari. . . . Ya, all right, I'll help you! Everything's going to be all right — I know it will! . . . Can you manage to get up?" He had untied the rope, and the woman had risen to her knees.

"O God!" she sighed, putting her hands to her head.

"Please come. That's right; I'll help you!" pleaded the man, as if he were trying to persuade a child.

She came down unsteadily. "Is this the place, Jakob?" she asked in a bewildered way. But now Beret ran up and put her arm around her; the women looked into each other's eyes and instantly a bond of understanding had been established. "You come with me!" urged Beret. . . . "O God! This isn't the place, either!" wailed the woman; but she followed Beret submissively into the house.

"Well, well!" sighed the man as he began to unhitch the horses. "Life isn't easy — no, it certainly isn't." . . .

Per Hansa watched him anxiously, hardly knowing what to do. Both the boys kept close to him. Then an idea flashed through his mind: "You boys run over to Hans Olsa's and tell him not to go to bed until I come. . . . No, I don't want him here. And you two stay over there tonight. Now run along!"

Turning to the man, he asked, "Aren't there any more in your party?"

"No, not now. We were five, you see, to begin with — five in all — but the others had to go on. . . . Haven't they been by here yet? Well, they must be somewhere over to the westward. . . . No, life isn't easy." . . . The man wandered on in his monotonous, blurred tone; he sounded all the time as if he were half sobbing.

"Where do you come from?" Per Hansa demanded gruffly.

The man didn't give a direct answer, but continued to ramble on in the same mournful way, stretching his story out interminably. . . . They had been wandering over the prairie for nearly six weeks. . . . Ya, it was a hard life. When they had started from Houston County, Minnesota, there had been five wagons in all. Strange that the others hadn't turned up here. Where could they be? It seemed to him as if he had traveled far enough to reach the ends of the earth! . . . Good God, what a nightmare life was! If he had only — only known! . . .

"Did the others go away and *leave you?*" Per Hansa hadn't intended to ask that question, but it had slipped out before he realized what he was saying. He wondered if there could be anything seriously wrong. . . .

"They couldn't possibly wait for us — couldn't have been expected to. Everything went wrong, you see, and I didn't know when I would be able to start again. . . . Turn the horses loose, John," he said to the boy. "Take the pail and see if you can squeeze some milk out of the cows. Poor beasts, they don't give much now!" Then he turned to Per Hansa again. "I don't know what would have become of us if we hadn't reached this place tonight! We'd have been in a bad hole, that I assure you! Womenfolk can't bear up." . . . The man stopped and blew his nose.

Per Hansa dreaded what might be coming next. "You must have got off your course, since you are coming down from the North?"

The man shook his head helplessly. "To tell the truth, I don't know where we've been these last few days. We couldn't see the sun."

"Haven't you got a compass?"

"Compass? No! I tried to steer with a rope, but the one I had wasn't long enough."

"You didn't!" exclaimed Per Hansa excitedly, full of a sudden new interest.

"Ya, I tried that rope idea — hitched it to the back of the wagon, and let it drag in the wet grass. But it didn't work — I couldn't steer straight with it. The rope was so short, and kept kinking around so much, that it didn't leave any wake."

"Uh-huh!" nodded Per Hansa wisely. "You must be a seafaring man, to have tried that trick!"

"No, I'm no sailor. But fisherfolk out here have told me that it's possible to steer by a rope. . . . I had to try *something.*"

"Where did you cross the Sioux?"

"How do I know where I crossed it? We came to a river a long way to the east of here — that must have been the Sioux. We hunted and hunted before we could find a place shallow enough to cross. . . . God! this has certainly been a wandering in the desert for me! . . . But if Kari only gets better, I won't complain — though I never dreamed that life could be so hard." . . .

"Is she — is she *sick,* that woman of yours?"

The man did not answer this question immediately; he wiped his face with the sleeve of his shirt. When he spoke again, his voice had grown even more blurred and indistinct. "Physically she seems to be as well as ever — as far as I can see. She certainly hasn't overworked since we've been traveling. I hope there's nothing wrong with her. . . . But certain things are hard to bear — I suppose it's worse for the mother, too — though the Lord knows it hasn't been easy for me, either! . . . You see, we had to leave our youngest boy out there on the prairie." . . .

"*Leave* him?" . . . These were the only two words that came to Per Hansa's mind.

"Ya, there he lies, our little boy! . . . I never saw a more promising man — you know what I mean — when he grew up. . . . But now — oh, well." . . .

Per Hansa felt faint in the pit of his stomach; his throat grew dry; his voice became as husky as that of the other; he came close up to him. " Tell me — how did this happen? "

The man shook his head again, in a sort of dumb despair. Then he cleared his throat and continued with great effort. " I can't tell how it happened! Fate just willed it so. Such things are not to be explained. . . . The boy had been ailing for some time — we knew that, but didn't pay much attention. We had other things to think of.·. . . Then he began to fail fast. We were only one day's journey this side of Jackson; so we went back. That was the time when the others left us. I don't blame them much — it was uncertain when' we could go on. . . . The doctor we found wasn't a capable man — I realize it now. He spoke only English and couldn't understand what I was said. He had no idea what was wrong with the boy — I could see that plainly enough. . . . Ya, well — so we started again. . . . It isn't any use to fight against fate; that's an old saying, and a true one, too, I guess. . . . Before long we saw that the boy wasn't going to recover. So we hurried on, day and night, trying to catch our neighbors. . . . Well, that's about all of it. One night he was gone — just as if you had blown out a candle. Ya, let me see — that was five nights ago."

" Have you got him there in the wagon? " demanded Per Hansa, grabbing the man by the arm.

" No, no," he muttered huskily. " We buried him out there by a big stone — no coffin or anything. But Kari took the best skirt she had and wrapped it all around him — we had to do *something,* you know. . . . But," he continued, suddenly straightening up, " Paul cannot lie there! As soon as I find my neighbors, I'll go and get him. Otherwise Kari . . ." The man paused between the sobs that threatened to choke him. " I have had to tie her up the last few days. She insisted on getting out and going back to Paul. I don't think she has had a wink of sleep for over a week. . . . It's just as I was saying — some people can't stand things." . . .

Per Hansa leaned heavily against the wagon. " Has she gone crazy? " he asked hoarsely.

" She isn't much worse than the rest of us. I don't believe . . . Kari is really a well-balanced woman . . . but you can imagine how it feels, to leave a child *that* way." . . .

The boy, John, had finished milking. He had put the pail down and was standing a little way off, listening to his father's story; suddenly, he threw himself on the ground, sobbing as if in convulsions.

" John! John! " admonished the father. " Aren't you ashamed of yourself — a grown-up man like you! Take the milk and carry it into the house! "

" That's right! " echoed Per Hansa, pulling himself together. " We'd better all go in. There's shelter here, and plenty to eat."

Beret was bustling around the room when they entered; she had put the woman to bed, and now was tending her. " Where are the boys? " she asked.

Per Hansa told her that he had sent them to Hans Olsa's for the night.

" That was hardly necessary; we could have made room here somehow." Beret's voice carried a note of keen reproach.

The man had paused at the door; now he came over to the bed, took the limp hand, and muttered, " Poor soul! . . . Why, I believe she's asleep already! "

Beret came up and pushed him gently aside. " Be careful! Don't wake her. She needs the rest."

" Ya, I don't doubt it — not I! She hasn't slept for a week, you see — the poor soul! " With a loud sniff, he turned and left the room.

When suppertime came, the woman seemed to be engulfed in a stupefying sleep. Beret did not join the others at the supper table, but busied herself, instead, by trying to make the woman more comfortable; she loosened her clothes, took off her shoes, and washed her face in warm water; during all this the stranger never stirred. That done, Beret began to fix up sleeping quarters for the strangers — in the barn. She carried in fresh hay and brought out all the bedding she had; she herself would take care of the woman, in case she awoke and needed attention. Beret did little talking, but she went about these arrangements with a firmness and confidence that surprised her husband.

Per Hansa came in from the barn, after helping the strangers settle themselves for the night. Beret was sitting on the edge of the bed, dressing the baby for the night; she had put And-Ongen [1] to bed beside the distracted woman.

"Did she tell you much?" he asked in a low voice.

Beret glanced toward the other bed before she answered.

"Only that she had had to leave one of her children on the way. She wasn't able to talk connectedly."

"It's a terrible thing!" he said, looking away from his wife. "I think I'll go over to Hans Olsa's for a minute. I want to talk this matter over with him."

"Talk it over with him?" she repeated coldly. "I don't suppose Hans Olsa knows everything!"

"No, of course not. But these people have got to be helped, and we can't do it all alone." He hesitated for a minute, as if waiting for her consent. "Well, I won't be gone long," he said as he went out of the door.

When he returned, an hour later, she was still sitting on the edge of the bed, with the baby asleep on her lap. They sat in silence for a long while; at last he began to undress. She waited until he was in bed, then turned the lamp low and lay down herself, but without undressing. . . . The lamp shed only a faint light. It was so quiet in the room that one could hear the breathing of all the others. Beret lay there listening; though the room was still, it seemed alive to her with strange movements; she forced herself to open her eyes and look around. Noticing that Per Hansa wasn't asleep, either, she asked:

[1] **And-Ongen** (ănd-ôn'gĕn): Beret's little daughter.

"Did you look after the boys?"

"Nothing the matter with them! They were fast asleep in Sofie's bed."

"You told them everything, at Hans Olsa's?"

"Of course!"

"What did they think of it?"

Per Hansa raised himself on his elbows and glanced at the broken creature lying in the bed back of theirs. The woman, apparently, had not stirred a muscle. "It's a bad business," he said. "We must try to get together a coffin and find the boy. We can't let him lie out there — that way." . . . As Beret made no answer, he briefly narrated the story that the man had told him. "The fellow is a good-for-nothing, stupid fool, I'm sure of that," concluded Per Hansa.

She listened to him in silence. For some time she brooded over her thoughts; then in a bitter tone she suddenly burst out, "Now you can see that this kind of a life is impossible! It's beyond human endurance."

He had not the power to read her thoughts; he did not want to know them; tonight every nerve in his body was taut with apprehension and dismay. But he tried to say, reassuringly, "Hans Olsa and I will both go with the man, as soon as the day breaks. If we only had something to make the coffin of! The few pieces of board that I've got here will hardly be enough. . . . Now let's go to sleep. Be sure and call me if you need anything!"

He turned over resolutely, as if determined to sleep; but she noticed that he was a long time doing it. . . . I wonder what's going through his mind? she thought. She was glad to have him awake, just the same; tonight there were strange things abroad in the room. . . .

[Perhaps you would like to know what happens later to these unfortunate travelers. During the night the crazed woman, Kari, thinking she must search for the body of her little boy, seized And-Ongen, Beret's child, and carried her out on the prairie. When their absence was discovered, Per Hansa rushed out in pursuit and was able to bring them back before any harm was done except for the terror suffered by Per and Beret. The next day the neighbors made a little coffin, and two of the men started out with the strangers to try to find the child's body. After four days they returned with the little coffin still empty. Then the strangers started out again on their westward trek, and this is the last we hear of them in the story. The whole incident, however, is a foreshadowing of the mental darkness that settled over Beret toward the end of the novel.]

## Suggestions for Study

1. Which hardships of pioneer days are more emphasized in this selection, the physical or the mental? What brighter side of the picture is given? Discuss the life of pioneers from all these angles.

2. How many different nationalities can you name that had a prominent part in the settlement of the West? Why were the Scandinavians particularly suited to build up the Northwest? How many of their characteristics can you gather from this selection?

3. Make a list, either individually or as a class, of all the books you have read or the movies you have seen which picture the covered-wagon days. Discuss the impressions of prairie life you have gained from these in comparison with the selection from *Giants in the Earth.*

4. If you live in a community where it is possible to collect actual experiences of pioneers from the older residents, assemble these for a storytelling hour or to put in a booklet for the school library.

5. Where in our modern world have large-scale migrations taken place? Have most of these been voluntary or forced? Investigate some one of these and write an incident of a migrating family; try to make the characters come alive.

## Bret Harte      1836–1902

### THE OUTCASTS OF POKER FLAT

Now that you are acquainted with the real West, see if you can detect for yourself the subtle changes that took place in literature about it when the local-color movement made capital of its many differences from other

BRET HARTE, in this picture, displays the affluence and easy confidence which became characteristic of the West. (Brown Brothers)

parts of the country. It will be easy to see why Bret Harte's stories swept the country, making him one of the most popular short-story writers the country has known.

As Mr. John Oakhurst, gambler, stepped into the main street of Poker Flat on the morning of the twenty-third of November, 1850, he was conscious of a change in its moral atmosphere since the preceding night. Two or three men, conversing earnestly together, ceased as he approached, and exchanged significant glances. There was a Sabbath lull in the air, which, in a settlement unused to Sabbath influences, looked ominous.

Mr. Oakhurst's calm, handsome face betrayed small concern in these indications. Whether he was conscious of any predisposing cause was another question. " I reckon they're after somebody," he reflected; " likely it's me." He returned to his pocket the handkerchief with which he had been whipping away the red dust of Poker Flat from his neat boots, and quietly discharged his mind of any further conjecture.

In point of fact, Poker Flat was " after somebody." It had lately suffered the loss of several thousand dollars, two valuable horses, and a prominent citizen. It was experiencing a spasm of virtuous reaction, quite as lawless and ungovernable as any of the acts that had provoked it. A secret committee had determined to rid the town of all improper persons. This was done permanently in regard to two men who were then hanging from the boughs of a sycamore in the gulch, and temporarily in the banishment of certain other objectionable characters. I regret to say that some of these were ladies. It is but due to the sex, however, to state that their impropriety was professional, and it was only in such easily established standards of evil that Poker Flat ventured to sit in judgment.

Mr. Oakhurst was right in supposing that he was included in this category. A few of the committee had urged hanging him as a possible example and a sure method of reimbursing themselves from his pockets of the sums he had won from them. " It's agin justice," said Jim Wheeler, " to let this yer young man from Roaring Camp — an entire stranger — carry away our money." But a crude sentiment of equity residing in the breasts of those who had been fortunate enough to win from Mr. Oakhurst overruled this narrower local prejudice.

Mr. Oakhurst received his sentence with philosophic calmness, nonetheless coolly that he was aware of the hesitation of his judges. He was too much of a gambler not to accept fate. With him life was at best an uncertain game, and he recognized the usual percentage in favor of the dealer.

A body of armed men accompanied the deported wickedness of Poker Flat to the outskirts of the settlement. Besides Mr. Oakhurst, who was known to be a coolly desperate man, and for whose intimidation the armed escort was intended, the expatriated party consisted of a young woman familiarly known as " The Duchess"; another who had won the title of " Mother Shipton "; and " Uncle Billy," a suspected sluice robber and confirmed drunkard. The cavalcade provoked no comments from the spectators, nor was any word uttered by the escort. Only when the gulch which marked the uttermost limit of Poker Flat was reached, the leader spoke briefly and to the point. The exiles were forbidden to return at the peril of their lives.

As the escort disappeared, their pent-up feelings found vent in a few hysterical tears from the Duchess, some bad language from Mother Shipton, and a Parthian [1] volley of expletives from Uncle Billy. The philosophic Oakhurst alone remained silent. He listened calmly to Mother Shipton's desire to cut somebody's heart out, to the repeated statements of the Duchess that she would die in the road, and to the alarming oaths that seemed to be bumped out of Uncle Billy as he rode forward. With the easy good humor characteristic of his class, he insisted upon exchanging his own riding horse, " Five-Spot," for the sorry mule which the Duchess rode. But even this act did not draw the party into any closer sympathy. The young woman readjusted her somewhat draggled plumes with a feeble, faded coquetry; Mother Shipton eyed the possessor of Five-Spot with malevolence, and Uncle Billy included the whole party in one sweeping anathema.

The road to Sandy Bar — a camp that, not having as yet experienced the regenerating influences of Poker Flat, consequently seemed to offer some invitation to the emigrants — lay over a steep mountain range. It was distant a day's severe travel. In that advanced season the party soon passed out

[1] **Parthian:** The Parthians were an ancient people who shot their arrows while fleeing.

of the moist, temperate regions of the foothills into the dry, cold, bracing air of the Sierras. The trail was narrow and difficult. At noon the Duchess, rolling out of her saddle upon the ground, declared her intention of going no farther, and the party halted.

The spot was singularly wild and impressive. A wooded amphitheater, surrounded on three sides by precipitous cliffs of naked granite, sloped gently toward the crest of another precipice that overlooked the valley. It was, undoubtedly, the most suitable spot for a camp, had camping been advisable. But Mr. Oakhurst knew that scarcely half the journey to Sandy Bar was accomplished, and the party were not equipped or provisioned for delay. This fact he pointed out to his companions curtly, with a philosophic commentary on the folly of " throwing up their hand before the game was played out." But they were furnished with liquor, which in this emergency stood them in place of food, fuel, rest, and prescience. In spite of his remonstrances, it was not long before they were more or less under its influence. Uncle Billy passed rapidly from a bellicose state into one of stupor, the Duchess became maudlin, and Mother Shipton snored. Mr. Oakhurst alone remained erect, leaning against a rock, calmly surveying them.

Mr. Oakhurst did not drink. It interfered with a profession which required coolness, impassiveness, and presence of mind, and, in his own language, he " couldn't afford it." As he gazed at his recumbent fellow exiles, the loneliness begotten of his pariah trade, his habits of life, his very vices, for the first time seriously oppressed him. He bestirred himself in dusting his black clothes, washing his hands and face, and other acts characteristic of his studiously neat habits, and for a moment forgot his annoyance. The thought of deserting his weaker and more pitiable companions never perhaps occurred to him. Yet he could not help feeling the want of that excitement which, singularly enough, was most conducive to that calm equanimity for which he was notorious. He looked at the gloomy walls that rose a thousand feet sheer above the circling pines around him, at the sky ominously clouded, at the valley below, already deepening into shadow; and, doing so, suddenly he heard his own name called.

A horseman slowly ascended the trail. In the fresh, open face of the newcomer Mr. Oakhurst recognized Tom Simson, otherwise known as " The Innocent," of Sandy Bar. He had met him sometime before over a " little game," and had, with perfect equanimity, won the entire fortune — amounting to some forty dollars — of that guileless youth. After the game was finished, Mr. Oakhurst drew the youthful speculator behind the door and thus addressed him: " Tommy, you're a good little man, but you can't gamble worth a cent. Don't try it over again." He then handed him his money back, pushed him gently from the room, and so made a devoted slave of Tom Simson.

There was a remembrance of this in his boyish and enthusiastic greeting of Mr. Oakhurst. He had started, he said, to go to Poker Flat to seek his fortune. " Alone? " No, not exactly alone; in fact (a giggle), he had run away with Piney Woods. Didn't Mr. Oakhurst remember Piney? She that used to wait on the table at the Temperance House? They had been engaged a long time, but old Jake Woods had objected, and so they had run away, and were going to Poker Flat to be married, and here they were. And they were tired out, and how lucky it was they had found a place to camp, and company. All this the Innocent delivered rapidly, while Piney, a stout, comely damsel of fifteen, emerged from behind the pine tree, where she had been blushing unseen, and rode to the side of her lover.

Mr. Oakhurst seldom troubled himself with sentiment, still less with propriety; but he had a vague idea that the situation was not fortunate. He retained, however, his presence of mind sufficiently to kick Uncle Billy, who was about to say something, and Uncle Billy was sober enough to recognize in Mr. Oakhurst's kick a superior power that would not bear trifling. He then endeavored to dissuade Tom Simson from delaying further, but in vain. He even pointed out the fact that there was no provision, nor means of making a camp. But, unluckily, the Innocent met this objection by assuring the party that he was provided with an extra mule loaded with provisions, and by the discovery of a rude attempt at a log house near the trail. " Piney can stay with Mrs. Oakhurst," said the Innocent, pointing to the Duchess, " and I can shift for myself."

Nothing but Mr. Oakhurst's admonishing foot saved Uncle Billy from bursting into a roar of laughter. As it was, he felt compelled to retire up the canyon until he could recover his gravity. There he confided the joke to the tall pine trees, with many slaps of his leg, contortions of his face, and the usual profanity. But when he returned to the party, he found them seated by a fire — for the air had grown strangely chill and the sky overcast — in apparently amicable conversation. Piney was actually talking in an impulsive girlish fashion to the Duchess, who was listening with an interest and animation she had not shown for many days. The Innocent was holding forth, apparently with equal effect, to Mr. Oakhurst and Mother Shipton, who was actually relaxing into amiability. " Is this yer a d——d picnic? " said Uncle Billy, with inward scorn, as he surveyed the sylvan group, the glancing firelight, and the tethered animals in the foreground. Suddenly an idea mingled with the alcoholic fumes that disturbed his brain. It was apparently of a jocular nature, for he felt impelled to slap his leg again and cram his fist into his mouth.

As the shadows crept slowly up the mountain, a slight breeze rocked the tops of the pine trees and moaned through their long and gloomy aisles. The ruined cabin, patched and covered with pine boughs, was set apart for the ladies. As the lovers parted, they unaffectedly exchanged a kiss, so honest and sincere that it might have been heard above the swaying pines. The frail Duchess and the malevolent Mother

Shipton were probably too stunned to remark upon this last evidence of simplicity, and so turned without a word to the hut. The fire was replenished, the men lay down before the door, and in a few minutes were asleep.

Mr. Oakhurst was a light sleeper. Toward morning he awoke benumbed and cold. As he stirred the dying fire, the wind, which was now blowing strongly, brought to his cheek that which caused the blood to leave it — snow!

He started to his feet with the intention of awakening the sleepers, for there was no time to lose. But, turning to where Uncle Billy had been lying, he found him gone. A suspicion leaped to his brain, and a curse to his lips. He ran to the spot where the mules had been tethered — they were no longer there. The tracks were already rapidly disappearing in the snow.

The momentary excitement brought Mr. Oakhurst back to the fire with his usual calm. He did not waken the sleepers. The Innocent slumbered peacefully, with a smile on his good-humored, freckled face: the virgin Piney slept beside her frailer sisters as sweetly as though attended by celestial guardians; and Mr. Oakhurst, drawing his blanket over his shoulders, stroked his mustaches and waited for the dawn. It came slowly in a whirly mist of snowflakes that dazzled and confused the eye. What could be seen of the landscape appeared magically changed. He looked over the valley, and summed up the present and future in two words, " Snowed in! "

A careful inventory of the provisions, which, fortunately for the party, had been stored within the hut, and so escaped the felonious fingers of Uncle Billy, disclosed the fact that with care and prudence they might last ten days longer. " That is," said Mr. Oakhurst *sotto voce* [1] to the Innocent, " if you're willing to board us. If you ain't — and perhaps you'd better not — you can wait till Uncle Billy gets back with provisions." For some occult reason, Mr. Oak-

[1] **sotto voce** (sŏt′tŏ vō′chȧ): in an undertone (Italian).

hurst could not bring himself to disclose Uncle Billy's rascality, and so offered the hypothesis that he had wandered from the camp and had accidentally stampeded the animals. He dropped a warning to the Duchess and Mother Shipton, who of course knew the facts of their associate's defection. "They'll find out the truth about us *all* when they find out anything," he added significantly, " and there's no good frightening them now."

Tom Simson not only put all his worldly store at the disposal of Mr. Oakhurst, but seemed to enjoy the prospect of their enforced seclusion. "We'll have a good camp for a week, and then the snow'll melt, and we'll all go back together." The cheerful gaiety of the young man and Mr. Oakhurst's calm infected the others. The Innocent, with the aid of pine boughs, extemporized a thatch for the roofless cabin, and the Duchess directed Piney in the rearrangement of the interior with a taste and tact that opened the blue eyes of that provincial maiden to their fullest extent. " I reckon now you're used to fine things at Poker Flat," said Piney. The Duchess turned away sharply to conceal something that reddened her cheeks through their professional tint, and Mother Shipton requested Piney not to " chatter." But when Mr. Oakhurst returned from a weary search for the trail, he heard the sound of happy laughter echoed from the rocks. He stopped in some alarm, and his thoughts first naturally reverted to the whisky, which he had prudently cached. " And yet it don't somehow sound like whisky," said the gambler. It was not until he caught sight of the blazing fire through the still blind storm, and the group around it, that he settled to the conviction that it was " square fun."

Whether Mr. Oakhurst had cached his cards with the whisky as something debarred the free access of the community, I cannot say. It was certain that, in Mother Shipton's words, he " didn't say ' cards ' once " during that evening. Haply the time was beguiled by an accordion, produced somewhat ostentatiously by Tom Simson

from his pack. Nothwithstanding some difficulties attending the manipulation of this instrument, Piney Woods managed to pluck several reluctant melodies from its keys, to an accompaniment by the Innocent on a pair of bone castanets. But the crowning festivity of the evening was reached in a rude camp-meeting hymn, which the lovers, joining hands, sang with great earnestness and vociferation. I fear that a certain defiant tone and Convenanters' [1] swing to its chorus, rather than any devotional quality, caused it speedily to infect the others, who at last joined in the refrain:

" I'm proud to live in the service of the Lord,
And I'm bound to die in His army."

The pines rocked, the storm eddied and whirled above the miserable group, and the flames of their altar leaped heavenward, as if in token of the vow.

At midnight the storm abated, the rolling clouds parted, and the stars glittered keenly above the sleeping camp. Mr. Oakhurst, whose professional habits had enabled him to live on the smallest possible amount of sleep, in dividing the watch with Tom Simson somehow managed to take upon himself the greater part of that duty. He excused himself to the Innocent by saying that he had " often been a week without sleep." " Doing what? " asked Tom. " Poker! " replied Oakhurst sententiously. " When a man gets a streak of luck, he don't get tired. The luck gives in first. Luck," continued the gambler reflectively, " is a mighty queer thing. All you know about it for certain is that it's bound to change. And it's finding out when it's going to change that makes you. We've had a streak of bad luck since we left Poker Flat — you come along, and slap, you get into it, too. If you can hold your cards right along you're all right. For," added the gambler, with cheerful irrelevance,

" I'm proud to live in the service of the Lord,
And I'm bound to die in His army."

[1] **Covenanters:** in seventeenth-century Scotland, adherents of the Presbyterian Covenant to resist the rule of the Anglican Church.

The third day came, and the sun, looking through the white-curtained valley, saw the outcasts dividing their slowly decreasing store of provisions for the morning meal. It was one of the peculiarities of that mountain climate that its rays diffused a kindly warmth over the wintry landscape, as if in regretful commiseration of the past. But it revealed drift on drift of snow piled high around the hut — a hopeless, uncharted, trackless sea of white lying below the rocky shores to which the castaways still clung. Through the marvelously clear air the smoke of the pastoral village of Poker Flat rose miles away. Mother Shipton saw it, and from a remote pinnacle of her rocky fastness hurled in that direction a final malediction. It was her last vituperative attempt, and perhaps for that reason was invested with a certain degree of sublimity. It did her good, she privately informed the Duchess. " Just you go out there and cuss, and see." She then set herself to the task of amusing " the child," as she and the Duchess were pleased to call Piney. Piney was no chicken, but it was a soothing and original theory of the pair thus to account for the fact that she didn't swear and wasn't improper.

When night crept up again through the gorges, the reedy notes of the accordion rose and fell in fitful spasms and long-drawn gasps by the flickering campfire. But music failed to fill entirely the aching void left by insufficient food, and a new diversion was proposed by Piney — storytelling. Neither Mr. Oakhurst nor his female companions caring to relate their personal experiences, this plan would have failed too, but for the Innocent. Some months before he had chanced upon a stray copy of Mr. Pope's ingenious translation of the *Iliad*. He now proposed to narrate the principal incidents of that poem — having thoroughly mastered the argument and fairly forgotten the words — in the current vernacular of Sandy Bar. And so for the rest of that night the Homeric demigods again walked the earth. Trojan bully and wily Greek wrestled in the winds, and the great

pines in the canyon seemed to bow to the wrath of the son of Peleus.[1] Mr. Oakhurst listened with great satisfaction. Most especially was he interested in the fate of " Ashheels," as the Innocent persisted in denominating the " swift-footed Achilles."

So, with small food and much of Homer and the accordion, a week passed over the heads of the outcasts. The sun again forsook them, and again from leaden skies the snowflakes were sifted over the land. Day by day closer around them drew the snowy circle, until at last they looked from their prison over drifted walls of dazzling white, that towered twenty feet above their heads. It became more and more difficult to replenish their fires, even from the fallen trees beside them, now half hidden in the drifts. And yet no one complained. The lovers turned from the dreary prospect and looked into each other's eyes, and were happy. Mr. Oakhurst settled himself coolly to the losing game before him. The Duchess, more cheerful than she had been, assumed the care of Piney. Only Mother Shipton — once the strongest of the party — seemed to sicken and fade. At midnight on the tenth day she called Oakhurst to her side. " I'm going," she said, in a voice of querulous weakness, " but don't say anything about it. Don't waken the kids. Take the bundle from under my head, and open it." Mr. Oakhurst did so. It contained Mother Shipton's rations for the last week, untouched. " Give 'em to the child," she said, pointing to the sleeping Piney. " You've starved yourself," said the gambler. " That's what they call it," said the woman querulously, as she lay down again, and, turning her face to the wall, passed quietly away.

The accordion and the bones were put aside that day, and Homer was forgotten. When the body of Mother Shipton had been committed to the snow, Mr. Oakhurst took the Innocent aside, and showed him a pair of snowshoes, which he had fashioned from the old packsaddle. " There's one chance in a hundred to save her yet," he

[1] son of Peleus (pē′lūs): Achilles (ȧ-kĭl′ēz), the hero of the *Iliad*.

said, pointing to Piney; "but it's there," he added, pointing toward Poker Flat. "If you can reach there in two days she's safe." "And you?" asked Tom Stimson. "I'll stay here," was the curt reply.

The lovers parted with a long embrace. "You are not going, too?" said the Duchess, as she saw Mr. Oakhurst apparently waiting to accompany him. "As far as the canyon," he replied. He turned suddenly and kissed the Duchess, leaving her pallid face aflame, and her trembling limbs rigid with amazement.

Night came, but not Mr. Oakhurst. It brought the storm again and the whirling snow. Then the Duchess, feeding the fire, found someone had quietly piled beside the hut enough fuel to last a few days longer. The tears rose to her eyes, but she hid them from Piney.

The women slept but little. In the morning looking into each other's faces, they read their fate. Neither spoke, but Piney, accepting the position of the stronger, drew near and placed her arm around the Duchess's waist. They kept this attitude for the rest of the day. That night the storm reached its greatest fury, and, rending asunder the protecting vines, invaded the very hut.

Toward morning they found themselves unable to feed the fire, which gradually died away. As the embers slowly blackened, the Duchess crept closer to Piney, and broke the silence of many hours: "Piney, can you pray?" "No, dear," said Piney simply. The Duchess, without knowing exactly why, felt relieved, and, putting her head upon Piney's shoulder, spoke no more. And so reclining, the younger and purer pillowing the head of her soiled sister upon her virgin breast, they fell asleep.

The wind lulled as if it feared to waken them. Feathery drifts of snow, shaken from the long pine boughs, flew like white-winged birds, and settled about them as they slept. The moon through the rifted clouds looked down upon what had been the camp. But all human stain, all trace of earthly travail, was hidden beneath the spotless mantle mercifully flung from above.

They slept all that day and the next, nor did they waken when voices and footsteps broke the silence of the camp. And when pitying fingers brushed the snow from their wan faces, you could scarcely have told from the equal peace that dwelt upon them which was she that had sinned. Even the law of Poker Flat recognized this, and turned away, leaving them still locked in each other's arms.

But at the head of the gulch, on one of the largest pine trees, they found the deuce of clubs pinned to the bark with a bowie knife. It bore the following, written in pencil in a firm hand:

BENEATH THIS TREE
LIES THE BODY
OF

## JOHN OAKHURST

WHO STRUCK A STREAK OF BAD LUCK
ON THE 23D OF NOVEMBER, 1850,
AND
HANDED IN HIS CHECKS
ON THE 7TH DECEMBER, 1850.

And pulseless and cold, with a Derringer by his side and a bullet in his heart, though still calm as in life, beneath the snow lay he who was at once the strongest and yet the weakest of the outcasts of Poker Flat.

## Suggestions for Study

1. What typically Western circumstances form the basis of this story? Do you know anything about the vigilante groups that kept order in the West before the law was well enough established to take over the job? What do you think of the arguments for merely banishing Oakhurst instead of hanging him?

2. Though the West has many authentic stories of noble unselfishness, this picture is extreme. Which of the characters acted realistically in the dilemma? What situation does Harte use to bring out the best in the other outcasts?

# THE WESTWARD MOVEMENT AND THE WAR

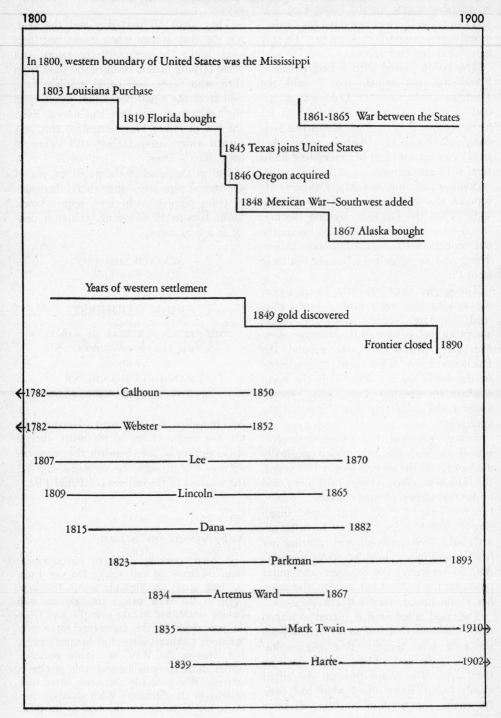

1800                                                          1900

In 1800, western boundary of United States was the Mississippi

1803 Louisiana Purchase

1819 Florida bought

1861-1865   War between the States

1845 Texas joins United States

1846 Oregon acquired

1848 Mexican War—Southwest added

1867 Alaska bought

Years of western settlement

1849 gold discovered

Frontier closed | 1890

1782 ———————— Calhoun ———————— 1850

1782 ———————— Webster ———————— 1852

1807 ———————— Lee ———————— 1870

1809 ———————— Lincoln ———————— 1865

1815 ———————— Dana ———————— 1882

1823 ———————— Parkman ———————— 1893

1834 ———————— Artemus Ward ———————— 1867

1835 ———————— Mark Twain ———————— 1910

1839 ———————— Harte ———————— 1902

3. One of Harte's assets was his humor. What evidence of it do you find in this story, one of his more serious ones? What characters furnish the humor?

4. Other of Harte's stories bring out other ways of the West. Read "Tennessee's Partner" and "The Luck of Roaring Camp" to fill out the picture he painted of the West.

5. For comparison with a genuine Western desperado and the vigilantes' handling of him, read Chapter XI of Mark Twain's *Roughing It*.

6. Vocabulary: category, equity, sluice, expletives, anathema, prescience, pariah, occult, hypothesis, defection, cached, irrelevance, malediction.

## For Your Vocabulary

CONTEXT. The outcasts take their expulsion in different ways that reveal their dispositions and characters, and Harte has some choice words to describe their reactions. With a whole story for context, you can master their meaning easily. One of the party is *bellicose* (bĕl'ĭ-kōs), inclined to " go to war " (see the relation to *belligerent?*). Another is *maudlin* (môd'lĭn), or tearfully emotional, a state often associated, as in this case, with drunkenness. Only one of them meets the crisis with *equanimity* (ē-kwá-nĭm'ĭ-tĭ), a calm, even state of mind. Think about the meaning of each word, and see if you can recall without looking back in the story which character's reaction it described. Check up if you need to. The words are used on page 715.

WORD ANALYSIS. If you think of the word *patriot*, one devoted to his own country, *expatriated* (page 714) will be easy to understand. Remember our current use of *felon* (fĕl'ŭn) to mean one who has committed a serious offense in the sight of the law and *felony* to designate a crime more serious than a misdemeanor, and *felonious* (fĕ-lō'nĭ-ŭs) is clear. *Intimidation* offers only a slight problem in deciding whether the *in-* means not or in, toward. To decipher *commiseration* (page 718) you need only to recall that *com-* means with.

REVIEW. Several words used in this story have been discussed in notes you have already studied. Did you recognize *malevolence*, *replenish*, *ostentatiously*, *malediction*, and *pallid?*

## For Further Reading on the Westward Movement

### BOOKS ABOUT THE PERIOD

#### Fiction

Adams, Andy: *The Log of a Cowboy*
Cable, G. W.: *Old Creole Days*
Hough, Emerson: *North of '36*
James, Will: *Home Ranch; Smoky*
Lane, R. W.: *Let the Hurricane Roar; Free Land*
Page, Elizabeth: *Wagons West*
Richter, Conrad: *The Trees*

#### Folklore

Bowman, J. C.: *Pecos Bill*
Chaplin, Henry: *The Adventures of Johnny Appleseed*
Lomax, John A.: *Cowboy Songs; Songs of the Cattle Trail and Cow Camp*
Lummis, C. F.: *Pueblo Indian Folk-Stories*
Thorp, N. H.: *Songs of the Cowboys*

#### Biography

Bruce, H. A. B.: *Daniel Boone and the Wilderness Road*
Dobie, J. Frank: *A Vaquero of the Brush Country*
Ellis, Anne: *The Life of an Ordinary Woman*
Rourke, Constance: *Davy Crockett*
Saxon, Lyle: *Lafitte the Pirate*
Vestal, Stanley: *Kit Carson; Sitting Bull*

#### Informal History

Chapman, Arthur: *The Pony Express*
Dobie, J. Frank: *Coronado's Children; Apache Gold and Yaqui Silver; The Longhorns*
Duffus, R. L.: *The Santa Fe Trail*
Garland, Hamlin: *The Book of the American Indian*
Hough, Emerson: *The Story of the Cowboy*
Orth, S. P.: *Our Foreigners*
Paine, R. H.: *Ships and Sailors of Old Salem; The Old Merchant Marine*
Radin, Paul: *The Story of the American Indian*
Sabin, E. L.: *Gold-Seekers of '49*
Saxon, Lyle: *Father Mississippi; Fabulous New Orleans*
Stockton, F. R.: *Buccaneers and Pirates of Our Coast*
Sullivan, O. M.: *The Empire Builder*
Vestal, Stanley: *Warpath; The Old Santa Fe Trail*

THE AUTOMOBILE was one of the important new inventions to bring a radical change in American life at the turn of the century when "realism" was the dominant trend in American Literature. (Culver)

# The Growth of Realism

WRITERS USUALLY don't know that they belong to a literary "movement." They write what they think, the best way they can write it, and let other people worry about what movement they belong to. Certainly Emerson or Mark Twain or Whitman couldn't have said whether he belonged to a literary movement or didn't.

But it sometimes helps us to understand the history of literature if we divide it into movements, and when a country gets older and more sophisticated, when it has more writers and they see more of each other, then it becomes easier to pick out and name those movements. In the case of this country, most historians say that a literary movement — or way of writing — called realism began about 1880, with William Dean Howells and Henry James, and has continued into our own time.

## THE MACHINE AGE

Realism came out of what was happening to the country. For one thing, it came out of an age of science and invention.

No country ever needed machines worse than the American West. Everything in the West was on such a vast scale — the farms so large, the mineral deposits so great, the distances so overwhelming, and the rewards so inviting to anyone who could claim them — that, from the beginning of settlement until today, the West has called for machinery to supplement the work of men. And the practical, inventive Americans have responded by devising machines powerful and wonderful enough to compete with nature itself.

Here are some of the machines developed during the century after the West was opened:

1787   John Fitch's steamboat (Robert Fulton's *Clermont* ran from New York to Albany and back in 1807.)

1791   Samuel Slater's spinning mill

1793   Eli Whitney's cotton gin

1798   David Wilkinson's machine tool for making machines

1802   Oliver Evans's new high-power steam engine

1831   Steam trains began to run in South Carolina. (Trains began to run from Philadelphia to Pittsburgh in 1852, the Baltimore and Ohio reached Ohio in 1853, and in that same year the Chicago and St. Louis line was opened.)

1833   McCormick's automatic reaper

1844   Samuel Morse's electric telegraph sent its first messages between Washington and Baltimore.

1847   Richard Hoe's new fast printing press

1851   William Kelly's new process of making steel

1858   First Atlantic cable laid

1868   C. L. Sholes's typewriter

1869   Westinghouse air brake

1875   G. F. Swift's refrigerator freight car

1876   Alexander Bell's telephone

1877   Thomas Edison's phonograph and electric light

1879   George Selden's patent for a "gasoline carriage" (First automobile ran on the streets in 1895.)

1880   Edison's electric railway

1882   Edison's electric power plant started operation in New York City.

1886   Mergenthaler Linotype

1894   First motion picture

1896   Langley's airplane made experimental flight.

Thanks to inventions like these, and especially to the internal combustion engine, which was much smaller than the old steam engine, and to the discovery that electric power from dynamos could be sent along wires, the country was able to multiply its human muscles manyfold and to reach out into far corners of the continent and take advantage of rich natural resources which otherwise would have been closed to human use. All over the country factories began to stick their smokestacks into the sky, while fast transportation brought raw materials to them and took manufactured goods away. Telegraph and telephone kept them in touch with their markets and with even their most remote sources of materials.

The master craftsmen of the industrial East were giving way to mass production in the factories. The gay West, where individual miners, trappers, and settlers could once strike it rich, was now being taken over by big operators and gigantic companies. As Paul Revere, the master silversmith, was the symbol of the old East, and Jim Bridger, the footloose scout, a symbol of the old West, so the big men of this new America were Andrew Carnegie, who made steel, John D. Rockefeller, who pumped petroleum, Commodore Vanderbilt, who owned railroads, and J. P. Morgan, whose money power extended into a dozen different industries.

The outlook for an individual operator was not so good as it had been a few decades before. The country had gone *big* business. Furthermore, by 1880, there was an inevitable reaction against the optimism and hope of the early West. For one thing, farmers had settled too far out on the prairie, on land that was really too dry for farming, and drought was beginning to drive them back. Furthermore, they were aware that most of the good Western land was already taken up and most of the rich minerals were now owned by companies. There was no longer the same chance of a " fresh start " which the West had offered for almost a century: if a man wasn't satisfied where he was, if he wasn't doing as well as he

thought he should be, he could move a little farther west and start over. Now there was no " farther west " to which they could move, no more get-rich-quick possibilities, no pot of gold behind the rainbow. Westerners began to realize that they had to fight it out where they were.

That was why late in the century the West was losing its symbolic quality as an American symbol of opportunity, and becoming a world of hard facts. And out of this setting, realism came to literature.

## WHAT IS REALISM?

There is nothing fancy about realism. It is simply a feeling on the part of an author that the thing worth writing about is the *real* thing. Let's forget the misty and glamorous past, people were saying. Let's forget our old optimism and hopefulness. Let's face things as they are. Let's quit writing about men who never existed — the ideal men, the unbeatable Americans, the Paul Bunyans, the great heroes. And let's write about the ordinary man, the average man, the little man. Let's tell about his defeats, as well as his victories; his disappointments, his moments of weariness and discouragement, as well as his high moments. Let's be " simple, natural, and honest," as Howells said; if man is a bore, let's show him as a bore; let's not pick out the one moment in his life when he acts like a hero. Men aren't Paul Bunyans or Napoleons very often; let's show them as they are. Our governments, our business, our economic lives aren't perfect, let's show them as they are. That was the spirit in which men like Howells and James began to write fiction.

## 1. WILLIAM DEAN HOWELLS AND HENRY JAMES

Howells was a talented young man who grew up in Ohio and knew just where he wanted to go and how to get there.

He went to work for Columbus newspapers until he got a chance to write a campaign biography of Lincoln. That got him a political appointment to the American consulate in Venice. And that in turn gave him a chance to settle in Boston when Boston was the center of American literary life.

He came to Boston first in 1866, twenty-nine years old, like a pilgrim. He went to see Lowell, because Lowell was editor of the *Atlantic Monthly*, in which Howells had published a poem. Lowell liked the young man, invited him to dinner with Holmes and James T. Fields, who later succeeded Lowell as editor of the *Atlantic Monthly*. They talked four hours. Finally, Holmes said to Lowell, " Well, James, this is something like the apostolic succession. This is the laying on of hands."

He was never more prophetic. In a few years, Howells was living in Cambridge. Those were the years when, people said, you couldn't fire a shot in that town without bringing down two or three writers, and when they told a delightful story of a little Cambridge girl who asked another, " Your grandfather's a poet, isn't he? " " Why, surely," said the second little girl. " Isn't yours? " Howells fitted into that group like an old hand. He catered to the vanities and the foibles of the great and elderly New Englanders. He was young, likable, talented, a good critic. When Fields retired from the *Atlantic Monthly*, Howells was the logical next editor. When it became evident that the center of publishing and writing was passing to New York, Howells moved there, as an editor and writer. When Holmes, Longfellow, and Lowell were the greatest names in American literature, he was their close friend in Boston. When Mark Twain became the best-known American writer, Howells was his bosom friend in Boston and New York. He had a talent for being in the right place at the right time.

But that is not to say that he rode on other men's reputation. He did very well by himself. He was an excellent editor, and his own books, when they were put together at the end of his sixty years of writing, totaled nearly one hundred volumes. Thirty-

WILLIAM DEAN HOWELLS was the friend of most of the authors of his time and a successful author and editor in his own right. (Brown Brothers)

six of them were novels, and you will doubtless want to read at least *The Rise of Silas Lapham* and *A Modern Instance* some day. Some of them were plays, some travel books, some criticism, several delightful pictures of his literary friends and acquaintances. He knew almost everyone worth knowing in American literature in his time, and he had a fine eye for character and appearance.

Howells's books, said Carl Van Doren, are " the most considerable transcript of American life yet made by one man." And Howells himself wrote the best account of the method of realism by which he transcribed that life. " The sincere observer of man," he said, " will not desire to look upon his heroic or occasional phases, but will seek him in his habitual moods of vacancy and tiresomeness. . . . It will not do to lift either houses or men *far* out of the average; they become spectacles, ceremonies; they cease to have charm, to have character."

Howells was born in Ohio, never went to college, went east to write. Henry James

HENRY JAMES, a writer's writer. He has received broader recognition in recent years. (Culver)

he had one great skill, perhaps above any other novelist who ever wrote in America. He had the ability to get into a character's mind and show what he was thinking and how he was reacting. The realism he sought was the realism of the *mind*. The more he dug for those treasures, the more subtle, involved, complicated his books became. Someone said that whereas his brother, the great psychologist William James, made psychology as interesting as novels, Henry James made novels as difficult as psychology.

James's novels fall into three distinct groups, the first and third representing different aspects of his favorite theme of contrasting European and American characters. To these groups belong some of his best-known novels, *The American, Daisy Miller, Portrait of a Lady,* and *The Ambassadors.* A middle group, containing some ·of his most subtle analyses and dealing more exclusively with English characters, includes *The Tragic Muse* and *The Awkward Age.* He also wrote over a hundred short stories, including the famous ghost story, " The Turn of the Screw."

was born in New York, went to Harvard and continued his education at Geneva, Paris, Bonn, London and everywhere else a wealthy and cultivated family might want to send a brilliant son. He too went east to write — to Europe. Most of his adult life he spent there, and finally became a British subject in protest against his native country's slowness in entering World War I.

He agreed with Howells in the thought that the fiction worth writing is a realistic fiction, and that one should write about people in ordinary moments, rather than in heroic or unusual moments. Unlike Howells, though, he had little experience with the average American. His acquaintances were of the upper classes, and especially of the wealthy international families. One problem interested him above all others. He would write about an American in European society, or a European in American society, and analyze the troubles resulting from their failure to understand each other. And

## 2. *THE ROMANTIC SURVIVAL*

Not all the new writers who appeared after the War between the States were realists.

One who was not was Sidney Lanier, the South's greatest poet after Poe. As in the case of most other Southern writers, the War between the States broke tragically into his career. He was only fifteen when it started, but he entered the blockade-running service so necessary to the South's survival. Captured, imprisoned by the Northern army, he developed tuberculosis and lived only sixteen years after the war's end. In that time, however, he became a great musician, and an interpreter of music in poetry. More important, he wrote poems of a lyrical and musical nature, and of deep feeling and keen imagination.

Emily Dickinson was writing poems in Amherst, Massachusetts, during the same years Lanier was writing in the South, but only a handful of her poems were published in her lifetime. She lived as a recluse. The reason why she did so is still rather mysterious, but it apparently involved an unfortunate love affair. Whatever the reason, she was very seldom seen by anyone except her immediate family. She sat at her desk and scribbled poems, on envelopes, on scratch paper, on anything that happened to be handy, with no thought of publishing them. When her literary executors found these scraps, some years after Emily's death, they got one of the great thrills of American literary history. For this girl who hid in her room and wrote on the back of envelopes was indisputably one of the great poets of her time. As simple and direct as a child, she nevertheless had a fresh and original way of putting an idea, a way of using words as sharply and exactly as a surgeon's knife, and a penetrating insight into the reasons why people act as they do. In our time, rather than hers, she became one of the most widely read of American poets.

James Whitcomb Riley wrote his way into the hearts of Americans in the late years of the century by poems of country and family life and childhood, written in a rustic Indiana dialect. Everyone has read " When the Frost Is on the Punkin " and " Little Orphant Annie." Eugene Field was another poet and columnist of this time who became popular through his children's poems, of which " Little Boy Blue " is the best known.

Thomas Bailey Aldrich, who succeeded Howells as editor of the *Atlantic Monthly,* also made his reputation with a children's book, *The Story of a Bad Boy*. This was the first realistic treatment of a boy in American literature, appearing seventeen years before Mark Twain's *Tom Sawyer*. But Aldrich, a romanticist at heart, was prouder of well-turned stories like " A Struggle for Life " and " Marjorie Daw," which popularized surprise endings, and of his long, elegant poems breathing oriental romance.

EMILY DICKINSON. Her small but unforgettable poems rank her as one of the great women poets of all literature. (Brown Brothers)

Not all these poets were in revolution against the realism that was coming in. Some of them had many realistic qualities in their own work. They were simply continuing the older tradition, or — especially in the case of Emily Dickinson and Lanier — writing fine poetry in the way they felt they could write it best. As was pointed out before, writers usually aren't aware that they are a part of a movement.

# Sidney Lanier 1842–1881

Of the Southern poets who passed through the War between the States, Sidney Lanier is decidedly the greatest. Besides, he has the distinction of being the only one of our important American poets who was also a professional musician. How fitting it is that the two talents should be linked together in one person! One of Lanier's famous lines is " Music is love in search of a word." As a boy in Macon, Georgia, Sidney had played both the violin and the flute,

SIDNEY LANIER. A talented musician and the South's greatest poet after Poe. (Brown Brothers)

but the latter became his real medium of expression. He carried his flute with him through the war, where he fought on the Confederate side, and even concealed it up his sleeve when he was sent to a Northern prison. Later, when he was a member of the Peabody Symphony Orchestra of Baltimore, he was considered by many the world's greatest flute player. So impressed was he with the close relation between music and poetry that he wrote *The Science of English Verse* to show the correspondence between the measures of poetry and the bars in music. He believed that by a nice selection of sounds and syllables and the proper "tuning" of his words the poet could produce unusual musical effects. Some of his longer poems have been worked out with the careful balancing of parts observed by the composer of a symphony. Lanier's technique is somewhat like Poe's in his use of liquid consonants, alliteration, and a smooth flow of sounds. But, unlike Poe, he has a strong spiritual and religious bent. He seeks the meaning of life; and the marshes, the cornfields, or the sunrise, as described in his long poems, are filled with a sense of the presence of God.

## SONG OF THE CHATTAHOOCHEE *

This is one of Lanier's most successful attempts at creating music in words and, therefore, perhaps his best-known poem. Even though you may have read it before just as a lovely song, there is an added pleasure in discovering how the poet worked out the pattern of the melody. After you have read it through first to get the idea — the temptations of the river to linger and the final call which it must answer — read the poem again (aloud, of course) and listen to the rippling sound of the lines.

Out of the hills of Habersham,°
  Down the valleys of Hall,
I hurry amain to reach the plain,
Run the rapid and leap the fall,
Split at the rock and together again,    5
Accept my bed, or narrow or wide,
And flee from folly on every side
With a lover's pain to attain the plain
  Far from the hills of Habersham,
  Far from the valleys of Hall.    10

All down the hills of Habersham,
  All through the valleys of Hall,
The rushes cried, *Abide, abide,*
The willful waterweeds held me thrall,
The laving laurel turned my tide,    15
The ferns and the fondling grass said *Stay,*
The dewberry dipped for to work delay,
And the little reeds sighed, *Abide, abide,*
  *Here in the hills of Habersham,*
  *Here in the valleys of Hall.*    20

High o'er the hills of Habersham,
  Veiling the valleys of Hall,
The hickory told me manifold
Fair tales of shade, the poplar tall
Wrought me her shadowy self to hold,    25
The chestnut, the oak, the walnut, the pine,
Overleaning, with flickering meaning and
    sign,
Said, *Pass not, so cold, these manifold*
  *Deep shades of the hills of Habersham,*
  *These glades in the valleys of Hall.*    30

* **Chattahoochee:** This river is in Georgia, Lanier's native state.  1. **Habersham** (hă′bĕr-shăm).

And oft in the hills of Habersham,
And oft in the valleys of Hall,
The white quartz shone, and the smooth
    brook-stone
Did bar me of passage with friendly brawl,
And many a luminous jewel lone    35
— Crystals clear or a-cloud with mist,
Ruby, garnet, and amethyst —
Made lures with the lights of streaming
    stone
  In the clefts of the hills of Habersham,
  In the beds of the valleys of Hall.    40

But oh, not the hills of Habersham,
  And oh, not the valleys of Hall
Avail: I am fain for to water the plain.
Downward the voices of Duty call —
Downward, to toil and be mixed with the
    main    45
The dry fields burn, and the mills are to
    turn,
And a myriad flowers mortally yearn,
And the lordly main from beyond the plain
  Calls o'er the hills of Habersham,
  Calls through the valleys of Hall.    50

## EVENING SONG

Addressed to his wife, this song is one of
Lanier's most beautiful lyrics. The second
stanza refers to a legend that Cleopatra actually drank a pearl in wine. Note how the poet
carries out his figurative idea.

Look off, dear Love, across the sallow sands,
  And mark yon meeting of the sun and sea,
How long they kiss in sight of all the lands.
  Ah! longer, longer, we.    4

Now in the sea's red vintage melts the sun,
  As Egypt's pearl dissolved in rosy wine,
And Cleopatra night drinks all. 'Tis done,
  Love, lay thine hand in mine.

Come forth, sweet stars, and comfort heav-
    en's heart;
  Glimmer, ye waves, round else-unlighted
    sands.    10
O night! divorce our sun and sky apart,
  Never our lips, our hands.

## A BALLAD OF TREES AND THE MASTER

This poem gives an unusual presentation of
Christ in the Garden of Gethsemane. It has
several musical settings, the most beautiful of
which, by George W. Chadwick, is often sung
by church choirs.

Into the woods my Master went,
Clean forspent, forspent.
Into the woods my Master came,
Forspent with love and shame.    4
But the olives they were not blind to Him,
The little gray leaves were kind to Him:
The thorn tree had a mind to Him
When into the woods He came.

Out of the woods my Master went,
And He was well content.    10
Out of the woods my Master came,
Content with death and shame.
When Death and Shame would woo Him
    last,
From under the trees they drew Him last:
'Twas on a tree they slew Him — last    15
When out of the woods He came.

## THE STIRRUP CUP

As a result of Lanier's imprisonment during
the war his health was greatly impaired, and
the last few years of his life showed a struggle
against tuberculosis which reminds one of
Robert Louis Stevenson. During this period he
was delivering a series of lectures on English
literature at Johns Hopkins University in Baltimore, and sometimes he kept his appointment when he was almost too weak to stand on
the platform. His wife testifies that when he
wrote the end of " Hymns of the Marshes " he
was so near death as to be unable to lift his
hand to his mouth, though he wrote it four
years before he died. " The Stirrup Cup " expresses the highhearted courage with which he
was able to meet death when it came to him at
the age of thirty-nine. In death he felt his spirit
would become blended with those of the great
poets whom he loved.

Death, thou'rt a cordial old and rare:
Look how compounded, with what care!
Time got his wrinkles reaping thee
Sweet herbs from all antiquity.

David° to thy distillage went,          5
Keats,° and Gotama° excellent,

Omar Khayyám,° and Chaucer° bright,
And Shakespeare for a king-delight.

Then, Time, let not a drop be spilt:
Hand me the cup whene'er thou wilt;          10
'Tis thy rich stirrup cup° to me;
I'll drink it down right smilingly.

5. **David:** King David, writer of the Psalms.
6. **Keats:** John Keats, the English poet, who died of consumption at twenty-six. 6. **Gotama:** another name for Buddha, the founder of Buddhism, who lived in India in the sixth century before Christ.

7. **Omar Khayyám** (kī-yäm'): a Persian poet of the twelfth century; author of the *Rubáiyát*. 7. **Chaucer:** Geoffrey Chaucer, the first notable English poet, who lived in the fourteenth century. 11. **stirrup cup:** the last drink taken by a horseman before he starts to ride.

## THE MARSHES OF GLYNN

Though this poem may appear difficult at first reading, it is most rewarding of careful study. It illustrates Lanier's idea of the close union between music and poetry, and like great music, it grows richer and more meaningful by repetition. The sound quality is unusual and of course the poem should be read aloud to bring this out. The lines vary greatly in length; you will see how greatly if you try to find which line has the greatest number of syllables. The rhythm is irregular. On first reading there may seem to be no regular pattern, but there is a basic rhythm and the variations from it are like variations in the rhythm of a great symphony. The rhythm of this poem is highlighted by the repetition of sounds and the rhymes within the lines.

The poem shows how Lanier found spiritual values in the great sweeps of forest and marsh to be found in his native state. The Marshes of Glynn are near Brunswick, Georgia.

Marginal notes are added to help you grasp the central idea of each section which may seem obscured by the figurative language.

Glooms of the live oaks, beautiful-braided and woven
With intricate shades of the vines that myriad-cloven
Clamber the forks of the multiform boughs —
          Emerald twilights —
          Virginal shy lights,          5
Wrought of the leaves to allure to the whisper of vows,
When lovers pace timidly down through the green colonnades
Of the dim sweet woods, of the dear dark woods,
          Of the heavenly woods and glades,
That run to the radiant marginal sand-beach within          10
          The wide sea-marshes of Glynn —

*The poet addresses the deep tangled shadows amid the live oaks, seeing in them a retreat for lovers,*

Beautiful glooms, soft dusks in the noonday fire —
Wildwood privacies, closets of lone desire,
Chamber from chamber parted with wavering arras of leaves —
Cells for the passionate pleasure of prayer for the soul that grieves,          15
Pure with a sense of the passing of saints through the wood,
Cool for the dutiful weighing of ill with good —

*and seeing in them a quiet retreat for prayer and solitary thought.*

O braided dusks of the oak and woven shades of the vine,
While the riotous noonday sun of the June day long did shine
Ye held me fast in your heart and I held you fast in mine;          20

*Through the heat of a June day he has relaxed in the shadows.*

But now when the noon is no more, and riot is rest,
And the sun is await at the ponderous gate of the West,
And the slant yellow beam down the wood-aisle doth seem
Like a lane into heaven that leads from a dream —
Ay, now, when my soul all day hath drunken the soul of the oak, 25
And my heart is at ease from men, and the wearisome sound of the
    stroke
    Of the scythe of time, and the trowel of trade is low,
    And belief overmasters doubt, and I know that I know,
    And my spirit is grown to a lordly great compass within,
That the length and the breadth and the sweep of the marshes of
    Glynn 30
Will work me no fear like the fear they have wrought me of yore
When length was fatigue, and when breadth was but bitterness sore,
And when terror and shrinking and dreary unnamable pain
Drew over me out of the merciless miles of the plain —

At evening he is
rested from the cares
of the world and
strong against fear,
no longer weary and
afraid of great spaces.

Oh, now, unafraid, I am fain to face 35
    The vast sweet visage of space.
To the edge of the wood I am drawn, I am drawn,
Where the gray beach glimmering runs, as a belt of the dawn,
    For a mete and a mark
    To the forest-dark — 40
        So:
Affable live oak, bending low —
Thus — with your favor — soft, with a reverent hand,
(Not lightly touching your person, Lord of the land!)
Bending your beauty aside, with a step I stand 45
On the firm-packed sand,
        Free
By a world of marsh that borders a world of sea.

So he steps out con-
fidently from the
protecting woods to
the open sweep of the
marshes.

Sinuous southward and sinuous northward the shimmering band
Of the sand-beach fastens the fringe of the marsh to the folds
    of the land. 50
Inward and outward to northward and southward the beach-lines
    linger and curl
As a silver-wrought garment that clings to and follows the firm sweet
    limbs of a girl.
Vanishing, swerving, evermore curving again into sight,
Softly the sand-beach wavers away to a dim gray looping of light.
And what if behind me to westward the wall of the woods stands
    high? 55
The world lies east: how ample, the marsh and the sea and the sky!
A league and a league of marsh-grass, waist-high, broad in the blade,
Green, and all of a height, and unflecked with a light or a shade,
Stretch leisurely off, in a pleasant plain,
To the terminal blue of the main. 60
Oh, what is abroad in the marsh and the terminal sea?
    Somehow my soul seems suddenly free

He rejoices in the
wide panorama of
curving marshes and
sea.

His soul is freed of
its care by the
sweeping views.

From the weighing of fate and the sad discussion of sin,
By the length and the breadth and the sweep of the marshes of Glynn.

Ye marshes, how candid and simple and nothing withholding and free
Ye publish yourselves to the sky and offer yourselves to the sea!    66
Tolerant plains, that suffer the sea and the rains and the sun,
Ye spread and span like the catholic man who hath mightily won
God out of knowledge and good out of infinite pain
And sight out of blindness and purity out of a stain.    70

*The marshes seem open, serene, and confident, like a man who has won greatness of soul after suffering and is in harmony with God.*

As the marsh-hen secretly builds on the watery sod,
Behold I will build me a nest on the greatness of God:
I will fly in the greatness of God as the marsh-hen flies
In the freedom that fills all the space 'twixt the marsh and the skies:
By so many roots as the marsh-grass sends in the sod    75
I will heartily lay me a-hold on the greatness of God:
Oh, like to the greatness of God is the greatness within
The range of the marshes, the liberal marshes of Glynn.

*The poet resolves to find refuge and strength in the greatness of God, which he senses in the greatness of the marshes.*

And the sea lends large, as the marsh: lo, out of his plenty the sea
Pours fast: full soon the time of the flood-tide must be:    80
Look how the grace of the sea doth go
About and about through the intricate channels that flow
  Here and there,
   Everywhere,
Till his waters have flooded the uttermost creeks and the low-lying
  lanes,    85
And the marsh is meshed with a million veins,
That like as with rosy and silvery essences flow
  In the rose-and-silver evening glow.
   Farewell, my lord Sun!
The creeks overflow; a thousand rivulets run    90
'Twixt the roots of the sod; the blades of the marsh-grass stir;
Passeth a hurrying sound of wings that westward whir;
Passeth, and all is still; and the currents cease to run;
And the sea and the marsh are one.

*The sea comes in with the rising tide, and the sun goes down.*

How still the plains of the waters be!    95
The tide is in his ecstasy;
The tide is at his highest height;
  And it is night.

And now from the Vast of the Lord will the waters of sleep
Roll in on the souls of men,    100
But who will reveal to our waking ken
The forms that swim and the shapes that creep
  Under the waters of sleep?
And I would I could know what swimmeth below when the tide
  comes in    104
On the length and the breadth of the marvelous marshes of Glynn.

*As the tide comes over the marshes, so sleep rolls over the souls of men. But mysterious life goes on beneath both quiet surfaces, and the poet broods over these mysteries.*

## Suggestions for Study of Lanier

SONG OF THE CHATTAHOOCHEE

1. Observe how neatly the second, third, and fourth stanzas each record a different kind of temptation to linger. Try to name a topic for each stanza. While there is no direct moral expressed, can you work out an implied parallel between the river and man's life?

2. How many examples of alliteration can you find in this poem? What particular consonants are used again and again? Where is refrain used? Do you like the variation of the refrain better than an exact refrain? Compare the sound of this poem with " Ulalume " (page 525). What similar devices are used? What marked differences are there between the two poems?

3. Read Tennyson's " The Brook," with which " Song of the Chattahoochee " has often been compared. Which do you prefer in rhythm? in idea?

4. Many other rivers in Georgia have musical names: Savannah, Willacoochee, Altamaha, Suwanee. What geographical names in your own state might have poems built around them? Try writing a short one.

THE SHORT LYRICS

5. In " Evening Song " show just what things about the sunset are compared to what things in the story of Cleopatra.

6. In " A Ballad of Trees and the Master " when and why was the Master " forspent "? Why was He " content with death and shame " when He came out of the woods? What is meant by " on a tree they slew Him "?

7. What do you think the poets mentioned in " The Stirrup Cup " had to do with Lanier's attitude toward death? Compare his feeling with that of Bryant in " Thanatopsis " (page 498) and of Whitman in " The Carol of Death " (page 621). Would you say that death is a common or uncommon subject among poets?

8. John Hay has written a poem called " The Stirrup Cup " (to be found in Jessie Rittenhouse's *Little Book of American Poets*). Contrast the attitude of the two poets. Which do you prefer?

THE MARSHES OF GLYNN

9. Study the poem line by line to be sure that you catch the poet's meaning and mood. Where do you think the spiritual quality of the poem reaches its greatest height?

10. Select some of the descriptive phrases and figures of speech that especially appeal to you; also lines that have a particularly musical sound. How does this poem compare with " Song of the Chattahoochee " in the use of liquid consonants?

11. If you live in a region where the live oak does not grow, try to find pictures of it to show how different live-oak groves of the South are from oak woods of the North.

12. Have you lived near marshes or plains? How do they affect you? Read if possible a poem called " From the Flats " which Lanier wrote just the year before " The Marshes of Glynn." You will be surprised to see what a different attitude he expresses toward flat lands and how he longed for hills. Can you account for such a change by any of the lines in " The Marshes of Glynn "?

13. Do you know other poems in which some element of nature has aroused yearning or produced satisfaction in the poet's mind?

14. If you have liked this poem, read " Sunrise," another of Lanier's four Hymns to the Marshes, with a dramatic approach of Dawn, and again a gathering of spiritual strength.

## Emily Dickinson 1830–1886

A few years ago an American anthologist called Emily Dickinson's poetry " perhaps the finest by a woman in the English language." An English critic in commenting on this remark said, " I quarrel only with his ' perhaps.' " The strange thing about Emily Dickinson is that during her lifetime no one outside of her small circle of friends had ever heard of her. None of her poems saw publication until after her death in 1886. Today she is recognized as a distinct genius.

It has been said that her whole life could be told in three lines:

> Born in Amherst
> Lived in Amherst
> Died in Amherst

It is true that outwardly her life was restricted by this little Massachusetts town, but the adventures of her mind and spirit knew no narrow bounds. To read the life written by her niece, Martha Dickinson Bianchi, is to realize how richly imaginative a life may be that bears no mark of outward adventure. Though her poems are all very short and rather similar in verse form, they have remarkable power to startle the mind and challenge the imagination. Once catch the fascination of them and you must read on to find out what original thing she will say next. In view of her retired life, an appropriate poem for an introduction is " I'm Nobody."

## I'M NOBODY

I'm nobody! Who are you?
  Are you nobody, too?
Then there's a pair of us -- don't tell!
  They'd banish us, you know.

How dreary to be somebody!
  How public like a frog
To tell your name the livelong day
  To an admiring bog!

## A WORD

A word is dead
When it is said,
  Some say.
I say it just
Begins to live
  That day.

## TO MAKE A PRAIRIE

To make a prairie it takes a clover
And one bee —
One clover, and a bee,
And reverie.
The reverie alone will do
If bees are few.

## THE STORM

It makes Emily Dickinson seem startlingly modern to know that a new volume of her hitherto unpublished poems came out in 1945. A careful reading of this *Bolts of Melody*, as it is called, shows that her best work had been gleaned in the earlier volume, but neverthe-less the amazing freshness and originality of her imagery is still there, as this little poem shows.

Like rain it sounded till it curved,
And then I knew 'twas wind;
It walked as wet as any wave
But swept as dry as sand.

When it had pushed itself away     5
To some remotest plain
A coming as of hosts was heard —
That was indeed the rain!

It filled the wells, it pleased the pools,
It warbled in the road,     10
It pulled the spigot from the hills
And let the floods abroad;

It loosened acres, lifted seas,
The sites of centers stirred,
Then like Elijah° rode away     15
Upon a wheel of cloud.

15. **Elijah** (ē-lī′jȧ): For this Bible story see II Kings 2:9–12.

## AN ALTERED LOOK ABOUT THE HILLS

An altered look about the hills;
A Tyrian° light the village fills;
A wider sunrise in the dawn;
A deeper twilight on the lawn;
A print of a vermilion foot;     5
A purple finger on the slope;
A flippant fly upon the pane;
A spider at his trade again;
An added strut in chanticleer;
A flower expected everywhere;     10
An ax shrill singing in the woods;
Fern odors on untraveled roads —
All this and more I cannot tell,
A furtive look you know as well,
And Nicodemus' mystery°     15
Receives its annual reply.

2. **Tyrian** (tĭr′ĭ-ăn): Ancient Tyre (tīr) was famous for its manufacture of purple dye. 15. **Nicodemus'** (nĭk-ō-dē′mŭs) **mystery:** John 3:1–12. Nicodemus' question was "How can a man be born again?" What is "the annual reply?"

## HOW HAPPY IS THE LITTLE STONE

How happy is the little stone
That rambles in the road alone,
And doesn't care about careers,
And exigencies never fears;
Whose coat of elemental brown          5
A passing universe put on;
And independent as the sun,
Associates or glows alone,
Fulfilling absolute decree
In casual simplicity.                  10


## SOME KEEP THE SABBATH

Some keep the Sabbath going to church;
 I keep it staying at home,
With a bobolink for a chorister,
 And an orchard for a dome.

Some keep the Sabbath in surplice;     5
 I just wear my wings;
And instead of tolling the bell for church,
 Our little sexton sings.

God preaches — a noted clergyman —
 And the sermon is never long;         10
So instead of getting to heaven at last,
 I'm going all along!


## I NEVER SAW A MOOR

I never saw a moor,
 I never saw the sea;
Yet know I how the heather looks,
 And what a wave must be.

I never spoke with God,
 Nor visited in heaven;
Yet certain am I of the spot
 As if the chart were given.


## THE SOUL SELECTS HER OWN SOCIETY

An experience of Emily Dickinson's girlhood colored her whole life and was largely responsible for her almost ascetic seclusion in her own home. While on a visit to Philadelphia — so we are told by her niece — she fell in love with a young man and he with her. The tragedy was that he was already married. Emily's decision was that they must never see each other again, and he took his wife and child across the continent. Except to her devoted sister-in-law she never referred directly to this painful experience, but many of her poems show the emotional scar which she covered up so unostentatiously with her charm and wit.

The soul selects her own society,
 Then shuts the door;
On her divine majority
 Obtrude no more.

Unmoved, she notes the chariot's pausing
 At her low gate;                      6
Unmoved, an emperor is kneeling
 Upon her mat.

I've known her from an ample nation
 Choose one;                           10
Then close the valves of her attention
 Like stone.


## MY LIFE CLOSED TWICE

My life closed twice before its close;
 It yet remains to see
If Immortality unveil
 A third event to me,

So huge, so hopeless to conceive,
 As these that twice befell.
Parting is all we know of heaven,
 And all we need of hell.


## WE NEVER KNOW HOW HIGH

We never know how high we are
 Till we are called to rise;
And then, if we are true to plan,
 Our statures touch the skies.

The heroism we recite
 Would be a daily thing,
Did not ourselves the cubits warp
 For fear to be a king.

## Suggestions for Study
### of Emily Dickinson

1. For each poem interpret the meaning in a sentence or two. Do you find them hard or easy to understand? Are there any upon the meaning of which the members of the class disagree?

2. How much can you gather from these poems of Emily Dickinson's attitude toward society? religion? nature? By reading further biographical details try to decide what she meant by " My life closed twice before its close."

3. Select some of the phrases she uses which seem especially original. Study the last line of each poem. What characteristic do they all seem to have in common?

4. Emily Dickinson never wrote very long poems. Can you see after reading these why she did not?

5. Her use of figures of speech is particularly interesting. How many can you find in this group of little poems? Explain four or five of the best ones.

6. Since her poems have no titles except their first lines, the best way to recommend further reading of her work is simply to say, " Get a volume of her poems and go on an exploring expedition."

## James Whitcomb Riley    1849–1916

James Whitcomb Riley was undoubtedly the most popular American poet of the end of the nineteenth century. His verse suggests a combination of some elements of Longfellow and Lowell; for like the former he was the poet of the children and of simple sentiment, while like the latter he immortalized the rural dialect of his state. Riley, " the Hoosier poet," was born in Greenfield, Indiana, and always made his home in or near Indianapolis. He was not a farmboy, but the son of a prosperous lawyer who wished his son to follow in his footsteps. Like many of his literary predecessors, the young man found the attempted study distasteful, and he ran away with a troupe of strolling actors. His services to the troupe were varied by coaching, poster painting, and drumbeating, as well as by acting. Then followed a newspaper career, and in his later life lecture tours and public readings from his poems.

At the age of thirty-three he began a series of dialect poems in the Indianapolis *Journal* signed by " Benj. F. Johnson, of Boone, the Hoosier poet." The pseudonym did not stick to the poet except for the last part — which seems to have become an invariable appositive to Riley's own name. The child dialect, pronounced rhythms, and homely vividness of such poems as " The Raggedy Man " and " Little Orphant Annie " make them popular with children, who today celebrate his birthday in schools throughout the country.

JAMES WHITCOMB RILEY, " the Hoosier poet." His dialect poems about country and family life and childhood have become a permanent part of American literature. (Brown Brothers)

## WHEN THE FROST IS ON THE PUNKIN

When the frost is on the punkin and the fodder's in the shock,
And you hear the kyouck and gobble of the struttin' turkey cock,
And the clackin' of the guineys, and the cluckin' of the hens,
And the rooster's hallylooyer as he tiptoes on the fence;
O, it's then the time a feller is a-feelin' at his best,                        5
With the risin' sun to greet him from a night of peaceful rest,
As he leaves the house, bareheaded, and goes out to feed the stock,
When the frost is on the punkin and the fodder's in the shock.

They's something kindo' harty-like about the atmusfere
When the heat of summer's over and the coolin' fall is here —                   10
Of course we miss the flowers, and the blossums on the trees,
And the mumble of the hummin'birds and buzzin' of the bees;
But the air's so appetizin'; and the landscape through the haze
Of a crisp and sunny morning of the airly autumn days
Is a pictur' that no painter has the colorin' to mock —                         15
When the frost is on the punkin and the fodder's in the shock.

The husky, rusty russel of the tossels of the corn,
And the raspin' of the tangled leaves, as golden as the morn;
The stubble in the furries — kindo' lonesomelike, but still
A-preachin' sermuns to us of the barns they growed to fill;                     20
The strawstack in the medder, and the reaper in the shed;
The hosses in theyr stalls below — the clover overhead! —
O, it sets my hart a-clickin' like the tickin' of a clock,
When the frost is on the punkin and the fodder's in the shock!

Then your apples all is gethered, and the ones a feller keeps                   25
Is poured around the celler floor in red and yeller heaps;
And your cider makin's over, and your wimmern folks is through
With theyr mince and apple butter, and theyr souse and sausage, too!
I don't know how to tell it — but ef sich a thing could be
As the Angels wantin' boardin', and they'd call around on *me* —               30
I'd want to 'commodate 'em — all the whole indurin' flock —
When the frost is on the punkin and the fodder's in the shock!

## Eugene Field          1850–1895

Though Field and Riley are often bracketed together because they were contemporary newspapermen and poets of childhood, their work shows numerous differences. Riley's dialect poems give us Midwestern domestic life, and are always decidedly local in flavor; Field shows the influence of foreign literature in his translations, his imitations of Horace, and his series of lullabies of all nations. Field was wittier than Riley and more original. He was one of the first newspaper columnists, and most of his poems were written primarily to fill his daily space. His newspaper connections were in St. Louis, the city of his birth, Chicago, and Denver. Himself the father of eight children, Field wrote many poems about childhood, of which the following is perhaps the best known.

## LITTLE BOY BLUE

The little toy dog is covered with dust,
  But sturdy and stanch he stands;
The little toy soldier is red with rust,
  And his musket molds in his hands.
Time was when the little toy dog was new
  And the soldier was passing fair;    6
And that was the time when our Little Boy
    Blue
  Kissed them and put them there.

" Now don't you go till I come," he said,
  " And don't you make any noise! "    10
So toddling off to his trundle bed,
  He dreamt of the pretty toys;
And, as he was dreaming, an angel song
  Awakened our Little Boy Blue —
Oh! the years are many, the years are long,
  But the little toy friends are true!    16

Ay, faithful to Little Boy Blue they stand,
  Each in the same old place,
Awaiting the touch of a little hand,
  The smile of a little face;    20
And they wonder, as waiting the long years
    through,
  In the dust of that little chair,
What has become of our Little Boy Blue
  Since he kissed them and put them there.

## Suggestions for Study
## of Riley and Field

1. Be sure you can interpret Riley's dialect to get the meaning, especially in words like " hallylooyer," " furries," " medder." Have you ever heard anyone speak a dialect similar to this? Do you like dialect poems?

2. How does autumn make the poet feel? Does it affect you the same way? What other poems on autumn do you know?

3. Riley " old favorites " are " The Old Man and Jim," " Knee-deep in June," " My Ruthers," " Wet-Weather Talk," " An Old Sweetheart of Mine," " A Life Lesson," " Out to Old Aunt Mary's," " The Old Swimmin-Hole." Read some of these and decide why they have a popular appeal.

4. Though " Little Boy Blue " is about a child, why is it definitely a poem for adults rather than children?

5. If possible, have " Little Boy Blue " presented in its musical setting. Find out by reading the life of Field if this poem was based on actual experience in his own family.

6. Two groups of Field's poems are strikingly different. One is a series of quaint and charming lullabies of different nations of which " Wynken, Blynken, and Nod " is the best known. The other is a group of humorous Western poems centered around the Colorado mining boom, of which " Casey's Table d'Hôte " is an excellent example. All of these are enjoyable reading.

7. After reading several poems by Riley and Field try to analyze why they are lesser poets than Lanier and Emily Dickinson. What is the difference between a popular poet and a great poet? Can you name any that are both popular and great?

# Thomas Bailey Aldrich
## 1836–1907

Aldrich is an old friend to those who have met him as Tom Bailey in the delightful pages of *The Story of a Bad Boy*. In his stories we find the compactness and directness of Poe seasoned with a Gallic spice that suggests the French masters who imitated Poe and whom in turn Aldrich followed.

In spite of the fact that Aldrich held the dignified position of editor of the *Atlantic Monthly*, he always remained a boy at heart; and it is, therefore, not surprising that his two chief contributions to American literature suggest perennial youthfulness. *The Story of a Bad Boy* is dear to the heart of every American boy; and Aldrich's second contribution, the surprise ending, is a kind of literary practical joke such as a boy would love to play.

## A STRUGGLE FOR LIFE

In " A Struggle for Life," published in the *Atlantic* in 1867, six years before the more famous " Marjorie Daw," Aldrich outdid himself with a double-barreled surprise; so as you read be prepared for anything.

One morning last April, as I was passing through Boston Common, which lies pleasantly between my residence and my office, I met a gentleman lounging along The Mall. I am generally preoccupied when walking, and often thrid [1] my way through crowded streets without distinctly observ- ing a single soul. But this man's face forced itself upon me, and a very singular face it was. His eyes were faded, and his hair, which he wore long, was flecked with gray. His hair and eyes, if I may say so, were seventy years old, the rest of him not thirty. The youthfulness of his figure, the elasticity of his gait, and the venerable appearance of his head were incongruities that drew more than one pair of curious eyes toward him. He was evidently an American — the New England cut of countenance is unmistaka- ble — evidently a man who had seen some- thing of the world; but strangely old and young.

Before reaching the Park Street gate, I had taken up the thread of thought which he had unconsciously broken; yet through- out the day this old young man, with his unwrinkled brow and silvered locks, glided in like a phantom between me and my duties.

The next morning I again encountered him on The Mall. He was resting lazily on the green rails, watching two little sloops in distress, which two ragged shipowners had consigned to the mimic perils of the Pond. The vessels lay becalmed in the middle of the ocean, displaying a tantalizing lack of sympathy with the frantic helplessness of the owners on shore. As the gentleman ob- served their dilemma, a light came into his faded eyes, then died out, leaving them drearier than before. I wondered if he, too, in his time, had sent out ships that drifted and drifted and never came to port; and if these poor toys were to him types of his own losses.

" I would like to know that man's story," I said, half aloud, halting in one of those winding paths which branch off from the quietness of the Pond, and end in the rush and tumult of Tremont Street.

" Would you? " replied a voice at my

[1] **thrid:** an archaic form of *thread*; to thread one's way is to move cautiously.

THOMAS BAILEY ALDRICH. His stories are noted for compactness, directness, and surprise endings. (Culver)

side. I turned and faced Mr. H——, a neighbor of mine, who laughed heartily at finding me talking to myself. " Well," he added, reflectively, " I can tell you this man's story; and if you will match the nar- rative with anything as curious, I shall be glad to hear it."

" You know him, then? "

" Yes and no. I happened to be in Paris when he was buried."

" Buried! "

" Well, strictly speaking, not buried; but something quite like it. If you've a spare half-hour," continued my interlocutor, " we'll sit on this bench, and I will tell you all I know of an affair that made some noise in Paris a couple of years ago. The gentleman himself, standing yonder, will serve as a sort of frontispiece to the romance — a full-page illustration, as it were."

The following pages contain the story that Mr. H—— related to me. While he was telling it, a gentle wind arose; the miniature sloops drifted feebly about the ocean; the wretched owners flew from point to point, as the deceptive breeze promised to waft the barks to either shore; the early robins trilled now and then from the newly fringed elms; and the old young man leaned on the rail in the sunshine, wearily, little dreaming that two gossips were discussing his affairs within twenty yards of him.

Three people were sitting in a chamber whose one large window overlooked the Place Vendôme.[1] M. Dorine, with his back half turned on the other two occupants of the apartment, was reading the *Moniteur,* pausing from time to time to wipe his glasses, and taking scrupulous pains not to glance toward the lounge at his right, on which were seated Mademoiselle Dorine and a young American gentleman, whose handsome face rather frankly told his position in the family. There was not a happier man in Paris that afternoon than Philip Wentworth. Life had become so delicious to him that he shrank from looking beyond today. What could the future add to his full heart? what might it not take away? In certain natures the deepest joy has always something of melancholy in it, a presentiment, a fleeting sadness, a feeling without a name. Wentworth was conscious of this subtle shadow, that night, when he rose from the lounge, and thoughtfully held Julie's hand to his lip for a moment before parting. A careless observer would not have thought him, as he was, the happiest man in Paris.

M. Dorine laid down his paper and came forward. " If the house," he said, " is such as M. Martin describes it, I advise you to close with him at once. I would accompany you, Philip, but the truth is, I am too sad at losing this little bird to assist you in selecting a cage for her. Remember, the last

train for town leaves at five. Be sure not to miss it; for we have seats for M. Sardou's [2] new comedy tomorrow night. By tomorrow night," he added laughingly, " little Julie here will be an old lady — 'tis such an age from now until then."

The next morning the train bore Philip to one of the loveliest spots within thirty miles of Paris. An hour's walk through green lanes brought him to M. Martin's estate. In a kind of dream the young man wandered from room to room, inspected the conservatory, the stables, the lawns, the strip of woodland through which a merry brook sang to itself continually; and, after dining with M. Martin, completed the purchase, and turned his steps toward the station, just in time to catch the express train.

As Paris stretched out before him, with its million lights twinkling in the early dusk, and its sharp spires here and there pricking the sky, it seemed to Philip as if years had elapsed since he left the city. On reaching Paris he drove to his hotel, where he found several letters lying on the table. He did not trouble himself even to glance at their superscriptions as he threw aside his traveling surtout for a more appropriate dress.

If, in his impatience to see Mademoiselle Dorine, the cars had appeared to walk, the fiacre which he had secured at the station appeared to creep. At last it turned into the Place Vendôme, and drew up before M. Dorine's residence. The door opened as Philip's foot touched the first step. The servant silently took his cloak and hat, with a special deference, Philip thought; but was he not now one of the family?

" M. Dorine," said the servant slowly, " is unable to see Monsieur at present. He wishes Monsieur to be shown up to the *salon.*"

" Is Mademoiselle — "

" Yes, Monsieur."

" Alone? "

" Alone, Monsieur," repeated the man,

---

[1] **Place Vendome** (plås' vän-dōm'): a famous square in Paris.

[2] **M. Sardou** (sár-dōō'): Victorien Sardou (1831–1908), popular French dramatist. "M." before all these names stands for *Monsieur* (mē-syû'), meaning *Mr.*

looking curiously at Philip, who could scarcely repress an exclamation of pleasure.

It was the first time that such a privilege had been accorded him. His interviews with Julie had always taken place in the presence of M. Dorine, or some members of the household. A well-bred Parisian girl has but a formal acquaintance with her lover.

Philip did not linger on the staircase; his heart sang in his bosom as he flew up the steps, two at a time. Ah! this wine of air which one drinks at twenty, and seldom after! He hastened through the softly lighted hall, in which he detected the faint scent of her favorite flowers, and stealthily opened the door of the *salon*.

The room was darkened. Underneath the chandelier stood a slim black casket on trestles. A lighted candle, a crucifix, and some white flowers were on a table near by. Julie Dorine was dead.

When M. Dorine heard the indescribable cry that rang through the silent house, he hurried from the library, and found Philip standing like a ghost in the middle of the chamber.

It was not until long afterward that Wentworth learned the details of the calamity that had befallen him. On the previous night Mademoiselle Dorine had retired to her room in seemingly perfect health. She dismissed her maid with a request to be awakened early the next morning. At the appointed hour the girl entered the chamber. Mademoiselle Dorine was sitting in an armchair, apparently asleep. The candle had burnt down to the socket; a book lay half open on the carpet at her feet. The girl started when she saw that the bed had not been occupied, and that her mistress still wore an evening dress. She rushed to Mademoiselle Dorine's side. It was not slumber. It was death.

Two messages were at once dispatched to Philip, one to the station at G——, the other to his hotel. The first missed him on the road, the second he had neglected to open. On his arrival at M. Dorine's house, the servant, under the supposition that Wentworth had been advised of Mademoiselle Dorine's death, broke the intelligence with awkward cruelty, by showing him directly to the *salon*.

Mademoiselle Dorine's wealth, her beauty, the suddenness of her death, and the romance that had in some way attached itself to her love for the young American, drew crowds to witness the final ceremonies which took place in the church in the Rue d'Aguesseau.[1] The body was to be laid in M. Dorine's tomb, in the cemetery of Montmartre.

This tomb requires a few words of description. First, there was a grating of filigrained [2] iron; through this you looked into a small vestibule or hall, at the end of which was a massive door of oak opening upon a short flight of stone steps descending into the tomb. The vault was fifteen or twenty feet square, ingeniously ventilated from the ceiling, but unlighted. It contained two sarcophagi; the first held the remains of Madame Dorine, long since dead; the other was new, and bore on one side the letters J. D., in monogram, interwoven with fleurs-de-lis.

The funeral train stopped at the gate of the small garden that enclosed the place of burial, only the immediate relatives following the bearers into the tomb. A slender wax candle, such as is used in Catholic churches, burnt at the foot of the uncovered sarcophagus, casting a dim glow over the center of the apartment, and deepening the shadows which seemed to huddle together in the corners. By this flickering light the coffin was placed in its granite shell, the heavy slab laid over it reverently, and the oaken door revolved on its rusty hinges, shutting out the uncertain ray of sunshine that had ventured to peep in on the darkness.

M. Dorine, muffled in his cloak, threw himself on the back seat of the carriage, too abstracted in his grief to observe that he

---

[1] **Rue d'Aguesseau** (rōō dȧ-gĕ-sō'): *Rue* means *street*. [2] **filigrained:** an unusual form of the word *filigreed*, which describes a delicate openwork design in metal.

was the only occupant of the vehicle. There was a sound of wheels grating on the graveled avenue, and then all was silence again in the cemetery of Montmartre. At the main entrance the carriages parted company, dashing off into various streets at a pace that seemed to express a sense of relief. The band plays a dead march going to the grave, but *Fra Diavolo* [1] coming from it.

It is not with the retreating carriages that our interest lies. Nor yet wholly with the dead in her mysterious dream; but with Philip Wentworth.

The rattle of wheels had died out of the air when Philip opened his eyes, bewildered, like a man abruptly roused from slumber. He raised himself on one arm and stared into the surrounding blackness. Where was he? In a second the truth flashed upon him. He had been left in the tomb! While kneeling on the farther side of the stone box, perhaps he had fainted, and in the last solemn rites his absence had been unnoticed.

His first emotion was one of natural terror. But this passed as quickly as it came. Life had ceased to be so very precious to him; and if it were his fate to die at Julie's side, was not that the fulfillment of the desire which he had expressed to himself a hundred times that morning? What did it matter, a few years sooner or later? He must lay down the burden at last. Why not then? A pang of self-reproach followed the thought. Could he so lightly throw aside the love that had bent over his cradle? The sacred name of mother rose involuntarily to his lips. Was it not cowardly to yield up without a struggle the life which he should guard for her sake? Was it not his duty to the living and the dead to face the difficulties of his position, and overcome them if it were within human power?

With an organization as delicate as a woman's, he had that spirit which, however sluggish in repose, can leap with a kind of

exultation to measure its strength with disaster. The vague fear of the supernatural, that would affect most men in a similar situation, found no room in his heart. He was simply shut in a chamber from which it was necessary that he should obtain release within a given period. That this chamber contained the body of the woman he loved, so far from adding to the terror of the case, was a circumstance from which he drew consolation. She was a beautiful white statue now. Her soul was far hence; and if that pure spirit could return, would it not be to shield him with her love? It was impossible that the place should not engender some thought of the kind. He did not put the thought entirely from him as he rose to his feet and stretched out his hands in the darkness; but his mind was too healthy and practical to indulge long in such speculations.

Philip chanced to have in his pocket a box of wax tapers which smokers use. After several ineffectual attempts, he succeeded in igniting one against the dank wall, and by its momentary glare perceived that the candle had been left in the tomb. This would serve him in examining the fastenings of the vault. If he could force the inner door by any means, and reach the grating, of which he had an indistinct recollection, he might hope to make himself heard. But the oaken door was immovable, as solid as the wall itself, into which it fitted airtight. Even if he had had the requisite tools, there were no fastenings to be removed; the hinges were set on the outside.

Having ascertained this, he replaced the candle on the floor, and leaned against the wall thoughtfully, watching the blue fan of flame that wavered to and fro, threatening to detach itself from the wick. " At all events," he thought, " the place is ventilated." Suddenly Philip sprang forward and extinguished the light. His existence depended on that candle!

He had read somewhere, in some account of shipwreck, how the survivors had lived for days upon a few candles which one of the passengers had insanely thrown into the

---

[1] **Fra Diavolo** (frà dē-ä′vō-lō): an opera with gay, vivacious music, based on the life of a famous Italian brigand.

longboat. And here he had been burning away his very life.

By the transient illumination of one of the tapers, he looked at his watch. It had stopped at eleven — but at eleven that day or the preceding night? The funeral, he knew, had left the church at ten. How many hours had passed since then? Of what duration had been his swoon? Alas! It was no longer possible for him to measure those hours which crawl like snails to the wretched, and fly like swallows over the happy.

He picked up the candle, and seated himself on the stone steps. He was a sanguine man, this Wentworth, but, as he weighed the chances of escape, the prospect did not seem encouraging. Of course he would be missed. His disappearance under the circumstances would surely alarm his friends; they would instigate a search for him; but who would think of searching for a live man in the cemetery of Montmartre? The Prefect of Police would set a hundred intelligences at work to find him; the Seine might be dragged, *les misérables* [1] turned over at the deadhouse; a minute description of him would be in every detective's pocket and he — in M. Dorine's family tomb!

Yet, on the other hand, it was here he was last seen; from this point a keen detective would naturally work up the case. Then might not the undertaker return for the candlestick, probably not left by design? Or, again, might not M. Dorine send fresh wreaths of flowers, to take the place of those which now diffused a pungent, aromatic odor throughout the chamber? Ah! what unlikely chances! But if one of these things did not happen speedily, it had better never happen. How long could he keep life in himself?

With unaccelerated pulse, he quietly cut the half-burned candle into four equal parts. " Tonight," he meditated, " I will eat the first of these pieces; tomorrow, the second; tomorrow evening, the third; the next day, the fourth; and then — then I'll wait! "

[1] **les misérables** (lā mē-zȧ-rȧ'bl'): the unfortunates.

He had taken no breakfast that morning, unless a cup of coffee can be called a breakfast. He had never been very hungry before. He was ravenously hungry now. But he postponed the meal as long as practicable. It must have been near midnight, according to his calculation, when he determined to try the first of his four singular repasts. The bit of white wax was tasteless; but it served its purpose.

His appetite for the time appeased, he found a new discomfort. The humidity of the walls, and the wind that crept through the unseen ventilator, chilled him to the bone. To keep walking was his only resource. A sort of drowsiness, too, occasionally came over him. It took all his will to fight it off. To sleep, he felt, was to die: and he had made up his mind to live.

Very strange fancies flitted through his head as he groped up and down the stone floor of the dungeon, feeling his way along the wall to avoid the sepulchers. Voices that had long been silent spoke words that had long been forgotten; faces he had known in childhood grew palpable against the dark. His whole life in detail was unrolled before him like a panorama; the changes of a year, with its burden of love and death, its sweets and its bitternesses, were epitomized in a single second. The desire to sleep had left him. But the keen hunger came again.

It must be near morning now, he mused; perhaps the sun is just gilding the pinnacles and domes of the city; or, maybe, a dull, drizzling rain is beating on Paris, sobbing on these mounds above me. Paris! It seems like a dream. Did I ever walk in its gay streets in the golden air? Oh, the delight and pain and passion of that sweet human life!

Philip became conscious that the gloom, the silence, and the cold were gradually conquering him. The feverish activity of his brain brought on a reaction. He grew lethargic, he sank down on the steps, and thought of nothing. His hand fell by chance on one of the pieces of candle; he grasped it and devoured it mechanically. This revived him. "How strange," he thought, "that I am not thirsty. Is it possible that the dampness of the walls, which I must inhale with every breath, has supplied the need of water? Not a drop has passed my lips for two days, and still I experience no thirst. That drowsiness, thank Heaven, has gone. I think I was never wide awake until this hour. It would be an anodyne like poison that could weigh down my eyelids. No doubt the dread of sleep has something to do with this."

The minutes were like hours. Now he walked as briskly as he dared up and down the tomb; now he rested against the door. More than once he was tempted to throw himself upon the stone coffin that held Julie, and make no further struggle for his life.

Only one piece of candle remained. He had eaten the third portion, not to satisfy hunger, but from a precautionary motive. He had taken it as a man takes some disagreeable drug upon the result of which hangs safety. The time was rapidly approaching when even this poor substitute for nourishment would be exhausted. He delayed that moment. He gave himself a long fast this time. The half inch of candle which he held in his hand was a sacred thing to him. It was his last defense against death.

At length, with such a sinking at heart as he had not known before, he raised it to his lips. Then he paused, then he hurled the fragment across the tomb, then the oaken door was flung open, and Philip, with dazzled eyes, saw M. Dorine's form sharply outlined against the blue sky.

When they led him out, half-blinded, into the broad daylight, M. Dorine noticed that Philip's hair, which a short time since was as black as a crow's wing, had actually turned gray in places. The man's eyes, too, had faded; the darkness had spoiled their luster.

"And how long was he really confined in the tomb?" I asked, as Mr. H—— concluded the story.

"*Just one hour and twenty minutes!*" replied Mr. H——, smiling blandly.

As he spoke, the little sloops, with their sails all blown out like white roses, came floating bravely into port, and Philip Wentworth lounged by us, wearily, in the pleasant April sunshine.

Mr. H——'s narrative made a deep impression on me. Here was a man who had undergone a strange ordeal. Here was a man whose sufferings were unique. His was no threadbare experience. Eighty minutes had seemed like two days to him! If he had really been immured two days in the tomb, the story, from my point of view, would have lost its tragic element.

After this it was but natural I should regard Mr. Wentworth with deepened interest. As I met him from day to day, passing through the Common with that same abstracted air, there was something in his loneliness which touched me. I wondered that I had not before read in his pale meditative face some such sad history as Mr. H—— had confided to me. I formed the resolution of speaking to him, though with what purpose was not very clear to my mind. One May morning we met at the intersection of two paths. He courteously halted to allow me the precedence.

"Mr. Wentworth — " I began.

He interrupted me.

"My name, sir," he said, in an offhand manner, "is Jones."

"Jo-Jo-Jones! " I gasped.

"Not Joe Jones," he returned coldly, "Frederick."

Mr. Jones, or whatever his name is, will never know, unless he reads these pages, why a man accosted him one morning as "Mr. Wentworth," and then abruptly rushed down the nearest path, and disappeared in the crowd.

The fact is, I had been duped by Mr. H——, who is a gentleman of literary proclivities, and has, it is whispered, become somewhat demented in brooding over the Great American Novel — not yet hatched. He had actually tried the effect of one of his chapters on me!

My hero, as I subsequently learned, is

no hero at all, but a commonplace young man who has some connection with the building of that pretty granite bridge which will shortly span the crooked little lake in the Public Garden.

When I think of the cool ingenuity and readiness with which Mr. H—— built up his airy fabric on my credulity, I am half inclined to laugh; though I feel not slightly irritated at having been the unresisting victim of his Black Art.

## Suggestions for Study

1. What was the author's purpose in writing this story?

2. In your case how successful was the double surprise? There are two tests of a good surprise ending: (a) You should not be able to see it coming; (b) You should be obliged to admit, on looking back over the story, that all the necessary clues were there.

3. Have you ever seen George M. Cohan's play *Seven Keys to Baldpate?* In what way is the play similar to Aldrich's story?

4. Of the French writers who influenced Aldrich the best known is Guy de Maupassant. You might be interested in his collection *The Odd Number.*

5. Read "Marjorie Daw" and others of Aldrich's surprise-ending stories. Are you always surprised? What stories with a surprise ending can you find in Part I of this volume?

6. Vocabulary: Mall, incongruities, dilemma, interlocutor, subtle, surtout, fiacre, sarcophagus, lethargic.

## For Your Vocabulary

WORD HISTORY. One of the interesting things about language is the way it makes common words from proper names. *Tantalizing* (page 739) is an example. Tantalus was a mythological character who was punished by being always thirsty, standing in water up to his shoulders, and having it ebb away whenever he stooped to drink. So *tantalizing* (tăn′tà-līz̆-ĭng) is not just teasing. It is offering something desperately wanted and then snatching it away. *Shanghai* (shăng-hī′) is another word developed the same way. When sailors could not be had for the long China voyage, usually to the port of Shanghai, they were dragged aboard ship drunk or drugged and awakened

to find themselves in for the trip. The verb is used for getting a fellow into something without letting him know what it's all about. De Kruif said some of the early yellow fever experiments may have been made on men who were *shanghaied* (page 168). In "Footfalls" (page 72) you found a voice described as *stentorian* (stĕn-tō′rĭ-ăn). Stentor was a herald in the Trojan War, who could make his call heard over any competition. Around any school you can find at least one teacher with a *stentorian* voice. What man's name has recently become a common noun meaning a traitor to his own people?

## 3. THE RISE OF SOCIAL CONSCIOUSNESS

Sidney Lanier and Emily Dickinson wrote poetry that is timeless and undated. It is as fresh and as interesting today as on the day it was first written. In a sense their poetry was not a part of the world they lived in but was rather apart from it. But as they wrote, history was moving past them. A social revolt was rising in the West.

The trouble was the old story that America was no longer the same land of opportunity it had been. Theodore Roosevelt explained it when he wrote about one of the coal strikes. "A few generations ago," he said, "an American workman could have saved money, gone west, and taken up a homestead. Now the free lands were gone. In earlier days a man who began with pick and shovel might have come to own a mine. That outlet too was now closed, as regards the immense majority." In other words, the pots of gold were farther away. There was little chance to get a fresh start somewhere else. Farmers could not so easily give up their dry lands and find homesteads elsewhere. Wage earners could not so easily quit their jobs and start in business for themselves. They had to stay where they were and face it out.

That meant that they were facing a different kind of frontier — not a geographic one, but a social and economic frontier. There was still plenty to be won, but it was in terms of improved working conditions, housing conditions, wages, prices, sanitation, schooling. There was plenty of money in the country, natural resources, strange and wonderful machines, elaborate facilities for transportation and communication. How could all these riches be used for the betterment of Americans? That was the new frontier.

In answer to that challenge, a whole series of reform movements, social reformers, and social programs arose in America beginning late in the nineteenth century. To describe them all would take too long. The important thing to remember is the challenge, because that is still with us.

WRITERS ON SOCIAL PROBLEMS

Fortunately, by the end of the century there were more writers to record what was happening. The selections in this book represent a good panorama.

First there is the eloquent address by the great Atlanta liberal editor, Henry Grady. He talks about the South, devastated by the war, and pleads for an understanding of Southern problems. But he does not rest on sympathy or on memories of the great past. He describes the new South in the making — small farms rather than plantations, industry along with the traditional agriculture. And he asks for friendship and a fair place in the American future.

Then there are two selections suggestive of some of the problems that came with the tremendous immigration from Europe and Asia — more than eight million in the single decade between 1901 and 1910. Mary Antin describes some of the feelings of a Russian girl coming to the land of freedom. Thomas A. Daly suggests in his dialect poem some of the problems of the melting pot, when unlike races were thrown in together, and the only answer was for all of them to become Americans. Unfortunately that process is not completed yet, as our race prejudices and occasional race riots indicate.

Edwin Markham's eloquent poem, " The Man with the Hoe," made such an impression in the 1890's because it seemed to typify

not only farmers, but all workers. It made people ask questions: Is this the best our land of opportunity can do? Is this what we dreamed about, and what Crèvecoeur told his European readers about when he described life in America? Is it for this kind of life that we settled the West, dug minerals out of the mountains, and built up industry? Are our workers really like this one, and if so what can we do for them? How can we distribute the wealth of the new land so that these men get a better share? How can we use the time so that these men have leisure to be more than working animals? How can we use our huge machines and our great companies for the little man's good? Those were the questions people were asking, and orators were shouting, at the end of the century.

The last of those questions is the one Peter Finley Dunne suggests in his dialect sketch on machinery. Underneath the assumed name " Mr. Dooley " and the humor of the sketch is a bitter accusation that all our wonderful new machinery is not really being used for man's good. Is the machine serving man, or man the machine? It is a question that echoed up and down the country.

The selection from Hamlin Garland is a warm and realistic picture of schooldays on the prairie. In the 1890's, however, Garland was known for a series of biting short stories about unfair living conditions on the prairie. He described later how he came to write them:

. . . My three years in Boston had given me perspective on the life of the prairie farmer. I perceived with new vision the loneliness and drudgery of the farmers' wives. All across northwestern Iowa and up through central Dakota I brooded darkly over the problem presented, and this bitter mood was deepened by the condition in which I found my mother on a treeless farm just above Ordway. It was in this mood of resentment that I began to write.

But perhaps no nineteenth-century novelist indicted our social system more bitterly than Frank Norris. He wrote two books of three he had planned on a challenging idea, the epic of the wheat. He was going to show how the great natural power of the crop was being perverted and not used for the good of man. His first book, *The Octopus,* was on the theme that the railroads were squeezing out the farmer who raised the wheat. The second book, *The Pit,* showed how the wheat was used for speculation in the Chicago grain pit. The third was to show how the wheat was finally used to combat a famine in India. Norris's idea is that nature is bigger than man, that if man doesn't use the wheat properly the wheat will ruin him. *The Octopus* ended with the death of the greedy railroad manager who fell into the hold of a grain boat and literally drowned in the wheat. *The Pit* ended with the financial ruin of the man who had sought to corner the grain market. But most Americans didn't wait for nature to punish the men who were responsible for bad conditions; they went out for new laws and new officeholders.

You ought to remember a few other names out of this period in our literature. One of these is Stephen Crane, a brilliant foreign correspondent, novelist, and story writer who died young but left such novels as *The Red Badge of Courage* and *Maggie,* and such memorable short stories as " The Open Boat," which you will surely want to read.

Then there was the name of a group and of a kind of writing which hit hard at social ills and inequalities. " Muckraking," it was called; the writers were " muckrakers." They were so called because they raked up the unsavory facts about some American businesses and businessmen. Upton Sinclair, for instance, told the story of the Chicago stockyards so vividly and malodorously that he forced the passage of a Pure Foods law. Most of these muckraking books and articles came out in the years between 1900 and 1910, when Theodore Roosevelt was waving his big stick at the trusts; much of the muckraking too was directed at the secrets of the beef trust, the copper trust, Standard Oil, and other trusts. The muckraking books accomplished minor reforms,

and did a great service in awakening the country to its social problems. The same social currents and anxieties which presented themselves to American writers when the frontier closed in 1890 have been a part of our literature and a challenge to us all — truly our new frontier — ever since.

## Henry Woodfin Grady
### 1850–1889

### THE NEW SOUTH

This oration was delivered by Grady before the distinguished membership of the New England Society in New York City at the banquet celebrating its eighty-first birthday, December 22, 1886. Among a number of brilliant after-dinner speeches given on this occasion, this one was pre-eminent; and at its conclusion the speaker was accorded a tremendous and sincere ovation. It is a skillfully constructed after-dinner talk, with all the necessary elements of flattery, humility, and humor. But it is much more — it is an honest and heartfelt plea for understanding of the New South.

" There was a South of slavery and secession — that South is dead. There is a South of union and freedom — that South, thank God, is living, breathing, growing every hour." These words, delivered from the immortal lips of Benjamin H. Hill, at Tammany Hall, in 1866, true then and truer now, I shall make my text tonight.

Mr. President and Gentlemen: Let me express to you my appreciation of the kindness by which I am permitted to address you. I make this abrupt acknowledgment advisedly, for I feel that if, when I raise my provincial voice in this ancient and august presence, it could find courage for no more than the opening sentence, it would be well if in that sentence I had met in a rough sense my obligation as a guest, and had perished, so to speak, with courtesy on my lips and grace in my heart.

Permitted, through your kindness, to catch my second wind, let me say that I appreciate the significance of being the first

Southerner to speak at this board, which bears the substance, if it surpasses the semblance, of original New England hospitality — and honors the sentiment that in turn honors you, but in which my personality is lost, and the compliment to my people made plain.

Pardon me one word, Mr. President, spoken for the sole purpose of getting into the volumes [1] that go out annually freighted with the rich eloquence of your speakers — the fact that the Cavalier as well as the Puritan was on the continent in its early days, and that he was " up and able to be about." I have read your books carefully and I find no mention of the fact, which seems to me an important one for preserving a sort of historical equilibrium, if for nothing else.

Let me remind you that the Virginia Cavalier first challenged France on the continent — that Cavalier John Smith gave New England its very name, and was so pleased with the job that he has been handing his own name around ever since — and that while Miles Standish was cutting off men's ears for courting a girl without her parents' consent, and forbade men to kiss their wives on Sunday, the Cavalier was courting everything in sight, and that the Almighty had vouchsafed great increase to the Cavalier colonies, the huts in the wilderness being as full as the nests in the woods.

But having incorporated the Cavalier as a fact in your charming little books, I shall let him work out his own salvation, as he has always done, with engaging gallantry, and we will hold no controversy as to his merits. Why should we? Neither Puritan nor Cavalier long survived as such. The virtues and good traditions of both happily still live for the inspiration of their sons and the saving of the old fashion. But both Puritan and Cavalier were lost in the storm of the first Revolution, and the American citizen, supplanting both and stronger than either, took possession of the republic bought by their common blood and fashioned to wisdom, and charged himself with teaching men government and establishing the voice of the people as the voice of God.

My friends, Dr. Talmage [2] has told you that the typical American has yet to come. Let me tell you that he has already come. Great types, like valuable plants, are slow to flower and fruit. But from the union of these colonists, Puritans and Cavaliers, from the straightening of their purposes and the crossing of their blood, slow perfecting through a century, came he who stands as the first typical American, the first who comprehended within himself all the strength and gentleness, all the majesty and grace of this republic — Abraham Lincoln. He was the sum of Puritan and Cavalier, for in his ardent nature were fused the virtues of both, and in the depths of his great soul the faults of both were lost. He was greater than Puritan, greater than Cavalier, in that he was American, and that in his honest form were first gathered the vast and thrilling forces of his ideal government — charging it with such tremendous meaning and elevating it above human suffering that martyrdom, though infamously aimed, came as a fitting crown to a life consecrated from the cradle to human liberty. Let us, each cherishing the traditions and honoring his fathers, build with reverent hands to the type of this simple but sublime life, in which all types are honored, and in our common glory as Americans there will be plenty and to spare for your forefathers and for mine.

Dr. Talmage has drawn for you, with a master's hand, the picture of your returning armies. He has told you how, in the pomp and circumstance of war, they came back to you, marching with proud and victorious tread, reading their glory in a nation's eyes! Will you bear with me while I tell you of another army that sought its home at the close of the late war — an army that marched home in defeat and not in victory — in pathos and not in splendor, but in

[1] volumes: the yearbooks containing reports of the speeches made before the society.

[2] Dr. Talmage: Thomas De Witt Talmage (1832–1902), clergyman, author, editor, and lecturer.

glory that equaled yours, and to hearts as loving as ever welcomed heroes home!

Let me picture to you the footsore Confederate soldier as, buttoning up in his faded gray jacket the parole which was to bear testimony to his children of his fidelity and faith, he turned his face southward from Appomattox in April, 1865. Think of him as, ragged, half-starved, heavyhearted, enfeebled by want and wounds, having fought to exhaustion, he surrenders his gun, wrings the hands of his comrades in silence, and lifting his tear-stained and pallid face for the last time to the graves that dot old Virginia hills, pulls his gray cap over his brow, and begins the slow and painful journey.

What does he find — let me ask you who went to your homes eager to find, in the welcome you had justly earned, full payment for four years' sacrifice — what does he find when, having followed the battle-stained cross against overwhelming odds, dreading death not half so much as surrender, he reaches the home he left so prosperous and beautiful? He finds his house in ruins, his farm devastated, his slaves free, his stock killed, his barns empty, his trade destroyed, his money worthless, his social system, feudal in its magnificence, swept away; his people without law or legal status; his comrades slain, and the burdens of others heavy on his shoulders. Crushed by defeat, his very traditions are gone. Without money, credit, employment, material, or training; and besides all this, confronted with the gravest problem that ever met human intelligence — the establishment of a status for the vast body of his liberated slaves.

What does he do — this hero in gray with a heart of gold? Does he sit down in sullenness and despair? Not for a day. Surely God, who had stripped him of his prosperity, inspired him in his adversity. As ruin was never before so overwhelming, never was restoration swifter.

The soldier stepped from the trenches into the furrow; horses that had charged Federal guns marched before the plow, and fields that ran red with human blood in April were green with the harvest in June; women reared in luxury cut up their dresses and made breeches for their husbands, and, with a patience and heroism that fit women always as a garment, gave their hands to work. There was little bitterness in all this. Cheerfulness and frankness prevailed. " Bill Arp " [1] struck the keynote when he said, " Well, I killed as many of them as they did of me, and now I'm going to work." So did the soldier returning home after defeat and roasting some corn on the roadside who made the remark to his comrades, " You may leave the South if you want to, but I'm going to Sandersville, kiss my wife, and raise a crop; and if the Yankees fool with me any more, I'll whip 'em again."

I want to say to General Sherman, who is considered an able man in our parts, though some people think he is a kind of careless man about fire, that from the ashes he left us in 1864 we have raised a brave and beautiful city; that somehow or other we have caught the sunshine in the bricks and mortar of our homes, and have builded therein not one ignoble prejudice or memory.

But what is the sum of our work? We have found out that in the summing up the free Negro counts more than he did as a slave. We have planted the schoolhouse on the hilltop and made it free to white and black. We have sowed towns and cities in the place of theories, and put business above politics. We have challenged your spinners in Massachusetts and your ironmakers in Pennsylvania. We have learned that the $400,000,000 annually received from our cotton crop will make us rich when the supplies that make it are home-raised. We have reduced the commercial rate of interest from 24 to 6 per cent, and are floating 4 per cent bonds. We have learned that one Northern immigrant is worth fifty foreigners and have smoothed the path to Southward, wiped out the place where Mason and Dixon's line used to be, and hung out the latchstring to you and yours.

---

[1] "Bill Arp": pen name of one of the humorists of the war period known as "crackerbox philosophers."

We have reached the point that marks perfect harmony in every household, when the husband confesses that the pies which his wife cooks are as good as those his mother used to bake; and we admit that the sun shines as brightly and the moon as softly as it did before the war. We have established thrift in city and country. We have fallen in love with work. We have restored comfort to homes from which culture and elegance never departed. We have let economy take root and spread among us as rank as the crab grass which sprung from Sherman's cavalry camps, until we are ready to lay odds on the Georgia Yankee as he manufactures relics of the battlefield in a one-story shanty and squeezes pure olive oil out of his cottonseed, against any down-Easter that ever swapped wooden nutmegs for flannel sausage in the valleys of Vermont. Above all, we know that we have achieved in these " piping times of peace " a fuller independence for the South than that which our fathers sought to win in the forum by their eloquence or compel in the field by their swords.

It is a rare privilege, sir, to have had part, however humble, in this work. Never was nobler duty confided to human hands than the uplifting and upbuilding of the prostrate and bleeding South — misguided, perhaps, but beautiful in her suffering, and honest, brave, and generous always. In the record of her social, industrial, and political institutions we await with confidence the verdict of the world.

But what of the Negro? Have we solved the problem he presents, or progressed in honor and equity toward solution? Let the record speak to the point. No section shows a more prosperous laboring population than the Negroes of the South, none in fuller sympathy with the employing and landowning class. He shares our school fund, has the fullest protection of our laws, and the friendship of our people. Self-interest, as well as honor, demand that he should have this. Our future, our very existence depends upon our working out this problem in full and exact justice. We understand that when Lincoln

signed the emancipation proclamation your victory was assured, for he then committed you to the cause of human liberty, against which the arms of man cannot prevail — while those of our statesmen who trusted to make slavery the cornerstone of the Confederacy doomed us to defeat as far as they could, committing us to a cause that reason could not defend or the sword maintain in sight of advancing civilization.

Had Mr. Toombs [1] said, which he did not say, " that he would call the roll of his slaves at the foot of Bunker Hill," he would have been foolish, for he might have known that whenever slavery became entangled in war it must perish, and that the chattel in human flesh ended forever in New England when your fathers — not to be blamed for parting with what didn't pay — sold their slaves to our fathers — not to be praised for knowing a paying thing when they saw it. The relations of the Southern people with the Negro are close and cordial. We remember with what fidelity for four years he guarded our defenseless women and children, whose husbands and fathers were fighting against his freedom. To his eternal credit be it said that whenever he struck a blow for his own liberty he fought in open battle, and when at last he raised his black and humble hands that the shackles might be struck off, those hands were innocent of wrong against his helpless charges, and worthy to be taken in loving grasp by every man who honors loyalty and devotion. Ruffians have maltreated him, rascals have misled him, philanthropists established a bank for him, but the South, with the North, protests against injustice to this simple and sincere people.

To liberty and enfranchisement is as far as law can carry the Negro. The rest must be left to conscience and common sense. It must be left to those among whom his lot is cast, with whom he is indissolubly connected, and whose prosperity depends upon

[1] **Mr. Toombs:** Robert Toombs (1810–1885), Secretary of State in the Confederacy under President Jefferson Davis. He was opposed to the Reconstruction measures and was one of the "unrelenting" Southerners.

their possessing his intelligent sympathy and confidence. Faith has been kept with him, in spite of calumnious assertions to the contrary by those who assume to speak for us or by frank opponents. Faith will be kept with him in the future, if the South holds her reason and integrity.

But have we kept faith with you? In the fullest sense, yes. When Lee surrendered — I don't say when Johnston surrendered, because I understand he still alludes to the time when he met General Sherman last as the time when he determined to abandon any further prosecution of the struggle — when Lee surrendered, I say, and Johnston quit, the South became and has since been, loyal to this Union. We fought hard enough to know that we were whipped, and in perfect frankness accept as final the arbitrament of the sword to which we had appealed. The South found her jewel in the toad's head of defeat. The shackles that had held her in narrow limitations fell forever when the shackles of the Negro slave were broken. Under the old regime the Negroes were slaves to the South; the South was a slave to the system. The old plantation, with its simple police regulations and feudal habit, was the only type possible under slavery. Thus was gathered in the hands of a splendid and chivalric oligarchy the substance that should have been diffused among the people, as the rich blood, under certain artificial conditions is gathered at the heart, filling that with affluent rapture but leaving the body chill and colorless.

The old South rested everything on slavery and agriculture, unconscious that these could neither give nor maintain healthy growth. The new South presents a perfect democracy, the oligarchs leading in the popular movement — a social system compact and closely knitted, less splendid on the surface, but stronger at the core — a hundred farms for every plantation, fifty homes for every palace — and a diversified industry that meets the complex needs of this complex age.

The new South is enamored of her new work. Her soul is stirred with the breath of a new life. The light of a grander day is falling fair on her face. She is thrilling with the consciousness of growing power and prosperity. As she stands upright, full-statured and equal among the people of the earth, breathing the keen air and looking out upon the expanded horizon, she understands that her emancipation came because through the inscrutable wisdom of God her honest purpose was crossed, and her brave armies were beaten.

This is said in no spirit of timeserving or apology. The South has nothing for which to apologize. She believes that the late struggle between the states was war and not rebellion; revolution and not conspiracy, and that her convictions were as honest as yours. I should be unjust to the dauntless spirit of the South and to my own convictions if I did not make this plain in this presence. The South has nothing to take back.

In my native town of Athens is a monument that crowns its central hill — a plain white shaft. Deep cut into its shining side is a name dear to me above the names of men — that of a brave and simple man who died in brave and simple faith. Not for all the glories of New England, from Plymouth Rock all the way, would I exchange the heritage he left me in his soldier's death. To the foot of that shaft I shall send my children's children to reverence him who ennobled their name with his heroic blood. But, sir, speaking from the shadow of that memory which I honor as I do nothing else on earth, I say that the cause in which he suffered and for which he gave his life was adjudged by higher and fuller wisdom than his or mine, and I am glad that the omniscient God held the balance of battle in His Almighty hand and that human slavery was swept forever from American soil — that the American Union was saved from the wreck of war.

This message, Mr. President, comes to you from consecrated ground. Every foot of soil about the city in which I live is sacred as a battleground of the republic. Every hill that invests it is hallowed to you by the blood of your brothers who died for your victory, and doubly hallowed to us by the blood of those who died hopeless, but undaunted, in defeat — sacred soil to all of us — rich with memories that make us purer and stronger and better — silent but stanch witnesses in its red desolation of the matchless valor of American hearts and the deathless glory of American arms — speaking an eloquent witness in its white peace and prosperity to the indissoluble union of American states and the imperishable brotherhood of the American people.

Now, what answer has New England to this message? Will she permit the prejudice of war to remain in the hearts of the conquerors, when it has died in the hearts of the conquered? Will she transmit this prejudice to the next generation, that in their hearts which never felt the generous ardor of conflict it may perpetuate itself? Will she withhold, save in strained courtesy, the hand which straight from his soldier's heart Grant offered to Lee at Appomattox? Will she make the vision of a restored and happy people, which gathered above the couch of your dying captain, filling his heart with grace, touching his lips with praise, and glorifying his path to the grave — will she make this vision on which the last sign of his expiring soul breathed a benediction, a cheat and delusion?

If she does, the South, never abject in asking for comradeship, must accept with dignity its refusal; but if she does not refuse to accept in frankness and sincerity this message of good will and friendship, then will the prophecy of Webster, delivered in this very society forty years ago amid tremendous applause, become true, be verified in its fullest sense, when he said, " Standing hand to hand and clasping hands, we should remain united as we have been for sixty years, citizens of the same country, members of the same government, united, all united now and united forever." There have been difficulties, contentions, and controversies, but I tell you that in my judgment

Those opposed eyes,
Which like the meteors of a troubled heaven,
All of one nature, of one substance bred,
Did lately meet in th' intestine shock,
Shall now, in mutual well beseeming ranks,
March all one way.

## Suggestions for Study

1. Point out the features of this address which make it an effective after-dinner speech.
2. What do you think of Grady's reference to his father? Do you think his remarks sincere? What effect was achieved by them?
3. What were the chief problems to be solved by the New South? Do any still remain?
4. What features of your own environment came from the Puritans? Which came from the Cavaliers? Read Vachel Lindsay's " The Virginians Are Coming Again " for another defense of the Cavalier and his contribution to America.
5. What effect did the assassination of Lincoln have on the problem of reconstruction in the South? What effect did the election of 1876 have? Look up the history of this problem from 1865 to the date of this speech.

## For Your Vocabulary

WORD POWER. When Grady speaks apologetically about raising his *provincial* (prŏ-vĭn'-shăl) voice (page 747), he is touching on the old issue of the city versus the country — more properly the big centers of civilization versus the outlying *provinces,* which are supposed to be narrower in their interests and knowledge. A *provincial* person may be quite at home in his own territory and yet awkward and out-of-place elsewhere. From the Latin word for city we get not only *urban,* of the city, which is usually applied to such definite matters as housing and finance, but also *urbane* (ûr-bān') meaning courteous, polished in manner. Washington Irving was compared to the *urbane* essayists of England. The general idea is that provincial people are *naïve* (nä-ēv'), natural and artless, while *urban* ones are more *sophisticated* (sŏ-fĭs-tĭ-kā'tĕd), or worldly-wise. The girl in " Sixteen " may be described as *naïve,* in spite of her assurance that she knows her way around. In another place you find Harvard men described as *sophisticated* (page 199). Youth always desires *sophistication,* but *naïveté* (nä-ēv-tā') has its charm.

Mary Antin    1881–

# FIRST IMPRESSIONS OF THE PROMISED LAND

America might be having trouble with its growing pains during the 1890's, but it was still the promised land to many a European immigrant who could find few opportunities open for him at home. What was America like to these eager newcomers? We can turn to Mary Antin's autobiographical book, *The Promised Land* (1912), and rediscover our own country with a little immigrant girl who was just thirteen when she came to Boston from Russia. In explaining why she was writing her autobiography when she was not yet thirty, Miss Antin said, " I am only one of the many whose fate it has been to live a page of modern history. We are the strands of the cable that binds the Old World to the New. As the ships that brought us link the shores of Europe and America, so our lives span the bitter sea of racial differences and misunderstandings. Before we came, the New World knew not the Old; but since we have begun to come, the Young World has taken the Old by the hand, and the two are learning to march side by side, seeking a common destiny." The eager little girl whom we find in the following chapter from *The Promised Land* successfully adapted her ways to those of the new country, finished the public schools of Boston, and later attended Columbia University. When she was twenty she married a professor on the faculty at Columbia.

And now for a look at the tenement section of Boston through the eyes of one to whom it was " The Promised Land."

By the time we joined my father,[1] he had surveyed many avenues of approach toward the coveted citadel of fortune. One of these, heretofore untried, he now proposed to essay, armed with new courage and cheered on by the presence of his family. In partnership with an energetic little man who had an English chapter in his history, he prepared to set up a refreshment booth on Crescent Beach. But while he was completing arrangements at the beach we remained in town, where we enjoyed the educational advantages of a thickly populated neighborhood; namely, Wall Street, in the West End of Boston.

Anybody who knows Boston knows that the West and North Ends comprise the chief tenement districts of Boston, where people who have never lived in the tenements are fond of going sight-seeing. He may know all this and yet not guess how Wall Street, in the West End, appears in the eyes of a little immigrant from Polotzk. What would the sophisticated sight-seer say about Union Place, off Wall Street, where my new home waited for me? He would say that it is no place at all, but a short box of an alley. Two rows of three-story tenements are its sides, a stingy strip of sky is its lid, a littered pavement is the floor, and a narrow mouth its exit.

But I saw a very different picture on my introduction to Union Place. I saw two imposing rows of brick buildings, loftier than any dwelling I had ever lived in. Brick was even on the ground for me to tread on, instead of common earth or boards. Many friendly windows stood open, filled with uncovered heads of women and children. I thought the people were interested in us, which was very neighborly. I looked up to the topmost row of windows, and my eyes were filled with the May blue of an American sky!

In our days of affluence in Russia we had been accustomed to upholstered parlors, embroidered linen, silver spoons and candlesticks, goblets of gold, kitchen shelves shining with copper and brass. We had feather beds heaped halfway to the ceiling; we had clothespresses dusky with velvet and silk and fine woolen. The three small rooms into which my father now ushered us, up one flight of stairs, contained only the necessary beds, with lean mattresses; a few wooden chairs, a table or two; a mysterious iron structure, which later turned out to be a stove; a couple of unornamental kerosene lamps; and a scanty array of cooking utensils and crockery. And yet we were all im-

---

[1] joined my father: He had been in America for three years before his family came.

ARRIVING AT THE PROMISED LAND. These families, like Mary Antin's, were among the thousands who came to America about the turn of the century with bright hopes for the future. (Brown Brothers)

pressed with our new home and its furniture. It was not only because we had just passed through our seven lean years, cooking in earthen vessels, eating black bread on holidays, and wearing cotton; it was chiefly because these wooden chairs and tin pans were American chairs and pans that they shone glorious in our eyes. And if there was anything lacking for comfort or decoration we expected it to be presently supplied — at least, we children did. Perhaps my mother alone, of us newcomers, appreciated the shabbiness of the little apartment and realized that for her there was as yet no laying down of the burden of poverty.

Our initiation into American ways began with the first step on the new soil. My father found occasion to instruct or correct us even on the way from the pier to Wall Street, which journey we made crowded together in a rickety cab. He told us not to lean out of the windows, not to point, and explained the word " greenhorn." We did not want to be " greenhorns," and gave the strictest attention to my father's instructions. I do not know when my parents found opportunity to review together the history of Polotzk in the three years past, for we children had no patience with the subject; my mother's narrative was constantly interrupted by irrelevant questions, interjections, and explanations.

The first meal was an object lesson of much variety. My father produced several kinds of food, ready to eat, without any cooking, from little tin cans that had printing all over them. He attempted to introduce us to a queer, slippery kind of fruit, which he called " banana," but had to give it up for the time being. After the meal he had better luck with a curious piece of furniture on runners, which he called "rocking chair." There were five of us newcomers, and we found five different ways of getting into the American machine of perpetual motion, and as many ways of getting out of it. One born and bred to the use of a rocking chair cannot imagine how ludicrous people can make themselves when attempting to use it for the first time. We laughed immoderately over our various experiments with the novelty, which was a wholesome way of letting off steam after the unusual excitement of the day.

In our flat we did not think of such a thing as storing the coal in the bathtub. There was no bathtub. So in the evening of the first day my father conducted us to the public baths. As we moved along in a little procession, I was delighted with the illumination of the streets. So many lamps, and they burned until morning, my father said, and so people did not need to carry lanterns. In America, then, everything was free, as we had heard in Russia. Light was free; the streets were as bright as a synagogue on a holy day. Music was free; we had been serenaded, to our gaping delight, by a brass band of many pieces, soon after our installation on Union Place.

Education was free. That subject my father had written about repeatedly, as comprising his chief hope for us children, the essence of American opportunity, the treasure that no thief could touch, not even misfortune or poverty. It was the one thing that he was able to promise us when he sent for us; surer, safer than bread or shelter. On our second day I was thrilled with the realization of what this freedom of education meant. A little girl from across the alley came and offered to conduct us to school. My father was out, but we five between us had a few words of English by this time. We knew the word school. We understood. This child, who had never seen us till yesterday, who could not pronounce our names, who was not much better dressed than we, was able to offer us the freedom of the schools of Boston! No application made; no questions asked; no examinations, rulings, exclusions; no machinations; no fees. The doors stood open for every one of us. The smallest child could show us the way.

This incident impressed me more than anything I had heard in advance of the freedom of education in America. It was a concrete proof — almost the thing itself. One had to experience it to understand it.

It was a great disappointment to be told by my father that we were not to enter upon our school career at once. It was too near the end of the term, he said, and we were going to move to Crescent Beach in a week or so. We had to wait until the opening of the schools in September. What a loss of precious time — from May till September!

Not that the time was really lost. Even the interval on Union Place was crowded with lessons and experiences. We had to visit the stores and be dressed from head to foot in American clothing; we had to learn the mysteries of the iron stove, the washboard, and the speaking tube; we had to learn to trade with the fruit peddler through the window, and not to be afraid of the policeman; and, above all, we had to learn English.

The kind people who assisted us in these important matters form a group by themselves in the gallery of my friends. If I had never seen them from those early days till now, I should still have remembered them with gratitude. When I enumerate the long list of my American teachers, I must begin with those who came to us on Wall Street and taught us our first steps. To my mother, in her perplexity over the cookstove, the woman who showed her how to make the fire was an angel of deliverance. A fairy godmother to us children was she who led us to a wonderful country called " uptown," where, in a dazzlingly beautiful palace called a " department store," we exchanged out hateful homemade European costumes, which pointed us out as " greenhorns " to the children on the street, for real American machine-made garments, and issued forth glorified in each other's eyes.

With our despised immigrant clothing

we shed also our impossible Hebrew names. A committee of our friends, several years ahead of us in American experience, put their heads together and concocted American names for us all. Those of our real names that had no pleasing American equivalents they ruthlessly discarded, content if they retained the initials. My mother, possessing a name that was not easily translatable, was punished with the undignified nickname of Annie. Fetchke, Joseph, and Deborah issued as Frieda, Joseph, and Dora, respectively. As for poor me, I was simply cheated. The name they gave me was hardly new. My Hebrew name being Maryashe in ful, Mashke for short, Russianized into Marya (*Mar-ya*), my friends said that it would hold good in English as *Mary;* which was very disappointing, as I longed to possess a strange-sounding American name like the others.

I am forgetting the consolation I had, in this matter of names, from the use of my surname, which I have had no occasion to mention until now. I found on my arrival that my father was " Mr. Antin " on the slightest provocation, and not, as in Polotzk, on state occasions alone. And so I was " Mary Antin," and I felt very important to answer to such a dignified title. It was just like America that even plain people should wear their surnames on weekdays.

## Suggestions for Study

1. What features of the new environment that were commonplace to Americans seemed wonderful to the newcomers? What evidence can you find that things seemed wonderful not because they were unusually splendid but just because they were American?

2. How did the immigrant family show their great desire to fit into the life of America? Do you think you could possibly be happy to make such great changes in your own ways if you went to another country to live?

3. Did you find yourself hoping that everyone would be kind to Mary and her family? Do you ever have opportunities to show similar kindness to other newcomers to America? or do you just laugh at them?

4. Do you believe that immigrants with such an attitude toward their new country as the Antins had will make just as good citizens as native-born Americans? What can we learn from them that will make us better citizens ourselves?

5. Make a list of " Immigrants Who Have Made Good." Include their nationality, their age when entering America, and their notable achievements. Discuss the value of what you have discovered in making this list.

## Thomas Augustine Daly 1871–

### TWO 'MERICANA MEN

In the foreign quarters of the larger American cities one can always hear English spoken with a variety of accents — accents often the source of amusement to native Americans. But the amusement is usually kindly, as in the poems of Thomas Augustine Daly. A man with an Irish name would hardly be expected to make his reputation with poems in Italian dialect, but that is what Daly has done. He is a native of Philadelphia and has been connected with several newspapers of his city, especially the *Evening Ledger*. His natural gift for reproducing the dialects of the many nationalities among the immigrant population of a great city proved valuable in verses for his newspaper columns. He tried various types of speech; but the Italian seemed his special forte, and the names of his volumes *Canzoni* and *Carmina* suggest the flavor of the poems within. He has published a number of other volumes, some containing poems in " pure " English. In recognition of his work he has been given an honorary degree of Doctor of Literature by Fordham University, which he had attended for two years before going into newspaper work. His poems are sometimes delightfully gay and lighthearted, at other times poignant with hidden tears. The following suggests the sentiment running through most of them — that human understanding makes all nations kin.

Beeg Irish cop dat walks hees beat
   By dees peanutta stan',
First two, t'ree week w'en we are meet
   Ees call me " Dagoman."
An' w'en he see how mad I gat,

Wheech eesa pleass heem, too,
Wan day he say: " W'at's matter dat,
Ain't ' Dago ' name for you?

Dat's 'Mericana name, you know,
For man from Eetaly;                    10
Eet ees no harm for call you so,
Den why be mad weeth me? "


First time he talka deesa way
I am too mad for speak,
But nexta time I justa say:              15
" All righta, Meester Meeck! "
O! my, I nevva hear bayfore
Sooch langwadge like he say;
An' he don't look at me no more
For mebbe two, t'ree day.                20
But pretta soon agen I see
Dees beeg poleecaman
Dat com' an' growl an' say to me:
" Hallo, Eyetalian!
Now, mebbe so you gon' deny             25
Dat dat's a name for you."
I smila back, an' mak' reply:
" No, Irish, dat'sa true."
" Ha! Joe," he cry, " you theenk dat we
Should call you 'Merican? "             30
" Dat's gooda 'nough," I say, " for me,
Eef dat's w'at you are, Dan."


So now all times we speaka so
Like gooda 'Merican:
He say to me, " Good morna, Joe,"       35
I say, " Good morna, Dan."


## Suggestions for Study

1. What does this little poem have in common with Mary Antin's narrative of her first
months in Boston? Do you think Daly must
have talked much with the immigrants in his
own city? Why?

2. Try reading the poem aloud. Daly's spelling of the dialect is remarkably clear and effective, and the dialect adds music and rhythm to
the poem.

3. If you read the dialect successfully, present other of Daly's popular Italian dialect
poems before the class.

## Edwin Markham 1852–1940

Edwin Markham, child of pioneer parents,
spent his boyhood in Oregon and California.
Not satisfied with his life of farming and
bronco riding on a cattle ranch, he determined
to be a teacher and entered a California normal
school, later acting as superintendent of schools
for many years. Though he had been writing
poetry of varying merit since childhood, he
suddenly became famous when he was forty-
seven years old with " The Man with the Hoe."
Partly because the poem was a splendid challenging thing in itself, partly because at the
end of the nineteenth century there was a great
wave of interest in common workers, the poem
had, and still has, tremendous vogue, being
quoted in papers from West to East. The poem
was suggested by Millet's notable painting of
a French peasant leaning on his hoe. Markham's own words best show the interpretation
he gave to the picture: " The Yeoman is the
landed and well-to-do farmer; you need shed
no tears for him. But here in the Millet picture
is the opposite — the Hoeman: the landless,
the soul-blighted workman of the world; the
dumb creature that has no time to rest, no
time to think, no time for the hopes that make
us men."

## THE MAN WITH THE HOE

WRITTEN AFTER SEEING MILLET'S WORLD-
FAMOUS PAINTING OF A BRUTALIZED
TOILER IN THE DEEP ABYSS OF
LABOR

God made man in his own image; in the
image of God made He him. — *Genesis*.

Bowed by the weight of centuries he leans
Upon his hoe and gazes on the ground,
The emptiness of ages in his face,
And on his back the burden of the world.
Who made him dead to rapture and de-
spair,                                   5
A thing that grieves not and that never
hopes,
Stolid and stunned, a brother to the ox?
Who loosened and let down this brutal jaw?
Whose was the hand that slanted back this
brow?
Whose breath blew out the light within this
brain?                                   10

THE MAN WITH THE HOE. This famous painting by the French painter, Jean François Millet, inspired Edwin Markham's poem. (Brown Brothers)

Is this the thing the Lord God made and
  gave
To have dominion over sea and land;
To trace the stars and search the heavens
  for power;
To feel the passion of eternity?
Is this the dream He dreamed who shaped
  the suns                                    15
And marked their ways upon the ancient
  deep?
Down all the caverns of hell to their last
  gulf
There is no shape more terrible than this —
More tongued with cries against the world's
  blind greed —
More filled with signs and portents for the
  soul —                                      20
More packed with danger to the universe.

What gulfs between him and the seraphim!
Slave of the wheel of labor, what to him
Are Plato° and the swing of Pleiades?°   24
What the long reaches of the peaks of song,
The rift of dawn, the reddening of the rose?
Through this dread shape the suffering ages
  look;
Time's tragedy is in that aching stoop;
Through this dread shape humanity be-
  trayed,
Plundered, profaned, and disinherited,   30
Cries protest to the Powers that made the
  world,
A protest that is also prophecy.

24. **Plato** (plā′tō): an ancient Greek philosopher whose idealistic views of man have greatly influenced the world. 24. **Pleiades** (plē′yà-dēz): a cluster of many stars, six of which are visible. It is often referred to by poets.

O masters, lords and rulers in all lands,
Is this the handiwork you give to God,
This monstrous thing distorted and soul-
    quenched?                                35
How will you ever straighten up this shape;
Touch it again with immortality;
Give back the upward looking and the light;
Rebuild in it the music and the dream;
Make right the immemorial infamies,      40
Perfidious wrongs, immedicable woes?


O masters, lords and rulers in all lands,
How will the future reckon with this man?
How answer his brute question in that hour
When whirlwinds of rebellion shake all
    shores?                                 45
How will it be with kingdoms and with
    kings —
With those who shaped him to the thing he
    is —
When this dumb Terror shall rise to judge
    the world,
After the silence of the centuries?

## Suggestions for Study

1. Point out words and details used to emphasize the picture of an utterly crushed being.
2. To whom are the questions of this poem addressed? In what way are these people held responsible?
3. Some critics have said that Millet never intended to portray such a hopeless creature but simply an honest workman resting. Refer to the copy of the picture on page 758 and discuss which interpretation it suggests to you.
4. What examples can you find in history of uprisings of peasants or other workers as suggested in "The Man with the Hoe" (line 45), "When whirlwinds of rebellion shake all shores"? Graphic pictures of such outbursts are to be found in Dickens's *Tale of Two Cities* and *Barnaby Rudge* and in Galsworthy's *Strife*.

## For Your Vocabulary

WORD POWER. Markham stresses the injustice done to "The Man with the Hoe" in such words as *profaned* (line 30) and *perfidious* (line 41). We *profane* (prŏ-fān') something when we debase it by wrong or unjust use. Does this definition throw any light on *profane* language? Similarly, a *perfidious* (pẽr-

fĭd'ĭ-ŭs) wrong is one that violates faith or obligation and is, therefore, base and ignoble. Such evils are well called *infamies* (ĭn'fà-mĭz) by the poet, for that which is *infamous* (ĭn'-fà-mŭs) is base or vile.

WORD ANALYSIS. Analyze *immedicable* (ĭm-mĕd'ĭ-kà-b'l). Then check it in context (line 41) to discover whether it is used literally or figuratively.

## Finley Peter Dunne     1867–1936

### MR. DOOLEY ON MACHINERY

Not all the writing about the rapid rise of industry in America was solemn and serious. One of the most popular and influential commentators between 1898 and 1910 was Finley Peter Dunne, a Chicago newspaperman who expressed his opinions in a humorous vein through the mouth of Martin Dooley, an Irish saloonkeeper who commented to his friend Hennessy on what he read in the newspapers. Dunne took up every important issue of his day, following no political party but simply expressing his own common-sense attitude. He had courage, too, for he often championed unpopular figures in the news, and during the muckraking era he criticized reformers as well as the bosses of political machines. You can measure his popularity by the fact that nine "Mr. Dooley" books were published between 1898 and 1911. In this article Mr. Dooley reflects on the rise of the machine in America and just how much good all our inventions do us.

Mr. Dooley was reading from a paper. "'We live,' he says, 'in an age iv wondhers. Niver befure in th' histhry iv th' wurruld has such pro-gress been made.'

"Thrue wurruds an' often spoken. Even in me time things has changed. Whin I was a la-ad Long Jawn Wintworth cud lean his elbows on th' highest buildin' in this town. It took two months to come here fr'm Pittsburgh on a limited raft an' a stagecoach that run fr'm La Salle to Mrs. Murphy's hotel. They wasn't anny tillygraft that I can raymimber an' th' sthreetcar was pulled be a mule an' dhruv be an engineer be th' name iv Mulligan. We thought we was a pro-grissive people. Ye bet we did. But look at us today. I go be Casey's house tonight an' there it is a fine story-an'-a-half frame house with Casey settin' on th' dure shtep dhrinkin' out iv a pail. I go be Casey's house tomorrah an' it's a hole in th' groun'. I rayturn to Casey's house on Thursdah an' it's a fifty-eight-story buildin' with a morgedge onto it an' they're thinkin' iv takin' it down an' replacin' it with a modhren sthructure. Th' shoes that Corrigan th' cobbler wanst wurruked on f'r a week, hammerin' away like a woodpecker, is now tossed out be th' dozens fr'm th' mouth iv a masheen. A cow goes lowin' softly in to Armour's an' comes out glue, beef, gelatin, fertylizer, celooloid, joolry, sofy cushions, hair restorer, washin' sody, soap, lithrachoor, an' bedsprings so quick that while aft she's still cow, for'ard she may be anything fr'm buttons to Pannyma hats. I can go fr'm Chicago to New York in twinty hours; but I don't have to, thank th' Lord. Thirty years ago we thought 'twas marvelous to be able to tillygraft a man in Saint Joe an' get an answer that night. Now, be wireless tillygraft ye can get an answer befure ye sind th' tillygram if they ain't careful. Me friend Macroni [1] has done that. Be manes iv his wondher iv science a man on a ship in mid-ocean can sind a tillygram to a man on shore, if he has a confid'rate on board. That's all he needs. Be mechanical science an' thrust in th' op'rator annywan can set on th' shore iv Noofoundland an' chat with a frind in th' County Kerry.[2]

" Yes, sir, mechanical science has made gr-reat sthrides. Whin I was a young man we used to think Hor'ce Greeley was th' gr-reatest livin' American. He was a gran' man, a gran' man with feathers beneath his chin an' specs on his nose like th' windows in a diver's hemlet. His pollyticks an' mine cudden't live in th' same neighborhood, but he was a gran' man all th' same. We used to

take th' Cleveland *Plain Daler* in thim days f'r raycreation an' th' New York *Thrybune* f'r exercise. 'Twas considhered a test iv a good-natured Dimmycrat if he cud read an article in th' *Thrybune* without havin' to do th' stations iv th' cross [3] aftherward f'r what he said. I almost did wanst, but they was a line at th' end about a frind iv mine be th' name iv Andhrew Jackson an' I wint out an' broke up a Methodist prayer meetin'. He was th' boy that cud put it to ye so that if ye voted th' Dimmycrat tickit it was jus' th' same as demandin' a place in purgatory. Th' farmers wud plant annything fr'm a rutybaga to a Congressman on his advice. He niver had money enough to buy a hat, but he cud go to th' Sicrety iv th' Threasury an' tell him who's pitcher to put on th' useful valentines we thrade f'r groceries.

" But if Hor'ce Greeley was alive today where'd he be? Settin' on three inches iv th' edge iv a chair in th' outside office iv me frind Pierpont Morgan [4] waitin' f'r his turn. In th' line is th' Imp'ror iv Germany, th' new cook, th' prisidint iv a railroad, th' cap'n iv th' yacht, Rimbrandt [5] th' painther, Jawn W. Grates,[6] an' Hor'ce. Afther a while th' boy at th' dure says, ' Ye're next, ol' party. Shtep lively, f'r th' boss has had a Weehawken Peerooginy [7] sawed off on him this mornin' an' he mustn't be kep' waitin'.' An' th' iditor goes in. ' Who ar-re ye? ' says th' gr-reat man, givin' him wan iv thim piercin' looks that whin a man gets it he has to be sewed up at wanst. ' I'm ye'er iditor,' says Hor'ce. ' Which wan? ' says Pierpont.

---

[3] **do th' stations iv th' cross:** say a prayer before each of the fourteen pictures placed in a Catholic church, representing stages of Christ's progress with the cross on the way to His crucifixion. The prayers are a special Lenten feature, but are also sometimes assigned as penance for sin. [4] **Morgan:** John Pierpont Morgan, Sr. (1837–1913), important American financier. [5] **Rimbrandt:** Rembrandt (1606–1669), famous Dutch painter, included humorously because Morgan was a great collector of art. [6] **Jawn W. Grates:** misspelling of John W. Gates, a famous speculator. [7] **Weehawken Peerooginy:** Perugino (1446–1524) was a famous Italian painter. Weehawken is a town in New Jersey. The combination suggests that Morgan has been cheated in supposing he had purchased an original old master that proved to be only a copy.

---

[1] **Macroni:** Of course he means Marconi (1874–1937), the Italian inventor who put wireless telegraphy on a commercial basis. [2] **County Kerry:** in southwest Ireland.

'Number two hundhred an' eight.' 'What's ye'er spishilty?' 'Tahriff an' th' improve-mint iv th' wurruld,' says Hor'ce. 'See Per-kins,' says Pierpont, an' th' intherview is over. Now what's made th' change? Me-chanical science, Hinnissy. Somewan made a masheen that puts steel billets within th' reach iv all. Hince Charlie Schwab.[1]

"What's it done f'r th' wurruld? says ye. It's done ivrything. It's give us fast ships an' an autymatic hist f'r th' hod, an' small flats an' a taste iv solder in th' peaches. If annybody says th' wurruld ain't betther off thin it was, tell him that a masheen has been invinted that makes honey out iv pethro-lyum. If he asts ye why they ain't anny Shakesperes today, say, 'No, but we no longer make sausages be hand.'

"'Tis pro-gress. We live in a cinchry iv pro-gress an' I thank th' Lord I've seen most iv it. Man an' boy I've lived pretty near through this wondherful age. If I was proud I cud say I seen more thin Julyus Caesar iver see or cared to. An' here I am, I'll not say how old, still pushin' th' malt acrost th' counther at me thirsty counthry-men. All around me is th' refinemints iv mechanical janius. Instead iv broachin' th' beer kag with a club an' dhrawin' th' beer through a fassit as me Puritan forefathers done, I have that wondher iv invintive sci-ence th' beer pump. I cheat mesilf with a cash raygisther. I cut off th' end iv me good cigar with an injanyous device an' pull th' cork out iv a bottle with a conthrivance that wud've made that frind that Hogan boasts about, that ol' boy Archy Meeds,[2] think they was witchcraft in th' house. Science has been a gr-reat blessin' to me. But amidst all these granjoors here am I th' same ol' an-tiquated combination iv bellows an' pump I always was. Not so good. Time has worn me out. Th' years like little boys with jack-knives has carved their names in me top. Ivry day I have to write off something f'r deprecyation. 'Tis about time f'r whoiver

owns me to wurruk me off on a thrust. Me-chanical science has done ivrything f'r me but help me. I suppose I ought to feel su-peeryor to me father. He niver see a high buildin' but he didn't want to. He cudden't come here in five days but he was a wise man an' if he cud've come in three he'd have stayed in th' County Roscommon.[3]

"Th' pa-apers tells me that midical sci-ence has kept pace with th' hop-skip-an'-a-jump iv mechanical inginooty. Th' doctors has found th' mikrobe iv ivrything fr'm lum-bago to love an' fr'm jandice to jealousy, but if a brick bounces on me head I'm crated up th' same as iv yore an' put away. Rockyfellar can make a pianny out iv a bar'l iv crude ile, but no wan has been able to make a blade iv hair grow on Rockyfellar. They was a doctor over in France that dis-covered a kind iv a thing that if 'twas pumped into ye wud make ye live till people got so tired iv seein' ye around they cud scream. He died th' nex' year iv prema-chure ol' age. They was another doctor cud insure whether th' nex' wan wud be a boy or a girl. All ye had to do was to decide wud it be Arthur or Ethel an' lave him know. He left a fam'ly iv unmarredgeable daughters.

"I sometimes wondher whether pro-gress is anny more thin a kind iv a shift. It's like a merry-go-round. We get up on a speckled wooden horse an' th' mechanical pianny plays a chune an' away we go, hollerin'. We think we're thravelin' like th' divvle but th' man that doesn't care about merry-go-rounds knows that we will come back where we were. We get out dizzy an' sick an' lay on th' grass an' gasp, 'Where am I? Is this th' meelin-yum?'[4] An' he says, 'No, 'tis Ar-rchey Road.' Father Kelly says th' Agyp-tians done things we cudden't do an' th' Romans put up skyscrapers an' aven th' Chinks had tillyphones an' phonygrafts.

"I've been up to th' top iv' th' very high-est buildin' in town, Hinnissy, an' I wasn't anny nearer Hivin thin if I was in th' sthreet.

---

[1] **Charlie Schwab:** Charles M. Schwab (1862–1939), president of two steel corporations and other industrial corporations. [2] **Archy Meeds:** Archimedes (är-kĭ-mē'dēz), a Greek mathema-tician and inventor (287–212 B.C.)

[3] **County Roscommon** (rŏs-kŏm'ŏn): in central Ireland. [4] **meelin-yum:** millennium, the thousand years during which, according to the Book of Revelations, Christ will return to rule on earth.

Th' stars was as far away as iver. An' down beneath is a lot iv us runnin' an' lapin' an' jumpin' about, pushin' each other over, haulin' little sthrips iv ir'n to pile up in little buildin's that ar-re called skyscrapers but not be th' sky; wurrukin' night an' day to make a masheen that'll carry us fr'm wan jack-rabbit colony to another an' yellin', ' Pro-gress! ' Pro-gress, oho! I can see th' stars winkin' at each other an' sayin', ' Ain't they funny! Don't they think they're playin' the divil! '

" No, sir, masheens ain't done much f'r man. I can't get up anny kind iv fam'ly inthrest f'r a steam dredge or a hydhraulic hist. I want to see skyscrapin' men. But I won't. We're about th' same hight as we always was, th' same hight an' build, composed iv th' same inflamable an' perishyable mateeryal, an exthra hazardous risk, unimproved an' li'ble to collapse. We do make pro-gress, but it's th' same kind Julyus Caesar made an' ivry wan has made befure or since an' in this age iv masheenery we're still burrid be hand."

" What d'ye think iv th' man down in Pinnsylvanya who says th' Lord an' him is partners in a coal mine? " asked Mr. Hennessy, who wanted to change the subject.

" Has he divided th' profits? " asked Mr. Dooley.

## Suggestions for Study

1. Does Mr. Dooley seem to have a good idea of the growing importance of machinery in American life? What kinds does he mention? Have we any still more astonishing machines today?

2. What is his conclusion about the importance of machinery? How does he back up his conclusion? Do you agree with him?

3. What dialect does Mr. Dooley use? Is it as clearly indicated by the spelling as Thomas Augustine Daly's Italian dialect (see page 756)? What does it contribute to the effect of the article?

4. Do you think you would read " Mr. Dooley " if he were appearing in your daily paper? Why? How is he different from most popular commentators of our own times? Does he have anything in common with any of the modern commentators?

5. Special assignment: Assemble a collection of examples or make a study of machinery as it appears today in one of the following: (a) literature; (b) art; (c) cartoons.

# Hamlin Garland    1860–1940

## SCHOOL LIFE

The literary historian of the pioneer farmer of the Middle West is Hamlin Garland. In 1917 he published *A Son of the Middle Border,* the greatest of his series of autobiographical books. It is not only a well-written autobiography, but also a significant document in the history of our national life. It is an epic portrayal of pioneer life on the farms of Wisconsin, Iowa, and Dakota. *A Daughter of the Middle Border* refers to Garland's mother, who figures prominently in the book. *Back-Trailers of the Middle Border* continues the story into his later life.

Before Garland's day those who wrote about farm life usually saw the country through the romantic haze of the city dweller and summer visitor. With the publication of *Main-Traveled Roads* (1890), his first volume of short stories, the voice of an actual farmer was heard in literature, and the story he told had the genuine touch of firsthand experience. He had no illusions about the farm.

Though the chapter here presented is called " School Life," its accounts of well-digging, threshing, prairie fires, and blizzards give varied aspects of the pioneering which is the core of *A Son of the Middle Border.* The description of the school life itself, with its rich detail of recess games, McGuffey's readers, feet itching from chilblains, and frozen lunches, illustrates the painstaking and vivid realism found throughout the entire book.

Our new house was completed during July but we did not move into it till in September. There was much to be done in way of building sheds, granaries, and corncribs and in this work father was both carpenter and stonemason. An amusing incident

"School Life," from *A Son of the Middle Border,* by Hamlin Garland. Reprinted by permission of The Macmillan Company, publishers.

comes to my mind in connection with the digging of our well.

Uncle David and I were " tending mason," and father was down in the well laying or trying to lay the curbing. It was a tedious and difficult job and he was about to give it up in despair when one of our neighbors, a quaint old Englishman named Barker, came driving along. He was one of these men who take a minute inquisitive interest in the affairs of others; therefore he pulled his team to a halt and came in.

Peering into the well, he drawled out, " Hello, Garland. W'at ye doin' down there? "

" Tryin' to lay a curb," replied my father, lifting a gloomy face, " and I guess it's too complicated for me."

" Nothin' easier," retorted the old man with a wink at my uncle, " jest put two atop o' one and one atop o' two — and the big end out " — and with a broad grin on his red face he went back to his team and drove away.

My father afterward said, " I saw the whole process in a flash of light. He had given me all the rule I needed. I laid the rest of that wall without a particle of trouble."

Many times after this Barker stopped to offer advice, but he never quite equaled the startling success of his rule for masonry.

The events of this harvest, even the process of moving into the new house, are obscured in my mind by the clouds of smoke which rose from calamitous fires all over the West. It was an unprecedentedly dry season, so that not merely the prairie but many weedy cornfields burned. I had a good deal of time to meditate upon this, for I was again the plowboy. Every day I drove away from the rented farm to the new land where I was crosscutting the breaking, and the thickening haze through which the sun shone with a hellish red glare produced in me a growing uneasiness which became terror when the news came to us that Chicago was on fire. It seemed to me then that the earth was about to go up in a flaming cloud

just as my granddad had so often prophesied.

This general sense of impending disaster was made keenly personal by the destruction of Uncle David's stable with all his horses. This building like most of the barns of the region was not only roofed with straw but banked with straw, and it burned so swiftly that David was trapped in a stall while trying to save one of his teams. He saved himself by burrowing like a gigantic mole through the side of the shed, and so, hatless, covered with dust and chaff, emerged as if from a fiery burial after he had been given up for dead.

This incident combined with others so filled my childish mind that I lived in apprehension of similar disaster. I feared the hot wind which roared up from the south, and I never entered our own stable in the middle of the day without a sense of danger. Then came the rains — the blessed rains — and put an end to my fears.

In a week we had forgotten all the " conflagrations " except that in Chicago. There was something grandiose and unforgettable in the tales which told of the madly fleeing crowds in the narrow streets. These accounts pushed back the walls of my universe till its far edge included the ruined metropolis whose rebuilding was of the highest importance to us, for it was not only the source of all our supplies, but the great central market to which we sent our corn and hogs and wheat.

My world was splendidly romantic. It was bounded on the west by THE PLAINS with their Indians and buffalo; on the north by THE GREAT WOODS, filled with thieves and counterfeiters; on the south by OSAGE [1] and CHICAGO; and on the east by HESPER, ONALASKA,[2] and BOSTON. A luminous trail ran from Dry Run Prairie to Neshonoc — all else was " chaos and black night."

For seventy days I walked behind my plow on the new farm while my father fin-

[1] **Osage** (ō-sāj'): a small town in northeastern Iowa, near which the Garland farm was located.
[2] **Hesper, Onalaska** (ŏn-à-lăs'kà): small towns in western Wisconsin, near which the Garlands had previously lived.

ished the harvest on the rented farm and moved to the house on the knoll. It was lonely work for a boy of eleven but there were frequent breaks in the monotony and I did not greatly suffer. I disliked crosscutting for the reason that the unrotted sods would often pile up in front of the colter and make me a great deal of trouble. There is a certain pathos in the sight of that small boy tugging and kicking at the stubborn turf in the effort to free his plow. Such misfortunes loom large in a lad's horizon.

One of the interludes, and a lovely one, was given over to gathering the hay from one of the wild meadows to the north of us. Another was the threshing from the shock on the rented farm. This was the first time we had seen this done and it interested us keenly. A great many teams were necessary and the crew of men was correspondingly large. Uncle David was again the thresher with a fine new separator; and I would have enjoyed the season with almost perfect contentment had it not been for the fact that I was detailed to hold sacks for Daddy Fairbanks, who was the measurer.

Our first winter had been without much wind but our second taught us the meaning of the word " blizzard," which we had just begun to hear about. The winds of Wisconsin were " gentle zephyrs " compared to the blasts which now swept down over the plain to hammer upon our desolate little cabin and pile the drifts around our sheds and granaries, and even my pioneer father was forced to admit that the hills of Green's Coulee had their uses after all.

One such storm which leaped upon us at the close of a warm and beautiful day in February lasted for two days and three nights, making life on the open prairie impossible even to the strongest man. The thermometer fell to thirty degrees below zero and the snow-laden air moving at a rate of eighty miles an hour pressed upon the walls of our house with giant power. The sky of noon was darkened, so that we moved in a pallid half-light, and the windows thick with frost shut us in as if with gray shrouds.

Hour after hour those winds and snows in furious battle howled and roared and whistled around our frail shelter, slashing at the windows and piping on the chimney, till it seemed as if the Lord Sun had been wholly blotted out and that the world would never again be warm. Twice each day my father made a desperate sally toward the stable to feed the imprisoned cows and horses or to replenish our fuel — for the remainder of the long pallid day he sat beside the fire with gloomy face. Even his indomitable spirit was awed by the fury of that storm.

So long and so continuously did those immitigable winds howl in our ears that their tumult persisted, in imagination, when on the third morning we thawed holes in the thickened rime of the windowpanes and looked forth on a world silent as a marble sea and flaming with sunlight. My own relief was mingled with surprise — surprise to find the landscape so unchanged. True, the yard was piled high with drifts and the barns were almost lost to view but the far fields and the dark lines of Burr Oak Grove remained unchanged.

We met our schoolmates that day, like survivors of shipwreck, and for many days we listened to gruesome stories of disaster, tales of stages frozen deep in snow with all their passengers sitting in their seats, and of herders with their silent flocks around them, lying stark as granite among the hazel bushes in which they had sought shelter. It was long before we shook off the awe with which this tempest filled our hearts.

The schoolhouse, which stood at the corner of our new farm, was less than half a mile away, and yet on many of the winter days which followed we found it quite far enough. Hattie was now thirteen, Frank nine, and I a little past eleven; but nothing, except a blizzard such as I have described, could keep us away from school. Facing the cutting wind, wallowing through the drifts, battling like small intrepid animals, we often arrived at the door moaning with pain yet unsubdued, our ears frosted, our toes numb in our boots, to meet others in similar case around the roaring hot stove.

Often after we reached the schoolhouse another form of suffering overtook us in the "thawing out" process. Our fingers and toes, swollen with blood, ached and itched, and our ears burned. Nearly all of us carried sloughing ears and scaling noses. Some of the pupils came two miles against these winds.

The natural result of all this exposure was, of course, chilblains! Every foot in the school was more or less touched with this disease, to which our elders alluded as if it were an amusing trifle; but to us it was no joke.

After getting thoroughly warmed up, along about the middle of the forenoon, there came into our feet a most intense itching and burning and aching, a sensation so acute that keeping still was impossible, and all over the room an uneasy shuffling and drumming arose as we pounded our throbbing heels against the floor or scraped our itching toes against the edge of our benches. The teacher understood and was kind enough to overlook this disorder.

The wonder is that any of us lived through that winter, for at recess, no matter what the weather might be, we flung ourselves out of doors to play "fox and geese," or "dare goal," until, damp with perspiration, we responded to the teacher's bell, and came pouring back into the entryways to lay aside our wraps for another hour's study.

Our readers were almost the only counterchecks to the current of vulgarity and baseness which ran through the talk of the older boys, and I wish to acknowledge my deep obligation to Professor McGuffey, whoever he may have been, for the dignity and literary grace of his selections. From the pages of his readers I learned to know and love the poems of Scott, Byron, Southey, Wordsworth, and a long line of the English masters. I got my first taste of Shakespeare from the selected scenes which I read in these books.

With terror as well as delight I rose to read "Lochiel's Warning," "The Battle of Waterloo" or "The Roman Captive."

Marco Bozzaris and William Tell were alike glorious to me. I soon knew not only my own reader, the fourth, but all the selections in the fifth and sixth as well. I could follow almost word for word the recitations of the older pupils and at such times I forgot my squat little body and my mop of hair, and became imaginatively a page in the train of Ivanhoe, or a bowman in the army of Richard the Lion Heart battling the Saracen in the Holy Land.

With a high ideal of the way in which these grand selections should be read, I was scared almost voiceless when it came my turn to read them before the class. " STRIKE FOR YOUR ALTARS AND YOUR FIRES. STRIKE FOR THE GREEN GRAVES OF YOUR SIRES — GOD AND YOUR NATIVE LAND," always reduced me to a trembling breathlessness. The sight of the emphatic print was a call to the best that was in me and yet I could not meet the test. Excess of desire to do it just right often brought a ludicrous gasp and I often fell back into my seat in disgrace, the titter of the girls adding to my pain.

Then there was the famous passage, " Did ye not hear it? " and the careless answer, " No, it was but the wind or the car rattling o'er the stony street." I knew exactly how those opposing emotions should be expressed but to do it after I rose to my feet was impossible. Burton was even more terrified than I. Stricken blind as well as dumb, he usually ended by helplessly staring at the words which, I conceive, had suddenly become a blur to him.

No matter, we were taught to feel the force of these poems and to reverence the genius that produced them, and that was worth while. Falstaff and Prince Hal, Henry and his wooing of Kate, Wolsey and his downfall, Shylock and his pound of flesh all became a part of our thinking and helped us to measure the large figures of our own literature, for Whittier, Bryant, and Longfellow also had place in these volumes. It is probable that Professor McGuffey, being a Southern man, did not value New England writers as highly as my grandmother did; nevertheless "Thanatopsis" was there and "The Village Blacksmith," and extracts from *The Deerslayer* and *The Pilot* gave us a notion that in Cooper we had a novelist of weight and importance, one to put beside Scott and Dickens.

A by-product of my acquaintance with one of the older boys was a stack of copies of the *New York Weekly*, a paper filled with stories of noble life in England and hairbreadth escapes on the plain, a shrewd mixture, designed to meet the needs of the entire membership of a prairie household. The pleasure I took in these tales should fill me with shame, but it doesn't — I rejoice in the memory of it.

I soon began, also, to purchase and trade "Beadle's Dime Novels" and, to tell the truth, I took an exquisite delight in *Old Sleuth* and *Jack Harkaway*. My taste was catholic. I ranged from *Lady Gwendolin* to *Buckskin Bill,* and so far as I can now distinguish, one was quite as enthralling as the other. It is impossible for any print to be as magical to any boy these days as those weeklies were to me in 1871.

One day a singular test was made of us all. Through some agency now lost to me my father was brought to subscribe for the *Hearth and Home* or some such paper for the farmer, and in this I read my first chronicle of everyday life.

In the midst of my dreams of lords and ladies, queens and dukes, I found myself deeply concerned with backwoods farming, spelling schools, protracted meetings, and the like familiar homely scenes. This serial (which involved my sister and myself in many a spat as to who should read it first) was *The Hoosier Schoolmaster,* by Edward Eggleston, and a perfectly successful attempt to interest Western readers in a story of the middle border.

To us Mandy and Bud Means, Ralph Hartsook, the teacher, Little Shocky, and sweet patient Hannah, were as real as Cyrus Button and Daddy Fairbanks. We could hardly wait for the next number of the paper, so concerned were we about Hannah and Ralph. We quoted old lady Means and we made bets on Bud in his fight with the villainous drover. I hardly knew where Indiana was in those days, but Eggleston's characters were near neighbors.

The illustrations were dreadful, even in my eyes; but the artist contrived to give a slight virginal charm to Hannah and a certain childish sweetness to Shocky, so that we accepted the more than mortal ugliness of old man Means and his daughter Mirandy (who simpered over her book at us as she did at Ralph) as a just interpretation of their worthlessness.

This book is a milestone in my literary progress, as it is in the development of distinctive Western fiction; and years afterward I was glad to say so to the aged author, who lived a long and honored life as a teacher and writer of fiction.

It was always too hot or too cold in our schoolroom and on certain days when a savage wind beat and clamored at the loose windows, the girls, humped and shivering, sat upon their feet to keep them warm, and the younger children with shawls over their shoulders sought permission to gather close about the stove.

Our dinner pails (stored in the entryway) were often frozen solid and it was necessary to thaw out our mince pie as well as our bread and butter by putting it on the stove. I recall, vividly, gnawing, doglike, at the mollified outside of a doughnut while still its frosty heart made my teeth ache.

Happily all days were not like this. There were afternoons when the sun streamed warmly into the room, when long icicles formed on the eaves, adding a touch of grace to the desolate building, moments when the jingling bells of passing wood sleighs expressed the natural cheer and buoyancy of our youthful hearts.

## Suggestions for Study

1. Point out marked contrasts between your own life and that of Hamlin Garland. What experiences have you had that are in any way

similar to his? Do you think the many hardships these boys and girls had to undergo to get an education were a help or a hindrance to them? Why?

2. Try to demonstrate Barker's rule for masonry, using books or other objects for stones.

3. Wherein lies the humor of the boy Hamlin's world? What are the boundaries of your " world "?

4. Do you think your literary taste is " catholic "? Can you name any " milestones " in your " literary progress "?

5. Describe some spectacular fire or storm that you have seen, either orally to the class or in writing as if it were a chapter in your autobiography.

6. A special report on the great Chicago fire of 1871 would be interesting.

7. Two good accounts of Midwestern blizzards in literature are Frances Gilchrist Wood's short story " Turkey Red " and Chapter IV in Part II of Rölvaag's *Giants in the Earth.* Whittier's *Snow-Bound* is the classic of the New England storm. Passages from these might be read aloud to the class — especially if you live in the South, where such storms are outside your experience.

8. If you read all of *A Son of the Middle Border* and would like to know more of this interesting family, read *A Daughter of the Middle Border* (about Hamlin's mother) and *Back-Trailers of the Middle Border* (contrasting life in the East and the West). Garland's stories in *Main-Traveled Roads* picture hard farm conditions of the early days. As a result of reading Garland's books, you might like to write on " Farm Life Then and Now."

## For Your Vocabulary

BASE-WORDS. Life on the middle border, where Garland grew up, developed strength of spirit as well as body. He calls his father's spirit *indomitable* (ĭn-dŏm′ĭ-tà-b'l), which means incapable of being mastered by outside forces. You probably know the related words *dominant,* ruling or controlling, and the verb *dominate.* All three come from *dominus,* a Latin word for lord or master. Horatio Alger suffered from his father's *dominations* (page 201), and George Washington feared the alternate *domination* of two rival political parties in this country (page 473). The children early developed the same strong spirit as their father, for they battled the storm " like small

*intrepid* (ĭn-trĕp′ĭd) animals " (page 764). *Intrepid* means without fear, literally without trembling from fear. *Trepidation* is a state of fear that sets one to trembling.

WORD ANALYSIS. Analyze *calamitous* and *unprecedentedly* (both on page 763). How many separate parts can you detect in the latter? It is a masterpiece of word-building, and you know all the prefixes and suffixes used.

## Frank Norris             1870–1902

### ALL THE TRAFFIC WILL BEAR

The early struggles of the Western farmers with railroad freight rates that often took all the profit out of their farming form the central theme of *The Octopus* (1901). We get a clear picture of the ruin a rise in rates could bring to a farmer in this little episode of a man who thought he could escape the general fate by raising another crop. S. Behrman all through the book personifies the cold, impersonal greed of the railroads that fattened off the struggling farmers.

The ex-engineer [1] reached the post office in Bonneville toward eleven o'clock; but he did not at once present his notice of the arrival of his consignment at Ruggles's office. It entertained him to indulge in an hour's lounging about the streets. It was seldom he got into town, and when he did he permitted himself the luxury of enjoying his evident popularity. He met friends everywhere, in the post office, in the drugstore, in the barbershop, and around the courthouse. With each one he held a moment's conversation; almost invariably this ended in the same way:

" Come on 'n have a drink."

" Well, I don't care if I do."

And the friends proceeded to the Yosemite bar, pledging each other with punctilious ceremony. Dyke, however, was a strictly temperate man. His life on the engine had trained him well. Alcohol he never touched, drinking instead ginger ale, sarsaparilla and iron — soft drinks.

[1] **ex-engineer:** Dyke, who had formerly worked for the railroad.

At the drugstore, which also kept a stock of miscellaneous stationery, his eye was caught by a " transparent slate," a child's toy, where upon a little pane of frosted glass one could trace with considerable elaboration outline figures of cows, plows, bunches of fruit, and even rural watermills that were printed on slips of paper underneath.

" Now, there's an idea, Jim," he observed to the boy behind the soda-water fountain; " I know a little tad that would just about jump out of her skin for that. Think I'll have to take it with me."

" How's Sidney getting along? " the other asked, while wrapping up the package.

Dyke's enthusiasm had made of his little girl a celebrity throughout Bonneville.

The ex-engineer promptly became voluble, assertive, doggedly emphatic.

" Smartest little tad in all Tulare County, and more fun! A regular whole show in herself."

" And the hops? " inquired the other.

" Bully," declared Dyke, with the good-natured man's readiness to talk of his private affairs to anyone who would listen. " Bully. I'm dead sure of a bonanza crop by now. The rain came *just* right. I actually don't know as I can store the crop in those barns I built, it's going to be so big. That foreman of mine was a daisy. Jim, I'm going to make money in that deal. After I've paid off the mortgage — you know I had to mortgage, yes, crop and homestead both, but I can pay it off and all the interest to boot, lovely — well, and as I was saying, after all expenses are paid off I'll clear big money, m' son. Yes, sir. I *knew* there was boodle in hops. You know the crop is contracted for already. Sure, the foreman managed that. He's a daisy. Chap in San Francisco will take it all and at the advanced price. I wanted to hang on, to see if it wouldn't go to six cents, but the foreman said, ' No, that's good enough.' So I signed. Ain't it bully, hey? "

" Then what'll you do? "

" Well, I don't know. I'll have a layoff for a month or so and take the little tad and Mother up and show 'em the city — 'Frisco — until it's time for the schools to open, and then we'll put Sid in the seminary at Marysville. Catch on? "

" I suppose you'll stay right by hops now? "

" Right you are, m' son. I know a good thing when I see it. There's plenty others going into hops next season. I set 'em the example. Wouldn't be surprised if it came to be a regular industry hereabouts. I'm planning ahead for next year already. I can let the foreman go, now that I've learned the game myself, and I think I'll buy a piece of land off Quien Sabe and get a bigger crop, and build a couple more barns, and, by George, in about five years' time I'll have things humming. I'm going to make *money*, Jim."

He emerged once more into the street and went up the block leisurely, planting his feet squarely. He fancied that he could feel he was considered of more importance nowadays. He was no longer a subordinate, an employee. He was his own man, a proprietor, an owner of land, furthering a successful enterprise. No one had helped him; he had followed no one's lead. He had struck out unaided for himself, and his success was due solely to his own intelligence, industry, and foresight. He squared his great shoulders till the blue gingham of his jumper all but cracked. Of late, his great blond beard had grown and the work in the sun had made his face very red. Under the visor of his cap — relic of his engineering days — his blue eyes twinkled with vast good nature. He felt that he made a fine figure as he went by a group of young girls in lawns and muslins and garden hats on their way to the post office. He wondered if they looked after him, wondered if they had heard that he was in a fair way to become a rich man.

But the chronometer in the window of the jewelry store warned him that time was passing. He turned about and, crossing the street, took his way to Ruggles's office, which was the freight as well as the land office of the P. and S. W. Railroad.

As he stood for a moment at the counter in front of the wire partition, waiting for the clerk to make out the order for the freight agent at the depot, Dyke was surprised to see a familiar figure in conference with Ruggles himself, by a desk inside the railing.

The figure was that of a middle-aged man, fat, with a great stomach, which he stroked from time to time. As he turned about, addressing a remark to the clerk, Dyke recognized S. Behrman. The banker, railroad agent, and political manipulator seemed to the ex-engineer's eyes to be more gross than ever. His smooth-shaven jowl stood out big and tremulous on either side of his face; the roll of fat on the nape of his neck, sprinkled with sparse, stiff hairs, bulged out with great prominence. His great stomach, covered with a light brown linen vest, stamped with innumerable interlocked horseshoes, protruded far in advance, enormous, aggressive. He wore his inevitable round-topped hat of stiff brown straw, varnished so bright that it reflected the light of the office windows like a helmet; and even from where he stood Dyke could hear his loud breathing and the clink of the hollow links of his watch chain upon the vest buttons of imitation pearl, as his stomach rose and fell.

Dyke looked at him with attention. There was the enemy, the representative of the Trust with which Derrick's League was locking horns. The great struggle had begun to invest the combatants with interest. Daily, almost hourly, Dyke was in touch with the ranchers, the wheat growers. He heard their denunciations, their growls of exasperation and defiance. Here was the other side — this placid fat man, with a stiff straw hat and linen vest, who never lost his temper, who smiled affably upon his enemies, giving them good advice, commiserating with them in one defeat after another, never ruffled, never excited, sure of his power, conscious that back of him was the Machine, the colossal force, the inexhaustible coffers of a mighty organization, vomiting millions to the League's thousands.

The League was clamorous, ubiquitous, its objects known to every urchin on the streets; but the Trust was silent, its ways inscrutable — the public saw only results. It worked on in the dark, calm, disciplined, irresistible. Abruptly Dyke received the impression of the multitudinous ramifications of the colossus. Under his feet the ground seemed mined; down there below him in the dark the huge tentacles went silently twisting and advancing, spreading out in every direction, sapping the strength of all opposition, quiet, gradual, biding the time to reach up and out and grip with a sudden unleashing of gigantic strength.

"I'll be wanting some cars of you people before the summer is out," observed Dyke to the clerk as he folded up and put away the order that the other had handed him. He remembered perfectly well that he had arranged the matter of transporting his crop some months before, but his role of proprietor amused him and he liked to busy himself again and again with the details of his undertaking.

"I suppose," he added, "you'll be able to give 'em to me. There'll be a big wheat crop to move this year, and I don't want to be caught in any car famine."

"Oh, you'll get your cars," murmured the other.

"I'll be the means of bringing business your way," Dyke went on; "I've done so well with my hops that there are a lot of others going into the business next season. Suppose," he continued, struck with an idea, "suppose we went into some sort of pool, a sort of shippers' organization, could you give us special rates, cheaper rates — say a cent and a half? "

The other looked up.

"A cent and a half! Say *four* cents and a half and maybe I'll talk business with you."

"Four cents and a half," returned Dyke; "I don't see it. Why, the regular rate is only two cents."

"No, it isn't," answered the clerk, looking him gravely in the eye, "it's five cents."

"Well, there's where you are wrong, m'

son," Dyke retorted genially. " You look it up. You'll find the freight on hops from Bonneville to 'Frisco is two cents a pound for carload lots. You told me that yourself last fall."

" That was last fall," observed the clerk. There was a silence. Dyke shot a glance of suspicion at the other. Then, reassured, he remarked, " You look it up. You'll see I'm right."

S. Behrman came forward and shook hands politely with the ex-engineer.

" Anything I can do for you, Mr. Dyke? "

Dyke explained. When he had done speaking, the clerk turned to S. Behrman and observed respectfully:

" Our regular rate on hops is five cents."

" Yes," answered S. Behrman, pausing to reflect; " yes, Mr. Dyke, that's right — five cents."

The clerk brought forward a folder of yellow paper and handed it to Dyke. It was inscribed at the top " Tariff Schedule No. 8," and underneath these words, in brackets, was a smaller inscription: " *Supersedes No. 7 of Aug. 1.*"

" See for yourself," said S. Behrman. He indicated an item under the head of " Miscellany."

" The following rates for carriage of hops in carload lots," read Dyke, " take effect June 1, and will remain in force until superseded by a later tariff. Those quoted beyond Stockton are subject to changes in traffic arrangements with carriers by water from that point."

In the list that was printed below, Dyke saw that the rate for hops between Bonneville or Guadalajara and San Francisco was five cents.

For a moment Dyke was confused. Then swiftly the matter became clear in his mind. The railroad had raised the freight on hops from two cents to five.

All his calculations as to a profit on his little investment he had based on a freight rate of two cents a pound. He was under contract to deliver his crop. He could not draw back. The new rate ate up every cent of his gains. He stood there ruined.

" Why, what do you mean? " he burst out. " You promised me a rate of two cents and I went ahead with my business with that understanding. What do you mean? "

S. Behrman and the clerk watched him from the other side of the counter.

" The rate is five cents," declared the clerk doggedly.

" Well, that ruins me! " shouted Dyke. " Do you understand? I won't make fifty cents. *Make!* Why, I will *owe* — I'll be — be — That ruins me, do you understand? "

The other raised a shoulder.

" We don't force you to ship. You can do as you like. The rate is five cents."

" Well — but — damn you, I'm under contract to deliver. What am I going to do? Why, you told me — you promised me a two-cent rate."

" I don't remember it," said the clerk. " I don't know anything about that. But I know this: I know that hops have gone up. I know the German crop was a failure and that the crop in New York wasn't worth the hauling. Hops have gone up to nearly a dollar. You don't suppose we don't know that, do you, Mr. Dyke? "

" What's the price of hops got to do with you? "

" It's got *this* to do with us," returned the other with a sudden aggressiveness, " that the freight rate has gone up to meet the price. We're not doing business for our health. My orders are to raise your rate to five cents, and I think you are getting off easy."

Dyke stared in blank astonishment. For the moment the audacity of the affair was what most appealed to him. He forgot its personal application.

" Great Scott," he murmured, " Great Scott! What will you people do next? Look here. What's your basis of applying freight rates, anyhow? " he suddenly vociferated with furious sarcasm. " What's your rule? What are you guided by? "

But at the words S. Behrman, who had kept silent during the heat of the discussion, leaned abruptly forward. For the only time in his knowledge, Dyke saw his face inflamed with anger and with the enmity and contempt of all this farming element with whom he was contending.

" Yes, what's your rule? What's your basis? " demanded Dyke, turning swiftly to him.

S. Behrman emphasized each word of his reply with a tap of one forefinger on the counter before him:

" All — the traffic — will — bear."

The ex-engineer stepped back a pace, his fingers on the ledge of the counter, to steady himself. He felt himself grow pale; his heart became a mere leaden weight in his chest, inert, refusing to beat.

In a second the whole affair, in all its bearings, went speeding before the eye of his imagination like the rapid unrolling of a panorama. Every cent of his earnings was sunk in this hop business of his. More than that, he had borrowed money to carry it on, certain of success — borrowed of S. Behrman, offering his crop and his little home as security. Once he failed to meet his obligations, S. Behrman would foreclose. Not only would the railroad devour every morsel of his profits, but also it would take from him his home; at a blow he would be left penniless and without a home. What would then become of his mother — and what would become of the little tad? She, whom he had been planning to educate like a veritable lady. For all that year he had talked of his ambition for his little daughter to everyone he met. All Bonneville knew of it. What a mark for gibes he had made of himself. The workingman turned farmer! What a target for jeers — he who had fancied he could elude the railroad! He remembered he had once said the great trust had overlooked his little enterprise, disdaining to plunder such small fry. He should have known better than that. How had he ever imagined the road would permit him to make any money?

Anger was not in him yet; no rousing of the blind, white-hot wrath that leaps to the attack with prehensile fingers moved him. The blow merely crushed, staggered, confused.

He stepped aside to give place to a coatless man in a pink shirt, who entered, carrying in his hands an automatic door-closing apparatus.

" Where does this go? " inquired the man.

Dyke sat down for a moment on a seat that had been removed from a worn-out railway car to do duty in Ruggles's office. On the back of a yellow envelope he made some vague figures with a stump of blue pencil, multiplying, subtracting, perplexing himself with many errors.

S. Behrman, the clerk, and the man with the door-closing apparatus involved themselves in a long argument, gazing intently at the top panel of the door. The man who had come to fix the apparatus was unwilling to guarantee it, unless a sign was put on the outside of the door warning incomers that the door was self-closing. This sign would cost fifteen cents extra.

" But you didn't say anything about this when the thing was ordered," declared S. Behrman. " No, I won't pay it, my friend. It's an overcharge."

" You needn't think," observed the clerk, " that just because you are dealing with the railroad you are going to work us."

Genslinger came in, accompanied by Delaney. S. Behrman and the clerk, abruptly dismissing the man with the door-closing machine, put themselves behind the counter and engaged in conversation with these two. Genslinger introduced Delaney. The buster had a string of horses he was shipping southward. No doubt he had come to make arrangements with the railroad in the matter of stock cars. The conference of the four men was amicable in the extreme.

Dyke, studying the figures on the back of the envelope, came forward again. Absorbed only in his own distress, he ignored the editor and the cowpuncher.

" Say," he hazarded, " how about this? I make out — "

" We've told you what our rates are, Mr. Dyke," exclaimed the clerk angrily. " That's all the arrangement we will make. Take it or leave it." He turned again to Genslinger, giving the ex-engineer his back.

Dyke moved away and stood for a moment in the center of the room, staring at the figures on the envelope.

" I don't see," he muttered, " just what I'm going to do. No, I don't see what I'm going to do at all."

Ruggles came in, bringing with him two other men in whom Dyke recognized dummy buyers of the Los Muertos and Osterman ranchos. They brushed by him, jostling his elbow, and as he went out of the door he heard them exchange jovial greetings with Delaney, Genslinger, and S. Behrman.

Dyke went down the stairs to the street and proceeded onward aimlessly in the direction of the Yosemite House, fingering the yellow envelope and looking vacantly at the sidewalk.

There was a stoop to his massive shoulders. His great arms dangled loosely at his sides, the palms of his hands open.

As he went along, a certain feeling of shame touched him. Surely his predicament must be apparent to every passer-by. No doubt everyone recognized the unsuccessful man in the very way he slouched along. The young girls in lawns, muslins, and garden hats, returning from the post office, their hands full of letters, must surely see in him the type of the failure, the bankrupt.

Then brusquely his tardy rage flamed up. No, it was not his fault; he had made no mistake. His energy, industry, and foresight had been sound. He had been merely the object of a colossal trick, a sordid injustice; a victim of the insatiate greed of the monster, caught and choked by one of those millions of tentacles suddenly reaching up from below, from out the dark beneath his feet, coiling around his throat, throttling him, strangling him, sucking his blood. For a moment he thought of the courts, but instantly laughed at the idea. What court was immune from the power of the monster? Ah, the rage of helplessness, the fury of impotence! No help, no hope — ruined in a brief instant — he a veritable giant, built of great sinews, powerful, in the full tide of his manhood, having all his health, all his wits. How could he now face his home? How could he tell his mother of this catastrophe? And Sidney — the little tad; how could he explain to her this wretchedness — how soften her disappointment? How keep the tears from out her eyes — how keep alive her confidence in him — her faith in his resources?

Bitter, fierce, ominous, his wrath loomed up in his heart. His fists gripped tight together; his teeth clenched. Oh, for a moment to have his hand upon the throat of S. Behrman, wringing the breath from him, wrenching out the red life of him — staining the street with the blood sucked from the veins of the people!

To the first friend that he met, Dyke told the tale of the tragedy, and to the next, and to the next. The affair went from mouth to mouth, spreading with electrical swiftness, overpassing and running ahead of Dyke himself, so that by the time he reached the lobby of the Yosemite House he found his story awaiting him. A group formed about him. In his immediate vicinity business for the instant was suspended. The group swelled. One after another of his friends added themselves to it. Magnus Derrick joined it, and Annixter.[1] Again and again Dyke recounted the matter, beginning with the time when he was discharged from the same corporation's service for refusing to accept an unfair wage. His voice quivered with exasperation; his heavy frame shook with rage; his eyes were injected, bloodshot; his face flamed vermilion, while his deep bass rumbled throughout the running comments of his auditors like the thunderous reverberation of diapason.

From all points of view the story was discussed by those who listened to him, now in the heat of excitement; now calmly, judicially. One verdict, however, prevailed. It was voiced by Annixter: " You're stuck. You can roar till you're black in the face, but you can't buck against the railroad. There's nothing to be done."

" You can shoot the ruffian; you can

[1] **Derrick . . . Annixter:** men prominent in the league formed to fight the railroad rates.

shoot S. Behrman," clamored one of the group. " Yes, sir, you can shoot him."

" Poor fool," commented Annixter, turning away.

Nothing to be done. No, there was nothing to be done — not one thing. Dyke, at last alone and driving his team out of the town, turned the business confusedly over in his mind from end to end. Advice, suggestion, even offers of financial aid had been showered upon him from all directions. Friends were not wanting who heatedly presented to his consideration all manner of ingenious plans, wonderful devices. They were worthless The tentacle held fast. He was stuck.

## Suggestions for Study

1. How does the author build up the impression of Dyke's optimism and good spirits in the early part of this narrative? What omen of trouble appears in the story before Dyke actually hears of the rate change? Why did the rate change mean ruin for him?

2. What is the purpose of introducing the incident about the door-closing gadget? of the broncobuster shipping his horses?

3. What passages refer to the title of the novel from which this selection was taken? Does the comparison strike you as being effective? Is it justified in so far as this incident is concerned?

4. Do you agree with Annixter that there was nothing Dyke could do about his predicament? How did the legislation putting freight rates under supervision of the Interstate Commerce Commission afford safety from such disaster?

## For Your Vocabulary

CONTEXT AND BASE-WORDS. You can find no better time to learn the words *tentacle* (page 769) and *prehensile* (page 771) than when the image of an octopus is fresh in your mind. Its *tentacles* (těn'tà-k'lz) are those waving arms, feeling about for a victim; and when they find one they are powerfully *prehensile* (prĕ-hĕn'-sĭl), able to seize. Do you know the word *tentative*, for feeling the way, or trying out? It comes from the same stem as *tentacle*. A *tentative* plan is only for trial and experiment, not something one is committed to hold to. *Pre-*

*hensile,* on the other hand, comes from a base-word meaning to seize and hold. A monkey has a *prehensile* tail. A child eating an ice-cream cone seems to have a *prehensile* tongue. We use many other words built on the same stem. An *apprehensive* person seizes on causes for alarm before they are justified. If he is mistaken, the idea is a *misapprehension* — as is any other idea we mistakenly hold. We *comprehend* what our minds can seize and hold, and new ideas are within our *comprehension* if we are able to grasp or understand them.

Check *chronometer* (krŏ-nŏm'ĕ-tēr) in its context (page 768). What other words can you recall built on the base-word *chronos,* time?

## For Further Reading on the Growth of Realism

### LITERATURE OF THE PERIOD
#### Fiction

Howells, William Dean: *The Rise of Silas Lapham; A Modern Instance*

James, Henry: *Roderick Hudson; The American; Daisy Miller; The Portrait of a Lady; The Bostonians*

Aldrich, Thomas Bailey: " Marjorie Daw," " Mlle. Olympe Zabriski," " Père Antoine's Date Palm," " Two Bites at a Cherry," " Goliath," *The Story of a Bad Boy*

Garland, Hamlin: *Main-Traveled Roads; Other Main-Traveled Roads*

Crane, Stephen: *The Red Badge of Courage,* " The Open Boat," " A Little Brown Dog," " The Bride Comes to Yellow Sky "

Norris, Frank: *The Octopus; The Pit*

#### Poetry

Lanier, Sidney: " Tampa Robins," " From the Flats," " Barnacles," " Life and Song," " The Revenge of Hamish "

Dickinson, Emily: *Poems of Emily Dickinson*

Riley, James Whitcomb: " Little Orphant Annie," " The Raggedy Man," " The Old Swimmin' Hole," " Out to Old Aunt Mary's," " The Old Man and Jim," " Knee-Deep in June," " My Ruthers," " A Life Lesson," " An Old Sweetheart of Mine," " My Fiddle "

Field, Eugene: " Jest 'fore Christmas," " Seein' Things," " Wynken, Blynken and Nod,"

# THE GROWTH OF REALISM

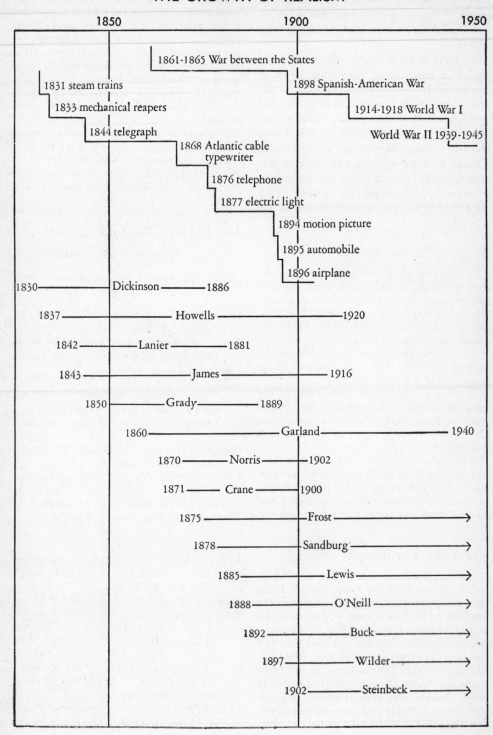

1850         1900         1950

1861-1865 War between the States

1898 Spanish-American War

1831 steam trains

1914-1918 World War I

1833 mechanical reapers

World War II 1939-1945

1844 telegraph

1868 Atlantic cable
typewriter

1876 telephone

1877 electric light

1894 motion picture

1895 automobile

1896 airplane

1830 —————— Dickinson —————— 1886

1837 —————— Howells —————— 1920

1842 ———— Lanier ———— 1881

1843 —————— James —————— 1916

1850 ———— Grady ———— 1889

1860 —————————— Garland —————————— 1940

1870 ———— Norris ———— 1902

1871 ———— Crane ———— 1900

1875 ———————— Frost ————————→

1878 ———————— Sandburg ————————→

1885 ———————— Lewis ————————→

1888 ———————— O'Neill ————————→

1892 ———————— Buck ————————→

1897 ———————— Wilder ————————→

1902 ———————— Steinbeck ————————→

"The Little Peach," "Casey's Table d'Hôte," "Our Two Opinions," "The Limitations of Youth"

Aldrich, Thomas Bailey: "Identity," "Memory," "A Snowflake," "Nocturne," Sonnets

Markham, Edwin: "Lincoln, the Man of the People," "In a Cornfield," "To Young America," Quatrains

### Nonfiction

Howells, William Dean: *A Boy's Town*
Garland, Hamlin: *A Son of the Middle Border; A Daughter of the Middle Border*

### Autobiographies of Successful Immigrants

Bok, Edward: *The Americanization of Edward Bok*
Muir, John: *My Boyhood and Youth*
Pupin, Michael: *From Immigrant to Inventor*
Riis, Jacob: *The Making of an American*
Stern, G. B.: *My Mother and I*

### BOOKS ABOUT THE PERIOD

Brooks, Van Wyck: *New England — Indian Summer*
Canby, H. S.: *The Age of Confidence; Life in the '90's*
Casson, Herbert: *The Romance of Steel; The Romance of the Reaper*
Hylander, C. J.: *American Inventors; American Scientists*
Patterson, J. C.: *America's Greatest Inventors*
Ticknor, Caroline: *Glimpses of Authors*
White, T. M.: *Famous Leaders of Industry*
Wildman, E.: *Famous Leaders of Industry*

### About the Authors

DICKINSON. Bianchi, Martha D.: *The Life and Letters of Emily Dickinson;* Benét, Laura: *Come Slowly, Eden;* Jenkins, M.: *Emily Dickinson, Friend and Neighbor*
LANIER. Mims, Edwin: *Sidney Lanier*
NORRIS. Walker, Franklin: *Frank Norris*
RILEY. Nolan, J. C.: *James Whitcomb Riley, Hoosier Poet*

LA GUARDIA FIELD, NEW YORK, where planes depart every hour to link the United States with all parts of the world. (Monkemeyer)

# America in the Modern World

IN THE FIRST part of this book there are many selections from the best writers of our own day. Comments on these writers have been placed with their stories, poems, or articles, so that it will not be necessary to discuss the rich American literature of the twentieth century so fully as we have discussed the literature of the nineteenth century.

It would not be possible, in any case, to put these new writers and their books into the pattern of history as we have put the writers and writings of preceding centuries. History is like a map. You can make a fairly good rough map of a wooded country by standing on a mountain and looking down over the forest. But if you stand in the midst of the woods, you can see only the few trees around you. Writing history, too, is much easier if you can stand up on the mountain of time. We are far enough from the nineteenth century that we can see it from the mountain, but whenever we write about the twentieth we run the risk of near-by trees blocking out our view of the forest as a whole.

And perhaps it is just as well to think of those modern books otherwise than as history, for they are not written primarily as history. They are written for *us*. They are written to bring us pleasure and to say something to us. If they can also do that for later readers, so much the better. But the poets and novelists who are writing today are thinking of what they want to say to *us,* and we ought to read them in that spirit.

It may help to read them if we try to draw out the bare outlines of the twentieth-century pattern, as we see it now, or at least enough of it to show some of the ways in which these new books are related to the books and men that have gone before. And let us start by taking a look at the road our literature has traveled since those first American books were written more than three centuries ago.

## THE AMERICAN HERITAGE

When this country was still a line of English colonies along the Atlantic coast, a farmer in the colony of New York tried to tell the people of his native France what life in America was like. His name was St. Jean de Crèvecoeur; you have read part of his letter in this book.

Crèvecoeur described the beauty and richness of the land, and the thrilling sight of men and women coming from every country in Europe to be forged together into a new nation. But he talked mostly about freedom. Nothing amazed him quite so much as how free a man could be in the New World. He was so afraid his friends in Europe could not comprehend this kind of freedom that he repeated it over and over.

In America, he said, a man is free to work for himself and keep what he earns; no prince or lord is going to take it away from him. In America, a man is free from hunger and servitude and abasement, because the country is not made up of great lords who have everything and common people who have nothing. In America, he noticed

Longfellow Building, Washington, D. C. William Lescaze, architect, 1941.

Modern design for public buildings emphasizes severe vertical and horizontal lines on the exterior, and lighter, better ventilated, more convenient rooms inside. Note the unusually large window areas of the Longfellow Building and the Crow Island School, which have been made possible through steel and reinforced concrete construction. The strong, dramatic appearance of the two buildings pictured at the top of the page is even more striking by comparison with the neighboring buildings of traditional styles.

*Above:* Daily News Building, New York City. Raymond Hood & John M. Howells, architects.

*Below:* Crow Island School, Winnetka, Illinois. Eliel Saarinen, architect, 1940.

Modern domestic architecture makes use of the outdoors in its floor plans. The Kaufmann house is elaborately arranged above a waterfall on the site. The low-cost home below manufactures a landscape to suit the pleasure of the owner.

*Above:* E. J. Kaufmann house, Bear Run, Pennsylvania, designed by Frank Lloyd Wright in 1937.

*Below:* Model of a two-story house designed by Carl Koch, 1945.

with amazement, even the dictionary is short in " words of dignity, and names of honor," because there are no inherited titles before which the common people must bow. In America, man is free to go to the church he prefers, because there is no state church. From all Europe, he said, come men who have been useless because they have had no freedom to grow, no incentive to work, and in the climate of American freedom they are reborn and remade.

Not every writer has written of America so favorably as Crèvecoeur did, but every writer who has tried to describe the American pattern has begun with freedom. Some have called it the American Way; others, the American Dream. Those who think of history as a stream have called it the Main Current. But all have seen the three and one half American centuries as, in one way or another, a quest of freedom.

The marks of the quest are all around us. When we sing our national anthems, we sing of " the land of the free " and " sweet land of liberty." The one quotation from American oratory that every schoolboy knows is " Give me liberty, or give me death." The Western star about which our poets have written so often has always been thought of as the star of freedom. Every one of our great wars has been fought to decide some point of freedom. One of our first legislative acts as a constituted nation was to add ten amendments to our Constitution, guaranteeing freedoms about which, it was felt, the framers of our Constitution had not been specific enough.

Americans have sought different kinds of freedom, and their quest has borne different names; but it has been the same quest. The first English-speaking Americans came in order to be free to own land, to profit from their hard work and skill, to be free to worship in public as their consciences told them to worship. They carved out a little strip of land between the angry sea and the mysterious forest. There wasn't much literature in that first century; there wasn't time. What was written, mostly, had to be: letters, records, sermons. But in the process of

winning that little strip of coast and fighting for those first freedoms, the settlers began to become Americans, rather than merely colonists. Soon they felt the need of political freedom — the right to make their own laws, elect their own governors, keep their tax money at home. In the fire of revolution and the heat of welding together a new nation, Americans produced their first writing that was as good as any nation had done in the same field — state papers like the Declaration of Independence, and political essays and orations that astonished the courts of Europe. In this time, too, appeared a man whom Europe took to be the first real American, no longer a colonial type but a new product of a new land, Benjamin Franklin.

Then in the nineteenth century these new-won freedoms flowered in the first great age of American literature, which we have called the Flowering of the East. Up and down the Atlantic coast appeared poets, novelists, and critics of a high order, concerned with cultural and artistic freedom. Boston and New York became literary centers comparable to London and Paris.

While the books were being written in the East, the frontier plunged westward, in search of elbow room and opportunity, the chance to start fresh and perhaps get rich quick. On the frontier, as in the first coastal settlements, there was little time for literature, but out of the kaleidoscopic westward movement emerged certain national characteristics which all the world began to recognize as American. In the midst of the westward movement, Americans had to stop and fight a bloody war to decide certain old differences and to determine what kind of racial and political freedom should be applied to the new West. Out of that war came a leader who was a symbol both of the new West and of the American nation, Abraham Lincoln. And out of the later frontier came Mark Twain, the most American of our writers up to that time.

The land filled up, and freedom of opportunity built a great industrial civilization across the continent. The frontier passed out of existence as a symbol of opportunity. Pessimism began to replace optimism, and the new spirit gave rise to a realistic tone in fiction and a strong current of social protest. Americans began to see that the frontier open to them was no longer a geographic one, that the freedom they wanted could be attained only by staking out claims on a social and scientific frontier. The questions before the people as the nineteenth century came to an end were how the great scientific advances of the last years could be made to serve man, and how the social and economic life of the nation could be made to bear out the promise of America's first three centuries. In other words, how could the individual best win freedom within the system?

Our American heritage is a tradition of adventurous pioneering on a frontier of freedom. " Freedom's a hard-bought thing," said Stephen Benét. To remember how hard, we have only to recall the early colonies in Virginia that disappeared before the ships could get back to them from England; the colony at Plymouth where more than half the company died in two or three months of cold and scurvy; the blood on the snow at Valley Forge; the graves which line the length of the Oregon Trail; and the monuments by which our towns pay tribute to their war dead.

The extraordinary thing is that Americans have always been willing to buy freedom with their blood. They fought the hardships of New England until they had beaten back the forests and the Indians, and had built some of our greatest universities to maintain the traditions of freedom of speech and freedom to learn. They kept coming back to Virginia until they could make a permanent colony; a century and a half later, it was a Virginian who wrote the Declaration of Independence and founded the first state university where a boy was free to study whether or not he had money. A few miles and a few years from Valley Forge, Americans prepared a Bill of Human Rights for a national Constitution. They buried their dead beside the Oregon Trail; they threw away their household goods in the salt desert to lighten the load; when their oxen sickened, the men themselves pulled the carts; but finally they planted the American flag and the American way at the farthest ends of the continent. And they have not liked to go to war, but have never hesitated if it seemed the road to freedom.

That is the tradition in which our great books have been written.

ROAD MAP OF THE NEW CENTURY

As the new century began, writers were aware that further freedom could be won only by pioneering on a new level.

In the first fifteen years of this century, the social and economic problems bothered our writers most. This was the period of the muckrakers, with their disclosures of unsavory conditions. Good poets like Robinson, powerful novelists like Dreiser, penetrating critics of civilization like Henry Adams, published in those years, along with a host of others, all concerned with whether America was traveling the right road.

And then the country, responding to its President's call to " keep the world safe for democracy," plunged with traditional American idealism into a great war. The aftermath was not good for idealism. Our statesmen did not find a suitable political climate in which to set up an organization against war, and finally our Senate repudiated the scheme. The country as a whole, once its idealism was spent in war, reacted like a rubber ball bouncing back from a wall.

For the next ten years we forgot internationalism, stayed at home, reminded ourselves that Washington had warned us against " entangling alliances," and enjoyed an economic boom. Those were fabulous years, the 1920's. There was so much wealth in the land that it seemed as though the old frontier promise of a pot of gold might come true for every man. And yet writers warned us that we were building a house on sand. Sinclair Lewis tried to show us that by producing successful and solid men we were not necessarily producing great or happy men. Lyric poets like Frost, novelists like Willa Cather called our attention to values we were neglecting. Some writers like Hemingway turned their backs on the age and went to Europe to write. Some dramatists like O'Neill and novelists like Sherwood Anderson analyzed in penetrating fashion the men of the day, and the results were not pretty. But the 1920's rolled on — speakeasies, Lindbergh, political scandals, Coolidge, new fast automobiles, radio broadcasting, home brew, hundreds of thousands playing the stock market, prices up to the skies and salaries up with them, and the country so rich and prosperous and dizzy with power that it seemed as though nothing could stop the American steam roller. It was a de luxe steam roller, of course; nothing was too good for America in the 1920's!

And then, in October, 1929, the bottom dropped out of the stock market. The country reeled like a flabby boxer hit in the stomach. It tried to rally, only to be knocked down again. It tried to whistle in the dark. It said there was nothing to worry about — while banks failed, farmers had their mortgages foreclosed, and city children stood in breadlines. Finally, it simply stood scared and bewildered while all the gingerbread castles of the 1920's crashed into little soggy crumbs.

Then began the third distinct period in this century of ours. It was a period of economic and social planning, but also a spiritual period, because America was trying to find its way back to the old ideals and goals from which it had turned. The reassuring voice of the President was heard on the radio — fireside chats, he called them. " The only thing we have to fear is fear itself," he said. The common man, the ordinary American, deserved a " new deal," he said. We argued about that new deal according to which party we belonged to, but we saw many steps taken along a path writers had talked about ever since the Western frontier closed, the path toward a new American homestead on the economic and

scientific frontier. Social security, for example . . . and bank deposit insurance. . . .

It was a stirring time for writers. Many of those who had run away to Europe came back and discovered America over again. Novelists like Steinbeck and Dos Passos tried to put down on paper what the depression really meant to people. Poets like Benét and MacLeish tried to reinterpret the American dream, the American tradition, so that the country could get back to it. Writers found that the radio was a new medium for serious art. A group of talented new poets and story writers arose, no longer self-conscious, no longer concerned over whether they were European or American, but mightily concerned over whether they were good writers and over what they had to say to America.

Then the war drums beat across the world again. The United States was drawn into the conflict, slowly, inevitably. We who had said in the 20's that we would never again fight outside our hemisphere sent our young men, our airplanes, our bright and shining materials of war to every corner of the globe. We entered unwillingly, yet grimly, knowing that this was a " fight for freedom " against aggressor nations representing everything we had opposed for three hundred years. We won a victory that was too solemn to be glorious in any light sense, too hard-bought to be celebrated except with gratitude to two hundred and fifty thousand dead and with prayers for the future. And now we are trying to " design this day " for peace, trying to apply what we have learned in three centuries of pioneering so that we can conquer a new frontier, deeper and more complex and more difficult than any we have yet faced.

## DESIGN THIS DAY

We have two great problems — you have, our writers have, our leaders have — and they must be solved in the same spirit with which our ancestors faced the problems of the forest and the desert.

One is: *How can we learn to live with our neighbors?*

We know now that our frontier is as big as the world and can never be smaller. Never again can we hope to turn our backs on Europe and lead a private national existence. Distance has shrunk. The airplane, the flying bomb, and radio have made the whole world our neighbors, taken away the ramparts which our oceans used to be, and shown us in a few years that our social, economic, and political problems are not simply American problems, but problems of *America in the world!* At home, our labor and our capitalists must learn to live together. Abroad, we as nations must learn to live together. This is now truly *One World*. A famine in China is dangerous to the economic health of America. Religious intolerance in Germany is dangerous to the peace of America. Trouble in South America may mean trouble in the Bronx. By that much has our problem grown. Henceforth our frontiers are world frontiers, and we must break our new Oregon Trail in co-operation with all the other frontier nations of this planet.

The other problem is: *How can we use what we know?*

The atomic bomb told us, with something of a shock, how much we know. Television, the sulfa drugs, penicillin, the new airplanes gave us that same message, in less shocking form. The atomic bomb told us that we now know enough to destroy civilization and write finis to the story of the human race. Or, on the other hand, we know enough to put the very force of the universe to work for man's betterment.

That is a more dramatic, more imperative way to say it, but it is still the same question that came up when the frontier closed: How can we make sure that science and industry are really working for man, not he for them? How can we best use our great skill in science? How can we best use our great command of natural forces and natural wealth? How can we design this day to insure us the freedom and good life which America has meant for more than three centuries?

That is the challenge which this day poses. It is not a challenge to be answered quickly or lightly.

In answering it, we shall do well to read carefully the books, magazines, and newspapers that are bringing us more information about our own times than any previous age has ever had. We shall do well to weigh conflicting opinions, look at all sides of arguments, read with open minds, to the end that we may understand the tremendous forces we have to deal with and can form an intelligent opinion of how to control them.

We shall also do well to ponder the meaning of our American heritage, our quest of freedom, our frontier spirit, our great books and our great men. No one has put that better than William Allen White, the great Kansas editor who died in 1944, and whose life and words are themselves a precious part of our heritage:

" Don't bemoan your lost frontier," he said in a radio talk to the young people of the country. " It is even now flashing on your horizon. A gorgeous land lies before you fair and more beautiful than man before has ever known. Out of the laboratories will come new processes to multiply almost infinitely material things for your America — but only if you will hold open the channels of free science, unfettered thought, and the right of a man to use his talents to the utmost, provided he gives honest social returns for the rewards he takes.

" Don't delude yourselves about your new frontier. For on that frontier which will rise over the laboratories you will find the same struggle, the same hardships, the same inequities that your forefathers have found on every frontier since the beginning of time. But don't let that discourage you.

" Finally, remember this: If you hang your horse thieves, if you jail your pirates of finance, and if you, indeed, make your new world worth while, it will be worth while not because of the material richness that the laboratories will bring you. All the regal wealth of this continent was here for countless centuries, before our English-speaking race came to develop the land. But they made it a noble civilization, not because of the fertile soil, the abundant mines, the illimitable forests, but because they, your forebears, transmuted into a livable approximate to a just society the physical blessings of nature — through the social forces that rise out of the humble virtues of man's heart: duty, tolerance, faith, and love. The American pioneers — your forefathers — institutionalized in American government, and somewhat in commerce, and certainly in their way of living, a neighborly consideration of the rights of others. They dedicated the products of our soil, the output of our mines, the wealth of our forests, to the establishment of a government of the people, by the people, and for the people, that the people may not perish from the earth.

" In closing let me say that your heritage is not in these great lovely cities, not this wide and fertile land, not the mountains full of undreamed-of riches. These you may find in other continents.

" What we bequeath to you that is precious are the few simple virtues which have stood us in good stead in the struggle of our generation. We leave you our enthusiasm, our diligence, our zeal for a better world, that were the lodestars of our fathers. As our legatees we assign you our tolerance; our patience; our kindness; our faith, hope, and love — which make for the self-respect of man. These qualities of heart and mind grow out of a conviction that the democratic philosophy as a mode of thinking will lead mankind into a nobler way of life."

## General Reference Books on American Literature

Cooper, F. T.: *Some American Short Story Tellers*

Foerster, Norman: *American Criticism; Nature in American Literature; The Reinterpretation of American Literature*

Gregory, Horace and Zaturenska, Marya: *A History of American Poetry 1900–1940*

Hart, J. D.: *Oxford Companion to American Literature*

Hazard, Lucy: *The Frontier in American Literature*

Lowell, Amy: *Tendencies in Modern American Poetry*

Macy, John: *The Spirit of American Literature*

Manly, J. M. and Rickert, Edith: *Contemporary American Literature*

Parrington, V. L.: *Main Currents in American Thought*

Pattee, F. L.: *The Development of the American Short Story; A History of American Literature since 1870; New American Literature; First Century of American Literature*

Perry, Bliss: *The American Spirit in Literature*

Phelps, W. L.: *Some Makers of American Literature; Essays on Modern Dramatists; Essays on Modern Novelists*

Rusk, R. L.: *The Literature of the Middle Western Frontier*

Smith, C. A.: *Southern Literary Studies; What Can Literature Do for Me?*

Untermeyer, Louis: *American Poetry since 1900*

Van Doren, Carl: *The American Novel; The Contemporary American Novel*

Williams, B. C.: *Our Short Story Writers*

# ACKNOWLEDGMENTS

THE EDITORS of *Adventures in American Literature,* fourth edition, are indebted to the following authors, periodicals, and publishers for permission to use the selections indicated, all rights in which are in all cases reserved by the owner of the copyright.

The American Folk-Lore Society. " The Sharpened Leg."

Stephen Vincent Benét. " The Mountain Whippoorwill " from *Ballads and Poems,* published by Doubleday & Company, Inc., copyright, 1918, 1920, 1923, 1925, 1929, 1930, 1931, by Stephen Vincent Benét; and " Mary Lou Wingate " from *John Brown's Body,* published by Farrar & Rinehart, copyright, 1927, 1928, by Stephen Vincent Benét.

The Bobbs-Merrill Company. " When the Frost Is on the Punkin " from *Neighborly Poems* by James Whitcomb Riley, copyright, 1891; " Sam Houston at San Jacinto " from *The Raven* by Marquis James. Both used by permission of the publishers.

Brandt and Brandt. " The Devil and Daniel Webster " by Stephen Vincent Benét, copyright, 1936, by Stephen Vincent Benét, from *Selected Works of Stephen Vincent Benét,* published by Farrar & Rinehart, Inc.; " Ballad of William Sycamore " by Stephen Vincent Benét, copyright, 1922, by Stephen Vincent Benét, from *Selected Works of Stephen Vincent Benét,* published by Farrar & Rinehart, Inc.

James Saxon Childers. " A Boy Who Was Traded for a Horse."

Charles W. Clark Company. " Jedediah Smith Explores the Far West " from *Jedediah Smith* by Maurice S. Sullivan.

Coward-McCann, Inc. " Our Town " by Thornton Wilder, copyright, 1938, by Coward-McCann, Inc.

J. Frank Dobie. " The Heraldry of the Range."

Doubleday & Company, Inc. " Those Two Boys " from *By and Large* by Franklin P. Adams, copyright, 1914; selections from *Leaves of Grass* by Walt Whitman, copyright, 1924; " All the Traffic Will Bear " from *The Octopus* by Frank Norris, copyright, 1901, 1929, by Doubleday & Company, Inc.; " freddy the rat perishes " from *archy and mehitabel* by Don Marquis, copyright, 1927, 1930, by Doubleday & Company, Inc.; " Ring Around a Rosy " from *American Omnibus* by Sinclair Lewis, copyright, 1933, by Doubleday & Company, Inc.; " The Cop and the Anthem " from *The Four Million* by O. Henry, copyright, 1904, by Doubleday & Company, Inc.

E. P. Dutton & Company, Inc. " Pershing at the Front " from *Lyric Laughter* by Arthur Guiterman, published and copyrighted by E. P. Dutton & Company, Inc., New York.

*Esquire.* " Split Cherry Tree " by Jesse Stuart from *Esquire,* January, 1939, copyright, 1939 by Esquire, Inc., 919 N. Michigan Avenue, Chicago, Illinois.

Harcourt, Brace and Company, Inc. " Walter Reed " from *Microbe Hunters* by Paul de Kruif; " Clean Curtains," and " Night Stuff " from *Smoke and Steel* by Carl Sandburg; selections from *The People, Yes* by Carl Sandburg, copyright, 1936, by Harcourt, Brace and Company, Inc.; selection from *Abraham Lincoln: The War Years* by Carl Sandburg, copyright, 1939, by Harcourt, Brace and Company, Inc.; " Two 'Mericana Men " from *Carmina* by Thomas Augustine Daly; " Barnum's American Museum " from *Barnum* by

M. R. Werner, copyright, 1923; " I Become a Reporter " from *The Autobiography of Lincoln Steffens,* copyright, 1931; " The Naming of Cats " from *Old Possum's Book of Practical Cats,* copyright, 1939, by T. S. Eliot, by permission of Harcourt, Brace and Company, Inc.; " Prelude " and Section I of " The Hollow Men " from *Collected Poems of T. S. Eliot,* copyright, 1936, by Harcourt, Brace and Company, Inc.; " Locomotive 38, the Ojibway " from *My Name Is Aram,* copyright, 1940, by William Saroyan. By permission of Harcourt, Brace and Company, Inc.

Harper & Brothers. " Boyhood " from *Autobiography* by Mark Twain; " Machinery " from *Observations of Mr. Dooley* by Finley Peter Dunne; " Prairie Doom " from *Giants in the Earth* by Ole E. Rölvaag; " Taming a Guide " from *Innocents Abroad* by Mark Twain; " Across the Plains by Stagecoach " from *Roughing It* by Mark Twain; " A Lightning Pilot " from *Life on the Mississippi* by Mark Twain; " The Storm," from *Bolts of Melody* by Emily Dickinson; " It's California " from *Anything Can Happen* by George and Helen Papashvily; " Once More to the Lake " from *One Man's Meat* by E. B. White.

Henry Holt and Company. " The Pasture," " A Minor Bird," " Stopping by Woods on a Snowy Evening," " Birches," and " The Death of the Hired Man " from *Poems* by Robert Frost; " Mending Wall " from *North of Boston* by Robert Frost; " Chicago," " Buttons," and " A Fence," from *Chicago Poems* by Carl Sandburg; and " Grass " and " Prayers of Steel " from *Cornhuskers* by Carl Sandburg; " Break-Through in Normandy " from *Brave Men* by Ernie Pyle; " Fog " from *Chicago Poems* by Carl Sandburg; " The Road Not Taken " and " A Considerable Speck " from *Collected Poems* by Robert Frost.

Houghton Mifflin Company. " A Lady," " Music," and " Patterns " by Amy Lowell; " The Outcasts of Poker Flat " by Bret Harte; selection from *The Promised Land* by Mary Antin; " It Is a Strange Thing — To Be an American " from *American Letter* by Archibald MacLeish; " John Colter's Race for Life " from *Mountain Men* by Stanley Vestal; " Eleven " by Archibald MacLeish.

P. J. Kenedy & Sons. " The Conquered Banner " by the Rev. Abram J. Ryan.

Alfred A. Knopf, Inc. " Velvet Shoes," " Pretty Words," " Nonsense Rhyme," and " Sea Lullaby " from *Collected Poems of Elinor Wylie;* " Father and His Hard Rocking Ship " from *Life with Father* by Clarence Day; " Atavism " from *Collected Poems* by Elinor Wylie, by permission of Alfred A. Knopf, Inc.; " The Armistice Is Signed " from *Berlin Diary* by William L. Shirer, by permission of Alfred A. Knopf, Inc. All used by permission of and special arrangement with Alfred A. Knopf, Inc., authorized publishers.

Little, Brown and Company. Selections from Emily Dickinson; " Nature Knows Best," copyright, 1936, the F–R. Publishing Corporation, and " This Is Going to Hurt Just a Little Bit," copyright, 1935, New York American, Inc., from *The Face is Familiar* by Ogden Nash.

Horace Liveright. " Where the Cross Is Made " by Eugene O'Neill.

Liveright Publishing Corporation. " Folk Tune " and " One Perfect Rose " from *Enough Rope* by Dorothy Parker, copyright, 1926.

David Lloyd. " The Enemy," copyright, 1942, by Pearl S. Buck, first published in *Harper's Magazine,* November 1942, and included in the *O. Henry Memorial Award Prize Stories of 1943;* " Will This Earth Hold," copyright, 1944, by Pearl S. Buck, published by Asia Magazine Inc., in *Asia and the Americas,* vol. xliv, No. 11; both by arrangement with the author's agent, David Lloyd, 49 E. 34th St., New York 16, N. Y.

Archibald MacLeish. " The Western Sky."

Edwin Markham. " The Man with the Hoe," copyright by Edwin Markham, and used by his permission.

Edgar Lee Masters. " Silence "; and " Anne Rutledge," " John Horace Burleson," " Mrs. George Reece," " George Gray," and " Lucinda Matlock " from *Spoon River Anthology*.

Harold Matson. " The Biscuit Eater " from *The Biscuit Eater* by James Street, published by The Dial Press, copyright, 1941, by James Street; permission granted by Harold Matson.

Edna St. Vincent Millay. " Lament " from *Second April*, published by Harper & Brothers, copyright, 1921 by Edna St. Vincent Millay; " The Spring and the Fall " from *The Harp-Weaver and Other Poems*, published by Harper & Brothers, copyright, 1920, 1921, 1922, 1923, by Edna St. Vincent Millay; " Dirge without Music " from *The Buck in the Snow*, published by Harper & Brothers, copyright, 1928, by Edna St. Vincent Millay; " Autumn Daybreak " and " If Still Your Orchards Bear " from *Wine from These Grapes*, published by Harper & Brothers, copyright, 1934, by Edna St. Vincent Millay.

*The New Yorker*. " The Atomic City " by Daniel Lang.

*The New York Times Book Review*: Review by Eudora Welty of *Names on the Land* by George Stewart.

Harold Ober. " Boone over the Pacific " by Wilbur Schramm, copyright, 1944, by The Curtis Publishing Company; " The Snow Goose " by Paul Gallico, copyright, 1940 by Paul Gallico, reprinted by permission of the author; " Justice and Mrs. Holmes Move to Washington " from *Yankee from Olympus* by Catherine Drinker Bowen, published by Little, Brown and Company, copyright, 1944, by Catherine Drinker Bowen; reprinted by permission of the author.

Howard Vincent O'Brien. " So Long, Son."

Random House, Inc. " Joy " by Robinson Jeffers, copyright, 1935, by Modern Library, Inc.; " To the Stone Cutters " by Robinson Jeffers from *Tamar and Other Poems;* " Hurt Hawks " by Robinson Jeffers from *Cawdor and Other Poems*. Reprinted by permission of Random House, Inc.

*The Saturday Review of Literature*. Review by William Rose Benét of *Up Front* by Bill Mauldin.

*Scholastic*. " Sixteen " by Maureen Daly, copyright by *Scholastic,* the American High School Weekly, 1938.

Charles Scribner's Sons. " Richard Cory," " Miniver Cheevy," and " The House on the Hill " by Edwin Arlington Robinson; " The Song of the Chattahoochee," " A Ballad of Trees and the Master," " Evening Song," " The Stirrup Cup," and " The Marshes of Glynn " by Sidney Lanier; " Little Boy Blue " by Eugene Field; " I Have a Rendezvous with Death " by Alan Seeger; " Lee in Defeat " from *Robert E. Lee, Man and Soldier* by Thomas Nelson Page; " An Old Story " from *Children of the Night* by Edwin Arlington Robinson; " Circus at Dawn " from *From Death to Morning* by Thomas Wolfe.

Wilbur Daniel Steele. " Footfalls."

James Stevens. " An American Hercules."

Booth Tarkington. " Henry the Great," copyright, 1936, by Curtis Publishing Company; reprinted by permission of the author.

James Thurber. " University Days " from *My Life and Hard Times* by James Thurber.

*Time Magazine*. Review of *Struggling Upward and Other Works* by Horatio Alger, Jr.

The Viking Press, Inc. " Let My People Go " from *The American Book of Negro Spirituals* by James Weldon Johnson, copyright, 1925, by permission of The Viking Press, Inc.; " Nobody Knows de Trouble I See " from *The Second Book of Negro Spirituals* by James Weldon Johnson, copyright, 1926, by permission of The Viking Press, Inc.; " The Creation " from *God's Trombones* by James Weldon Johnson, copyright, 1927, by permission of The Viking Press, Inc.; " Flight " from *The Long Valley* by John Steinbeck, copyright, 1938, published by The Viking Press, Inc.; " Résumé " from *The Portable Dorothy Parker*, copyright, 1926, 1944, by Dorothy Parker; reprinted by permission of The Viking Press, Inc.

William Allen White. " Mary White."

Grateful acknowledgment is also due the Whitney Museum of American Art for permission to reproduce the paintings by Morgan Russell, Man Ray, and Thomas Benton, on pages 278 and 279; to An American Place, for permission to reproduce the Georgia O'Keeffe painting on page 278, and to Earle Horter for the Charles Sheeler painting on page 279. Credit is due Hedrich-Blessing, photographers, for their prints of the Crow Island School on page 778 and the E. J. Kaufmann house on page 779, to Mr. William Lescaze for permission to reproduce The Longfellow Building on page 778, and to the Museum of Modern Art for the Daily News Building on page 778 and the Model House on page 779. Credit is also due Ann Watkins, Inc., for permission to reproduce the Bill Mauldin cartoon on page 196; copyright, 1944, United Feature Syndicate, Inc.

The editors wish to thank cordially the following teachers who on the basis of their classroom use of *Adventures in American Literature,* third edition, contributed helpful suggestions regarding this fourth edition: Miss Elizabeth Griffin, Miss Ernestine Moore, and Miss Barbara Pollard under the direction of Mrs. Cecelia M. Mahoney, High School, Willimantic, Connecticut; Miss Ethel M. Parkinson, Decatur High School, Decatur, Illinois; Mr. R. Paul Hibbs, DuQuoin Township High School, DuQuoin, Illinois; Mr. Henry J. Firley, Glenbard Township High School, Glen Ellyn, Illinois; Miss Hetty Pick, Community High School, District #149, Granite City, Illinois; Miss Isabel Hoover, Western Illinois State Teachers College, Macomb, Illinois; Miss Alverda Doxey, Miss Media Hankins, Miss Sarah Laraway, Miss Esca Rodger, Miss Carolee Schutz, Miss Cora L. Stoddard, and Miss Margaret Winbigler under the direction of Miss Ada Blanche Lauck, Senior High School, Rock Island, Illinois; Miss Margaret Adams, Sycamore High School, Sycamore, Illinois; Miss Audrey Banner, Miss Louise Busche, Miss Ruth Howell, Miss Dorothy Kelly, Miss Margaret Lake, and Mr. J. F. Wiley under the direction of Miss Ruth Broughton, Elkhart High School, Elkhart, Indiana; Miss M. E. Ford and Miss Hortense L. Harris, Gloucester High School, Gloucester, Massachusetts; Miss L. Winifred Terry, Northampton High School, Northampton, Massachusetts; Mr. Otto H. Olsen and Miss Evelyn Pugh, Dearborn High School, Dearborn, Michigan; Miss Frances G. Barrett, Miss Annette Cummings, and Miss Mary Lila Zang, Fordson High School, Dearborn, Michigan; Mr. John R. Barnes, Assistant Superintendent of Schools, Grosse Pointe, Michigan; Miss Mildred Toogood, Eastern High School, Lansing, Michigan; Miss Lulu B. Utley, Central High School, Minneapolis, Minnesota; Mr. Blandford Jennings, Clayton High School, Clayton, Missouri; Miss Mary Howard, Webster Groves High School, Webster Groves, Missouri; Mr. J. Arthur Ferner, Collingswood Senior High School, Collingswood, New Jersey; Miss Jessie W. Boutillier, Central High School, Newark, New Jersey; Miss Olga Achtenhagen, High School, Plainfield, New Jersey; Miss Carolyn Fanning and Miss Isabella J. Kennan, High School, Amityville, Long Island, New York; Miss Frances C. Waight, High School, Babylon, Long Island, New York; Mr. Paul R. Sweitzer, High School, Manhasset, Long Island, New York; Mr. Warren W. Read, Flushing High School, New York City; Miss Dorothy C. Bunker, Hunter College High School, New York City; Miss Lucile Foreman, Harding High School, Marion, Ohio; Miss Bess Marie Hoover, High School, Middletown, Ohio; Miss Dorothy Hanson, Instructor in Education, Miami University, Oxford, Ohio; Miss Annabelle Hartle, Public School, Wyoming, Ohio; Mr. Harold C. Stearns, The Hill School, Pottstown, Pennsylvania; Miss Princess Martin, Highland Park High School, Dallas, Texas; Miss Anna Turgasen, Horlick High School, Racine, Wisconsin.

# GLOSSARY

This glossary contains pronunciations and definitions for the words and phrases of some difficulty which occur in this book, exclusive of those explained in footnotes. For each word the definition is limited to the use of that word in this volume. For words with more than one accepted pronunciation, the most usual one is given. Closely related words are grouped under one entry, with pronunciation given for each word when accent or vowel sound changes.

Words explained in vocabulary studies are printed in boldface with references to the pages where the studies appear.

The diacritical markings are simple: āce, senāte, râre, băt, fäther, or sofà; ēven, ĕvent, hęre, ĕnd, mothēr; fīnd, sĭt, rōpe, ŏmit, côrd, hŏt, sŏft; ūnit, ûnite, bûrn, cŭt; bōōt, fŏŏt; naṭure; ṭhen; boN (French nasal). In a few foreign words, only approximate pronunciation is achieved.

## A

abalone (ăb-à-lō′nĕ). A shellfish

abasement (à-bās′mĕnt). A lowering or degrading

abate (à-bāt′). To reduce

abeyance (à-bā′ăns). Temporary inactivity; suspension

abhor (ăb-hôr′). To detest; to regard with horror

**aboriginal,** page 625

absolve (ăb-sŏlv′). To clear of blame

abstracted (ăb-străk′tĕd). Withdrawn

abyss (à-bĭs′). Bottomless gulf or pit; hence, a boundless space

academic (ăk-à-dĕm′ĭk). Pertaining to colleges or universities

academicians (à-kăd-ē-mĭsh′ănz). Men devoted to study of the arts or sciences

accelerated (ăk-sĕl′ĕr-āt-ĕd). Speeded up

acquisitive (à-kwĭz′ĭ-tĭv). Strongly desirous of acquiring and possessing

**acrid,** page 156

adduce (ă-dūs′). To offer as an argument

admonish (ăd-mŏn′ĭsh). To give a gentle, friendly reproof or warning. *Noun,* admonition (ăd-mô-nĭsh′ŭn)

**adolescent,** page 319

adroit (à-droit′). Skillful; nimble

adversity (ăd-vûr′sĭ-tĭ). Hardship

**advert,** page 471

affable (ăf′à-b'l). Pleasant; sociable; easy to speak to or get along with

affinity (à-fĭn′ĭ-tĭ). A natural mutual liking

**affluence,** page 284

alewives (āl′wīvz). Shad-like fish

Algonquin (ăl-gŏn′kwĭn). The largest group of American Indian tribes, according to language

**allegation,** page 244

**allege,** page 244

**alleviate,** page 174

allopathic (ăl-ŏ-păth′ĭk). Pertaining to allopathy, a system of medical practice.

alms (ämz). A charitable gift

Alsace-Lorraine (ăl′säs-lō-rān′). Provinces taken from France by Germany in 1871 and restored after World War I

amain (à-mān′). With full force; at full speed

ambiguous (ăm-bĭg′ŭ-ŭs). Capable of being understood in more than one sense

ambuscade (ăm-bŭs-kād′). A body of troops lying in wait for the enemy

amendment (à-mĕnd′mĕnt). A change for the better; an improvement

amicable (ăm′ĭ-kà-b'l). Peaceable; friendly

amulet (ăm′ŭ-lĕt). An ornament worn as a charm

anathema (à-năth′ē-mà). A curse

animosity (ăn-ĭ-mŏs′ĭ-tĭ). Hostility; enmity

**annihilate,** page 212

anodyne (ăn′ō-dīn). Any medicine that relieves pain

anonymous (à-nŏn′ĭ-mŭs). Giving no name; of unidentified authorship

**anthem,** page 528

anthracite (ăn′thrà-sīt). Hard coal

anthropological (ăn-thrŏ-pŏ-lŏj′ĭ-kăl). Pertaining to the scientific study of mankind

antipathy (ăn-tĭp′à-thĭ). Dislike; distaste

**antonym,** page 284

apathetically (ăp-à-thĕt′ĭ-kăl-ĭ). Without interest or feeling

aperture (ăp′ēr-tūr). An opening

apex (ā′pĕks). The highest point

aphid (ā′fĭd). A small insect that lives on plants and sucks their juices

apostolic succession (ăp-ŏs-tŏl′ĭk sŭk-sĕsh′ŭn). The passing on of office in a select group

apparition (ăp-à-rĭsh′ŭn). A ghost; a phantom

appease (ă-pēz′). To pacify, often by satisfying; to soothe or calm

appellation (ăp-ĕ-lā′shŭn). Name; title

appendage (ă-pĕn'dĭj). Something hung on or added to; a limb or external organ

**apportioned,** page 654

**apprehensive,** page 773

apprentice (ă-prĕn'tĭs). A beginner learning a skill or trade

appropriate (ă-prō'prĭ-āt). To take exclusive possession of

**aquiline,** page 365

arabesque (ăr-à-bĕsk'). A fanciful ornament

arbitrament (är-bĭt'rà-mĕnt). Authoritative decision

arbitration (är-bĭ-trā'shŭn). Settlement of a dispute by a mutually agreed upon authority

ardent (är'dĕnt). Glowing; warm; eager

arduous (är'dů-ŭs). Difficult; laborious

argument (är'gů-mĕnt). Evidence; reason for believing (page 562)

**arraign,** page 244

arras (ăr'ás). A tapestry; a wall hanging

arrogance (ăr'ô-găns). Overbearing pride

articulate (är-tĭk'ů-lăt). Clear; separate; distinct

artifice (är'tĭ-fĭs). An artful deception for a specific purpose

artisan (är'tĭ-zăn). One trained in some mechanic art or trade

**asinine,** page 365

assiduously (ă-sĭd'ů-ŭs-lĭ). With care and close attention

assimilated (ă-sĭm'ĭ-lāt-ĕd). Absorbed; made like

atrocious (ă-trō'shŭs). Savagely cruel or brutal; very bad, abominable (colloquial). *Noun*, atrocity (ă-trŏs'ĭ-tĭ)

attribute (ăt'rĭ-bůt). A quality or characteristic firmly associated with a person, state, or thing

attrition (ă-trĭsh'ŭn). The process of wearing down; state of being worn down

audacity (ô-dăs'ĭ-tĭ). Daring; boldness. *Adj.*, audacious (ô-dā'shŭs)

august (ô-gŭst'). Possessing stately grandeur; exalted

aura (ô'rà). A distinctive surrounding atmosphere

auroral (ô-rō'răl). Pertaining to the dawn; rosy; radiant

austere (ôs-tēr'). Harsh; hard; strict

**avalanche,** page 698

**avarice,** page 494

aversion (à-vûr'zhŭn). Dislike, nearing disgust; act of turning away

**avert,** page 471

avid (ăv'ĭd). Keenly eager, as for food or gain; greedy. *Noun*, avidity (à-vĭd'ĭ-tĭ)

avocation (ă-vô-kā'shŭn). A hobby

# B

bagatelle (băg-à-tĕl'). A trifle

baneful (bān'fööl). Evil and damaging in influence

barouche (bà-röösh'). A four-wheeled carriage

bauble (bô'b'l). A trifling bit of finery

bayou (bī'öö). A slow, stagnant stream

beachcomber (bēch'cōm-ēr). One who lives by picking up waste on a seashore

beams and carlines (bēmz, kär'lĭnz). Main supporting timbers for the deck of a ship.

belay (bĕ-lā'). To make fast or stop by winding a rope around a pin or cleat in order to hold secure.

**bellicose,** page 720

**beneficiary,** page 570

**benevolence,** page 570

**benign,** page 570

bibliophile (bĭb'lĭ-ô-fīl). A lover of books

binnacle (bĭn'à-k'l). A case, box, or stand containing a ship's compass and a lamp for use at night

bland (blănd). Smooth and soothing in manner; gentle

blatant (blā'tănt). Clamorous; noisy

blazed (blāzd). Marked clearly, as a trail

bonanza (bŏ-năn'zà). A rich ore pocket; hence, a source of quick riches

boodle (bōō'd'l). Quick, easy money; graft

boon-doggle (bōōn'dŏg''l). A useless occupation

Boreas (bō'rĕ-ăs). The north wind. *Adj.*, boreal, pertaining to the north in general

**bovine,** page 365

bow (bou). The forward part of a ship

brusque (brŭsk). Rough and short in manner

buccaneer (bŭk-à-nēr'). A pirate

**buoyant,** page 253

burden (bûr'dĕn). A refrain (page 523)

burlesque (bûr-lĕsk'). A mocking imitation

# C

cabal (kà-băl'). A number of persons united in some secret design

cabalistic (kăb-à-lĭs'tĭk). Secret; mysterious

cache (kăsh). *Noun*, a hiding place for stores to be recovered later. *Verb*, to store supplies in such a manner; to hide

cadaver (kà-dăv'ēr). A dead body, especially a human one

calaboose (kăl'à-bōōs). A prison; a jail

**calamitous,** page 767.

caldron (kôl'drŭn). A large kettle

calliope (kă-lī'ô-pē). A musical instrument made of whistles operated by keys calumnious (kă-lŭm'nĭ-ŭs). Slanderous

camembert (kăm'ĕm-bâr). A soft cheese

candid (kăn'dĭd). Frank

canny (kăn'ĭ). Shrewd; thrifty

cant (kănt). Tilt

Canuck (kȧ-nŭk'). Slang term for a Canadian

capitulation (kȧ-pĭt-ŭ-lā'shŭn). A surrender upon terms agreed to

cardinal (kär'dĭ-năl). Of primary importance

**caricaturist,** page 70

carlines. *See* beams and carlines.

carnage (kär'nĭj). Slaughter

carrion (kăr'ĭ-ŭn). Dead or decaying flesh

caste (kăst). A rigid division or class of society, such as is found in India

catamount (kăt'ȧ-mount). A wildcat

catastrophe (kȧ-tăs'trȯ-fê). A sudden calamity

category (kăt'ê-gō-rĭ). A class or division

cater (kā'tēr). To supply what is desired, often food

catholic (kăth'ȯ-lĭk). Universal or general; affecting mankind as a whole

cavalcade (kăv-ăl-kād'). A company of persons on the march

celerity (sê-lĕr'ĭ-tĭ). Speed; quickness

celestial (sê-lĕs'chăl). Heavenly; divine

celibacy (sĕl'ĭ-bȧ-sĭ). State of being unmarried, especially that of one bound by vows not to marry

censer (sĕn'sēr). A vessel for burning perfume or incense

Chablis (shȧ-blē'). A white wine

chaff (chȧf). The husks of grain separated from the seed by threshing. *Verb,* to joke

chalice (chăl'ĭs). A drinking cup, especially the one Christ used at the Last Supper

chancery (chȧn'sēr-ĭ). A state of control by the courts pending legal settlement

chanticleer (chăn'tĭ-klēr). A rooster

chaparral (chăp-ȧ-răl'). Dwarf evergreen oaks, or a thicket of such growth

charnel (chär'nĕl). Pertaining to a burial place

chasten (chās'n). To correct by punishment

chattel (chăt''l). Any item of movable property

cherub (chĕr'ŭb). An angel, usually represented as a child. *Plural,* cherubim (chĕr'ŭ-bĭm)

Chickamauga (chĭk-ȧ-mô'gȧ). A river in Tennessee, scene of a bitter but indecisive battle in the War between the States

chilblain (chĭl'blān). Itching sore or bruise caused by exposure of the hands or feet to cold

chronic (krŏn'ĭk). Constant; of long duration

**chronometer,** page 773

**churlish,** page 601

cicada (sĭ-kā'dȧ). A locust

cipher (sī'fēr). *Noun,* the figure for zero; hence, a person of no importance. *Verb,* to do a problem in arithmetic (colloquial)

circuitous (sēr-kū'ĭ-tŭs). Roundabout; indirect

circumjacent (sûr-kŭm-jā'sĕnt). Bordering on every side

cistern (sĭs'tērn). An underground reservoir

citadel (sĭt'ȧ-dĕl). A fortress; stronghold

citation (sī-tā'shŭn). A legal summons to appear before a court or other legal authority

Citroen (sē-trȯ-än'). The manufacturer of France's leading small motor car

claim (klām). A tract of government land claimed by a settler

**clarification,** page 83

clarion (klăr'ĭ-ŭn). Loud and clear; a trumpet call

cleft (klĕft). A crack; a split

clipper (klĭp'ēr). A fast sailing vessel

clique (klēk). A small and exclusive set of persons

clown (kloun). A rustic person

coffer (kŏf'ēr). A chest for storing valuables

cognizant (kŏg'nĭ-zănt). Aware of from observation. *Noun,* cognizance

coherent (kȯ-hēr'ĕnt). Sticking together; logically consistent

collectivistic (kȯ-lĕk-tĭ-vĭs'tĭk). Accepting socialistic theories and regarding individuals only as parts of the mass

**colloquial,** page 540

colonnade (kŏl-ȯ-nād'). A series of evenly spaced columns

colossal (kȯ-lŏs'ăl). Huge; tremendous. *Noun,* colossus, a huge and powerful organization

colter (kōl'tēr). A cutter on a plow

combine (kŏm'bīn). A machine that harvests and threshes grain while moving over the field

combustible (kŏm-bŭs'tĭ-b'l). Capable of being burned

commensurability (kȯ-mĕn-shŏŏ-rȧ-bĭl'ĭ-tĭ). State of being reducible to a common measure

commiseration (kȯ-mĭz-ēr-ā'shŭn). Sorrow, or expressions of sympathy, for the distress of another

commissary (kŏm'ĭ-sēr-ĭ). Those whose duty it is to furnish food and supplies for an army

companionway (kŏm-păn'yŭn-wā). Steps leading from the deck of a ship to a cabin below

compass (kŭm'păs). Range; sweep

complaisant (kŏm-plā'zănt). Courteous; agreeable

complex (kŏm'plĕks). An exaggerated emotional attitude without logical basis

**comprehend,** page 773

concoct (kŏn-kŏkt'). To compose or make up, as a plan or intrigue

condescendingly (kŏn-dē-sĕnd'ĭng-lĭ). With a courteous but superior manner

condescension (kŏn-dē-sĕn'shŭn). Bestowing courtesies with an air of superiority

configuration (cŏn-fĭg-û-rā'shŭn). Form; shape

congenial (kŏn-jēn'yăl). Kindred in spirit or tastes

conglomerate (kŏn-glŏm'ēr-ĭt). Made up of parts collected from various sources or of assorted natures

conjecture (kŏn-jĕk'tûr). A supposition; a guess

consignment (kŏn-sīn'mĕnt). A quantity of goods turned over to an agent for shipment or sale

**constant,** page 164

constituted (kŏn'stĭ-tût-ĕd). Made up; formed

constraint (kŏn-strānt'). Repression

contiguity (kŏn-tĭ-gū'ĭ-tĭ). Nearness

contrive (kŏn-trīv'). To plan; manage; bring about

**convalescent,** page 319

**convert,** page 471.

convolutions (kŏn-vô-lū'shŭnz). Windings or whorls in an intricate design

cordial (kôr'jăl). A fragrant, sweetened alcoholic beverage

coronet (kŏr'ŏ-nĕt). A small crown

**correct,** page 468

cosmopolitan (kŏz-mô-pŏl'ĭ-tăn). At home in any country; without local prejudices

cosmos (kŏz'mŏs). The universe

cottonmouth (kŏt'′n-mouth). A poisonous water snake

coulee (kōō'lĭ). A long, narrow, steep-walled valley

countinghouse (kount'ĭng-hous). The accounting or bookkeeping office of a merchant

course (kōrs). To run (page 572); chase (page 574)

craven (krā'vĕn). A confessed coward

credence (krē'dĕns). Belief

cringe (krĭnj). To draw back or shrink, especially in fear or base humility

crotchety (krŏch'ĕ-tĭ). Full of contrary or whimsical notions

crypt (krĭpt). A vault partly or wholly underground

cryptic (krĭp'tĭk). Hidden; mysterious

cryptographer (krĭp-tŏg'rà-fēr). One who specializes in coded writing

crystalline (krĭs'tăl-ĭn). Shiningly clear, like crystal

cubit (kū'bĭt). An ancient measure of length, usually from the tips of the fingers to the elbow

culinary (kū'lĭ-nēr-ĭ). Relating to cooking

culminate (kŭl'mĭ-nāt). To reach the highest point. *Noun,* culmination (kŭl-mĭ-nā'shŭn)

cult mongers (kŭlt mŭng'gērz). People devoted to spreading intellectual fads

**curative,** page 174

cut (kŭt). To separate an animal from the main cattle roundup herd for special grouping (page 699).

**cynic,** page 194

## D

dais (dā'ĭs). A raised platform in a large room

dank (dăngk). Cold and moist.

dear (dēr). Expensive (page 456)

debris (dē-brē'). Rubbish, especially from wreckage

**decadent,** page 35

decolletage (dà-kôl-tàzh'). Dress that leaves the arms and shoulders bare; a low-backed or low-necked dress

decorum (dē-kō'rŭm). Propriety; good form

**decrepit,** page 552

decry (dē-krī'). To express disapproval of

deduction (dē-dŭk'shŭn). Reasoning from a generally accepted truth to a particular case

defalcation (dē-făl-kā'shŭn). A misappropriation of money by one who has it in trust

defection (dē-fĕk'shŭn). Desertion

defective (dē-fĕk'tĭv). A person lacking in some respect, usually in intelligence

deference (dĕf'ēr-ĕns). Courteous regard for another's wishes. *Adj.,* deferential (dĕf-ēr-ĕn'shăl)

deft (dĕft). Skillful, especially in use of the hands

degenerate (dē-jĕn'ēr-ĭt). Degraded; lowered in quality

deification (dē-ĭ-fĭ-kā'shŭn). The procedure of making a god of, or treating as a god

deity (dē'ĭ-tĭ). A god; divine nature

delectable (dē-lĕk'tà-b'l). Highly pleasing; delightful

deleterious (dĕl-ē-tēr'ĭ-ŭs). Hurtful; damaging

delirium (dē-lĭr'ĭ-ŭm). A temporary state of mental disturbance

deluge (dĕl'ûj) A flood; to flood

demean (dē-mēn'). To lower; debase

demented (dē-mĕnt'ĕd). Mentally unbalanced

demitasse (dĕm'ĭ-tăs). A small cup for or of black coffee

**demoniac,** page 577

denim (dĕn'ĭm). A coarse cotton cloth used for work clothes

denizen (děn'ĭ-zěn). Inhabitant

**denominate,** page 184

**denomination,** page 184

**denuded,** page 83

deploy (dě-ploi'). To spread out wide, especially troops

deprecate (děp'rě-kāt). To express disapproval of; to belittle

dereliction (děr-ē-lĭk'shŭn). A failure in duty

derision (dě-rĭzh'ŭn). Contemptuous laughter

Derringer (děr'ĭn-jēr). A short-barreled pocket pistol of large caliber

**despicable,** page 35

devastate (děv'ăs-tāt). To lay waste; ravage

devil (děv'ĭl). An apprentice in a printer's shop (page 605)

**devilish,** page 577

**diabolical,** page 577

diadem (dī'à-děm). A crown

dialect (dī'à-lěkt). A local form of a language

diapason (dī-à-pā'zŭn). The full range of a musical instrument

didactic (dī-dăk'tĭk). Designed to teach a lesson

diffident (dĭf'ĭ-děnt). Lacking confidence

diffuse (dĭ-fūz'). To scatter; spread

digression (dĭ-grěsh'ŭn). A departure from the main path or subject

dilemma (dĭ-lěm'à). A state so beset with obstacles that there seems to be no satisfactory way out

dilettante (dĭl-ě-tăn'tĭ). One who dabbles in an art or branch of knowledge

diminutive (dĭ-mĭn'ū-tĭv). Below average size; very small

**dirge,** page 528

**disconsolate,** page 35

discountenance (dĭs-koun'tě-nǎns). To discourage by open disapproval

disengage (dĭs-ěn-gāj'). To free from; release

disinterested (dĭs-ĭn'tēr-ěs-těd). Not influenced by personal advantage

disparagement (dĭs-pǎr'ĭj-měnt). Expression of low esteem

dispensation (dĭs-pěn-sā'shŭn). The dealing of good or evil by God to man

dissemble (dĭ-sěm'b'l). To pretend an attitude not sincerely felt or taken

dissimulation (dĭ-sĭm-ū-lā'shŭn). False pretension; deception

distillage (dĭs-tĭl'ǎj). A distilled liquor

**ditty,** page 528

diverge (dĭ-vûrj'). To go out in different directions

divers (dī'vērz). Of different kinds

**divert,** page 471

divest (dī-věst'). To strip

docile (dŏs'ĭl). Easy to manage. *Noun,* docility (dŏ-sĭl'ĭ-tĭ)

doggerel (dŏg'ēr-ěl). A sort of loose, irregular verse, often comic

**dogie,** page 700

**dogmatic,** page 457

dole (dōl). Woe; grief

**domination,** page 767.

dominion (dŏ-mĭn'yŭn). Rule; power over

**dotage,** page 552

dowry (dou'rĭ). The money or goods a woman brings to her husband in marriage

dross (drŏs). Waste matter, especially as mixed with valuable

drover (drō'vēr). A dealer in cattle or other domestic animals

dualism (dū'ăl-ĭz'm). State of having a double nature

ductile (dŭk'tĭl). Capable of being drawn into wire or thread

duenna (dů-ěn'à). A chaperone

dulcet (dŭl'sět). Melodious

dungaree (dŭng-gà-rē'). A coarse cotton fabric used for work clothes

## E

eccentric (ěk-sěn'trĭk). Irregular; odd. *Noun,* eccentricity (ěk-sěn-trĭs'ĭ-tĭ)

echelon (ěsh'ě-lŏn). A military arrangement of troops or planes in diagonal lines

ecstatic (ěk-stăt'ĭk). In a state of intense joy or delight. *Noun,* ecstasy (ěk'stà-sĭ)

edelweiss (ā'děl-vīs). A small Alpine flower

edible (ěd'ĭ-b'l). Fit to be eaten as food

edify (ěd'ĭ-fī). To instruct and improve. *Noun,* edification (ěd-ĭ-fĭ-kā'shŭn)

effable (ěf'à-b'l). Capable of being expressed in words

efface (ě-fās'). To wipe out; to erase

effervescent (ěf-ēr-věs'ěnt). Bubbling; showing high spirits

efficacy (ěf'ĭ-kà-sĭ). Power to produce effects

egress (ē'grěs). An exit; outlet

Eldorado (ěl-dŏ-rä'dō). A place rich in gold

eleemosynary (ěl-ě-mŏs'ĭ-něr-ĭ). Relating to or supported by charity

elixir (ě-lĭk'sēr). The refined spirit

elusive (ě-lū'sĭv). Difficult to catch or understand clearly

embellish (ěm-běl'ĭsh). To adorn; to beautify

embezzlement (ěm-běz''l-měnt). Theft of funds entrusted to one's care

embryo (ěm'brĭ-ō). A beginning or undeveloped stage

emissaries (ĕm'ĭ-sĕr-ĭz). Agents sent on a special mission

emporium (ĕm-pō'rĭ-ŭm). A place of trade; store

emulous (ĕm'ū-lŭs). Ambitious to equal another

enfranchisement (ĕn-frăn'chĭz-mĕnt). Liberation; admission to citizenship

engender (ĕn-jĕn'dēr). To cause to develop

enigma (ē-nĭg'mà). Something perplexing, hard to get the meaning of

ensign (ĕn'sīn). Flag on a Navy ship

ensue (ĕn-sū'). To follow as a consequence

enthrall (ĕn-thrôl'). To charm; to hold spellbound

epic (ĕp'ĭk). Great; heroic

epicure (ĕp'ĭ-kŭr). One of exacting taste in food or drink. *Adj.*, epicurean (ĕp-ĭ-kŭ-rē'ăn)

**epitome,** page 264

**equanimity,** page 720

equestrian (ē-kwĕs'trĭ-ăn). Mounted on horseback

equilibrium (ē-kwĭ-lĭb'rĭ-ŭm). Balance

equinox (ē'kwĭ-nŏks). The time when the sun crosses the equator and day and night everywhere are of equal length

equitable (ĕk'wĭ-tà-b'l). Impartial; fair

equity (ĕk'wĭ-tĭ). Fairness in dealing

**eradicate,** page 457

erratic (ē-răt'ĭk). Wandering; queer

esoteric (ĕs-ō-tĕr'ĭk). Confined to a select group; belonging only to an inner circle

Esperanto (ĕs-pĕ-rän'tō). An artificial international language

estrangement (ĕs-trānj'mĕnt). A turning away in feelings or affection

ethics (ĕth'ĭks). Moral principles

etymology (ĕt-ĭ-mŏl'ō-jĭ). The origin of a word as shown by its parts

euchre (ū'kēr). A card game

eupeptic (ū-pĕp'tĭk). Pertaining to good digestion

euphony (ū'fō-nĭ). Harmonious sound

evaluation (ē-văl-ū-ā'shŭn). Process of weighing merits and faults to reach a judgment

evanescent (ĕv-à-nĕs'ĕnt). Tending to fade away like vapor; fleeting

evicted (ē-vĭk'tĕd). Put out by legal process

evince (ē-vĭns'). To show

**excruciating,** page 58

execrated (ĕks'ē-krāt-ĕd). Despised; cursed

**exhilarating,** pages 253–254

exhortations (ĕg-zôr-tā'shŭnz) Expressions of encouragement

exigencies (ĕk'sĭ-jĕn-sĭz). The special requirements or needs of a situation or occasion

expatiate (ĕks-pā'shĭ-āt). To talk at length

**expatriated,** page 720

**expedient,** page 475

**expedite,** page 475

expletive (ĕks'plĕ-tĭv). An oath or exclamation

explicable (ĕks'plĭ-kà-b'l). Capable of being explained

explicit (ĕks-plĭs'ĭt). Distinctly stated; clear

exponent (ĕks-pō'nĕnt). An interpreter; one who fully stands for a group or principle

expostulation (ĕks-pŏs-tū-lā'shŭn). Earnest protest

extemporize (ĕks-tĕm'pō-rīz). To compose on the spur of the moment without previous planning

extenuate (ĕks-tĕn'ū-āt). To excuse; to represent as less serious

**exterminate,** page 212

**extort,** page 494

extricate (ĕks'trĭ-kāt). To free; to clear of entanglement

**extrovert,** page 471

exuberance (ĕgz-ū'bēr-ăns). Unlimited supply of energy and high spirits

exultant (ĕg-zŭl'tănt). Rejoicing in triumph

## F

fabulous (făb'ū-lŭs). Like a fable; fictitious, astonishing

facilitate (fà-sĭl'ĭ-tāt). To make easier

faction (făk'shŭn). A party within a state

faculty (făk'ŭl-tĭ). Any one power of the mind

**fallacious,** page 465

**fallacy,** page 465

fantastic (făn-tăs'tĭk). Unreal; hard to believe

fathomless (făth'ŭm-lĕs). Immeasurable

fatuous (făt'ū-ŭs). Foolish, especially in being pleased with oneself

feign (fān). To pretend

felicity (fē-lĭs'ĭ-tĭ). Well-founded happiness; complete comfort. *Adj.*, felicitous

**feline,** page 365

**felonious,** page 720

fermentation (fûr-mĕn-tā'shŭn). The working of yeast; hence, upheaval, unrest

ferocity (fē-rŏs'ĭ-tĭ). Fierceness

**fervid,** page 314

**fervor,** page 314

fiacre (fē-ä'kēr). A small French hackney coach

fidelity (fī-dĕl'ĭ-tĭ). Loyalty; faithfulness to a trust

**fiendish,** page 577

filament (fĭl'à-mĕnt). A thread

fillip (fĭl'ĭp). Something serving to excite or arouse

firmament (fûr'mà-mĕnt). The arch of the sky

fissure (fĭsh'ēr). A crack or other such long narrow opening

flamboyant (flăm-boi'ănt). Flamelike in color; strikingly colored

fleur-de-lis (flûr-dē-lē'). The iris, or a conventional representation of it

flippant (flĭp'ănt). Treating serious matters lightly

flotsam (flŏt'săm). Anything drifting about on the surface of water

fodder (fŏd'ēr). Coarse food for cattle, horses, and sheep

foible (foi'b'l). A failing; weakness

folio (fō'lĭ-ō). A large-paged book

foppery (fŏp'ēr-ĭ). Foolish and extravagant concern with dress

forecastle (fōr'kăs'l). Forward part of a ship where sailors are quartered

forspent (fŏr-spĕnt'). Exhausted

fortitude (fôr'tĭ-tūd). Courageous endurance

fowler (foul'ēr). One hunting wild fowl

fowling piece (foul'ĭng pēs). A light gun for shooting birds

fratricidal (frăt-rĭ-sīd'ăl). Involving, or like, the murder of one's own brother

fresco (frĕs'kō). A painting or decoration applied directly to a wall

fretwork (frĕt'wûrk). Ornamental work with ridges or open spaces

frond (frŏnd). A leaf, usually a large one

**frugality,** page 494

furl (fûrl). To wrap or roll, as a flag or a sail

furtive (fûr'tĭv). Sly

fustian (fŭs'chăn). In pioneer times, a heavy cotton and linen cloth

futile (fū'tĭl). Useless; to no avail

## G

galley (găl'ĭ). The kitchen of a ship

galvanic (găl-văn'ĭk). Relating to a current of electricity

gangrene (găng'grēn). Diseased state in which the flesh decays

Garand (găr'ănd). A light semiautomatic rifle, named for its inventor

**gargoyle,** page 71

garrulous (găr'ū-lŭs). Talkative

Gethsemane (gĕth-sĕm'à-nē). A garden near Jerusalem where Christ endured his agony and was betrayed; hence any place or occasion of great mental or spiritual suffering

glade (glād). A grassy open space in a forest

glib (glĭb). Easy, smooth in manner or speech

gorse (gôrs). A spiny, evergreen shrub common in Europe

gossamer (gŏs'à-mēr). A thread of spider silk, or a filmy tangle of such threads; hence, a gauzelike fabric

grackle (grăk'l). A blackbird with a harsh call

grandiose (grăn'dĭ-ōs). Impressive; pompous

gratuitous (grà-tū'ĭ-tŭs). Given freely, regardless of merit; unwarranted

grimace (grĭ-mās'). A wry face

groined (groind). Built so as to form intersecting arches.

gruesome (grōō'sŭm). Horrifying

gudgeon. *See* stem to gudgeon.

guerrilla (gĕ-rĭl'à). Acting in an independent, irregular manner, as in guerrilla warfare

guile (gīl). Crafty or deceitful cunning

guise (gīz). External appearance or dress

gullibility (gŭl-ĭ-bĭl'ĭ-tĭ). Tendency to believe anything one is told

## H

harass (hăr'ås). To disturb or torment continuously; to wear out with worry

harpsichord (härp'sĭ-kôrd). An old-fashioned stringed instrument, forerunner of the piano

harpy (här'pĭ). A fabulous winged monster which fed on shipwreck victims

haymaker (hā'mā-kēr). A knockout blow (slang)

hegira (hĕ-jī'rà). A flight

helgramite (hĕl'grà-mīt). A larva used as fish bait

helm (hĕlm). The apparatus by which a ship is steered

helves (hĕlvz). Handles of tools

heraldry (hĕr'ăld-rĭ). The representation of family history by coats of arms

hibernatorial (hī-bēr-nà-tō'rĭ-ăl). Spending the winter in sleep or an inactive state

hieroglyphic (hī-ēr-ō-glĭf'ĭk). A character in ancient picture writings; hence, an obscure symbol

**hilarious,** page 254

**hilarity,** page 254

hoary (hōr'ĭ). White with age

**hoax,** page 654

hobgoblin (hŏb'gŏb-lĭn). Any imaginary cause of terror or dread

holocaust (hŏl'ō-kôst). Destruction by fire of a large number of human beings

hostelry (hŏs'tĕl-rĭ). A lodginghouse

hostler (hŏs'lēr). One who takes care of horses

hove to (hōv). Of ships, stopped by bringing the head of the vessel into the wind and setting the sails to act against each other

hull (hŭl). The frame or body of a ship

hummock (hŭm'ŭk). A little hill

**hyperbole,** page 152

**hypnotic,** page 152

hypothesis (hī-pŏth'ē-sĭs). Something assumed or conceded merely for the purposes of argument or action

hysterical (hĭs-tĕr'ĭ-kăl). Emotionally out of control

## I

icon (ī'kŏn). An image of Christ, the Virgin Mary, or a saint

idiom (ĭd'ĭ-ŭm). The language peculiar to a group of people or community

idiosyncrasy (ĭd-ĭ-ō-sĭng'krá-sĭ) A distinctive peculiarity

idyllic (ī-dĭl'ĭk) Pleasing in natural simplicity

ignified (ĭg'nĭ-fīd). Set on fire

ignominious (ĭg-nō-mĭn'ĭ-ŭs). Dishonorable; shameful

illimitable (ĭl-lĭm'ĭt-á-b'l). Not capable of being limited; immeasurable

illusion (ĭ-lū'zhŭn). A false impression; deceptive appearance

image (ĭm'ĭj). A likeness; a reflection

imbecility (ĭm-bē-sĭl'ĭ-tĭ). A feeble-minded state

imbibe (ĭm-bīb'). To drink

**immedicable,** page 759

immemorial (ĭm-mē-mō'rĭ-ăl). Beyond the reach of memory

immersion (ĭ-mûr'shŭn). Act of plunging something completely under water

imminent (ĭm'ĭ-nĕnt). Threatening to occur immediately

immitigable (ĭ-mĭt'ĭ-gá-b'l). Not capable of being softened or made easier

**immobility,** page 83

immunize (ĭm'ŭ-nīz). To protect against completely

immure (ĭ-mūr'). To shut within walls; to entomb

impairment (ĭm-pâr'mĕnt). Decline in quality

impassive (ĭm-păs'ĭv). Showing no emotion

impediment (ĭm-pĕd'ĭ-mĕnt). That which obstructs or hinders

impedimenta (ĭm-pĕd-ĭ-mĕn'tá). The supplies and supply train of an army

imperceptible (ĭm-pēr-sĕp'tĭ-b'l). Not capable of being noticed by the senses; extremely slight

imperious (ĭm-pē̤r'ĭ-ŭs). Urgent; compelling

imperturbable (ĭm-pēr-tûr'bá-b'l). Incapable of being disturbed; calm; serene

impervious (ĭm-pûr'vĭ-ŭs). Incapable of being penetrated

impetuosity (ĭm-pĕt-ŭ-ŏs'ĭ-tĭ). Hastiness and rashness in action or feeling

impious (ĭm'pĭ-ŭs). Irreverent

implacable (ĭm-plā'ká-b'l). Not to be pacified; relentless

implicate (ĭm'plĭ-kāt). To involve

implicit (ĭm-plĭs'ĭt). Understood or implied rather than stated

imponderable (ĭm-pŏn'dēr-á-b'l) Not capable of being weighed or accurately measured

**importance,** page 206

**impoverished,** page 71

impregnable (ĭm-prĕg'ná-b'l). Unconquerable

impregnate (ĭm-prĕg'nāt). To fill or saturate one substance with another substance, usually contrasting with the first substance in physical properties.

impute (ĭm-pūt'). To ascribe

inaccessible (ĭn-ăk-sĕs'ĭ-b'l). Not to be reached; inapproachable

inalienable (ĭn-āl'yĕn-á-b'l). Not to be transferred or taken away

inanition (ĭn-á-nĭsh'ŭn). Emptiness; exhaustion from lack of food

inarticulate (ĭn-är-tĭk'ŭ-lăt). Without the power of intelligible speech

**incalculably,** page 83

**incarnated,** page 264

incensed (ĭn-sĕnst'). Inflamed with anger

incentive (ĭn-sĕn'tĭv). Motive

**incessantly,** page 625

inclemency (ĭn-klĕm'ĕn-sĭ). Harshness; of weather, storminess

incompatible (ĭn-kŏm-păt'ĭ-b'l). Incapable of harmonious association because of contradictions in nature

incongruity (ĭn-kŏn-grōō'ĭ-tĭ). That which is out of harmony, unsuitable, or inconsistent

**inconstancy,** page 164

**incorrigible,** page 457

**incorruptibility,** page 83

increase (ĭn'krēs). Offspring (page 748)

incredulous (ĭn-krĕd'ŭ-lŭs). Not believing

incumbent (ĭn-kŭm'bĕnt). Imposed as an obligation

indefatigable (ĭn-dē-făt'ĭ-gá-b'l). Incapable of being fatigued; untiring

**indictment,** page 244

**indigence,** page 284

**indispensable,** page 654

**indisputable,** page 71

**indomitable,** page 767

ineffable (ĭn-ĕf'á-b'l). Beyond one's power to express

inequity (ĭn-ĕk'wĭ-tĭ). Injustice

inert (ĭn-ûrt'). Lacking the power to move

inexorable (ĭn-ĕk'sō-rá-b'l). Relentless

inexplicably (ĭn-ĕks'plĭ-ká-blĭ). Not capable of being explained inextricably (ĭn-ĕks'trĭ-kȧ-blĭ). In such a manner that untangling is impossible

**infallible,** page 465

**infamous,** page 759

**infamy,** page 759

infidel (ĭn'fĭ-dĕl). An unbeliever

**infinitesimal,** page 83

infirmity (ĭn-fûr'mĭ-tĭ). Feebleness

infringe (ĭn-frĭnj'). To trespass

**infuriating,** page 71

ingenious (ĭn-jēn'yŭs). Cleverly inventive

ingratiate (ĭn-grā'shĭ-āt). To win one's way into favor

inhibition (ĭn-hĭ-bĭsh'ŭn). Restraint of free activity

innovation (ĭn-ȯ-vā'shŭn). A novelty; a new thing or course of action

insatiable (ĭn-sā'shĭ-ȧ-b'l). Incapable of being satisfied

inscrutable (ĭn-skrōō'tȧ-b'l). Incapable of being searched into and understood

**insensibility,** page 575

insidious (ĭn-sĭd'ĭ-ŭs). Sly; treacherous; doing damage without arousing suspicion

**insolvency,** page 570

instancy (ĭn'stăn-sĭ). Urgency; insistence

instigate (ĭn'stĭ-gāt). To urge another to action

insular (ĭn'sŭ-lēr). Pertaining to an island

insurgent (ĭn-sûr'jĕnt). Rebellious

intangible (ĭn-tăn'jĭ-b'l). Not perceptible to touch

integral (ĭn'tē-grăl). Essential to completeness

integrity (ĭn-tĕg'rĭ-tĭ). Honesty; state of being undivided, in complete harmony with oneself

**integument,** page 83

intelligentsia (ĭn-tĕl-ĭ-jĕnt'sĭ-ȧ). Intellectuals collectively; the educated class

interim (ĭn'tēr-ĭm). Interval; time between happenings

**interlocutor,** page 540

interlude (ĭn'tēr-lūd). A space of time between events

**interminable,** page 625

internecine (ĭn-tēr-nē'sĭn). Involving mutual slaughter; deadly

interspersed (ĭn-tēr-spûrst'). Scattered among other things

**intimidation,** page 721

**intrenched,** page 570

**intrepid,** page 767

intrinsic (ĭn-trĭn'sĭk). Essential in the nature of something

**introvert,** page 471

intuitive (ĭn-tū'ĭ-tĭv). Possessing or operating by insight; understanding without needing to know facts

**iridescent,** page 319

irised (ī'rĭst). Colored like the rainbow

irrelevant (ĭr-rĕl'ē-vȧnt). Unrelated; unessential. *Noun,* irrelevance

## J

Jack (jăk). A nickname for a sailor

jackanapes (jăk'ȧ-nāps). An impertinent fellow

japanned (jȧ-pănd'). Covered with hard, bright varnish

jasper (jăs'pēr). A semi-precious stone, usually dark green

jeopardy (jĕp'ēr-dĭ). Serious danger

jerbilla (jēr-bĭl'lȧ). Belonging to the mouse family; usually jerboa (jēr-bō'ȧ)

jerky (jûr'kĭ). Strips of dried, smoked meat

jocose (jȯ-kōs'). Joking; jesting

jocular (jŏk'ū-lēr). Sportive; merry

jodhpurs (jŏd'pŏŏrz). Riding breeches that fit closely from knee to ankle

johnny (jŏn'ĭ). English slang for "fellow"

jubilant (jūb'ĭ-lănt). Shouting with joy; exulting. *Noun,* jubilation (jū-bĭ-lā'shŭn)

## K

kaleidoscopic (kȧ-lī-dȯ-skŏp'ĭk). In an ever-changing pattern

ken (kĕn). Sight or insight

kill (kĭl). A creek or stream (local N.Y.)

## L

labyrinthian (lăb-ĭ-rĭn'thĭ-ăn). Intricate; involved

lacteal (lăk'tē-ăl). Milky

**languid,** page 314

**languor,** page 314

lassitude (lăs'ĭ-tūd). Sluggishness; listlessness

lave (lāv). To wash; to bathe

laxity (lăk'sĭ-tĭ). Lack of tenseness or strictness

lay (lā). Not professional

leeward (lē'wērd). On or toward the side away from the wind

legacy (lĕg'ȧ-sĭ). An inheritance

**leonine,** page 365

lethargy (lĕth'ēr-jĭ). Morbid drowsiness; dull inactivity. *Adj.,* lethargic (lē-thär'jĭk)

levee (lĕv'ē). A miscellaneous gathering of guests

**levity,** page 174

liaison (lē-ā'zŭn). The linking or co-ordinating of activities

libation (lī-bā'shŭn). Ceremonious pouring out of wine; humorously, the drinking of alcoholic liquors

libel, page 244

libretto (lĭ-brĕt'ō). The words of an opera or musical comedy

limbo (lĭm'bō). A place of confinement or neglect, especially of those forgotten

limpid (lĭm'pĭd). Clear; transparent

linsey (lĭn'zĭ). A coarse cloth of pioneer days

liquescent (lĭ-kwĕs'ĕnt). Becoming liquid; melting

literate (lĭt'ẽr-ĭt). Able to read and write; educated

locoed (lō'kōd). Of cattle, crazed by effects of eating loco weed

locution, page 540

lodestar (lōd'stär). A star that leads and guides, especially the polestar; hence, a guiding idea or principle

loquacious, page 540

ludicrous (lū'dĭ-krŭs). Provoking laughter

luminous (lū'mĭ-nŭs). Shining; brilliant

lustrous (lŭs'trŭs). Having sheen or brilliance

# M

machination (măk-ĭ-nā'shŭn). An artful scheme or plot

Mackinaw (măk'ĭ-nô). A short, heavy coat, usually plaid

magnanimity (măg-nà-nĭm'ĭ-tĭ). Generous and courageous spirit. *Adj.*, magnanimous (măg-năn'ĭ-mŭs)

mail (māl). Armor made of linked metal rings

mainmasthead (mān'màst-hĕd). The top of the tallest mast on a ship

malediction, page 570

malevolence, page 570

mali (mòl). Public walk; promenade

maneuver (mà-nōō'vẽr). Management with artful design

manifold (măn'ĭ-fōld). Numerous; many

manipulator (mà-nĭp'ū-lā-tẽr). One who manages skillfully, often for purposes of fraud

manzanita (măn-zä-nē'tà). A shrub common in California

marge (märj). Margin, as of a stream

marquee (mär-kē'). A large field tent

martial (mär'shăl). Warlike

masher (măsh'ẽr). Slang for a man who tries to make an impression on women to whom he is a stranger

mast (màst). Feed for livestock

mattock (măt'ŭk). An implement for digging or grubbing

maudlin, page 720

maverick, page 700

meager (mē'gẽr). Thin; barren; scanty

mediator (mē'dĭ-ā-tẽr). One who acts as a go-between, especially to effect a reconciliation

mendicant (mĕn'dĭ-kănt). A beggar

meridian (mē-rĭd'ĭ-ăn). The highest point reached by the sun

metamorphosis (mĕt-à-môr'fō-sĭs). A striking change in appearance or character

metaphor (mĕt'à-fẽr). A figure of speech presenting an implied comparison

metate (mà-tä'tā). A hollowed-out stone used by Mexicans to grind corn by hand

mete (mēt). A boundary

meteor (mē'tĕ-ẽr). A starlike body in rapid motion

meteorological (mē-tĕ-ŏr-ô-lŏj'ĭ-kăl). Pertaining to the atmosphere and weather

meticulous (mē-tĭk'û-lŭs). Excessively careful of small details

mettle (mĕt'l). Spirit

mien (mēn). Manner; bearing

minion (mĭn'yŭn). A lowly servant; one who does another's bidding without question

mirage (mĭ-räzh'). An optical illusion caused by reflection, usually on heat rays

mitigation, page 438

mizzen (mĭz'n). A designated mast on a vessel, third from the bow

moiety (moi'ĕ-tĭ). A part, roughly half

Mojave (mô-hä'và). A desert in southern California

mollify (mŏl'ĭ-fī). To soften; pacify

morass (mô-răs'). A tract of soft, wet ground; marsh

moribund (môr'ĭ-bŭnd). In a dying state

morose (mô-rōs'). Gloomy, sullen

mortar (môr'tẽr). A cannon that throws its shells in a high curve

mortification, page 654

mortised. *See* tenoned and mortised.

motley (mŏt'lĭ). Composed of widely varying colors or parts

muster (mŭs'tẽr). An assembly

mutiny (mū'tĭ-nĭ). A rebellion against formal authority, especially military or on shipboard

myriad (mĭr'ĭ-ăd). A great but indefinite number

# N

naïve, page 752

naïveté, page 752

napery (nā'pẽr-ĭ). Table linen

nebulous (nĕb'û-lŭs). Cloudy; hazy; misty

nice (nīs). Discriminating; sometimes, too particular

niche (nĭch). A recess in a wall

nocturne (nŏk'tûrn). A musical composition dealing with night noisome (noi'sŭm). Offensive to the senses

**nomenclature,** page 184

**nominal,** page 184

nonchalance (nŏn'shȧ-lăns). Lack of concern; gay carelessness

**nonconformist,** page 570

**nondescript,** page 264

nonplussed (nŏn'plŭst). Puzzled; perplexed

nullify (nŭl'ĭ-fī). To make ineffective, of no value

## O

obdurate (ŏb'dŭ-rȧt). Stubborn; unyielding

obeisance (ȯ-bā'sȧns). A gesture, usually a low bow, in token of respect or homage

oblique (ŏb-lēk'). Slanting; indirect

**obliterate,** page 212

oblivion (ŏb-lĭv'ĭ-ŭn). State or fact of being forgotten

obscene (ŏb-sēn'). Foul; disgusting

obsequious (ŏb-sē'kwĭ-ŭs). Fawning; unbecomingly servile

**obsolete,** page 227

obtrude (ŏb-trōōd'). To thrust oneself upon attention

obviate (ŏb'vĭ-āt). To make unnecessary

occult (ŏ-kŭlt'). Secret; hidden

odium (ō'dĭ-ŭm). The reproach and discredit attached to something hated

**oligarchy,** page 502

ominous (ŏm'ĭ-nŭs). Foreshadowing evil

omnipotence (ŏm-nĭp'ȯ-tĕns). State of being all-powerful

omnipresent (ŏm-nĭ-prĕz'ent). Present everywhere

omniscient (ŏm-nĭsh'ĕnt). Knowing everything

omnivorous (ŏm-nĭv'ȯ-rŭs). Eating any kind of food; greedy

onerous (ŏn'ēr-ŭs). Burdensome; oppressive

opacity (ȯ-păs'ĭ-tĭ). Quality of not reflecting or transmitting light

**opalescent,** page 319

opulent (ŏp'ů-lĕnt). Wealthy; luxuriant

oracular (ȯ-răk'ů-lēr). Forecasting the future with solemnity and dignity

orb (ôrb). A circle or sphere; an object in this shape

orbit (ôr'bĭt). The path of a heavenly body in its revolutions; a fixed circle of activity

orphic (ôr'fĭk). Prophetic; wise

oscillation (ŏs-ĭ-lā'shŭn). Rhythmic movement backward and forward

**ostensible,** page 47

**ostentatious,** page 47

## P

pacific (pȧ-sĭf'ĭk). Calm; peaceful; peace-loving

pacify (păs'ĭ-fī). To appease; calm; quiet

padre (pä'drĭ). Spanish for "father"; priest

padrone (pä-drō'nȧ). Italian for "master"

**paean,** page 528

palatable (păl'ĭt-ȧ-b'l). Agreeable to the taste; hence, pleasing

pall (pôl). A covering for a coffin; hence, any dark and gloomy overcast

**pallid,** page 314

**pallor,** page 314

palpable (păl'pȧ-b'l). Capable of being touched or felt

palpitate (păl'pĭ-tāt). To throb

**palsied,** page 552

panegyrize (păn'ē-jĭ-rīz). To speak or write high praise

panhandler (păn'hănd-lēr). A beggar (slang)

panorama (păn-ȯ-rä'mȧ). A wide view of a whole region in every direction

pantheon (păn-thē'ŏn). All the gods of a people, collectively

pantomime (păn'tȯ-mīm). To act out without speaking

**paradox,** page 190

paraphrase (păr'ȧ-frāz). A free translation or restatement in another manner

pariah (pȧ-rī'ȧ). An outcast; a person despised by society

parlance (pär'lăns). Manner of speech

parley (pär'lĭ). Conversation; often a formal discussion between enemies

parody (păr'ȯ-dĭ). An imitation in a humorous or feeble manner

parole (pȧ-rōl'). Release of a military prisoner on his word not to take up arms again

paroxysm (păr'ŏk-sĭz'm). A convulsion; spasm

parry (păr'ĭ) and fend. To ward off blows by meeting them before they reach their object

**parsimony,** page 494

partisan (pär'tĭ-zăn). A devoted follower

paternoster (pä'tēr-nōs'tēr). The Lord's Prayer, from the opening Latin words

pathology (pȧ-thŏl'ȯ-jĭ). Scientific study and treatment of disease

**patriarch,** page 502

patrician (pȧ-trĭsh'ăn). A person of high birth or breeding

patrimony (păt'rĭ-mō-nĭ). An inheritance from one's father

pedigree (pĕd'ĭ-grē). A table representing a line of ancestors

pellicle (pĕl'ĭ-k'l). A thin skin or film

peltry (pĕl'trĭ). Pelts or furs, collectively

pennon (pĕn′ŭn). A flag; a banner

pensive (pĕn′sĭv). Thoughtful

penury (pĕn′ū-rĭ). Extreme poverty

perambulation (pĕr-ăm-bŭ-lā′shŭn). Walking around or over

perdition (pĕr-dĭsh′ŭn). Ruin; eternal death

peremptory (pĕr-ĕmp′tŏ-rĭ). Leaving no chance for refusal or denial

**perfidious,** page 759

perfunctory (pĕr-fŭngk′tŏ-rĭ). Done mechanically by way of routine; careless; indifferent

peroration (pĕr-ŏ-rā′shŭn). The concluding part of an oration

perpetuating (pĕr-pĕt′ŭ-āt-ĭng). Causing to last forever

persiflage (pûr′sĭ-fläzh). Frivolous or bantering talk

pertinacity (pûr-tĭ-năs′ĭ-tĭ). Unyielding perseverance. *Adj.,* pertinacious (pûr-tĭ-nā′shŭs)

pertinence (pûr′tĭ-nĕns). A fact related to the matter in hand

perturbation (pûr-tĕr-bā′shŭn). A state of great alarm or agitation

perusal (pĕ-rōōz′ăl). A careful, slow reading

petrol (pĕt′rŏl). In England, gasoline

petulant (pĕt′ŭ-lănt). Cross; fretful

phantom (făn′tŭm). A delusion; a specter

phenomenon (fĕ-nŏm′ĕ-nŏn). An exceptional, unusual, or abnormal thing or occurrence. *Plural,* phenomena

philanthropy (fĭ-lăn′thrŏ-pĭ). Love and good will for all mankind

phthisic (tĭz′ĭk). A wasting disease, usually tuberculosis

pillage (pĭl′ĭj). To plunder or loot; the act of plundering

pinnacle (pĭn′á-k′l). The highest point

piquant (pē′kănt). Having a lively charm

piqued (pēkt). Excited or aroused by a provocation

pithy (pĭth′ĭ). Saying much in few words

placatingly (plā′kăt-ĭng-lĭ). In a soothing manner

placidity (plă-sĭd′ĭ-tĭ). Calmness; serenity

plashy (plăsh′ĭ). Abounding in puddles; splashy

**plenipotentiary,** page 206

plutonium (plŭ-tō′nĭ-ŭm). One of the chemicals used in making the atomic bomb; from Pluto, lord of the infernal regions

**poignant,** page 58

polyphonic (pŏl′ĭ-fŏn′ĭk). Consisting of many sounds

pommel (pŭm′ĕl). The rounded knob at the front and top of a saddle

pontifical (pŏn-tĭf′ĭ-kăl). Having the dignity of a high church official

pontificate (pŏn-tĭf′ĭ-kăt). The term of office of a pope

poop (pōōp). An upper deck on a ship, against the mizzenmast

portend (pōr-tĕnd′). To give a warning; foreshadow. *Noun,* portent (pōr′tĕnt); *adj.,* portentous (pōr-tĕn′tŭs)

posteriors (pŏs-tēr′ĭ-ērz). The buttocks

posterity (pŏs-tĕr′ĭ-tĭ). Offspring or descendants

**potent,** page 206

**potential,** page 206

poultice (pōl′tĭs). A soft preparation spread over a sore or inflamed spot to reduce pain or combat infection

precarious (prĕ-kâr′ĭ-ŭs). Uncertain; insecure

precedence (prĕ-sē′dĕns). Rank above or ahead of another

precept (prē′sĕpt). A rule of action or conduct

precipitate (prĕ-sĭp′ĭ-tăt). Acting with unwise haste

precocious (prĕ-kō′shŭs). Exceptionally early in development

predicament (prĕ-dĭk′á-mĕnt). An unpleasant or trying situation

predominant (prĕ-dŏm′ĭ-nănt). Outstanding

**prehensile,** page 773

**premise,** page 190

premonitory (prĕ-mŏn′ĭ-tō-rĭ). Giving advance notice or warning. *Noun,* premonition (prē-mŏ-nĭsh′ŭn)

preoccupation (prĕ-ŏk-ŭ-pā′shŭn). State of being lost in thought about matters other than those immediately before one. *Adj.,* preoccupied (prĕ-ŏk′ŭ-pīd)

prerogative (prĕ-rŏg′á-tĭv). Of first rank or importance

prescient (prē′shĕnt). Knowing in advance what will happen. *Noun,* prescience (prē′shĕns)

**presentiment,** page 35

**primal,** page 625

primeval (prī-mē′văl). Belonging to the first ages of history

**primitive,** page 625

probity (prōb′ĭ-tĭ). Honesty; tried virtue

proclivity (prŏ-klĭv′ĭ-tĭ). Inclination or tendency

**procrastinate,** page 698

prodigy (prŏd′ĭ-jĭ). A marvel; someone or something out of the ordinary. *Adj.,* prodigious (prŏ-dĭj′ŭs)

**profane,** page 759

progenitor (prŏ-jĕn′ĭ-tēr). A forefather

proletarian (prō-lĕ-târ′ĭ-ăn). A laborer for day wages, not possessed of capital

prolific (prŏ-lĭf′ĭk). Fruitful; productive

promiscuous (prŏ-mĭs′kŭ-ŭs). Undiscriminating; irregular

propitiate (prō-pĭsh'ĭ-āt). To make favorable

proscenium (prō-sē'nĭ-ŭm). The curtain and its framework in a theater

prostrate (prŏs'trāt). Fallen; lying helpless

protoplasm (prō'tō-plăz'm). The essential substance of living cells

protozoa (prō-tō-zō'à). Tiny animals, mostly too small to be seen with the naked eye

protracted (prō-trăk'tĕd). Long drawn out

**provincial, page 752**

prowess (prou'ĕs). Valor; bravery

pseudonym (sū'dō-nĭm). A pen name

puerperal (pŭ-ûr'pēr-ăl). Pertaining to childbirth

pugnaciousness (pŭg-nā'shŭs-nĕs). Disposition to fight

puncheon (pŭn'chŭn). A short piece of timber

punctilious (pŭngk-tĭl'ĭ-ŭs). Scrupulously exact in details, or careful about codes of conduct

**pungent, page 156**

punitive (pū'nĭ-tĭv). Punishing

purgatory (pûr'gà-tō-rĭ). A place or state of temporary punishment; torment by uncertainty as to the future

purloin (pûr-loin'). To steal

pursed (pûrst). Puckered

## Q

quagmire (kwăg'mīr). Soft, wet, miry land

querulous (kwĕr'ū-lŭs). Complaining

quest (kwĕst). In medieval times, a knight's search for adventure

quien sabe (kyĕn sä'bā). *Spanish,* who knows?

quizzical (kwĭz'ĭ-kăl). Bantering; teasing

quorum (kwō'rŭm). A sufficient assembly to transact official business

## R

ramification (răm-ĭ-fĭ-kā'shŭn). A branch or subdivision

rapid-transit (răp'ĭd-trănz'ĭt). The name of a New York subway; literally fast passage

rapier (rā'pĭ-ēr). A straight two-edged sword having a narrow, pointed blade

rational (răsh'ŭn-ăl). Having the power of reasoning or understanding

rationalization (răsh-ŭn-ăl-ĭ-zā'shŭn). A mental process of assigning for actions or attitudes reasons which are more pleasing to the ego than the real reasons involved

raucous (rô'kŭs). Disagreeably harsh

**rebuffed, page 601**

recalcitrance (rē-kăl'sĭ-trăns). Stubborn rebelliousness or resistance

receding (rē-sēd'ĭng). Moving back or away

reciprocal (rē-sĭp'rō-kăl). Shared, felt, or shown by both sides

recluse (rē-klōōs'). A person who by choice lives shut away from others

reconnoiter (rĕk-ō-noi'tēr). To make a preliminary survey

**rectangle, page 468**

**rectify, page 468**

**rectitude, page 468**

recumbent (rē-kŭm'bĕnt). Lying down; resting

redoubtable (rē-dout'à-b'l). Formidable; worthy of respect as a foe

redress (rē-drĕs'). Amends for a wrong

reef (rēf). To reduce a sail by rolling or folding up a part of it; the resulting roll or fold

refectory (rē-fĕk'tō-rĭ). A dining hall, especially in a convent or monastery

regimenting (rĕj'ĭ-mĕnt-ĭng). Reducing individuals to mere parts of a group under strict control

reimburse (rē-ĭm-bûrs'). To pay back

reiterate (rē-ĭt'ēr-āt). To repeat over and over again

rejuvenescent (rē-jūv-ĕn-ĕs'ĕnt). Becoming young again

relegate (rĕl'ē-gāt). To banish; to dismiss by putting out of mind

relevancy (rĕl'ē-văn-sĭ). Proper application to the matter at hand

remuneration (rē-mū-nēr-ā'shŭn). Payment; pay

rendezvous (rän'dē-vōō). An appointed meeting or meeting place

renegade (rĕn'ē-gād). One who turns against his own group

repartee (rĕp-ēr-tē'). A clever retort; conversation marked by such retorts

**replenish, page 206**

repletion (rē-plē'shŭn). Fullness to capacity

replevin (rē-plĕv'ĭn). To recover

repulsion (rē-pŭl'shŭn). A feeling of intense dislike; drawing back because of such dislike

**requiem, page 528**

requisite (rĕk'wĭ-zĭt). Required by circumstances or nature; something so required

respite (rĕs'pĭt). Temporary relief from strain or pain

retching (rĕch'ĭng). Straining to vomit

reverberation (rē-vûr-bēr-ā'shŭn). Re-echo

revile (rē-vīl'). To speak of abusively

ribald (rĭb'ăld). Coarse; offensive

rigging (rĭg'ĭng). The ropes, chains, etc., that serve to lower and raise the spars and masts of a vessel or to set and trim the sails

**roundup, page 700**

rudimentary (rōō-dĭ-měn'tȧ-rĭ). Elementary; immature; not developed

rusty (rŭs'tĭ). A defective animal cut out of a cattle roundup (colloquial)

ruthless (rōōth'lĕs). Without pity or mercy

## S

sable (sā'b'l). Intensely black

sacked (săkt). Invaded and robbed

sagacity (sȧ-găs'ĭ-tĭ). Keen penetration and judgment. *Adj.*, sagacious (sȧ-gā'shŭs)

sage (sāj). One distinguished for wisdom

salutary (săl'ū-těr-ĭ). Promoting health

samovar (săm'ō-vär). A Russian urn for making tea

sanative (săn'ȧ-tĭv). Curative; healing

sanctified (săngk'tĭ-fīd). Devoted to holy things

sanction (săngk'shŭn). To confirm or approve

sanguinary (săng'gwĭ-něr-ĭ). Bloody

sanguine (săng'gwĭn). Optimistic; hopeful

sarcophagus (sär-kŏf'ȧ-gŭs). A large coffin exposed to view in the open air or in a tomb

sardonic (sär-dŏn'ĭk). Scornful; mocking

sarsaparilla (sär-sȧ-pȧ-rĭl'ȧ). A carbonated beverage flavored with the root for which it is named

satirist, page 71

savanna (sȧ-văn'ȧ). A grassy plain with few trees

savor, page 156

scantling (skănt'lĭng). A small piece of timber

schism (sĭz'm). A division or separation

scimitar (sĭm'ĭ-tēr). A curved sword, used chiefly by Moslems

scion (sī'ŭn). An offshoot; descendant

scoriac (skō'rĭ-ăk). Full of rock refuse

scotching (skŏtch'ĭng). Stamping out

scourge (skûrj). To whip or flog; to afflict; a sore affliction

scrounge (skrounj). To get possession by whatever means are necessary (slang)

scurvy (skûrv'ĭ). A disease of the digestive tract, caused by lack of vitamin C

scutter (skŭt'ēr). A low-down, mean creature (colloquial)

scuttle (skŭt''l). A covered opening on the deck of a ship

seance (sā'äns). A meeting of spiritualists to receive messages from spirits

secular (sěk'ū-lēr). Worldly rather than spiritual; not under church control

sedative (sěd'ȧ-tĭv). Tending to calm or make tranquil

seer (sēr). A prophet; wise man

selectman (sĕ-lĕkt'măn). A member of a community council in New England

semblance (sěm'blăns). Outward appearance

senescent, page 319

sententiously (sěn-těn'shŭs-lĭ). Emphasizing a meaning or moral

sepulcher (sěp'ŭl-kēr). A tomb; burial vault

seraph (sěr'ăf). A type of angel. *Plural*, seraphim (sěr'ȧ-fĭm)

sere (sēr). Dry; withered

serried (sěr'ĭd). Pressed together; dense

servile (sûr'vĭl). Behaving like a slave; abject

servitude (sûr'vĭ-tūd). Slavery; bondage

shackles (shăk''lz). Fetters; that which binds a prisoner

shambles (shăm'b'lz). A place of slaughter; hence, of great disorder

Shanghai, page 745

sheeted (shēt'ĕd) home. Spread a sail as wide and flat as possible

shrive (shrīv). To pardon the sins of one confessing them

shroud (shroud). One of the ropes leading from a vessel's mastheads to give lateral support to the masts

sibyl (sĭb'ĭl). A prophetess

siesta (sĭ-ĕs'tȧ). A short rest or nap after the midday meal

silicate (sĭl'ĭ-kȧt). A compound containing silica, the basis of glass

simper (sĭm'pēr). A silly smile

sinister (sĭn'ĭs-tēr). Boding evil

sinuous (sĭn'ū-ŭs). Winding; of wavy form

skeptic (skěp'tĭk). One who doubts. *Noun for the quality*, skepticism (skěp'tĭ-sĭz'm)

slatternly (slăt'ērn-lĭ). Slovenly; untidy

slough (slŭf). To cast off as a snake does its skin; also (sloō), a swamp

sluice (sloōs). An artificial waterway used by miners to wash gold out of sand

solicitor general (sȯ-lĭs'ĭ-tēr jěn'ēr-ăl). A high law officer in the British government

solicitous (sȯ-lĭs'ĭ-tŭs). Full of concern. *Noun*, solicitude

soliloquy, page 540

solstice (sŏl'stĭs). The day on which the sun is farthest from the equator, north or south

sombrero (sŏm-brā'rō). A broad-brimmed felt hat worn in the Southwest

sophisticated, page 752

soporific (sō-pȯ-rĭf'ĭk). Causing sleepiness

sordid (sôr'dĭd). Vile; base

span (spăn). The distance measured by the spread hand (page 602); to stretch across a given space (page 732)

spar (spär). A mast or yard on a sailing vessel

sparse (spärs). Thinly scattered

spavins (spăv'ĭnz). Bony enlargements on a horse's leg, caused by strain

specious (spē'shŭs). Deceptively appearing to be fair, just, or correct

spherule (sfĕr'ōōl). A little sphere or globe

spigot (spĭg'ŭt). A faucet

spontaneous (spŏn-tā'nĕ-ŭs). Self-acting; voluntary

sporadic (spŏ-răd'ĭk). Occurring in scattered instances

spurious (spū'rĭ-ŭs). Counterfeit; false

squalid, page 314

squalor, page 314

staggers (stăg'ērz). A nervous disease of horses, marked by staggering and falling

stamina (stăm'ĭ-nà). Vigor; endurance

stampede, page 700

stanch (stänch). To check the flowing of blood

stanchion (stăn'shŭn). Upright bars to secure cattle in their stalls

stay (stā). A support; prop

steerage (stēr'ĭj). The poorest and cheapest accommodations on a passenger vessel

stem to gudgeon (gŭj'ŭn). From one end to the other; all the way

stentorian, page 745

stereotyped (stĕr'ĕ-ô-tīpt). Lacking originality

stigma (stĭg'mà). A mark of disgrace

stipulate (stĭp'ŭ-lāt). To arrange definitely

stoic (stō'ĭk). A member of an early Greek school of thought who believed in unemotional acceptance of events, good or bad

stolid (stŏl'ĭd). Dull; not easily excited

stratagem, page 654

strategist, page 654

suave (swäv). Smoothly polite. *Noun*, suavity

subjugation, page 463

subsequent (sŭb'sĕ-kwĕnt). Following in time; later

subservient (sŭb-sûr'vĭ-ĕnt). Meekly obedient

subsidized (sŭb'sĭ-dīzd). Aided by outside funds, not earned by the enterprise in its regular operations

subtle (sŭt''l). Cunningly made; artful; delicate. *Noun*, subtlety, a thing or remark so made

subversion, page 471

succor (sŭk'ēr). To aid or help

succulence, page 156

suffice (sŭ-fīs'). To be sufficient

suffuse (sŭ-fūz'). To overspread

supercilious (sū-pĕr-sĭl'ĭ-ŭs). Haughtily contemptuous

supernal (sŭ-pûr'năl). Coming from the skies

supervene (sū-pēr-vēn'). To happen as something extra, unexpected

supinely, page 463

supplication, page 463

surcease (sŭr-sēs'). End

surly, page 601

surmise (sûr-mīz'). To imagine on slight grounds; guess

surplice (sûr'plĭs). Outer vestment worn by Anglican or Catholic clergy

surtout (sûr-tōōt'). An overcoat

surveillance (sûr-vāl'ăns). Close supervision; constant guard

sustenance (sŭs'tĕ-năns). Means of support, often food

swain (swān). A country lad

sylvan (sĭl'văn). Pertaining to the woods

symphony (sĭm'fô-nĭ). A harmony of sounds

synagogue (sĭn'à-gŏg). A Jewish place of worship

synchronize (sĭng'krô-nīz). To time in harmonious relation with

## T

tacit (tăs'ĭt). Implied though not expressed

Tally (tăl'ĭ) Book. Record of the cattle on a ranch

talons (tăl'ŭnz). Claws

tantalizing, page 745

tariff (tăr'ĭf). Schedule of rates or charges

tarn (tärn). A small mountain lake

tartar (tär'tēr). An opponent who proves too strong for his attacker; a crust that forms on teeth (page 125)

tawdry (tô'drĭ). Cheap and gaudy

tawny (tô'nĭ). Of a deep tan color

temporize, page 698

tenacious (tĕ-nā'shŭs). Holding firmly

tenement (tĕn'ĕ-mĕnt). A dwelling place; often, a crowded apartment house in the poorer section of a city

tenet (tĕn'ĕt). An opinion or principle

tenoned and mortised (tĕn'ŭnd, môr'tĭst). Joined firmly, with projections of one part fitted into shaped cavities in the other part

tensile (tĕn'sĭl). Pertaining to stretching or straining

tentacle, page 773

tentatively (tĕn'tà-tĭv-lĭ). Experimentally

termagant (tûr'mà-gănt). A quarrelsome, scolding woman

terminate (tûr'mĭ-nāt). To end. *Adj.*, terminal

terrain (tĕ-rān'). A tract of ground immediately under observation

tether (tĕth'ēr). A rope or leash on which an animal is confined to a small range thermal (thûr'măl). Pertaining to heat

thrall (thrôl). A slave

thwart (thwôrt). A rower's seat across a boat

tiller (tĭl'ẽr). The lever by which the rudder is turned to steer a boat

timothy (tĭm'ô-thĭ). A grass grown for hay

tintinnabulation (tĭn-tĭ-năb-ŭ-lā'shŭn). The tinkling sound of ringing bells

topsail (tŏp'sāl). The sail just above the lowest one on a mast

torpid (tôr'pĭd). Sluggish

torso (tôr'sō). The trunk of the human body.

tortilla (tôr-tē'yà). A thin cake of baked corn-meal (Mexican)

transient (trăn'shĕnt). Of short duration

transition (trăn-zĭ'shŭn). Change from one state to another

transitory (trăn'sĭ-tō-rĭ). Temporary; not last-ing

transmute (trăns-mūt'). To change from one nature, form, or substance to another

transpire (trăn-spīr'). To happen; to occur

travail (trăv'āl). Toil, especially painful effort or exertion

trek (trĕk). A trip or journey

**trepidation,** page 767

tympanum (tĭm-păn'ŭm). The eardrum

# U

ubiquitous (ŭ-bĭk'wĭ-tŭs). Being everywhere at the same time

ultimate (ŭl'tĭ-măt). Last; final; farthest

unadulterated (ŭn-à-dŭl'tẽr-āt-ĕd) McCoy. The genuine article; the real thing (slang)

**unattainable,** page 35

**unavailing,** page 35

uncanny (ŭn-kăn'ĭ). Ghostly; weird; unnatu-rally strange

unconscionable (ŭn-kŏn'shŭn-à-b'l). Not guided, or controlled by conscience; unscrupulous

unction (ŭngk'shŭn). Affected earnestness in talking

undeviating (ŭn-dē'vĭ-āt-ĭng). Holding firmly to a course

undulation (ŭn-dŭ-lā'shŭn). A rising and falling motion, as of waves

unequivocal (ŭn-ê-kwĭv'ô-kăl). Not doubtful; clear

**unfalteringly,** page 625

**unique,** page 164

**unmitigated,** page 438

**unprecedentedly,** page 767

**unquenchable,** page 83

unremitting (ŭn-rê-mĭt'ĭng). Without stopping or pausing

unrequited (ŭn-rê-kwīt'ĕd). Not returned

**urbane,** page 752

**usurer,** page 494

usurpation (ū-zŭr-pā'shŭn). Unauthorized ex-ercise of powers belonging to another

**usury,** page 494

utilization (ū-tĭl-ĭ-zā'shŭn). Practical use

# V

vacillation (văs-ĭ-lā'shŭn). Wavering in purpose or conduct

variegated (vâr'ĭ-ĕ-gāt-ĕd). Of different colors combined

vehement (vē'ê-mĕnt). Acting with great force

vellum (vĕl'ŭm). Fine parchment

**venerable,** page 552

veracious (vê-rā'shŭs). Truthful

verdure (vûr'dŭr). Greenness; vegetation

veritable (vĕr'ĭ-tà-b'l). Real; true; actual

vermilion (vẽr-mĭl'yŭn). A brilliant red, the color or the pigment

verminous (vûr'mĭ-nŭs). Infested with vermin; hence, cluttered with undesirable matter

vernacular (vẽr-năk'ŭ-lẽr). The common mode of speech in a particular locality

**vestige,** 227

vestryman (vĕs'trĭ-măn). A member of the church board

viand (vī'ănd). An article of food

vicissitude (vĭ-sĭs'ĭ-tūd). A complete change or reversal of fortune

victualed (vĭt''ld). Supplied with food

vigilance (vĭj'ĭ-lăns). Watchfulness; caution

vindication (vĭn-dĭ-kā'shŭn). Justification against blame

vintage (vĭn'tĭj). Wine

**virulent,** page 174

**virus,** page 174

visage (vĭz'ĭj). Face

vitreous (vĭt'rê-ŭs). Like glass, as in color

vituperative (vī-tū'pẽr-ā-tĭv). Scolding; abu-sive

vixen (vĭk's'n). An ill-tempered woman

vociferate (vô-sĭf'ẽr-āt). To talk or cry out loudly

volcanic (vŏl-kăn'ĭk). Like a volcano; seething with strong emotion

voluble (vŏl'ŭ-b'l). Talkative

voluptuous (vô-lŭp'tŭ-ŭs). Luxurious; highly pleasing to the senses

voracity (vô-răs'ĭ-tĭ). Greediness

votive (vō'tĭv). Given or done as an act of con-secration

vouchsafe (vouch-sāf'). To condescend to grant or bestow

## W

wanton (wŏn′tŭn). Undisciplined or unrestrained

weal (wēl). Prosperity; happiness

weir (wēr). A type of fish trap

welkin (wĕl′kĭn). The sky

werewolf (wĕr′wŏŏlf). A person who can assume at will a wolf's shape and appetite

whitlow (hwĭt′lō). An inflammation of a finger or toe

windrows (wĭnd′rōz). Rows, as in a raked hay-meadow

winnow (wĭn′ō). To sift or scatter

withe (wĭth). A slender, flexible twig or branch used as a rope or band

wold (wōld). An open lowland

## Y

yawl (yôl). A light boat

yearling (yēr′lĭng). An animal one year old, or in the second year of its life

yucca (yŭk′à). A spike-leafed plant found in arid sections

## Z

zephyr (zĕf′ĭr). A gentle breeze

zone (zōn). The waistline (page 602)

# INDEX

## DATE DUE

| | | | |
|---|---|---|---|
| FEB 2 1953 | MR 8 '68 | | DE 5 '75 |
| FEB 3 1953 | FEB | | OCT 14 1994 |
| MAR 2 1953 | | | |
| NOV 12 1953 | MR 26 '69 | | |
| MAR 21 | SEP 30 1994 | | |
| DEC 7 | | | |
| DEC 17 | | | |
| JAN 18 1947 | | | |
| NO 24 66 | MR 10 | | |
| MR 13 '67 | | | |
| MR 14 67 | | | |
| OC 18 '67 | | | |
| DE 3 '67 | | | |
| MR 12 68 | | | |
| OCT 30 1981 | | | |
| | | | |
| | | | |
| | | | |

170 Issco                                    Printed